BARRON'S

HOW TO PREPARE FOR THE

GED

HIGH SCHOOL EQUIVALENCY EXAM CANADIAN EDITION

4TH EDITION

Murray Rockowitz, Ph.D.
Former Chairman, Board of Examiners,
New York City Board of Education

Former Principal, John Philip Sousa Junior High School, New York City

Former Chairman, English Department,
Charles Evans Hughes High School,
New York City

Dale E. Shuttleworth, Ph.D.
Executive Director, The Training Renewal Foundation, GED Preparation Centre

Former Superintendent, City of York Board of Education, Ontario, Canada

Murray Shukyn
Associate Director, GED Preparation Centre
Toronto, Ontario, Canada

Samuel C. Brownstein
Former Chairman, Biology Department,
Wingate High School, Brooklyn, New York

Max Peters
Former Chairman, Mathematics Department,
Wingate High School, Brooklyn, New York

BARRON'S

All inquiries should be addressed to:
Barron's Educational Series, Inc.
250 Wireless Boulevard
Hauppauge, New York 11788
http://www.barronseduc.com

Library of Congress Catalog Card No. 2001043246

International Standard Book No. 0-7641-1789-0

Library of Congress Cataloging-in-Publication Data

How to prepare for the Canadian GED high school equivalency exam / Murray Rockowitz . . . [et al.].—4th ed.
p. cm.
At head of title: Barron's.
Rev. ed. of: How to prepare for the GED high school equivalency exam. c1998.
ISBN 0-7641-1789-0 (alk. paper)
1. General educational development tests—Study guides. 2. High school equivalency examinations—Canada—Study guides. I. Title: GED. II. Title: Barron's how to prepare for the Canadian GED high school equivalency exam. III. Rockowitz, Murray. IV. How to prepare for the GED high school equivalency exam.
LB3060.33.G45 H69 2002
373.126'2—dc21 2001043246

PRINTED IN THE UNITED STATES OF AMERICA
9 8 7

Contents

The 2002 GED Examination

Standardized tests change from time to time. The GED Examination, as you may already know, will change this year. While much of the 2002 exam will test the same concepts in the same way as past GED Exams, the new exam will also differ from its predecessors in some significant respects. As you prepare for your GED Exam, you must familiarize yourself with these differences.

The purpose of the following test update is to outline these changes as they affect each part of the exam: Writing Skills, Parts I and II; Social Studies; Science; Literature and the Arts; and Mathematics. This test update describes in detail the changes to each part of the exam. It also provides some examples of new question types. As you work your way through this book, therefore, you should consult this test update regularly.

If you revisit this test update regularly in conjunction with the rest of the book, you will be well prepared for the GED Exam. Good luck on test day!

TEST 1: THE LANGUAGE ARTS, WRITING, PART I (WRITING SKILLS, PART I) TEST

As in the past, Test 1: Writing Skills, Part I, will test your knowledge of the content of written English—sentence structure, the ability to recognize correct and incorrect sentences—sentence fragments and run-on sentences; correct usage, agreement, case of pronouns, verb forms; mechanics of capitalization and punctuation. Passages 12–20 sentences long will continue to be used. Within each passage there will be errors you will have to find and correct, or recognize as correct; sentences you will be asked to combine; and alternative ways to write sentences, all of these in a multiple-choice format. In some you will be given the sentence to be corrected and five possible answers. One possible answer will be, in some questions, "no correction is necessary." Three types of errors will be retained from the current test: errors in sentence structure, errors in usage, and errors in mechanics: punctuation and capitalization. The three types of items will be the same as in the current test: correction of errors in a sentence or a number of sentences; revision of a stem with an underlined part that may be correct or incorrect; construction shift, the rewriting of a stem that is correct but that you will be asked to write in a different way.

WHAT IS NEW IN GED 2002?

1. The current Test I weights sentence structure at 35%, usage 35%, and mechanics 30%. Mechanics includes spelling, punctuation, and capitalization. GED 2002 drops spelling except for homonyms, contractions, and possessives. Sentence structure is now weighted 30%, usage 30%, and mechanics 25%. Tested will be homonyms (words with the same sound as another word or words but with a different spelling and meaning, such as *to, two, too*); possessives (form of a noun or pronoun that shows ownership, such as *boy's hat, ladies' hats*), and contractions (shortened form of a word or words by omission of a letter, such as *do not, don't; they are, they're*). Fewer uses of the comma will be tested, emphasizing only those that prevent confusion in meaning, as in "Let's eat Frank before we go to work." "Let's eat, Frank, before we go to work."

2. GED 2002 has a change in the weight of the three question types. Correction questions are now weighted at 45%, down from 50%. You are asked to correct errors in organization, sentence structure, usage, and mechanics in one sentence, a number of sentences, or a complete paragraph. Construction shift items have been raised to 20%. These test only mechanics and sentence structure. You are asked to rewrite a stem using an alternate structure (another way to write the sentence). Revision questions test skills in sentence structure, usage, and mechanics by having part of the stem underlined and having you choose from five possible corrections. These remain weighted at 25%.

3. Sentence structure, usage, and mechanics are now worth 85%. A new content area, **organization**, is now weighted at 15%, an important change. This involves moving sentences in a

paragraph to improve logic and clarity; removing irrelevant sentences; identifying, moving, inserting topic sentences (a statement of the main idea or unifying thought); and joining or dividing paragraphs to improve clarity. Here is a sample question on organization:

(1) People know little about this fascinating game. (2) A common saying among those who know this game best is that the winner of the game is the one who makes the next-to-the-last mistake. (3) Even among grandmasters, the secret of success is not superior strategy but the failure to make tactical errors. (4) The purpose of the game is the opponent's skillful exploitation of a mistake made at any point in the game. (5) It is rare, nonetheless, that a game lasts for 100 moves. (6) The average number of moves is usually somewhere around 45, and the shortest game can consist of only two moves.

1. **The topic sentence of this paragraph is**

   (1) sentence 1
   (2) sentence 2
   (3) sentence 3
   (4) sentence 4
   (5) sentence 5

2. **Sentence 1 should be**

   (1) left as it is
   (2) placed last
   (3) placed after sentence 3
   (4) placed after sentence 6
   (5) omitted

3. **A new paragraph can**

   (1) be started after sentence 2
   (2) be started after sentence 3
   (3) be started after sentence 4
   (4) be started after sentence 5
   (5) not be started

ANSWER ANALYSIS

1. **2** The main idea of the paragraph is the role of errors in the playing of chess.
2. **5** The sentence is irrelevant to the topic.
3. **3** The paragraph shifts from its main idea to a subordinate one after sentence 4—the length of games.

4. The content of the passages that are the basis for the questions in the Writing Skills Test, Part I has been broadened to include, in addition to informational passages, "how to" (practical subjects) and business documents.

TEST 1: THE LANGUAGE ARTS, WRITING, PART II (WRITING SKILLS, PART II) TEST

In this part, as in the current test, you will be asked to write an expository essay in 45 minutes. The length of the essay is now 250 words rather than the 200 words as in the current test. In the essay you are asked to explain, describe, or interpret a particular idea, situation, or experience by using your own personal life and information, as in the current test.

The essay directions will be thorough and specific:

- You must write on the assigned topic ONLY.
- You will have 45 minutes to write on your assigned essay topic.

Two evaluators will score your essay according to its overall effectiveness. Their evaluation will be based on:

- Well-focused main points
- Clear organization
- Specific development of your ideas
- Control of sentence structure, punctuation, grammar, word choice, spelling

1. Do not leave any blank pages.
2. Write legibly *in ink* so that the evaluators will be able to read your writing.
3. Write on the assigned topic. If you write on a topic other than the one assigned, you will not receive a score for the Writing Skills Test.
4. Write your essay on the lined pages of the separate answer sheet booklet.

Part II is a test to determine how well you can use written language to explain your ideas. In preparing your essay, take the following steps:

1. Read the DIRECTIONS and the TOPIC carefully.
2. Plan your essay before you write. Use the scratch paper to make any notes. These notes will be collected but not scored.
3. Before you turn in your essay, reread what you have written and make any changes that will improve your essay.
4. Your essay should be long enough to develop the topic adequately and should be approximately 250 words.

The assigned topic will be clearly indicated. Here are some sample topics to practice on.

1. If you could choose to spend a day with a particular person, whom would you choose? In your essay, indicate the reasons you would choose that person.
2. If you had a choice of a travel destination, indicate the place and the reasons why you chose it.
3. All of us have beliefs we hold dear. Choose one such belief and indicate the reasons why you chose it.
4. We all have favourite memories. Choose the memory you most cherish and give the reasons why it is dear to you.
5. "A friend in need is a friend indeed," goes the saying. Choose an experience you had helping a friend or being helped by a friend. Indicate why the experience is memorable.

SOCIAL STUDIES TEST

The following will indicate the four main changes or new emphases.

1. The test will emphasize history and government including civics; 40% will be history with Canadian history 25% and world history 15%.
2. More questions will be based on maps, tables, and cartoons—the graphic and visual.
3. Each test will include part of at least one *historical* document, for example, the United States Constitution, and at least one *practical* document chosen from sources dealing with your life as a citizen and a consumer. Both global (international) and Canadian (national) settings will be included.
4. Questions requiring analysis of prose and graphic materials will be emphasized.

The multiple-choice questions will be based on both *prose* (texts, speeches, newspapers, news magazines, and documents) and *visuals* (maps, graphs, tables, and political cartoons). Both single-question items and sets of questions based on the selections will be included.

Four types of thinking will be tested as in previous versions of the examination:

1. Questions requiring comprehension—understanding of information and ideas and the meaning they may imply (20%).
2. Questions requiring application—ability to use the information and ideas you understand in new situations (20%).
3. Questions involving analysis—ability to go beyond mere comprehension and application to recognize cause and effect, to determine the writer's point of view, assumptions, and errors, and to distinguish fact from opinion (40%).
4. Questions involving evaluation—determine how the facts presented lead to the conclusions reached, their accuracy, and how they are influenced by the author's point of view or bias (20%).

THE SCIENCE TEST

There have been some changes made to the GED Science test. You will find that this book still provides you with an excellent preparation for the test and most of the material in this study guide is highly relevant to the new test as well. Many things will remain the same on the new version of the test.

The test is still a multiple-choice format with five choices per question. The scoring for the test is the same as in previous years. All of the test-taking hints that this book provides will still be valuable. For example, if the correct answer to a question is not immediately obvious, it is still a good strategy to try to eliminate incorrect choices to narrow down the choices.

There is no need for you to memorize any equations. There are very few calculations on the GED science section and those that do exist involve some basic calculations such as addition, subtraction, or multiplication. In the event that a formula is needed, it will be provided to you.

Probably the biggest difference between previous versions of the test and the new one is that there will be fewer lengthy passages followed by several questions and more brief passages followed by a single question. This is to allow each question to focus on a specific topic or concept. While this may seem like a major change, you will find that all of the strategies you have learned in using this study guide still work. You will also find that the new test tries to make use of more practical examples. For instance, instead of a question that describes the motion of a pendulum, you might find a question, or series of questions, that deals with a swing. The concept is the same, but you are using a common object to illustrate it.

There will be a slight redistribution of the topic contents as well: a greater emphasis on life sciences and environmental topics on the newer version of the GED. On the newer version of the test, more questions will deal with the life sciences—mainly biology—or environmental science—including ecology. There will still be questions from all areas of the physical science as well, including chemistry, physics, and earth and space science.

The test does not seek to see how much vocabulary you have memorized or how much science you may recall from school. Instead, the emphasis is on applying basic concepts and thinking things through. In this respect, the test remains unchanged.

The newer version of the GED uses the National Science Education Standards as a guideline. Below you will find a short summary of the standards and some of the examples of each.

CONTENT STANDARD A: SCIENCE AS INQUIRY

- Abilities needed to perform scientific inquiry
- Understanding the nature of scientific inquiry

This section refers to the ability to understand a well-planned experiment, including the use of control (or comparison) groups.

CONTENT STANDARD B: PHYSICAL SCIENCE

- The structure of atoms
- The properties and structure of matter
- Chemical reactions
- Motion and forces
- Conservation of energy and the concept of entropy
- Interactions of energy and matter

This standard deals mainly with the physical sciences such as chemistry and physics.

The science practice sections on chemistry and physics cover these topics, and there are many more questions in the practice exams.

CONTENT STANDARD C: LIFE SCIENCE

- The cell
- The molecular basis of heredity
- Evolution of life
- The interdependence of organisms
- Matter, energy, and organization in living systems
- Behavior

The science practice section on biology covers these topics. Keep in mind that not every biology question fits exactly into each of the topics above. The new standards are general guidelines that can be used to help organize information for you.

CONTENT STANDARD D: EARTH AND SPACE SCIENCE

- Energy in the earth
- Geochemical cycles (rock and mineral cycles)
- Origin and evolution of the earth and the moon
- Origin and evolution of the universe

This topic area also includes meteorology and the water cycle.

CONTENT STANDARD E: SCIENCE AND TECHNOLOGY

- Technological design
- General understanding about science and technology

This section deals with the applications of science.

CONTENT STANDARD F: SCIENCE IN PERSONAL AND SOCIAL PERSPECTIVES

- Personal and community health
- Population growth
- Natural resources
- Environmental quality
- Natural and human-induced hazards
- Local, national, and global challenges in science and technology

Many of the questions dealing with this content standard are those that stress some real-world applications. Questions dealing with water or air quality would be good examples of topics covered under this content standard.

CONTENT STANDARD G: HISTORY AND NATURE OF SCIENCE

- Science as a human endeavor
- Nature of scientific knowledge
- Historical perspectives

This content standard deals with the manner in which scientific knowledge is gained (through experimentation) and some historical perspectives on the acquisition of this knowledge. Keep in mind that you will not be expected to have memorized any names of scientists or dates regarding discoveries. Instead, you are more likely to see a passage dealing with the history of a concept, such as models or the structure of the atom, and then to see a few questions dealing with that passage. Remember that all of the information you will need to answer the questions will be contained in the passage.

As you study for the new GED, it may help to see into which content standard questions or groups of questions fit. Keep in mind that not every question or passage will fit neatly into a single category, but you should find that paying close attention to the study material, the questions, and answers with explanations will allow you to be successful on the science section of the GED.

THE LANGUAGE ARTS, READING (INTERPRETING LITERATURE AND THE ARTS) TEST

This test will keep a number of features of the current GED Examination, but the title will be changed to Language Arts: Reading from Interpreting Literature and the Arts.

1. Selections of 300 to 400 words will be drawn from respected writers of prose fiction and nonfiction, poetry, and drama. The texts will have been written from pre-1920 to after 1960 to date, both classical and modern.
2. The subject matter and authors will continue to reflect many different cultural backgrounds. Diversity will be emphasized as in the past.
3. Each selection will continue to be introduced by a purpose question to help you, the reader, focus on the meaning and intent of the passage. It will be of the "why" and the "how" variety.
4. The questions will be in the same multiple-choice format.
5. The test will include prose, poetry, and drama with four to eight questions designed to test your reading comprehension on several levels of difficulty to understand, to apply your understanding, to analyze specific parts of a passage, and to synthesize the parts of the passage into a whole.
6. As is now the case, 75% of the questions will be literary texts divided among prose, poetry, and drama with at least one selection from each. Various passages from classical and modern writing will continue to be represented; 25% will be nonfiction prose.

WHAT'S NEW?

1. In *content* and *context* there will be greater emphasis on diversity of the selections. Various ethnic groups and more women will be included. To help you prepare for these kinds of texts, a number of authors of different backgrounds are represented in the current edition.
2. Another change in the literary texts comprising 75% of the test will be a broader range of time periods in which the texts were written, and the time periods will be more specifically defined into three, more classical passages written pre-1920, passages written between 1920 and 1960, and more modern passages written after 1960.

   In addition there will be an 8 to 25-line poem and one drama selection.
3. Nonfiction questions will be based on three selections chosen from nonfiction prose. They deal with a variety of subjects.
4. A completely new feature will be a business-related document such as a company bulletin or an annual report. One such selection will be on the test.

READING SKILLS

The emphasis on reading skills has shifted to higher and more difficult levels. Comprehension and application questions are now only 35% of the test—20% comprehension and 15% application. Analysis questions (reference to specific parts of a passage) are allocated 30–35%, and synthesis questions (drawing on the passage as a whole) are similarly allocated 30–35%.

Comprehension

Comprehension tests a basic understanding of the meaning and purpose of the writing. It tests your ability to restate information in other words (paraphrase), summarize the main idea, and explain the thought conveyed by the text.

Application Questions

Application questions test your ability to use information and ideas from the passage in a different situation.

Analysis Questions

Analysis questions ask you to break down the information in the text to its parts and make several references to specific parts of a passage. You will have to draw conclusions, understand consequences (cause and effect), or arrive at other ideas suggested or implied by the passage. In addition, you may be asked to identify such qualities as tone and mood or arrive at what is suggested from language sometimes used in an unusual way.

Synthesis Questions

Synthesis questions, the most difficult kind, require putting parts together to make a whole from different parts of a text or from two texts. You will have to make connections between the parts, determine how the text is organized, the overall tone or purpose of the text, or bring to the passage outside knowledge to integrate with it.

A major change is the inclusion of expanded synthesis questions, combining information from two parts within a passage.

MATHEMATICS TEST

The 2002 Mathematics section of the GED Exam will be somewhat different than previous exams. Here's a summary of the important changes:

1. ***Fewer questions.*** The number of questions will be reduced from 56 to 50 and will be split into Parts I and II, each of the parts having 25 questions.

2. ***Use of a calculator.*** For Part I, you will be given a Casio fx-260SOLAR calculator at the testing site, which you have the option of using to help solve all questions in this part only.

3. ***Use of an answer grid.*** For 10 of the 50 questions on the test, you will not be offered multiple choice but must come up with answers on your own. You will then be required to "bubble in" these answers on an answer grid.

The good news is that the "new" test doesn't appear to be any more difficult than the "old" one. The concepts tested and the level of complexity of the questions are virtually the same as those included in past exams, and are covered thoroughly in this book. With the added privilege of being able to use a calculator for Part I, you will almost certainly find the 2002 test easier.

USING THE CASIO FX-260SOLAR CALCULATOR

Before taking Part I, you will be issued a Casio fx-260SOLAR calculator and then given a few minutes to practice using it. You don't have to use the calculator, but it is strongly recommended that you do so. It can really help you to avoid computational errors that lead to incorrect answers and can dramatically reduce the time it takes to solve certain problems, giving you more time to spend on the tougher questions. After Part I is over, you must return the calculator and complete Part II without it.

If you have had some past experience using a calculator, it will help you in operating the Casio fx-260, which works like virtually all hand-held calculators. If you have never used a calculator, however, it is a good idea to purchase or borrow one to practice on prior to taking the GED. The most effective way to practice is to use the fx-260, which is available in retail stores for about $10 or can be ordered from the GED Fulfillment Center by calling (301) 604-9073.

As you take the practice exams in this book, use the calculator to help solve only about half the questions. Because you will still be required to do your own calculations for many of the questions, it's important to keep your computational skills strong and avoid overdependence on the calculator.

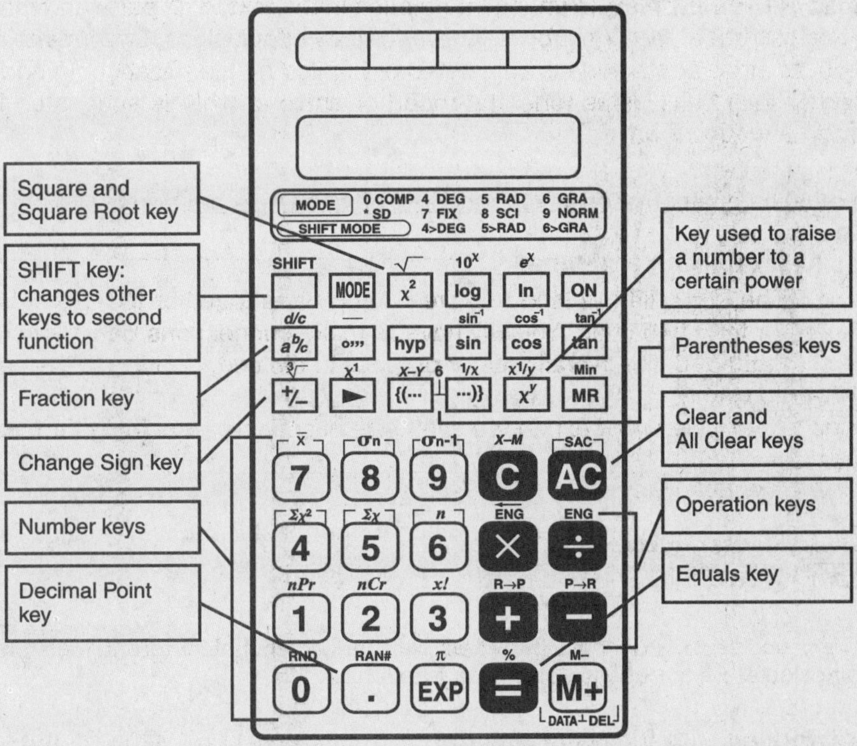

Above is a basic diagram of the Casio fx-260SOLAR calculator that will be issued to you. Please note that the calculator has a lot more function keys than you will need to use on the test.

Here are some basic rules to keep in mind when using a calculator:

- Press the keys firmly, checking the display window to make sure you have entered numbers accurately.
- Press [AC] (or similar key) after completing each problem to completely clear it. Pressing [C] will erase just the last number entered.
- Numbers and the decimal point will appear on the display window, but operations signs (like [+] or [×] or [+]) will not.

Example One (Basic Operations)

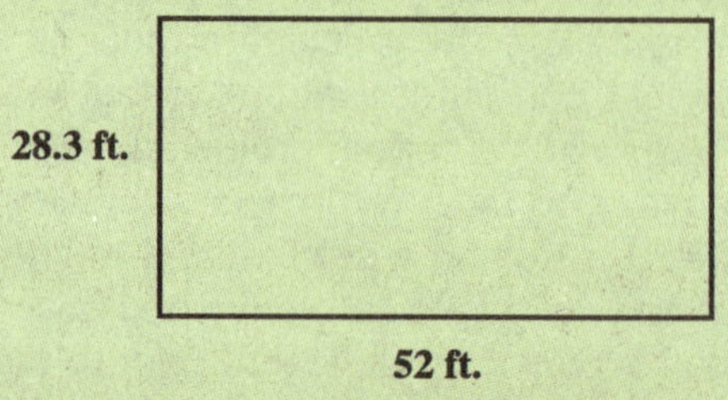

How many square feet of carpet are required to cover the entire office floor in the diagram above?

PRESS *28.3*, then [×], then *52*, then [=]

Answer: 1471.6 sq. ft.

Example Two (Working with Parentheses)

Find: 12(117 + 13) – 68

PRESS *12* [×] [[(···] *117* [+] *13* [···)]] [–] *68* [=]

Answer: 40

Note: The fx-260 has parentheses keys, but some other calculators don't.

Example Three (Working with Fractions)

Broadway	3/4 mile
Alice Avenue	2 1/2 miles
Stockton Street	4 miles

According to the highway exit sign above, how much further past Broadway is Alice Avenue?

PRESS *2* [a b/c] *1* [a b/c] *2* [–] [a b/c] *3* [a b/c] *4* [=]

Answer: 1 3/4 miles

Note: Not all calculators are able to compute fractions.

Example Four (Working with Signed Numbers)

What is the value of the following expression?

–3(–6 + 8) – (–12)

PRESS *3* [+/–] [×] [[(···] *6* [+/–] [+] *8* [···)]] [–] *12* [+/–] [=]

Answer: 6

Note: Some calculators allow you to enter negative numbers using the [–] key.

Example Five (Working with Exponents)

A container that holds crushed gravel is in the shape of a cube, with each side measuring 17 feet. What is the volume of the container?

PRESS *17* [×] *3* [X^y] [=]

Answer: 4,913 cu. ft.

Example Six (Working with Square Roots)

The square root of 138 is between what two whole numbers?

PRESS *138* [SHIFT] [X^y]

Answer: between 11 and 12

FINDING AN ANSWER AND USING AN ANSWER GRID

On 10 questions out of the 50 on the test, multiple-choice answers will not be provided. You must come up with an answer yourself and then record it on a grid (see illustration).

Example One (Recording Whole Numbers)

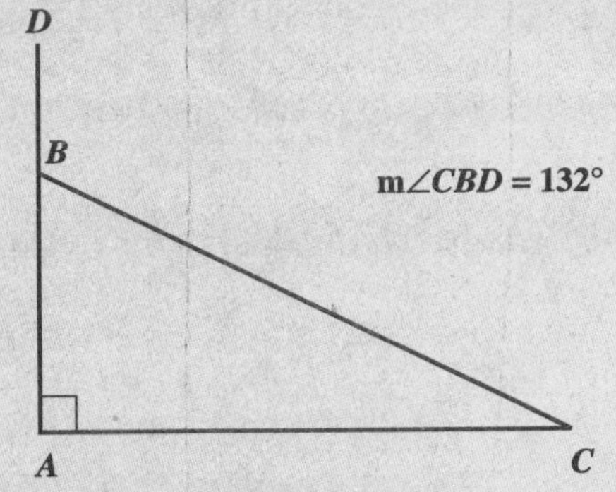

What is the measure in degrees of $\angle ACB$?
(Using what you've learned about triangles and supplemetary angles in Chapter 23, you calculate the correct answer to be 42°.)

Answer: 42°

You can fill in the answer grid for this response in four different ways; all are correct (see illustration). Make sure to write the answer in the top horizontal row of boxes and then "bubble in" the corresponding numbers below. Don't worry about including the degrees sign (°); it's unnecessary.

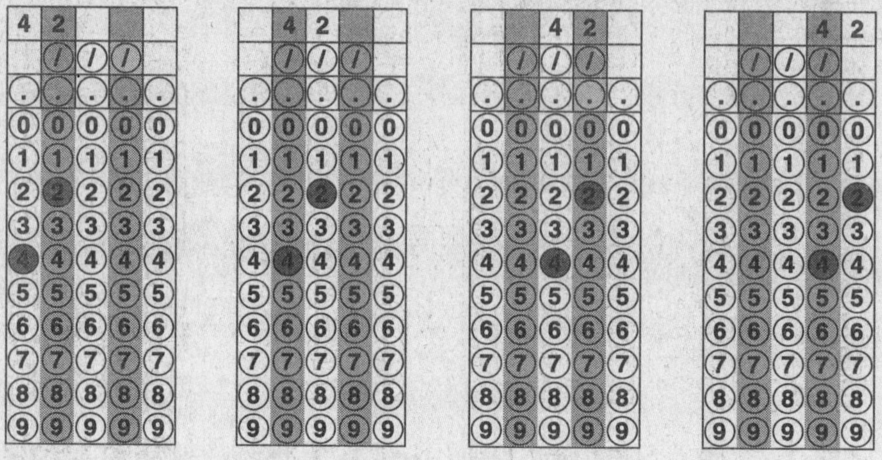

Example Two (Recording Numbers with Decimals)

Sharon and her coworkers want to purchase a portable CD player as a going-away present for their boss. The player costs \$86.99. Sharon collects \$47.35 from her coworkers and contributes \$20 herself. How much more does she need to make the purchase?

Answer: \$19.64

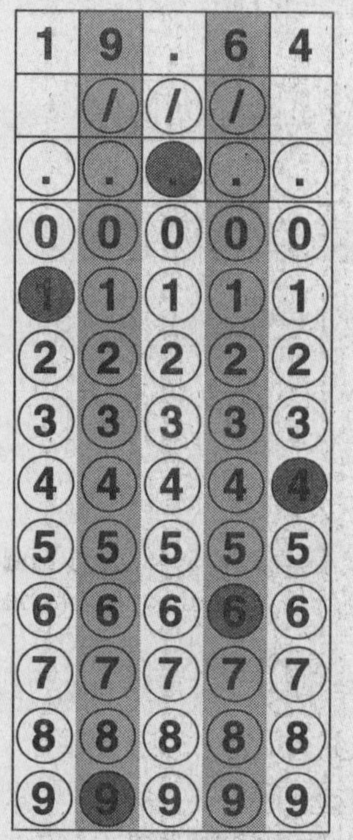

Here, there is only one way to complete the grid. Note that the decimal point *must* be recorded and takes up an entire column. Recording the $ sign is unnecessary.

Example Three (Recording Fractions)

A plumber measures a piece of pipe to be 1 5/8 inches. How much does he need to trim from the pipe to make it fit a connection that is 1 3/8 inches long?

Answer: 2/8 or **1/4**

The grid can be completed in the following ways, all of which are correct.

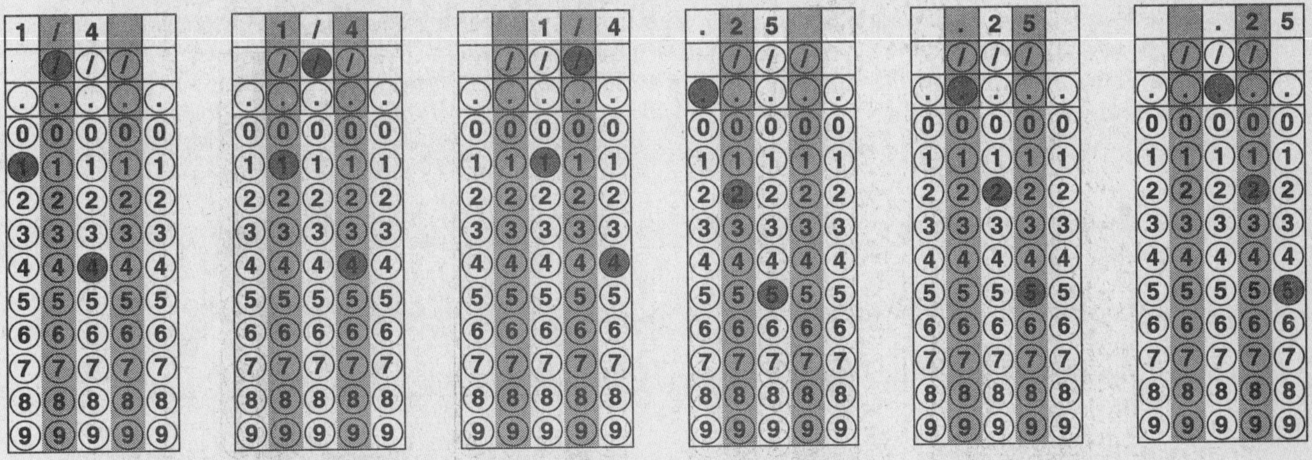

Example Four (Recording Points on a Coordinates Plane Grid)

Two lines intersect at a point with coordinates of (5, –3). Show the location of the intersecting point on the grid below.

Answer: see grid

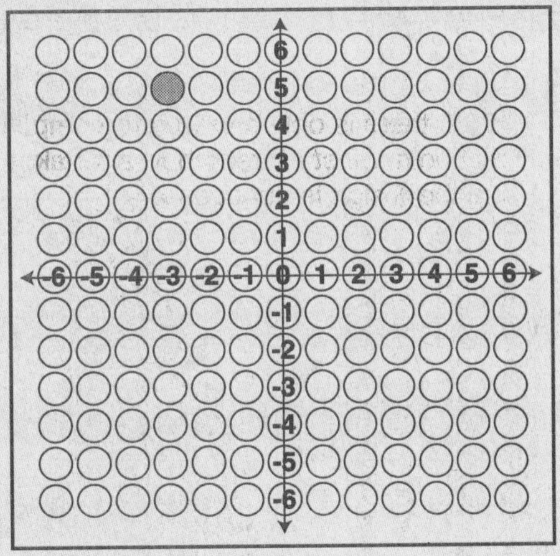

Note: The coordinate plane grid illustrated is just like a rectangular coordinate grid. However, the *x* and *y* axes are not labeled, so it's essential that you memorize which is which. There will most probably be only two questions out of the 50 requiring you to fill in this type of grid.

PRACTICE STRATEGIES FOR QUESTIONS WITHOUT MULTIPLE CHOICE

Learning to fill in the answer grid is rather easy. The challenging part of the 2002 test is feeling confident about the answers you calculate without actually seeing them confirmed with a multiple choice.

Much of the practice in the instructional chapters requires you to come up with answers on your own, so that kind of practice should help instill confidence in your work. Except when using the method of "Plugging In," you should always calculate an answer first and then compare it to the multiple-choice offerings.

For additional practice, try this: Before you take any of the practice tests or exams in this book, decide on ten questions per exam to which you will write out answers instead of using the multiple-choice offerings. Before taking each test, quickly scan the multiple-choice answers and use your common sense when deciding—only some of the questions can be answered properly in the grid format. Circle these questions in advance. When you come to them, cover the multiple-choice answers with a sheet of paper, write out the answer on another paper, and move to the next problem. Carefully compare your answers with the correct answers provided. Practice entering some answers in the blank grids below.

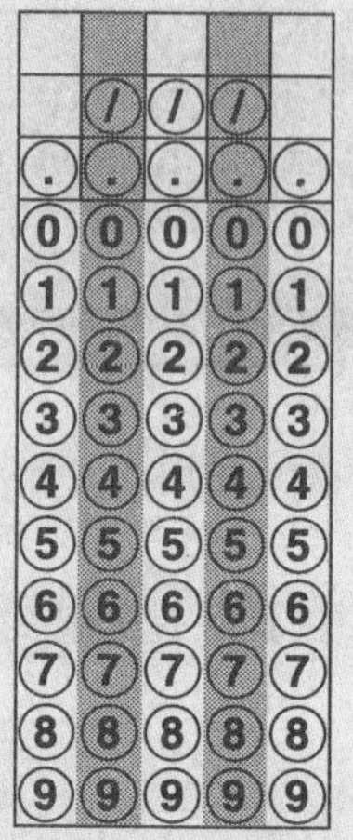

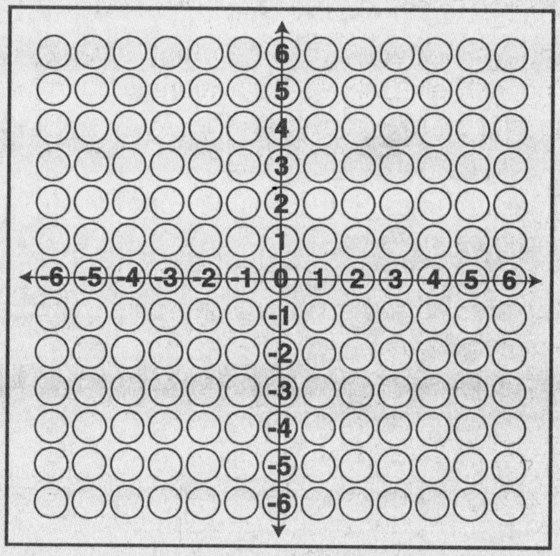

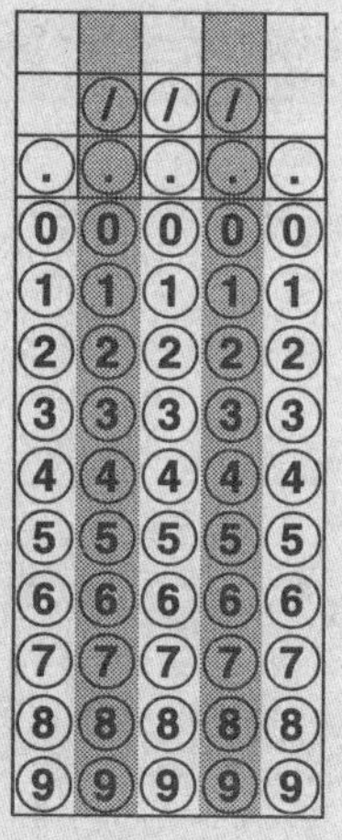

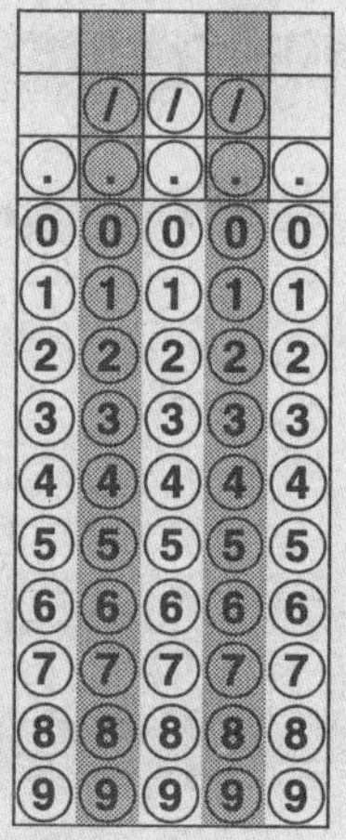

Preface

This edition includes the most recent changes in the content and format of the tests of General Educational Development (GED) required to qualify for a High School Equivalency Certificate. The authors, all specialists in various areas of the high school curriculum, have developed practice exercises and tests which reflect these changes and provide extensive preparation for the GED test.

To the Reader

"Until recently, all we asked of job applicants was that they be able to sign their name and find their way to the time clock. Now they've got to have a high school diploma." These words of an electronics manufacturer are a warning to the student and jobseeker of today.

IF you want an interesting job—one that does not lead to a dead end;
IF you want to be accepted in a good company's apprenticeship program;
IF you want to advance on the job to technician or troubleshooting levels from a one-operation task;
IF you want to continue your studies at a community college or university;
IF you want to get a technical or junior professional Civil Service position;
IF you want to be accepted in a specialized assignment in the Armed Forces;

You Must Have a High School Diploma

If you have not yet completed high school, this book will help you earn that precious diploma by passing a High School Equivalency Examination. Most Canadian provinces/territories have programs that enable you to do this.

To Help You

We have carefully analyzed the GED test.

We have carefully prepared materials that provide:
—explanations of key ideas
—concise summaries of each topic
—thorough drill exercises
—realistic practice tests

All you need add is the determination to use these materials according to the schedule we have suggested. If you do, you will gain the confidence and knowledge you need to pass the High School Equivalency Examination and earn your high school equivalency certificate.

Acknowledgments

The authors gratefully acknowledge the kindness of all organizations concerned with the granting of permission to reprint passages, charts, graphs, and outlines.

We are indebted to Scholastic Magazines, Inc. for their kind permission to reproduce passages from *Senior Scholastic* which formed the basis for original questions interpreting items to be analyzed in social studies. Sources and permissions for charts and graphs appear on the appropriate pages throughout the book through the courtesy of the following organizations: U.S. Department of Agriculture; U.S. Department of Health, Education and Welfare—Office of Education; U.S. Bureau of the Budget; Social Security Administration and Statistics Canada.

Dr. Andrew Hughes contributed to the social studies chapter, and was assisted in the preparation of the 1992 social studies materials by his research assistants, Barbara Corbett and Cynthia Manderville; and in the 1994 revision by Kim Lynch.

The copyright holders and publishers of quoted materials are listed below.

Page 45, Passage for Items 13–14: from "The 51st Syndrome," by Robert J. Taylor, *Canada and the World*, Copyright © September 1989. Reprinted with the permission of *Canada and the World* magazine, Oakville, Ontario.

Pages 45–46, Passage for Items 15–16: from P. Waite, *Putting Canada Together*. Copyright © 1985 by Grolier, Toronto.

Page 48, Passage for Items 29–31: adapted from J. Hudson, J.P. Hornick, and B.A. Burrows (eds) *Justice and the Young Offender in Canada*. Copyright © 1988, 1993, Thompson Educational Publishing, Inc., Canada.

Page 50, Map and chart for items 38–39: *Globe & Mail*, Nov. 1993.

Pages 67–68, Passage for Items 16–20: from *A Raisin in the Sun*, by Lorraine Hansberry. Copyright © 1959, 1966, 1984 by Robert Nemiroff. Reprinted by permission of Random House, Inc.

Pages 284–285, Passage for Illustration 2: from *Politics in Canada* by Jackson, Jackson, and Baxter-Moore. Copyright © 1986 by Prentice Hall Canada Inc.

Page 289, Illustration 4: from Arthur H. Doerr and J.L. Guernsey, *Principles of Geography—Physical and Cultural*, Second Edition Revised. Copyright © 1975 Barron's Educational Series, Inc.

Page 294, Cartoon: Paul Lachine, *Portfoolio 15*. © Macmillan, Canada, 1999, p. 37.

Page 294, Cartoon: Cameron Cardow, *Portfoolio 15*. © Macmillan, Canada, 1999, p. 22

Page 295, Cartoon: Dusan Petricic, *Portfoolio 15*. © Macmillan, Canada, 1999, p. 8

Page 307, Passage for Item 8: From *Canadian Studies: Self and Society* by Munro, Doughty, and King. Copyright © 1975 Wiley of Canada.

Page 331, Passage for Items 7–9: from "Take Notice: An Introduction to Canadian Law," 2nd edition by Steven N. Spetz and Glenda S. Spetz, Copyright © 1984, Copp Clark Pitman Ltd. Used by permission of the publisher.

Page 332, Passage for Items 10–12: from *Politics in Canada* by Jackson, Jackson, and Baxter-Moore. Copyright © 1986 Prentice-Hall Canada Inc.

Page 339, Passage for Items 35–37: from Hutchinson B. *Mr. Prime Minister 1867–1964*. Copyright © 1964 Longmans, Toronto.

Pages 341–342, Passage for Items 44–46: from Erwin Rosenfeld and Harriet Geller, *Afro-Asian Culture Studies*, Second Revised Edition. Copyright © 1976 Barron's Educational Series, Inc.

Pages 342–343, Map and Passage for Items 47–49: from Erwin Rosenfeld and Harriet Geller, *Afro-Asian Culture Studies*, Second Revised Edition. Copyright © 1976 Barron's Educational Series, Inc.

Page 347, Passage for Items 62–64: Gordon H. Bower, "How to . . . Uh . . . Remember!" reprinted with permission from *Psychology Today Magazine*. Copyright © 1973 (Sussex Publishers, Inc).

Page 394, Passage for Items 18–20: from Baker-Allen, *Matter, Energy, and Life*. Third Edition. Copyright © 1974, Benjamin/Cummings Publishing Company, Menlo Park, California.

Page 398, Passage for Items 37–39: from Carl P. Swanson/Peter L. Webster, THE CELL, 5e, © 1985, p. 176. Reprinted by permission of Prentice Hall, Englewood Cliffs, New Jersey.

Page 465, Passage for Illustration of Commentary on the Arts: from "He Made Us Feel Like Dancing" by Brad Darrach in the July 6, 1987 issue of PEOPLE WEEKLY Magazine, by special permission. Copyright © 1987 by Time, Inc. All rights reserved.

Page 481, Passage for Items 51–55: from "Television," *The Twentieth Century: An Almanac*, p. 337. Copyright © 1985 by Bison Books Corp.

Page 752, Map for Items 21–24: From CANADA: PROFILE OF A NATION by John Molyneux and Eric Jones. Copyright © McGraw-Hill Ryerson Limited, 1974. Used by permission.

Page 778, Drawing for Item 9: from *What Was New France Like* by R. Craig and R. Noonan. Copyright © 1979 New Star Books.

Page 783, Passage for Item 39: from Cardinal H. *The Unjust Society: The Tragedy of Canada's Indians*. Copyright © 1969 Hurtig, Edmonton.

Page 857, Passage for Items 4–6: from *Politics in Canada* by Jackson, Jackson, and Baxter-Moore. Copyright © 1986 Prentice-Hall Canada, Inc.

Page 861, Passage for Items 27 and 28: from Arthur H. Doerr and J.L. Guernsey, *Principles of Geography—Physical and Cultural*, Second Edition Revised. Copyright © 1975 Barron's Educational Series, Inc.

1

THE GED HIGH SCHOOL EQUIVALENCY EXAMINATION

THE IMPORTANCE OF THE GED TESTS

The GED Tests give you the opportunity to earn an equivalency diploma. This diploma will enable you to continue your education, enhance your chances of finding a job, or even secure a job promotion.

WHAT ARE THE GED TESTS?

The emphasis in the GED Tests is on comprehension, application, analysis, and evaluation of reading materials and their data. We have incorporated this emphasis in our treatment of the five test areas: Writing Skills (Parts I and II), Social Studies, Science, Interpreting Literature and the Arts, and Mathematics. Each of these tests is described in detail.

TIMETABLE OF A HIGH SCHOOL EQUIVALENCY EXAMINATION

This timetable presents in chart form the sections of the examination, time allowed, number of test items in each section, and a description of the major parts of each test.

COMMONLY ASKED QUESTIONS ABOUT THE GED TESTS

Eight common questions about the GED Tests are answered. You learn who can take them, where they are given, what score is required for the diploma, how the required standard score relates to the number of correct answers, what types of questions appear, how experience outside school helps you, how to use your maturity and motivation, and how to determine when you are ready to take the GED Tests.

TO THE STUDENT

Throughout this book, we have decided to call the word given by the provincial testing authorities for passing all of the GED Tests by a standard name, "diploma." This is the name used for the award in Alberta, Manitoba, New Brunswick, Newfoundland, Northwest Territories, Nova Scotia, and Saskatchewan. British Columbia, Ontario, Prince Edward Island, and the Yukon use the word "certificate." No matter what you call it, after being granted this award a whole world of opportunities can open up to you. This piece of paper is worth all the effort.

The testing process also is called by many names. In some areas, the final evaluation is called an "exam," in others a "test." Rather than go back and forth and use both, we shall use the word "test" in this book. Remember that no matter what you choose to call it, this test is a series of multiple-choice questions, and, in order to complete it successfully, you must score above a specific number. The test is to be taken in a specific length of time, which means that you should be very much aware of time during all your preparation.

The GED Testing program is an international program introduced in Canada in 1969, and is designed for adults who have been unable to complete high school, but who have continued to learn through life and work experiences. Many adults learn through a variety of experiences encountered in everyday life. It is the purpose of the GED Testing program to provide a means by which learning acquired from such educational experiences can be evaluated and recognized. The GED Tests make it possible for qualified individuals to earn high school equivalency diplomas that enable them to obtain certain jobs, gain promotions, or pursue higher educational or other personal goals.

If you left high school without graduating, the GED Tests provide a way for you to earn your high school equivalency diploma. This book has been written especially to help you prepare for the GED Tests. The reviews, practice exercises, and practice tests will familiarize you with the content and format of the test sections. Over one million successful candidates have found this book helpful in earning a high school equivalency diploma.

Good luck in your studies. Keep one eye on the book and the other on the clock.

THE IMPORTANCE OF THE GED TESTS

By the age of 30, most of us have acquired about 30,000 transferrable skills. Since the GED Tests are tests of prior learning, everything we have learned will help us in passing the tests. Most of us, however, are not sure that we have learned much in the years since leaving school. For us, then, we have prepared a few worksheets. Work through them carefully and you will come to realize how much you really have learned. After each skill try to relate it to one of the test areas in the GED.

Let us look at work first. For each job you have held, describe the job, list the responsibilities you had and the skills you needed to do the job and whether they were learned or you had them before being hired, and what you learned on-the-job.

Position:
Job Description:

Responsibilities:		
Skills Required:	Learned Prior to Employment	Learned on-the-Job
1		
2		
3		
4		

What did I learn on-the-job:

Skill:	Literature	Mathematics	Science	Social Studies	Writing
1					
2					
3					
4					

For example, if you worked as a clerk in a pharmacy:

Position: *Clerk*

Think back to this position and list all the tasks you were required to perform.
Job Description: *I performed the following tasks:*
a *assisted customers in finding items*
b *accepted cash, charge, and debit card payments*
c *wrapped or bagged purchases*

What were your responsibilities in this job? What would not get done if you didn't do it?		
Responsibilities: *I was responsible for*		
a *maintaining a neat and tidy store*		
b *customer assistance*		
c *accepting cash and making change*		
d *completing credit card vouchers and checking totals*		
e *accepting debit card payments*		
f *entering amounts correctly into register*		
g *balancing register at end of each day*		
h *creating and maintaining restocking lists*		
i *writing reports on any issues that arose during the day*		
What skills were required and where did you learn them? Skills Required:	Learned Prior to Employment	Learned on-the-Job
1 *keeping store neat and tidy*		✓
2 *making change*		✓
3 *completing credit card vouchers*		✓
4 *writing reports*		✓

What did I learn on-the-job:

What subject area would have taught you skills similar to these?					
Skill:	Literature	Mathematics	Science	Social Studies	Writing
1 *keeping store neat and tidy*					
2 *making change*		✓			
3 *completing credit card vouchers*		✓			
4 *writing reports*					✓

From this simple example you can see that you did learn skills from doing this job; most were learned on-the-job and some related to school subjects. Make copies of this simple table and try it for each of the jobs that you have held.

WHAT ARE THE GED TESTS?

The GED Tests are a rigourous seven hour and thirty-five minute battery of tests in the core high school curriculum areas of writing skills, social studies, science, literature and the arts, and mathematics. The tests measure your ability to understand and apply information; to evaluate, analyze, and draw conclusions; and to express ideas and opinions in writing. The tests do not test how well you can remember minute facts, details, or exact definitions. If you have not completed high school, the tests give you the opportunity to demonstrate that you have achieved mastery of academic skills and concepts equal to that of a high school graduate. If you can successfully demonstrate that you have achieved this equivalent of education by passing the GED Tests, your achievement will be recognized with a formal certificate of "High School Equivalency."

With the exception of the essay part of the Writing Skills Test, all questions use a multiple-choice format in which a brief statement or short passage is given and then one or more questions are asked based on that statement or passage. On some of the tests, questions are also based on maps, graphs, tables, diagrams, or charts.

A brief description of each of the five GED Tests and of the changes for 2002 follow. More detailed information on each test can be found in later chapters.

THE TRANSITION TEXT

On January 1, 2002, a new series of tests will be administered to candidates for the secondary school equivalency certificate. The changes introduced in these tests will be evolutionary and are summarized in Chart A (page 6).

People using this book to prepare for the GED Tests should know that the tests will still be testing skill areas. The text presented may differ from test to test, but the basic skill set being tested will be the same. Any differences in test formats are noted here. For this transition text, both the new and old test names will be used, with the new names coming first.

THE LANGUAGE ARTS, WRITING (WRITING SKILLS) TEST

This test has been renamed "Language Arts, Writing" and will consist of two parts: Part I, the multiple-choice section, and Part II, the essay section. The scores for each section will be combined

Chart A: Charting the Course to 2002: A Summary of Changes to the GED Tests

Test	What's the Same	What's Been Eliminated	What's Included for 2002
Writing Skills (renamed Language Arts, Writing)	45-minute essay. Three item types (correction, revision, and construction shift). Sentence structure, usage, and mechanics. Informational documents (passages). Part I, multiple-choice, and Part II, essay. Examinee must complete both parts.	Spelling—except for homonyms, possessives, and contractions. Commas—tested only when they are used to eliminate confusion.	Business communications (letters, memos, reports, applications, etc.); "how to" texts (dressing for success, leasing a car, planning a trip, etc.); both 200–300 words, 12–18 sentences. Organization—transitions, text divisions, topic sentences, and unity/coherence. Essay scoring rubric changes from 6- to 4-point scale.
Social Studies	Multiple choice in sets and single items. Measures comprehension, application, analysis, and evaluation. Covers history, geography, civics, government, and economics. National, global, and adult contexts. Text and visual sources.	Behavioral science—psychology, sociology, anthropology—not tested as separate content areas. Some concepts tested within context of other areas.	More history, civics, and government. More graphics, photographs. More clearly defined content on U.S. and world history. More analysis. Different content areas tested within same item set. More single-item questions. At least one "practical" document (voter's guide, tax form, etc.). At least one excerpt from *U.S. Constitution*, *Declaration of Independence*, *Federalist Papers*, or landmark Supreme Court case.
Science	Multiple choice in sets and single items. Text and visual sources.	More single items. Fewer item sets.	Integrated with National Science Education Content Standards. Earth science includes space science. Physical science includes physics and chemistry. Increased focus on environmental and health topics (recycling, heredity, disease prevention, pollution, climate) and on science's relevance to everyday life. 50% Conceptual understanding, 50% problem-solving. Increase in graphic stimuli from 30% to 50%.
Interpreting Literature and the Arts (renamed Language Arts, Reading)	Reflect diversity—gender, ethnicity, age, region. Passages range from 300 to 400 words. One poem (8–25 lines) and one piece of drama represented. No graphics. Viewing addressed in textual manner.	Definitions: popular text and classical literature redefined as time periods; "Literal comprehension" now "comprehension." "Inferential comprehension" now "synthesis."	Content areas defined by type of text: literary (75%) and nonfiction (25%). At least one comparison/contrast question. Nonfiction will include one business document and one selection about visual representation. 20% Comprehension, 15% application, 30–35% analysis, 30–35% synthesis.
Mathematics	Measures algebra, geometry, number relations, and data analysis. 25% Setup questions—examinee must identify correct way to solve problem.	"Not sufficient information" questions decreased from 12% to 4%.	More emphasis on data analysis and statistics. Two parts: Part I permits calculator; Part II does not. Candidate will have practice time with calculator prior to test. Alternate-format items approximately 20%: item sets in which candidate must access multiple pieces of information—pie charts, bar graphs, tables. All candidates will use Casio fx-260 Solar.

and reported as a single score. Thus, you must finish both parts to complete this test and receive a satisfactory score.

PART I

In the multiple-choice section, spelling will no longer be tested except for homonyms, possessives, and contractions. Since this book is also used for preparation for other standardized exams, such as a section of the TOEFL tests, and for remedial work by secondary school students, these sections have been left in but are marked with an asterisk (*) to denote that they can be lightly covered by those studying for the GED Tests. Commas will be tested only in some circumstances, for example, when a comma is used to eliminate confusion.

In this book new types of material are presented as examples. Material from business and "how-to" texts is included in the questions. The skills being tested will still be from the areas of sentence structure, usage, and mechanics. In addition, however, the content area of organization will be tested. Organization involves developing a smooth transition between paragraphs, separating text into sections that effectively communicate the author's intention, effective topic sentences, and unity and coherence. The new additions are included in this text.

PART II

All candidates will continue to write a focussed, developed essay, which may require writing 250 words at least. Candidates will be asked to draw on their personal knowledge and experience in writing the essay. This section of the book prepares you to write the essay, but you will still need extensive practice. The ability to write a short essay is something that does not develop overnight. The three rules for writing good essays are practice and mark, practice and mark, and practice and mark.

THE SOCIAL STUDIES TEST

This test will consist of a series of prose texts from the areas of history, geography, civics and government, and economics. It will measure comprehension, application, analysis, and evaluation. The test will cover these skill areas. The texts presented may be different, but the tested skills are the same.

Psychology, sociology, and anthropology will not be tested as a separate content area, but the essence of these subjects will be tested in the context of other areas. The understanding and use of concepts related to human health and development will not be measured. However, people using this book should still work through all the questions, as the skills acquired will assist them in passing other tests. There will be more single-item questions. All practice is beneficial when preparing for tests.

More material on history, geography, economics, and government and civics will be presented.

There will be more emphasis on analysis as a skill area. Visual processing as a skill will be tested. There is a section on the visual presentation of content in this book which should be studied carefully.

THE SCIENCE TEST

The new science test has been made more relevant to modern life, and several topics have been combined to form new areas presented as text. Half of the new test will involve conceptual understanding, and half problem solving. There will be an increase in the graphic content of test questions. This book covers most of these areas, but it would be a good idea for candidates to read some additional material on modern science to become familiar with the concepts and vocabulary used in test questions. No test will require you to become a scientist to pass but will ask you to understand what scientists say and how they think.

THE LANGUAGE ARTS, READING (INTERPRETING LITERATURE AND THE ARTS) TEST

This test has been renamed "Language Arts, Reading." The content areas of popular text and classical literature will be displayed as time periods instead of as content areas, with 1950 as the transition time. The new periods will be pre-1920, 1920 to 1960, and 1960 to the present. Commentary on the arts has been integrated into nonfiction prose. There will be some technical redefinitions of skill areas, but they are not relevant to the preparation in this book.

THE MATHEMATICS TEST

The basics will still be tested on the new mathematics test. The emphasis will change somewhat, but the mathematics will still be the same. The major difference in the test is that it will be divided into two parts with the first part allowing the use of a calculator. Readers should remember that a calculator permits them to calculate faster but does not tell them what to calculate or whether to add, subtract, multiply, or divide. The reader must decide based on the question. In order to give the reader some experience with this option, the transitional edition of this book has some problems marked with a "C" at the end of the problem. A calculator can be used with these questions for practice. There will be an increased emphasis on visual material. Readers should remember to complete the chapter on visual material.

The scores for each section will be combined and reported as a single score. Thus, you must finish both parts to complete the test and receive a satisfactory score.

FINAL THOUGHTS

In general, although the tests are changing, this book is still a useful preparation tool. A single source may not be enough for thorough preparation, however, courses on preparation for the GED Tests are helpful. Setting up study groups to work on preparation will help you get ready. Writing the sample tests under controlled conditions will reduce your anxiety about tests. Whatever you can do to increase your skill levels will be helpful and worthwhile.

For more information check the GED website *http://www.acenet.edu/calec/ged/whatsNew* where additional information is posted.

This book gives the reader practice in the skills required to pass the GED Tests, but anyone planning on writing the tests should keep up-to-date by regularly consulting the GED website or entering "GED" into any of the popular search engines.

TIMETABLE OF A HIGH SCHOOL EQUIVALENCY EXAMINATION

Total: 7 hours, 5 minutes

	SECTION	TIME ALLOWED*	NUMBER OF TEST ITEMS*
Test 1	Language Arts, Writing		
	Part I	75 minutes	50
	Part II	45 minutes	1 Essay
Test 2	Social Studies Test	70 minutes	50
Test 3	Science Test	80 minutes	50
Test 4	Language Arts, Reading	65 minutes	40
Test 5	Mathematics Test	90 minutes	50

**Note:* Format and timing are subject to change with the introduction of the new series of tests.

A SPECIAL NOTE

Most provincial administrators will make special arrangements for applicants who have special needs. This may require some documentation that you would have to provide. Before contacting the proper authority, make sure that you have at least some documentation so that it can be sent early. It takes time to make special arrangements, and we do not all have the patience to wait.

The GED Tests are usually given over two days, Friday evening and all day Saturday. For some people, religious customs prevent them from taking exams on those days. If this is a problem for you, contact your provincial GED administrator immediately. Special arrangements can usually be made to take the examinations on other days, but you will have less selection of dates to take the examinations.

COMMONLY ASKED QUESTIONS ABOUT THE GED TESTS

1. ***Who can take the GED Tests?*** Adults who have not graduated from high school may take the GED Tests. In addition, you must meet the eligibility requirements established by your province or territory. Refer to Chapter 12 for the specific requirements in your area.

2. ***Where are the GED Tests given?*** The address and phone number of your provincial or territorial GED administrator can be found in Chapter 12. Contact the office in your area for further information regarding specific writing locations, dates, and times.

3. ***How are the GED Tests scored?*** GED Test scores are established by administering the tests to a national random sample of graduating high school seniors. This makes it possible to compare GED graduates with traditional high school graduates. Your GED Test scores are reported in two ways—in standard scores and in percentile ranks.

   Standard Scores

   The highest possible standard score on any of the five tests is 80. A score of 50 represents the average performance of graduating high school seniors. The standard score has been set so that only three quarters of graduating high school seniors would pass the GED Tests. **Remember, a standard score of 48 for example does not mean that you scored 48% out of a possible 100% as in high school.**

   Percentile Rank

   Percentile ranks are used to compare your test scores to those of a national graduating class of high school seniors. A percentile rank shows the percentage of graduating high school seniors who earned a certain standard score.

   For example, if your percentile rank on a test is 71, this means that 71% of graduating high school seniors did not do as well as you on that test, and 29% did better. In other words, you did better on the test than 71% of graduating high school seniors.

4. ***What score is required to earn a high school equivalency diploma?*** In each province across the country, you must get a minimum standard score of 45 to pass that test. Refer to Chapter 12 for specific score requirements.

5. ***What types of questions are on the GED Tests?*** Part II of the Writing Skills Test requires a written essay. In all other test sections a multiple-choice format is used. Five answer choices are offered for each question. There are sets of questions based on written selections, illustrations, graphs, charts, or tables. There are also single questions in many test areas. Chapters 4 through 9 will further discuss and give examples of the individual test questions. In Chapters 3 and 11, three full-length examinations exemplify the format and question types you will encounter on the actual examination.

6. ***How can experience outside the classroom help?*** Instead of thinking positively, many adults overemphasize their reasons for leaving school, the gap of years since attending school, and their inability to concentrate: In fact, learning continues after you leave school. You read newspapers and follow political events; you travel and converse with people; you listen to the radio, watch television programs, and go to the movies. These experiences add to your educational background and provide a base for new learning.

7. ***How are maturity and motivation strong assets?*** More mature students are better able to comprehend or visualize a situation that may be part of a problem. Older students also understand the need for proper study habits. With the mature decision to study for the GED Tests, half the battle is over. Many educators regard motivation, the desire to learn, as the first step toward success.

8. ***When will I be ready to take the GED Tests?*** After reviewing and doing practice exercises, take the practice tests in Chapter 11. Score your results. If your scores are in the categories Good or Excellent, you are probably ready to walk into the examination room with confidence. If you did not attain such scores, do not apply for the GED Tests until you have studied further.

Concentrate on the areas in which you are weak. A 30-session study schedule is part of Chapter 2.

9. ***Who accepts the GED Tests?*** The tests are widely accepted as a basis for awarding high school equivalency credentials. The credentials issued on the basis of GED Tests scores are generally considered satisfactory high school graduation requirements for purposes of employment, promotion, and licencing. For admissions purposes, most colleges and universities accept GED scores in place of a completed high school transcript although, as with a traditional high school graduate, some post-secondary programs require the successful completion of certain subjects to supplement your high school credentials.

10. ***If I don't pass the GED Tests, can I take them again?*** Yes, you may take any test(s) again in which the required standard score was not attained. If your grade was between 40 and 44, there are no restrictions, but you will be charged another fee. If your grade was less than 40, you must wait at least 3 months. This gives you a chance to review and relearn to prepare for the next test(s). If a second exam is needed, there is another waiting period. In some cases that may be as long as 6 months or as short as 3 months. The waiting period is to ensure that you do not take the same test twice. Although Canadian jurisdictions are attempting to coordinate their annual introduction of the new tests to be in September of each year, that is still not the case as of the writing of this section. If a student's first test was at the end of the previous year, and their second test was at the beginning of the next year, a shorter waiting period is possible. The best course of action if you must take any or all of the tests is to contact your local GED coordinator to get a ruling on when you may schedule a new exam date.

11. ***What should I take to the examinations?*** You will have to bring satisfactory identification. Some provinces require identification bearing your photograph. Other jurisdictions require that the identification bear your signature. Determine before arriving at the test centre, what must be brought, and bring it. Everything else you need, such as pens, pencils, and paper will be provided. No reference material, notes, or formulae may be brought into the examination room. Formulae are provided for you in the Mathematics test. If you think you need a particular skill or knowledge, prepare ahead of time to ensure that you know it. What is part of your knowledge always travels with you.

12. ***What can I expect at the test centre?*** You can expect to take all five exams within the times listed unless special arrangements have been made on the basis of special needs. You will have to arrive at least a half hour early to ensure time for identification to be checked and for other administrative duties to be performed. Except for Part II of the Writing Skills examination, all questions are multiple choice and must be answered on the answer sheet. No one will mark your rough work for extra answers. Make sure that you have left enough time at the end to ensure that each question is answered.

13. ***Is guessing a good idea?*** The best answer is to know the work and to mark the correct answer. The world, however, is not perfect and you will find questions whose answers elude you. It is better in these cases to guess. If you can eliminate some of the answers as obviously wrong, your chances of guessing the right answer are improved. If you can eliminate four of the answers as obviously wrong, you will always get the right answer. You receive no marks for a blank answer and no points are deducted for wrong answers.

14. ***What if I still have questions on taking the test?*** If you are preparing on your own, contact the GED administrator for your area and ask. If you are enrolled at a preparation centre, ask your instructor. If you are still unsure, ask the GED administrator for the area. Make sure that you get an answer well in advance of taking the test. Going into the test is not the best time to have a lot of unanswered questions on your mind.

15. ***How can I handle the stress of taking the examinations?*** Examinations cause stress in most people. You can look upon the stress of preparing for and taking the GED Tests as a motivation. The better you are prepared . . . the more confident you are of your abilities . . . the less stress you will feel. However, even the best prepared, most confident student feels stress around examinations. Learn to relax. There are good books in the library on relaxation techniques. Read a few and see if there are any lessons about relaxation you can learn before the examinations.

2

ORGANIZING YOUR PLAN OF STUDY

SOME STUDY HINTS

Nine study hints relate to physical conditions of studying, timing, a workable study schedule, efficiency of study time, review periods, writing while studying, reading, and use of the dictionary.

THE DICTIONARY

We identify four essential dictionary skills and seven benefits of dictionary use.

BEFORE THE TEST DATE

This advice pertains to using this book, practicing reading and writing, setting the right test time, and relaxing.

TACTICS AND STRATEGIES IN THE EXAMINATION ROOM

Twelve suggestions cover reading directions, handing questions, checking answers, using examination time, guessing, and marking answers properly.

SUGGESTED STUDY TACTICS

Thirty home-study sessions are planned for you. Following the schedule prevents you from omitting essential areas and not devoting proper amounts of time to them. The schedule covers all material on the examination and in this book.

SOME STUDY HINTS

Educators agree that in order for learning to be efficient certain steps must be followed. As a mature person, you will probably appreciate the value of carefully following these rules for successful study.

1. **PHYSICAL CONDITIONS.** Find a quiet place. Have no distractions—noise or music. Do not work in an overheated room.

2. **TIMING.** You will learn faster and remember longer if you study in several short sessions rather than in one long session. Do not attempt to study for an entire weekend. Fatigue will set in after a few hours. It is wiser to spend some time each day rather than to "cram" your work into one or two days.

3. **SCHEDULE FOR STUDY.** A study schedule must be workable, realistic, practical, and above all suited to you and your other obligations. Decide which days and hours you can spare for study. Make a schedule, and stick to it.

4. **USING ODD MOMENTS.** Put spare time and wasted moments to work. Riding in the bus or train may be a good time to memorize troublesome spelling words and to study rules of grammar or definitions of newly acquired terms.

5. **EFFICIENCY.** Most people find that learning occurs faster in the early part of the day. Perhaps you can work into your schedule some time for study before your day's work begins or on weekend mornings. Certainly you should not schedule yourself for study in the later hours of the evening.

6. **REVIEW PERIODS.** On certain days, plan to review. Take stock of yourself in these study periods. Check up on yourself. This will serve at least two purposes. It will definitely reinforce the learning, and the gratification of knowing that you have acquired new material will stimulate you to go on to learn more.

7. **WRITE WHILE YOU LEARN.** Wherever possible, write what you are studying. Spelling can best be learned by writing. Get into the habit of writing down key ideas of the passages you read. It will focus attention on your learning. It will avoid distractions that may cause your mind to wander. It will give you an opportunity to check up on yourself. Also, educators believe that the more senses employed in studying, the more effective the learning will be.

8. **READ, READ, READ.** The best way to improve reading comprehension is by practicing reading. You will find that a great part of the test involves the interpretation of reading material. Read your newspaper very carefully. Make it a habit to read the editorials. If possible, engage a member of your family or a friend in frequent discussions of the ideas presented in your newspaper. Of course, this book has specific reading exercises on the various phases of the test. But remember, there is no substitute for general reading.

9. **THE DICTIONARY.** The most important single book, in addition to this one, that can help you prepare for the High School Equivalency Examinations is the dictionary. It is important for you to have one nearby as you study.

THE DICTIONARY

What You Must Know to Use the Dictionary

You must know:

1. **How to Alphabetize.** These words are taken from the page of a widely used dictionary.

fuel
fugitive
fugue
Fuhrer
fulcrum
fulfill
fulgent
full
fullback

All these words begin with "fu . . ." and, to locate *fugue*, your eye must be able to pick out "fug" as coming between "fue" and "Fuh" on the page.

2. **How to Use Guide Words.** All dictionaries have two words at the top of each page. All words on that page come alphabetically between the words given. For example, on the page mentioned in item 1, the guide words are "fuel" and "funny." You can locate the word *funeral* a lot faster if your eye moves over the two guide words at the top of the page ("funeral" comes between "fuel" and "funny") rather than all the words on that page.

   Try your hand at the following. The guide words are "heartache" and "hedge." Which of these words are found on that page: Hebrew, height, heathen, headquarters, heaven, heckle, helicopter, heavy?

3. **Certain Abbreviations.** Most dictionaries give you a list of the abbreviations they use on the page or pages immediately preceding the *first* page of definitions. The abbreviations, for the most part, concern grammatical parts of speech (*v.*, verb) and countries where words originated (*Scot.*, Scottish).

4. **How to Choose the Suitable Definition.** Take this dictionary entry as an example:

   sheer *adj.* **1.** very thin, transparent: said of textiles **2.** absolute, downright: as, *sheer* folly **3.** extremely steep

   It is obvious that the three definitions have no relationship to one another. You must match one of the definitions to the phrase, clause, or sentence in which the word appears. Try to choose the suitable definition for each of the following sentences:

   (1) She wore *sheer* stockings.
   (2) He fell over the *sheer* cliff.
   (3) They spoke *sheer* nonsense.

What the Dictionary Can Do for You

1. **It Can Help You with Spelling.** You find that you have to use the word *embar?as?ed?* in some writing you are doing. You're not sure of the spelling. Are there two *r*'s or one? Two *s*'s or one? Your dictionary has the answer. Check it and you won't be *embarrassed*.

   In addition, your dictionary will help you to divide the word into syllables. You note that the word is broken up as follows: *em bar rassed*. You now know where to put the hyphen when you come to the end of a line of writing and you must break up the word.

2. **It Can Help You with Meaning.** You find that you cannot understand a passage you are reading because you do not know the meaning of a key word. Let us take, for example, a passage in biology that uses the word *nucleus* again and again. Your dictionary will list all the meanings of the word in order of the frequency in which they are used, the most frequent first, the least frequent last. The dictionary we have been referring to lists four meanings, the fourth definition reading "**4.** in *biology*, the central mass of protoplasm in a cell." You now can make sense of the paragraph or selection you are reading.

3. **It Can Help You with Pronunciation.** You find you have to use the name of the city, *Detroit*, in a talk you are giving. You are not sure where the accent falls. Is it on the first syllable *De-* or on the second syllable *-troit*? You look up the name in the dictionary and find next to the word the markings (di-troit′) and you know that the name of the city is accented on the second syllable. By the way, the key to the sounds represented by these markings (called diacritical marks) is generally found on the bottom of the page.

4. **It Can Help You with Grammar.** You find you have to use the past tense of the verb *lie* meaning "to be in a reclining position." You look up the word and you find the part of speech *v.i.* (indicating verb, intransitive) as well as the principal parts *lay*, *lain*, *lying*. You now know that the sentence you want to use should read "I lay under the tree for four hours."

You can also find the plural for some very troublesome nouns. Is it *heros* or *heroes*? The dictionary leaves no doubt. It indicates (*pl. -roes*).

5. **It Can Help You with Usage.** You find that you'd like to use the word *cop* meaning "policeman" in a formal letter you are writing to a city official. You dictionary indicates (Slang) before the definition, so you know that good form does not allow you to use the word as you had wanted.

   You find you want to use the word *girl* in the sense of sweetheart—"introducing my girl to my parents." You check the dictionary and you find (Colloq.) before the definition. This means you may use the word when speaking but it is not advisable that you use it in formal writing:

   > *A word of caution:* Dictionaries often disagree on levels of usage. What may be *Slang* to one is *Colloquial* to another. What is *Colloquial* to one may be completely acceptable to another. Always be certain to check a good dictionary and be guided by it.

6. **It Can Help You Build Your Vocabulary by Providing the Origin of Words and by Indicating Word Families.** You check the word *telescope*. You learn it comes from the Greek *tele*, "far off," and *scope*, "to view." You notice that other words on the page use the combing form *tele*: telecast, telegram, telegraph, telephone, telephoto, teletype, television. You have learned a whole family of words. In addition, you can add the family of *scope* words: horoscope, kinescope, microscope, periscope, as well as just plain *scope*.

7. **It Can Help You with Information on Literature and Social Studies.** You can find references to mythology (Midas) and to literature (*Hamlet*). You can find place names in geography (New York) and in history (Valley Forge). You can find references to biblical names (Babel). You can find the meaning of such well-known phrases as "auld lang syne."

BEFORE THE TEST DATE

1. **Use this book wisely.** This book can help you achieve your goal—the High School Equivalency Diploma. After you take the diagnostic Pre-Test, you will discover your specific weaknesses and concentrate your review on these areas. Study the examination strategies, and apply them when you do the exercises and take the practice tests.

2. **Practice reading and writing.** Besides using the material in this book, spend more time reading. Give yourself more time with the daily newspaper and with magazines. Take sides on issues as they appear in editorials. Also practice writing. Write letters to friends and relatives. Instead of using the telephone, use your pen.

3. **Don't rush to take the test.** Don't apply for the examination prematurely. Make certain that you are adequately prepared by testing yourself with the exercises and tests in this book. It is far better to postpone taking the examination until success can reasonably be expected than to go into the test at an earlier date trusting to good fortune. Although many provinces have arrangements for retesting after a waiting period, the notice of failure is an unpleasant experience and may discourage you from further success. Last-minute cramming seldom leads to success. It is advisable to extend your preparation for the test over a reasonably long period of time.

4. **Know what to expect.** By the time you finish the preparation material in this book, you will be familiar with all the kinds of questions that are going to appear on the GED Tests. The exercises and practice test questions in this book are very similar to the actual test questions. Knowing what to expect will relieve some of your anxiety about taking the exam.

5. **Be relaxed.** It is highly desirable to relax the night before the test. A good night's sleep will put your body in a better condition to think logically. You'll be well rested and alert.

TACTICS AND STRATEGIES IN THE EXAMINATION ROOM

1. Take one form of identification to the test centre. You will be required to produce a form of identification that includes a photo so that the examiner has no doubt as to who you are. You will be asked to sign a sheet to verify your attendance. All other supplies such as paper, pens, pencils, etc., will be provided at the testing centre.

2. Allow plenty of time for getting to the test centre. Taking a test is pressure enough. You don't need the extra tension that comes from worrying about whether you will get there on time.

3. Read all directions and questions carefully. Answer the question given, not what you expected it to be. Look for key words, such as except, exactly, and not. Carefully examine charts, tables, graphs and illustrations so you don't miss important information.

4. Don't expect trick questions. A straightforward presentation is used in all test sections.

5. When you have difficulty finding your answer, eliminate those that are definitely wrong. Then consider the remaining choices.

6. Don't let one or two challenging questions upset you. Some questions are definitely harder than others. Remember you do not have to get 100% on this test. No one does.

7. Don't get bogged down on any one question. If a question is taking too much time, circle it and make a guess. Then, if you have time at the end of the test, go back and review those answers.

8. Change answers only if you have a good reason for doing so. Don't change your answer on a hunch or a whim. Most often the first judgment that you make is correct.

9. As you go through the test, be sure that the number on your answer sheet matches the corresponding number for the question you are answering. This is extremely important; the test will be machine-graded, and the computer will assume that you have marked your answers in the correct position.

10. Use your time wisely. After taking the practice tests in this book, you will become familiar with the proper pace needed to complete each test.

11. Be careful not to make stray pencil marks on the answer sheet. These may interfere with the rating of your performance. If you wish to change an answer, be sure to erase your first mark completely. The rating machine will automatically mark an answer wrong if more than one choice is made. Also, do not fold or crease the answer sheet.

12. Answer all questions, even if you have to guess. Your score will be determined by the number of correct answers; no points are deducted for wrong answers. It is better to guess at an answer than not to respond at all because there is a chance of getting some questions right. Of course, wherever possible, eliminate as many wrong answers as you can before guessing. Every answer you eliminate improves your chances of guessing correctly.

13. Remain as calm as possible. If you consider yourself a person who "goes to pieces" on tests, cheer up! Psychologists claim that more than 90% of us think we don't perform well on tests *of any kind.* Nobody likes tests. But more than 80% of the people who have taken the High School Equivalency Tests in the Toronto area, for example, have passed them. They must be doing something right. And so can you—with the right attitude and careful preparation.

SUGGESTED STUDY TACTICS

AN INDIVIDUAL STUDY METHOD

Looking at this book and at the task of preparing for five tests is enough to frighten most people. But, you are determined to use your knowledge to gain that high school equivalency diploma that you want and/or need. The only way to do that is to be methodical in your preparation. You do not have enough time to concentrate on everything you know well as well as everything you need extra help with. You need a system.

1. **Use the Pre-Test:** Each subject area has a diagnostic Pre-Test. If you do this test within the time limits set, you will discover the extent of your strengths and weaknesses.
   In order to use your time efficiently, you should spend the most time on your weak areas and the least time on your strengths. Mark each Pre-Test using the answers provided. Using the chart at the end of the Pre-Test, circle each item number that you had incorrect. Calculate the percentage of correct answers and put a mark in the appropriate box. This will give you a representation of your initial levels in each content area.

2. **Develop a Personal Prescription and Schedule:** After marking your Pre-Test, use the charts at the end of each diagnostic Pre-Test to develop a list of the pages and exercises in the book that will help you achieve your goal. We have included Prescription Charts to help you organize this task. Check each content area in which you scored below 80%. These are your areas of weakness. Wherever you have scored over 80%, congratulate yourself and go on. Wherever you have scored less than 80%, go through the explanations for the items in those content areas and proceed with the prescription suggested.

MARK	DIAGNOSTIC
below 80%	Areas of Weakness a. go through the explanations for each question you missed b. proceed with the prescription suggested
above 80%	Areas of Strength Carry on

Make sure that you check every answer, and if you made a mistake, find out why and correct it. The first choice of material to help you find out why you made a mistake is the book. The second is people around you who may have more educational experience than you. If these are not an option or if you are more comfortable learning in groups, consider enrolling in a preparation course. Preparation courses are offered by some school boards, community colleges, community agencies, and private preparers. Shop around until you find one that suits your needs and your budget.

To develop a schedule, you have to know the last date to finish your preparation and the first day you can begin working towards your goal. After considering whether or not you wish to work on weekends, count the number of days you have to meet your goal. We would suggest leaving the weekends for a safety valve. If you finish all the work you had planned for that week by Friday evening, you deserve a rest. If not, you have two days to catch up.

A. Number of Days to Reach My Goal = __________

Realistically think through the number of hours you can spend on preparation each day. Double-check this figure to ensure you have not forgotten anything that takes time like working, eating, or sleeping.

B. Number of Hours Each Day for Preparation = __________

By multiplying the number of hours each day by the number of days, you will reach a possible number of hours for preparation. Assume that things will come up without warning, and multiply the number of hours by 0.8. This gives you a safety factor. If things often come up unexpectedly in your life, multiply by 0.6. It is always better to have some time left before the tests than to have some studying left after the tests.

C. Number of Hours I Have to Prepare for the GED Exams = A × B × 0.8 = __________

This number is the number of hours we have to work with for scheduling. Since there are five exams, if you were equally as strong or weak in each, you could just divide the total number of hours by five, and that would be the number of hours to spend preparing. However, you will probably score differently in each test. Use the scheduling sheets to figure out the amount of time to spend on each subject area. Allow the most time for the subject area test with the lowest score.

3. **Carry Out Your Preparation Plan:** You have to work on your plan each day, and modify it. If you need additional schedules, copy the one you used and make modifications in a different colour. That way, you will see the changes.

4. **Try a Sample Test:** Try a sample test within the time limits recommended. Compare this score with the score on your Pre-Test. If you are improving, keep reviewing your weakest areas. If you are not improving, consider trying a course or class. You may need an instructor and others around you to prepare successfully for the exams.

5. **The Final Test:** Before the tests, try the last test in the book. Analyze your mistakes and review any weak areas. Then relax and wait for your test date. Keep telling yourself not to panic. You have reviewed all the work that was marginal, learned all the work that was unknown, and prepared yourself to take a multiple-choice test. There is little else you can do except take the tests.

6. **A Reminder:** To achieve success in these exams, you are preparing by changing your weaknesses into strengths by persistent practice, review, and learning.
   Good Luck!

PREPARATION WORK SHEET

A. NUMBER OF DAYS TO REACH MY GOAL = ____________
B. NUMBER OF HOURS EACH DAY FOR PREPARATION = ____________
C. NUMBER OF HOURS I HAVE TO PREPARE FOR THE GED EXAMS = $A \times B \times 0.8 =$ ____________

MY DIAGNOSTIC PRE-TEST SCORES

Subject Area	Score	Rank	Hours Allocated
1. Language Arts, Writing (Writing Skills), Part I			
2. Language Arts, Writing (Writing Skills), Part II			
3. Social Studies			
4. Science			
5. Language Arts, Reading (Interpreting Literature and the Arts)			
6. Mathematics			

If your score in a diagnositic Pre-Test is:	Allocate the following percentage of your time to that area:
80 to 100%	just review
50 to 80%	up to 20%
under 50%	CONSIDER REMEDIAL OR PREPARATION CLASSES

NOTE: Any remaining time can be spent in reviewing the general skills for Reading comprehension, Science vocabulary, or Mathematics concepts, depending on which is your weakest subject area.

PLANNING SCHEDULE

Look over your study plans. Use the chart to decide which area you should concentrate on for each period. Make sure that you block out periods of time that are not available to you for study and preparation.

Each person has a unique schedule. This is a schedule for a 24-hour-day. Block out areas that you cannot or will not study. Thus, you will end up with a few blocks each day that you can use to prepare for the GED tests.

	MONDAY	TUESDAY	WEDNESDAY	THURSDAY	FRIDAY	SATURDAY	SUNDAY
Midnight							
1:00							
2:00							
3:00							
4:00							
5:00							
6:00							
7:00							
8:00							
9:00							
10:00							
11:00							
Noon							
1:00							
2:00							
3:00							
4:00							
5:00							
6:00							
7:00							
8:00							
9:00							
10:00							
11:00							

Preparation Planning Flow Diagram

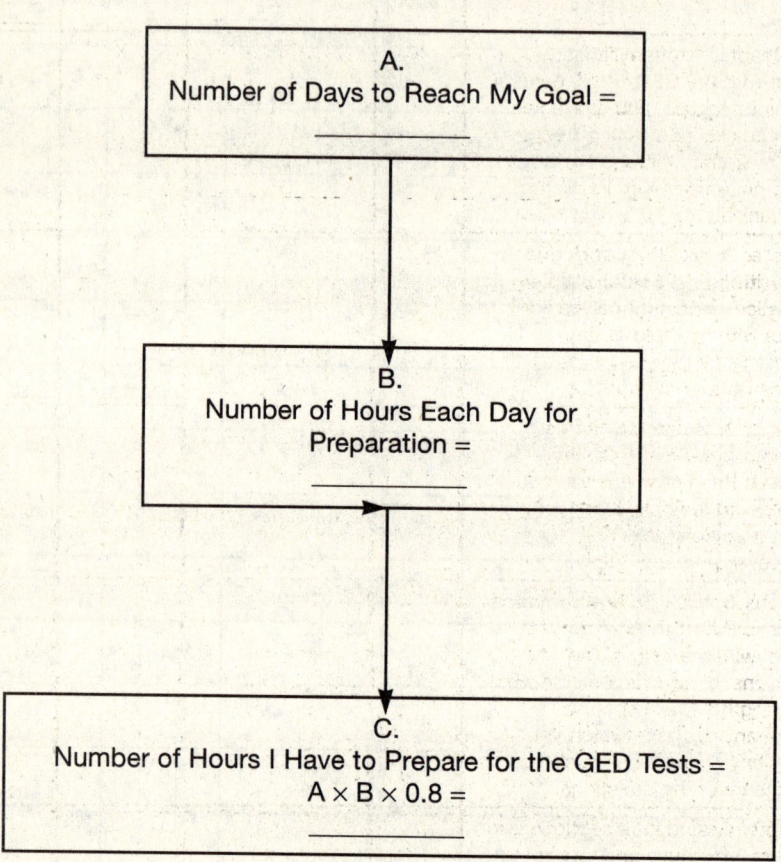

A.
Number of Days to Reach My Goal =
____

B.
Number of Hours Each Day for Preparation =
____

C.
Number of Hours I Have to Prepare for the GED Tests =
$A \times B \times 0.8 =$
____

Instructions:

A. Determine the number of days you have available to reach your goal. You might consider omitting weekends, and leaving those days for relaxation or as a safety valve if you run into problems during the week.

B. Determine the number of hours you have available for preparation each day. Do this realistically so that you can actually work this number of hours each day.

C. Multiply the number of days by the number of hours to calculate the ideal number of hours. Multiply by 0.8 because we are just human beings and will be distracted some of the time.

A STUDY PLAN

This plan will be most useful if you use it as a planning aid after taking the diagnostic Pre-Tests. Each session can be of varying length. You may find that an hour session in one area is too long, while a four-hour session is too short in another area. Adjust the time to fit your individual needs. For areas of weakness, plan longer study sessions, or divide the study session into parts. For areas of strength use shorter study sessions and use the extra time for review. If you are weak in this area, emphasize sessions indicated.

SESSION NUMBER	ACTIVITY	READ-ING	MATHEMATICS	SCIENCE	SOCIAL STUDIES	WRITING
1	Read Chapter 1 to familiarize yourself with the GED Tests, general study hints, tactics, and strategies. Plan a specific individual schedule for study. Glance through the book to become familiar with the setup and organization.	X	X	X	X	X
2	In Chapter 3, take the **Language Arts, Writing and Social Studies** diagnostic Pre-Tests. Analyze your answers with the help of the instructions. Note your weaknesses and strengths.				X	X
3	In Chapter 3, take the **Science and Language Arts, Reading** diagnostic Pre-Tests. Analyze your answers with the help of the instructions. Note your weaknesses and strengths.	X		X		
4	In Chapter 3, take the **Mathematics** diagnostic Pre-Test. Analyze your answers with the help of the instructions. Note your weaknesses and strengths. Make specific notes of any topics in which you made many errors or in which you were unsure of the questions.		X			
5	In Chapter 4, study the sections on **sentence structure and usage.** If you were weak in this section on the diagnostic Pre-Test, do all the practice exercises. If you did well, do every other question. Check your answers and the answer analysis. If you did not score over 80%, review the section and do any questions you left out.					X
6	In Chapter 4, study the sections on **mechanics and additional writing skills**. If you were weak in this section on the diagnostic Pre-Test, do all the practice exercises. If you did well, do every other question. Check your answers and the answer analysis. If you did not score over 80%, review the section and do any questions you left out.					X

SESSION NUMBER	ACTIVITY	READ-ING	MATHEMATICS	SCIENCE	SOCIAL STUDIES	WRITING
7	In Chapter 4, work on the sample **paragraphs**. Do all the practice exercises if your diagnostic Pre-Test mark was low. If not, do every other question. Mark your answers carefully and study the answers. If you scored less than 80%, do and correct any questions you omitted.					X
8	Study and do all practice exercises in Chapter 5. Write several **essays** using the suggested topics and mark them using the scoring guide on page 271. If you score low on any essay, review the guide to see where you could improve.					X
9	In Chapter 11, take the **Language Arts, Writing Tests, Parts I and II** (Practice Test One). Check your answers and analyze your errors. Study the analysis of the answers for the questions you got wrong. If you scored less than 80%, go back and review the section.					X
10	In Chapter 6, study the analyzed passages on the basics in **Social Studies**.				X	
11	Study the **Glossary** of Social Studies Terms in Chapter 6. Do the **Concept** questions as well as the **Reading Passage** questions. If you scored well in the diagnostic Pre-Test, do every other question. Check and analyze your errors. If you scored less than 80%, do any questions that you omitted. Analyze your errors.				X	
12	In Chapter 11, take the **Social Studies Test** (Practice Test One). Check your answers and analyze your errors. Study the analysis of the answers for the questions you got wrong. If you scored less than 80%, go back and review the section.				X	
13	In Chapter 10, study the basics for interpreting **tables, graphs, diagrams, and maps**. Begin the practice exercises. Check your answers. For any incorrect answers, return to the section to review it.		X	X	X	

SESSION NUMBER	ACTIVITY	READ-ING	MATHEMATICS	SCIENCE	SOCIAL STUDIES	WRITING
14	In Chapter 7, read about the **Science Test**. Study the sample questions. Examine the outline of Science topics. Check the diagnostic Pre-Test for your areas of weakness. Concentrate on these areas. Review the Glossary of terms. Look up any unfamiliar terms in the library.			X		
15	In Chapter 7, do the practice exercises in **Biology**. If you scored high in the diagnostic Pre-Test, do every other question. Mark your answers and study the correct answers. If you got less than 80%, go back and do any questions you omitted. If you still are making mistakes review the section again. Look up any unfamiliar terms in the Glossary, and note the ones you may need to review before the final test.			X		
16	In Chapter 7, do the practice exercises in **Earth Science**. If you scored high in the diagnostic Pre-Test, do every other question. Mark your answers and study the correct answers. If you got less than 80%, go back and do any questions you omitted. If you still are making mistakes review the section again. Look up any unfamiliar terms in the Glossary, and note the ones you may need to review before the final test.			X		
17	In Chapter 7, do the practice exercises in **Chemistry** and **Physics**. If you scored high in the diagnostic Pre-Test, do every other question. Mark your answers and study the correct answers. If you got less than 80%, go back and do any questions you omitted. If you still are making mistakes review the section again. Look up any unfamiliar terms in the Glossary, and note the ones you may need to review before the final test.			X		
18	In Chapter 11, take the **Science Test** (Practice Test One). Check your answers and analyze your errors. Study the analysis of the answers for the questions you got wrong. If you scored less than 80%, go back and review the section.			X		

SESSION NUMBER	ACTIVITY	READ-ING	MATHEMATICS	SCIENCE	SOCIAL STUDIES	WRITING
19	In Chapter 8, study the material on **reading skills and skills in interpreting classical and popular literature**. Do all the practice exercises on **popular literature** if your diagnostic Pre-Test mark was low. If not, do every other question. Mark your answers carefully and study the answers. If you scored less than 80%, do and correct any questions you omitted.	X				
20	In Chapter 8, review the material on **classical literature**. Do all the practice exercises if your diagnostic Pre-Test mark was low. If not, do every other question. Mark your answers carefully and study the answers. If you scored less than 80%, do and correct any questions you omitted.	X				
21	In Chapter 8, study the material on **commentary about literature**. Do all the practice exercises if your diagnostic Pre-Test mark was low. If not, do every other question. Mark your answers carefully and study the answers. If you scored less than 80%, do and correct any questions you omitted.	X				
22	In Chapter 11, take the **Language Arts, Reading Test** (Practice Test One). Check your answers and analyze your errors. Study the analysis of the answers for the questions you got wrong. If you scored less than 80%, go back and review the section.	X				
23	In Chapter 9, review the basics of the **Mathematics** section. Check for unfamiliar terms and learn their meanings. Review the section on **Arithmetic**. Do all the practice exercises if your diagnostic Pre-Test mark was low. If not, do every other question. Mark your answers carefully and study the answers. If you scored less than 80%, do and correct any questions you omitted.		X			
24	In Chapter 9, review the basics of **Algebra**. Check for unfamiliar terms and learn their meanings. Review the section on **Algebra**. Do all the practice exercises if your diagnostic Pre-Test mark was low. If not, do every other question. Mark your answers carefully and study the answers. If you scored less than 80%, do and correct any questions you omitted.		X			

SESSION NUMBER	ACTIVITY	READ-ING	MATHEMATICS	SCIENCE	SOCIAL STUDIES	WRITING
25	In Chapter 9, review the basics of **Geometry and Graphs** (see also Chapter 11). Check for unfamiliar terms and learn their meanings. Review the section on **Geometry and Graphs**. Do all the practice exercises if your diagnostic Pre-Test mark was low. If not, do every other question. Mark your answers carefully and study the answers. If you scored less than 80%, do and correct any questions you omitted.		X			
26	In Chapter 9, take the **Mathematics** practice tests. Mark your answers carefully and study the answers. If you scored less than 80%, do and correct any questions you omitted.		X			
27	In Chapter 11, take the **Language Arts, Writing, Parts I and II and Reading Tests** (PracticeTest Two). Keep within the specified times. Check your answers carefully. Analyze your errors. Refer to the analysis of the correct answers.					X
28	In Chapter 11, take the **Social Studies Test** (Practice Test Two). Keep within the specified times. Check your answers carefully. Analyze your errors. Refer to the analysis of the correct answers.				X	
29	In Chapter 11, take the **Science Test** (Practice Test Two). Keep within the specified times. Check your answers carefully. Analyze your errors. Refer to the analysis of the correct answers.			X		
30	In Chapter 11, take the **Mathematics Tests** (Practice Test One and Two). Keep within the specified times. Check your answers carefully. Analyze your errors. Refer to the analysis of the correct answers.		X			

A WORD ABOUT TIME

Don't try to learn everything or take every test in one session. Go at your own speed and in your own way. A book can't be completely flexible—but we urge you to be flexible in using this book to suit your individual needs. If you need review in math but feel pretty confident about English, concentrate on the math. If you want to try the exams first and skip a study section, do it. Remember that High School Equivalency Exams are given frequently. Remember especially that, if you fail one test, you can take another. But you probably will take only one test in each of the five parts—and pass the first time! That is what this book aims to help you do.

3

DIAGNOSTIC PRE-TESTS

DIAGNOSTIC PRE-TESTS

These Diagnostic Pre-Tests are designed to help you define your strengths and weaknesses before beginning to prepare to take the GED tests. An efficient plan of study concentrates on remediating weaknesses. Test times are indicated on each test. Complete the test within that time. If you need much more time to complete any section, you have a very good indication that either you are very uncertain about this section, you are having problems with the vocabulary, or you need help in taking multiple-choice exams.

The questions in this Pre-Test are similar in style and difficulty to the questions on the actual tests. There are fewer questions on each test because we want to help you devise an efficient study plan by diagnosing your strengths and weaknesses. This book has been designed for self-study, and these Diagnostic Pre-Tests will help you become your own best tutor.

ANSWER KEYS, SUMMARIES OF RESULTS, AND SELF-APPRAISAL CHARTS

For each of the five tests, you will find answer keys to score yourself. Our charts enable you to summarize your results according to content areas so you can locate where most errors occurred. In effect, you are diagnosing your strengths and weaknesses.

ANSWER ANALYSIS

The answer analysis contains *two complete model essays* found in no other book. They are based on the assigned topic and include outlines of the arguments presented. Each essay takes one side of the issue so you can choose. Explanations for all answers to the multiple-choice questions are also provided. Following the advice in Chapter 2, you can develop a study plan to improve your weaknesses.

The direction sheets, mathematics formulae, and question formats of these tests are like the actual test you will take.

	TESTS	QUESTIONS	TIME ALLOWANCE
Test 1:	The Language Arts, Writing (Writing Skills) Test, Part I	37	60 minutes
	The Language Arts, Writing (Writing Skills) Test, Part II	Essay	45 minutes
Test 2:	The Social Studies Test	49	65 minutes
Test 3:	The Science Test	66	1 hour, 35 minutes
Test 4:	The Language Arts, Reading (Interpreting Literature and the Arts) Test	25	38 minutes
Test 5:	The Mathematics Test	36	1 hour, 55 minutes
		Total:	5 hours, 58 minutes

For these tests we have included answer sheets and diagnostic and prescription charts. Mark yourself on each test, checking your answers against the answer key. Read the answer explanations to be sure you understand the correct answer choices. After you have calculated the scores for all five tests, refer to the self-appraisal materials to determine your subject area strengths and weaknesses.

The main purpose of the test is to help you discover your strengths and your weaknesses. IMPORTANT: You should spend more time studying those chapters which deal with the tests in which you are weakest. In that way, you will improve your score when you take the two practice examinations at the end of this book.

SIMULATE TEST CONDITIONS

To make conditions similar to those on the actual examination:

- do not take more time than that allowed for each test
- follow all directions for each test
- read the questions carefully to determine what is asked for
- answer *all* questions
- choose the *one* correct answer from the five choices available after you have read all five
- if a question seems difficult to you, eliminate as many choices as you can and then decide on the one that seems most likely to be correct
- do *not* spend too much time on any one question.

Here is some additional advice on handling the test answer sheet:

- fill in only *one* answer space for every question as the machine will not give you credit if you fill in more than one space
- since the machine may pick up any marks you make on the answer sheet, keep your pencil away from the sheet until you fill in the space of your choice
- if you change your mind about your answer, erase completely the answer you do *not* want and fill in the space you *do* want
- handle your answer sheet carefully so that you do not wrinkle, crease, or fold it.

TO THE STUDENT

The Diagnostic Pre-Tests are designed to give you information about your strengths and weaknesses. They are not a definitive diagnosis of every strength and weakness. On the other hand, even with the limited questions, they will give you a very good idea of where to put your emphasis in your studies. For simplicity, the content areas are the ones used in the rest of the book.

Answer Sheet—Diagnostic Pre-Tests

Test 1: The Language Arts, Writing (Writing Skills) Test ______________________

1. ① ② ③ ④ ⑤
2. ① ② ③ ④ ⑤
3. ① ② ③ ④ ⑤
4. ① ② ③ ④ ⑤
5. ① ② ③ ④ ⑤
6. ① ② ③ ④ ⑤
7. ① ② ③ ④ ⑤
8. ① ② ③ ④ ⑤
9. ① ② ③ ④ ⑤
10. ① ② ③ ④ ⑤
11. ① ② ③ ④ ⑤
12. ① ② ③ ④ ⑤
13. ① ② ③ ④ ⑤
14. ① ② ③ ④ ⑤
15. ① ② ③ ④ ⑤
16. ① ② ③ ④ ⑤
17. ① ② ③ ④ ⑤
18. ① ② ③ ④ ⑤
19. ① ② ③ ④ ⑤
20. ① ② ③ ④ ⑤
21. ① ② ③ ④ ⑤
22. ① ② ③ ④ ⑤
23. ① ② ③ ④ ⑤
24. ① ② ③ ④ ⑤
25. ① ② ③ ④ ⑤
26. ① ② ③ ④ ⑤
27. ① ② ③ ④ ⑤
28. ① ② ③ ④ ⑤
29. ① ② ③ ④ ⑤
30. ① ② ③ ④ ⑤
31. ① ② ③ ④ ⑤
32. ① ② ③ ④ ⑤
33. ① ② ③ ④ ⑤
34. ① ② ③ ④ ⑤
35. ① ② ③ ④ ⑤
36. ① ② ③ ④ ⑤
37. ① ② ③ ④ ⑤

Test 2: The Social Studies Test ______________________

1. ① ② ③ ④ ⑤
2. ① ② ③ ④ ⑤
3. ① ② ③ ④ ⑤
4. ① ② ③ ④ ⑤
5. ① ② ③ ④ ⑤
6. ① ② ③ ④ ⑤
7. ① ② ③ ④ ⑤
8. ① ② ③ ④ ⑤
9. ① ② ③ ④ ⑤
10. ① ② ③ ④ ⑤
11. ① ② ③ ④ ⑤
12. ① ② ③ ④ ⑤
13. ① ② ③ ④ ⑤
14. ① ② ③ ④ ⑤
15. ① ② ③ ④ ⑤
16. ① ② ③ ④ ⑤
17. ① ② ③ ④ ⑤
18. ① ② ③ ④ ⑤
19. ① ② ③ ④ ⑤
20. ① ② ③ ④ ⑤
21. ① ② ③ ④ ⑤
22. ① ② ③ ④ ⑤
23. ① ② ③ ④ ⑤
24. ① ② ③ ④ ⑤
25. ① ② ③ ④ ⑤
26. ① ② ③ ④ ⑤
27. ① ② ③ ④ ⑤
28. ① ② ③ ④ ⑤
29. ① ② ③ ④ ⑤
30. ① ② ③ ④ ⑤
31. ① ② ③ ④ ⑤
32. ① ② ③ ④ ⑤
33. ① ② ③ ④ ⑤
34. ① ② ③ ④ ⑤
35. ① ② ③ ④ ⑤
36. ① ② ③ ④ ⑤
37. ① ② ③ ④ ⑤
38. ① ② ③ ④ ⑤
39. ① ② ③ ④ ⑤
40. ① ② ③ ④ ⑤
41. ① ② ③ ④ ⑤
42. ① ② ③ ④ ⑤
43. ① ② ③ ④ ⑤
44. ① ② ③ ④ ⑤
45. ① ② ③ ④ ⑤
46. ① ② ③ ④ ⑤
47. ① ② ③ ④ ⑤
48. ① ② ③ ④ ⑤
49. ① ② ③ ④ ⑤

Test 3: The Science Test ______

1. ① ② ③ ④ ⑤
2. ① ② ③ ④ ⑤
3. ① ② ③ ④ ⑤
4. ① ② ③ ④ ⑤
5. ① ② ③ ④ ⑤
6. ① ② ③ ④ ⑤
7. ① ② ③ ④ ⑤
8. ① ② ③ ④ ⑤
9. ① ② ③ ④ ⑤
10. ① ② ③ ④ ⑤
11. ① ② ③ ④ ⑤
12. ① ② ③ ④ ⑤
13. ① ② ③ ④ ⑤
14. ① ② ③ ④ ⑤
15. ① ② ③ ④ ⑤
16. ① ② ③ ④ ⑤
17. ① ② ③ ④ ⑤
18. ① ② ③ ④ ⑤
19. ① ② ③ ④ ⑤
20. ① ② ③ ④ ⑤
21. ① ② ③ ④ ⑤
22. ① ② ③ ④ ⑤
23. ① ② ③ ④ ⑤
24. ① ② ③ ④ ⑤
25. ① ② ③ ④ ⑤
26. ① ② ③ ④ ⑤
27. ① ② ③ ④ ⑤
28. ① ② ③ ④ ⑤
29. ① ② ③ ④ ⑤
30. ① ② ③ ④ ⑤
31. ① ② ③ ④ ⑤
32. ① ② ③ ④ ⑤
33. ① ② ③ ④ ⑤
34. ① ② ③ ④ ⑤
35. ① ② ③ ④ ⑤
36. ① ② ③ ④ ⑤
37. ① ② ③ ④ ⑤
38. ① ② ③ ④ ⑤
39. ① ② ③ ④ ⑤
40. ① ② ③ ④ ⑤
41. ① ② ③ ④ ⑤
42. ① ② ③ ④ ⑤
43. ① ② ③ ④ ⑤
44. ① ② ③ ④ ⑤
45. ① ② ③ ④ ⑤
46. ① ② ③ ④ ⑤
47. ① ② ③ ④ ⑤
48. ① ② ③ ④ ⑤
49. ① ② ③ ④ ⑤
50. ① ② ③ ④ ⑤
51. ① ② ③ ④ ⑤
52. ① ② ③ ④ ⑤
53. ① ② ③ ④ ⑤
54. ① ② ③ ④ ⑤
55. ① ② ③ ④ ⑤
56. ① ② ③ ④ ⑤
57. ① ② ③ ④ ⑤
58. ① ② ③ ④ ⑤
59. ① ② ③ ④ ⑤
60. ① ② ③ ④ ⑤
61. ① ② ③ ④ ⑤
62. ① ② ③ ④ ⑤
63. ① ② ③ ④ ⑤
64. ① ② ③ ④ ⑤
65. ① ② ③ ④ ⑤
66. ① ② ③ ④ ⑤

Test 4: The Language Arts, Reading (Interpreting Literature and the Arts) Test ______

1. ① ② ③ ④ ⑤
2. ① ② ③ ④ ⑤
3. ① ② ③ ④ ⑤
4. ① ② ③ ④ ⑤
5. ① ② ③ ④ ⑤
6. ① ② ③ ④ ⑤
7. ① ② ③ ④ ⑤
8. ① ② ③ ④ ⑤
9. ① ② ③ ④ ⑤
10. ① ② ③ ④ ⑤
11. ① ② ③ ④ ⑤
12. ① ② ③ ④ ⑤
13. ① ② ③ ④ ⑤
14. ① ② ③ ④ ⑤
15. ① ② ③ ④ ⑤
16. ① ② ③ ④ ⑤
17. ① ② ③ ④ ⑤
18. ① ② ③ ④ ⑤
19. ① ② ③ ④ ⑤
20. ① ② ③ ④ ⑤
21. ① ② ③ ④ ⑤
22. ① ② ③ ④ ⑤
23. ① ② ③ ④ ⑤
24. ① ② ③ ④ ⑤

Test 5: The Mathematics Test ______

1. ① ② ③ ④ ⑤
2. ① ② ③ ④ ⑤
3. ① ② ③ ④ ⑤
4. ① ② ③ ④ ⑤
5. ① ② ③ ④ ⑤
6. ① ② ③ ④ ⑤
7. ① ② ③ ④ ⑤
8. ① ② ③ ④ ⑤
9. ① ② ③ ④ ⑤
10. ① ② ③ ④ ⑤
11. ① ② ③ ④ ⑤
12. ① ② ③ ④ ⑤
13. ① ② ③ ④ ⑤
14. ① ② ③ ④ ⑤
15. ① ② ③ ④ ⑤
16. ① ② ③ ④ ⑤
17. ① ② ③ ④ ⑤
18. ① ② ③ ④ ⑤
19. ① ② ③ ④ ⑤
20. ① ② ③ ④ ⑤
21. ① ② ③ ④ ⑤
22. ① ② ③ ④ ⑤
23. ① ② ③ ④ ⑤
24. ① ② ③ ④ ⑤
25. ① ② ③ ④ ⑤
26. ① ② ③ ④ ⑤
27. ① ② ③ ④ ⑤
28. ① ② ③ ④ ⑤
29. ① ② ③ ④ ⑤
30. ① ② ③ ④ ⑤
31. ① ② ③ ④ ⑤
32. ① ② ③ ④ ⑤
33. ① ② ③ ④ ⑤
34. ① ② ③ ④ ⑤
35. ① ② ③ ④ ⑤
36. ① ② ③ ④ ⑤

DIAGNOSTIC PRE-TESTS

TEST 1: LANGUAGE ARTS, WRITING (WRITING SKILLS) TEST, PART I

Directions

Allotted Time: 60 minutes

This part of the Writing Skills test contains **37 multiple-choice questions** that test your ability to write English correctly and effectively.

The multiple-choice questions are based on numbered sentences in paragraphs. These sentences may be correct as written (if so, choose option 5), or they will contain an error in sentence structure, grammar and usage, punctuation, capitalization, or spelling. You must choose the option that either corrects the error, indicates the best way to write a portion of the sentence, combines two sentences effectively, or provides another way in which the sentence can be rewritten.

Since 37 questions must be answered in 60 minutes, do not devote more than a few minutes to any one question. If there is time left, you may go back to a question.

Answer all questions. Do not leave any blanks since there is no penalty for incorrect answers. Your score will be the number of your correct responses. Decide which is the best answer and mark the numbered space on the answer sheet beside the number that corresponds to the question in the test.

You may go on to Writing Skills, Part II, the essay, when you complete Part I.

Make no mark on your answer sheet other than your choice of the correct answer. If you change your answer, erase your first mark completely. Only *one* answer space should be marked for each question.

EXAMPLE:

In the future, people will need to learn to turn to their computer for assistence.

What correction should be made to this sentence?

(1) remove the comma after future
(2) change will need to need
(3) change the spelling of their to they're
(4) change the spelling of assistence to assistance
(5) no correction is necessary

① ② ③ ● ⑤

In this sentence, the correct spelling is "assistance," so mark answer 4 on the answer sheet.

Directions: Choose the one best answer to each item.

Items 1 to 9 refer to the following paragraph.

(1) A combination of attributes make vegetable gardening a national hobby with both young and old. (2) For an ever-increasing number of individuals seed catalogues and the thoughts of spring gardening provide a happy escape from the winter doldrums. (3) Vegetable gardeners unanimously agree that many home-grown vegetables picked at their peak of maturity have quality. seldom found in vegetables purchased from commercial markets. (4) From Spring to late Fall, a well-planned and maintained garden can provide a supply of fresh vegetables, thus increasing the nutritional value of the family diet. (5) Freezers make it possible to preserve some of the surplus vegetables to be enjoyed at a later date other vegetables can be stored for a few months in a cool area. (6) Not to be overlooked is the finger-tip convenience of having vegetables in the backyard; this in itself justifies home gardening for many individuals. (7) In addition, vegetable gardening provides exercise and recreation for both urban and suburban families. (8) Although your initial dollar investment for gardening may be nominal, one cannot escape the fact that gardening requires manual labour and time. (9) Neglecting jobs that should be performed on a regular basis may result in failure and a negative feeling towards gardening.

1. Sentence 1: **A combination of attributes make vegetable gardening a national hobby with both young and old.**

   What correction should be made to this sentence?

   (1) insert a comma after attributes
   (2) change make to makes
   (3) capitalize vegetable gardening
   (4) reverse with and both
   (5) no correction is necessary

2. Sentence 2: **For an ever-increasing number of individuals seed catalogues and the thoughts of spring gardening provide a happy escape from the winter doldrums.**

   What correction should be made to this sentence?

   (1) remove the hyphen from ever-increasing
   (2) change number to amount
   (3) insert a comma after individuals
   (4) insert a comma after catalogues
   (5) no correction is necessary

3. Sentence 3: **Vegetable gardeners unanimously agree that many home-grown vegetables picked at their peak of maturity have quality. seldom found in vegetables purchased from commercial markets.**

   Which of the following is the best way to write the underlined portion of this sentence? If you think the original is the best way, choose option (1).

   (1) quality. seldom
   (2) quality. Seldom
   (3) quality seldom
   (4) quality; seldom
   (5) quality, seldom

4. Sentence 4: **From Spring to late Fall, a well-planned and maintained garden can provide a supply of fresh vegetables, thus increasing the nutritional value of the family diet.**

   What correction should be made to this sentence?

   (1) remove capitals from Spring and Fall
   (2) remove the hyphen from well-planned
   (3) remove the comma after vegetables
   (4) change thus to however
   (5) no correction is necessary

5. Sentence 5: **Freezers make it possible to preserve some of the surplus vegetables to be enjoyed at a later date other vegetables can be stored for a few months in a cool area.**

   Which of the following is the best way to write the underlined portion of this sentence? If you think the original is the best way, choose option (1).

   (1) date other
   (2) date, other
   (3) date. Other
   (4) date, while other
   (5) date; while other

6. Sentence 6: **Not to be overlooked is the finger-tip convenience of having vegetables in the backyard; this in itself justifies home gardening for many individuals.**

   What correction should be made to this sentence?

   (1) insert a comma after overlooked
   (2) change the spelling of vegetables to vegetabless
   (3) replace the semicolon after yard with a comma
   (4) change the spelling of gardening to gardning
   (5) no correction is necessary

7. Sentence 7: **In addition, vegetable gardening provides exercise and recreation for both urban and suburban families.**

   What correction should be made to this sentence?

   (1) remove the comma after addition
   (2) change the spelling of excercise to exercise
   (3) insert a comma after recreation
   (4) change for both to both for
   (5) no correction is necessary

8. Sentence 8: **Although your initial dollar investment for gardening may be nominal, one cannot escape the fact that gardening requires manual labour and time.**

   What correction should be made in this sentence?

   (1) change Although to Because
   (2) remove the comma after nominal
   (3) change one to you
   (4) change requires to require
   (5) no correction is necessary

9. Sentence 9: **Neglecting jobs that should be performed on a regular basis may result in failure and a negative feeling towards gardening.**

   What correction should be made to this sentence?

   (1) insert a comma after jobs
   (2) insert a comma after basis
   (3) change may result to results
   (4) change and to despite
   (5) no correction is necessary

Items 10 to 19 refer to the following paragraph.

(1) In coming years, families will need to learn to turn to their computer for assistence. (2) With the increasing amounts of information a family is required to process, the home computer will become a necessity for both decision making and family record storage and retrieval. (3) A home communications revolution is predicted with the arrival of the home computer. It will serve as a source and processor of information. (4) A virtually infinite amount of information from many sources will be at the instantaneous disposal of the family for more efficient decision making. (5) The computer will plan meals, turn lights on at appropriate times keep track of family members' schedules, calculate budget information, and oversee credit, spending, and bank accounts. (6) Just as home equipment frees the homemaker from the labour of house-

keeping, the computer releases family members from some repetitious managerial duties. (7) The home terminal may serve as a home education centre for children's homework and part of the lifelong learning program of parents and elderly family members. (8) The change which will have the most immediate effect on family decision making will be increased discretionary time. (9) For economic reasons, many families will decide to use they're "free" time to hold a second job. (10) With the increasing interest in personal development, a segment of the time might be chosen by some to develop alternative interests through lifelong educational programs that will facilitate career changes, to increase skills for effective citizenship, and learning new skills to enhance their family living.

10. Sentence 1: **In coming years, families will need to learn to turn to their computer for assistence.**

    What correction should be made to this sentence?

    (1) remove the comma after years
    (2) change will need to need
    (3) change the spelling of their to they're
    (4) change the spelling of assistence to assistance
    (5) no correction is necessary

11. Sentence 2: **With the increasing amounts of information a family is required to process, the home computer will become a necessity for both decision making and family record storage and retrieval.**

    What correction should be made to this sentence?

    (1) change With the to Despite
    (2) change is to are
    (3) remove the comma after process
    (4) change the spelling of necessity to neccesity
    (5) no correction is necessary

12. Sentence 3: **A home communications revolution is predicted with the arrival of the home computer. It will serve as a source and processor of information.**

    Which of the following is the best way to write the underlined portion of the sentence? If you think the original is the best way, choose option (1).

    (1) computer. It
    (2) computer, It
    (3) computer, it
    (4) computer it
    (5) computer; It

13. Sentence 4: **A virtually infinite amount of information from many sources will be at the instantaneous disposal of the family for more efficient decision making.**

    What correction should be made to this sentence?

    (1) insert a comma after information
    (2) insert a comma after sources
    (3) insert a comma after family
    (4) change the spelling of efficient to eficient
    (5) no correction is necessary

14. Sentence 5: **The computer will plan meals, turn lights on at appropriate times keep track of family members' schedules, calculate budget information, and oversee credit, spending, and bank accounts.**

    What correction should be made to this sentence?

    (1) remove comma after meals
    (2) insert comma after times
    (3) change members' to member's
    (4) change the spelling of schedules to skedules
    (5) no correction necessary

15. Sentence 6: **Just as home equipment frees the homemaker from the labour of housekeeping, the computer releases family members from some repetitious managerial duties.**

What correction should be made to this sentence?

(1) Change Just as to Although
(2) change the spelling of equipment to equipment
(3) remove the comma after housekeeping
(4) change releases to will have released
(5) no correction is necessary

16. Sentence 7: **The home terminal may serve as a home education centre for children's homework and part of the lifelong learning program of parents and elderly family members.**

If you rewrote sentence 7 beginning with

Children's homework and part of the lifelong learning program of parents and elderly family members

the next words should be

(1) are served
(2) may serve
(3) may be served
(4) serve
(5) will serve

17. Sentence 8: **The change which will have the most immediate effect on family decision making will be increased discretionary time.**

What correction should be made to this sentence?

(1) change will have to having
(2) change the spelling of effect to affect
(3) change family to family's
(4) change will be to is
(5) no correction is necessary

18. Sentence 9: **For economic reasons, many families will decide to use they're "free" time to hold a second job.**

What correction should be made to this sentence?

(1) remove the comma after reasons
(2) change the spelling of families to familys
(3) change the spelling of they're to their
(4) change to to and
(5) no correction is necessary

19. Sentence 10: **With the increasing interest in personal development, a segment of the time might be chosen by some to develop alternative interests through lifelong educational programs that will facilitate career changes, to increase skills for effective citizenship, and learning new skills to enhance their family living.**

What correction should be made to this sentence?

(1) change the spelling of development to developement
(2) change the spelling of through to thorough
(3) remove the comma after changes
(4) change learning to to learn
(5) no correction is necessary

Items 20 to 28 refer to the following paragraphs.

(1) To lessen the threat of faulty car repair work or repair frauds, they're a number of constructive steps you can take. (2) While these measures can't offer full protection they are wise insurance against dented pocketbooks and time schedules.

(3) First, never wait until a small problem becomes a big and costly one. (4) Always take your car in for a check at the first sign of trouble.

(5) But before you take the car in, make a list of all problems and "symptoms" so you are prepared to describe the trouble as accurately and specifically as possible.

(6) Don't just ask to have the car put in "working order," (7) that kind of general statement can lead directly to unnecessary work.

(8) On your initial visit, make certain you get a copy of the work authorization that you sign or a general estimate of the total cost of the repairs. (9) Don't leave until you do.

(10) Ask the repair garage to telephone you when the exact work to be done is determinned. (11) When you recieve the call, say you now want to return to the station to obtain another work order itemizing the cost of each repair to be made.

20. Sentence 1: **To lessen the threat of faulty car repair work or repair frauds, they're a number of constructive steps you can take.**

What correction should be made to this sentence?

(1) change lessen to lesson
(2) remove the comma after frauds
(3) change the spelling of they're to there are
(4) change can to might
(5) no correction is necessary

21. Sentence 2: **While these measures can't offer full protection they are wise insurance against dented pocketbooks and time schedules.**

What correction should be made to this sentence?

(1) change while to nevertheless
(2) insert a comma after protection
(3) change insurance to insurence
(4) insert a hyphen in pocketbooks
(5) no correction is necessary

22. Sentence 3: **First, never wait until a small problem becomes a big and costly one.**

What correction should be made to this sentence?

(1) change first to firstly
(2) remove the comma after first
(3) change the spelling of until to untill
(4) change becomes to will become
(5) no correction is necessary

23. Sentence 4: **Always take your car in for a check at the first sign of trouble.**

What correction should be made to this sentence?

(1) change always to allways
(2) change take to you should take
(3) change your to your'e
(4) insert a comma after check
(5) no correction is necessary

24. Sentence 5: **But before you take the car in, make a list of all problems and "symptoms" so you are prepared to describe the trouble as accurately and specifically as possible.**

What correction should be made to this sentence?

(1) change take to will take
(2) remove the comma after in
(3) change are to will be
(4) change the spelling of specifically to specificaly
(5) no correction is necessary

25. Sentences 6 and 7: **Don't just ask to have the car put in "working order," that kind of general statement can lead directly to unnecessary work.**

Which of the following is the best way to write the underlined portion of these sentences? If you think the original is the best way, choose option (1).

(1) order," that
(2) order" that
(3) order": that
(4) order". that
(5) order." That

26. Sentence 8: **On your initial visit, make certain you get a copy of the work authorization that you sign or a general estimate of the total cost of the repairs.**

What correction should be made to this sentence?

(1) change the spelling of initial to initail
(2) remove the comma after visit
(3) insert a comma after sign
(4) change the spelling of estimate to estemate
(5) no correction is necessary

27. Sentence 10: **Ask the repair garage to telephone you when the exact work to be done is determinned.**

What correction should be made to this sentence?

(1) insert a comma after you
(2) change when to while
(3) change is to will have been
(4) change the spelling of determinned to determined
(5) no correction is necessary

28. Sentence 11: **When you recieve the call, say you now want to return to the station to obtain another work order itemizing the cost of each repair to be made.**

What correction should be made to this sentence?

(1) change the spelling of recieve to receive
(2) remove the comma after call
(3) insert a comma after order
(4) change to be made to that will have been made
(5) no correction is necessary

Items 29 to 37 refer to the following paragraphs.

(1) Total dollars available, family tastes storage and preparation facilities, end use, and item cost all affect a buying decision. (2) Unit pricing can help by taking the guesswork out of the price factor and simplifying cost comparisons.

(3) Unit pricing is just what its name implies—the price per unit. (4) To be more specific, it gives you the cost per gram or per kilogram or per 100 or per square metre. (5) This price per unit enables you to readily find the best buy dollarwise among several items in different size packages with different total prices.

(6) Thousands of retail food chain stores now have unit pricing programs. (7) Such programs are required by local laws in several areas, but generally the programs are voluntary.

(8) Stores that offer unit pricing generally use a shelf tag system—a label on the shelf edge below the item gives the name of the item, the size, the total price, and the unit price.

(9) When unit pricing was first introduced there were some problems with the shelf tag system since just keeping the tags on the shelves in the right location can be difficult. (10) But as unit pricing has gained acceptance, some of these mechanical problems have been overcome, and the label information has become more usable from the shoppers standpoint.

29. Sentence 1: **Total dollars available, family tastes storage and preparation facilities, end use, and item cost all affect a buying decision.**

If you rewrote sentence 1 beginning with

A buying decision is affected

the next words should be

(1) because of
(2) by
(3) depending on
(4) however
(5) therefore

30. Sentence 1: **Total dollars available, family tastes storage and preparation facilities, end use, and item cost all affect a buying decision.**

What correction should be made to this sentence?

(1) insert a comma after tastes
(2) change all to each
(3) change affect to effect
(4) change the spelling of buying to bying
(5) no correction is necessary

31. Sentence 2: **Unit pricing can help by taking the guesswork out of the price factor and simplifying cost comparisons.**

What correction should be made to this sentence?

(1) change can to could
(2) change by taking to to take
(3) insert a hyphen in guesswork
(4) insert a comma after factor
(5) no correction is necessary

32. Sentences 3 and 4: **Unit pricing is just what its name implies—the price per unit. To be more specific, it gives you the cost per gram or per kilogram or per 100 or per square metre.**

Which of the following is the best way to write the underlined portion of these sentences? If you think the original is the best way, choose option (1).

(1) . To be more specific
(2) , To be more specific
(3) ; To be more specific
(4) : To be more specific
(5) —To be more specific

33. Sentence 5: **This price per unit enables you to readily find the best buy dollarwise among several items in different size packages with different total prices.**

What correction should be made to this sentence?

(1) change readily find to find readily
(2) insert comma before and after dollarwise
(3) change among to between
(4) change size to sized
(5) no correction is necessary

34. Sentences 6 and 7: **Thousands of retail food chain stores now have unit pricing programs. Such programs are required by local laws in several areas, but generally the programs are voluntary.**

The most effective combination of sentences 6 and 7 would include which of the following groups of words?

(1) and such programs
(2) although such programs
(3) whereas such programs
(4) programs which are
(5) programs some being

35. Sentence 8: **Stores that offer unit pricing generally use a shelf tag system—a label on the shelf edge below the item gives the name of the item, the size, the total price, and the unit price.**

Which of the following is the best way to write the underlined portion of this sentence? If you think the original is the best way, choose option (1).

(1) system—a label
(2) system. a label
(3) system; a label
(4) system: a label
(5) system, a label

36. Sentence 9: **When unit pricing was first introduced there were some problems with the shelf tag system since just keeping the tags on the shelves in the right location can be difficult.**

What correction should be made to this sentence?

(1) change was to had been
(2) insert a comma after introduced
(3) change there to their
(4) insert commas before and after in the right location
(5) no correction is necessary

37. Sentence 10: **But as unit pricing has gained acceptance, some of these mechanical problems have been overcome, and the label information has become more usable from the shoppers standpoint.**

What correction should be made to this sentence?

(1) change the spelling of acceptance to acceptence
(2) remove the comma after acceptance
(3) change the spelling of usable to useable
(4) add an apostrophe after shoppers
(5) no correction is necessary

TEST 1: LANGUAGE ARTS, WRITING (WRITING SKILLS) TEST, PART II

Directions

Allotted Time: 45 minutes

Part II of the Writing Skills Test will test your ability to write by having you write an essay in which you either take and defend a position on a debatable topic or explain how something affects our lives.

Remember to:

- follow the directions
- read the topic on which your essay will be based
- be careful to write your essay on the separate answer sheet, confining your notes to scratch paper
- reread your essay, revising it where necessary to improve what you have written
- correct any errors you find in paragraphing, sentence structure, capitalization, punctuation, spelling and usage.

You must:

- write the letter of the topic in the box at the upper right corner of the answer sheet where you write your essay
- write your essay on the given topic legibly on the lined pages of the answer sheet in the 45 minutes allotted. Use a ballpoint pen. Your notes on scratch paper will not be considered.

You will have 45 minutes to write on the topic below.

In the decades since the end of World War II, air travel has become an increasingly important part of our way of life.

In many ways, mankind has benefited from air travel; in others, it has proved to be harmful. Write a composition of about 200 words in which you present your view of air travel, for or against, with appropriate reasons and examples to support that view.

END OF TEST

Air travel has done great things for mankind; 1 you can get a cross the world in hours, 2 it is comfortale. and Also, 3 a great convience.

-1 flying compared to driving or ~~train~~ ~~car~~ ride is a big deal of time and

-2 it is more comfortables then sitting on a train for extra time which is ton neccassary

-3 the convience of flying compared to any other way of travel, is a great deal.

TEST 2: SOCIAL STUDIES

Directions

Allotted Time: 65 minutes

This test consists of **49 multiple-choice questions** designed to measure your knowledge of the general ideas or concepts of social studies: history, geography, economics, political science, and behavioural sciences.

You will be given information in the form of readings, some of which will be accompanied by a map, chart, or graph. Study the given information and answer the questions based on it.

Since you are allowed 65 minutes, be careful not to spend too much time on each question.

Make no mark on the answer sheet other than your choice of the correct answer. If you change your answer, erase your first mark completely. Only *one* answer space should be marked for each question.

EXAMPLE:

Changes in occupational titles from busboy to dining room attendant and stewardess to flight attendant illustrate an attempt to deal with the problem of

(1) racism
(2) ethnocentrism
(3) sexism
(4) age bias
(5) unionism

① ② ● ④ ⑤

The changes in occupational titles are evidence that sex indications, such as boy and stewardess, are being removed and that sexism, the exploitation and domination of one sex by the other, is being given attention. Therefore, the correct answer is 3 and 3 should be marked on the answer sheet.

Directions: Choose the one best answer to each item.

Items 1 to 3 are based on the following passage.

Although bills can be introduced in the Senate, most bills originate in the House of Commons. This applies to all bills except those concerned with how the government raises and spends revenue. These are commonly called money bills and must originate in the Commons. The government introduces most of the bills, but bills can be presented by any member of the House of Commons as private members' bills. However, the chance of a private member's bill becoming law is remote and they rarely survive the three-readings process. The main purpose of a private member's bill is to provide a way for an ordinary member of Parliament to criticize the government, or to influence its decisions.

Once a bill is introduced, it has to pass through a number of stages. The general procedure is that bills receive three readings in the House of Commons, three in the Senate and then go to the Governor General to be signed and to receive royal assent. In the first reading, the bill is introduced and no debate is allowed. In the second reading the bill is debated but the focus is only on the general concept or principles of the bill rather than specific details. The bill is then referred to the Committee stage for examination, clause by clause, and for the consideration of amendments. The amended bill is then voted on as a whole. The bill then moves to the other house where it must negotiate the same process before going to the Governor General.

1. This passage indicates that

   (1) members of Parliament are not allowed to criticize the government
   (2) private members' bills do not usually become law
   (3) only cabinet ministers may introduce legislation
   (4) members must pay a fee to introduce legislation into Parliament
   (5) private members' bills may only be introduced in the Senate

2. The main purpose of private members' bills is

   (1) to allow ordinary members of Parliament some say in the less important legislation
   (2) to help the government get new ideas
   (3) to reduce the influence of the opposition parties
   (4) to help the Prime Minister identify possible new cabinet members
   (5) to allow ordinary members to influence the government's legislative program

3. At which stage in the legislative process would the opposition be most likely to force the government to change some of the specific details of a bill?

   (1) first reading
   (2) second reading
   (3) Committee stage
   (4) third reading
   (5) when the bill goes to the Governor General

Items 4 to 6 are based on the following passage.

The consumer's first line of defence is information. Before you buy any product—especially before you make a major purchase of any kind—get all the information you can about the manufacturer's guarantee or warranty provisions.

Remember, a guarantee is a statement by the manufacturer or vendor that he stands behind his product or service. Guarantees and warranties usually have limitations or conditions, so get all promises in writing.

Before you buy any product or service covered by a guarantee or warranty, make sure you resolve these questions:

—What, exactly, is covered?

—Whom should you call when you need repairs under the warranty?

—Must repairs be made at the factory or by an "authorized service representative" to keep the warranty in effect?

—Who pays for parts, for labour, for shipping charges?

—How long does the warranty last?

—If pro rata reimbursement is provided, what is the basis for it?

—If the warranty provides for reimbursement, is it in cash or credit toward a replacement?

Keep the warranty and sales receipt for future reference.

4. The advice given to the consumer in this passage deals chiefly with

   (1) business ethics
   (2) unconditional guarantees
   (3) product safety
   (4) unwarranted promises
   (5) pre-purchase information

5. Guarantees and warranties, the passage implies, should be

   (1) conditional
   (2) in writing
   (3) made by the salesman
   (4) cancelable
   (5) dependent on the use of the product

6. Warranties usually include all of the following EXCEPT

   (1) what is covered
   (2) who does the repairs
   (3) where the repairs are made
   (4) who pays for expenses incurred in doing the repairs
   (5) return of monies if consumer is dissatisfied

Items 7 and 8 are based on the following chart.

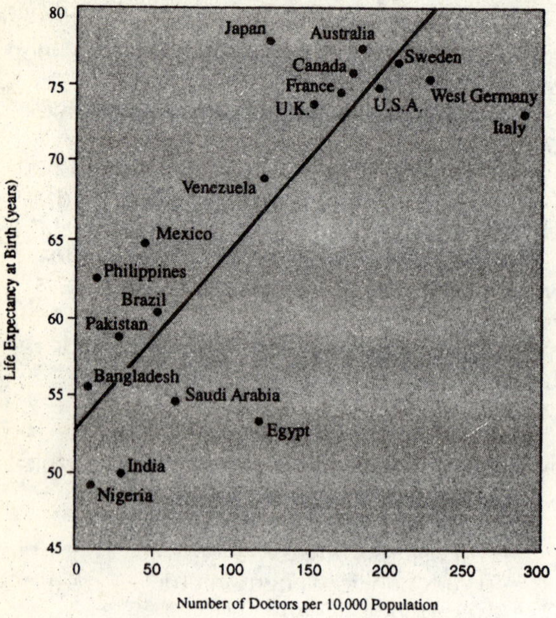

7. According to the chart, in which ONE of the countries listed below do people generally live longest?

(1) Canada
(2) Nigeria
(3) Italy
(4) Japan
(5) USA

8. Which ONE of the following generalizations is best supported by information from the chart?

(1) Middle East countries have the lowest proportion of doctors and the highest life expectancies.
(2) The more doctors, the lower the life expectancy.
(3) European countries have the highest life expectancy rates.
(4) The more doctors, the higher the life expectancy rates.
(5) There is no relationship between the proportion of doctors in the population and the life expectancy rates.

9. Government policies designed to foster economic growth by encouraging greater consumption would probably meet with the greatest opposition from which group?

(1) labour leaders
(2) business executives
(3) military leaders
(4) environmentalists
(5) individual entrepreneurs

Items 10 and 11 are based on the following cartoon.

10. What is the main idea of the cartoon?

(1) The world lacks sufficient energy resources to survive much longer.
(2) Concerns of environmentalists have had little impact on the actions of industrialists.
(3) The struggle between energy and the environment cannot be resolved.
(4) The need to produce energy comes into conflict with the need to preserve the environment.
(5) A stalemate has been arrived at between industrialists and environmentalists.

11. In dealing with the situation referred to in the cartoon, which of the following statements best reflects Canadian public opinion during the 1990s?

    (1) Canadians are becoming less likely to support energy projects that may cause significant environmental damage.
    (2) Canadians want cheap energy, no matter what the cost to the environment.
    (3) Canadians want less attention paid to the environment.
    (4) Canadians want energy sources to be imported so that there is no threat to the Canadian environment.
    (5) Canadians blame damage to the environment on pollution from the United States.

Item 12 is based on the following statement.

"You have a choice. I can destroy you painlessly, or I can make you Minister of Finance." (Attributed to Prime Minister Trudeau in a sketch by the Royal Canadian Air Farce, CBC Radio, December 24, 1977.)

12. Which of the following comments best captures the idea in the above statement?

    (1) The Prime Minister did not like the Minister of Finance.
    (2) Mr. Trudeau was a difficult man to please.
    (3) The Ministry of Finance can be damaging to political careers.
    (4) The problem of stereotyping is found in many political positions.
    (5) The Prime Minister has power over life and death.

Items 13 and 14 are based on the following passage.

For decades many Canadians have had a fear of becoming the fifty-first state of the United States. This has been called the "fifty-first syndrome." Those worried about this particular problem, fashion their arguments this way:

—Canada is so small economically, compared to the United States, that its businesses will be swallowed up by huge competitors.
—Our culture will be submerged under the tidal wave of American soap operas, game shows, and shoot-em-up dramas. U.S. movies, books, magazines, even sports will close down their Canadian counterparts.
—With our independent economy gone, and our culture swamped, the next step will see Prince Edward Islanders and Albertans sending two Senators to the United States Congress, while the House of Commons is turned into a combination hotel/theme park.
—Goodbye Canada!

13. Which issue in the 1980s brought the fifty-first syndrome to the forefront in national debates?

    (1) the Free Trade Agreement
    (2) the Meech Lake Accord
    (3) the Goods and Services Tax
    (4) acid rain
    (5) the General Agreement on Tariffs and Trade

14. The major concern expressed in the passage is

    (1) to negotiate Canada's admission to the United States as the fifty-first state
    (2) to obtain Canadian representation in the U.S. Congress
    (3) to prevent foreign ownership of Canadian business
    (4) to maintain Canada's status as a sovereign nation
    (5) to protect Canadian culture from being overwhelmed by its American counterparts

Items 15 and 16 are based on the following passage.

In 1867, Canada was a convenient name for the newly united provinces of New Brunswick, Nova Scotia, Quebec, and Ontario. But the very convenience of the name masked a highly diverse and complicated reality. There were differences between Nova Scotians and Ontarians in outlook, attitudes, and ways of doing things. Many of these differences still exist. Nor were the Acadians of New Brunswick the same as the Quebecois;

though many Acadians still cherished the illusion they had much in common, they would soon learn that they could expect no help from their French-speaking compatriots in Quebec in their struggles to maintain their heritage. Canadian society was not one; it was a series of provincial worlds, among which there were considerable differences.

15. This passage discusses circumstances related mainly to

    (1) Confederation
    (2) the Constitution
    (3) the national policy
    (4) the national dream
    (5) nationalism

16. According to the passage, the provinces of Canada in 1867 had

    (1) a strong sense of national unity
    (2) stronger ties to foreign countries
    (3) a strong sense of provincial identity
    (4) compatible economic interests
    (5) populations with similar outlooks

<u>Items 17 to 19</u> are based on the following chart, which lists some characteristics of *Nations A* and *B*.

Factors of Production	*Nation A*
Land (natural resources)	Relative scarcity
Labour	Relative abundance
Capital	Relative abundance
Business management	Relative abundance

Factors of Production	*Nation B*
Land (natural resources)	Relative abundance
Labour	Relative abundance
Capital	Relative scarcity
Business management	Relative scarcity

17. Which economic decision would most probably be in the best interests of *Nation A*?

    (1) Permitting an unfavourable balance of payments
    (2) seeking foreign markets
    (3) attracting investments from foreign nations
    (4) encouraging immigration
    (5) increasing imports

18. During the early 19th century, which nation most nearly resembled *Nation A*?

    (1) Canada
    (2) Great Britain
    (3) Russia
    (4) Turkey
    (5) China

19. If *Nation B* wishes to industrialize, how could it best encourage its own citizens to invest their capital in domestic industries?

    (1) by permitting an unfavourable balance of payments and seeking colonies
    (2) by permitting an unfavourable balance of payments and encouraging immigration
    (3) by attracting investments from foreign nations and encouraging immigration
    (4) by instituting high protective tariffs and giving tax concessions to business
    (5) by lowering taxes on imports

<u>Item 20</u> is based on the following passage.

In 1991, the German Chancellor, Mr. Kohl, explained that change in a reunited Germany would be gradual and carried out in cooperation with other European and world nations. However, some leaders have expressed anxiety that a reunited Germany will emerge as the most powerful country in Europe and will soon be capable of exercising not only great economic power but also political and military power.

20. The most valid conclusion to be drawn from this statement is that

    (1) Germany intends to become the most powerful military force in Europe
    (2) a united Germany will withdraw from the European Economic Community
    (3) Germany exercises too much economic power
    (4) some countries fear a resurgence of the militarism and nationalism of the past
    (5) Germany is not interested in cooperation with other countries in Europe or elsewhere

Items 21 and 22 are based on the following graph.

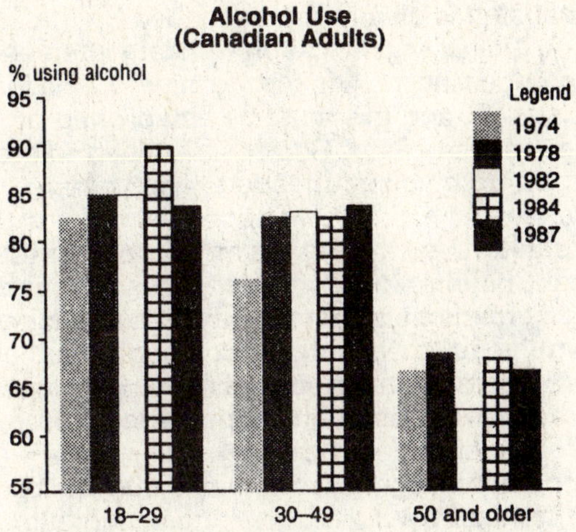

21. Which research technique was most likely used to gather the information in the graph?

(1) direct observation
(2) controlled experiment
(3) case study
(4) sample survey
(5) census

22. Which of the following is a valid conclusion based on the trends indicated on the graph?

(1) Alcohol use declined between 1974 and 1987.
(2) The 18 to 29 age group continues to be the heaviest user of alcohol.
(3) People are turning to drugs instead of alcohol.
(4) Older Canadians are less likely to use alcohol than younger ones.
(5) Between 1974 and 1987, older Canadians reduced their alcohol consumption.

23. Ethnocentrism is a belief that one's own ethnic group, nation, or culture is inherently superior to all others. An example of ethnocentrism is

(1) the use of the term "barbarian" to describe people of differing backgrounds
(2) the singing of a country's national anthem at sports events
(3) Japanese acceptance and imitation of Western culture
(4) the spread of Chinese culture to Southeast Asia
(5) a liberal immigration policy

Item 24 is based on the following diagram.

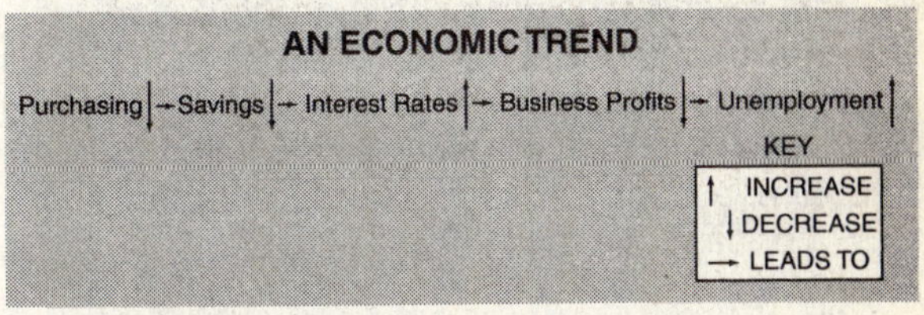

24. Which is occurring in the economy illustrated above?

(1) increase in real income
(2) devaluation of currency
(3) growth
(4) recession
(5) recovery

25. "All forms of life developed from earlier forms. In every case the fittest survived and the weak died out. It is the same for people and nations."

This passage expresses a view most often found in

(1) fundamentalism
(2) social Darwinism
(3) liberalism
(4) utopian socialism
(5) egalitarianism

Items 26 to 28 are based on the following passage.

The problems we face in conserving natural resources are labourious and complex. The preservation of even small bits of marshlands or woods representing the last strands of irreplaceable biotic communities is interwoven with the red tape of law, conflicting local interests, the overlapping jurisdiction of governmental and private conservation bodies, and an intricate tangle of economic and social considerations. During the time spent in resolving these factors, it often happens that the area to be preserved is swallowed up. Even more formidable is the broad-scale conservation problem raised by the spread of urban belts in such places as Southern Ontario. The pressures of human growth are so acute in such instances that they raise issues which would tax the wisdom of Solomon.

26. The author of this passage is primarily concerned with

    (1) biotic communities
    (2) legal red tape
    (3) obstacles to conservation
    (4) private conservation organizations
    (5) encroaching suburbs

27. The most perplexing problem of conservationists is the one involving

    (1) population growth
    (2) public indifference
    (3) favourable legislation
    (4) division of authority
    (5) increased taxes

28. The author's attitude toward the situation he describes is

    (1) optimistic
    (2) realistic
    (3) apathetic
    (4) illogical
    (5) combative

Items 29 to 31 are based on the following passage.

The Young Offenders Act, which came into force in 1984, constitutes a clear departure from the Juvenile Delinquents Act which preceded it. There is a uniform national age jurisdiction of 12 through 17 years, as of the date of the offense, and the YOA is unmistakably criminal law, not child welfare legislation. The discretion of police, judges, and correctional staff is clearly circumscribed by the YOA. The only justification for state intervention under the YOA is the violation of criminal legislation, and this must be established by due process of law. Society is entitled to protection from young offenders, and young offenders are to be held accountable for their acts. However, the YOA is not simply a "Kiddies' Criminal Code." It establishes a justice and corrections system separate and distinct from the adult system, and it recognizes that young persons have special needs as compared with adults, require special legal protection, and are not to be held as fully accountable as adults for their violations of the criminal law.

29. According to the passage

    (1) young offenders are not responsible for their actions
    (2) the detention of young offenders is not necessary
    (3) courts must place young offenders in correctional institutions
    (4) young offenders cannot lead productive lives
    (5) young offenders are to be held accountable for their actions

30. The main purpose of the Young Offenders Act is to

    (1) introduce a uniform national age jurisdiction for young offenders
    (2) support alternatives to the imprisonment of young offenders
    (3) establish a justice and corrections system separate from the adult system
    (4) take away the rights of young people who commit offenses
    (5) make young people the responsibility of their parents

31. The emphasis in the Young Offenders Act is upon

    (1) diagnosis and research
    (2) protection and accountability
    (3) prevention and rehabilitation
    (4) treatment and diagnosis
    (5) rehabilitation and research

Items 32 and 33 are based on the following cartoon.

COLLINS IN MONTREAL GAZETTE

32. Which statement best summarizes the main idea of the cartoon?

(1) Prices should be regulated by a committee of private business people.
(2) Competition among major industries has led to economic chaos.
(3) Strict price-and-wage controls would assure a stable economy.
(4) Government has been unable to deal effectively with a major economic problem.
(5) Deregulation leads to lower prices.

33. A likely response to the problem of inflation referred to in the cartoon would be an increase in the

(1) interest rates on bank loans
(2) amount of Government spending
(3) amount of money in circulation
(4) number of loans approved by banks
(5) number of housing starts

34. Humanism as an intellectual and cultural movement stressed human values and welfare rather than religious interests.

The statement most in agreement with the humanist view is

(1) Life on earth is only a preparation for another life.
(2) Individuals are important and should be treated with dignity.
(3) Degree of faith is an accurate measure of a person's worth.
(4) The best education comes from a thorough understanding of religious doctrines and values.
(5) Man does not have the free will to determine his own destiny.

Items 35 to 37 are based on the following passage.

It is the opinion of some historians that Louis Riel, who led the rebellions of the Metis people in western Canada, was not really a great man. These historians believe that it was only by accident that Louis Riel came to symbolize the divisions between the French and the English cultures north of the forty-ninth parallel. In spite of the fact that the Prime Minister at that time, as well as other leading politicians, saw the rebellions on the Red River and the Saskatchewan as simply the continuation of the historical hostilities that were evident in old Canada, they were not that at all. Rather, they were the results of the extension of the frontier. They were the last attempts of the Metis to stem the flow of progress and to halt the westward extension of civilization that would inevitably obliterate or absorb the last vestiges of their culture.

35. According to the author of the passage, some historians think that the Riel rebellions were

(1) historical accidents
(2) battles for the survival of the Metis culture
(3) the struggle of the Metis against the harsh Canadian frontier
(4) a demonstration of the leadership of Louis Riel
(5) a continuation of the traditional hostilities between the French and the English

36. The Metis referred to in the quotation are

(1) people of mixed French and Native Indian background
(2) immigrants from Europe
(3) refugees from France
(4) people of mixed French and English background
(5) people of mixed Native Indian and English background

37. The author of the passage probably believed that Prime Minister Macdonald viewed the Riel Rebellions as

(1) battles between East and West
(2) a determined people's struggle to maintain their culture
(3) rekindled hostilities between the French and the English
(4) the result of the creation of the North West Mounted Police
(5) a discrepancy between Old and New World values

Items 38 and 39 are based on the following map and chart.

NAFTA ECONOMIES AND TRADE

$Canadian

1992	Canada	United States	Mexico
Population, million	28.8	256	89.5
GDP, million	$688.5	$7,200	$400
Economic growth	0.7%	2.6%	2.7%
Inflation	1.5%	2.6%	14.5%
Share of world exports	4%	13%	1%

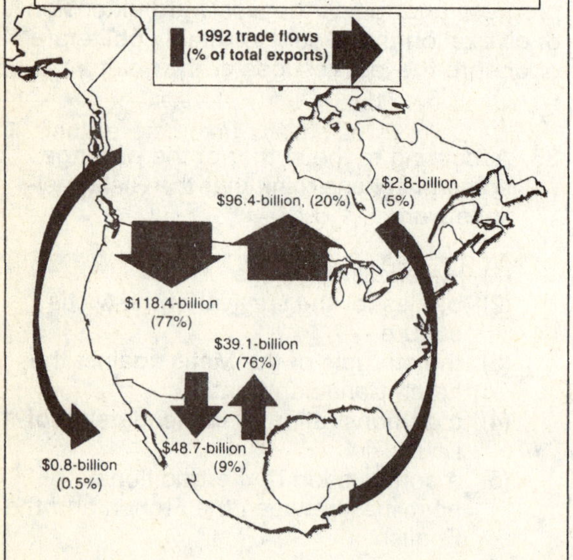

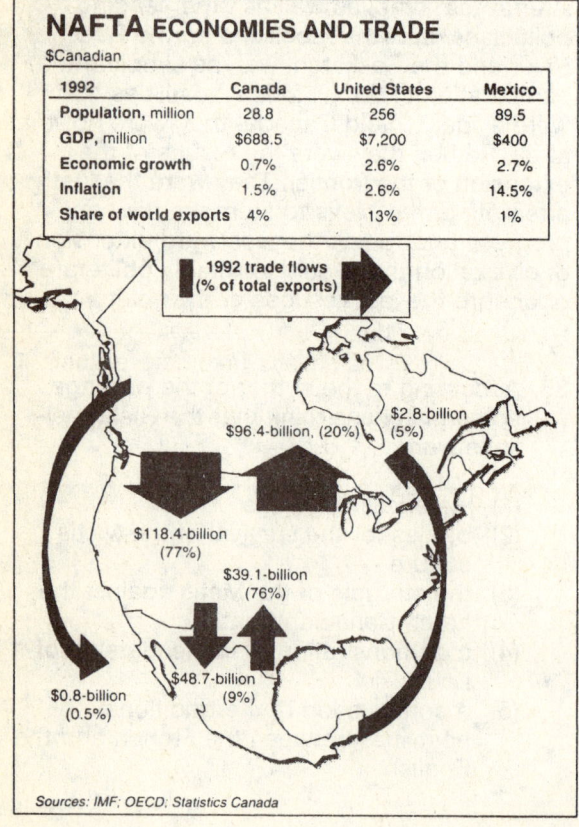

Sources: IMF; OECD; Statistics Canada

38. The North American Free Trade Agreement came into effect on January 1, 1994. Which of the following statements about the three NAFTA countries is supported by information from the map?

(1) Canada had a trade surplus with the United States and a trade deficit with Mexico in 1992.
(2) Canada had a trade surplus with both Mexico and the United States in 1992.
(3) Canada had a trade deficit with both Mexico and the United States in 1992.
(4) Mexico had a trade surplus with both the United States and Canada in 1992.
(5) The United States had a trade deficit with both Canada and Mexico in 1992.

39. Which of the following statements is not supported by the above data?

(1) The gross domestic product per capita is greatest in the United States.
(2) Mexico experienced greater economic growth in 1992 than either Canada or the United States.
(3) Canada had the lowest inflation rate of the three in 1992.
(4) Twenty percent of Canada's exports went to the United States in 1992.
(5) The United States contributed more of the world's share of exports in 1992 than Canada and Mexico combined.

---

40. A primary source is an eyewitness account of an event or events in a specific time period.

Which would be an example of a primary source of information about life in the 18th century North American colonies?

(1) a diary of a colonial shopkeeper
(2) a painting of the colonial period by a 20th century artist
(3) a novel about the flight of the Loyalists from the newly independent American colonies to Canada
(4) a reproduction of furniture used during the colonial period
(5) a social history of the period

Items 41 to 43 are based on the statements made by Speakers A, B, C, D, and E.

Speaker A: Government could not function very well without them. The flow of information they provide to Parliament and the federal agencies is vital to the functioning of a democratic system.

Speaker B: Yes, but the secrecy under which they generally operate makes me suspicious that they are influencing lawmakers in improper ways.

Speaker C: Don't forget that they not only try to influence opinion in Ottawa, but they also try to shape public opinion across the nation in order to create a favourable climate for their views.

Speaker D: That's true! Any politician who chooses to ignore hundreds or perhaps thousands of letters does so at great risk. We have to pay attention to them whether we accept their views or not.

Speaker E: I agree with Speaker C. Public opinion is essential to the functioning of our political system.

41. Which group are the speakers most likely discussing?

(1) lawyers
(2) reporters
(3) government workers
(4) media analysts
(5) lobbyists

42. Which speaker is most concerned about the impact of the methods used by this group upon democratic government?

(1) A
(2) B
(3) C
(4) D
(5) E

43. Which speaker implies that lawmakers frequently must deal with a great many issues about which they know very little?

(1) A
(2) B
(3) C
(4) D
(5) E

Item 44 is based on the following cartoon.

"I'm sorry, Wilson. After 16 years of loyal service, you're being replaced by this microchip."

44. Which statement best summarizes the main point of the above cartoon?

(1) Technological change can be a threat to everyone's job.
(2) Companies always take care of their loyal employees.
(3) Computers are changing the nature of the workplace.
(4) Companies would rather have computers than people.
(5) Older employees are losing their jobs.

Items 45 to 47 are based on the following passage.

The people and groups that provide the stimulation and contact necessary for social development—the socializing agents—usually fall into two classes: (1) those people with authority over the individual, such as parents and teachers, and (2) those in positions of equality with him—age peers, such as playmates or a circle of friends. Since the family is the socializing agent during the critical first years of life, it naturally has great influence. But because of the increased specialization of the functions of the family, the rapidity of social change that tends to divide the generations, and the high degree of mobility and social fluidity, the peer group is perhaps of growing importance in modern urban life.

45. Parents, teachers, and age peers share the role of

(1) people with authority over the individual
(2) peer group members
(3) the friendly circle
(4) the family circle
(5) socializing agents

46. All of these reasons are given for the increased role of peers in an individual's social development EXCEPT

(1) social mobility
(2) social fluidity
(3) generation gap
(4) growing number of peers
(5) specialization of family functions

47. The family, in modern urban life, is

(1) exerting great influence
(2) growing in importance
(3) being replaced by the peer group
(4) filling a broadening role
(5) influential only in the early years of life

Items 48 and 49 refer to the following statements made by Speakers A, B, and C.

Speaker A: Increased contact among nations and peoples is characteristic of our times. A single decision of OPEC or a multinational corporation can send ripples of change throughout our global society.

Speaker B: If we are to survive, all passengers on our Spaceship Earth must participate in efforts to solve the issues that threaten mankind—poverty, resource depletion, pollution, violence, and war.

Speaker C: We must understand that no single culture's view of the world is universally shared. Other people have different value systems and ways of thinking and acting. They will not see the world as we do.

48. Which concept is discussed by both Speakers A and B?

(1) self-determination
(2) nationalism
(3) conservation
(4) interdependence
(5) protectionism

49. Speaker C indicates a desire to reduce

(1) ethnocentrism
(2) globalism
(3) social mobility
(4) religious tolerance
(5) interdependence

END OF TEST

TEST 3: SCIENCE

Directions

Allotted Time: 95 minutes

The **66 multiple-choice questions** in this test measure the general concepts in science. You may find a graph, a chart, or a table included with some questions.

Study the information given. Decide which is the best answer and mark the numbered space on the answer sheet beside the number that corresponds to the question in the test.

Answer all questions. Do not leave any blanks since there is no penalty for incorrect answers. Your score will be determined by the number of your correct responses.

EXAMPLE:

Which of the following is the smallest unit:

(1) element
(2) compound
(3) atom
(4) mixture
(5) molecule

① ② ● ④ ⑤

The correct answer is "atom"; therefore, answer space 3 would be marked on the answer sheet.

Directions: Choose the one best answer to each item.

Items 1 to 4 refer to the following article.

Scientists may differ in their explanation of the method by which evolution has occurred but there is little disagreement among them in regard to the doctrine that all living things have evolved from less complex forms. The paleontologists have studied enough fossils to justify this conclusion. In addition, evidence from other branches of science points to the fact that organic change has occurred and is still going on.

The origin of humanity has been the subject of study for many years by the anthropologist. Also, important knowledge has been added about ancient humans and their civilizations by the archaeologist. Within the study of humanity, anthropologists specialize in their research. One may study the history of a language; another may investigate various types of pottery. Physical anthropology makes a study of the anatomy of various vertebrates, particularly the primates, which is the group of mammals that includes humans, apes, monkeys, and chimpanzees. Comparisons of the anatomy of present forms are made with structures of animals of the past using information gained in the study of fossils.

1. Which of the following terms includes all the others?

(1) human
(2) primate
(3) monkey
(4) ape
(5) chimpanzee

2. Evolution is the biological process by which

(1) fossils are produced in the rock
(2) the anatomy of vertebrates is compared
(3) ancient human life is studied
(4) new kinds of living things arise
(5) chimpanzees give rise to humans

3. Which of the following gives the most direct evidence that different forms of life existed in the past?

(1) organic chemistry
(2) fossils
(3) comparative anatomy
(4) archeology
(5) laboratory experiments

4. Which of the following discoveries would suggest that the human species is still evolving?

   (1) The human brain is much larger than the brain of a gorilla.
   (2) In early stages of development, human embryos have a large tail.
   (3) There is a strong similarity between the chemistry of humans and that of chimpanzees.
   (4) The armour of medieval knights is too small for today's average man.
   (5) Tractors have replaced horses for farm work.

Items 5 to 8 refer to the following article.

Water is so widely distributed that scientists have used it to establish several standards of scientific measurement. The fixed points of a thermometer are set at the boiling and freezing points of water. The calorie is defined in terms of the specific heat of water: a calorie is the amount of heat energy needed to raise the temperature of a gram of water by one degree Celsius. Specific gravity is the density of a substance compared with the density of water. The density of water is just one gram per millilitre because the gram was originally defined as the mass of a millilitre of water.

5. What property of water has made it so useful in defining a variety of scientific standards?

   (1) Its specific heat is exactly one.
   (2) Its density is just one gram per millilitre.
   (3) It boils at a definite temperature.
   (4) It is common and widely distributed.
   (5) Its specific heat is exceptionally high.

6. The calorie is a unit of

   (1) specific heat
   (2) energy
   (3) specific gravity
   (4) temperature
   (5) density

7. Sulphuric acid has a specific gravity of 1.84. This indicates that a litre of sulphuric acid

   (1) is a liquid at room temperature
   (2) will boil at a higher temperature than water
   (3) absorbs more heat than a litre of water
   (4) weighs more than a litre of water
   (5) is widely distributed

8. The density of water is exactly one gram per millilitre because

   (1) the specific heat of water is just one calorie per gram degree Celsius
   (2) the specific gravity of water is exactly one
   (3) the gram was first defined by the density of water
   (4) water boils at exactly 100 degrees Celsius
   (5) water is the most widespread liquid

Items 9 and 10 refer to the following article.

The Swedish scientist, Svante Arrhenius, formulated a theory to explain why water solutions of certain substances conduct electricity. He coined the term *ion* (which means wanderer) to explain why solutions of electrolytes, which are substances like acids, bases, and salts, conduct an electric current. Electrolytes in solution dissociate or ionize into ions. Substances that do not ionize do not conduct an electric current.

9. Which of the following is a nonelectrolyte?

   (1) HNO_3 (nitric acid)
   (2) HCl (hydrochloric acid)
   (3) $Ba(OH)_2$ (barium hydroxide)
   (4) C_3H_8 (propane gas)
   (5) NaCl (table salt)

10. Which of the following compounds in the liquid phase best conducts electricity?

    (1) NaOH (sodium hydroxide)
    (2) H_2O (distilled water)
    (3) H_2O_2 (hydrogen peroxide)
    (4) CuO (rusting copper)
    (5) CO_2 (carbon dioxide)

Items 11 to 13 refer to the following article.

Can you imagine how the thirsty desert traveler who believes he sees water ahead feels when it turns out be a mirage? In dry desert areas during hot summer days, temperatures at the ground reach very high values. In the absence of water, no evaporation takes place to cool the soil. Evaporation is a cooling process as the liquid becomes gaseous. Also, other heat transfer mechanisms, such as convection (the movement of liquids and gases) and condensation (formation of a liquid from a gas) are absent. Thus, the decrease in temperature with height is very great and a mirage occurs. This optical effect occurs when the light rays are bent upward as the air density increases with height. The sky appears to be below and the very hot air is in turbulent motion. This shimmering appearance of the sky makes it look like water.

11. The heat transfer mechanism or mechanisms that act to transport heat upward from the ground include

(A) evaporation
(B) condensation
(C) convection

(1) A only
(2) B only
(3) C only
(4) A and B only
(5) A, B, and C

12. Driving on a very hot road, you may sometimes see what appears to be a large body of water instead of the surface of the approaching road. What explains this mirage?

(1) slow evaporation of vapour in the air and rapid condensation
(2) rapid evaporation of vapour in the air and slow condensation
(3) evaporation of water from a nearby body of water
(4) turbulent motion of the hot air and its effect on light rays
(5) extreme difference of temperature of the air and temperature of the ground

13. Why do you feel cool when you get out of the surf on a dry day?

(1) The water takes heat from your body as it evaporates from your wet skin.
(2) Evaporation produces heat.
(3) Condensation cools the body.
(4) The air is cooler than the surf water.
(5) Sea breezes make you feel cooler.

Items 14 to 16 refer to the following article.

The German engineer, Rudolf Diesel, wondered whether he could develop an engine without spark plugs. He realized that the function of the plugs is to explode the mixture of gasoline and air and that the compression stroke of the gasoline engine squeezes the fuel-air mixture, making it very hot. In the engine named for him, the intake stroke admits air only, not fuel and air. The heavy fuel, such as the oil in diesel engines, is exploded by the high temperature resulting from the compression of air when the tight-fitting piston moves upward in the cylinder. Because of the strong compression stroke, diesel engines are heavy engines and need the strength of a thick-walled cylinder to function. Diesel engines get more energy out of the fuel they burn because they can operate hotter than a gasoline engine.

14. What is true of the diesel engine but not of the gasoline engine?

(1) It needs no air supply.
(2) It has no cylinders.
(3) It has no spark plugs.
(4) It uses less expensive types of gasoline.
(5) It has no pistons.

15. Why are diesel engines used on locomotives?

(1) They can get more heat energy from a less expensive fuel.
(2) Coal-burning engines pollute the air.
(3) It is difficult to store large quantities of gasoline safely in the locomotive.
(4) Electric power is not easily available in remote, rural areas.
(5) Diesel fuel is available in remote, rural areas.

16. Why aren't diesel engines used in airplanes?

(1) Diesel engines are heavy engines.
(2) Diesel oil is very explosive.
(3) Airplanes do not need the power of diesel engines.
(4) Housing the cylinders would take up too much space.
(5) Diesel oil produces more pollutants than other fuels.

Items 17 to 19 refer to the following article.

All nations agree that cooperative efforts are needed to share in research to study and predict earthquakes. In July 1956 the first World Conference on Earthquake Engineering was held in Tokyo. Its purpose was to share information about the prediction of earthquakes and methods of constructing buildings and bridges that can withstand the shocks. What causes earthquakes? The crust of the earth is a broken mosaic of pieces, bounded by deep cracks called faults. When forces deep inside the earth move these pieces, tremendous shock waves start from the faults. The waves can be detected by seismographs all over the world. If the earthquake occurs beneath the ocean, it produces an enormous wave, called a tsunami, that can do much damage when it arrives at a shore.

17. What is the most frequent cause of major earthquakes?

(1) faulting
(2) folding
(3) landslides
(4) submarine currents
(5) tsunamis

18. How can some earthquake destruction be minimized?

(1) more frequent use of seismographs
(2) better construction of buildings
(3) quicker methods of evacuation
(4) international cooperation
(5) better control of tsunamis

19. Nuclear explosions can be detected by seismographs because they

(1) cause tsunamis
(2) occur on geologic faults
(3) cause earthquakes
(4) produce shock waves in the crust
(5) compress the rock

Items 20 to 23 refer to the following article.

All matter is made up of atoms. Atoms contain protons which have positive charges, electrons which have negative charges, and neutrons which are neither positively nor negatively charged. Since the atom has the same number of protons and electrons, the atom as a whole is neutral. The centre of the atom, the nucleus, holds protons and neutrons while the electrons move around in orbits called shells. Each shell has a capacity to hold a maximum number of electrons. The first shell can hold no more than two electrons while the second shell is complete with eight electrons. The third shell can hold eighteen electrons except when it happens to be the outer shell in which case its capacity is only eight electrons. In some atoms, additional shells carry additional electrons.

An atom tends to complete the outer shell either by borrowing electrons, lending electrons, or sharing electrons. The number of electrons available for such action is called valence. For example, a valence of +2 means an atom has two electrons to lend. An atom with a valence of −1 is an atom that needs one electron to complete its outer ring. The borrowing, lending, and sharing of electrons gives rise to the formation of compounds. The atomic mass of an atom is the sum of the total mass of its protons and neutrons. The proton has a mass of one atomic mass unit. The neutron also has a mass of one atomic mass unit, but the electron adds almost nothing to the mass of an atom and so does not have to be considered in calculating atomic mass. The atomic number tells you the number of protons in the atom.

20. The valence of calcium (Ca) is +2. The valence of chlorine(Cl) is −1. When these elements combine to form calcium chloride, the correct formula for this compound is

(1) $CaCl$
(2) Ca_2Cl
(3) $CaCl_2$
(4) Ca_2Cl_2
(5) Ca_4Cl_2

21. Lithium has an atomic mass of 7 and an atomic number of 3. How many neutrons are there in the lithium atom?

(1) none
(2) two
(3) three
(4) four
(5) ten

22. The atomic number of an atom is always equal to the total number of

(1) neutrons in the nucleus
(2) neutrons and protons in the atom
(3) protons and electrons in the atom
(4) electrons in the orbits
(5) protons in the nucleus

23. What is the valence of an element that has 11 protons?

(1) +11
(2) −11
(3) +8
(4) +1
(5) −1

Items 24 to 29 refer to the following article.

Photosynthesis is a complex process with many intermediate steps. Ideas differ greatly as to the details of these steps, but the general nature of the process and its outcome are well established. Water, usually from the soil, is conducted through the xylem of root, stem, and leaf to the chlorophyll-containing cells of a leaf. Carbon dioxide, diffusing from the air through the stomata and into the intercellular spaces of the leaf, comes into contact with the water. The carbon dioxide becomes dissolved in the water, and in solution diffuses through the walls and the plasma membranes into cells. By the agency of chlorophyll in the chloroplasts of the cells, the energy of light is transformed into chemical energy. This chemical energy is used to decompose the carbon dioxide and water, and the products of their decomposition are recombined into a new compound. The compound first formed is successively built up into more and more complex substances until finally a sugar is produced and oxygen is given off as a by-product of the process.

24. Which plant structure is directly involved in the making of sugar?

(1) stoma
(2) xylem
(3) cell wall
(4) plasma membrane
(5) chloroplast

25. To carry on photosynthesis, the water of the soil must be transported to the leaf. Which structure conducts soil water to the leaf?

(1) chlorophyll
(2) stoma
(3) xylem
(4) phloem
(5) chloroplasts

26. Why is chemical energy needed for photosynthesis?

(1) to bring water to the leaf
(2) to decompose chlorophyll
(3) to decompose water
(4) to change the form of light energy
(5) to recombine the products of photosynthesis

27. Sugar is composed of carbon, hydrogen, and oxygen. In the process of photosynthesis, what is the source of these chemical elements?

(1) carbon dioxide alone
(2) water alone
(3) either the carbon dioxide or the water
(4) both the carbon dioxide and the water
(5) neither the carbon dioxide nor the water

28. What is the function of chlorophyll in photosynthesis?

(1) source of carbohydrate
(2) produces carbon dioxide
(3) changes light energy to chemical energy
(4) supplies chemical energy
(5) provides the green colour

29. Carbon dioxide enters a plant by way of the

(1) roots
(2) xylem
(3) plasma membrane
(4) stomata
(5) intercellular spaces

30. In photosynthesis, green plants produce the carbohydrates that become the energy supply of the plants and of the animals that eat them. Photosynthesis can take place only when the plants are in sunlight. Which statement below is a summary of this process?

(1) Light and chemical energy are used for growth.
(2) Chemical energy is converted to light energy.
(3) Light energy is used for growth.
(4) Chemical energy is used for growth.
(5) Light energy is converted to chemical energy.

31. Green plants, in sunlight, absorb carbon dioxide to produce glucose, releasing oxygen in the process. Which of the following would be most likely to increase the rate at which this process goes on?

(1) Increase the amount of oxygen in the air.
(2) Add glucose to the soil.
(3) Move the plants into the shade.
(4) Reduce the amount of carbon dioxide in the air.
(5) Increase the amount of carbon dioxide in the air.

32. In the process of evolution, organisms undergo long-range changes that cause them to become better adapted to the environment in which they live. What is the probable reason that African hornbills closely resemble the South American toucans, even though they are unrelated?

(1) The resemblance is purely a coincidence.
(2) There has been an interchange of genetic material between the two kinds of birds.
(3) The two kinds of birds have evolved from a common ancestor.
(4) Both kinds of birds are fruit eaters in tropical rain forests.
(5) The toucans have migrated from Africa.

33. Green plants, like animals, produce the energy they need by the reaction of sugar with oxygen. Under what conditions do they use more oxygen than they produce?

(1) when the atmosphere has a lot of carbon dioxide
(2) when the atmosphere has a lot of oxygen
(3) when the soil is extremely wet
(4) when the sunlight is unusually strong
(5) at night, in the dark

34. A daily dose of 8000 units of vitamin A is recommended for expectant mothers. The chemical compound 13-cisretinoic acid, chemically related to vitamin A, is found to be responsible for certain birth defects. What recommendation should be made to pregnant mothers?

(1) Avoid vitamins.
(2) Take larger doses of vitamin A.
(3) Take no vitamin A.
(4) Wait for further research results before modifying vitamin intake.
(5) Avoid doses of more than 8000 units of vitamin A.

35. Potassium is receiving special attention as an important nutritional requirement. Potassium conducts an electric charge and is important in the transmission of nerve impulses and muscle contraction. Such foods as banana and dried apricots are rich in potassium. These foods are recommended for those whose medication involves the loss of body water because they also lose potassium. Why would the heart malfunction with the loss of potassium?

(1) The heart needs banana and apricot.
(2) The heart absorbs much potassium.
(3) High blood pressure can be treated.
(4) Low blood pressure can be treated.
(5) Contraction of heart muscles requires potassium.

36. Oxides of carbon, sulphur, and nitrogen, which occur in the stack gases of coal-burning plants, react with water to form acids. The pollution caused by stack gases might be responsible for all the following forms of environmental damage EXCEPT

(1) physical deformity of developing fish
(2) corrosion of buildings
(3) death of many forest trees
(4) damage to human lungs
(5) sewage contamination of water supplies

37. The laws that control recombination of genes seem to be much the same for all sexually reproducing organisms. The laws are studied by statistical analysis of large numbers of offspring for several generations. Which of the following organisms would be most useful in experiments to study the laws of recombination of genes?

(1) bacteria
(2) human beings
(3) mice
(4) dogs
(5) oak trees

38. The early atmosphere of the earth had no oxygen. It was first produced when bacteria developed the green pigment that made photosynthesis possible. Which of the following groups represent the sequence in which the organisms appeared on earth?

(1) animals, green bacteria, non-green bacteria
(2) green bacteria, animals, non-green bacteria
(3) animals, non-green bacteria, green bacteria
(4) non-green bacteria, green bacteria, animals
(5) non-green bacteria, animals, green bacteria

39. The diagram below shows the changes in the populations of wolves and moose in a northern forest for a period of six years. What is the most reasonable explanation of the facts?

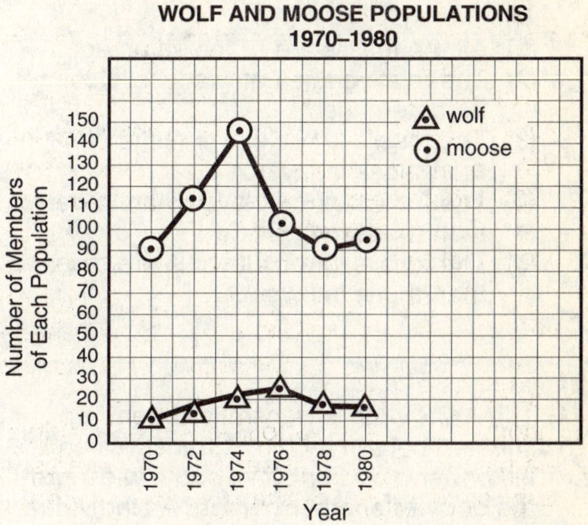

(1) Moose produce more offspring when there are few wolves.
(2) When there are many wolves, they kill many more moose.
(3) Wolves produce more offspring when there are many moose.
(4) Both wolf and moose populations vary according to the weather conditions.
(5) Wolf populations have no relationship to the availability of moose.

Item 40 is based on the following diagram.

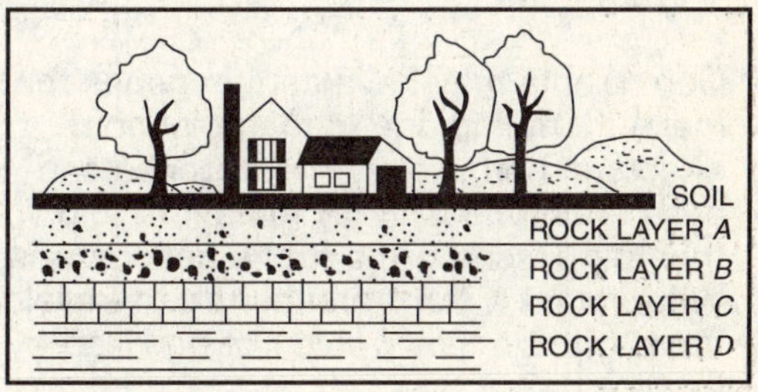

40. When sediments are deposited in the ocean, new layers form on top of preexisting layers. The sediments may eventually turn into fossil-bearing rocks. What might a geologist conclude about fossils found in the rock layers shown in the diagram?

(1) All the fossils are of the same age.
(2) The relative ages of the fossils cannot be determined.
(3) The fossils in rock layer *D* are older than those in layer *A*.
(4) The fossils in rock layer *B* are older than those in layer *C*.
(5) The fossils in rock layer *A* are older than those in layer *B*.

---

41. The AIDS virus is transmitted from an infected person by direct transmission of his or her blood or other body fluids into the body of another person. An individual can contract AIDS by any of the following means EXCEPT

(1) breathing the air expelled by a person with the disease
(2) sexual intercourse with an infected person
(3) using a hypodermic needle that had been used by someone with the disease
(4) receiving a blood transfusion from an infected person
(5) passage of the virus from a pregnant woman into the fetus she is carrying

42. Corn plants may have certain genes that make them immune to the poisonous effects of herbicides. These genes can arise spontaneously by mutation, and will then be passed on to future generations. What might a plant breeder do to develop a line of corn that would not be killed by herbicides?

(1) Apply herbicides to cause mutations.
(2) Prevent mutations by careful control of environmental conditions.
(3) Find immune plants by applying herbicides and breeding the survivors.
(4) Withhold all fertilizers and breed those plants that survive.
(5) Withhold all herbicides and breed whichever plants mutate.

43. Since World War II, new varieties of rice have been developed that produce two or three times as much grain when they are grown with heavy doses of chemical fertilizers. A farmer should decide not to use these varieties if

(1) he is accustomed to growing more familiar varieties of rice
(2) he is cultivating only a small plot
(3) his farm is in an unusually wet climate
(4) there is no way he can get access to the seed of the new varieties
(5) the fertilizer needed costs more than the value of the extra grain

44. When alcohol is heated, it releases a heavy, flammable vapour. What precaution should be taken in heating alcohol in a test tube?

(1) Cork the test tube, and then heat it gently near the bottom only.
(2) Heat the open test tube gently near the bottom only.
(3) Cork the test tube and place it in a beaker of water; then heat the water in the beaker.
(4) Place the open test tube in a beaker of water, and then heat the water in the beaker.
(5) Heat the open test tube in the middle and then the bottom.

<u>Items 45 to 49</u> refer to the following article.

Today some plants are cloned to produce millions of offspring from a small piece of the original plant. Plant cloning is possible because the plant's diploid cells have the same genetic potential as the zygote that originally produced the plant and because of the action of the plant hormones auxin and cytokinin. These hormones are combined with other organic and inorganic substances in a growth medium that stimulates the production of new plants. The cloning process occurs in a sterile environment. The new plants produced are genetically identical to the original plant and to each other.

The process and equipment for cloning are more expensive than for other forms of vegetative propagation. The advantage of cloning is that large numbers of desirable plants are produced in a short period of time. For example, a million plants of a new variety can be cloned in about six months.

45. For which reason is cloning used to reproduce plants?
    (1) Plants with a large degree of genetic variability are produced.
    (2) Plants are produced more cheaply than by other vegetative methods.
    (3) Plants are produced by the sexual process, resulting in seeds.
    (4) A large number of plants are produced in a short period of time.
    (5) Plants with large degrees of variation are produced.

46. If the diploid chromosome number of a cloned plant is 12, what is the chromosome number of the plant cell used to produce the cloned plant?
    (1) 3
    (2) 6
    (3) 12
    (4) 24
    (5) 36

47. Which statement describes the hormones auxin and cytokinin?
    (1) They are forms of vegetative propagation.
    (2) They can develop into a zygote.
    (3) They stimulate the production of new plants.
    (4) They inhibit the production of new plants.
    (5) They are forms of asexual reproduction.

48. How is cloning defined?
    (1) a form of sexual reproduction
    (2) a form of vegetative propagation
    (3) an inorganic hormone
    (4) an inorganic component of the growing medium
    (5) an auxin

49. An important difference between plants produced by cloning and plants grown from seed is that
    (1) cloned plants are healthier
    (2) cloned plants are identical to the parent plant
    (3) plants grown from seed are identical to the parent plant
    (4) plants grown from seed are better adapted to the conditions in which the plants are grown
    (5) cloned plants do not need as much care

50. Liquid solutions are clear. The particles are the size of molecules and do not sink. Why do we find on the label on some medicines, "Shake well before using"?
    (1) The liquid is a solution.
    (2) The mixture is not a solution.
    (3) The particles are the size of molecules.
    (4) The particles are not visible.
    (5) Light goes through the solution.

<u>Items 51 to 53</u> refer to the following article.

Compounds known as bases are bitter to the taste and have a slippery feel. Acids taste sour. Litmus paper is used to determine whether a substance is acid or basic; the paper turns blue in a base and red in an acid. If exactly correct quantities of an acid and a base are combined, they react chemically to produce a salt, which is neither acid nor basic.

51. All of the following are acids EXCEPT
    (1) oranges
    (2) vinegar
    (3) sour cream
    (4) apples
    (5) butter

52. Which of the following would turn litmus paper blue?
    (1) alcohol
    (2) soap
    (3) grapefruit
    (4) pure water
    (5) cream soda

53. Either a base such as ammonia or an acid like vinegar can clean accumulated dirt from glass. Knowing this, a housekeeper makes a mixture of ammonia and vinegar to clean windows. How would this work?
    (1) There is no way to predict how well this works.
    (2) The mixture would work better than either substance alone.
    (3) The ammonia would still be effective, but the vinegar would not improve the material.
    (4) The vinegar would still be effective, but the ammonia would not improve the material.
    (5) The mixture would probably not work well at all.

54. Which of the following general rules is the best explanation of the way an ice cube cools down a drink?

(1) Cold moves to objects of higher temperature.
(2) Heat moves to objects of higher density.
(3) Heat moves to objects of lower density.
(4) Cold moves to objects of lower temperature.
(5) Heat moves into objects of lower temperature.

Items 55 to 58 are based on the following passage and diagram.

When air rises, it expands, and this makes it cool down. Conversely, when air sinks, it is compressed and it gets warmer. As air cools down, its relative humidity rises, and when the relative humidity gets to 100%, moisture condenses out of the air.

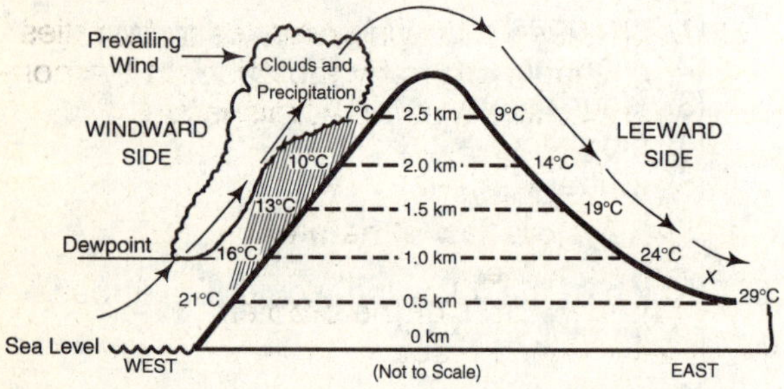

The diagram shows the prevailing wind direction and air temperatures at different elevations on both sides of the mountain.

55. What would be the approximate air temperature at the top of the mountain?

(1) 12°C
(2) 10°C
(3) 0°C
(4) 7°C
(5) 4°C

56. On which side of the mountain and at what elevation is the relative humidity probably 100%?

(1) on the windward side at 0.5 km
(2) on the windward side at 1.5 km
(3) on the leeward side at 1.0 km
(4) on the leeward side at 2.5 km
(5) on the leeward side at 1.5 km

57. How does the temperature of the air change as the air rises on the windward side of the mountain between sea level and 0.5 kilometres?

(1) The air is warming owing to compression of the air.
(2) The air is warming owing to expansion of the air.
(3) The air is cooling owing to compression of the air.
(4) The air is cooling owing to expansion of the air.
(5) The air is warmed and cooled owing to expansion of the air.

58. Which feature is probably located at the base of the mountain on the leeward side (location *X*)?

(1) an arid region
(2) a jungle
(3) a glacier
(4) a large lake
(5) a river

---

59. Human activities produce or add all these pollutants except

(1) sound
(2) pollen
(3) radiation
(4) smoke
(5) carbon oxides

Items 60 and 61 are based on the following passage and diagram.

The block marked A is being pulled uphill at constant speed by the falling weight. Since its speed is constant, the force pulling it uphill must be equal in magnitude to the force holding it back.

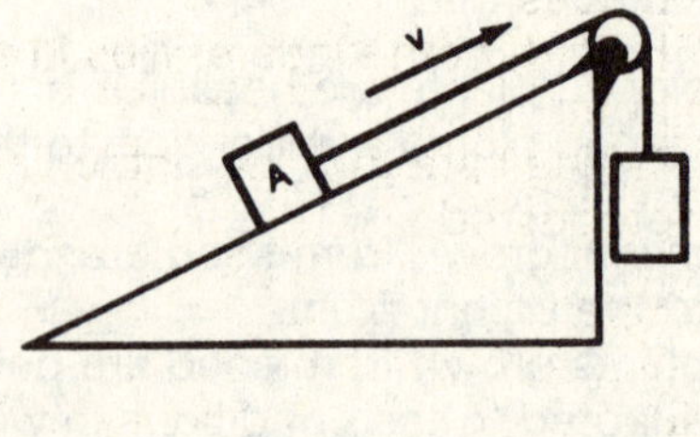

60. How would the situation change if a larger weight were used?

(1) Nothing would be different.
(2) Both the block and the weight would accelerate instead of going at a constant speed.
(3) Both the block and the weight would be going at a higher constant speed.
(4) The weight would accelerate, but the block would still travel at constant speed.
(5) Both the block and the weight would slow down.

61. Which arrow best represents the direction of the force of friction on the block?

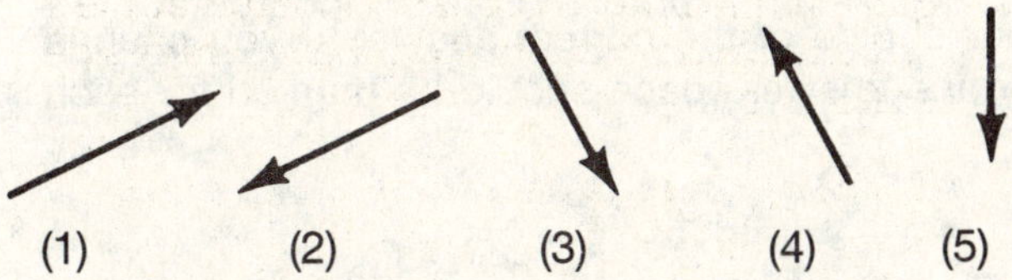

Items 62 to 66 refer to the following information.

An experiment was performed to find out whether there are any circumstances in which an abnormal type of fruit fly has a selective advantage over the normal kind. Two culture bottles were prepared, using the same kind of food, and they were kept next to each other for the entire period of the experiment. Bottle A has a small strip of flypaper suspended from its stopper, and B did not. Four kinds of flies were introduced into each bottle: 10 males and 10 females each of wingless and normal fruit flies.

62. Which of the following is an important control in this experiment?

(1) The use of both males and females
(2) Placing the flypaper in one bottle only
(3) Using the same kind of food in both bottles
(4) Putting both kinds of flies in each bottle
(5) Taking care that the bottles are well-stoppered

63. What is the hypothesis being tested?

(1) Male fruit flies have a better survival rate than females.
(2) Flies with wings have a better survival rate than those without.
(3) There are circumstances in which winglessness confers an advantage in survival.
(4) Wingless flies have a better survival rate than those with wings.
(5) All kinds of flies are equally likely to survive.

64. The experiment started with equal numbers of the four kinds of flies in each jar. This is a(n)

(1) irrelevant fact
(2) detail of experimental design
(3) assumption
(4) general law of nature
(5) experimental finding

65. It is known that winglessness in fruit flies sometimes arises by mutation. In the context of this experiment, this is a(n)

(1) assumption
(2) general law of nature
(3) hypothesis
(4) statement of the problem
(5) irrelevant fact

66. What general principle of nature would be exemplified by the finding that most of the flies with wings dies on the flypaper?

(1) Flypaper is an effective means of control of insects.
(2) Fruit flies exist in nature in many different forms.
(3) Evolution favours those forms with the best survival value.
(4) Survival value of a trait depends on the environment in which the organism lives.
(5) Processes in natural ecosystems cannot be simulated in the laboratory.

END OF TEST

TEST 4: LANGUAGE ARTS, READING (INTERPRETING LITERATURE AND THE ARTS) TEST

Directions

Allotted Time: 45 minutes

This test consists of **24 multiple-choice questions** based on passages from classical and popular literature, prose, poetry, and drama, as well as from articles about literature and the arts—music, dance, and mass media, such as television.

Each passage is introduced by a question designed to help you locate the main purpose of the selection and to focus on the ideas presented to achieve that purpose.

Since you are allowed 45 minutes, be careful not to spend too much time on each question.

Make no mark on the answer sheet other than your choice of the correct answer. If you change your answer, erase your first mark completely. Only *one* answer space should be marked for each question.

EXAMPLE:

I went to the woods because I wished to live deliberately, to front only the essential facts of life, and see if I could not learn what it had to teach, and not, when I came to die, discover that I had not lived.

The author

(1) wishes to learn from nature
(2) is afraid of death
(3) has little regard for life
(4) seeks life's pleasures
(5) wishes to avoid life's problems.

● ② ③ ④ ⑤

The author states that he wanted to "learn what it (the woods, that is, nature) had to teach" so 1 is the correct answer and 1 should be marked on the answer paper.

Directions: Choose the one best answer to each item.

Items 1 to 5 refer to the following excerpt from a work of prose nonfiction.

WHAT WAS MARY WHITE'S LAST HOUR LIKE?

The last hour of Mary White's life was typical of its happiness. She came home from a day's work at school, topped off by a hard grind with the copy on the high school annual, and felt that a ride would refresh her. She climbed into her khakis, chattering to her mother about the work she was doing, and hurried to get her horse and be out on the dirt roads for the country air and the radiant green fields of the spring. As she rode through the town at an easy gallop, she kept waving at passersby. She knew everyone in town. For a decade the little figure with the long pigtail and the red hair ribbon had been familiar on the streets of Emporia, and she got in the way of speaking to those who nodded at her. She passed the Kerrs, walking the horse, in front of the Normal Library, and waved at them; passed another friend a few hundred feet farther on, and waved at her. The horse was walking, and as she turned into North Merchant Street, she took off her cowboy hat, and the horse swung into a lope. She passed the Tripletts and waved her cowboy hat at them, still moving gaily north on Merchant Street. A *Gazette* carrier passed—a high school boyfriend—and she waved at him, but with her bridle hand; the horse veered quickly, plunged into the parking lot where a low-hanging limb faced her, and while she still looked back waving, the blow came. But she did not fall from the horse; she slipped off, dazed a bit, staggered, and fell in a faint. She never quite recovered consciousness.

1. The passage gives details which create a picture of a(n)

   (1) sad death
   (2) bookish lady
   (3) active girl
   (4) boy-crazy kid
   (5) pathetic child

2. Mary White was

   (1) small of stature
   (2) big-boned
   (3) tall
   (4) husky
   (5) pretty

3. The picture contains such details as

   (1) jeans, a green ribbon, a pigtail
   (2) riding clothes, sombrero, plait
   (3) overalls, cowboy hat, short hair
   (4) khakis, cowboy hat, red hair ribbon
   (5) bridle, saddle, spurs

4. The death of Mary White can be said to have been caused indirectly by her

   (1) poor horsemanship
   (2) small size
   (3) fast riding
   (4) friendliness
   (5) failure to take proper precautions

5. The main purpose of the author is to

   (1) report the tragic end of a happy life
   (2) stress that it was an accident that killed Mary White
   (3) inform us of the mistake she made in waving with the wrong hand
   (4) show Mary White's bravery in not falling from the horse
   (5) emphasize the unexpectedness of the fatal blow

Items 6 to 10 refer to the following excerpt from a work of prose fiction.

WHAT CAN A BEREAVED FATHER DO?

Iona sees a hall porter with some sacking, and decides to talk to him.

"Friend, what sort of time is it?" he asks.

"Past nine. What are you standing here for? Move on."

Iona moves on a few steps, doubles up, and abandons himself to his grief. He gives a tug at the reins; he can bear it no longer. "The stables," he thinks, and the little horse, as if it understood, starts off at a trot.

One of the cabdrivers around the stove half gets up, grunts sleepily, and stretches toward a bucket of water.

"Do you want a drink?" Iona asks him.

"Don't I want a drink!"

"That's so? Your good health! But listen, mate—you know, my son is dead . . . Did you hear? This week, in the hospital . . . It's a long story."

Iona looks to see what effect his words have, but sees none—the young man is fast asleep again. Just as much as the young one wants to drink, the old man wants to talk. Is it nothing to tell?

"I'll go and look after my horse," thinks Iona; "there's always time to sleep. No fear of that!"

When he is alone, he dares not think of his son; he can speak about him to anyone, but to think of him, and picture him to himself, is unbearably painful.

"That's how it is, my old horse. There's no more Kuzma Ionitch. Now let's say, you had a foal, you were the foal's mother, and suddenly, let's say, that foal went out and left you to live after him. It would be sad, wouldn't it?"

The little horse munches, listens, and breathes over its master's hand . . .

Iona's feelings are too much for him, and he tells the little horse the whole story.

6. In this story it is ironic that

(1) the cabdriver wants a drink
(2) the hall porter tells Iona to move on
(3) Iona tells his story to his horse
(4) Iona has run out of food for his horse
(5) the horse had a foal

7. Iona goes to take care of his horse. He does so most probably to

(1) have something to do
(2) protest the high cost of feed
(3) show his great love for his horse
(4) prove that he does not resent the cab-driver's action
(5) remove his feelings of guilt

8. The setting for this story is probably a nineteenth-century

(1) American city
(2) eastern European city
(3) northern European farm
(4) American small town
(5) English city

9. The author's purpose in using the present tense is most probably to

(1) make the story seem modern
(2) increase the length of the story
(3) heighten the reader's sense of immediacy
(4) write the story as consciously as possible
(5) reinforce the first person point of view

10. Iona's situation is brought home to the reader when he

(1) asks the hall porter for the time
(2) asks the cab driver for a drink
(3) talks to himself
(4) fights off sleep
(5) compares himself to a foal's mother

Items 11 to 15 refer to the following excerpt from a work of prose fiction.

WHAT WAS ANNA WORRIED ABOUT?

Having been seen at the window, having been waved to, made Anna step back instinctively. A face at the window for no reason is a face that should have a thumb in its mouth: there is something only-childish about it. Or, if the face is not foolish, it is threatening—blotted white by the darkness inside the room, it suggests a malignant indoor power. Would Portia and Thomas think she had been spying on them?

Also, she had been seen holding a letter—not a letter that she had got today. It was to escape from thoughts out of the letter that she had gone to the window to look out. Now she went back to her escritoire which, in a shadowed corner of this large light room, was not suitable to write more than notes at. In the pigeonholes she kept her engagement pad, her account books; the drawers under the flap were useful because they locked. At present, a drawer stood open, showing packets of letters; and more letters, creased from folding, exhaling an old smell, lay about among slipped-off rubberbands. Hearing Thomas's latchkey, the hall door opening, Portia's confident voice, Anna swept the letters into the drawer quickly, then knelt down to lock everything up. But this sad little triumph of being ready in time came to nothing, for the two Quaynes went straight into the study; they did not come upstairs.

11. Anna's treatment of her possessions suggests that she

(1) is disorganized
(2) cherishes accuracy
(3) values her privacy
(4) dislikes everyone
(5) lives only for the present

12. In this passage, the author's chief purpose seems to be to

    (1) describe the room clearly
    (2) determine Anna's likes and dislikes
    (3) create sympathy for the Quaynes
    (4) predict Anna's relationships
    (5) indicate Anna's concerns

13. Which most probably happened prior to the events in this passage?

    (1) The Quaynes had been away from the house.
    (2) The Quaynes mailed a letter to Anna.
    (3) The Quaynes delivered Anna's mail to her.
    (4) Anna saw a face at the window.
    (5) Anna tried to open the window.

14. The point of view in this passage gives the reader

    (1) only what Anna knows and experiences
    (2) Anna's thoughts and the author's understanding of them
    (3) an objective picture of the entire household
    (4) the thoughts of several characters
    (5) the Quaynes' opinion of Anna

15. Anna has gone to the window to

    (1) look for Portia and Thomas
    (2) get away from what she read in a letter
    (3) get ready for the Quaynes
    (4) spy on the Quaynes
    (5) relieve the darkness in the room

Items 16 to 20 refer to the following excerpt from a play.

HOW DOES THE FAMILY RESPOND TO LINDNER'S OFFER?

WALTER: I mean—I have worked as a chauffeur most of my life—and my wife here, she does domestic work in people's kitchens. So does my mother, I mean—we are plain people . . .

LINDNER: Yes, Mr. Younger—

WALTER: [*Really like a small boy, looking down at his shoes and then up at the man*] And—uh—well, my father, well, he was a labourer most of his life.

LINDNER: [*Absolutely confused*] Uh, yes—

WALTER: [*Looking down at his toes once again*] My father almost beat a man to death once because this man called him a bad name or something, you know what I mean?

LINDNER: No, I'm afraid I don't.

WALTER: [*Finally straightening up*] Well, what I means is that we come from people who had a lot of pride. I mean—we are very proud people. And that's my sister over there and she's going to be a doctor—and we are very proud—

LINDNER: Well—I am sure that is very nice, but—

WALTER: [*Starting to cry and facing the man eye to eye*] What I am telling you is that we called you over here to tell you that we are very proud and that this is—this is my son, who makes the sixth generation of our family in this country, and that we have all thought about your offer and we have decided to move into our house because my father—my father—he earned it. [MAMA *has her eyes closed and is rocking back and forth as though she were in church, with her head nodding the amen yes*] We don't want to make no trouble for nobody or fight no causes—but we will try to be good neighbours. That's all we got to say. [*He looks the man absolutely in the eyes*] We don't want your money. [*He turns and walks away from the man*]

LINDNER: [*Looking around at all of them*] I take it then that you have decided to occupy.

BENEATHA: That's what the man said.

LINDNER: [*To* MAMA *in her reverie*] Then I would like to appeal to you, Mrs. Younger. You are older and wiser and understand things better I am sure . . .

MAMA: [*Rising*] I am afraid you don't understand. My son said we was going to move and there ain't nothing left for me to say. [*Shaking her head with double meaning*] You know how these young folks is nowadays, mister. Can't do a thing with 'em. Good-bye.

LINDNER: [*Folding up his materials*] Well—if you are that final about it . . . There is nothing left for me to say. [*He finishes. He is almost ignored by the family who are concentrating on* WALTER LEE, *At the door* LINDNER *halts and looks around*] I sure hope you people know what you're doing. [*He shakes his head and exits*]

—Lorraine Hansberry, *A Raisin in the Sun*

16. The story Walter tells about his father almost beating a man to death for calling him a name is a(n)

(1) anecdote
(2) lie
(3) warning
(4) dream
(5) allusion

17. From this point on, the family will

(1) stay in the ghetto
(2) try for a new life
(3) sell their house
(4) retreat to the South
(5) fight for causes

18. After this incident, the head of the house will be

(1) Travis
(2) Mama
(3) Walter
(4) Ruth
(5) Beneatha

19. Mr. Lindner

(1) understands the Youngers
(2) despises the Youngers
(3) is sympathetic to the Youngers
(4) is tolerant of the Youngers
(5) disagrees with the Youngers

20. The word that best describes Walter's family is

(1) plain
(2) vicious
(3) proud
(4) trouble-making
(5) uncooperative

Items 21 to 24 refer to the following commentary on the plays Romeo and Juliet and West Side Story.

HOW DO ROMEO AND JULIET AND WEST SIDE STORY COMPARE?

What glorious verse falls from the lips of Shakespeare's boys and girls! True, there is a rollicking jazzy vigour in such songs of West Side Story as the one of Officer Krupke, but it pales alongside the pyrotechnical display of Mercurio's Queen Mab speech. There is tenderness in "Maria," but how relatively tongue-tied is the twentieth-century hero alongside the boy who cried, "He jests at scars that never felt a wound." "Hold my hand and we're halfway there," say Maria and Tony to each other, and the understatement touches us. But "Gallop apace, you fiery-footed steeds" and the lines that follow glow with a glory that never diminishes. The comparisons of language could be multiplied, and always, of course, Shakespeare is bound to win.

Without its great poetry Romeo and Juliet would not be a major tragedy. Possibly it is not, in any case; for as has frequently been remarked, Shakespeare's hero and heroine are a little too slender to carry the full weight of tragic grandeur. Their plight is more pathetic than tragic. If this is true of them, it is equally true of Tony and Maria: for them, too, pathos rather than tragedy. But there is tragedy implicit in the environmental situation of the contemporary couple, and this must not be overlooked or underestimated. Essentially, however, what we see is that all four young people strive to consummate the happiness at the threshold on which they stand and which they have tasted so briefly. All four are deprived of the opportunity to do so, the Renaissance couple by the caprice of fate, today's youngsters by the prejudice and hatred engendered around them. All four are courageous and lovable. All four arouse our compassion, even though they may not shake us with Aristotelian fear.

Poets and playwrights will continue to write of youthful lovers whom fate drives into and out of each other's lives. The spectacle will always trouble and move us.

21. In comparing the language of Romeo and Juliet with that of West Side Story the author

(1) takes no position
(2) likes each equally
(3) favours that of Romeo and Juliet
(4) favours that of West Side Story
(5) downplays the differences

22. Both plays share a common weakness. That weakness is

(1) the stature of their heroes and heroines
(2) the absence of deep emotion
(3) their dramatic construction
(4) the lack of substance of their themes
(5) the lack of linguistic power

23. The couples in the two plays share all of the following EXCEPT

(1) a pathetic situation
(2) lack of opportunity to achieve happiness
(3) courage
(4) inability to instill fear in the reader
(5) inability to arouse pity in the reader

24. The couples in the two plays differ in the nature of

(1) their plight
(2) their ultimate fate
(3) the cause of their tragic situation
(4) their attractiveness
(5) their love for one another

END OF TEST

TEST 5: MATHEMATICS

Directions

Allotted Time: 55 minutes

This test consists of **36 multiple-choice questions** designed to measure general mathematics skills and problem-solving ability. Some questions include a graph, chart, or figure, along with a short reading upon which the question is based. You may not use a calculator during the test.

Some questions require the application of a formula. Page 71 has any of the formulae you may need.

There will be some questions that give more information than you need to solve the problem. Other questions do not furnish enough information to solve the problem. In such cases, choose the answer "Not enough information is given."

Work carefully but do not spend too much time on any one question. Record your answer on the answer sheet by marking the numbered space beside the number that corresponds to the question in the test. Answer all questions since there is no penalty for incorrect answers. Your score will depend on the number of correct responses.

EXAMPLE:

I purchased five 45¢ postage stamps with two $2 bills. How much change should be returned? (Do not calculate GST.)

(1) $.29
(2) $.54
(3) $1.45
(4) $1.55
(5) $1.75

① ② ③ ④ ●

The correct answer is $1.75; therefore, answer space 5 should be marked on the answer sheet.

FORMULAE

Description	Formula
AREA (A) of a:	
square	$A = s^2$; where s = side
rectangle	$A = lw$; where l = length, w = width
parallelogram	$A = bh$; where b = base, h = height
triangle	$A = \frac{1}{2} bh$; where b = base, h = height
circle	$A = \pi r^2$; where $\pi = 3.14$, r = radius
PERIMETER (P) of a:	
square	$P = 4s$; where s = side
rectangle	$P = 2l + 2w$; where l = length, w = width
triangle	$P = a + b + c$; where a, b, and c are the sides
circumference (C) of a circle	$C = \pi d$; where $\pi = 3.14$, d = diameter
VOLUME (V) of a:	
cube	$V = s^3$; where s = side
rectangular container	$V = lwh$; where l = length, w = width, h = height
cylinder	$V = \pi r^2 h$; where $\pi = 3.14$, r = radius, h = height
Pythagorean relationship	$c^2 = a^2 + b^2$; where c = hypotenuse, a and b are legs of a right triangle
distance (d) between two points in a plane	$d = \sqrt{(x_2 - x_1)^2 + (y_2 - y_1)^2}$; where (x_1, y_1) and (x_2, y_2) are two points in a plane
slope of a line (m)	$m = \frac{y_2 - y_1}{x_2 - x_1}$; where (x_1, y_1) and (x_2, y_2) are two points in a plane
mean	$mean = \frac{x_1 + x_2 + \cdots + x_n}{n}$; where the x's are the values for which a mean is desired, and n = number of values in the series
median	median = the point in an ordered set of numbers at which half of the numbers are above and half of the numbers are below this value
simple interest (i)	$i = prt$; where p = principal, r = rate, t = time
distance (d) as function of rate and time	$d = rt$; where r = rate, t = time
total cost (c)	$c = nr$; where n = number of units, r = cost per unit

<u>Directions:</u> Choose the <u>one best answer</u> to each item.

1. One-half of the students at Lester B. Pearson High School walk to school. One-fourth of the remainder go to school by bicycle. What part of the school population travels by some other means?

   (1) 1/8
   (2) 3/8
   (3) 3/4
   (4) 1/4
   (5) Not enough information is given.

2. For which value of x is the inequality $2x > 9$ true?

   (1) 0
   (2) 2
   (3) 3
   (4) 4
   (5) 5

3. A purse contains 6 nickels, 5 dimes, and 8 quarters. If one coin is drawn at random from the purse, what is the probability that the coin drawn is a dime?

   (1) 5/19
   (2) 5/14
   (3) 5/8
   (4) 5/6
   (5) 19/5

4. The leaders in the Peninsula Golf Tournament finished with scores of 272, 284, 287, 274, 275, 283, 278, 276, and 281. What is the median of these scores?

   (1) 273
   (2) 274
   (3) 276
   (4) 278
   (5) 280

5. The cost of a dozen ballpoint pens and 8 pencils is \$4.60. If the cost of the pens is 3 for \$.97, what is the cost of one pencil, in cents?

   (1) 8
   (2) 8.5
   (3) 9.5
   (4) 6
   (5) 9

6. The scale on a map is 1 cm to 150 km. The cities of Benton and Dover are 3.5 cm apart on this map. What is the distance between Benton and Dover in kilometres?

   (1) 525
   (2) 545
   (3) 580
   (4) 625
   (5) Not enough information is given.

<u>Item 7</u> is based on the following figure.

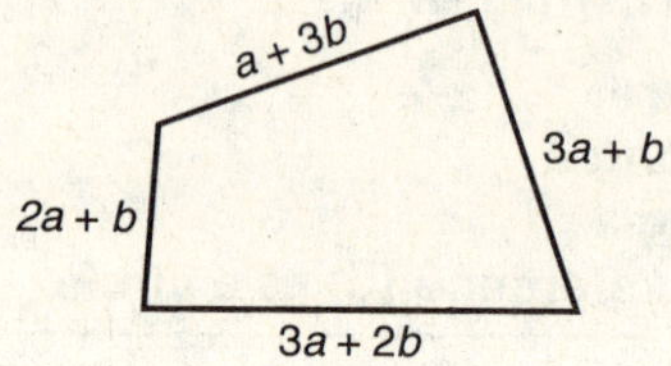

7. What is the perimeter of the figure?

   (1) $8a + 5b$
   (2) $9a + 7b$
   (3) $7a + 5b$
   (4) $6a + 6b$
   (5) $8a + 6b$

<u>Item 8</u> is based on the following number line.

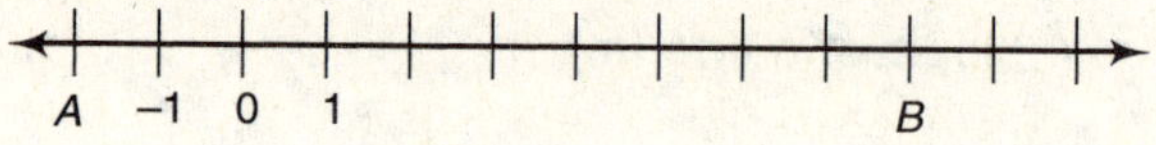

8. On the number line, what is the coordinate of the midpoint of $\overline{AB}$?

   (1) –11
   (2) 0
   (3) 2
   (4) 3
   (5) 8

---

9. The Men's Shop advertised a spring sale. David Morris was especially interested in the following sale items.
   3 ties for \$23, or \$8 each
   3 shirts for \$43, or \$15 each
   slacks \$32.75 each pair
   jackets \$58.45 each
   David bought 6 ties, 3 shirts, 2 pairs of slacks, and one jacket. What was his bill excluding tax?

   (1) \$157.20
   (2) \$180.20
   (3) \$189.95
   (4) \$202.95
   (5) \$212.95

10. Consider the following arrangements of the given set of numbers.

A. 0.80, 19%, 0.080, 1/2, 3/5
B. 0.80, 1/2, 0.080, 3/5, 19%
C. 0.80, 3/5, 1/2, 19%, 0.080
D. 1/2, 0.80, 3/5, 19%, 0.080
E. 3/5, 1/2, 19%, 0.080, 0.80

Which one of the above arrangements places the numbers in order from the greatest to the smallest?

(1) A
(2) B
(3) C
(4) D
(5) E

11. If an airplane completes its flight of 880 km in 5 hours and 30 minutes, what is its average speed, in kilometres per hour?

(1) 155
(2) 156
(3) 160
(4) 180
(5) 280

12. The distance between two heavenly bodies is 85 000 000 000 km. This number, written in scientific notation, is

(1) 8.5×10^{-10}
(2) 8.5×10^{10}
(3) 85×10^{9}
(4) 0.85×10^{-9}
(5) 850×10^{7}

Item 13 is based on the following figure.

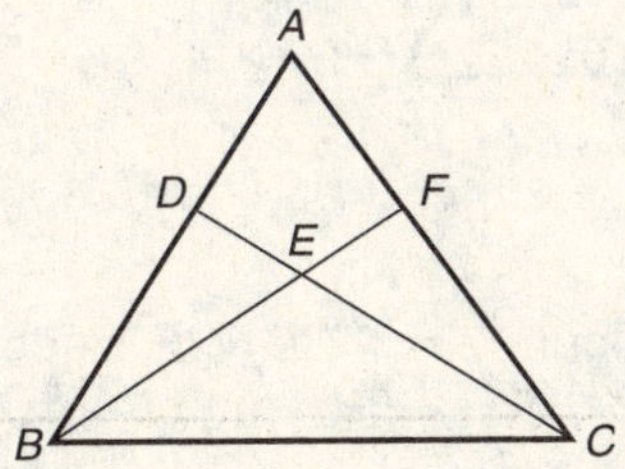

13. If $\overleftrightarrow{BF}$ bisects $\angle ABC$, $\overleftrightarrow{CD}$ bisects $\angle ACB$, $m\angle ABC = 68°$, and $m\angle ACB = 72°$, then $m\angle BEC =$

(1) 90°
(2) 98°
(3) 100°
(4) 110°
(5) 120°

14. Luba has $5 more than Jack, and Jack has $3 less than Marcus. If Marcus has $30, how many dollars does Luba have?

(1) $30
(2) $27
(3) $32
(4) $36
(5) Not enough information is given.

15. John Davis had a mass of 100 kg. His doctor put him on a diet, which enabled him to lose at least 4 kg per month. What was John's mass after 6 months on the diet?

(1) 76 kg
(2) 78 kg
(3) 80 kg
(4) 88 kg
(5) Not enough information is given.

16. Ms. Ames bought a bond for $10 000. The bond yields interest at $8\frac{1}{2}$% annually. If the interest is paid semi-annually, how much is Ms. Ames paid every six months?

(1) $400
(2) $425
(3) $475
(4) $500
(5) $850

17. A group of guides wish to determine the distance between points *A* and *B* on opposite sides of a pond. They measure a distance of 15 units from point *A* to point *C*. The distance from point *C* to point *B* is 25 units. What is the distance from *A* to *B*?

(1) 10 units
(2) 18 units
(3) 19 units
(4) 21 units
(5) 20 units

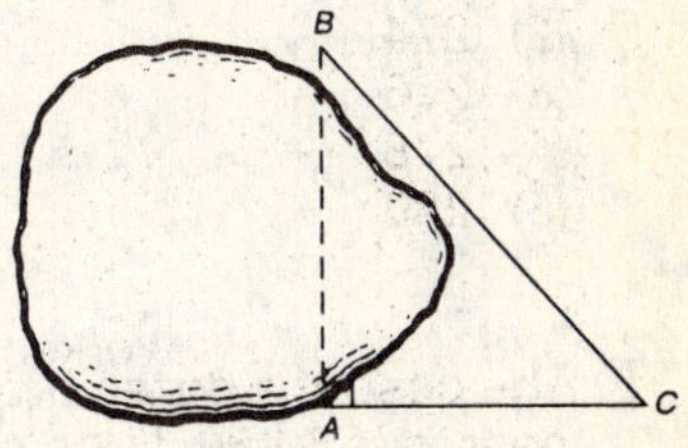

18. The ratio of men to women at a professional meeting was 9:2. If there were 12 women at the meeting, how many men were at the meeting?

(1) 33
(2) 44
(3) 54
(4) 66
(5) Not enough information is given.

19. What is the slope of the line joining point *A* (2,1) and point *B* (4,7)?

(1) 1/3
(2) 2/3
(3) 3/2
(4) 2
(5) 3

Items 20 and 21 are based on the following table.

ANNUAL PREMIUM AND INSTALLMENT PAYMENTS PER $1000 ON ORDINARY LIFE INSURANCE AT AGES FROM 21 THROUGH 25

AGE	ANNUAL PREMIUM	SEMIANNUAL INSTALLMENT	QUARTERLY INSTALLMENT
21	$16.62	$8.48	$4.32
22	17.08	8.71	4.44
23	17.55	8.95	4.56
24	18.04	9.20	4.69
25	18.56	9.47	4.83

According to the schedule, Vida (age 24) decides to make quarterly payments on a $10 000 policy, while Philip (age 25) decides to make semiannual payments on his $10 000 policy.

20. How much does Vida pay per year for her $10 000 policy?

(1) $18.76
(2) $182.40
(3) $184.00
(4) $187.60
(5) $193.20

21. How much does Philip pay for his policy over a 5-year period?

(1) $947.00
(2) $950.00
(3) $966.00
(4) $968.00
(5) $970.50

22. One week Marie worked 42 hours and earned $12 per hour. The following week she worked 37 hours and earned $12 per hour. Which of the following indicates the number of dollars earned for the two weeks?

(1) $12 \times 2 + 37$
(2) $12 \times 42 + 42 \times 37$
(3) $12 \times 37 + 42$
(4) $12 + 42 \times 37$
(5) $12(42 + 37)$

Item 23 is based on the following figure.

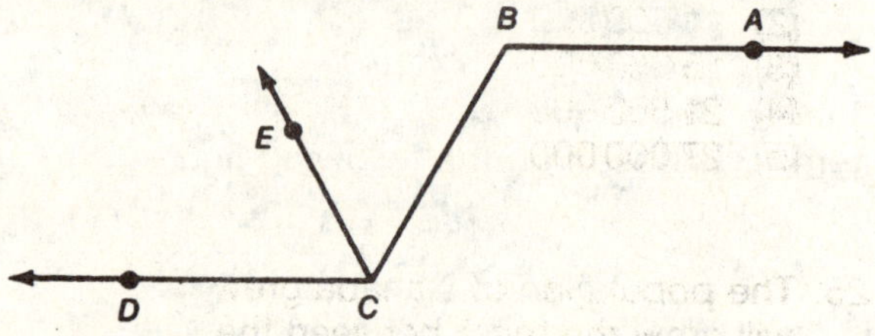

23. In the figure $\overleftrightarrow{AB} \parallel \overleftrightarrow{CD}$, $\overleftrightarrow{CE}$ bisects $\angle BCD$, and $m\angle ABC = 112°$. Find $m\angle ECD$.

(1) 45°
(2) 50°
(3) 56°
(4) 60°
(5) Not enough information is given.

Items 24 and 25 are based on the following graph.

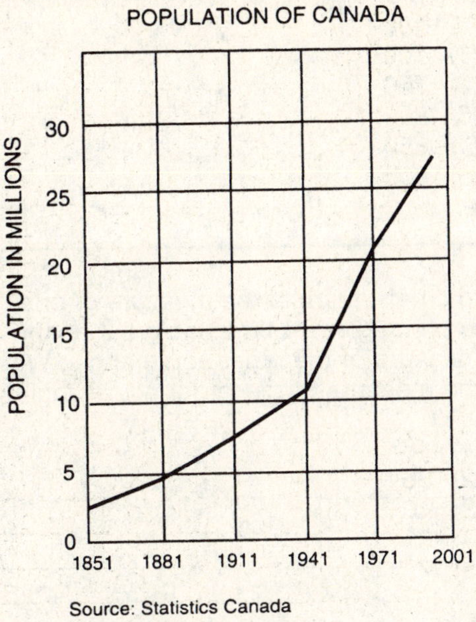

The graph shows the growth in population in Canada from 1851 to the 1990s.

24. What was the approximate population of Canada in the year 1971?

(1) 7 500 000
(2) 11 500 000
(3) 15 000 000
(4) 21 500 000
(5) 27 000 000

25. The population of Canada grew or will grow the most between the years

(1) 1851 and 1881
(2) 1881 and 1911
(3) 1911 and 1941
(4) 1941 and 1971
(5) 1971 and 2001

26. A box is in the form of a rectangular solid with a square base of side x units in length and a height of 8 units. The volume of the box is 392 cubic units. Which of the following equations may be used to find the value of x?

(1) $x^2 = 392$
(2) $8x = 392$
(3) $8x^3 = 392$
(4) $8x^2 = 392$
(5) $8 + x^2 = 392$

27. A cyclist rides 12 km due north. Then he turns and rides 16 km due east. At this point, how many kilometres is the cyclist from his starting point?

(1) 12
(2) 16
(3) 18
(4) 20
(5) Not enough information is given.

28. The square root of 30 is between which of the following pairs of numbers?

(1) 3 and 4
(2) 4 and 5
(3) 5 and 6
(4) 6 and 7
(5) 15 and 16

Item 29 is based on the following figure.

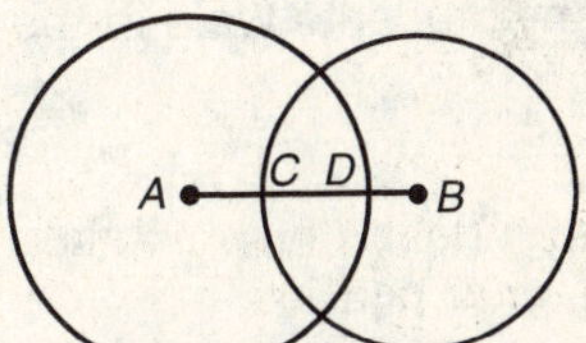

29. The radius of circle A measures 20 cm and the radius of circle B measures 8 cm. If CD = 6 cm, find AB, in centimetres.

(1) 22
(2) 24
(3) 25
(4) 28
(5) Not enough information is given.

Item 30 is based on the following figure.

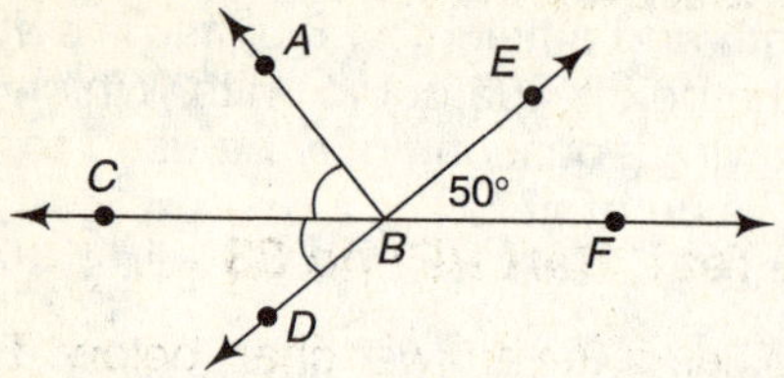

30. $\overleftrightarrow{CF}$ and $\overleftrightarrow{ED}$ intersect at *B*, m∠*EBF* = 50°, and $\overleftrightarrow{CB}$ bisects ∠*ABD*. Find m∠*ABC*.

(1) 30°
(2) 32°
(3) 40°
(4) 50°
(5) 60°

---

31. A woman buys *n* kilograms of sugar at *c* cents a kilogram. She gives the clerk $1. The change she receives, in cents, is

(1) $nc - 100$
(2) $n + c - 100$
(3) $100 - (n + c)$
(4) $100 - nc$
(5) Not enough information is given.

32. In a high school graduating class 85% of the class planned to go to university. If 170 graduates planned to go to university, how many students were in the graduating class?

(1) 200
(2) 250
(3) 340
(4) 400
(5) 500

Item 33 is based on the following figure.

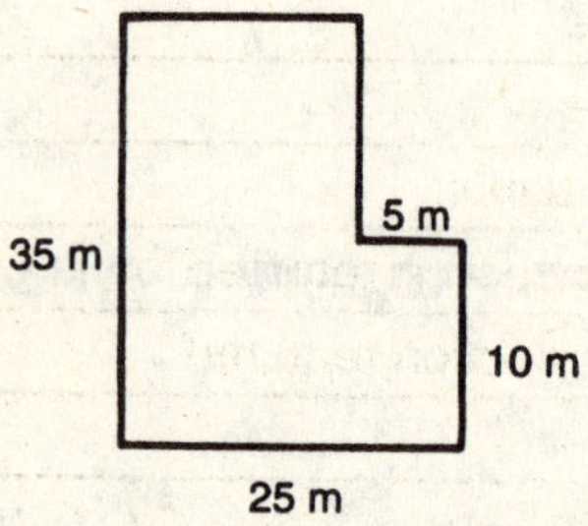

33. Mr. Chin planned to build a house on the plot of ground shown. What is the area of this plot of ground, in square metres?

(1) 700
(2) 750
(3) 800
(4) 850
(5) 900

---

34. In a right triangle the measure of one acute angle is 4 times as great as the measure of the other acute angle. What is the measure of the larger acute angle?

(1) 18°
(2) 36°
(3) 40°
(4) 65°
(5) 72°

Item 35 is based on the following figure.

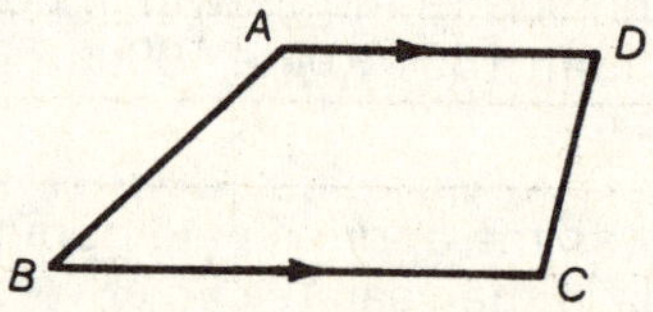

35. If $\overleftrightarrow{AD} \parallel \overleftrightarrow{BC}$ and m∠*A* exceeds m∠*B* by 50°, then m∠*A* equals

(1) 65°
(2) 105°
(3) 115°
(4) 125°
(5) Not enough information is given.

---

36. The PWX Corporation employs 150 clerks, each of whom is paid *x* dollars per week, and 6 managers, each of whom is paid *y* dollars per week. The average weekly pay per employee is

(1) $\dfrac{150x + 6y}{156}$
(2) $150x + 6y$
(3) $156xy$
(4) $156(x + y)$
(5) $\dfrac{150}{xy}$

END OF TEST

ANSWER KEYS, SUMMARIES OF RESULTS, AND SELF-APPRAISAL CHARTS

TEST 1: The Language Arts, Writing (Writing Skills) Test, Part I/Page 33

After you have completed your Pre-Test, mark your answers using the answer chart below. The column to the right of each question number indicates the correct answer. If you answered the question incorrectly, place an "X" over the question number. Remember to check the explanation of the answers for any questions you answered incorrectly.

In the column to the right of the correct answers is a list of the sections of Chapter 4 to which you should pay special attention. The entire section is an excellent review of the skills needed to pass the exam. Work your way through the sections that require review, always checking your work as soon as you complete it.

ANSWER CHART

QUESTION NUMBER	CORRECT ANSWER	SECTIONS FOR SPECIAL EMPHASIS
1	2	Usage—Agreement—Subject and Verb
2	3	Punctuation
3	3	Sentence Structure
4	1	Punctuation
5	4	Sentence Structure
6	5	No correction required
7	2	Spelling
8	3	Usage
9	5	No correction required
10	4	Spelling
11	5	No correction required
12	1	Sentence Structure
13	5	Sentence Structure
14	2	Punctuation
15	2	Spelling
16	3	Sentence Structure
17	5	No correction required
18	3	Spelling
19	4	Usage
20	3	Usage
21	2	Punctuation
22	5	No correction required
23	5	No correction required
24	3	Usage
25	5	Sentence Structure
26	5	Punctuation
27	4	Spelling

QUESTION NUMBER	CORRECT ANSWER	SECTIONS FOR SPECIAL EMPHASIS
28	1	Spelling
29	2	Sentence Structure
30	1	Punctuation
31	5	No correction required
32	1	Sentence Structure
33	2	Punctuation
34	4	Sentence Structure
35	3	Punctuation
36	2	Punctuation
37	4	Punctuation

TEST 1: The Language Arts, Writing (Writing Skills) Test, Part II/Page 41

To mark your essay, use this chart. The left column contains general areas to be considered when marking the essay. Mark the box that contains words that describe your work. For example, consider the first row.

	0	1	2	3	4	5	6
Ideas	irrelevant	no planning evident	superficial	average planning	planned and well-chosen	worthwhile	mature

Read your essay, looking for the ideas presented. If after reading, you feel that your ideas exhibit "Average Planning," put a mark in the box in column 3.

	0	1	2	3	4	5	6
Ideas	irrelevant	no planning evident	superficial	✓ average planning	planned and well-chosen	worthwhile	mature

After doing this as objectively as possible, give your paragraph to someone else who can be objective and ask them to mark it in a different colour. Wherever there is disagreement, discuss the reasons for each choice until a choice acceptable to both is reached. Circle the final selections in a third colour and look at where most of them fall.

A portion of your chart may begin to look like this.

	0	1	2	3	4	5	6
Ideas	irrelevant	no planning evident	superficial	✓ average planning ✗	planned and well-chosen	worthwhile	mature
Presentation	none	no planned presentation evident	little planned presentation evident	some planning in presentation evident ✗	generally effective presentation ✓	clear and effective presentation	clear, effective, and well-organized presentation related to topic
Organization	no evidence of organization	disorganized	not well-organized	less well-organized	organized ✓ ✗	well-organized	well-organized
Coherence	incoherent	minimal	ideas undeveloped	coherent ✓	coherent and under-standable ✗	coherent and under-standable	coherent and under-standable

These marks fall between 3 and 4. The mark for this essay would be between 3 and 4. Look for patterns. Not every essay will fall into one column for marks. The majority of boxes in a column should be used to indicate your mark on the paragraph. Any boxes that fall below 4 need attention.

	0	1	2	3	4	5	6
Ideas	irrelevant	no planning evident	superficial	average planning	planned and well-chosen	worthwhile	mature
Presentation	none	no planned presentation evident	little planned presentation evident	some planning in presentation evident	generally effective presentation	clear and effective presentation	clear, effective, and well-organized presentation related to topic
Organization	no evidence of organization	disorganized	not well-organized	less well-organized	organized	well-organized	well-organized
Coherence	incoherent	minimal	ideas undeveloped	coherent	coherent and under-standable	coherent and under-standable	coherent and under-standable
Argument	none	none	not developed	some evidence of development	generally effective	clear and effective	well developed, clear, and effective
Illustrations and Examples	none	none	few	some relevant	appropriate and relevant	sound and supporting	well-chosen and appropriate
Details	none	few unrelated	superficial	some relevant and thorough	relevant	relevant and thorough	specific, relevant, and thorough
Usage	mostly incorrect	numerous errors	many weaknesses	some weaknesses	usually correct	generally correct	few minor errors
Vocabulary	elementary	elementary	simple	average	above average	well-chosen	well-chosen and mature
Evidence	none	very little	little	less relevant and thorough	appropriate and relevant	appropriate, relevant, and clearly presented	appropriate, relevant, specific, and maturely presented
Penmanship	illegible	sloppy	legible	legible	legible	legible	legible

TEST 2: The Social Studies Test/Page 42

After you have completed your Pre-Test, mark your answers using the answer chart below. To the right of each number is the correct answer. If you answered the question incorrectly, place an "X" over the question number. Remember to check the explanation of the answers for any questions you answered incorrectly.

In the column to the right of the correct answer is a list of the sections of Chapter 6 to which you should pay special attention. These sections will help you get additional practice in areas in which you made errors. If you have made errors in "Interpreting Graphs, Tables, Maps, and Diagrams," review Chapter 10.

The remaining sections of Chapter 6 are an excellent review of the skills needed to answer the questions on the Social Studies test. Work your way through them, always checking your work as soon as you complete it.

ANSWER CHART

QUESTION NUMBER	CORRECT ANSWER	SECTIONS FOR SPECIAL EMPHASIS
1	2	Passages in Political Science
2	5	Passages in Political Science
3	3	Passages in Political Science
4	5	Passages in Economics
5	2	Passages in Economics
6	5	Passages in Economics
7	4	Passages in Political Science Interpreting Graphs, Tables, Maps, and Diagrams (Chapter 10)
8	4	Passages in Political Science Interpreting Graphs, Tables, Maps, and Diagrams (Chapter 10)
9	4	Passages in Economics
10	4	Basics of Interpreting Political Cartoons
11	1	Basics of Interpreting Political Cartoons
12	3	Passages in Political Science
13	1	Passages in Economics
14	4	Passages in Economics
15	1	Passages in History
16	3	Passages in History
17	2	Passages in Economics Interpreting Graphs, Tables, Maps, and Diagrams (Chapter 10)
18	2	Passages in Economics Glossary Interpreting Graphs, Tables, Maps, and Diagrams (Chapter 10)
19	4	Passages in Economics Interpreting Graphs, Tables, Maps, and Diagrams (Chapter 10)
20	4	Passages in History
21	4	Passages in Behavioural Science Glossary Interpreting Graphs, Tables, Maps, and Diagrams (Chapter 10)

QUESTION NUMBER	CORRECT ANSWER	SECTIONS FOR SPECIAL EMPHASIS
22	4	Passages in Behavioural Science Interpreting Graphs, Tables, Maps, and Diagrams (Chapter 10)
23	1	Passages in Behavioural Science
24	4	Passages in Economics Glossary Interpreting Graphs, Tables, Maps, and Diagrams (Chapter 10)
25	2	Passages in History
26	3	Passages in Geography Glossary
27	1	Passages in Geography Glossary
28	2	Passages in Geography
29	5	Passages in Behavioural Science
30	3	Passages in Behavioural Science
31	2	Passages in Behavioural Science Glossary
32	4	Passages in Economics Basics of Interpreting Political Cartoons
33	1	Passages in Economics Basics of Interpreting Political Cartoons
34	2	Passages in History
35	2	Passages in History
36	1	Passages in History
37	3	Passages in History
38	1	Passages in History Glossary Interpreting Graphs, Tables, Maps, and Diagrams (Chapter 10)
39	4	Passages in Geography Glossary Interpreting Graphs, Tables, Maps, and Diagrams (Chapter 10)
40	1	Passages in Geography
41	5	Passages in Political Science
42	2	Passages in Political Science
43	1	Passages in Political Science
44	1	Passages in Political Science
45	5	Passages in Behavioural Science
46	4	Passages in Behavioural Science
47	1	Passages in Behavioural Science
48	4	Passages in Economics Glossary
49	1	Passages in Behavioural Science Glossary

TEST 3: The Science Test/Page 53

After you have completed your Pre-Test, mark your answers using the answer chart below. To the right of each number is the correct answer. If you answered the question incorrectly, place an "X" over the question number. Remember to check the explanation of the answers for any questions you answered incorrectly.

In the column to the right of the correct answer is the chapter number. The review material for Science may be found in either Chapter 7 or Chapter 10. The Reading Comprehension material and the review on each of the subjects in Science are in Chapter 7. Review on Graphs, Tables, and Diagrams is in Chapter 10. The next column to the right indicates the headings in the chapter on which you should concentrate. These sections will help you get additional practice in areas in which you made errors.

If you have any difficulties with the words used in the questions or the readings, study the Glossary and learn the words. Learning new words is best accomplished a few at a time. This is not something to leave to the last minute. Plan your time so that you can learn a few words each day that you prepare for the exam.

The Science test is a test of Reading Comprehension with a specialized vocabulary. To build your Reading Comprehension skills, review "Skills Analysis" in Chapter 7. The Science test also has questions based on extracting information from Graphs, Tables, and Diagrams. The review for these questions is found in Chapter 10. As you work your way through these sections, always check your work as soon as you complete it.

ANSWER CHART

QUESTION NUMBER	CORRECT ANSWER	SELECTION FOR SPECIAL EMPHASIS	
		CHAPTER	TOPIC
1	2	7	Biology Single-Item Questions
2	4	7	Biology Single-Item Questions
3	2	7	Biology Single-Item Questions
4	4	7	Biology Single-Item Questions
5	4	7	Physics Multiple-Item Questions based on Reading
6	2	7	Physics Multiple-Item Questions based on Reading
7	4	7	Physics Multiple-Item Questions based on Reading
8	3	7	Physics Multiple-Item Questions based on Reading
9	4	7	Chemistry Multiple-Item Questions based on Reading
10	1	7	Chemistry Multiple-Item Questions based on Reading
11	5	7	Earth Science Multiple-Item Questions based on Reading
12	4	7	Earth Science Multiple-Item Questions based on Reading

QUESTION NUMBER	CORRECT ANSWER	SELECTION FOR SPECIAL EMPHASIS	
		CHAPTER	TOPIC
13	1	7	Earth Science Multiple-Item Questions based on Reading
14	3	7	Physics Multiple-Item Questions based on Reading
15	1	7	Physics Multiple-Item Questions based on Reading
16	1	7	Physics Multiple-Item Questions based on Reading
17	1	7	Earth Science Multiple-Item Questions based on Reading
18	2	7	Earth Science Multiple-Item Questions based on Reading
19	4	7	Earth Science Multiple-Item Questions based on Reading
20	3	7	Chemistry Multiple-Item Questions based on Reading
21	4	7	Chemistry Multiple-Item Questions based on Reading
22	5	7	Chemistry Single-Item Questions
23	4	7	Chemistry Multiple-Item Questions based on Reading
24	5	7	Biology Multiple-Item Questions based on Reading
25	3	7	Biology Multiple-Item Questions based on Reading
26	3	7	Biology Multiple-Item Questions based on Reading
27	4	7	Biology Multiple-Item Questions based on Reading
28	3	7	Biology Multiple-Item Questions based on Reading
29	4	7	Biology Multiple-Item Questions based on Reading
30	5	7	Biology Single-Item Questions
31	5	7	Biology Single-Item Questions
32	4	7	Biology Single-Item Questions
33	5	7	Biology Single-Item Questions
34	5	7	Biology Single-Item Questions

QUESTION NUMBER	CORRECT ANSWER	SELECTION FOR SPECIAL EMPHASIS	
		CHAPTER	TOPIC
35	5	7	Biology Single-Item Questions
36	5	7	Biology Single-Item Questions
37	3	7	Biology Single-Item Questions
38	4	7	Biology Single-Item Questions
39	3	7 10	Biology Single-Item Questions based on Graph
40	3	7 10	Earth Science Single-Item Questions based on Diagram
41	1	7	Biology Single-Item Questions
42	3	7	Biology Single-Item Questions
43	5	7	Biology Single-Item Questions
44	4	7	Chemistry Single-Item Questions
45	4	7	Biology Multiple-Item Questions based on Reading
46	3	7	Biology Multiple-Item Questions based on Reading
47	3	7	Biology Multiple-Item Questions based on Reading
48	2	7	Biology Multiple-Item Questions based on Reading
49	2	7	Biology Multiple-Item Questions based on Reading
50	2	7	Chemistry Single-Item Questions
51	5	7	Chemistry Multiple-Item Questions based on Reading
52	2	7	Chemistry Multiple-Item Questions based on Reading
53	5	7	Physics Multiple-Item Questions based on Reading
54	5	7	Physics Single-Item Questions
55	5	7 10	Earth Science Multiple-Item Questions based on Reading Questions based on Diagram

QUESTION NUMBER	CORRECT ANSWER	SELECTION FOR SPECIAL EMPHASIS	
		CHAPTER	TOPIC
56	2	7 10	Earth Science Multiple-Item Questions based on Reading Questions based on Diagram
57	4	7 10	Earth Science Multiple-Item Questions based on Reading Questions based on Diagram
58	1	7 10	Earth Science Multiple-Item Questions based on Reading Questions based on Diagram
59	2	7	Biology Single-Item Questions
60	2	7	Physics Multiple-Item Questions based on Reading Questions based on Diagram
61	2	7 10	Physics Multiple-Item Questions based on Reading Questions based on Diagram
62	3	7	Biology Multiple-Item Questions based on Reading
63	3	7	Biology Multiple-Item Questions based on Reading
64	2	7	Biology Multiple-Item Questions based on Reading
65	5	7	Biology Multiple-Item Questions based on Reading
66	4	7	Biology Multiple-Item Questions based on Reading

TEST 4: The Language Arts, Reading (Interpreting Literature and the Arts) Test/Page 64

After you have completed your Pre-Test, mark your answers using the answer chart on the next page. To the right of the question number is the correct answer. If you answered the question incorrectly, place an "X" over the question number. Remember to check the explanation of the answers for any questions you answered incorrectly.

In the column to the right of the correct answer is the skill area or areas tested by this question. These sections of Chapter 8 are the ones on which you should concentrate as you review for the exam. As you work your way through the sections, always check your work as soon as you complete it.

This test is a test of Reading Comprehension. Some of the terms used are specific to this subject area. If you are unfamiliar with the terms or feel that you need a review, begin with the "Glossary of Literary Terms."

ANSWER CHART

QUESTION NUMBER	CORRECT ANSWER	SECTIONS FOR SPECIAL EMPHASIS
1	3	Classical Literature Prose Non-Fiction Making Inferences
2	1	Classical Literature Prose Non-Fiction Finding Details
3	4	Classical Literature Prose Non-Fiction Finding Details
4	4	Classical Literature Prose Non-Fiction Making Inferences
5	1	Classical Literature Prose Non-Fiction Locating the Main Idea
6	3	Popular Literature Prose Fiction Determining Tone and Mood
7	1	Popular Literature Prose Fiction Making Inferences
8	2	Popular Literature Prose Fiction Inferring Setting
9	3	Popular Literature Prose Fiction Determining Tone and Mood
10	5	Popular Literature Prose Fiction Making Inferences
11	3	Popular Literature Prose Fiction Inferring Character
12	5	Popular Literature Prose Fiction Locating the Main Idea
13	1	Popular Literature Prose Fiction Making Inferences
14	2	Popular Literature Prose Fiction Determining Tone and Mood
15	2	Popular Literature Prose Fiction Finding Details

QUESTION NUMBER	CORRECT ANSWER	SECTIONS FOR SPECIAL EMPHASIS
16	3	Popular Literature Drama Determining Tone and Mood
17	2	Popular Literature Drama Determining Tone and Mood
18	3	Popular Literature Drama Inferring Character
19	5	Popular Literature Drama Inferring Character
20	3	Popular Literature Drama Inferring Character
21	3	Commentary Making Inferences
22	1	Commentary Finding Details
23	4	Commentary Finding Details
24	3	Commentary Finding Details

TEST 5: The Mathematics Test/Page 70

After you have completed your Pre-Test, mark your answers using the answer chart below. To the right of the question number is the correct answer. If you answered the question incorrectly, place an "X" over the question number. Remember to check the explanation of the answers for any questions you answered incorrectly.

In the column to the right of the correct answer is the area of Mathematics that the question is testing. If you make a mistake in an Arithmetic question, it would be wise to review the entire Arithmetic section. For your information, we have included the specific topic covered by the question, should you decide to review only that topic. In Mathematics, the more practice you get, the better you will do. Work your way through the sections, checking your answers as soon as you complete the question.

ANSWER CHART

QUESTION NUMBER	CORRECT ANSWER	SECTIONS FOR SPECIAL EMPHASIS
1	2	Arithmetic—Fractions Verbal Problems
2	5	Algebra—Inequalities
3	1	Algebra—Probability
4	4	Algebra—Mean and Median
5	5	Arithmetic—Whole Numbers Verbal Problems

QUESTION NUMBER	CORRECT ANSWER	SECTIONS FOR SPECIAL EMPHASIS
6	1	Map—Scale (See Chapter 10)
7	2	Geometry—Perimeter, Area, and Volume
8	4	Algebra—Signed Numbers
9	5	Arithmetic—Decimals Verbal Problems
10	3	Arithmetic—Fractions
11	3	Verbal Problems
12	2	Algebra—Operations with Exponents and Scientific Notation
13	4	Geometry—Geometric Figures
14	3	Verbal Problems
15	5	Verbal Problems
16	2	Arithmetic—Percent
17	5	Algebra—Formulae
18	3	Algebra—Ratio and Proportion Verbal Problems
19	5	Geometry—Coordinate Geometry
20	4	Arithmetic—Insurance, Investment, Taxation
21	1	Arithmetic—Insurance, Investment, Taxation
22	5	Verbal Problems
23	3	Geometry—Geometric Concepts and Relationships
24	4	Graphs (See Chapter 10)
25	4	Graphs (See Chapter 10)
26	4	Verbal Problems
27	4	Geometry—Congruence and Similarity Verbal Problems Co-Ordinate Geometry
28	3	Arithmetic—Properties of Operations
29	1	Geometry—Geometric Figures
30	4	Geometry—Geometric Concepts and Relationships
31	4	Arithmetic—Decimals
32	1	Arithmetic—Percent
33	2	Geometry—Areas
34	5	Geometry—Geometric Figures
35	3	Geometry—Geometric Figures
36	1	Verbal Problems

ANSWER ANALYSIS

TEST 1: The Language Arts, Writing (Writing Skills) Test, Part I/Page 33

1. **2** There is an error in usage. The subject of the sentence is *combination* which is singular. A singular verb, *makes*, is required for agreement.
2. **3** The error is in punctuation. A comma is needed to set off an introductory phrase.
3. **3** There is a sentence fragment beginning with *seldom*. This is corrected by removing the period and joining the fragment to the rest of the sentence.
4. **1** There is an error in capitalization. Seasons are *not* capitalized.
5. **4** The run-on sentence can be corrected by subordinating the second idea to the first. *Some . . . vegetables* can be frozen while *other vegetables can be stored . . . in a cool area.*
6. **5** No correction is necessary.
7. **2** The correct spelling is *exercise*.
8. **3** The usage error is in the shift in person in two pronouns which refer to the same person. The pronoun, *your*, in the second person in the introductory clause requires a continuation of the second person, *you*, in the main clause.
9. **5** No change is necessary.
10. **4** The correct spelling is *assistance*.
11. **5** No correction is necessary.
12. **1** The original is correct. Two sentences are needed.
13. **5** No correction is necessary.
14. **2** A comma is required to set off items in a series.
15. **2** *Equipment* is the correct spelling.
16. **3** The meaning of the sentence requires *may be* served.
17. **5** No correction is necessary.
18. **3** The correct spelling is *their* rather than *they're* which is a contraction of *they are*.
19. **4** There is an error in usage. Parallel structure requires the use of infinitives: *to develop, to increase, to learn* (rather than *learning*).
20. **3** The sentence requires the use of *there are* rather than *they are*. *They are a number of . . . steps* doesn't make sense.
21. **2** A comma is required after the introductory clause "While . . . protection."
22. **5** No correction is necessary.
23. **5** No correction is necessary.
24. **3** The future tense should be used for an action taking place in the future, i.e., when you take the car in.
25. **5** Two sentences are necessary to correct the run-on sentence. To accomplish this, a period after *order* and a capitalized *That* are needed.
26. **5** No correction is necessary.
27. **4** The correct spelling is *determined*.
28. **1** The correct spelling is *receive*.
29. **2** The rewritten sentence should read "A buying decision is affected by total dollars . . ."
30. **1** A comma is needed to set off items in a series.
31. **5** No correction is necessary.
32. **1** The original way is the best among the choices offered.
33. **2** Commas are used to set off phrases which are inserted in the sentence and which interrupt the normal word order.
34. **4** The relative adjective, *which*, avoids the unnecessary use of the words *such programs*.
35. **3** A semicolon is used to separate independent clauses in a sentence.
36. **2** A comma is used after an introductory clause.
37. **4** An apostrophe must be added after the plural noun *shoppers'* to show possession.

TEST 1: The Language Arts, Writing (Writing Skills) Test, Part II/Page 41

SAMPLE ESSAYS

For *air travel*

Air travel is the best way to travel.

Thanks to air travel, we now have the opportunity to reach places within and outside of Canada in a matter of hours rather than in weeks and months. This allows the businessperson to transact business or the traveler to go to distant places in a relatively short time.

Larger planes and lower fares have made the benefits of travel available to large numbers of people who might not otherwise have had the opportunity to travel.

Travel by air has become increasingly safe. Per kilometre traveled, there are fewer injuries and fatalities in airplane travel than there are in travel by automobile and railroad.

Airlines have also coped well with the comfort and possible boredom of the air traveler. In-flight movies, music, and reading matter have helped to make the hours pass more quickly. Airline food has been greatly improved.

All of these are practical considerations. But there is another, more intangible benefit—the beauty and serenity of flight. Once the plane reaches thousands of kilometres into the skies, the passenger experiences the majesty of flying above the clouds and the thrill of looking down at the earth below with its mighty mountains and puny people.

Air travel has indeed been a blessing to mankind.

Summary of reasons <u>for</u> air travel:

1. Air travel has made distant places accessible to the businessperson and the traveler.
2. Air travel has brought greater opportunity to travel to many.
3. Air travel is safer than other forms of travel.
4. Air travel has been made more comfortable.
5. Flight is a beautiful experience.

Against *air travel*

Air travel has too many disadvantages for this traveler.

At 1000 kilometres per hour, there is a kaleidoscope of places whizzing by which allows the passenger little time to enjoy the sights and sounds that make travel an enriching experience. Hour after hour of flight above the earth's atmosphere can indeed be boring.

Many people fear air travel because the passengers are subjected to the vagaries of weather. Pockets of air turbulence can upset even the most seasoned traveler.

A recently added concern is the matter of air safety. Maintenance of aircraft has become less efficient. Near misses of collisions between commercial and private aircraft occur daily. Security from attacks by terrorists has become a major problem for airlines around the world.

There is always the nagging feeling that, should an accident take place, it probably would result in fatalities.

Then there are the not so minor inconveniences. While the flight itself is swift, jet lag can linger for days while the body attempts to adjust to the new time zone that has been reached. Add to this, the traditionally poor airline food, the crowded seating, and the overutilized lavatories the air traveler has to endure and one wonders why anyone would travel by air.

These are the reasons why this traveler prefers to remain grounded.

Summary of reasons against air travel:

1. Speed of air travel does not allow the traveler to enjoy the sights.
2. The passenger is subject to unpredictable weather conditions.
3. There has been a deterioration in air safety conditions because of poorer maintenance, flight control, and terrorism.
4. Accidents usually result in fatalities.
5. Air travel is uncomfortable and produces jet lag.

TEST 2: The Social Studies Test/Page 42

1. **2** The first paragraph states clearly that "the chance of a private member's bill becoming law is remote . . ."
2. **5** This is a straightforward question requiring you to locate the main idea of the passage. In this case, the task is made easier because the question uses exactly the same language as the passage. See the last sentence of the first paragraph, beginning "The main purpose . . ." The other choices may be purposes of private members' bills or may be the result of them, but the "main purpose" is clearly choice 5.
3. **3** This question requires you to interpret a specific detail in the passage. The second paragraph points out that it is during the Committee stage that a bill is examined in detail ("clause by clause") and for "the consideration of amendments."
4. **5** Nearly all of the selection deals with a plan of action before the consumer buys. See the second sentence and again the first words of the third paragraph.
5. **2** The consumer is advised to get all promises in writing.
6. **5** Return of monies or credit toward a replacement may or may not be part of a warranty.
7. **4** In this question you need to focus on only one of the two types of information presented on the graph. The question asks you about where people live longest. Note that the vertical axis of the chart is labelled "Life Expectancy at Birth (years)." From the chart, you can then read that life expectancy at birth in Japan is 77 years and that in no other country is there a higher life expectancy. Australia is second at 76 years.
8. **4** This question requires you to combine information on life expectancy with the number of doctors in the population. Note that the nine countries with the highest life expectancies also have the highest proportion of doctors in their populations.
9. **4** Persons concerned with the natural environment fear that an emphasis on greater production and consumption will mean further pollution of the air (by factory smokestacks and apartment house incinerators) and of rivers, lakes, and streams (by industrial wastes and sewage disposal); and increased problems of solid waste disposal and rising noise levels.
10. **4** There is no movement toward a solution to the energy problem as long as the two cyclists representing energy and environment keep pedaling in different directions.
11. **1** Here you need to understand the broad issue. During the past decade, Canadians have supported legislation that requires study of the environmental effects of energy projects before work commences.
12. **3** This question directly relates to the difficulties experienced by the Canadian economy during the past two decades. Often, the Minister of Finance has been the member of the government most clearly associated with increases in taxes and severe unemployment. The resulting unpopularity has often damaged political careers.
13. **1** Here you need to apply your knowledge of current political and economic conditions in Canada to help you analyze the "fifty-first syndrome." The Free Trade Agreement between the United States and Canada that became law in 1989 raised, for public discussion, many of the issues referred to in the passage.
14. **4** The major concern expressed here is not just that Canada will have difficulty in competing successfully in cultural and economic arenas but that the consequences of this could be a loss of our independence as a sovereign nation.
15. **1** This question requires you to recognize that the passage is dealing with a specific historical event, namely the unification of the British North American Colonies in 1867, an event that we normally refer to as Confederation.

16. **3** The whole theme of the passage focuses on the differences that existed between and among the four original provinces.
17. **2** Lacking land for agriculture, Nation A will use its abundant labour, capital, and management skills to develop industry. The resulting products can be sold to domestic and foreign markets.
18. **2** In the 1800s, Great Britain led the world in manufacturing and resembled Nation A in factors of production.
19. **4** Nation B, with is natural resources and labour, must encourage new industries by protectionist tariffs and by tax concessions to attract capital investment.
20. **4** The purpose of Chancellor Kohl's statement was to reassure Germany's neighbours of Germany's continued friendship and economic cooperation. He felt that he had to make such a statement because of the fears that were being expressed about a possible resurgence of German militarism and nationalism.
21. **4** Personal interviews and questionnaires are used to gather this kind of information from a representative sample of the population.
22. **4** This question requires you to examine trends over a period of time. The graph clearly shows that older Canadians were less likely to use alcohol than younger Canadians in all of the years reported on the graph. You will have to examine some of the other choices carefully to see that there is no evidence to support them. For example, choice 1 is not a valid conclusion since the graph shows that alcohol usage actually increased for the 18–29 and the 30–49 age groups.
23. **1** The Chinese of the Middle Kingdom and the ancient Greeks held the belief that their cultures were superior to those of any other group. The word barbarian comes from the term used by the Greeks of antiquity to describe foreigners who did not speak Greek.
24. **4** A recession takes place in the economy when purchasing, saving, and business profits go down. The result is an increase in unemployment and a recession.
25. **2** Social Darwinism became popular in the second half of the 19th century. It applied Darwin's theory of natural selection to people and nations, attempting thereby to justify the widening gap between the rich and the poor.
26. **3** The focus of the paragraph is the "problems we face in conserving natural resources."
27. **1** "The pressures of human growth" are identified in the passage as being "acute."
28. **2** The author recognizes the problems realistically and does not minimize them.
29. **5** Choice 5 is a direct quotation from the passage. Do not confuse the statement in the last sentence that they are not to be held "as fully accountable as adults" to mean they they are not to be held accountable at all. None of the other choices is even implied from the information provided.
30. **3** The focus of the Young Offenders Act is upon the creation of a "justice and corrections system" and not upon child welfare legislation.
31. **2** The emphasis in the passage is upon holding young offenders accountable for their actions and protecting society from young offenders. The other choices are not necessarily excluded by the Young Offenders' Act but they are not where the emphasis lies.
32. **4** The cartoon shows the Prime Minister of the day struggling to control inflation while juggling a host of other problems. It proved to be too much.
33. **1** Higher interest rates discourage bank loans by businesspeople and consumers, decreasing the amount of money in circulation and reducing the rate of inflation.
34. **2** Humanists stressed human concerns rather than problems of the next world.
35. **2** The advance of the frontier inevitably posed a threat to the Metis way to life and so the author sees the rebellions as battles for the survival of Metis culture.
36. **1** The Riel period is an important one in Canadian history and the question requires you to show an understanding of a central concept.
37. **3** The author says that "the politicians" saw the rebellions as continuations of the old hostilities. Macdonald, of course, was the leading politician of the day.
38. **1** In 1992 Canada exported goods and services to the United States worth $118.4 billion and imported goods and services worth $96.4 billion, giving a trade surplus of some $22 billion. On the other hand, Canada exported only $0.8 billion but imported $2.8 from Mexico giving a trade deficit of $2 billion.

39. **4** 20 percent of the United States exports went to Canada in 1992 but 77% of all of Canada's exports went to the United States.
40. **1** A primary source is an eyewitness account of an event or an artifact constructed in a specific time period.
41. **5** Lobbyists are representatives of special interest groups who attempt to influence Members of Parliament by providing information, proposing legislation, and presenting briefs at parliamentary hearings.
42. **2** Speaker B expresses concern about how lobbyists operate. Sometimes they may offer gifts or make campaign contributions; the legislation they support may be of more benefit to the group they represent than to the Canadian public at large.
43. **1** Speaker A points out that lobbyists often provide information that is helpful to legislators who must often consider many complex issues about which it is difficult to always remain fully informed.
44. **1** The key issue in the cartoon is the relationship between technological change and employment. It is also true that computers are changing the nature of the workplace (choice 3) but much of this change does not pose a direct threat to individuals' jobs.
45. **5** Parents, teachers, and age peers are mentioned in the two classes of socializing agents.
46. **4** In the last sentence, all of the reasons are mentioned except the *number* of peers. The group is mentioned as being of increasing importance.
47. **1** The passage, in the second sentence, refers to the great influence of the family.
48. **4** Speaker A is talking about a world made smaller by modern technology. Speaker B agrees and adds that the problems of any area now become the problems of all mankind. Both feel that, as the world becomes one community, interdependence is a factor in world survival.
49. **1** Ethnocentrism is the view that one's own culture is superior to all others. The speaker is calling for the appreciation of other people's value systems and ways of life.

TEST 3: The Science Test/Page 53

1. **2** Human, monkey, ape, and chimpanzee belong to the primate group of mammals.
2. **4** Evolution is a process in all of life, not just humans or chimpanzees. Fossils and anatomy provide some of the evidence for evolution.
3. **2** Fossils are the remains of the actual living things of the past, so they give detailed knowledge.
4. **4** When it is found that today's men are different from those of only a few hundred years ago, it suggests that evolution has not stopped.
5. **4** Water is surely everywhere, and this suggests that anyone has access to it for purposes of standardization.
6. **2** The passage implies that heat is a form of energy, and this is what is measured in calories.
7. **4** Specific gravity is density compared with the density of water. A specific gravity of 1.84 means that any given volume of sulphuric acid weighs 1.84 times as much as an equal volume of water.
8. **3** Any unit must be defined arbitrarily and the inventors of the metric system used water as a standard.
9. **4** Propane (C_3H_8) is an organic compound. $Ba(OH)_2$ is a base. HNO_3 and HCl are acids. NaCl is a salt.
10. **1** Sodium hydroxide (NaOH) is an ionic compound made up of an active metal, sodium, and the hydroxide ion OH^-.
11. **5** In the atmosphere, energy is transferred by means of water vapour carried by air currents. When water evaporates, it consumes energy. The humid air rises by convection and then forms clouds of condensation with the release of energy (heat) to the air at high altitudes. By condensation, rain is formed but the heat is left in the upper part of the atmosphere.
12. **4** The passage describes the optical illusion that occurs when hot air near the surface is in turbulent motion because cooling effects are not present.
13. **1** When evaporation occurs, heat is required to change a liquid to a gas. Evaporation is a cooling process.

14. **3** In diesel engines the tight-fitting pistons compress air and thus cause the temperature to rise above the kindling temperature of the heavy fuels used. This serves the same purpose as the spark plugs in the gasoline engine.
15. **1** Locomotives can easily carry the heavy diesel engine and thus take advantage of using the less expensive fuel.
16. **1** Because of the strong compression stroke, diesel engines are very heavy engines. Diesel engines need the strength of a thick-walled cylinder to function.
17. **1** Earthquakes are the result of rapid movement of rock masses below the earth's surface, resulting in breaking rock layers and displacement (fault) of segments of the layer at the breaking point. The folding of rock layers results from the action of lesser forces acting over a longer period of time. The forces produced by landslides are too small to create an earthquake.
18. **2** In severe earthquakes many people are killed because older buildings and roadways are not built to withstand such a severe shock. The more modern buildings will stand.
19. **4** It is shock waves in the crust that a seismograph detects, whether they are produced by earthquakes or by nuclear explosions.
20. **3** A calcium atom with a valence of +2 has two electrons in its outer ring. Chlorine with a valence of −1 needs one electron to complete its outer ring. Two chlorine atoms can combine with one atom of calcium to form calcium chloride ($CaCl_2$).
21. **4** Atomic mass (number of protons plus number of neutrons) minus atomic number (number of protons) equals number of neutrons. Therefore, $7 - 3 = 4$.
22. **5** The atomic number is equal to the number of protons.
23. **4** This element sodium, which has 11 protons, must have 11 electrons in its shells. The first shell holds 2, the second shell holds 8, leaving one electron in its outer shell. Since it can lend this electron to another atom, it has a valence of +1.
24. **5** Many parts of the plant are involved, but it is in the chloroplasts that the actual chemical process takes place.
25. **3** Water from the soil is conducted through the xylem.
26. **3** Chemical energy is needed to split water into H^+ (combined in the glucose) and O_2.
27. **4** Hydrogen and carbon dioxide are successively built up into sugars.
28. **3** Chlorophyll in the chloroplasts of the cells transforms the energy of light into chemical energy.
29. **4** The stoma are openings through which carbon dioxide enters the leaf.
30. **5** The energy put into the plant is in the form of light; the output is the chemical energy stored in the carbohydrates. The passage says nothing about growth.
31. **5** Since carbon dioxide is used in photosynthesis, increasing the supply would speed the process up.
32. **4** The birds have come to resemble each other because they have evolved to adapt to the same life style. Choices (2), (3), and (5) contradict the statement that the birds are unrelated.
33. **5** In the dark, there is no photosynthesis and the plants can produce no oxygen.
34. **5** Vitamins are prescribed for expectant mothers. Vitamin A is necessary for health but doses in excess may be harmful.
35. **5** Since the heart is a muscle with nerves that conduct impulses, potassium is an important nutrient consideration. Many prescription drugs that heart patients take have a tendency to remove excess water. Dissolved potassium is thus lost.
36. **5** Stack gases combine with atmospheric water to produce acid rain, which can damage embryos, buildings, trees, and lungs.
37. **3** Mice have many offspring and short time between generations. Choice (1) is wrong because bacteria do not reproduce sexually. Choices (2) and (4) are wrong because dogs and humans, while of great practical interest, are not as prolific as mice. Oak trees are extremely prolific, but they have to grow for many years before they produce acorns.
38. **4** The passage implies that green bacteria evolved from non-green forms, which must have been on earth first. Animal life requires oxygen, so it must have come after the green bacteria changed the atmosphere.
39. **3** The wolf population peaked a year after the peak of the moose population, so many wolves must have been born when the moose population was at its highest.

40. **3** The fossils in rock layer *D* are older than those in layer *A*. Fossils are found in sedimentary rocks. Sedimentary rocks are formed as layer upon layer of material is deposited. The oldest sediment layer was laid down first and appears at the bottom. The youngest layer is at the top.
41. **1** Breathing air is not a form of direct transmission of body fluids. In sexual intercourse, each person has intimate contact with the body fluids of the other, so choice (2) is wrong. Choices (3), (4), and (5) all involve transmission of blood from person to person.
42. **3** The breeder's problem is to locate the immune plants, which will be those that survive when herbicides are applied.
43. **5** Choice (1) is wrong; a farmer might follow this practice, but it is not what he *should* do. Choice (4) is wrong because you are asked the basis on which he should decide. There is no reason to suspect that Choices (2) and (3) are relevant.
44. **4** In all incorrect choices explosion is possible. The safe procedure calls for slow, careful heating, with no cork on the test tube.
45. **4** Cloning is used to produce a large number of plants in a short period of time. According to the passage, one million plants can be cloned in about six months.
46. **3** If the chromosome number of the cloned plant is 12, the chromosome number of the plant used to produce the clone is 12. The cells of the cloned plant reproduce by the process of mitosis. All mitotically produced cells have the same amount of genetic material.
47. **3** The hormones auxin and cytokinin stimulate the production of new plants. Hormones are substances that regulate the growth and reproduction of organisms.
48. **2** Cloning is defined as a form of vegetative propagation. Vegetative propagation is a form of asexual reproduction, only one parent is required.
49. **2** Sexual processes mix the heredity of the two parents, and produce offspring different from both. In cloning or other vegetative methods, there is no change in the genotype.
50. **2** The medicine is a suspension. All incorrect choices are characteristic of solutions.
51. **5** All other choices have a sour taste, so they are acid.
52. **2** The slippery feel of soap gives away its nature as a base.
53. **5** Mixing an acid and a base would produce a product that is neither.
54. **5** Heat is a form of energy that moves spontaneously from regions of higher temperatures to lower. Cold is not a thing; the word is an adjective.

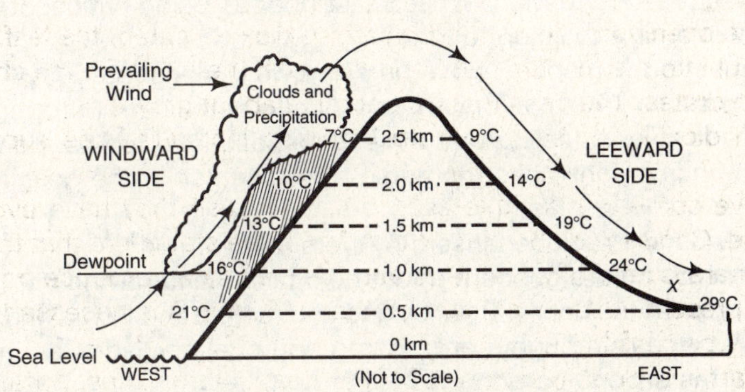

55. **5** On the west side of the mountain, the temperature is dropping 3°C for each 0.5 km. At 2.5 km the temperature is 7°C. At the top it would be 3° less, or 4°C. The same results would be obtained by using data from the east side of the mountain, where the temperature is dropping 5°C for each 0.5 km.
56. **2** When precipitation occurs, the relative humidity is 100%. In the diagram, precipitation is occuring on the windward side of the mountain. There is precipitation at 1.5 km elevation.
57. **4** As the air rises, it expands. When it expands, it cools. You may have noticed that the air rushing out of a tire feels cool. This is because the air is expanding.
58. **1** As the air descends on the leeward side of the mountain, it becomes warmer. As a result, there will rarely be precipitation here. The lack of precipitation will produce an arid region. The deserts in the southwestern part of the United States are located on the leeward side of mountain ranges.

59. **2** Some plants release pollen to the atmosphere. Human activity does not greatly affect the amount of pollen in the atmosphere. Substances are usually considered pollutants when they are added to the environment by human activity. Any portion of the environment can become polluted, including the atmosphere, the hydrosphere, or the lithosphere. The environment is said to be polluted when more of some substance is added than would normally be present. If, for example, large amounts of waste are dumped into a river, the water becomes polluted. Fish and other living organisms in the river may die if the pollution level becomes too great.
60. **2** The block and the weight are tied together, so they must always have the same speed. If the force moving the block is larger than the friction, the block must accelerate.
61. **2** The friction on an object that slides along a surface is in the direction opposite to that of the motion. In this question the object slides up along the incline; therefore the friction on the block is directed down along the incline. This is shown by choice (2).
62. **3** If the experiment is to test the effect of the flypaper, there must be no other difference between the two bottles; all properties that are the same in both are controls.
63. **3** The experimenter is clearly using flypaper in the bottle because it will trap flies that can fly, but not the others.
64. **2** The experimenter must decide in advance what to put in his bottles in order that the outcome will give him a meaningful answer to the question.
65. **5** The source of winglessness has nothing to do with the experimental problem.
66. **4** In most circumstances in nature, it must be expected that wings are useful. This experiment sets up an artificial environment in which the survival values are reversed. Some such environment might well exist in nature.

TEST 4: The Language Arts, Reading (Interpreting Literature and the Arts) Test/Page 64

1. **3** Her activities included school work, volunteer editorial work, and riding.
2. **1** She is referred to as a "little figure."
3. **4** All three are mentioned: she wore khakis and a red hair ribbon, and waved her cowboy hat.
4. **4** Because she waved to a friend with the wrong hand, the horse veered.
5. **1** The topic sentence refers to Mary White's last hour as being typical of her happiness.
6. **3** Only an animal is awake to listen to Iona.
7. **1** Iona feels he must do something since he can always sleep later.
8. **2** The name of Iona's son, Kuzma Ionitch, is a clue to an eastern European setting.
9. **3** The present tense gives a feeling that the events described are happening now.
10. **5** In talking to the horse, Iona asks the horse to put herself in the position of a foal's mother who loses her foal.
11. **3** Anna valued certain drawers because they were locked.
12. **5** The author presents Anna's concern about being seen and having her letters seen.
13. **1** Since Thomas opened the door with a key and entered, he and Portia had probably been away.
14. **2** The author gives Anna's thoughts only (paragraph one) and adds an interpretation of them near the end of the second paragraph.
15. **2** The passage states that it was to escape from thoughts out of the letter that she had gone to the window.
16. **3** Walter indirectly indicates that Lindner can expect the same treatment if he insults him.
17. **2** It can be inferred that a better home will be part of a new life.
18. **3** Mama says, "My son said we was going to move," so Walter will be the head of the house.
19. **5** As he leaves, Lindner shakes his head in disagreement.
20. **3** Walter says, "We are very proud people."
21. **3** The author says that the songs of *West Side Story* pale next to the speech of Mercutio among other unfavourable comparisons.
22. **1** The passage states that Romeo and Juliet "are a little too slender" to carry the play and this is "equally true of Tony and Maria."
23. **4** The passage observes that the heroes and heroines do "not shake us with . . . fear."

24. **3** Romeo and Juliet suffer from "the caprice of fate" while Tony and Maria suffer from prejudice and hatred.

TEST 5: The Mathematics Test/Page 70

1. **2** 1/2 of the students walk to school
   1 – 1/2 = 1/2 of the students represent the remainder
   1/4 of the remainder = 1/4 × 1/2 = 1/8 of the students use bicycles.
   1/2 = 4/8
   4/8 + 1/8 = 5/8 of the students either walk or use bicycles.
   Therefore, 1 – 5/8 = 3/8 use other means.

2. **5** $2x > 9$
   If we divide both sides of this inequality by 2 we have $x > 9/2$, or 4 1/2.
   The only choice which is greater than 4 1/2 is 5.
   An alternative method is to replace x by each of the choices given. The only choice that makes the inequality true is $x = 5$.

3. **1** The purse contains 6 + 5 + 8 = 19 coins.
   5 coins are dimes.
   $$\text{Probablity} = \frac{\text{number of successful outcomes}}{\text{number of possible outcomes}}$$
   In this case, there are 5 successful outcomes since there are 5 dimes. And the number of possible outcomes is 19 since there are 19 coins in all.
   Thus, $P = \frac{5}{19}$.

4. **4** If we arrange the scores in order of magnitude the number in the middle is called the median.
   In this case, there are 9 scores. If we arrange them in order of magnitude the fifth scores is the median. Notice that we will obtain the same result whether we arrange the scores from lowest to highest or from highest to lowest.
   Scores arranged from lowest to highest—
   272, 274, 275, 276, 278, 281, 283, 284, 287
   ↓
   median

5. **5** The pens cost 3 for $.97.
   The cost of 1 dozen pens = 4($.97) = $3.88.
   The cost of 8 pencils = $4.60 – $3.88 =$.72.
   The cost of 1 pencil = $.72 ÷ 8 = 9 cents.

6. **1** 1 cm on the map = 150 km
   3 1/2 cm on the map = (3 1/2)(150) = 7/2×150 = 525 cm

7. **2** To find the perimeter of the figure we find the sum of the lengths of the four sides
   $2a + b + a + 3b + 3a + b + 3a + 2b = 9a + 7b$.

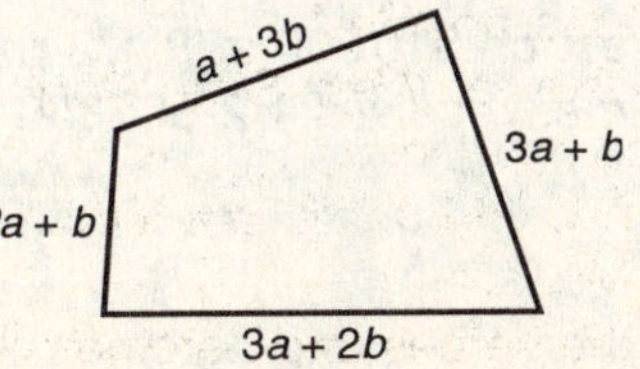

8. **4** The distance between point A and point B is 10 units. Thus, the midpoint of $\overline{AB}$ is located at 5 units to the right of point A.
The coordinate of the midpoint of $\overline{AB}$ is 3.

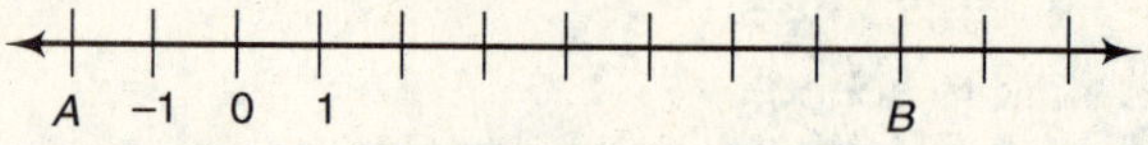

9. **5** 3 ties sold for \$23, 6 ties cost 2(\$23) = \$46
3 shirts sold for \$43
slacks sold for \$32.75 per pair, 2 pairs of slacks
sold for 2(\$32.75) = \$65.50
1 jacket sold for \$58.45
\$46 + \$43 + \$65.50 + \$58.45 = \$212.95

10. **3** If we write all the numbers as decimals, it is easier to arrange the numbers in order of size.
19% = .19, 1/2 = .50, 3/5 = .60, and .080 may be written as .08.
The correct order from greatest to smallest is
.80, .60, .50, .19, .08, or
.80, 3/5, 1/2, 19%, .080
The correct choice is (3).

11. **3** Average speed = Distance covered ÷ time of flight
Average speed = 880 km ÷ 5 1/2 hours
880 ÷ 5 1/2 = 880 ÷ 11/2 = 880 × 2/11

$$\overset{80}{(\cancel{880})}\left(\frac{2}{\cancel{11}}\right) = 160$$

12. **2** To write number in scientific notation we write it as the product of a number between 1 and 10 and a power of 10. In this case, the number between 1 and 10 is 8.5. In going from 8.5 to 85 000 000 000 we move the decimal point 10 places to the right. Therefore
$85\,000\,000\,000 = 8.5 \times 10^{10}$

13. **4** Since m∠ABC = 68° and $\underline{BF}$ bisects ∠ABC, then m∠EBC = 1/2(68°) = 34°.
Since m∠ACB = 72° and $\underline{CD}$ bisects ∠ACB, then m∠ECB = 1/2(72°) = 36°.
Since the sum of the measure of the angles of a triangle is 180°,
m∠EBC + m∠ECB + m∠BEC = 180°
34° + 36° + m∠BEC = 180°
70° + m∠BEC = 180°
m∠BEC = 180° – 70° = 110°

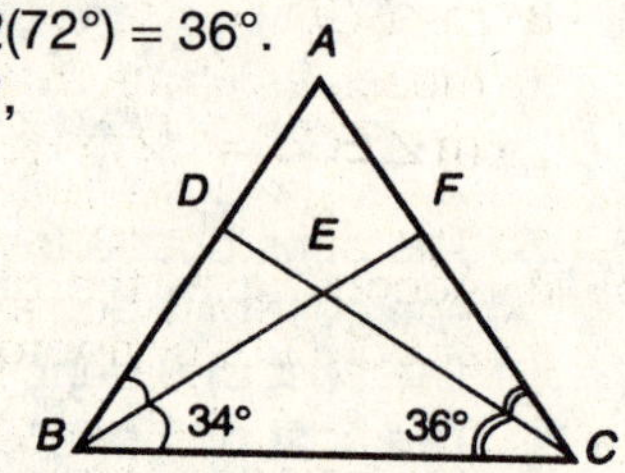

14. **3** Marcus has \$30.
Jack has \$3 less, or \$30 – \$3 = \$27.
Luba has \$5 more than Jack, or Luba has \$27 + \$5 = \$32.

15. **5** We know that John Davis lost at least 4 kg each month. But he may have lost 4 kg during one month, or even more. Not enough information is given to determine John Davis's exact mass after the 6-month period.

16. **2** To compute the annual interest on \$10 000 at 8 1/2 percent we find \$10 000 × .085 = \$850.
Thus, every 6 months Ms. Ames receives 1/2 of \$850 = \$425.

17. **5** Use the Pythagorean Theorem.

$$BC^2 = AC^2 + AB^2$$
$$(25)^2 = (15)^2 + (AB)^2$$
$$625 - 225 = (AB)^2$$
$$400 = (AB)^2$$
$$20 = AB$$

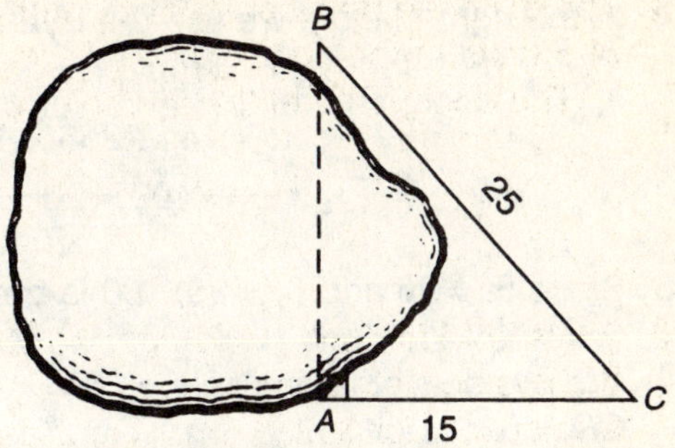

18. **3** Let $9x$ = the number of men at the meeting.
And $2x$ = the number of women at the meeting.

$$2x = 12$$
$$x = 6$$
$$9x = 9(6) = 54$$

19. **5** The slope of $\overleftrightarrow{AB} = \dfrac{\text{change in } y \cdot \text{coordinates}}{\text{change in } x \text{ - coordinates}}$

Slope of $\overleftrightarrow{AB} = \dfrac{7-1}{4-2} = \dfrac{6}{2} = 3$

20. **4** According to the table Vida pays \$4.69 per \$1000 quarterly, or 10(\$4.69) = \$46.90 per quarter. Vida's annual payments are 4(\$46.90) = \$187.60.

21. **1** Philip pays \$9.47 per \$1000 semiannually, or 10(\$9.47) = \$94.70 per half year.
Philip's annual payment is 2 × \$94.70 = \$189.40.
Over a period of 5 years Philip pays 5(\$189.40) = \$947.00.

22. **5** To find Marie's earnings we must multiply 42 by 12 and add this to the product of 37 and 12. From the choices we must select the equivalent of 42 × 12 + 37 × 12.

$$42 \times 12 + 37 \times 12 = 12(42 + 37)$$

23. **3** m$\angle BCD$ = m$\angle ABC$ since pairs of alternate interior angles of parallel lines have equal measures. Thus m$\angle BCD$ = 112°.
$\text{m}\angle ECD = 1/2\,\text{m}\angle BCD = 1/2(112°) = 56°$

24. **4** According to the graph the population in 1971 was more than 20 000 000 but less than 25 000 000, or approximately 21 500 000.

25. **4** According to the graph the population shows the greatest growth between 1941 and 1971 where the line has the greatest slope.

26. **4** We use the formula $V = lwh$ to represent the volume of the rectangular solid. The volume of the rectangular solid is

$$x \cdot x \cdot 8 = 8x^2$$
$$8x^2 = 392$$

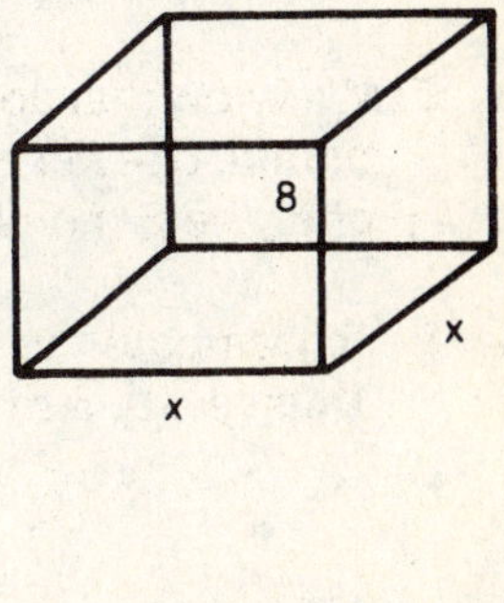

27. **4** In the right triangle we use the Pythagorean Theorem to obtain

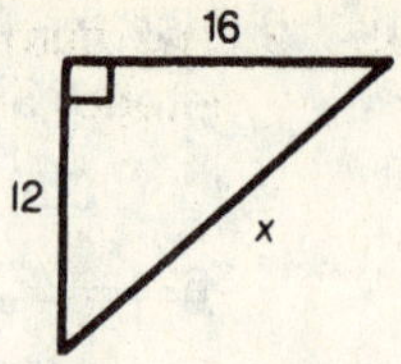

$$x^2 = (12)^2 + (16)^2$$
$$x^2 = 144 + 256 = 400$$
$$x = \sqrt{400} = 20$$

28. **3** Since $5^2 = 25$ and $6^2 = 36$, $\sqrt{30}$ is between 5 and 6.

29. **1** AD = radius of large circle = 20
$CD = 6$
$AC = AD - CD = 20 - 6 = 14$
BC = radius of small circle = 8
$CD = 6$
$BD = BC - CD = 8 - 6 = 2$
$AB = AC + CD + DB = 14 + 6 + 2 = 22$

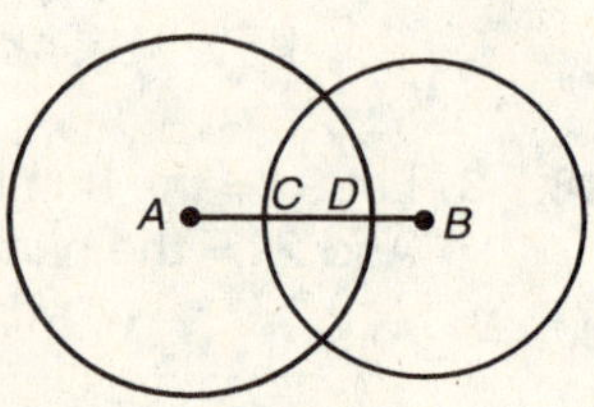

30. **4** $m\angle EBF = m\angle CBD = 50°$ since opposite angles have equal measures.
Since $\overleftrightarrow{CB}$ bisects $\angle ABD$, $m\angle ABC = m\angle CBD$.
Thus, $m\angle ABC = 50°$.

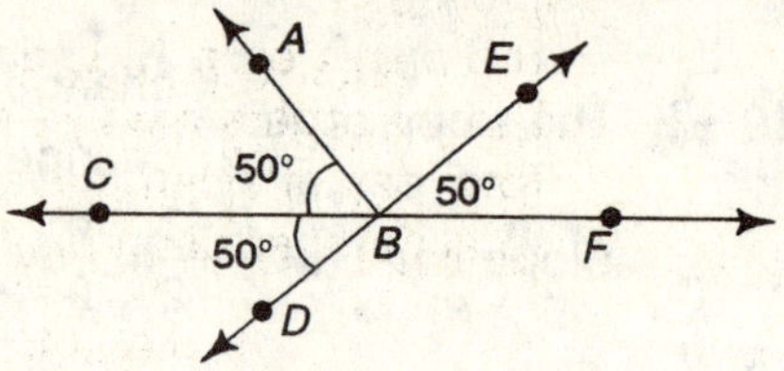

31. **4** To find the cost of n kilograms of sugar at c cents per kilogram we multiply n by c to obtain nc. To find the change received we subtract nc from $1, or 100 cents. The result is $100 - nc$.

32. **1** Let x = the number of students in the graduating class.
$.85x$ plan to go to university.

$$.85x = 170$$
$$x = \frac{170}{.85} = \frac{17000}{85} = 200$$

33. **2** We divide the figure into two rectangles by drawing the dotted line.
The width of rectangle $A = 25 - 5 = 20$ m
The length of rectangle $A = 35$ m
The area of rectangle $A = (20)(35) = 700\ m^2$
The area of rectangle $B = (5)(10) = 50\ m^2$
Area of figure $= 700 + 50 = 750\ m^2$

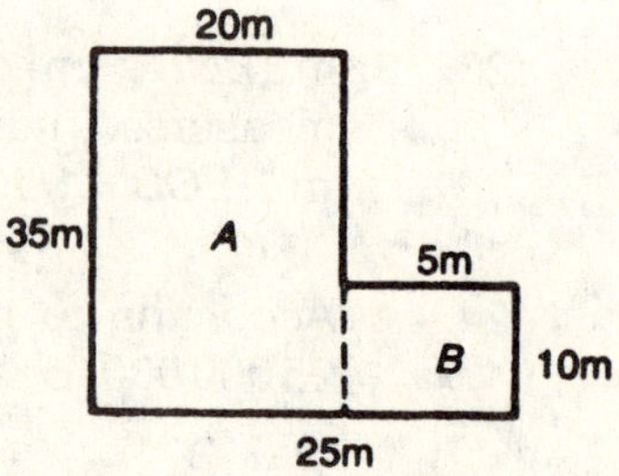

34. **5** Let x = measure of smaller acute angle.
And $4x$ = measure of larger acute angle.

$$x + 4x = 90$$
$$5x = 90$$
$$x = 90 \div 5 = 18$$
$$4x = 4(18) = 72°$$

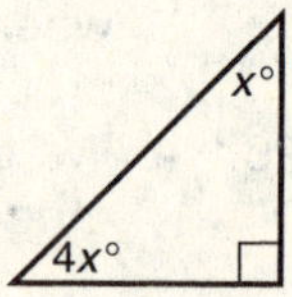

35. **3** The sum of the measures of $\angle A$ and $\angle B$ is 180° since $\overline{AD} \parallel \overline{BC}$ and $\angle A$ and $\angle B$ are interior angles on the same side of the transversal.

$$\text{Let } x = m\angle B.$$
$$\text{And } x + 50 = m\angle A.$$
$$m\angle B + m\angle A = 180$$
$$x + x + 50 = 180$$
$$2x + 50 = 180$$
$$2x = 180 - 50 = 130$$
$$x = 65$$
$$x + 50 = 65 + 50 = 115$$
$$m\angle A = 115°$$

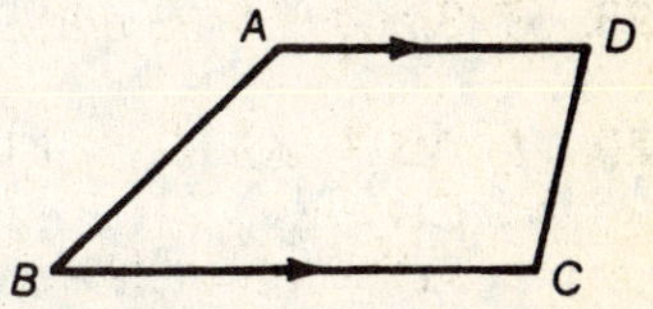

36. **1** To obtain the average weekly pay we divide the total pay of all employees by the number of employees.

The clerks earn 150*x* dollars.
The managers earn 6*y* dollars.
Total pay of all employees is $150x + 6y$.
Total number of employees is 150 + 6 = 156.

$$\text{Average pay} = \frac{\text{Total pay of all employees}}{\text{Total number of employees}} = \frac{150x + 6y}{156}$$

4

LANGUAGE ARTS, WRITING (WRITING SKILLS), PART I

AN OVERVIEW

The three content areas in the Writing Skills Test are sentence structure, usage, and mechanics which includes capitalization and punctuation. Additional writing skills such as diction and tone are described, as are the kinds of practice materials provided.

SENTENCE STRUCTURE

We identify *seven* kinds of run-on sentences and *six* kinds of sentence fragments. Parallel structure, misplaced, dangling, and squinting modifiers are thoroughly covered. *Seven* frequent violations of logic in sentences are shown.

USAGE

A glossary defines over a hundred usage terms and provides examples of each. Key areas of usage are limited to agreement, case of nouns and pronouns, and errors in verb form and tense.

MECHANICS

Fourteen basic rules of capitalization are listed. Basic rules are presented for each of the nine major punctuation marks.

ADDITIONAL WRITING SKILLS

You will learn the importance of context, the difference between denotation and connotation, and the difference between 46 pairs of words frequently confused or misused. Tone and styles of writing are described. *Five* kinds of wordiness are demonstrated. Idioms are listed.

SAMPLE PARAGRAPHS

We have analyzed all possible answers to a sample paragraph. We have provided two additional sample paragraphs for practice. All answers are analyzed.

AN OVERVIEW

The Language Arts, Writing (Writing Skills), Part I, covers three content areas divided into five parts on the examination.

Content

The content areas include
Sentence Structure weighted at about 35%
Usage weighted at about 35%
Mechanics (which includes capitalization, punctuation, and some spelling) weighted at about 30%

Format

The three areas will be tested in 75 minutes by 50 multiple-choice items. These questions, unlike those in previous GED examinations, will be based on paragraphs about 150–200 words in length comprising 10–12 sentences. You will be asked to locate errors contained in sentences in the paragraph and choose the answers which either correct the errors or state that no error exists in the sentence on which the question is based. The kind of error will *not* be identified as has been the case in the past. Instead, you will be required to determine whether the error is in sentence structure, agreement, verb tense or form, pronoun reference, spelling, punctuation, or capitalization.

Types of Questions

There will be three types of questions. The *sentence correction* type (50% of the examination) repeats one of the sentences from the paragraph and asks what correction, if any, should be made. The *sentence revision* type (35%) presents a sentence with a portion underlined that may or may not contain an error. The error, if there is one, may be in sentence structure, agreement, reference, or punctuation. The final type of question, *construction shift*, (15%) requires you to rewrite a sentence which, while correct as it stands, can be improved in logic or combined with other sentences more effectively.

You will be answering 50 questions based on about six different paragraphs containing errors in sentence structure, usage, and mechanics.

The materials in this chapter will thoroughly prepare you for the content, format, and item types which are used on the examination. At the end of the chapter, you will find four sample paragraphs and 36 multiple-choice questions based on them, *exactly as you will find them* on the GED examination. If you study those, with the answers and explanations provided, you should have no trouble on the actual test.

Sentence Structure

The sentence is the basic unit of communication. It's the means by which you express your thoughts for others to understand. We identify five kinds of errors in sentence structure: run-on sentences (including comma splices), incomplete sentences (sentence fragments), sentences lacking parallel structure, sentences containing incorrect modifiers, and sentences containing violations of logic.

Usage

To make certain you can follow our careful explanation of the major problems of usage, we start with a basic glossary (small dictionary) of 104 words used in explaining three of the areas which cause trouble: agreement (of subject and verb, pronoun and antecedent); case of nouns and pronouns (including pronoun reference); and verb form and tense errors.

Mechanics (Capitalization and Punctuation)

For capitalization, 14 basic rules are given, with applications for each. In addition, basic rules are given for each of the major punctuation marks: period, question mark, exclamation point, comma, semicolon, colon, apostrophe, parentheses, and quotation marks, all with appropriate examples. We have compiled three lists of spelling words for you to study: "The Basic 100"; "201 Often Used Easy Words"; and "666 More Frequently Used Words." These 967 words are the ones you will most likely meet on the test. They have been analyzed for you, with the most frequently made spelling errors identified. In addition, the 3 basic skills of a good speller are presented, and the 13 most helpful spelling rules are listed, with examples of how each is applied.

Additional Writing Skills

Some elements of writing, such as diction and tone, are touched on occasionally on the examination. They are, however, essential to good overall performance. There is a section "Words Confused and Misused" which contains 46 pairs of frequently used and confused words. These are carefully explained, with examples of their correct use. Ten DON'Ts are included, with ways to avoid the errors involved. These will help you with questions which deal with correct usage. Other elements such as idioms and economy in writing (how to get rid of unnecessary words) are useful in handling possible responses in the multiple-choice questions.

Practice

Two kinds of practice materials are provided. The traditional individual items dealing with sentence structure, usage, and mechanics will help you master the basic principles.

In addition, sample paragraphs and questions based on them, similar to those you will meet on the GED, will be provided at the end of the chapter. These will enable you to experience the kind of materials you will actually face on the examination and will contain, with explanations, examples of sentence correction, sentence revision, and construction shift items used on the GED.

SENTENCE STRUCTURE

RUN-ON SENTENCES AND SENTENCE FRAGMENTS

A sentence may be defined as a group of words having a subject and a predicate and expressing a complete thought. Each sentence should be separated from the sentence which follows it by some form of end punctuation such as a period, a question mark, or an exclamation point.

Types of Run-on Sentences

In one important group of errors, the writer fails to separate two or more sentences by using the proper end (or terminal) punctuation, either using no punctuation at all or incorrectly using a comma.

This group of errors is called by the general term *run-on sentence* or if a comma is incorrectly used, a comma splice. Here are frequently made errors and the ways they may be corrected.

1. ***Cause-and-effect relationship incorrectly expressed***. This can result from an incorrectly used conjunction or adverb; see the "Glossary of Usage" for definitions of these terms.

Incorrect or Missing Conjunction

EXAMPLE:

WRONG: Joe was elected class president $_x$ he is very popular.
CORRECT: Joe was elected class president because he is very popular.
EXPLANATION:

"Joe was elected class president" and "he is very popular" are both independent sentences. The two sentences have been run together because there is no end punctuation between them. This error can be corrected by simply placing a period between the two sentences. A better way to correct this error is to look for a relationship between the two sentences. The first sentence, "Joe was elected class president," happened because of the second, the fact that "he is very popular"; the first sentence is a result of the second. It is, therefore, possible to join the two sentences using the conjunction "because." Joe was elected president *because* he is very popular.

Incorrect Use of Adverb

EXAMPLE:

WRONG: Joe is very popular $_x$ therefore he was elected president.
WRONG: Joe is very popular $_x$ so he was elected president.
CORRECT: Joe is very popular and, as a result, he was elected president.
CORRECT: Joe is very popular. Therefore, he was elected president.
CORRECT: Joe is very popular; therefore, he was elected president.
EXPLANATION:

To correct this type of error, you must

- *substitute a conjunction for the adverbs "therefore" and "so" or*
- *break the run-on sentence at the point marked x with either a period or a semicolon.*

Important Directions: **Some of the sentences in all the practice exercises have errors. Others are correct. Rewrite correctly the sentences which contain errors. Write "correct" for those that have no errors.**

Practice

1. Hector studied very hard. He passed the test.
2. Maria was very beautiful therefore she was chosen queen of the prom.
3. Céline has lots of friends she is very good-natured.

Answers

1. Correct.
2. Maria was very beautiful. Therefore, she was chosen queen of the prom.
3. Céline is very good-natured and, as a result, she has lots of friends.

2. ***Result incorrectly related to the cause.***

EXAMPLE:

WRONG: Joe worked hard $_x$ he was bound to succeed.
CORRECT: Joe worked *so* hard *that* he was bound to succeed.
WRONG: Joe worked hard $_x$ consequently he was bound to succeed.
CORRECT: Joe worked hard. *Consequently*, he was bound to succeed.
CORRECT: *Since* Joe worked hard, he was bound to succeed.

Practice

1. Since the employer required a high school diploma, I had to pass the GED test.
2. Helena was a good shopper she saved lots of money.

Answers

1. Correct.
2. Helena was a good shopper. Consequently, she saved lots of money.

3. *Opposite idea incorrectly connected to the idea it apparently contradicts.*

EXAMPLE:

WRONG: Joe disliked English $_x$ he got a good mark anyhow.
CORRECT: Joe disliked English *but* he got a good mark anyhow.
WRONG: Joe disliked English $_x$ nevertheless he got a good mark.
CORRECT: Joe disliked English. *Nevertheless*, he got a good mark.
CORRECT: Although Joe disliked English, he got a good mark.
WRONG: Joe disliked English $_x$ however he got a good mark.
CORRECT: Joe disliked English. *However*, he got a good mark.

Practice

1. The politician did not do much campaigning nevertheless he was elected.
2. Although the team rallied, it lost the game.

Answers

1. The politician did not do much campaigning. Nevertheless, he was elected.
2. Correct.

4. *Additional idea incorrectly connected to the idea to which it is added.*

EXAMPLE:

WRONG: Joe is excellent in mathematics $_x$ he is also good in English.
CORRECT: Joe is excellent in mathematics *and* he is also good in English.
WRONG: Joe is excellent in mathematics $_x$ furthermore he is good in English.
CORRECT: Joe is excellent in mathematics. *Furthermore*, he is good in English.
WRONG: Joe is excellent in mathematics $_x$ besides he is good in English.
CORRECT: Joe is excellent in mathematics. He is *also* good in English.
CORRECT: Joe is excellent in mathematics. *Besides*, he is good in English.

Practice

1. Fernando is an excellent violinist he is a fine violist as well.
2. The telecast raised much money for muscular dystrophy research, furthermore it was very entertaining.

Answers

1. Fernando is an excellent violinist; he is a fine violist as well.

or Fernando is an excellent violinist. Besides, he is a fine violist.

2. The telecast raised much money for muscular dystrophy research. Furthermore, it was very entertaining.

5. *Descriptive (adjective) clause incorrectly connected to the word (noun) described.*

EXAMPLE:

WRONG: Joe is always imitating the coach, he respects him greatly.
CORRECT: Joe is always imitating the coach, *whom* he respects greatly.
EXPLANATION:

In the above example, *coach* is the word (noun) described and *whom he respects greatly* is the descriptive clause.

Practice

1. The class elected René president of the class they liked him best of all the candidates.
2. Anna was the best student the class admired her.

Answers

1. The class elected René, whom they liked best of all the candidates, president of the class.
2. Anna, whom the class admired, was the best student.

6. ***Two different sentences incorrectly run together because there is a change in the kind of sentence.***

EXAMPLE:

WRONG: Did Joe win $_x$ he was the best candidate.
CORRECT: Did Joe win? He was the best candidate.
EXPLANATION:
"Did Joe win?" is an interrogative sentence. "He was the best candidate" is a declarative sentence. Often students combine, in error, the question and the answer given to it.

Practice

1. Is Connie home? I have to speak to her.
2. Did you go to see the play it was very entertaining.

Answers

1. Correct.
2. Did you go to see the play? It was very entertaining.

7. ***Two different sentences run together improperly because there is a divided quotation.*** This type of run-on sentence error is difficult to correct because it also involves the punctuation of quotations. Therefore, refer to "Basic Rules of Punctuation" beginning on page 164.

EXAMPLE:

WRONG: "Joe won," he said, "I thought he was the best runner."
CORRECT: "Joe won," he said. "I thought he was the best runner."
CORRECT: "Joe won." He said, "I thought he was the best runner."

Practice

1. "Come in," said the hostess, "I'm happy to see you."
2. "Study hard," advised the teacher. "You'll pass the test."

Answers

1. "Come in," said the hostess. "I'm happy to see you."
2. Correct.

Types of Sentence Fragments

In another important group of errors, the student does not complete the sentence. (You will remember that a sentence is defined as a group of words having a subject and a predicate and expressing a complete thought.) In the kind of error called a *sentence fragment*, either the subject is left out so that a predicate is left standing by itself (e.g., "Wish you were here.") or a part of the predicate is broken off from the sentence and made to stand by itself. (e.g., "Walking down the street.")

1. *Subject of the sentence is improperly left out.*

EXAMPLE:

WRONG: Am having a wonderful time. Wish you were here.

CORRECT: *I* am having a wonderful time. *I* wish you were here.

EXPLANATION:

In each case, without the subject it is impossible to know who is doing the action indicated in the predicate.

Practice

1. Miss you. Will be home tomorrow.
2. Great idea. Wish you luck.

Answers

1. We miss you. We'll be home tomorrow.

or I miss you. I'll be home tomorrow.

or They miss you. They'll be home tomorrow.

2. That's a great idea. I (We) wish you luck.

2. *Parts of a compound predicate are improperly made independent.*

EXAMPLE:

WRONG: Joe studied hard. Passed all his tests and graduated.

CORRECT: Joe studied hard, passed all his tests and graduated.

EXPLANATION:

Note that *studied hard*, *passed all his tests*, and *graduated* are all parts of the predicate, and they all tell us something about Joe.

Practice

1. Don collected baseball cards. Played the piano and excelled in sports.
2. Donna went to school. Worked as a babysitter.

Answers

1. Don collected baseball cards, played the piano, and excelled in sports.
2. While Donna went to school, she worked as a babysitter.

3. *Part of the predicate, a clause, is incorrectly detached from the sentence to which it belongs and is made independent.*

EXAMPLE:

WRONG: Joe got a good mark in English. Although he doesn't like the subject. *(Adverbial clause)*

CORRECT: Joe got a good mark in English, although he doesn't like the subject.

EXAMPLE:

WRONG: Joe has an English teacher. Whom he likes very much. *(Adjective clause)*

CORRECT: Joe has an English teacher whom he likes very much.

Practice

1. Fern is popular. Because she is considerate.
2. I enjoy being with Jill. Who is very amusing.

Answers

1. Fern is popular because she is considerate.
2. I enjoy being with Jill, who is very amusing.

4. ***Part of the predicate, a phrase, is incorrectly detached from the sentence to which it belongs and is made independent.***

EXAMPLE:

WRONG: Joe got up early. To go to school. *(Infinitive phrase)*
CORRECT: Joe got up early to go to school.

EXAMPLE:

WRONG: Joe worked hard. Studying his lessons. *(Participial phrase)*
CORRECT: Joe worked hard studying his lessons.

EXAMPLE:

WRONG: Walking down the street. Joe thought about his job. *(Participial phrase)*
CORRECT: Walking down the street, Joe thought about his job.

> ***Important Note:***
> A clause and a phrase can be detached in error either at the *beginning* or at the *end* of the sentence.

EXAMPLE:

WRONG: Joe went to the movies. With his friend.
CORRECT: Joe went to the movies with his friend.
WRONG: Joe enjoyed himself. At the movies.
CORRECT: Joe enjoyed himself at the movies.

Practice

1. Looking around the room. Cynthia saw her friend.
2. Frances practiced daily, doing her exercises on the piano.
3. I was too tired. To go to the supermarket.

Answers

1. Cynthia, looking around the room, saw her friend.
2. Correct.
3. I was too tired to go to the supermarket.

5. ***Part of the predicate, one or more nouns in apposition with a noun in the predicate, is incorrectly detached from the sentence to which it belongs and is made independent.***

EXAMPLE:

WRONG: Joe enjoys all sports. Baseball, football and swimming.
CORRECT: Joe enjoys all sports: baseball, football and swimming.
EXPLANATION:

Sports is the predicate; baseball, football, and swimming are nouns in apposition. Note that the colon is used to introduce listings. See the section "Basic Rules of Punctuation" beginning on page 164.

EXAMPLE:

WRONG: Joe admires the captain of the team. Ron Jones.
CORRECT: Joe admires the captain of the team, Ron Jones.

Practice

1. Michel collects antiques. Stamps and coins.
2. Dick met his fiancée's mother, Mrs. Ellis.

Answers

1. Michel collects antiques, stamps, and coins.
2. Correct.

6. ***Part of the predicate, one or more nouns in a series, is incorrectly detached from the sentence to which it belongs and is made independent.***

EXAMPLE:

WRONG: Joe has excelled in his studies. Also in sports and extracurricular activities.

CORRECT: Joe has excelled in his studies, in sports, and in extracurricular activities.

Practice

1. Noel spent his spare time at the movies. Also at the pool and at the gym.

2. Sheila helped at home, in school, and at church.

Answers

1. Noel spent his spare time at the movies, the pool, and the gym.

2. Correct.

PRACTICE WITH RUN-ON SENTENCES AND SENTENCE FRAGMENTS

Directions: **Beneath each sentence you will find five ways of writing the underlined part. Choose the answer that makes the best sentence and mark the number of that answer. Answer 1 is always the same as the underlined part and is sometimes the right answer. This is the sentence revision type of multiple-choice item.**

1. Anna had a passion for fruits; melons, pineapples, grapefruits and pears.

(1) fruits; melons,
(2) fruits. melons,
(3) fruits, melons,
(4) fruits: melons,
(5) fruits. Melons,

1. 1 2 3 4 5

2. "Take your umbrella," suggested the boy's mother. "It might rain."

(1) mother. "It
(2) mother," it
(3) mother,". It
(4) mother: "it
(5) mother:" it

2. 1 2 3 4 5

3. "Why he didn't come home on time." stated the parent, "is beyond me."

(1) time." stated
(2) time? "stated
(3) time"? stated
(4) time, "Stated
(5) time," stated

3. 1 2 3 4 5

4. If Jean would have come on time she would have been able to see her friend.

(1) would have come
(2) would come
(3) came
(4) had come
(5) should have come

4. 1 2 3 4 5

5. The teacher told her student to bring his books to class every day.

(1) student to bring his
(2) student that he should bring his
(3) student he should bring his
(4) student: bring your
(5) student—bring your

5. 1 2 3 4 5

6. Arnold studied hard he wanted to make the honour roll.

(1) hard he
(2) hard because he
(3) hard: He
(4) hard, he
(5) hard. since he

6. 1 2 3 4 5

7. Have you been to the museum it has an excellent exhibition.

(1) museum it
(2) museum, it
(3) museum? it
(4) museum? It
(5) museum which

7. 1 2 3 4 5

8. "The Blue Jays won the pennant," said the sportscaster, "I thought they were the best team."

(1) pennant," said the sportscaster, "I
(2) pennant." said the sportscaster, "I
(3) pennant", said the sportscaster, "I
(4) pennant," said the sportscaster. "I
(5) pennant." said the sportscaster. "I

8. 1 2 3 4 5

9. They decided to honour Mr. Wilson, who will have been president of the club ten years next Tuesday.

(1) will have been
(2) shall have been
(3) has been
(4) had been
(5) will be

9. 1 2 3 4 5

10. The student replied that he is living here for the last three years.

(1) that he is
(2) that "He is
(3) that, "He is
(4) that he was
(5) that he has been

10. 1 2 3 4 5

11. If he would have played in every game, he would have won the scoring championship.

(1) would have played
(2) would play
(3) had played
(4) should play
(5) should have played

11. 1 2 3 4 5

12. I should agree to the proposal if I were in your situation.

(1) I should agree to the proposal if I were
(2) I would agree to the proposal if I would be
(3) I would agree to the proposal if I was
(4) I would agree to the proposal, if I was
(5) I would agree to the proposal; if I were

12. 1 2 3 4 5

13. Neither Kim nor she will have arrived by the time you come.

(1) nor she will have arrived
(2) nor her will have arrived
(3) or she will have arrived
(4) nor she arrived
(5) nor her arrived

13. 1 2 3 4 5

14. The employer refused the worker the raise besides, he threatened to fire him.

(1) raise besides,
(2) raise, besides,
(3) raise: besides,
(4) raise. besides
(5) raise. Besides,

14. 1 2 3 4 5

15. Studying hard. Miss you. Write.

(1) Studying hard. Miss you. Write.
(2) I am studying hard. Miss you. Write.
(3) I am studying hard. I miss you. Write.
(4) Studying hard; miss you; write.
(5) Studying hard: miss you. Write.

15. 1 2 3 4 5

16. To succeed in school: Jean attended regularly, did his homework, and studied hard.

(1) school: Jean
(2) school. Jean
(3) school, Jean
(4) school—Jean
(5) school Jean

16. 1 2 3 4 5

17. Why didn't you come I waited for hours for your arrival.

(1) come I
(2) come, I
(3) come; I
(4) come: I
(5) come? I

17. 1 2 3 4 5

18. Joanne didn't like to study she passed the examination anyhow.

(1) study she
(2) study and she
(3) study, and she
(4) study: but she
(5) study, but she

18. 1 2 3 4 5

19. They objected to me staying. Nevertheless, I remained at the gathering.

(1) me staying. Nevertheless, I
(2) me staying, nevertheless I
(3) my staying, nevertheless, I
(4) my staying. Nevertheless I
(5) my staying. Nevertheless, I

19. 1 2 3 4 5

20. Can't be at your wedding send all our love.

(1) Can't be at your wedding send
(2) Can't be at your wedding: send
(3) Can't be at your wedding; we send
(4) Can't be at your wedding, we send
(5) We can't be at your wedding, but we send

20. 1 2 3 4 5

21. Although Vincent and Giuseppe, buddies during the Gulf War, hadn't met for over five years.

(1) Giuseppe, buddies during the Gulf War, hadn't met
(2) Giuseppe buddies during the Gulf War hadn't met
(3) Giuseppe, buddies during the Gulf War didn't meet
(4) Giuseppe were buddies during the Gulf War yet hadn't met
(5) Giuseppe were buddies during the Gulf War, they hadn't met

21. 1 2 3 4 5

22. Will you come to my party I'd be happy to have you there.

(1) party I'd
(2) party. I'd
(3) party; I'd
(4) party: I'd
(5) party? I'd

22. 1 2 3 4 5

23. "This is most unusual," said George," the mail has never come late before."

(1) George," the
(2) George, "The
(3) George. "The
(4) George; "The
(5) George: "The

23. 1 2 3 4 5

24. Judy wanted to have gone to the movies.
(1) wanted to have gone
(2) wanted to go
(3) had wanted to have gone
(4) wanted to have went
(5) had wanted to have went

24. 1 2 3 4 5

25. My doctor inspires confidence because he is practicing twenty years already.
(1) he is practicing twenty years already
(2) he was practicing twenty years already
(3) he has already been practicing twenty years
(4) already he is practicing twenty years
(5) already he has been practicing twenty years

25. 1 2 3 4 5

Turn to the answer key and the answer analysis which follow.

What's Your Score?

______ right,	______ wrong
Excellent	23–25
Good	20–22
Fair	17–19

If you scored lower, study the kinds of run-on sentences and sentence fragments illustrated in this section.

ANSWER KEY

Practice with Run-on Sentences and Sentence Fragments/Page 111

1. **4**	6. **2**	11. **3**	16. **3**	21. **5**
2. **1**	7. **4**	12. **1**	17. **5**	22. **5**
3. **5**	8. **4**	13. **1**	18. **5**	23. **3**
4. **4**	9. **1**	14. **5**	19. **5**	24. **2**
5. **1**	10. **5**	15. **3**	20. **5**	25. **3**

ANSWER ANALYSIS

Practice with Run-on Sentences and Sentence Fragments/Page 110

1. **4** See Type 5 under "Types of Sentence Fragments" (page 110). The nouns in apposition with fruits should be preceded by a colon. See Rule 1 under "The Colon" (page 166).
2. **1** No error.
3. **5** See Rule 7 under "The Comma" (page 164), as it refers to the divided quotation where commas are used to set off the speaker.
4. **4** See the discussion of the proper sequence of tenses under "Troublesome Verbs" (page 150).
5. **1** No error.
6. **2** See Type 1 under "Types of Run-on Sentences" (page 106). The explanation given there applies to this sentence. A cause for Arnold's studying hard is needed to bring the two sentences together.
7. **4** See Type 6 under "Types of Run-on Sentences" (page 108). The two sentences are improperly run together because there is a change in the kind of sentence.
8. **4** See Type 7 under "Types of Run-on Sentences" (page 108). The two sentences are improperly run together because there is a divided quotation.

9. **1** No error.
10. **5** The present perfect tense is required since the student has been living here up to the present time.
11. **3** The sequence of tenses requires the past perfect tense in the dependent clause beginning with *If*.
12. **1** No error.
13. **1** No error.
14. **5** See Type 4 under "Types of Run-on Sentences" (page 107). This is a run-on sentence where an additional idea is incorrectly connected to the idea to which it is added.
15. **3** See Type 1 under "Types of Sentence Fragments" (page 109). The subjects of the first two sentences are improperly left out. In *Write*, the subject *you* is understood.
16. **3** See Type 4 under "Types of Sentence Fragments" (page 110). The important note mentions that a phrase may, in error, be detached at the beginning of the sentence. Here, it is "To succeed in school." The colon detaches it; the comma connects it to the sentence. (Also, see Rule 4 under "The Comma," page 164.)
17. **5** See Type 6 under "Types of Run-on Sentences" (page 108). The discussion explains this error.
18. **5** See Type 3 under "Types of Run-on Sentences" (page 107). The opposite idea is incorrectly connected to the idea it apparently contradicts.
19. **5** See Problem 3 under "Some Special Problems" of "Case of Nouns and Pronouns" (page 147).
20. **5** See Type 1 under "Types of Sentence Fragments" (page 109). The subject of the sentence is improperly left out. In addition, see Type 3 under "Types of Run-on Sentences" (page 107). An opposite idea is incorrectly connected to the idea it apparently contradicts.
21. **5** See Type 4 under "Types of Sentence Fragments" (particularly in the IMPORTANT NOTE—page 109). This is an example of a detached clause at the beginning of the sentence.
22. **5** See Type 6 under "Types of Run-on Sentences" (page 108). This is a case of two sentences being incorrectly run together because of a change in the kind of sentence. "Will you come to my party?" is an interrogative sentence; "I'd be happy to have you there" is a declarative sentence.
23. **3** See Type 7 under "Types of Run-on Sentences" (page 108). Two different sentences are run together improperly because there is a divided quotation.
24. **2** The sequence of tenses is incorrect. According to the meaning of the sentence, Judy's wanting comes *before*, not *after*, Judy's going.
25. **3** The present perfect tense is required.

PARALLEL STRUCTURE

A major error in sentence structure is the failure to keep elements of the sentence which perform the *same purpose* in the *same form.* This is called an error in parallel structure.

Here is an example of such an error.

WRONG: Joe likes *swimming*, *fishing*, and, if he has the time, *to take* a long walk.

The sentence tells us three things Joe likes. They are related to us by words which are the object of the verb *likes.* They serve the same purpose. But are their forms alike? Let us line them up vertically.

Joe likes swimming
fishing
to take a long walk

No, they are not. *Swimming* and *fishing* are gerunds (verbs used as nouns in the *-ing* form). *To take* is an infinitive. Words having the same function should have the same form. Then, they would be parallel in structure. The sentence should read:

Joe likes swimming
fishing
taking a long walk

CORRECT: Joe likes *swimming*, *fishing*, and, if he has the time, *taking a long walk.*

Practice

1. Irene enjoys baking, cooking, and to prepare meals.
2. Julie excels at embroidering, crocheting, and hooking rugs.

Answers

1. Irene enjoys baking, cooking, and preparing meals.
2. Correct.

Here is another example of lack of parallel structure.

WRONG: Jane and Jim took part *in* baseball *games*, *in* swimming *contests*, and *in learning* about golf.

The sentence tells us three things in which Jane and Jim took part. All three are objects of the preposition *in.* They serve the same purpose, yet the form of one of them is different.

Jane and Jim took part in baseball *games*
in swimming *contests*
in *learning* about golf

Two are nouns; the third is a gerund (a verb used as a noun in the *-ing* form). To maintain parallel structure, the third must also be a noun.

Jane and Jim took part in baseball *games*
in swimming *contests*
in golf *lessons*

Lessons is a noun. The structure of the items in the sentence is now parallel.

CORRECT: Jane and Jim took part *in* baseball *games*, *in* swimming *contests*, and *in* golf *lessons.*

Practice

1. Ben took courses in computers, in mathematics, and in learning about fine arts.
2. Jesse couldn't decide on a career in education, in business, or becoming a doctor.

Answers

1. Ben took courses in computers, in mathematics, and in fine arts.
2. Jesse couldn't decide on a career in education, in business, or in medicine.

Here is another type of error in parallel structure.

WRONG: The backers failed to realize *the success of the show* or *how long it would run.*

Two things were realized: both are objects of the verb *realize.* Yet one is a noun, *success*; the other a noun clause, *how long it would run.* Since both fill the same purpose in the sentence, they should have the same form. Either both should be nouns or both should be noun clauses. You may correct this sentence in either of two ways to achieve parallel structure.

CORRECT: The backers failed to realize the *success* of the show or the *length* of its run. (Two nouns)

CORRECT: The backers failed to realize *how successful the show would be* or *how long it would run.* (Two noun clauses)

Practice

1. Jane needed financial support and being encouraged.
2. Arnold was not aware of his strength or how good-looking he was.
3. The movie was entertaining and it instructed us as well.

Answers

1. Jane needed financial support and encouragement.
2. Arnold was not aware of how strong or how good-looking he was.
3. The movie was entertaining and instructive.

Here is another type of error in parallel structure.

Note: Certain pairs of words in the English language are called correlatives. They connect parts of a sentence which are equal in importance—*parallel elements*. You are familiar with a number of them:

both . . . and
either . . . or
neither . . . nor
not only . . . but also
whether . . . or

Remember to use these *immediately before* the parallel element each accompanies.

A few examples will make this point clear.

WRONG: Camille was *both* asked to work the switchboard *and* to address envelopes.

Note that only one of the correlatives, *and*, precedes an infinitive, *to address.* Both correlatives should precede the infinitives, *to work* and *to address*

Camille was asked *both* to work
and to address

CORRECT: Camille was asked *both* to work the switchboard *and* to address envelopes.

Here is another example.

WRONG: The basketball star *not only* was popular *but also* modest.

The basketball star was *not only* popular
but also modest

CORRECT: The basketball star was *not only* popular *but also* modest.

Practice

1. Carmen was interested neither in sports nor in books.
2. He was not only smart but also handsome.

Answers

1. Correct
2. Correct

If you want to remember the idea behind parallel structure, here is an example.

Something *old*
Something *new*
Something *borrowed*
Something *blue*

(Note that *Something* is followed by four different adjectives.)

PRACTICE WITH PARALLEL STRUCTURE

Directions: **Beneath each sentence you will find five ways of writing the underlined part. Choose the answer that makes the best sentence and mark the number of that answer. Answer 1 is always the same as the underlined part and is sometimes the right answer. These are included in the sentence correction type of multiple-choice item.**

1. To strive for perfection, to serve one's fellow man, to help the needy are ideals all should try to follow.
(1) To strive for perfection, to serve one's fellow man, to help
(2) To strive for perfection, serving one's fellow man, helping
(3) Striving for perfection, serving one's fellow man, and to help
(4) Striving for perfection, to serve one's fellow man, helping
(5) To strive for perfection. To serve one's fellow man. To help

1. 1 2 3 4 5
‖ ‖ ‖ ‖ ‖

2. Jones, the president of the union and who is also a member of the community group, will be in charge of the negotiations.
(1) who is also a member of the community group,
(2) since he is a member of the community group
(3) a member of the community group,
(4) also being a member of the community group
(5) , in addition, who is a member of the community group

2. 1 2 3 4 5
‖ ‖ ‖ ‖ ‖

3. Marie is good-looking, with intelligence, and has youth.
(1) with intelligence, and has youth
(2) intelligent, and has youth
(3) intelligent, youthful
(4) , with intelligence, and youthful
(5) intelligent, and youthful

3. 1 2 3 4 5
‖ ‖ ‖ ‖ ‖

4. He is rude, gruff, and doesn't think of the feelings of others or of showing consideration to others.
(1) and doesn't think of the feelings of others or of showing consideration to
(2) and doesn't think of or show consideration to
(3) thoughtless, and inconsiderate of
(4) thoughtless of others and of showing consideration to
(5) thoughtless of others' feelings, and lacking in consideration to

4. 1 2 3 4 5
‖ ‖ ‖ ‖ ‖

5. The instructor told the student to hold the club lightly, keeping his eye on the ball and drawing the club back quickly, but too much force should not be used on the downward stroke.
(1) to hold the club lightly, keeping his eye on the ball and drawing the club back quickly, but too much force should not be used
(2) to hold the club lightly, keep his eye on the ball, and drawing the club back quickly, and too much force should not be used

5. 1 2 3 4 5
‖ ‖ ‖ ‖ ‖

(3) to hold the club lightly, keep his eye on the ball, draw the club back quickly and not use too much force
(4) to hold the club lightly, keep his eye on the ball, draw the club back quickly and too much force should not be used
(5) he should hold the club lightly, keeping his eye on the ball, drawing the club back quickly, and not using too much force

Turn to the answer key and the answer analysis which follow.

What's Your Score?

______ right,	______ wrong
Excellent	5
Good	4
Fair	3

If you scored lower, review this section and study the examples of correct parallel structure.

ANSWER KEY

Practice with Parallel Structure/Page 118

1. **1** 2. **3** 3. **5** 4. **3** 5. **3**

ANSWER ANALYSIS

Practice with Parallel Structure/Page 118

1. **1** No error.
2. **3** While verbs are not involved, nouns in apposition are, and they must be parallel to one another. "Jones, the *president* . . . and a *member* . . ."
3. **5** This is a case of parallel structure involving three adjectives.
4. **3** Parallel structure requires the use of four adjectives (*rude*, *gruff*, *thoughtless*, and *inconsiderate*) instead of two adjectives (*rude*, *gruff*) and two phrases (*of the feelings . . . of showing . . .*) following an unnecessary verb *doesn't think.*
5. **3** Four infinitives are in parallel form and much clearer than the mixture of an infinitive (*to hold*), two verbals (*keeping* and *drawing*), and a clause (*too much force should not be used*).

MUDDLED MODIFIERS

A modifier is a word or a group of words which help describe another word or group of words by giving a more exact meaning. The modifier may be an adjective (a *big* house) or an adverb (walk *slowly*), an adjective clause (the man *who came to dinner*) or an adjective phrase (Jeanie *with the light brown hair*), an adverbial clause (he arrived *when the clock struck twelve*) or an adverbial phrase (he arrived *on time*). Very often, confusion in meaning takes place when a modifier is used incorrectly.

Misplaced Modifiers

A modifier which is misplaced in a sentence may cause confusion in meaning.
Here is an example.

WRONG: Fred cut himself while shaving *badly.*

The word *badly* is a misplaced modifier. It is an adverb which modifies the meaning of the verb *cut* and, therefore, should be placed where there is no doubt about what it modifies. (it certainly isn't intended to modify *shaving*.)

CORRECT: Fred cut himself *badly* while shaving.

The meaning is completely changed by the placement of the modifier. Now the sentence means what the writer intended it to mean.

Here is another example.

WRONG: The fire was put out before any damage was done *by the firefighters.*

The phrase *by the firefighters* is a misplaced modifier. It is an adverbial phrase which modifies the verb *put out* and, therefore, should be placed near the verb it modifies. The writer certainly did not mean to say that the firefighters did any damage, yet this is the message conveyed. Once again, the misplaced modifier completely confuses the meaning.

CORRECT: The fire was put out *by the firefighters* before any damage was done.

> By now, you may have figured out the rule that will save you from misplacing modifiers. *Always place the modifier, be it a word or a group of words, as near as possible to the word it is modifying* so that the reader will not be in any doubt about the meaning of the sentence.

Here's a humourous example of a misplaced modifier to help you remember the rule.

WRONG: They were *almost* married for five years.

To save the couple from living in sin, you must place the modifier, *almost*, near the word it modifies, *five.*

CORRECT: They were married for *almost* five years.

Practice

1. Julia almost won all the prizes that were awarded.
2. The girl was dancing with her boyfriend in the red dress.
3. What do you think of Shakespeare as an English teacher?

Answers

1. Julia won almost all the prizes that were awarded,
2. The girl in the red dress was dancing with her boyfriend.
3. As an English teacher, what do you think of Shakespeare?

Dangling Modifiers

In our previous examples, the modifier was misplaced. It should have been placed clearly and unmistakably near the word or words it modified. But at least there was a word in the sentence with which the modifier belonged. In the case of the *dangling modifier*, the problem is that there is no word or words to which the modifier clearly refers.

Here are some examples.

EXAMPLE 1.

WRONG: *Standing* on the corner, *the car* passed me by.

It is important to note that merely turning the incorrect sentence around will not keep the modifier from dangling.

WRONG: *The car* passed me by, *standing* on the corner.

The sentence has to be rewritten to read:

CORRECT: While I was *standing* on the corner, *the car* passed me by.

Standing is now part of the verb in the subordinate clause and is no longer dangling.

EXAMPLE 2.

WRONG: *Speeding* down the track at one hundred and thirty kilometres an hour, *the stalled car* was demolished by the train.

The stalled car obviously can't be speeding. The dangling modifier, *speeding,* can only refer to the train. This is an easy one to correct.

CORRECT: *Speeding* down the track at one hundred and thirty kilometres an hour, the *train* demolished the stalled car.

EXAMPLE 3.

WRONG: *At ten,* my parents took me on a trip to British Columbia.

The phrase *at ten* is dangling since it does not have a noun it clearly modifies. Who was ten? Surely not the parents. The phrase has to be converted into a clause to correct the error.

CORRECT: *When I was ten,* my parents took me on a trip to British Columbia.

How can dangling modifiers be avoided? *Dangling modifiers can be avoided by following an introductory phrase immediately with the word it modifies*. Note that the dangling modifier need not be a particular grammatical form. It can be

—a prepositional phrase
—an infinitive phrase
—a gerund phrase
—a participial phrase
—a clause

Note the following examples.

EXAMPLE 4. (Infinitive phrase)

WRONG: *To get* good grades, *lessons* must be prepared carefully.
CORRECT: *To get* good grades, *you* must prepare your lessons carefully.

EXAMPLE 5. (Gerund phrase)

WRONG: *After graduating from school, my father* got me a good job.
CORRECT: *After I graduated from school, my father* got me a good job.

EXAMPLE 6. (Participial phrase)

WRONG: *Watching the baseball game, the hot dogs* tasted delicious.
CORRECT: *Watching the baseball game, I* ate delicious hot dogs.

EXAMPLE 7. (Clause)

WRONG: *His leg* was injured *while playing* tennis.
CORRECT: *He* injured his leg *while playing* tennis.

EXAMPLE 8. (A humourous one)

WRONG: *Walking around in the zoo, my eye* was caught by the gorilla. Did you ever see an eye walking?
CORRECT: *As I* was *walking around in the zoo*, the gorilla caught my eye.

Practice

1. Sightseeing in Ottawa, the Parliament was my first stop.
2. Swimming in the water, the lifeguard saw me.
3. To earn an equivalency diploma, the GED test must be passed.

Answers

1. When I was sightseeing in Ottawa, the Parliament was my first stop.
2. The lifeguard saw me when I was swimming in the water.
3. To earn an equivalency diploma, you must pass the GED test.

Two-Way, or Squinting, Modifiers

We have discussed the case of the modifier which is so placed that it modifies the wrong word or phrase. We have also dealt with the case of the modifier which actually doesn't modify any word or phrase in the sentence clearly. Now we come to the case of the modifier which can modify not one but two words or phrases. Although it is most frequently called a squinting modifier, we prefer to call it a two-way modifier because it can modify in two ways, only one of which is correct.

Here's an example.

EXAMPLE 1.

WRONG: Does a man live here with a wife and a child *named Johnny*?

Who is named Johnny, the man or the child? The sentence is unclear as it stands. If the man is named Johnny, then this is how it should have been written.

CORRECT: Does a man *named Johnny* live here with a wife and a child?

If the child is indeed named Johnny, the sentence has to be changed to put the name, Johnny, in apposition with child, thus making them equivalent.

CORRECT: Does a man live here with a wife and a child, *Johnny*?

Here are some other two-way modifiers.

EXAMPLE 2.

WRONG: Plans for withdrawing troops *gradually* were drawn up by the government.

Gradually has two meanings here. It can mean that the troops will be withdrawn gradually *or* that the plans were drawn up gradually. The writer probably meant:

CORRECT: Plans for the gradual withdrawal of troops were drawn up by the government.

EXAMPLE 3.

WRONG: Because we studied hard *for a week* we were ready for the examination. Did we study hard for a week, or were we ready for the examination for a week? It is not clear from the sentence what the writer intended. A comma, put in the right place, will help get rid of the two-way modifier.

CORRECT: Because we studied hard for a week, we were ready for the examination.

Practice

1. Because we had no classes for a week we were on vacation.
2. After I passed the GED test with the help of the teacher I got a job.
3. Hopes for recovering from the operation quickly were dashed by the doctor.

Answers

1. Because we had no classes, for a week we were on vacation.
or Because we had no classes for a week, we were on vacation.

2. After I passed the GED test, with the help of my teacher I got a job.
or After I passed the GED test with the help of my teacher, I got a job.

3. Hopes for recovering quickly from the operation were dashed by the doctor.
or Hopes for recovering from the operation were quickly dashed by the doctor.

PRACTICE WITH MUDDLED MODIFIERS

Directions: **Beneath each sentence you will find five ways of writing the underlined part. Choose the answer that makes the best sentence and mark the number of that answer. Answer 1 is always the same as the underlined part and is sometimes the right answer.**

1. Turning the corner, my eye caught sight of the house where I used to live.

(1) Turning
(2) After turning
(5) Having turned
(4) When turning
(5) When I turned

1. 1 2 3 4 5

2. The horse, ridden by the experienced jockey with the broken leg, had to be destroyed.

(1) horse, ridden by the experienced jockey with the broken leg, had
(2) horse ridden by the experienced jockey with the broken leg had
(3) horse with the broken leg ridden by the experienced jockey had
(4) horse with the broken leg ridden by the experienced jockey, had
(5) horse with the broken leg, ridden by the experienced jockey, had

2. 1 2 3 4 5

3. The interviewee was asked, "What is your opinion of "Gone with the Wind" as a movie critic?"

(1) asked, "What is your opinion of "Gone with the Wind" as a movie critic?"
(2) asked his opinion of "Gone with the Wind" as a movie critic.
(3) asked "What his opinion was of "Gone with the Wind" as a movie critic?"
(4) asked, "As a movie critic, what is your opinion of "Gone with the Wind"?"
(5) asked as a movie critic "What is your opinion of "Gone with the Wind"?"

3. 1 2 3 4 5

4. Wagging its tail, the dog food was quickly consumed by the happy puppy.

(1) Wagging its tail, the dog food was quickly consumed by the happy puppy.
(2) Wagging it's tail, the dog food was quickly consumed by the happy puppy.
(3) The happy puppy quickly consumed the dog food wagging its tail.
(4) Wagging its tail, the happy puppy quickly consumed the dog food.
(5) The dog food was quickly consumed by the happy puppy wagging it's tail.

4. 1 2 3 4 5

5. At the age of ten, my parents took me to Canada's Wonderland.
(1) At the age of ten, my parents took me
(2) At the age of ten my parents took me
(3) My parents took me at the age of ten
(4) My parents took me aged ten
(5) At the age of ten, I was taken by my parents

5. 1 2 3 4 5
|| || || || ||

6. The secretary located the picture of Lester Pearson looking through the files.
(1) The secretary located the picture of Lester Pearson looking through the files.
(2) The secretary located Lester Pearson's picture looking through the files.
(3) Looking through the files, Lester Pearson's picture was located by the secretary.
(4) Looking through the files, the secretary located the picture of Lester Pearson.
(5) Looking through the files the picture of Lester Pearson was located by the secretary.

6. 1 2 3 4 5
|| || || || ||

7. The Smiths were almost married ten years before they had their first child.
(1) were almost married
(2) were married almost
(3) almost were married
(4) had been almost married
(5) had been married almost

7. 1 2 3 4 5
|| || || || ||

8. We finally agreed on a price for the picture of the ship which hung in the balcony.
(1) picture of the ship which hung
(2) picture of the ship which was hung
(3) picture of the ship which hanged
(4) ship's picture which hung
(5) ship's picture which hanged

8. 1 2 3 4 5
|| || || || ||

9. Our guest let us know that he would be arriving next week in his last letter.
(1) that he would be arriving next week in his last letter
(2) that he was arriving next week in his last letter
(3) that he will arrive next week in his last letter
(4) in his last letter that he would be arriving next week
(5) in his last letter that he was arriving next week

9. 1 2 3 4 5
|| || || || ||

10. My mother lives in the house on the hill that she just bought.
(1) house on the hill that she just bought
(2) house on the hill she just bought
(3) house she just bought on the hill
(4) house on the hill which she just bought
(5) house, she just bought, on the hill

10. 1 2 3 4 5
|| || || || ||

Turn to the answer key and the answer analysis which follow.

What's Your Score?

_______ right,	_______ wrong
Excellent	9–10
Good	8
Fair	7

If you scored lower, review the corrected examples in this section.

ANSWER KEY

Practice with Muddled Modifiers/Page 123

1. **5**	3. **4**	5. **5**	7. **5**	9. **4**
2. **5**	4. **4**	6. **4**	8. **4**	10. **3**

ANSWER ANALYSIS

Practice with Muddled Modifiers/Page 123

1. **5** The way the sentence reads with the dangling modifier, the eye is *turning the corner.*
2. **5** *With the broken leg* is a misplaced modifier. Also see Rule 8 under "The Comma" (page 165). In this sentence, commas are required to set off the clause *ridden . . . jockey.*
3. **4** Again there is a misplaced modifier. The modifier, *movie critic,* should be placed near the word it modifies—*interviewee.*
4. **4** The dangling modifier gives the impression that the *dog food was wagging its tail.* The possessive pronoun *its* does not have an apostrophe.
5. **5** The dangling modifier, *At the age of ten,* erroneously modifies *parents.*
6. **4** The dangling modifier *looking through the files* gives the mistaken impression that *the picture* was doing the looking.
7. **5** The modifier, *almost,* is misplaced. It should be near *ten years* which it modifies. Also see "Some Special Problems" of "Verb Sequences" (page 153). The past perfect tense, *had been married,* is needed because the years of marriage in the past *preceded* the birth of the child in the past.
8. **4** The modifier, *which hung in the balcony,* should be near the noun, *picture*, which it modifies. See "Muddled Modifiers" (page 119). The past tense of *hang* (an object) is *hung.*
9. **4** The misplaced modifier, *in his last letter,* gives the mistaken impression that the guest would be arriving *in* the letter. The phrase should be near *know* which it modifies.
10. **3** *She just bought* modifies *house* and should be placed next to it.

SEVEN FREQUENT VIOLATIONS OF LOGIC

1. ***Logic may be violated by introduction of irrelevant ideas.*** One of the most frequent violations of logic is including in a paragraph sentences or clauses which are irrelevant, having nothing to do with the topic under discussion.* Technically, we can say that these sentences or clauses do not relate to the topic sentence.

How can this happen? When you write on a subject, you may know so much about it, you may get so enthusiastic, that you want to include everything, whether it belongs or not. In other instances, you may be unaware that a particular idea is not relevant to the topic or does not fit in with the other sentences in the paragraph.

Here are some examples. Each of the sentences looks correct enough, yet each contains some weakness in logic.

EXAMPLES:

1. Pierre Trudeau was the fifteenth Canadian prime minister and one of the most influential men of his time.
EXPLANATION:
This sentence contains *two unrelated ideas.* Trudeau was both our fifteenth prime minister and an influential man, but the conjunction *and* gives equal importance to two facts which really do not belong together. Only one idea should be included in a sentence if a second one is unrelated to it. The familiar opening sentence of many book reports is another example of this error. "This book was about married life and I liked it very much." Was the fact that the reader liked the book a *result* of the fact that it was about married life? If so, the sentence should be changed completely. As it stands, one idea does not relate to the other.

2. American professional athletes get higher salaries, even though their cost of living is higher than Europe's, than any other athletes in the world.
EXPLANATION:
This sentence contains *one idea and an unrelated secondary idea.* The sentence is about the salaries of American professional athletes, not the cost of living. That clause can safely be dropped.

3. The man-on-the-moon program of NASA, which was extremely costly, greatly advanced our knowledge of the universe.
EXPLANATION:
This sentence also contains a main idea and an unrelated secondary idea. Why get into the cost of the NASA program when the main purpose of the sentence is to stress its contribution to our knowledge of outer space? That clause, too, should be dropped or placed in another sentence.

4. The teacher, experienced and neatly dressed, had difficulty disciplining the class.
EXPLANATION:
This sentence contains *irrelevant details*. What does the fact that the teacher was experienced and neatly dressed have to do with discipline? Indeed, it distracts the reader from the main idea of the sentence and even causes him to wonder why an experienced and neatly dressed person would have discipline problems with a class.

The point is that, while the additional ideas and details *can* be made relevant, as the sentences now stand, they are not. The logic is either missing or weak.

2. *Logic may be violated by incorrect subordination or by lack of subordination of ideas*. You will recall that an independent clause can stand alone, whereas a dependent clause cannot. In the sentence, "He played well although he was hurt," *He played well* is an independent clause that can stand alone; *although he was hurt* is a dependent adverbial clause which cannot. The

*Remember to review the section "Writing Effective Sentences" (beginning on page 242) very carefully.

important thing to remember is that, if two ideas are included in a single sentence, the more important one should be placed in the independent clause. The more important idea is *he played well* despite the less important fact that he was injured. The less important idea, therefore, should be put in the dependent clause.

The error in logic arises when the more important idea is placed in the dependent clause, the less important part of the sentence. Going back to our illustration, compare these two sentences:

EXAMPLE:
He played well although he was hurt.
He was hurt although he played well.

The second sentence is a violation in logic because the main idea is in the dependent clause introduced by *although*, instead of in the main clause. Here is another example:

EXAMPLE:
He was returning home from work when he suffered a heart attack.
He suffered a heart attack when he was returning home from work.

Surely the idea of a heart attack is more important than the return from work; therefore, the second sentence is correct.

Another major violation of logic is the failure of the writer to subordinate less important ideas. The tendency is to treat important and less important ideas alike. It's what a child does when he strings ideas together with a series of *and*'s.

EXAMPLE:
WRONG: My parents took me to the Music Hall and then we had lunch and then we took a walk and we had a good time.

The most important idea is the good time. The visit to the Music Hall, lunch, and a walk contributed to this. Therefore, the fact of the good time should be in the main or independent clause and the causes of this good time should be in the subordinate or dependent clause. The sentence should read:

CORRECT: I had a good time with my parents because we went to the Music Hall, had lunch, and took a walk.

The sentence now presents the ideas in their proper relative importance.

Try to correct these sentences which fail to subordinate the less important idea.

EXAMPLE 1.
WRONG: Not enough people vote in local elections and now we are suffering from corrupt politicians.

In this sentence, the more important idea is that we are suffering from corruption. The failure to vote should be placed in a subordinate clause which shows its relationship to the main idea.

CORRECT: Because not enough people vote in local elections, we are now suffering from corrupt politicians.

EXAMPLE 2.
WRONG: Devote more time to our children and we shall decrease juvenile delinquency.

Here, again, both ideas are not equally important. Combatting juvenile delinquency should be emphasized by placing it in the main clause and subordinating the other idea in the sentence.

CORRECT: If we devote more time to our children, we shall decrease juvenile delinquency.

EXAMPLE 3.

WRONG: People are better educated than ever, but they are not any happier.

In this example, the subordinate idea is education; the main idea is happiness or the lack of it. The sentence, therefore, should read as follows:

CORRECT: Although people are better educated than ever, they are not any happier.

Practice

1. We economize on police protection and now crime is increasing.
2. Theirs was a happy marriage although they were poor.
3. I studied hard and participated in student activities and I had a good education.

Answers

1. Crime is increasing because we economize on police protection.
2. Correct.
3. I had a good education because I studied hard and participated in student activities.

3. ***Logic may be violated by incorrect relationships between ideas in a sentence or sentences.*** Ideas are joined by words or phrases called connectives precisely because their function is to connect. Connectives may be any of the following:

Connectives

General Usage

Conjunctions:	and	if
	but	when
	or	as
	for	although
	nor	because
Conjunctive adverbs:	therefore	likewise
	moreover	besides
	however	also
	nevertheless	accordingly
Transitional phrases:	on the other hand	
	in addition	
	for example	
	in the first place	
	in other words	
	as a matter of fact	
	at the same time	
	For Specific Purposes	
To add ideas:	furthermore	
	moreover	
	in addition	

To connect ideas of equal Importance:	and also in other words	
To show opposing ideas:	but on the other hand nevertheless conversely	
To show a result:	therefore because since	as a result consequently so
To show a definite order:	first next then	in the second place finally

An error in logic occurs when two ideas have a definite relationship and *the wrong connective is used* to show that relationship. For example, you cannot use a connective that joins similar ideas to connect ideas that are opposite to one another.

EXAMPLE:
WRONG: The critics liked the movie *and* I found it boring.

The two ideas indicate liking on the one hand and disliking on the other. The ideas are in opposition. Therefore, logically, they should not be joined by a connective like *and* that indicates similarity. Instead a connective like *but*, *on the other hand*, or *nevertheless* should be used.

CORRECT: The critics liked the movie *but* I found it boring.

Here's another sentence which contains faulty logic:

EXAMPLE:
WRONG: When I came late, I failed to see the whole movie.

The two ideas indicate lateness and missing a part of the movie. One idea is a result of the other. Therefore, the connective *when* is inappropriate since it indicates time rather than cause.

CORRECT: *Because* I came late, I failed to see the whole movie.

A final example will further clarify the point.

EXAMPLE:
WRONG: *While* I have few possessions, I am happy.

The ideas focus on possessions and happiness. Since the writer wants to contrast the fact that he is happy despite his having few possessions, the ideas are in opposition. "While" does not perform this function. Therefore, it is illogical and should be replaced by a connective that shows opposition or contrast.

CORRECT: *Although* I have few possessions, I am happy.

In sum, to avoid errors in the use of connectives, determine the logical relationship between the ideas they connect and choose the proper connective to show that relationship.

Practice

1. Since I practiced very little, I played well at the concert.
2. The teacher recommended the book and I didn't agree with her.

Answers

1. Although I practiced very little, I played well at the concert.
2. The teacher recommended the book but I didn't agree with her.

4. ***Logic may be violated by failing to complete the statement about the subject of the sentence.*** Poorly constructed or awkward sentences are often confusing because they fail to finish what they start. There are many varieties of awkward sentences, but a look at a few should give you an idea of the kinds of incompleteness to avoid. The error in logic will be pointed out in each case. As you will see, correcting this kind of error is more difficult than correcting the others we have studied thus far.

EXAMPLE:

WRONG: A depression is $_x$ when there is widespread unemployment, falling prices and wages, and a lessening of business activity.

The reader expects to find out *what* a depression is, not *when*. The sentence is incomplete because a word is missing (technically, a predicate nominative) which is the equivalent of the subject *depression*. Why is an equivalent necessary? Because the verb *is* requires it. Words are omitted where the $_x$ appears.

CORRECT: A *depression* is an economic *condition* characterized by widespread unemployment, falling prices and wages, and a lessening of business activity.

Another example of an awkward sentence which results from an illogical complement (predicate) is the following:

EXAMPLE:

WRONG: The most unusual food I ever ate was when I had a dish of enchiladas.

Again the sentence requires a word which is the equivalent of the word *food*, and the reader expects that word to follow immediately after the verb *was*.

CORRECT: The most unusual *food* I ever ate was a dish of *enchiladas*.

Here are some additional awkward sentences.

EXAMPLE:

WRONG: The main reason I quit my job is $_x$ the work was long and uninteresting.

In this sentence, the subject *reason* has been made equal to the complement *work* when clearly the two are not equivalent. There is an incompleteness at the point indicated by the $_x$. The reason for quitting is really the long and uninteresting work. One way to correct this sentence is to make the whole complement the reason.

CORRECT: The main *reason* I quit my job is *that the work was long and uninteresting*.

EXAMPLE:

WRONG: I was successful in business is the reason I left school.

In this sentence, the same error is made but this time the omission is at the start of the sentence.

CORRECT: *The fact that I was successful in business* is the *reason* I left school.

EXAMPLE:

WRONG: Before I was graduated from school, everything I learned about life was studying books.

This sentence is somewhat different. Here, the subject *everything* is equated with *studying books*. But, logically, everything that was learned was not *studying books* but the information that was contained in the books. There are a number of ways to correct this error. Here are two.

CORRECT: Before I was graduated from school, everything I learned about life I learned from the books I studied.

CORRECT: Before I was graduated from school, everything I learned about life was learned from the books I studied.

To avoid these kinds of awkwardness, always be certain that the statement about the subject of the sentence is completed. If a subject is said to be something, that something should be indicated.

Practice

1. An error is when the fielder doesn't handle the ball properly.
2. Because I didn't study hard, I passed the test.

Answers

1. An error is made when the fielder doesn't handle the ball properly.
2. Although I didn't study hard, I passed the test.

5. ***Logic may be violated by omitting words needed to complete the meaning of the sentence.*** This kind of error is similar to the one just discussed since necessary words are omitted. Let us look at some omissions which take place when comparisons are made.

Why is logic involved? Because a comparison involves two items and both have to be considered. If one is left out or left incomplete, then the comparison is no longer logical.

There are a number of kinds of omissions involving comparisons.

1. *Omission of* ***than*** *or* ***as*** *in a comparison.*

EXAMPLE:

WRONG: Deborah is as bright $_x$ if not brighter than her sister.

If the words *if not brighter than* are temporarily removed from the sentence, the sentence reads "Deborah is as bright . . . $_x$ her sister," clearly a sentence which makes no sense. If *as* is added at the point indicated, the sentence makes sense.

CORRECT: Deborah is as bright as, if not brighter than, her sister.

OR BETTER STILL

CORRECT: Deborah is as bright as her sister, if not brighter.

2. *Omission of one part of the comparison.*

EXAMPLE:

WRONG: I like Mary better than $_x$ Susan $_x$.

This omission causes a confusion in meaning. Do you mean that you prefer Mary to Susan? Or do you mean that you like Mary more than Susan likes her?

CORRECT: I like Mary better than I like Susan. (First $_x$)

OR

CORRECT: I like Mary better than Susan does. (Second $_x$)

3. *Omission of the part of the comparison to which another person or object is being compared.*

EXAMPLE:

WRONG: The Expos played better baseball last year $_x$.

Better than who? You must indicate what the Expos are being compared to. A possible correction is:

CORRECT: The Expos played better baseball last year than any other team in the National League.

4. *Omission of* ***other*** *after* ***than*** *or* ***as*** *in comparing two things or groups of things in the same category.*

In the correct sentence above dealing with the Expos, notice the inclusion of the word *other.* If *other* is omitted, the meaning is changed.

EXAMPLE:

WRONG: The Expos played better baseball last year than any team in the National League.

Since the Expos are in the National League, this sentence indicates that the Expos played better baseball than themselves!

5. *Omission of words that prevent a false or impossible comparison.*

EXAMPLE:

WRONG: According to Ray, the legal profession is better than a doctor.

You cannot compare a profession with a person. You can only compare a profession with a profession, or a person with a person.

CORRECT: According to Ray, the legal profession is better than the medical profession.

CORRECT: According to Ray, being a lawyer is better than being a doctor.

Other kinds of illogical omissions do not involve comparisons.

1. *Omission of a noun necessary to complete the meaning of the sentence.*

EXAMPLE:

WRONG: Some people consider him one of the best $_x$, if not the best athlete, in the world.

One of the best athlete or athletes? Clearly something is missing. You must supply the suitable noun after the first "best."

CORRECT: Some people consider him one of the best *athletes,* if not the best athlete, in the world.

2. *Omission of a preposition necessary to complete the meaning of the sentence.*

EXAMPLE:

WRONG: Canadians should show their faith $_x$ and loyalty to the democratic way of life.

As the sentence reads, the noun *faith* is followed by the preposition *to,* a preposition with which it does not belong. One has faith *in* something. The sentence should read:

CORRECT: Canadians should show their faith *in* and loyalty *to* the democratic way of life.

3. *Omission of part of a verb necessary to complete the meaning of a sentence.*

EXAMPLE:

WRONG: We always have $_x$ and always will try to do our best.

Two ideas are contained in the sentence, but one of them is indicated incompletely.

We always *have tried* to do our best.
We always *will try* to do our best.

You will notice that *will* is properly followed by *try* but *have* is followed by nothing in the incorrect sentence. The word *tried,* the past participle, must be added.

CORRECT: We always *have tried* and always *will try* to do our best.

Here's another example.

EXAMPLE:

WRONG: As children, we were happy and $_x$ brought up strictly.

The word *were* should be added before *brought* because the first *were* is a verb in itself and the word *brought* is only part of the verb *were brought.*

CORRECT: As children, we *were* happy and *were* brought up strictly.

4. *Omission of other parts of speech necessary to complete the meaning of the sentence.*

EXAMPLE:

WRONG: He asked both the secretary and $_x$ treasurer to stand.

As written, the secretary and treasurer is one person. If they are actually two people, the article *the* must be repeated.

CORRECT: He asked both the secretary and *the* treasurer to stand.

Practice

1. I like Montreal's monuments more than I like Toronto.
2. Elaine is as good-looking if not better looking than Jane.
3. The parents expressed their admiration and confidence in their child.
4. John Diefenbaker was one of the finest if not the finest orator of his time.
5. The candidate stated that he always had and always would vote for his principles.

Answers

1. I like Montreal's monuments more than I like Toronto's.
2. Elaine is as good-looking as, if not better looking, than Jane.
3. The parents expressed their admiration for and confidence in their child.
4. John Diefenbaker was one of the finest orators, if not the finest orator, of his time.
5. The candidate stated that he always had voted and always would vote for his principles.

6. *Logic may be violated by unnecessary shift in sentence construction.* All good writers keep the reader in mind. Good writing is easy to read. Anything, therefore, which causes difficulty for the reader should be avoided.

One of the most frequent reasons that readers become perplexed is that the writer needlessly shifts the construction of his sentences or his point of view. This happens in a number of ways.

1. *The subject may be unnecessarily shifted when the writer moves from the main clause to a coordinate or subordinate clause.*

EXAMPLE:

WRONG: Jim was a loyal friend, but self-discipline was lacking in him.

In this sentence, the subject of the main clause is Jim. For some reason, the writer chose to shift to another subject in the coordinate clause although it was not necessary to do so.

CORRECT: Jim was a loyal friend, but he lacked self-discipline.

EXAMPLE:

WRONG: We traveled in Israel, where archeological sites interested us.

Here, again, there is an unnecessary shift, this time from the subject of the main clause to the subject of the subordinate clause.

CORRECT: We traveled in Israel, where we were interested in archeological sites.

2. *The verb may be shifted unnecessarily from the active to the passive voice, from the imperative mood to the indicative mood, or from one tense to another.*

EXAMPLE:

WRONG: Alice enjoyed the movies, and television was also enjoyed by her.

We indicated earlier that, wherever possible, the active verb should be used in preference to the passive because it expresses an idea more effectively. Having correctly started with an active verb, it is simply illogical to shift to a passive. In the first sentence, Alice *enjoyed* movies actively in the main clause, but then television was *enjoyed* (the passive verb) in the coordinate clause.

CORRECT: Alice enjoyed movies and also television.

EXAMPLE:

WRONG: First do the required homework, and then you should try to do the optional assignment.

In this sentence, the imperative mood (command) *do* is used in the main clause, but then there is a shift to the indicative mood (statement) in the coordinate clause *you should try.* Actually, the words *you should* are unnecessary and both parts of the sentence will be in the imperative if they are dropped.

CORRECT: First do the required homework, and then try to do the optional assignment.

EXAMPLE:

WRONG: When her son did not return for hours after the agreed-on time, the mother begins to get worried and then she called the police.

In this sentence, the mother *begins* to worry (present tense) and then she *called* the police (past tense). If you are telling what happened, you must use tense consistently.

CORRECT: . . . , the mother began to worry and then she *called* the police.

Another shift in verb tense is shown in this sentence.

EXAMPLE:

WRONG: I told my fiancée I will call for her at six.

Here the tenses for direct and indirect conversation are being confused. There is a shift from *told* to *will.*

CORRECT: I told my fiancée I would call for her at six.

CORRECT: I told my fiancée, "I will call for you at six."

Sometimes indirect and direct conversation are mixed.

EXAMPLE:

WRONG: Frank asked whether I knew Lola and will she come to the party.

To correct this shift, use either indirect or direct discourse throughout.

CORRECT: Frank asked whether I knew Lola and whether she would come to the party.
(Indirect conversation is used in both clauses.)

CORRECT: Frank asked, "Do you know Lola? Will she come to the party?"
(Direct conversation is used in both clauses.)

Practice

1. Come home on time and then you should help with the dishes.
2. Stuart is a good baseball player and tennis is also played by him.
3. The employee was certain he can get the job done.

Answers

1. Come home on time and help with the dishes.
2. Stuart is a good baseball and tennis player.
3. The employee was certain he could get the job done.

3. *The number and person of the pronoun may be shifted unnecessarily.*

EXAMPLE:

WRONG: If one wishes to succeed, they should work hard.

In this sentence, there is a shift in number from the singular pronoun *one* to the plural pronoun *they.* The number of the pronoun should be kept consistent.

CORRECT: If *one* wishes to succeed, *one* should work hard.

OR

CORRECT: If *they* wish to succeed, *they* should work hard.

7. ***Logic is violated when figures of speech such as metaphors are mixed.*** *A mixed figure of speech* results when the picture you are trying to create has confusing elements.
Here is an example.

WRONG: The couple waded into the *sea* of matrimony and found it a very *rocky road.*

The writer has to choose either water or land as a comparison or else the reader will get a mixed picture. The use of metaphors (implied comparisons between two objects with the word *like* or *as* omitted) must be consistent. Here marriage is being compared to two different objects in the same sentence—a sea and a road. The couple can either wade into the troubled waters of matrimony or plod along the rocky road of marriage but not both in the same sentence.

USAGE

Usage, which includes grammar, causes much concern among those taking the GED examination. We have limited the key areas of study to just three: agreement (of subject and verb, of pronoun and antecedent); case of nouns and pronouns (including pronoun reference); and errors in verb form and tense.

For best test results, study the "Glossary of Usage" (which follows immediately) in conjunction with our treatment of the three key areas of usage. The glossary not only defines the most frequently used terms, but also includes an example of each. Refer to it each time you encounter a term in grammar or usage which causes you difficulty.

GLOSSARY OF USAGE

ACTIVE VERB A verb is active when its subject is the doer of the action the verb is indicating. (The batter *hit* the ball.)

ADJECTIVE A part of speech which helps describe a noun or pronoun by giving it a more exact meaning. (*big* house; *many* friends; *this* pencil)

ADJECTIVE CLAUSE A group of words having a subject and a predicate which is unable to stand alone and which helps describe a noun or pronoun by giving it a more exact meaning. (the pen *which has red ink*; the food *I like*—"that" or "which" is understood)

ADVERB A part of speech which helps describe a verb, an adjective, or another adverb by giving it a more exact meaning. (walks *slowly*; *very* pretty)

ADVERBIAL CLAUSE A group of words having a subject and a predicate which is unable to stand alone and which helps describe a verb, an adjective, or another adverb by giving it a more exact meaning. (He played *although he had a broken leg*. She was prettier *than I had imagined*. He was so busy *that he didn't answer*.)

AGREEMENT This refers to parts of a sentence which are alike in gender, number, and person such as a subject and its verb and a pronoun and its antecedent. (*I study*. *He studies*. The *dog* wagged *its* tail.)

ANTECEDENT Noun which is replaced with a pronoun. (EVERYONE will please remove *his* hat. WALKING is what I like to do most.)

ANTONYM Word that is opposite in meaning to another word. (happy, sad)

APPOSITION Condition describing two nouns, next to each other in a sentence, which are equivalent in meaning. (my brother, Joe; Mrs. Brown, the secretary)

ARTICLE Special kind of adjective which refers to these three words: the, a, an. (*the* book; *a* house; *an* egg)

AUXILIARY VERB Verb which helps another word show voice or tense. (I *would have* forgotten. She *had* left.)

CASE Form of a noun or pronoun which shows its relation to the other words in a sentence.

Nominative case of pronouns has the forms *I*, *you*, *he*, *she*, *we*, *they*, *who*, and is used as the subject of a verb or as a predicate noun. (*They* go. It is *we*.)

Possessive case shows possession. In nouns, it is formed with the apostrophe: (Frank's). Possessive pronouns include *mine*, *yours*, *his*, *hers*, *its*, *ours*, *theirs*, *whose*. (*Note:* There are no apostrophes in any possessive pronoun.)

Objective case of pronouns has the forms *me*, *you*, *him*, *her*, *us*, *them*, *whom*, and is used as object of a verb, object of a preposition, subject or object of an infinitive. (They hit *him*. They gave it to *him*. I want *him* to go. I want to hit *him*.)

CLAUSE Group of words in a sentence which contains a subject and a predicate.

Independent clauses can stand alone. (He played well.)

Dependent clauses, adverb, adjectives or noun clauses, cannot stand alone. (He played well *although he was hurt*. The book *which I read* was very interesting. *That he recovered* was a miracle.)

CLICHÉ An expression used so often that it loses effectiveness. ("bigger and better"; "let's put our shoulders to the wheel")

COMMON NOUN Noun which refers to a group of persons, places, or things and not to any individual person, place, or thing. (pupils; states; schools)

COMPARISON Change of form in adjectives and adverbs to show increase in amount or quality. (strong, strong*er*, strong*est*; good, *better*, *best*)

Comparative refers to a greater degree in quality or quantity of one item with respect to another. (smart*er* of the two)

Superlative refers to a greater degree in quality or quantity of one item with respect to two or more other items. (larg*est* of the three)

COMPLEX SENTENCE Sentence which has one independent clause and at least one dependent clause. (We are happy *that you* came.)

COMPLIMENTARY CLOSE That part of a letter just before the signature where the writer takes polite leave of the reader. (In formal letters, "Yours truly,"; in informal letters, "Cordially,")

COMPOUND-COMPLEX SENTENCE Sentence which has two independent clauses and at least one dependent clause. (*Joe sang* and *Joan played the song which she had been studying*.)

COMPOUND PREDICATE Two or more predicates usually joined by "and" or "or." (*He goes to school by day* and *works at night*.)

COMPOUND SENTENCE Sentence which has two independent clauses. (*Joe sang* and *Joan played the piano*.)

COMPOUND SUBJECT Two or more subjects that take the same verb. (*Frank* and *I* will come.)

CONJUNCTION Part of speech which connects words, phrases or clauses. (bread *and* butter; "to be *or* not to be"; She came *when* I left.)

CONNOTATION The suggested meaning of a word beyond the specific meaning it conveys. (He was warned by the flashing red signal. Red is a colour which has the connotation of danger.)

CONSONANT Letter other than *a, e, i, o, u* (which are considered vowels) or *y* (which is considered a semi-vowel).

CONTEXT Other words with which a given word is associated in a sentence and which determine the meaning of that word. (sheer *nonsense*; sheer *cliff*; sheer *stockings*)

DASH Punctuation mark which shows a pause or break in a sentence. (He may not come—but why should I worry.)

DECLARATIVE SENTENCE Sentence which makes a statement. (Sue loves Greg.)

DENOTATION Direct specific meaning of a word. (red as a colour rather than as a sign of danger or, when capitalized, as a Communist)

DICTION Effectiveness with which words are chosen by a writer or speaker to express his or her thougts.

DIRECT OBJECT Noun or pronoun which receives the action of the verb. (Jon struck *him.* Give *it* to Gerry.)

DIRECT QUOTATION Use of the exact words of the speaker. (The teacher said, "Do your homework.")

EUPHEMISM Roundabout expression used instead of a more direct one which might have too harsh an effect on the reader or listener. ("short of funds" instead of "bankrupt")

FIRST PERSON Pronoun and verb forms which refer to the person speaking. (*I, we; my, our; me, us; am, are*)

FUTURE TENSE Time of verb which shows a happening yet to take place. (He *will retire* next year.)

GENDER Classification of nouns and pronouns into three groups: masculine, feminine and neuter. A *masculine* pronoun is *he*; a *feminine* pronoun is *she*; a pronoun in the *neuter* gender is *it*.

GERUND Verb form ending in "ing" which is used as a noun. It can be used as a subject (*Walking* is fun) or as an object (I hate *walking*).

GLOSSARY Listing of difficult or unusual words occurring in a book with their definitions. It is usually found in the back of the book.

HEADING In an informal letter, this contains the address of the sender and the date the letter is written. In a formal letter, this contains the date the letter is written since the address is on the letterhead.

HOMONYM Word with the same sound but a different spelling and meaning from another word. (to, too, two, pear, pair, pare)

HYPHEN Mark (-) used to join compound words (two-faced), to join certain prefixes to words (ex-president) or to separate words into syllables (En-glish).

IDIOM Group of words which, taken together, has a different meaning from the individual words used separately (once upon a time).

IMPERATIVE SENTENCE A sentence which gives a command. The subject is "you" although it may not be stated. (Study hard for your test.)

INDEFINITE ARTICLE Refers to "a" and "an."

INDIRECT OBJECT Word that shows, without any preposition, to whom or for whom the action in the sentence is taking place. (He gave *me* a pen.)

INDIRECT QUOTATION Quotation which does not use the exact words of the speaker. (The candidate said [that] he would accept the nomination.)

INFINITIVE Verb form which is usually indicated by "to" before the verb. Sometimes the "to"' is understood. (I want to go. He made me *laugh.*)

INSIDE ADDRESS Name and address of the person to whom the letter is written.

INTERJECTION Independent word which expresses strong feeling. (ah!; oh!; alas!)

INTERROGATIVE ADJECTIVE Adjective which is used before a noun in a question. (*Which* boy came? *What* book did you read?)

INTERROGATIVE ADVERB Adverb which is usually used at the beginning of a question. (*When* did you come? *Where* did you eat?)

INTERROGATIVE PRONOUN Pronoun which is usually used at the beginning of a question. (*Who* came? *Whom* did you see?)

INTERROGATIVE SENTENCE Sentence that asks a question. (Did he leave?)

INTRANSITIVE VERB Verb that has no object. (He *stands.* I *sit.*)

MODIFIER Word or group of words which help describe another word or group of words by giving a more exact meaning. See ADJECTIVE, ADJECTIVE CLAUSE, ADVERB, ADVERBIAL CLAUSE.

NOMINATIVE ABSOLUTE Independent group of words containing a noun and a participle which are included as part of a sentence. (*The sun shining,* we left for the park.)

NOMINATIVE CASE Case of the subject or predicate noun in a sentence. (*Frank* is *president*.)

NOUN Part of speech which is the name of a person, place, or thing. (George Washington; New York; toy)

NOUN CLAUSE Group of words having a subject and a predicate which is unable to stand alone and which is either the subject or object in a sentence. (*That Washington was our first president* is a fact. He knew *that Washington was our first president*.)

NUMBER Change in the form of a noun, pronoun, adjective, or verb to show whether there is one (*singular*) or more than one (*plural*) (man, men; he, they; this, these; is, are).

OBJECT Noun or pronoun which shows the person or thing acted upon by the verb. (She brought the *book.* I hate *her*.)

OBJECTIVE CASE Form of the noun or pronoun which shows it is the person or thing which receives the action. (I hit *him*.)

OBJECT OF THE PREPOSITION Noun or pronoun which follows a preposition and which is controlled by it. (with *me*; between *you* and *me*; among *him* and *them*; behind the *hill*)

PARALLELISM Two parts of a sentence which have equal importance and are given the same form (and therefore the same importance) in the sentence. (He eats *both* meat *and* vegetables. *Not only* the relatives were invited *but also* the friends.)

PARTICIPLE Form of a verb which is used both as an adjective and as part of a verb. (the *sleeping* child; am *going*)
present participle (going)
past participle (gone)
perfect participle (having gone)

PART OF SPEECH One of eight categories into which words in a sentence are assigned: *noun, pronoun, verb, adjective, adverb, preposition, conjunction, interjection.*

PASSIVE Form of verb which is used when the subject of the sentence receives the action. (The watch *was given* to Joe. The man *was laid* to rest.)

PAST PERFECT TENSE Time of verb which shows that an action had been completed in the past before another completed action. (The train *had left* when I arrived.)

PAST TENSE Time of verb which shows that an action has been completed. (He *went.* We *did* go.)

PERSON Form of pronoun or verb which tells that a person (or persons) is speaking or is doing the action (*first person*); a person (or persons) is being spoken to or is doing the action (*second person*); a person (or persons) spoken about is doing the action (*third person*). (*We* left for home. *You* stayed here. *They* arrived late.)

PHRASE Group of words without a subject and predicate, usually introduced by a preposition, which has a use in a sentence like that of a noun, adjective, or adverb. (*In the park* is where I like to sit. Jeanie *with the light brown hair.* He ran *to first base.*)

PLURAL Form of noun, pronoun, adjective, or verb which indicates that more than one person, place or thing is being spoken about in the sentence. (boys; they; these; are)

POSSESSIVE Form of noun or pronoun which shows that something belongs to it. (*girl's* pencil; *ladies'* hats; *its* paw)

PREDICATE Part of the sentence which tells something about the subject (what the subject does, what is done to the subject, or what is true about the subject). (The boy *went home quickly.*)

PREDICATE ADJECTIVE Adjective in the predicate which describes the subject by giving it a more exact meaning. (He is *honest.*)

PREDICATE NOUN Noun in the predicate which is the same in meaning as the subject and can sometimes be interchanged with it. (He is *president.* She became an *actress.*)

PREFIX Part added to the beginning of a word which adds to or changes its meaning. (*im*possible; *ex*-president; *re*view; *pre*fix)

PREPOSITION Part of speech which shows the relationship between a noun or pronoun which it controls (and which is its object) and some other word in the sentence. (Mary went *to* the library.)

PRESENT PERFECT TENSE Time of verb which shows an action which started in the past and is continuing or has just been completed in the present. It requires the use of an auxiliary verb in the present tense and the past participle. (He *has been* our friend for years.)

PRESENT TENSE Time of verb which shows an action which is going on now. There are three forms of the verb—he *says,* he *is saying,* he *does say.*

PRINCIPAL PARTS OF THE VERB Three parts which include verb forms in the present tense, past tense, and the past participle. (go, went, gone; walk, walked, walked)

PRONOUN Part of speech which is used in place of a noun. (John came. He *was* welcome.) The four main kinds of pronouns are:
demonstrative (this, that, these, those);
personal (I, you, he, she, it, we, they);
possessive (mine, yours, his, hers, ours, theirs);
relative (that, what, who, which).

PROPER NOUN Noun that refers to an individual person, place or thing. (George Washington; New York City; City Hall)

REDUNDANCY Use of unnecessary words. (cooperate ~~together~~, return ~~back~~).

REFLEXIVE PRONOUN Pronoun which accompanies a noun in the same sentence and refers back to it. (The president *himself* was there. She dressed *herself* quickly.)

ROOT Basic part of a word without prefixes or suffixes which gives the main meaning of the word. ("cred"—believe; with prefix "in" and suffix "ible"—"in *cred* ible"—unbelievable)

RUN-ON (or COMMA FAULT) SENTENCE Two sentences which are made into one by mistake They are separated either by a comma or by no punctuation at all (Wrong: Kay is class president, she is my friend. Correct: Kay is class president. She is my friend.)

SALUTATION Part of a letter where the writer greets the reader. It usually is "Dear Sir:" in formal letters or "Dear [*name of friend*]," in informal letters.

SENTENCE Group of words containing a subject and a predicate and expressing an independently complete thought. (*He came early.*) Three chief kinds of sentences are:
declarative (makes a statement);
interrogative (asks a question);
imperative (gives a command).

SENTENCE FRAGMENT Group of words which may contain a subject and a predicate but which fails to express a complete thought and is, by error, punctuated as if it did. (Wrong: Hoping to hear from you. Correct: I am hoping to hear from you.)

SIMPLE SENTENCE Sentence which contains no dependent clauses and only one independent clause. (The sun shone all day.)

SINGULAR Form of noun, pronoun, adjective, or verb which refers to one person, place, or thing in a sentence. (boy; he; this; is)

SUBJECT Part of the sentence which does the action or is spoken about. (*He* hit the ball. *The watch* was given to the man.)

SUBJECT OF AN INFINITIVE Noun or pronoun in the objective case which does the action indicated by the infinitive. (I want *him* to go.)

SUFFIX Part added to the ending of a word which adds to or changes its meaning. (hand*ful*; quick*ly*; act*or*)

SYLLABICATION Division into syllables. (En-glish)

SYLLABLE Smallest group of sounds consisting of a vowel sound and one or more consonant sounds which are pronounced as a unit. (con-so-nant)

SYNONYM Word that is very similar in meaning to another word. (happy—glad)

TENSE Time of an action indicated by the verb as *present, past, future, past perfect,* etc. These are the most widely used tenses in English.

TRANSITIVE VERB Verb which can take an object of the action it indicates. (He *hit* the ball.) An *intransitive verb* has no object. (He was *lying* in bed.)

USAGE Actual use of language by the people at large. *Good usage* is the actual use of language by educated persons and persons in positions of importance. Good usage is constantly subject to the changes made in the use of language by these persons.

VERB Part of speech which indicates the action carried out by the subject or which tells something about the subject. (He *hit* the ball. She *was* in the garden.)

VOICE Form of the verb which shows whether the subject is doing the action (*active voice*) or is receiving the action (*passive voice*). (He *hit* the boy. He *was hit* by the boy.)

VOWELS Letters representing the sounds *a, e, i, o, u.* The letter *y* is considered a semi-vowel as in "slowly."

AGREEMENT

Subject and Verb

A frequently made error is the failure to provide agreement between subject and verb. The basic rule is:

The **VERB** must agree with its **SUBJECT** in *number* and in *person*.

Number

1. If the subject is *singular* (there is only one person or thing spoken about), the verb must be *singular*.
2. If the subject is *plural* (there is more than one person or thing spoken about), the verb must be *plural*.

Person

The verb must agree with the subject in *person*.

EXAMPLE:

Singular	
I study	—First Person
You study	—Second Person
He / She / It } studies	—Third Person
Plural	
We study	—First Person
You study	—Second Person
They study	—Third Person

(See the "Glossary of Usage" (page 136) for a complete definition of *person*.)

There are two difficulties to be overcome.

1. ***What is the subject?***
   Ask yourself, "What is spoken about?" Ordinarily, you should have no trouble. Sometimes, however, *the subject and the verb are separated* by a number of intervening words.

EXAMPLE: *Joe*, despite the fact that many of his friends were absent, was elected president. (*Joe* is still the subject—singular.)

The intervening words may contain a plural.

EXAMPLE: *Joe*, together with all his friends, *came* in. (*Joe* is still the subject—singular.)

2. ***Is the subject singular or plural?***

EXAMPLE: A *box* of chocolates *is* on the table. (*Box*, the subject, is singular.)

Most of the time, *pronouns* will be involved. Some of those which can cause confusion are:

Singular Pronouns		Singular or Plural Pronouns
anybody	neither	any
anyone	nobody	all
each	no one	more
either	one	most
everybody	somebody	none
everyone	someone	some

However, *compound subjects* may also be involved. When a subject has more than one part and the parts are connected by *and* or a word or groups of words similar in meaning to *and,* it is considered a *compound subject* and is plural. A compound subject can consist of more than one group of words, of more than one phrase or one clause.

EXAMPLE: Joe *and* his friend *are* here.
EXAMPLE: To study hard, to play hard, to enjoy life are desirable aims.
EXAMPLE: Her outstanding contribution to school athletics, her service as class officer, and her excellent scholastic record make her qualified for the position of president.

Nevertheless, when a compound subject consists of two singular subjects connected by *either . . . or, neither . . . nor*, it is considered a singular subject.

EXAMPLE: Neither Joe nor his friend is here.

> ***Note:***
> Agreement is always with the number of the part of the subject nearest the verb.
>
> **EXAMPLE:** Neither Joe nor I *am* voting for Frank.

Sometimes the subject comes after the verb. It is still the subject and may be singular or plural.

EXAMPLE: Pasted in the upper right-hand corner of the envelope were two twenty-cent stamps.

(*Stamps* is the subject, even though it is the last word in the sentence. The verb is plural because the subject, *stamps,* is plural.)

Some Special Problems

We have touched on the problems of words coming between the subject and verb, of pronouns singular and plural, of compound subjects and of subjects appearing after the verb. We pointed out the exception of the "either . . . or," "neither . . . nor" subject. Now let us turn to some additional special problems.

1. ***Agreement of subject and certain irregular verbs.*** The addition of the negative contraction, "n't," should not result in an error you would not make if the "n't" were omitted.

   EXAMPLE:
   WRONG: It don't matter.
   CORRECT: It doesn't matter.

   You would never say, "It do matter." You would say, "It does matter."

   Sometimes the reversal of subject and verb in a question causes an error that would not be made in a declarative sentence.

   EXAMPLE:
   WRONG: Was you there?
   CORRECT: Were you there?

2. ***Use of singular or plural after "there" at the opening of a sentence.*** The form of "is" or "are" depends on the *noun or pronoun that follows* the verb.

   EXAMPLE:
   WRONG: There's many ways to skin a cat.
   CORRECT: There are many ways to skin a cat.

3. ***Subjects that are plural in form but singular in meaning***. Just because a noun ends in "s" doesn't make it plural.

Nouns with Singular Meanings

economics	mumps
mathematics	news
measles	physics

4. ***Subjects that are singular in form but plural in meaning***. Despite what you might think, these subjects take a *singular* verb when the group involved is thought of as a single unit.

Nouns with Plural Meanings

army	group
class	orchestra
club	team
crowd	

EXAMPLE: The crowd *was* dispersed by the police.

Practice

1. Economics is my most difficult subject.
2. The group of students are gathering at the office.
3. Neither Jules nor I are coming to the meeting.
4. There's a great many problems to be solved.
5. The teacher, together with her students, are going to the theatre.

Answers

1. Correct.
2. The group of students is gathering at the office.
3. Neither Jules nor I am coming to the meeting.
4. There are a great many problems to be solved.
5. The teacher, together with her students, is going to the theatre.

Pronoun and Antecedent

Another frequently made error is the failure to provide agreement between a pronoun and the noun it is replacing, its *antecedent*. The basic rule is:

A **PRONOUN** must agree with its **ANTECEDENT** in *number*, *gender*, and *person*.

Number

If the antecedent is singular, the pronoun replacing it is singular

EXAMPLE: Joe does *his* homework.
(The pronoun *his* takes the place of Joe. *Joe* is singular (one person); therefore, the pronoun is singular.)

Gender

If the antecedent is masculine, the pronoun replacing it is masculine. If the antecedent is feminine, the pronoun replacing it is feminine.

EXAMPLE: Susan does *her* homework.

Person

Note above that both *Joe* and *Susan* are in the third person. Therefore, the pronouns replacing each must be in the third person—*his*, *her*.

How do you find the antecedent? Sometimes it is not easy to determine what noun the pronoun is replacing. The *antecedent may be separated from the pronoun* which takes its place by a number of words or a phrase.

EXAMPLE: Joe is a *boy* who does *his* work.
(*boy*—antecedent; *his*—pronoun)

EXAMPLE: *One* of the boys who walked to school was late to *his* class.
(*One*—antecedent; *his*—pronoun)

The same procedure should be used to *determine the number of the pronoun when it replaces a compound subject*.

EXAMPLE: *Joe and* his *friend* brought *their* books.

When *either . . . or* or *neither . . . nor* connects singular subjects, the pronoun is singular.

EXAMPLE: *Neither* Joe *nor* his friend brought *his* book.

However, a pronoun that refers to a singular and a plural antecedent connected by *or* or *nor* agrees in number with the closer antecedent.

EXAMPLE: *Either* Kathy *or* the boys should explain *their* reasons.

Some Special Problems

1. ***Pronouns which appear to be plural but are, in fact, singular.*** Some pronouns appear to refer to more than one person, but they never refer to more than one person *at a time*. Others may be either singular or plural.

Singular Pronouns		Singular or Plural Pronouns
anybody	neither	any
anyone	nobody	all
each	no one	more
either	one	most
everybody	somebody	none
everyone	someone	some

It may sound a little strange to you, but the following sentence is correct.

EXAMPLE: Every student must do *his* homework every day.

2. ***Pronouns which refer to nouns that appear to be plural but are singular in form.*** These require a verb in the singular.

EXAMPLE: The team continued *its* winning streak.

3. ***Pronouns with indefinite antecedents.*** The antecedent must be clear or the sentence rephrased.

EXAMPLE:

WRONG: Frank told Joe to take *his* books to school.
(To whom does *his* refer—to Frank or to Joe? The sentence must be rewritten to clear up this confusion.)

CORRECT: Frank told Joe to take Frank's books to school for him.

OR BETTER:

CORRECT: Frank said to Joe: "Take my books to school for me."

Practice

1. Will everyone who has the right answer raise his hands?
2. Every participant must do his best.
3. The mother told her daughter to take her laundry to the laundromat.
4. One of my friends who went to school with me lost his mother.
5. Either the workers or the supervisor are expected to attend.

Answers

1. Will everyone who has the right answer raise his hand?
2. Correct.
3. The mother told her daughter, "Take my laundry to the laundromat."
4. Correct.
5. Either the workers or the supervisor is expected to attend.

PRACTICE IN AGREEMENT

Directions: **In each sentence, five parts are underlined and numbered. Where there is an error in agreement, blacken the number of the underlined part which contains the error. If there is no error, mark answer space 5. <u>No sentence contains more than one error</u>. These are included.**

1. Jean, accompanied by his (1) friend, are (2) waiting to see whether you and I (3) are (4) joining them. No error (5)

   1. 1 2 3 4 5

2. There (1), Mr. Chairman, is (2) all the reports which the committee prepared in its (3) work as well as the notes that (4) were taken. No error (5)

   2. 1 2 3 4 5

3. There's (1) several ways for the city to solve its (2) fiscal problems but one (3) of them is not to lose its (4) integrity. No error (5)

   3. 1 2 3 4 5

4. News from abroad is (1) that each country is supporting its (2) own policies despite the fact that ours (3) are (4) superior to theirs. No error (5)

   4. 1 2 3 4 5

5. Let everyone who agrees (1) raise his (2) hand so that neither George nor I am (3) in doubt about what the majority opinion is (4). No error (5)

   5. 1 2 3 4 5

6. Margaret asked Rosa to take her (1) clothes to the cleaners and to make certain that none (2) of them (3) were (4) in need of repair. No error (5)

   6. 1 2 3 4 5

7. Watching our (1) game were (2) Fred, his father and his mother, together with their (3) children and their (4) neighbours. No error (5)

   7. 1 2 3 4 5

8. Each (1) Canadian must ask himself (2): "Don't (3) it matter if we pollute our (4) environment?" No error (5)

   8. 1 2 3 4 5

9. "Neither I (1) nor they (2) are (3) attending the game," we said to its (4) promoter. No error (5)

   9. 1 2 3 4 5

10. Everyone (1) gave her (2) opinion that a blue and white suit was (3) the best choice for Liz to wear although there were (4) exceptions. No error (5)

    10. 1 2 3 4 5

Turn to the answer key and the answer analysis which follow.

What's Your Score?

_______ right,	_______ wrong
Excellent	9–10
Good	8
Fair	7

If you scored lower, restudy this section, concentrating on the rules and examples.

ANSWER KEY

Practice in Agreement/Page 143

1. **2**	3. **1**	5. **5**	7. **5**	9. **5**
2. **2**	4. **5**	6. **1**	8. **3**	10. **5**

ANSWER ANALYSIS

Practice in Agreement/Page 143

1. **2** Jean, the subject of the sentence, is singular, so the verb should be singular: *is* instead of *are*.
2. **2** The actual subject of the sentence, *reports*, follows the verb. Since the subject is plural, the verb should be plural.
3. **1** The actual subject is *ways*, which follows the verb. The verb must be plural to agree with the plural subject. *There's* should be *There are*.
4. **5** No error.
5. **5** No error.
6. **1** The antecedent of *her* is not clear. Is it Margaret or Rosa? Depending on the answer, *her* should be changed to *Margaret's* or *Rosa's*.
7. **5** No error.
8. **3** The correct form in the third person singular of the verb *do* is *does*. *Doesn't it . . .* is correct.
9. **5** No error.
10. **5** No error.

CASE OF NOUNS AND PRONOUNS

Nouns

In English, the form of a noun rarely changes because of its *case* (its relation to other words in the sentence). Only in the *possessive case* does the form of most nouns change.

Nominative Case

EXAMPLE: *Frank* hit Joe.
(*Frank* is the subject.)

Objective Case

EXAMPLE: Joe hit *Frank*.
(*Frank* is the object.)

EXAMPLE: Ellen ate the *salad*.
(*Salad* is the object.)

Possessive Case

EXAMPLE: Claude's friend went away.
(Nouns require an apostrophe to indicate possession.)

Pronouns

Nearly all pronouns have different forms in the nominative, objective and possessive cases. Only the pronoun forms *you* and *it* do NOT change when their case changes from *nominative* to *objective* or vice versa.

NOMINATIVE CASE (for subjects)	POSSESSIVE CASE	OBJECTIVE CASE (for objects)
I	my, mine	me
you	your, yours	you
he	his	him
she	her, hers	her
it	its	it
we	our, ours	us
they	their, theirs	them
who	whose	whom
whoever	—	whomever

BASIC RULES FOR THE CASE OF PRONOUNS

RULES	EXAMPLES
Nominative	
1. The subject of a verb (a noun or a pronoun) is in the nominative case. This is true whether the subject is singular or compound.	**WRONG:** Me and Frank are good friends. **CORRECT:** Frank and I are good friends.
2. A predicate pronoun, whether singular or plural, is in the nominative case.	They thought that the visitor was *he*. Frank and Joe knocked on the door. "It is *they*," Sue said.
3. Pronouns in apposition with nouns in the nominative case are also in the nominative case.	The two contestants, she and I, were tied for first place.
Objective	
4. The object of a verb (a noun or pronoun) is in the objective case. This is true whether the object is singular or compound.	They applauded him and her. Did they face Frank and us in the contest?
5. The object of a preposition is in the objective case. This is true whether the object is singular or compound.	Everyone but *her* did the homework. Between *you* and *me*, Sue is my best friend.
6. Pronouns in apposition with nouns in the objective case are also in the objective case.	They gave the prizes to the *winners*, *her and me*. For *us amateurs*, it is fun to watch professionals perform.

BASIC RULES FOR THE CASE OF PRONOUNS

7. The subject of an infinitive is in the objective case; the same is true for the object of an infinitive.	We asked *him* to go. We wanted him to ask *them* to come along.
Possessive **8.** Pronouns in the possessive case *never* have an apostrophe, unlike nouns in the possessive case.	The dog wagged *its* tail. We have met the enemy and they are *ours*. She has *hers*; they have *theirs*.

Some Special Problems

As you have realized by now, the case of pronouns is one of the most troublesome topics in the study of English grammar. After you have mastered the eight rules, turn to these three tricky problems.

1. *The case of pronouns coming after a comparison involving* than *or* as.

EXAMPLE: Joe received more votes than *I*.

The problem of deciding the case, and therefore the form, of the pronoun is complicated by the fact that the verb following "I" is understood.

EXAMPLE: Joe received more votes than I (did).

This is, therefore, a special instance of Rule 1: The subject of a verb is in the nominative case. This rule is true even if the verb is understood.

2. *The case of the relative pronoun who or whom.* (See the "Glossary of Usage" on page 136.) Determine whether the relative pronoun is the subject or the object in its clause, and don't be fooled by the words which come between the subject and the verb.

EXAMPLE: *Who* do you think *was elected* president?

(*Who* is the subject of *was elected* and is therefore in the nominative case.)

EXAMPLE: *Whom did you invite* to the party?

(*Whom* is the object of *did you invite* and is therefore in the objective case.)

The same rule applies to *whoever* and *whomever*.

EXAMPLE: Give the book to *whoever asks* for it.

(*Whoever* is the subject of *asks* and is in the nominative case.)

EXAMPLE: He impressed *whomever he approached*.

(*Whomever* is the object of *he approached* and is in the objective case.)

3. *The case of pronouns (or nouns) coming before verbs ending in "ing" and used as nouns.*

EXAMPLE: I do not object to *his* going with me.

Going is a verb ending in "ing" and used as a noun—object of the preposition "to." The possessive case, *his*, must be used. This is a fine point, but it often appears on tests.

Here are several more examples:

EXAMPLE: Fatigue was the cause of *Frank's* falling asleep at the wheel.
EXAMPLE: *My* going to school daily helped my work.
EXAMPLE: The television program interfered with *Sue's* and *Joe's* doing their homework.

4. *The case of shift in pronoun reference.* Shift in pronoun reference is another common error. This is an unnecessary shift in pronouns which refer to the same person in the same sentence. There is an inconsistency in the use of an impersonal pronoun such as *one* with other pronouns in the first, second, and third person.

EXAMPLE:
WRONG: If *one* has a good sense of humour, *you* will probably be popular.
CORRECT: If *one* has a good sense of humour, *one* will probably be popular.
CORRECT: If *you* have a good sense of humour, *you* will probably be popular.

Remember to be consistent in your use of pronouns. Do not shift from a pronoun in one person (*one* is in the third person) to another pronoun in another person (*you* is in the second person) unless the two pronouns refer to different people.

Practice

1. Dolores was prettier than her.
2. Jocelyne didn't like us asking her all those questions.
3. Who can you trust with your money these days?
4. Whoever thought of this idea is a genius.
5. Who do you feel deserves the prize?
6. When one works hard, he feels he deserves a raise.

Answers

1. Dolores was prettier than she.
2. Jocelyne didn't like our asking her all those questions.
3. Whom can you trust with your money these days?
4. Correct.
5. Correct
6. When one works hard, one feels one deserves a raise.

PRACTICE WITH NOUNS AND PRONOUNS

***Directions:* In each sentence, five parts are underlined and numbered. Where there is an error in case, blacken the number of the underlined part which contains the error. If there is no error, mark answer space 5. No sentence contains more than one error.**

1. If I (1) were she (2), I would not exchange hers (3) for mine (4). No error (5)

1. 1 2 3 4 5

2. Whom (1), do you think, should be asked to send his (2) regrets to them (3) and me (4)? No error (5)

2. 1 2 3 4 5

3. It is they (1) whom (2) we invited, not him (3) and her (4). No error (5)

3. 1 2 3 4 5

4. She (1) and I (2) decided to give ours (3) to whoever (4) we pleased. No error (5)

4. 1 2 3 4 5

5. They (1) and I (2) gave the prize to the winners, him (3) and her (4). No error (5)

5. 1 2 3 4 5

6. The winners, he (1) and she (2), were welcomed to the society by us (3) and them (4). No error (5)

6. 1 2 3 4 5

7. Did Joe and him (1) meet John and her (2) in the finals when they eliminated their (3) opponents and ours (4)? No error (5)

7. 1 2 3 4 5

8. Between you (1) and I (2), it's (3) their problem, not ours (4). No error (5)

8. 1 2 3 4 5

9. Whose (1) going to get more votes than I (2), he (3) or she (4)? No error (5)

9. 1 2 3 4 5

10. For us (1) newcomers, his (2) going upset us (3), me (4) particularly. No error (5)

10. 1 2 3 4 5

Turn to the answer key and the answer analysis which follow.

What's Your Score?

______ right,	______ wrong
Excellent	9–10
Good	8
Fair	7

If you scored lower, restudy this section, concentrating on the rules and examples.

ANSWER KEY

Practice with Nouns and Pronouns/Page 148

1. **5**	3. **5**	5. **5**	7. **1**	9. **1**
2. **1**	4. **4**	6. **5**	8. **2**	10. **5**

ANSWER ANALYSIS

Practice with Nouns and Pronouns/Page 148

1. **5** No error.
2. **1** The relative pronoun which begins the sentence is the subject of *should be asked* and should therefore be in the nominative case, *who*.
3. **5** No error.
4. **4** This is the object of the preposition *to*, so it should be in the objective case. *Whomever* is correct.
5. **5** No error.
6. **5** No error.
7. **1** This is part of the subject and should be in the nominative case, *he*.
8. **2** *Me* is correct since the objective case is required for the object of the preposition *between*.
9. **1** A subject and verb are required, not a possessive pronoun. *Who's* is correct.
10. **5** No error.

VERBS

Troublesome Verbs

The *verb*, the part of the sentence which indicates the action carried out by the subject, *also indicates* when the action was carried out. It does so by its tense.

Tense

The most widely used tenses are the

present,
past, and
future.

Two additional tenses, less frequently used, sometimes cause difficulty. These are the

present perfect and
past perfect.

Both of the perfect tenses require the use of a helping verb (have, had) and the past participle of the verb.

Verb: *to live*	
Present Tense:	live
Past Tense:	lived
Future Tense:	shall live
Present Perfect Tense:	have lived
Past Perfect Tense:	had lived

Examples of the use of tense:

Note the way in which the rest of each sentence is affected.

Present Tense:	I *live* in Toronto *now*.
Past Tense:	I *lived* in Toronto *last year*.
Future Tense:	I *shall live* in Toronto *next year*.
Present Perfect Tense:	I *have lived* in Toronto for *five years*.
Past Perfect Tense:	I *had lived* in Toronto *before moving to Winnipeg*.

Verb Forms

The principal parts of the *regular verb* are easy to recognize. The principal parts of *to live*, *to see*, *to do*, and *to lie* are:

Verb	*Past*	*Past Participle*
live	lived	lived
see	saw	seen
do	did	done
lie	lay	lain

Many of the difficulties you have with verbs are with the *irregular* verbs. These change form in either the past or the past participle or both. The most frequent error is the use of the wrong part of the verb, most often the use of the past participle for the simple past.

EXAMPLE:
WRONG: I seen him do it.
CORRECT: I *saw* him do it.

EXAMPLE:
WRONG: I done it.
CORRECT: I *did* it.

EXAMPLE:
WRONG: I laid under the tree for an hour.
CORRECT: I *lay* under the tree for an hour.

Note: The present perfect tense is formed with *have* plus the past participle; the past perfect tense is formed with *had* plus the past participle.

EXAMPLE: I *had seen.*

To avoid these errors in tense and in use of the principal parts of irregular verbs, study these forty-nine most frequently confused verbs.

Frequently Used Irregular Verbs

VERB	PAST TENSE	PRESENT PERFECT TENSE
be	I was	I have been
beat	I beat	I have beaten
become	I became	I have become
begin	I began	I have begun
bite	I bit	I have bitten
blow	I blew	I have blown
break	I broke	I have broken
bring	I brought	I have brought
buy	I bought	I have bought
catch	I caught	I have caught
choose	I chose	I have chosen
come	I came	I have come
dig	I dug	I have dug
do	I did	I have done
draw	I drew	I have drawn
drink	I drank	I have drunk
eat	I ate	I have eaten
fall	I fell	I have fallen
fly	I flew	I have flown
freeze	I froze	I have frozen
get	I got	I have got *or* gotten
give	I gave	I have given
go	I went	I have gone
grow	I grew	I have grown
have	I had	I have had
know	I knew	I have known
lay	I laid (place)	I have laid
lead	I led	I have led
lie	I lay (recline)	I have lain
lose	I lost	I have lost
make	I made	I have made
ride	I rode	I have ridden

VERB	PAST TENSE	PRESENT PERFECT TENSE
ring	I rang	I have rung
rise	I rose	I have risen
run	I ran	I have run
say	I said	I have said
see	I saw	I have seen
shake	I shook	I have shaken
sink	I sank	I have sunk
speak	I spoke	I have spoken
swim	I swam	I have swum
swing	I swung	I have swung
take	I took	I have taken
teach	I taught	I have taught
tear	I tore	I have torn
think	I thought	I have thought
throw	I threw	I have thrown
win	I won	I have won
write	I wrote	I have written

50 Other Irregular Verbs That Can Cause Trouble

VERB	PAST TENSE	PRESENT PERFECT TENSE
arise	I arose	I have arisen
awake	I awaked *or* awoke	I have awaked *or* awoke
bear	I bore	I have borne *or* born
bend	I bent	I have bent
bind	I bound	I have bound
build	I built	I have built
creep	I crept	I have crept
deal	I dealt	I have dealt
dive	I dived, dove	I have dived
drive	I drove	I have driven
drown	I drowned	I have drowned
feed	I fed	I have fed
feel	I felt	I have felt
fight	I fought	I have fought
find	I found	I have found
flee	I fled	I have fled
forget	I forgot	I have forgotten
forgive	I forgave	I have forgiven
hang (an object)	I hung	I have hung
hang (a person)	I hanged	I have hanged
hide	I hid	I have hidden
hold	I held	I have held
kneel	I knelt	I have knelt
leave	I left	I have left
lend	I lent	I have lent
meet	I met	I have met
mistake	I mistook	I have mistaken
pay	I paid	I have paid
prove	I proved	I have proved *or* proven
seek	I sought	I have sought
sell	I sold	I have sold
send	I sent	I have sent
sew	I sewed	I have sewed *or* sewn

VERB	PAST TENSE	PRESENT PERFECT TENSE
shine	I shone	I have shone
shrink	I shrank	I have shrunk
sing	I sang	I have sung
slay	I slew	I have slain
slide	I slid	I have slid
sleep	I slept	I have slept
spend	I spent	I have spent
spring	I sprang	I have sprung
steal	I stole	I have stolen
strike	I struck	I have struck
swear	I swore	I have sworn
sweep	I swept	I have swept
swing	I swung	I have swung
wake	I waked *or* woke	I have waked *or* woken
wear	I wore	I have worn
weep	I wept	I have wept
wind	I wound	I have wound

Practice

1. They begun to improve after much practice.
2. Aaron brung the book I needed to school.
3. My friends had drunk all the lemonade at the party.
4. The valise which had lain out in the rain was soaked.
5. The batter swang the bat at the wild pitch.
6. The hostess had laid out the cookies on the table beautifully.
7. The rower almost drownded when the winds blew up.
8. The choir sung all the songs on the program.
9. The sun shined all day.
10. The guest awoked before I did.

Answers

1. They began to improve after much practice.
2. Aaron brought the book I needed to school.
3. Correct.
4. Correct.
5. The batter swung the bat at the wild pitch.
6. Correct.
7. The rower almost drowned when the winds blew up.
8. The choir sang all the songs on the program.
9. The sun shone all day.
10. The guest awoke before I did.

Some Special Problems

The irregular verbs you have just studied present difficulties when used in simple sentences. Even more difficult are complex sentences (see the "Glossary of Usage" on page 136). In these, you have to figure out the time (or tense) relationship between the verbs in the two clauses.

1. ***What is the proper sequence of tenses for verbs in the main and dependent clauses of a complex sentence?*** This can vary, but some common sequences follow.

VERB SEQUENCES

	MAIN CLAUSE	DEPENDENT CLAUSE
	PRESENT TENSE	**PRESENT TENSE**
EXAMPLE:	I *gain* weight	when I *eat* too much.
	PRESENT TENSE	**PAST TENSE**
EXAMPLE:	I *believe*	that he *studied* for the examination.
	PAST TENSE	**PAST TENSE**
EXAMPLE:	the audience *applauded*	when the soloist *finished*.
	PAST TENSE	**PAST PERFECT TENSE**
EXAMPLE:	I *played* my first concert	after I *had studied* piano for three years.
	Note: The action of the dependent clause (the studying) had taken place *before* the action in the main clause. This is a difficult sequence.	
	FUTURE TENSE	**PRESENT TENSE**
EXAMPLE:	I *shall leave*	when he *comes*.
	PAST CONDITIONAL TENSE	**PAST PERFECT TENSE**
EXAMPLE:	Joe *would have been elected*	if he *had received* my vote.
	Note: Never use the past conditional tense in a dependent clause starting with "if." "If he would have been there . . ." is wrong. It must read, "If he *had been there* . . ."	

Here is a *special case*. Study it carefully.

EXAMPLE: He *wanted to go* before dark.

Sometimes the sentence is written incorrectly as, "He wanted to have gone before dark." This is wrong, because, according to the meaning of the sentence, he hasn't left yet. Therefore, the present tense of the infinitive *to go* must be used.

2. ***The special case of an assumption which isn't true.*** The technical term for the type of error we are going to try to avoid next is the failure to use the subjunctive in a condition contrary to fact. The problem becomes clear if you study this example.

EXAMPLE: If I *were* Joe, *I'd accept* the offer. ("If I *was* Joe . . ." would be incorrect.)

The verb *were* is in the subjunctive mood because it isn't true that *I* and *Joe* are one and the same person. It is only an assumption that isn't true; it's an *if* that is contrary to fact. This is probably the one form in which you will meet this special problem. Here's another example:

EXAMPLE: They *would vote* for her only if she *were* older.

Practice

1. If Douglas would have campaigned, he would have been elected.
2. After he attended high school for four years, he earned a diploma.
3. If my father was here, he'd be proud of me.

Answers

1. If Douglas had campaigned, he would have been elected.
2. After he had attended high school for four years, he earned a diploma.
3. If my father were here, he'd be proud of me.

VERB PRACTICE

Directions: **In each sentence, five parts are underlined and numbered. When there is an error in the form of the verb, blacken the number of the underlined part which contains the error. If there is no error, mark answer space 5. No sentence contains more than one error.**

1. He was suppose to lay the book on the table after he had brought
(1) (2) (3)
it home from the man from whom he had taken it. No error
(4) (5)

1. 1 2 3 4 5

2. After the pitcher had thrown a fast ball, the batter swung the bat
(1) (2)
and hit the ball to left field, where it was caught. No error
(3) (4) (5)

2. 1 2 3 4 5

3. The child awoke when the parent brung the gift he had chosen and
(1) (2) (3)
gotten into the bedroom. No error
(4) (5)

3. 1 2 3 4 5

4. After he drunk his milk, the athlete dived into the pool and swam
(1) (2) (3)
ten laps more than he had said he would. No error
(4) (5)

4. 1 2 3 4 5

5. I lay in bed dreaming of the places I had seen, the friends I had not
(1) (2)
forgotten, and the new friends I had met. No error
(3) (4) (5)

5. 1 2 3 4 5

6. After I had wrote her I wanted it done, Rita hung the picture that
(1) (2) (3)
had lain on the floor. No error
(4) (5)

6. 1 2 3 4 5

7. The entertainer sung the song I had sung when you saw me, and I
(1) (2) (3)
was shaken by the coincidence. No error
(4) (5)

7. 1 2 3 4 5

8. He would have drownded, had I not bent the board which pinned
(1) (2)
him down and then broken it with the tool I had found. No error
(3) (4) (5)

8. 1 2 3 4 5

9. I arose; I sprang after the mugger; I struck him; I threw him to the
(1) (2) (3) (4)
ground. No error
(5)

9. 1 2 3 4 5

10. The suspect admitted: "I done it. I crept into the apartment. I
(1) (2)
fought with the man. I tore his clothes." No error
(3) (4) (5)

10. 1 2 3 4 5

Turn to the answer key and the answer analysis which follow.

What's Your Score?

_____ right,	_____ wrong
Excellent	9–10
Good	8
Fair	7

If you scored lower, restudy this section, concentrating on the rules and examples.

ANSWER KEY

Verb Practice/Page 155

1. **1**	3. **2**	5. **5**	7. **1**	9. **5**
2. **5**	4. **1**	6. **1**	8. **1**	10. **1**

ANSWER ANALYSIS

Verb Practice/Page 155

1. **1** The past participle of *suppose* is *supposed*.
2. **5** No error.
3. **2** The past participle of *bring* is *brought*.
4. **1** The past tense of *drink* is *drank*.
5. **5** No error.
6. **1** The past participle of *write* is *written*.
7. **1** The past tense of *sing* is *sang*.
8. **1** The past participle of *drown* is *drowned*.
9. **5** No error.
10. **1** The past tense of *do* is *did*.

TROUBLESOME ADJECTIVES AND ADVERBS

Most of the time, it is easy to decide whether an adjective or an adverb is required in a given sentence. *The **adjective** is used to describe a noun or pronoun.*

EXAMPLE: He wore a *dark* hat.

*The **adverb** is used to modify a verb, adjective or another adverb.*

EXAMPLE: He played *very poorly.* (*poorly* modifies *played: very* modifies *poorly*)

There are times, however, when adjectives and adverbs can be confused. This confusion can be caused by:

1. ***Use of a verb describing a condition, not an action.*** If the verb is not used as an action verb, or if the verb describes a condition, then an *adjective rather than an adverb* must follow it. Why? Because the adjective really modifies the subject and not the verb.

Examples:

look	be
feel	am
taste	is
seem	are
become	was
smell	were
grow	has been
sound	had been

EXAMPLE: He looks *sick*.
(*sick* describes *he*)

EXAMPLE: I feel *good*.
(*good* describes *I*)

EXAMPLE: The fruit tastes *sweet*.
(*sweet* decribes *fruit*)

2. *Adjectives or adverbs having the same form.*

Adjectives and Adverbs with the Same Form	
fast	long
slow	ill
deep	sharp

EXAMPLE: He worked very *fast*.

EXAMPLE: He cut *deep* into the skin.

Some Special Problems

1. *Adjectives indicate the degree to which they describe nouns.* They do this in one of two ways:

—the adverb *more* or *most* is placed before the adjective;

—the form of the adjective changes to "—er" or "—est."

EXAMPLE: He was *more quiet* than she.
He was *quieter* than she.

EXAMPLE: He was the *most friendly* person there.
He was the *friendliest* person there.

What is the problem? It is that you must use the "more" *or* "—er" form where two and only two persons are involved. Similarly, you must use the "most" *or* "—est" form where three or more persons are involved. Never use *both* in the same sentence.

EXAMPLE: He was the *shyer* of the two.

EXAMPLE: He was the *most shy* among the three of them.

Note:

Some irregular adjectives do not follow these rules. The most frequently used are:

	Comparative (Comparison between two people or things)	**Superlative (Comparison among more than two people or things)**
bad	worse	worst
far	farther	farthest
good	better	best
many, much	more	most

2. *The use of two negative adverbs in the same sentence, or a negative adverb and a negative adjective in the same sentence, is incorrect.* Here are some examples:

EXAMPLE:

WRONG: He had*n't scarcely* a friend.
(Two negative adverbs —*n't* [*not*] and *scarcely*)

CORRECT: He had *scarcely* a friend.

EXAMPLE:

WRONG: He does*n't* do *no* work.
(A negative adverb —*n't* [*not*] and a negative adjective —*no*)

CORRECT: He doesn't do *any* work.

Practice

1. The orchestra sounded superb.
2. Alfredo waited long for his reward.
3. Henri was the most noisy student in the class.
4. Ricky had hardly any friends.
5. Of the three children, the youngest was the worst.

Answers

1. Correct.
2. Correct.
3. Correct.
4. Correct.
5. Correct.

PRACTICE WITH ADJECTIVES AND ADVERBS

Directions: **In each sentence, five parts are underlined and numbered. Where there is an error in the use of an adjective or an adverb, blacken the number of the underlined part which contains the error. If there is no error, mark answer space 5. No sentence contains more than one error.**

1. Hardly hadn't (1) he quietly (2) and painfully (3) built the sand castle than it was swiftly (4) torn down. No error (5)

1. 1 2 3 4 5

2. Although I feel good, (1) I look sick (2) because I ate sparingly (3) and improperly (4). No error (5)

2. 1 2 3 4 5

3. Gladly (1) I'll say that he surely (2) shot the puck real (3) well (4). No error. (5)

3. 1 2 3 4 5

4. Anita was the most (1) pretty (2) girl although she didn't dress well (3) or act properly (4). No error (5)

4. 1 2 3 4 5

5. The lunch, which was lovingly (1) and carefully (2) prepared, tastes deliciously (3) and is healthful (4). No error (5)

5. 1 2 3 4 5

6. He worked fast (1); I worked slow (2). He rested frequently (3); I worked continuously (4). No error (5)

6. 1 2 3 4 5

7. It doesn't seem right (1) that some flowers that look ugly (2) smell sweet (3) while others that look pretty smell bad (4). No error (5)

7. 1 2 3 4 5

8. Doesn't Gilles succeed just as good (1) as Carl though he isn't as hard-working (2), serious (3), and conscientious (4)? No error (5)

8. 1 2 3 4 5

9. The worse (1) of the two storms ended as quickly (2) and suddenly (3) as it had begun, leaving us ill (4) with fear. No error (5)

9. 1 2 3 4 5

10. He spoke deliberately (1) and chose his words carefully (2), with the result that his speech cut deep (3) and he was the more (4) effective of the two speakers. No error (5)

10. 1 2 3 4 5

Turn to the answer key and the answer analysis which follow.

What's Your Score?

_______ right,	_______ wrong
Excellent	9–10
Good	8
Fair	7

If you scored lower, restudy this section, concentrating on the rules and examples.

ANSWER KEY

Practice with Adjectives and Adverbs/Page 158

1. **1**	3. **3**	5. **3**	7. **5**	9. **5**
2. **5**	4. **5**	6. **5**	8. **1**	10. **5**

ANSWER ANALYSIS

Practice with Adjectives and Adverbs/Page 158

1. **1** To avoid a double negative, the correct word is *had*.
2. **5** No error.
3. **3** The word modifies the adverb *well*, so it should be an adverb—*really*.
4. **5** No error.
5. **3** The verb *tastes* requires a predicate adjective. *Delicious* is correct.
6. **5** No error.
7. **5** No error.
8. **1** This word modifies the verb *Doesn't succeed*, so an adverb, *well*, is required.
9. **5** No error.
10. **5** No error.

MECHANICS

Mechanics deals with the areas of capitalization, punctuation, and spelling. While these are annoying to many, they follow definite rules which, if mastered, can enable you to do well on the parts of the GED examination which test your knowledge of mechanics.

Capitalization. Fourteen basic rules are provided with applications for each.

Punctuation. Basic rules and appropriate examples are given for each of the major punctuation marks: period, question mark, exclamation point, comma, semicolon, colon, comma, apostrophe, parentheses and quotation marks.

Spelling. The 967 words that are most likely to be tested have been broken down into three lists for you to study: "The Basic 100"; "201 Often Used Easy Words"; and "666 More Frequently Used Words." We have analyzed these for you with the difficult parts underlined.

In addition, we identify the 3 basic skills of a good speller and the 13 most helpful spelling rules. Applications of these rules are provided. Although spelling is not directly tested, it is important for your writing and reading.

BASIC RULES OF CAPITALIZATION

RULES	EXAMPLES
1. Capitalize the first word of a sentence.	We went to the theatre.
2. Capitalize the first word of a direct quotation.	He said, "Don't give up."
3. Capitalize the first word of a line of poetry.	"Poems are made by fools like me . . ."
4. Capitalize proper nouns (names of specific persons, places or things).	Winston Churchill; Mr. James Jones; Toronto; Queen Street; City Hall
5. Capitalize proper adjectives (adjectives formed from proper nouns).	Canadian; Shakespearean

BASIC RULES OF CAPITALIZATION

RULES	EXAMPLES
6. Capitalize names of specific organizations or institutions.	Marc Garneau Junior High School; Dalhousie University; Canadian Red Cross; Royal Canadian Mounted Police
7. Capitalize days of the week, months of the year and holidays. (*Note:* Do *not* capitalize seasons; e.g., winter.)	Sunday; June; Canada Day
8. Capitalize languages. (*Note:* These are the *only* school subjects which are capitalized.)	French; Hebrew I study English, French, biology, mathematics and social studies.
9. Capitalize races and religions.	Black; Christian
10. Capitalize references to the Deity and to titles of holy books.	the Almighty; the Old Testament; the Koran
11. Capitalize titles of people when they are followed by a name, being careful to capitalize both the title and the name. (*Note:* If a specific person is meant, the name may, at times, be omitted.)	Governor-General LeBlanc; Dr. Schweitzer
12. Capitalize titles of works of literature, art and music.	*War and Peace* (note that articles, short prepositions, and conjunctions like "and" are not capitalized in titles); *American Gothic*; Beethoven's *Fifth Symphony*
13. The pronoun "I" is capitalized at all times.	I walked one mile south to the school.
14. Sections of the country are capitalized, but directions are not.	I lived in the North for five years.
15. Capitalize specific places and addresses.	Queen's Park; 317 Dundas Street

Practice

1. Junior belongs to the Boy scouts.
2. My favorite subject in school is English.
3. Cobourg is about 112 kilometres east of Toronto.
4. The bible is a holy book to millions.
5. Saskatoon is in Saskatchewan.
6. My cousin shouted, "be careful!"
7. Donna's cat was named sandy.
8. My home is located near Broadway.
9. Most inhabitants of Israel are jewish.
10. Labour day occurs in September.

Answers

1. Junior belongs to the Boy Scouts.
2. Correct.
3. Correct.

4. The Bible is a holy book to millions.
5. Correct.
6. My cousin shouted, "Be careful!"
7. Donna's cat was named Sandy.
8. My home is located near Broadway.
9. Most inhabitants of Israel are Jewish.
10. Labour Day occurs in September.

CAPITALIZATION PRACTICE

Directions: **The following sentences contain problems in capitalization. If there is an error, select the one underlined part that must be changed to make the sentence correct. *No sentence contains more than one error.* If there is no error, mark answer space 5. These are included in the sentence correction type of multiple-choice item.**

1. Peter Winkle of Alberta (1), the last doubtful conservative (2) name to be called on May (3) 16, was, like Ross (4), a "nobody." No error (5)

1. 1 2 3 4 5

2. We visited Mackenzie House (1) on Bond Street (2), the completely restored 19th-century home of Toronto's (3) first Mayor (4). No error (5)

2. 1 2 3 4 5

3. As the 800-foot-long tanker *Houston* (1) entered Toronto (2) Harbour (3), the captain (4) ordered its speed reduced. No error (5)

3. 1 2 3 4 5

4. The English (1) teacher assigned the Poe (2) story "Murders (3) in The (4) Rue Morgue." No error (5)

4. 1 2 3 4 5

5. He lived on Twenty (1)-First (2) Street (3), at the corner of Broadway (4). No error (5)

5. 1 2 3 4 5

6. Canada's (1) Wonderland (2) is located North (3) of Toronto (4). No error (5)

6. 1 2 3 4 5

7. He failed Chemistry (1) and French (2) but passed English (3) and Spanish (4). No error (5)

7. 1 2 3 4 5

8. I attended Dawson School and McGill University. No error
(1) Dawson (2) School (3) McGill (4) University (5) No error

8. 1 2 3 4 5

9. Mr. and Mrs. Jones and Family invite you to a party at their home. No error
(1) Mr. (2) Mrs. (3) Jones (4) Family (5) No error

9. 1 2 3 4 5

Turn to the answer key and the answer analysis which follow.

What's Your Score?

_______ right,	_______ wrong
Excellent	9
Good	8
Fair	7

If you scored lower, restudy this section, concentrating on the rules and examples.

ANSWER KEY

Capitalization Practice/Page 162

1. **2**	4. **4**	7. **1**
2. **4**	5. **2**	8. **5**
3. **5**	6. **3**	9. **4**

ANSWER ANALYSIS

Capitalization Practice/Page 162

1. **2** See Rule 6 on page 161. Capitalize names of specific organizations.
2. **4** See Rule 11 on page 161. Only capitalize titles of people if a specific person is meant.
3. **5** No error.
4. **4** Unimportant words in the title of a literary work are not capitalized.
5. **2** In an address, the second part of a hyphenated number is not capitalized.
6. **3** Directions are not capitalized.
7. **1** Only languages, among school subjects, are capitalized.
8. **5** No error.
9. **4** This is a word which refers to a general group and, therefore, is not capitalized.

BASIC RULES OF PUNCTUATION

RULES	EXAMPLES
THE PERIOD *is used after* **1.** a sentence which makes a statement; **2.** a sentence which gives a command; **3.** some abbreviations and contractions.	 He arrived on time. Sit up straight. Mr., lb., A.M., etc.
THE QUESTION MARK *is used after* a sentence which asks a question.	 Did you like the game?
THE EXCLAMATION POINT *is used after* a sentence which emphasizes a command or which conveys strong feeling.	 Stop writing immediately! What a pleasant surprise!
THE COMMA *is* **1.** used to separate words that indicate the person to whom a remark is addressed;	 John, please come here. You may come, John, if you like.
2. used to separate words that are in apposition with a noun; that is, add information about the noun;	Nancy, my accountant, is very efficient.
3. used to set off expressions or phrases which are inserted in the sentence and which interrupt the normal word order;	Regina, in my opinion, will win the championship. Joan, on the other hand, disagrees with us.
Note: **Rules 4 and 5 do not apply to short introductory phrases and clauses and short independent clauses.**	
4. used after introductory phrases and clauses, particularly when they are long or when the meaning may be temporarily confused if the comma is omitted;	When the dog jumped up, Darryl's parents became frightened. After a long but exciting trip through the Alps, Amy returned tired but happy. Springing into action, the constable caught the bandit.
5. used to separate independent clauses of a compound sentence joined by a conjunction such as *and*, *but*, *for*, *nor*, *or*, *so*, or *yet*;	Joe decided to attend the game, but I remained at home. **but** Joe returned but I remained.
6. used to separate items in a series but is omitted between the last two items unless the meaning might be confused or whenever the phrase before the final item contains a conjunction (note that some authorities recommend the use of the comma in a series consistently even if there is no possibility of confusion);	The box contained books, toys, games and tools. Jason, Meghan, and Sarah are going to the office today. (If the comma is omitted after "Meghan," it might seem that Jason was being told that Meghan and Sarah were going to the office.) For breakfast he had juice, ham and eggs, and coffee.
7. used before the text of a quotation; in a divided quotation, commas are used to set off the speaker.	The teacher said, "Return to your seats." "Return to your seats," said the teacher, "so we may continue the lesson."

RULES	EXAMPLES
8. used to set off clauses and phrases which are not essential to the meaning of the sentence. (*No commas are needed if the clause or phrase is essential to the meaning intended by the speaker or writer.*)	Jan, who was seated beside me, left early. (Note that the clause "who was seated beside me" is not essential to the sentence, which, without it, would read, "Jan left early.") **but** The students who studied hard passed the test. (The clause "who studied hard" is essential since only those students who studied hard passed. Without this clause the meaning intended by the writer—that the others who did not study hard failed—would not be clear to the reader.)
The comma also has a number of uses which are the result of custom:	
9. after the salutation in a friendly letter;	Dear Dad,
10. after the complimentary close in all letters;	Very truly yours,
11. between the day of the month and the year in writing a date;	May 24, 1919
12. between the city and province in writing an address.	North York, Ontario M6M 2L7

Note:

Do NOT use a comma

—between a subject and its verb when the verb immediately follows the subject;

EXAMPLE: The boys on the team celebrated their victory.

—to separate parts of a compound predicate.

EXAMPLE: They wanted to have a good dinner and see a play.

Practice

1. Invite Constance my sister to the dance.
2. What nonsense!
3. Eli, if you ask me, is the smartest of them all.
4. After Ruth rested at home she felt better.
5. Exercising daily getting a good night's sleep and eating the proper food are three ways to good health.

Answers

1. Invite Constance, my sister, to the dance.
2. Correct.
3. Correct.
4. After Ruth rested at home, she felt better.
5. Exercising daily, getting a good night's sleep, and eating the proper food are three ways to good health.

RULES	EXAMPLES
THE SEMICOLON *is used to* **1.** separate independent clauses in a sentence; either a semicolon or a comma may be used when the clauses are short;	I came; I saw; I conquered. (*or* I came, I saw, I conquered.)
2. separate items in a series when these items contain commas.	The guests included William H. Rehnquist, Chief Justice of the United States; George Schultz, Secretary of State; and Jim Wright, Speaker of the House.
THE COLON *is used* **1.** to introduce a series or a list of items;	These items were included on the shopping list: fruit, vegetables, meat, fish and ice cream.
2. before a restatement, an illustration or an explanation of the main idea of the sentence;	I have but one rule of conduct: do unto others as you would be done by.
3. after the salutation of a business letter.	Dear Sir:
THE APOSTROPHE *is used to* **1.** indicate possession a. in general, to make a singular noun possessive, add an apostrophe and "s" ('s) to words not ending in "s."	boy's hat
b. To make a plural noun possessive, add an apostrophe if the plural noun ends in "s." If it does not end in "s," add an apostrophe and "s";	ladies' hats men's coats
2. indicate that one or more letters have been omitted in a contraction;	He didn't come.
3. indicate the plural of letters or numbers.	There are 4 s's in Mississauga.

Note:

—Before adding the apostrophe to make the possessive, first form the plural of the noun;

EXAMPLE: child—children—children's

—Do *not* break up a word by using the apostrophe. The apostrophe can be added only at the end of a word.

EXAMPLE: WRONG: ladie's hats
CORRECT: ladies' hats

RULES	EXAMPLES
PARENTHESES *are used to* *enclose any words that explain or add to an idea or ideas contained in a sentence.*	*Parentheses are always used in pairs (that is, one opens and the other closes the included word or words).*

RULES	EXAMPLES
QUOTATION MARKS *are used to*	
1. indicate the titles of works that are *part* of a book (*Note:* The titles of whole books are underlined to indicate that the title should be italicized when what is written is printed);	"Trees" is a poem by Joyce Kilmer.
2. set off a direct quotation of the speaker or the writer. (*Note:* Only the speaker's or writer's exact wording may be used.) Indirect quotations, quotations which do not use the exact words of the speaker or writer, do *not* require quotation marks.	Kim Campbell said: "Charisma without substance is a dangerous thing." They boy said that he would be late. **but** The boy said, "I will be late."

Note:
In almost every case, the comma and the period are enclosed *within* the quotation marks.

Practice

1. The childrens' clothing department was well stocked.
2. Your country expects only one thing from you citizens; do your duty.
3. Present at the meeting were General Smith, Army Chief of Staff: Admiral Jones, Chief of Naval Operations: and General Gray, Commanding General of the Marine Corps.
4. Maria indicated that she wouldnt come.
5. My parents warned me, "Dont be late".

Answers

1. The children's clothing department was well stocked.
2. Your country expects only one thing from you citizens: do your duty.
3. Present at the meeting were General Smith, Army Chief of Staff; Admiral Jones, Chief of Naval Operations; and General Gray, Commanding General of the Marine Corps.
4. Maria indicated that she wouldn't come.
5. My parents warned me, "Don't be late."

PUNCTUATION PRACTICE

***Directions:* The following sentences contain problems in punctuation. If there is an error, select the one underlined part that must be changed to make the sentence correct. <u>No sentence contains more than one error.</u> If there is no error, mark answer space 5. These are included in the sentence correction type of multiple-choice item.**

1. Consider, (1) for example, (2) the widespread notion that a clean environment can be obtained by reducing our dependence on "technology" (3). (4) No error (5)

1. 1 2 3 4 5

2. However, (1) we often get careless; (2) we say, "It's close enough," (3) or "Who cares anyway." (4) No error (5)

2. 1 2 3 4 5

3. Gasoline and whisky have much in common: they're both blended, both distilled—and both have something of a kick. No error
(1) : (2) they're (3) , (4) — (5) No error

3. 1 2 3 4 5

4. The object_therefore, is to clean up the air: the higher the vapour pressure, the more likely it is that gasoline will evaporate. No error
(1) _ (2) , (3) : (4) , (5) No error

4. 1 2 3 4 5

5. At 6 PM tomorrow, however, they will be fed into a 30-cm diameter pipeline, each entering at a different point. No error
(1) PM (2) , (3) , (4) , (5) No error

5. 1 2 3 4 5

6. Woodrow Wilson, when he was president of the United States, said that "he made the world safe for democracy. No error
(1) , (2) , (3) " (4) . (5) No error

6. 1 2 3 4 5

7. Mr. James Smith, President
(1)
The Line company_
(2)
16 Fifth Street_
(3)
Lasing, Arizona 47962
Dear Mr. Smith,
(4)
No error
(5)

7. 1 2 3 4 5

8. 1413 Sixth Street_
(1)
Columbus_Florida_
(2) (3)
March 5, 1984
(4)
No error
(5)

8. 1 2 3 4 5

9. "Are you coming?" he asked.
(1)
"Yes."
(2)
"When?"
(3)
"Now."
(4)
No error
(5)

9. 1 2 3 4 5

10. "You take care of your problems," said those to whom we addressed our questions, "and we'll take care of ours". No error
(1) (2)(3) (4) (5)

10. 1 2 3 4 5

Turn to the answer key and the answer analysis which follow.

What's Your Score?

_______ right,	_______ wrong
Excellent	9–10
Good	8
Fair	7

If you scored lower, restudy this section, concentrating on the rules and examples.

ANSWER KEY

Punctuation Practice/Page 167

1. **4**	3. **5**	5. **1**	7. **4**	9. **5**
2. **4**	4. **1**	6. **3**	8. **2**	10. **4**

ANSWER ANALYSIS

Punctuation Practice/Page 167

1. **4** At the end of a sentence, the period should be placed between the quotation marks and the word (*technology*.").
2. **4** The question mark is used after a sentence which asks a question.
3. **5** No error.
4. **1** See Rule 3 under "The Comma" (page 164). The comma is used to set off expressions or phrases which are inserted in the sentence and which interrupt the normal word order.
5. **1** See Rule 3 under "The Period" (page 164). The period is used after most abbreviations.
6. **3** See Rule 2 under "Quotation Marks" (page 167). Indirect quotations do not require quotation marks.
7. **4** A colon is required after the salutation of a business letter.
8. **2** In an address, a comma is used to separate a state from the city located in it.
9. **5** No error.
10. **4** The period should be enclosed within the quotation marks.

SPELLING (Not tested in the 2002 test)

If you are one of the thousands of people in Canada who simply can't spell, take heart. You needn't be. Modern educational research has made the job of becoming a good speller a lot easier than it used to be. We now know which words are used most frequently in print. In fact, the words on these lists, if thoroughly mastered, will prepare you to spell correctly approximately two thirds of the words you need.

Note

There are a few common differences in spelling between American and Canadian words:

1. Words ending in "or" (American) become **"our"** in (Canadian)
   e.g., color vs. colour
   neighbor vs. neighbour

2. Words ending in "er" (American) become **"re"** in (Canadian)
   e.g., center vs. centre
   theater vs. theatre

3. Words ending in "k" (American) become **"que"** in (Canadian)
   e.g., check vs. cheque
   mark vs. marque

THE BASIC 100

The first list contains 100 basic words that all students should know thoroughly.

ache	done	making	there
again	don't	many	they
always	early	meant	though
among	easy	minute	through
answer	enough	much	tired
any	every	none	tonight
been	February	often	too
beginning	forty	once	trouble
believe	friend	piece	truly
blue	grammar	raise	Tuesday
break	guess	read	two
built	half	ready	used
business	having	said	very
busy	hear	Saturday	wear
buy	heard	says	Wednesday
can't	here	seems	week
choose	hoarse	separate	where
colour	hour	shoes	whether
coming	instead	since	which
cough	just	some	whole
could	knew	straight	women
country	know	sugar	won't
dear	laid	sure	would
doctor	loose	tear	write
does	lose	their	writing

How do you go about studying this list?
One way involves the following steps.

1. Fold a sheet of paper into three parts, holding the paper lengthwise.
2. Fold the left third of the paper over so that it covers the centre part.
3. Look at the word, noticing the difficult spot or spots. Say it aloud carefully.
4. Look at the word again, spelling it aloud by syllables. We'll help you with the problem of dividing words into syllables later on.
5. Spell the word aloud by syllables again, without looking at it this time.
6. Look at the word a third time, copying the letters on the folded part of the paper while you say them aloud by syllables.
7. Turn the fold back, this time writing the letters on the right-hand part of the paper while you again say them aloud by syllables.

8. Fold the left third of the paper over again so that you can compare the word you originally copied with the word you wrote from memory. If it is spelled correctly, turn the fold back and write the word twice more, being careful to spell the word aloud by syllables each time. If you made an error, the word will require more study, particularly of the letter or syllable you misspelled.
9. Master this list before turning to the next list. This second word list contains 201 words which are somewhat more difficult than the basic 100, but which are still rated "Easy" by those who test spelling ability. We've tried to help you by underlining the letters or parts of the words which cause difficulty.

201 OFTEN USED EASY WORDS

absence
accept
accident
address
adjourn
advice
advise
airplane
allowed
almost
already
altogether
American
amount
annual
anxious
around
aroused
arrival
article
asked
athletic
attacked
attention
author
because
before
brakes
breathe
Canadian
careful
carrying
certain
changing
chief
children
choice
chosen
climbed
cloth
clothes
cloud
coarse
collar
common
conceal
confident
conquer
corner
course
crowd
curtain
customer
decided
delivery
destroy
determine
device
dictator
didn't
different
dining
discussed
divided
doesn't
dropped
due
dying
earliest
easily
effect
eighth
eliminate
English
entirely
envelope
etc.
everybody
evidently
excellent
expense
experience
extremely
fatigue
formerly
forth
forward
fourteen
fourth
future
generally
genius
gentlemen
good-bye
guard
handful
handle
handsome
hasn't
height
hoping
hundred
hungry
hurrying
interesting
invitation
its
it's
jealous
ladies
later
latter
led
library
losing
lying
magazine
merely
minutes
movable
neither
nevertheless
nickel
niece
ninety
ninth
o'clock
officer
operate
owing
paid
partner
passed
past
perform
perhaps
permanent
planning
politics
possible
presence
probably
prominent
promptly
proved
purpose
quarter
quiet
quite
quizzes
realize
really
receipt
received
recognize
reference
safety
salary
sandwich
scarcely
secretary
sentence
shining
shriek
speech
stopped
stories
strength
stretched
strictly
striking
studying
succeed
success
summer
surely

surround
terrible
than
they're
thorough
those
threw
together
toward
tries
twelfth
until
unusual
useful
varied
wasn't
weather
weird
welfare
whose
wonderful
wouldn't
written
you're
yours

666 MORE FREQUENTLY USED WORDS

This list contains 666 additional words which occur frequently in print. Each appears on several well-known spelling lists of words often misspelled by high school students. Each appears regularly on examinations.

a lot
ability
absolutely
abundance
acceptable
accidentally
accommodate
accompanied
accomplish
accordance
accordingly
accumulation
accurately
accuse
accustomed
achievement
acknowledge
acquainted
acquired
across
actually
additional
adequate
advantageous
advertisement
advisable
aerial
affectionately
against
aggravate
aggressive
agreement
aisle
allege
all right
although
amateur
analysis
analyze
angel
angle
another
antiseptic
apologize
apparatus
apparently
appearance
appetite
application
apply
appreciation
approaching
appropriate
approval
approximately
arctic
arguing
argument
arrangements
artificial
ascend
ascertain
assistance
assistant
association
attaching
attempt
attendance
audience
August
automobile
autumn
auxiliary
available
avenue
aviator
awful
awkward
bachelor
balance
balloon
bargain
basic
beautiful
become
beggar
being
benefited
between
bicycle
board
bored
borrow
bottle
bottom
boundary
breadth
brilliant
Britain
building
bulletin
bureau
buried
bushes
cafeteria
calculator
calendar
campaign
Canada
candidate
capital
capitol
captain
career
careless
carriage
category
ceiling
celebrity
cemetery
cereal
changeable
chaos
character
charity
chocolate
cigarette
circumstances
citizen
coffee
collect
college
colonel
column
comedy
comfortable
commission
commitment
committed
committee
communication
community
company
comparative
compel
competent
competition
complement
completely
compliment
conceit
conceivable
concentration
conception
condition
conference
congratulate
connection
conscience
conscientious
conscious
consequently
considerable
consideration
consistency
constable
consul
continually

continuously
controlled
convenience
conversation
coolly
corporal
correspondence
corroborate
council
counsellor
courageous
courteous
courtesy
criticism
crucial
crystal
curiosity
cylinder
daily
daughter
daybreak
death
deceive
December
deception
decision
decisively
deed
definite
delicious
dependent
deposit
derelict
descend
descent
description
desert
desirable
despair
desperate
dessert
destruction
develop
development
died
difficulty
dilemma
dinner
direction
disappeared
disappointed
disapproval
disastrous
discipline
discover
discriminate
disease
disposition
dissatisfied
dissection
dissipate
distance
distinction
division
dollar
doubt
dozen
duly
earnest
ecstasy
education
efficiency
either
eligible
embarrass
embarrassment
emergency
eminent
emphasize
enclosure
encouraging
endeavour
enemies
engineer
enormous
entrance
environment
equipment
equipped
especially
essentially
evening
exaggeration
examination
exceedingly
except
exceptional
excitement
exercise
exhausted
exhilaration
existence
exorbitant
experiment
explanation
extension
facility
factory
familiar
fascinating
finally
financial
financier
flourish
forcibly
forehead
foreign
foresee
formal
fortunate
freight
frequent
frightening
fugitive
fundamental
further
gallon
gardener
government
governor
grateful
great
grievance
grocery
guarantee
guardian
guidance
hammer
handkerchief
happiness
harassed
healthy
heavy
heroes
heroine
hideous
himself
holiday
hopeless
hospital
humourous
hurriedly
identity
ignorance
imaginary
imbecile
imitation
immediately
immigrant
incidentally
increase
indefinitely
independence
indispensable
individual
inevitable
influence
influential
ingenious
initiate
innocence
inoculate
inquiry
insistent
instinct
integrity
intellectual
intelligence
intercede
interfere
interpreted
interrupt
irrelevant
irresistible
irritable
island
itself
January
jewelry
journal
judgment
kindergarten
kitchen
knock
knowledge
laboratory
language
laugh
legible
leisure
length
lesson
license
lieutenant
lightning
likelihood
likely
literal
literature
livelihood
loaf
loneliness
loveliness
loyalty
maintenance
manoeuver
marriage
married
match
material
mathematics
meanness
measure
medicine

memorandum
merchandise
million
miniature
minimum
miracle
miscellaneous
mischievous
misspelled
mistake
momentous
monkey
monotonous
moral
morale
mortgage
mountain
mournful
murmur
muscle
mutual
mysterious
narrative
naturally
necessary
needle
negligence
neighbour
newspaper
newsstand
noticeable
obedient
oblige
obstacle
occasion
occurred
ocean
offer
omission
omitted
opinion
opportunity
optimistic
organization
origin
original
oscillate
ought
ounce
overcoat
pamphlet
panicky
parallel
particular
pastime
patience
peaceable
pear
peculiar
pencil
people
perceive
perception
perfectly
performance
period
perpendicular
perseverance
persistent
personally
personnel
persuading
pertain
physically
picture
plain
playwright
pleasant
pleasure
pocket
poison
population
portrayed
positive
possesses
possibility
post office
potatoes
practically
prairie
preceding
precise
predictable
preference
preferred
prejudice
preparations
prescription
president
prevalent
primitive
principal
principle
privilege
procedure
proceeded
produce
professional
professor
profitable
promise
pronunciation
propeller
prophecy
prophesy
prophet
prospect
psychology
pursuing
quality
quantity
quarreling
realistic
reason
rebellion
recede
recipe
recommend
recuperate
referee
referred
refugee
regretting
rehearsal
repeat
repetition
replying
representative
requirements
resemblance
reservoir
resistance
resources
respectability
response
responsibility
restaurant
rhyme
rhythm
ridiculous
right
role
roommate
sacrifice
satisfactory
scene
schedule
scientific
scissors
season
seize
seminar
sergeant
service
several
severely
shepherd
sheriff
shoulder
siege
sight
signal
significance
similar
sincerely
site
skiing
soldier
solemn
sophomore
soul
source
souvenir
special
specified
specimen
stationary
stationery
statue
stockings
stomach
strenuous
substantial
suddenness
sufficient
suggestion
superintendent
suppress
surprise
suspense
sweat
sweet
syllable
symmetrical
synonym
technical
telegram
telephone
temperament
temperature
temporary
tenant
tendency
tenement
therefore
title
tobacco
tomorrow
tongue
tragedy

transferred	unnecessary	vicinity	weak
treasury	unusually	vicious	weight
tremendous	vacuum	view	while
twelve	valley	village	wholly
typical	valuable	villain	woman
tyranny	vegetable	visitor	wretched
undoubtedly	vein	voice	yield
United States	vengeance	volume	
university	versatile	waist	

MOST FREQUENTLY MADE ERRORS

To help you study these lists, modern research has identified the five most frequent types of spelling errors.

1 and 2. *Over sixty percent of all spelling errors are caused by either leaving out a letter that belongs in a word or substituting one letter for another (usually because of incorrect pronunciation of the word).*

An example of a word misspelled because of a letter left out is the word *recognize.* Many students mispronounce the word by leaving out the "g"; they also, therefore, leave out the "g" when they spell the word.

An example of a word misspelled because one letter is substituted for another is the word *congratulations.* Many students mispronounce the word by substituting the voiced "d" sound for the unvoiced "t" sound; they also, therefore, substitute a "d" for the "t" when they spell the word. Other words which are misspelled because of the omission or substitution of letters are:

accidentally	environment	library	surprise
arctic	escape	partner	temperature
candidate	February	postpone	tragedy
chocolate	government	prejudice	tremendous
diphtheria	laboratory	probably	usually

3 and 4. *Over twenty percent of all errors are caused by either adding letters to a word or reversing two letters within the word.*

An example of a word to which a letter is added is the word *equipment.* Some people incorrectly pronounce the word with a "t" after the "p." As a result, they add a "t" to the word when they spell it.

An example of a reversal of letters within the word is the simple word *doesn't.* Very often, the letters "e" and "s" are reversed and the student spells the word incorrectly—"dosen't." Other words which are misspelled because of the addition or reversal of letters are:

asparagus	(*not* gras)	percent	(*not* pre)
athletics	(*no* e after the th)	performance	(*not* pre)
barbarous	(*no* i after the second bar)	perspire	(*not* pre)
chimney	(*no* i after the m)	produce	(*not* per)
disastrous	(*no* e after the t)	profession	(*not* per)
hundred	(*not* derd)	pronounce	(*not* per)
introduce	(*not* ter)	protect	(*not* per)
lightning	(*no* e after the t)	remembrance	(*no* e after the b)
mischievous	(*no* i after the v)	secretary	(*not* er)
modern	(*not* dren)	umbrella	(*no* e after the b)

5. *The next most common error is the confusion of two words having the same pronunciation but different spellings and meanings.* These are called *homonyms.* In this humourous

sentence—"A doctor must have lots of patients (patience)"—there is no way of our knowing which word the speaker means if the sentence is spoken. Therefore, we don't know how to spell the word. The words "patients" and "patience" are homonyms.

Forty of the most frequently used groups of homonyms follow. Be certain to check the meaning of each word in each group so that you can figure out the spelling from the meaning of the word as it is used in a sentence.

air; ere; heir
ate; eight
blew; blue
bough; bow
brake; break
buy; by
cent; scent; sent
coarse; course
for; four
forth; fourth
grate; great
groan; grown
hear; here
him; hymn
hole; whole
hour; our
knew; new
know; no
lead; led
mail; male
meat; meet
pail; pale
pair; pare; pear
peace; piece
principal; principle
read; red
right; write
road; rode
sew; so; sow
stationary; stationery
steal; steel
straight; strait
some; sum
son; sun
their; there; they're
threw; through
to; too; two
way; weigh
wood; would
your; you're

How to Become a Good Speller

There are three things you can do to help eliminate these errors and to equip yourself with the skills you will need to become a good speller.

1. **LEARN HOW TO SYLLABICATE.** Knowing how to syllabicate—divide a word into syllables—will help you avoid many kinds of errors. This skill is particularly helpful with words of more than average length. Here are some simple rules that will help you to syllabicate properly.

HOW TO SYLLABICATE

RULES	EXAMPLES		
1. When a word has more than one vowel sound, it is broken into parts or syllables.	**strength** **metal**	*strength* *me/tal*	(one syllable) (two syllables)
2. Every syllable contains a sounded vowel or pair of vowels sounded as one vowel (digraph).	**going** **breakout**	*go/ing* *break/out*	(sounded vowel in each syllable) (pairs of vowels sounded as one vowel in each syllable)
3. Sometimes a sounded vowel forms a syllable by itself.	**again**	*a/gain*	
4. Double consonants usually are separated.	**mitten** **possesses**	*mit/ten* *pos/ses/ses*	
5. A consonant between two vowels usually is joined to the vowel that follows it.	**local** **final**	*lo/cal* *fi/nal*	
6. When the suffix "ed" is added to a word ending in "d" or "t," it forms a separate syllable.	**added**	*add/ed*	

Applying these rules to the words listed earlier will help you avoid many of the common type of errors, particularly in the omission and addition of letters.

EXAMPLES: ath / le / tics
chim / ney
um / brel / la
ac / ci / den / tal / ly

2. LEARN THE CORRECT PRONUNCIATION OF THE WORD YOU MUST SPELL. Mispronunciation is known to be one of the most common causes of misspelling. Your best ally in learning the pronunciation of a word is the dictionary. Knowing the correct pronunciation will help you attack successfully such words as:

Feb / ru / a / ry (the first "r" is often not pronounced)
gov / ern / ment (the first "n" is often not pronounced)
choc / o / late (the second "o" is often not pronounced)

3. LEARN THE THIRTEEN MOST HELPFUL SPELLING RULES AND HOW TO APPLY THEM.

BASIC RULES OF SPELLING

RULES	EXAMPLES
1. Plurals of most nouns are formed by adding "s" to the singular.	house, hous*es*
2. When the noun ends in "s," "x," "ch," or "sh," the plural generally is formed by adding "es."	gas, gas*es* box, box*es* witch, witch*es* dish, dish*es*
3. a. *Plural of a noun ending in "y" preceded by a consonant* is formed by changing "y" to "i" and adding "es." b. *Plural of a noun ending in "y" preceded by a vowel* does not change "y" to "i" EXCEPT for words ending in "quy."	lady, lad*ies* toy, toy*s* **but** soliloquy, soliloqu*ies*
4. a. *A word ending in "y" preceded by a consonant* usually changes "y" to "i" before a suffix unless the suffix begins with "i." b. *A word that ends in "y" preceded by a vowel* usually keeps the "y" when a suffix is added.	beauty, beauti*ful* coy, coy*er*
5. a. *A word that ends in silent "e" generally keeps the "e" when a suffix beginning with a consonant is added.* b. *A word that ends in silent "e" generally drops the "e" when a suffix beginning with a vowel is added.*	care, care*ful* believe, believ*able* move, mov*ing*
6. Exceptions to Rule 5. Words ending in "ce" and "ge" keep the letter "e" before "able" and "ous."	notice, notic*eable* change, change*able* courage, courag*eous*

RULES	EXAMPLES
7. A one-syllable word that ends in one consonant following a short vowel generally doubles the consonant before a suffix that begins with a vowel.	big, big*gest* thin, thin*ner*
8. A word of more than one syllable that ends in one consonant following one short vowel generally doubles the final consonant before a suffix beginning with a vowel *if* the accent is on the last syllable.	omít, omit[t]*ed* regrét, regret[t]*ing* allót, allot[t]*ed*
9. The letter "i" is generally used before "e" except after "c." **There Are Many Exceptions**, as: either neither neighbourhood weigh leisure	bel*ie*ve, rec*ei*ve
10. An apostrophe is used to show that a letter has been omitted in a contraction.	it is, it's they are, they're
11. An abbreviation is always followed by a period.	etc.
12. Nouns of Latin origin ending —in "us" become "i" in the plural, —in "a" become "ae" in the plural, —in "um" become "a" in the plural, —in "is" become "es" in the plural.	rad*ius*, rad*ii* formul*a*, formul*ae* medi*um*, medi*a* ax*is*, ax*es*
13. The suffix "ful" is spelled with a single "l." (Note: the word "full" itself is the only exception.)	help*ful* tablespoon*ful*

SPELLING PRACTICE

***Directions:* In each set of words, find the misspelled word if there is one. No set has more than one misspelled word. If there is no misspelled word, mark answer space 5. This kind of error is included in the sentence correction type of multiple-choice item.**

1. (1) rein
(2) conceited
(3) cheif
(4) shield
(5) no error

1. 1 2 3 4 5

2. (1) greif
(2) wield
(3) relieve
(4) besiege
(5) no error

2. 1 2 3 4 5

3. (1) proceed
(2) succeed
(3) preceed
(4) exceed
(5) no error

3. 1 2 3 4 5

4. (1) illegal
(2) illegible
(3) unatural
(4) uncivilized
(5) no error

4. 1 2 3 4 5

5. (1) prespective
(2) present
(3) proceed
(4) proposal
(5) no error

5. 1 2 3 4 5
|| || || || ||

6. (1) combustible
(2) intelligible
(3) perceptable
(4) taxable
(5) no error

6. 1 2 3 4 5
|| || || || ||

7. (1) tangible
(2) lamentible
(3) considerable
(4) separable
(5) no error

7. 1 2 3 4 5
|| || || || ||

8. (1) logically
(2) typically
(3) verbally
(4) globally
(5) no error

8. 1 2 3 4 5
|| || || || ||

9. (1) practically
(2) exceptionally
(3) significantly
(4) intelligently
(5) no error

9. 1 2 3 4 5
|| || || || ||

10. (1) advantagous
(2) perilous
(3) desirous
(4) adventurous
(5) no error

10. 1 2 3 4 5
|| || || || ||

11. (1) mischievious
(2) previous
(3) poisonous
(4) mountainous
(5) no error

11. 1 2 3 4 5
|| || || || ||

12. (1) murderous
(2) slanderous
(3) grievous
(4) beauteous
(5) no error

12. 1 2 3 4 5
|| || || || ||

13. (1) momentous
(2) marvelous
(3) outragous
(4) hazardous
(5) no error

13. 1 2 3 4 5
|| || || || ||

14. (1) channal
(2) acquittal
(3) flannel
(4) kernel
(5) no error

14. 1 2 3 4 5
|| || || || ||

15. (1) sparkle
(2) disciple
(3) thimbal
(4) clerical
(5) no error

15. 1 2 3 4 5
|| || || || ||

16. (1) corpuscle
(2) muscle
(3) proposal
(4) morsel
(5) no error

16. 1 2 3 4 5
|| || || || ||

17. (1) nickle
(2) pickle
(3) logical
(4) neutral
(5) no error

17. 1 2 3 4 5
|| || || || ||

18. (1) signal
(2) medical
(3) swivel
(4) shuttel
(5) no error

18. 1 2 3 4 5
|| || || || ||

19. (1) senator
(2) investigator
(3) inventer
(4) stenographer
(5) no error

19. 1 2 3 4 5
|| || || || ||

20. (1) actor
(2) ancestor
(3) purchaser
(4) elevater
(5) no error

20. 1 2 3 4 5

21. (1) begger
(2) bookkeeper
(3) regular
(4) singular
(5) no error

21. 1 2 3 4 5

22. (1) calender
(2) passenger
(3) collar
(4) hangar
(5) no error

22. 1 2 3 4 5

23. (1) spectator
(2) educator
(3) dollar
(4) receiver
(5) no error

23. 1 2 3 4 5

24. (1) pendant
(2) brilliant
(3) superintendent
(4) permanent
(5) no error

24. 1 2 3 4 5

25. (1) descendant
(2) repentant
(3) defendent
(4) president
(5) no error

25. 1 2 3 4 5

26. (1) lieutenent
(2) sergeant
(3) resident
(4) tenant
(5) no error

26. 1 2 3 4 5

27. (1) appearance
(2) endurance
(3) persistance
(4) remembrance
(5) no error

27. 1 2 3 4 5

28. (1) presence
(2) absence
(3) hindrance
(4) attendance
(5) no error

28. 1 2 3 4 5

29. (1) cemetary
(2) imaginary
(3) dictionary
(4) boundary
(5) no error

29. 1 2 3 4 5

30. (1) stationery
(2) secondary
(3) elementery
(4) honorary
(5) no error

30. 1 2 3 4 5

31. (1) revolutionary
(2) infirmary
(3) vocabulary
(4) voluntary
(5) no error

31. 1 2 3 4 5

32. (1) advise
(2) capsize
(3) despise
(4) surprize
(5) no error

32. 1 2 3 4 5

33. (1) supervise
(2) exercise
(3) disguize
(4) baptize
(5) no error

33. 1 2 3 4 5

34. (1) hypnotize
(2) antagonize
(3) patronize
(4) authorize
(5) no error

34. 1 2 3 4 5

35. (1) merchandise (2) dramatise (3) centralize (4) neutralize (5) no error

35. 1 2 3 4 5

36. (1) specialize (2) franchize (3) arise (4) enterprise (5) no error

36. 1 2 3 4 5

37. (1) realize (2) recognize (3) compromise (4) advertise (5) no error

37. 1 2 3 4 5

38. (1) emphasise (2) revise (3) modernize (4) fertilize (5) no error

38. 1 2 3 4 5

39. (1) agonize (2) analyze (3) generalize (4) paralyze (5) no error

39. 1 2 3 4 5

40. (1) houses (2) classes (3) waltzs (4) businesses (5) no error

40. 1 2 3 4 5

41. (1) sopranos (2) torpedos (3) vetoes (4) echoes (5) no error

41. 1 2 3 4 5

42. (1) chiefs (2) loaves (3) beliefs (4) handkerchieves (5) no error

42. 1 2 3 4 5

43. (1) rooves (2) calves (3) hoofs (4) proofs (5) no error

43. 1 2 3 4 5

44. (1) thiefs (2) briefs (3) knives (4) shelves (5) no error

44. 1 2 3 4 5

45. (1) radios (2) tangos (3) silos (4) cameos (5) no error

45. 1 2 3 4 5

46. (1) valleys (2) monkeys (3) attorneys (4) alleys (5) no error

46. 1 2 3 4 5

47. (1) allies (2) journeys (3) dormitorys (4) armies (5) no error

47. 1 2 3 4 5

48. (1) spagheti (2) ravioli (3) confetti (4) bacilli (5) no error

48. 1 2 3 4 5

49. (1) carrying (2) hurrying (3) tragedys (4) chimneys (5) no error

49. 1 2 3 4 5

50. (1) desirable
(2) knowledgeable
(3) lovable
(4) advisable
(5) no error

50. 1 2 3 4 5

51. (1) desirous
(2) advantageous
(3) porous
(4) courageous
(5) no error

51. 1 2 3 4 5

52. (1) suddeness
(2) genuineness
(3) vagueness
(4) likeness
(5) no error

52. 1 2 3 4 5

53. (1) pursuing
(2) relieving
(3) canoeing
(4) toeing
(5) no error

53. 1 2 3 4 5

54. (1) truely
(2) carefully
(3) solemnly
(4) purely
(5) no error

54. 1 2 3 4 5

55. (1) wholy
(2) duly
(3) sincerely
(4) freely
(5) no error

55. 1 2 3 4 5

56. (1) agreeable
(2) noticeable
(3) changable
(4) serviceable
(5) no error

56. 1 2 3 4 5

57. (1) vengence
(2) insurance
(3) manageable
(4) desirable
(5) no error

57. 1 2 3 4 5

58. (1) occuring
(2) preferring
(3) conference
(4) admittance
(5) no error

58. 1 2 3 4 5

59. (1) traveled
(2) controlled
(3) annulment
(4) compelled
(5) no error

59. 1 2 3 4 5

60. (1) dinning
(2) committing
(3) equipping
(4) omitting
(5) no error

60. 1 2 3 4 5

61. (1) regretable
(2) transferable
(3) comparable
(4) controllable
(5) no error

61. 1 2 3 4 5

62. (1) beginning
(2) admitting
(3) benefiting
(4) rebeling
(5) no error

62. 1 2 3 4 5

63. (1) awful
(2) beautiful
(3) hopefuly
(4) usefully
(5) no error

63. 1 2 3 4 5

64. (1) its
(2) your's
(3) ours
(4) there's
(5) no error

64. 1 2 3 4 5

65. (1) childrens' (2) women's (3) girls' (4) mothers' (5) no error

65. 1 2 3 4 5

66. (1) alltogether (2) all right (3) already (4) allot (5) no error

66. 1 2 3 4 5

67. (1) labratory (2) licorice (3) privilege (4) diamond (5) no error

67. 1 2 3 4 5

68. (1) athletic (2) February (3) libary (4) interesting (5) no error

68. 1 2 3 4 5

69. (1) Wednesday (2) goverment (3) kindergarten (4) handkerchief (5) no error

69. 1 2 3 4 5

70. (1) arctic (2) choclate (3) environment (4) partner (5) no error

70. 1 2 3 4 5

71. (1) probably (2) usually (3) temperture (4) tragedy (5) no error

71. 1 2 3 4 5

72. (1) tremendous (2) postpone (3) diphtheria (4) supprise (5) no error

72. 1 2 3 4 5

73. (1) performance (2) perspire (3) pertect (4) percent (5) no error

73. 1 2 3 4 5

74. (1) mischievous (2) lightning (3) disastrous (4) chimney (5) no error

74. 1 2 3 4 5

75. (1) hundred (2) childern (3) modern (4) laundry (5) no error

75. 1 2 3 4 5

76. (1) Britain (2) villian (3) captain (4) crucial (5) no error

76. 1 2 3 4 5

77. (1) fascinating (2) ascertain (3) discipline (4) descent (5) no error

77. 1 2 3 4 5

78. (1) attendence (2) audience (3) assistance (4) balance (5) no error

78. 1 2 3 4 5

79. (1) carriage (2) marriage (3) morgage (4) college (5) no error

79. 1 2 3 4 5

80. (1) harass (2) embarass (3) across (4) success (5) no error

80. 1 2 3 4 5

81. (1) arguement (2) advertisement (3) requirement (4) agreement (5) no error

81. 1 2 3 4 5

82. (1) courtesy (2) hypocrisy (3) prophecy (4) delinquent (5) no error

82. 1 2 3 4 5

83. (1) appreciate (2) definate (3) syndicate (4) adequate (5) no error

83. 1 2 3 4 5

84. (1) aqueduct (2) aquaintance (3) acquire (4) acknowledge (5) no error

84. 1 2 3 4 5

85. (1) accommodate (2) recommend (3) committee (4) ammendment (5) no error

85. 1 2 3 4 5

86. (1) paralell (2) unusual (3) colonel (4) additional (5) no error

86. 1 2 3 4 5

87. (1) allege (2) knowlege (3) oblige (4) siege (5) no error

87. 1 2 3 4 5

88. (1) remedy (2) medecine (3) vegetable (4) repetition (5) no error

88. 1 2 3 4 5

89. (1) doubt (2) endeavor (3) bureau (4) amature (5) no error

89. 1 2 3 4 5

90. (1) foward (2) forehead (3) toward (4) foresee (5) no error

90. 1 2 3 4 5

91. (1) familiar (2) miniture (3) religious (4) similar (5) no error

91. 1 2 3 4 5

92. (1) tobacco (2) accross (3) macaroni (4) occasion (5) no error

92. 1 2 3 4 5

93. (1) necessary (2) professor (3) possesses (4) success (5) no error

93. 1 2 3 4 5

94. (1) develop (2) envelope (3) equiptment (4) interrupt (5) no error

94. 1 2 3 4 5

95. (1) proceeded (2) proceedure (3) preceding (4) precedent (5) no error

95. 1 2 3 4 5

96. (1) tenth (2) lenth (3) strength (4) height (5) no error

96. 1 2 3 4 5

97. (1) attatched (2) watched (3) detached (4) stomach (5) no error

97. 1 2 3 4 5

98. (1) studying (2) lying (3) hoping (4) planning (5) no error

98. 1 2 3 4 5

99. (1) murmer (2) gutter (3) conquer (4) neither (5) no error

99. 1 2 3 4 5

100. (1) mistake (2) disease (3) passtime (4) dessert (5) no error

100. 1 2 3 4 5

Turn to the answer key and the answer analysis which follow.

What's Your Score?

______ right,	______ wrong
Excellent	91–100
Good	81–90
Fair	71–80

If you scored lower, turn back to the section giving the rules that can help to make you a good speller. Then try the test again, possibly having someone dictate to you the words you missed.

ANSWER KEY

Spelling Practice/Page 178

1. **3**	16. **5**	31. **5**	46. **5**	61. **1**
2. **1**	17. **1**	32. **4**	47. **3**	62. **4**
3. **3**	18. **4**	33. **3**	48. **1**	63. **3**
4. **3**	19. **3**	34. **5**	49. **3**	64. **2**
5. **1**	20. **4**	35. **2**	50. **2**	65. **1**
6. **3**	21. **1**	36. **2**	51. **5**	66. **1**
7. **2**	22. **1**	37. **5**	52. **1**	67. **1**
8. **5**	23. **5**	38. **1**	53. **5**	68. **3**
9. **5**	24. **5**	39. **5**	54. **1**	69. **2**
10. **1**	25. **3**	40. **3**	55. **1**	70. **2**
11. **1**	26. **1**	41. **2**	56. **3**	71. **3**
12. **5**	27. **3**	42. **4**	57. **1**	72. **4**
13. **3**	28. **5**	43. **1**	58. **1**	73. **3**
14. **1**	29. **1**	44. **1**	59. **5**	74. **5**
15. **3**	30. **3**	45. **5**	60. **1**	75. **2**

76. **2**
77. **5**
78. **1**
79. **3**
80. **2**
81. **1**
82. **5**
83. **2**
84. **2**
85. **4**
86. **1**
87. **2**
88. **2**
89. **4**
90. **1**
91. **2**
92. **2**
93. **1**
94. **3**
95. **2**
96. **2**
97. **1**
98. **5**
99. **1**
100. **3**

ANSWER ANALYSIS

Spelling Practice/Page 178

1. **3** chief
2. **1** grief
3. **3** precede
4. **3** unnatural
5. **1** perspective
6. **3** perceptible
7. **2** lamentable
8. **5** no error
9. **5** no error
10. **1** advantageous
11. **1** mischievous
12. **5** no error
13. **3** outrageous
14. **1** channel
15. **3** thimble
16. **5** no error
17. **1** nickel
18. **4** shuttle
19. **3** inventor
20. **4** elevator
21. **1** beggar
22. **1** calendar
23. **5** no error
24. **5** no error
25. **3** defendant
26. **1** lieutenant
27. **3** persistence
28. **5** no error
29. **1** cemetery
30. **3** elementary
31. **5** no error
32. **4** surprise
33. **3** disguise
34. **5** no error
35. **2** dramatize
36. **2** franchise
37. **5** no error
38. **1** emphasize
39. **5** no error
40. **3** waltzes
41. **2** torpedoes
42. **4** handkerchiefs
43. **1** roofs
44. **1** thieves
45. **5** no error
46. **5** no error
47. **3** dormitories
48. **1** spaghetti
49. **3** tragedies
50. **5** no error
51. **5** no error
52. **1** suddenness
53. **5** no error
54. **1** truly
55. **1** wholly
56. **3** changeable
57. **1** vengeance
58. **1** occurring
59. **5** no error
60. **1** dining
61. **1** regrettable
62. **4** rebelling
63. **3** hopefully
64. **2** yours
65. **1** children's
66. **1** altogether
67. **1** laboratory
68. **3** library
69. **2** government
70. **2** chocolate
71. **3** temperature
72. **4** surprise
73. **3** protect
74. **5** no error
75. **2** children
76. **2** villain
77. **5** no error
78. **1** attendance
79. **3** mortgage
80. **2** embarrass
81. **1** argument
82. **5** no error
83. **2** definite
84. **2** acquaintance
85. **4** amendment
86. **1** parallel
87. **2** knowledge
88. **2** medicine
89. **4** amateur
90. **1** forward
91. **2** miniature
92. **2** across
93. **1** necessary
94. **3** equipment
95. **2** procedure
96. **2** length
97. **1** attached
98. **5** no error
99. **1** murmur
100. **3** pastime

ADDITIONAL WRITING SKILLS

DICTION

Words can be powerful weapons. Just think of the effect on you of such words as Mother, baby and American; or cancer, blindness and poverty. Used well, words not only communicate to others the ideas you want them to share, but also make a deep impression if you use them effectively. On the other hand, failure to use the proper word can confuse your reader and result in a complete breakdown in communication.

EXAMPLE: *Leave* him out.
VERSUS
Let him out.

Which sentence would apply to a dog scratching at the door in the hope of being taken for a walk? The truth is that you know the meaning of the words "leave" and "let." *Let* him out, of course. Yet their use in the sentences above may very well be confusing.

It is not the *meaning* of the words with which we are dealing now, but their *use. The correct choice and use of words is what is meant by* ***diction.***

Synonyms

There are times when you have difficulty choosing the right word because *two or more words have the same or very nearly the same essential meaning*, and only one really fits.

Do you *slay* or *execute* a murderer?
Is an explorer *adventurous* or *rash*?
Was it an optical *delusion* or *illusion?*
Was she *childish* or *childlike* in her behaviour?
Are you flattering someone when you call him *fat* instead of *stout*?

You *execute* a murderer because he has been found guilty by a jury in a legal trial. It is possible for any individual to *slay* another person. Is the explorer *adventurous*? He may be if he likes new experiences. He is *rash* only if he attempts adventures which are unwise. It is an optical *illusion* because it appears to be real even if it isn't. A *delusion* is brought about by others who wish to deceive or by mental illness. Whether the behaviour is childish or childlike depends on the attitude toward it. *Childlike* behaviour may be admirable. Childish behaviour is not. If you call someone *fat*, you are definitely not flattering that person. *Stout* is far less offensive.

Context

A word about the importance of context is in order. The meaning of a word is frequently changed by the other words in the phrase or sentence in which it appears. As we have seen, the word *sheer* has different meanings when it is associated with *stocking* (transparently thin), *cliff* (steep), or *nonsense* (complete).

You will have to identify those words which are out of place in the given sentence because their *context* (the words they appear with) makes them so. For example, it might be said that a price is exorbitant (unreasonable) but behaviour never is.

You *ride* a horse but *drive* a car.
You *celebrate* a wedding but *conduct* a funeral.
You *return* a favour but *retaliate* an insult.

What this all adds up to is—you never really know a word unless you also know how it fits in with the other words near it.

Note the *different* uses of the *same* word in the following sentences:

1. When the *baby* was awake, I told my husband not to *baby* her.
2. She is *cold* to me when I catch a *cold.*
3. The actor made a *scene* when his performance in the last *scene* of the play was poorly received by the audience.

4. Hotel accommodations sometimes *trip* up the person who is planning a *trip.*
5. The man was *game* to try hunting big *game.*
6. I have to *hand* it to him since I never expected him to win her *hand* in marriage.
7. The fans *scored* the manager because the game ended in a tie *score.*
8. The *run* of the train took it past many historical sites and it made the *run* in three hours.
9. The *plain* fact is that she has a *plain* face.
10. Her *set* ways *set* her apart from her friends.
11. The politician was *open* to criticism because of his *open* mind on some issues.
12. I *love* to win a set in tennis, six-*love.*

Shades of Meaning: Denotation and Connotation

Sometimes your choice of words is complicated by the fact that very many words in English have an implied meaning, a meaning beyond the specific one that appeals to our mind, one that affects our feelings and our imagination. The ***specifically stated meaning*** *is the one you find in a dictionary.* It is generally exact, leaving little to the imagination. We call that the word's *denotation.* The extra ***implied meaning***, *the meaning suggested by or associated with a word in addition to its specific meaning* is its *connotation.* This additional suggested meaning may affect people in different ways so its effect is sometimes unpredictable, but most connotations are either favourable or unfavourable. This little rhyme should help make the meaning of connotation clear.

> Call a woman a *lamb*, but never a *sheep;*
> *Economical* she likes, but you can't call her *cheap.*
> You can say she's a *vision*, but don't say she's a *sight;*
> And no woman is *skinny;* she's *slender* and *slight.*

Sheep has a connotation of stupidity, defencelessness, and meekness, an unfavourable connotation. *Lamb* has a connotation of a loved person, a dear one. *Cheap* connotes stinginess; *economical* means thrifty. A *sight* suggests someone or something that is most unpleasant or unusual in appearance. A *vision*, when referring to a woman, connotes extraordinary beauty. Finally, *skinny* implies an unattractive thinness or lack of flesh as contrasted with the attractive connotation of a *slender* or *slight* slim, trim figure.

Here are a number of pairs of expressions which have varying connotations, all of which can be favourable. Which do you prefer in the suggested context? (Our preferences will follow, although they need not be yours.)

1. craftsmanship—proficiency (in car manufacture)
2. smooth on—apply (makeup)
3. styling—design (of furniture)
4. treasured—valuable (traditions)
5. subtle—suggestive (colours)
6. exotic—rare (ingredients)
7. create—make (a product)
8. vital—important (contribution)
9. astounded—surprised (by the change)
10. texture—surface (of the skin)
11. modern—up-to-date (kitchen)
12. glowing—shining (look)
13. tangy—tasty (food)
14. gleaming—bright (stemware)
15. old-fashioned—conservative (dress)

Our preferences are:

1. craftsmanship
2. smooth on
3. design
4. treasured
5. subtle
6. exotic
7. create
8. vital
9. astounded
10. texture
11. modern
12. glowing
13. tangy
14. gleaming
15. conservative

Try to choose the word in the following pairs with the more favourable connotation.

1. colourful—gaudy
2. firm—stubborn
3. fat—portly
4. shy—sullen
5. politician—statesman
6. promoter—impresario
7. impartial—straddling
8. crusader—agitator
9. flabby—loose
10. feminine—effeminate
11. opponents—antagonists
12. lazy—idle
13. defeat—rout
14. unusual—outlandish
15. gruff—rude
16. neat—fussy
17. lie—fib
18. spend—squander

The more favourable connotations are associated with these words:

1. colourful
2. firm
3. portly
4. shy
5. statesman
6. impresario
7. impartial
8. crusader
9. loose
10. feminine
11. opponents
12. idle
13. defeat
14. unusual
15. gruff
16. neat
17. fib
18. spend

WORDS CONFUSED AND MISUSED

Many pairs of words, for one reason or another, are frequently confused or misused. It may be that they look alike or sound alike, or it may be that they are similar in meaning but have widely differing suitable contexts.

We have selected those pairs which are most widely confused and misused. Study the distinctions between them. Examples of the correct use of each member of the pair are given.

Accept, Except

Accept is most frequently used as a verb meaning "to receive something" or "to agree to something." **Except** is most frequently used as a preposition meaning "leaving out." The use of *except* as a verb meaning "to leave out" is rare.

EXAMPLE: He was chosen to *accept* the gift.
EXAMPLE: Everyone came *except* him.

Adapt, Adopt

You **adapt** something when you change it or adjust it to fit or work in a new situation. You **adopt** something when you take it over completely without any change or adjustment.

EXAMPLE: The immigrant *adapted* his habits to the way of life in his new country.
EXAMPLE: The Senate *adopted* the proposal without modification.

Affect, Effect

Affect is most frequently used as a verb meaning "to influence." **Effect** is most frequently used as a noun meaning "result." (The use of effect as a verb meaning "to bring about" is rare.)

EXAMPLE: Climate and topography *affect* the life of people everywhere.
EXAMPLE: The war had a far-reaching *effect* on the entire people.

Aggravate, Irritate

The verb **aggravate** means to make worse. The verb **irritate** means to annoy. In general, a person is *irritated;* a situation or a condition is *aggravated.*

EXAMPLE: Constant rubbing tended to *aggravate* the already painful wound.
EXAMPLE: The behaviour of the child *irritated* all the guests.

Allusion, Illusion

An **allusion** is an indirect reference to something, often a literary work or a literary character. An **illusion** is a wrong idea or a misconception.

EXAMPLE: He made an *allusion* to the herculean efforts of the leader.
EXAMPLE: The loser continued under the *illusion* that he won the contest.

Already, All Ready

Already is an adverb of time meaning previously. **All ready** means exactly what the two words indicate—all prepared.

EXAMPLE: When I arrived, he had *already* left.
EXAMPLE: When I arrived, I found them *all ready* for the meeting.

Altogether, All Together

Altogether is an adverb of degree meaning completely. **All together** means exactly what the two words indicate—all the persons in a group.

EXAMPLE: He was *altogether* unprepared for the assignment.
EXAMPLE: We found the team *all together* in the locker room.

Among, Between

Among is used when more than two persons or things are involved. **Between** is used when only two persons or things are involved. (You needn't be concerned with the rare exceptions to these rules.)

EXAMPLE: Frank, Joe, and Ed shared the expenses *among* them.
EXAMPLE: Jane and Joan shared the expenses *between* them.

Amount, Number

Amount is used for things or ideas which cannot be counted, and is usually followed by a singular noun—money, talent, courage. **Number** is used for things which can be counted.

EXAMPLE: Sue carried a large *amount* of cash.
EXAMPLE: The *number* of accidents this year is greater than we thought.
EXAMPLE: I needed a large *amount* of money.
EXAMPLE: I needed a large *number* of dollars to pay my bills.

In the one sentence, the word *money* is thought of as a single unit. In the other, the word *dollars* is thought of as individual items which can be counted.

Around, About

Around is correctly used to indicate direction in a circle around an object. **About** should be used when number or size is indicated.

EXAMPLE: They walked *around* the house.
EXAMPLE: There were *about* 50,000 fans in the stadium.
EXAMPLE: The rug was *about* three metres wide.

As, Like

Only **as** can introduce a clause. **Like** cannot serve as a conjunction to introduce a clause; it is most frequently used as a preposition meaning "similar to."

EXAMPLE:
WRONG: This cereal tastes good *like* a cereal should.
CORRECT: This cereal tastes good *as* a cereal should.
EXAMPLE:
CORRECT: He wanted everyone to be *like* him.

Avenge, Revenge

Avenge is used where the intention is to right a wrong; there is a moral purpose involved. **Revenge** involves inflicting punishment in return for insult or injury, thus receiving personal satisfaction.

EXAMPLE: He set out to *avenge* the wrong done his father.
EXAMPLE: In the feud between the families, the McCoys set out to *revenge* the death of one of their number.

Beat, Bet

Beat means to defeat. **Bet** means to wager, or to gamble something of value, on the result of a game.

EXAMPLE: Frank *beat* Jacques in straight sets in their tennis match.
EXAMPLE: I *bet* five dollars that Joan would outrun Jane.

Beside, Besides

Beside means "at the side of." **Besides** means "in addition."

EXAMPLE: He came over to sit *beside* me.
EXAMPLE: There were nine others present *besides* Joe.

Borrow, Lend

Borrow means that the borrower is on the taking end of the transaction. **Lend** means that the lender is on the giving end of the transaction.

EXAMPLE: Please let me *borrow* ten dollars from you.
EXAMPLE: I'll be glad to *lend* the ten dollars to you.

Both, Each

Both refers to two objects taken together. **Each** refers to one or more objects taken individually.

EXAMPLE: *Both* my pens cost ten dollars.
(*Note:* Don't use *both* in the above example if you mean that the cost of the two pens was twenty dollars. *Both* means the pair of pens.)
EXAMPLE: *Each* of my pens cost five dollars.

Bring, Take

Bring is used when the movement in the sentence is towards the speaker or the writer. **Take** is used when the movement in the sentence is away from the speaker or the writer.

EXAMPLE: *Bring* the pencils to me, please.
EXAMPLE: *Take* these books to the principal's office.

Can, May

Can is used to indicate the knowledge or ability to do something. **May** is used when permission is sought to do something, most frequently in the form of a question.

EXAMPLE: I *can* tie a slip knot.
EXAMPLE: *May* I have the car tonight?

Capital, Capitol

Capital refers to a city where a national or state government is located. **Capitol** refers to a building where the governing body meets.

EXAMPLE: London is the *capital* of Great Britain
EXAMPLE: The *Capitol* is located in Washington, D.C., the *capital* of the United States.

Continual, Continuous

Continual refers to something which is repeated often with stops in between. **Continuous** refers to something which goes on without interruption.

> **EXAMPLE:** The game was *continually* interrupted by showers.
> **EXAMPLE:** The sun shone *continuously* for eight hours.

Counsel, Council

A **counsel** refers to a lawyer or a consultant who gives advice. As a verb, to *counsel* means "to give advice." A **council** is a group of people brought together to discuss and/or take action on a given matter.

> **EXAMPLE:** Jules was *counsel* to the investigating commission.
> **EXAMPLE:** The city *council* met to take up the problem of vandalism.

Disinterested, Uninterested

Disinterested refers to someone who has nothing to gain personally from a particular activity. He may be very much interested (concerned) in the matter. **Uninterested** refers to someone who is lacking interest or concern in an activity.

> **EXAMPLE:** The referee was a *disinterested* participant in the game.
> **EXAMPLE:** The students were *uninterested* in the work of the class.

Dumb, Stupid

Dumb properly means not having the power of speech, as in "deaf and dumb." **Stupid** means not having normal intelligence.

> **EXAMPLE:** The *dumb* man had to use sign language to communicate.
> **EXAMPLE:** The mute was not *stupid* by any means.

Emigrate, Immigrate

Emigrate means to leave one country permanently to settle in another; one who does so is an *emigrant.* **Immigrate** means to enter a new country to settle there; one who does so is an *immigrant.*

> **EXAMPLE:** Because they were being persecuted for their religious beliefs, the family decided to *emigrate* from their country.
> **EXAMPLE:** The persecuted family *immigrated* to Canada to begin a new life in freedom.

Fever, Temperature

A **fever** is an abnormally high body temperature, generally a symptom of some kind of illness. A **temperature** is the degree of heat of a person's body. (Don't use *temperature* when you mean *fever.* "Does the patient have a *fever*?" Everyone has a body temperature.)

EXAMPLE: The baby ran a high *fever* because of the infection.
EXAMPLE: His *temperature* was a normal 37° Celsius.

Fewer, Less

The correct use of these words follows the same rules as those indicated for **amount** and **number.** **Fewer** is used for things which can be counted. **Less** is used for things or ideas which cannot be counted. (Note that *less* is usually followed by a singular noun, *fewer* by a plural noun.)

EXAMPLE: The number of accidents this year is *fewer* than we thought.
EXAMPLE: We enjoyed *less* freedom this year than last.

Flaunt, Flout

Flaunt means to show something off boldly and conspicuously in an offensive way. **Flout** means to show scorn for something, usually an established custom or rule.

EXAMPLE: The rich man *flaunted* his wealth by driving expensive cars.
EXAMPLE: The man *flouted* tradition by walking under a ladder.

Hanged, Hung

Hanged refers to a specific kind of execution which has taken place. **Hung** refers to something which has been suspended from an object.

EXAMPLE: The murderer was *hanged.*
EXAMPLE: The picture was *hung* on the hook attached to the wall.

Healthy, Healthful

Healthy refers to a condition of people. **Healthful** refers to anything which helps to produce or maintain health.

EXAMPLE: The doctor found the patient to be *healthy.*
EXAMPLE: The doctor recommended lots of *healthful* exercise.

Imply, Infer

Imply is used to indicate that the speaker or the writer is making a hint or suggestion. **Infer** is used to indicate that the hint or suggestion made by the speaker was taken by the audience, which drew a conclusion from it.

EXAMPLE: I mean to *imply* that he didn't get the job done.
EXAMPLE: I *infer* from your remarks that he was lazy.

In, Into

In is used to indicate that something is already at a place. **Into** is used to indicate that someone or something is moving from the outside to the inside of a place.

EXAMPLE: The dog is *in* the living room.
EXAMPLE: The dog dashed *into* the living room from the kitchen.

Latest, Last

Latest means the most recent in a series. **Last** means final.

EXAMPLE: The popular candidate was seen talking with his *latest* rival.
EXAMPLE: He appeared on television for the *last* time before his retirement.

Learn, Teach

Learn is used to indicate that knowledge or behaviour is being acquired. **Teach** is used to indicate that knowledge or behaviour is being provided.

EXAMPLE: He tried to *learn* how to speak softly.
EXAMPLE: I tried to *teach* him how to speak softly.

Liable, Likely

Likely is used to indicate the probability that something will happen. **Liable** is used in two ways. It can indicate legal responsibility; it can also indicate an undesirable possibility.

EXAMPLE: He is *likely* to receive the medal.
EXAMPLE: If you drive too quickly, you are *liable* to a fine.
EXAMPLE: If you don't study, you are *liable* to fail the course.

Myself, Me

Myself may be used properly in one of two ways. It can be used for emphasis, or it can be used as the object of an action verb with "I" as the subject. (*Never* use "myself" when "I" or "me" should be used.)

EXAMPLE: I *myself* will attend to this matter.
EXAMPLE: I hit *myself* in the hand.
EXAMPLE:
WRONG: He gave the awards to Frank and myself.
CORRECT: He gave the awards to Frank and me.
EXAMPLE:
WRONG: Frank and myself will get the awards.
CORRECT: Frank and I will get the awards.

Persecute, Prosecute

Persecute means to oppress a person or a people deliberately. **Prosecute** means to take court action against someone.

EXAMPLE: Dictatorships *persecute* minority groups which oppose the government.
EXAMPLE: The constable decided to *prosecute* the drug dealer.

Pour, Spill

Pour means to cause a liquid to flow deliberately. **Spill** means to cause a liquid to flow accidentally or unintentionally.

EXAMPLE: The host *poured* coffee for her guests.
EXAMPLE: The host was embarrassed when she *spilled* the coffee on her guest's dress.

Practical, Practicable

Practical refers to something which can be made to serve a useful purpose. **Practicable** refers to something which can be made to operate but which may not be practical.

EXAMPLE: He found it *practicable* to extract gold from ocean water but the costs involved made the whole procedure not a *practical* one.

Precede, Proceed

Precede means "to come or go before" something or someone. **Proceed** means "to go on," particularly after an interruption.

EXAMPLE: Kim Campbell *preceded* Jean Chrétien as Prime Minister of Canada.
EXAMPLE: The speaker *proceeded,* after he was interrupted by a heckler.

Principal, Principle

Principal may be used in two ways. It can denote the head of a school, or it can be used as an adjective meaning "the main" or "the most important." **Principle** may be used to indicate a law or a rule of conduct.

EXAMPLE: The *principal* addressed the teachers and the parents.
EXAMPLE: He was the *principal* speaker at the graduation exercises.
EXAMPLE: We are dedicated to the *principle* that all men are created equal.

Quite, Quiet

Quite may be used as an adverb meaning "completely" or "very." **Quiet** may be used only as an adjective meaning "still" or "calm."

EXAMPLE: He was *quite* angry when he lost the game.
EXAMPLE: After his fit of temper, he became *quiet.*

Raise, Rise

Raise means to lift or bring up something or someone. **Rise** means to get up or go up; it does not take an object.

EXAMPLE: The guard *raised* his rifle when he heard a sound.
EXAMPLE: He *rises* in the morning when the sun rises.

Rob, Steal

One is said to **rob** a person or an *institution* such as a bank by taking property or valuables from it. One is said to **steal** *an object* such as personal property or valuables from someone or some institution.

EXAMPLE: The criminal was caught in the act of trying to *rob* the bank.
EXAMPLE: The criminal tried to *steal* the man's wallet.

Set, Sit

Set means to put something in a certain place. **Sit** means to be seated.

EXAMPLE: The delivery person *set* the packages on the kitchen floor.
EXAMPLE: Please *sit* in this chair.

Stand, Stay

You **stand** when you are on your feet. (The past tense is *stood*.) You **stay** when you remain at a given place. (The past tense is *stayed*.)

EXAMPLE: He *stood* all the way home in the bus.
EXAMPLE: He *stayed* at the stadium until the game was over.

Stationary, Stationery

Stationary means not moving or still. **Stationery** refers to writing paper, envelopes, and other office supplies.

EXAMPLE: The *stationary* animal provided an excellent target for the hunter.
EXAMPLE: The student bought his notebooks at the *stationery* store.

AVOID 10 FREQUENT ERRORS IN DICTION

RULES	EXAMPLES	
1. **DON'T USE** the expression *being that*. Instead, use a conjunction such as *because* or *since*.	**WRONG:**	Being that he was first, he won the prize.
	CORRECT:	*Since* he was first, he won the prize.
2. **DON'T USE** the expressions *could of*, *should of*, or *would of*. Instead, use the correct expressions (using *have*) for which these aural distortions are the incorrect substitutions.	**WRONG:**	He could of been the winner if he had tried.
	CORRECT:	He *could have* been the winner if he had tried.
3. **DON'T USE** the expression *different than*. Instead, use *different from*.	**WRONG:**	Playing baseball is different than playing softball.
	CORRECT:	Playing baseball is *different from* playing softball.

RULES	EXAMPLES
4. DON'T USE idioms with incorrect prepositions.	WRONG: May I borrow a dollar off you? CORRECT: May I borrow a dollar *from* you? WRONG: Come over our house for a party. CORRECT: Come *to* our house for a party.
5. DON'T USE *don't* in the third person singular. Use *doesn't* since it is the contraction of *does not*.	WRONG: He don't belong here. CORRECT: He *doesn't* belong here.
6. DON'T use *due to* as part of an adverbial phrase. Use *due to* as an adjective which modifies or is the predicate adjective referring to a noun.	WRONG: Due to overeating, he was heavy. CORRECT: His heaviness was *due to* overeating. WRONG: He was late due to the traffic. CORRECT: He was late *because of* the traffic.
7. DON'T USE the expression *had ought*. Use *ought* alone since it expresses obligation or duty without the need for any other word.	WRONG: I had ought to write to my parents. CORRECT: I *ought* to write to my parents.
8. DON'T USE any article after the expressions *kind of* and *sort of*.	WRONG: He's not the kind of a person I like. CORRECT: He's not the *kind of* person I like.
9. DON'T USE the expression *the reason is because*. Use *the reason is that* since the words *reason* and *because* both have similar meanings; a *reason* is indeed a cause.	WRONG: The reason he left is because he did not get a raise. CORRECT: The *reason* he left *is that* he did not get a raise.
10. DON'T USE *who's* when you want to use *whose*. *Whose* should be used to show possession. *Who's* is a contraction of *who is*.	WRONG: I know who's book this is. CORRECT: I know *whose* book this is.

PRACTICE WITH CONFUSED AND MISUSED WORDS

Directions: **In each sentence, five parts are underlined and numbered. Where there is an error in usage, blacken in the answer grid the number of the underlined part which contains the error. If there are no errors, blacken number 5. This kind of error is included in the sentence correction type of multiple-choice item.**

1. "Have no allusions (1) about getting something for nothing" was (2) the advice given us (3) by the principal (4) speaker. No error (5)

1. 1 2 3 4 5 || || || || ||

2. The number (1) of persons present this time was (2) much different than (3) the number which (4) came last time. No error (5)

2. 1 2 3 4 5 || || || || ||

3. Fewer visitors were allowed in our hospital than yours. No error
(1) (2) (3) (4) (5)

3. 1 2 3 4 5

4. We were already to leave as we had been instructed had it not been for him and her. No error
(1) (2) (3) (4) (5)

4. 1 2 3 4 5

5. Bring this book to whoever you think is most deserving besides me. No error
(1) (2) (3) (4) (5)

5. 1 2 3 4 5

6. He awoke to find less people at the party than he thought he had invited. No error
(1) (2) (3) (4) (5)

6. 1 2 3 4 5

7. The speaker tried to infer that the uninterested audience had hardly been fair to the manner in which he had dealt with the topic. No error
(1) (2) (3) (4) (5)

7. 1 2 3 4 5

8. The disinterested student laid the book down beside him and dozed off while the teacher spoke. No error
(1) (2) (3) (4) (5)

8. 1 2 3 4 5

9. The consensus of us fans was that Bobby Orr had broken the record we thought was most liable to stand. No error
(1) (2) (3) (4) (5)

9. 1 2 3 4 5

10. Louis and I asked Yolande and him whether they'd except the gift. No error
(1) (2) (3) (4) (5)

10. 1 2 3 4 5

11. Of him and myself, he was the brighter and the more shy. No error.
(1) (2) (3) (4) (5)

11. 1 2 3 4 5

12. I have been living in Toronto continuously for the past five years because of the healthy climate. No error
(1) (2) (3) (4) (5)

12. 1 2 3 4 5

13. Anyone may ask a question about any problem bothering him because it's the kind of situation which is most aggravating. No error.
(1) (2) (3) (4) (5)

13. 1 2 3 4 5

14. "Ours is better than yours" was the disinterested consensus of
(1) (2) (3) (4)
those gathered to consider the problem. No error
(5)

14. 1 2 3 4 5

15. She and I decided to add on the number of people required to
(1) (2) (3)
provide continuous supervision. No error
(4) (5)

15. 1 2 3 4 5

16. The principal speaker was all together unprepared to effect the
(1) (2) (3)
necessary contact with those who disagreed with him, including
me. No error
(4) (5)

16. 1 2 3 4 5

17. Francine is the kind of a person whom everyone likes despite the
(1) (2)
fact that it is she who is least likely to do anyone a favour. No error.
(3) (4) (5)

17. 1 2 3 4 5

18. Enclosed herein are cheques which cover all the expenses except
(1) (2) (3)
hers. No error
(4) (5)

18. 1 2 3 4 5

19. The obnoxious child aggravated his babysitter by crying
(1)
continuously, by lying on the floor and by dragging the dog by its
(2) (3) (4)
tail. No error
(5)

19. 1 2 3 4 5

20. Give the book to whoever asks for it despite the large number of
(1) (2)
requests and say it is a gift from him and myself. No error
(3) (4) (5)

20. 1 2 3 4 5

21. My plans, alas, failed to provide a practicable answer to the
(1) (2)
problem whose solution I had sought for many years. No error
(3) (4) (5)

21. 1 2 3 4 5

22. She insists it is I who am mistaken about the effect of an order on
(1) (2)
those who have less responsibilities than I. No error
(3) (4) (5)

22. 1 2 3 4 5

23. He considered it altogether likely that less accidents would occur
(1) (2) (3)
this year than last since the speed limit was changed. No error
(4) (5)

23. 1 2 3 4 5

24. Hector felt that, among (1) the three of us who ran for office, the number (2) of votes should have proven (3) that the winners were Henri and myself (4). No error (5).

24. 1 2 3 4 5

25. Inside of (1) the house, besides (2) my brother and me (3), were (4) two guests and a friend. No error (5)

25. 1 2 3 4 5

Turn to the answer key and the answer analysis which follow.

What's Your Score?

______ right,	______ wrong
Excellent	24–25
Good	21–23
Fair	17–20

If you scored lower, restudy this section, concentrating on the differences between the pairs of words and the ten errors in diction to avoid.

ANSWER KEY

Practice with Confused and Misused Words/Page 198

1. **1**	6. **2**	11. **2**	16. **2**	21. **5**
2. **3**	7. **1**	12. **4**	17. **1**	22. **3**
3. **2**	8. **1**	13. **4**	18. **1**	23. **3**
4. **1**	9. **4**	14. **5**	19. **1**	24. **4**
5. **1**	10. **4**	15. **2**	20. **4**	25. **1**

ANSWER ANALYSIS

Practice with Confused and Misused Words/Page 198

1. **1** The word required here is *illusions* or *wrong ideas*.
2. **3** Use *different from* rather than *different than*.
3. **2** *Into* must be used to indicate that the visitors are moving from the outside to the inside of the hospital.
4. **1** *All ready* must be used in the meaning of *all* prepared.
5. **1** *Take* should be used when the movement in the sentence is away from the speaker or writer.
6. **2** *Fewer* is used for things that can be counted.
7. **1** *Imply* is used to indicate that the speaker is making a hint.
8. **1** *Uninterested* refers to someone who is lacking in interest in an activity.
9. **4** *Likely* is used to indicate the probability that something will or will not happen.
10. **4** *Accept* is used to mean *receive something*.
11. **2** Never use *myself* when *me* should be used.
12. **4** *Healthful* refers to anything that helps to maintain health.
13. **4** The verb *irritate* should be used since the required meaning is *annoying*.
14. **5** No error.

15. **2** Don't use extra words, such as *on*.
16. **2** *Altogether* is an adverb meaning *completely*, and describes *unprepared.*
17. **1** Don't use an article after the expression *kind of*.
18. **1** Don't use extra words. The use of *enclosed* makes the word *herein* unnecessary. Similarly, the use of *herein* makes *enclosed* unnecessary. Use either, but not both.
19. **1** The verb *irritate*, meaning to *annoy*, should be used.
20. **4** Since neither emphasis nor an object of an action verb is required, *me* should be used.
21. **5** No error.
22. **3** *Fewer* is used for things that can be counted.
23. **3** *Fewer* should be used since the number of accidents can be counted.
24. **4** Since neither emphasis nor an object of an action is needed in this sentence, *I* should be used.
25. **1** The word *of* is not needed.

BUILDING YOUR VOCABULARY

To help you build your vocabulary, you should try to use the English language as much as possible both in writing essays and stories and in speaking to others. Another essential aid is a thesaurus (e.g., Roget's *Thesaurus*) or a good dictionary (such as the *Canadian Dictionary of the English Language*). They will provide both the literal and other meanings of each word. Both books should be your constant companions as you improve your writing skills and expand your vocabulary.

A BASIC 1,100-WORD VOCABULARY

To help you build your vocabulary, we have selected 1,100 words which every high school graduate should know. They are grouped into lists of nouns, verbs, and adjectives. You should use these lists and the definitions together with a good dictionary such as *Webster's New World Dictionary of the American Language.* (See page 14 for hints on using the dictionary.) For each new word, we have provided a definition which is most widely used but is often far removed from the first or literal meaning. You may wish to study other meanings of each word. We have also provided many words, sentences or phrases to show you the context in which the particular word should be used.

300 Useful Nouns

ACCESS (means of) approach or admittance (e.g., to records)

ACCORD agreement

ADAGE proverb (as "Better late than never")

AFFLUENCE abundance; wealth (e.g., age of _____)

AGENDA list of things to be done or discussed (e.g., at a meeting)

ALACRITY brisk willingness (e.g., agreed with _____)

ALIAS assumed name (e.g., Fred Henry, _____ John Doe)

ANIMOSITY great hatred (e.g., towards strangers)

ANTHOLOGY collection of writings or other creative work such as songs

APATHY indifference (e.g., toward poverty)

APEX the highest point (e.g., _____ of a triangle)

ATLAS book of maps

AUDACITY boldness

AVARICE greed for wealth

AWE feeling of respect and wonder (e.g., in _____ of someone's power)

BEACON guiding light (e.g., of knowledge)

BENEDICTION blessing

BIGOTRY unwillingness to allow others to have different opinions and beliefs from one's own

BLEMISH defect (e.g., on one's record)

BONDAGE slavery

BOON benefit (e.g., a _____ to business)

BRAWL noisy fight

BREVITY shortness

BROCHURE pamphlet (e.g., a travel _____)

BULWARK strong protection (e.g., a _____ against corruption)

CALIBER quality (e.g., a person of high _____)

CAMOUFLAGE disguise, usually in war, by changing the appearance of persons or material

CASTE social class or distinction

CATASTROPHE sudden disaster (e.g., an earthquake)

CHAGRIN feeling of deep disappointment

CHRONICLE historical record

CLAMOUR uproar

CLEMENCY mercy (e.g., toward a prisoner)

CONDOLENCE expression of sympathy (e.g., extended _____ to a bereaved)

CONNOISSEUR expert judge (e.g., of paintings, food)

CONSENSUS general agreement

CONTEXT words or ideas just before or after a given word or idea (e.g., meaning of a word in a given _____)

CRITERION standard of judgment (e.g., good or poor by this _____)

CRUX the essential point (e.g., the _____ of the matter)

CYNIC one who doubts the good intentions of others

DATA known facts (e.g., _____ were found through research)

DEARTH scarcity (e.g., of talent)

DEBACLE general defeat (e.g., in a battle)

DEBUT first appearance before an audience (e.g., actor, pianist)

DELUGE great flood (e.g., rain or, in a special sense, mail)

DEPOT warehouse

DESTINY predetermined fate (e.g., it was his _____ to)

DETRIMENT damage or loss (e.g., it was to his _____)

DIAGNOSIS determining the nature of a disease or a situation

DICTION manner in which words are used in writing and speech (e.g., the radio announcer's _____ was excellent)

DILEMMA situation requiring a choice between two unpleasant courses of action (e.g., he was in a _____)

DIN loud continuing noise

DIRECTIVE a general order (e.g., from an executive or military commander)

DISCORD disagreement

DISCREPANCY inconsistency (e.g., in accounts, in testimony)

DISCRETION freedom of choice (e.g., he was given _____ to spend the money as he saw fit)

DISSENT difference of opinion (e.g., from a decision)

DROUGHT long spell of dry weather

EGOTIST one who judges everything only as it affects his own interest; a self-centered person

ELITE choice part (e.g., of society)

ENTERPRISE an important project

ENVIRONMENT surrounding influences of conditions

EPITOME typical representation (e.g., she was the _____ of beauty)

EPOCH period of time identified by an important person or event (e.g., the _____ of spaceflight)

ERA period of time marked by an important person or event (e.g., the Napoleonic _____)

ESSENCE basic nature (e.g., of the matter)

ETIQUETTE rules of social behaviour which are generally accepted

EXCERPT passage from a book or a document

EXODUS departure, usually of large numbers

FACET side or aspect (e.g., of a problem)

FACSIMILE exact copy

FALLACY mistaken idea; reasoning which contains an error

FANTASY imagination (e.g., he indulged in _____)

FEUD continued deadly hatred (e.g., between two families)

FIASCO complete humiliating failure

FIEND inhumanly cruel person

FINALE last part or performance

FLAIR natural talent (e.g., for sports)

FLAW defect

FOCUS central point (e.g., of attention)

FOE enemy

FORMAT physical appearance or arrangement (e.g., of a book)

FORTE one's strong point (e.g., school grades)

FORTITUDE steady courage (e.g., when in trouble)

FORUM a gathering for the discussion of public issues

FOYER entrance hall (e.g., to a building or dwelling)

FRAUD deliberate deception

FRICTION rubbing of the surface of one thing against the surface of another

FUNCTION purpose served by a person, object, or organization

FUROR outburst of excitement (e.g., over a discovery)

GAMUT the whole range (e.g., of experiences)

GAZETTEER geographical dictionary; usually accompanying an atlas

GENESIS origin (e.g., of a plan)

GHETTO section of a city where members of a particular group (formerly religious, now racial) live

GIST essential content (e.g., of a speech or an article)

GLUTTON one who overeats or who indulges in anything to excess

GRIEVANCE complaint made against someone responsible for a situation believed to be unjust

HAVOC great damage and destruction (e.g., wreak _____ on)

HAZARD danger

HERITAGE inheritance either of real wealth or of a tradition

HOAX deliberate attempt to trick someone either seriously or as a joke

HORDE crowd

HORIZON limit (of knowledge, experience, or ambition)

HUE shade of colour

HYSTERIA wild emotional outburst

IDIOM expression peculiar to a language which has a different meaning from the words which make it up (e.g., hit the road)

ILLUSION idea or impression different from reality

IMAGE likeness or reflected impression of a person or object

IMPETUS moving force

INCENTIVE spur or motive to do something (e.g., profit _____)

INCUMBENT present holder of an office

INFIRMITY physical defect

INFLUX flowing in (e.g., of money into banks, tourists into a country)

INFRACTION violation of a rule or a law

INITIATIVE desire or ability to make the first step in carrying out some action (often a new plan or idea)

INNOVATION introduction of a new idea or method

INTEGRITY moral and intellectual honesty and uprightness

INTERIM meantime (e.g., in the _____)

INTERLUDE period of time between two events (e.g., _____ between the acts of a play)

INTRIGUE secret plot

INTUITION knowledge through instinct rather than thought

IOTA very small amount

ITINERARY route followed on a trip, actual or planned

JEOPARDY risk of harm (e.g., put into _____)

KEYNOTE main theme (e.g., He sounded the _____ of the convention)

LARCENY theft (e.g., They couldn't decide whether it was grand or petty _____)

LAYMAN one who is not a member of a particular profession (e.g., from the point of view of a _____)

LEGACY material or spiritual inheritance (e.g., _____ from a parent)

LEGEND story or stories passed on from generation to generation and often considered to be true

LEGION large number

LIAISON contact between two or more groups (e.g., _____ between headquarters and field units)

LORE body of traditional knowledge (e.g., nature _____)

MALADY disease (e.g., incurable _____)

MANEUVER skillful move (e.g., a clever _____)

MANIA abnormal absorption (e.g., She had a _____ for clothes)

MARATHON contest requiring endurance

MAVERICK one who acts independently rather than according to an organizational pattern

MAXIM saying which provides a rule of conduct (e.g., Look before you leap)

MEDIUM means of communication (e.g., _____ of radio)

MEMENTO object which serves as a reminder (e.g., a _____ of the war)

METROPOLIS main city of a state or region (or any large city)

MILIEU surroundings

MORALE state of mind as it affects possible future action (e.g., The troops had good _____)

MORES well-established customs (e.g., the _____ of a society)

MULTITUDE a large number

MYRIAD a large number of varied people or things

MYTH a story which is a traditional explanation of some occurrence, usually in nature (e.g., the _____ of Atlas holding up the heavens)

NICHE a suitable and desirable place (e.g., He found his _____ in the business organization)

NOMAD wanderer

NOSTALGIA desire to return to past experiences or associations

OASIS a place which provides relief from the usual conditions (e.g., an _____ of peace in a troubled world)

OBLIVION place or condition in which one is completely forgotten

ODYSSEY long journey

OMEN something which is believed to predict a future event (e.g., an evil _____)

OPTIMUM the best possible quantity or quality (e.g., He participated to the _____)

OVATION enthusiastic reception usually accompanied by generous applause (e.g., He received a tumultuous _____)

OVERSIGHT failure to include something through carelessness (e.g., His name was omitted because of an _____)

OVERTURE first step which is intended to lead to others in either action or discussion (e.g., He made a peace _____)

PAGEANT public spectacle in the form of a stage performance or a parade (e.g., a historical _____)

PANACEA something considered a cure for all diseases or problems

PANORAMA a clear view of a very broad area

PARADOX statement of a truth which appears to contradict itself (e.g., a 20-year-old who had only five birthdays because he was born on February 29)

PASTIME way of spending leisure time (e.g., He took up golf as a _____)

PAUCITY scarcity (e.g., a _____ of nuclear scientists)

PAUPER very poor person

PEER an equal in age, social standing, ability or other feature

PHENOMENON an event that can be scientifically described, such as the tides

PHOBIA fear of something which is so great as to be unreasonable (e.g., _____ against cats)

PHYSIQUE build (of the human body)

PILGRIMAGE long trip to some place worthy of respect or devotion

PINNACLE highest point (e.g., the _____ of power)

PITFALL trap

PITTANCE very small sum of money (e.g., He survived on a _____)

PLATEAU area of level land located at a height

PLIGHT condition, usually unfavourable (e.g., the sorry _____ of the refugees)

POISE calm and controlled manner of behaviour (e.g., He showed _____ in difficult situations)

POPULACE the common people

POSTERITY future generations (e.g., leave a peaceful world to our _____)

PRECEDENT event or regulation which serves as an example or provides the basis for approval of a later action (e.g., set a _____)

PREDICAMENT unpleasant situation from which it is difficult to free oneself (e.g., He found himself in a _____)

PREFACE introductory statement to a book or speech

PRELUDE something which is preliminary to some act or work which is more important

PREMISE statement from which a conclusion is logically drawn (e.g., Granted the _____ that . . . , we may conclude . . .)

PREMIUM amount added to the usual payment or charge (e.g., He paid a _____ for the seats)

PRESTIGE respect achieved through rank, achievement, or reputation

PRETEXT reason given as a cover-up for the true purpose of an action (e.g., He gave as a _____ for stealing it, his sentimental attachment to the ring)

PRIORITY something which comes before others in importance (e.g., He gave _____ to his studies)

PROCESS step-by-step system for accomplishing some purpose (e.g., the _____ of legislation)

PROSPECT outlook for the future (e.g., the _____ of peace)

PROVISO requirement that something be done, usually made in writing

PROWESS superior ability (e.g., _____ in athletics)

PROXIMITY nearness

PSEUDONYM assumed name, usually by an author (e.g., Mark Twain, _____ of Samuel Clemens)

PUN play on words depending on two different meanings or sounds of the same word (e.g., Whether life is worth living depends on the *liver*)

QUALM uneasy doubt about some action (e.g., He had a _____ about running for office)

QUANDARY uncertainty over a choice between two courses of action (e.g., He was in a _____ between the careers of law or medicine)

QUERY question

QUEST search (e.g., _____ for knowledge)

RAPPORT harmonious relationship (e.g., _____ between teacher and pupil)

RARITY something not commonly found (e.g., A talent like his is a _____)

REFUGE place to which one can go for protection (e.g., He found _____ in the church)

REMNANT remaining part (e.g., _____ of the troops)

REMORSE deep feeling of guilt for some bad act (e.g., He felt _____ at having insulted his friend)

RENDEZVOUS a meeting or a place for meeting

RENOWN fame (e.g., an actor of great _____)

REPAST meal

REPLICA an exact copy (e.g., _____ of a painting)

REPRIMAND severe criticism in the form of a scolding (e.g., He received a _____ from his superior)

REPRISAL return of something in kind (e.g., _____ for an injury—"An eye for an eye")

RESIDUE remainder

RESOURCES assets, either material or spiritual, which are available for use

RESPITE temporary break which brings relief (e.g., from work)

RÉSUMÉ summary

REVERENCE feeling of great respect (e.g., _____ for life)

ROBOT one who acts mechanically or like a mechanical man

ROSTER list of names (e.g., _____ of guests)

SABOTAGE deliberate damage to vital services of production and supply, usually to those of an enemy in wartime

SAGA long tale, usually of heroic deeds

SALUTATION greeting, written or spoken (e.g., The _____ of a letter may be "Dear Sir")

SANCTION approval, usually by proper authority

SARCASM use of cutting remarks

SATIRE attack upon evil or foolish behaviour by showing it to be ridiculous

SCAPEGOAT someone who is blamed for the bad deeds of others

SCENT distinctive smell

SCOPE entire area of action or thought (e.g., the _____ of the plan)

SCROLL roll of paper or parchment containing writing

SECT group of people having the same beliefs, usually religious

SEGMENT part or section of a whole (e.g., _____ of a population)

SEMBLANCE outward appearance (e.g., He gave the _____ of a scholar)

SEQUEL something that follows from what happened or was written before (e.g., _____ to a novel)

SHAM false imitation (e.g., His devotion was a _____ of true love)

SHEAF bundle either of grain or of papers

SHEEN luster (e.g., of furniture)

SILHOUETTE outline drawing in black

SITE location of an object or an action (e.g., original _____ of a building)

SLANDER untruth spoken or spread about someone which damages his reputation

SLOGAN motto which is associated with an action or a cause (e.g., Pike's Peak or Bust!)

SLOPE slant (e.g., _____ of a line)

SNARE trap

SOLACE comfort (e.g., She found _____ in work)

SPONSOR one who endorses and supports a person or an activity

SPUR something which moves one to act (e.g., a _____ to sacrifice)

STAMINA ability to fight off physical difficulties such as fatigue

STATURE height reached physically or morally (e.g., a man of great _____)

STATUS standing, social or professional

STIGMA mark of disgrace

STIMULUS any encouragement to act

STRATEGY skillful planning and execution (e.g., the _____ in a battle)

STRIFE conflict (e.g., _____ between labour and management)

SUMMIT the highest point (e.g., the _____ of his career)

SUPPLEMENT amount added to complete something (e.g., _____ to a budget)

SURVEY broad study of a topic (e.g., a _____ of employment)

SUSPENSE tenseness brought about by uncertainty as to what will happen

SYMBOL something which is used to stand for something else (e.g., Uncle Sam is a _____ of the United States)

SYMPTOM indication of something (e.g., _____ of disease)

SYNOPSIS brief summary

TACT ability to say and do the right thing socially

TACTICS skillful actions to achieve some purpose (e.g., The _____ he used to win were unfair)

TALLY record of a score or an account (e.g., the _____ of the receipts)

TANG strong taste or flavor

TECHNIQUE method or skill in doing work (e.g., the _____ of an artist)

TEMPERAMENT natural disposition, often to act in a contrary manner (e.g., He displayed a changeable _____)

TEMPO pace of activity (e.g., The _____ of life is increasing)

TENSION mental or emotional strain (e.g., He was under great _____)

THEME topic of a written work or a talk

THRESHOLD the starting point (e.g., the _____ of a career)

THRIFT ability to save money (e.g., He became wealthy because of _____)

TINT a shade of colour

TOKEN sign which stands for some object or feeling (e.g., a _____ of esteem)

TONIC something which is a source of energy or vigor

TRADITION customs and beliefs which are received by one generation from another

TRAIT distinguishing feature (e.g., _____ of character)

TRANSITION movement from one situation to another (e.g., _____ from dictatorship to democracy)

TRIBUNAL place of judgment such as a court

TRIBUTE showing of respect or gratitude (e.g., He paid a _____ to his parents)

TURMOIL disturbance (e.g., great _____ at the meeting)

TUTOR a private teacher

TYCOON wealthy and powerful businessman

ULTIMATUM a final ("Take it or leave it") offer

UNREST restless dissatisfaction

UPHEAVAL sudden overthrow, often violent

USAGE established practice or custom

UTENSIL implement which is of use (e.g., a kitchen _____)

UTOPIA ideal place or society

VALOUR courage

VENTURE something involving risk

VICINITY neighbourhood

VICTOR winner

VIGOUR vitality

VIM energy

VOW solemn pledge

WAGER bet

WHIM sudden notion or desire

WOE great sorrow (e.g., He brought _____ to his friends)

WRATH intense anger (e.g., He poured his _____ on his enemies)

ZEAL eager desire

ZENITH the highest point

ZEST keen enthusiasm (e.g., _____ for competition)

300 Useful Verbs

ABHOR hate

ABSOLVE free from guilt (e.g., for a crime)

ACCEDE agree to (e.g., a request)

ACCELERATE speed up

ACCOST go up and speak to

ADHERE give support to (e.g., a cause)

ADJOURN put off to a later time (e.g., a meeting)

ADVOCATE act in support of (e.g., revolution)

ALLAY calm (e.g., fears)

ALLEGE claim

ALLOT assign (e.g., a share)

ALLUDE refer to (e.g., a book)

ALTER change

ASSENT agree

ATONE make up for (e.g., a sin)

AUGMENT add to

AVERT prevent

BAFFLE puzzle

BAN forbid

BAR exclude

BEFALL happen to

BERATE scold

BESEECH plead

BESTOW grant (used with on or upon)

CEDE give up (e.g., territory)

CENSURE blame

CHAR scorch

CHASTISE punish

CHIDE scold

CITE mention in order to prove something

COERCE force

COLLABORATE work with someone

COMMEND praise

COMPLY act in answer to (e.g., a request)

CONCEDE admit that something is true (e.g., an argument)

CONCUR agree

CONSTRICT squeeze

CULL pick out

CURTAIL cut short or reduce

DEDUCE make a conclusion from given facts

DEEM consider

DEFER postpone

DEFRAY pay (e.g., the costs)

DELETE remove or erase (e.g., a word)

DELVE investigate

DEPLETE use up

DEPLORE be sorry about

DEPRIVE keep someone from having or getting something

DESPISE scorn

DETAIN delay temporarily

DETECT uncover something that is not obvious

DETER keep someone from doing something

DETEST hate

DETRACT take away from

DEVOUR eat up greedily

DIGRESS depart from the subject under consideration

DILUTE weaken by adding something less strong to the original (e.g., a mixture)

DISBURSE pay out

DISCERN make out clearly (e.g., a pattern)

DISDAIN look down on with scorn

DISINTEGRATE fall apart

DISMAY dishearten

DISPEL drive away

DISPERSE scatter

DISRUPT break up

DISTORT present incorrectly (e.g., facts)

DIVERGE go in different directions

DIVERT turn from a course (e.g., a stream)

DIVULGE reveal

DON put on (e.g., clothing)

EFFACE blot out

EFFECT bring about

EJECT throw out

ELATE make happy

EMIT give forth (e.g., sounds)

ENCOUNTER meet

ENCROACH intrude on (e.g., property)

ENDEAVOR try

ENDOW provide with (e.g., a desirable quality)

ENHANCE increase the value of

ENSUE follow as a result

ENTREAT plead

ERR make a mistake

ERUPT break out

ESTEEM value

EVADE avoid or escape from someone or something

EVICT expel

EXALT raise to greater heights

EXCEED surpass

EXPEDITE speed up the handling of

EXPLOIT take advantage of a situation or a person

EXTOL praise highly

FALTER stumble

FAMISH starve

FEIGN pretend

FLAUNT show off

FLOURISH thrive

FLOUT defy mockingly

FOIL prevent

FORGO do without

FORSAKE abandon

FRUSTRATE prevent someone from achieving something

GAUGE estimate

HARASS disturb constantly

HEAVE lift and throw

HEED pay attention to (e.g., advice)

HINDER keep back

HOVER hang in the air above a certain spot

HURL throw with force

IGNITE set fire to

IMMERSE plunge into a liquid

IMPAIR damage

IMPEDE stand in the way of

IMPLY suggest

INCITE arouse

INCUR bring upon oneself (e.g., criticism)

INDUCE persuade

INDULGE satisfy (e.g., a desire)

INFER come to a conclusion based on something known

INHIBIT restrain

INSTIGATE spur to action

INSTILL put a feeling into someone gradually (e.g., fear)

INTERCEPT interrupt something (or someone) which is on its way

INTERROGATE question

INTIMIDATE frighten by making threats

INVOKE call upon

IRK annoy

JAR shake up (e.g., as in a collision)

JEER poke fun at (e.g., by sarcastic remarks)

LAMENT feel sorrow for

LAUNCH set in motion

LOOM appear in a threatening manner

LOP cut off

LURE tempt

LURK remain hidden

MAGNIFY make larger

MAIM cripple

MIMIC imitate

MOCK ridicule

MOLEST bother

NARRATE tell (e.g., a story)

NAVIGATE steer (e.g., a ship)

NEGATE deny

ORIENT adjust oneself or someone to a situation

OUST expel

PARCH make dry

PEER look closely

PEND remain undecided

PERFECT complete

PERPLEX puzzle

PERSEVERE continue on a course of action despite difficulties

PERTAIN have reference to

PERTURB upset to a great extent

PERUSE read carefully

PINE long for

PLACATE make calm

PONDER think through thoroughly

PRECLUDE prevent something from happening

PRESCRIBE order (e.g., for use or as a course of action)

PRESUME take for granted

PREVAIL win out over

PROBE investigate thoroughly

PROCURE obtain

PROFESS claim with doubtful sincerity

PROSPER be successful

PROTRUDE project

PROVOKE arouse to action out of irritation

PRY look closely into

QUELL subdue

RAVAGE ruin

REBATE give back, usually part of an amount paid

REBUFF repulse

REBUKE disapprove sharply

RECEDE move backward

RECOMPENSE repay

RECONCILE bring together by setting differences

RECOUP make up for (e.g., something lost)

RECTIFY correct

RECUR happen again

REDEEM buy back; make good a promise

REFRAIN keep from

REFUTE prove false

REIMBURSE pay back

REITERATE repeat

REJECT refuse to take

RELINQUISH give up

REMINISCE recall past happenings

REMIT send (e.g., money)

REMUNERATE pay for work done

RENOUNCE give up (e.g., a claim)

RENOVATE restore (e.g., a house)

REPENT feel regret for (e.g., a sin)

REPLENISH make full again

REPOSE rest

REPRESS hold back (e.g., a feeling)

REPROACH blame

REPUDIATE refuse to recognize

REPULSE drive back (e.g., an attack)

RESCIND cancel (e.g., a rule or regulation)

RESPIRE breathe

RESTRAIN hold back

RETAIN keep

RETALIATE return in kind (e.g., a blow for a blow)

RETARD delay

RETORT answer sharply

RETRACT take back (e.g., something said)

RETRIEVE get back

REVERE have deep respect for

REVERT to back to a former condition

REVOKE withdraw (e.g., a law)

RUPTURE break

SALVAGE save something out of a disaster such as fire

SCALD burn painfully with steam or hot liquid

SCAN look at closely

SCOFF mock

SCORN treat with contempt

SCOUR clean thoroughly; move about widely in a search

SCOWL make an angry look

SECLUDE keep away from other people

SEEP ooze

SEETHE boil

SEVER divide

SHEAR cut with a sharp instrument

SHED throw off (e.g., clothing)

SHIRK seek to avoid (e.g., duty or work)

SHRIVEL contract and wrinkle

SHUN avoid

SHUNT turn aside

SIFT sort out through careful examination (e.g., evidence)

SIGNIFY mean

SINGE burn slightly

SKIM read over quickly

SMITE hit hard

SMOLDER burn or give off smoke after the fire is out

SNARL tangle

SOAR fly high in the air

SOJOURN live temporarily in a place

SOLICIT plead for (e.g., help)

SPURN reject scornfully

STARTLE surprise

STIFLE suppress (e.g., feelings)

STREW scatter

STRIVE try hard

STUN daze

SUBSIDE lessen in activity

SUBSIST continue to live with difficulty

SUCCUMB yield to

SUFFICE be enough

SUPPRESS put down (e.g., a revolt)

SURGE increase suddenly

SURMOUNT overcome (e.g., an obstacle)

SUSTAIN support

SWARM move in great numbers

SWAY move back and forth

TAMPER meddle with

TARNISH discolour

TAUNT reproach mockingly

THAW melt

THRASH defeat thoroughly

THRIVE prosper

THROB beat insistently

THROTTLE choke

THRUST push forcefully and suddenly

THWART prevent someone from achieving something

TINGE colour slightly

TORMENT afflict with pain

TRANSFORM change the appearance of

TRANSMIT send along

TRANSPIRE come to light

TRAVERSE cross over

TRUDGE walk with difficulty

UNDERGO experience

UNDO return to condition before something was done

USURP seize power illegally

UTILIZE make use of

UTTER speak

VACATE make empty

VANQUISH conquer

VARY change

VEND sell

VERGE be on the point of

VERIFY prove the truth of

VEX annoy

VIBRATE move back and forth

VIOLATE break (e.g., a law)

VOUCH guarantee

WAIVE give up (e.g., a right or privilege)

WANE decrease in strength

WARP twist out of shape

WAVER sway back and forth

WHET sharpen

WIELD put to use (e.g., power or a tool such as a club)

WILT become limp

WITHER dry up (e.g., a flower)

WITHSTAND hold out against (e.g., pressure)

WREST pull violently

WRING force out by squeezing

WRITHE twist and turn about

YEARN long for

YIELD give up

500 Useful Adjectives

ACRID sharp to taste or smell (e.g., odour)

ADAMANT unyielding

ADEPT skilled

ADROIT skillful

AESTHETIC having to do with beauty

AGILE nimble

AMBIDEXTROUS equally skilled at using both hands

AMENABLE disposed to follow (e.g., advice)

AMIABLE friendly

APT suitable

AQUATIC living in or practiced on water

ARDENT passionate

ARROGANT overly proud

ARTICULATE able to express oneself clearly (e.g., an _____ person)

ASTUTE shrewd

AUSPICIOUS favourable (e.g., circumstances)

AUSTERE harsh

AUTHENTIC genuine

AUXILIARY helping

BARREN unfruitful

BIZARRE strange

BLAND gentle

BLATANT overly loud

BOISTEROUS rambunctious

BRUSQUE rudely brief

CALLOUS unfeeling

CANDID honest

CASUAL offhand

CHIC stylish

CHRONIC continuing over a long period of time

CIVIC municipal

CIVIL courteous

COGENT convincing (e.g., argument)

COHERENT clearly holding together

COLLOQUIAL conversational

COLOSSAL huge

COMPATIBLE capable of getting along together

COMPLACENT satisfied with oneself

CONCISE brief but complete

COPIOUS plentiful

CRAFTY sly

CREDIBLE believable

CREDULOUS given to believing anything too easily

CUMBERSOME bulky

CURSORY done quickly but only on the surface (e.g., a _____ examination)

CURT rudely brief

DEFT skillful

DEFUNCT dead

DEMURE overly modest

DEROGATORY belittling

DESOLATE lonely

DESPONDENT depressed

DESTITUTE poverty-stricken

DETERGENT cleansing

DEVIOUS indirect

DEVOID completely free of (e.g., feeling)

DEVOUT very religious

DIFFIDENT shy

DIMINUTIVE tiny

DIRE dreadful

DISCREET careful

DISCRETE distinctly separate

DISINTERESTED impartial

DISMAL gloomy

DISTRAUGHT driven to distraction

DIVERSE varied

DOCILE easily led

DOGMATIC stubbornly positive (e.g., opinion)

DOMESTIC having to do with the home

DOMINANT ruling

DORMANT sleeping

DRASTIC extreme (e.g., changes)

DREARY gloomy

DUBIOUS doubtful

DURABLE lasting

DYNAMIC energetic

EARNEST intensely serious

EBONY black

ECCENTRIC peculiar (e.g., behaviour)

EDIBLE fit to be eaten

EERIE weird

ELEGANT tastefully fine

ELOQUENT powerfully fluent in writing or speech

ELUSIVE hard to get hold of

EMINENT distinguished (e.g., author)

EPIC heroic in size

ERRATIC not regular

ETERNAL everlasting

ETHNIC having to do with race

EXORBITANT unreasonable (e.g., price)

EXOTIC foreign

EXPEDIENT suitable in a given situation but not necessarily correct

EXPLICIT clearly indicated

EXQUISITE extremely beautiful

EXTEMPORANEOUS spoken or accomplished with little preparation

EXTENSIVE broad

EXTINCT no longer existing

EXTRANEOUS having nothing to do with the subject at hand

FANATIC extremely emotionally enthusiastic

FEASIBLE possible to carry out (e.g., a _____ plan)

FEEBLE weak

FERTILE productive

FERVENT warmly felt

FESTIVE in the spirit of a holiday (e.g., celebration)

FICKLE changeable

FLAGRANT noticeably bad (e.g., violation)

FLEET swift

FLIMSY not strong (e.g., platform)

FLUENT smooth (e.g., speech)

FORLORN hopeless

FORMIDABLE fear-inspiring because of size or strength (e.g., enemy)

FRAGILE easily broken

FRAIL delicate

FRANK outspoken

FRATERNAL brotherly

FRIGID extremely cold

FRUGAL thrifty

FUTILE useless

GALA festive

GALLANT courteously brave (e.g., conduct)

GAUDY tastelessly showy

GAUNT overly thin and weary-looking

GENIAL kindly

GERMANE pertinent

GHASTLY frightful (e.g., appearance)

GIGANTIC huge

GLIB fluent but insincere

GLUM gloomy

GORY bloody

GRAPHIC vividly realistic

GRATIS free

GRIEVOUS causing sorrow

GRIM sternly forbidding (e.g., future)

GROSS glaringly bad (e.g., injustice)

GROTESQUE distorted in appearance

GRUESOME horrifying

GULLIBLE easily fooled

GUTTURAL throaty (e.g., sound)

HAGGARD worn-looking

HALE healthy

HAPHAZARD chance

HARDY having endurance

HARSH disagreeably rough

HAUGHTY overly proud

HEARTY friendly (e.g., welcome)

HECTIC feverish

HEINOUS outrageous (e.g., crime)

HIDEOUS extremely ugly

HILARIOUS very gay

HOMOGENEOUS of like kind (e.g., group)

HORRENDOUS horrible

HOSTILE unfriendly (e.g., unwelcome)

HUMANE merciful

HUMBLE modest

HUMID damp

ILLICIT illegal

IMMACULATE spotlessly clean

IMMENSE very large

IMMINENT about to happen (e.g., storm)

IMPARTIAL unbiased

IMPERATIVE necessary

IMPERTINENT rude

IMPETUOUS acting on impulse

IMPLICIT implied

IMPROMPTU without any preparation (e.g., remarks)

IMPUDENT rudely bold

INANE silly

INCENDIARY causing fire (e.g., bomb)

INCESSANT uninterrupted

INCLEMENT rough (e.g., weather)

INCOGNITO with real identity hidden

INCOHERENT not clearly connected

INDELIBLE unable to be erased

INDIFFERENT showing no interest

INDIGENT poor

INDIGNANT very angry

INDISPENSABLE absolutely necessary

INDUSTRIOUS hard-working

INEPT ineffective

INFALLIBLE unable to make a mistake

INFAMOUS having a bad reputation

INFINITE endless

INFINITESIMAL very, very small

INFLEXIBLE unbending

INGENIOUS clever

INGENUOUS naturally simple

INHERENT existing in someone or something

INNATE inborn

INNOCUOUS harmless

INSIPID uninteresting (e.g., conversation)

INSOLENT boldly rude

INTEGRAL essential to the whole

INTENSIVE thorough (e.g., study)

INTERMITTENT starting and stopping (e.g., rain)

INTOLERANT unwilling or unable to respect others or their beliefs

INTRICATE complicated

INVINCIBLE unable to be conquered

IRATE angry

IRRATIONAL unreasonable

JOVIAL good humoured

JUBILANT joyous

JUDICIOUS showing good judgment (e.g., decision)

LABOURIOUS demanding a lot of work

LANK tall and thin

LATENT hidden (e.g., talent)

LAUDABLE worthy of praise

LAVISH extremely generous (e.g., praise)

LAX loose (e.g., discipline)

LEGIBLE easily read (e.g., print)

LEGITIMATE lawful (e.g., claim)

LETHAL fatal

LISTLESS lacking in spirit

LITERAL following the exact words or intended meaning of the original (e.g., translation)

LITERATE educated to the point of being able to read and write (e.g., person)

LIVID discoloured by a bruise (e.g., flesh)

LOATH reluctant

LOFTY very high

LOQUACIOUS talkative

LUCID clear

LUCRATIVE profitable (e.g., business)

LUDICROUS ridiculous

LURID shockingly sensational (e.g., story)

LUSTY vigourous

MAJESTIC grand (e.g., building)

MALICIOUS spiteful

MALIGNANT harmful

MAMMOTH gigantic

MANDATORY required

MANIFEST evident

MANUAL done by the hands (e.g., labour)

MARINE of the sea (e.g., life)

MARTIAL warlike

MASSIVE bulky and heavy

MEAGER scanty

MENIAL lowly (e.g., task)

MERCENARY working only for financial gain (e.g., soldier)

METICULOUS extremely careful

MILITANT aggressive

MOBILE movable (e.g., home)

MOOT debatable (e.g., question)

MORBID unhealthily gloomy

MUTUAL reciprocal (e.g., admiration)

NAIVE innocently simple

NAUSEOUS disgusting

NAUTICAL having to do with ships and sailing

NEGLIGENT neglectful

NEUROTIC describing the behaviour of a person suffering from an emotional disorder

NIMBLE moving quickly and easily

NOCTURNAL of the night (e.g., animal)

NOMINAL small in comparison with service or value received (e.g., fee)

NONCHALANT casual and unexcited

NOTABLE important (e.g., person)

NOTORIOUS well-known in an unfavourable way (e.g., criminal)

NULL having no effect

OBESE overly fat

OBJECTIVE free from prejudice (e.g., analysis)

OBLIQUE indirectly indicated (e.g., suggestion)

OBNOXIOUS extremely unpleasant (e.g., behaviour)

OBSOLETE out-of-date (e.g., machine)

OBSTINATE stubborn

OMINOUS threatening (e.g., clouds)

ONEROUS burdensome (e.g., task)

OPPORTUNE timely

OPULENT wealthy

ORNATE elaborately decorated

ORTHODOX usually approved (e.g., religious beliefs)

OSTENSIBLE apparent

OUTRIGHT complete

OVERT open

PALTRY insignificant (e.g., sum of money)

PARAMOUNT chief (e.g., importance)

PASSIVE not active (e.g., participation)

PATENT obvious

PATHETIC pitiful

PEDESTRIAN unimaginative (e.g., ideas)

PEEVISH irritable

PENITENT repentant

PENSIVE thoughtful

PERENNIAL lasting for a long time (e.g., problem)

PERILOUS dangerous

PERTINENT relevant

PETTY relatively unimportant

PICAYUNE petty

PIOUS devoutly religious

PLACID calm (e.g., waters)

PLAUSIBLE apparently true (e.g., argument)

PLIABLE flexible

POIGNANT keenly painful to emotions

POMPOUS self-important (e.g., person)

PORTABLE capable of being carried (e.g., radio)

POSTHUMOUS taking place after a person's death (e.g., award)

POTENT powerful (e.g., drug)

POTENTIAL possible (e.g., greatness)

PRACTICABLE capable of being done (e.g., plan)

PRAGMATIC practical

PRECARIOUS risky

PRECISE exact

PRECOCIOUS advanced to a level earlier than is to be expected (e.g., child)

PREDOMINANT prevailing

PREPOSTEROUS ridiculous

PREVALENT widespread

PRIMARY fundamental (e.g., reason)

PRIME first in importance or quality

PRIMITIVE crude (e.g., tools)

PRIOR previous (e.g., appointment)

PRODIGIOUS extraordinary in size or amount (e.g., effort)

PROFICIENT skilled

PROFUSE abundantly given (e.g., praise)

PROLIFIC producing large amounts (e.g., author)

PRONE disposed to (e.g., accident)

PROSAIC ordinary

PROSTRATE laid low (e.g., by grief)

PROVINCIAL narrow (e.g., view of a matter)

PRUDENT discreet (e.g., advice)

PUGNACIOUS quarrelsome (e.g., person)

PUNGENT sharp to taste or smell (e.g., odor)

PUNITIVE inflicting punishment (e.g., action)

PUNY small in size or strength (e.g., effort)

PUTRID rotten

QUAINT pleasantly odd (e.g., custom)

RADIANT brightly shining

RAMPANT spreading unchecked (e.g., violence)

RANCID having the bad taste or smell of stale food (e.g., butter)

RANDOM decided by chance (e.g., choice)

RANK complete (e.g., incompetency)

RASH reckless

RAUCOUS harsh (e.g., sound)

RAVENOUS extremely hungry

REFLEX of an involuntary response (e.g., action)

REGAL royal

RELENTLESS persistent (e.g., chase)

RELEVANT pertinent

REMISS careless (e.g., in one's duty)

REMOTE far distant (e.g., time or place)

REPLETE filled (e.g., with thrills)

REPUGNANT extremely distasteful

REPULSIVE disgusting

REPUTABLE respectable (e.g., doctor)

RESIGNED submitting passively to (e.g., one's fate)

RESOLUTE firmly determined

RESONANT resounding (e.g., sound)

RESTIVE restless (e.g., pupils)

RETICENT speaking little (e.g., child)

RIGID stiff

ROBUST strong and healthy

ROWDY rough and disorderly (e.g., mob)

RUGGED rough

RUSTIC of the country (e.g., life)

RUTHLESS pitiless (e.g., dictator)

SAGE wise (e.g., advice)

SALIENT prominent (e.g., points)

SALUTARY healthful (e.g., climate)

SANE mentally sound

SANGUINARY bloody

SANGUINE cheerfully hopeful

SCANTY meager

SCHOLASTIC having to do with school and education (e.g., record)

SCRAWNY thin

SCRUPULOUS careful and honest (e.g., accounting)

SECRETIVE given to secrecy

SECULAR not religious (e.g., education)

SEDATE dignified

SERENE calm

SHEER very thin (e.g., stockings); utter (e.g., nonsense)

SHIFTLESS lazy

SHIFTY tricky

SHODDY inferior in quality (e.g., material)

SHREWD clever in one's dealings (e.g., businessman)

SIMULTANEOUS happening at the same time (e.g., events)

SINGULAR remarkable; strange (e.g., behaviour)

SINISTER threatening evil

SKEPTICAL showing doubt (e.g., attitude)

SLACK not busy (e.g., business season); loose (e.g., rope)

SLEEK smooth and glossy (e.g., appearance)

SLENDER small in size or amount (e.g., contribution)

SLOVENLY untidy

SLUGGISH slow-moving

SMUG self-satisfied

SNUG comfortable

SOBER serious

SOLEMN grave (e.g., occasion)

SOLITARY lone

SOMBER dark and gloomy (e.g., outlook)

SOPHISTICATED wise in the ways of the world

SORDID wretched (e.g., condition)

SPARSE thinly scattered

SPIRITED lively

SPIRITUAL of the spirit or soul

SPONTANEOUS happening as a result of natural impulse (e.g., reaction)

SPORADIC happening at irregular times (e.g., shooting)

SPRY nimble

STACCATO with breaks between successive sounds

STAGNANT dirty from lack of movement (e.g., water)

STALWART robust

STARK bleak (e.g., outlook)

STATELY dignified

STATIC stationary

STATIONARY not moving

STAUNCH firm (e.g., friend)

STEADFAST firm

STERN severe (e.g., look)

STOCKY short and heavily built

STODGY uninteresting

STOICAL unmoved emotionally

STOUT fat; firm (e.g., resistance)

STRAIGHTFORWARD honest (e.g., answer)

STRENUOUS demanding great energy (e.g., exercise)

STUPENDOUS amazing (e.g., effort)

STURDY strongly built

SUAVE smoothly polite (e.g., manner)

SUBLIME inspiring admiration because of noble quality (e.g., music)

SUBSIDIARY of less importance (e.g., rank)

SUBSTANTIAL of considerable numbers or size

SUBTLE suggested delicately (e.g., hint)

SULLEN resentful

SULTRY extremely hot and humid (e.g., weather)

SUMPTUOUS costly (e.g., meal)

SUNDRY various

SUPERB of a high degree of excellence

SUPERFICIAL not going beyond the obvious (e.g., examination)

SUPERFLUOUS beyond what is needed

SUPERLATIVE superior to all others (e.g., performance)

SUPPLE limber (e.g., body)

SURLY offensively rude

SUSCEPTIBLE easily affected by

SWARTHY dark-skinned

TACIT not openly said but implied (e.g., approval)

TANGIBLE capable of being touched; actual (e.g., results)

TARDY late (e.g., student)

TART having a sharp taste (e.g., food)

TAUT tightly stretched (e.g., rope)

TEDIOUS long and tiresome (e.g., study)

TEMPERATE moderate (e.g., climate)

TENACIOUS holding fast (e.g., grip)

TENTATIVE for a temporary period of trial (e.g., agreement)

TEPID lukewarm (e.g., water)

TERMINAL concluding

TERSE brief but expressing a good deal (e.g., comment)

THANKLESS unappreciated (e.g., task)

TIDY neat (e.g., appearance)

TIMELESS eternal (e.g., beauty)

TIMELY happening at a desirable time (e.g., arrival)

TIMID shy

TIRESOME tiring

TITANIC of enormous size or strength

TORRID intensely hot

TRANQUIL calm (e.g., waters)

TRANSIENT passing away after a brief time

TRIFLING of little importance

TRITE ordinary (e.g., remark)

TRIVIAL insignificant

TURBULENT agitated

ULTIMATE final (e.g., conclusion)

UNANIMOUS in complete agreement (e.g., decision)

UNASSUMING modest

UNCANNY unnatural (e.g., accuracy)

UNCONDITIONAL absolute (e.g., surrender)

UNCOUTH crude and clumsy (e.g., individual)

UNDAUNTED not discouraged

UNDERHAND sly

UNDULY overly (e.g., concerned)

UNEASY disturbed

UNGAINLY awkward (e.g., person)

UNIQUE only one of its kind (e.g., specimen)

UNKEMPT not combed

UNRULY disorderly (e.g., crowd)

UNSCATHED uninjured

UNWIELDY clumsy to use, usually because of size (e.g., implement)

UPRIGHT honest (e.g., citizen)

UTMOST most extreme (e.g., in distance, height or size)

UTTER complete (e.g., failure)

VAIN futile (e.g., attempt); conceited (e.g., person)

VALIANT brave

VALID (legally) sound (e.g., argument)

VAST very large in extent or size (e.g., distances)

VEHEMENT violent in feeling (e.g., protest)

VERBATIM word for word (e.g., report)

VERSATILE able to perform many tasks well (e.g., athlete)

VIGILANT watchful (e.g., sentry)

VILE highly disgusting (e.g., conduct)

VISIBLE able to be seen (e.g., object)

VITAL essential (e.g., contribution)

VIVACIOUS lively

VIVID bright (e.g., colour)

VOID not binding legally (e.g., contract)

VOLUMINOUS very great in size (e.g., writings)

VORACIOUS greedy for food (e.g., appetite)

VULNERABLE open to attack (e.g., position)

WARY cautious

WEARY tired

WEE very small

WEIGHTY important (e.g., decision)

WHOLESOME causing a feeling of well-being (e.g., entertainment)

WILY cunning (e.g., magician)

WISHFUL showing desire that something be so (e.g., thinking)

WITTY amusingly clever (e.g., remark)

WORDY using too many words (e.g., reply)

WORLDLY enjoying the pleasures and experiences of this world (e.g., person)

WORTHY deserving (e.g., choice)

WRETCHED miserable

Tone

Tone in writing is very difficult to define. It refers to the manner of the writer that reveals his purpose or attitude toward his topic or his reader by such techniques as choice of words and sentence structure. Tone can be humourous or serious, natural or affected, calm or angry, satirical or appreciative, factual or emotional. One can identify over 30 different ways in which tone can be described (or, if you prefer, 30 different tones). We've added descriptions to help.

affected (artificial; not natural)
bantering (good-natured teasing)
bitter (showing feelings of hatred or resentment)
colloquial (conversational; chatty)
cynical (showing a lack of belief in man's goodness or sincerity)
devotional (showing sincere faith)
didactic (teaching moral values)
elegaic (mournful)
eulogistic (praising someone or something highly)
fanciful (playfully imaginative)
fervent (showing warmth of feeling)
flippant (disrespectful)
grave (showing heavy responsibility)
indignant (showing anger)
intemperate (extreme; unrestrained)
ironical (stating the opposite of what is really meant)

light-hearted (cheerful)
matter of fact (sticking strictly to facts)
meditative (showing deep thought)
nostalgic (showing longing for the past)
patronizing (talking down to someone who is considered inferior)
reminiscent (remembering past experiences)
resigned (showing acceptance of an unhappy situation)
rhapsodic (showing great enthusiasm)
sarcastic (sneering and cutting with the intention to hurt)
satirical (holding up to ridicule the foolish behaviour of people)
sentimental (showing feelings that are open or exaggerated)
solemn (impressively serious)
tender (showing warm affection and concern)
whimsical (full of sudden changes of mood)
wry (showing a twisted kind of humour)

Other words to describe tone are *stiff* and *formal* (as contrasted with *colloquial* and *informal*), *relaxed* and *familiar, simple* and *direct.*

Why all this fuss about tone? On the examination, you will be given sentences or passages in which a certain tone is set and then you will be asked to identify a word or words that violate the tone, that do not belong because they destroy the mood that has been set.

Here are some examples, a bit exaggerated to make the point:

1. The dignified guest *gulped* down her food during the dinner in her honour.
2. The hikers *glared* at the mountains in awe.
3. I introduced my *pappy* to the minister of my church.
4. The distinguished statesman pulled up to the Parliament in his *buggy.*
5. "Mom," said my son, "I'd like you to meet my *inamorata.*"

In sentence 1, *gulped* clearly violates the tone set by the word *dignified.* ". . . ate her food hastily" would be more suitable. In sentence 2, the verb *glared* is out of place in connection with an awesome feeling. Instead of a fierce stare (glare), *contemplated* would be more in keeping with the tone. In the third sentence, *pappy* is out of place in the sentence. *Father* should be used since a minister is involved. Nor is *buggy* the right word for a statesman's automobile in sentence 4. Finally, *inamorata* is much too formal a word for the tone required in a sentence depicting an introduction to a parent. *Sweetheart* is more in keeping with the tone of the sentence.

These words vary greatly in their degree of formality and informality. Our next concern in dealing with diction and the choice of the right word is with distinguishing between formal and informal styles of writing.

Formal and Informal: Two Styles of Writing

You may not realize it, but each of us uses many kinds of English when we write. (The same is true of speaking, by the way.) We are most casual and informal with our family and friends whenever we write notes or letters. For the few occasions when we have to deal with important matters in our writing, we are somewhat more serious and choose our words more carefully. When we write to people outside our circle, we tend to be much more formal, especially if we are writing for business reasons.

To see how this is reflected in our writing let us examine some groups of words that will make the distinction between formal and informal writing clear.

Formal	**Less Formal**	**Informal**
spouse	wife	old lady
expire	die	kick off
officer	constable	the cop

boast	brag	shoot one's mouth off
inebriated	drunk	blotto
entered into matrimony	got married	got hitched
celebration	party	bash
automobile	car	wheels
taken into custody	arrested	busted
abode	home	pad

It is unlikely that you would use the words listed under "formal" with your family and friends. Nor would you use the informal words in letters written to strangers or for business purposes.

One way, then, to distinguish formal style from informal style in writing is by the kinds of words that are used. Terms used to describe these distinctions include *literary* for "formal" and *colloquial* or *slang* for "informal." Because it is often difficult to distinguish among these—where colloquial leaves off and slang begins, for example—it is better to think in terms of degrees of formality or informality (in our word lists above, going from left, most formal, to right, most informal).

Is more formal preferable to less formal? Not at all. It depends on the person to whom you are writing and the reasons why. At times, a less formal word might be more effective for your purpose—*broke,* for example, instead of *short of funds.* Try the following as examples.

1. The president of the corporation invited the members of the board to bring their wives and *kids* to the holiday party.
2. My family asked me to send them *epistles* from time to time when I was on my travels.
3. "I must differ with my learned colleague," said the senator, "if he expects me to believe that *bunk*."
4. The gangster accused his accomplice of lacking *intestinal fortitude.*
5. The mother told the child to *masticate* its food properly.

In the first sentence, the term *kids* is too informal for the formality of an office party: *children* is more appropriate. The reverse is true in the next sentence. The word *epistle,* which means a long, formal letter of instruction, is much too formal for a family situation. In the third sentence, the use of *bunk* in a formal parliamentary setting is improper. *Nonsense* or some other synonym should be used. No gangster would use the term *intestinal fortitude.* The informal term *guts* is much more likely. Finally, the word *masticate* is much too difficult for a child to understand. Why not use the simple word *chew*?

While we are dealing with the varying degrees of formality, let us turn to the problem of the unnecessary use of big words where simpler words will do. The big word for the use of such long words, by the way, is sesquipedalian! (The word itself means "a foot and a half.") To illustrate the problem, try restating these well-known proverbs in simpler English.

1. A male adult's most highly regarded companion is his canine.
2. At no time do drops of condensed moisture fall to earth except in a deluge.

The first is obviously, "A man's best friend is his dog." The second is, "It never rains but it pours." Another example is the use of a phrase such as "improved financial support and less onerous work loads" instead of "more pay and less work."

The point is that if a question contains a sentence which includes an obviously inappropriate long or technical word, one that is readily replaced by a simple one, that sentence should be identified as having poor diction. The sentence above in which the word masticate appears is an excellent illustration.

Ways to Set Tone

1. Distinguish between the *kinds of words* that are used (as above) to determine the level of formality.

2. Note the use of *other elements* that contribute to a colloquial (conversational, chatty) informal tone versus a formal tone.
   — The writer can use informal personal pronouns such as "you" or "I" instead of the nouns they replace. "This writer suggests to the reader . . ." or "It is suggested that the reader" are much more formal than "You should . . ." where "you" stands for the reader.
   — Contractions such as "isn't" for "is not," "don't" for "do not," and "I'm" for "I am," among others can be used. "I'm sure you'll agree" is less formal than "I am sure you will agree."
3. Vary the kinds of sentences that are used. Informal writing uses questions as well as statements. "The reader would agree that . . ." is much more formal than "Don't you agree?"
4. Note that writing which includes quotations or sustained conversation tends to be less formal than a solid page of printed matter.

We shall return to these techniques used in informal writing when we deal with style.

WORDINESS: THE PROBLEM OF TOO MANY WORDS

Wordiness, the use of more words than is necessary, is a frequent weakness of many speakers and writers. This verbosity, as it is called, is particularly undesirable when it confuses the reader. Wordiness often reflects a fuzziness in thinking which requires the writer to add words to or restate ideas which he feels are unclear to the reader, probably because he is not clear about them himself.

1. *Some sentences contain words or phrases which are grammatically unnecessary.*

EXAMPLES:

1. My friend *he* is a hockey fan.
   EXPLANATION:
   In this sentence, both the noun, *friend,* and the pronoun, *he,* are unnecessary when referring to the same person. A pronoun takes the place of a noun. The sentence should read:
   "My friend is a hockey fan."
   OR
   "He is a hockey fan."

2. This *here* pen writes better than that *there* one.
   EXPLANATION:
   Both *here* and *there* are not needed. *This* means nearer than another person or thing referred to as *that.*

3. Take your feet off *of* the table.
   EXPLANATION:
   Off means "so as to be no longer on." The word *of* in the sentence is superfluous.

4. Whatever he does, he does *it* well.
   EXPLANATION:
   The pronoun *it* isn't needed. In fact, it replaces nothing in the sentence and what the *it* refers to isn't clear.

2. *Some sentences contain words which are repetitive since they restate parts of the meaning of other words in the sentence.*

EXAMPLES:

1. I have a friend *of mine* who helps me with my housework.
   EXPLANATION:
   In this sentence, *mine* means "belonging to me," and the idea is already contained in the words *I have.* Therefore, *of mine* can be eliminated from the sentence.

2. The shoe store had boots, sneakers, slippers *and* et cetera in stock.
   EXPLANATION:
   Et cetera is a Latin phrase meaning "and others." Since the *and* is already contained in *et cetera,* the *and* is unnecessary and should be left out of the sentence.

3. I have to be at work at 9 A.M. *in the morning.*
   EXPLANATION:
   In this sentence, A.M. means "ante meridiem" or "before noon." It contains the idea *morning.* Therefore, the phrase "in the morning" isn't needed.

4. Cabbage is *more* preferable to potatoes for people on a diet.
   EXPLANATION:
   Preferable means "more desirable." Since the idea of *more* is already in the word, including the word *more* is unnecessary.

5. The consensus of *opinion* is that the prisoner is guilty.
   EXPLANATION:
   Consensus already contains the idea "opinion." It means "an opinion held by most or all people." The words *of opinion* are, thus, extra.

6. The Commons has decided to refer the matter *back* to committee.
   EXPLANATION:
   The word *refer* in the sentence contains a prefix (*re-*) which means "back." Therefore, the word *back* is unnecessary. Another similar incorrect expression is "return back."

3. *Some sentences contain words which unnecessarily repeat other words in the sentence.*

EXAMPLES:

1. We left after *the conclusion of* the concert.
   EXPLANATION:
   After means "later than," so the words *the conclusion of* are unnecessary.

2. Helen Keller wrote an autobiography *of her life.*
   EXPLANATION:
   An *autobiography* is the story of one's life; *of her life* can be dropped.

3. The husband and wife had nothing in common *with each other.*
   EXPLANATION:
   In common means "shared by each member of a group of two or more," so *with each other* is a phrase that is not needed.

4. In my opinion, *I think* the criminal should be pardoned.
   EXPLANATION:
   In this sentence, *think* means to "hold an opinion," so either *in my opinion* or *I think* can safely be dispensed with.

5. The fashion show was presented exclusively for women *only.*
   EXPLANATION:
   Exclusively means "excluding all others," so *only* is not needed.

4. ***Some sentences express ideas clumsily because too many words are used.*** This problem can be corrected by omitting unnecessary words, recasting the sentence, or substituting a single word for a phrase or clause.

EXAMPLES:

1. Everyone wondered *as to* what the gunman was going to do.
   EXPLANATION:
   As to should be omitted; it is unnecessary.

2. The reason I joined the club was *on account of the fact* that I needed a place to go to in my spare time.
   EXPLANATION:
   On account of the fact should be omitted, as it is unnecessary.

3. The secretary prepared the letter in a manner that showed that she didn't care.
   This sentence should be rephrased to read:
   "The secretary prepared the letter carelessly."

4. There were five of us present at the ceremony.
   This sentence should be recast to read:
   "Five of us were present at the ceremony."

5. The constable, who had lots of experience, was honoured for his work.
   This sentence should be rephrased to read:
   "The experienced constable was honoured for his work."

6. To improve your style, omit words which aren't necessary.
   This sentence should be rephrased to read:
   "To improve your style, omit unnecessary words."

Practice

1. That there book belongs to me.
2. Despite the rain, the umpires decided to continue on with the game.
3. Please refer back to page 12 in the book.
4. My parents they are completely devoted to me.
5. I usually go to bed at 11 P.M. at night.
6. Each and every student should pay attention.
7. Felicia doesn't want for you to date her anymore.
8. When I was eighteen years old, I was graduated from high school.
9. There were a hundred people attending the affair.
10. The firefighter, who was very brave, saved the children from the burning house.

Answers

1. That book belongs to me.
2. Despite the rain, the umpires decided to continue the game.
3. Please refer to page 12 in the book.
4. My parents are completely devoted to me.
5. I usually go to bed at 11 P.M.
6. Each student should pay attention.
   Every student should pay attention.
7. Felicia doesn't want you to date her anymore.
8. When I was eighteen, I was graduated from high school.
9. A hundred people were attending the affair.
10. The very brave firefighter saved the children from the burning house.

5. ***Some roundabout expressions are used to express thoughts that the writer finds disagreeable.*** These are called euphemisms, words or phrases that are less direct but considered less distasteful or less offensive than others.

Examples include expressions for death. Rather than say *die,* the writer uses "pass away," "go to his reward," or "enter into rest." The *toilet* becomes the "rest room" or the "powder room" "Termination of employment" requires more words but it sounds better than *fired.* "An institution for the mentally ill" is preferable to *asylum* for many writers. The *drunk* may be described as being "under the weather." A *liar* is said to be "one who is far from the truth." Euphemisms may be included in some of the sentences in the questions which you will be asked.

PRACTICE WITH WORDINESS

Directions: **Beneath each sentence you will find five ways of writing the underlined part. Choose the answer that makes the best sentence and mark the number of that answer. Answer 1 is always the same as the underlined part and is sometimes the right answer.**

1. After the conclusion of the game, my friend, he decided to return back home.

1. 1 2 3 4 5

(1) After the conclusion of the game, my friend, he decided to return back
(2) After the conclusion of the game, my friend decided to return back
(3) After the conclusion of the game, my friend decided to return
(4) After the game, my friend decided to return back
(5) After the game, my friend decided to return

2. At this point in time, type up five copies of this here contract.

2. 1 2 3 4 5

(1) point in time, type up five copies of this here
(2) point in time, type five copies of this here
(3) time, type five copies of this
(4) time, type five copies of this here
(5) time, type up five copies of this

3. Because we cooperated together, we divided up the work on the report which was assigned.

3. 1 2 3 4 5

(1) together, we divided up the work on the report which was assigned
(2) together, we divided the work on the report which was assigned
(3) , we divided up the work on the report which was assigned
(4) , we divided the work on the assigned report
(5) , we divided up the work on the assigned report

4. Write down each and every true fact.

4. 1 2 3 4 5

(1) down each and every true fact
(2) down each true fact
(3) each true fact
(4) each fact
(5) down each fact

5. Mr. Steele, who was president of the company, repeated again what he had said while we were having dinner.

(1) who was president of the company, repeated again what he had said while we were having
(2) who was president of the company, repeated what he had said while we were having
(3) president of the company, repeated what he had said while we were having
(4) president of the company, repeated again what he had said during
(5) president of the company, repeated what he had said during

5. 1 2 3 4 5

6. At 8:00 P.M. in the evening, he continued on his walk which was enjoyable.

(1) in the evening, he continued on his walk which was enjoyable
(2) he continued on his walk which was enjoyable
(3) he continued on his enjoyable walk
(4) in the evening, he continued his enjoyable walk
(5) he continued his enjoyable walk

6. 1 2 3 4 5

7. A large crowd of people who had nothing in common with each other waited outside of the building.

(1) A large crowd of people who had nothing in common with each other waited outside of
(2) A crowd which had nothing in common waited outside
(3) A large crowd which had nothing in common waited outside of
(4) A crowd who had nothing in common with each other waited outside of
(5) A crowd which had nothing in common with each other waited outside

7. 1 2 3 4 5

8. I don't want for you to meet up with my friend until the time I tell you.

(1) for you to meet up with my friend until the time
(2) for you to meet my friend until the time
(3) for you to meet my friend until
(4) you to meet my friend until
(5) you to meet my friend until the time

8. 1 2 3 4 5

9. The senator rose up to say that, in his opinion, he thought the bill should be referred back to committee.

(1) rose up to say that, in his opinion, he thought the bill should be referred back to
(2) rose up to say that he thought the bill should be referred back
(3) rose up to say that he thought the bill should be referred
(4) rose up to say that, in his opinion, the bill should be referred
(5) rose to say that he thought the bill should be referred

9. 1 2 3 4 5

10. My wife wanted <u>that I should return to school when I was thirty years of age</u>.
(1) that I should return to school when I was thirty years of age
(2) that I should return back to school when I was thirty years of age
(3) me to return back to school when I was thirty years of age
(4) me to return to school when I was thirty years of age
(5) me to return to school when I was thirty

10. 1 2 3 4 5

Turn to the answer key and the answer analysis which follow.

What's Your Score?

_____ right,	_____ wrong
Excellent	9–10
Good	8
Fair	7

If you scored lower, review the five kinds of wordiness illustrated in this section.

ANSWER KEY

Practice with Wordiness/Page 222

1. **5**	3. **4**	5. **5**	7. **2**	9. **5**
2. **3**	4. **4**	6. **5**	8. **4**	10. **5**

ANSWER ANALYSIS

Practice with Wordiness/Page 222

1. **5** The *conclusion of*, *he* and *back* are all included in the meanings of other words in the sentence.
2. **3** *Point in*, *up* and *here* are all included in the meanings of other words in the sentence.
3. **4** *Together* and *up* are included in the meanings of other words in the sentence. The adjective *assigned* is preferable stylistically to the adjective clause *which was assigned*.
4. **4** *Down*, and *every*, and *true* are unnecessary.
5. **5** *Again* is unnecessary. The appositive, *president*, is preferable stylistically to the adjective clause *who was president*. The preposition *during* is preferable to the adverb clause *while we were having*.
6. **5** *In the evening* and *on* are included in the meanings of other words in the sentence. The adjective *enjoyable* is preferable to the adjective clause *which was enjoyable*.
7. **2** The words *large*, *with each other*, and *of* are unnecessary. *Which* is preferable to *who* when it refers to a neuter noun such as *crowd*.
8. **4** The words *up* and *the time* are included in the meanings of other words in the sentence. The word *for* is awkward and unnecesary.
9. **5** The words *up*, *in his opinion*, and *back* are unnecessary.
10. **5** The words *years of age* are unnecessary. The expression *that I should* is clumsy and can easily be replaced by the words *me to*.

A Word About Idioms

Idioms are expressions which are peculiar to a language. English has more than its share. "She caught my eye" is one example. You can tell that idioms do not deal with literal meanings although they might. The slang idiom "tie one on" (to get drunk) is such an example.

Most frequently, errors in idiomatic English occur when the wrong preposition is used after a given verb or adjective. This is the problem you will face in examination questions.

EXAMPLE:
WRONG: His view of the world situation was different than mine.
CORRECT: His view of the world situation was different from mine.

EXAMPLE:
WRONG: Don't blame it on me!
CORRECT: Don't blame me for it!

Frequently Misused Prepositions

Here is a list of frequently misused prepositions. Study them carefully so you will be able to identify unidiomatic use of prepositions if you have to. *These are the correct forms.*

abstain from
accede to
accompanied by
accuse of
acquaint with
acquiesce in
acquit of
addicted to
adept in
adhere to
adjust to
agree in (an opinion)
agree to (a suggestion or plan)
agree with (a person)
angry at (an object)
angry with (a person)
apprehensive for (someone)
apprehensive of (danger)
approve of
assure of
averse to
blame for
capable of
careless about (unimportant details)
careless of (worth)
careless with (an object)
characteristic of
charge with
coincide with
compare to (indicate similarities)
compare with (examine similarities or differences)
compatible with
concerned for (anxious)
concerned with (involved)
concur in (an opinion)
concur with (a person)
contend about (an issue)
contend with (a person)
contrast with
convict of
cured of
deprive of
desire for
desirous of
desist from
despair of
devoid of
differ from (things)
differ with (a person)
different from
disagree with
dissatisfied with
dissent from
distaste for
distrustful of
divest of
emerge from
empty of
envious of
exclude from
expel from
expert in
fond of
fondness for
forbid to
foreign to
guard against
hinder from
hindrance to
hint at
inconsistent with
independent of
infer from
inferior to
inseparable from
insight into
instill into (a person)
instruct in
involve in
jealous of

know that (*not* know as)
lacking in
lag behind
mastery of (a subject)
neglectful of
obedient to
oblivious of
observant of
opposition to
peculiar to
persevere in
pertinent to
prior to
prohibit from
protest against
responsibility for
revel in
rich in
rid of
separate from
similar to
substitute for
superior to
thoughtful of
try to (*not* try and)
vary from
wary of
yield to

Unidiomatic Expressions

Avoid these frequently found unidiomatic expressions.

WRONG	CORRECT
aim at winning	aim to win
and etc.	etc.
as a fact	as a matter of fact
be sure and	be sure to
choose between good or evil	choose between good and evil
doubt if it will rain	doubt whether it will rain
in search for	in search of
in the meanwhile	meanwhile
irregardless	regardless
kind of a	kind of
lest it fails	lest it fail
off of	off
plan on staying	plan to stay
try and go	try to go

PRACTICE WITH IDIOMS

***Directions:* Beneath each sentence you will find five ways of writing the underlined part. Choose the answer that makes the best sentence and mark the number of that answer. Answer 1 is always the same as the underlined part and is sometimes the right answer.**

1. Frank was angry <u>at Charlie for having agreed with my plan in opposition to</u> his.
(1) at Charlie for having agreed with my plan in opposition to
(2) at Charlie for having agreed to my plan in opposition with
(3) at Charlie for having agreed with my plan in opposition with
(4) with Charlie for having agreed to my plan in opposition to
(5) with Charlie for having agreed with my plan in opposition to

1. 1 2 3 4 5
|| || || || ||

2. The prisoner was acquitted <u>of the murder with which he was charged and for</u> which he was blamed.
(1) of the murder with which he was charged and for
(2) from the murder he was charged and with
(3) from the murder he was charged with and with
(4) of the murder for which he was charged and with
(5) of the murder of which he was charged and for

2. 1 2 3 4 5
|| || || || ||

3. Jim's work was independent <u>and superior to Fred's from</u> which it differed.
(1) and superior to Fred's from
(2) and superior to Fred's with
(3) and superior than Fred's from
(4) of and superior to Fred's with
(5) of and superior to Fred's from

3. 1 2 3 4 5

4. I don't know <u>as I concur with your decision to try and</u> run for office.
(1) as I concur with your decision to try and
(2) that I concur in your decision to try to
(3) as I concur in your decision to try and
(4) that I concur with your decision to try to
(5) as I concur with your decision to try to

4. 1 2 3 4 5

5. Can you rid yourself <u>of your desire to substitute your insight into the case for</u> mine?
(1) of your desire to substitute your insight into the case for
(2) from your desire to substitute your insight into the case instead of
(3) from your desire to substitute your insight of the case for
(4) of your desire to substitute your insight into the case with
(5) of your desire to substitute your insight of the case of

5. 1 2 3 4 5

Turn to the answer key and answer analysis which follow.

What's Your Score?

_____ right,	_____ wrong
Excellent	5
Good	4
Fair	3

If you scored lower, review the lists of idiomatic and unidiomatic expressions.

ANSWER ANALYSIS

Practice with Idioms/Page 226

1. **4** 2. **1** 3. **5** 4. **2** 5. **1**

ANSWER KEY

Practice with Idioms/Page 226

1. **4** One is angry *with* a person. One agrees to a plan but *with* a person.
2. **1** No error.
3. **5** The adjective *independent* requires the preposition *of* which was omitted. One differs *with* a person; an object differs *from* another object.
4. **2** *As* is an incorrect vulgarism after the verb *know*. One concurs *in* a decision. The infinitive *try* should be followed by *to*.
5. **1** No error.

SAMPLE PARAGRAPHS

This section of the chapter presents sample paragraphs of the type you will encounter on the actual examination. We have included a direction sheet for TEST 1: Writing Skills, Part I. This is followed by a fully analyzed sample test paragraph and three additional paragraphs for practice with answers.

TEST 1: WRITING SKILLS, PART I

Directions

Allotted Time: 75 minutes

This part of the Writing Skills test contains **55 multiple-choice questions** that test your ability to write English correctly and effectively.

The multiple-choice questions are based on numbered sentences in paragraphs. These sentences may be correct as written (if so, you choose option 1), or they will contain an error in sentence structure, grammar and usage, punctuation, capitalization, or spelling. You must choose the option that either corrects the error, indicates the best way to write a portion of the sentence, combines two sentences effectively, or provides another way in which the sentence can be rewritten.

Since 55 questions must be answered in 75 minutes, if there are six paragraphs, spend no more than 12 minutes on each set of questions based on each paragraph. Do not devote more than a few minutes to any one question. If there is time left, you may go back to a question.

Answer all questions. Do not leave any blanks since there is no penalty for incorrect answers. Your score will be the number of your correct responses.

You may go on to Writing Skills, Part II, the essay, when you complete Part I.

Decide which is the best answer and mark the numbered space on the answer sheet beside the number that corresponds to the question in the test.

Make no mark on the answer sheet other than your choice of the correct answer. If you change your answer, erase your first mark completely. Only *one* answer space should be marked for each question.

EXAMPLE:

In the future, people will need to learn to turn to their computer for assistence.

What correction should be made to this sentence?

(1) remove the comma after future
(2) change will need to need
(3) change the spelling of their to they're
(4) change the spelling of assistence to assistance
(5) no correction is necessary

① ② ③ ● ⑤

In this sentence, the correct spelling is "assistance," so mark answer 4 on the answer sheet.

SAMPLE TEST PARAGRAPH

Directions: **The following items are based on a paragraph which contains numbered sentences. Some of the sentences may contain errors in sentence structure, usage, or mechanics. <u>A few sentences, however, may be correct as written</u>. Read the paragraph and then answer the items based on it. For each item, choose the answer that would result in the most effective writing of the sentence or sentences. The best answer must be consistent with the meaning and tone of the rest of the paragraph.**

(1) Savings has been refered to as the tool for accomplishing future goals. (2) After a family has decided on a savings plan the decision on how to invest wisely must be made. (3) Life insurance is a way to provide immediate financial protection for the loss of income through the death of the breadwinner. (4) Once children are expected, the need arises for life insurance. (5) Life insurance is purchased to cover the cost of the funeral, the expenses of the last illness, and to provide income for the survivors. (6) When planning for this type of financial protection, be sure to consider all resources the survivors will have to use (earning ability as well as financial) the amount of income that will meet necessities, and finally the cost of such a program. (7) Concentrate insurance dollars on the breadwinner and buy the type of insurance that will give the most protection for the cost. (8) A savings account is the second leg of the stool for a savings program. (9) It is here where a family keeps the money that it may need immediately or plans to use within the near future. (10) After the family will protect itself with insurance for the survivors and with a savings account, it is then ready to invest in other possible channels. (11) At this point a family needs to consider these channels in line with its distant goals, and the economy.

1. Sentence 1. **Savings has been refered to as the tool for accomplishing future goals.**
What correction should be made to this sentence?
(1) change <u>has</u> to <u>have</u>
(2) change the spelling of <u>refered</u> to <u>referred</u>
(3) insert a comma after <u>to</u>
(4) change the spelling of <u>accomplishing</u> to <u>acomplishing</u>
(5) no correction is necessary

1. 1 2 3 4 5
|| || || || ||

2. Sentence 2. **After a family has decided on a savings plan the decision on how to invest wisely must be made.**
What correction should be made to this sentence?
(1) change <u>has</u> to <u>have</u>
(2) insert an apostrophe after <u>savings</u>
(3) insert a comma after <u>plan</u>
(4) change the spelling of <u>decision</u> to <u>descision</u>
(5) change <u>how to invest</u> to <u>how to have invested</u>

2. 1 2 3 4 5
|| || || || ||

3. Sentence 3. **Life insurance is a way to provide immediate financial <u>protection for the</u> loss of income through the death of the breadwinner.**
Which of the following is the best way to write the underlined portion of this sentence? If you think the original is the best way, choose option (1)
(1) protection for the
(2) protection. For
(3) protection, for
(4) protection; for
(5) protection—for

3. 1 2 3 4 5
|| || || || ||

4\. Sentences 4 and 5. **Once children are expected, the need arises for life insurance. Life insurance is purchased to cover the cost of the funeral, the expenses of the last illness, and to provide income for the survivors.**
The most effective combination of these sentences would include which of the following groups of words?
(1) insurance, life insurance is
(2) insurance which is purchased
(3) insurance, in fact life insurance
(4) insurance, that is to say life insurance
(5) insurance life insurance is then purchased

4\. 1 2 3 4 5

5\. Sentence 6. **When planning for this type of financial protection, be sure to consider all resources the survivors will have to use (earning ability as well as financial) the amount of income that will meet necessities, and finally the cost of such a program.**
What correction should be made to this sentence?
(1) change <u>when planning</u> to <u>having planned</u>
(2) insert a comma after the second parenthesis
(3) substitute quotation marks for the parentheses
(4) change the spelling of <u>necessities</u> to <u>neccessities</u>
(5) remove the comma after <u>necessities</u>

5\. 1 2 3 4 5

6\. Sentence 7. **Concentrate insurance dollars on the breadwinner and buy the type of insurance that will give the most protection for the cost.**
What correction should be made to this sentence?
(1) capitalize <u>breadwinner</u>
(2) insert a hyphen between <u>bread</u> and <u>winner</u>
(3) change <u>will give</u> to <u>gives</u>
(4) remove <u>the</u> before <u>most protection</u>
(5) no correction is necessary

6\. 1 2 3 4 5

7\. Sentences 8 and 9. **A savings account is the second leg of the stool for a savings program. It is here where a family keeps the money that it may need immediately or plans to use within the near future.**
The most effective combination of these sentences would include which of the following groups of words?
(1) program where a family
(2) program for which a family
(3) program here where a family
(4) program in which a family
(5) program to which a family

7\. 1 2 3 4 5

8\. Sentence 10. **After the family will protect itself with insurance for the survivors and with a savings account, it is then ready to invest in other possible channels.**
What correction should be made to this sentence?
(1) change <u>will protect</u> to <u>protects</u>
(2) insert a comma before <u>and</u>
(3) remove the comma after <u>account</u>
(4) change <u>then</u> to <u>therefore</u>
(5) no correction is necessary

8\. 1 2 3 4 5

9. Sentences 10 and 11. **After the family protects itself with insurance for the survivors and with a savings account, it is then ready to invest in other possible channels. At this point a family needs to consider these channels in line with its distant goals, and the economy.**
The most effective combination of these sentences would include which of the following groups of words?
(1) channels in line with
(2) channels which are considered in line with
(3) channels a family needs to consider in line with
(4) channels at this point in line with
(5) channels to be considered in line with

9. 1 2 3 4 5
|| || || || ||

ANALYSIS OF QUESTIONS AND ANSWERS

Important: **Do not answer any question until you have read and analyzed all the possible choices.**

1. The correct answer is **(2)**. (1) is not correct because *savings* may be considered a singular noun. (2) is correct because "r" is doubled in *referred* because the accent is on the second syllable. See rule 8 on page 178. (3) is wrong because no comma is needed here. (4) is wrong because *accomplishing* is correctly spelled. (5) is wrong because a correction *is* necessary.
2. The correct answer is **(3)**. (1) is not correct because *family* may be considered a collective noun in the singular. (2) is wrong because no apostrophe is necessary since the idea of possession is not involved. (3) is correct because a comma *is* necessary after an introductory clause. See rule 4 on page 164. (4) is incorrect because *decision* is spelled correctly. (5) is wrong because *to invest* is the correct tense since the investment has not yet taken place.
3. The correct answer is **(1)**. This is so because the original is the best way. In (2), a period would result in a sentence fragment. In (3), (4), and (5), no punctuation is necessary after protection.
4. The correct answer is **(2)**. In (1) the correction would result in a run-on sentence. (2) is correct because *which is purchased* is an adjective clause describing insurance. In (3), (4), and (5), all the corrections would result in run-on sentences.
5. The correct answer is **(2)**. In (1), the present tense is correct and should not be changed. In (2), a comma should be inserted in a series according to rule 6, page 164, so this is correct. (3) is wrong because no one is being quoted. (4) is incorrect because *necessities* is the correct spelling. In (5), the comma is needed because it helps punctuate a series.
6. The correct answer is **(5)** because no correction is necessary. (1) is incorrect because breadwinner is not a proper noun and should not be capitalized. (2) is wrong because breadwinner is a single word that does not need a hyphen. In (3), *will give* is the correct tense because the future tense is required and, therefore, there should be no change. In (4), *the* is necessary because a definite article is needed. Therefore (5) is the correct answer.
7. This is a tricky question because it calls for the *most effective combination.* The correct answer is **(1)**. It is the most effective combination because the adjective clause immediately follows the noun, *program,* which it describes. (2), (4), (5) are awkward and not as effective. (3) is incorrect because an adjective clause is required.
8. The correct answer is **(1)**. The family protects itself in the *present* so the present tense, not the future tense, is needed. In (2), no comma is needed where only two items are involved: insurance and savings. In (3), the comma after *account* is necessary after an introductory clause. (4) is wrong because *then* is correct since it means "at that time." (5) is incorrect because there is an error in the sentence.
9. Again the most effective combination is called for. In this case, an adverbial clause with the unnecessary words eliminated is best. That choice is **(1)** which eliminates ten unneeded words after *channels* in the first sentence. All the other choices have superfluous words which reduce the effectiveness of the combination.

***Remember.* Test out each choice before you answer. You will have to draw on your knowledge of sentence structure, usage, and mechanics, all of which may be involved in a single question.**

THREE ADDITIONAL SAMPLE TEST PARAGRAPHS

Refer to page 229 for directions in answering the questions based on these paragraphs.

SAMPLE TEST PARAGRAPH 1

(1) To improve consumer choice use good buying strategies and tactics to carry out the basic plan. (2) Prices, quality and conveniance can vary greatly in buying food, auto insurance, or dandruff treatments. (3) A watermelon is a better buy at certain times of the year because of transportation costs. (4) Air conditioning may be a good buy at other times. (5) A used car may be adequate for many purposes. (6) A turnip is nutritious. (7) The variety and choice available makes your personal consumer decision process complex, but the potential savings and improvements is huge compared to poor results from not shopping harder. (8) A great deal of sorrow can be avoided by obtaining reliable information in consumer education courses consumer magazines, and numerous books and pamphlets. (9) Unfair and deceptive practices of a few businesses would largely disappear, if consumers practiced self-defence. (10) Such defence means being well informed. (11) Consumers can assist in improving product safety, help maintain reasonable prices, and raising the quality of goods not only by buying wisely, but by addressing themselves to economic and consumer problems. (12) Its a mutual responsibility among consumers to seek and to improve the ways in which producers make and sell their products and services.

1. Sentence 1. **To improve consumer choice use good buying strategies and tactics to carry out the basic plan.**
What correction should be made to this sentence?
(1) insert a comma after choice
(2) change strategies to stratagies
(3) insert a comma after strategies
(4) change to to and
(5) no correction is necessary

1. 1 2 3 4 5

2. Sentence 2. **Prices, quality, and conveniance can vary greatly in buying food, auto insurance, or dandruff treatments.**
What correction should be made to this sentence?
(1) remove the comma after quality
(2) change the spelling of conveniance to convenience
(3) change can to could
(4) remove the comma after food
(5) no correction is necessary

2. 1 2 3 4 5

3. Sentences 3 and 4. **A watermelon is a better buy at certain times of the year because of transportation costs. Air conditioning may be a good buy at other times.**
The most effective combination of sentences 3 and 4 would include which of the following words?
(1) costs, although air
(2) costs, and air
(3) costs, but air
(4) costs, however air
(5) costs, whereas air

3. 1 2 3 4 5

4. Sentence 7. **The variety and choice available makes your personal consumer decision process complex, but the potential savings and improvements is huge compared to poor results from not shopping harder.**
What correction should be made to this sentence?
(1) change the spelling of variety to veriety
(2) remove the comma after complex
(3) change but to and
(4) change is to are
(5) no correction is necessary

4. 1 2 3 4 5

5. Sentence 8. **A great deal of sorrow can be avoided by obtaining reliable information in consumer education courses consumer magazines, and numerous books and pamphlets.**
What correction should be made to this sentence?
(1) change can to could
(2) change by obtaining to if you obtained
(3) insert a comma after courses
(4) remove the comma after magazines
(5) no correction is necessary

5. 1 2 3 4 5

6. Sentence 9. **Unfair and deceptive practices of a few businesses would largely disappear, if consumers practiced self-defense.**
What correction should be made to this sentence?
(1) change the spelling of businesses to busineses
(2) change would to should
(3) remove the comma after disappear
(4) change the spelling of disappear to disapear
(5) no correction is necessary

6. 1 2 3 4 5

7. Sentences 9 and 10. **Unfair and deceptive practices of a few businesses would largely disappear, if consumers practiced self-defense. Such defense means being well-informed.**
Which of the following is the best way to write the underlined portion of this sentence? If you think the original is the best way, choose option (1).
(1) self-defense. Such
(2) self-defense such
(3) self-defense, such
(4) self-defense; such
(5) self-defense, nevertheless such

7. 1 2 3 4 5

8. Sentence 11. **Consumers can assist in improving product safety, help maintain reasonable prices, and raising the quality of goods not only by buying wisely, but by addressing themselves to economic and consumer problems.**
What correction should be made to this sentence?
(1) remove the comma after safety
(2) change help to helping
(3) change but to and
(4) change the spelling of addressing to adressing
(5) no correction is necessary

8. 1 2 3 4 5

9. Sentence 12. **Its a mutual responsibility among consumers to seek and to improve the ways in which producers make and sell their products and services.**
What correction should be made to this sentence?
(1) change the spelling of Its to It's
(2) change among to between
(3) change to seek to and seek
(4) change and to or
(5) no correction is necessary

9. 1 2 3 4 5

SAMPLE TEST PARAGRAPH 2

(1) Household insects seem to have an incredible ability to escape extinction. (2) Cockroaches for example which have been on earth millions of years longer than man, can subsist on any kind of food. (3) They thrive in all parts of the world, some species prefer man's home to other habitats. (4) Once they enter it they use countless instinctive tricks to keep from being killed or evicted. (5) You can control household pests. (6) Do systematic house cleaning. (7) The best way to rid your home of practically all insect pests is by a combination of good housekeeping practices and proper use of the right insecticide. (8) It is easier to prevent pests from infesting your home than it is to get rid of them after they are established. (9) Household insects seek available food in places where they can hide and breath. (10) If one eliminates these attractions from your home, the insects will look elsewhere for them. (11) Keep storage cabinets, kitchen drawers, and washtubs clean. (12) Frequent scrubbings with hot water and soap will do the job.

1. Sentence 2. **Cockroaches for example which have been on earth millions of years longer than man, can subsist on any kind of food.**
What correction should be made to this sentence?
(1) insert commas before and after for example
(2) change which to who
(3) remove the comma after man
(4) change can subsist to have subsisted
(5) no correction is necessary

1. 1 2 3 4 5

2. Sentence 3. **They thrive in all parts of the world, some species prefer man's home to other habitats.**
Which of the following is the best way to write the underlined portion of this sentence? If you think the original is the best way, choose option (1).
(1) world, some species
(2) world. Some species
(3) world some species
(4) world but some species
(5) world because some species

2. 1 2 3 4 5

3. Sentence 4. **Once they enter it they use countless instinctive tricks to keep from being killed or evicted.**
What correction should be made to this sentence?
(1) change it to man's home
(2) insert a comma after it
(3) change being killed to having been killed
(4) change or to and
(5) no correction is necessary

3. 1 2 3 4 5

4. Sentences 5 and 6. **You can control household pests. Do systematic house cleaning.**
The most effective combination of sentences 5 and 6 would include which of the following groups of words?
(1) pests and do
(2) pests if they try to do
(3) pests while doing
(4) pests by doing
(5) pests having done

4. 1 2 3 4 5

5. Sentence 7. **The best way to rid your home of practically all insect pests is by a combination of good housekeeping practices and proper use of the right insecticide.**
If you rewrote sentence 7 beginning with
A combination of good housekeeping practices and proper use of the right insecticide is
the next word(s) would be
(1) indeed
(2) therefore
(3) furthermore
(4) for example
(5) however

5. 1 2 3 4 5

6. Sentence 8. **It is easier to prevent pests from infesting your home than it is to get rid of them after they are established.**
Which of the following is the best way to write the underlined portion of this sentence? If you think the original is the best way, choose option (1).
(1) them after
(2) them. After
(3) them, after
(4) them; after
(5) them, and after

6. 1 2 3 4 5

7. Sentence 9. **Household insects seek available food in places where they can hide and breath.**
What correction should be made to this sentence?
(1) change the spelling of available to availible
(2) insert a comma after places
(3) change can to could
(4) change the spelling of breath to breathe
(5) no correction is necessary

7. 1 2 3 4 5

8. Sentence 10. **If one eliminates these attractions from your home, the insects will look elsewhere for them.**
What correction should be made to this sentence?
(1) change your to one's
(2) remove the comma after home
(3) change will to would
(4) change elsewhere to somewhere else
(5) no correction is necessary

8. 1 2 3 4 5

9. Sentences 11 and 12. **Keep storage cabinets, kitchen drawers, and washtubs clean. Frequent scrubbings with hot water and soap will do the job.**
The most effective combination of sentences 11 and 12 would include which of the following groups of words?
(1) and frequent scrubbings
(2) by frequent scrubbings
(3) because frequent scrubbings
(4) since frequent scrubbings
(5) as a matter of fact frequent scrubbings

9. 1 2 3 4 5
|| || || || ||

SAMPLE TEST PARAGRAPH 3

(1) Among your important records are a thorough household inventory. (2) Before this can be of much value, in case of fire or burglary, youll need to supply some details. (3) Be sure to list the date item bought, purchase price, model number if it applies, brand name, dealer's name. (4) And general description (colour, size, style, electric or gas, etc.) (5) Don't forget to include a realistic lump sum in your list for clothes and jewelry if you don't itemize these. (6) This information serves a triple purpose. (7) It helps you to determine the value of your possessions so you can have adequate insurance protection. (8) It helps you if it becomes necessary for you to make an insurance claim. (9) Some families take pictures of their rooms to help identify posessions. (10) One copy of the household inventory should be put in your safe deposit box; you may wish to give a copy to your insurance company.

1. Sentence 1. **Among your important records are a thorough household inventory.**
What correction should be made to this sentence?
(1) change your to you're
(2) change are to is
(3) change thorough to through
(4) change the spelling of inventory to inventary
(5) no change is necessary

1. 1 2 3 4 5
|| || || || ||

2. Sentence 2. **Before this can be of much value, in case of fire or burglary, youll need to supply some details.**
What correction should be made to this sentence?
(1) remove the comma after value
(2) remove the comma after burglary
(3) change youll to you'll
(4) change to supply to to have supplied
(5) no correction is necessary

2. 1 2 3 4 5
|| || || || ||

3. Sentence 3. **Be sure to list the item date bought, purchase price, model number if it applies, brand name, dealer's name.**
What correction should be made to this sentence?
(1) insert a comma after item
(2) capitalize date bought
(3) remove the comma after applies
(4) change dealer's to dealers
(5) no correction is necessary

3. 1 2 3 4 5
|| || || || ||

4. Sentences 3 and 4. **Be sure to list the date item bought, purchase price, model number if it applies, brand name, dealer's name. And general description (colour, size, style, electric or gas, etc.)**
Which is the best way to write the underlined portion of this sentence? If you think the original is the best way, choose option (1).
(1) name. And
(2) name. and
(3) name and
(4) name, and
(5) name, And

4. 1 2 3 4 5

5. Sentence 5. **Don't forget to include a realistic lump sum in your list for clothes and jewelry if you don't itemize these.**
What correction should be made to this sentence?
(1) change Don't to Dont
(2) change the spelling of realistic to reelistic
(3) insert a comma after sum
(4) change the spelling of clothes to cloths
(5) no correction is necessary

5. 1 2 3 4 5

6. Sentences 6 and 7. **This information serves a triple purpose. It helps you to determine the value of your possessions so you can have adequate insurance protection.**
Which of the following is the best way to write the underlined portion of this sentence? If you think the original is the best way, choose option (1).
(1) purpose. It
(2) purpose it
(3) purpose It
(4) purpose, so it
(5) purpose although it

6. 1 2 3 4 5

7. Sentence 8. **It helps you if it becomes necessary for you to make an insurance claim.**
What correction should be made to this sentence?
(1) insert a comma after you
(2) change you to one
(3) change becomes to will become
(4) change the spelling of necessary to neccessary
(5) no correction is necessary

7. 1 2 3 4 5

8. Sentence 9. **Some families take pictures of their rooms to help identify posessions.**
What correction should be made to this sentence?
(1) change the spelling of their to they're
(2) insert a comma after rooms
(3) change to help to which helps
(4) change the spelling of posessions to possessions
(5) no correction is necessary

8. 1 2 3 4 5

9. Sentence 10. **One copy of the household inventory should be put in your safe deposit box; you may wish to give a copy to your insurance company.**
What correction should be made to this sentence?
(1) change should be to is to be
(2) change the semicolon after box to a colon
(3) change may to might
(4) capitalize insurance company
(5) no correction is necessary

9. 1 2 3 4 5
|| || || || ||

Turn to the answer key and the answer analysis which follow.

What's Your Score?

Total your score on the three sample test paragraphs (the analyzed paragraph and the three additional sample test paragraphs).

______ right,	______ wrong
Excellent	32–36
Good	27–31
Fair	22–26

ANSWER KEY

Sample Test Paragraph 1/Page 232

1. **1**
2. **2**
3. **2**
4. **4**
5. **3**
6. **5**
7. **1**
8. **2**
9. **1**

ANSWER ANALYSIS

Sample Test Paragraph 1/Page 232

1. **1** There is an error in punctuation. A comma is used after an introductory phrase.
2. **2** There is an error in spelling. *Convenience* is the correct spelling.
3. **2** A coordinating conjunction is required because both independent clauses are equally important.
4. **4** There is an error in usage. A plural subject, *savings and improvement*, requires a plural verb, *are*.
5. **3** There is an error in punctuation. A comma is required to separate items in a series.
6. **5** No correction is necessary.
7. **1** The original is correct. All other choices result in run-on sentences.
8. **2** There is an error in usage. The use of the participle *helping* is required to parallel the participles *improving* and *raising*.
9. **1** There is an error in spelling. *It's* is a contraction of *it is*, the subject and verb needed to make this sentence.

ANSWER KEY

Sample Test Paragraph 2/Page 234

1. **1**
2. **2**
3. **2**
4. **4**
5. **5**
6. **1**
7. **4**
8. **1**
9. **2**

ANSWER ANALYSIS

Sample Test Paragraph 2/Page 234

1. **1** There is an error in punctuation. Commas are used to set off phrases which are inserted into a sentence.
2. **2** There is an error in sentence structure. As it is, there is a run-on sentence. A period is needed to divide the two sentences and the second sentence must start with capital letter.
3. **2** There is an error in punctuation. A comma is needed to set off the introductory clause.
4. **4** The sentences are best combined by changing the second sentence into an adverbial clause modifying the verb *control*.
5. **5** *However* is used when the idea in its sentence differs from the idea in the previous sentence. In this case, the previous sentence had one method of control. This sentence refers to a combination of methods.
6. **1** The original is correct, since *after they are established* is an adverbial clause modifying *get rid of*.
7. **4** *Breathe* is the correct spelling of the verb which is needed here. *Breath* is a noun.
8. **1** There is an error in the use of the pronouns. There is a needless shift from the third person *one* to the second person *your*. If you use more than one pronoun to refer to the same person, you must be consistent. The sentence refers to *If one eliminates*. Therefore, it must be followed by *from one's home*.
9. **2** The best combination is *by frequent scrubbings*. It modifies the verb *keep* and makes the words *will do the job* unnecessary.

ANSWER KEY

Sample Test Paragraph 3/Page 236

1. **2**
2. **3**
3. **1**
4. **4**
5. **5**
6. **1**
7. **5**
8. **4**
9. **5**

ANSWER ANALYSIS

Sample Test Paragraph 3/Page 236

1. **2** There is an error in usage. The subject of the sentence is *inventory* which is singular. The verb, therefore, must be singular *is*, since subject and verb must agree in number.
2. **3** The error is in spelling. The proper contraction of *you will* is *you'll* with the apostrophe indicating that letters are omitted.
3. **1** There is a punctuation error. Commas are needed to set off items in a series.
4. **4** Inclusion of the phrase *and general description* in the previous sentence removes the sentence fragment. A comma is necessary because the phrase is one of a series of phrases.
5. **5** No correction is necessary.
6. **1** The original is correct. Two separate sentences are required.
7. **5** No correction is necessary.
8. **4** There is a spelling error. *Possessions* is the correct spelling.
9. **5** No correction is necessary.

5

LANGUAGE ARTS, WRITING (WRITING SKILLS), PART II

THE ESSAY TEST

We introduce you to the essay with a detailed description of what is required.

PLAN OF THE CHAPTER

We outline the chapter which takes you from the sentence to the completed essay.

THE SENTENCE—THE BASIC UNIT OF WRITING

The essential skills of writing *effective*, *suspenseful*, *emphatic*, *interesting*, *colourful*, and *varied* sentences are discussed.

THE PARAGRAPH—THE BASIC WAY TO DEVELOP IDEAS

We demonstrate *eight* ways to develop paragraphs—by details, illustration and example, time sequence, space sequence, definition, classification, comparison and contrast, and reasons and proof. *Seven* ways to write effective paragraphs are discussed. You are given the opportunity to write paragraphs of your own according to specific models.

THE ESSAY—AT THE TEST CENTRE

You are shown how to plan the essay using the 45 minutes allotted. We show you how to transform your notes into an outline. We proceed from the outline to the final essay with advice on how to improve a satisfactory essay to a superior one. An explanation of how the essay is scored is presented. Finally, 27 topics are suggested for further practice.

THE ESSAY TEST

What is the Language Arts, Writing (Writing Skills), Part II test? You must write a composition based on a single topic. The topic will be brief, presenting an issue or situation familiar to you and asking a question about it.

The purpose of the Language Arts, Writing (Writing Skills), Part II, the GED Essay Test, is to test directly your ability to write. It does this by requiring you to write an essay of about 250 words in which you either present your opinion on an issue, a problem which has positive and negative sides, or explain a situation about which you have some general knowledge. The purpose is *not* to test *how much you know but* rather *your ability to express in writing what you already know* about the issue or situation presented. No specialized information is necessary to write on the topic.

PLAN OF THIS CHAPTER

Writing well requires a great many difficult skills, many of which you may have already mastered. Before we take you to a test centre and run you through a dress rehearsal for the actual essay you will write, it is worth reviewing the elements essential to your demonstrating your ability to write.

The building blocks to a well-written essay are good sentence structure and carefully developed paragraphs. We will review the two most important ways to write effective sentences. We shall go beyond that to an introduction to suspenseful, emphatic, interesting, colourful, and varied sentences. Then we will review the elements of a good paragraph including topic and summary sentences, illustrating eight different ways in which effective paragraphs can be developed. We shall then take you step by step through the actual experience of writing an essay at the test centre, tell you how it will be rated, and provide opportunity for you to have ample practice before you take the actual test.

THE SENTENCE—THE BASIC UNIT OF WRITING

The basic unit of communication is the sentence. The *sentence* is a complete thought expressed in words. It must be independent of other words or groups of words. It must have a *subject*, the person or thing spoken about, and a *predicate* which makes a statement about the subject. The subject is a noun or pronoun which is stated or a noun or pronoun which is understood, as in a command. *Stop!* (*You* or the *name of the person addressed* may be understood.) The predicate must contain at least one verb form.

EXAMPLE: Mario likes food.

Mario is the subject and the predicate makes a statement about Mario—that he likes food. The predicate contains the verb—likes.

Sentences may serve many purposes. They may make a statement, as in the case of Mario. Such a sentence is termed *declarative.* They may indicate a command—*Don't go*. This is an *imperative* sentence. The sentence may ask a question—*Does Mario like food*? This is an example of an *interrogative* sentence. Finally, an *exclamatory* sentence may show extreme emotion—*I can't believe it!*

Sentences may be simple, with one main, independent clause.

EXAMPLE: Dahlia has many friends.

Or they may be *compound* with two or more main, independent clauses linked together.

EXAMPLE: <u>I stayed home last night</u> and <u>my brother helped me with my homework</u>.

They may also be *complex* with one main clause and one or more dependent clauses, groups of words which cannot stand independently.

EXAMPLE: <u>Consuela got a job</u> <u>after she graduated.</u>

<u>Consuela got a job</u> is the independent clause and <u>after she graduated</u>, which cannot stand by itself, is the dependent clause.

WRITING EFFECTIVE SENTENCES

> A most important element of good sentence structure is the *ability to relate ideas to one another effectively*.

There are *two* ways to do this.

1. ***Relate an idea in one sentence to an idea in another sentence.*** The word used depends, of course, on the nature of the relationship between the ideas. In general, there are *seven* different kinds of relationships.

   1. *Add other ideas to an idea already expressed, using words or phrases which indicate addition.* Since more than one sentence may be involved, be careful not to commit a run-on sentence error. (Review the section "Types of Run-On Sentences" on page 105.)

Words and Phrases That Indicate Addition

also	again
too	likewise
in addition	similarly
moreover	what's more
furthermore	

Words That Emphasize or Call Special Attention to the Idea Being Added

indeed	certainly
in fact	truly
as a matter of fact	

EXAMPLE: The work I do is interesting. *Moreover*, it pays well.
EXAMPLE: Mr. Jones was wealthy. *In addition*, he was generous to a fault.
EXAMPLE: The quarterback was an excellent passer. *In fact*, he was an all-round athlete.

   2. *Illustrate an idea or explain it further*. This is considered a special case of addition.

Words That Help Illustrate an Idea

for example	to illustrate
for instance	thus

Words That Help Explain an Idea Further

in other words	that is to say
as has been said	

EXAMPLE: Athletes in some sports earn huge sums of money. *For example*, the heavyweight boxing champion earns millions of dollars in one fight.
EXAMPLE: Politics often ignores ethics. *That is to say*, political decisions are based on practical considerations rather than principles of right or wrong.

3. *Establish an order in the ideas expressed in either time or space.*

Words That Establish Time Order	
first, second, etc.	later
next	before this
further	after
then	after this
then again	afterwards
finally	last

Words That Establish Space Order	
above	in front
beyond	to the right
nearby	to the left
far off	

EXAMPLE: The father spanked his son for misbehaving. *Afterwards*, he felt sorry that he had.

EXAMPLE: *Beyond* the house stood the barn and *to the left* was the silo.

4. *Contrast ideas or show how they differ from each other.* Be careful not to commit a run-on sentence error. (Review the section on "Types of Run-On Sentences" on page 105.)

Words That Indicate Contrast	
although	yet
but	however
nevertheless	rather
on the other hand	still
on the contrary	

EXAMPLE: My father is advanced in years. *Still*, he likes to participate actively in sports.

EXAMPLE: My son is independent in most respects where money is concerned. *On the other hand*, he comes to me for advice about clothes.

5. *Admit that an already expressed idea has some limitations.*

Words That Indicate Limitation of an Idea	
of course	granted that
to be sure	I admit

EXAMPLE: Presidents in the United States are popularly elected. Gerald Ford, *of course*, was an exception.

6. *Show that one idea results from another.*

Words That Indicate Results	
as a consequence	so
therefore	hence
consequently	accordingly
as a result	

EXAMPLE: At the baseball game, the fan ate too many hot dogs. *As a result*, he got an upset stomach.

EXAMPLE: The student prepared thoroughly. *Therefore*, he got a high grade.

7. *Summarize briefly ideas contained in a previous sentence or previous sentences.*

Words That Summarize	
in brief	in short
in sum	to sum up
in summary	

EXAMPLE: The doctor recommended swimming, jogging, tennis, and handball. *In sum*, she preferred active sports.

Practice

Directions: **Using words that**

indicate addition
emphasize the added part
illustrate or explain an idea further
establish time or space order
contrast ideas
limit ideas
indicate results
summarize

relate the ideas in the following pairs of sentences. Use an appropriate word from the preceding boxes. In each pair of sentences, the word(s) in parentheses indicates the relationship.

1. (Contrast) I have a wealthy friend. His tastes are simple.
2. (Result) The athlete put in long hours of practice. He won the trophy.
3. (Summary) The teenager ate lots of potato chips, french fries, candy bars, and cookies. She likes junk foods.
4. (Time order) The child spoke disrespectfully to his parents. He felt sorry.
5. (Time order) The worker hurt his leg when he fell. The pain subsided.
6. (Example) Many handicapped persons achieve greatness. Helen Keller was a great writer.
7. (Emphasis) Anne Murray has a very broad repertoire. She can sing a wide variety of popular songs.
8. (Explain further) Our village is a microcosm. It is a miniature of the world.
9. (Addition) My parents are good parents. They are my friends.
10. (Contrast) My father spends little on himself. He is very generous to us children.

Answers

There are several possible answers to each of the questions. Two are provided for each question, but others can be found in the same box from which these two are taken.

1. I have a wealthy friend, *but* his tastes are simple.
   I have a wealthy friend; *however* his tastes are simple. (Note important change in punctuation).
2. The athlete put in long hours of practice. *Therefore*, he won the trophy.
   The athlete put in long hours of practice. *As a result*, he won the trophy.
3. The teenager ate lots of potato chips, french fries, candy bars, and cookies. *In brief*, she likes junk foods.
   The teenager ate lots of potato chips, french fries, candy bars, and cookies. *In sum*, she likes junk foods.
4. The child spoke disrespectfully to his parents. *After*, he left sorry.
   The child spoke disrespectfully to his parents. *Then* he felt sorry.
5. The worker hurt his leg when he fell. *Later* the pain subsided.
   The worker hurt his leg when he fell. *Afterwards* the pain subsided.
6. Many handicapped persons achieve greatness. *For example*, Helen Keller was a great writer.
   Many handicapped persons achieve greatness. *For instance*, Helen Keller was a great writer.
7. Anne Murray has a very broad repertoire. *Indeed*, she can sing a wide variety of popular songs.
   Anne Murray has a very broad repertoire. *In fact*, she can sing a wide variety of popular songs.
8. Our village is a microcosm. *In other words*, it is a miniature of the world.
   Our village is a microcosm. *That is to say*, it is a miniature of the world.
9. My parents are good parents. *What's more*, they are my friends.
   My parents are good parents. *Furthermore*, they are my friends.
10. My father spends little on himself, *yet* he is very generous to us children.
    Although my father spends little on himself, he is very generous to us children.

Practice

Directions: **Here are some more pairs of sentences. Figure out the relationship between them and use one of the appropriate words from the preceding boxes to show that relationship. (Several of the pairs of sentences can be joined into a single sentence.)**

1. In high school, I studied mathematics. I studied English.
2. The farm worker was very poor. He didn't know where his next meal was coming from.
3. Frank was slight of build and rather short. He was a fine athlete.
4. Deena was graduated from high school. She went on to college.
5. Mother recently underwent surgery. She feels extremely weak.
6. The nutritionist recommended dairy foods, fruits, cereals, and proteins. She advised a balanced diet.
7. Exercising regularly is important. Walking is healthy.
8. The baby had a fever. Her parents called the doctor.
9. My grandmother is over ninety years old. She is quite alert.
10. My car needs gas. It needs oil.

Answers

There are several possible answers to the questions. Two are given for each.

1. In high school, I studied mathematics. I *also* studied English.
   In high school, I studied mathematics. *In addition*, I studied English.
2. The farm worker was very poor. *Indeed*, he didn't know where his next meal was coming from.
   The farm worker was very poor. *In fact*, he didn't know where his next meal was coming from.
3. Frank was slight of build and rather short; *yet* he was a fine athlete.
   Frank was slight of build and rather short. *Nevertheless*, he was a fine athlete.
4. *After* Deena was graduated from high school, she went on to college.
   Deena was graduated from high school. *Next* she went on to college.

5. Mother recently underwent surgery. *Hence* she feels extremely weak.
   Mother recently underwent surgery, *so* she feels extremely weak.
6. The nutritionist recommended dairy foods, fruits, cereals, and proteins. *To sum up*, she advised a balanced diet.
   The nutritionist recommended dairy foods, fruits, cereals, and proteins. *In short*, she advised a balanced diet.
7. Exercising regularly is important. *Thus* walking is healthy.
   Exercising regularly is important. *To illustrate*, walking is healthy.
8. The baby had a fever. *As a consequence*, her parents called the doctor.
   The baby had a fever. *Consequently*, her parents called the doctor.
9. My grandmother is over ninety years old, *but* she is quite alert.
   My grandmother is over ninety years old. *However*, she is quite alert.
10. My car needs gas. It *also* needs oil.
    My car needs gas. *In addition*, it needs oil.

2. ***Relate ideas within a single sentence.*** There are a number of possible kinds of relationships.
   1. *Connect two ideas of equal importance.*

Connecting Words

and	nor
or	for
but	

EXAMPLE: I enjoy my work *and* look forward to each working day.
EXAMPLE: She does housework *or* goes shopping on the days she does not go to work.

   2. *Combine two sentences by subordinating the less important action pertaining to a person or object described in a separate sentence*. This may be done by using a relative clause that is introduced by a relative pronoun.

Relative Pronouns Used to Introduce Relative Clauses

who	whom	which

EXAMPLE: I married Mary. She is the girl I met at your house.
COMBINED: I married Mary *whom* I met at your house.

Whom I met is the relative clause which enables you to subordinate the idea of meeting (less important) to the idea of marrying (more important).

EXAMPLE: The children left their clothes strewn about the room. The mother had to pick them up.
COMBINED: The mother had to pick up the clothes *which* the children left strewn about the room.

Which the children left strewn is the relative clause which subordinates the idea of leaving about (less important) to the idea of picking up (more important).

Not only do you save unnecessary words at times in this manner, but you express your ideas more effectively by indicating their relative importance to your reader.

   3. *Combine sentences by subordinating a less important action described in one sentence to a related more important action described in another, using a subordinate conjunction.*

Subordinate Conjunctions

Showing Time Relationships

when	before
while	after

Showing Causal Relationships

because	since

Showing Opposite Relationships

although

Showing dependent relationships

if

A number of examples indicating these relationships follows. In each case, the second action is subordinate (less important) to the first.

EXAMPLE:

ORIGINAL:	I was happy. I had a good job.
COMBINED:	
(Time relationship)	I was happy *when* I had a good job.
	I was happy *while* I had a good job.
	I was happy *before* I had a good job.
	I was happy *after* I had a good job.
(Causal relationship)	I was happy *because* I had a good job.
	I was happy *since* I had a good job.
(Opposite relationship)	I was happy *although* I had a good job.
(Dependent relationship)	I was happy only *if* I had a good job.

4. *Combine sentences by using a phrase to subordinate a less important action described in one sentence to a related more important action described in another.* Note the italicized phrases that follow. In each case, the idea expressed in the phrase is less important than the idea in the sentence in which it appears.

EXAMPLE:

ORIGINAL: There are many famous goal scorers in hockey. Maurice Richard is the most colourful.

COMBINED: *Of the many famous goal scorers in hockey*, Maurice Richard is the most colourful.

EXAMPLE:

ORIGINAL: I took the baby out of the stroller. I entered the supermarket to shop.

COMBINED: *Taking the baby out of the stroller*, I entered the supermarket to shop.

EXAMPLE:

ORIGINAL: The Careys decided to hire a housekeeper. She had to take care of the baby while they were at work.

COMBINED: *To take care of the baby while they were at work*, the Careys decided to hire a housekeeper.

Note: In each example, the subordinate or less important idea is first in the sentence, with the more important idea kept for last.

5. *Combine sentences by substituting a word or words for an entire subordinate (less important) sentence which describes a related action*. Note the italicized words.

EXAMPLE:

ORIGINAL: The student prepared his lesson. He did so, however, in a way that showed he wasn't careful.

COMBINED: The student prepared his lesson *carelessly*.

EXAMPLE:

ORIGINAL: The young lady caught my eye. She was an extraordinary beauty.

COMBINED: The *extraordinarily beautiful* young lady caught my eye.

EXAMPLE:

ORIGINAL: He had one important quality. It was that he was extremely intelligent.

COMBINED: *Intelligence* was his one important quality.

6. *Combine sentences by placing a description of a person or object in one sentence in* <u>*apposition*</u> *(see the "Glossary of Usage" on page 136) with the word identifying that person in another*. (The words in apposition are italicized.)

EXAMPLE:

ORIGINAL: My mother is very active in community affairs. She is president of the Parents' Association.

COMBINED: My mother, *president of the Parents' Association*, is very active in community affairs.

> ***Important note:*** With the exception of item 1 on page 243—to "connect two ideas of equal importance"—it is also possible to use *phrases* instead of clauses and sentences.

Here are some examples:

EXAMPLE 1.

My mother, *who is president* of the Parents' Association, is very active in community affairs.

BECOMES

My mother, *president* of the Parents' Association, is very active in community affairs.

EXAMPLE 2.

Jet airplanes, *which are a twentieth-century phenomenon*, have brought the world's nations closer together.

BECOMES

Jet airplanes, *a twentieth-century phenomenon*, have brought the world's nations closer together.

EXAMPLE 3.

While we were having lunch, I got a telephone call from the office.

BECOMES

During lunch, I got a telephone call from the office.

EXAMPLE 4.

He studied hard *so that he could* get into medical school.

BECOMES

He studied hard *to* get into medical school.

EXAMPLE 5.

The hero of the game was given an ovation *which was heart-warming*.

BECOMES

The hero of the game was given a *heart-warming* ovation.

Practice

Directions: **Combine into a single sentence the ideas contained in the following pairs of sentences.**

1. Claudia introduced me to Fred. He is the president of the club.
2. I had few responsibilities. I was young.
3. George could go to college. He had saved up enough money.
4. The actor gave a magnificent performance. He was handsome.
5. Celia likes to swim. She likes to play tennis.
6. Sue and Joe got married. They met at a party.
7. Jennifer failed the test. She had studied very hard.
8. Dwight was given a diploma. It was well earned.
9. Let me introduce Shira. I spoke to you about her.
10. Many women do not like housework. They do not like marketing.

Answers

1. Claudia introduced me to Fred *who* is the president of the club.
   Claudia introduced me to Fred, the president of the club.
2. I had few responsibilities *when* I was young.
3. *Because* he had saved up enough money, George could go to college.
4. The *handsome* actor gave a magnificent performance.
5. Celia likes to swim *and* play tennis.
   Celia likes to swim *and* she likes to play tennis.
6. Sue and Joe got married *after* they met at a party.
7. *Although* she had studied very hard, Jennifer failed the test.
8. Dwight was given a *well-earned* diploma.
9. Let me introduce Shira about *whom* I spoke to you.
10. Many women like *neither* housework *nor* marketing.

Practice

Directions: **Using phrases or words in apposition (see #6) instead of clauses make the following sentences shorter and more effective.**

1. George rushed home so that he could see his favourite television program.
2. Mother prepared a dinner for the family which was tasty.
3. Charlie, who is an outstanding athlete, contributed much to his team's success.
4. As we were driving home, we saw an accident.
5. Our home, which is located on a quiet street, is my favourite place to relax.

Answers

1. George rushed home *to see* his favourite television program.
2. Mother prepared *a tasty dinner* for the family.
3. Charlie, *an outstanding athlete*, contributed to his team's success.
4. *Driving home*, we saw an accident.
5. Our home, *located on a quiet street*, is my favourite place to relax.

WRITING SUSPENSEFUL SENTENCES

A famous English writer of mystery stories once summed up his technique in three brief words. "Make 'em wait." That is a good definition of suspense. The dictionary is more detailed: "the growing interest and excitement felt while awaiting a climax."

You can create suspense in your writing by using sentences which either postpone the most important idea or put off its completion until the very end. These sentences are effective because they keep the reader on the alert, waiting to find out the main idea or person discussed. That makes the conclusion much more powerful when the reader reaches it.

Here is an example of a suspenseful sentence:

> If there is no change in his condition by next week, and if, unfortunately, the laboratory tests show no improvement, the doctor will have to operate.

How to Write a Suspenseful Sentence

1. ***Where ideas are involved, save the main clause for the end of the sentence.*** This means simply that the independent clause, the one that can stand alone, should follow the subordinate clause or clauses. In our example, "the doctor will have to operate" is the main clause. It is preceded by two adverbial subordinate clauses. By holding the main clause until the end, you keep the reader in suspense as to what will happen, and the word *operate*, the most important word in the sentence, is emphasized.

   A famous example by a famous writer who used the technique of the suspenseful sentence to perfection is found in this sentence from an address by Winston Churchill: "I would say to the House, as I said to those who have joined this Government: 'I have nothing to offer but *blood*, *toil*, *tears*, and *sweat*."' The key words are in italics.

2. ***Where the identity of people or objects is involved, save the identity for the end of the sentence.*** In the following situations, the identification of the person as a proper noun (referring to an individual person, place, or thing) or as a common noun (referring to a group of persons, places, or things) is kept to the end of the sentence.
   Here are two examples, the first using a proper noun, the second a common noun.

   PROPER NOUN EXAMPLE:

   Of all the persons I have met in my lifetime, persons who have left an indelible impression, the most remarkable was that blind, deaf-mute sensitive artistic genius *Helen Keller.*

   COMMON NOUN EXAMPLE:

   With her jet-black hair, her high cheekbones, her slanting eyes, her hands with their long, tapered fingers, the woman suggested a *Chinese princess.*

   Here is a slightly humourous example.

   EXAMPLE:

   There are few more obvious, natural, apparent, plain, intelligible, literal, and down-right objects on this earth than *a boiled potato.*

3. ***Where several ideas are involved, save the most important one for last.*** Often, sentences contain a number of ideas. To create suspense, build up to the most important idea by mentioning the others first and holding the most important one till the end of the sentence.

   EXAMPLE:

   America is not just a country, nor is it merely a democracy, but it is, without any doubt, "the last best hope of earth."

   The progression from the simple word *country* to the phrase which emphasizes America's importance to the world illustrates this way of keeping your reader involved until the end of the sentence.

WRITING EMPHATIC SENTENCES

Writing suspenseful or periodic sentences is but one way of giving emphasis to an important idea or person. There are other ways of achieving the emphasis you wish to give.

Ways to Achieve Emphasis

1. ***Repeat an important idea you want to impress on your reader.*** Do not hesitate to use the same word over and over if you want to hammer home your point. A famous example of this technique is Abraham Lincoln's "government of the *people*, by the *people*, for the *people*." Another is Winston Churchill's promise, made during World War II: *We shall fight* on the beaches, *we shall fight* on the landing grounds, *we shall fight* in the fields and in the streets, *we shall fight* in the hills.

2. ***Reverse the usual order of elements of the sentence, putting the word to be emphasized first.*** This technique is known as *inversion.*

   EXAMPLE:
   Home is where the heart is.

   Home is emphasized by reversing the order; *Where the heart is is home.*

   EXAMPLE:
   Advice I did not want.

   The normal order here is *I did not want advice.* The word *advice* is emphasized.

3. ***Place the idea to be emphasized either first or last.*** If you place it last, you are using the technique we discussed in creating suspense through periodic sentences. But you can also place it first, and then discuss and develop it.

4. ***Tell the reader directly that the idea is important.*** The simplest way to emphasize a thought is to identify it as being important. You can do this in any number of ways.

Ways to Identify an Important Thought

—Use certain words or phrases to emphasize a thought:

mainly	above all
principally	in the main
chiefly	most important
mostly	foremost

—Use the word *first* to indicate that this idea leads others.

—Use superlatives of adjectives to indicate importance, e.g.,

biggest
most significant

—State that an idea is important, e.g.,

I think it most important that . . .
. . . is most significant.
. . . should be emphasized.

These are your ways of conveying what is most important to you, the writer. They are signals which say "Pay close attention. This is important."

Practice

Directions: **Using the techniques listed under writing suspenseful and emphatic sentences, rewrite the following sentences either to inject suspense or to emphasize important ideas or people.**

1. Serious steps will have to be taken if productivity is not improved and profit margins widened.
2. Every citizen must be interested, well informed, and active in the voting process.

3. Of all my friends, Laura is the one I like best.
4. Pierre Trudeau, for his outspokenness, his unbridled energy, his enthusiasm, and his intellect, is the twentieth century prime minister I most admire.
5. The family is a refuge for many troubled people and it is also the basic unit of society.

Answers

1. If productivity is not improved and profit margins widened, serious steps will have to be taken.
2. Every citizen must be interested; every citizen must be well informed; every citizen must be active in the voting process.
3. Of all my friends, the one I like best is Laura.
   Laura, of all my friends, is the one I like best.
4. For his outspokenness, his unbridled energy, his enthusiasm, and his intellect, the twentieth century prime minister I most admire is Pierre Trudeau.
5. A refuge for many troubled people and the basic unit of society is the family.
   The family, the basic unit of society, is a refuge for many troubled people.

WRITING INTERESTING SENTENCES

It is worth indicating briefly a number of additional ways to make your sentences, and, therefore, your writing, more interesting.

1. ***Use personal pronouns where possible.*** You will recall that the personal pronouns are

Singular	Plural
I	we
you	you
he	they
she	
it	

Using these, instead of the more formal nouns, creates interest.

EXAMPLE:
The reader will find this book helpful in studying for the examination.
How much better is the simple, direct "*You* will find . . ." *You* replaces the more formal *The reader.*

EXAMPLE:
It is expected that you . . .
IS MORE FORMAL THAN
You are expected to . . .

EXAMPLE:
The writer feels that . . .
IS LESS INTERESTING THAN
I feel that . . .

2. ***Use active verbs in preference to passive verbs.*** Active verbs, verbs that usually take an object, add power to your writing.

EXAMPLE:
PASSIVE: The examination *was passed by* me. (weak)
ACTIVE: *I passed* the examination. (much stronger)

EXAMPLE:
PASSIVE: Diane *is loved by everyone.*
HAS LESS POWER THAN
ACTIVE: *Everyone loves* Diane.

Not only are passive verbs weaker, but because they require two words where one will do, they result in longer sentences which get bogged down with such meaningless words as *it is*, *it was*, *is being*, *have been*, *has been*, and other forms of the verb *to be* which are necessary in the passive.

3. ***Use conversation wherever it belongs naturally in your writing.*** You know how you feel when you see unbroken pages of print. Conversation breaks up the printed page and makes what you have to say more interesting.
Compare these two passages.

I told my friend, John, that I was going to the ball game. I asked if he would come along. He answered, thanking me for the invitation but he added that he would have to check to see if he was needed at home by his mother.

"John, I'm going to the ball game. Would you like to come along?"
"Thanks for the invitation but I have to check to see if my mother needs me at home."

There is no doubt that the passage with the direct conversation is far more interesting (and easier to read) than the passage with the wordier indirect conversation.

Practice

Directions: **Rewrite the following sentences using personal pronouns and/or active verbs.**

1. All the food served to me was eaten by me.
2. The book was enjoyed by my father.
3. It is certain that you will be invited.
4. The writer of this letter wishes to comfort you.
5. Robert was admired by his classmates.

Answers

1. *I ate* all the food / was served.
2. My father *enjoyed* the book.
3. *You* are certain to be invited.
4. *I wish* to comfort you.
5. His classmates *admired* Robert.

WRITING COLOURFUL SENTENCES

You will recall that, in discussing word choice, we made a distinction between denotative (more exact) words and connotative (more suggestive) words. In poetic language, words or expressions are used which appeal to the reader's imagination, to his emotions. They do so because they are used in an unusual way or in an unusual context. These expressions are called figures of speech. You will meet them again when you read poetry or poetic prose.

You can write colourful sentences by using *figurative language*—language which creates pictures. The two principal figures of speech are the *simile* and the *metaphor.* Both involve comparisons, sometimes unlikely ones. In the simile, the comparison is stated; in the metaphor, the comparison is implied (not stated outright with such words as *like* or *as*.)

SIMILES:
Her eyes were flashing *like* a railroad-crossing signal.
He spoke *as if* he were fastening each word with a thumbtack.
The crickets sound *like* a thousand tiny sleigh bells.
Cornstalks were rustling *like* taffeta.

METAPHORS:
Pussy willows were purring in the wind.
Tulip goblets were catching rays of sunshine.
Lightning was cracking its whip.
Water lilies were lying at anchor.

Using figurative language well will add colour to your sentences as will adding a touch of humour to the figures of speech you use.

Here are examples.

1. Her mouth opened like a folding bed.
2. She not only reads her husband like a book, she gives the neighbours reviews.
3. He had a voice like a coyote with bronchitis.

WRITING VARIED SENTENCES

There are two kinds of sentences that have little place in adult writing. Examples will make them clear.

1. "I got up at 7:00 A.M. I had breakfast. I got dressed. I left my house. I took the bus to work. I got there by 9:00 A.M."
2. "I got up at 7:00 A.M. and I had breakfast and I got dressed and I left my house and I took the bus to work and I got there by 9:00 A.M."

In the first case, the series of short sentences is monotonous and childish. The second sentence goes on and on, making it difficult for the reader to follow. In neither case is any sense of relative importance given to the ideas. Each is treated in the same way as the other. We shall now turn to some effective ways of achieving one of the most important ingredients of style—variety in sentence patterns.

Four Basic Ways to Achieve Sentence Variety

1. ***Vary the types of sentences within a paragraph.*** Sentences may be simple, compound, complex, and compound-complex.

—A *simple sentence* contains one independent clause and no dependent clauses.

EXAMPLE:

Joan played the piano.

—A *compound sentence* contains two independent clauses.

EXAMPLE:

Joan played the piano and John sang. (They are joined by the coordinating conjunction *and*.)

—A *complex sentence* contains one independent and at least one dependent clause.

EXAMPLE:

Joan played the piano while John sang. (The second clause is dependent,)

—A *compound-complex sentence* contains two independent clauses and at least one dependent clause.

EXAMPLE:

Joan played the piano and Joe sang the song which recalled their meeting. (The last clause is dependent.)

Sentence variety can be achieved by mixing these types of sentences in a paragraph. Here is an example.

I like submarine sandwiches. (Simple sentence) Although I like all kinds, a cold meat sandwich is my favourite. (Complex sentence) My brother, Frank, likes eggplant with Parmesan cheese and my sister likes meatballs which are drowned in tomato sauce. (Compound-complex sentence)

2. ***Vary the purposes of the sentences.*** Most sentences are statements. "I got up at 7:00 A.M. I had breakfast . . ."

A series of statements can become very boring. *Why not vary the purpose of one or more of the sentences?* You can do this in a number of ways.

1. *Ask a question.* We just asked you a question in the previous paragraph. This technique has the advantage of making the reader think of an answer. Indeed, the author can also proceed to answer the question.

2. *Give a command.* This is another way to vary sentences.

   EXAMPLE:

   "Don't give up the ship."

   The command may be phrased, "Let us . . ."

   EXAMPLE:

   "Let us look at the problem from a different angle."

3. *Make an exclamation.* The exclamation adds variety and life when interspersed once in a while in a group of sentences which make statements.

   EXAMPLE:

   "I got up at 7:00 A.M. I had my usual breakfast. *What a dull way to start the day! . . .*"

4. *Use a direct quotation*. Instead of the indirect quotation, use a direct one. It adds variety and is much more interesting. Compare these two sentences:

   My brother said it was a good idea and that he would join us at the party.

   AND

   My brother said, "That's a good idea. I'll join you at the party."

3. ***Vary the elements which make up the sentences.*** The usual monotonous order of elements is subject, verb, object.

I had breakfast.

I is the subject; *had* is the verb; *breakfast* is the object. It is possible to vary this order in a number of ways.

1. *Start the sentence with the predicate*, the part of the sentence which tells something about the subject, and have the subject follow it. This technique is known as *inversion*, reversing the customary order of the sentence. Used occasionally and naturally, inversion adds variety.

   EXAMPLE:

   Black is the colour of my true love's hair.

   The subject *hair* follows the predicate which consists of the verb is and the predicate adjective *black.*

   EXAMPLE:

   Hiding in the closet was the frightened child.

2. *Place a word, phrase, or clause before the subject*, if you keep the usual order of the elements of a sentence.

   EXAMPLES:

   Slowly I ate the whole cake.

   Across the street, the crowd was threatening the mugger.

   While he was studying, he munched a sandwich.

   In the first sentence, an adverb precedes the subject; in the second, an adverbial phrase is used; in the final sentence, an adverbial clause is placed first.

3. *Place a phrase or clause between the subject and the verb* if you keep the usual order of the elements of a sentence.

   EXAMPLES:

   One way *to become successful* is to work hard.

   The athlete *who received the most* votes got the award.

Frank, *anxious to please his employer*, worked overtime.
Sir John A. Macdonald, *the first prime minister of Canada*, served about eighteen years.
My parents, *oddly enough*, had never flown in an airplane.

4. ***Vary sentence length.*** A short sentence of two or three words following a more lengthy one is an effective way to get sentence variety. Here is an example.

   After a long flight from Vancouver, the soldier on leave dashed through the airport terminal anxiously searching the crowd for his fiancée. At the end of the long corridor impatiently standing at the information desk was the object of his search. *It was Anna.*

   The short, three-word sentence at the end not only serves to vary sentence length (the first two sentences are 23 words and 19 words) but also focuses the reader's attention on the subject of the paragraph, the soldier's fiancée Anna.

Practice

Directions: **Vary the following sentences using the techniques in paragraph 3.**

1. The precious jewel was hidden in the corner of the box.
2. The crowd rose to its feet at the crucial moment in the ball game.
3. Kim paid close attention, wanting to get a good grade.
4. The series of events unfolded rapidly.
5. Her relatives were waiting to greet Jean at the airport.

Answers

1. Hidden in the corner of the box was the precious jewel.
   In the corner of the box was hidden the precious jewel.
2. At the crucial moment in the ball game, the crowd rose to its feet.
3. Kim, wanting to get a good grade, paid close attention.
4. Rapidly the series of events unfolded.
   Rapidly unfolded the series of events.
5. At the airport, her relatives were waiting to greet Jean.
   Waiting at the airport to greet Jean were her relatives.

THE PARAGRAPH—THE BASIC WAY TO DEVELOP IDEAS

A paragraph is a group of related sentences which develop a single central idea or a single important aspect of a central topic. Its purpose is to help the reader follow the organization of the writer's thoughts.

At its simplest, a paragraph may be considered a visual device to help the reader follow and understand the ideas of the writer. Mechanically it is set off from the rest of the printed page by an indentation of its first sentence and perhaps by some extra space between it and the previous and succeeding paragraphs.

Depending on the topic and its difficulty, the kind of reader doing the reading, and the purpose of the writing, the number of paragraphs in an essay will vary.

HOW THE PARAGRAPH IS CONSTRUCTED

The Topic Sentence

Each paragraph contains a *topic sentence* which states the main idea or unifying thought. (Rarely, the topic sentence may be missing, and the entire paragraph itself becomes the main idea.) It is best to limit each paragraph to one main idea.

Here are some examples of typical topic sentences:

Many television programmes contain too much violence. (Which?)
There is a great deal of humour in everyday life. (When and where?)
Jogging is a good way to keep fit. (Why?)
Sewing is quite different from knitting. (How?)
Wilfrid Laurier was an all-around Canadian. (For example?)

Each of these topics contains a main thought which can be developed in a suitable way to answer the question placed after it.

Must every paragraph have a topic sentence?
No, but it is desirable to have one if you are not a professional writer and your audience is not especially skilled in reading. A topic sentence focuses on the main point you wish the reader to understand.

Where should the topic sentence be placed?
Most often, it should be at the *beginning of the paragraph*, but not necessarily so. The sentence, "Sewing is quite different from knitting" can come in the *middle of the paragraph* after sewing has been discussed and before knitting is described. Frequently, you may wish to hold off the topic sentence until the very *end of the paragraph* in order to create suspense or to hammer home your main idea. The following paragraph is a good example.

> If you enjoy the strategy of games, tic-tac-toe, backgammon or poker; if you like to solve codes and ciphers or are interested in crossword puzzles; if you like to fool around with numbers —then you will enjoy logic. Those who take up logic, you should be warned, join a fanatical sect. But they have a good time. Theirs is one of the most lasting, interesting, and inexpensive pleasures. Logic is fun.

The brief *final* sentence of the paragraph is the *topic sentence*.

How can a topic sentence be created from the essay question?
Let us assume that you are asked to write an essay on computers indicating your views on the ways they have affected our lives.
The best way to turn the essay topic into a topic sentence is to make "computers" (or whatever subject is given to you) the subject of the topic sentence and make a general statement about it that tells how you feel about it. Here are some examples.

General: Computers have greatly affected our lives.
More specific: Computers have had a positive (or negative) influence on our lives.

Or if the essay assigned deals with nuclear energy, these topic sentences can be used.

General: Nuclear energy has greatly affected our lives.
More specific: Nuclear energy has been a boon (or bane) to civilization.

These topic sentences give unity to the entire essay which follows.
Having written a good topic sentence, your next task is to select the best way to develop the topic sentence into a paragraph.

EIGHT WAYS TO DEVELOP PARAGRAPHS

1. ***The paragraph may be developed by details.*** The most frequent method of paragraph development is by the use of further details. In the paragraph which follows, details help put together the picture of a famous adventurer.

> Who is that short, sturdy, plainly dressed man who stands with legs a little apart, hands behind his back, looking up with keen gray eyes into the face of each speaker? His cap is in his hands, so you can see the bullet head of crisp brown hair and the wrinkled forehead, as well as the high cheekbones, the short square face, the broad temples, the thick

lips, which are set firm as granite. A coarse plebeian stamp of a man: yet the whole figure and attitude are that of boundless determination, self-possession, energy; and when at last he speaks a few blunt words, all eyes turn respectfully to him. He is *Sir Francis Drake.*

In a dozen and a half details, the author, Charles Kingsley, has created a paragraph word picture of the man who traveled around the globe in the sixteenth century and led the English fleet in its defeat of the Spanish Armada in 1588.

2. ***The paragraph may be developed by illustration and example.*** A paragraph's topic sentence may be developed by means of examples or typical instances. This is not only a relatively easy method of paragraph development, but it is also a delightful kind of paragraph to read if the examples are well chosen. Take this paragraph for example:

> Even before the war, French had borrowed generously from English. It had adopted baby, bridge, club, sandwich, film, and wagon. Then came such words as gangster, steak (used in place of the older loan-word bifteck), des shorts, un bikini, boyfriend, bestseller, groggy, racket, covergirl.

Be certain that the examples are accurate and are actual illustrations of the statement in the topic sentence.

3. ***The paragraph may be developed by events presented in time sequence.*** Sometimes the events described in a paragraph must be listed in a certain order. This is important when you explain a process. For example, a paragraph dealing with a recipe for a particular dish would have to give the steps in order of the time they would have to be taken. You must do one thing first, another next, and so on. Here is an example of a typical recipe.

> ***Recipe for Tuna Creole***
>
> Sauté green pepper, onion, and celery in butter for about five minutes. Add flour and blend. Add tomatoes gradually while stirring constantly. Add salt, pepper, sugar, bay leaf and parsley; cook gently 30 minutes. Remove bay leaf and parsley. Add tuna fish and heat. Prepare rice. Serve tuna creole over rice.

There are eight steps, and the paragraph presents them in chronological sequence. If the time order is violated, your recipe will end in disaster.

Time sequence is also important in paragraphs which narrate a series of events. In a story, certain events happen before others. To rearrange the sequence would destroy the logic of the story. Take this famous scene from *Robinson Crusoe* where Crusoe finds a footprint on the sand on an island he believes is uninhabited.

> It happened one day about noon, going towards my boat, I was exceedingly surprised with the print of a man's naked foot on the . . . sand. I stood like one thunderstruck, or as if I had seen a ghost. I listened, I looked around me, but I could hear nothing, nor see anything. I went up to a rising ground to look further. I went up the shore and down the shore, but it was all one. I could see no other impression but that one.

Crusoe's actions are presented in time sequence: he saw the footprint; he stood amazed; he listened; he looked around; he climbed a rise; he went up and down the beach. The order is chronological and psychological. He acted just as anyone would who has been taken by surprise.

Often, such time sequence words as *first*, *next*, *then*, *finally*, *meanwhile*, *later*, *afterwards* will be included to serve as chronological signposts. The skeleton of such a paragraph would look like this.

> There were four people who influenced my life most. *First*, there were my parents. *Next*, when I got a job in my chosen profession, there was my boss. *Last*, and certainly not least, came my wife.

4. ***The paragraph may be developed by placing objects in space sequence.*** Another way to develop paragraphs is by placing things in some kind of spatial order. Just as time sequence starts at one point in time and ends in another, so space sequence starts at one point in space and ends in another. You may begin at the right or at the left and work toward the opposite direction. You may start at a nearby point and end at a distant one, or you may reverse that procedure. Finally, you may start at the top and work your way down or vice versa. These space sequences are particularly important in description. The important thing to remember is not to jump back and forth. The progression of the description should be logical in most instances. (Great writers often violate this rule when they try to give you a main impression of a sight, but you are best advised to follow a definite order.)

What order do you find in the following passage?

> Down below on the right are green slopes blooming with heather. Lower and nearer the centre are cultivated (tilled) fields; then, toward the left, some woods; and beyond, just in the picture, a glimpse of a tiny church, some cottages, and the ruin of a large house. Further off, but dominating the scene, is a long chalk cliff.

First you establish that the writer is looking down on the scene (*down below*, *lower*). Then you realize that he is looking through a window (*just in the picture*). The space sequence is indicated for you by the phrases *on the right*, *nearer the centre*, *toward the left*, *beyond* and *further off.* So the writer's eye is moving; first, from right to left, then, from near to far. Notice how important the place words are in setting the objects seen in a definite space order: *to the right, to the left, in the centre, in front, beyond, nearby, above, below.*

It would be illogical to violate these space sequences by moving from east to west and then back to centre. While this example is obviously simple, the principle is the same.

5. ***The paragraph may be developed by defining or stating what something or some idea is.*** A definition answers the question: What is meant by this? The paragraph which tries to define something explains what it is and what makes it different from other similar or different things.

How important is definition? It is really the basis for any discussion dealing with a challenging subject. How can you talk about democracy unless you define what it is? Here is one such definition.

> The term democracy refers primarily to a form of government by the many as opposed to government by the one—government by the people as opposed to government by a dictator or an absolute monarch.

This general definition serves as a basis for a discussion. It tells what democracy is so that the reader understands at the start, before the discussion begins.

What makes a definition a definition? Every definition has two parts: a classification or kind and a distinguishing characteristic. The term democracy refers primarily to *a form of government*; this is the classification to which democracy belongs. What distinguishes this form of government from others? The distinguishing characteristic is that it is run by *many* as distinguished from governments which are run by *one person.*

Here are some brief definitions. See if you can find the classification and distinguishing characteristic of each term which is defined.

> A child is someone who passes through your life and then disappears into an adult.
> Kindness is a language which the deaf can hear and the blind can see.
> The most powerful weapon on earth is the human soul when it is on fire.

The classifications are: child-someone; kindness-language; soul-weapon. The rest of the sentences give the distinguishing characteristics.

6. ***The paragraph may be developed by classifying persons or objects.*** Once the terms to be used in a discussion or a piece of writing have been logically defined, the writer frequently goes on to classify the terms involved. For example, after defining democracy, he may go on to

describe different kinds of democracies. His topic sentence in the next paragraph might read: "There are three different kinds of democracies functioning today." Or following the definition of leadership, there may be a paragraph beginning, "There are three different kinds of leaders—democratic, authoritarian, and laissez-faire."

Classification is important because it groups ideas and makes them easier for the reader to grasp; people remember better if they can put things into categories or classifications. There are a number of things to keep in mind when classifying:

1. *Select one basis for your classification.* In the leadership example, the classification is by kind of leadership.

2. *Make these bases for classification mutually exclusive.* What falls into one category should not fall into another. A democratic leader cannot be confused with an autocratic (dictatorial) one.

3. *Make these bases for classification complete.* Try to fit all possible kinds of leaders into as few categories as possible. A leader involves the people he leads in deciding what to do (*democratic*), tells them what to do (*authoritarian*), or takes no part in the decision-making process, leaving them to do as they choose (*laissez-faire*). These three bases include all leaders.

Another way to define classification is to say that it is a logical way of dividing persons or things into a complete system of categories that do not overlap.

Here is an example.

A humourous piece of writing by a college student classifies a number of men that women should avoid on a date.

Type 1. The Party Boy. This one simply isn't himself until he gets outside of a little alcohol. Then he manages to be so much himself you are bored to death.
Type 2. The Lover. He is a ball of fire with women. He overwhelms you with attention.
Type 3. The Great Mind. You have to prepare ahead of time for a date with one of these. You sit down in a corner and solve world problems.
Type 4. The Artist. He knows he's a genius and dresses accordingly.
Type 5. The Dud. He isn't funny; he isn't interesting; he isn't clever.
Type 6. The Missing Link. Not that we object to muscles, but there is a type that has too much of a good thing.

The basis for classification is kinds of *dates.* The categories do not overlap and they cover the whole spectrum of men who date.

7. ***The paragraph may be developed by comparison and contrast.*** After two or more ideas have been defined and/or divided into subcategories, the writer might wish to compare or contrast them. In *comparison*, similarities between two or more things are pointed out. In *contrast*, differences between two or more things are noted.

Why do we compare or contrast?

1. We may want to compare an unknown idea or object with a known one in order to help the reader understand it better. In describing a game of skill like Othello, the writer might compare it with checkers, with which most readers are more familiar.

2. We may want to help the reader understand some quality of two objects or two persons that is not known in relation to a well-known principle which applies to both. For example, we may not know much about family life in two societies in distant lands, but we could learn about it by comparing and contrasting their family life with our own.

3. Finally, taking the second reason a step further, we may want to compare or contrast several ideas or persons to arrive at some general principle. For example, we can compare Martina Navratilova, Don Mattingly, and Wayne Gretzky to determine the qualities that make an outstanding athlete.

Basically, there are two ways to organize a paragraph that compares or contrasts two items. One is to describe the first item thoroughly and then turn to the second, indicating similarities and differences between them, The second is to move back and forth from one to the other, comparing or contrasting specific aspects of each.

Both methods are effective, but they have to be consistent.

8. ***The paragraph may be developed by reasons and proof.*** Very often we write not only to explain (by details, by examples, by definition, by classification, by comparison and contrast), to describe (by space sequence), or to narrate (by time sequence), but also to persuade, to convince the reader of our point of view.

Daily we make statements of either fact or opinion which we have to justify. A child will try to convince his or her parents to let him or her stay up late. A worker will try to persuade the boss to give him or her a raise. A wife or husband will try to convince a tired spouse to go out for the evening.

In *argument*, you try to win someone over to a belief or opinion; in *persuasion*, you present arguments to bring about some action you want someone to take. How do you do this?

In argument, you start with a proposition, something you will attempt to prove. How do you prove a proposition? Like a lawyer, you have to present evidence that will convince others of the validity of your proposition. You may cite facts; you may bring in the opinion of authorities; you may bring to bear beliefs which are widely held. In this manner, you establish your proof—proof being a string of related reasons as to why some position or proposition is true. Here are some propositions to be argued:

Women deserve equal rights with men.
Wealth does not bring happiness.
Education is essential in a democracy.
The United Nations has failed to prevent war.
Urban living is preferable to rural living.

In *persuasion*, you continue from the proposition you have established to an action you want to convince someone to take. Here are some actions which people might be persuaded to take:

All people should stop smoking cigarettes.
All citizens should vote in national and local elections.
Education, through college, should be compulsory.
Drivers should be reexamined periodically and relicensed.
Juvenile offenders should be treated in the same way as other offenders.

In these instances, reasons must be given to persuade either positive or negative courses of action: smoking is unhealthy; therefore, people should stop smoking; voting is important; therefore, people should vote. (Note that *argument* may lead to *persuasion*, but it is not necessary for this to happen.)

One special case deserves mention. A paragraph may attempt to establish the fact that one thing causes another, that one event is responsible for a certain effect. This involves giving reasons why one thing led to another, why the effect would not have taken place without the cause, or why, whenever a certain cause is present, a certain effect must take place. This is a special kind of proof which is used by social scientists and scientists alike. Where poverty exists, life spans of people are shorter. Reasons would have to be given to show that poverty causes people to die sooner. Where alcoholism is present, diseases of the liver result. Evidence would have to be given that liver disease is caused by excessive drinking.

WRITING EFFECTIVE PARAGRAPHS

1. ***Vary the types of sentences within the paragraph.*** Use simple, compound, complex, and compound-complex sentences, mixing them according to the complexity of the ideas you wish to express.

2. ***Vary the purposes of the sentences within the paragraph.*** Ask questions. Use commands. Make exclamations. Do not hesitate to use direct quotations.
3. ***Vary the elements which make up the sentences within the paragraph.*** Use inversions. Precede the subject with appropriate words, phrases, or clauses. Introduce suitable phrases, clauses, and appositives between the subject and the verb which follows it.
4. ***Vary the length of sentences within the paragraph.*** Throw in a two- or three-word sentence to break up a series of longer ones, particularly if you have something you wish to emphasize.
5. ***Vary paragraph length.*** If not overused, one of the most effective means of drawing the reader's attention to a key idea is the single sentence paragraph.
6. ***Organize the paragraph carefully to emphasize the most important idea.*** You have a choice between starting the paragraph with a sentence that contains the main idea to be developed in the paragraph (the topic sentence) or building up to the main idea by using the technique for the suspenseful sentence. Either method can be effective.
7. ***Since paragraphing is a convenience to the reader, break up pages of solid paragraphs by using dialogue where appropriate.*** In writing dialogue, begin a new paragraph each time the speaker changes. Thus, each exchange of conversation requires two paragraphs and serves to make it easier for the reader to follow the conversation.

A word about summary sentences. Although the summary sentence may seem to be repetitive, it is more often better than not to have one.

If your paragraph has dealt with the United Nations, it helps to have a summary sentence such as "The United Nations has indeed had (failed to have) great influence on the world we live in."

Summary sentences reinforce for the reader what you set out to do in your essay, what views you wanted to get across.

Practice

Directions: **Of the eight ways to develop paragraphs, several are most likely to be used on the actual test because they lend themselves to allowing you to present your views. Here are some topics for paragraphs and a suggested way to develop them.**

1. (By illustration) Computers: Magicians or Monsters
2. (By details) My Idea of Sportsmanship
3. (By reasons and proof) The Changing Role of Women in the Family
4. (By definition) Genocide: Defined
5. (By reasons and proof) It Pays to Dress Well

Answers

Possible sample paragraphs are presented for each of the five topics given.

1. Computers: Magicians or Monsters

   Computers are the latest and the most effective tool man has developed to make his world a better one. Consider how and where computers are used in our world. Our use of electricity is controlled by a computer. The type in our daily newspaper is set by computer. The automobile we drive is the product of computer machinery. Our banking services rely on the computer, and cheques are issued and reviewed by one. Most of our bankbook transactions are handled by computers, including our withdrawing and depositing money by using a plastic card.

   Note: The above paragraph is developed by illustration.

2. My Idea of Sportsmanship

A good sport is a combination of hero, martyr, and humourist, with a deep sense of justice in acknowledging the rights of others at the cost of his own disadvantage and discomfort. He can smile when it rains on a picnic day, laugh at a joke about himself, shake hands with a man who mistakenly knocks him down with his car, forgive the friend who marries the girl he loves, and die on the battlefield for his country with a smile on his lips.

Note: The above paragraph is developed by detail.

3. The Changing Role of Women in the Family

The role of women in the family is changing rapidly in today's society. Many women are discovering great personal satisfaction in the wife-mother role in the family. This role is taking on greater economic significance as society begins to place dollar value on family functions such as caring for children and providing services for family members. The contribution by women is becoming more important and complex because of the information they need for decision making and the knowledge that the health and productivity of family members depend upon the quality of the choices they make.

Note: The above paragraph is developed by reasons and proof.

4. Genocide: Defined

The term "genocide" was coined in 1946 by the international legal scholar, Professor Raphael Lemkin. The mass murder of six million Jews by the Nazis is the most vivid, violent, and tragic example of genocide. But this century alone has seen others—Armenians, gypsies, Chinese, Slavs. Some twenty million people have been slaughtered because of their racial, religious or ethnic backgrounds. In the language of the United Nations Convention on the Prevention and Punishment of the Crime of Genocide, genocide means certain specifically defined acts "committed with intent to destroy, in whole or in part, a national, ethnical, racial or religious group, as such."

Note: The above paragraph is developed by building a definition out of examples, word origin, and official language of a governmental body.

5. It Pays to Dress Well

At every stage of your life, clothes can help you establish your identity for yourself and for those with whom you interact. Many roles in life can't be carried off successfully without the aid of the props of costume. The degree to which you choose clothes that fit a role will affect your performance in that role. Clothes are, moreover, an important factor in developing your feelings of self-confidence and self-respect. When you look good, you feel good.

Note: The above paragraph is developed by reasons and proof.

You have reviewed the basics of writing—the sentence and the paragraph. Now you are ready to tackle the writing of the essay.

THE ESSAY—AT THE TEST CENTRE

You open the test booklet and, under Writing Skills, Part II, you see the following essay topic:

> Television plays a very important part in Canadian life. As an entertainment and educational medium, it has brought the world into the average home. It has its advantages and disadvantages.
>
> Write an essay of about 250 words giving your views on television, indicating its positive effects, its negative effects, or both. Support your views by giving specific examples.

This is a topic requiring you to *present your opinion and defend it*. How do you go about doing this? This section will help you with a step by step analysis, showing you exactly what to do and how to do it.

BEFORE YOU BEGIN

Note the following important facts:

1. The essay must be *about 250 words*, or a minimum of about 32 lines for the average writer.
2. You are allowed 45 minutes to write the essay.
3. You must write your essay on the answer sheet provided to you, legibly in ink.

Read the instructions carefully. You will learn additional important information, including advice on how to take the test.

Essentially there are three major steps:

1. Planning the essay
2. Writing the essay
3. Revising the essay

You are advised to plan carefully, write your essay, and revise your essay to improve what you have written before handing in your paper

Finally, you are told how your essay will be rated. Two evaluators will read it, judging how clearly you express your opinions, how well you support your opinions by examples and/or arguments, and how effectively and correctly you write.

PLANNING THE ESSAY

The first thing to do is to:

1. ***Plan your time.*** Remembering that you have a 45-minute maximum, allow the following amounts of time:

   1. For reading the instructions: 3 minutes
   2. For reading the topic and planning your outline: 7 minutes
   3. For writing the 200-word essay: 20–25 minutes
   4. For reading and revising the essay: 5–10 minutes

   These limits are not compulsory, but they will prevent you from failing to finish your essay (and be penalized) or from handing in a paper containing errors you did not have time to correct.

2. ***Plan your essay.*** It is essential to read the topic carefully and write on the given topic. *Your essay will receive a failing grade if you write on a topic different from the one you are given.*

   Let us return to our sample topic: television. Reread the topic carefully, noting on your scrap paper what is required. You are asked to do two things: *give your opinions* and *support them by specific examples and proof.* You are given a choice of the aspects of television on which you will write: *its good points, its bad points, or both.* You must plan your essay to do just this.

   Think through the topic, briefly jotting down your ideas. Your *notes* might took like this.

   TV is entertaining.
   Too much violence.
   Public TV is educational.
   Sitcoms.
   Informative news programmes.

Cost of programmes.
Reruns waste time.
Overdone game shows
"Sesame Street"
Baseball, hockey, and other sports

To organize them into an *outline* or *plan*, combine ideas that belong together, eliminating those that don't fit in.

The notes *TV is entertaining*, *Public TV is educational*, *Informative news programmes*, *"Sesame Street,"* and *Baseball, hockey, and other sports* might be positive examples of programming. *Too much violence*, *Reruns waste time*, *and Overdone game shows* are negative aspects of programming. *Cost of programmes* is irrelevant to the other notes, so drop it.

After you have gathered related ideas from your notes, put them into a paragraph which has a suitable topic sentence. Simple sentences like "Television has many good points" and "Television has its bad points" can serve as headings under which to put your related notes.

Warning: Notes are just that—notes. Your outline or plan should be *written in full sentences* so you can go directly from the outline into your essay. A sample plan from the notes would look like this.

Sample Plan

1. Television affects the lives of all Canadians. It has its good points and its bad points. (*Restatement of the given topic can serve as a topic sentence*. You have chosen to deal with the positive *and* negative aspects of television.)

2. Television has many good points.
   a. There are educational programmes on public TV.
   b. There are informative news programmes.
   c. There are entertaining comedies, adventures, and mysteries.
   d. There are exciting sports events.

3. Television also has its bad points.
   a. It often portrays violence.
   b. Its situations are unrealistic.
   c. Its programmes are often a waste of time.

4. Despite its good/bad points, television is a medium which enriches/impoverishes our lives. (You may choose either conclusion.)
This serves as a concluding summary sentence.

WRITING THE ESSAY

This plan can easily be expanded into an essay of about 250 words. All you need to do is:

1. ***Give more reasons:*** it brings good movies into our homes; it provides excellent programmes for children; it features important sports events. Or negatively, it has too many and too annoying commercials; it has too many reruns of movies; its dramas are tasteless. (Review 8 under Eight Ways to Develop Paragraphs.)

2. ***Give more examples.*** Under 2 of the Sample Plan, you can give examples of nature programmes (National Geographic specials), politics (election coverage), theatre (Shakespeare), and music (Metropolitan Opera). (Review 2 under Eight Ways to Develop Paragraphs.)

Here is a sample essay in which you present your opinion and defend it.

Television: A Force for Good or Evil

Television affects the lives of most people. It has its good points and bad points.

Television programming has much to recommend it. It features excellent educational programmes on public television and the specialty channels. Well-known programmes include "Masterpiece Theatre," which, although in reruns, still presents important dramas, the National Geographic specials featuring natural history, "Biography," which tells stories about the lives of notable people in our time, and educational children's programmes like "Mr. Dressup." News programmes keep us well informed. Nightly newcasts include international and local news, and programmes like "Pamela Wallin" bring us face to face with newsmakers. Entertainment is provided by comedies such as "This Hour Has 22 Minutes," by contemporary drama programmes like "Traders," by adventure programmes like "Nikita," and police dramas like "Due South." The television viewer has the best seats in the house for sports specials.

Unfortunately, television programming has its negative side. It often portrays violence in its ugliest forms. Viewing is often a waste of time when tasteless dramas, overdone reruns of sitcoms, and poor movies are presented. Viewers are frustrated when they see game show participants instantly win huge prizes.

(There are two possible endings depending on your own feelings.)

Despite its bad points, television can be a powerful force for enriching our lives since its weaknesses can be improved if the public insists.

OR

Despite its good points, television's weaknesses make it an evil influence on the viewing public. The Canadian public would be better off without it.

Writing a Superior Essay

Although this sample essay would easily receive a good grade, the reasons and examples deal only with programming. Television, however, has deeper sociological effects on Canadian life. *If you treat these less obvious but more important aspects of the topic, you will get a superior grade.* What do we mean by this?

Television affects the use of our leisure time. If we watch television as *spectators*, we cannot be *participants* in other activities. We have less time for reading, less time for physical activity, and less time for conversation and socialization. These are some of the negative sociological effects of television.

On the other hand, television can have deeper positive effects. Those who must endure long periods of forced inactivity such as shut-ins or the elderly, have, because of television, an entertaining and sometimes constructive way to use their time. Furthermore, viewers can experience vicariously many things that they cannot know firsthand, such as faraway places, underwater exploration, and scientific discoveries.

These kinds of reasons are more mature, more sophisticated than discussions dealing merely with programming. Therefore, this kind of essay will receive a higher grade.

Any topic can be treated on both levels, the surface level and the deeper, more mature level. If you plan, if you use relevant reasons and pertinent examples, you will receive a passing grade, but a more mature treatment will earn you an even higher one.

Explanatory Topics

Another kind of topic you might be given is an explanatory topic. This requires you to explain something. There are four major kinds of explanatory topics and we shall analyze each of these in turn. One might be a *process* (example, How to Prepare a Budget); another might be a *term to be defined* (example, Being a Good Citizen). Still another might be a *comparison*, explaining *similarities* (example, Big Cities Are All Alike), *or* differences, explaining a *contrast* (example, Urban and Suburban Ways of Life). Finally the topic might call for *classification* (example, The Basic Four of a Good Diet).

1. ***Explaining a Process.*** This involves a series of steps each of which is a part of a total process. These steps must be presented in order so that an exact sequence is followed. For the explanation to be clear, each paragraph must be developed in a definite time sequence.

   Note that the four steps of the budget process are presented in a definite order. All must be included and one step must follow the other in time sequence. A good idea is to review page 241 for time sequence words such as *first*, *next*, *then*, *meanwhile*, *last* and *finally.*

Here is a sample essay which explains a process.

How to Prepare a Budget

Preparing a budget involves a definite series of steps.

First, determine the total amount of money you have available to spend. It can be a single amount, money from a single wage earner, or it can be money earned by both husband and wife. It can include wages, dividends, and interest from bank accounts or investments.

After you have determined your income, list your necessary expenditures. These fall into several categories. Most important are food, rent, clothing, health care, transportation, entertainment, education, insurance, and miscellaneous. Some of these expenses are daily (carfare); weekly (food marketing); monthly (rent or mortgage payments); quarterly (income tax payments), or yearly (insurance premiums). The miscellaneous category includes extraordinary expenses such as unusual medical expenses or automobile repair bills.

The next step is to allocate the proper percentage to each category, for example, 25% for shelter. These allocations fall into two categories. They are either necessary or optional expenditures. Food and lodging are necessities. Entertainment is an optional expenditure. It is also important not to forget savings, an important part of every budget.

Finally, total the expenditures and compare them with your income to make certain the budget is balanced and you are not sending more than is available. If you are, you must go back and revise the allocations you have made.

These are the essential steps in preparing a budget.

2. ***Defining a Term.*** The best way to write an essay which defines a term is to list the component parts that make up the idea being defined and give an example of each. For example, good citizenship may be explained by a number of behaviours that make up a definition. A *sample outline* of this topic follows.

Being a Good Citizen

1. Every Canadian wants to be a good citizen. But what is good citizenship?
2. A good citizen is well informed. To be a good citizen, one must read newspapers and magazines, listen to radio newscasts and telecasts, and keep in touch with public officials.
3. A good citizen not only is well informed, but also acts on the information obtained. The good citizen votes and expresses his or her views to legislative representatives and the press.
4. A good citizen contributes his or her time, talents, and wealth to the public good. The good citizen is active in community organizations and contributes to worthy causes, thereby showing concern for fellow citizens.
5. A good citizen displays the personal qualities that make our democracy strong. Such a citizen is a good family member, law-abiding, and loyal to his or her country.
6. These are the qualities that make a good citizen. (Note this final summary sentence.)

It would be easy to expand this outline of 148 words to 200 words by adding examples to outline items 2, 3, 4, and 5, e.g., expresses his or her views on pending legislation, does jury duty, pays his taxes, serves in the armed forces when called upon, and supports such local service organizations as the police, the firefighters, and the public library.

3. ***Making a Comparison or a Contrast.*** In a comparison, you discuss the similarities in two or more items. You can follow a simple outline such as this:

1. Topic sentence: *Big cities are alike in many ways.*
2. Similarity 1: *Big cities are crowded (have a high population density).*
3. Similarity 2: *Big cities are burdened by traffic congestion.*
4. Similarity 3: *Big cities have higher crime rates.*
5. Closing summary sentence: *These are some of the ways in which big cities are alike.*

Sandwiched between a topic sentence and a closing summary sentence, the three paragraphs make up an essay that would, when expanded to 200 words, receive a passing grade.

In making a *contrast* between two ideas or objects, use the same plan, but point out the differences. Your topic sentence might read: *Urban and suburban living differ in many ways.* Then these paragraphs indicating differences can follow.

One difference between urban and suburban living is population density. Suburbia is less crowded and, therefore, tends to have fewer problems caused by inner city overcrowding. Although an automobile is more often a necessity in suburbia, traffic problems are less frequent. Crime, while it certainly exists, occurs at a much lower rate than in a big city.

In addition, inhabitants of suburbia tend to have higher incomes. They have more money to spend. Housing is generally more luxurious. Unemployment and poverty levels are lower than those of urban areas.

Finally, suburbia usually has few of the problems that industry brings to the city. Air pollution is lower and problems of industrial waste are fewer.

It can safely be said that life in suburbia and in urban centres is vastly different.

Note: The final sentence is the concluding or summary sentence.

4. ***Making a Classification.*** Classification is an important mental process that groups ideas or objects making them easier for people to use. For example, we classify people according to personality types. The outgoing person is an extrovert; the shy, retiring person is an introvert. We also classify people according to their values. One who pursues money and acquires objects of worth is a materialist; one who is interested in things of the mind and heart is an idealist. Animals may be carnivorous (meat-eaters) or herbivorous (plant-eaters).

A sample essay dealing with the classification of foods follows:

The Four Groups of Foods

A balanced diet requires you to eat a carefully planned menu of varied foods that will provide your body with the four essentials: energy, repair materials, growth materials, and vitamins and other special substances. These foods fall into four main groups: dairy, fruits and vegetables, breads and cereals, and proteins.

Dairy foods include milk and milk products such as cottage cheese, yogurt, cheeses, butter and ice cream. These provide vitamins A, B_2, B_{12}, and D.

Fruits include citrus fruits as oranges and grapefruits, rich in vitamin C, and noncitrus fruits such as melons, berries, and peaches. Green leafy and yellow vegetables include lettuce, spinach, carrots and squash, excellent sources of vitamins A, B, and E. Potatoes, broccoli, and cauliflower contribute vitamin C.

Bread, cereals, and pasta provide us with B vitamins, iron, and carbohydrates among others. They are also sources of critically needed fiber.

Finally, the protein foods include meat, fish, and poultry, with fish and poultry containing less fat. Eggs and liver are nutritious, but they contain cholesterol. Protein-rich foods are essential for muscle building and the health of vital organs.

The important thing to remember is that, if you and your family eat one or more foods from each of these groups daily, you will be providing yourselves with a healthy, balanced diet.

Note: The first paragraph introduces the idea of a balanced diet and the four food groups. Paragraphs 2 through 5 describe the foods in the various groups, giving examples and the contribution each makes to good health. The final sentence returns to the idea of a balanced diet.

REVISING THE ESSAY

You read the directions and the topic carefully; you planned what you would say; you have written your essay. You may think you are finished, but in reality, you are not.

It is essential that you read the essay you have written, revising it where necessary. You will recall that you left 5 to 10 minutes for doing this when you planned your time.

What do you look for when you read your essay?

Checklist for Revision

Content

1. Are your ideas pertinent to the topic?
2. Are your ideas clearly stated?
3. Are they properly organized?
4. Are they logically developed? Have you used the proper connecting and transitional words?
5. Is the purpose of your essay achieved? If you had to make a judgment, did you do so? Did you explain the process? Did you define the term? Did you make the comparison or contrast? Did you make the proper classification?

Organization

1. Does each paragraph have a good topic sentence?
2. Is each key idea developed in a separate paragraph?
3. Is each paragraph finished with a clear summary sentence?

Correctness (Review Writing Skills Part I Chapter)

1. Is your essay free of sentence errors (run-on sentences and sentence fragments)?
2. Are agreement, case of pronouns, and verb forms correct?
3. Have you punctuated and capitalized correctly?
4. Have you chosen your words with proper usage in mind?
5. Have you spelled them correctly?

Only after you have read and revised your essay can you feel you have completed the test. Don't hesitate to make changes or corrections on your paper. As long as *your writing is legible*, neatness is not a factor.

HOW TO RATE YOUR ESSAY

In order to mark your essay, use this chart. Circle the box that contains words that describe your work. After doing this as objectively as possible, give your paragraph to someone who can be objective and ask them to mark it in a different colour. Wherever there is disagreement, discuss the reasons for each choice until a choice acceptable to both is reached. Circle the final selections in a third colour and look at where most of them fall. The majority of boxes in a column should be used to indicate your mark on the paragraph. Any boxes that fall below 4 need attention.

	0	1	2	3	4	5	6
Ideas	irrelevant	no planning evident	superficial	average planning	planned and well-chosen	worthwhile	mature
Presentation	none	no planned presentation evident	little planned presentation evident	some planning in presentation evident	generally effective presentation	clear and effective presentation	clear, effective, and well-organized presentation related to topic
Organization	no evidence of organization	disorganized	not well-organized	less organized	organized	well-organized	well-organized
Coherence	incoherent	minimal	ideas undeveloped	coherent	coherent and understandable	coherent and understandable	coherent and understandable
Argument	none	none	not developed	some evidence of development	generally effective	clear and effective	well-developed, clear, and effective
Illustrations and Examples	none	none	few	some relevant	appropriate and relevant	sound and supporting	well-chosen and appropriate
Details	none	few, unrelated	superficial	some relevance and thoroughness	relevant	relevant and thorough	specific, relevant, and thorough
Usage	mostly incorrect	numerous errors	many weaknesses	some weakness	usually correct	generally correct	few minor errors
Vocabulary	elementary	elementary	simple	average	above average	well-chosen	well-chosen and mature
Evidence	none	very litle	little	less relevant and thorough	appropriate and relevant	appropriate, relevant, and clearly presented	appropriate, relevant, specific, and maturely presented
Penmanship	illegible	sloppy	legible	legible	legible	legible	legible

6

SOCIAL STUDIES

AN OVERVIEW

This section describes the five social studies test areas: economics, history, geography, political science, and behavioural sciences.

WHAT THE TEST IS LIKE

This section introduces you to the format and types of test questions as well as the basic and specific skills you will need to do well on the social studies test.

HOW TO READ AND INTERPRET SOCIAL STUDIES MATERIALS

Each of *ten* basic skills in reading social studies materials is thoroughly treated. *Five* passages are thoroughly analyzed in each of the social studies, sociology, and anthropology. An additional section deals with interpreting political cartoons with analyses of two of the most famous cartoons and a contemporary one.

HOW TO HANDLE SOCIAL STUDIES SKILLS QUESTIONS

The four basic kinds of skills questions, including the new item format sets, are analyzed with examples of each. An outline of study for all the social studies is included. Twenty questions offer practice in dealing with questions testing comprehension, application, analysis, and evaluation.

GLOSSARY OF SOCIAL STUDIES TERMS

This is a mini-dictionary of 688 words with clear and simple definitions.

SOCIAL STUDIES PRACTICE

The 64 questions based on 32 passages, tables, and maps provide ample practice in reading and interpreting social studies materials.

AN OVERVIEW

The social studies in the 2002 Social Studies Test are *history*, *geography*, *civics, government,* and *economics. Behavioural Science* is tested within the context of the other areas.

History

This is the chronological record (in time sequence) of human events and an analysis of their significance. The interdependence of individuals and nations is included. These items comprise about 25% of the test.

Economics

This deals with the description and analysis of the production, distribution, and consumption of goods and services. These questions comprise about 20% of the test.

Geography

This is the study of the size and distribution of land masses, seas, and natural resources; of climatic zones and plant and animal life—all in their relationship to human beings. About 20% of the questions are based on geography.

Political Science

This is concerned with the description and analysis of the institutions and processes of government. About 20% of the items are based on political science.

Behavioural Sciences

This discipline includes the areas of sociology, anthropology, and psychology. It examines human activity to discover patterns and to formulate rules about human social behaviour. About 15% of the items relate to this area.

SOCIOLOGY studies society, social institutions, and social relationships among human groups such as the family and the community.

ANTHROPOLOGY studies human beings with respect to race, physical characteristics, customs and culture; as well as their origin, development, and distribution throughout the world.

SOCIAL PSYCHOLOGY studies the mind and the mental and emotional processes of humans and animals, as well as human and animal behaviour.

These are working definitions to help you distinguish among the social studies. They are not complete, and experts will differ among themselves as to the definitions of each or all of the major social sciences.

WHAT THE TEST IS LIKE

FORMAT

All of the social studies items are multiple-choice questions. They will be based on

—written passages chosen from various sources such as historical documents, quotations from speeches, parts of newspaper editorials, and newspaper and magazine articles.

—graphics such as charts, diagrams, graphs, tables, maps, cartoons, or newspaper headlines.

Approximately two-thirds of the 64 questions will be based on written passages; one third will be based on graphics. These are further broken down into

—single item questions based on brief written passages or on graphics. You may be asked to interpret a statement by a Prime Minister (Sir John A. Macdonald's "A British subject I was born, a

British subject I will die.") or to decide whether a statement based on a map is correct ("Which of the following statements is supported by the information in the map?").

—sets of item questions, several items based on a longer written passage of up to 250 words or on a more complicated graphic such as a table, graph, or chart. A new item type requires you to apply to current issues or events, ideas, or principles provided in the question. These items test your ability to work with categories of ideas—political, economic, social, or other systems in the social studies and with complex issues that cut across social studies lines (economics and political science, or history and political science).

Approximately two-thirds of the questions will be in sets of two or more items and one-third will be single or stand-alone questions. In addition, all items can be divided into the social studies skills they seek to test: your ability to understand, to apply, to analyze, or to evaluate the written or graphic bases for the questions.

Sound confusing? It won't be after you have studied this chapter and worked on the many practice exercises and answer analyses provided.

SKILLS

Basic Skills

All written passages on which questions are based test your ability to read and interpret the content of the passages. These skills are common to all reading materials. We will apply the principles of reading and interpretation to the social studies content of this test. These principles include locating the main idea of a passage, finding details, determining patterns of writing, drawing conclusions and making inferences, reading critically, separating fact from opinion, determining cause and effect, comparing and contrasting ideas and organizations, and deriving the meaning of social studies terms from the context of the passage.

Five illustrative readings in the five social studies areas with thorough analyses of the answers to the questions based on them will provide you with practice in these basic skills.

There is also a special section dealing with political cartoons, cartoons that present the cartoonist's view on some event or issue in the social studies. These will be analyzed for you.

Specific Skills

These skills involve comprehension, application, analysis, and evaluation. Each of these reading and thinking processes will be described, examples of these types of questions will be analyzed, and ample practice in dealing with typical questions will be provided.

HOW TO READ AND INTERPRET SOCIAL STUDIES MATERIALS

BASICS ON POLITICAL SCIENCE, HISTORY, ECONOMICS, GEOGRAPHY, BEHAVIOURAL SCIENCES

Reading in the social studies requires a number of skills that are common to all reading materials. It is only natural that when you read in any subject, you want to get the *main ideas* of the writer. So, too, in social studies you need to get at the key thoughts being expressed.

The main idea can be difficult to determine at times. If you read too slowly, you may miss the main point because you have gotten too involved in details. It is important, therefore, that you first read the selection through to the end rather quickly *before* you turn to the questions.

Where do you look for the main idea? Most often you will find it in the topic sentence, usually the first sentence in the selection. Sometimes, however, the writer will withhold the main idea until the last sentence, building up to it throughout the entire selection. At other times, the writer will include both a main idea and an important secondary (or subordinate) idea. Finally, it does happen (fortunately not often) that the main idea is not expressed in the selection directly, but is implied by the contents of the entire passage. This is the most difficult kind of passage to handle.

To train yourself in **locating the main idea**, ask yourself the same questions that will be asked of you in the examination.

1. What is the main idea of the passage?
2. What is the best title for the passage?
3. If I were choosing a suitable headline for the article in a newspaper, what headline would I choose?
4. What is the *topic sentence* of this paragraph or paragraphs; *that is, the sentence that includes the ideas contained in all the other sentences?*

FINDING DETAILS

After you have determined the main idea, the next step is to *locate the facts supporting the main idea or details* that flow from the main idea. If, for example, the main idea of a selection is that democracy is the best form of government for man, the author will undoubtedly provide facts or reasons to support this statement or include facts that show the superiority of democracy to other forms of government. If the main idea is a general conclusion that many persons have overcome physical disabilities to become famous, details would probably include such examples as Helen Keller, President Franklin D. Roosevelt, or Rick Hansen.

How do you locate a detail? You go back to the selection a second or third time to dig it out of the passage. It most frequently will come in the middle or toward the end of a selection. Sometimes clues are contained in the selection which steer you to the detail or fact in question. These clues for locating details might read:

An example is . . .	An argument in support of (or against) . . . is . . .
One reason is . . .	A reason for . . . is . . .

To train yourself in **locating details**, ask yourself these questions:

1. What examples are given to illustrate the main point?
2. What reasons are offered to support the author's position?
3. What arguments for or against a proposal does the author present?
4. When, where, how did something happen?
5. What did someone do?
6. Why did he or she do it?

To find the proper detail, it will be necessary for you to *learn how to skim*, that is, read rapidly to locate the piece of information you are seeking. You can do this only if you know specifically what it is you need to find in a given selection and limit your reading to finding only that fact.

DETERMINING ORGANIZATIONAL PATTERNS OF WRITING

Note the manner in which the writer organizes his or her material. This is helpful to follow the author's thoughts effectively. The writer may organize his or her material chronologically; that is, in the order in which a series of events happened. The writer may organize it logically by presenting the arguments *for* a position in one paragraph and the arguments *against* in another. Or the writer may present his or her ideas in the order of their importance, with the most important ideas first. This, in fact, is the way a newspaper article is wrltten—"from the top down"—in case the reader doesn't have time to finish it all.

If you can determine the organization of a passage, you can zero in on the relationship between the main parts of a passage.

Clues to Finding the Relationship between the Main Parts of a Passage

Sequence of Ideas is clued by such words as:

first	next	finally
second	further	

Additional Ideas are indicated by such words as:

and	furthermore	likewise
besides	also	in addition

Opposing or Contrasting Ideas are indicated by such words as:

on the other hand	but	yet
however	still	although

DRAWING CONCLUSIONS

Another step involves *drawing conclusions from the material presented*. Conclusions are often indicated by such words as:

thus	accordingly	consequently
therefore	so	as a result

Sometimes, however, the author does not draw the conclusion, but leaves it to you, the reader, to do so. You infer the conclusion from the materials presented; you draw the inference as a result of details you have noted and the relationships you have determined (time sequence, logical order, cause-and-effect, among others). Thus, if an author indicates that a particular provincial government has introduced a series of clean air laws even though such legislation has been opposed by local industry, you might infer that the government attached greater importance to protecting the environment than to ensuring local business support.

To train yourself to make inferences properly in order to draw a conclusion, ask yourself these questions:

1. What do I think will happen next? (inference or prediction as to the outcome)
2. Putting these arguments together, what conclusion can I reach?
3. If one result was caused by something, will a similar effect take place in another situation where the same cause is operating?
4. What is the writer suggesting, rather than saying outright?

READING CRITICALLY

In addition to drawing conclusions and making inferences, it is essential in social sciences that you react to what you have read. Often you must judge the material you are reading, not merely understand it. Historians, geographers, political scientists, economists, sociologists, and anthropologists often present one side of the story, their side. There is almost always another side. In other words, they may "slant" the material to show their bias by including only facts and arguments favourable to their own view and omitting everything else. It is essential for you to read *critically.* Do *not* accept everything that is written just because it appears in print.

You must develop the habit of challenging the author, raising questions, judging the completeness and truth of the information, and distinguishing fact from opinion.

A *statement of fact* is one that can be proven true by using a reliable source of information such as an encyclopedia, an almanac, or an official government document. Here is an example.

EXAMPLE: The Federal Government spends billions of dollars each year helping provinces with aid to those in need due to unemployment, disability, or family troubles.

This can be proved by consulting the official Federal budget.

A *statement of opinion or belief* is one that expresses the feelings, thoughts, or beliefs of a person or persons, and that cannot be proven to be true in any reliable source at the present time.

EXAMPLE: It is believed by the year 2005, population will have outstripped food production and starvation will be widespread.

This is a prediction in the form of a statement or belief attributed to an unidentified source ("It is believed . . .") which cannot be provided until the year 2005. It is possible that others may have another belief. In any case, the statement is definitely not a fact. Note that certain words are clues to statements of opinion.

Words That Are Clues to Statements of Opinion

claim	probably
believe	possibly
think	might
consider	should (have)
will be	could (have)
likely	ought

Words That Probably Reflect Opinion Rather Than Fact

better	undesirable
worse	necessary
desirable	unnecessary

REMEMBER: Always apply the test, "Can it be proved by reference to a reliable source?"

It is important to distinguish fact from opinion in the printed word when the writer unconsciously allows his opinion or bias to enter into his writing. It is even more important to do so when the writer does it deliberately.

You can **read critically** if you ask yourself the following questions:

1. Why is the author writing this selection?
2. What is he trying to get me, the reader, to believe?
3. Is he presenting a balanced or one-sided view of the situation?
4. Is he omitting essential information?
5. Is he appealing to my mind or to my emotions and prejudices?
6. Does he have some hidden reason for writing what he writes?
7. Is he accurate? Or does he deal in half-truths?
8. Is he using words with specific agreed-upon meanings, or is he using words which are "loaded" because they have special meanings for certain readers?

DETECTING PROPAGANDA AND PROPAGANDA TECHNIQUES

When a writer deliberately spreads ideas or opinions to benefit himself or an institution to which he belongs or to damage an opponent or opposing institution, he is engaging in propaganda. The writer is trying to influence your thinking or behaviour and turn your opinions and actions in a certain direction. He or she is using words to appeal to your emotions—your fears, your loves, your hates—rather than to your reason, to your ability to think clearly and, ultimately, to make you do things in a way you never ordinarily would do.

Seven common techniques in propaganda are:

1. *Name-calling.* The writer tries to influence you by attaching a bad name to an individual, group, nation, race, policy, practise, or belief.

> **EXAMPLE:** It would be wise to pay no attention to that loony liberal (or retarded reactionary, depending upon the writer's point of view).

Names are loaded with emotional overtones: Fascist, Red, Nazi, Commie. You must note carefully *how* these words are used and for what purpose. Name-calling is a frequently used propaganda technique.

2. *Glittering generalities.* This is a device used by a writer to attach "good" names to people and policies, so you will accept them without really looking into the facts.

> **EXAMPLE:** The writer appeals to our emotions by using such "good" words as "forward-looking," "peace-loving," "straight-shooting," and "idealistic."

We all love progress, peace, honesty, and idealism so we tend to accept rather than challenge. Always ask the questions "why" and "how" when these terms are applied to people and policies.

3. *Transfer.* This is a device used by a writer who tries to carry over the approval and prestige of something or some institution we respect to get us to accept something else in which he is interested.

> **EXAMPLE:** Canadians are law-abiding. They respect their police officers. One who writes on behalf of an athletic league supported by the local police will try to get you to transfer your approval of the police to the athletic league he or she is sponsoring.

Always examine the person or institution receiving the transfer on its own merits of the original institution you love and respect.

4. *Testimonial.* Advertisements on television and radio make wide use of testimonials. A top athlete endorses a breakfast cereal. A beautiful actress recommends a cosmetic cream. A prominent businessman testifies to the value of a credit card. A testimonial is a recommendation made by someone on behalf of a person, a product, or an institution.

But is the athlete an expert on nutrition? Is the actress an expert on skin care? Is the politician an expert on personal money management? REMEMBER: these people are being paid to make these testimonials. You must ask yourself whether the person making the testimonial is expert enough to do so before you believe what you read or hear.

More subtle is newspaper reporting that is based on *indirect* testimonials.

> **EXAMPLE:** Official circles report . . . ; It was learned from a senior government official . . . ; A reliable source stated . . .

Always ask *which* circles, *which* official, *which* source. Be careful of any information which comes from an *unidentified* source.

5. *Plain-folks.* This technique appears in print infrequently, but, before elections, politicians kiss babies and eat ethnic foods just like the rest of us. They go to church and share activities with their families in public. In these ways they hope to appeal to our emotional identification ("He's just like me") and gain our confidence and our vote. Again, always look beyond appearances to the *real* office-seeker, labour leader, businessman to the extent you can.

6. *Card-stacking.* This is an attempt by a writer to get you to see only one side of a particular issue. To do so, he will use half-truths and omit the other side of the argument. Examples of this occur frequently in "authorized" biographies that tell a person's life in glowing terms, presenting all the good qualities while omitting or toning down the poor ones. When reading about an issue, always note whether both sides have been discussed or whether the cards have been stacked by the writer on one side of the issue only, in an effort to appeal to our feelings.

7. *Bandwagon.* This is a device used to make you go along with the crowd. Since most people like to follow the trend, they will respond favorably to such statements as "Nine out of ten Canadians prefer . . ." or ". . . sells more . . . than all other companies put together." In politics, the bandwagon technique is often seen in action in national political conventions. "Join the swing to . . ."

This bandwagon approach does not want you to think clearly for yourself. You should always ask *why* you should join the others, and not do so because your emotions have gotten the better of you.

REMEMBER

A critical reader
—does not believe everything he reads simply because it is in print;
—accepts as true only those statements which can be proved or which are made by reliable authorities;
—separates fact from opinion, recognizes emotional language and bias; is aware of slanting by omission.

DETERMINING CAUSE-AND-EFFECT

A reading skill frequently used in social studies involves determining the relationship between events. Events rarely occur in isolation. They are generally the result of other events that happened earlier.

EXAMPLE: The Japanese bombed Pear Harbor on December 7, 1941. The United States then declared war on Japan.

The bombing of Pearl Harbor was the cause; the declaration of war was the result or effect of the bombing. Always try, when reading of an event, to determine its cause or causes. *Here is a question involving cause-and-effect:*

EXAMPLE: In 1960 Quebec entered the period of the "Quiet Revolution" that dispelled somewhat the long-held Anglo-Saxon concept of Quebec as a rural, backward, priest-ridden, homogeneous society. One major result of this "Quiet Revolution" was that

(1) only French-speaking immigrants were permitted to come to Quebec
(2) the Olympic Games were held in Montreal
(3) Quebecers became more willing to examine the Separatist option
(4) Quebec became a hotbed of international terrorism
(5) all children in Quebec had to attend French schools

The question asks for a result of the reforms known as the "Quiet Revolution." Choices 1 and 5 are simply not true. While French-speaking immigrants are welcome in Quebec, so are those who speak no French. Similarly, while there have been restrictions on school choice, all children do not have to attend French schools. Choice 2 is true in the sense that the Olympic Games were indeed held in Montreal in 1976, but this was not a direct consequence of the "Quiet Revolution" so the choice is not correct. There were some acts of terrorism in Quebec during the 1960s and 1970s but they were rare. Quebecers who believe in separatism have used the democratic institutions of the country to advance their viewpoint, so choice 4 is not correct. Only choice 3 is correct since the reforms of the period created a political, economic, and cultural atmosphere that encouraged examination of the separatist option.

COMPARING AND CONTRASTING IDEAS AND ORGANIZATIONS

Another frequently needed skill in social studies reading involves that ability to compare and contrast institutions and events. You may be asked to compare Canadian and American democracy, contrast democracy with communism, compare the platforms of the Liberal and Conservative parties, or contrast the role of women in the eighteenth century with the role of women in the twentieth century.

EXAMPLE: The careers of Prime Ministers Trudeau and Clark were similar because each man
(1) was elected to Parliament from the same province
(2) was Prime Minister for only a short time
(3) believed in sovereignty association for Quebec
(4) led his party to a victory over the other
(5) represented the same political party

One of the important differences between Prime Ministers Trudeau and Clark was that the former was from Quebec and the latter from the West. They were elected to Parliament from their home provinces; so choice 1 cannot be correct. Prime Minister Clark was in office for less than a year while Mr. Trudeau served for almost 16 years, so choice 2 is not correct. Neither one of them believed in sovereignty association so choice 3 is not correct. Mr. Trudeau was a Liberal and Mr. Clark a Conservative, so choice 5 is not correct. Choice 4 is the correct response. In 1979 Mr. Clark led the Conservatives to office over Mr. Trudeau's Liberals. Less than a year later, Mr. Trudeau was back in office when his party defeated the Conservatives in a general election.

LEARNING SOCIAL STUDIES VOCABULARY AND DERIVING MEANING FROM CONTEXT

In social studies as in science, vocabulary is of critical importance. Words found in social studies may

—represent complicated ideas, such as *nationalism*, *referendum*, *mercantilism*;
—imply a whole set of ideas, such as *feudalism*, *militarism*, *bimetallism*;
—have meanings specific to the social studies although they have other meanings as well, such as *Axis*, *act*, *shop*;
—come from foreign languages, such as *apartheid*, *junta*, *laissez-faire*;
—have meanings that go beyond what they actually say, such as *dove*, *plank*, *scab*.

Try to derive the correct meanings from the *context*—the words with which the terms appear in a sentence.

You can **check your understanding of the meaning of the vocabulary** in a given selection by asking yourself:

1. What is the key word in the sentence (paragraph, selection)?
2. What is the meaning of the word in *this* sentence (context)?
3. What is the exact meaning (denotation) of the word in this selection?
4. What is the extended meaning (connotation) of the word in this selection? (What does it *suggest* as well as say?)
5. What is the effect of a given word on me?
6. What is the special meaning of this word in social studies?

A representative selection in each of the social studies follows, together with questions based on it. Read each of the selections and try to answer the questions *without* referring to the answer analyses that follow. Then check your answers by carefully reading the analyses. Each of the sets of questions following the selections contain a question that

—is aimed at testing whether you can *locate the main idea* ("The best title for the selection is . . .");
—is designed to test your ability to *locate details* ("One difference between ___ and ___ is . . .");
—requires you to show your *knowledge of* social studies vocabulary ("All of the following words used in economics are correctly paired with their meanings except . . .");
—forces you to *make a conclusion or predict an outcome* ("We can conclude that . . ." "It is most likely that . . .").

In addition, there are questions designed to test your ability to

—*find reasons* that the author uses to support an argument;
—*follow the organization* of a selection;
—*identify the position taken by the author* (or any bias he or she may have).

BASICS ON SOCIAL STUDIES READINGS

> ***Note:***
> The following five illustrative readings in social studies are longer than the passages in the actual examination. This was done to make possible the broadest range of questions for practice and thorough analysis. Passages on the examination rarely exceed 250 words.

POLITICAL SCIENCE ILLUSTRATION

Illustration 1

Elections play an important role in the Canadian political process. According to the Constitution, the Prime Minister must call an election before the end of the government's five-year term. Usually, Canadian governments go to the polls in the fourth year of their mandate. Once the election is called it is the Chief Electoral Officer who sets the electoral machinery in motion.

The Chief Electoral Officer issues the writs of election to the returning officers who, in turn, supervise the collation of the voters' lists and receive the nominations of candidates. Canvassers visit every residence in the country in order to register voters.

On election day, the voting is overseen by the Deputy Returning Officers and their polling clerks, together with scrutineers for each candidate. Voters identity themselves to the polling clerk who checks the name against the list of eligible voters. The voter is given an official ballot, written in both French and English, listing the candidates in alphabetical order along with their party affiliation. The voter marks the ballot in a private booth and returns it to the Deputy Returning Officer who checks that it is a valid ballot before it is placed in the official box.

1. The main idea of the above selection is
(1) electing the Prime Minister
(2) representative democracy in action
(3) election procedures in Canada
(4) key workers in elections
(5) elections: a Canadian political drama

1. 1 2 3 4 5
|| || || || ||

2. According to the passage an election must be called when one of the following happens:
(1) the Prime Minister dies
(2) the term of the government is about to expire
(3) the government has entered the fourth year of its mandate
(4) the people are clearly unhappy with the government's performance
(5) public opinion polls show that the government could increase its majority by holding an election

2. 1 2 3 4 5

3. A government elected at the beginning of 1992 would be most likely to go to the polls in
(1) 1993
(2) 1994
(3) 1995
(4) 1996
(5) 1997

3. 1 2 3 4 5

4. The scrutineers at each poll are working for the
(1) Prime Minister
(2) Chief Electoral Officer
(3) Returning Officer
(4) candidates
(5) voters

4. 1 2 3 4 5

5. Which one of the following is INCORRECTLY paired?
(1) The Prime Minister—calling the election
(2) The Chief Electoral Officer—supervising the election
(3) Canvassers—registering voters
(4) Returning Officers—receiving the nominations of candidates
(5) Polling clerks—checking the validity of ballots

5. 1 2 3 4 5

6. Evidence that Canada is an officially bilingual country can be found in the fact that
(1) voters mark their ballots in a private booth
(2) the ballot is printed in both French and English
(3) there are two scrutineers working at each polling station
(4) only bilingual citizens are eligible to vote
(5) voters must ask for a ballot printed in either English or French

6. 1 2 3 4 5

7. The writer of the passage has organized the information
(1) logically
(2) psychologically
(3) chronologically
(4) argumentatively
(5) critically

7. 1 2 3 4 5

Note:

The words in the illustration and questions that are defined in the "Glossary of Social Studies Terms" under Political Science (page 312) are: *ballot*, *bilingual*, *Constitution*, *election*, *nominate* and *vote*.

ANSWER KEY

1. **3** 2. **2** 3. **4** 4. **4** 5. **5** 6. **2** 7. **3**

ANSWER ANALYSIS

1. **3** Question 1 calls for the main idea of the passage. The possible answers generally fall into several categories. *One of the choices* will possibly be incorrect or irrelevant; that is, it will have nothing to do with the question. *Other choices* will focus on details and not on the main idea. *Still another choice* will be too general, too vague. *The correct answer* will be broad in scope yet specific enough to indicate the main idea or purpose of the article. Choice 3 is correct because it gives the main idea of the passage which is to give an account of how federal elections in Canada are conducted. Choice 1 is incorrect since Prime Ministers are not chosen directly through popular election. Choices 2 and 5 are too broad and would extend greatly beyond the scope of the passage. Choice 4 is too narrow since the passage goes beyond simply identifying key workers.
2. **2** Question 2 requires you to locate an important detail in the passage. In skimming (reading rapidly) through the passage you will note reference to when the Prime Minister must call an election in the first paragraph. What is important here is to distinguish between when an election *must* be called and when it *may* be called. Only the expiration of the term of office is mentioned in the passage as the time when an election *must* be called. The other choices can be recognized as incorrect from information contained in the passage or are not mentioned at all.
3. **4** Question 3 requires you to predict what is likely to occur in the future. The passage tells you that governments usually go to the polls in the fourth year of their mandate. Therefore, it is reasonable to presume that a government elected in the spring of 1992 would be likely to go to the polls during its fourth year in office, which would be 1995—1992 would be its first year, 1993 its second, 1994 its third, and 1995 its fourth.
4. **4** Question 4 requires you to pinpoint the relationship between one group of workers in the election and other important personnel. Skimming through the passage, looking for the word scrutineer, we find it in the third paragraph. Here we see that the scrutineers are explicitly linked with the candidates. The correct choice, therefore, is 4.
5. **5** Question 5 is somewhat tricky. Each of the choices contains correct associations in all instances but one. Thus, the Prime Minister calls the election; the Chief Electoral Officer supervises it; the canvassers register voters; the Returning Officers receive the nominations of candidates. Only choice 5 is in error. It is the Deputy Returning Officers who check the validity of ballots.
6. **2** Question 6 requires you to make an inference based on evidence contained in the passage. Information about choices 1 and 3 is contained in the passage but there is no basis in either case for establishing a connection with bilingualism. There is no mention in the passage of the information contained in choices 4 and 5, and, in any case, neither one is true. The printing of the official ballot in both French and English, referred to in choice 2, is explicitly mentioned in the passage and would be some evidence of Canada's official bilingual status.
7. **3** Question 7 calls your attention to the organization of the passage. To find the answer you must note how the information is organized. The second paragraph here shows what the Chief Electoral Officer has to do after the Prime Minister has called the election. The third paragraph focuses on what has to happen, step by step, on election day. Since the passage focuses on what generally happens first, then second, then third, and so on in a time sequence, it is organized chronologically. Choice 3 is the correct answer.

HISTORY ILLUSTRATION

Illustration 2

In May 1980 Premier René Levesque's Parti Québecois *indépendantiste* government sought sovereign political status but continued economic association with the rest of Canada for Quebec.

Federalist opponents of this proposal—including the federal Liberal party—pledged during the referendum campaign that Canada would begin a process of "renewal" and constitutional change to address the concerns of Quebec citizens if they rejected the referendum. Quebec voters ultimately did reject Levesque's plan by a convincing margin, 60% to 40%. Patriation of the Constitution was thereby given new momentum, with Prime Minister Trudeau and the Liberal party urging Canadians and their political leaders to renew federalism in order to return Quebec's gesture of confidence in Canadian federalism.

That summer, the federal government and the provinces conducted a series of meetings, culminating in a major conference in Ottawa. However, government leaders made no progress on the agenda items, which included patriation, an amending formula, a *Charter of Rights and Freedoms*, the principle of equalization, reform of the Senate and the Supreme Court and redistribution of powers between the two levels of government. At length, Prime Minister Trudeau, faced with an intransigent group of provincial premiers and frustrated by the many previous attempts of constitutional negotiation, decided that the federal government should proceed unilaterally.

1. The main issue for the federal government following the defeat of the Quebec referendum in 1980 was
(1) reforming the Senate
(2) negotiating the terms of Quebec's Independence
(3) developing a Charter of Rights and Freedoms
(4) renewing Canadian federalism
(5) defeating the Parti Québecois

1. 1 2 3 4 5

2. An important goal of Prime Minister Trudeau mentioned in the passage concerns
(1) weakening the power of the provinces
(2) patriation of the Constitution
(3) balancing the federal budget
(4) improving economic conditions
(5) winning the next election

2. 1 2 3 4 5

3. Which one of the following would the Parti Québecois have supported?
(1) recognition of Quebec as a distinct national society
(2) bilingualism and biculturalism
(3) patriation of the Constitution
(4) strengthening the role of the federal government
(5) the Charter of Rights and Freedoms

3. 1 2 3 4 5

4. According to the passage, which one of the following statements is true?
(1) At the 1980 Ottawa Conference, only the Quebec government was opposed to the federal proposals.
(2) Most Canadians wanted the Senate to be abolished.
(3) The other provinces ganged up against Quebec.
(4) There was a general agreement on the need to patriate the Constitution.
(5) Most Quebecers were opposed to independence from Canada.

4. 1 2 3 4 5

5. If the responsibility for the postal service were to be transferred from the federal government to the provinces, this would be an example of
(1) the principle of equalization
(2) use of the amending formula
(3) redistribution of power between the two levels of government
(4) strengthening the power of the federal government
(5) application of the Charter of Rights and Freedoms

5. 1 2 3 4 5

6. When politicians talked of patriating the Constitution they referred to
(1) the need for all Canadians to be more patriotic
(2) treating all regions of the country equally
(3) encouraging citizens to be more public spirited
(4) bringing control over the Constitution under the Canadian parliament
(5) severing international relations with Great Britain

6. 1 2 3 4 5

7. The author's view of the actions of the federal government during this period is best described as
(1) cautious
(2) neutral
(3) favourable
(4) qualified
(5) critical

7. 1 2 3 4 5

ANSWER KEY

1. **4** 2. **2** 3. **1** 4. **5** 5. **3** 6. **4** 7. **2**

ANSWER ANALYSIS

1. **4** This question requires you to identify a major theme of the passage and to differentiate it from other themes on the basis of chronology or sequence ("following the defeat of the Quebec referendum"). The major issue here is "to renew federalism" rather than any of the details associated with it, such as reforming the Senate.
2. **2** Here you have to differentiate general goals that the Prime Minister may have had from specific goals discussed in the passage. The goal that receives particular attention in the passage is that of patriation of the Constitution.
3. **1** This question requires you to apply your knowledge of the Parti Québecois to a number of specific policies. Only the recognition of Quebec as a distinct national society works toward the party's goal of political sovereignty and economic association.
4. **5** Involved here are four statements that are false or about which the passage provides no direct information. Each statement has to be considered in light of what is said in the passage. Four have to be discarded and one retained. The passage provides information to support only choice 5. It is explicitly stated that the voters of Quebec rejected Levesque's plan by 60% to 40%.
5. **3** The passage refers to the idea of the redistribution of powers between the federal and the provincial governments. This question examines your understanding of the concept by asking you to recognize choice 3 as an example of this.

> **Note:**
> *It will be necessary for you to return to the passage each time you wish to locate specific details. This is not only the correct way, but the absolutely necessary method for you to find the right answers.*

6. **4** The passage refers to the patriation of the Constitution. This question requires you to recognize that the issue involved here was the formal assumption of authority over the Constitution by the Canadian Parliament. Up until this time, the laws that made up the Constitution were passed by the British Parliament. Many people were of the view that until the Constitution was brought home, Canada would remain a colony in many respects.

7. **2** While this passage describes a very critical and emotional time in Canadian history, the author has not made judgments concerning the legitimacy or the value of the positions taken by the federal and provincial governments. We cannot tell from the way the events are described what position the author would have supported. We can, therefore, describe the author's view as "neutral."

Thus far, we have thoroughly analyzed the answers to two passages in political science and history. We *have located the main ideas* of each selection. We have dealt with the problem of *identifying* various kinds of *details*. In each selection, your *knowledge of social studies vocabulary* was tested. Finally, you were required to *draw inferences and predict outcomes*. The remaining four selections will give you further practice in these reading skills. We will analyze only those questions that introduce new reading techniques or that present special problems. Be certain to check your answers against the correct answers that follow the questions. If you make an error, do not hesitate to go back to the selection and read it through once more.

ECONOMICS ILLUSTRATION

Illustration 3

In 1935, in the depths of the Great Depression, and with an election approaching, Prime Minister Bennett announced his "New Deal" patterned after President Roosevelt's New Deal in the United States.

Here was a sweeping program of government intervention in the nation's economy, a significant departure from the long-held view of the proper role of the government in the economy. The promised reforms included unemployment insurance, social security, minimum wages, stock market regulation, a shorter work week and laws to control price-fixing.

Mr. Bennett addressed the nation by radio and announced that "great changes have taken place in the world. The old order is gone. It will not return . . ." He went on to say, ". . . in my mind, reform means government intervention. It means government control and regulation . . . Selfish men," he continued, "and this country is not without them . . . fearful that this government might impinge on what they have grown to regard as their immemorial right of exploitation, will whisper against us. They will call us radicals. They will say that this is the first step on the road to socialism. We fear them not . . . We invite their cooperation . . . all the parts of the capitalist system, have only one purpose and that is to work for the welfare of the people. And when any of these instruments in any way fails, it is the plain duty of government which represents the people to remove the cause of failure."

1. This selection emphasizes
(1) the effects of the Great Depression
(2) how to avoid economic disaster
(3) weaknesses of the Canadian economy
(4) the government's plan to combat the Depression
(5) the importance of federal-provincial cooperation

1. 1 2 3 4 5
|| || || || ||

2. All of the following are associated with Bennett's New Deal EXCEPT
(1) social security
(2) family allowances
(3) unemployment insurance
(4) stock market regulation
(5) minimum wage laws

2. 1 2 3 4 5
|| || || || ||

3. All of the following were characteristics of the Great Depression which economists sought to correct EXCEPT
(1) stock market speculation
(2) unemployment
(3) bank failures
(4) soaring inflation
(5) poverty

3. 1 2 3 4 5
|| || || || ||

4. Critics of the New Deal claimed that Bennett's government was introducing
(1) laissez-faire policies
(2) capitalist policies
(3) socialist policies
(4) communist policies
(5) fascist policies

4. 1 2 3 4 5
|| || || || ||

5. Which ONE of the following policies would Bennett have been least likely to support?
(1) forming the Bank of Canada to control the monetary system
(2) setting up the CBC with a monopoly in radio broadcasting
(3) creating the Wheat Board to guarantee producers a minimum price for their product
(4) forming an Unemployment Insurance Commission
(5) allowing market forces to dictate the shape of the economy

5. 1 2 3 4 5
|| || || || ||

6. Which statement best reflects Bennett's attitude about the role of the government in the economy?
(1) The government should take control of all essential services.
(2) No aspect of the economy should be left free of government supervision.
(3) The government should interfere in the economy only when it is clearly in the best interests of its citizens.
(4) Governments should only interfere when specifically requested to do so by the business community.
(5) Governments should never interfere in the economy under any circumstances.

6. 1 2 3 4 5
|| || || || ||

ANSWER KEY

1. **4** 2. **2** 3. **4** 4. **3** 5. **5** 6. **3**

ANSWER ANALYSIS

Let us look at questions 3 and 6.

3. **4** Question 3 gives you five statements, one of which is false. You have to check each statement against the passage. You can also use your knowledge of the period to help you make the correct choice. Note that there is no reference in the passage to "soaring inflation" so you may wonder if inflation was a problem during the Depression. Your own knowledge of the period may also cause you to infer that periods of high unemployment and widespread poverty are not periods that are likely to place inflationary pressure on the economy.

6. **3** Question 6 asks you to make an inference, one of the most difficult reading skills. Choices 1 and 5 provide two extreme positions that do not reflect Bennett's position. Choice 2 is simply a restatement of choice 1. Choice 3 reflects Bennett's position that governments should interfere in the economy only when it is in the best interests of the citizens and, therefore, excludes choice 4 which emphasizes the business community over the interests of the people in general.

GEOGRAPHY ILLUSTRATION

Illustration 4

Geography may be subdivided into several areas of study.

Physical Geography The study of physical geography emphasizes elements of the natural environment. These include topography, soils, earth materials, earth-sun relationships, surface and underground water, weather and climate, and native plant and animal life. Physical geography also includes the impact of humans on the physical environment as well as those influences omnipresent in nature.

Cultural Geography In cultural geography emphasis is placed upon the study of observable features resulting from human occupation of the earth. These features include population distribution and settlement, cities, buildings, roads, airfields, factories, railroads, farm and field patterns, communication facilities, and many other examples of human work. Cultural geography is one of the very significant fields of geographic inquiry.

Economic Geography In economic geography, the relationship between human efforts to gain a living and the earth's surface on which they are conducted are correlated. In order to study how people make a living, the distribution of materials, production, institutions, and human traits and customs are analyzed.

Regional Geography In regional geography the basic concern is with the salient characteristics of areas. Emphasis is placed upon patterns and elements of the natural environment and their relationships to human activities. By using the regional technique in studying geographic phenomena, what otherwise might be a bewildering array of facts is brought into focus as an organised, cohesive pattern.

Systematic Geography It is also feasible to study the geography of a small area or the entire surface of the earth in systematic fashion. Settlement, climates, soils, landforms, minerals, water, or crops, among others, may be observed, described, analyzed, and explained. Research in systematic geography has proved to be very valuable.

1. This passage describes geography's
(1) growth
(2) scope
(3) importance
(4) role in the social sciences
(5) principles

1. 1 2 3 4 5
|| || || || ||

2. The difference among the five areas of geography described is one of
(1) method
(2) importance
(3) emphasis
(4) recency
(5) objectivity

2. 1 2 3 4 5
|| || || || ||

3. A student interested in the influence of a geographical feature of a region on available jobs would study
(1) physical geography
(2) cultural geography
(3) economic geography
(4) regional geography
(5) systematic geography

3. 1 2 3 4 5
|| || || || ||

4. A meteorologist would likely be most interested in
(1) physical geography
(2) cultural geography
(3) economic geography
(4) regional geography
(5) systematic geography

4. 1 2 3 4 5
|| || || || ||

5. An urban sociologist would probably study
(1) physical geography
(2) cultural geography
(3) economic geography
(4) regional geography
(5) systematic geography

5. 1 2 3 4 5
|| || || || ||

6. A person studying the problems of the Middle East will use the approach found in
(1) physical geography
(2) cultural geography
(3) economic geography
(4) regional geography
(5) systematic geography

6. 1 2 3 4 5
|| || || || ||

7. A conservationist studying the effects of such activities of man as strip mining and land erosion would turn to
(1) physical geography
(2) cultural geography
(3) economic geography
(4) regional geography
(5) systematic geography

7. 1 2 3 4 5
|| || || || ||

8. The aspect of geography that seeks to study in a planned and orderly way the geography of a small area is
(1) physical geography
(2) cultural geography
(3) economic geography
(4) regional geography
(5) systematic geography

8. 1 2 3 4 5
|| || || || ||

ANSWER KEY

1. **2** 2. **3** 3. **3** 4. **1** 5. **2** 6. **4** 7. **1** 8. **5**

ANSWER ANALYSIS

Four of the questions deal with definitions: questions 3, 6, 7, and 8. Two call for knowing terms in addition to those defined in the passage.

2. **3** Question 2 is a little tricky, but, if you read closely, you will notice that the author uses the words *stress* and *emphasis* in his definitions of the various aspects of geography.

Questions 4 and 5 are, in effect, two-step questions. First, you must define the term in the question. Then, you must recall the definition of the area of geography to which it relates.

4. **1** In question 4, you must know that a meteorologist is concerned with weather. Only then can you identify physical geography as his primary interest.
5. **2** In this question, an urban sociologist studies cities, an area of interest to the cultural geographer.

BEHAVIOURAL SCIENCES ILLUSTRATION

Illustration 5

Urbanization has been a persistent feature of Canada's demographic history since Confederation. Migration from rural to urban areas has occurred largely in response to perceived greater economic opportunities in cities. At the same time it has led to growing societal problems such as crime.

Population has grown in both urban and rural Canada since 1851 but the major trend has been toward urbanization. In fact, the change from a mainly rural society to an urban one took place during the 1920s.

By 1986 the 19 million people living in urban areas accounted for 77% of the total Canadian population. This contrasts sharply with 1851 when only 13% of Canadians lived in urban areas.

Urban population growth from 1951 to 1986 varied by the size of the urban area. Large centres grew more quickly than small centres. By 1986 more than half of the Canadian population lived in only nine metropolitan areas. Between 1981 and 1986 almost two thirds of the total population growth took place in three cities: Toronto, Montreal, and Vancouver.

Canada has become a nation of city dwellers. Most of us live in organized built-up areas of more than 1,000 people where the population density is greater than 400 per square kilometre. Of course, it also depends on which part of Canada we are examining. While over 80% of the people in Ontario and Quebec may be urban dwellers, over 50% of the people in Prince Edward Island and Saskatchewan are not.

1. This selection is mainly concerned with
(1) the attractions of cities
(2) defining urbanization
(3) the increasing rate of urbanization
(4) the growing importance of cities
(5) Canada's urban character

1. 1 2 3 4 5

2. All of the following are characteristic of urban areas EXCEPT
(1) high density population
(2) communities of over 1,000
(3) organized, built-up areas
(4) population density greater than 400 per square kilometre
(5) low density population

2. 1 2 3 4 5

3. Which one of the following is cited as a reason for the growth of urban areas?
(1) lack of arable land
(2) the lure of the city life-style
(3) greater economic opportunity
(4) the pressure of rural population growth
(5) more things to do for young people

3. 1 2 3 4 5

4. Which of the following statements is NOT supported by the selection?
(1) Rural population has declined continuously since Confederation.
(2) Between 1920 and 1930 the population was divided about equally between urban and rural areas.
(3) Most Canadians live in large metropolitan areas.
(4) Urbanization has led to increased social problems.
(5) Urbanization has led to concern about the viability of rural areas.

4. 1 2 3 4 5

5. Given that electoral boundaries in Canada are adjusted infrequently, it would be reasonable to infer from the selection that
(1) urban areas are suitably represented in Parliament
(2) urban areas are overrepresented in Parliament
(3) urban areas are underrepresented in Parliament
(4) rural areas are underrepresented in Parliament
(5) rural areas are suitably represented in Parliament

5. 1 2 3 4 5

6. Which ONE of the following conclusions cannot be drawn from the information presented in the selection?
(1) At the time of Confederation, Canada was a predominantly rural society.
(2) All Canadian provinces are mainly urban in character.
(3) Urban growth has proceeded unabated since Confederation.
(4) While the rural population has grown, the rate of growth has been slow when compared with urban growth.
(5) The recent growth in the Canadian population is found mainly in a few large cities.

6. 1 2 3 4 5

ANSWER KEY

1. **5** 2. **5** 3. **3** 4. **1** 5. **3** 6. **2**

ANSWER ANALYSIS

Questions 3 and 6 are of interest.

3. **3** This question requires you to find a reason that the author cites to explain the growth of urban areas. The reason is cited in the opening paragraph: namely, "perceived greater economic opportunities in cities."

6. **2** Question 6 is tricky. This requires you to identify a conclusion that cannot be drawn from the information in the paragraph. It also requires you to correctly interpret some numerical information. In the last sentence, it says, "over 50% of the people in Prince Edward Island and Saskatchewan are not (urban dwellers)." This means that most people in these two provinces live in rural areas and the provinces are, therefore, better described as rural rather than urban. Thus, it would be incorrect to say that "all Canadian provinces are mainly urban in character."

Since study of the social sciences involves the gathering and interpretation of fact, you will frequently encounter various methods for presenting the facts you need. Most often, these facts will be presented in the form of tables or charts, graphs, or maps.

For a study of these methods, please refer to Chapter 10.

BASICS IN INTERPRETING POLITICAL CARTOONS

Political cartoons, as a distinct art, first became important in the second half of the nineteenth century and they remain an important vehicle of political, economic and social commentary. Throughout Canadian history, an enduring concern has been our relationship with our United States neighbour, and this has often been the subject of the cartoonist's wrath. Two of the best of these are the Jack Canuck cartoon of 1884 and the contemporary Andy Donato cartoon of "Americanus Economus."

1. Most cartoons deal with a single important issue, usually an election campaign issue, questions of peace and war, or corruption in the government.
2. The cartoonist frequently uses an exaggerated likeness, or caricature, of some well-known person or institution as the main focus of attention, for example, Uncle Sam or Johnny Canuck. Or he may use or create a symbol known to all his readers to represent an important idea, e.g., a dove for peace, a beaver or maple leaf for Canada, a bulldog for Great Britain.
3. Reading is kept to a minimum so that the appeal is largely visual. A few words at most are used in a caption to drive home an idea, so the visual appeal of the political cartoon is universal. Boss Tweed, an American nineteenth-century political figure pointed out that, even if his followers could not read, they could "look at the d__n pictures." Thus, cartoonists present the issue in simplified form, stripped of all the relatively unimportant details, in a way that their readers can understand.
4. Cartoonists graphically present their own point of view or that of their newspaper or magazine. They are usually openly anticorruption or antiwar, and they portray the object of their criticism in the ugliest manner possible.

Because of the visually appealing use of caricature and/or symbol focusing critically on a single important issue, the political cartoon is a powerful means of shaping public opinion. Its appeals to the emotions is difficult to equal and its influence continues to the present.

How, then, do you interpret a political cartoon when you encounter it on the High School Equivalency Examination?

Here are a few suggestions using the Paul Lachine and the Cameron Cardow (CAM) cartoons.

Step 1. *Identify the caricatures or symbols used in the cartoon.* In historical cartoons, you may have to have some social studies background. In contemporary cartoons, the caricatures and symbols will be easier to identify.

In the Paul Lachine cartoon, the top-hatted Uncle Sam (President Clinton) wearing the pince-nez and the striped shorts represents a strong and more productive United States. The diminutive Canadian Prime Minister (Jean Chrétien) wears maple leaf shorts on his false body which is propped up by a bag of lower-value Canadian dollars.

Step 2. *Identify the issue being exposed or criticized by the cartoonist.* Here it is what Canadians perceive to be American ignorance of everything to do with Canada. In the Cameron Cardow (CAM) cartoon it is the impact that the American economy inevitably has upon economic conditions in Canada.

Step 3. *Determine the point of view being expressed by the cartoonist.* The two hulking American hockey teams, symbolizing lower US taxes and a stronger US dollar, are squeezing the small economically-challenged Canadian hockey teams' in their ability to compete in the National Hockey League (NHL).

LACHINE, Paul, *Portfoolio15*, Toronto, Macmillan Canada, 1999, p. 37.

Cardow, Cameron, *Portfoolio15*, Toronto, Macmillan Canada, 1999, p. 22.

Now turn to a contemporary cartoon, study it, and try to answer the questions based on it.

DUSAN, *The Toronto Star*

Petricic, Dusan, *Portfoolio15*, Toronto, Macmillan Canada, 1999, p. 8.

1. What does the ship in the cartoon represent?
2. What does the wave symbolize?
3. Why is the location of the ship important?
4. Who do the passengers on the ship represent?
5. What is the issue depicted by the cartoonist?
6. What is the point of view of the cartoonist?

ANSWER ANALYSIS

1. The ship represents Noah's Ark, which in turn represents computers in the world.
2. The wave represents the uncertainty that exists because many computers were not originally programmed to recognize the year 2000 (Y2K).
3. The ship (computers) is perched on a cliff and is in danger of being swept in to the unknown.
4. Noah and animals represent mankind throughout the world dependent on computers.
5. The issue is the sense of uncertainty of whether mankind will survive the Y2K flood.
6. The cartoonist feels that there is a potential disaster of world-wide proportions.

On the examination, the questions on cartoons will be similar to the following. Answer them and then continue to the analysis of the answers.

Questions

1. The main purpose of the cartoon is to show that
   (1) The Bible foretold a Year 2000 (Y2K) disaster.
   (2) Noah was a very good ship builder.
   (3) The fact that many computers were not programmed to read the Year 2000 may put the world in danger.
   (4) Noah and the animals on the Ark are frightened.
   (5) Noah built the world's first computer.

1. 1 2 3 4 5
|| || || || ||

2. The dark wave stands for
(1) the power of nature
(2) the destruction of mankind
(3) indifference
(4) the ship's location
(5) patience

2. 1 2 3 4 5

ANSWER KEY

1. **3** 2. **2**

ANSWER ANALYSIS

1. **3** Choice 1 is wrong because the story of Noah's Ark in the Bible was not about computers. Choices 2, 4 and 5 are wrong because the story of Noah's Ark is just used as a source of symbolism. Only choice 3 refers to the potential disaster the world faced because many computers (symbolized by Noah's Ark) were not prepared for Y2K.
2. **2** The dark wave represents the lack of preparedness of many computer systems for Y2K which could have been very destructive to mankind who depends upon these systems.

HOW TO HANDLE SOCIAL STUDIES SKILLS QUESTIONS

The social studies test no longer tests your ability to recall information such as dates, isolated facts, or events. It now emphasizes higher level skills. It does so by testing your ability to understand the written word or graphics, to apply the information and ideas given in the question, to analyze the given information and ideas, and to evaluate the accuracy of the information and the conclusions based on it.

1. ***Comprehension items*** (20% of the test or about 13 items) require you to understand the meaning and purpose of written material, passages or quotations, and information contained in maps, graphs, tables, and political cartoons. They test your ability to restate information, summarize ideas, and identify incorrectly stated ideas. The question will usually include a quotation and be followed by the words "This most nearly means" or "The best explanation of this statement is" or "The author believes or suggests." Here is an example.

EXAMPLE:

A CODE

Never DO, BE, or SUFFER, anything in soul or body, less or more, but what tends to the glory of God.

Resolved, never to lose one moment of time; but improve it the most profitable way I possibly can.

Resolved, to think much, on all occasions, of my own dying, and of the common circumstances which attend death.

Resolved, to maintain the strictest temperance in eating and drinking.

The author of the code believes that people should be mainly concerned with
(1) monetary issues
(2) luxuries
(3) patriotism
(4) spiritual matters
(5) politics

The passage reflects the ideas of Puritanism, a code that stresses spiritual concerns.

You can answer this question correctly if you read the passage carefully and decide what is being emphasized. Then, look for the answer which identified that emphasis. In this question, the emphasis is on living for the glory of God, concern for one's manner of dying, and discipline in such material concerns as eating and drinking. The spiritual is stressed. Indeed, you can answer the question even if you do not know it is the Puritan Code that is being quoted. The correct choice is 4.

2. ***Application items*** (30% of the test or about 19 items) require you to use information and ideas in a situation other than that indicated to you in the question. Applying information and ideas is a high-level skill because you must not only understand the general content, but be able to transfer it to the context of a particular situation. You must go from the general information you are given to a specific case.

EXAMPLE:

Under the Constitution all Canadians are equal before the law and are entitled to equal protection and benefit of the law without discrimination based on race, national, or ethnic origin, colour, religion, sex, age, or mental or physical disability.

A company seeking to recruit new workers decides to place some newspaper advertisements directed at particular groups. Under the Constitution only which one of the following groups could be specifically named?

(1) Christian persons of good reputation
(2) highly qualified women
(3) strong, physically fit men
(4) persons under the age of 30
(5) high school graduates

Choice 5 addresses only an earned qualification whereas all of the others refer to physical attributes or beliefs of applicants that are expressly prohibited as criteria for selecting employees.

A new form of question or item now appears in the High School Equivalency Examination social studies test. Its purpose is to test your ability to apply information given in the question that defines ideas in historical documents, divisions of subject matter in the social studies, systems of government, economics, psychology, and groups of basic concepts in the five areas of the social studies. You will have to

1. understand information that is presented in defined categories, usually five in number;
2. relate a situation, action, or event to those categories;
3. arrive at an application of the information in the categories to the given situation, action, or event.

An illustration will make this clear.

In this example, the information presented in defined categories is each of five important sections of the Canadian Charter or Rights and Freedoms, 1982. The question follows.

EXAMPLE:

Listed here are five of the important sections of the Canadian Charter of Rights and Freedoms, 1982.

(1) Section 2 (b) Everyone is entitled to freedom of thought, belief, opinion, and expression, including freedom of the press and other media of communication.
(2) Section 2 (c) Everyone is entitled to freedom of peaceful assembly.
(3) Section 3 Every citizen of Canada has the right to vote in an election of members of the House of Commons or of a legislative assemble, and to be qualified for membership therein.
(4) Section 11 (c) Any person charged with an offence has the right not to be compelled to be a witness in proceedings against him- or herself.
(5) Section 12 Everyone has the right not to be subjected to an unusual treatment or punishment.

This is followed by three ways in which the information can be used by three individuals in three different situations.

Indicate the section most likely to be cited in support of his or her position by
(1) an opponent of capital punishment
(2) a union leader on a picket line
(3) a person accused of a criminal act testifying at his own trial

You must apply the categorized information to the above situations.

An opponent of capital punishment will cite section 12's prohibition against any unusual treatment or punishment, so choice 5 is correct.

A labour union leader on a picket line will cite Section 2(c) concerning the right of peaceful assembly, so choice 2 is correct.

A person on trial will site section 11(c) so that he/she will not have to be a witness against himself/herself, so choice 4 is correct.

Try another item set in the new format.

EXAMPLE:

Psychology is the science of behaviour and of human thought processes. There are a number of closely interrelated branches of human psychology.

(1) Social psychology investigates the effect of the group on the behaviour of the individual.
(2) Applied psychology puts to practical use the discoveries and theories of psychology as in industrial psychology.
(3) Clinical psychology diagnoses and treats mental disorders and mental illness.
(4) Comparative psychology deals with different behavioural organizations of animals including man.
(5) Physiological psychology attempts to understand the effects of body functions on human behaviour.

Each of the following describes a proposed study. Indicate which branch of psychology is most involved.

(1) A company wants to study the effects of music piped into a factory where workers are on an assembly line.
  (1) Social psychology
  (2) Applied psychology
  (3) Clinical psychology
  (4) Comparative psychology
  (5) Physiological psychology

(2) A drug rehabilitation centre wants to study the role of peer pressure on a teenager in a drug prevention program.
  (1) Social psychology
  (2) Applied psychology
  (3) Clinical psychology
  (4) Comparative psychology
  (5) Physiological psychology

(3) A grant is available for a study of schizophrenia characterized by hallucinations and delusions.
  (1) Social psychology
  (2) Applied psychology
  (3) Clinical psychology
  (4) Comparative psychology
  (5) Physiological psychology

The correct answer to question (1) is 2. Applied psychology puts to practical use the findings of industrial psychologists, in this case to people who work on an assembly line.

The correct answer to question (2) is 1. Social psychologists are concerned with the effects of groups, in this case teenagers, who put pressure on their teenaged peers to use drugs.

The correct answer to question (3) is 3. Clinical psychologists would apply for the grant because of their interest in schizophrenia, a mental disorder.

3. ***Analysis items*** (30% of the test or about 19 items) require you to break down information into its parts to find out their interrelationships. They involve the ability to identify cause and effect relationships, separate fact from opinion, separate conclusions from supporting statements, and show that you can recognize assumptions on which conclusions are based.

EXAMPLE:

On October 17, 1970, in the midst of the FLQ crisis, Prime Minister Trudeau announced that the government had invoked the War Measures Act. In addition to giving the government a variety of sweeping powers, this had the effect of suspending the Canadian Bill of Rights. Here are some of the rights provided in Section One of the Bill:

(a) the right of the individual to life, liberty, security of the person . . .
(b) the right of the individual to equality before the law
(c) freedom of religion
(d) freedom of speech
(e) freedom of assembly
(f) freedom of the press

Which of the following powers granted to the government under the War Measures Act seems to be directly opposed to section 1(a) of the Bill of Rights?

(1) seizure, censorship, or closure of newspapers, radio and television stations
(2) arrest of anyone without being charged with a crime, indefinite detention without trial . . .
(3) search and seizure of private homes
(4) seizure of private property to include all factories, ships, every means of transportation
(5) seizure of all privately owned weapons

Not only must you understand the meaning of each possible answer, but you must analyze it to determine which is *contrary* to section 1(a) of the Canadian Bill of Rights. First you must understand; then you must analyze.

You have to go through the following steps, keeping in mind the provisions of section 1(a) of the Canadian Bill of Rights: the key features of this are that a person's well-being cannot be threatened through danger to his or her life, being placed in jail except through due process of law, or being held in jail without being brought quickly to trial.

Choice 1: allows the government to take over and control the media but says nothing about individuals

Choice 2: refers directly to holding individuals without being charged with a crime or without any provision being made for a speedy trial. This is the choice that is contrary to section 1(a)

Choice 3: refers to people's dwellings rather than to their persons

Choice 4: refers to property such as cars being searched and confiscated

Choice 5: refers to the right of the government to have the police or army confiscate any guns or knives or other weapons whether or not the owner seems to pose any threat

It is important to consider every choice carefully and ask yourself how it relates to the principle, issue, or question raised in the passage.

4. ***Evaluation items*** (20% of the test or about 13 items) are the most difficult. You must make judgments about the soundness or accuracy of information. They test your ability to determine whether facts are adequately documented or proven, whether they are appropriately used to support conclusions, and whether they are used correctly or incorrectly in the presentation of opinions or arguments.

EXAMPLE:

Which statement is an opinion rather than a fact?
(1) France was involved in the Vietnam conflict before the United States entered it.
(2) There are tensions between mainland China and the former Soviet Union.
(3) Arms limitation agreements between the United States and the former Soviet Union will lead to worldwide peace.
(4) Great Britain has become a full member of the European Common Market.
(5) The United States is a member of the North Atlantic Treaty Organization.

Five statements are presented. Four are facts that can be proved or verified by evidence—that France was involved in Vietnam; that mainland China and the former Soviet Union have tensions; that Great Britain is a member of the European Common Market; that the United States is a member of the North Atlantic Treaty Organization. That arms limitation agreements between the United States and the former Soviet Union *will* lead to worldwide peace is an opinion or a hypothesis—not a fact—and it remains to be proved.

These, then, are the four kinds of questions you will be asked to deal with on the social studies test.

OUTLINE OF STUDY FOR THE SOCIAL STUDIES

Although the social studies test does not ask you to recall specific facts, it does take the reading passages and other material from the topics that are covered in the high school curriculum. The more you know about these topics, the easier it will be for you to understand the material.

You can use the following outline of topics that may appear on the social studies test to guide you in your review. Remember that, even though you will not have to remember dates or definitions, the better you understand the important areas of social studies, the easier you will find the test.

Economics

I. The meaning of economics and the theme of scarcity

II. Comparison of modern economic systems: capitalism, communism, socialism (free market versus command)

III. How businesses behave
- A. How business is organized
- B. Economic markets
- C. Capitalism
- D. Supply and demand
- E. How prices are determined
- F. Competition and monopoly

IV. Production
- A. Role of production
- B. Deciding what and how to produce and distribute
- C. Production of goods and services
- D. Uses and rewards of factors of production

V. Consumers
   A. The key role of the consumer in the economy
   B. Money management: spending, investing, saving; the effects of inflation
   C. Advertising: its role; government regulations
   D. Consumer protection: legislation; Canadian Standards Association; grading and labelling regulations
   E. Consumer budgeting: credit and contracts

VI. Economics and Financial Institutions
   A. The concept of money
   B. The Bank of Canada and monetary policy
   C. Banking and interest
   D. Financial institutions other than banks

VII. Government's role in the economy
   A. Sources of revenue
   B. Expenditures (including servicing the national debt)
   C. Monetary and fiscal policies; stimulating and stabilizing the economy; government regulations affecting the economy

VIII. How the overall economy behaves
   A. Measuring the economy: G.N.P., Consumer Price Index, wages
   B. How the economy grows: industrialization, development, expanding markets
   C. Inflation and deflation; unemployment

IX. Labour and the economy
   A. The rights and responsibilities of labour and management
   B. The labour market: unionized and non-union labour
   C. The origins and growth of trade unions
   D. Collective bargaining
   E. Productivity

X. Canada and the World Economy
   A. International trade
   B. Foreign Exchange; the balance of trade; the balance of payments
   C. Foreign ownership
   D. Competition in a global market

Canadian History

I. Native Canadian peoples before the Europeans

II. European exploration
   A. The Norse
   B. The English, Portuguese, and French explorers

III. Colonization
   A. The fur trade
   B. The exploration and development of New France (government, church, social, and economic systems)

IV. Growth and Change
  A. The clash of British and French Empires
  B. British imperial policy
  C. Royal Proclamation (1763)
  D. Quebec Act (1774); Constitutional Act (1791)
  E. British North America and the American Revolution
  F. The Loyalists
  G. The War of 1812

V. The Expanding Frontier
  A. Western trade and settlement
  B. Canals, railways, and migrations

VI. Political Reform
  A. The reform movements in Lower Canada, Upper Canada, and the Maritimes
  B. Responsible government
  C. Lord Durham's Report

VII. Confederation
  A. The British North America Act, 1867
  B. National policy
  C. The development of political parties
  D. The Canadian Pacific Railway
  E. The Riel Rebellions
  F. The Macdonald-Cartier alliance

VIII. Canada and the early twentieth century
  A. The prime ministries of Laurier and Borden
  B. Reciprocity
  C. World War I and the conscription crisis
  D. Canada and the League of Nations
  E. Canada and the British Empire
  F. Increasing independence; the Statute of Westminster, 1931

IX. Economic Development
  A. The Great Depression; the prime ministries of Bennett and Mackenzie King
  B. World War II
  C. The growth of the welfare state

X. Canada and the World
  A. The Cold War
  B. The United Nations
  C. Canada and the United States
  D. Canada and the Commonwealth

XI. Contemporary challenges
  A. Federal-provincial relations
  B. Separatism in Quebec; the problem of the "distinct" society
  C. The native Canadian peoples
  D. The role of women
  E. Global interdependence

Geography

I. The individual's relationship to the Earth
  A. The Earth as a globe: principal features, size, shape, the relative size and position of the land masses and the oceans, the atmosphere
  B. Location: maps and globes, latitude and longitude
  C. Topography: the chief topographical features of the Earth, soils, vegetation, water supply. Effects upon transportation and communication
  D. Climate: factors affecting climate; effects of climate upon human activity
  E. Topics: agriculture, mining, forestry, fishing, transportation, energy
  F. Sustainable development and issues of non-renewable resources

II. Canadian Regions
  A. Regional differences: population, income, resources
  B. Foreign investment
  C. The cultural mosaic
  D. The urban/rural dichotomy
  E. Pollution and waste
  F. Native land claims

III. Major cultural regions of the world: North America, Latin America, Western Europe including the Mediterranean, the former Soviet Union, the Middle East, the Far East, all regions of Africa, the Pacific and Southeast Asia
  A. Physical aspects
  B. Economic development
  C. Climate
  D. Cultural dimensions

IV. Using the world's resources
  A. Resources and development
  B. Comparisons between the developed and the developing world
  C. Preserving the world's environments
  D. International trade
  E. Urbanization

Political Science

I. Political systems
  A. Government and society—importance and basic role of government
  B. Types of modern governments
  C. Meaning of democracy

II. The Canadian political system
  A. The foundations of Canadian Government; the British North America Act, 1867; the Constitution Act, 1982
  B. The nature of federalism

III. The Canadian political process
  A. The party system
  B. The right to vote and voter behaviour
  C. Nominations and elections
  D. Public opinion, pressure groups, lobbying
  E. Citizenship

IV. National executive branch
  A. The Crown and the Governor General
  B. The Prime Minister
  C. Cabinet government

V. National legislative branch
   A. Legislative powers and processes
   B. Parliament: House of Commons, Senate

VI. National judicial branch
   A. the Canadian system of justice
   B. Federal courts
   C. the Supreme Court of Canada
   D. Charter of Rights and Freedoms

VII. Provincial governments
   A. The division of authority between federal and provincial governments
   B. The particular responsibilities of provincial governments
   C. Regional disparity

VIII. Municipal governments
   A. Roles and responsibilities
   B. Financing
   C. Special Services: local roads, transit, sanitation, water supply

IX. Government and general welfare
   A. Federal revenues and expenditures
   B. Money and banking policies
   C. Government and business: Crown Corporations, DRIE, ACOA
   D. Labour and social security
   E. Federal Agencies: Wheat Board, Environment Canada, Transport Canada, CRTC

X. Canada in the world today
   A. Canadian foreign policy
   B. Canada and international organisations—the United Nations, the Commonwealth, La Francophonie
   C. Population explosion; technological revolution; meeting social responsibilities—health, education, welfare, crime, and other social issues

Behavioural Sciences

I. Introduction to behavioural sciences

II. From the psychologist's view
   A. What psychology is
   B. Humans as individuals
   C. Primary needs for survival and well-being
   D. Understanding human behaviour—measures of personality and intellect
   E. Heredity and environment
   F. Principles of learning
   G. Humans' beliefs, feelings, attitudes—male/female roles

III. From the sociologist's view
   A. What sociology is
   B. Humans in groups
      1. Family
      2. Schools
      3. Peer group
      4. Behaviour in small groups
      5. Other social institutions

C. Social stratification
   1. Social class
   2. Occupational scale
   3. Ethnic background—minority, immigrant, and ethnic experiences
   4. Norms and values

IV. From the anthropologist's view
   A. What anthropology is
   B. Humans in culture
      1. Social relationships
      2. Problems of society
      3. When cultures meet
      4. Race and prejudice
   C. The search for identify

PRACTICE IN SOCIAL STUDIES SKILLS QUESTIONS

—That Test Comprehension

1. During the last 150 years, immigrants were attracted to Canada because the demand for workers increased. This occurred when Canada was experiencing periods of

(1) economic expansion
(2) economic depression
(3) war
(4) political change
(5) stability

1. 1 2 3 4 5

2. The original idea behind it was that it should act as a restraint upon democratic government. It was thought that the elected representatives of the people might rush too quickly to some judgments. Here, every piece of legislation could be given "a second sober look."

To which body does this passage refer?

(1) the Office of the Governor General
(2) the Cabinet
(3) the Senate
(4) the Opposition
(5) the Supreme Court

2. 1 2 3 4 5

3. Which is a basic assumption of the graduated income tax?

(1) The ability to pay increases as wealth increases.
(2) Each wage earner should contribute the same percentage of his or her income.
(3) The middle class should bear the burden of financing the government.
(4) Citizens should pay the costs of government services in proportion to their use of such services.
(5) Taxes on the wealthy should not be too great.

3. 1 2 3 4 5

4. "In a sense the people of the Third World were forced to help pay for the Industrial Revolution in the West."
Which statement most clearly supports this viewpoint?
(1) The colonizing power encouraged industries in their colonies.
(2) Western nations depended upon raw materials from their colonies.
(3) Financial centres of the world blocked investments in these new nations.
(4) The Third World is now experiencing an Industrial Revolution.
(5) The Third World supplied most of the manpower needed by the West.

4. 1 2 3 4 5

5. "Public opinion is of major significance in social control." The author of this statement most probably meant that
(1) the influence of public opinion on government leaders is very limited
(2) problem solving is simplified when public opinion is not known
(3) public opinion may be predicted accurately especially in the time of national crisis
(4) government officials must pay attention to public opinion in the formulation of policies
(5) polls provide little help to lawmakers

5. 1 2 3 4 5

—That Test Analysis

The Business Cycle

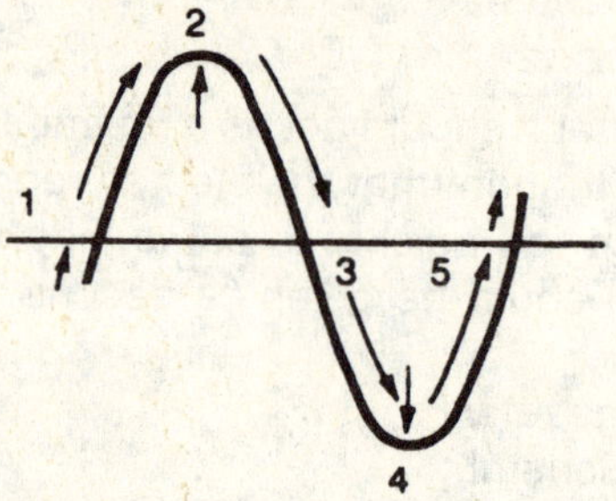

6. If economic indicators place the economy at a point on the cycle between 1 and 2, the government's economic advisors would most likely suggest which action to the Cabinet?
(1) planned deficit spending
(2) increasing income tax rates
(3) lowering interest rates
(4) increasing government expenditures
(5) encouraging higher wages

6. 1 2 3 4 5

7. A Swiss survey of nineteen nations showed that Canada is tops (or should it be bottoms) in foreign penetration of its insurance industry. In 1969, the last year for which the Swiss Reinsurance Co. of Zurich has figures, foreign companies creamed off 42% of all premiums paid by Canadians. Forty-two percent is almost double the next highest; in Pakistan it is 24%.
Which of the following statements best represents the point of view of the author of the passage?

7. 1 2 3 4 5

(1) Insurance rates are too high worldwide.
(2) It is hard to conduct international surveys.
(3) Pakistan has an excellent insurance industry.
(4) Too much of Canada's insurance industry is controlled by foreign companies.
(5) Swiss Reinsurance is the largest insurance company in the world.

8. No matter how distant each of us may seem from the critical problems that face the world's poor, we should never forget that we all travel on "Spaceship Earth" together. Their problems are also our problems. We can ignore them, but we can never wish them away, regardless of how many fingers we cross. When we eventually are forced to open our eyes, these difficulties will have only become much worse. Canada's wealth and technology advance demand that we assume a major leadership role for the betterment of our "universal" fraternity.
Which action by the Canadian government best reflects the philosophy expressed in this passage?
(1) passage of legislation restricting immigration
(2) legislation increasing aid to developing countries
(3) approval of the United Nations Charter
(4) participation in the North Atlantic Treaty Organization
(5) legislation permitting immigration by highly qualified Third World personnel.

8. 1 2 3 4 5
|| || || || ||

9. "If a nation expects to be ignorant and free, in a state of civilization, it expects what never was and never will be."
Which idea is most strongly supported by this statement?
(1) the government's right to tax
(2) universal suffrage
(3) a strong central government
(4) compulsory education
(5) free medical care

9. 1 2 3 4 5
|| || || || ||

10. "We have a society which is based on arbitrary and strictly enforced sex roles . . . Through her upbringing and education a girl's sense of self is progressively crushed."
This quotation most clearly supports the idea that
(1) women, in Canada, often find themselves in positions of inferiority to men
(2) there should be a strict division of labour between men and women
(3) education is not as powerful an influence on women as their upbringing
(4) men and women have equal opportunity in Canada
(5) some jobs should be reserved for women only

10. 1 2 3 4 5
|| || || || ||

—That Test Application

11. Which is the most valid statement concerning the problem of balancing human wants with limited resources?

(1) It exists only in societies with a free enterprise economy.
(2) It has been solved in nations with strong governmental controls over economic activity.
(3) It has become less of a problem with the advancements in technology.
(4) It exists in all societies, no matter what the economic system.
(5) It was solved by the year 2000.

11. 1 2 3 4 5

12. An advocate of decentralized government, one who would support the increasing share of governmental responsibility that the provinces have gained since Confederation, would favour which of the following?

(1) a National Pollution Control Act
(2) transferring control over education to Ottawa
(3) increasing the powers of the federal government
(4) increasing the powers of the provinces
(5) abolition of the monarchy

12. 1 2 3 4 5

Listed below are some principles which are important to the operations of parliamentary democracy:

—the Privilege of Parliament which means that members of Parliament may speak openly and criticize the government for its shortcomings
—the Supremacy of Parliament means that, within the limits imposed by the Constitution, Parliament may enact any legislation—without regard for property, human rights or tradition
—the Independence of the Judiciary means that judges are free to interpret the law as they see fit without any form of interference
—Due Process of Law means that all law enforcement must adhere to proper procedure as a safeguard of individual rights
—the Right to Dissent means that citizens can oppose passage of a law or even petition for a law to be changed or abolished.

Each of the following is a threat to one of these principles. Identify which one.

13. In seventeenth-century England, the King tells Parliament, "You are here to hear my demands, not to present yours."

(1) the Privilege of Parliament
(2) the Supremacy of Parliament
(3) the Independence of the Judiciary
(4) Due Process of Law
(5) the Right to Dissent

13. 1 2 3 4 5

14. A Cabinet Minister calls a judge to tell him that a witness at a trial has worked for him and was not very reliable.

(1) the Privilege of Parliament
(2) the Supremacy of Parliament
(3) the Independence of the Judiciary
(4) Due Process of Law
(5) the Right to Dissent

14. 1 2 3 4 5

15. A police chief is fed up with vandalism caused by young people at night and announces a 10:00 P.M. curfew for everyone under 18.
(1) the Privilege of Parliament
(2) the Supremacy of Parliament
(3) the Independence of the Judiciary
(4) Due Process of Law
(5) the Right to Dissent

15. 1 2 3 4 5

—That Test Evaluation

16. Which statement would be most *difficult* to prove?
(1) Japan's emperors have reigned but have seldom ruled.
(2) The workers of the United States are better workers than those of Japan.
(3) In the post-World War II period, the United States was the source of much cultural borrowing by the Japanese.
(4) Japanese technology in the 1970s is more advanced than it was in the 1940s.
(5) The cost of living in Japan has been rising since World War II.

16. 1 2 3 4 5

17. Which statement would be most *difficult* to prove?
(1) The major political parties in Canada sometimes adopt popular measures proposed by minor parties.
(2) The Constitution Act of 1867 rendered more authority to the federal government than to the provinces.
(3) In 1975, Bill C-58 set standards of Canadian content for magazines published in Canada.
(4) World War II was necessary in order to end the Great Depression.
(5) The right to vote has been extended in the twentieth century.

17. 1 2 3 4 5

18. Which information about country X would be most useful to the head of a government establishing a foreign policy toward country X?
(1) an analysis of the national resources and goals of country X
(2) a file containing the major public statements made by the leaders of country X concerning their nation's foreign policies
(3) an analysis by religious leaders of the major religious groups and beliefs of the people of country X
(4) a newspaper report summarizing the treaties and international agreements of country X
(5) the party to which leaders of country X belong

18. 1 2 3 4 5

19. Which statement expresses an opinion rather than a fact?
(1) After World War I, Canada became a member of the League of Nations.
(2) At one time, Canada was on the gold standard.
(3) The Canadian negotiators made unnecessary concessions to the United States in the 1988 Free Trade Negotiations.
(4) In 1846, the Oregon Treaty established the 49th parallel as the northern boundary of the United States.
(5) Canada is a member of NATO.

19. 1 2 3 4 5

20. The privilege of conducting a business in any manner that one sees fit is not guaranteed by the Canadian Charter of Rights. Businesses must abide by a variety of laws such as those that relate to consumer protection and to the conditions of work. The courts have accepted no justification to reject these limitations on the conduct of business.
Which concept is being rejected in the above passage?
(1) laissez-faire
(2) welfare
(3) competition
(4) profit motive
(5) antitrust legislation

20. 1 2 3 4 5
|| || || || ||

Turn to the answer key and the answer analysis which follow.

What's Your Score?

________right, ________wrong

Excellent	19–20
Good	15–18
Fair	13–14

If your score was low, the explanation of the correct answers below will help. Analyze your errors. Reread the appropriate section "How to Handle Social Studies Skills Questions" (page 296). There are more skills questions in the two full-length practice examinations at the end of this book.

ANSWER KEY

Practice in Social Studies Skills Questions/Page 305

1. **1**	6. **2**	11. **4**	16. **2**
2. **3**	7. **4**	12. **4**	17. **4**
3. **1**	8. **2**	13. **1**	18. **1**
4. **2**	9. **4**	14. **3**	19. **3**
5. **4**	10. **1**	15. **4**	20. **1**

ANSWER ANALYSIS

Practice in Social Studies Skills Questions/Page 305

1. **1** Immigrants have been attracted when there were opportunities for cheap, fertile land to farm; and for jobs in factories and mines and in building transportation lines. Immigration has fallen off during wars, when it was dangerous and difficult to travel, and during depressions, when jobs were not available.
2. **3** Since all legislation introduced and passed by the elected representatives of the people in the House of Commons must also be passed by the Senate, there is a second opportunity for examination and amendment, or even rejection. Hence, the Senate has come to be considered a body which provides a "second sober look" at legislation.
3. **1** Such a tax raises the rate of taxation as one's income increases. For example, a family of four earning $50 000 pays a federal income tax at a higher rate than a similar family having a taxable income of $25 000.
4. **2** The growth of European industrialization from about 1870 on increased the search for African copper, precious woods, diamonds, gold and (later) uranium; and the development of rubber and cocoa plantations by North American and Western European firms. In Asia, areas like Malaya and Indonesia furnished rubber, tin, and petroleum to the West.

5. **4** Social controls are composed of two parts. There are first the laws against what society defines as criminal actions, such as malicious destruction of property or the sale of narcotics. Those laws are enforced by police and courts to the extent of their ability and efficiency. Then there are the informal controls that society exerts upon its members based upon one's desire to keep the good opinion of others. Teenage fads illustrate the control exerted by group conformity. Public opinion in general is a powerful factor in social control. Political leaders know that they cannot get too far away from public opinion without risking loss of control, e.g., with respect to keeping or eliminating price and wage controls; pardoning convicted criminals, or introducing new taxes.
6. **2** A major economic aim of government is to smooth out the extremes of the business cycle in order to avoid "boom and bust." During this period of economic expansion and prosperity, a rise in income tax rates would reduce disposable income, slowing down the rate of inflation that can shorten the period of expansion. Another reason for higher tax rates under these conditions is to create a budget surplus to repay part of the national debt.
7. **4** Foreign control of Canadian-based businesses has been a major concern at certain periods in Canadian history. The control of a significant proportion of the insurance industry was typical of this concern in the late sixties. The prevailing opinion at the time was that too much control lay in the hands of foreign businesses.
8. **2** In the second part of this century, people have come to appreciate that we are all citizens of a "global village" and that what affects one country is also likely to have effects upon others. In particular, we have become increasingly aware of the plight of the poor in Third World countries. Increasing aid to these countries would be one way that Canada could use its wealth and technology for the betterment of all people.
9. **4** This statement by an early President of the United States, Thomas Jefferson, strongly supports compulsory education. It is a point of view that has become widely accepted in democratic societies where free, universal and compulsory public education have become the norm.
10. **1** Even though the law may require that men and women be treated equally, there are sometimes features of a society beyond the control of the law that result in differences in how men and women are treated and what they can achieve. This quotation from Bonnie Kreps indicates that young women, through their upbringing and education, may place more emphasis on their roles in relation to men, for example, wives and mothers, than upon their own individual identity.
11. **4** The central problem of all economic systems is how best to use those limited resources to meet unlimited human needs and desires.
12. **4** In 1867, the fathers of Confederation had the intention of creating a system of government with a strong central or federal government. Over the years there have been many advocates of decentralization who sought to reduce the power of the federal government and increase the powers of the provinces.
13. **1** The principle of the privilege of Parliament has evolved over the centuries. When Charles I stormed into Parliament to arrest members who where critical of him, he was greeted with cries of "Privilege! privilege!" His quarrel with Parliament led to the outbreak of the English Civil War.
14. **3** Although judges are appointed by the government, an important principle of Canadian parliamentary tradition has been that they should be free to carry out their duties without any interference from the government. This principle is so important, that any Minister who approached a judge in order to exert influence in a matter before the courts would be required to resign.
15. **4** The responsibility for making laws in Canada rests with Parliament, the provincial legislatures, and municipal councils, each with its own area of jurisdiction. Laws cannot be made on the whim and fancy of one individual. A police chief would not make laws. By imposing a curfew, the chief would be acting without proper authority.
16. **2** The term "better" would involve many factors, and it would be difficult to come to agreement about what was to be measured, let alone how to measure the many varieties.

17. **4** Each of the other choices can be substantiated by objective factual evidence. Such evidence will be generally accepted and agreed upon. This is not true for the statement about World War II and the Great Depression. Some historians and economists will argue that the Great Depression would have come to an end without the impact of the war.
18. **1** One nation should understand the purposes and abilities of another in order to carry on intelligent dealings with it. An analysis of those items is particularly valuable.
19. **3** We may define a fact as a statement that can be proved or verified and about which most people agree. An opinion is a personal conclusion which may be based on factual information, one's own biases and background, and even wishful thinking. It is not verifiable, and people tend to disagree about opinions; e.g., which team will win next year's World Series, Stanley Cup, or Super Bowl, and who is the world's greatest musician.
20. **1** The paragraph approves of laws which regulate business in the public interest. Laissez-faire is an economic policy which provides for little or no interference by government in the affairs of business, so the author of this passage would most likely reject it.

GLOSSARY OF SOCIAL STUDIES TERMS

In social studies as in science, vocabulary is of critical importance. The selected subject area vocabulary lists consist of 688 words from the five social sciences—Canadian history (page 312), political science (page 315), economics (page 318), geography (page 323), and behavioural sciences (page 326). The definitions have been simplified and, in the simplification, some aspects of the identification have been omitted. If the definition is not clear, be certain to consult a dictionary. In any event be sure to review the section "Learning Social Studies Vocabulary and Deriving Meaning from Context" (page 281).

Don't forget: The glossary defines a number of terms which are likely to be used on the test. Do not forget to consult the glossary when you meet unfamiliar terms in the questions.

Canadian History and World Backgrounds

A

ABOLITIONIST one who favoured abolishing Black slavery in the United States prior to the Civil War

ABORIGINAL PEOPLE the native Indian and Inuit peoples who inhabited much of North America before the arrival of the Europeans

ABORIGINAL RIGHTS rights claimed by the aboriginal people in Canada because they are the original inhabitants of the country

ABSOLUTISM form of government in which unlimited power is put in the hands of a ruler

AGGRESSION attack by one country on another without any provocation

ANNEXATION adding of territory to an already existing country or state

APARTHEID policy of racial segregation and discrimination against Blacks, and other non-Europeans, practised by the Republic of South Africa

APPEASEMENT policy of giving into the demands of an enemy power in an effort to maintain peace

ARMISTICE temporary stopping of war by agreement of both sides before a peace treaty is signed

ARYAN term wrongly used by the Nazis to mean a person of German or northern European descent

AUTHORITARIANISM policy of complete obedience to the authority of a ruler

AXIS in World War II, the countries who fought against the United States and her allies—Nazi Germany, Fascist Italy, and Japan

B

BLACKLIST a list of people or organizations to avoid in trade or to deny employment to because of government policy or suspected disloyalty

BLOCKADE action taken to cut off trade and communication with an enemy

BOLSHEVIK follower of Lenin and member of the Communist party who took part in the Russian Revolution

BOONDOGGLE spending of public money to create unnecessary jobs

BOURGEOISIE the middle class

BOYCOTT refuse to deal with a country or an organization for political or economic reasons

C

CARPETBAGGER Northern politician or businessman who went to the South during the Reconstruction Era to take advantage of conditions there

CHARTER in colonial times, a grant from the English ruler to a person or corporation giving certain rights and privileges of settlement

CIVIL WAR American war between the northern and southern states (1861–1865)

COLD WAR diplomatic and economic conflict between nations short of actual warfare

COLONY settlement in a distant land which remains under control of the country from which its settlers came

COMPROMISE agreement in which each side gives up some things it wanted

CONSERVATION policies and practises which aim at preservation of natural resources such as forests

COUP D'ETAT sudden overthrow of a government by force

D

DECREE an order of a government or a church

DESEGREGATION removal of separation of races in public places such as schools

DESPOT a ruler with unlimited powers

DISARMAMENT reduction in arms and armed forces as a result of agreement between nations

DISCRIMINATION prejudice in the treatment of one group compared with another in such things as jobs, housing, etc.

DOCTRINE a principle or belief or a set of principles or beliefs; sometimes identified with a person

DOVE one who is identified as espousing the cause of peace and/or pursuing a conciliatory policy in foreign affairs

DYNASTY successive series of rulers from the same family

E

ECCLESIASTICAL having to do with the church or the clergy

EDICT official proclamation or decree

EMANCIPATION the setting free of a slave or anyone in bondage

EMBARGO official order preventing ships from entering or leaving the ports of a country for the purpose of commerce

EMIGRATION movement of a person or persons from one country to settle in another

EMPIRE a unit of a group of states, colonies, or territories joined together under the rule of one dominant power

ENTENTE informal, friendly agreement between nations which calls for cooperation in policy or action

EVOLUTION theory of Darwin which states that plants and animals develop from earlier forms by transmitting variations which help them better to survive

EXPROPRIATION taking away of property from a private owner in the public interest for public use

EXTRATERRITORIALITY removal from control of the country in which he lives of a foreign person such as a diplomat

F

FAIR DEAL continuation and development of the principles of the New Deal by the Truman administration

FEMINISM movement to win for women rights equal to those of men in political, social, and economic areas

FEUDALISM medieval social and economic organization of society (ninth and fifteenth centuries) in Europe in which land worked by serfs was held by vassals in return for service to their lords

G

GENOCIDE systematic killing off of an entire national, racial, or cultural group

GREENBACK U.S. political party after the Civil War which advocated government paper money as the only money to be used

H

HAWK one who advocates an aggressive and warlike approach to his country's foreign policy

HEGEMONY dominance of one country over others in the same league or in the same geographic area

HERESY a religious belief opposed to doctrine established by the church

HUMANISM intellectual and cultural movement stressing human (as opposed to natural or religious) interests and the study of classical literature which led to the Renaissance

I

IMMIGRATION movement of a person into a new country to settle there

IMPERIALISM policy of a nation to extend its power by establishing colonies, controlling territories, raw materials, and world markets

INDUSTRIAL REVOLUTION social and economic changes brought about by the development of large-scale industrial production

INTERVENTION interference of one country in the affairs of another

ISOLATIONISM policy of a country which is based on unwillingness to take part in international affairs

L

LOYALIST term used to describe many immigrants to Canada following the American Revolutionary War (War of Independence); called loyalists because they remained loyal to the British Crown during the course of the Revolution

M

MANDATE authority given by the League of Nations to one nation to administer some territory or geographic region

MANIFESTO public declaration by a government or any person or persons of intention to act or of action taken

MARITIME having to do with the sea, navigation, and shipping

MEDIEVAL referring to the period in Europe between the fifth and fifteenth centuries A.D.

METIS a person of mixed Indian and European, usually French, background; they played an important part in Canadian history at the time of the Riel rebellions

MILITARISM belief that the military should dominate the government and that military efficiency is the ideal of the state

MONARCHY government where supreme power is placed in a king, queen, or emperor and where such power may be absolute or limited

MONOTHEISM doctrine that there is only one God

MORATORIUM legal permission, in an emergency, to delay the payment by one nation of its debt to another

MUCKRAKER in the late nineteenth and early twentieth centuries, one who, in America, sought to expose corruption by politicians or businessmen

N

NATIONALISM doctrine that the interests and security of one's own country are more important than those of other nations or international groups

NAZISM system in Germany (1933–1945) which controlled all activities of the people, fostered belief in the supremacy of Hitler as Fuhrer and the German people as a master race, and its establishment as the dominant world power

NEW DEAL principles of the liberal democrats as advocated under the leadership of President Franklin Roosevelt

NONAGGRESSION referring to an agreement between two nations not to attack one another

P

PACIFISM belief that conflicts between nations should be settled by peaceful means rather than by war

PACT an agreement or treaty between nations

PAN-AMERICANISM belief in political, economic, social, and cultural cooperation and understanding between the nations of North, Central, and South America

PANIC in the United States, specific periods in which fear of economic collapse results in wild attempts to convert property, goods, and securities into cash

PARLIAMENT the legislative body of Canada consisting of the House of Commons and Senate; also the legislative body of Great Britain consisting of the House of Lords and the House of Commons

PARTITION division of a geographic area into two or more countries or into areas annexed to already existing countries

PATROON in colonial areas under the Dutch, one who held a landed estate

PLEBISCITE direct vote of all eligible voters on an important political issue

PROHIBITION in the United States, the period between 1920 and 1933 when the manufacture and sale of alcoholic drinks was forbidden by federal law

PROPAGANDA systematic spread of ideas or doctrines with a view to convincing others of their truth, using repetition and, in some cases, distortion

PROTECTORATE weaker state protected and in some instances controlled by a stronger state

PROTOCOL signed document containing points of agreement between nations before a final treaty is negotiated

PROVISIONAL referring to a government which functions temporarily until a permanent government is established

PURGE getting rid of persons in a nation or political party who are considered disloyal or who hold views other than those of the majority of the party

PURITAN Protestant in sixteenth and seventeenth century England and America who sought greater reform in the Church of England

Q

QUOTA the greatest number of persons who may be admitted, as to Canada or to an institution like a college

R

RATIFICATION the giving of formal approval, as to a constitution or a treaty

REACTIONARY extreme conservative, one who opposes progress or liberalism

RECIPROCAL applying by mutual agreement to both parties or countries concerned, as in trade

RECONSTRUCTION the period, after the U.S. Civil War (1865–1877), during which the Confederate states were controlled by the federal government and recognized prior to readmission to the Union

RENAISSANCE period of revival in learning and the arts in Europe (fourteenth through sixteenth centuries)

REPARATION payment by a defeated nation for damages done to persons and property of the victorious country in a war

S

SANCTIONS measures taken by a group of nations to force another to stop a violation of international law it is considered to have made

SATELLITE a small state that is dependent on a larger, more powerful state and must, as a result, keep its policies in line with it

SCHISM split in a group or institution such as the church which results from a difference of opinion in thought or doctrine

SECTIONALISM an important theme in Canadian history and an important dimension of political life; this refers to the varying interests of the different regions of the country and their efforts to adjust political, economic and cultural relations between the regions and the central government

SEDITION acts which tend to foment rebellion against the existing government

SELF-DETERMINATION right of a people to determine its own form of government independently

SHARECROPPER farmer who does not own his land but who works it for a share of the crop

SOVEREIGNTY a state's supreme and independent political authority

STATUS QUO the existing condition at a given time, as the present political, social and economic order

SUFFRAGETTE woman who works actively for the right of women to vote

SYNDICALISM political movement which advocates the use of any direct action, including violence, to bring production and distribution of goods under the control of labour unions

T

THEOCRACY government ruled by religious officials on behalf of divine authority

TOLERATION freedom to hold religious beliefs different from those in authority

TRIPARTITE agreement or treaty made among three parties or nations

TRUSTEESHIP authority from the United Nations to one country to administer a territory or region

Z

ZIONIST supporter of the movement to establish a Jewish national state in Palestine; now, a supporter of the State of Israel

Political Science

A

ACT document made into law by a legislative body

ADMINISTRATION term of office of the executive branch of government

AGENCY bureau which administers a governmental function

ALIEN one who owes allegiance to a government or country other than the country in which he resides

ALLEGIANCE formal agreement between nations to achieve a common purpose

AMENDMENT change or revision made in a constitution or a law

AMNESTY general pardon to a group of persons freeing them from punishment usually for offenses against a government

ANARCHY complete absence of government and law with resulting disorder

APPELLATE court that can receive appeals and reverse the decisions of lower courts

APPORTIONMENT allotting representatives to a group in proportion to their members

APPROPRIATION money made available by formal act of a legislative body for a specific public purpose

AUTOCRACY government in which one person has supreme power and is accountable to no one

AUTONOMY self-government

B

BALLOT refers both to the paper on which a vote is recorded and to the vote itself

BICAMERAL legislature which is made up of two houses, such as a Senate and an Assembly or a Senate and a House of Commons

BILINGUALISM a Canadian policy that recognizes two official languages for the country and guarantees that the services of the federal government will be available to citizens in their choice of either French or English

BILL preliminary form of a law proposed to a legislative body

BIPARTISAN representing or composed of members of two parties

BLOC combination of legislators or nations which acts as a unit for a common interest or purpose

BOSS politician who controls a political machine and has influence over legislation and appointments to office

BUREAUCRACY government which functions through departments which follow given rules and have varying degrees of authority in the organization

C

CABINET in Canada, a group of members of Parliament, chosen by the Prime Minister to develop policies to govern the country; in the United States, it consists of a group of advisors to the President. They are chosen by the President and are not members of the Congress.

CAMPAIGN program of activities designed to elect a candidate to political office

CAUCUS closed meeting of party members to decide policy or to select candidates for office

CENSURE reprimand voted by a governmental body of one of its members or of the government or its cabinet

CENTRE in politics, a party or group which follows policies between the left (which advocates change) and the right (which opposes it)

CHECKS AND BALANCES system of government that provides for each branch of the government (executive, legislative, and judicial) to have some control over the others

CIVIL LIBERTIES rights of thinking, speaking, and acting without interference (except for the public welfare) guaranteed to the individual by law and custom

CIVIL RIGHTS rights guaranteed to the individual by the Constitution and by acts of Congress; e.g., right to vote

CIVIL SERVICE those in the employ of government who received their positions through open competitive examination on the basis of merit; also the process involved

CLOSURE procedure which results in closing off debate and in bringing up for a vote the matter under discussion

COALITION temporary alliance of countries or parties for action to achieve some purpose

COMMISSION government agency with administrative, judicial, or legislative powers

COMMITTEE group chosen by a legislative body to consider a particular law or topic

COMMONWEALTH sometimes used as shorthand for the British Commonwealth of Nations; it is an association of "equal and autonomous" nations that have a link to Great Britain and that nation's former empire

CONFEDERATION a term used to refer to the uniting of Ontario, Quebec, Nova Scotia, and New Brunswick in 1867 to form Canada

CONFERENCE meeting of committees from two branches of a legislature to settle differences in a bill they have enacted

CONFIDENCE in politics, a vote of confidence is evidence of legislative support

CONFIRMATION approval by a legislative body of an act or appointment by an executive

CONGRESS the legislature of the United States made up of the Senate and the House of Representatives

CONSERVATIVE person or party which tends to oppose change in government and its institutions; also refers to a political party in Great Britain

CONSTITUTION system of fundamental laws and principles, written or unwritten, by which a people is governed

CONSTITUTIONAL MONARCHY a form of government that has an hereditary head of state whose powers are limited by a democratic Constitution

CONVENTION a gathering of members or delegates of a political group for a specific purpose as choosing a candidate for office

D

DE FACTO GOVERNMENT the actual government, whether legal or not

DE JURE GOVERNMENT the legal government

DELEGATE representative to a convention; person empowered to act on behalf of those who choose him

DEMOCRACY government by the people directly or through representatives chosen in free elections

DICTATORSHIP state ruled by one who has absolute power and authority

DISSOLUTION formal dismissal of a legislative body

E

ELECTION choosing by vote among candidates for public office

ELECTORAL referring to a college or group elected by the voters to formally elect the President and Vice-President of the United States

ELECTORATE those qualified to vote in an election considered as a group

EXECUTIVE that branch of government charged with administering the laws of a nation

F

FASCISM a system of government in which there is power in the hands of a dictator, suppression of opposition parties, and aggressive nationalism (Italy, 1922–1945)

FEDERAL referring to a system of government in which a constitution divides powers between the central government and such political subdivisions as states

FEDERATION a union of states or other groups which are part of a federal system of government

FELONY a major crime such as murder for which the law punishes more severely than any other

FILIBUSTER tactics used by a minority in a legislative body to delay action on a bill in the hope that it will be withdrawn

FOREIGN POLICY course of action adopted by a country in its dealings with other nations

FRANCHISE either (1) the right to vote or (2) a special right or privilege granted to an individual or group by a government

FREEDOM civil or political liberty

FRENCH CANADA term used to refer to the community of French descent; it usually emphasizes the French community in Quebec but includes all people in Canada whose first language is French, especially, the Acadians of the Maritime provinces

G

GERRYMANDER action by the party in power to divide unfairly a voting area in such a way that it will win a majority of the districts

GOVERNMENT established system of political administration by which a country or its subdivisions is ruled

H

HEARING session of a legislative committee in which evidence is obtained from witnesses bearing on possible legislation

I

IMPEACH(MENT) bring(ing) charges against a public official for wrongdoing prior to possible trial and removal from office, if a conviction is obtained

INAUGURATION formal induction into office of a public official

INDICTMENT formal accusation of someone with the commission of a crime, usually after investigation of charges made by a prosecutor

INITIATIVE the right of a citizen to bring up a matter for legislation, usually by means of a petition signed by a designated number of voters

INJUNCTION court order preventing a person or a group from taking an action which might be in violation of the law and do irreparable damage to other persons or property

J

JUDICIAL having to do with the courts and their functions or with the judges who administer these functions

JUNTA group which controls a government usually after seizing power by revolution or coup d'état

JURISDICTION the authority of a government or court to interpret and apply the law

L

LAW bill that has been approved by a legislative body and signed by the chief executive; all the rules established by legislation, interpretation of legislation, and authority of a given government or other community

LEFT members of a legislative body who take more radical and liberal political positions than the others

LEGISLATION the laws made by a legislative body

LEGISLATIVE having to do with making laws

LEGISLATURE a group of persons having the responsibility and authority to make laws for a nation or a political subdivision of it

LIBERAL an individual or political party whose beliefs stress protection of political and civil liberties, progressive reform, and the right of an individual to govern himself

LICENSE formal legal permission to carry on an activity

LOBBY work to influence legislators to support bills which favour some special group or interest

LOGROLLING agreement between legislators to support bills in which each one has a separate interest ("You vote for mine; I'll vote for yours.")

M

MACHINE political organization under the leadership of a boss and his lieutenants that controls party policy and job patronage

MAJORITY number of votes for a candidate that is greater than the votes for all the other candidates put together; party in a legislative body that commands the largest number of votes

MINORITY political group that is smaller than the controlling group in a government or legislature; group that does not have the necessary votes to gain control

MISDEMEANOR a minor offense, usually the breaking of a local law such as loitering

MULTICULTURALISM a policy of the Canadian government to promote the retention of characteristic cultural features of ethnic groups that want to maintain their identify

MUNICIPAL having to do with local government such as that of a city, town, or village

MUNICIPALITY a city or town which has the power to govern itself

N

NATURALIZE give the rights of citizenship to a noncitizen or alien

NEUTRALITY policy of a government which avoids taking sides directly or indirectly in disputes between other nations

NOMINATE name a candidate for election to public office

O

OLIGARCHY government in which power is in the hands of a very few

ORDINANCE law enacted by local government authority

OVERRIDE action taken by a legislative body to enact a law which has been disapproved (vetoed) by the chief executive of a political unit such as a nation or state

P

PARDON official release from (continued) legal punishment for an offense

PARTISAN a position or vote that follows party policy ("the party line")

PARTY an organization of persons who work to elect its candidates to political office to further the governmental philosophy and causes in which they believe

PATRONAGE the power of a political organization or its representative to give political or other jobs to persons who supported that party in an election

PETITION request for specific legal or judicial action that is initiated and signed by an interested individual or group of individuals

PLANK one of the items or principles in a party program or platform

PLATFORM statement of the policies and principles of a political party or its candidate for office

PLURALITY number of votes by which the winning candidate in an election defeats his nearest opponent

POLL vote as recorded by a voter; the count of these votes; the place where the votes are cast; questioning of a group of people chosen at random on their views on political and other matters

PORK BARREL the grant of money by a governmental agency to a locality in order to further the political ends of a party or its local representatives

PRECINCT subdivision of a town or city that serves as an election unit

PRESSURE GROUP group of people that seeks to change government law or policy through the use of lobbies, propaganda, and media

PRIMARY vote by members of a political party to choose candidates for political office or for some other political purpose

PROGRESSIVE a person or party who stands for moderate political and social change or reform

PUBLIC OPINION views of a people generally as they influence social and political action

Q

QUORUM the minimum number of a legislative body that must be present before it can legally conduct business

R

RADICAL a person or party who stands for extreme political and social change or reform

RATIFY give formal approval to a document such as a treaty or constitution

RECALL the right of or action taken by vote of the people or by petition to remove a public official from office

REFERENDUM the principle or practise of submitting to direct popular vote a proposed law or one that has been passed by a legislative body; the right of the people to such a vote

REFORM political movement designed to correct abuses in government by changes in the law

REGIME form or manner of government or rule

REGISTRATION signing up of a person in his election district to enable him to vote

REGULATE be or bring under control of government or a government agency

REPRESENTATIVE member of a legislative body chosen to act on behalf of those who elected him or her to represent them

REPRIEVE postpone the punishment of a person convicted of a crime

REPUBLIC government in which power remains with all the citizens who are entitled to vote and who elect representatives who act for them and who are responsible to them

RESOLUTION formal statement of opinion or intention voted by a legislative or other group

REVIEW reexamination by higher judicial authority of the proceedings or decision of a lower court

REVOLUTION complete overthrow of an established government or political system

RIGHT members of a legislative body who hold more conservative views than the other members, opposing change in current practise; that which belongs to an individual by law or tradition; such as the right to free speech

S

SELF-GOVERNMENT government of a people by its own members or their representatives instead of by some outside power

SENIORITY consideration given to length of service in a legislative body in making assignments to important positions or to membership in committees of that body

SOCIAL SECURITY federal system of old age, unemployment, or disability insurance for employed and dependent persons

SOVEREIGNTY supreme and independent power of authority in government

SOVEREIGNTY-ASSOCIATION a policy of the Parti Quebecois. Instead of emphasizing complete independence for Quebec, it promotes political independence but with economic association.

SPEAKER public official who presides over a law-making body such as the U.S. House of Representatives or an assembly

STATE any of the political units that constitute the federal government

STATUTE law passed by a legislative body

SUBPOENA a written order to a person to appear in court or before a legislative body to give evidence

SUBVERSIVE an act or a person that would tend to overthrow the existing government

SUFFRAGE the right to vote in political elections or on political matters

SUMMONS a written order to appear in court to a person who may be involved in or has knowledge of a crime

SUPREME COURT highest federal court of Canada whose decisions are final and take precedence over those of all other courts

SURROGATE judge who acts in place of another person to see to it that guardians are appointed, wills approved, and estates settled

T

TARIFF tax imposed by a country on imported goods (usually to protect manufacturers in that country)

TENURE length of time a person holds office, his right to hold that office until retirement or death

TESTIFY present evidence in a court under oath

TICKET list of candidates nominated for election by a political party

TOTALITARIAN kind of government in which one political party is in power to the exclusion of all others

TREASON betrayal of one's country by actively helping its enemies in their attempt to overthrow it or defeat it in war

TREATY formal agreement dealing with commerce or policies entered into by two or more nations

U

URBAN having to do with a town or a city

V

VETO the act or power of a chief executive to turn down or temporarily prevent from taking effect a bill passed by a legislative body by actually rejecting it or refusing to sign it

VOTE casting a ballot or taking any other necessary action to express one's choice in an election of a candidate for office or of any proposal for legislative change

W

WHIP member of a political party in a legislative body such as Congress whose duty it is to enforce party discipline

Economics

A

AGGREGATE DEMAND the total spending capacity of a nation and its people

AGGREGATE SUPPLY capacity of a nation's resources to produce real goods and services

ARBITRATION attempt to settle or settlement of a dispute, generally between labour and management, by submitting it to a third party designated to decide it after hearing evidence presented by both sides on their own behalf

ASSET property and resources of all kinds of a person or a corporation

AUTOMATION in business and industry, the method whereby production and distribution of goods is made to take place automatically by mechanical and electronic rather than human means

B

BALANCE OF PAYMENTS the relationship between a nation's outflow of money (imports, foreign aid) and inflow of money (exports, gifts)

BALANCE SHEET a financial statement summarizing the assets, liabilities, and net worth of an individual or a business with the sum of the assets equaling the total of the liabilities plus the net worth

BANKING the practise of receiving, keeping, lending, or issuing money and making easier the exchange of funds

BANK RATE (BANK OF CANADA) the interest rate charged by the Bank of Canada on loans it makes to the chartered banks; as the bank rate changes so do the interest rates charged by the chartered banks to their customers

BANKRUPTCY financial condition in which a person or company is found legally unable to pay off the creditors who then may share the assets of the bankrupt person or company

BARGAINING more properly, collective bargaining, refers to negotiation between representatives of management and labour on wages, hours, working conditions, and other benefits

BARTER a system of trading in which one item is exchanged for another without the use of money

BIMETALLISM use of two metals (for example, gold and silver) as the legal monetary standard of a country with each in a fixed ratio of value to the other (for example 16:1)

BOND certificate indicating the obligation of a business or government to pay the holder certain interest or principal plus interest at indicated time or times

BUDGET statement of an individual, business, or government in which expected incomes are allocated as expenses in designated necessary areas

BUSINESS buying and selling of commodities and services for a profit

C

CAPITALISM an economic system based on private ownership of the means of production with freedom of private enterprise to earn a profit under free market (competitive) conditions

CARTEL combination of businesses to establish a national or, more frequently, an international monopoly by limiting competition through such means as price fixing

CENSUS an official count of the population of a country

CERTIFICATE a document that shows that someone owns stock and is entitled to benefits and liabilities of a stockholder

CHECK-OFF system, usually arranged under collective bargaining, in which the employer deducts union dues from the member's wages and turns them over to the union

CLOSED describes a shop in which, by agreement the employer hires only members of a union

COLLECTIVE BARGAINING a right of workers to negotiate their conditions of employment through labour unions rather than as individuals

COMMERCE large-scale buying and selling of goods usually involving transportation of the goods between cities or countries

COMMODITY any good that is bought or sold in a commercial transaction

COMMUNISM economic system based on the ownership of all property by the community as a whole or the state and, in Marx's view, by equal distribution of economic goods through revolutionary means

COMPENSATION payment given to make up for an injury or loss, as to a worker who has been hurt on the job

COMPETITION in a free enterprise system, the attempt by rival businesses to get customers for the goods they manufacture or distribute

CONCILIATION in a dispute, the attempt to settle differences between parties (for example, labour and management) in a friendly manner

CONSUMER one who uses goods or services out of need

CONSUMER PRICE INDEX single number which compares consumer prices in one year with prices paid by consumers in previous years

CONTRACT agreement between two or more people to do something as set forth in writing or orally and which is enforceable by law

CORPORATION a group of individuals who possess shares and which, as a group, has the privileges and obligations of a single person (for example, to make contracts and borrow money) with liability limited to the amount invested by the shareholders

COST the amount of money, labour, and other expenses involved in producing or obtaining goods or services

COSTS expense needed to produce an output of goods and services

CRAFT (members of) a trade requiring special skills, such as printers

CRASH sudden failure of a business or decline in market values of shares in a business

CREDIT based on a person's economic standing, the money a person is allowed to borrow and repay at a later date

CREDITOR someone to whom money is owed

CURRENCY money, such as coin or bank notes, which is in circulation in a country

CUSTOMS duty or tax levied by a government on imported and, in some instances, exported goods

CYCLE in business, a sequence of events that occurs and recurs in a given order involving boom, downturn, depression or recession, and recovery

D

DEBENTURE certificate or bond signifying that a debt is owed by the signer who may be an individual or a corporation

DEBT an obligation of an individual or corporation to pay something to a creditor

DEFICIT the amount by which a corporation's or a government's debts are greater than its credits or assets (in government, for example, where expenditures are greater than taxes collected)

DEFLATION fall in prices brought about by a decrease in the amount of spending

DEMAND desire and ability to pay for certain goods and services, usually within a given price range at a given time

DEPLETION using up of natural resources such as oil and timber

DEPOSIT money put in a bank or given in partial payment for something purchased

DEPRECIATION decrease in value of business property or equipment through "wear and tear," money set aside as a reserve to meet the cost of repairing or replacing this equipment

DEPRESSION period of low business activity, wide unemployment, and falling prices

DEVALUATION lowering of the exchange value of one currency with respect to another by lowering the amount of gold backing it

DIRECTORATE board chosen to run the affairs of a corporation

DIRECT TAX a tax that cannot be passed along to another party; for example, if a property tax is increased, the person responsible for paying it, the property owner, can simply raise the rents of the tenants. The rent then includes provision for paying the taxes. This is an indirect tax. On the other hand, personal income tax cannot be passed along and is a good example of a direct tax

DISCOUNT amount deducted from the original price of something sold; amount of interest deducted in advance in a business transaction; the rate of interest charged in a transaction

DISTRIBUTION the process of making goods and services available to consumers, as well as the promotion of the buying and selling of these goods and services

DIVISION OF LABOUR use of the labour force so that each is engaged in producing that good or service for which the worker is best suited or in which the worker has been trained

E

ECONOMIC EFFICIENCY greater output for a given input of resources

ECONOMIC GROWTH development of human and natural resources to produce more goods and services

ECONOMICS the science that deals with the production, distribution, and consumption of goods and services

ECONOMIC SYSTEM the manner in which a nation's resources are used, and goods and services are produced and distributed

ECONOMY the structure and functioning of a nation's economic system

ENTREPRENEUR a person who enters into business and risks his or her skills, time, and money for the sake of earning a profit

EQUILIBRIUM market price at which supply equals demand

EXCISE tax on the production, sale, or use of certain commodities within a country; for example, tobacco and liquor

EXPORT refers to goods sold by one country to another

F

FEATHERBEDDING limiting of work or hiring of more employees than are necessary to prevent or limit unemployment in an industry

FISCAL having to do with taxes, public revenues, or public debt

FISCAL POLICY method of bringing aggregate demand into balance with aggregate supply centering on governmental budget surplus or deficit

FISCAL YEAR refers to an accounting period of twelve months (for the United States, the year ending June 30)

FOREIGN EXCHANGE currency that can be used to pay international debts

FREE TRADE a trade arrangement whereby tariffs and other customs duties are removed and goods and services flow freely between nations; the arrangement of the European Economic Community and the Canada/United States Free Trade Agreement represent attempts to move toward free trade

FRINGE refers to a benefit given by an employer that is not paid directly as wages, but has a cost to him nonetheless

G

GOODS merchandise

GROSS NATIONAL PRODUCT (GNP) the total value of a nation's annual output of goods and services

H

HARD CURRENCY one of the world's more stable currencies, in which most international transactions are carried out; for example, American dollars, German marks, Japanese yen, or British pounds

HOLDING refers to a company organized to control other companies by holding their stocks and bonds

I

IMPORT goods brought in, usually by purchase, by one country from another

INCOME money received by a person or a business organization for work or services or from investment or property; also refers to a tax on these receipts or earnings, usually levied by the government or a division of it, such as a state

INDIRECT TAX (see DIRECT TAX)

INDUSTRY businesses as a group which are engaged in manufacturing

INFLATION rise in prices brought about by an increase in the amount of money in circulation or by an increase in the amount of spending resulting from greater aggregate demand than aggregate supply

INPUT amount of money and/or manpower invested in a project or process

INSTALLMENT a system of credit in which goods purchased are paid for over a period of time by partial payments

INTEREST charge for money borrowed, usually expressed as a percentage of the money lent; also money paid to a depositor for money left in a bank for a stated period

INTERLOCKING refers to boards of directors (directorates) of several corporations which have some directors in common, with the result that they control the corporations involved

INVESTMENT money put into a business or property in the hope of receiving income or earning a profit

K

KEYNESIAN THEORY theory holding that full employment and a stable economy depend on government stimulation of spending and investment through adjustment of interest and tax rates, money supply, etc.

L

LAISSEZ-FAIRE economic policy that provides for little or no interference by government in the affairs of business which is allowed to operate under its own regulations

LEVY tax imposed or collected by a government or other authority

LIABILITY debt owed by a business, corporation, or an individual

LOCKOUT prevention by an employer of his workers from working, by shutting down the business partly or completely until the workers settle a dispute on the employer's terms

LOSS amount by which the cost of an article sold is greater than the selling price

M

MACROECONOMICS branch of economics developed about 1930 which deals with the economic activity of a nation as a whole as distinct from that of individual businesses

MALTHUSIAN THEORY theory that the population of the world tends to increase faster than the food supply and, therefore, must be checked by social and moral restraints

MANAGEMENT those who direct the affairs of a business or industry considered as a group

MARGIN the smallest return that allows a business to continue to operate profitably; the difference between the cost and the selling price of a product

MARKET the buying and selling of goods or property; the location where the buying and selling takes place

MARXISM doctrine that the state's ruling class exploits the masses, that class struggle is inevitable, and that capitalism will give way to classless socialism after a dictatorship of the proletariat

MEDIATION entry into a dispute between management and labour, with the intention of settling it fairly

MERCANTILISM economic policy that prevailed from the sixteenth to the eighteenth century that put the economic welfare of the nation above that of the individual citizen and in which a nation sought to accumulate gold by having greater exports than imports

MERGER combination of two or more businesses or corporations in which one of them ends by controlling the other(s)

MICROECONOMICS the study of individual businesses within a national economy with emphasis on the determination of prices and the distribution of income

MONETARY having to do with the money of a country

MONETARY POLICY method of bringing aggregate demand into balance with aggregate supply centering on changing the supply and cost of money

MONEY coin or paper stamped by government authority generally used as a medium of exchange and measure of value

MONOPOLY exclusive control of a product or service in a market through group action, legal authority, or cornering of supply so that prices for the product or service can be fixed and competition eliminated

N

NEGOTIABLE refers to something that can be transferred legally from one person to another in return for something of equal value, usually through the use of such instruments as cheques or notes

NON-RENEWABLE RESOURCES resources such as oil or coal that, once used, are lost forever

NOTE written promise to pay a debt, such as a promissory note

O

OBSOLESCENCE the process by which the plant and equipment of a business become outdated and cannot be used efficiently to produce the goods needed today

OPEC the Organization of Petroleum Exporting Countries; an association of Third World oil-producing nations, formed in 1960 to counteract the influence of Western oil internationals such as Exxon, Shell, and Gulf

OPPORTUNITY COST the cost of producing one thing rather than another that has to be sacrificed

OUTPUT work done or amount produced by a person, machine, assembly line in a given period

OVERHEAD the cost involved in running a business, such as rent, electricity, etc.

P

PARITY the farmer's current purchasing power as compared with that of a selected earlier period used to determine the degree of the government's support of farm prices; the equivalent value of money in one currency as compared with that of another

PARTNERSHIP form of business organization in which two or more people put money or property into a business and share the profits or losses

POVERTY extreme lack of the things necessary to sustain life, as food, shelter, and clothing

PREFERRED refers to stock on which dividends must be paid before they can be paid on common stock; holders of this stock also receive preference when a company's assets are distributed

PRICE the amount of money or its equivalent for which anything is bought, sold, or offered for sale

PRODUCER one who produces goods and services for consumers

PRODUCTION creation of economic value by making goods and services available to meet the needs of consumers

PRODUCTIVITY degree of ability to produce goods and services of economic value

PROFIT amount by which the selling price of an article sold is greater than the cost

PROLETARIAT the working class, especially the workers in industrial jobs

PROPERTY possessions that may be personal (movable), land or real estate, or securities (stocks and bonds)

PROPRIETORSHIP legal and exclusive right to ownership of some property or business

PROSPERITY condition in which the economy of a country and/or its business enjoys a state of well-being

PROTECTIONISM the practise of protecting the manufacturers of goods produced at home by taxing goods imported from abroad

R

RECESSION period of temporarily reduced business activity

REGRESSIVE refers to a tax whose rate decreases as the amount taxed increases

RENEWABLE RESOURCES resources such as wheat, fish, and wood that can be harvested year after year if managed properly

RENT income received by a land or property owner for the use of his or her land or property

RESERVE money or other assets kept available by a bank or other business to meet possible demands

RESOURCES natural and human assets that can be used to produce economic goods or provide services

REVENUE income that a country or a political subdivision of a country receives from taxes and other sources so that it is available for use on behalf of the public

S

SAVINGS total money saved by an individual or a nation; bank whose principal business it is to receive savings and pay interest for the use of these savings from income it earns

SCAB a worker who works during a strike

SCARCITY the gap between the supply of goods produced and human needs

SECURITIES documents, usually bonds or stock certificates, which are evidence of either indebtedness (bonds) or ownership (stocks)

SERVICES duties performed or work done for others that has economic value

SHAREHOLDER someone who has become an owner of part of a company by purchasing shares in it, usually through the stock market

SHOP if *open*, a business establishment where workers are employed regardless of union membership; if *union*, one in which labour and management agree that only employees who are union members or who join the union may continue to work there

SLUM highly crowded area in which housing is rundown, sanitary conditions are poor, and poverty is widespread

SOCIALISM ownership and operation of the means of production and distribution by society rather than by private persons, with all members sharing in the work and the products

SPECIALIZATION division of a productive function to allow each worker or region to use to the best advantage specific differences in skill and resources

SPECIE money in coin as distinguished from paper money

SPECULATION use of capital to buy and sell stocks, property, commodities, and businesses where above average risk is taken in the hope of above average gains

STANDARD OF LIVING a level of subsistence of a country or an individual which takes into account possession of the necessities and comforts of life

STOCK shares held by an individual in a corporation which give him an interest in its earnings and assets and the right to vote on matters concerning it

STRIKE work stoppage carried out by workers to force the employer to improve working conditions and benefits and to increase wages

SUBSIDY sum of money given by a government to a private individual or business in the public interest

SUBSISTENCE the lowest level of food, clothing, and shelter needed to sustain life

SUPPLY amount of goods and services available for sale, usually within a given price range at a given time

SURPLUS amount of goods over and above what is needed; the amount that the assets of a business are greater than its liabilities

SURTAX a tax that is added on to an already existing tax

T

TAX sum that an individual or corporation is required by the government to pay on income or property or an object purchased

TECHNOLOGY use of scientific knowledge in industry and commerce

TENDER something that is generally acceptable to be offered as payment

TRADE the buying and selling of economic goods; an occupation involving skilled work, manual, or mechanical

TRUST combination of corporations in an industry to control prices and eliminate competition

U

UNDERDEVELOPED NATION country inadequately developed economically and industrially with a relatively low standard of living

UNDERWRITER one who guarantees the purchase of stocks and bonds made available to the public in an offering

UNEMPLOYMENT the condition of being out of work; the level at which this condition exists for workers generally

UNION organization of workers that seeks to protect and advance the interests of its members with respect to working conditions and wages, usually through collective bargaining

UTILITY the capacity of an object to satisfy the needs or wants of society

W

WAGES money paid to an employee for work done; the share of industrial production that goes to labour in general

WEALTH everything having economic value measurable in price; ability of a nation to produce real goods and services

WELFARE refers to a state or nation in which government rather than private organizations assumes the primary responsibility for the well-being of its citizens

WILDCAT refers to a strike that takes place without the permission of the union representing the striking workers

Geography

A

ALLUVIAL SOIL soil containing clay, sand, gravel, or similar material produced by the wearing-down action of water, collected by rivers and deposited by them

ALPINE referring to high altitudes

ALTITUDE elevation of an object above sea level

ANTARCTIC relating to the region near the South Pole

AQUIFER an underground layer of porous rock, such as sandstone or limestone, that contains water and allows it to percolate; when blocked by nonporous layers, an aquifer may become a groundwater reservoir

ARABLE LAND land used for ploughing and growing crops

ARCTIC relating to the region around the North Pole to approximately 65°N

ATMOSPHERE the envelope of gases that surrounds the earth, containing mostly nitrogen, oxygen, and carbon dioxide

ATOLL coral island consisting of a reef surrounding a lagoon

B

BADLANDS an area in a semi-arid environment where deep gullies and ravines have been formed by water erosion; in Canada, the largest area of badlands is in southern Alberta

BASIN a body of water partly or fully enclosed

BAY an inlet of the sea or other body of water usually smaller than a gulf

BAYOU a lake occupying the abandoned part of a stream channel

BLUFF steep rises of ground between bottom lands and higher lands or high banks on the shore of a river, sea, or lake

BUTTE steep-sided, round-topped hill or mountain

C

CANADIAN INTERNATIONAL DEVELOPMENT AGENCY (CIDA) government organization formed to assist developing nations with technical advice and loans of both money and personnel

CANADIAN SHIELD an area of Precambrian rock, mostly igneous, that covers almost half of Canada; the dominant physical feature of the Near North region

CANYON a deep narrow valley with steep sides cut by a river

CLEAR CUTTING the harvesting of all trees in a given area that are large enough for commercial use

CLIMATE average weather condition at a given place over a period of years as evidenced by temperature, precipitation, and winds

CONSERVATION planned management of our natural resources to prevent exploitation, destruction, or neglect

CONTAINERIZATION a method of shipping materials by packing them into containers of a specific size and shape; they fit directly onto trucks or trains without having to be unpacked

CONTINENT one of the great land areas of the earth

CONTINENTAL DRIFT the movement of the large, rigid plates in the earth's lithosphere.

CONTINENTAL SHELF a shallow underwater plain that borders a continent and ends in a steep slope to the ocean depths

COOPERATIVE an organization involved with the production or sale of a product or service; the organization is owned collectively by its members who share the profits

CROWN LAND land owned by the nation; any income from its sale or lease goes to the government

CYCLONE violent storm or system of winds rotating about a calm centre of low atmospheric pressure, traveling at a speed of 32 to 48 kilometres (20 to 30 miles) per hour and accompanied by rain

D

DELTA triangular or fan-shaped areas of low-lying land formed by deposits at the mouth of a river

DESERT a dry, barren expanse of land unable to support normal plant and animal life and therefore any sizeable population without an artificial water supply

DEVELOPED COUNTRIES countries with a high degree of economic development as indicated by GNP, income, literacy rates, energy use, quantity and quality of food, etc.

DEVELOPING COUNTRIES countries with a lesser degree of economic development; determined in comparison with developed countries

DOLDRUMS belt or zone within 15° north or south of the equator characterized by calms, light shifting winds and high temperature and humidity

DROUGHT prolonged period of lack of rainfall

E

EARTHQUAKE shaking or trembling of the earth that is volcanic in origin or involves the earth's crust

ECOLOGY science concerned with interrelationship of organisms and their environments

ELEVATION height above the level of the sea

ENVIRONMENT the climatic, soil, and living factors that influence an organism or an ecological community

EQUATOR a great circle of the earth that is equidistant from the North and South Poles and divides the earth's surface into the northern and southern hemispheres

EQUINOX one of two times each year when day and night are everywhere of equal length

EROSION wearing away by the action of water, wind, or glacial ice of the surface features of the earth—mountains, plateaus, valleys, coasts

F

FAR EAST countries of east Asia including China, Japan, and Korea and southeast Asia and the Malay Archipelago

FAULT a break in the earth's crust accompanied by a displacement of one side of the break with respect to the other in a direction parallel to the break; any displacement along a fissure, or series of fissures, in any kind of rock

FAUNA animals or animal life of a region

FJORD narrow inlet of the sea between steep cliffs and extending far into the land

FLORA plant life of a region or special environment

FRONT boundary between differing air masses in temperature

G

GEYSER a hot spring that from time to time, violently ejects boiling water and steam

GLACIER large mass of ice and snow moving slowly down a mountain or valley

GLOBE spherical model of the earth

GRASSLAND an area of grass or grasslike vegetation, such as a prairie

GROWING SEASON the period of the year with enough warmth and moisture for crops to grow

GULF a large area of a sea or ocean partially enclosed by land

H

HABITAT the region where a plant or animal naturally lives

HARD WOOD wood generally produced from broadleaf trees, including maple, oak and elm

HIGH a centre of high atmospheric pressure

HUMIDITY moisture or water vapour in the atmosphere

HUMUS dark part of the soil resulting from the partial decay of leaves

HURRICANE severe tropical cyclone with winds over 120 kilometres (75 miles) per hour and usually involving heavy rains

I

ICE CAP a large mass of ice, smaller than an ice sheet

ICE FLOE an area of floating ice detached from the main polar ice mass

ICE SHEET a very large mass of ice; the last continental ice sheet to cover parts of North America was the Wisconsin Ice Sheet

INSHORE FISHERY the sector of the fishing industry that usually operates less than 15 kilometres (9 miles) from the shore and involves small boats that return to shore each day

INTENSIVE FARMING a type of farming that obtains very high yields per hectare by using much labour and capital; in Canada, examples include market gardening of vegetables, and the use of greenhouses, feed-lots or irrigation

ISLAND land mass, smaller than a continent, entirely surrounded by water

ISOBAR line on a map connecting points of equal barometric pressure

ISOTHERM points of equal average temperature

ISTHMUS a narrow strip of land having water at each side and connecting two larger bodies of land

J

JUNGLE land densely overgrown with tropical vegetation and trees

L

LAKE a relatively large inland body of water, usually fresh

LANDLOCKED surrounded by land, as a bay; cut off from the sea and confined to fresh water

LATIN AMERICA part of the Western Hemisphere south of the United States: Mexico, Central America, the West Indies and South America where Spanish, Portuguese, and French are officially spoken

LATITUDE distance north or south from the equator, measured in degrees

LEACH lose soluble matter (e.g., soil) as a result of the filtering through of water

LEGEND title or key accompanying an illustration or map

LOESS a fine-grained, yellowish-brown, extremely fertile soil deposited mainly by the wind and found widely in North America, Asia, and Europe

LONGITUDE distance in degrees or time east or west of the prime meridian

LOW a region of depressed barometric pressure

M

MAGNETIC POLE either point on the earth's surface toward which the needle of the magnetic compass points: the north and south magnetic poles do not coincide with the geographical poles, and are not exactly opposite each other

MAP representation on a flat surface of all or part of the earth's area

MARITIME on, near, or living near the sea

MARKETING BOARD an organization that buys products from producers and then collectively distributes these products to wholesalers or retailers; Canada has marketing boards for wheat, eggs, and dairy products

MEDITERRANEAN CLIMATE climate characterized by warm dry summers and rainy winters

MERIDIAN any of the lines of longitude

MESA a high, broad, and flat plateau bounded at least on one side, and sometimes on all sides, by a steep cliff

METROPOLIS any large or important city; a major city, especially the capital of a country, state, or region

MIDDLE EAST lands from the eastern shores of the Mediterranean and Aegean seas to India

MIGRATION moving of people from one region or country to another, with the intention to settle there

MIXED FARMING a type of farming in which both livestock and crops are produced

MONSOON a seasonal wind, one which blows over the Indian Ocean from Australia to India

MORAINE accumulation of boulders, stones, or other debris carried and deposited by a glacier

N

NATURAL RESOURCES forms of wealth supplied by nature, as coal, oil, water power, etc.

NEAP TIDE tide that occurs when the difference is smallest between high and low tides

O

OASIS a fertile place in a desert, due to the presence of water

OCEAN any of the five main divisions of the body of salt water that covers over 70% of the earth's surface: Atlantic, Pacific, Indian, Arctic, or Antarctic

OCEANIA term used frequently to refer to the islands of the South Pacific; it includes major countries such as Australia and New Zealand

P

PADDY an irrigated or flooded field where rice is grown

PARALLEL imaginary line parallel to the equator and representing degrees of latitude on the earth's surface

PARKLAND a transitional vegetation region between grassland and boreal forest

PENINSULA land area almost entirely surrounded by water and connected with the mainland by a narrow strip of land

PERMAFROST permanently frozen subsoil

PLAIN an extent of level country

PLATEAU an elevated tract of fairly level land

POLAR (ICE CAP) a mass of glacial ice that lies on a plain or plateau and spreads slowly out in all directions from the poles

POPULATION DENSITY number of people in a given area

POPULATION EXPLOSION the very great and continuing increase in human population in modern times

PRAIRIE large area of level or slightly rolling grassland that occupies the region between the Ohio and the Mississippi-Missouri rivers

PRECIPITATION rain, snow, sleet deposited on the earth

PRIME MERIDIAN a great circle on the earth's surface passing through Greenwich, England, from which longitude is measured both east and west; 0° longitude

R

RAINFALL amount of water falling in the form of rain, snow, etc., over a given area in a given period of time

RAIN FOREST dense, evergreen forest occupying a tropical region having abundant rainfall throughout the year

RANGE a series of connected mountains forming a single system

RAW MATERIAL material still in its natural or original state before processing or manufacture

REGION a large, indefinite part of the earth's surface

RELATIVE HUMIDITY the amount of moisture in the air expressed as a percentage, as compared with the maximum amount that the air could contain at the same temperature

RELIEF the general physical variations in the land

REVOLUTION movement of a body, as a star or planet, in an orbit or circle

RIFT a large fault along which movement was mainly lateral

ROTATION turning around a centre point or axis

RURAL the areas outside cities and towns

S

SAVANNA a treeless plain or a grassland characterized by scattered trees, especially in tropical or subtropical regions having seasonal rains

SCALE proportion that a map bears to the thing that it represents

SEA a large body of salt water wholly or partly enclosed by land

SEASON any of four divisions of the year, characterized chiefly by differences in temperature, precipitation, amount of daylight, and plant growth

SILT fine-grained unconsolidated sediment, with particles between sand and clay in size, carried by moving water

SOFT WOOD wood produced by most conifers such as pine

SOLSTICE either of two points on the sun's path at which it is farthest north or farthest south of the equator

SOUND a wide channel or strait linking two large bodies of water or separating an island from the mainland

STEPPE vast usually level plain of Europe and Asia having few trees

STRAIT narrow waterway connecting two large bodies of water

SUBARCTIC the area surrounding the Antarctic Circle

SUBCONTINENT large land mass subdivision of a continent, considered a geographic or political unit

SUBTROPICAL regions bordering on the tropical zone

T

TAIGA forests of cone-bearing trees in the far north of Europe, Asia, and North America

TEMPERATE ZONE one of two zones between the tropics and the polar circles

TERRACE any of a series of flat platforms of earth with sloping sides, rising one above the other, as on a hillside; or flat lands bordering the main channel of a river

TERRAIN ground considered for its natural or surface features or fitness for some use

THUNDERSTORM storm accompanied by thunder and lightning

TIDAL WAVE an unusually great wave sent inshore by an earthquake or a very strong wind

TIDES alternating rise and fall of the surface of oceans and waters connected with them, caused by the attraction of the moon and sun, occurring twice in approximately 24 hours (lunar day)

TOPOGRAPHY surface features of a region, including its relief and rivers, lakes, etc., and with man-made features, such as canals, bridges, roads, etc.

TORNADO violently whirling column of air extending down from a mass of storm clouds that usually destroys everything in its rapid advance along a narrow path

TORRID ZONE area of the earth's surface between the Tropic of Cancer and the Tropic of Capricorn, and divided by the equator

TRADE WIND wind that blows steadily toward the equator from the NE in the tropics north of the equator, and from the SE in the tropics south of the equator

TRIBUTARY a stream or river flowing into a larger stream or river

TROPICS area between the two tropics of Cancer and Capricorn, 23 1/2° north and south of the equator

TUNDRA any of the vast, nearly level, treeless plains, and often marshy plains of the arctic and extreme northern regions

TYPHOON violent tropical cyclone originating in the west Pacific, especially in the South China Sea, principally from July to October

U

URBAN a city or town; in Canada, an urban area is defined as one with 1,000 people and a population density of 400 or more per square kilometre

V

VALLEY stretch of low land lying between hills or mountains and usually having a river or stream flowing through it

VELD(T) South African open grassy country with few bushes and trees

VOLCANO cone-shaped hill or mountain built up around a vent to form a crater with lava, cinders, ashes, and gases escaping through the vent from the earth's interior when the volcano is active

W

WEATHER the general condition of the atmosphere at a particular time and place with regard to the temperature, moisture, cloudiness, etc.

WEATHERING breaking up of surface rock by the action of the atmosphere

WESTERLIES winds blowing primarily from the west

WIND air naturally in horizontal motion at the earth's surface, coming from any direction, with any degree of velocity

Behavioural Sciences

A

ACCOMMODATION adjustment of feelings and patterns of behaviour to fit the demands made

ACCULTURATION the process of becoming adapted to a new or different culture that is in an advanced state; the process of learning a culture different from the one in which a person was originally raised

ACHIEVEMENT accomplishment or attainment of a goal

ADAPTIVE BEHAVIOUR the way in which an organism acts to satisfy its own needs and to meet the demands of its environment

ADJUSTMENT the achievement of harmony between an individual and his or her environment

AGGRESSION angry or hostile feelings and behaviour

AMBIVALENCE the holding of conflicting reactions toward a person or object

ANAL PERSONALITY in psychoanalysis, the second stage of development with interest in feces; residual adult behaviour traits are orderliness, stinginess and stubbornness

ANGER emotion arising from frustration

ANXIETY fear or apprehension

APATHY indifferent and listless behaviour

APTITUDE capacity for skillful performance on an as yet unlearned task

ASSIMILATION acceptance of an outsider as a genuine member of a new social group

ATTITUDES a predisposition to respond positively or negatively to particular objects or issues

AVOIDANCE motive that results from the desire to flee from harmful or potentially harmful stimulation

AWARENESS consciousness; cognizance of one's surroundings

B

BEHAVIOUR any activity of an organism

BEHAVIOURAL SCIENCES the study of anthropology, psychology, and sociology (including social geography, and behavioural elements of economics, political science and law—without archaeology and physical anthropology)

BEHAVIOURISM school of psychology that holds that the proper object of study in psychology is behaviour alone, with reference to consciousness

C

CASTE a social class or group formed on the basis of birth, wealth, etc. and existing under strict rules within a social system with little or no movement in or out

CATHARSIS release of tensions through the expression of pent-up emotions or through the reliving of traumatic experiences

CHANNELING finding a new goal object for a drive

CHRONOLOGICAL AGE age in years

CLASS a group of people considered as a unit according to economic, occupational, or social status with a similar ranking in the community or society

CLIQUE a small, exclusive circle of people

COGNITION knowing or understanding

COMPENSATION counterbalancing failure in one area by excelling in another

COMPULSION irrational and irresistible impulse to perform some act repeatedly

CONDITIONED RESPONSE any response to an action or agent (person or object) that becomes associated with that action or agent

CONDITIONED STIMULUS any action or agent (person or object) that causes or changes a response in a person, or part of the person that comes to be associated with the action

CONDITIONING pairing a conditional stimulus and an unconditional stimulus

CONFLICT simultaneous arousal of two or more incompatible motives

CONFORMITY response governed by prevailing attitudes and opinions

CREATIVITY seeking and discovering of new relationships and new solutions to problems

CULTURAL ANTHROPOLOGY study of the structure and function of societies

CULTURAL DIFFUSION spreading of culture over additional areas

CULTURE the sum of the activities—skills, arts, customs, ideas—of a people at a given time in history; the whole that includes knowledge, belief, arts, morals, law, custom, and any other capabilities and habits acquired by man as a member of society

D

DEFENCE MECHANISM reaction to frustration or conflict in which the individual deceives himself about his real motives and goals to avoid anxiety or loss of self-esteem

DELINQUENCY, JUVENILE behaviour by minors under a given age, usually 18 years, that is antisocial or in violation of the law

DEMOGRAPHY, SOCIAL the distribution, density, and vital statistics of populations within a society; the growth and the character of populations and their distribution, as it is affected by birth and death rate and migrations

DEVELOPMENT maturation of the individual from conception to adulthood; the orderly, progressive changes in behaviour that accompany the growth of all normal human beings

DEVIANT BEHAVIOUR behaviour departing from the general norms of society, such as crime and alcoholism

DISCRIMINATION unfavorable treatment of persons based on unfavorable prejudgments made without regard to fact; disadvantageous treatment of an ethnic group

DISPLACEMENT OF AGGRESSION transference of emotion from the original object to a replacement which is more acceptable

DIVORCE legal and formal termination of a marriage

E

EGO that part of personality corresponding most closely to the perceived self

EMOTIONS changes resulting from a person's response to a given stimulus that represent an experiencing of his or her estimate of the stimulus' harmful or beneficial effect

EMPATHY realization, understanding, and vicarious participation in another person's feelings and attitudes

ETHNICITY classification or affiliation with one of the basic races of mankind as distinguished by customs, language, common history, et al; identification of groups by race (a common biological heritage), religion (a common and different system of worship), and nationality (a distinctive language)

EXTENDED FAMILY group that includes other relatives—grandparents, uncles and aunts, cousins, in-laws—outside one's immediate, nuclear family

EXTINCTION OF BEHAVIOUR procedure where responses previously reinforced are no longer reinforced resulting in their decreasing frequency

F

FAMILY the basic unit in society having as its nucleus two or more adults living together and cooperating in the care and rearing of their children

FRUSTRATION state resulting from the blocking of behaviour that is seeking achievement of a goal

G

GROUP a number of persons classified together because of common characteristics, interests, or needs

GROUP DYNAMICS the forces interacting within a human group

GUILT painful feeling of self-reproach resulting from a belief that one has done something wrong or immoral

H

HABITS actions occurring in an accustomed set of circumstances that become virtually automatic

HEREDITY passing along of qualities from parents to offspring through a biological mechanism involving the germ cells

HUMAN RELATIONS interaction between persons or groups of persons

I

IDENTIFICATION process where a person takes over the features of another person and makes them part of his own personality

IDENTITY the characteristics or qualities that set one person apart from others

INHIBITION mental or psychological suppression of an action, emotion, or thought

INSIGHT sudden grasping of the solution of a problem after other attempts—thought out or trial and error—have failed

INSTINCT unlearned behaviour, based on a biological urge

INSTITUTIONS organizations formed by a society to fill an educational, religious, or social need

INTEGRATION the bringing of different racial or ethnic groups into free and equal association; bringing as equals into society or an organization, individuals of different racial or ethnic groups

INTELLECT ability to reason, understand, or perceive relationships between ideas and objects

INTELLIGENCE ability to form concepts and to grasp relationships

INTERACTION communication between people through talking, listening, writing, reading, and gestures

INTERGROUP RELATIONS relations between different ethnic or racial groups in a society

IQ index of the rate of mental growth of a child, obtained by a numerical relationship between actual age and score achieved on a test

K

KINSHIP the nuclear and the extended family together

L

LABOUR an economic group made up of wage-earning workers

LEADERSHIP quality of guidance provided by the person or persons who direct a group in its activities

LEARNING modification of behaviour resulting from reinforced practise; effects of experience, either direct or symbolic, on subsequent behaviour

M

MARRIAGE state of, or relation between, a man and woman who have become husband and wife; institution whereby men and women are joined in a special kind of social and legal dependence for the purpose of founding and maintaining a family

MATRILINEAL society in which descent is traced through the maternal line

MATURATION behaviour changes that take place while the body is completing the process of growth; the biological development of the bodily machinery: musculature, nervous system, etc.

MEMORY body of information that has been learned and retained

MENTAL AGE mental level of a person determined by a test that enables comparison of his score with that of average scores obtained by others

MIGRATION movement of a people from one region or country to another with the intention of settling there

MINORITY GROUP a racial, religious, ethnic, or political group smaller than and differing from the larger, controlling group in a community or nation

MOBILITY movement or shifting of membership between or within social classes, either from place to place within the same class or from one class to another

MOTIVATION factors that arouse and maintain behaviour directed toward satisfying needs, drives, desires, wishes, and the like

N

NEED an essential or desirable requirement that is lacking in a living being

NEUROSIS mental disorder where anxiety and partial loss of functioning prevents the person from dealing effectively with reality

NORM standard of achievement as represented by the average achievement of a group

NUCLEAR FAMILY the immediate group of father, mother, and child(ren) living together

O

OPERANT CONDITIONING conditioning where the organism's response helps obtain reinforcement

OPINIONS, ATTITUDES AND BELIEFS a person's preference or position on a controversial matter in the public arena based on rational and/or emotional judgments; opinions being short-term judgments on specific topics, attitudes more lasting and general, and beliefs dealing with the more basic values of life

ORGANIZATION a sizeable body of persons having a formal set of goals, policies, procedures, and rules governing the behaviour of its members with varying levels of authority and power and having an existence usually beyond that of its members at any given time

P

PARANOIA behaviour featuring delusions of either grandeur or persecution

PEER GROUP all those of about the same age and status in a society having a similar system of values

PERCEPTION awareness of the outside world through interpreting sense impressions; the process by which people select, organize, and interpret stimulation of the senses into a meaningful picture of the world

PERSONALITY characteristic pattern of behaviour and thought; patterns and qualities of behaviour and any individual as expressed by physical and mental activities and attitudes

PHOBIA unreasonable, strong fear of some particular thing or situation

PREJUDICE a hostile attitude toward an ethnic group, or any member of it; an attitude that is preconceived and without foundation in fact or knowledge

PROJECTION seeing one's own traits and motives in others; the unconscious act or process of ascribing to others one's own ideas, impulses, or emotions especially when they are considered undesirable or cause anxiety

PROPAGANDA systematic spreading and promotion of particular ideas

PSYCHIATRY branch of medicine that specializes in the diagnosis and treatment of mental illness

PSYCHOANALYSIS treatment of mental and emotional disorders that tries to give the patient insight into his unconscious conflicts and motives

PSYCHOLOGY the science dealing with the mind and with mental and emotional processes as well as human and animal behaviour

PSYCHOSIS severe mental disorder in which the personality is very seriously disorganized, and contact with reality is usually weakened

PSYCHOTHERAPY treatment of mental and emotional disorders by using psychological methods such as suggestion, counseling, psychoanalysis, etc.

R

RACE one of three primary major divisions of mankind—Caucasian, Black, and Mongoloid—differing in hair, colour of skin and eyes, stature, bodily proportions, among others

RATIONALIZATION justification of impulsive or irrational behaviour by presenting false but seemingly acceptable reasons for that behaviour to oneself or to others

RECIDIVISM relapse into crime or antisocial behaviour

REGRESSION immature behaviour appropriate only to an earlier stage of development; reversion to earlier or more infantile behaviour patterns

REINFORCEMENT procedure of immediately following a response with a consequence that results in the repetition of the behaviour that produces it

REPRESSION forcefully ejecting unpleasant memories or impulses from conscious awareness

RESPONSE behavioural result brought about by particular stimuli

ROLE behaviour pattern of a person in a particular social situation

ROTE learning by memory alone, without understanding or thought

S

SCHIZOPHRENIA abnormal behaviour in which the patient becomes withdrawn and apathetic, with hallucinations and delusions

SEGREGATION policy or practise of compelling racial groups to live apart from each other, go to separate schools, use separate social facilities, etc.

SELF-ACTUALIZATION full development of one's abilities

SELF-ESTEEM belief in oneself, self-respect

SIBLING RIVALRY competition between persons born of the same parent or having one parent in common

SOCIAL CHANGE broad and basic changes in the nature of a society, particularly shifts in the basic institutions and organizations within it

SOCIALIZATION process of learning the values and customs of the culture in which one exists; the training by which an individual is made a member of a particular society including learning its customs, skills, etc.

SOCIETY a group of people that is self-sustaining, that has a definite location and a long continuity and that shares a way of life

SOCIOECONOMIC STATUS position in society based on social and economic factors

STATUS position or rank with respect to others in society

STEREOTYPE an unchanging pattern, a fixed or conventional notion or belief as of a person, group, idea, etc., held by a number of people, and allowing for no individuality, critical judgment, etc.

STIGMA a mark or sign indicating that something is not considered normal or standard

STIMULUS any form of environmental energy capable of affecting the organism

STRATIFICATION the ranking of people in a society by other members of the society into higher and lower social positions (with a resultant hierarchy)

SUBCULTURE a group (within a society) of persons of the same social or economic status, ethnic background, etc., having its own distinct cultural patterns

SUBLIMATION process whereby socially or personally unacceptable impulses are diverted into constructive, acceptable forms, consciously or unconsciously

SUBLIMINAL below the level of conscious awareness, specifically involving stimuli that become effective subconsciously by repetition

T

TABOO forbidding of an act in order to protect a cultural group against supernatural retaliation

THINKING process of forming ideas involving the integrating of mental impressions, percepts, grasping relationships, and the seeking of further clarification

TRADITION handing down information, beliefs, and customs by word of mouth from one generation to another

TRANSFER OF TRAINING the extent to which the learning of one skill helps or hinders the learning of another one

U

UNCONDITIONED RESPONSE answer to a stimulus that, without training, elicits a response

URBANIZATION creating population areas that include one or more cities and adjoin densely settled urban places

V

VALUES the social principles, goals or standards held or accepted by an individual, class, society, etc.

SOCIAL STUDIES PRACTICE IN ITEM SETS BASED ON

PASSAGES IN POLITICAL SCIENCE

Directions: **Read each of the following selections carefully. After each selection, there are questions to be answered or statements to be completed. Select the best answer. Then blacken the appropriate space in the answer column to the right.**

Questions 1–3 are based on the following passage.

When more prominent Tory lieutenants announced their departure, the succession seemed to fall almost inevitably to a forty-five-year-old Vancouver woman Mulroney had promoted to defence minister only weeks earlier. Kim Campbell was an attractive alternative, because she was much that Mulroney was not: a Westerner, twice divorced, witty but abrasive, a newcomer elected only in 1988, unconnected with Tory old-boy networks. It was not clear that she had many friends, but suddenly she had a bandwagon, and hundreds of ambitious Tories clambering aboard. The media and some Tories had second thoughts, and Jean Charest, an impeccably bilingual environment minister from Sherbrooke, was the beneficiary. He was too late. On June 13, 1993, Campbell took the leadership convention on the second ballot, and on June 25, she became Canada's nineteenth prime minister.

1. This passage deals chiefly with
(1) reorganizing the Conservative party
(2) appointing a new defence minister
(3) finding a replacement for Brian Mulroney
(4) promoting the career of Jean Charest
(5) challenging the old-boy networks

1. 1 2 3 4 5
|| || || || ||

2. Why was Campbell seen as a good choice?
(1) she was the new defence minister
(2) she was impeccably bilingual
(3) she had many qualities Mulroney lacked
(4) she was attractive to the old guard
(5) the media liked her

2. 1 2 3 4 5
|| || || || ||

3. What was the result of the convention?
(1) Mulroney lost the election
(2) Campbell became Canada's first woman prime minister
(3) Charest won the leadership of the party
(4) the old guard was victorious
(5) the Tories were defeated

3. 1 2 3 4 5
|| || || || ||

Questions 4–6 are based on the following passage.

By the words *public duty* I do not necessarily mean *official duty*, although it may include that. I mean simply that constant and active practical participation in the details of politics without which, upon the part of the most intelligent citizens, the conduct of public affairs falls under the control of selfish and ignorant or crafty and venal men. I mean that personal attention—which, as it must be incessant, is often wearisome and even repulsive—to the details of politics, attendance at meetings, service upon committees, care and trouble and expense of many kinds; patient endurance of rebuffs, chagrins, ridicules, disappointments, defeats—in a word, all those duties and services which, when selfishly and meanly performed, stigmatize a man as a mere politician; but whose constant, honourable, intelligent, and vigilant performance is the gradual building, stone by stone and layer by layer, of that great temple of self-restrained liberty which all generous souls mean that our government should be.

4. The paragraph is primarily concerned with
(1) the public duty of intelligent men
(2) the evils of indifference
(3) characteristics of the mere politician
(4) the imaginary democracy
(5) true patriotism

4. 1 2 3 4 5

5. Public duty stresses
(1) craftiness
(2) mean performance
(3) venal acts
(4) official duty
(5) attention to details

5. 1 2 3 4 5

6. Which one of the following statements best expresses an idea found in the passage?
(1) Politics has never been under the control of selfish men.
(2) Personal attention of officeholders insures democratic principles.
(3) Genuine public spirit demands personal sacrifice.
(4) *Public duty* is synonymous with *official duty*.
(5) Liberty is based upon constant legislation

6. 1 2 3 4 5

Questions 7–9 are based on the following passage.

Much of the system of law in Canada revolves around what is called *the rule of precedent*. This refers to the principle that like cases should be decided alike. A judge attempting to reach a decision in one case relies upon previous cases involving the same kind of circumstances. If the judge can find such a case, the decision made in it will be followed provided that the cases are on "all fours." This expression means that the legal issues are very similar. A case that becomes an important precedent for many other cases is a landmark case.

Precedent provides many benefits to our legal system, including:

—Uniformity: Without precedent, similar cases could result in unlike decisions. This would be unfair to those people who did not receive such favourable decisions as others.

—Predictability: A lawyer can advise a client as to the probable outcome of a case based on the way similar cases were decided in the past.

—Impartiality: The judge cannot show favouritism when guided by accepted principles of law established over a long period of legal history.

7. As used in line 8 of the passage, the word landmark most nearly means
(1) exciting
(2) just
(3) significant
(4) publicized
(5) legal

7. 1 2 3 4 5

8. This passage deals mainly with
(1) judges and juries
(2) client-lawyer privilege
(3) how to defend oneself in court
(4) a key principle in the legal system
(5) favouritism in the courts

8. 1 2 3 4 5

9. Which ONE of the following cases deals primarily with the benefit of uniformity?
(1) The defence claims that the prosecution witnesses are not credible.
(2) A convicted defendant is sentenced to probation for a crime that usually attracts a prison sentence.
(3) The judge belongs to the same golf club as the defendant.
(4) Most witnesses say that the defendant is innocent.
(5) The defendant's wife provides an alibi.

9. 1 2 3 4 5

<u>Questions 10–12</u> are based on the following passage.

Party identification refers to the degree to which citizens identify with particular political parties. It is thought by some that the most important influence in shaping a person's political loyalties are the views transmitted by parents. Some researchers feel that this sort of socialization has long-term effects on voting behaviour, filtering the effects of short-term factors such as party leaders or campaign issues.

Studies of electoral behaviour indicate that party identification is widespread in Canada but is relatively low in intensity. The impact of specific issues and the image of the leader are credited with many recent defections from party loyalty. While there continues to be a relatively stable core of loyalists, a significant proportion (20% in 1979) shifted from one party affiliation to another.

10. This passage deals mainly with influences of
(1) regionalism on voting
(2) party leadership on voting
(3) political issues on voting
(4) party identification on voting
(5) political ideology

10. 1 2 3 4 5

11. The author suggests that Canadian voters
(1) change party loyalties regularly
(2) tend to be loyal to a single party
(3) consider how to vote based solely on the issues
(4) vote for the leader rather than the party
(5) are not influenced by family traditions

11. 1 2 3 4 5

12. Based on the passage, which of the following terms could not likely be used to describe the author's attitude toward political parties?
(1) unprejudiced
(2) objective
(3) impartial
(4) detached
(5) biased

12. 1 2 3 4 5
|| || || || ||

Turn to the answer key on page 348 and the answer analysis on page 348.

PASSAGES IN ECONOMICS

Directions: **Read each of the following selections carefully. After each selection, there are questions to be answered or statements to be completed. Select the best answer. Then blacken the appropriate space in the answer column to the right.**

Questions 13–15 are based on the following passage.

As we open the 1990s with a global recession, Western economies are facing the grim reality of seeing traditional sources of employment in manufacturing, construction, or natural resources downsize their work forces, automate their operations, relocate to low-wage zones or simply go out of business. What social theorists have characterized as the "postindustrial age" (Toffler, 1980) began to be sharply felt in the 1981–82 recession when jobs lost were never replaced. The recession of the 1990s promises to have an even more profound effect on the nature of employment in Western industrialized countries.

For example, fewer than 20 percent of Canadians now earn their livelihood by actually producing goods such as automobiles, buildings, food products, or fuel. By far the majority, more than 80 percent, are employed by governments, commercial enterprises, or not-for-profit organizations that provide wide-ranging services (Statistics Canada). Unfortunately, employment opportunities related to business and personal services may be low-paying and structurally unstable.

13. The main topic of this passage is
(1) new jobs in manufacturing
(2) the effect of the recession of the 1990s
(3) the decline of employment opportunities in the postindustrial age
(4) employment in not-for-profit organizations
(5) low-paying service jobs

13. 1 2 3 4 5
|| || || || ||

14. The postindustrial age refers to
(1) the nineteenth century
(2) the age of automation
(3) the global recession
(4) replacement of traditional employment by low-paying business and service jobs
(5) government and commercial enterprises

14. 1 2 3 4 5
|| || || || ||

15. The effect of automation and relocation will be
(1) more manufacturing employment
(2) movement to low-wage zones
(3) more wide-ranging services
(4) fewer well-paying production jobs
(5) more enterprises in Western countries

15. 1 2 3 4 5

Questions 16–18 are based on the following passage.

Schooling has long been criticized for its role in creating a sense of dependency among students and teachers inhabiting those institutions. As manufacturing increasingly moves "offshore" in search of cheaper labour pools and to escape unionization, our economies have been forced to adjust to a new age of service employment and global interdependency.

Our formal educational systems, however, have most often stressed an abstract, academic style of institutional learning that has resulted in an average school-leaving rate of 46 percent (18 years and older) among eleven Western nations (OECD, 1989). It is estimated that the majority of workers at all levels will require substantial retraining every five to eight years, regardless of whether they change careers or stay in existing jobs.

Because education and employment are both facing this "crisis in confidence" at the same time, it would seem that only a massive joint campaign that mobilizes the resources of the governmental, commercial, and voluntary sectors to attack the problem at the local level will result in a more enterprising culture. Such a culture should recycle existing resources; embrace appropriate technologies; and encourage innovative design, cooperation and sharing. Education for employability in the postindustrial era will need to incorporate these values in an experience-based service that is responsive to the needs of all learners and consumers.

16. This passage chiefly describes
(1) movement of manufacturing "offshore"
(2) the need for ongoing retraining
(3) the inability of education to keep pace with economic change
(4) the academic style of institutional schooling
(5) the school-leaving rate among Western nations

16. 1 2 3 4 5

17. The "crisis of confidence" may be resolved by
(1) changing the schools
(2) creating a more enterprising culture
(3) a new age of service employment
(4) increasing manufacturing
(5) global interdependency

17. 1 2 3 4 5

18. Education for employability depends upon
(1) recycled resources
(2) appropriate technologies
(3) innovative design
(4) cooperation among governmental, commercial, and voluntary sectors
(5) local enterprise

18. 1 2 3 4 5

Questions 19–21 are based on the following passage.

Opposition to free trade stems from the unwillingness of some Canadian producers to face the rigours of foreign competition. This is often complicated by charges that foreign competitors are dumping their products in the Canadian market; that is, they are charging a lower price here than they charge in their home market. Furthermore, many Canadians believe that we should not let foreign goods into our country if our goods are excluded from theirs.

From the viewpoint of the ordinary Canadian, the long-run advantages to be gained from free trade are enormous. Greater access to imports will increase domestic efficiency and ensure competition, thereby leading to lower prices for both imported and domestic products, as well as providing new ideas and developing new tastes that often create new demands. Exports to large foreign markets will reduce costs, will help create employment, and will ultimately lead to better salaries for Canadian workers.

Protectionism is simply self-defeating. It leads to Canadians subsidizing weakly competitive industries while those industries that are competitive have to pay higher costs for their raw materials and then pass on their higher costs to the Canadian consumer in the form of higher prices.

19. Which ONE of the following statements would the author of this passage accept as characterizing free trade?
(1) increased imports, increased exports, increased tariffs
(2) decreased imports, increased exports, increased tariffs
(3) decreased imports, decreased exports, decreased tariffs
(4) increased imports, decreased exports, decreased tariffs
(5) increased imports, increased exports, decreased tariffs

19. 1 2 3 4 5
|| || || || ||

20. The author of the passage attempts to counter the argument that free trade will
(1) adversely affect Canada's highest paid industries
(2) adversely affect the skill of Canadian workers
(3) result in lower wages for Canadian workers
(4) affect total labour costs
(5) create difficulties between the First World and the Third World

20. 1 2 3 4 5
|| || || || ||

21. The passage argues that free trade will have all of the following results EXCEPT
(1) new ideas
(2) new tastes
(3) assured competition
(4) greater efficiency
(5) more costly Canadian products

21. 1 2 3 4 5
|| || || || ||

Questions 22–25 are based on the following passage.

The whole question of industrialism is a complex one. For labourers, it means that greater skills are required, and, in the last analysis, that the work may prove more difficult than in the past, where the time element had less importance. The positive benefits, however, outweigh these considerations. The labourer today has greater leisure, is less provincial, and enjoys the fruits of his labours to a far greater degree than was hitherto possible. In a way, we may say that we have reached the end of the Industrial Revolution. We may call it today a technological revolution, in that science has found ways to utilize the efforts of a man beyond the dreams of yesteryear. The dawn of the Atomic Age presages further benefits for all of us. Some have called the dawning age the Power-Metal Age. The term is significant, for in these two elements our country is rich and, if not self-sufficient, at least we have shown ourselves alert in exploiting these two elements to a degree hitherto unseen in the world.

22. The author's chief purpose in writing this passage seems to be to
(1) point out the difficulties of industrialism
(2) defend the work of scientists
(3) explain why modern man has considerable leisure time
(4) explain why the Industrial Revolution came to an end
(5) describe certain manifestations of industrialism

22. 1 2 3 4 5

23. The author implies that the future strength of his country will be found in its
(1) vast numbers of labourers
(2) skilled technicians
(3) plentiful sources of power and metal
(4) more effective use of leisure time
(5) mobile labour force

23. 1 2 3 4 5

24. When the author states that "work may prove more difficult than in the past" (line 3), he implies that
(1) back-breaking physical labour is going to return
(2) workers will feel the pressure of time
(3) wartime conditions will make work difficult
(4) the labourer is going to have to spend more time on the job
(5) many labourers are going to be out of jobs

24. 1 2 3 4 5

25. The first positive proof that the author has a specific country in mind is in line
(1) 1
(2) 5
(3) 6
(4) 7
(5) 12

25. 1 2 3 4 5

Turn to the answer key on page 348 and the answer analysis on page 349.

PASSAGES IN HISTORY

Directions: **Read each of the following selections carefully. After each selection, there are questions to be answered or statements to be completed. Select the best answer. Then blacken the appropriate space in the answer column to the right.**

Questions 26–28 are based on the following passage.

Under such conditions, the *Half Moon* set sail from Amsterdam and left the Texel, an island barrier of the Zuider Zee, on April 6, 1609.

Juet's log of the transatlantic passage describes some of the rigours of the voyage. The rocky shores of the Faroe Islands north of the British Isles made the landing there hazardous; and storms with heavy seas were responsible for the loss of the foremast and other damage to the tiny vessel. Also, the sighting of a "sayle" on June 25 must go down as a hazard, in the days when any strange ship was assumed to be hostile, until proven to the contrary. Truly, it must have been a relief when Hudson made a landfall at Newfoundland. In fact, the men were able to take 118 cod in five hours.

Their coasting trip went southward, while their interest in the lands and in their wealth, as well as in the Indians, suggests that Hudson may have been as anxious to explore these shores as he was to gain a new route to the East.

26. The chief aims of the voyage were to
(1) explore the new lands and chart the icebergs
(2) find a new route to the East and find a source of codfish
(3) find a new route to the East and explore the new lands
(4) become acquainted with the Indians and see how far north they could go
(5) discover the Hudson River and reach Virginia

26. 1 2 3 4 5
|| || || || ||

27. All of the following are mentioned in the passage EXCEPT
(1) Amsterdam
(2) Zuider Zee
(3) the Faroe Islands
(4) Newfoundland
(5) the Hudson River

27. 1 2 3 4 5
|| || || || ||

28. All of the following difficulties on the trip are mentioned EXCEPT
(1) hazardous landing
(2) storms
(3) heavy seas
(4) a strange ship
(5) Indians

28. 1 2 3 4 5
|| || || || ||

Questions 29–31 are based on the following passage.

Four times in a row, Canada has been labeled internationally as one of the world's finest places to live. Few Canadians credit the climate or even the scenery for their standing; it must be what people have done with the land and each other. Canadians do live at relative peace with each other, and they practice, imperfectly, those virtues of neighbourliness and compromise their politicians and diplomats urge on the rest of the world. Satisfaction with Canada is surprisingly widespread, among French and English, among old-stock immigrants and newcomers, and even, more surprisingly, among native peoples. Even among Quebec sovereignists, most also consider themselves Canadian, seek and expect a significant association with Canada, and expect to carry its passport and to use Canadian money. Aboriginal self-government would be a third order of Canadian government and not, in the eyes of its architects, a bid for independence.

29. Why is Canada considered a fine place to live?
(1) it has a good climate
(2) Canadians are accomplished farmers
(3) it has many immigrants
(4) it is peaceful, neighbourly, and compromising
(5) even Quebec sovereignists expect association

29. 1 2 3 4 5

30. Satisfaction is widespread among
(1) Quebec sovereignists
(2) old-stock, newcomers, and natives
(3) the founding cultures
(4) politicians and diplomats
(5) architects of independence

30. 1 2 3 4 5

31. Aboriginal people are seeking
(1) independence
(2) sovereignty
(3) self-government
(4) more land
(5) peace and compromise

31. 1 2 3 4 5

Questions 32–34 are based on the following passage.

Underlying historical events which influenced two great American peoples, citizens of Canada and of the United States, to work out their many problems through the years with such harmony and mutual benefit constitute a story which is both colourful and fascinating. It is a story of border disputes, questions and their solutions, for certainly the controversies and wars of the early years of Canada and the northern colonies of what now is the United States, and after 1783 their continuation through the War of 1812, scarcely constituted a sound foundation for international friendship.

Yet it is a fact that solutions were found for every matter of disagreement that arose and, as it is, the two nations have been able to work out a peaceful result from the many difficulties naturally arising in connection with a long and disputed boundary line, in many cases not delineated by great natural barriers.

32. The title that best expresses the ideas of this passage is
(1) “A Proud Record”
(2) “Our Northern Neighbour”
(3) “Cooperation with the United States”
(4) “Our Boundary with the United States”
(5) “The Role of the Loyalists in Canada”

32. 1 2 3 4 5

33. Disagreements between Canada and the United States
(1) did not occur after 1800
(2) were solved in every case
(3) constituted a basis for friendship
(4) were solved principally to America’s advantage
(5) resulted from the presence of natural barriers

33. 1 2 3 4 5

34. The writer considers the period before 1812
(1) an insurmountable barrier
(2) a time of geographical disputes
(3) the definer of our differences
(4) a cementer of our friendship with the United States
(5) the period that settled our boundary with the United States

34. 1 2 3 4 5

Questions 35–37 are based on the following passage.

The first Canadian to sense the meaning of his arrival (St. Laurent as the new Prime Minister) may have been a nameless elevator attendant in the East Block.

After taking his oath of office, St. Laurent had worked until nearly eight o'clock and, when he started for home, was astonished to find his humble functionary awaiting his departure, as he had been instructed to await King's (the former P.M.). The unfairness of such arrangements outraged the new Prime Minister. "From now on," he said, "you'll leave with the others at the regular time. I can walk downstairs."

. . . (in November 1948) the new government held its first cabinet meeting. . . . Seated at the head of the table, St. Laurent drew out his silver cigarette case, fitted a cigarette into his holder, and lit it. Other ministers followed suit. That, too, was a symbolic move: under Mackenzie-King, smoking had been forbidden in the Council Chamber.

35. The main idea of the passage is best stated as
(1) better working conditions in Parliament
(2) life styles of the Prime Ministers
(3) reduced elevator service
(4) beginning of a new era
(5) new smoking regulations

35. 1 2 3 4 5

36. When St. Laurent lit the cigarette at the Cabinet meeting, he was
(1) showing that he was comfortable in his new position
(2) providing a signal that an important change was taking place
(3) demonstrating his support for the tobacco lobby
(4) opposing the no smoking regulations
(5) simply enjoying a smoke

36. 1 2 3 4 5

37. From reading this selection, we might reasonably infer that Prime Minister St. Laurent was
(1) arrogant
(2) imperious
(3) pompous
(4) self-important
(5) kind

37. 1 2 3 4 5

Questions 38–40 are based on the following passage.

The Parliament Buildings in Ottawa present one of Canada's most visually striking and historically important structures. They were first built in 1865 and the first Federal Parliament of Canada met there in November, 1867. The original building was destroyed by fire in 1916 except for the Library (designed by Fuller and Jones who also designed the Centre Block). The Library was saved when the librarian closed the iron doors leading into it before the fire could take hold.

The new building which opened in 1926 houses the House of Commons and the Senate as well as providing offices and committee rooms for the Members. Four main elements make up the complex: the Centre Block with its tower, the flanking East and West Blocks, and the picturesque library at the rear.

The central feature and most important symbol of the Parliament Buildings is the Peace Tower. It houses the Memorial Chamber that contains that Book of Remembrance. Together they commemorate the sacrifice of those Canadians who died in the service of their country.

38. Which of the following is not located in the Parliament Buildings? **38.** 1 2 3 4 5 || || || || ||
(1) the Parliamentary Library
(2) the Supreme Court
(3) the House of Commons
(4) the Senate
(5) the Memorial Chamber

39. The design for the Parliamentary Library was **39.** 1 2 3 4 5 || || || || ||
(1) suggested by Sir John A. Macdonald
(2) selected by the Cabinet
(3) approved by Parliament
(4) created by the same architects who designed the original Centre Block
(5) created by the same architects who designed the rest of the Buildings

40. The chief symbol of the Parliament Buildings is **40.** 1 2 3 4 5 || || || || ||
(1) the Peace Tower
(2) Centre Block
(3) the Parliamentary Library
(4) the Memorial Chamber
(5) the East Block

Turn to the answer key on page 348 and the answer analysis on page 350.

PASSAGES IN GEOGRAPHY

***Directions:* Read each of the following selections carefully. After each selection, there are questions to be answered or statements to be completed. Select the best answer. Then blacken the appropriate space in the answer column to the right.**

Questions 41–43 are based on the following table.

SIZE, POPULATION, AND DENSITY OF THE WORLD'S LARGEST NATIONS AND REGIONS

Country	Size (sq. miles)	Population (U.N. Estimate) (in millions)		People Per Sq. Mi.	
		1992	2000	1992	2000
Canada	3 850 000	27.36	30.42	7.1	7.9
China	3 700 000	1187.99	1309.74	321.1	353.98
USA	3 600 000	255.16	275.32	70.88	76.48
Brazil	3 300 000	154.11	172.77	46.7	52.36
India	1 200 000	879.55	1018.67	732.96	848.89
Japan	143 000	124.49	128.06	870.57	895.57
Southeast Asia	1 692 000	461.5	531.01	272.75	313.83
Western Asia	1 830 817	139.27	171.43	76.07	93.64
Africa	11 700 000	681.69	836.15	58.26	71.47

(Note the estimated increase of population in the eight years that separate the two sets of figures. Scientists estimate that the earth's population will double in less than 50 years.)

Current annual population growth rates for world regions

Africa	2.9%	Latin America	2.0%	Oceania	1.6%
Asia	1.9%	Europe	0.4%	World	1.7%
North America	1.0%	former Soviet Union	0.8%		

41. From the table, it can be inferred that population growth is
(1) greatest in Europe
(2) greatest in developed countries
(3) led by the United States and the former Soviet Union
(4) greatest in the Middle East
(5) greatest in China

41. 1 2 3 4 5

42. Which ONE of the following countries is projected to have a population growth of less than 10 percent between 1992 and 2000?
(1) Japan
(2) China
(3) India
(4) Canada
(5) Brazil

42. 1 2 3 4 5

43. It can be inferred from the table that
(1) islands have low population densities
(2) Canada has primarily a friendly environment
(3) Japan is highly industrialized
(4) India has an unhealthy climate
(5) Puerto Rico has the same population density as the United States

43. 1 2 3 4 5

Questions 44–46 are based on the following passage.

The conference members often broke down into two groups. On one side were the 120 developing nations ranging in size from China (population 800 million) to the South Pacific island of Nauru (population 6500). They saw the conference as a chance to divide the oceans' wealth. To them the idea of "freedom of the seas" gave an unfair advantage to the developed nations. On the other side was a group of 29 modern industrial nations including the U.S., the former Soviet Union, the European nations, Canada, Australia, and Japan. They felt that freedom of the seas and the development of the seas was open only to limited negotiation.

However, the less developed nations were not completely united. The less developed nations who are landlocked and shelf-locked (little sea) did not like the idea of other nations dividing the richest parts of the oceans.

The outcome of this Third World Conference on the Law of the Sea and future conferences on the sea—for it is not expected that agreements will be easily reached—is of great importance to all people.

44. Freedom of the seas, as used in this passage, refers to freedom
(1) geographically
(2) politically
(3) economically
(4) legally
(5) historically

44. 1 2 3 4 5

45. It can be inferred from the passage that
(1) industrial nations outnumber developing nations
(2) landlocked nations outnumber shelf-locked nations
(3) industrial nations are largely landlocked
(4) developing nations are less developed industrially
(5) all nations see the need to change the current arrangement

45. 1 2 3 4 5

46. The evidence presented in the passage indicates an outlook toward future control of the oceans' use which is
(1) optimistic
(2) pessimistic
(3) cooperative
(4) indifferent
(5) idealistic

46. 1 2 3 4 5

Questions 47–49 are based on the following map and passage.

THE MIDDLE EAST AND NORTH AFRICA

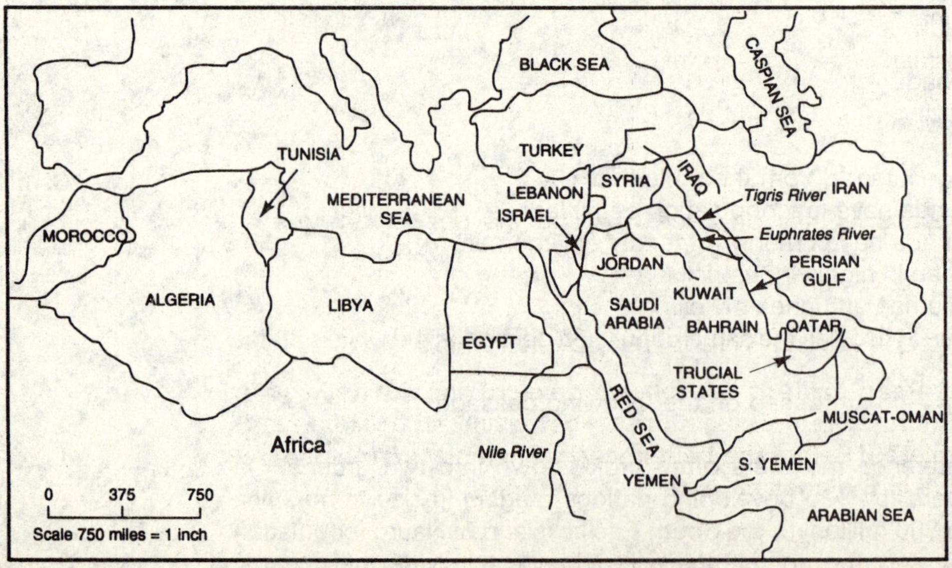

It is important to know about the Middle East for many reasons.

1. The Middle East is very rich in oil. It is believed that two-thirds of the world's total oil reserves lie in the Middle East. Oil is vital to industry throughout the world.
2. The Middle East has always been of great importance because it is located at the crossroads of three continents. Trade between Asia, Africa, and Europe has had to pass through the Middle East, and its waterways have been used as trade routes since the beginning of civilization. . . .
3. Some of the earliest civilization developed in the Middle East. . . .
4. Three of the world's great religions—Judaism, Christianity, and Islam—began in this part of the world. Many places in Israel, Jordan, and Saudi Arabia are thought of as holy by Christians, Muslims, and Jews.
5. Finally, the Jewish state of Israel stands in the middle of the Arab countries of the area. Israel is a democracy in a part of the world where most people have very little voice in their own government. . . .

47. The map reveals that among the following the country with the smallest area is
(1) Egypt
(2) Saudi Arabia
(3) Iran
(4) Jordan
(5) Israel

47. 1 2 3 4 5
|| || || || ||

48. Of the reasons given for knowing about the Middle East, the most important are
(1) political
(2) economic
(3) historical
(4) religious
(5) cultural

48. 1 2 3 4 5
|| || || || ||

49. According to the map and the text, the bodies of water accessible for trade from the Mediterranean Sea include all of the following EXCEPT the
(1) Black Sea
(2) Caspian Sea
(3) Persian Gulf
(4) Arabian Sea
(5) Red Sea

49. 1 2 3 4 5
|| || || || ||

Turn to the answer key on page 348 and the answer analysis on page 350.

PASSAGES IN BEHAVIOURAL SCIENCES

Directions: **Read each of the following selections carefully. After each selection, there are questions to be answered or statements to be completed. Select the best answer. Then blacken the appropriate space in the answer column to the right.**

Questions 50–52 are based on the following passage.

Every Hindu is born into a caste from which he must take his wife and which often determines how he shall earn a living. All together there are some 2,000 castes and subcastes.

Today, as the highest caste, the Brahmans stand at the top of the social ladder. They often are the priests and the scholars of Hindu society. Brahmans may carry the honourary title of Pandit (learned man), as Pandit Nehru, from which our term pundit (meaning "heavy-duty thinker") derives. Brahmans also are found in many occupations, ranging from farming to accountancy. You will see them everywhere wearing a sacred thread over the left shoulder as insignia of their rank. All Brahmans are vegetarian, as are most Hindus of the higher castes.

The present caste system is by no means fixed. There are many subdivisions within each caste, and new ones are constantly being formed.

There are a large number of Hindus who are outside the caste structure. They are called the "Untouchables" or in official documents the "Depressed Classes," and are often pitifully poor.

50. According to the article, Brahmans may be all of the following EXCEPT
(1) priests
(2) scholars
(3) vegetarians
(4) "Untouchables"
(5) farmers

50. 1 2 3 4 5
|| || || || ||

51. A sacred thread over the left shoulder may have been worn by
(1) a former regiment of the Indian Army
(2) the "Untouchables"
(3) those outside the caste structure
(4) the four main caste groups
(5) Pandit Nehru

51. 1 2 3 4 5
|| || || || ||

52. The passage indicates that
(1) the caste system is fixed
(2) subcastes are rare
(3) all Hindus belong to a specific caste
(4) Hindus outside the caste structure suffer from poverty
(5) the "Depressed Classes" are better off than the "Untouchables"

52. 1 2 3 4 5
|| || || || ||

Questions 53–55 are based on the following passage.

During the late 1940s and early 1950s, a religious sect known as Jehovah's Witnesses often found themselves in conflict with the authorities in the Province of Quebec. At one point the police raided an apartment in the town of Sherbrooke and confiscated religious material that some political leaders were describing as seditious. It turned out that the apartment had been rented from a Montreal restaurateur called Roncarelli who, as a Jehovah's Witness himself, had often paid for legal assistance to other Witnesses who found themselves in trouble with the law. It was never established, however, that Roncarelli knew of or supported any illegal activity.

In 1956, Roncarelli's licence to sell liquor in his restaurant was revoked. In a radio interview, the premier of the Province, Maurice

Duplessis, claimed that he personally was responsible for this. Roncarelli brought an action against Duplessis which, after going through a number of lower courts, ended up in the Supreme Court of Canada which found in favour of Roncarelli. The justices concluded that Duplessis had used his personal power to bring economic ruin upon a citizen without trial.

53. The Roncarelli-Duplessis case resulted from what type of discrimination?
(1) ethnic
(2) racial
(3) linguistic
(4) religious
(5) sexual

53. 1 2 3 4 5

54. Roncarelli verses Duplessis sets an example for future cases involving discrimination: What type of case is this?
(1) harbinger
(2) forerunner
(3) precursor
(4) illustration
(5) precedent

54. 1 2 3 4 5

55. What was the basis of the Supreme Court's decision in favour of Roncarelli?
(1) He had not violated Quebec's liquor laws.
(2) He had not known what was happening in the apartment he rented to the Jehovah's Witnesses.
(3) He had been denied due process.
(4) Duplessis had been prejudiced.
(5) The Supreme Court wished to weaken the power of the provincial government.

55. 1 2 3 4 5

Questions 56–58 are based on the following passage.

Voluntary assistance has had a long tradition in the Western world. Perhaps it has been exemplified best in agrarian societies, where people learned to pull together to survive climatic conditions or an inhospitable environment. The history of the early pioneers in North America and Australia produces many tales of neighbours helping neighbours in rural areas to clear the land, bring in the harvest, raise the buildings, or rebuild after a fire. These elements of community service became part of the hands-on culture of the agricultural age that passed by example from parents to children.

Voluntary action in rural areas resulted in the creation of the first public schools in North America. In fact many of the social and health-related services grew out of the experience of volunteers responding to local needs as "good neighbours." This pioneering spirit of neighbours working together to share resources and solve mutual problems did not always survive rural-urban migration, however. The state gradually seized control of schools, hospitals, and social welfare agencies in both cities and rural areas as they became more institutionalized and dependent on tax revenue.

56. This passage deals chiefly with
(1) contributions of the pioneers
(2) culture of the Agricultural Age
(3) the importance of volunteers in our society
(4) the creation of public schools
(5) learning to be good neighbours

56. 1 2 3 4 5

57. Community service might be described as
(1) surviving climatic conditions
(2) neighbours helping neighbours
(3) bringing in the harvest
(4) health-related services
(5) rural-urban migration

57. 1 2 3 4 5

58. The decline of voluntary assistance was chiefly caused by
(1) the decline of pioneering spirit
(2) the culture of the Agricultural Age
(3) movement to the cities
(4) mutual problem-solving
(5) control of services by the state

58. 1 2 3 4 5

<u>Questions 59–61</u> are based on the following passage.

Much has sometimes been made of the great importance for human evolution of the hand with its opposable thumb; it was important, certainly, but only as the servant of a growing brain. The hands of the higher monkeys would be perfectly capable of the finest skills had they a mind to set them to work; monkeys could be watchmakers had they ever conceived the notion of time.

A further stimulus to mental growth was given our ancestors when they left the trees and a mainly vegetarian diet and began to adapt themselves to living in relatively open country and eating meat. Undoubtedly meat's nutritive value, so much greater than that of herbs and fruit, relieved them of the necessity of perpetual eating. More important, the need for a creature with a relatively flat muzzle and no sharp claws or canine teeth to kill, skin, and break up animal food must have led first to the use and then to the manufacture of tools.

59. Man's beginning to eat meat had as its first direct consequence
(1) a flat muzzle
(2) canine teeth
(3) the use of tools
(4) the manufacture of tools
(5) increased barbarity

59. 1 2 3 4 5

60. It can be inferred that when man learned to eat meat, he
(1) improved his brain
(2) spent less time eating
(3) suffered nutritionally
(4) was equipped to obtain animal food
(5) developed an opposable thumb

60. 1 2 3 4 5

61. The most important element in human evolution, according to the author, was a(n)
(1) sharpening of sight
(2) flexible hand
(3) opposable thumb
(4) more varied diet
(5) growing brain

61. 1 2 3 4 5

Questions 62–64 are based on the following passage.

One mnemonic technique . . . consists simply of searching for or elaborating some vivid connection between . . . two items. One way to establish a connection is to imagine the two elements interacting in some way. . . .

Consider learning a series of word pairs such as *dog-hat*, *man-pencil*, *clock-woman*, *sofa-floor*, and *pipe-clown*. People usually learn a list such as this by rapidly repeating each pair as often as possible in the allotted time. The method is reasonably satisfactory for short lists and over short retention intervals. But extend either the length of the list or the retention interval, and the rehearsal method falters seriously. People who have lerned to use mental imagery to relate the items of a pair perform much better. They visualize a dog wearing a hat, a man resting a large pencil on his shoulder like a rifle, a woman wearing a clock on a chain around her neck, a section of floor resting on a sofa, and a clown smoking a pipe. . . . This procedure can improve recall by as much as 100 to 150 percent.

62. The selection deals mainly with
(1) the value of mental imagery in remembering
(2) the learning of word pairs
(3) improvement of recall
(4) learning rapidly
(5) foreign-language vocabulary

62. 1 2 3 4 5

63. It can be inferred from the passage that
(1) mental imagery is inferior to repetition
(2) rehearsal and repetition are essentially similar
(3) learners prefer repetition to rehearsal
(4) repetition is effective in mastering lengthy lists
(5) memorization is an effective technique

63. 1 2 3 4 5

64. Retention, as used in this passage, is most similar in meaning to
(1) recall
(2) repetition
(3) rehearsal
(4) image
(5) connection

64. 1 2 3 4 5

See the answer key on the next page and the answer analysis on page 350.

What's Your Score?

________right,	________wrong
Excellent	58–64
Good	51–57
Fair	44–50

If your score is low in the section "Social Studies Practice," you may need more social studies review. The explanations of the correct answers which follow will help you determine where your weaknesses lie. Analyze your errors. Then reread the section "How to Read and Interpret Social Studies Materials" at the beginning of this chapter and review the areas in which you had the most trouble.

ANSWER KEY

Social Studies Practice

Passages in Political Science/Page 330

1. **3**	4. **1**	7. **3**	9. **2**	11. **2**
2. **3**	5. **5**	8. **4**	10. **4**	12. **5**
3. **2**	6. **2**			

Passages in Economics/Page 333

13. **3**	16. **3**	19. **5**	22. **5**	24. **2**
14. **4**	17. **2**	20. **3**	23. **3**	25. **5**
15. **4**	18. **4**	21. **5**		

Passages in History/Page 336

26. **3**	29. **4**	32. **3**	35. **4**	38. **2**
27. **5**	30. **2**	33. **2**	36. **2**	39. **5**
28. **5**	31. **3**	34. **2**	37. **5**	40. **1**

Passages in Geography/Page 340

41. **5**	43. **3**	45. **4**	47. **5**	49. **2**
42. **1**	44. **3**	46. **2**	48. **2**	

Passages in Behavioural Sciences/Page 343

50. **4**	53. **4**	56. **3**	59. **3**	62. **1**
51. **5**	54. **5**	57. **2**	60. **2**	63. **2**
52. **4**	55. **3**	58. **5**	61. **5**	64. **1**

ANSWER ANALYSIS

Social Studies Practice

Passages in Political Science/Page 330

1. **3** Brian Mulroney had resigned and the Tory party needed to find a replacement.
2. **3** The fact that she was a Westerner, witty, and an unconnected newcomer were qualities that Mulrooney lacked.

3. **2** Campbell won the leadership on the second ballot to become Canada's first female prime minister.
4. **1** The paragraph stresses public duty, as opposed to official duty, of men whose performance is "constant, honourable, intelligent, and vigilant."
5. **5** The paragraph stresses the personal attention to detail which lifts servants above the level of mere politicians.
6. **2** Personal attention to the details of politics is indicated as the foundation of the "great temple of . . . liberty" which is our government.
7. **3** "Landmark" refers to a distinguishing feature which guides someone on his or her way. It is, therefore a "significant" object.
8. **4** While there are references to a number of details and examples, the passage focuses primarily on "a key principle in the legal system"; namely, the rule of precedent.
9. **2** If a convicted defendant were sentenced to probation for a crime that usually holds a prison sentence, it would not be a "like" decision. A "like" decision would require the same sort of punishment for a "like" crime.
10. **4** The passage deals with various aspects of party identification but especially its influence upon voting.
11. **2** The last sentence points out that a proportion of voters will switch between parties in elections and cites the figure of 20% for the 1979 election. This means that a much larger percentage does not change party affiliation. Canadian voters, then, tend to be loyal to a single party.
12. **5** Nowhere in the passage does the author express a personal preference for one political party over another. Nor does the author express any views about the value of political parties in general. Consequently, the term "biased" could not be used to describe the author's attitude toward political parties.

Passages in Economics/Page 333

13. **3** There were fewer production jobs available.
14. **4** Production jobs were replaced by service employment.
15. **4** The number of well-paying production jobs are decreasing.
16. **3** The passage indicates, as characteristics of the factory system, that workers became proficient at the particular work done by the machine, i.e., specialization, and that a division of labour was set up.
17. **2** The passage implies that hand production of goods, the domestic system, preceded the factory system where goods were produced with the use of machinery.
18. **4** Choice 4 incorrectly states that the factory system encouraged worker versatility, whereas the reverse was true: instead, each worker became proficient at the specialized job done by the machine he or she tended.
19. **5** Paragraph 2 emphasizes a greater international trade both in the form of imports and in the form of exports. The argument is that this would be the result of free trade which requires the reduction and/or elimination of tariffs.
20. **3** The author argues that free trade will "ultimately lead to better salaries for Canadian workers," so he is attempting to counter the argument that free trade will "result in lower wages for Canadian workers."
21. **5** The argument is that free trade will reduce the price of Canadian products, not that it will result in "more costly Canadian products."
22. **5** Building on the statement in the first sentence, the writer proceeds to list the positive and negative aspects of industrialism with some indication of its future.
23. **3** The writer mentions that his country is rich in both power and metal and, since the dawning age will require both, his country will be strong.
24. **2** Since greater skills will be required to run the machines, time pressure becomes a more important factor.
25. **5** On line 12, the author refers to "our country" for the first time.

Passages in History/Page 336

26. **3** Although Hudson was primarily interested in gaining a new route to the East, the last sentence of the passage indicates that he was also interested in exploring the new lands that he visited.
27. **5** Nowhere in the passage is the Hudson River mentioned. All the other places are.
28. **5** Hazardous landing in the Faroe Islands, storms, heavy seas, and "the sighting of a 'sayle' of a strange ship" are mentioned as difficulties. Indians are not.
29. **4** People from other countries admire the peaceful, neighbourly, and compromising nature of Canadian society.
30. **2** Canadians of French and English origin, immigrants, and natives all seem satisfied to be Canadian.
31. **3** The aboriginal people seek self-government within Canada.
32. **3** The passage emphasizes the fact that, despite their many problems, Canada and the United States have cooperated to solve them.
33. **2** The passage states that solutions have been found for every matter of disagreement.
34. **2** The passage mentions border disputes that occurred through the War of 1812.
35. **4** The emphasis in the passage is upon how the new Prime Minister is different from his predecessor. Hence, it is the beginning of a new era.
36. **2** By smoking in the Cabinet room, St. Laurent provided a very powerful signal that change was taking place.
37. **5** By allowing the elevator operator to go home rather than wait until the Prime Minister had left, St. Laurent showed himself to be kind. Certainly, this was not the act of a man who was arrogant or self-important. Indeed, his kindness earned him the nickname "Uncle Louis."
38. **2** The passage identifies all of the choices except the Supreme Court as being located in the Parliament Buildings.
39. **5** In the first paragraph, Fuller and Jones are identified as the designers of both the Library and the Centre Block.
40. **1** The first sentence of the third paragraph identifies the Peace Tower as the most important symbol of the Parliament Buildings.

Passages in Geography/Page 340

41. **5** From 1968 to 1973, the population of China increased by 70 000 000, over twice the number of any of the countries or areas listed.
42. **1** Only the population of Japan, with a projected growth of less than 4%, will grow less than 10% between 1992 and 2000.
43. **3** Since Japan has the highest number of people per square mile and high population densities frequently occur in areas of heavy industrialization, it can be inferred that Japan is highly industrialized.
44. **3** "Freedom of the seas" is equated in the passage with the oceans' wealth, which the developing nations wish to share.
45. **4** Developing nations are "on the other side" from industrial nations so they must be lacking industry.
46. **2** The evidence includes unsuccessful fishery management, difficulty in reaching agreements, and the possibility that development of ocean resources will not occur.
47. **5** Israel, about the size of the state of New Jersey, is by far the smallest with an area of 12,784 kilometres, less than one quarter the size of Jordan, one fiftieth the size of Egypt, and one eightieth the size of Iran, and one hundredth the size of Saudi Arabia.
48. **2** Oil and trade are mentioned first.
49. **2** The Caspian Sea is an inland sea.

Passages in Behavioural Sciences/Page 343

50. **4** The second paragraph describes the status of the Brahman caste. As the highest caste, Brahmans are well above the "Untouchables," who are the lowest.

51. **5** As an insignia of their rank, Brahmans may carry a sacred thread over their left shoulder, as is mentioned in the second paragraph. Pandit Nehru was a Brahman (see the second paragraph).
52. **4** The "Untouchables" or the "Depressed Classes" are outside the caste structure, and they "are often pitifully poor."
53. **4** The case resulted from the animosity felt toward a particular religious group.
54. **5** Cases that serve as examples or references for future cases are referred to as precedents.
55. **3** The premier of Quebec had used the power of his office to take action against a citizen without that citizen ever having been charged or tried for a violation of the law. Roncarelli had been denied due process.
56. **3** The passage describes the different ways in which volunteer action has contributed to our society.
57. **2** Neighbours helping neighbours is the essence of voluntary community service.
58. **5** The state has assumed control of many of the functions previously performed by volunteers.
59. **3** The passage states that the need to break up animal food, i.e., meat, must have first led to the use of tools.
60. **2** Because meat provided greater nutrition than herbs and fruit, men did not have to eat as often as previously.
61. **5** The passage mentions that a waxing (growing) brain was more important even than the hand with its opposable thumb.
62. **1** The author states that people who use mental imagery can associate items better.
63. **2** The passage states that rapid repetition (the rehearsal method) is helpful for short lists and time intervals but that this method falters for long lists and/or intervals.
64. **1** Both mean "remembering" or "memory."

7

SCIENCE

AN OVERVIEW

This section answers your questions abut content, format, and skill levels of the Science Test.

READING AND INTERPRETING SCIENCE QUESTIONS

Science questions may be based on reading passages, graphs, diagrams, or tables. Test-taking tactics are presented by means of 31 explained examples.

OUTLINE OF STUDY FOR THE SCIENCES

The Science Test emphasizes broad concepts. Study outlines in biology, earth science, physics, and chemistry identify topics found in typical science questions.

GLOSSARY OF SCIENTIFIC TERMS

This comprehensive glossary of over 700 terms enables you to review terms pertaining to the science articles upon which questions are based.

SKILLS ANALYSIS

The skill levels of comprehension, application, analysis, and evaluation are discussed using 20 explained examples.

PRACTICE EXERCISES

There are 150 questions arranged by subject (biology, earth science, chemistry, and physics). Articles, charts, graphs, and diagrams are presented in the actual GED format. Conveniently placed answer keys and full explanations follow exercises in each subject.

AN OVERVIEW

CONTENT

The Science Test questions may be drawn from any of four content areas. About half will be in the field of biology, and the rest in physics, chemistry, and earth science. Some questions may be of such a general nature that they apply to more than one of the scientific disciplines.

The examiners are not looking for detailed, specific knowledge of facts. You will, however, be expected to be familiar with general scientific principles. For example, you might be expected to know that gases are composed of molecules in motion; you will *not* be expected to know that an oxygen molecule has 16 times the mass of a hydrogen molecule.

Many of the questions will involve familiar life situations, rather than something that happens only in a laboratory. You might be asked, for example, a question about the pressure and temperature changes that occur when you inflate an automobile tire. Your will *not* be asked about the pressure and temperature changes observed when a cathode-ray tube is being evacuated.

The science questions are designed to test your ability to understand and to interpret scientific information. Reasoning and problem-solving skills are important aspects of the test. If you have learned the skills of reading diagrams, graphs, and scientific statements and interpreting what they mean, you are well prepared for this test. See Chapter 10.

FORMAT

Each of the 50 questions begins by giving some kind of information about a scientific subject. The information may be given in a sentence or two, a full paragraph, or a graph, diagram, or table. A typical question might start with a graph showing how the production of gas by the yeast in rising bread dough varies with time, and then ask when the rate is greatest. You will *not* be expected to supply this sort of information unless you are first given some source for deriving it.

The questions are of the multiple-choice type. You will be asked to select the best answer from five choices, only one of which will be correct. Sometimes you will have to discriminate carefully to choose the *best* answer, because more than one choice could reasonably be considered.

Some of the questions may be grouped; in other words, there may be several questions based on a single paragraph, graph, or table. In this case, you must read the instructions carefully so that you will know just which questions apply to which piece of information.

SKILLS

The examiners are looking for several specific kinds of ability. You should refer back to the introduction to review the National Science Education Standards. In particular, they define four levels of skills that are tested by these questions.

Comprehension

This is the simplest and most basic skill. It means the ability to understand the question. Sometimes you will be asked nothing more than to restate the information presented in a paragraph or graph. You might, for example, be given a graph of speed as a function of time, and asked at what time the speed was increasing at the fastest rate. Or you might be given a short paragraph describing the germination of a seed and asked which of five choices best summarizes the paragraph.

Application

If you fully understand the information given, you ought to be able to apply it to a real situation. The information given may be some kind of general rule, which you will have to apply to a particular case. For example, you could be given the general rule that mushrooms and other fungi live by digesting organic material. Then you could be asked to select an example of this process from a list of five choices. Questions of this kind may call for some judgment, and therefore may be a little more difficult than the simple comprehension type of question.

Analysis

These questions call for understanding the relationships between any of several items of information given. Some statements may be fact and others opinion, and you will have to tell which is which.

Observations are facts that may lead to a conclusion, and you must be able to tell whether a given statement is a fact or conclusion. If one event causes another, you must be able to distinguish between cause and effect. If you are told, for example, that fast-flowing rivers carry larger particles in suspension, you should realize that the fast flow is the cause, and the larger particles are the effect.

Evaluation

This high-level skill is probably the most important outcome of good science education. We are constantly faced with statements that purport to be general conclusions. Consider this one, for example: A psychologist states that people who do crossword puzzles retain their mental abilities further into old age than those who do not. A person well educated in science should think of several problems with this generalization. How was the evidence obtained, and how reliable is it? Is the evidence sufficient to support the conclusion? Did the experimenter have some prior belief that prejudiced his conclusions? Is there any reason to believe that doing crossword puzzles is the cause, rather than the effect, of better mental capacity in old age? Your ability to evaluate evidence and decide what it means will be tested in some questions of the test.

READING AND INTERPRETING SCIENCE QUESTIONS

There are several types of questions in the Science Test, and each calls for a specific skill.

SINGLE-ITEM QUESTIONS

In these, a short paragraph of one or two sentences is followed by a single question. Your first task in dealing with this kind of question is to identify the main idea or ideas presented, and the best way to do this is to start by reading the paragraph and the questions quickly, without stopping to be sure you understand every point, This will given you some sense of the content of the question, and of the kind of information you will need to answer it. Fix in your mind the main idea of the paragraph.

After you have done this, reread the question carefully. You may be able to select the correct answer at once. If you have any doubt, go back to the paragraph and reread it carefully, searching for the answer to the question.

Practice this technique on the following question:

EXAMPLE: **1.** Growing plants will not develop their green colour, the chlorophyll in their leaves, unless they have both sunlight and the necessary genetic system.

If a seeding growing in dim light turns out to be colourless, what could be done to find out why?

(1) Give it a new set of genes.
(2) Add chlorophyll to the soil.
(3) Graft it onto a green plant.
(4) Move it into the sunlight.
(5) Add fertilizer to the soil.

A quick reading tells you that the main idea deals with the factors involved in the development of a plant's green colour. Now go back to the paragraph and read it again. After rereading, you known that the crucial factors are sunlight and genes. This narrows the answer possibilities to choices 1 and 4. Since there is no way to give the plant a new set of genes, the answer is choice 4.

Here is another sample of this kind of question:

EXAMPLE: **2.** There are no bubbles in a sealed bottle of soda water. When the cap is removed, the liquid foams up with the release of bubbles of gas. The foaming is much more violent if the soda water is warm.

What general rule would explain these observations?

(1) Warmer water tends to lower the pressure of the dissolved gas.
(2) Gases are more soluble at low temperature and high pressure.
(3) Gases do not dissolve in water when the pressure is too high.
(4) Gases are not as soluble when the pressure and temperature are high.
(5) High pressure tends to keep the temperature low.

A quick reading tells you that the main idea concerns the solubility of gases and its dependence on pressure and temperature. Now you have to reread carefully to find out just what this dependence is.

This question introduces a type of difficulty that you may meet often—the *unstated assumption*. To get the answer to this question, you will have to realize that the pressure in a sealed soda bottle is high. This should be obvious to you: when you remove the cap from the bottle of soda, gas rushes out. You will often be expected to supply, for yourself, bits of information that are commonly and widely known.

Adding this piece of information, you can now go back to the passage to find out how temperature and pressure affect the solubility of the gas in the soda. When you take the cap off, you reduce the pressure and the gas comes out of solution, so it is clear that the gas is more soluble when the pressure is high. Since there is more foaming when the soda is warm, the gas is more soluble at lower temperatures. Thus the answer is choice 2.

MULTIPLE-ITEM QUESTIONS BASED ON READING

Here you will have to read a passage consisting of several paragraphs, and answer up to six questions about it. The strategy for this kind of question is somewhat different from that used when there is only one question per passage.

In answering this kind of question, you should study the passage carefully before going on to the questions. As you read, you should note the two or three main ideas. Only then should you go on to the questions.

To find the main ideas, look for key words. Ignore common words like *process* or *definite* or *increase*. It is words like *aorta* or *nucleus* or *ecosystem*, which are used in restricted scientific contexts, that tell you what the passage is about. When you have found these words, you can be sure that each will lead you to one of the main ideas of the passage.

As an example, start by reading this passage:

EXAMPLE: The annual migration of birds is a complex process that is only partly understood. Some birds that are born in the Arctic fly thousands of miles to South America and then return to the place where they were born. The adults migrate earlier than the newborn young. The young birds find their way to the wintering grounds even though no adult shows them the route.

It is now fairly well established that in the temperate zones the urge to migrate is prompted by changes in the length of the day. As the days grow shorter in the fall, certain definite physiological changes occur in the birds, such as degeneration of the ovaries or testes. This is accompanied by restlessness and the urge to fly south.

There is some evidence that birds navigate using many clues, including the earth's magnetic field, the position of the sun in the sky, visible land forms, and even the pattern of the stars at night. How they know the route, however, is a complete mystery. It can be called instinct, but that is simply a word that explains nothing.

As you read this passage through for the first time, you should identify several key words such as *migration*, *degeneration*, *navigate*, *ovaries*, *magnetic field.* Now use these words to locate the main ideas in the passage. They will probably lead you to three main ideas: (1) the changing length of daylight is the signal that prompts migration; (2) birds use a number of clues to navigate; and (3) how they know the route is completely unknown.

Once you have these main ideas firmly fixed in your mind, you are ready to read the questions. As needed, refer to the passage to find the answers.

EXAMPLE: **3.** What is the most probable factor that prompts birds to migrate north in the spring?

(1) depletion of the food supply during the winter
(2) the disappearance of snow from the ground
(3) the coming of warmer weather
(4) the increase in the amount of daylight
(5) the instinct to fly north

One of the main ideas tells you that, in the fall, migration is prompted by the decreasing length of daylight. It is surely reasonable to suppose that the reverse is true in the spring, so the answer is choice 4. It should not be necessary for you to reread the passage.

EXAMPLE: **4.** Which of the following provides evidence for one of the modes of navigation used by birds?

(1) Birds can be trained to find their way home.
(2) Certain birds cannot find their way on cloudy nights.
(3) There is a great deal of northward migration when the wind is from the south.
(4) A bird that cannot see the ground can still find its way.
(5) Many large birds migrate in the daylight hours.

You will probably have to go back to the passage, but you now know where to look. You will find in the third paragraph a list of the modes of navigation. Since one of them is navigation by the stars, the answer is choice 2. Choices 1, 3, and 5 are true statements, but they give no information about the mode of navigation. Choice 4 is wrong because it eliminates one possible mode (navigation by visible land forms), but leaves open several other possibilities.

EXAMPLE: **5.** In an experiment, the testes are removed from birds in the Arctic in the summertime. It is found that they then show the typical restlessness that precedes migration. What hypothesis does this suggest?

(1) Early migration causes the testes to degenerate.
(2) The length of the day has nothing to do with migration.
(3) The immediate physiological factor that initiates migration is the degeneration of the testes.
(4) Increasing length of daylight causes the testes to degenerate.
(5) Restlessness is not a sign that migration is about to begin.

This question requires you to analyze a cause-and-effect relationship. Since it deals with the factors that initiate migration, your attention is drawn to the second paragraph, where you find that degeneration of the testes (or ovaries) always precedes migration. The experiment tests whether loss of the testes is an actual cause of the urge to migrate. When it is found that removal of the testes produces premigratory restlessness, the cause-and-effect relationship is established. The answer is choice 3. Choice 1 is wrong because a cause cannot come after an effect. Choice 2 is wrong because it introduces a factor not tested for in the experiment. Choice 4 is wrong because the length of daylight decreases, not increases, as the summer advances toward fall. Choice 5 is wrong because it violates one of the assumptions on which the experiment was based.

EXAMPLE: **6.** What has the study of migration revealed about how birds know what route to follow?

(1) Young birds learn by following their parents.
(2) Birds are born with an instinct that tells them the route.
(3) Birds use several different means of navigation.
(4) The changing length of daylight gives birds the necessary clues.
(5) So far, investigation has not given any answers to the question.

One of the main ideas, already extracted from the passage, is choice 5—the answer. The text says that choice 1 is not true, and choice 2 offers a word, but not an explanation. Choices 3 and 4 are true, but irrelevant to this particular question.

EXAMPLE: **7.** In the tropics, some birds migrate for short distances between wet and dry seasons. How do we know that they do not use the same seasonal clues as temperate-zone birds?

(1) There is no marked temperature variation between winter and summer in the tropics.
(2) Food is available all year round in the tropics.
(3) The testes and ovaries of tropical birds do not change cyclically during the year.
(4) In the tropics, the length of daylight is much the same all year.
(5) Since it is always warm in the tropics, the birds have no definite nesting season.

It is the changing length of daylight that stimulates migration in the temperate zone. The answer is choice 4, which rules out this factor in the tropics.

Here is another passage for you to practice on:

EXAMPLE: Sicklemia is a hereditary disease of the erythrocytes (red blood cells) that is found chiefly in the people of tropical Africa and their descendants in America. It is characterized by abnormal hemoglobin, the red protein in erythrocytes.

People afflicted with this condition are subject to repeated attacks, brought on by conditions in which the erythrocytes receive insufficient oxygen in their passage through the lungs. This may happen during periods of intense physical exertion, or at high altitudes where the oxygen pressure is low. Under these conditions, the abnormal hemoglobin gels, distorting the erythrocytes into a rigid sickle shape. They are then unable to pass through the capillaries. Blockage of the circulation produces a variety of severe symptoms and may result in death.

The gene that produces the abnormal hemoglobin confers a certain benefit on its carriers. Children of a mating between a person with sicklemia and one with normal hemoglobin have some damaged erythrocytes, but not enough to make them ill except under very severe conditions. They benefit by being immune to malaria, which is a devastating and often fatal disease in tropical Africa.

This is a complex passage containing many key words: *sicklemia*, *Africa*, *erythrocyte*, *hemoglobin*, *hereditary*, *oxygen*, *capillary*, *malaria.* Some of these words may be unfamiliar, but you should note that three of them are defined for you. You are told that erythrocytes are red blood cells, hemoglobin is the red protein in these cells, and malaria is a devastating disease. Sicklemia is described in detail through the passage. You are expected to know the meaning of *Africa*, *hereditary*, *oxygen*, and *capillary*.

Using these words, you should find the following key ideas: (1) sicklemia is hereditary; (2) it occurs in Africa, where malaria is common; (3) it involves abnormal hemoglobin; (4) attacks occur in conditions of low oxygen supply; (5) it protects against malaria.

Now you are ready to look at the questions.

EXAMPLE: **8.** Which of the following might be an appropriate treatment for a person suffering an acute attack of sicklemia?

(1) Administer antimalarial medication.
(2) Move the person to a high altitude.
(3) Administer oxygen.
(4) Make the person exercise strenuously to open the capillaries.
(5) Remove the sickled erythrocytes.

One of the key ideas tells you that attacks are provoked by shortage of oxygen in the blood, so the answer is choice 3. It should not be necessary to refer to the passage to get this answer.

EXAMPLE: **9.** Why does sicklemia produce some benefit in Africa, but not in the United States?

(1) There is no malaria in the United States.
(2) The United States has a temperate climate.
(3) There is more oxygen in the air in the United States.
(4) The gene for sicklemia is not found in the United States.
(5) The United States has a lower altitude than Africa.

The last paragraph of the passage details the only benefit of sicklemia: protection against malaria in the carriers of the gene. Where there is no malaria, this benefit disappears, and the answer is choice 1. Choices 3, 4, and 5 are not true, and choice 2 is irrelevant.

EXAMPLE: **10.** Of the following, in which group is sicklemia likely to appear most frequently?

(1) Americans living in Africa
(2) Americans of African descent
(3) people who have been exposed to malaria
(4) all people living in the tropics
(5) people who have been in close contract with individuals who have sicklemia

One of the key points is that sicklemia is hereditary; another is that it is common in Africa. It follows that people of African descent are most liable to get it. The answer is choice 2.

EXAMPLE: **11.** A test is available to determine whether an individual is a carrier of sicklemia. Someone might take such a test to help him or her decide whether to

(1) move to a tropical climate
(2) take an office job
(3) work at manual labour at a high altitude
(4) go to a hospital for treatment
(5) make a will

This is a difficult question, which cannot be answered except by careful reading of the passage. The last paragraph tells you that under severe conditions a carrier may become ill. In the second paragraph you learned that severe conditions mean a limited supply of oxygen, brought on by hard physical exercise or high altitude. The answer is choice 3, a combination of both these factors.

EXAMPLE: **12.** Natural selection tends to eliminate genes that produce serious illness and no benefit. Which of the following would result in long-range reduction of the amount of sicklemia in the world?

(1) improved sanitation in tropical countries
(2) a new vaccine against the disease
(3) restriction of immigration from Africa
(4) quarantine of affected individuals
(5) complete elimination of malaria in the world

Since the disease is hereditary rather than infectious, choice 1, 2, or 4 would have no effect. Choice 3 would have no effect in Africa. The answer is choice 5 because, if there were no malaria, the sicklemia gene would have no benefit, and its frequency would gradually be reduced by natural selection.

OUTLINE OF STUDY FOR THE SCIENCES

The science questions on the GED place emphasis on broad concepts and principles. You must realize that you have acquired useful information in your reading books, magazines, and newspapers. Bear in mind that your science background has profited from radio and television. Running a home requires science background. Often, job experience is based on concepts and principles in science. Your science background may be richer than you realize.

The following study outline may help you organize your study plan.

I. BIOLOGY

(1) Unity and Diversity Among Living Things
  a. cell theory
  b. chemistry of living things
  c. life functions
  d. photosynthesis
  e. types of nutrition, nutritional relationships

(2) Diversity of Life
  a. classification of living things
  b. genetics
  c. changes in living things, evolution
  d. fossils
  e. interdependence of living things, balance of nature, conservation

II. EARTH SCIENCE

(1) The Earth in Space
  a. structure, magnetism, gravity
  b. rocks, minerals, and ores
  c. fossils and geologic time
  d. planetary motion, rotation, revolution, seasons, the moon

(2) The Universe
  a. the solar system
  b. stars and galaxies

(3) Destructional Forces
  a. weathering
  b. erosion

(4) Constructional Forces
  a. earthquakes
  b. volcanos
  c. earth movements

(5) Movements of Air Masses

(6) Climate and Weather
  a. humidity
  b. air pressure
  c. winds

(7) Sources of Energy
  a. wind
  b. solar
  c. nuclear
  d. geothermal

III. PHYSICS

(1) Mechanics of Solids
  a. concurrent forces and velocities, composition at any angle, resolution, components at any angle
  b. motion as a result of force, uniform and accelerated
  c. work and its measurements
  d. force, energy, power, and work
  e. machines as principles of work

(2) Nature of Waves
  a. heat—conduction, convection, radiation
  b. sound—origin, velocity, reflection
  c. light—illumination, colour, reflection, refraction

(3) Magnetism
  a. natural, artificial, permanent
  b. polarity
  c. induction

(4) Electricity
  a. static
  b. current
  c. induction

(5) Nuclear Physics
  a. rays
  b. radiation
  c. fission, fusion
  d. reactors

IV. CHEMISTRY

(1) Matter and Energy
  a. substances—elements, compounds
  b. mixtures
  c. atomic theory—electrons
  d. measurement of energy—calorie, thermometry
  e. forms of energy
  f. energy changes

(2) Atomic Structure
  a. the nucleus, electrons
  b. subatomic particles

(3) Bonding

(4) Chemical Equilibrium
  a. factors affecting rate
  b. solubility
  c. acids, bases, salts
  d. oxidation—reduction
  e. electrochemistry

GLOSSARY OF SCIENTIFIC TERMS

In your preparation for the Science Test you may on occasion find a term, an expression, or a reference that is not familiar to you. This handy glossary may save you trips to another source of reference. On some occasions your idea of a term may be hazy. It may be an item you knew well in the past but have now forgotten. Make it a habit to turn to this glossary to locate clear, succinct definitions. Some students have used the glossary as a tool for checking up on science information. Your science background will greatly improve if you can find time to develop this habit.

A

ABDOMEN the part of the body between the thorax and pelvis in higher animals

ABIOGENESIS belief that living things may develop from lifeless matter

ABSOLUTE HUMIDITY the amount of water vapour actually contained in a given quantity of air

ABSOLUTE ZERO the lowest possible temperature, –273.16°C

ABSORPTION the passage of digested food through the walls of the villi of the small intestine into the surrounding lymph and blood vessels

ACCELERATION the rate at which velocity changes

ACCRETION increase in size of nonliving things by the addition of molecules around a centre

ACETYLCHOLINE one of the substances secreted by the endings of many neurons at certain synapses and nerve endings

ACID a compound that dissociates in water to produce hydrogen ions; usually tastes sour

ACID RAIN rain with an excessive acidic composition that has a harmful effect on fish, animal, and plant life

ACTH adreno-corticotropic hormone, a hormone produced by the anterior lobe of the pituitary gland, the master gland of the body; stimulates the adrenal glands to secrete a hormone known as cortisone

ACTIVE SITES regions on the cell membranes to which enzymes become attached

ACTIVE TRANSPORT process by which a cell uses metabolic energy to move substances through its membrane

ADAPTATION change in a living thing that better fits it for survival in its environment

ADENOSINE DIPHOSPHATE (ADP) a compound containing a ribose and two phosphate groups; stores energy

ADENOSINE TRIPHOSPHATE (ATP) a substance that acts as a storehouse for respiration energy

ADIPOSE TISSUE tissue in which fat or oil is stored

ADRENAL CORTEX outer part of the adrenal gland, the source of cortisone and other hormones

ADRENALINE another term for epinephrine

ADRENAL MEDULLA core of the adrenal glands, which secretes adrenaline

ADSORPTION concentration of a solid, liquid, or gas on the surface of a solid or liquid

AEROBIC RESPIRATION respiration with the use of oxygen

AGAR a gelatinlike substance obtained from seaweed; used in making culture media for growing microorganisms

AGGLUTININ plasma protein that reacts with a corresponding agglutinogen in clumping blood

AGONIC LINE a line connecting locations of zero magnetic variation

AILERON a flap in the edge of the wings of an airplane that controls its course

AIR MASS a very large body of air with uniform temperature, pressure, and humidity at any given level

AIR SAC microscopic structure (alveolus) in the lungs where gas exchange takes place

ALBINISM hereditary trait in which there is a lack of pigment in the skin, hair, and eyes

ALCHEMY the pseudo-science of the Middle Ages in which the primary goal was to change ordinary metals to gold

ALGA (ALGAE) one of a group of simple chlorophyll-containing protists

ALKALI a soluble base (containing the OH radical)

ALLANTOIS a membranous sac that in mammals helps form the placenta

ALLELE any of the various forms taken by a given gene

ALLERGY tendency to develop antibodies against otherwise harmless substances

ALLOTROPE one of two different forms of the same element (or compound) having different physical and chemical properties

ALLOY a substance composed of two or more metals

ALLUVIAL soil, sand, or gravel deposited by running water

ALPHA PARTICLE composed of two protons and two neutrons; the nucleus of a helium atom

ALTERNATING CURRENT an electric current that changes its direction in regular cycles

ALTIMETER an instrument used to measure height above the earth's surface

ALVEOLUS an air sac in the lungs

AMALGAM an alloy containing mercury

AMBER fossilized resin from trees often containing fossil insects

AMINO ACIDS compounds containing an amine group and a carboxyl group; the building blocks of protein molecules

AMMETER a device that measures electric current

AMNION liquid-filled membranous sac protecting the embryo in higher vertebrates

AMOEBA a type of protozoan that has no permanent shape

AMORPHOUS without definite shape

AMPERE the unit for measuring the intensity of an electric current

AMPHIBIANS class of vertebrates that included frogs and salamanders

AMPLIFIER a device that makes weak electric currents stronger

AMPLITUDE the maximum value of a wave or vibration

AMYLASE any enzyme that digests starch

ANAEROBIC RESPIRATION fermentation, or respiration in the absence of oxygen

ANATOMY branch of biology that studies the structure of organisms

ANEMIA condition in which the blood has insufficient red blood cells

ANEMOMETER an instrument used for measuring the velocity of the wind

ANEROID BAROMETER a type of barometer that does not use mercury or any other liquid

ANNULAR ECLIPSE a partial eclipse of the sun in which a ring of the sun appears around the black disk of the moon

ANODE the positive electrode of an electrolytic cell; the positive terminal of a battery; the plate of a vacuum tube

ANOPHELES MOSQUITO a mosquito that carries the protozoan cause of malaria

ANTHER the part of the flower in which the pollen is produced

ANTHRACITE the hardest form of coal

ANTIBIOTIC any substance made by a microorganism that destroys germs

ANTIBODY a substance, usually in the blood of an organism, that serves to counteract the effects of disease-producing bacteria

ANTICLINE an arch of rock in which the layers bend down in opposite directions from the crest

ANTICYCLONE known as a "high"; a large mass of high-pressure air with winds moving out from it clockwise

ANTIDOTE a substance used to counteract the effects of poison

ANTIGEN a foreign substance that stimulates the body to produce antibodies

ANTISEPTIC a substance that prevents the growth or activity of germs

ANTITOXIN any substance in the body the neutralizes toxins

AORTA the largest artery; carries blood from the left ventricle of the heart to all of the body except the lungs

APHELION the point on a planet's orbit farthest from the sun

APOGEE the position of a satellite at the point in its orbit when it is farthest from the earth

APPENDIX a wormlike, narrow part of the alimentary canal, in the lower right-hand part of the human abdomen

AQUA REGIA mixture of nitric acid and hydrochloric acid

ARCHIMEDES' PRINCIPLE a law stating that an object is buoyed upward by a force equal to the weight of the displaced liquid or gas

ARMATURE a piece of metal or a coil of wire that moves back and forth, or rotates, in a magnetic field

ARTERIOSCLEROSIS hardening of the arteries

ARTERY a muscular vessel carrying blood away from the heart to the periphery of the body

ARTHROPODS the phylum of animals with non-living external skeletons and jointed appendages; insects, spiders, crustaceans

ARTIFACTS implements of structures made by humans

ASCORBIC ACID vitamin C; found in citrus fruits, tomatoes, and green vegetables

ASEPTIC free of live germs

ASEXUAL REPRODUCTION producing offspring without union of individuals or germ cells

ASSIMILATION process by which digested food is utilized by the body to build up or repair cells

ASTEROID one of a group of "minor planets" between Mars and Jupiter, of which about 1,500 are known

ATMOSPHERE the whole mass of air surrounding the earth

ATMOSPHERIC PRESSURE the force per unit area exerted by the atmosphere against all surfaces

ATOLL a circular coral reef that encloses a lagoon

ATOM the smallest unit of an element, consisting of a nucleus surrounded by electrons

ATOMIC FISSION the breaking down of an atomic nucleus, into two or more parts, with a great release of energy

ATOMIC FUSION the joining of atomic nuclei to form heavier nuclei, such as deuterium (heavy hydrogen) and tritium (another form of heavy hydrogen) to make helium, resulting in the release of enormous quantities of energy

ATOMIC MASS UNIT the number of protons and neutrons in any atom

ATOMIC NUMBER total number of protons in the nucleus of an atom

ATOMIC PILE a mass of uranium rods, embedded in pure carbon, that produces a chain reaction and releases atomic energy

ATOMIC WEIGHT the mass of an atom, expressed in daltons

AUREOMYCIN an antibiotic produced by certain soil bacteria

AURICLE an upper chamber of the hearth that receives blood from the veins—also called the atrium

AUTONOMIC NERVOUS SYSTEM part of the human nervous system that regulates the involuntary activities of the body

AUTOTROPH an organism, such as a green plant, that nourishes itself by making organic materials out of inorganic

AUXIN a plant hormone

AXIS an imaginary line through the earth's poles

AXON the part of a nerve cell that carries impulses away from the cyton (cell body)

B

BACILLUS a rod-shaped bacterium

BACTERIA the smallest one-celled organisms, having neither nucleus nor other organelles

BALANCE IN NATURE the interdependence of all plants and animals with their environment

BANDING practice of attaching a band or tag to an animal or bird to study its travel habits

BAROGRAPH an instrument that measures and records changes in air pressure

BAROMETER an instrument that measures air pressure

BASAL METABOLISM the rate of the body's activities when it is at rest

BASE a chemical compound that produces a salt when it reacts with an acid; an alkali

BEDROCK the solid surface of the earth's crust, often overlaid by soil or sediments

BENIGN TUMOR a growth that, although abnormal, does not spread but remains localized and does no particular harm unless it presses upon a vital organ

BERIBERI a disease caused by a diet lacking vitamin B_1 (thiamine)

BETA PARTICLES high-speed electrons released in the radioactive breakdown of nuclei

BILE a fluid that is secreted by the liver and passes into the small intestine, where it aids in the digestion of fats

BINARY FISSION equal division of nucleus and cytoplasm in one-celled organisms

BINOMIAL NOMENCLATURE double name used to identify a living organism by genus and species

BIOME a community of plants and animals

BIOPSY the removal of a small part of living tissue for microscopic examination to see if it is malignant

BITUMINOUS soft coal that, unlike anthracite coal, has not been subjected to heat and pressure

BLASTULA the hollow ball stage of cleavage

BLOOD BANK a place in which whole blood may be kept for future use in transfusions

BLOOD PLATELET cell that assists in clotting of blood

BRAIN the main centre of the human nervous system, made up of cerebrum, cerebellum, and medulla

BREEDER REACTOR a nuclear reactor in which more atomic fuel is made than is used up

BRONCHIAL TUBE one of the two branches of the windpipe

BROWNIAN MOVEMENT the random movement of particles in liquid or gas

BUDDING a form of asexual reproduction in which a small part of the organism develops into a new individual

BUFFER a substance that tends to keep the pH (hydrogen ion concentration) constant

BULB a leafy underground stem that produces a new plant

BUOYANCY an upward force exerted by a liquid or gas on a submerged object

C

CALCIUM an element found in many vegetables and in milk; important in building healthy bones and teeth

CALORIE a unit of measure of heat or other forms of energy

CALORIMETER an instrument that measures the heat energy released by the oxidation of food

CAMBIUM the actively growing layer of cells in the stems of higher plants

CANCER an abnormal growth that, if not detected early and removed or destroyed, will usually, in time, spread widely throughout the body and ultimately cause death

CAPACITOR a device that stores electric charge

CAPILLARY a thin-walled tube; one of the tiny blood vessels in the network connecting the arteries and the veins

CAPILLARY ACTION the upward movement of water through a tube

CARBOHYDRATE a compound made up of carbon, hydrogen, and oxygen (for example, starch or sugar)

CARBON DIOXIDE colourless, odourless gas present in the air in small amounts; breathed out from the lungs

CARBON MONOXIDE a poisonous gas that prevents oxygen from entering the red blood cells; produced when gasoline is not completely burned

CARBOXYL GROUP the —COOH group of organic acids

CARCINOMA cancerous growth

CARNIVORE a flesh-eating mammal with long eye-teeth and sharp claws, like the cat, lion, and dog

CAROTENE a yellow substance that is changed to vitamin A in the human body

CARTILAGE an elastic, yet hard, tissue composing most of the skeleton of the very young of all vertebrates and breastbone of adults

CARTOGRAPHY science of mapmaking

CAST IRON brittle iron that is usually cast in moulds

CATABOLISM the life processes that break down protoplasm for the release of energy

CATALYST a substance that affects the rate of a chemical reaction without any change in itself

CATHODE the negative electrode of an electrolytic cell; the negative terminal of a battery; the electron source in a vacuum tube

CATION positive ion

CELL the basic unit of plant and animal life, consisting of a small mass of protoplasm, including a nucleus, surrounded by a semipermeable membrane

CELL MEMBRANE the thin outer layer of cytoplasm acting as a cell boundary

CELLULOSE a complex carbohydrate found in the wall of plant cells

CELL WALL the non-living, rigid wall surrounding the cells of plants, algae, fungi, and bacteria

CELSIUS temperature scale on which 0° is the freezing point of water and 100° is the boiling point; this is the term now used instead of centigrade

CENTRE OF GRAVITY the point in an object from which the torque produced by gravity can be calculated

CENTROSOMES structures found in the cytoplasm of animal cells that form asters during mitosis

CEREBELLUM the part of the brain lying behind and below the cerebrum; controls muscular coordination

CEREBRUM the part of the brain concerned with thought and judgment

CHAIN REACTION the reaction in which the splitting of one atom causes other atoms to undergo fission

CHEMICAL BOND linkage between atoms produced by transfer or sharing of electrons

CHEMICAL CHANGE a reaction during which substances lose their identify and change their composition

CHEMISTRY the science that deals with the makeup of substances and how they are changed into other substances

CHEMOTHERAPY treatment of illness by the use of chemicals (drugs)

CHITIN the material forming the exoskeleton of anthropods

CHLORINATION the treatment of water with chlorine to kill germs

CHLOROPHYLL a green substance that enables green plants to make glucose by the process of photosynthesis

CHLOROPLAST a small green body that contains chlorophyll

CHOLESTEROL crystalline fatty substance found in animal fats

CHORDATES the phylum of animals, including the vertebrates, which have a living, internal skeleton with a notochord in the embryo

CHORION outermost membrane protecting the embryo in higher vertebrates; in mammals, helps form the placenta

CHROMATID one of the two strands that make up the chromosome

CHROMATIN an obsolete name for the substance of the chromosomes

CHROMOSOME one of several small more or less rod-shaped bodies in the nucleus of a cell; contains the hereditary factors (genes)

CHRONOMETRE an extremely accurate clock used in navigation

CHRYSALIS the pupa of the butterfly

CILIUM one of many microscopic, waving, hairlike structures projecting from a cell

CIRRUS CLOUD a white, filmy type of cloud, usually formed at high altitudes, generally consisting of ice crystals

CLAY finely ground quartz, feldspar, and mica resulting from the erosion of rocks

CLEAVAGE repeated division of an embryo's cells, without an increase in the total mass; also, the splitting of a mineral

CLIMATE a composite of weather conditions over a long period of time

CLIMAX COMMUNITY final stable stage in a succession within a particular area

CLOUD SEEDING artificial method of producing precipitation from clouds

COAGULATION the clumping of smaller particles into larger particles

COBALT 60 radioactive cobalt used mainly for the treatment of internal cancers

COCCUS a spherical bacterium

COCHLEA a coil-like structure in the inner ear

COENZYME substance that together with enzymes controls the chemical reactions of protoplasm

COLCHICINE chemical applied to plant tissue that causes doubling of number of chromosomes, often producing new varieties

COLD FRONT contact zone in which cold air displaces warm air

COLLOID a state of matter between true solution and suspension

COLOUR SPECTRUM a band of colours (red, orange, yellow, green, blue, violet) into which white light can be split

COMBUSTION rapid oxidation caused by the chemical union of a substance with oxygen

COMET a heavenly body with a head and tail, traveling in a long, oval orbit around the sun

COMMENSALISM symbiotic relationship in which one organism benefits by consuming the food of the other organism without harming or helping it

COMPOUND a substance composed of two or more elements chemically united

COMPRESSIBILITY a property of gases that permits large volumes of gases to be forced into a small space

CONCAVE LENS a lens that is thinner in the centre than at the edges, so that it makes light rays diverge

CONDENSATION the process of forming a liquid or solid from a vapour or gas

CONDENSER an obsolete name for a capacitor; a tube in which a vapour is cooled to liquefy it

CONDITIONED REFLEX an acquired automatic response

CONDUCTOR a material, such as copper wire, that carries a flow of electrons (electricity)

CONE CELL light-sensitive cell in the retina, capable of distinguishing colours in bright light

CONGLOMERATE sedimentary rock made up of a mixture of rounded fragments cemented together by natural substances, such as clay

CONJUGATION sexual reproduction by identical gametes

CONSERVATION the wise and careful use of our natural resources

CONSTELLATION any one of the groups of stars and the area of the sky in its vicinity to which a definite name has been given, such as Ursa Major, the Great Bear

CONTINENTAL SHELF the submerged extension of the continent that slopes to the ocean floor

CONTOUR INTERVAL the difference in elevation between two successive contour lines

CONTOUR PLOWING plowing in which the furrows go around the hill instead of up and down

CONVECTION CURRENT a current in air, or in water or other fluid resulting from a difference in temperature

CONVEX LENS a lens that is thicker in the middle than at the edges so that it makes light rays diverge less strongly or converge

COPROLITE fossil excrement

CORNEA the transparent tissue in front of the iris and the pupil of the eye

CORONA a bright white light that appears to surround the sun in an eclipse of the moon

CORONARY pertaining to the blood vessels of the heart muscle

CORPUSCLES red or white cells found in that blood

CORROSION the wearing away of a metal by chemical action, such as oxidation

COSMIC RAY various high-energy subatomic particles coming to earth from outer space

COTYLEDON seed leaf of the embryo plant that provides food for the growing seedling

COVALENT BOND chemical bond formed by a pair of shared electrons

CRACKING a process by which the petroleum oils of different boiling points are separated from one another and from other petroleum compounds

CRETIN a person showing physical stunting and mental deficiency due to improper functioning of the thyroid gland

CREVASSE a deep crack in a glacier

CROSS-POLLINATION the transfer of pollen from the anther of one blossom to the stigma of another flower

CRYOGENICS the branch of physics dealing with the production of very low temperatures

CUMULUS CLOUD a type of cloud between 1700 and 5000 metres above the earth, having a flat base and rounded masses piled up like a mountain

CUTTING a piece of root, stem, or leaf that can be planted to produce a new plant

CYCLONE winds blowing counterclockwise about a nearly circular region of low air pressure in the Northern Hemisphere over an area covering thousands of square kilometres

CYCLOTRON an instrument used to study the properties of atoms by increasing the speed of atomic particles

CYTOPLASM that part of the cell that lies outside the nucleus; carries on all life activities except reproduction

D

DARK REACTION the stage of photosynthesis in which carbon dioxide fixation occurs

DECIBEL unit for measuring the relative loudness of a sound

DECIDUOUS vegetation that regularly loses its leaves with the change in seasons

DECOMPOSERS organisms that feed on dead organic material, returning inorganic compounds to the environment in a form used again by other living things

DEHYDRATION the loss of water

DELIQUESCENCE property of certain substances to take up water from the air to form a solution

DELTA a deposit of silt at the mouth of a river

DENDRITE fine branches of a nerve cell that receive impulses

DENTINE material under the enamel of the tooth

DEOXYRIBONUCLEIC ACID (DNA) nucleic acid that controls the metabolism of the cell and stores the hereditary information of the cell

DEPLETION removal of organic matter and minerals from the soil

DESALINATION removal of salt from a solution, as in the purification of seawater

DEUTERIUM hydrogen-2, with nuclei composed of one proton and one neutron

DEW moisture condensed on the surfaces of cool bodies, especially at night

DEW POINT temperature at which the air becomes saturated with moisture

DEXTROSE the form of glucose used as an energy source by all cells

DIABETES a disease in which the body cannot utilize sugar because of lack of insulin

DIAPHRAGM a sheet of muscle that separates the chest cavity from the abdomen and by its movement helps in breathing; the name also used for the vibrating disk of metal in a telephone

DIATOMIC ELEMENT a molecule formed when two atoms of the same element are bonded together

DICK TEST a test to determine immunity to scarlet fever

DICUMAROL a drug used to retard blood clotting

DIESEL ENGINE an internal combustion engine in which the fuel is ignited by heat generated in the compression of air in the cylinders

DIFFERENTIATION development of specialized tissues in the embryo

DIFFUSION the process whereby the molecules of substances tend to intermingle, as when two gases or solutions are brought into contact

DIGESTION a process of chemical change that prepares food for absorption by breaking down complex molecules into simpler ones

DIHYBRID an organism known to be heterozygous for two different genes

DILUTE referring to solution containing a relatively small amount of solute

DIRECT CURRENT an electric current flowing in one direction only (as contrasted with alternating current)

DISACCHARIDE a sugar whose molecule is formed by combination of two simple sugar molecules

DISINFECTANT a chemical that kills microbes

DISPLACEMENT the volume of a fluid removed by an immersed solid

DISSOLVE cause to pass into solution

DISTILLATION the process of heating a substance until it turns into a gas and condensing this gas by cooling

DNA deoxyribonucleic acid, the material of the genes, whose function is to specify the composition of proteins in a cell

DOLDRUMS a part of the ocean near the equator with calms, squalls, and light shifting winds

DOMINANT describing an allele that produces its full effect on development even when it is present in only a single dose

DOPPLER EFFECT the sudden drop or rise in pitch when the source of a sound and the listener approach, pass each other, and move away

DOUBLE DISPLACEMENT chemical reaction in which metals in two compounds trade nonmetal partners

DOUBLE HELIX describing the shape of a DNA molecule, two long spirals wrapped around each other

DRAG the force exerted to reduce the forward motion of an airplace

DRIFT material left by a glacier after the ice has receded

DUCTLESS GLAND an endocrine gland that has no duct to carry away its secretions; therefore the secretion (hormone) is deposited directly into the bloodstream

DUNE hill or ridge of sand deposited by wind erosion

DUODENUM the part of the small intestine immediately past the stomach

DYNAMO a mechanical device used to produce an electric current by rotating an armature coil in a magnetic field

E

EARTHSHINE illumination of the darker portion of the moon by reflection of light from the earth

EBB TIDE the outgoing tide

ECHO a reflected sound wave

ECLIPSE cutting off of light from one celestial body by another

ECOLOGICAL SUCCESSION the orderly process by which one biotic community is replaced by another

ECOLOGY the study of the relations of living things with each other and with their environment

ECTODERM the outermost layer of the primary germ tissue from which the skin and the nervous system develop

EFFECTORS parts of the body (muscles and glands) that respond to stimuli

EFFERVESCENCE rapid escape of a gas from a liquid in which it is dissolved

EFFICIENCY the ratio of useful work done by a machine to work put into it

EFFLORESCENCE property of hydrated crystals to lose water of hydration when exposed to air

EFFORT applied force

EGG the female sex cell that may be fertilized by a sperm

ELECTRIC CIRCUIT a complete path in which electricity travels from its source out into a wire and back to its source

ELECTRIC CURRENT the flow of electric charge, such as electrons in a wire or ions in a solution

ELECTRIC GENERATOR a device that produces electric energy by turning a coil through a magnetic field

ELECTRIC MOTOR a device that transforms electric energy into mechanical work

ELECTRODE conductor by which current enters (or leaves) an electrolyte

ELECTROLYSIS chemical breakdown of a compound due to the passage of an electric current through it

ELECTROLYTE a substance that, when dissolved in water, will conduct electricity

ELECTROMAGNET a core of soft iron surrounded by a coil of wire through which an electric current passes, thus magnetizing the core

ELECTRON a particle with extremely small mass and a unit electric charge, occurring in the outer part of every atom

ELECTRON MICROSCOPE an optical instrument using a beam of elections directed through an object to produce an enlarged image of about 200,000 magnification on a fluorescent screen or photographic plate

ELECTROPLATING the process by which electricity is used to deposit metal ions on another metal

ELEMENT a chemical substance made up of one kind of atom; cannot be decomposed by ordinary means

ELEVATOR the movable part of an airplane attached to the stabilizer controlling climbing and diving

EMBRYO an organism in its early stage of development

EMULSIFIER a substance, such as soap, that can break large fat droplets into many smaller droplets suspended in water

EMULSION a mixture of liquids that are not soluble in each other

ENAMEL the hard outer covering of the crown of a tooth

ENDOCRINE GLAND a ductless gland that secretes its hormone directly into the bloodstream

ENDODERM the innermost layer of the primary germ tissue from which the digestive and respiratory systems develop

ENDOPLASTIC RETICULUM a network of submicroscopic canals in cells

ENDOTHERMIC referring to a chemical reaction accompanied by the absorption of heat

ENERGY a quantity taking various forms, such as motion, heat, etc., whose sum remains unchanged in all interactions

ENERGY LEVEL the specific amount of energy possessed under various conditions by an electron in an atom, by an atomic nucleus, etc.

ENTOMOLOGY the study of insects

ENZYME an organic substance that speeds up the reaction of chemicals without itself being changed

ENZYME SPECIFICITY the ability of an enzyme to activate one particular substrate

EPINEPHRINE hormone of the adrenal gland that functions in emergencies, also called ADRENALINE

EPITHELIAL CELLS covering or lining cells

EQUINOX a moment, occurring twice each year on or about March 21 and September 23, when the sun appears to cross the celestial equator and day and night are of equal length

EROSION the wearing away of the earth's surface by water, ice, and winds

ERYTHROCYTES red blood cells

ESOPHAGUS (gullet) tube that connects the mouth with the stomach

ESTROGEN female hormone secreted by the ovaries

EVAPORATION escape of molecules from the surface of liquids or solids

EVOLUTION the process by which living things change into other kinds through the generations

EXCRETION elimination of wastes of metabolism: carbon dioxide and water

EXHAUST STROKE the stroke of an engine in which the piston pushes the burned gases out of the cylinder

EXFOLIATION the splitting off of scales or flakes or rock as a result of weathering

EXHALATION the phase of breathing that expels air out of the lungs

EXOSKELETON an exterior body covering, usually made of chitin

EXOTHERMIC referring to a chemical change that produces heat

EXTERNAL-COMBUSTION ENGINE an engine in which the fuel is burned outside the engine

F

FAHRENHEIT SCALE a scale on a thermometer graduated so that the freezing point of water is at 32° above zero, and the boiling point is at 212° above zero

FALLOUT radioactive particles that fall to earth as the result of an atomic or hydrogen bomb explosion

FARSIGHTEDNESS a defect of the eye that forms sharper images of objects at a distance than of things nearby

FATTY ACID an organic substance whose molecule is a long hydrocarbon chain with a carboxyl group at the end; a component of molecules of fats and oils

FAULTING vertical or horizontal movements between great masses of bedrock

FAUNA animal life typical for a particular region

FERMENTATION a chemical change brought about by enzymes produced by microbes; in the making of beer or wine, yeasts ferment sugars into alcohol and carbon dioxide

FERTILIZATION a process that occurs in sexual reproduction when the gametes, a sperm and an egg, unite

FIBRIN threadlike protein that forms the meshwork of a blood clot

FIBRINOGEN a blood protein that can form a clot by turning into fibrin

FILAMENT the fine wire inside an electric light bulb that gives off light and heat when electricity is passed through it

FILTRATE the fluid that has passed through a filter

FILTRATION BEDS layers of sand and gravel that catch soil and other particles as water passes through them

FISSION splitting of the nucleus of an atom with the release of tremendous amounts of energy

FJORD a narrow inlet of the sea between cliffs or steep slopes

FLOWER reproductive organ of seed plant

FLUORESCENCE the emission of light when an object is struck by electrons or by visible or ultraviolet light

FOCUS the point at which light rays are brought together or seem to be brought together by a lens or mirror

FOG a cloud of condensed water vapor formed on or near the ground

FOLIC ACID one of the B-complex vitamins

FOLLICLE the site of egg maturation in the ovary

FOOD CHAIN the pathway of energy through an ecosystem from producer to consumers

FOOD WEB the complex feeding relationships within a biological community

FOOT-POUND a unit of work or energy, the product of the distance an object moves multiplied by the force moving it

FORCE a push or a pull on an object

FOSSIL remains or impression of a plant or animal in rock or amber

FOSSIL FUEL the remains of organisms that lived hundreds of millions of years ago; used to release energy on burning, coal, oil, natural gas

FRATERNAL TWINS twins that result from the fertilization of two ova simultaneously by two different sperm

FREEZING the change in the state of matter from a liquid to a solid

FRICTION the force exerted on an object by its motion in contact with something else

FRONT boundary between two air masses

FROST a deposit of ice crystals that forms on objects that are colder than the freezing point of water

FRUIT ripened seed-containing structure formed from the ovary of a flower

FULCRUM the point of rest upon which a lever turns in moving an object

FUNGUS a kingdom of plantlike organisms that lack chlorophyll and therefore cannot make their own food

FUSE a device to break an electric circuit that is overloaded

FUSELAGE the body of an airplane that holds the engine, passengers, and cargo

FUSION an atomic reaction in which the nuclei of atoms combine and energy is released

G

GALAXY a large group of billions of stars

GALLBLADDER sac attached to the liver that stores bile

GALVANIZE to coat iron with zinc to protect the surface of the iron

GALVANOMETER an instrument used to detect small electric currents

GAMETE one of the two cells that unite in sexual reproduction: egg or sperm, or isogamete

GAMMA GLOBULIN a protein in blood plasma that protects against such diseases as polio

GAMMA RAYS rays similar to X-rays given off by exploding atoms

GANGLIA a group of neurons that lie outside the brain and spinal cord

GAS the phase of matter in which the substance spreads out to fill all the space in its container

GASOHOL a motor fuel that consists of nine parts gasoline and one part ethanol

GASOLINE ENGINE an internal-combustion engine that uses the heat energy of gasoline for its operation

GASTRIC JUICE the acid digestive fluid given off by the glands in the walls of the stomach

GASTRULA the stage in cleavage during which the ingrowth of cells occurs

GEIGER COUNTER an instrument that detects the presence of radioactive material by giving off clicks when radioactive particles strike its tube

GENE a part of a DNA molecule that controls the manufacture of a specific protein. Since it is copied and passed on in every cell division, it forms the unit of heredity

GENERATOR a machine that changes mechanical energy into electrical energy by cutting magnetic lines of force with coils of wire

GENOTYPE the gene makeup

GEOTHERMAL ENERGY great amounts of heat produced in the earth's interior

GEOTROPISM response to gravity by movement or growth of an organism

GERM a microorganism, especially one causing disease

GESTATION the period of time necessary for embryo development; pregnancy

GLACIER a slow-moving mass of ice

GLAND a part of the body that makes secretions, such as enzymes or hormones

GLUCOSE a simple, soluble sugar oxidized in the body to give energy

GLUTATHIONE substance released by an injured animal that stimulates a Portuguese man-of-war to eat it

GOITER an enlargement of the thyroid gland

GONADS sex glands; testes and ovaries

GRAFTING joining the cut branch of one plant to that of a rooted plant that supplies water and minerals

GRAVITY the force that holds everything to the earth; the attraction between any two masses of matter

GROUND WATER water that saturates the soil, filling all the space between particles

GUARD CELLS cells that regulate the opening and closing of the stomata in the leaf epidermis

GULLET regions of the alimentary canal that connects the mouth and the stomach

H

HABIT an acquired type of behaviour resulting from practice until it is done automatically

HALF-LIFE time required for half of any sample of a radioactive material to undergo transformation into something else

HARD WATER water containing a large quantity of dissolved mineral salts

HEAT OF FUSION the amount of heart required to melt a gram of a pure solid substance

HEAT OF VAPORIZATION the amount of heat required to turn a gram of substance from a liquid into a gas

HEAVY WATER water in which the hydrogen is deuterium, the isotope of mass 2

HEMOGLOBIN an iron-rich chemical found in the red blood cells, which unites with oxygen

HEMOPHILIA physical condition in which blood fails to clot properly; inherited by sons from mothers who are carriers

HEREDITARY the tendency of offspring to resemble parents due to the passage of genes in the reproduction process

HERMAPHRODITE an organism that possesses both testes and ovaries

HETEROTROPH an organism that cannot synthesize food from inorganic material

HETEROZYGOTE an organism with non-identical alleles of a given gene

HIBERNATION a torpid or resting state throughout some or all or the winter season

HOMEOSTASIS maintenance of a stable internal environment in an organism

HOMOGENIZE to distribute the solute in a solution to form a permanent emulsion

HOMO SAPIENS the scientific name for a human being

HOMOZYGOTE an organism with identical alleles of a given gene

HORMONES chemical messengers produced by endocrine glands; help in controlling and coordinating the activities of the body

HORSE LATITUDE belts of calm air under high pressure, 35° north or south of the equator

HORSEPOWER a unit for measuring the rate of work, equal to 550 foot-pounds per second

HOST a plant or animal on which a parasite grows or feeds

HUMIDITY the amount of water vapour in the air

HUMUS dead and decaying organic matter found in the soil

HURRICANE a tropical cyclone with winds of at least 74 miles per hour

HYBRID a cross between species; an organism with dissimilar genes for a trait

HYDRATES a compound or complex ion that contains water

HYDROCARBON compound containing only hydrogen and carbon atoms

HYDROELECTRIC referring to the generation of electric energy from falling water

HYDROGEN BOMB a bomb consisting of deuterium and tritium (forms of heavy hydrogen) that are fused into helium, releasing a great deal of energy

HYDROGEN ION the H^+ ion of acids

HYDROLYSIS decomposition of large molecules into smaller units by combining them with water

HYDROMETER an instrument used to measure the density (specific gravity) of a liquid

HYDRONIUM ION hydrated proton; the H_3O^+ ion

HYDROPONICS soilless growth of plants

HYDROTROPISM response to moisture by the growth of a plant root

HYDROXIDE chemical compound containing at least one hydroxyl group

HYDROXIDE ION the OH^- ion of bases

HYGROMETER an instrument used to measure relative humidity

HYPOTHESIS an assumption made as a basis for further investigation or research

I

IDENTICAL TWINS twins that result from the division of a single fertilized egg

IGNEOUS ROCK rock formed by the cooling and hardening of hot molten rock

IMMUNITY the body's ability to resist or overcome infection

IMPULSE message that travels along nerve cells or fibres

INERTIA the property of a body at rest remaining at rest or a body in motion remaining in motion

INFECTION invasion of the body by a foreign microbe

INFECTIOUS DISEASE illness caused by microorganisms

INGESTION the taking in of food

INHALATION the phase of breathing that draws air into the lungs

INORGANIC COMPOUND substance that contains any combination of elements except carbon

INSOLATION the total energy received by the earth from the radiation of the sun

INSOLUBLE incapable of being dissolved in a liquid

INSTINCT complex inborn pattern of involuntary responses

INSULATION any material used to reduce the transfer of heat or to shield a conductor of electricity

INSULIN hormone secreted by the pancreas that enables cells to use glucose

INTERNAL-COMBUSTION ENGINE an engine in which the fuel is burned inside the cylinders

INTERNATIONAL DATE LINE a map line, mostly on the 180th meridian; travelers must change the date when they cross this line

INTESTINE a section of the digestive system below the stomach in which digestion and absorption of substances take place

INTRACELLULAR DIGESTION digestion that occurs inside the cells

INTRUSION invasion of liquid magma into or between rock

INVERTEBRATES animals without a backbone

ION electrically charged atom or group of atoms

IONIC BOND chemical bond between ions, resulting from a transfer of electrons

IONIZATION process of separation into ions

IONOSPHERE the part of the atmosphere 40–300 miles above the earth

IRIS muscular, coloured part of the eye, surrounding the pupil

IRRIGATION the supplying of land with water by means of canals and ditches

IRRITABILITY the ability to respond to stimuli of the environment

ISLETS OF LANGERHANS clusters of cells in the pancreas that secrete the hormone insulin

ISOBAR a line on a weather map connecting observatories reporting the same barometric pressure

ISOGAMETES two identical cells that unite to initiate sexual reproduction by conjugation

ISOGONIC LINE a line connecting locations of equal magnetic variation

ISOMERS chemical compounds with the same empirical (molecular) formula but different structural formulas

ISOTHERM a line on a weather map connection places having the same temperature

ISOTOPES forms of the same element differing from each other in the number of neutrons within the nucleus and therefore in atomic mass

J

JEJUNUM in mammals, part of the small intestine between the duodenum and the ileum

JET STREAMS swift, high altitude winds at heights of about 12 000 metres

JOULE unit of energy equivalent to 1 newton-metre

K

KAME a mound of stratified drift deposited by streams running off a glacier

KETTLE a depression remaining after the melting of large blocks of ice buried in glacial drift

KIDNEY one of a pair of bean-shaped organs in the back part of the abdomen that collect the wastes of metabolism from the blood

KILOMETRE unit of distance, equal to about ⅝ mile

KILOWATT-HOUR a unit of energy equal to 1000 watts used for one hour

KINETIC ENERGY the energy possessed by an object because of its motion, depending on its mass and velocity

KOCH'S POSTULATES rules used to prove that a particular organism causes a certain disease

L

LACTATION secretion of milk by the mammary glands

LACTEAL one of the small vessels in the villi of the small intestine that absorbs digested fats

LAGOON a shallow body of water near or communicating with a larger body of water

LARVA the young, usually wormlike stage of an invertebrate

LARYNX the voice box, located in the upper part of the windpipe, in which the vocal cords are found

LASER device in which atoms, when stimulated by focused light waves, amplify and condense these waves and emit them in a narrow, intense beam

LATEX a milky substance from which rubber is made

LATITUDE the distance due north or south from the equator, measured in degrees and marked by an imaginary line parallel to the equator

LAVA liquid rock material that flows out on the surface of the earth from underground sources

LEACHING process by which water washes dissolved minerals from the soil

LEGUME a member of the pea family; peas, beans, clover, alfalfa; roots contain nodules with nitrogen-fixing bacteria

LENTICELS opening in the stems of plants for passage of air

LEUKEMIA a disease of the blood-forming organs, bone, lymph glands, spleen, etc., characterized by uncontrolled multiplication of white blood cells

LEVEE the raised bank of a stream

LEVER a rigid rod turning around a fulcrum to increase the force or distance moved of the work input

LICHEN a complex organism composed of a fungus and an alga in intimate connection, able to live in highly unfavourable conditions

LIFT air pressure under the wing of a plane

LIGAMENT tissue joining two or more bones

LIGHT REACTION the phase of photosynthesis in which light energy is used to split water

LIGHT-YEAR the distance that light, traveling at about 116 250 kilometres each second, travels in one year

LIMESTONE a type of sedimentary rock rich in calcium carbonate that yields lime when burned

LINES OF FORCE imaginary lines in a field of force of any magnet that show the amount and direction of the field

LINKAGE the tendency of two genes to pass together to offspring because they are located on the same chromosome

LIPASE any fat-digesting enzyme

LIPIDS fats, oils, and waxes

LIQUID the phase of matter in which the material has a definite volume, but no shape, so that it takes the shape of its container up to a definite upper surface.

LIQUID AIR air that has been made into a liquid by cooling it to –312°F

LITMUS paper or liquid that turns red in acid solutions and blue in alkaline solutions

LITRE the metric unit of volume, equal to 1000 cubic centimetres, a little more than a quart

LIVER the largest gland in the body; makes bile, stores extra sugar as glycogen

LOAM ordinary garden soil; a loose soil made up mainly of clay and sand and a small amount of humus

LODESTONE a natural rock magnet occurring in the earth

LONGITUDE distance on the earth's surface measured in degrees east or west of the meridian of Greenwich

LOW an area of low air pressure (in the centre of a cyclone or hurricane, for example)

LUNAR ECLIPSE an eclipse that occurs when the full moon crosses the plane of the earth's umbra

LYMPH a nearly colorless liquid containing proteins, found in the lymphatic vessels of the body

LYMPHOCYTE type of white blood cell involved in immunity

LYSIN an antibody that dissolves the cells of a pathogenic microorganism

M

MACHINE any device that transmits force

MAGGOT larva of a fly

MAGMA molten material from which igneous rocks are derived

MAGNETIC FIELD a region around a magnet or an electric current in which another magnet or current experiences a force

MAGNETISM the phenomenon by which electric currents exert forces on each other

MAGNETO a generator that uses permanent magnets

MAIZE the grain called corn in the United States

MALARIA a disease of the blood caused by a protozoan; transmitted by the female *Anopheles* mosquito

MALIGNANT TUMOR a cancerous growth

MALLEABILITY the property of a metal that allows it to be extended or shaped

MAMMAL a vertebrate that suckles its young

MAMMARY GLANDS glands capable of secreting milk

MANOMETRE an instrument used to measure the pressure of gas

MARINE referring to saltwater environments

MARSUPIALS mammals whose young continue development in a pouch after birth

MASS quantity of matter in a substance, compared by weighing

MATTER any substance that occupies space

MECHANICAL ADVANTAGE the ratio between the force exerted by a machine and the force input

MEDULLA the lower part of the brain, which connects the brain to the spinal cord; controls breathing, circulation, and all involuntary physiological activities

MEGACYCLE a unit of frequency equal to a million cycles per second

MEIOSIS reduction division in which the diploid number of chromosomes is reduced to the haploid number

MELTING POINT the temperature at which the solid and liquid phases of a pure substance can exist together in equilibrium

MEMBRANE a thin sheet of tissue; also the outer edge of the cytoplasm of a living cell

MERIDIAN a line running north and south on a map, numbered according to its degree of longitude

MESODERM middle tissue layer of an animal embryo and all tissues derived from it

MESOSPHERE zone above the stratosphere

MESOZOIC the geologic era from about 190 to 60 million years ago when life colonized all land areas; dominated by reptiles, dinosaurs, non-flowering plants

METABOLISM the sum total of all chemical activity in an organism

METAMORPHIC ROCK rock formed by heat and pressure from igneous or sedimentary rock

METAMORPHISM the process by which heat and pressure in the earth's crust cause recrystallization of rock

METAMORPHOSIS the change from larval to adult form, as in insect and amphibian development

METASTASIS spreading of cancer cells throughout the body

METEOR the streak of light in the sky caused by the burning of a meteoroid as it enters the earth's atmosphere

METEOROID a small stony or metallic body in outer space

METEORITE a meteoroid that strikes the earth's surface

METRE a unit of length in the metric system, equal to 39.37 inches

MICROBE (MICROORGANISM) any simple organism, microscopic in size

MILT the material produced by the testes of male fish; sperm cells

MINERAL any chemical element or compound occurring free or in rocks

MITOSIS process by which the nucleus duplicates during cell division

MIXTURE two or more substances mixed together in no definite proportions and not chemically united

MOULD a filamentous fungus

MOLECULE the smallest unit of any pure chemical substance

MOLLUSK a soft-bodied invertebrate; usually has a shell outside the body; includes the snail, the octopus, and the clam

MOLTING the process by which an animal sheds its shell, skin, feathers, or other outer covering and grows a new one

MOMENTUM motion; product of velocity and mass

MONOSACCHARIDE a sugar that cannot be broken down into simpler sugars by hydrolysis

MONOTREME an egg-laying mammal

MONSOON seasonal wind that is more pronounced over large continental areas near the equator

MORAINE landforms composed of minerals deposited by glaciers

MOTOR NEURON a nerve cell that carries impulses from the brain or spinal cord to muscles or glands

MUSCLE TISSUE animal tissue with the ability to contract

MUTATION permanent change in a gene, transmitted to the offspring

N

NARCOTICS habit-forming drugs that relieve pain and produce sleep or stupor

NATURAL IMMUNITY resistance to disease produced without medical intervention, as by exposure to the causative organism or by passage of antibodies from mother to offspring

NATURAL SELECTION survival of certain organisms that are best adjusted to the conditions in which they live

NEANDERTHAL MAN an extinct type of human being with a large brain, heavy brow ridges, and a sloping forehead

NEAP TIDE a tide having small range and occurring between spring tides

NEARSIGHTEDNESS a defect of the eye that forms sharper images of things nearby than of things at a distance

NEBULA an immense area of gases in space

NEMATOCYSTS stinging cells located on the tentacles of members of the jellyfish group and other organisms

NEPHRIDIA excretory organs of earthworms

NERVE bundle of nerve fibres held together by connective tissue

NERVE CELL an animal cell that is sensitive to a stimulus and carries an impulse

NERVE FIBER a threadlike band of tissue that carries impulses

NEUROHUMOR a secretion of nerve endings that transfers impulses from a nerve cell to another cell or an effector

NEURON nerve cell

NEUTRALIZATION reaction between an acid and a base, producing a salt and water

NEUTRON uncharged particle found in the nucleus of the atom

NEWTON the unit force that accelerates a one kilogram mass at one m/s^2

NIACIN a member of the B-complex vitamins that prevents pellagra

NIGHT BLINDNESS a condition in which a person does not see well in dim light, sometimes due to a deficiency of vitamin A

NIMBUS CLOUD a low-level cloud covering the whole sky, from which rain is falling

NITROGEN an element which makes up 80 percent of the air

NITROGEN CYCLE the cycle in which nitrogen passes from the air through organisms and soil and back to the air

NITROGEN-FIXING BACTERIA bacteria (usually found in the roots of peas, clover, and alfalfa) that can take in nitrogen and change it to a form useful to green plants

NONELECTROLYTE substance whose water solution does not conduct electric current

NOVA a star that suddenly becomes brighter than normal and then fades again

NUCLEAR DECAY the breakdown of the nucleus of an atom

NUCLEAR FISSION the breakup of a nucleus of an atom into two or more smaller nuclei

NUCLEAR FUSION the joining of two or more atomic nuclei

NUCLEAR REACTOR a device for splitting the atom so that it can be made to produce useful energy or valuable radioactive materials

NUCLEOLUS structure in the nucleus where RNA is stored

NUCLEOTIDE the unit of structure and function of a DNA molecule

NUCLEUS (BIOLOGICAL) a specialized chromosome-containing portion of the protoplasm of cells; coordinates cell activities

NUCLEUS (PHYSICAL SCIENCE) positively charged, dense part of an atom

NUTRIENT one of a group of substances in food used in nourishing and repairing body tissue

NYMPH an immature stage of certain insects resembling the adult

O

OPTIC NERVE the nerve that carries impluses from the eye to the brain

ORBIT path of a revolving object

ORE a rock from which one or more minerals can be extracted

ORGAN any group of tissues performing a special function in a plant or in an animal

ORGANIC COMPOUND compound containing carbon and hydrogen

ORGANISM any individual living animal or plant

OSCILLATOR anything that vibrates rapidly, particularly a radio transmitter that sends out radio waves

OSCILLOSCOPE an instrument used in the study of any oscillating system, such as a sound wave or an alternating current

OSMOSIS diffusion of water through a semipermeable membrane between solutions of different concentrations

OVARY an egg-producing organ in a female

OVIDUCT a tube through which eggs pass from the ovary

OVULATION the release of an egg from an ovary

OVULE the part containing the egg nucleus in flowering plants; after fertilization, each ovule develops into a seed

OXIDATION union of oxygen with some other substance; a reaction involving the loss of electrons from an atom

OXYGEN a colourless, odourless gas that makes up 20 percent of the air; needed by cells to burn food for energy

OZONE a form of oxygen (O_3) usually formed by an electrical charge

P

PALEONTOLOGY the study of fossils

PALEOZOIC the geologic era from about 630 to 190 million years ago, when multicellular life originated and developed into all modern phyla

PANCREAS a dual gland, near the beginning of the small intestine, which makes the pancreatic juice; also produces the hormone insulin in the cells of the islets of Langerhans

PARAMECIUM a common protozoan found in ponds; moves by means of cilia

PARASITE an animal or plant that obtains its food by living inside or on another living thing; includes the tapeworm, hookworm, louse, ringworm, and many harmful bacteria

PARATHYROIDS four small ductless glands embedded in the thyroid gland; produce a hormone that regulates the amount of calcium and phosphorus in the blood

PARTHENOGENESIS development of an unfertilized egg

PARTIAL ECLIPSE the incomplete darkening of one body in space by another

PASTEURIZATION process of heating to kill pathogenic microorganisms

PATHOGEN any organism that causes an infectious or parasitic disease

PAYLOAD the contents of an earth satellite or rocket useful in gathering information

PELLAGRA a deficiency disease caused by the lack of the vitamin niacin

PENDULUM an object suspended from a fixed point so that it may swing back and forth

PENICILLIN an antibiotic obtained from a type of mould; used effectively in the treatment of many diseases, such as pneumonia

PENUMBRA the lighter portion of a shadow

PEPSIN an enzyme found in the gastric juice that helps break down proteins into simpler proteins

PEPTONE an intermediate product in the digestion of proteins to amino acids

PERIGEE the position of an earth satellite at the point in its orbit when it is nearest to the earth

PERIHELION the point on the orbit of a planet when the planet is closest to the sun

PERISTALSIS waves of contraction in a muscular tube, like those that move food through the intestines or urine through the ureter

PERITONEUM a serous membrane that lines the abdominal walls and the organs contained in the abdomen

PETALS the coloured parts of a flower that help attract insects

PETRIFIED referring to plant or animal remains that have become like stone

PHAGOCYTE a type of white blood corpuscle capable of engulfing bacteria

PHARYNX the throat—common passageway for air and food

PHENOTYPE the observable traits of an organism

PHLOEM the part of the fibrovascular bundle of a plant that conducts food downward

PHOSPHOR a chemical that gives off visible light when struck by electrons, ultraviolet light, or other radiation

PHOSPHORESCENCE the capacity of a substance to emit visible light when simulated by electrons

PHOSPHORUS an element important in making proteins, bones, and teeth

PHOTON a particle of light

PHOTOSYNTHESIS the process by which a green plant makes sugar in the presence of light, from water and carbon dioxide

PHOTOTROPISM responses of a plant in which the direction of its growth is controlled by light

PHYLUM any of the largest groupings within the animal kingdom

PHYSICAL CHANGE any change that does not involve changes in the composition of the molecules or ions of a substance

PHYSIOLOGY the branch of biology concerned with the study of functions or life processes of living things

PIG IRON iron that is made in a blast furnace

PISTIL the female reproductive organ of a flower, which contains an ovary with its ovules

PITCH the property of a sound represented by the notes of a scale, depending on the frequency

PITUITARY GLAND endocrine gland located in the middle of the head, called the master gland

PLACEBO an inactive substance given to patients in the controlled evaluation of drugs

PLACENTA structure by means of which the young are nourished in the body of a mammal

PLANET one of the nine bodies circling around the sun; the earth is a planet

PLANETOID one of the many small bodies between the orbits of the planets Mars and Jupiter

PLANKTON minute floating organisms that live at the surface of the ocean and serve as food for large animals

PLASMA the liquid part of the blood; contains antibodies, hormones, and digested foods

PLASTIC a synthetic substance capable of being moulded, such as cellophane

PLATELETS tiny particles in the blood that help the blood to clot

PLEURA tissue covering the lungs and lining the chest cavity

PLUTONIUM an element produced from uranium in an atomic pile

POLAR BODIES in the maturation of an egg cell, the tiny cells that remove those chromosomes that do not enter the egg after meiosis

POLIO a virus disease that injures the nerve cells in the brain or spinal cord; may result in paralysis of the diaphragm or other muscles

POLLEN GRAIN the cell, formed in the anther of a flower, that produces the sperm nucleus

POLLINATION transfer of pollen from the stamen of a flower to a pistil

POLLUTANT substance that contaminates air, water, or earth

POLLUTION accumulation of harmful substances in air or water

POLYMER a giant molecule formed by smaller molecules joining together

POLYSACCHARIDE a polymer formed of many simple sugar molecules; starch, cellulose, glycogen

PORTUGUESE MAN-OF-WAR member of the jellyfish group with specialized organs

POTENTIAL ENERGY the energy that something has because of its position, such as the energy of an object at high altitude

POWER the rate of doing work, expressed, for example, in watts (= joules per second)

PRECIPITATE insoluble solid formed by a reaction between two liquids

PRECIPITATION all forms of moisture falling from the sky; hail, snow, rain, and sleet

PREVAILING WIND a wind that almost always blows from one direction

PRIMARY LIGHT COLOURS a group of three colours, usually red, green, and blue, that can be combined to produce all the colour sensations possible to the human eye

PRIMATES order of mammals that includes lemurs, monkeys, apes, and humans

PROGESTERONE a hormone produced by the ovaries, regulates the menstrual cycle and regulates the uterus during pregnancy

PROTEIN one of a group of nitrogen-containing organic compounds of large molecular size; important constituents of protoplasm

PROTON positively charged particle found in the nuclei of all atoms

PROTOPLASM all the living substance of a cell

PROTOZOA single-celled organisms that nourish themselves by ingesting organic material

PSYCHIATRIST a medical doctor who specializes in mental illness

PSYCHOLOGY the study of behaviour and learning

PSYCHROMETRE an instrument used to determine relative humidity

PTOMAINE poisonous substance formed by the action of certain bacteria

PTYALIN enzyme in saliva that changes starches to sugar

PULLEY a wheel with a grooved rim, used with a rope or chain to change direction of a pulling force; a simple machine

PULMONARY CIRCULATION circulation of blood from the heart through the lungs and back to the heart

PULSE the beat of an artery, produced by the surging of blood out of the heart

PUPA the young stage of an insect, which is enclosed in a protective covering

PURE CULTURE growth of one type of microbe

PUS yellowish white matter made of dead tissue, white blood cells, and bacteria, present in an abscess or boil

Q

QUARANTINE isolation of an individual carrying a contagious disease

QUININE a drug used in preventing and treating malaria

R

RABIES a dangerous disease of the nervous system caused by a virus; transmitted in the saliva of infected dogs, foxes, and similar animals when they bite a victim

RADAR abbreviation for radio detection and ranging, the device used for the detection of objects by radio waves

RADIANT ENERGY energy in the form of light or other kinds of radiation

RADIANT HEATING a heating system in which hot water or steam pipes set in floors or walls send out heat into rooms

RADIATION the process by which energy is transferred in space

RADIOACTIVITY the property of large atomic nuclei in which the nuclei are unstable and break down spontaneously, emitting particles and radiation

RADIOSONDE a radio transmitter attached to a balloon and sent aloft by observers seeking information about weather conditions in the upper atmosphere

RADIUM an intensely radioactive metallic element found in minute quantities in pitchblende and other uranium minerals

RECEPTORS the endings of nerves; sensitive to touch, chemicals, taste, sound, temperature, and other stimuli

RECESSIVE of an allele that affects development only if it is present in double dose, in the absence of the corresponding dominant allele

RECESSIVE TRAIT a trait that does not show up in a hybrid, hidden by the dominant trait

RECTUM the lowest part of the intestine from which solid food wastes leave the body

RECYCLE to save and return material so that it can be used again

REDUCTION gain of electrons, or a gain of hydrogen atoms by an atom or a molecule

REFLECTED LIGHT light that is cast back or returned by an object

REFLEX an inborn immediate response to a stimulus; done without thinking

REFRACTION bending of light rays as they pass from one medium into another

REFRIGERANT a liquid, such as ammonia that evaporates easily and therefore is useful in the cooling coils of a refrigerator

REGENERATION regrowth of lost body parts

RELATIVE DENSITY the density of a substance compared to an equal mass of water; also referred to as specific gravity

RELATIVE HUMIDITY the ratio of the amount of water vapour present in the air compared with the greatest amount that would be possible at a given temperature

REPLICATION process by which the DNA molecules make exact copies of themselves

REPRODUCTION the process by which an organism produces others like itself

REPTILES class of scaly-skinned vertebrates that includes snakes and turtles

RESISTANCE the weight to be lifted or moved by a simple machine; also, the physical condition in which a person is able to fight off infection

RESONANCE the violent vibration produced when a system is stimulated by a wave of its own natural frequency, as an object stimulated by sound waves or an electric circuit by an AC

RESPIRATION the process in cells by which nutrients are oxidized to release energy; also, the movement of air in and out of the lungs

RESPIRATORY SYSTEM the breathing system

RESPONSE any action or reaction of an organism resulting from a stimulus

RETINA light-sensitive layer of the eye that enables us to see

REVOLUTION a single cycle of body in space about another body in space; for example, the earth's yearly revolution about the sun

Rh FACTOR a blood protein present in most people; incompatible Rh factors cause damage to the blood of newborns

RIBOFLAVIN vitamin B_2; found in milk, lean meat, eggs, and many vegetables; necessary for normal growth

RICKETS a condition caused by lack of vitamin D; results in a softening of the bones

RICKETTSIA disease germs intermediate in size and structure between bacteria and viruses

RNA ribonucleic acid, a cell component that carries genetic information from the nucleus

ROCKET projectile propelled by recoil from burning gases escaping at one end of the rocket

ROD CELL modified sensory neutron in the retina, adapted for vision in dim light and for motion detection

ROOT HAIR a plant root cell from which a hairlike extension grows; it increases absorption of water and minerals

ROOT PRESSURE the osmotic pressure generated in roots

ROTATING CROPS a farming method in which different plants are sown in the same soil in succeeding years

ROUGHAGE the parts of food that cannot be digested; adds bulk to the diet and prevents constipation

RUDDER a flat piece of fabric-covered wood or a piece of metal hinged to the vertical fin of an airplane to control its direction to the right or left.

RUNNERS reproductive stems that grow close to the ground

RUNOFF surface water that runs to the sea without entering the underground water supply

RUST a fungus, related to the smuts, different forms of which cause plant diseases, such as wheat rust

S

SALINITY degree of saltiness

SALIVA a secretion made by three pairs of glands near the tongue; contains an enzyme that changes starch into sugar

SALK VACCINE a vaccine made of polioviruses grown on living cells and killed by chemicals

SALT a compound composed of a positive (metallic) ion and a negative ion, other than OH^-

SANCTUARY a haven for wild animals where hunting is prohibited or regulated

SANDSTONE a type of sedimentary rock formed from compacted sand

SAPROPHYTE plant that feeds on dead organic matter

SARCOMA cancer in connective tissue

SATELLITE natural or artificial body circling the earth or some other planet

SATURATED SOLUTION a solution containing the maximum amount of dissolved material

SCHICK TEST a test to determine if a person is immune to diphtheria

SCURVY a disease characterized by weakness of the capillaries, caused by vitamin C deficiency

SEDIMENTARY ROCK rock layers that were formed from sediment

SEDIMENTATION the settling out of particles in a liquid

SEED a developed ovule consisting of a protective coat, stored food, and an embryo plant

SEISMOGRAPH a sensitive instrument used to record vibrations of the earth's crust and to detect earthquakes

SELECTION process of choosing certain desired organisms for breeding

SELECTIVE PERMEABILITY ability of a membrane to allow certain kinds of particles to diffuse through it more easily than other kinds

SEMIPERMEABLE MEMBRANE plasma membrane that allows certain substances to pass through its boundary

SENSE ORGAN a part of the body that senses, or receives, stimuli coming from the surroundings

SENSORY NEURON nerve cell that carries signals from sense organs toward the nerve centres

SEPALS the tiny, green, leaflike parts found below the petals

SERUM blood plasma from which certain factors necessary for clotting have been removed

SERUM ALBUMIN a protein substance making up a large part of blood plasma, used to treat shock and severe burns

SEXUAL REPRODUCTION production of new organism from the union of two cells

SHALE rock formed by the hardening of clay

SHORT CIRCUIT an accidental direct connection between the two sides of an electric circuit, producing a destructive surge of current

SILT soil particles intermediate in size between clay particles and sand grains

SLATE metamorphic rock formed from shale

SLOW OXIDATION the slow burning of a substance, or the burning of food that takes place in cells; rusting of iron

SMALL INTESTINE longest region of the food tube, where most digestion and absorption take place

SMOG a layer of fog that contains smoke and irritating gases

SOFT COAL bituminous coal that yields illuminating gas, coal tar, and coke upon being heated without air

SOFT WATER water that is relatively free of mineral salts

SOLAR CELL a device that produces electricity from the energy of sunlight

SOLAR SYSTEM the sun with the group of bodies in space that, held by its attraction, revolve around it

SOLDER an alloy of lead and tin; used in joining pieces of metal because of its low melting point

SOLID the phase of matter in which the substance has a definite shape and size

SOLSTICE a time when the sun seems to reverse its apparent movement north or south of the equator

SOLUBLE capable of being dissolved

SOLUTE substance dissolved in a solution

SOLUTION a mixture in which molecules or ions of a substance are dispersed in a liquid

SOLVENT the part of a solution in which the substance is dissolved

SONAR the detection apparatus that can locate objects under water by sound waves

SOUND BARRIER the speed at which an airplane overtakes its own sound waves, resulting in violent vibration

SPAWNING the shedding of eggs and milt into the water during the reproductive process of fish

SPECIES a group of similar organisms, consisting of populations that can interbreed with each other freely

SPECIFIC GRAVITY density of a substance compared with the density of water

SPECTRUM the array of colours or wavelengths into which light is divided, usually by the action of a prism or diffraction grating

SPERMATOGENESIS process of production of sperm, including meiosis, by which the number of chromosomes is reduced by half

SPERM CELLS the sex cells produced in the testis of the male; sperm are microscopic and are able to swim and unite with the egg

SPINAL CORD a mass of nerve cells and their fibres running down a canal in the backbone and acting as a centre for reflexes

SPINDLE FIBER one of the threads attached to chromosomes during mitosis

SPIRACLES breathing openings in the bodies of insects

SPIRILLUM a type of bacterium, so named because of its spiral shape

SPLEEN a small organ near the stomach in which red blood cells are stored

SPONGE a simple invertebrate animal, consisting of only two cell layers and permanently attached to a substrate

SPONTANEOUS COMBUSTION the bursting into flame of a substance due to the accumulated heat of slow oxidation

SPONTANEOUS GENERATION the concept, no longer believed, that living things can arise automatically from non-living matter

SPORE heavy-walled structure, probably protective, that forms within certain bacteria; also, an asexual reproductive cell

SPRING TIDE the highest of high tides and the lowest of low tides

STALACTITE iciclelike mass of calcium carbonate hanging from the roof of a limestone cave

STALAGMITE mass of calcium carbonate rising from the floor of a limestone cave

STAMEN the male organ of the flower, in which the pollen is made

STAPHYLOCOCCI spherical bacteria that grow in clusters

STARCH complex, insoluble carbohydrate compound

STATIC ELECTRICITY electric charge accumulated on an object

STEEL iron to which enough carbon, manganese, silicon, etc., have been added to give it hardness and strength

STERILITY complete absence of microscopic life; or, inability to have offspring

STIGMA the part of the pistil of a flower upon which the pollen germinates

STIMULUS any form of energy to which protoplasm is sensitive

STOMACH muscular region of the food tube that stores food and begins the digestion of proteins

STOMATE pore in the leaf epidermis of a seed plant through which gases diffuse

STORAGE BATTERY a battery that stores electricity on plates of different chemical composition

STRATOSPHERE the middle region of the atmosphere between the troposphere and the ionosphere

STRATUM layer of rock

STRATUS CLOUD a cloud that extends horizontally over a large area and is at low altitude

STREPTOCOCCI spherical bacteria that grow in chains

STREPTOMYCIN an antibiotic used to combat infections, such as tuberculosis

STRIATED MUSCLE voluntary, skeletal muscles composed of long, multinucleate fibres with cross striations

STRIP CROPPING alternation of crops in narrow strips along land contours to protect the soil from erosion

STRUCTURAL FORMULA diagram to show bonds between atoms and the arrangement of the atoms in the molecule

SUBATOMIC PARTICLE particles that make up the atom

SUBLIMINATION the change from solid to gas or gas to solid without going through the liquid phase

SUBLIME to pass from solid to gaseous state without liquefying

SULFA DRUGS synthetic drugs used to combat certain bacterial infections

SUPERSATURATED referring to a solution in which the amount of solute that can be held has been increased

SUSPENSION a cloudy mixture composed of a finely divided solid in a liquid

SWEAT GLAND a gland in the skin that excretes a fluid made of water, salts, and urea onto the skin surface

SYMBIOSIS beneficial relationship between organisms living closely together

SYNAPSE space between the ending of one neuron and the dendrites of the next across which the nerve impulse travels

SYNTHESIS the building up of compounds from simpler compounds or elements

SYSTEM group of organs in an organism that deal with the same function

T

TADPOLE the fishlike embryonic form of a frog, toad, or salamander

TAGGED ATOMS radioactive atoms that may be detected by a Geiger counter

TENDON tough tissue binding muscles to bones

TERRACING a method of farming used on steep hillsides; reduces erosion by catching water in ditches

TESTIS organ that produces sperm cells

THALLOPHYTE in an obsolete classification, plants with no stems, such as algae and fungi

THEORY a scientific principle that is more or less acceptable, which is offered in explanation of observed facts

THERMODYNAMICS study of laws governing heat

THERMOGRAPH a device used to make an automatic and continuous record of temperature changes

THERMOMETER an instrument for measuring the temperature

THERMONUCLEAR referring to a nuclear reaction that requires heat in order to take place

THERMOSTAT a device on a heating system that automatically controls temperature

THIAMINE the chemical name for vitamin B_1

THORAX the chest region of the body

THRUST the forward motion given to an airplane by its propeller or jet engine

THUNDER the sound following a flash of lightning due to the sudden expansion of air in the path of the discharge

THYROID a large, ductless or endocrine gland in front of and on either side of the trachea in the lower part of the neck

THYROXINE the hormone made by the thyroid gland; rich in iodine

TIDAL WAVE destructive wave caused by an earthquake or very strong winds; a tsunami

TIDES regular movements of the oceans caused by the gravitational pull of the moon and sun upon the earth's waters

TISSUE a group of similar cells and intercellular material that perform similar work

TOPSOIL the upper fertile layer of soil, containing humus, which is necessary to plant life

TORNADO one of the most violent of windstorms, noted for its funnel-shaped clouds, high-speed winds, and great destructiveness over a short path and a small area

TOTAL ECLIPSE the complete hiding of one heavenly body by another or by the umbra of the shadow cast by another

TOXIN any poisonous substance of microbial origin

TOXOID a chemically treated toxin; injected to make a person form antitoxin against a disease

TRACHEA tube through which air passes from the throat or pharynx toward the lungs (windpipe)

TRADE WINDS winds that blow toward the equator

TRAIT a distinguishing quality of a person or thing

TRANSFORMER a device for transforming high voltage to low voltage, or low voltage to high voltage

TRANSISTOR an electronic device that controls the flow of electrons

TRANSPARENT capable of being seen through

TRANSPIRATION the process by which water evaporates through the stomata of a leaf

TRICHINOSIS a disease cause by a parasitic roundworm in the muscles of animals, usually hogs

TRIPLE BOND a chemical tie formed when three pairs of electrons are shared by two atoms

TRITIUM hydrogen-3, with nuclei composed of one proton and two neutrons

TROPICAL HURRICANE a violent storm originating in the tropics, often called a cyclone or typhoon

TROPISM growth movement of a part of a plant toward or away from a stimulus

TROPOSPHERE the lowest region of the atmosphere, about 8 km thick, in which weather changes take place

TSUNAMI a violent wave in the ocean, caused by an earthquake, which can do great damage when it arrives on a shore

TUBER an underground storage stem that produces new plants; an example is the white potato

TUMOR an abnormal swelling or enlargement, either benign or malignant

TUNDRA far-northern type of ecological community; water soaked, with permanently frozen ground, bogs, and low plants

TURBINE a rotary engine moved by steam, water, or gas

TYPHOON tropical storm in the region of the Philippines or the China sea

U

ULTRASONIC SOUND high-pitched sound above the range of human hearing

ULTRAVIOLET RAY electromagnetic radiation with wavelengths too short to be seen

UMBILICAL CORD structure that connects a mammalian embryo with the placenta

UMBRA the darker portion of a shadow

URANIUM a heavy, radioactive element occurring in an ore called pitchblende

UREA a compound containing nitrogen; the chief part of urine

URETER tube connecting each kidney with the bladder

URETHRA tube connecting the bladder with the outside of the body

URINE a liquid containing wastes removed from the blood by the kidneys

UTERUS the organ of female mammals inside which the embryo develops

V

VACCINATE to inoculate with dead or weakened germs, causing a light attack of a disease in order to prevent a serious attack of the same disease, as in smallpox

VACCINE a substance consisting of dead or weakened bacteria or viruses; used to produce immunity

VACUOLE a tiny cavity inside a plant or animal cell; filled with liquid

VACUUM a condition that exists in the absence of matter

VALENCE number of electrons gained, lost, or shared by an atom in bonding with one or more atoms

VALVES flaplike structures in the heart and large veins that keep the blood flowing in one direction

VAPOUR the gaseous phase of a substance more familiar as a liquid

VECTOR a quantity that has magnitude and direction

VEGETATIVE REPRODUCTION reproduction by means of vegetative organs that are usually concerned with nutrition

VEIN a blood vessel that drains the other organs of the body and carries the blood toward the heart

VELOCITY the time rate of traversing a distance in a particular direction

VENA CAVA either of the two large veins that carry blood directly into the right atrium of the heart

VENEREAL DISEASE disease transmitted through sexual intercourse

VENTRICLE one of the two muscular chambers of the heart that pump blood to parts of the body

VERTEBRATE an animal having a backbone

VESTIGES structures in organisms that do not appear to have any function but seem to be derived from structures that were useful in ancestral forms

VIBRATION movement due to the effect of waves on a membrane; caused by sound waves, among others

VILLUS one of the many tiny tubelike structures on the inside wall of the small intestine that serve to absorb food

VIRUS a submicroscopic disease-causing organism, consisting of a DNA or RNA molecule surrounded by a protein coat

VITAMIN a chemical found in foods and needed in small quantities for special body functioning

VOLATILE describing a liquid that evaporates at room temperature

VOLCANO an opening in the earth's crust from which molten rock and steam are thrown forth

VOLT the unit of electric potential, equal to a joule per coulomb

VOLTMETER an instrument for measuring electric potential difference

VULCANIZATION process by which raw rubber is mixed with other substances to improve its properties

W

WARM FRONT the boundary between a mass of advancing warm air and a retreating mass of relatively cooler air

WATER CYCLE path through which water moves from the atmosphere, to the surface of the earth, and back to the atmosphere

WATERSHED area from which a river or lake draws its water

WATER TABLE the level below which the soil is saturated with water

WATER VAPOUR water in the gas phase

WATT a unit of power, equal to a joule per second

WAVELENGTH the distance between two points in the same phase on a wave, such as from one crest to the next

WEATHERING the gradual destruction of material exposed to the weather

WEIGHT measure of the pull of gravity on an object

WEIGHTLESSNESS the condition in which there is an apparent absence of gravity, as inside an orbiting spacecraft

WHITE BLOOD CELL leukocyte; blood cell that helps destroy bacteria and other foreign particles that enter the body

WIDAL TEST used to determine whether a person has typhoid fever

WILSON CLOUD CHAMBER a device used to study the path of nuclear particles

WORK the product of the distance an object moves multiplied by the force acting in the direction of motion, measured in foot-pounds or joules (newton-meters)

X

X CHROMOSOME the chromosome that appears in pairs in female cells but singly in male cells; called a sex chromosome

XEROPHTHALMIA a dry, lusterless condition of the eyeball, sometimes caused by lack of vitamin A

XEROPHYTE a plant that can survive in an environment with a scanty available supply of water

XYLEM the part of the fibrovascular bundle of a plant that conducts water from the root upward

Y

Y CHROMOSOME the chromosome that appears only in cells of males; called a sex chromosome

YEAST a single-celled fungus, responsible for many kinds of fermentation and certain infections

YOLK the supply of food found inside the egg cells

Z

ZENITH the point in the sky directly above the observer

ZYGOTE cell formed by the union of two gametes; capable of developing into an adult organism

SKILLS ANALYSIS

The makers of the GED test try to test you for a wide range of skills. You can be asked something as simple as restating an idea from the passage, or something as complex as evaluating the scientific validity of an experiment. The questions are generally grouped into four skill levels, as stated on pages 354–355.

It is probably not worth your while to try to determine to which of the four levels any question belongs, or to develop special strategies for each of the four levels. In taking the test, this sort of approach would probably consume valuable time and use a part of your thinking ability that is best reserved for answering questions. Nevertheless, it is a good idea to become familiar with the four levels of skill that are investigated in the test.

COMPREHENSION

This is the simplest level. What is comes down to is this: Do you understand the passage, graph, or diagram? Can you rephrase some of the information in it? Can you summarize it? Can you identify a simple implication of the information given?

Here are some examples of the simple, comprehension type of question:

EXAMPLE: **1.** Energy expressed in joules is the product of power in watts and time in seconds. How much energy is used by a 10-watt bulb burning for 20 minutes?

(1) 200 joules
(2) 1200 joules
(3) 2000 joules
(4) 12 000 joules
(5) 120 000 joules

If you understood the passage, you know that you have to multiply the number of watts by the number of seconds. Twenty minutes is 1200 seconds, so the answer is choice 4, 12 000 joules.

EXAMPLE: **2.** The scientific name of an animal has two parts. The first word (capitalized) is the name of the genus to which the animal belongs. The second word (lower case) is the name of its species within the genus. Here are the English and scientific names of five birds:

A. American Robin, *Turdus migratorius*
B. European Robin, *Erithacus rubecula*
C. European Blackbird, *Turdus merula*
D. Military Macaw, *Ara militaris*
E. Red-breasted Blackbird, *Sturnella militaris*

Of the following pairs, which belong to the same genus?

(1) A and B only
(2) D and E only
(3) B and C only
(4) A and C only
(5) C and E only

The passage deals only with scientific names, so you can ignore the English names. The first word of the scientific name will be the same for two birds in the same genus, so the answer is choice 4. If you understood the passage, you got the answer.

EXAMPLE: **3.** The diagram below represents the result of spinning a suspension of broken cells in an ultracentrifuge. Which is a correct conclusion?

(1) Ribosomes are more dense than mitochondria.
(2) Nuclei are more dense than mitochondria.
(3) Mitochondria and ribosomes are equal in density.
(4) The cell consists of only solid components.
(5) Nuclei are less dense than mitochondria.

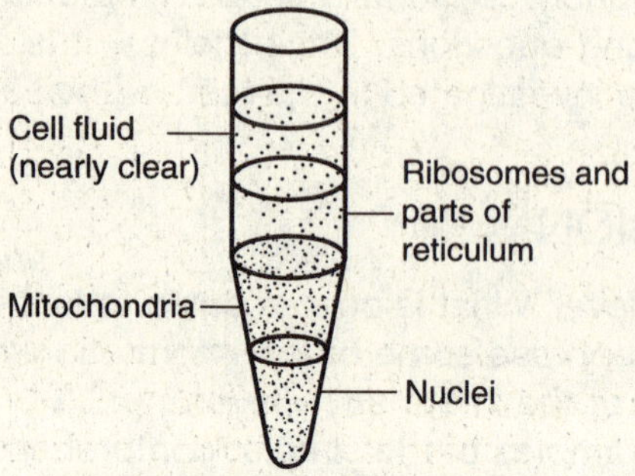

Ultracentrifuge Tube, Showing Various Layers

The correct choice is 2 because the most dense articles settle at the bottom after spinning.

EXAMPLE: **4.** The soft body feathers of a bird are useful as insulation, while the stiff feathers of the wings and tail form airfoil surfaces, like those of an airplane wing. If a new species of bird is found that has no stiff feathers, it is safe to assume that it

(1) cannot fly
(2) lives in a tropical country
(3) migrates to the south in winter
(4) lives mainly in the water
(5) is able to run rapidly

This question calls for you to make a simple deduction. If the stiff feathers are used in flight, a bird without them cannot fly, so the answer is choice 1.

EXAMPLE: **5.** The chart below gives the densities of four kinds of materials found in the earth:

Substance	Density (g/cm^3)
water	1.00
petroleum	0.86
wood chips	0.75
sand	2.10

If a mixture of all four materials is placed in a cylinder, shaken, and allowed to stand, the materials will settle out with the most dense on the bottom. What will the cylinder look like?

(1) The sand and wood chips will be mixed together on the bottom, and the water will be on top of the petroleum.
(2) The sand will be on the bottom; above will be the water with the wood chips in the layer between the petroleum and the water.
(3) The wood chips will form a layer above the sand on the bottom, and the water will form a layer over the petroleum.
(4) The sand will be on the bottom; the petroleum will form a layer over the water, with the wood chips floating on top.
(5) The water will be on the bottom, with the wood chips floating on it; the petroleum and sand will be mixed above the water.

The materials, top to bottom must be in the sequence of increasing density: wood chips, petroleum, water, sand, so the answer is choice 4.

APPLICATION

If you have thoroughly understood the information provided in the passage, graph, or diagram, you ought to be able to apply what you have learned. The application questions ask you to use the general principle contained in the information, but you will have to apply that principle to a different situation.

Here are some examples:

EXAMPLE: **6.** Study the graph which shows the percentage distribution of the earth's surface elevation above and depth below sea level.

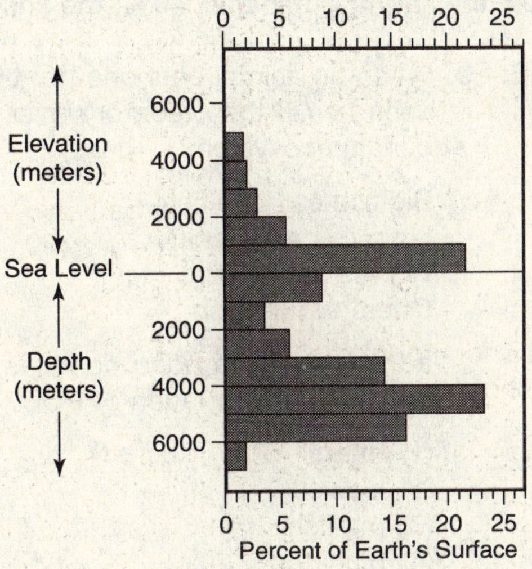

Approximately what total percentage of the earth's surface is below sea level?

(1) 30%
(2) 50%
(3) 70%
(4) 80%
(5) 90%

There are more shaded bars below sea level than above sea level on the graph. Adding up the lengths of all the shaded bars below sea level yields a total percentage of about 70%. This represents the total percentage of the earth's surface below sea level.

EXAMPLE: 7. High-energy sound waves are known to produce long term damage to the ears, resulting in loss of ability to hear high frequencies. Which of the following individuals is most likely to have good high-frequency hearing after many years of work?

(1) a rock musician
(2) an aircraft mechanic
(3) a riveter
(4) an accountant
(5) a sawmill operator

Again, you cannot get the answer just by looking back at the information. You have to look at the list of choices to figure out who is least likely to have been exposed to loud noise. The answer is choice 4; a pencil and a calculator are not noisy.

EXAMPLE: 8. A 20-watt fluorescent lamp produces as much light as a 100-watt incandescent bulb. The lighting in a factory is redesigned to provide the same amount of light when half of the incandescent lamps are replaced with fluorescents. What percentage of the cost of lighting is saved?

(1) 10%
(2) 20%
(3) 25%
(4) 40%
(5) 80%

A complete change to fluorescents would save 80 out of 100 watts or 80%. Since only half of the lamps are changed, the saving is half this, 40%; the answer is choice 4.

EXAMPLE: 9. When an animal eats another that contains PCB pollutants, the PCB concentrates in the predator's liver. The following food relationships exist in a certain ecosystem:

Big fish eat little fish.
Little fish eat plankton.
Wolves eat otters.
Otters eat big fish.

If the water of a pond contains PCB, which of the following will have the greatest concentration of PCB?

(1) otters
(2) wolves
(3) big fish
(4) plankton
(5) little fish

The concentration of PCB must increase in the sequence plankton, little fish, big fish, otters, wolves, so the answer is choice 2.

EXAMPLE: 10. Many foods, such as bread, potatoes, and spaghetti, contain a great deal of starch. An enzyme in saliva slowly changes starch to sugar. Which of the following statements is most probably true?

(1) A piece of bread held in the mouth for a long time becomes sweet.
(2) Spaghetti in the mouth causes an increase in the flow of saliva.
(3) If you eat a potato, the enzyme is in your saliva.
(4) If you eat sugar, it can turn to starch in the mouth.
(5) A cookie tastes sweet because it contains starch.

If the saliva in the mouth changes the starch in the bread to sugar, you might expect that the bread would begin to taste sweet. Choice 1 is correct. None of the other choices is suggested by the information given.

ANALYSIS

These questions are more complicated. To answer them, you will have to find a relationship between several different items of information. Some of them will not be given to you; you will be expected to know the sorts of things that are general knowledge. It is possible to identify five somewhat different kinds of skills that belong to the general category of analysis:

Recognizing unstated assumptions.
Using several related pieces of information.
Distinguishing fact from opinion.
Distinguishing cause from effect.
Distinguishing conclusions from data.

Here are some examples:

EXAMPLE: **11.** A doctor discovers that a patient has a blood pressure of 170/110. He tells the patient that medication, accompanied by a reducing diet and limited exercise, will bring the blood pressure down. What has the doctor assumed without actually stating it?

(1) Blood pressure of 170/110 is dangerous to the health of the patient.
(2) Medication can bring down blood pressure.
(3) Medication will reduce the patient's weight.
(4) The patient has not been exercising at all.
(5) Blood pressure varies greatly in the population at large.

Surely the doctor would not bother with the problem if he did not assume that the patient's blood pressure is too high for continued good health, so the answer choice is 1. Choice 2 is true, but it is not unstated; the doctor told the patient that medication would work. Since there is no reason to believe that the medication is used for weight reduction, choice 3 is wrong. Choice 4 is wrong because the prescription for limited exercise might just as easily mean that the patient has been doing too much. Choice 5 is true, but irrelevant.

If you are asked to find an unstated assumption, do not select one that is (a) stated in the information given; (b) untrue; (c) ambiguous; or (d) irrelevant.

EXAMPLE: **12.** Corals are tiny animals that obtain their energy from their close association with green algae. Fishes that eat corals do not live in deep water because

(1) the pressure is too great in deep water
(2) the fishes in deep water eat them
(3) sunlight does not penetrate into deep water
(4) there are no currents in deep water to carry nutrients to them
(5) it is too cold in deep water

This is one of the questions in which you are expected to know a few things and to put some ideas together. You should know that green algae need sunlight to grow, and that corals use energy for growth. The answer is choice 3. Some of the other answers may be true, but they are irrelevant.

EXAMPLE: **13.** Someone sees a high waterfall on the side of a cliff, and comments about it. Which of the following comments is probably based on opinion rather than fact?

(1) The waterfall is about 30 metres high.
(2) The valley into which it falls was carved by a glacier.
(3) The rock in the mountain is a form of granite.
(4) The speed of the water at the bottom of the fall is about 25 metres per second.
(5) A photograph of the fall would be really beautiful.

"Based on fact" is not the same as "factual." A statement is probably based on fact if it can be derived from one or more facts. Choices 1 and 4 could be determined by measurement or calculation—facts. Choices 2 and 3 could be determined from facts by any competent geologist. Since beauty is in the eye of the beholder, choice 5 is an opinion.

EXAMPLE: **14.** It is found that, when a stream becomes more muddy, the population of catfish increases. Three possible explanations are offered:

A. More catfish tend to make the water muddy.
B. Catfish thrive on invertebrates that live in mud.
C. Other fish cannot live in muddy water, so that catfish have less competition.

Which of these explanations is (are) feasible?

(1) A only
(2) B only
(3) C only
(4) A and B only
(5) B and C only

This question requires you to tell the differences between cause and effect. Is it possible that explanation A is true? No; the water became muddy before the catfish population increased. A cause can never come after its effect. In both explanation B and explanation C the water is already muddy, and both are reasonable hypotheses, so the answer is choice 5.

This type of question can be tricky. If one event follows another, the one that occurs first may or may not be the cause of the second. This is true even if the second invariably follows the first. It is not the crowing of the rooster that makes the sun rise. In the example given, the sequence of the two events establishes only that B and C are possible explanations, not that they must necessarily be true.

EXAMPLE: **15.** A chemical factory producing a detergent discovers that the output contains too many contaminating materials. Of the following, which is a conclusion based on the data?

(1) The amount of reactant A is twice as great as that of reactant B.
(2) The temperature of the reaction is 140°C.
(3) The pH of the reaction mixture is 5.4.
(4) The problem can be solved by adding an alkali.
(5) There is a contaminant in reactant A.

Fact or conclusion? All the statements except choice 4 are data, testable and presumably confirmed by measurement. Putting all the known facts together, the engineer might use his knowledge of the process to get an overall picture of what is happening. He can then draw the conclusion in choice 4.

A conclusion is a general statement that is not obtained from direct observation. It comes from an intelligent application of known principles to measurement data.

EVALUATION

We all have beliefs and ideas about many things. Most of our beliefs and general thinking are not scientific. Science cannot tell you what career to choose, whom to marry, whom to vote for, or what kind of music is best. In general, what science can do is to provide highly reliable, accurate, and testable answers to simple questions. To get these answers, you have to know the rules.

The evaluation questions test your ability to apply the rules of scientific analysis. The first step is to understand that there are many kinds of knowledge. Here is an analysis of the kinds of knowledge and the ways in which you may have to use them in answering the evaluation questions.

Facts or **data** are definite bits of information acquired by specific observation or measurement. If you are told that a ball is rolling along at 12 metres per second, that is a measurement. If true, it is a fact. You may be asked to determine whether some statement is a valid fact supported by the method of finding it. Sloppy experimental technique produces statements that look like facts, but are not dependable.

A **hypothesis** is a proposition, based on facts, that explains why the facts are as they are. It is a purely tentative statement, subject to modification or disproof when more facts are available. If you find that a shrub in the sunshine grows better than one of the same kind in the shade, you may advance the hypothesis that shrubs of that variety need sunshine for optimum growth. This can be tested by a carefully controlled experiment. The most common error that people make in evaluating scientific information is to accept a hypothesis as proof, without realizing the need for experimental confirmation. You may well be asked questions about whether certain given facts lead to a stated hypothesis.

A **control** is a necessary part of any experiment. The shrub mentioned above might be growing better than its counterpart in the shade because it had more water or better soil or better genes. To do the experiment, you would have to grow several genetically identical shrubs, all planted in the same soil and given the same water, fertilizer, and so on. The experiment will be valid only if all conditions are identical except one. Therefore one plant—the control—is grown in the shade, and the other in the sunshine. If the one in the sunshine grows better, it will then be valid to conclude that the operational factor is sunshine. In every experiment, the experimental system and the control differ by only one factor.

A **conclusion** can be the result of a controlled experiment, or of an intelligent application of known principles to the facts. A hypothesis becomes a conclusion when the data are strong enough to result in action. If that shrub really does do better in the sunshine, with all controls in place, it is reasonable to conclude that this particular plant should be grown in sunshine. You may be asked whether a certain conclusion can reasonably follow from the data given. You will have to distinguish between a conclusion and a hypothesis.

A **generalization** is a conclusion that applies in a wide variety of circumstances. Many experiments with green plants, for example, could produce the generalization that all of them need light in some degree or other. If you are asked whether a particular generalization is reasonable, look to see whether it applies widely.

A **value judgment** is an opinion based on cultural or emotional factors, rather than on scientific evidence. Opinions about esthetics, morality, religion, and interpersonal relationships play important and valid roles in our lives. Such opinions may improperly intrude, however, into the process of reaching scientific conclusions. You will be asked to distinguish value judgments from scientifically valid statements.

A **logical fallacy** is an erroneous conclusion reached by using data incorrectly. The commonest one is known as *post hoc ergo propter hoc*, which means "followed by, therefore caused by." Here is an example: I drink a glass of milk for breakfast every morning, and I always get sleepy. Does the milk make me sleepy? Maybe. Or maybe I would get sleepy even if I didn't drink the milk. The way out of this fallacy is a controlled experiment.

The example below will give you some idea of the sorts of questions that will test your ability to evaluate scientific statements.

EXAMPLE: **16.** A proposal to build a dam on a river is opposed by a group of citizens, offering various reasons. Which of the following reasons is based on a value judgment rather than scientific information?

(1) The river should be preserved because it is a habitat for much beautiful wildlife.
(2) The cost of the dam will be too high for the amount of electricity it produces.
(3) It is not possible to dam the river at the site selected because of the surface features of the land.
(4) The proposed site is on a fault, and the dam could be destroyed by an earthquake.
(5) The river carries so much silt that the lake formed by it would soon fill up and render the dam useless.

The word *beautiful* in choice 1 is a giveaway, specifying a value judgment. Whoever makes that argument sees an esthetic value in the preservation of wildlife. All the other objections are based on arguments that can be subjected to rigid testing, using established scientific principles.

EXAMPLE: **17.** The graph below shows the average growths of two groups of rats. The solid line represents a group grown under standard conditions by a supplier of laboratory animals; the dash line, a group raised in a laboratory and treated with pituitary extract.

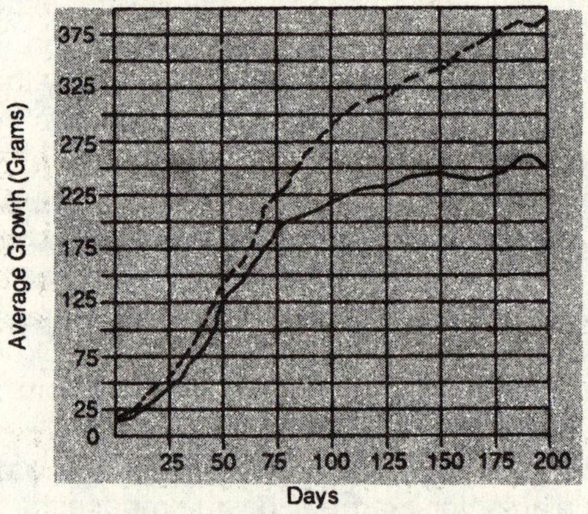

——Average growth of 38 untreated rats (control)
--- Average growth of 38 rats injected with anterior pituitary extract (experimental)

What is a proper conclusion from the experiment?

(1) It is known that pituitary extract stimulates growth, and the experiment confirms it.
(2) The difference between the control group and the experimental group is so clear that it can be concluded that pituitary extract stimulates growth.
(3) The difference between the two groups is insufficient to show that there is any difference in average growth.
(4) The experiment is useless because there is no reason to believe that the same result would be obtained with human beings.
(5) The experiment is inconclusive because there was no attempt to control the heredity of the animals or the conditions of their nurture.

Whether an experiment should have some obvious use is a value judgment that is not at issue here, so choice 4 is wrong. Choice 1 is wrong because it suggests that the outcome of the experiment was prejudiced in advance. At first this looks like a nice, neat experiment; the difference is marked, and so choice 3 is wrong. However, choice 2 is wrong because the controls are inadequate. The rats were not necessarily of the same breed, nor were they raised in the same place. They could differ also in their hereditary endowments, their feeding, and any number of other factors. The results of this experiment could lead to a hypothesis, but not a conclusion, and the answer is choice 5.

EXAMPLE: **18.** Which graph best represents what most likely happens to the temperature of the earth's atmosphere as the amount of carbon dioxide in the atmosphere increases over a period of many years?

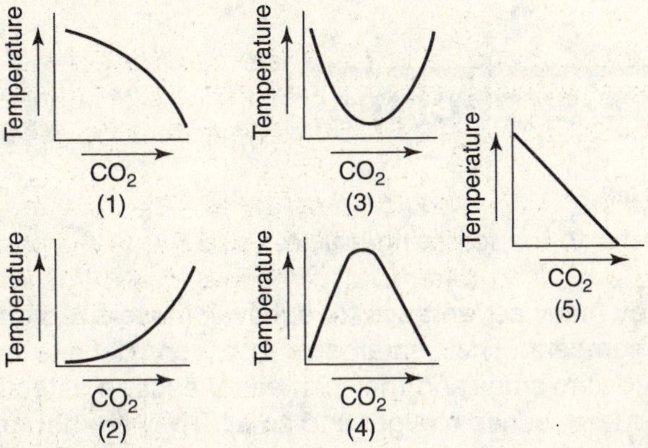

Carbon dioxide is a good absorber of infrared radiation. Energy radiated back to the atmosphere by the earth contains a large amount of infrared radiation. When this radiation is absorbed by the carbon dioxide in the atmosphere, the temperature of the atmosphere rises. As more infrared radiation is added to the atmosphere, the average temperature of the atmosphere will continue to rise. Graph (2) shows that, as the amount of carbon dioxide increases, the average temperature of the atmosphere increases.

EXAMPLE: **19.** Which of the following advertising claims for a toothpaste could not be confirmed or contradicted by laboratory tests?

(1) It contains 2% stannous fluoride.
(2) It removes plaque.
(3) It has a fresh taste.
(4) It is not abrasive.
(5) It prevents cavities.

Taste is a highly subjective value judgment, and what is a fresh taste for one person might be revolting to another, so the answer is choice 3.

EXAMPLE: **20.** A field biologist finds that for three successive winters the beavers in a pond were unusually active and the water in the pond was exceptionally high in the following spring.

Which of the following is an appropriate response?

(1) She concludes that the winter activity of the beavers raises the water level.
(2) She decides to see what happens to the water level in years in which the beavers are less active.

(3) She suggests the possibility that the high water level makes the beavers more active.
(4) She proposes limiting the winter activity of the beavers so as to avoid flooding.
(5) She suggests that there is no connection between the water level and the activity of the beavers.

Choice 1 is wrong because the evidence is insufficient for a conclusion; the fact that the rising water level followed the activity does not prove a cause-and-effect relationship. Choice 3 is wrong because an effect can never come before a cause. Choice 4 is wrong because there has been no suggestion that flooding is a problem, or that limiting the activity of the beavers will prevent it. Choice 5 is wrong because the evidence is sufficient to suggest the hypothesis that winter activity of beavers raises the water level. More investigation is called for, and choice 2 is a good idea.

PRACTICE EXERCISES

BIOLOGY

Items 1 to 3 refer to the following article.

Insects enjoy many advantages for survival. Insects reproduce often and in large numbers. Their small size is a very definite advantage. Their food needs are small and they can easily escape detection, especially with their keen sense of sight and smell. They are not fussy about diet and can adapt to changes, as illustrated by the new forms that have reproduced that defy human poisons. Camouflage helps many insects blend with the environment. The names assigned to such insects as the "walking stick" and the "dead leaf" are illustrations. Mimicry is another device used for protection and ultimate survival. Birds often turn down a meal of a viceroy butterfly that mimics the unpleasant-tasting monarch butterfly.

Let us bear in mind that we need some members of the insect world. For example, when other factors are absent, some species of insects transfer pollen from anthers of stamens to pistils of blossoms. Without pollination, fruit formation is impossible. Our pure silk comes from the material of the cocoon of an insect. Our honey is the result of the work of the honeybee.

1. Flowers of grasses consist of stamens and pistils only, with neither petals nor odor. Which of the following is a reasonable assumption about these flowers?
(1) Insects need excellent eyesight to find these flowers.
(2) These flowers do not have to be pollinated.
(3) The flowers are pollinated by wind.
(4) The flowers do not form seed.
(5) Grasses reproduce only by asexual means.

1. 1 2 3 4 5
|| || || || ||

2. What accounts for the survival of insects through the ages?
(A) mimicry and camouflage
(B) ability to pollinate blossoms
(C) body size

(1) A and B
(2) B and C
(3) C only
(4) A and C
(5) A, B, and C

2. 1 2 3 4 5
|| || || || ||

3. Without the insect world, all of the following are possible EXCEPT
(1) disease
(2) fruits
(3) nylon
(4) beeswax
(5) natural syrups

3. 1 2 3 4 5

Items 4 to 7 refer to the following information.

Plant hormones (auxins) can be produced in the laboratory. NAA is used on blossoms to produce fruit without pollination. These resulting seedless fruits have great economic value. The use of 2,4-D in killing weeds without damaging the grass on lawns is widespread. Botanists classify seedbearing plants into dicots and monocots. Interestingly enough, it has been found that in certain concentrations 2,4-D is more effective on dicots than on monocots. Actually they cause such abnormal growth that the dicot plant dies. Since most weeds are dicots and grass is a monocot, an effective chemical weed killer has been developed from our knowledge of plant hormones and taxonomy.

4. Which of the following is necessary in order for a flower to produce seeds?
(1) pollination
(2) hormones
(3) abnormal growth
(4) weed killers
(5) grass

4. 1 2 3 4 5

5. Taxonomy (the science of classification) has contributed to agronomy by
(1) producing new plant hormones
(2) devising more effective weed killers
(3) making seedless fruits possible
(4) producing better quality grass
(5) distinguishing which plants respond to weed killers

5. 1 2 3 4 5

6. How does 2,4-D effectively kill weeds?
(1) abnormal rapid growth of dicots
(2) abnormal rapid growth of monocots
(3) retarded growth of monocots
(4) retarded growth of dicots
(5) retarded growth of leaves

6. 1 2 3 4 5

7. A newly introduced plant may or may not be affected by 2,4-D. Which of the following will most probably be destroyed by 2,4-D?
(1) a weed
(2) a parasite
(3) a dicot
(4) an auxin
(5) a hormone

7. 1 2 3 4 5

Items 8 to 10 refer to the following information.

When a new individual is produced from a single parent cell or from two parent cells, the process of reproduction occurs. This life function differs from all the other life processes in that it preserves the species rather than ensuring the survival of the individual. To understand how a cell divides, one must consider the behaviour of the nuclear material and the cytoplasmic division. Mitosis is the process by which the hereditary material of the nucleus is doubled and then distributed into the daughter cells. This is accompanied by the division of the cytoplasmic material so that, as a result of cell division, normally two cells similar to the parent cell are produced. This is the basis of all forms of asexual reproduction in which a single parent is involved, as is the case in binary fission in single-celled organisms, such as amoebas, paramecia, and bacteria, or in the process of budding in yeast cells or sporulation in bread mould.

8. Which life function is more essential to the species than the individual?

(1) growth
(2) movement
(3) food manufacture
(4) reproduction
(5) protection

8. 1 2 3 4 5
|| || || || ||

9. Which of the following terms does NOT belong with the others?

(1) fertilization
(2) budding
(3) sporulation
(4) asexual reproduction
(5) binary fission

9. 1 2 3 4 5
|| || || || ||

10. Which of the following processes is a part of all the others?

(1) binary fission
(2) asexual reproduction
(3) sporulation
(4) budding
(5) mitosis

10. 1 2 3 4 5
|| || || || ||

<u>Items 11 to 13</u> refer to the following information.

Insects are so well adapted to survive that humans have to modify chemical warfare against them. Not too many years ago, dichlorodiphenyl-trichlorethane (DDT) was a potent weapon. But insects have a newly evolved immunity to DDT. Also, as a result of the criticism of the side effects of this chemical, chemists had to search for new insecticides. A good insecticide must destroy insects, but must not accumulate in the bodies of the fish and birds that feed on insects. An apparently effective insecticide that protected crops was recently found to drain off into rivers where the chemical killed fish.

11. Why is DDT no longer considered a good insecticide?

(1) Insects cannot adapt to DDT.
(2) DDT does not accumulate in the bodies of fish.
(3) DDT has bad side effects.
(4) DDT is a potent weapon.
(5) Birds do not feed on insects treated with DDT.

11. 1 2 3 4 5
|| || || || ||

12. In addition to the ability to destroy harmful insects, what other characteristic should a good insecticide have?

(1) It must be easily researched.
(2) It should not cause harm to other living forms.
(3) It must drain off into rivers.
(4) It should kill harmful birds.
(5) It must cause insects to develop immunity.

12. 1 2 3 4 5
|| || || || ||

13. What causes an insecticide to suddenly lose its effectiveness?
(1) Insects learn to avoid old poisons.
(2) DDT is no longer effective.
(3) Insects have keen senses.
(4) Valuable insects are often destroyed by a particular poison.
(5) Insects give rise to new poison-resistant forms.

13. 1 2 3 4 5

Items 14 and 15 refer to the following information.

Asepsis refers to a technique that avoids the introduction of viable microorganisms. Sterilization and disinfection are processes that eliminate viable microbes; the terms are essentially synonymous, but the latter is usually limited to the use of chemicals that render infectious organisms non-viable. Antibacterial effects are divided into bacteriostasis, or reversible inhibition of the multiplication of bacteria, and irreversible bactericidal action, which "kills" them. The terms *disinfectant*, *germicide*, and *bactericide* are synonymous for bactericidal agents. Antiseptics are antibacterial substances that can be applied to body surfaces, cavities, or wounds to prevent or combat bacterial infection; these compounds do not necessarily completely sterilize the treated surface. Chemotherapeutics are antibacterial (or, more generally, antimicrobial) substances that are sufficiently nontoxic within the tissues as well as on body surfaces.

14. The process of preventing the reproduction of bacteria without killing them is called
(1) asepsis
(2) disinfection
(3) bacteriostasis
(4) antisepsis
(5) chemotherapy

14. 1 2 3 4 5

15. All of the following are antibacterial substances EXCEPT
(1) germicide
(2) bactericide
(3) asepsis
(4) disinfectant
(5) antiseptic

15. 1 2 3 4 5

Items 16 and 17 refer to the following information.

It is well known that plants tend to grow toward the light, a process known as phototropism. Research with plant hormones, known as auxins, has disclosed the mechanisms at work. One such mechanism results in the bending of a stem toward the light. In the grass family, the tip of the growing stem produces an auxin. When the light strikes one side of the tip, the auxin moves to the other side. It then diffuses down the stem, where it promotes the elongation of the cells below the tip. As the cells on the dark side elongate, the stem bends toward the light.

16. What causes a stem to turn toward the light?
(1) phototropism
(2) the need for light for photosynthesis
(3) an auxin that controls cell elongation
(4) the effect of light in stimulating growth
(5) a plant hormone produced in the dark

16. 1 2 3 4 5

17. Which of the following best describes auxins?
(1) leaf structures
(2) stem tips
(3) tropisms
(4) plant hormones
(5) light filters

17. 1 2 3 4 5
|| || || || ||

Items 18 to 20 refer to the following article.

Why are proteins so distinctive? To answer this question, attention must be given to the *nucleic acids*. Either directly or indirectly, *nucleic acids assemble proteins* from amino acids. Today, one of the most exciting areas of biological research centres around trying to discover just *how* nucleic acids perform this protein-building function.

Like proteins, nucleic acids are large molecules with high molecular weights. They are, perhaps, the most fascinating of all macromolecules. Nucleic acids are found in all living organisms from viruses to humans. They received their name because of their discovery in the nuclei of white blood cells and fish sperm by Miescher in 1869. However, it is now well established that nucleic acids occur outside of the cell nucleus as well.

Nucleic acids serve two main functions. First, they are a sort of molecular "paper" upon which the blueprint for the construction of a new individual is written. This, essentially, is the function of *deoxyribonucleic acid*, or DNA.

But nucleic acids are more than carriers of the hereditary message. They also serve to put this message into action. This active phase is carried out by *ribonucleic acid*, or RNA.

DNA is generally found within the cell combined with protein to form *nucleoprotein*. In cells of higher plants and animals, nucleoprotein is found within the cell nucleus as rod-shaped bodies called *chromosomes*. Where there is no definite nuclear area, as in bacterial cells, nucleoprotein is scattered throughout the entire cell. RNA, depending upon its specific molecular type, is found both inside and outside of the cell nucleus. In *cells without nuclei*, RNA may be found anywhere within the cell.

18. What are the building blocks of proteins?
(1) DNA
(2) RNA
(3) nucleoprotein
(4) amino acids
(5) nucleic acids

18. 1 2 3 4 5
|| || || || ||

19. Where are nucleic acids found?
(1) only in human cells
(2) only in viruses
(3) in all living cells
(4) only in white blood cells
(5) only in fish sperm

19. 1 2 3 4 5
|| || || || ||

20. All of the following describe nucleic acids EXCEPT
(1) They are found in all living things.
(2) They have a high molecular weight.
(3) They are micromolecular.
(4) They are carriers of hereditary traits.
(5) They are assemblers of proteins.

20. 1 2 3 4 5
|| || || || ||

Items 21 to 25 refer to the following article.

The timber wolf occupies an important position in the food chain. Like any other large carnivore, it plays a major role in keeping populations of smaller animals in balance. Its diet includes many rodents. Even as a deer killer, it is more helpfully selective than its rival predator, the human.

The human hunter kills for sport and pride, most often shooting the finest member of the deer herd, but the wolf kills for food alone, picking off the weakest, the oldest, and the sickliest. Thus, humans lower the quality of the herd, but the wolf preserves its health and keeps its numbers geared to the sustaining support of the land. The result is good for the deer, good for the wolf, and good for the browsing area.

Recently a project was launched in Minnesota to extend the range of the wolf. The plan is to trap a small pack of wolves there and transplant them to a new wild environment in northern Michigan. At one time wolves inhabited this area but are now almost extinct there. The purpose of the project is to have the wolves breed and preserve the species. In this way, Northern Michigan University and several wildlife organizations that are sponsoring the experiment will be doing a service to preserve a creature that is useful in the natural environment. They hope also to explode the myth of the wolf's wickedness.

21. Which deer are killed by the wolf?
(1) weakest
(2) strongest
(3) best specimens
(4) those that eat rodents
(5) fastest

21. 1 2 3 4 5

22. In connection with deer population why is the human race more destructive than the wolf?
(1) The wolf destroys only browsing areas.
(2) The hunter preserves the health of the herd.
(3) The hunter shoots deer for food alone.
(4) The hunter shoots the weakest, the oldest, and the sickliest deer.
(5) The hunter shoots the finest members of the herd.

22. 1 2 3 4 5

23. What is the purpose of the Northern Michigan University Project?
(1) trap the wolves in Michigan and export them to Minnesota
(2) increase the range of the wolf in Michigan
(3) increase the number of deer in Michigan
(4) keep wolves out of Michigan
(5) prove the wolf's wickedness

23. 1 2 3 4 5

24. Which of the following best describes the wolf's position in the food chain?
(1) important because it keeps the population of its prey in balance
(2) unimportant because it preys mostly on rodents
(3) unimportant because it is a large carnivore
(4) unimportant because it leaves healthy deer alone
(5) important because it lives in the midst of tall timber

24. 1 2 3 4 5

25. Two examples of predators mentioned in the selection are
(1) wolf and man
(2) wolf and deer
(3) man and deer
(4) wolf and rodent
(5) rodent and deer

25. 1 2 3 4 5

Items 26 to 28 refer to the following information.

The food energy in a food chain may be transferred by predators, scavengers, or symbionts. A *predator* kills prey and then eats it. *Scavengers* consume dead animals or plants. Many bacteria, yeasts, and molds live on dead organic material. They are known as saprophytes as contrasted with parasites that live on living things. A *symbiont* is a member of a nutritive relationship (symbiosis) in which neither partner causes harm to the other. The lichen, which grows on a rock and may ultimately erode the rock, is an alga and a fungus. The alga with its chlorophyll carries on photosynthesis, and the fungus absorbs water for itself and the alga. Such a symbiotic relationship is known as mutualism. Where only one member benefits, with no harm to the other member of the symbiotic relationship, the term *commensalism* is applied.

26. Which term describes the type of nutritional relationship in which both symbionts benefit from the association?
(1) commensalism
(2) autotrophism
(3) parasitism
(4) saprophytism
(5) mutualism

26. 1 2 3 4 5
|| || || || ||

27. Many orchids live rooted high in trees, where they can receive the effects of sunlight but do not damage the trees. The orchids would be classified as
(1) parasites
(2) saprophytes
(3) commensals
(4) scavengers
(5) mutual symbionts

27. 1 2 3 4 5
|| || || || ||

28. In a lichen, why does the fungus need the alga to survive?
(1) the fungus cannot absorb enough water
(2) neither the alga nor the fungus alone can grow on rock
(3) the fungus provides the alga with protection against drying
(4) the fungus cannot carry on photosynthesis
(5) the fungus cannot absorb nutrients from the soil

28. 1 2 3 4 5
|| || || || ||

Items 29 to 33 refer to the following information.

The higher forms of plants and animals, such as seed plants and vertebrates, are similar or alike in many respects but decidedly different in others. For example, both of these groups of organisms carry on digestion, respiration, reproduction, conduction, and growth and exhibit sensitivity to various stimuli. On the other hand, a number of basic differences are evident. Plants have no excretory systems comparable to those of animals. Plants have no heart or similar pumping organ. Plants are very limited in their movements. Plants have nothing similar to the animal nervous system. In addition, animals cannot synthesize carbohydrates from inorganic substances. Animals do not have special regions of growth, comparable to terminal and lateral meristems in plants, which persist throughout the life span of the organism. And finally the animal cell has no wall, only a membrane, but plant cell walls are more rigid, usually thicker, and may be composed of such substances as cellulose, lignin, pectin, cutin, and suberin. These characteristics are important to an understanding of living organisms and their functions and should, consequently, be carefully considered in plant and animal studies.

29. Which of the following do animals lack?
(1) ability to react to stimuli
(2) ability to conduct substances from one place to another
(3) reproduction by gametes
(4) a cell membrane
(5) a terminal growth region

29. 1 2 3 4 5

30. Plants have rigid cell walls, but animals do not. This is probably related to the difference between animals and plants in the function of
(1) respiration
(2) photosynthesis
(3) excretion
(4) responsiveness
(5) locomotion

30. 1 2 3 4 5

31. Which of these do only plants possess?
(1) specialized organs for circulation
(2) excretory organs
(3) organs of locomotion
(4) the ability to manufacture carbohydrates
(5) specialized nerve tissue

31. 1 2 3 4 5

32. Which of the following do plants lack?
(1) rigid cell walls
(2) pumping structures
(3) special regions of growth
(4) structures for reproduction
(5) a digestive process

32. 1 2 3 4 5

33. Which of these processes are carried on by plants and animals?
(1) the synthesis of carbohydrates
(2) conduction
(3) the manufacture of cellulose
(4) the production of cutin
(5) excretion through excretory organs

33. 1 2 3 4 5

<u>Items 34 to 36</u> refer to the following information.

The natural successions of plant and animal communities refer to the changes in animal and plant life of a region as a result of environmental changes. The study of organisms in relation to their environment is known as *ecology*. With changes in environment, the previous animal and plant life disappears and is succeeded by new types, adapted to new conditions. Thus, a bare rock area can support the primitive algae and lichens. Gradually, as the rock decomposes to become soil, the mosses, grasses, and quick-growing weeds appear, followed by small shrubs. As the soil becomes deeper and more porous, the larger evergreens appear, crowding out the grasses and shrubs. If these rocky, shallow soils change to deeper ones of firmer loam, the evergreens are replaced with hardwoods, such as maple and beech.

34. Which of these is the main concern of ecology?
(1) methods of preventing runoff of water
(2) erosion of land
(3) the relationship between the environment and living things
(4) the effect of living things on the environment
(5) changes in plants

34. 1 2 3 4 5

35. After a lava flow produces new rock, which of the following would be the first to appear?
(1) insects
(2) grasses
(3) mosses
(4) rodents
(5) lichens

35. 1 2 3 4 5

36. Which of the following represents the most probable order of natural succession of plants in a barren rocky area?
(1) mosses, grasses, shrubs, trees
(2) lichens, mosses, grasses, shrubs
(3) lichens, grasses, shrubs, mosses
(4) grasses, shrubs, trees, mosses
(5) mosses, lichens, grasses, shrubs

36. 1 2 3 4 5

Items 37 to 39 refer to the following information.

Chloroplats may assume many forms, and vary widely in number per cell, in different plants. In some algae, such as the filamentous *Spirogyra*, only a single chloroplast is present in each cell. When the cell divides, it divides at the same time. In contrast, a cell in the spongy part of a grass leaf may have 30–50 chloroplasts. Their division, which occurs in the immature, or proplastid, state, is not correlated with cell division in any exact way. The grana may be missing in some chloroplasts, as in some brown algae, to be replaced by long membranes running the length of the chloroplast, but these presumably function in the same manner as the grana. The blue-green algae, on the other hand, lack definite chloroplasts; instead they possess loosely arranged membranes in the cytoplasm on which the photosynthetic pigments are layered. Only in bacterial cells do we find a photosynthetic capacity associated with a nonmembranous structure. Here the vacuolarlike *chromatophores* are the photosynthetic units, but we know little about the molecular arrangement of the light-absorbing pigments. However, bacteria kept in the dark lose their chromatophore and are no longer photosynthetic; the chromatophore thus behaves as the chloroplast of *Euglena* and is its functional, but not structural, equivalent.

37. Chloroplasts are important to the cell because they control
(1) cell division
(2) grana
(3) photosynthesis
(4) pigmentation
(5) filamentation

37. 1 2 3 4 5

38. Which of the following is a correct statement?
(1) Brown algae have no chlorophyll.
(2) No bacteria are photosynthetic.
(3) All algae have cells with chloroplasts.
(4) Cells of a grass leaf have chloroplasts.
(5) All chloroplasts are composed of grana.

38. 1 2 3 4 5

39. How are chromatophores and chloroplasts similar?

(A) structure (B) function (C) location

(1) A only
(2) B only
(3) C only
(4) A and B
(5) A, B, and C

39. 1 2 3 4 5

Items 40 to 46 refer to the following article.

Whenever microorganisms have successfully invaded the body and are growing at the expense of the tissues, the process is called an infection. The term *infection* should always imply the existence of an abnormal state or unnatural condition resulting from the harmful action of microorgansims. In other words, the simple presence of an organism is not sufficient to cause disease.

Infection may arise from the admission of microorganisms to the tissues through the gastrointestinal tract, through the upper air passages, through wounds made by contaminated teeth or claws of animals or by contaminated weapons, and by the bite of suctorial insects. Another type of infection sometimes occurs when for some reason the body has become vulnerable to the pathogenic action of bacteria whose normal habitat is the body.

The reaction of the body to the attack of an invading organism results in the formation of substances of a specific nature. Those reaction bodies that circulate mainly in the blood serum are known as antibodies and are classified according to their activity. Some, known as antitoxins, neutralize poisonous substances produced by the infecting organism. Others, called bacteriolysins, destroy bacteria by dissolving them. Opsonins or bacteriotropins prepare the bacteria for destruction by phagocytes; precipitins and agglutinins have the property of grouping the invading agents into small clumps of precipitates. The formation of defensive substances is specific for each organism.

40. Which of the following conditions illustrates an infection?

(1) A guinea pig is exposed to diphtheria toxin.
(2) A nurse taking care of a tubercular patient inhales some tuberculosis bacilli.
(3) A man cuts his finger with a dirty knife. He uses no antiseptic.
(4) A student examines his saliva with a microscope. Under high power he observes some streptococci.
(5) Malaria parasites in the blood cause chills and fever.

40. 1 2 3 4 5

41. Since each antibody is specific for the invading organism, it follows that

(1) the body can produce only a small number of different kinds of antibodies
(2) the anti-diphtheria antibody will not protect against tetanus
(3) there are many kinds of invading organisms that cannot be attacked by antibodies
(4) an individual cannot be immune to more than one kind of disease organism at a time
(5) immunity to some diseases weakens the body's ability to protect itself against others

41. 1 2 3 4 5

42. Which of the following statements is true of phagocytes?
(1) Opsonins are also called phagocytes.
(2) Opsonins prepare bacteria for destruction by phagocytes.
(3) Phagocytes destroy opsonins.
(4) Bacteriotropins destroy phagocytes.
(5) Phagocytes prepare bacteria for destruction by opsonins.

42. 1 2 3 4 5
|| || || || ||

43. Which of the following is a correct statement?
(1) The white blood corpuscles help ward off infection by distributing antibodies to all parts of the body.
(2) A disease organism that lives in the body of a person always has a bad effect on the person.
(3) Antibodies are classified according to the type of organism they attack.
(4) Infection is usually accompanied by an abnormal state of the body.
(5) Antitoxins are formed against every organism that enters the body.

43. 1 2 3 4 5
|| || || || ||

44. All of the following are antibodies EXCEPT
(1) phagocytes
(2) antitoxins
(3) bacteriolysins
(4) opsonins
(5) precipitins

44. 1 2 3 4 5
|| || || || ||

45. All of the following might result in infection EXCEPT
(1) inhalation of dust particles
(2) a drink of contaminated water
(3) a bite from a mosquito
(4) a cut with a knife
(5) a fly landing on the skin

45. 1 2 3 4 5
|| || || || ||

46. By what process do agglutinins destroy invading organisms?
(1) dissolving
(2) neutralizing
(3) clumping
(4) engulfing
(5) digesting

46. 1 2 3 4 5
|| || || || ||

<u>Items 47 to 49</u> are based on the following information.

Relationships between organisms are classified according to the way they affect each other. Below are five types of relationships.

(1) parasitism—a relationship in which an organism lives on another organism and harms the organism that it lives on.
(2) commensalism—a relationship in which one organism is benefited and the other is neither harmed nor benefited.
(3) saprophytism—a relationship in which an organism feeds on the dead remains or product of other organisms.
(4) mutualism—a relationship between two organisms in which both organisms benefit from the association.
(5) cannibalism—a relationship in which an organism feeds on the flesh of its own kind.

Each of the following statements describes a relationship that refers to one of the categories just defined. For each item, choose the one category that best describes the relationship.

47. The relationship between athlete's foot fungus and humans is best classified as

(1) parasitism
(2) commensalism
(3) saprophytism
(4) mutualism
(5) cannibalism

47. 1 2 3 4 5

48. Nitrogen-fixing bacteria enrich the soil by producing nitrates beneficial to green plants. The bacteria live in nodules located on the roots of legumes. These nodules provide a favourable environment for the bacteria to grow and reproduce. The relationship between these bacteria and the leguminous plant is an example of

(1) parasitism
(2) commensalism
(3) saprophytism
(4) mutualism
(5) cannibalism

48. 1 2 3 4 5

49. Bacteria of decay decompose dead plants and animals, releasing ammonia into the environment. This relationship would best be described as

(1) parasitism
(2) commensalism
(3) saprophytism
(4) mutualism
(5) cannibalism

49. 1 2 3 4 5

Items 50 to 55 refer to the following statement.

At the beginning of the nineteenth century, it was generally believed that any features of an individual could be inherited by offspring. Thus, if a man lifted weights and developed muscles, he might expect his children to be muscular. Jean Lamarck developed a theory of evolution in which the inheritance of acquired characters was the main driving force for change through the generations.

Charles Darwin accepted the concept of inheritance of acquired characters, but he believed that it played only a minor role. The main driving force of evolution, he said, is natural selection. This means that the individuals that survive and reproduce are those that are best adapted to the environment in which they live. Adaptation improves generation by generation because the best adapted individuals pass on their favorable traits to their offspring.

Later, August Weismann's theory of the continuity of the germ plasm denied that acquired characters could be inherited. He said that reproductive cells are somehow isolated from the rest of the body, and cannot be affected by any changes in the environment. This means that only features that were inherited by an individual can be passed on to offspring. Modern genetics has substantiated this theory; genes that combine at fertilization remain unaffected by the environment throughout life and pass into the gametes. The theory of inheritance of acquired characters is dead, and Darwin's idea of natural selection remains a cornerstone of all theories of evolution.

50. Why was Darwin able to accept the theory of inheritance of acquired characters?
(1) He did not know of Lamarck's work.
(2) He had not gathered enough information.
(3) There was good experimental evidence for it.
(4) There was then no knowledge of the gene.
(5) Weismann had developed a theory to explain it.

50. 1 2 3 4 5

51. How would someone using Lamarck's theory of evolution probably explain the development in South American monkeys of a strong prehensile tail?
(1) There was a mutation that made the tails strong.
(2) The gene for a strong tail was dominant.
(3) The monkeys interbred with other kinds.
(4) The tail muscles were strengthened by use.
(5) Strong-tailed monkeys left more offspring.

51. 1 2 3 4 5

52. Which of these theories has been discredited by the development of modern genetics?
(1) There is variation within a species.
(2) The best-adapted individuals survive.
(3) Inherited features are passed on to offspring.
(4) Acquired characters are inherited.
(5) Development is controlled by genes.

52. 1 2 3 4 5

53. Why have certain strains of bacteria that were susceptible to penicillin in the past now become resistant?
(1) The mutation rate must have increased naturally.
(2) The strains have become resistant because they needed to do so for survival.
(3) A mutation was retained and passed on to succeeding generations because it had high survival value.
(4) The principal forces influencing the pattern of survival in a population are isolation and mating.
(5) Penicillin strains became less effective.

53. 1 2 3 4 5

54. Which of the following statements is a modern expression of the theory of the continuity of the germ plasm?
(1) Acquired characters may be inherited.
(2) Genes are not altered to suit environmental demands.
(3) Natural selection is an important factor in evolution.
(4) Evolution produces better-adapted forms.
(5) Heredity changes by gene mutation.

54. 1 2 3 4 5

55. In any species, which organisms are most likely to survive and reproduce?
(1) the largest
(2) the strongest
(3) the best adapted
(4) the most prolific
(5) the most intelligent

55. 1 2 3 4 5

Items 56 to 60 refer to the following information.

Cholesterol is a fatty substance that is manufactured by the liver and has many important functions in the human body. It is found in all animal fats, but not in any plant product. Cholesterol circulates in the blood, combined with proteins, in two forms: HDL and LDL. Research has shown that if there are high levels of LDL, fatty material is deposited inside the arteries, restricting the flow of blood. This is especially dangerous in the arteries of the heart and the brain. HDL is a form in which the deposits are removed from the arteries. Saturated fats and oils such as coconut oil and the solid fats of animals tend to raise the LDL level in the blood. On the other hand, exercise and unsaturated vegetable oils, such as olive oil, tend to raise the HDL level.

56. All of the following foods would tend to raise the LDL level in the blood EXCEPT
(1) bacon
(2) coconut candy
(3) corn oil
(4) beefsteak
(5) pepperoni pizza

56. 1 2 3 4 5
|| || || || ||

57. How does exercise benefit the arteries?
(1) It lowers the cholesterol level.
(2) It raises the LDL level.
(3) It strengthens the artery walls.
(4) It strengthens the body muscles.
(5) It raises the HDL level.

57. 1 2 3 4 5
|| || || || ||

58. What is a dangerous result of fatty deposits on arteries?
(1) high cholesterol levels
(2) lipid deposits
(3) dietary deficiencies
(4) heart attacks
(5) obesity

58. 1 2 3 4 5
|| || || || ||

59. What kind of evidence probably led to the conclusion that high blood cholesterol levels are undesirable?
(1) People with high cholesterol levels suffer from indigestion.
(2) The rate of heart attack is greater in people with high cholesterol levels.
(3) Statistics show that people with high cholesterol levels are often overweight.
(4) Cholesterol is a main ingredient of blood clots.
(5) Saturated fats in the diet tend to elevate the blood cholesterol level.

59. 1 2 3 4 5
|| || || || ||

60. According to modern medicine, which of these should most definitely be avoided to prevent heart attacks and strokes?
(1) candy
(2) raisins
(3) animal fats
(4) nuts
(5) all oily foods

60. 1 2 3 4 5
|| || || || ||

<u>Items 61 to 65</u> refer to the following information.

The nuclei of body cells contain two complete sets of chromosomes, on which the genes are located. In the process of mitosis, every chromosome is exactly copied so that each exists in duplicate. When the cell divides, the duplicates separate into different daughter cells so that each daughter cell still has two sets. In meiosis, on the other hand, reproductive cells are formed that have only one set of chromosomes per cell.

61. A plant cell with 12 chromosomes undergoes normal mitosis. What is the total number of chromosomes in each of the resulting daughter cells?

(1) 4
(2) 6
(3) 12
(4) 18
(5) 24

61. 1 2 3 4 5

62. In what specialized organ would meiotic cell division occur in a multicellular animal?

(1) kidneys
(2) gametes
(3) cytoplasmic organelles
(4) chromosomes
(5) gonads

62. 1 2 3 4 5

63. Which of the following statements describes the two daughter cells that result from the normal mitotic division of the original parent cell?

(1) the same number of chromosomes but genes different from those of parent cell
(2) the same number of chromosomes and genes identical to those of parent cell
(3) one-half of the number of chromosomes but genes different from those of the parent cell
(4) one-half of the number of chromosomes and genes identical to those of the parent cell
(5) different number of chromosomes and genes that are similar

63. 1 2 3 4 5

64. What process changes the number of sets of chromosomes from one per cell to two?

(1) mitosis
(2) gamete formation
(3) fertilization
(4) gene duplication
(5) meiosis

64. 1 2 3 4 5

65. Mitosis is a complex and elaborate process. Why is it important for the life of the organism?

(1) It places genetic information in all cells.
(2) It distributes chromosomes into different cells.
(3) It assures that each kind of tissue will get the special genes it needs.
(4) It controls the passage of materials into the cells.
(5) It produces enough cells to make up the body.

65. 1 2 3 4 5

---

66. Which assumption is the basis for the use of the fossil record as evidence for evolution?

(1) Fossils have been found to show a complete record of the evolution of all mammals.
(2) In undisturbed layers of the earth's crust, the oldest fossils are found in the lowest layers.
(3) All fossils can be found embedded in rocks.
(4) All fossils were formed at the same time.
(5) All fossils are found in sedimentary rock.

66. 1 2 3 4 5

67. The graph shows the relationship between the number of cases of children with Down's syndrome per 1000 births and maternal age.

67. 1 2 3 4 5

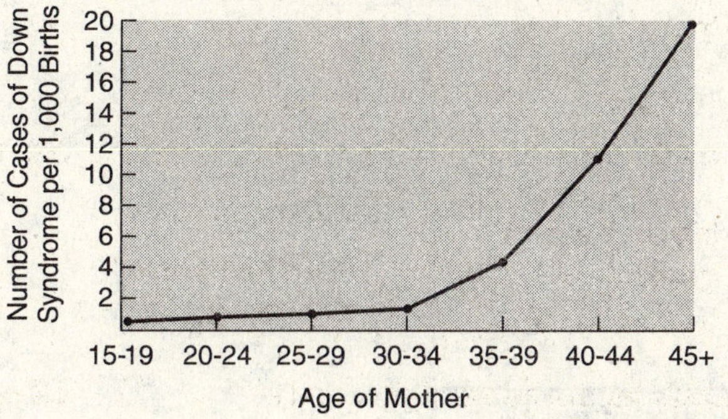

According to the graph, the incidence of Down's syndrome
(1) generally decreases as maternal age increases
(2) is about nine times less at age 45 than at age 30
(3) stabilizes at 2 per 1000 births after age 35
(4) is greater at age 15 than at age 35
(5) is about nine times greater at age 45 than at age 30

Items 68 to 70 are based on the following graphs.

The graphs show data on some environmental factors acting in a large lake.

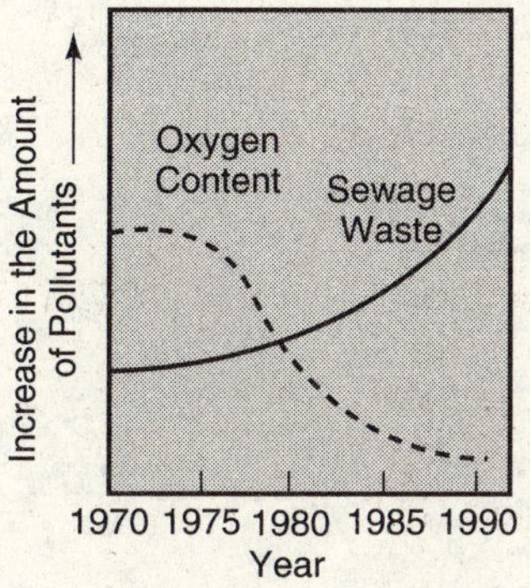

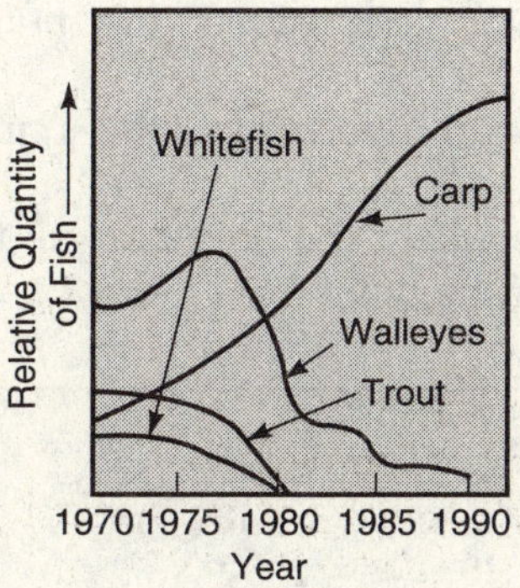

68. Which relationship can be correctly inferred from the data presented?
(1) As oxygen content decreases, the carp population decreases.
(2) As oxygen content decreases, the trout population increases.
(3) Sewage waste and oxygen content are not related.
(4) As sewage waste increases, the oxygen content increases.
(5) As sewage waste increases, the oxygen content decreases.

68. 1 2 3 4 5

69. Between what years did the greatest change in the lake's whitefish population occur?
(1) 1970 and 1975
(2) 1975 and 1980
(3) 1980 and 1982
(4) 1983 and 1985
(5) 1986 and 1990

69. 1 2 3 4 5

70. Which of the fish species appears able to withstand the greatest degree of oxygen depletion?
(1) trout
(2) trout and walleye
(3) walleye
(4) whitefish
(5) carp

70. 1 2 3 4 5

Item 71 is based on the following information.

A green plant was placed in a test tube, and a light illuminated the plant. The light was placed at varying distances from the plant. The bubbles of O_2 given off by the plant were counted. The table shows the data collected during this experiment.

Distance of light from plant (cm)	Number of bubbles per minute produced by plant
10	60
20	25
30	10
40	5

71. Which conclusion can be drawn from this investigation?
(1) As the distance from the light increases, the number of bubbles produced decreases.
(2) As the distance from the light increases, the number of bubbles produced increases.
(3) As the distance from the light decreases, the number of bubbles decreases.
(4) As the distance from the light decreases, the number of bubbles produced increases.
(5) There is no relationship between the number of bubbles produced and the distance of the plant from the light.

71. 1 2 3 4 5

Item 72 is based on the following graph.

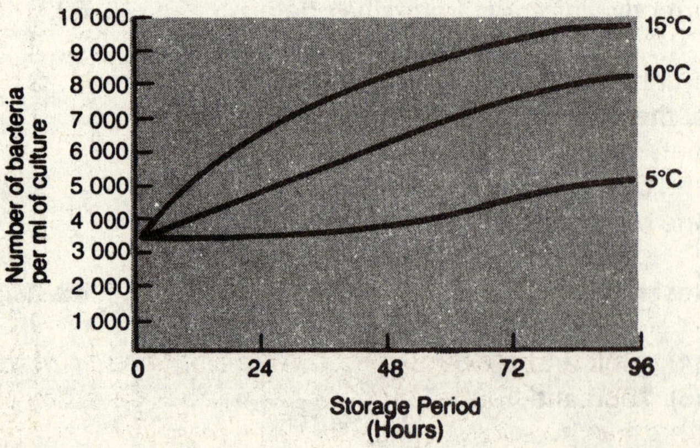

72. The graph was developed as a result of an investigation of bacterial counts of three identical cultures grown at different temperatures. Which conclusion may be correctly drawn from this graph?
(1) The culture contains no bacteria.
(2) Refrigeration retards bacterial reproduction.
(3) Temperature is unrelated to the bacterial reproduction rate.
(4) Bacteria cannot grow at a temperature of 5°C.
(5) Refrigeration increases bacterial reproduction.

72. 1 2 3 4 5
|| || || || ||

73. A drug company tested a new medication before putting it on the commercial market. Pills without medication were given to 500 test subjects in group A and pills containing medication were given to 500 test subjects in group B. In this experiment, the individuals in group A served as the
(1) host
(2) variable
(3) control
(4) hypothesis
(5) generalization

73. 1 2 3 4 5
|| || || || ||

Turn to the answer key and answer analysis which follow.

What's Your Score?

________ right, ________ wrong

Excellent	65–73
Good	48–64
Fair	37–47

If your score is low, don't get discouraged. Perhaps biology is a difficult subject for you. Try to find out why you failed. The analysis of correct answers which follows will help you to pinpoint your errors. If your mistake was lack of information, turn to the "Glossary of Scientific Terms" (page 362) and look up the meanings of the words you did not understand. If it was a mistake in interpretation, review the analysis of the question.

ANSWER KEY

1. **3**	10. **5**	18. **4**	26. **5**	34. **3**	42. **2**	50. **4**	58. **4**	66. **2**
2. **4**	11. **3**	19. **3**	27. **3**	35. **5**	43. **4**	51. **4**	59. **2**	67. **5**
3. **4**	12. **2**	20. **3**	28. **4**	36. **2**	44. **1**	52. **4**	60. **3**	68. **5**
4. **1**	13. **5**	21. **1**	29. **5**	37. **3**	45. **5**	53. **3**	61. **3**	69. **2**
5. **5**	14. **3**	22. **5**	30. **5**	38. **4**	46. **3**	54. **2**	62. **5**	70. **5**
6. **1**	15. **3**	23. **2**	31. **4**	39. **2**	47. **1**	55. **3**	63. **2**	71. **1**
7. **3**	16. **3**	24. **1**	32. **2**	40. **5**	48. **4**	56. **3**	64. **3**	72. **2**
8. **4**	17. **4**	25. **1**	33. **2**	41. **2**	49. **3**	57. **5**	65. **1**	73. **3**
9. **1**								

ANSWER ANALYSIS

1. **3** With neither petals nor odor, these flowers would not attract insects, so pollination must be by some other means.
2. **4** Insects can escape enemies by mimicry and camouflage. The small body size of insects permits them to hide from enemies and also reduces food requirements. The ability to pollinate blossoms may help the plant but has no survival value for the insect.

3. **4** Not all causative agents of disease are carried by insects. Some fruits would develop without insects by wind pollination or self-pollination. Nylon is synthetic. Syrups are usually products of sugar.
4. **1** The passage says flowers that are not pollinated produce no seed.
5. **5** Taxonomy distinguishes dicots from monocots, which are immune to the weed killer.
6. **1** The weed killer 2,4-D causes an abnormal growth of the dicot plant.
7. **3** See item 6.
8. **4** Reproduction preserves the species.
9. **1** Fertilization is a sexual process, while all the others are asexual.
10. **5** All reproductive processes must include the division of cells by mitosis.
11. **3** DDT is responsible for many undesirable side effects.
12. **2** One of the reasons DDT had to be replaced was its effect on fish and birds.
13. **5** Insects that have immunity to DDT survive and produce offspring with this immunity. This produces a large population of insects that can resist the insecticide.
14. **3** Bacteriostasis means stopping the reproduction of bacteria without killing them.
15. **3** Asepsis is the condition of preventing the introduction of harmful microorganisms. All of the other choices are chemicals that destroy harmful microorganisms.
16. **3** It is the effect of the auxin on the dark side of the stem that bends the stem. Choice 1 is merely the name of the process, not a statement of causation. Choice 2 tells why the bending is useful, but does not explain how it happens.
17. **4** An auxin is a chemical substance that moves through the plant and carries instructions for growth. This is a hormone.
18. **4** Nucleic acids assemble proteins from amino acid building blocks.
19. **3** Nucleic acids are present in all living things.
20. **3** Nucleic acids are large molecules (macromolecular).
21. **1** The wolf kills only for food and eliminates the weakest, the oldest, and the sickliest deer.
22. **5** Humans kill for sport and pride and try to pick off the finest specimen of the herd.
23. **2** The project is aimed at exporting wolves from Minnesota into northern Michigan to preserve the species and extend their range there.
24. **1** The wolf occupies an important position in the food chain by keeping populations of smaller animals in balance. In addition, the wolf keeps the number of deer geared to the sustaining support of the land.
25. **1** The end of the first paragraph compares the wolf to its rival predator, man. It thus identifies both as predators.
26. **5** Mutualism refers to a type of symbiotic relationship in which both members benefit from the relationship. Commensalism is a relationship wherein only one member benefits, with no harm to the other member of the symbiotic relationship. In parasitism and saprophytism, only one member benefits, but at the expense of the other. An independent organism, such as a green plant, is an example of autotrophism.
27. **3** Orchids benefit from their position in the tree, but do not harm the tree. This is the definition of commensalism.
28. **4** The passage says that it is the alga that performs photosynthesis for the benefit of both.
29. **5** Animals do not have special regions of growth, comparable to terminal and lateral meristems in plants, which persist throughout the life span of the organism.
30. **5** The rigid cell walls severely limit the flexibility of the plant body, so that it is unable to move freely.
31. **4** Green plants have the ability to synthesize carbohydrates from inorganic substances (carbon dioxide and water) in the presence of light.
32. **2** Plants have no heart or similar pumping organ.
33. **2** Food, wastes, and other substances are conducted from one part of a plant or animal to another.
34. **3** Ecology is the study of the relations of living things with each other and with their environment. The incorrect choices are factors relating to ecology.
35. **5** Only lichens can survive on bare, dry rock.

36. **2** One kind of plant succeeds another when the soil is thick enough to support the newcomer. In choice 2, the plants are in order of increasing soil depth.
37. **3** Chloroplasts are involved in the process of photosynthesis.
Choice 1 is incorrect; the passage traces the division of chloroplasts as the cell divides. Choice 2 is incorrect; grana are units that make up some chloroplasts. Choice 4 is incorrect; although chloroplasts give the green color to plants, their function is to carry on photosynthesis. Choice 5 is incorrect; spirogyra, a filamentous algae, is mentioned as an illustration of a cell with a single chloroplast.
38. **4** All higher plants have chloroplasts composed of grana. The passage tells that brown algae have chlorophyll, some bacteria photosynthesize, and some algae have chlorophyll without chloroplasts or chloroplasts without grana.
39. **2** The chromatophore has the same function as the chloroplast, but they do differ in structure. They are not similar in regard to location. Chromatophores are found in some bacterial cells, and chloroplasts are found in the green cells of higher plants.
40. **5** Only in this choice is there evidence that the invading organism has produced a disease process.
41. **2** An antibody is produced in response to a specific invading organism, and will protect only against that one. The body can produce an unlimited variety of antibodies, and the blood usually has many of them.
42. **2** Opsonins prepare bacteria for destruction by phagocytes.
43. **4** Microorganisms that cause an infection produce an abnormal state or unnatural condition.
44. **1** Phagocytes are white blood cells that destroy bacteria by engulfing them.
45. **5** The unbroken skin is an excellent barrier against the invasion of microorganisms.
45. **5** In some cases, microorganisms may enter through normal body openings; in other cases, through wounds or bites.
46. **3** Agglutinins clump invading organisms.
47. **1** The relationship between athlete's foot fungus and humans is known as *parasitism*. A parasite is an organism that lives in or on another organism. The parasite harms the organism that it lives off.
48. **4** The relationship between nitrogen-fixing bacteria and the leguminous plant is an example of *mutualism*. Mutualism is an association between two organisms in which both are benefited from the association. The plant gets nitrogen, and the bacteria have a place to live.
49. **3** In a saprophytic relationship, an organism feeds on the dead remains of other organisms.
50. **4** After Darwin's day, the work of Weismann and others showed that genes pass unchanged by environmental influences from generation to generation.
51. **4** The theory of use and disuse said that any organ that is used becomes stronger. While this is true of some organs, the changes are not hereditary and thus have no effect on evolution.
52. **4** With the discovery that heredity is controlled by genes that are sequestered in the germ cells, it became clear that there is no mechanism by which acquired characters could be inherited.
53. **3** Bacteria resistant to penicillin developed as a result of mutation. Those organisms that did not receive the mutated gene were killed by the antibiotic. Those in which gene mutation occurred survived and passed the mutation on to succeeding generations.
54. **2** Continuity of the germ plasm occurs because no environmental influence affects the genes.
55. **3** Being larger, or stronger, or more prolific, or more intelligent may or may not promote survival. The general statement (3) is the only one that applies universally.
56. **3** All animal fats, and coconut oil, have saturated fat and tend to raise the LDL level. Most vegetable oils are unsaturated.
57. **5** The passage says that exercise raises the HDL level and that higher HDL tends to clean the arteries.
58. **4** Blood flow is not normal through clogged arteries. If the arteries that feed the heart are affected, heart disease results.
59. **2** The crucial evidence is the relationship between high cholesterol level and the state of the arteries, which is a factor in heart disease.
60. **3** Not all oily foods contain cholesterol, but most animal fats are rich in cholesterol.

61. **3** Chromosomes are structures in the nucleus. During mitosis, two cells with identical chromosomes are formed. Since the cell had 12 chromosomes, the daughter cells must also have 12 chromosomes.
62. **5** *Gonads* are sex glands. Gametes or sex cells are produced in these organs. Gametes are produced from primary sex cells that undergo meiosis, also known as reduction division. Male gonads are called *testes*; female gonads are called *ovaries*.
63. **2** *Mitosis* is the process by which two identical cells are formed. The chromosomes are duplicated. Each cell receives the same number of chromosomes and the identical genes.
64. **3** Each gamete has one set of chromosomes, and fertilization puts the chromosomes of the sperm into the egg.
65. **1** Every time a cell divides, mitosis puts an exact copy of each chromosome, with its genes, into the daughter cells.
66. **2** *Fossils* are the remains of organisms of the past. When an organism dies, it may be covered by sediment. Sediments are deposited in layers. The layers are compacted into rock. The oldest fossils are found in the lowest layers.
67. **5** According to the graph, the maximum number of Down's syndrome cases occurs at age 45. At age 45, 18 cases per 1000 births occur. At age 30 two cases per 1000 births occur. Therefore at age 45, there are nine times as many cases than at age 30.
68. **5** According to the graph, oxygen content decreases as the sewage waste increases. The organisms that decompose sewage are aerobic organisms. They consume oxygen.
69. **2** There was the greatest change in the whitefish population between 1975 and 1980. The whitefish population disappeared from the lake by 1980.
70. **5** The carp appears to be able to withstand oxygen depletion. The number of carp has increased as the oxygen content decreased.
71. **1** According to the table of results, the number of bubbles produced by the plant decreases as the distance from the light increases. The results from the table indicate that there is a relationship between the number of bubbles produced and the distance of the plant from the light.
72. **2** According to the graph, refrigeration retards (slows down) bacterial reproduction. There were bacteria in all three cultures. The higher the temperature, the more the bacteria reproduced.
73. **3** A control is a part of an experiment in which no changes have been made. Group *A* was the control. The individuals in the group did not receive pills containing medication.

EARTH SCIENCE

Items 1 to 4 refer to the following information.

Ganymede, one of the 16 moons of Jupiter, has a diameter of 5300 km, making it the largest moon of the solar system. Mars has two small moons—Deimos and Phobos. The former moves around Mars in 30 hours, but the latter takes only eight hours. Our satellite, the moon, is about 3476 km in diameter and about 384 000 km from the earth. It revolves around the earth from west to east, completing its orbit in 27⅓ days. Actually, the moon takes 29½ days to come back to the same place, since the earth, moving around the sun in the same direction as the moon moves around the earth, is always pulling ahead of the moon.

Actually, we always see the same side of the moon because the period of rotation of the moon is equal to its own period of revolution. Thus, as the moon rotates a given number of degrees on its axis, it will have revolved the same number of degrees about the earth, leaving the same portion of the moon always facing the earth.

1. Of the following, which most nearly expresses (in earth days) the moon's period of rotation?

(1) 1
(2) 7
(3) 8
(4) 28
(5) 365

1. 1 2 3 4 5

2. Traveling at an average velocity of 38 400 km per hour, how long would it take a spacecraft launched from the moon to reach the earth?

(1) 10 hours
(2) 47 hours
(3) 10 days
(4) 15 days
(5) 20 days

2. 1 2 3 4 5

3. Why do we always see the same side of the moon?

(1) Rotation of the earth is equal to the period of rotation of the moon.
(2) Rotation of the earth is equal to the revolution of the moon.
(3) Rotation of the moon is equal to the revolution of the moon.
(4) Rotation of the moon is greater than the revolution of the moon.
(5) Rotation of the moon is less than the revolution of the moon.

3. 1 2 3 4 5

4. Which of the following terms is LEAST related to the other four terms?

(1) Ganymede
(2) Mars
(3) Deimos
(4) moon
(5) Phobos

4. 1 2 3 4 5

Items 5 to 7 refer to the following article.

The moon goes through a cycle of four major phases in a period of four weeks. As it revolves around the earth, its orbit takes it first between the sun and the earth and then to the other side of the earth away from the sun. When the moon is in the area between the earth and sun, the side of the moon toward us is not lighted directly by the sun. However, the moon is slightly visible because of sunlight reflected by the earth. The light is called earthshine.

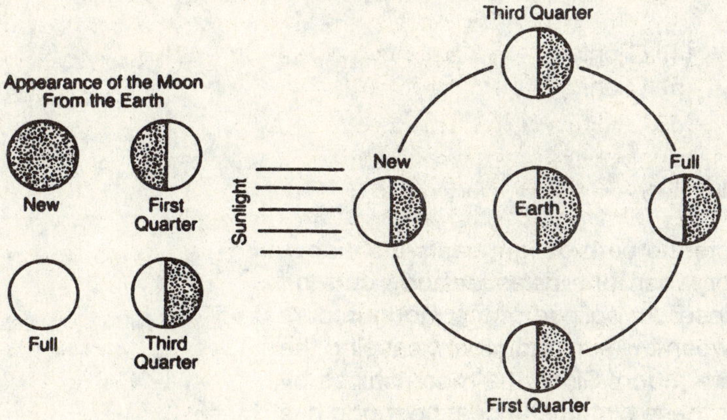

Tides are the result of the gravitational pull of the moon and the sun of the freely moving waters of the earth. Since the moon is so much closer to the earth than is the sun, the moon has a much greater effect on the tides than does the sun. The greatest effect is during the periods of the full and new moon when the moon and sun are in direct line with the earth and exert a pull in the same direction. The result is a *spring tide* or tide of great range. At the periods of the first and third quarter the sun and moon pull at right angles and thus oppose each other. Thus the pull of the moon is lessened, the result being a *neap tide* or tide of small range.

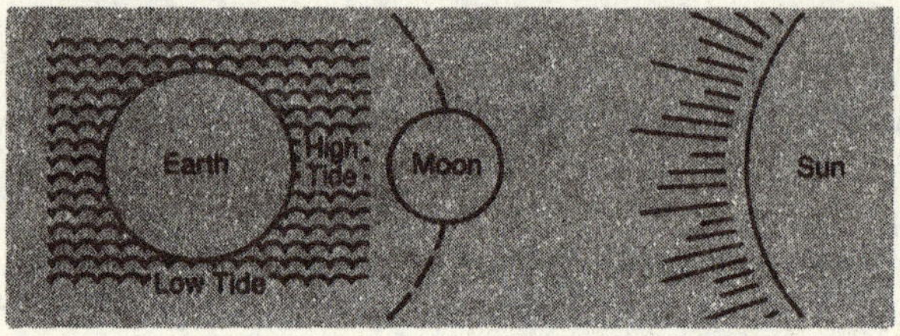

5. Earthshine is illumination seen during which phase of the moon?
(1) full
(2) new
(3) first quarter
(4) crescent
(5) last quarter

5. 1 2 3 4 5

6. Why is it possible for an observer on earth to see the phases of the moon?
(1) The moon revolves around the sun.
(2) The moon rotates on its axis.
(3) The earth revolves around the sun.
(4) The earth rotates on its axis.
(5) The moon revolves around the earth.

6. 1 2 3 4 5

7. During what phase(s) of the moon does it happen that we have a very high tide and a very low tide?
(A) new moon
(B) full moon
(C) first quarter
(D) third quarter

(1) A only
(2) B only
(3) A and B
(4) C only
(5) D only

7. 1 2 3 4 5

<u>Items 8 to 10</u> refer to the following article.

Any opaque object that intercepts the path of light casts a shadow. Basically this explains eclipses, for when one celestial body cuts off light from another we have an eclipse. An eclipse of the moon occurs when the earth comes directly between the sun and moon, causing the earth's shadow (umbra) to fall on the moon. Since the moon shines by the reflected light of the sun, under these circumstances the moon has been eclipsed.

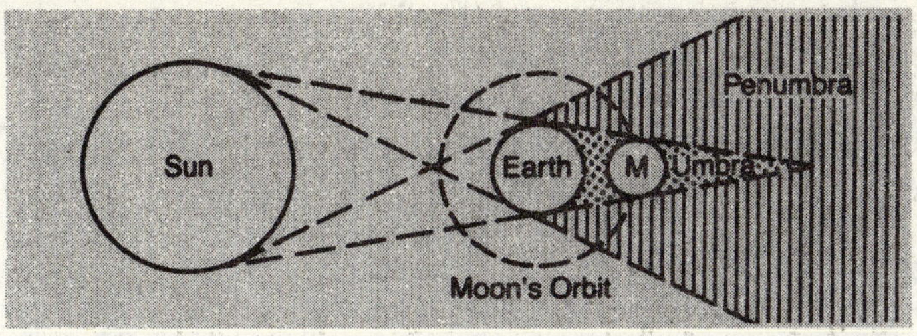

In a total solar eclipse, the moon is directly between the earth and the sun so that the umbra of the moon touches the earth. However, since the moon is a much smaller body than the earth, the narrow tip of the umbra barely reaches the earth. Thus, the path of the shadow that sweeps across the earth is very narrow, having a maximum width of about 274 km.

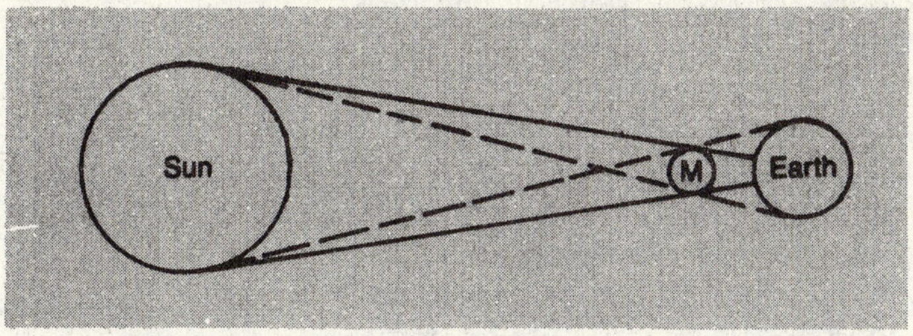

8. When does a total solar eclipse occur?
(1) The earth casts its shadow on the moon.
(2) The sun casts its shadow on the moon.
(3) The moon casts its shadow on the sun.
(4) The moon casts its shadow on the earth.
(5) The sun casts its shadow on the earth.

8. 1 2 3 4 5 || || || || ||

9. During which phase of the moon would an eclipse of the moon occur?
(1) new
(2) first quarter
(3) full
(4) third quarter
(5) any phase

9. 1 2 3 4 5 || || || || ||

10. Which of the following best describes penumbra?
(1) a ray of light
(2) a total lunar eclipse
(3) a total solar eclipse
(4) the lighter, outer part of a shadow
(5) the darker part of a shadow

10. 1 2 3 4 5 || || || || ||

<u>Items 11 to 13</u> refer to the following article.

Toward the end of the year 1973, the comet Kohoutek began to make newspaper headlines as it moved toward the sun at great speed. Predictions were made that it would be more spectacular than Halley's comet, which was last seen in 1910, as well as Ikeya-Seki of 1965 and Bennett's of 1970. It was first discovered in March 1973 by a Czech astronomer, Dr. Lubos Kohoutek, when it was still more than 800 million kilometres from the sun. Astronomers reasoned that if it was visible that far out, it would probably prove to be spectacular when it streaked to within 20 million kilometres of the sun on December 28. Thus, it was expected to be the third brightest object in the sky, after the sun and the moon.

Measurements indicated that Kohoutek's nucleus was 32–40 kilometres across, its coma about 16 000 kilometres in diameter, and its tail about 32 million kilometres in length. The nucleus of a comet is thought to be composed of a clump of "dirty ice"—dust particles, stony matter, and frozen gases, such as water, methane, and ammonia. The coma is a large, hazy cloud formed when the sun's heat liberates dust and gases from the nucleus as the comet enters the inner part of the solar system. The tail is a long cloud of ions and molecules that may become fluorescent under the influence of the solar wind.

Despite the predictions made for it, the comet Kohoutek turned out to be of such minimum brightness that few people were actually able to see it. The reason for its disappointing appearance may be traced to the fact that it was not the typical "dirty snowball" astronomers had predicted. Where the icy head of Halley's comet released streams of dust particles on melting as it approached the sun, catching the sunlight and reflecting it in orange and yellow bands, Kohoutek turned out to be a relatively clean, blue-white comet.

Astronomers have identified in Kohoutek the complex molecule methyl cyanide, which is believed essential in star formation; this substance was previously detected only in the vast dust clouds toward the center of the galaxy. Consequently, the conclusion is drawn by some astronomers that comet Kohoutek originated in a dust cloud outside of the solar system.

11. What is the composition of the comet Kohoutek?
(1) a nucleus, a coma, and a tail
(2) a nucleus, a comet, and a tail
(3) only a nucleus and a tail
(4) only a tail
(5) star dust

11. 1 2 3 4 5
|| || || || ||

12. Why was Kohoutek not as bright as predicted?
(1) It originated within the solar system.
(2) It originated outside the solar system.
(3) It originated in a dust cloud.
(4) It did not release streams of dust particles on approaching the sun.
(5) It contained too much ice.

12. 1 2 3 4 5
|| || || || ||

13. Why was Kohoutek expected to be spectacularly bright?
(1) Its appearance coincided with the Christmas season.
(2) It would pass within 20 million kilometres of the sun.
(3) It was first visible when more than 800 million kilometres from the sun.
(4) It was the third brightest object in the sky.
(5) Its nucleus was very large, about 16 000 kilometres in diameter.

13. 1 2 3 4 5
|| || || || ||

Items 14 to 18 refer to the following article.

One of the contributions of the space age has been a new vantage point for viewing the earth's surface from distant heights. The earth can now be viewed by remote sensing, which can be defined as detecting an object from afar without direct contact. All our lives could be influenced by the results of the new era of accomplishment that makes possible such activities as immediate observation of natural and human-made disasters; continuous study of the ocean; monitoring and more efficient management of land, food, and water resources; discovery of additional natural resources; identification of pollution; tracing current flow along coastlines; studying the distribution of fish; and mapmaking.

In July 1972, the Earth Resources Technology Satellite (ERTS-1) was launched to make a systematic surveillance of North America and other areas from space. This unmanned satellite follows a near-polar orbit at an altitude of 920 kilometres and circles the earth 14 times daily. As it passes overhead, images are transmitted through its various cameras to a number of receiver stations. It also collects and relays information dealing with water quality, snow depth, rainfall, and earthquake activity from about 100 stations located in remote parts of the continent.

In addition to the advantages of viewing the earth's surface from high altitudes is the value of using infrared photography to study features that would not be visible with ordinary photography. These include plant growth, fungus infections of plants, circulation of sewage in lakes, spread of oil slicks, spawning grounds of sea life, identification of bedrock, surveys of mineral deposits, volcanic activity, and temperature differences in warm water currents, such as the Gulf Stream. It is highly probable that the ultimate benefits to be derived from this program will far exceed the original cost.

14. Which of the following best defines "remote sensing"?
(1) study of fish distribution by the use of sensitive currents
(2) release of a rowboat to see its path in an ocean current
(3) study of the earth's features without direct contact
(4) measurement of the effect of an atom bomb in causing an earthquake
(5) measurement of the depth of snow without the use of snowshoes

14. 1 2 3 4 5
|| || || || ||

15. The space age has contributed all of the following values of remote sensing in view of the earth's surface EXCEPT the
(1) immediate observation of natural disasters
(2) continuous surveillance of the oceans
(3) identification of pollution
(4) monitoring of food resources
(5) making accurate observations of the land features of the planet Mars

15. 1 2 3 4 5
|| || || || ||

16. Which of the following describes the orbit of ERTS?
(1) 14 times daily, at an altitude of 920 kilometres
(2) 14 times daily, at an altitude of 920 miles
(3) 41 times daily, at an altitude of 290 miles
(4) 290 times daily, at an altitude of 41 kilometres
(5) an orbit around the equator

16. 1 2 3 4 5
|| || || || ||

17. What can be accomplished by infrared photography?
(1) Fungus infections of plants can be sterilized.
(2) Circulation of sewage in lakes can be speeded up.
(3) The spread of oil slicks can be absorbed.
(4) The location of mineral deposits can be surveyed.
(5) The direction of the Gulf Stream can be influenced.

17. 1 2 3 4 5

18. Which statement gives correct information about the Earth Resources Technology Satellite?
(1) The Russians were the first to launch their ERTS in 1954.
(2) The ERTS was launched in 1972 to make a study of North America.
(3) In 1972, the Soviet Union applied for permission to survey North America with its ERTS.
(4) The Apollo project to the moon was equivalent to the use of the ERTS around the earth.
(5) The next use of ERTS is to study the surface of the planet Venus.

18. 1 2 3 4 5

<u>Items 19 to 23</u> are based on the following information.

The diagrams show the general effect of the earth's atmosphere on insolation from the sun at middle latitudes during both clear-sky and cloudy-sky conditions. The graph shows the percentage of insolation reflected by the earth's surface at different latitudes in the Northern Hemisphere in winter.

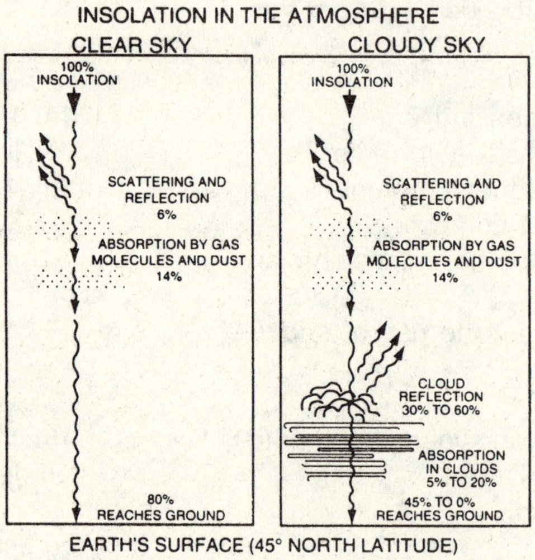

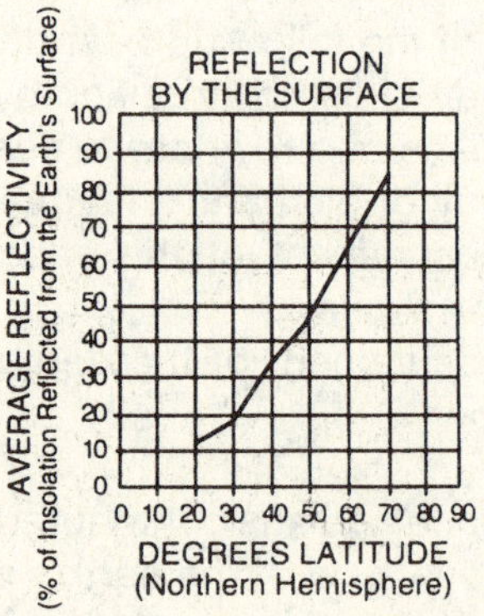

19. Approximately what percentage of the insolation actually reaches the ground at 45° North latitude on a clear day?
(1) 100%
(2) 80%
(3) 60%
(4) 45%
(5) 85%

19. 1 2 3 4 5

20. Which factor keeps the greatest percentage of insolation from reaching the earth's surface on cloudy days?
(1) absorption by cloud droplets
(2) reflection by cloud droplets
(3) absorption of clear-air gas molecules
(4) reflection by clear-air gas molecules
(5) refraction by cloud droplets

20. 1 2 3 4 5

21. According to the graph, on a winter day at 70° North latitude, what approximate percentage of the insolation is reflected by the earth's surface?
(1) 50%
(2) 65%
(3) 85%
(4) 100%
(5) 90%

21. 1 2 3 4 5

22. Which statement best explains why, at high latitudes, reflectivity of insolation is greater in winter than in summer?
(1) The North Pole is tilted toward the sun in winter.
(2) Snow and ice reflect almost all insolation.
(3) The colder air holds much more moisture.
(4) Dust settles quickly in cold air.
(5) Snow and ice absorb all insolation.

22. 1 2 3 4 5

23. The radiation that passes through the atmosphere and reaches the earth's surface has the greatest intensity in the form of
(1) visible-light radiation
(2) infrared radiation
(3) ultraviolet radiation
(4) radio-wave radiation
(5) invisible light radiation

23. 1 2 3 4 5

Items 24 to 27 are based on the information in the table which shows the physical properties of nine minerals.

Mineral	Colour	Luster	Streak	Hardness	Density (g/mL)	Chemical Composition
biotite mica	black	glassy	white	soft	2.8	$K(Mg,Fe)_3(AlSi_3O_{10})(OH_2)$
diamond	varies	glassy	colourless	hard	3.5	C
galena	grey	metallic	grey-black	soft	7.5	PbS
graphite	black	dull	black	soft	2.3	C
kaolinite	white	earthy	white	soft	2.6	$Al_4(Si_4O_{10})(OH)_8$
magnetite	black	metallic	black	hard	5.2	Fe_3O_4
olivine	green	glassy	white	hard	3.4	$(Fe,Mg)_2SiO_4$
pyrite	brass yellow	metallic	greenish-black	hard	5.0	FeS_2
quartz	varies	glassy	colourless	hard	2.7	SiO_2

Definitions
Luster: the way a mineral's surface reflects light
Streak: colour of a powdered form of the mineral
Hardness: resistance of a mineral to being scratched (soft—easily scratched; hard—not easily scratched)

Chemical Symbols

Al —Aluminum	Pb —Lead
C —Carbon	Si —Silicon
Fe —Iron	K —Potassium
H —Hydrogen	S —Sulfur
Mg —Magnesium	
O —Oxygen	

24. Which mineral has a different colour in its powdered form than in its original form?
(1) pyrite
(2) graphite
(3) kaolinite
(4) magnetite
(5) galena

24. 1 2 3 4 5

25. Which mineral contains iron, has a metallic luster, is hard, and has the same colour and streak?
(1) biotite mica
(2) galena
(3) kaolinite
(4) magnetite
(5) graphite

25. 1 2 3 4 5

26. Why do diamond and graphite have different physical properties, even though they are both composed entirely of the element carbon?
(1) Only diamond contains radioactive carbon.
(2) Only graphite consists of organic material.
(3) The minerals have different arrangements of carbon atoms.
(4) The minerals have undergone different amounts of weathering.
(5) The minerals have similar arrangements of carbon atoms.

26. 1 2 3 4 5

27. Which mineral would most likely be weathered most after being placed in a container and shaken for 10 minutes?
(1) pyrite
(2) quartz
(3) magnetite
(4) kaolinite
(5) olivine

27. 1 2 3 4 5

<u>Items 28 and 29</u> refer to the following information.

Since the land heats up more rapidly than the water, the air pressure over the land is less. As the heated air rises, it moves out to the ocean and is replaced by the cooler air blowing in from the ocean. The diagram represents a coastal region with daytime wind direction as indicated.

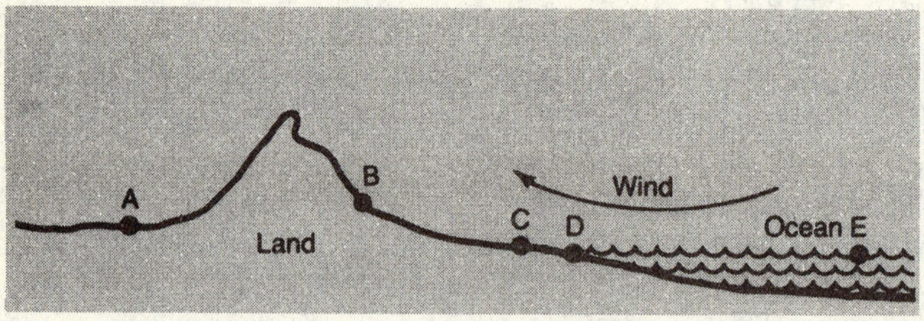

28. Which of the following best explains the direction of the wind?
(1) the land being cooled during a clear night
(2) more water vapour in the air over the ocean than in the air over the land
(3) low pressure over the land and high pressure over the ocean
(4) warm ocean currents
(5) high pressure over the land and low pressure over the ocean

28. 1 2 3 4 5

29. If the wind indicated in the diagram shows the prevailing wind direction, which location probably records the highest annual precipitation?
(1) A
(2) B
(3) C
(4) D
(5) E

29. 1 2 3 4 5

<u>Items 30 to 33</u> are based on the following graph.

At the Wednesday noon broadcast, the weather forecaster predicted that a cold front was heading in this vicinity and the warm weather would end by Thursday night. The graph is the one he studied to verify his forecast.

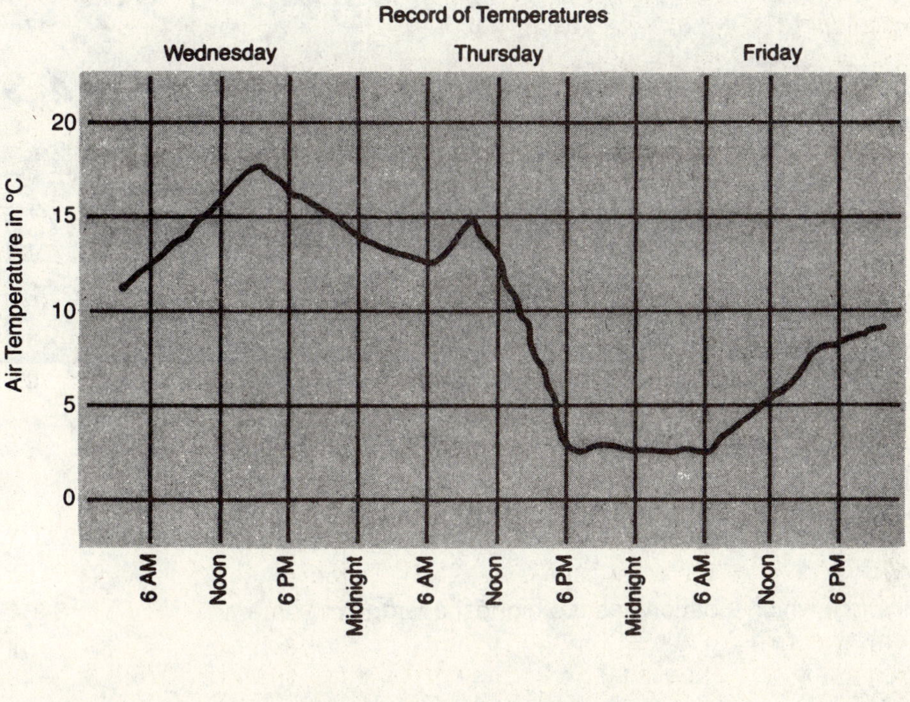

30. What is the lowest temperature indicated by the graph?
(1) 0°C
(2) 3°C
(3) –3°C
(4) 5°C
(5) 7°C

30. 1 2 3 4 5

31. During which interval of time did the temperature vary LEAST?
(1) 6 P.M. Wednesday to 6 A.M. Thursday
(2) 6 A.M. to 6 P.M. Thursday
(3) 6 P.M. Thursday to 6 A.M. Friday
(4) 6 A.M. to 6 P.M. Friday
(5) 6 A.M. to noon on Thursday

31. 1 2 3 4 5

32. For Thursday from 9 A.M. to 6 P.M., which approach and passage was most probably responsible for the change in temperature?
(1) warm front
(2) cold front
(3) stationary air
(4) warm air mass
(5) combination of any of these

32. 1 2 3 4 5

33. Which period showed a difference of more than 12 degrees?
(1) Thursday morning to Friday morning
(2) Wednesday noon to Thursday noon
(3) Wednesday morning to Wednesday evening
(4) Thursday morning to Thursday noon
(5) Friday morning to Friday evening

33. 1 2 3 4 5

Items 34 to 37 are based on the following graph.

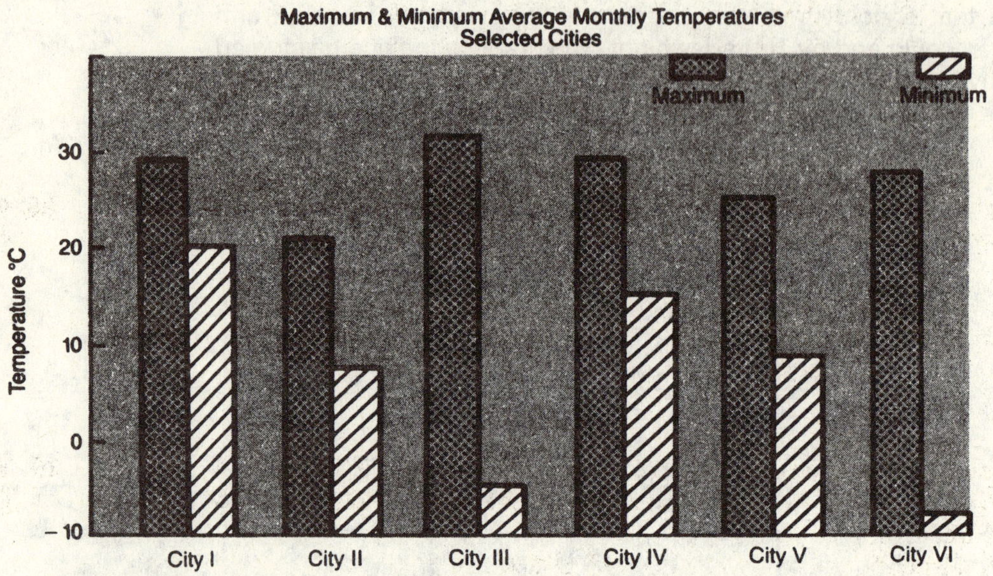

The graph represents data collected from six cities showing the average maximum and the average minimum temperatures for a 12-month period.

34. Of the following, which location has the highest average maximum monthly temperature?
(1) I
(2) II
(3) III
(4) IV
(5) V

34. 1 2 3 4 5

35. Of the following, which location has the greatest difference in average monthly temperatures?
(1) I
(2) II
(3) IV
(4) V
(5) VI

35. 1 2 3 4 5

36. Between City II and what other city is the variation in temperature extremes greatest?
(1) City I
(2) City IV
(3) City III
(4) City V
(5) any of the above

36. 1 2 3 4 5

37. To the climate of which city is the climate of City VI most similar?
(1) I
(2) II
(3) III
(4) IV
(5) VI

37. 1 2 3 4 5

<u>Items 38 and 39</u> are based on the following graph.

This graph shows the measurements of air pollutants as recorded in a large city for a two-day period—July 10 and 11.

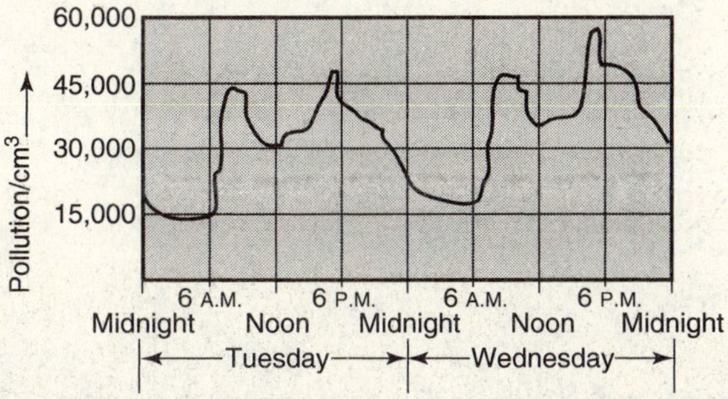

38. What is a probable cause for the increase in pollutants at 8 A.M. and 5 P.M. on the two days?
(1) change in insolation
(2) occurrence of precipitation
(3) high wind velocity
(4) heavy automobile traffic
(5) any of these

38. 1 2 3 4 5

39. On the basis of the trends indicated by the graph, at what time on Thursday, July 12, will the greatest amount of pollutants probably be observed?
(1) 12 noon
(2) 5 P.M.
(3) 3 A.M.
(4) 8 A.M.
(5) midnight

39. 1 2 3 4 5

---

40. An explosion occurs at the upper surface of an ocean. The sound returns to the original site of the explosion four seconds later, after having been reflected from the ocean bottom. If the speed of sound in ocean water is 1460 metres per second, how deep (in metres) is the water?
(1) 1460
(2) 2930
(3) 4380
(4) 5850
(5) 29300

40. 1 2 3 4 5

Turn to the answer key and answer analysis which follow.

What's Your Score?

_________ right, _________ wrong

Excellent	35–40
Good	25–34
Fair	20–24

If your score is low, don't get discouraged. Perhaps earth science is a difficult subject for you. Try to find out why you failed. The analysis of correct answers that follows will help you to pinpoint your errors. If your mistake was lack of information, turn to the "Glossary of Scientific Terms" (page 363) and look up the meanings of the words you did not understand. If it was a mistake in interpretation, review the analysis of the question.

ANSWER KEY

1. **4**	11. **1**	21. **3**	31. **3**
2. **1**	12. **4**	22. **2**	32. **2**
3. **3**	13. **3**	23. **1**	33. **1**
4. **2**	14. **3**	24. **1**	34. **3**
5. **2**	15. **5**	25. **4**	35. **5**
6. **5**	16. **1**	26. **3**	36. **3**
7. **3**	17. **4**	27. **4**	37. **3**
8. **4**	18. **2**	28. **3**	38. **4**
9. **3**	19. **2**	29. **2**	39. **2**
10. **4**	20. **2**	30. **2**	40. **2**

ANSWER ANALYSIS

1. **4** The moon revolves around the earth in $27\frac{1}{3}$ days. The rotation of the moon is equal to its own period of revolution.

2. **1** This question involves using a basic mathematical formula: distance ÷ rate = time. The passage tells us that the average distance from the moon to earth is 384 000 km. This question assumes that the average velocity of the spacecraft is 38 400 km per hour. Substitute these values in the formula

$$\frac{384\,000\text{ km}}{38\,400\text{ km per hour}} = 10\text{ hours}$$

3. **3** The period of rotation of the moon is equal to its own period of revolution.

4. **2** Mars is a planet; the other choices are satellites of planets.

5. **2** Note that in discussing the new moon phase, earthshine is explained.

6. **5** The diagram illustrates that the phases of the moon result from the illumination of the moon's surface by the sun. Note that about half of the moon's surface is always facing the sun. Since the moon revolves around the earth, the angle between the sun, earth, and moon changes. This results in different phases of the moon.

7. **3** This question refers to spring tide when the gravitational pull of the moon and sun causes tides of great range.

6. **4** Observe the diagram accompanying the discussion of total solar eclipse. The shadow of the moon falls on one part of the earth.

9. **3** Observe the diagram accompanying the discussion of an eclipse of the moon. Note that only when the earth is directly between the sun and the moon is it possible for the shadow of the earth to fall on the moon. Under these circumstances, we would ordinarily have a full moon.

10. **4** If this term is not part of your science vocabulary, observe the diagram explaining the eclipse of the moon. Note that the darker part of the shadow is labeled *umbra* and the lighter part is labeled *penumbra*.

11. **1** A comet consists of three parts—a tightly packed nucleus consisting of frozen gases, dust particles, and stony matter, about 32–40 km across; a hazy coma around the nucleus, composed of dust transformed into a glowing vapour under the sun's influence, and 16 000 km or more in diameter; and the tail, composed of ions and molecules, which stretches out millions of miles in length.

12. **4** A comet with lots of dust is spectacularly visible to the naked eye when it is near the sun. Light and electrified particles from the sun blast the dust out of the comet's head, and the dusty tail reflects the yellow sunlight. Apparently Kohoutek did not release much dust.

13. **3** Astronomers reasoned that since comet Kohoutek was already visible at such a great distance from the sun in March, it would be spectacular by the time it streaked to within 16 million kilometres of the sun on December 28.

14. **3** *Remote sensing* is a contribution of the space age in viewing the earth's surface from the vantage point of distance heights.

15. **5** No mention is made of studying other planets in this project.

16. **1** The ERTS (Earth Resource Technology Satellite) follows a near-polar orbit at an altitude of 920 km and circles the earth 14 times daily.
17. **4** The use of infrared photography permits the study of features of the earth's surface that would not be visible with ordinary photography.
18. **2** ERTS was launched to make a systematic surveillance of North America and other areas from space.
19. **2** The first diagram shows that, when there is a clear sky, 80% of the insolation reaches the ground.
20. **2** The second diagram indicates that, when the sky is cloudy, cloud reflection returns 30% to 60% of the insolation. This is greater than the percentage scattered and reflected by the atmosphere (6%), absorbed by gas molecules and dust (14%), or absorbed in clouds (5% to 20%).
21. **3** Find 70° North latitude on the horizontal axis of the graph. Trace upward until you reach the curve. The average reflectivity (vertical axis) is 85% for this latitude.
22. **2** Compared to other ground surfaces, snow and ice are both very good reflectors of insolation. This fact explains why surfaces covered with snow or ice do not heat up as quickly.
23. **1** The atmosphere is a better absorber of infrared, ultraviolet, or radio-wave radiation than of visible light. As a result, the greatest intensity of insolation passing through the atmosphere and reaching the earth's surface represents the visible part of the electromagnetic spectrum.
24. **1** The streak of a mineral is the colour of its powdered form. This property is shown in the table. A sample of pyrite has a brass-yellow colour. When pyrite is powdered, however, the colour is greenish black. The others have the same or nearly the same colour in both crystal and powdered form, according to the table.
25. **4** Biotite mica contains iron (Fe), but it is soft. Galena is metallic, but it does not contain iron and is soft. Kaolinite has the same colour in mineral and powdered form, but is earthy and soft and does not contain iron. Magnetite contains iron and is hard. It has a metallic luster, and both the mineral sample and the powdered form are black. Graphite contains carbon.
26. **3** The arrangement of the atoms in a mineral can affect the properties of the mineral. The close-knit structure of the atoms of carbon in a sample of diamond makes the diamond very hard and transparent. In graphite the carbon atoms are loosely arranged, so graphite is more brittle and opaque.
27. **4** According to the table, pyrite, quartz, olivine, and magnetite are hard minerals. Hence they are resistant to weathering. Kaolinate is soft and therefore would weather the most over the same period of time.
28. **3** As the air above the land heats up, its pressure becomes lower than the air above the water. The difference in pressure explains the direction of wind.
29. **2** As the air blowing in from the ocean reaches the mountainous area, it tends to rise. As it rises, it cools, causing moisture in the air to condense. This condensation tends to cause location *B* to record the highest annual precipitation.
30. **2** The lowest temperature occurred during the period of time between 6 P.M. Thursday and 6 A.M. Friday. At this time, the temperature remained fairly constant (at about 3°C).
31. **3** The temperature remained almost constant from 6 P.M. Thursday to 6 A.M. Friday, as indicated by the horizontal line on the graph.
32. **2** On Thursday from 9 A.M. to 6 P.M. the temperature dropped steadily. This may have been caused by the approach of a cold front. As the cold front approached, it brought cold air to replace the warm air.
33. **1** At 9 A.M. Thursday the temperature was 15°C. On Friday at 6 A.M. the temperature was 25°C.
34. **3** The solid bar is tallest for City III, indicating that it has the highest average maximum monthly temperature.
35. **5** In City I, the average maximum temperature is about 29° and the average minimum is about 20°: 29° – 20°C = 9°. In City II, the average maximum temperature is about 20° and the average minimum is about 7°: 20° – 7° = 13°. In City IV, the average maximum temperature is about 30° and the average minimum is about 15°: 30° – 15° = 15°. In City V, the average maximum temperature is about 26° and the average minimum is about 9°: 26° – 9° = 17°. City VI has the greatest difference since the average maximum temperature is about 29° and the average minimum is –8°: 29° – (–8°) = 37°.

36. **3** Except for City VI (which is not one of the choices), the difference between the length of the two bars is greatest for City III.
37. **3** Cities III and VI have similar maximum and minimum temperatures and would therefore *probably* have similar climates. However, since climate also depends upon the amount of moisture, it is possible that the two cities have different climates.
38. **4** Automobile emission adds pollutants to the atmosphere. Traffic is heaviest at 8 A.M. and 5 P.M. in most large cities. Changes in the amount of insolation generally have little or no effect on pollution levels. Precipitation tends to remove some pollutants, such as particulate matter. High winds decrease pollution levels by blowing away polluted air and replacing it with fresh clean air.
39. **2** Since the pattern indicates that the highest pollution level occurs at 5 P.M., it is reasonable to assume that the highest level will also be reached at that time the following day.
40. **2** One-half of the four seconds is the time spent by the sound vibrations to reach the bottom of the ocean: (2 seconds)(1460 metres/second) ≈ 2930 metres.

CHEMISTRY

Items 1 to 4 refer to the following information.

A student floated a lighted candle on a cork in a shallow pan of water. He carefully inverted a bottle over the burning candle. He measured the time required for the candle to stop burning. He then removed the bottle, relit the candle, filled the bottle with exhaled air, and again inverted it over the candle. When the candle went out, he repeated this second part of his demonstration, but before filling the bottle with exhaled air, he ran 30 m at top speed.

1. What was the procedure attempting to demonstrate?
(1) Inhaled and exhaled air differ in composition.
(2) Exhaled air contains less carbon dioxide than inhaled air.
(3) Combustion releases heat.
(4) Respiration produces heat.
(5) Combustion produces carbon dioxide.

1. 1 2 3 4 5

2. In regard to the candle going out, what observation would the student make?
(1) The candle stopped burning most quickly in the first trial.
(2) The candle went out most quickly in the last trial.
(3) The candle stopped burning at the same time in all three trials.
(4) Only in the first trial did the candle stop burning.
(5) The candle stopped burning after a long waiting period in all three trials.

2. 1 2 3 4 5

3. What conclusion can be reached about exhaled air?
(1) It contains carbon dioxide.
(2) It contains no oxygen.
(3) It has less carbon dioxide than inhaled air.
(4) It has less oxygen than inhaled air.
(5) It contains as much oxygen as inhaled air.

3. 1 2 3 4 5

4. Which of the following is a justified conclusion of the demonstration?

(1) Activity results in a higher percentage of oxygen in exhaled air.
(2) Activity results in a higher percentage of carbon dioxide in exhaled air.
(3) Respiration is similar to burning.
(4) Respiration produces more carbon dioxide than burning.
(5) The rate of respiration remains constant.

4. 1 2 3 4 5
|| || || || ||

Items 5 to 10 are based on the following information.

Solubility is a property that describes the amount of one substance that will dissolve in another substance. Table 1 describes the solubility in water of several salts at different temperatures. The temperatures are given on the Celsius scale. The degree of solubility is expressed in the number of grams of substance that will dissolve in 100 mL of water. The abbreviation mL is for millilitre. A millilitre is one-thousandth part of a litre, which is equal to one cubic centimetre. Some substances will not dissolve in water regardless of temperature changes. These are said to be insoluble. Those substances that dissolve to a slight degree are considered slightly soluble. Table 2 describes these general characteristics for some 165 chemical substances.

TABLE 1
SOLUBILITY CURVES

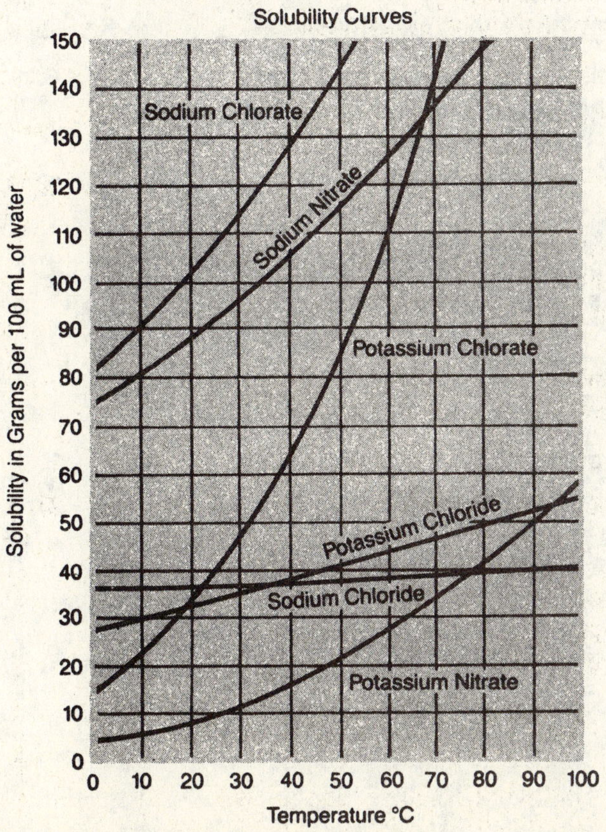

TABLE 2

Table of Solubilities in Water

i-nearly insoluble
Ss-slightly soluble
S-soluble
d-decomposes

	ACETATE	BROMIDE	CARBONATE	CHLORIDE	HYDROXIDE	IODIDE	NITRATE	OXIDE	PHOSPHATE	SULFATE	SULFIDE
aluminum	S	S		S	i	S	S	i	i	S	d
ammonium	S	S	S	S	S	S	S		S	S	S
barium	S	S	i	S	S	S	S	S	i	i	d
calcium	S	S	i	S	Ss	S	S	Ss	i	Ss	d
copper II	S	S	i	S	i		S	i	i	S	i
iron II	S	S	i	S	i	S	S	i	i	S	i
iron III	S	S		S	i	S	S	i	i	Ss	d
lead	S	Ss	i	Ss	i	Ss	S	i	i	i	i
magnesium	S	S	i	S	i	S	S	i	i	S	d
mercury I	Ss	S	i	i		i	S	i	i	Ss	i
mercury II	S	Ss	i	S	i	i	S	i	i	d	i
potassium	S	S	S	S	S	S	S	S	S	S	S
silver	Ss	i	i	i		i	S	i	i	Ss	i
sodium	S	S	S	S	S	S	S	d	S	S	S
zinc	S	S	i	S	i	S	S	i	i	S	i

5. At 50°C, how many grams of sodium chlorate will dissolve in 100 mL of water?
(1) 100
(2) 120
(3) 130
(4) 140
(5) 150

5. 1 2 3 4 5

6. Which of the following salts, when dissolving in water, would show the least difference in solubility as the temperature increases?
(1) sodium nitrate
(2) potassium chlorate
(3) sodium chloride
(4) potassium chloride
(5) potassium nitrate

6. 1 2 3 4 5

7. How many additional grams of sodium nitrate will dissolve in 100 mL of water if the temperature is raised from 10°C to 40°C?
(1) 25
(2) 55
(3) 80
(4) 105
(5) 185

7. 1 2 3 4 5

8. Which of the following salts has the greatest change in solubility (in grams per 100 mL of water) between 30°C and 60°C?
(1) potassium chlorate
(2) sodium chloride
(3) potassium chloride
(4) potassium nitrate
(5) sodium nitrate

8. 1 2 3 4 5

9. Which of the following exhibit the greatest solubility in water?
(1) aluminum compounds
(2) ammonium compounds
(3) barium compounds
(4) silver compounds
(5) zinc compounds

9. 1 2 3 4 5

10. Which of the following types of compounds are the least water soluble?
(1) sulfates
(2) nitrates
(3) bromides
(4) acetates
(5) carbonates

10. 1 2 3 4 5

Items 11 to 14 refer to the following article.

All living things need proper temperature. Our body stays at 37°C in good health. To survive in cold or hot climates special protection is required. The same is true for plants and animals. Roses will not grow in the icelands and polar bears cannot thrive near the equator.

Temperatures vary. In Antarctica temperatures colder than 73°C below zero have been recorded. A temperature of above 65°C has been recorded in Death Valley, California. Even greater variations have been recorded in the laboratory and in industry. The lowest possible temperature is 273°C below zero.

These low temperatures are of interest to the scientist who specializes in cryogenics. Cryogenic temperatures start at the point where oxygen liquefies (–183°C) and go down to the lowest temperature possible according to scientists. This point, known as absolute zero, is 273°C below zero on the Celsius scale. Physicists are approaching this temperature by modern methods of removing most heat from solids. At low temperatures, atoms and molecules move slowly. It is as though one is watching a slow-motion replay of a football game that offers an ideal way of analysing a specific occurrence. Scientists have thus found many clues to the nature of atoms and molecules. From the physicist's point of view, temperature is a measure of the average kinetic energy, or energy of motion, of these particles.

At high temperatures, atoms and molecules move faster and thus turn into liquids or gases. The human body cannot survive high temperatures partly because the proteins in our protoplasm would coagulate.

11. What is the lowest temperature recorded outside the laboratory?
(1) –73°C
(2) 65°C
(3) –273°C
(4) –183°C
(5) 38°C

11. 1 2 3 4 5

12. Death Valley is not suitable for constant, successful human existence. What does the high temperature affect most?
(1) shape of atoms
(2) number of molecules
(3) protoplasm
(4) sweat glands
(5) liquids

12. 1 2 3 4 5

13. What is required in order to liquefy air?
(1) adding heat
(2) adding pressure and heat
(3) reducing pressure and adding heat
(4) decreasing the movement of atoms
(5) removing the heat

13. 1 2 3 4 5

14. Which of the following best describes cryogenics?
(1) the supercold world
(2) the science of atomic structure
(3) crystallography
(4) the study of Celsius and Fahrenheit
(5) physical chemistry

14. 1 2 3 4 5

Items 15 to 20 refer to the following article.

Without human interference, nature has its own ways of purifying water. These may be physical, chemical, or biological.

As streams flow, they become purer. This process is open to question since some dangerous components may remain. Communities that wish to use water from "self-purified" streams now use added precautions, including filtration and chlorination.

Aeration, which may be accompanied by wind action, turbulent flow, and waterfalls, causes an exchange of gases between the atmosphere and the water. Hydrogen sulphide, carbon dioxide, and methane are liberated from the water, and oxygen is absorbed from the atmosphere.

Light has an important effect on water. Light stimulates photosynthesis in aquatic plant life by which carbon dioxide is absorbed and oxygen is liberated. Furthermore, this plant life utilizes organic material that may be dissolved in the water for its own maintenance and thus removes substances from the water. Also, light has a germicidal effect on the surface of the water although its effect on water below the immediate surface is slight.

Sedimentation of suspended particles removes organic bacterial food from the water. This process, caused by gravity, is most effective in quiet waters.

Oxidation and reduction are two important chemical processes by which water is naturally purified. Some bacteria oxidize organic material, thus converting it to mineral substances. In the absence of oxygen, other organisms, known as anaerobic bacteria, can split organic compounds and prepare the way for subsequent oxidation. These anaerobic bacteria thrive at the bottom of bodies of water where there is a great deal of concentrated pollution.

Biological cycles also purify water. Protozoa, one-celled animals, thrive on bacteria. As these are reduced in the population, green algae appear. They in turn consume carbon dioxide, nitrates, and ammonia and produce oxygen. Large invertebrate animals, such as worms and mollusks, appear and feed on the deposits at the bottom. All of these reduce the bacterial population.

15. Which of the following prevents streams from purifying themselves?
(1) humanity
(2) evaporation
(3) condensation
(4) filtration
(5) chlorination

15. 1 2 3 4 5

16. What is accomplished by aeration of water?
(1) loss of oxygen
(2) loss of methane
(3) gain of carbon dioxide
(4) gain of hydrogen
(5) gain of carbon dioxide and loss of oxygen

16. 1 2 3 4 5

17. Which of these causes sedimentation?
(1) wind action
(2) bacterial residue
(3) turbulent water
(4) gravity
(5) organic material

17. 1 2 3 4 5

18. Which of the following statements correctly refers to the process of photosynthesis?
(1) It is carried on by all protozoa.
(2) Oxygen is necessary for the process to occur.
(3) Light is necessary for the process to occur.
(4) Carbon dioxide is given off during this process.
(5) The process has a germicidal effect on deep stagnant water.

18. 1 2 3 4 5

19. Which of these would best remove wastes at the bottom of ponds?
(1) fish
(2) aerobic bacteria
(3) green plants
(4) anaerobic bacteria
(5) algae

19. 1 2 3 4 5

20. All of the following tend to purify water EXCEPT
(1) oxidation
(2) reduction
(3) light
(4) aquatic plants
(5) bacteria

20. 1 2 3 4 5

Turn to the answer key and the answer analysis which follow.

What's Your Score?

_______ right, _______ wrong

Excellent	16–20
Good	13–15
Fair	10–12

If your score is low, don't get discouraged. Perhaps chemistry is a difficult subject for you. Try to find out why you failed. The analysis of correct answers which follows will help you to pinpoint your errors. If your mistake was lack of information, turn to the "Glossary of Scientific Terms" (page 362) and look up the meanings of the words you did not understand. If it was a mistake in interpretation, review the analysis of the question.

ANSWER KEY

1. **1**	6. **3**	11. **1**	16. **2**
2. **2**	7. **1**	12. **3**	17. **4**
3. **4**	8. **1**	13. **5**	18. **3**
4. **2**	9. **2**	14. **1**	19. **4**
5. **4**	10. **5**	15. **1**	20. **5**

ANSWER ANALYSIS

1. **1** In the first trial, the student used ordinary air, which is the same as inhaled air. In the second and third trials, he used exhaled air. He compared the time necessary for the candle to go out in each case. The difference was due to the difference in composition of the inhaled and exhaled air.
2. **2** In the last trial, the candle would go out most quickly because the exhaled air would contain the least amount of oxygen. The act of running required the use of more oxygen for the body cells.

3. **4** Since the candle would not burn as long in exhaled air, it is obvious that it contained less oxygen than inhaled air.
4. **2** As a result of respiration, carbon dioxide is given off. With strenuous exertion, a higher percentage of carbon dioxide is exhaled.
5. **4** In Table 1, follow the horizontal line at the base. At the point marked 50 (to indicate 50°C), move up along the vertical line until it intersects the curve for sodium chlorate. Move horizontally to the left to the point marked 140 to indicate that at that temperature 140 grams of this salt will dissolve in 100 millilitres of water.
6. **3** Observe that the solubility curve of sodium chloride is almost parallel to the baseline, which means that an increase in temperature makes little or no change in the number of grams that dissolve in water.
7. **1** At 10°C, 80 grams of sodium nitrate will dissolve in 100 millilitres of water. At 40°C, 105 grams of sodium nitrate will dissolve in 100 millilitres of water. The difference is 105 – 80, or 25 grams.
8. **1** Table 1 reveals the following:

Salt	Grams per 100 ml of water at 30°C	Grams per 100 ml of water at 60°C	Difference (in grams)
potassium chlorate	47	110	63
potassium nitrate	11	27	16
sodium chloride	38	39	1
potassium chloride	35	45	10
sodium nitrate	96	126	30

9. **2** Observe in Table 2 that all ammonium compounds are soluble in water.
10. **5** Table 2 reveals that of the carbonates, only ammonium carbonate, potassium carbonate, and sodium carbonate are soluble in water. All nitrates and acetates are soluble in water. Most sulfates and bromides are soluble in water.
11. **1** Observe the temperature recorded for Antarctica.
12. **3** Proteins of protoplasm coagulate at very high temperatures.
13. **5** Removing heat from a substance causes molecules to move more slowly. States of matter (solid, liquid, gas) depend on this factor.
14. **1** Cryogenic temperatures are 183°C below zero.
15. **1** Humans are responsible for many forms of water pollution, including industrial processes.
16. **2** During aeration of water, methane and carbon dioxides are liberated, and oxygen is absorbed from the air.
17. **4** Objects heavier than water will drop to the bottom of water. This is an effect of gravity.
18. **3** Green plants absorb carbon dioxide and liberate oxygen during photosynthesis. Light is needed by the plant in order to carry on the process.
19. **4** Anaerobic bacteria thrive in environments that do not have oxygen.
20. **5** While bacteria of decay may at times decompose organic wastes, in this question the other four choices are definite methods of water purification. Another justification for this choice is that bacteria may be pathogenic.

PHYSICS

<u>Items 1 and 2</u> refer to the following information.

As you break a beam of light, in one case you may be operating an automatic door opener and in another case you may be setting off a burglar alarm system. Actually your body is breaking a beam of light that is focused on a photoelectric cell.

That beam has been producing a flow of electrons from the photoelectric cell. When your body interrupts the beam, the current stops. This closes a relay that starts a motor.

Almost a hundred years ago Heinrich Hertz found that certain substances give off a weak electric current when struck by a beam of light. This is the basis for the electric eye in which light energy is changed into electricity.

1. Which of the following illustrates the change from mechanical energy to electrical energy? **1.** 1 2 3 4 5
   (1) electric iron
   (2) steam engine
   (3) flourescent lamp
   (4) electric eye
   (5) electric generator

2. A photoelectric cell is a device that **2.** 1 2 3 4 5
   (1) opens doors
   (2) sets off burglar alarms
   (3) breaks a beam of light
   (4) produces electric energy from light
   (5) starts a motor

---

3. An object travels for 8.00 seconds with an average speed of 160 metres per second. The distance traveled by the object is **3.** 1 2 3 4 5
   (1) 20 m
   (2) 200 m
   (3) 1280 m
   (4) 2560 m
   (5) more than 2560 m

4. People who live close to major airports are most likely to complain about which form of pollution? **4.** 1 2 3 4 5
   (1) sound
   (2) heat
   (3) radioactivity
   (4) particulates
   (5) none of these

5. Which diagram best represents the reflection of an object *O* by plane mirror *M*? **5.** 1 2 3 4 5

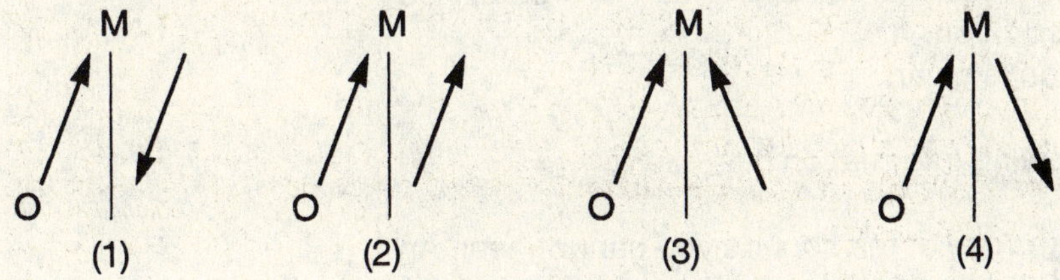

(5) none of these

6. The graph on the next page represents the relationships between temperature and time as heat is added at a constant rate to equal masses of four substances labeled *A*, *B*, *C*, and *D*. The temperature of which substance increased most rapidly? **6.** 1 2 3 4 5
   (1) *A*
   (2) *B*
   (3) *C*
   (4) *D*
   (5) Not enough information is given

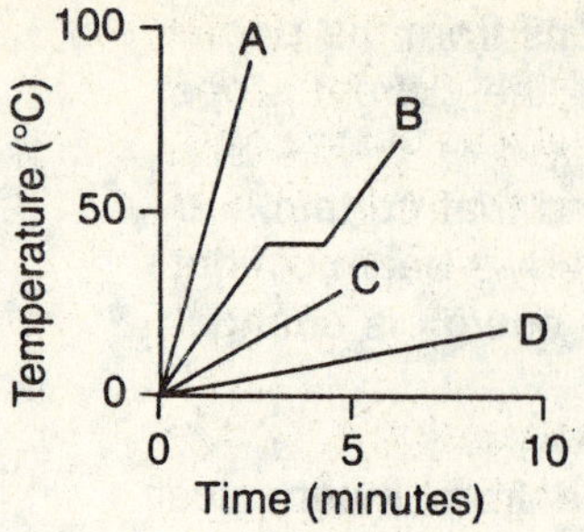

7. Which graph represents the relationship between the mass of an object and its distance from the earth's surface?

7. 1 2 3 4 5

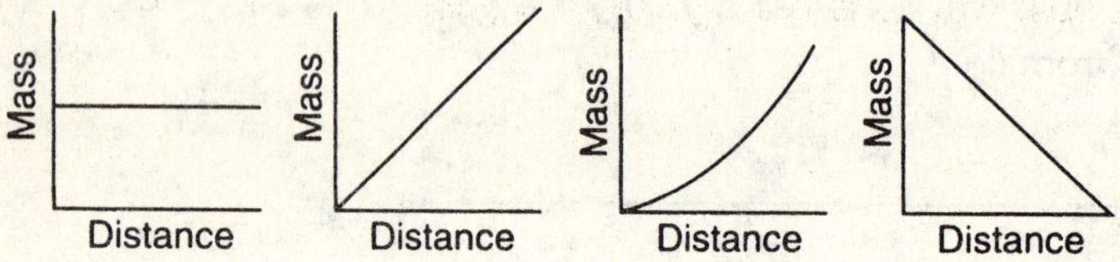

(1) (2) (3) (4)

(5) none of these

8. The climates of densely populated industrial areas tend to be warmer than similarly located sparsely populated rural areas. From this observation, what can be inferred about the human influence on local climate?

8. 1 2 3 4 5

(1) Local climates are not affected by increases in population density.
(2) The local climate in densely populated areas can be changed by human activities.
(3) In densely populated areas, human activities increase the amount of natural pollutants.
(4) In sparsely populated areas, human activities have stabilized the rate of energy absorption.
(5) Not enough information is given.

Items 9 to 11 refer to the following information.

The field of ultrasonics makes use of the sounds you cannot hear. An object must vibrate at least 16 times per second to make sound vibrations that the human ear can detect. The human ear cannot hear sounds made by vibrations of more than 20 000 per second. Sounds beyond the range of our hearing are called ultrasonic sounds. Bats use these sounds to avoid whatever is in the path of flight. The bat sends out a sound, and hearing no echo indicates that the path is clear. An echo makes the bat change the direction of flight.

Sound waves can be absorbed by soft material, but they will reflect when they strike a rigid surface. This principle is used in a device called *sonar* (SOund Navigation And Ranging), which is used to detect submarines and other underwater objects. Sound waves are sent out. The time for the waves to return gives a measure of the distance of the object that produces the echo.

9. What principle explains why test explosions made underwater can be picked up by instruments hundreds of kilometres away?
(1) Sound waves travel through water.
(2) Special instruments can pick up sound waves out of the range of human hearing.
(3) Sound waves bounce.
(4) Echoes can be silences by acoustics.
(5) Sonar can find objects beyond the range of ordinary sight and hearing.

9. 1 2 3 4 5

10. Of the following, which is the best way to avoid echoes in a busy room?
(1) Keep all windows closed.
(2) Use air-conditioning.
(3) Hang curtains and draperies.
(4) Lower all ceilings.
(5) Adjust the sound of rings on the telephone and door bells.

10. 1 2 3 4 5

11. Which term describes a reflected sound?
(1) frequency
(2) wave
(3) echo
(4) pitch
(5) vibration

11. 1 2 3 4 5

Items 12 to 17 refer to the following information.

Although a jet engine and a rocket engine operate on the principle of Newton's Third Law, they differ in that a jet must take in oxygen from the air to burn its fuel, but a rocket must carry its own oxygen. Gases escaping under great pressure in one direction exert a push on the engine in the opposite direction. According to Newton's Third Law, to each action there is an equal and opposite reaction. You can illustrate the principle by blowing up a rubber balloon and then allowing the air to escape. Notice that the balloon moves forward as the air escapes in the opposite direction.

12. Which of the following describes Newton's Third Law?
(1) an object at rest
(2) gravitational force
(3) objects in uniform motion
(4) falling bodies
(5) action equals reaction

12. 1 2 3 4 5

13. What characteristic of rocket engines is not characteristic of jet engines?
(1) method of obtaining oxygen
(2) method of using oxygen
(3) reaction to the escaping gases
(4) application of Newton's Third Law
(5) methods involved in the burning process

13. 1 2 3 4 5

14. Which of the following would be best explained by Newton's Third Law?
(1) A balloon with a lower density than air rises.
(2) A bat strikes a ball and the bat breaks.
(3) A sled accelerates while sliding downhill.
(4) A boat slows down when its engines are turned off.
(5) A rock, thrown horizontally, falls to the ground.

14. 1 2 3 4 5

15. Which of the following is (are) not found in an airplane with a jet engine?
(1) ailerons
(2) fuselage
(3) propellers
(4) rudders
(5) flaps

15. 1 2 3 4 5

16. What propels jet planes?
(1) the thrust of hot gases
(2) propeller blades
(3) rocket motors
(4) steam turbines
(5) any of these

16. 1 2 3 4 5

17. Imagine that you are standing on a frictionless ice rink, holding a medicine ball. What will happen if you throw the ball forward?
(1) You will move backwards.
(2) You will move forward, following the ball.
(3) You will not move at all.
(4) How you move depends on how you are standing.
(5) How you move depends on how the ball is caught.

17. 1 2 3 4 5

<u>Items 18 to 20</u> refer to the following information.

The extreme cold of last winter has made us more conscious of the need for heat conservation. Canadians have become aware that new fuels should be sought and, perhaps just as important, new ways of preventing heat loss should be developed. In the operation of engines we are concerned with the problem of getting rid of excess heat, so that the engine does not overheat. How is heat transferred? By conduction, heat energy is transferred through a substance by increased movement of its molecules. In convection, air is heated so that it expands and rises; it is then replaced by cooler air. When heat energy is transferred through space, the process is called radiation. The wave motion in radiation is similar to that of light. The higher the temperature of an object, the greater the amount of heat it radiates. Hot black objects radiate more heat than light objects at the same temperature.

18. Why can the vacuum bottle (thermos) keep hot liquids hot and cold liquids cold?
(1) Cork is a conductor.
(2) Glass is a poor insulator.
(3) The silvered inside surfaces reflect electromagnetic waves.
(4) The double-walled glass bottle helps heat transfer by conduction.
(5) The double-walled glass bottle helps heat transfer by convection.

18. 1 2 3 4 5

19. To heat a room efficiently, you should place a radiator near the floor. What principle is being put into operation?
(1) convection
(2) radiation
(3) conduction
(4) direct heat transfer
(5) condensation

19. 1 2 3 4 5

20. To which of the following is the thermos bottle similar in principle?
(1) the freezing unit in an electric refrigerator
(2) radiant heaters
(3) solar heating systems
(4) storm windows
(5) a thermostatically controlled heating system

20. 1 2 3 4 5

Turn to the answer key and the answer analysis which follow.

What's Your Score?

________ right, ________ wrong

Excellent	16–20
Good	13–15
Fair	10–12

If your score is low, don't get discouraged. Perhaps physics is a difficult subject for you. Try to find out why you failed. The analysis of correct answers which follows will help you to pinpoint your errors. If your mistake was lack of information, turn to the "Glossary of Scientific Terms" (page 362) and look up the meanings of the words you did not understand. If it was a mistake in interpretation, review the analysis of the question.

ANSWER KEY

1. **5**	6. **1**	11. **3**	16. **1**
2. **4**	7. **1**	12. **5**	17. **1**
3. **3**	8. **2**	13. **1**	18. **3**
4. **1**	9. **1**	14. **2**	19. **1**
5. **3**	10. **3**	15. **3**	20. **4**

ANSWER ANALYSIS

1. **5** An electric generator is driven by steam or water power. This rotary mechanical energy is converted into electrical energy. In the electric iron, electrical energy is converted into heat energy when electricity passing through the core heats the element. In the steam engine, steam expands and pushes a piston that is attached to a drive shaft. Thus, heat energy is converted into mechanical energy. In the fluorescent lamp electrical energy is converted into light energy. The electric current vapourizes some mercury in the lamp, and ultraviolet rays are produced. These rays strike the inner coating of the lamp and cause the chemical phosphorous in it to glow. The electric eye or photoelectric cell and its operation are described in the selection. Light energy is converted into electric energy.
2. **4** All of the events occur, but the photoelectric cell does nothing but produce electricity when light strikes it.
3. **3** The *average speed* with which an object moves is equal to the distance moved divided by the time it takes to move that distance:

$$v = \frac{s}{t}$$

$$16\,m/sec = s/8\,sec$$

$$s = 1280\,m$$

4. **1** Modern technology has been producing faster and faster jet planes. In general these faster planes tend to produce more engine noise than earlier models. As jets approach an airport for landing, they descend to lower altitudes. People who live near these landing approaches are exposed to high noise levels.
5. **3** The reflection of light from an object by a *plane mirror* results in a virtual image behind the mirror. The image is erect (if the object is erect), the same size as the object, and the image is as far behind the mirror as the object is in front. This last part means that every point of the image is as far behind the mirror as the corresponding point of the object is in front. We eliminate choices 1 and 4 immediately because in them the image is upside down. In choice 2 the image is erect, but its top is far from the mirror although the top of the object is close, and the bottom of the image is close to the mirror although the bottom of the object is far. In choice 3 everything looks right. The image is erect, it is the same size as the object, and every point on it is as far behind the mirror as the corresponding point of the object is in front.
6. **1** For line A the temperature rises amost 100° in about two minutes. By comparison the temperature rise for line D in two minutes is only about ten degrees. Line A has the steepest slope. This indicates that its temperature is increasing the most rapidly.

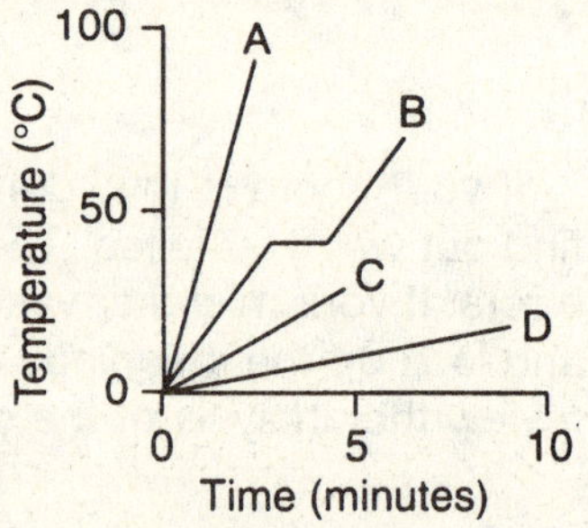

7. **1** The mass of an object is not affected by its distance from the earth's surface. It has the same value in a valley as on the top of a mountain. The horizontal graph on a plot of mass against distance shows this correctly; the mass value does not change as the distance changes. (*Weight* decreases as the distance from the earth increases, but not in accordance with any of the graphs.)
8. **2** There is less vegetation in densely populated areas. This can cause an increase in the amount of energy absorbed. The discharge of gases into the air from some industrial plants would also increase the amount of energy absorbed. Greater energy absorption would cause warmer temperatures.
9. **1** Some liquids carry sound waves better than air. At normal room temperature sound travels at 340 metres per second in air and 1500 metres per second in water.
10. **3** In order to catch sound waves before they can become echoes, curtains and draperies can be used to absorb the sound waves.
11. **3** In sound, the frequency of the wave is the number of complete vibrations back and forth per second. A wave is disturbance in a medium as a result of transfer of energy. An echo is a reflected sound. Pitch is one of the basic characteristics of musical sounds. Vibration is a rapid movement to and fro.
12. **5** To each action there is an equal and opposite reaction.
13. **1** The passage mentions that a rocket must carry its own oxygen supply, but the jet uses the oxygen of the air.
14. **2** When the bat strikes the ball, the ball strikes the bat, causing it to break.
15. **3** In jet engines the force of hot, expanding gases provides the energy that drives the plane forward. In other engines, the blades of the propeller pull against the air as they whirl. Ailerons are flaps on the rear edge of the wing of the plane that help change the direction of the plane in flight. The fuselage is the body of the plane. The rudder is the part used to swing

the nose of the plane and prevent it from slipping when making a turn. The flaps act as brakes in the air and slow down the motion for a smooth landing.

16. **1** According to Newton's Third Law, the action of the ejected gases produces a reaction that thrusts the plane forward.
17. **1** If you push the ball forward, the ball pushes you backward.
18. **3** Since a shiny surface reflects electromagnetic waves, it minimizes heat loss by radiation.
19. **1** Radiators heat rooms by convection.
20. **4** The basic principle of the thermos bottle is to prevent heat loss. The cork is a good insulator, thus preventing heat loss by conduction. The space between the double walls is evacuated, minimizing heat transfer by convection or conduction. The inside surfaces are silvered to reflect electromagnetic waves and prevent heat transfer by radiation.

8

LANGUAGE ARTS, READING (INTERPRETING LITERATURE AND THE ARTS)

AN OVERVIEW

The overview provides a complete description of each of the content areas: Popular Literature, Classical Literature, and Commentary on the Arts.

WHAT THE TEST IS LIKE

This section introduces you to the *purpose questions* preceding each selection as well as types of test questions: comprehension, application, and analysis questions.

BASIC READING SKILLS

The three basic reading skills are finding the main idea, finding details, and making inferences.

BASICS ON READING LITERATURE—PROSE, POETRY, DRAMA

In this section, basic reading skills are applied to reading of prose, poetry, and drama selections. Detailed analyses are made of five selections, two each in prose and poetry, and one in drama.

BASICS ON READING COMMENTARY ON THE ARTS

The new content area, Commentary on the Arts, is thoroughly treated.

GLOSSARY OF LITERARY TERMS

This is a mini-dictionary of 73 terms with definitions and illustrations of each.

PRACTICE IN INTERPRETING LITERATURE AND THE ARTS

There are 60 questions on interpreting literature and the arts. All of the arts are tested—literature, art, music, theatre, dance, film, and television.

AN OVERVIEW

The Language Arts, Reading (Interpreting Literature and the Arts) Test consists of questions based on materials drawn from three areas: Popular Literature, Classical Literature, and Commentary on the Arts.

Literature selections are mostly by American authors. English, Canadian, and world literature are also represented.

Materials in the commentary area include prose excerpts *about* literature and the arts: published comments, reviews, and criticism of art, music, television, film, theatre, dance, and literature.

Items in this test measure your ability to understand, apply, and analyze literary selections and selections that deal with the arts. They are weighted as follows:

Content Area	Percentage of Test
Popular Literature	50%
Classical Literature	25%
Commentary about Literature and the Arts	25%

Popular Literature

Popular literature ranges from contemporary literary works to the popular press. The popular literature used on the test is of such quality that it can be considered a model of good writing that is likely to be read for a long time to come. The selections include fiction, prose nonfiction, poetry, and drama.

Fiction selections are excerpts from novels or short stories found in popular books and magazines. Prose nonfiction includes excerpts from journals, travelogues, essays, criticism, biography, and major newspapers. Other sources for prose nonfiction include columns that serve as social commentary, well-written biographies of men and women in this century, articles from news periodicals, essays from journals, and essays and other materials that have already appeared in books.

Poetry selections consist of short contemporary poems or excerpts from longer poems. Drama selections are chosen from the work of contemporary playwrights.

Good writers whose work is represented in the questions on this test in the popular literature category include Maya Angelou, James Baldwin, Betty Friedan, William Golding, Ken Kesey, John LeCarré, Toni Morrison, Joyce Carol Oates, and Studs Terkel, among others.

Classical Literature

Classical literature includes fiction, prose, prose nonfiction, poetry, and drama. Classical literature is defined as "a piece of literature which has achieved a recognized position in literary history for its superior qualities."

Materials for this section of the test may be drawn from nineteenth- and twentieth-century works considered classics. The writers represented in the classical category include Stephen Crane, Ralph Waldo Emerson, William Faulkner, F. Scott Fitzgerald, Robert Frost, Ernest Hemingway, Eugene O'Neill, Carl Sandburg, John Steinbeck, Henry David Thoreau, and Tennessee Williams, among others.

Commentary on the Arts

Commentary selections consist of writing about literature and the arts, and are comments, criticism, or reviews of art, music, television, film, literature, dance, and theatre. These are drawn from popular magazines and newspapers and are informational and descriptive. The selections will give you all the information you need to know to answer the questions.

WHAT THE TEST IS LIKE

Reading selections on which the questions are based range in length from 200 to about 400 words. There will be nine or ten such selections on the test. A brief question will precede each selection. This question will give you a lead as to what the selection is about and help you focus your attention on the main idea of the selection.

The 40 questions you will have to answer in the allotted 65 minutes fall into four categories:

Comprehension	20%
Application	15%
Analysis	30–35%
Synthesis	30–35%

All questions are of the multiple-choice type.

Comprehension Questions

These questions are of two kinds.

1. The first kind refers to ideas that are clearly stated in the selection. These questions test your ability to understand the information and ideas, to restate them, and to summarize them.

2. They are easier than the second kind which refers to ideas that are implied from what is stated in the selection. This tests your ability to draw conclusions, identify implications, and understand the consequences of what is stated in the selection. Because you must add your own thinking to what the selection states, these questions are more difficult.

Application Questions

These test your ability to use information and ideas gathered from the selection in a situation *different* from the one described in the test. You have to transfer those ideas and principles to a new context.

Analysis Questions

These test your ability to examine elements of diction, style, and structure we studied in the chapter on Writing Skills, Part I as they are found in each of the selections in this test: tone, diction, logical organization, sentence structure, figurative language, principles of paragraph development, among others. Not only will you have to identify these techniques of style but you will have to be able to know which produce a particular effect and identify that effect. If you mastered Writing Skills, Part I, you should have no trouble with these questions.

BASIC READING SKILLS

Reading consists of a complex number of skills. The writer sets forth his or her ideas using the medium of language consisting of printed words. If the writer has stated the ideas clearly, they have been well organized and well developed. You, the reader, must draw meaning from the ideas expressed on the printed page. In addition, there may be ideas which are implied and not openly stated. For example, a woman dressed in black is described as *grieving*. The implication is that she has lost a loved one, even if it is not exactly so stated.

Reading requires the use of a number of skills so you can decode or derive from the language used the meaning intended by the writer, whether it is explicitly stated or suggested by implication. These skills are basically three in number.

1. ***You read to find the main idea of the selection.*** You find it in a variety of places. It may be stated directly in the first sentence (easy to find). It may be stated in the final sentence to which the others build up (a bit harder to find). It may have to be discovered within the passage (most difficult). An example of this (note the underscored words) may be found in the following paragraph:

    Several students were seriously injured in football games last Saturday. The week before, several more were hospitalized. Football has become a dangerous sport. The piling up of players in a scrimmage often leads to serious injury. Perhaps some rule changes would lessen the number who are hurt.

    You may also find that the main idea is not expressed at all, but can only be inferred from the selection as a whole.

    The plane landed at 4 P.M. As the door opened, the crowd burst into a long, noisy demonstration. The waiting mob surged against the police guard lines. Women were screaming. Teenagers were yelling for autographs or souvenirs. The visitor smiled and waved at his fans.

    The main idea of the paragraph is not expressed, but it is clear that some popular hero, movie or rock star is being welcomed enthusiastically at the airport.

> ***To find the main idea of a passage***, ask yourself any or all of these questions:
> 1. What is the *main idea* of the passage? (Why did the author write it?)
> 2. What is the *topic sentence* of the paragraph or paragraphs (the sentence that the other sentences build on or flow from)?
> 3. What *title* would I give this selection?

2. ***You read to find the details that explain or develop the main idea.*** How do you do this? You must determine how the writer develops the main idea. Either he will give examples to illustrate that idea, or he may give reasons why the statement which is the main idea is true. Or he may give arguments for or against a position stated as the main idea. The writer may define a complex term and give a number of qualities of a complicated belief (such as democracy). He may also classify a number of objects within a larger category. Finally, he may compare two ideas or objects (show how they are similar) or contrast them (show how they are different).

    In the paragraph immediately above, you can see that the sentence "You must determine how the writer develops the main idea" *is* the main idea. Six ways in which the writer can develop the main idea follow. These are the details that actually develop the main idea of the paragraph.

> ***To find the main details of a passage***, the questions to ask yourself are these:
> 1. What examples illustrate the main point?
> 2. What reasons or proof support the main idea?
> 3. What arguments are presented for or against the main idea?
> 4. What specific qualities are offered about the idea or subject being defined?
> 5. What classifications is a larger group broken down into?
> 6. What are the similarities and differences between two ideas or subjects being compared or contrasted?

3. ***You read to make inferences by putting together ideas which are expressed to arrive at other ideas which are not.*** In other words, you draw conclusions from the information pre-

sented by the author. You do this by locating relevant details and determining their relationships (time sequence, place sequence, cause and effect).

How do you do this? You can put one fact together with a second to arrive at a third which is not stated. You can apply a given fact to a different situation. You can predict an outcome based on the facts given.

To make inferences from a passage, ask yourself the following questions:
1. From the facts presented, what conclusions can I draw?
2. What is being suggested, in addition to what is being stated?
3. What will be the effect of something which is described?
4. What will happen next (after what is being described)?
5. What applications does the principle or idea presented have?

Reading Popular Literature

The basic reading skills apply to popular and classical literature alike. Popular literature is easier to read. It presents fewer problems in content since you are more likely to have shared the same experiences as the writer. Also you are generally more familiar with the language of the writer. True, the content and style of the writer may cause difficulties, but, since the selections are drawn from sources which you read quite frequently—newspapers and magazines, for example—they should be no more difficult than the usual materials geared to the high school graduate.

Reading Classical Literature

Classical literature differs from popular literature in a number of ways. The settings are certainly different because they go back at least fifty to two hundred years. The style of writing is different. Sentences are longer and more complicated. The vocabulary is less familiar. Some of the subject matter may be dated for today's reader. On the other hand, fine classical literature deals with the eternal emotions of love, hate, greed, loyalty, self-sacrifice, joy, fear, among others. And many themes are eternal—the relationship of man to his fellow man and woman, of man to God, of man to nature, of man to his family, of man to his country.

Reading classical literature requires patience but it can be greatly rewarding. Try to imagine the unfamiliar setting. Reread the difficult sentences. Get the meaning of the unfamiliar word from its context. Find the application to life today of the theme of the selection. Continued practice will make these worthwhile tasks easier and the literature more satisfying.

BASICS ON READING LITERATURE—PROSE, POETRY, DRAMA

In addition to the reading skills required in general reading, to read literary material, whether popular or classical, additional special skills are necessary, namely the ability to: recognize the mood of the selection and the purpose for which it was written; deal with involved sentences and sentence structure; figure out unusual word meanings from the sentences in which they appear; interpret figures of speech (see the "Glossary of Literary Terms" beginning on page 467).

Read carefully the following treatment of these special skills and then go to the sample reading passages and the questions and analyzed answers based on them to get a feeling for these special, and necessary, skills.

LOCATING THE MAIN IDEA

Depending upon the type of passage—poetry, fiction, essay, drama—the technique of finding the main idea may vary. In the essay, for example, the main idea may very well appear as a straightforward statement, usually expressed in the topic sentence. In this particular case, the trick is to find the topic sentence. In works of fiction, poetry, or drama, the main idea might be found in a line of dialogue or exposition, or within a long, flowing line of verse.

Prose

In reading *prose*, the main unit is the paragraph. Since the paragraphs you will encounter on the examination have all been chosen for their "loaded" content—that is, because they contain a number of ideas offering possibilities for questions—it is important that you learn how to locate the main idea. This, in turn, will enable you to understand many of the subordinate, that is, less important elements of the paragraph—all of which may be the basis for examination questions.

The topic sentence containing the main idea is used in five standard patterns:

1. The topic sentence, expressing the main idea, may introduce the paragraph and be followed by sentences containing details that explain, exemplify, prove, or support the idea, or add interest.

EXAMPLE:
In *Alice in Wonderland*, Lewis Carroll has created a world of fantasy out of essentially real creatures, transformed into whimsy by the odd patterns of a dream. Sitting with her sister by a stream, Alice sees a rabbit; as she dozes off, the rabbit becomes larger, dons a waistcoat and a pocket watch, and acquires human speech.

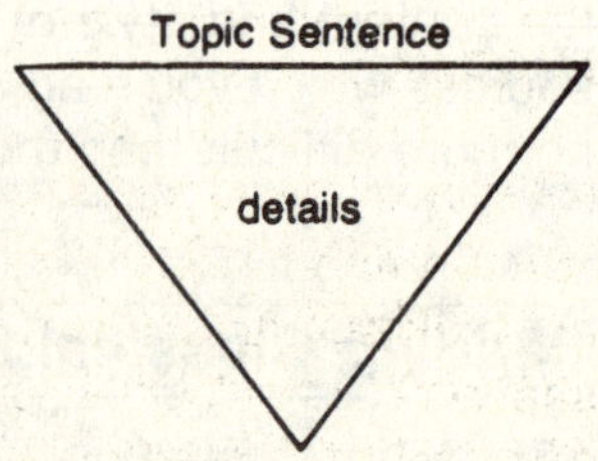

2. The topic sentence may appear at the end of the paragraph, with a series of details leading to the main idea.

EXAMPLE:
The small, darting rabbit on the riverbank becomes a huge White Rabbit, complete with waistcoat and pocket watch. The cards in a discarded deck become the Queen of Hearts and her court. The real world of Alice Liddell becomes, through the odd patterns of the dream, the fantasy world of *Alice in Wonderland.*

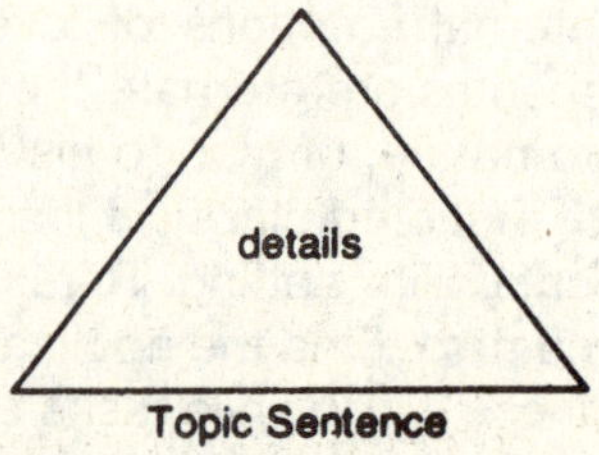

3. The selection may begin with a broad generalization (topic sentence) followed by details that support the main idea and lead to another, broad generalization which is called the "summary sentence" (conclusion).

EXAMPLE:
The elements of the real world become, through the strange, shifting patterns of the dream, objects and creatures of curiosity and whimsy. A scurrying rabbit becomes a humanized White Rabbit, a deck of cards becomes the court of the Queen of Hearts, a kitten becomes a chess Queen. In *Alice in Wonderland* reality becomes fantasy and, for a while, fantasy becomes reality.

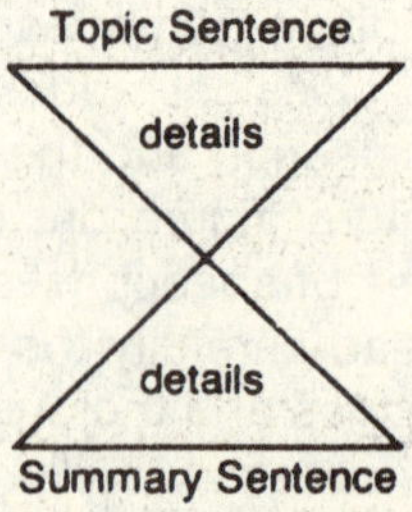

4. The topic sentence may appear in the body of the paragraph.

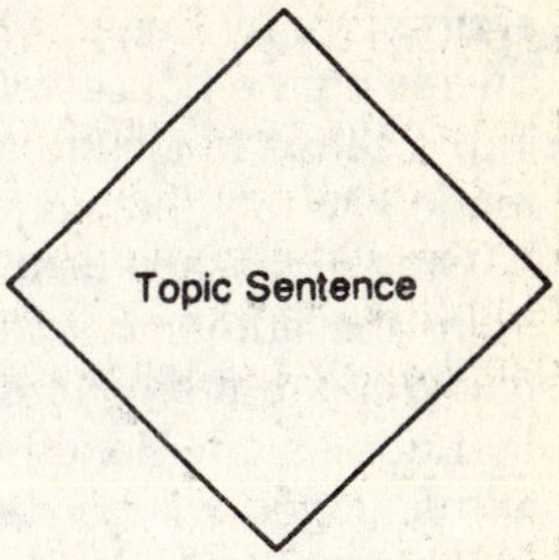

EXAMPLE:

When Alice goes through the looking glass, she enters a garden where the flowers speak. In a dark forest, a fawn befriends her. The dream world reverses the events of the real world. The Lion and the Unicorn come off their shield and do battle. The Red Queen, originally a kitten of Alice's pet cat Dinah, gives Alice instructions in etiquette.

5. The selection may contain *no expressed topic sentence* but consist of a series of sentences concerning details and implying a central thought.

EXAMPLE:

A deck of cards becomes a royal court. A kitten becomes a chess Queen. A scurrying wild creature becomes a sophisticated courtier, a White Rabbit in vest and pocket watch. A proper Victorian tea-party becomes the setting for rude remarks and outrageous behaviour.

Poetry

Finding the main idea of a poem can be particularly difficult because of a special kind of language surrounding it. This language, known as "imagery," is one of the main characteristics of poetry. Do not make the mistake of thinking that imagery is just put there by the poet to obscure meaning or to show off his or her facility with language. In the best poems, imagery is a very important and integral part of the work. Take, for example, the following lines by John Donne:

Go, and catch a falling star,
  Get with child a mandrake root,
Tell me where all past years are,
  Or who cleft the Devil's foot.
Teach me to hear mermaids singing . . .
    And swear
    No where
Lives a woman true and fair.

A close look at the imagery in this poem will give us an important key to understanding Donne's meaning. Four images in these lines all have one thing in common, and they are very important to the understanding of the poem.

These images include: (1) a falling star, (2) a mandrake root (a large, forked root believed by the superstitious to have human qualities), (3) the Devil's cloven hoof, and (4) mermaids. All these images have one thing in common: they are the objects of the imagination, of mythology, of superstition. No one can catch a falling star, impregnate a root, hear mermaids singing, or say who cleft the Devil's foot. All of these objects and actions are *impossible*. The *only possible act* in these lines is the ability to swear that nowhere can be found a loyal and beautiful woman. But the poet has already asked the reader, several times, to do the impossible—and there is nothing in these lines to indicate that there is any difference between the ability to catch a star and to swear that no good woman exists.

FINDING DETAILS

Very often questions on reading passages will test your ability to locate relevant details. In a descriptive passage, the author may give a general impression of a scene. Take, as an example, the famous short story by Edgar Allan Poe, "The Fall of the House of Usher." The narrator conveys his reaction on seeing the house with the words: "I know not how it was, but, with the first glimpse of the building, a sense of insufferable gloom pervaded my spirit." Two sentences later you get the details that made him feel that way.

Or in a passage dealing with the character of the subject of a biography, details will document the point the author is making. Sandburg's biography of Abraham Lincoln is full of passages which follow this pattern. To show the industriousness of Lincoln, Sandburg writes: "Abe knew the sleep that comes after long hours of work outdoors. . . ." You can almost feel certain that the "work" that is mentioned will be described in detail and it is. Among the jobs listed are "clearing timberland," "splitting rails," "harrowing," "planting," "pulling fodder," "helping . . . house raisings, log-rollings, corn-huskings."

Details are also used to move the plot or story interestingly and smoothly along the way. In Hawthorne's "The Ambitious Guest," we find the sentence, "The simplest words must intimate, but not portray, the unutterable horror of the catastrophe." Immediately there follow details which tell us just how horrible the catastrophe was.

Finally, details are often used to provide reasons for a conclusion that has been reached. Sherlock Holmes is talking to Dr. Watson about his solution of the case, "The Adventure of the Speckled Band." "I had come to these conclusions before ever I had entered his room," and Holmes proceeds to give us the details of why he reached them.

How do you locate a detail? It may be necessary for you to return to the reading passage many times to dig out the details required to answer a given question. In your search, a number of clues may help you. These involve the location of what are called *transitional words*, words which point out the purpose of the details presented.

Transitional Words

These words may indicate *illustrations* of a general idea or impression:

for example	in such cases	
for instance	in the same manner	
in other words	just as	

Or they may signal *additional items:*

again	another	second
also	as well as	third
and	besides	

Or they may point to *opposite evidence:*

but	nevertheless	although
however	otherwise	despite

Sometimes they *identify an important detail:*

don't overlook	notice that	most important

Finally, they may announce a helpful *conclusion* which the details document:

accordingly	finally	in conclusion
as a result	hence	in short

INFERRING WORD MEANING

It is not necessary to memorize an extensive vocabulary to understand the meaning of an unfamiliar word. Quite often the clue to a word's meaning may be found by carefully reading the sentence in which the word appears. For example:

EXAMPLE:

It is easy to understand how the author's *misogyny* developed. His mother abandoned him at the age of five; the aunt who raised him tended to treat him as if he were one of the crosses all good "Christians" must bear; and his wife, whom he adored, ran off with his best friend.

What information are we given in this sentence? We are told that the author had a series of bad experiences in his childhood and young manhood involving people who were very important to him at those times. All of these people—mother, aunt, and wife—are women. We can assume that his treatment by these women led to the author's dislike or mistrust—even hatred—of women because of the way he was treated by some of them. Therefore, we can infer that *misogyny* means "a hatred and mistrust of women," which is, in fact, the dictionary meaning of the word.

Let's try another. Here's a double challenge.

EXAMPLE:
She took *umbrage* at his critical remarks and left in a *dudgeon*.

The key to the meaning of these unfamiliar words is the phrase "critical remarks" which obviously implies that "he" was saying certain things that were unpleasant to "her." The fact that she left, rather than staying to hear him out, tells us that she resented what he was saying, and was very likely quite angry with him. In other words, she *took umbrage* at his remarks, which is the same as saying she *took offense*.

To understand the word *dudgeon*, we must assume, first of all, that the second part of the sentence has some direct relation to the first. We cannot infer that a dudgeon is, for example, some sort of vehicle, since to say that she took offense at his words and left in a carriage, for example, adds an entirely new idea which has no relation to the rest of the sentence. We know, however, that her mood was affected by his remarks, and we may logically conclude that she went away angry. In fact, *dudgeon* means ill humour or resentment, a state of mind which fits in with her having taken offense in the first place. In other words, she got angry and she left in a huff.

The fact to remember, whether you are taking an examination or merely reading for your own pleasure or information, is that unfamiliar words should not be disturbing, or appear to present obstacles that cannot be overcome. While it is true that many big words are used much more frequently in written than in spoken language, there is often a very good reason for this. Spoken language is reenforced with gestures, facial expressions, tone of voice of the speaker. Because written language can rely on none of these, it must be much more specific; and the more words there are to express a particular idea, the more easily the author can choose those which convey his or her exact meaning. A mechanic with a large selection of good tools can accomplish much more, and do the job much better, than a man with only a wrench and a crowbar. Words are the tools of the writer, and the more he or she has and knows how to use properly, the better he or she can do the job.

DETERMINING TONE AND MOOD

Tone is the aspect of the author's style that reveals attitude toward the subject. *Mood* is the atmosphere, or emotional effect, created by the manner in which the author presents the material.

To determine the tone or mood of a passage, consider the feelings or attitudes that are expressed. Examine, for example, the following passages:

EXAMPLE 1:
The room was dark—so dark that even after giving her eyes a while to accustom themselves to the blackness, she could still see nothing. Something soft—she hoped it was only a cobweb—brushed her lip. And the throbbing sound, attuned to her own heavy heartbeat, became stronger and faster.

EXAMPLE 2:
The room was dark—not dark as it is when your eyes are just not used to it, but really *dark* dark. Then there was some soft creepy thing brushing her lip, and she found herself hoping very hard that it was only a cobweb. And then there was that sound—baBoom, baBoom, baBoom—getting faster and louder all the time like her own heart going thump, thump, thump.

Consider the contrasting moods of the two passages above. The first passage presents a sustained mood of suspense and fear. The woman in the room can see nothing; something strange touches her; she hears a heavy and mysterious sound. We have the feeling that something terrible is going to happen; the indication is that something will happen that is dangerous, evil, or deadly.

The second paragraph relates essentially the same event. But we are distracted somewhat from what is happening by several devices. First, we are brought informally into the story—we know what it's like when it's really dark. And the quality of darkness is also expressed informally—it is not pitch dark, or night dark, but "*dark* dark." Then something "creepy" is felt, and the sounds of the noise *and* the woman's heart are described—"baBoom" and "thump." The feeling conveyed by these devices is somehow made less frightening by the familiarity of the language, and the general impression is less one of total fear than of "scariness"—an easier emotion to deal with. Thus we have the impression from this second passage that whatever happens will probably not be all that bad or, if it is, it will somehow be easier to overcome.

Satire and Irony

One way of expressing a particular tone in relation to what is being described is the use of *satire*. Satire is a form of wit, at times disrespectful, which has, as its main purpose, exposing the foolishness of a person, an idea, or a social custom or institution. Political cartoonists use satire to express their views on the stupidity or silliness of world events which, under other circumstances, might appear to be of earth-shaking importance. The following passage, from Voltaire's *Candide*, one of the world's great satirical masterpieces, will help you better understand satire.

EXAMPLE:

The Baron was one of the most powerful lords in Westphalia, for his castle possessed a door and windows. The dogs in his stable-yards formed a pack of hounds when necessary; his grooms were his huntsmen; the village curate was his Grand Almoner. They all called him "My Lord," and laughed heartily at his stories. The Baroness weighed about three hundred and fifty pounds, was therefore greatly respected; and did the honours of the house with a dignity which rendered her still more respectable.

Obviously, the passage above is not intended as a serious or respectful description of the "powerful" Baron and his way of life. On the contrary, his castle is distinguished only by the commonplace—a door and windows. His "hunting pack"—the purebred hunting dogs kept by wealthy and aristocratic men who hunted more for pleasure than out of necessity—is composed of the mongrels which hang about the stables on the off chance of finding a scrap of food. His stablehands double as well-trained men-at-arms attached to many noble households; probably, when necessary, they go out after the odd deer or boar whenever the meat supply starts to get a little low. The village priest (probably the only person in the village who can read or write) handles the Baron's bookkeeping, such as it may be. The Baroness is distinguished mostly by her enormous size; her dignity is due mainly to the fact that she probably has difficulty moving from one place to the other and therefore appears dignified when she is merely slow and clumsy. The author is, in fact, poking fun at certain well-to-do farmers who pose as landed gentry; and, by implication, at those who are impressed by such types as well.

Often confused with satire, but quite different from it, is *irony*. The confusion may result from the fact that, as a figure of speech, irony, like satire, often says one thing and means something entirely different. Mark Antony's calling Julius Caesar's assassin, Brutus, "an honourable man" is such an example. But, unlike satire, irony is often not at all amusing.

Irony may be more than a figure of speech; a sense of irony may pervade an entire piece of literature. One famous example is Guy de Maupassant's short story "The Diamond Necklace," which concerns a vain and pretty woman who borrows a fabulous necklace from a wealthy friend to wear to a ball—hoping, of course, to impress the other guests with her own wealth. Upon returning home, she discovers the necklace is missing. To purchase a replacement, she borrows an enormous sum of money at staggering interest rates, and spends the rest of her life slaving away to repay the loan.

Many years later she meets her wealthy friend, who at first hardly recognizes her because she has aged so badly. When she admits to the friend what had happened, the friend is stunned. "You poor thing," she exclaims. "The necklace you borrowed was an imitation—it was made of paste!" The irony consists of the fact that the woman's life was spent in earning money to pay for an object which was worthless.

Irony may occur on all levels. The de Maupassant story is sad and bitter, but it concerns only a person of little importance. Irony also appears in high tragedy. The great Greek dramatist Sophocles uses irony to crucial effect in his play *Oedipus the King*. As the play opens, the city of which Oedipus is the ruler is cursed by a plague. When Oedipus consults a fortuneteller as to the cause, he is told that the gods are angry because there is a man in the city who has committed a horrible crime, and only that man's punishment will lift the curse. Oedipus vows to find and destroy the culprit. What he does not know is that he is the guilty one, having, unknowingly, murdered his father many years before and subsequently married his own mother. Through his own overwhelming pride in his own righteousness, he has, ironically, sworn to destroy himself.

INFERRING CHARACTER

Character is often implied by a person's words or actions, rather than by direct description. This has always been particularly true of drama, where the reader of the play is often called upon to interpret a character's personality without benefit of stage directions or other descriptive material. In the modern novel, too, the trend has been away from utilizing long descriptive passages and more toward allowing the characters' actions, speech, or thoughts (often called "inner dialogue") to reveal their personalities. The reader must rely, therefore, on the hints offered by the playwright or novelist to interpret character—and even then, a wide range of interpretation may be possible.

The following scene, from Oscar Wilde's comedy *The Importance of Being Earnest*, offers a good sketch of two minor characters. They are Miss Prism, a governess, and Canon (or Doctor) Chasuble, a clergyman.

EXAMPLE:

MISS PRISM: You are too much alone, dear Dr. Chasuble. You should get married. A misanthrope, who hates everyone, I can understand—a womanthrope, never!

CANON CHASUBLE: Believe me, I do not deserve such a new-fangled phrase. The teaching as well as the practice of the early church was distinctly against marriage.

MISS PRISM: That is obviously the reason why the early church has not lasted up to the present day. And you do not seem to realize, dear Doctor, that by persistently remaining single, a man converts himself into a permanent public temptation. Men should be more careful; this very condition of remaining unmarried leads weaker persons astray.

CANON CHASUBLE: But is a man not equally attractive when married?

MISS PRISM: No married man is ever attractive except to his wife.

CANON CHASUBLE: And often, I've been told, not even to her.

MISS PRISM: That depends on the intellectual sympathies of the woman. Maturity can always be depended on. Ripeness can be trusted. Young women are green. (Canon Chasuble shows surprise.) I spoke horticulturally. My metaphor was drawn from fruits.

What do we learn about Miss Prism? First, she is quickwitted. She quickly demolishes the Canon's argument about the teachings and practices of the church. Then, we are given an example of her intellectual prowess. Her argument that bachelors become a permanent temptation to weaker women is a brilliant comment and, when Chasuble questions it, she also disposes of his observation that a married man might also be attractive. Finally, she marshals all the arguments on her own behalf since she is intelligent and no longer a youngster. She stresses "intellectual sympathies"; she mentions her doubts about the trustworthiness of young wives—only maturity and ripeness can really be trusted; young women do not make dependable wives. The conclusion: Miss Prism, who is no longer in the first flush of her youth, thinks she would make an ideal wife.

What has been revealed of Canon Chasuble? First, he is obviously something of a stuffed shirt; his first response to Miss Prism's unusual vocabulary—"womanthrope"—is to scold her for it. He then launches into a speech on the practices of the ancient Church regarding marriage of the clergy. Finally, Miss Prism manages to draw from him a more human response to the idea of marriage: the Canon sadly remarks that married men are not often attractive even to their wives. We can conclude from this remark that he is also somewhat shy, or frightened, by the idea of marriage, although not from personal experience; when a man like Dr. Chasuble says "I've been *told*," he means it. He is a man who speaks, and who must be spoken to, quite precisely; thus, when Miss Prism says "Young women are green," she feels obliged to explain that she is using the word *green* in a special sense.

Briefly, we may draw the following inferences from this passage: (1) the two characters are no longer youthful; (2) they have known each other for a long time; (3) Miss Prism is determined to marry Dr. Chasuble; (4) she understands his personality and has apparently made up her mind that she can adjust to it; and (5) the Canon is a stuffy, somewhat impractical man who is probably no match for a woman of Miss Prism's determination. If asked to draw any conclusions, we might well decide that Miss Prism will probably have her way, and that the two will probably make the necessary adjustments to a married life of limited happiness and total respectability.

Obviously, some ways of portraying character are easier to understand than others, and the personalities described may be more or less complex. The examination questions, however, do not delve too deeply into the characters discussed; the answers can readily be found in the reading passages. You merely have to pick up the author's clues.

INFERRING SETTING

A number of factors are involved in the setting of a selection. These include not only *place* (physical location, type of locale—noisy, crowded, tranquil, etc.), but *time* (of day, of season, of historical period). See what clues you can find in the following passage.

EXAMPLE:

He knew she would be late, but he could not keep himself from hurrying, pushing his way impatiently through the strolling, multilingual crowd. The Germans, their sunburned necks garlanded with camera straps, bargained gutturally with the indifferent women at their stalls, thinking to strike a sharp bargain on the price of a straw handbag or a painted box. The women let them struggle with the unfamiliar numbers, knowing exactly how much they would ultimately settle for. Three American girls, distinguishable by their short hair and madras skirts above sandalled feet and bare legs, dawdled along, giggling at the pleadings of two persistent *pappagalli* who seemed determined to improve international relations at all costs.

The sidestreet leading to the Signoria was hardly less busy, and he found it easier to dodge the small motorbikes bouncing noisily along the cobbled roadway than to struggle against the crowds pouring out of the great museum and onto the narrow sidewalks. He hated these annual floods of holiday-makers and culture-seekers who jammed the streets, the hotels, and the small restaurants so that the year-round residents found it necessary to retreat more than ever to the interiors of their cool, stone houses and their small, closed social circles. The more fortunate natives, of course, headed for Viareggio or the beaches of the South or the Riviera.

He finally found a table at the back of the cafe—a little too close to the bar but partially screened by a box hedge—and ordered a drink. The ancient *piazza* was mostly in shade now, except for the very tops of the towers which had been turned by the sun from the faded buff of the old stone to a rich gold against the blue sky.

What can we tell of the setting described?

Place: We can immediately pick up a number of clues. Obviously, the setting is a city (crowds, sidewalks, a market, a museum). It is also not in the United States, since American girls are particularly distinguishable. By the mention of the Riviera as a nearby vacation spot, we know that we are somewhere in Western Europe—but not Germany (the Germans are not familiar with the language).

We can narrow the location down even further (although you are not expected to have all this extra information): two foreign words, *pappagalli* and *piazza*, might lead to the educated guess that the country is Italy.

Time: (1) Period—Although the city itself is old (cobbled streets, narrow sidewalks, towers in an ancient piazza), the period is more recent. Motorbikes, barelegged girls, camera-carrying tourists all indicate the modern era. (2) Season—we can assume by the dress of the tourists, and by the fact that the natives usually head for the beach during this season, that it is summer. (3) Time of day—The piazza is in shade, except for the tops of the towers. It is unlikely, therefore, to be midday. Since the main character orders a drink in a cafe-bar, and since we have nowhere been given to understand that he has a drinking problem, we can assume it is late afternoon (cocktail time) and he has an appointment with someone for a predinner drink.

You should be made aware that the above passage was prepared solely to give you practice in inferring setting, and that you are not likely to find too many passages on the actual examination that concentrate on such description. However, you should learn to pick up small clues here and there that will give you an idea of the setting in a descriptive passage. Remember that, more often than not, the locale will be inferred rather than actually stated.

Now let us turn to two representative passages from prose literature. Read these carefully; answer the six questions based on each; compare your answers with those in the answer key; then study the analysis of the answers, particularly those which you may have answered incorrectly.

Prose Illustration—Popular

WHAT IS ABOUT TO HAPPEN TO BORIS?

The light carriage swished through the layers of fallen leaves upon the terrace. In places, they lay so thick that they half covered the stone balusters and reached the knees of Diana's stag. But the trees were bare; only here and there a single golden leaf trembled high upon the black twigs. Following the curve of the road, Boris's carriage came straight upon the main terrace and the house, majestic as the Sphinx herself in the sunset. The light of the setting sun seemed to have soaked into the dull masses of stone. They reddened and glowed with it until the whole place became a mysterious, a glorified abode, in which the tall windows shone like a row of evening stars.

Boris got out of the britska in front of the mighty stone stairs and walked toward them, feeling for his letter. Nothing stirred in the house. It was like walking into a cathedral. "And," he thought, "by the time that I get into that carriage once more, what will everything be like to me?"

1. The title below that expresses the main idea of this passage is
(1) "The Lure of Autumn"
(2) "Sphinx in the Sunset"
(3) "A Mysterious Cathedral"
(4) "A Terrifying Surprise"
(5) "An Important Visit"

1. 1 2 3 4 5

2. From the description of the house, we may most safely conclude that the house
(1) is sometimes used as a place of worship
(2) is owned by a wealthy family
(3) was designed by Egyptian architects
(4) is constructed of modern brick
(5) is a dark, cold-looking structure

2. 1 2 3 4 5

3. This story probably takes place in
(1) the British Isles
(2) the Far East
(3) eastern Europe
(4) southern United States
(5) the Mediterranean

3. 1 2 3 4 5

4. We may most safely conclude that Boris has come to the house in order to
(1) secure a job
(2) find out about his future
(3) join his friends for the holidays
(4) attend a hunting party
(5) visit his old family home

4. 1 2 3 4 5

5. In this passage, which atmosphere does the author attempt to create?
(1) pleasant anticipation
(2) quiet peace
(3) carefree gaiety
(4) unrelieved despair
(5) vague uncertainty

5. 1 2 3 4 5

6. From this passage, which inference can most safely be drawn?
(1) The house is topped by a lofty tower.
(2) Boris is tired from his journey.
(3) There is only one terrace before the house is reached.
(4) The most imposing feature of the house is the door.
(5) Boris intends to stay at the house for only a short time.

6. 1 2 3 4 5

ANSWER KEY

1. **5** 2. **2** 3. **3** 4. **2** 5. **5** 6. **5**

ANSWER ANALYSIS

1. **5** Boris has come to the house and, as he enters, he wonders what changes may take place for him as a result of his visit. To Boris, this will be "an important visit." Choice 1 cannot be correct. Going back to the passage, we find on lines 3–5 that "the trees were bare; only here and there a single golden leaf trembled high upon the black twigs." This and a reference to "layers of fallen leaves" in line 1 are the only indications of season. And "the lure" of attraction of the season is not even mentioned. We reject this because it is only the setting for the main idea of the selection and background detail at best. It is not the *main* idea. Choices 2 and 3 are incorrect for similar reasons. In each case, a *detail* has been picked out of the selection and offered as the *main* idea. Choice 2 is taken from line 6 where the house is compared to the Sphinx. Choice 3 is a combination of words taken from lines 9 and 13, both also involving a comparison—this time of the house with a cathedral. Choice 4 is completely incorrect. There is no surprise, nor is the selection's mood one of terror. There is anticipation of something about to happen rather than something surprising which has happened.
2. **2** We can conclude that the house is owned by a wealthy family because there are several terraces, the stone stairs are "mighty," the windows are tall, and there are "masses of stone." Of the possibilities offered, this is the one "we may most safely conclude" is correct. Choices 1 and 3 are both incorrect, again for similar reasons. Each is based on a figure used in the passage, the implied comparison between the house and a cathedral and the stated comparison of the house to the Sphinx. These are comparisons in the mind of the writer. Choice 4 is incorrect because it flatly contradicts the passage. The house is built of stone. Choice 5 is incorrect because it, too, contradicts the selection. The stone is not dark; it glows with the light of the setting sun.
3. **3** This question calls on you to draw an inference. The chief character is named Boris, a Russian name. He gets out of a britska, and, even if you don't know that it is a kind of open carriage used in eastern Europe, the word suggests a conveyance that immediately eliminates the possibilities of "the British Isles" and "southern United States." It is safe to conclude because of the name, Boris, that the story "probably takes place in eastern Europe."
4. **2** The purpose of the question is to see whether you can determine the purpose of Boris' visit from the *evidence given*. While choices 1, 3, and 4 may possibly be correct, there is *no*

evidence in the passage that they are. Choice 5 must be considered along with choice 2. If the selection ended just before the final sentence, the two choices would be equally correct. But Boris is not merely making a visit. The question he asks himself in the final sentence makes it clear that the visit promises to change his future. Therefore, choice 2 is the better of the two.

5. **5** Usually this type of question can be quite difficult. It involves not only locating details but deciding the feeling that the author wishes these details to create in you, the reader. Choices 5 and 2 remain possibilities. While "quiet peace" could describe the situation, "vague uncertainty," choice 5, is clearly superior as the answer. The whole place became "mysterious." Boris feels for his letter, the contents of which we are forced to guess. The uncertainty is climaxed by Boris' question, which asks, in effect, "What will become of me?" Choices 1, 3, and 4 are inadequate. They involve some indication of Boris' feelings—of pleasure, of gaiety, of despair. But the passage contains no such indications.

6. **5** This question again calls for an inference, a conclusion which you, the reader, must draw from the facts which are presented. Choice 5 is correct because it represents the inference which "can most safely be drawn." Boris mentions getting back into the carriage. From this *fact* in the passage, we can *infer* that he intends to stay at the house for only a short time. Choices 1, 2, and 4 cannot be based on any facts in the passage. No tower is mentioned. Neither is the door. And Boris' feelings are not described. Choice 3 contradicts the facts in the passage. One terrace is mentioned in line 2 and a main terrace is mentioned in line 6. Clearly there are two terraces.

Prose Illustration—Classical

WHAT IS A CAMP OF WAR-WOUNDED LIKE?

Then the camps of the wounded—O heavens, what scene is this?—is this indeed humanity—these butchers' shambles? There are several of them. There they lie, in the largest, in an open space in the woods, from 200 to 300 poor fellows—the groans and the screams—the odour of blood, mixed with the fresh scent of the night, the grass, the trees—that slaughter-house! O well is it their mothers, their sisters cannot see them—cannot conceive, and never conceiv'd these things. One man is shot by a shell, both in the arm and leg—both are amputated—there lie the rejected members. Some have their legs blown off—some bullets through the breast—some indescribably horrid wounds in the face or head, all mutilated, sickening, torn, gouged out—some in the abdomen—some mere boys—many rebels, badly hurt—they take their regular turns with the rest, just the same as any—the surgeons use them just the same. Such is the camp of the wounded—such a fragment, a reflection afar off of the bloody scene—while all over the clear, large moon comes out at times softly, quietly shining. Amid the woods, that scene of flitting souls—amid the crack and crash and yelling sounds—the impalpable perfume of the woods—and yet the pungent, stifling smoke—the radiance of the moon, looking from heaven at intervals so placid—the sky so heavenly—the clear-obscure up there, those buoyant upper oceans—a few large placid stars beyond, coming silently and languidly out, and then disappearing—the melancholy, draperied night above, around. And there, upon the roads, the fields, and in those woods, that contest, never one more desperate in any age or land—both parties now in force—masses—no fancy battle, no semi-play, but fierce and savage demons fighting there—courage and scorn of death the rule, exceptions almost none.

—Walt Whitman

1. The author's main purpose in writing this selection is to
(1) express his sympathy for the wounded
(2) point out the brutal treatment of the rebels
(3) praise the courage of the fighters
(4) deplore the horrors of war
(5) describe the camps of the wounded

1. 1 2 3 4 5

2. The author shows his emotions in all of the following ways EXCEPT by
(1) asking unanswerable questions
(2) effective use of epithets
(3) contrasting the battle with its peaceful setting
(4) including gruesome details
(5) sympathizing with the surgeons

2. 1 2 3 4 5

3. All of the following relate to our sense of smell EXCEPT
(1) "the fresh scent of the night"
(2) "the odour of blood"
(3) "the radiance of the moon"
(4) "the pungent, stifling smoke"
(5) "the impalpable perfume of the woods"

3. 1 2 3 4 5

4. The soldiers are referred to by all of the following EXCEPT
(1) butchers
(2) poor fellows
(3) mere boys
(4) flitting souls
(5) savage demons

4. 1 2 3 4 5

5. The reader can infer from the final sentence that, for the soldiers, the author has a feeling of
(1) pity
(2) contempt
(3) indifference
(4) admiration
(5) resignation

5. 1 2 3 4 5

6. That the author is also a poet may be inferred from his
(1) description of the wounded
(2) comments on the camps
(3) conclusions about war
(4) awareness of the night's beauty
(5) indignation at what he sees

6. 1 2 3 4 5

ANSWER KEY

1. **4** 2. **5** 3. **3** 4. **1** 5. **4** 6. **4**

ANSWER ANALYSIS

1. **4** The key word in the question is the word "main." The question calls for you to identify the "main purpose" of the author. While it is true that the author expresses his sympathy for the wounded ("poor fellows") and while he does describe the camps of the wounded, his main purpose is to use the camps of the wounded as "a reflection" of the "bloody scene" to express his disgust at the horrors of war. Choice 2 is obviously wrong since the author indicates that the rebel soldiers got the same treatment as the rest. He mentions the courage of the fighters almost incidentally in the last sentence of the selection, so choice 3 cannot be the main purpose of the author.
2. **5** This question requires you to go back to the selection and to ferret out the details in it that the possible answers identify. Choices 5 is correct because the one thing the author does *not* do is sympathize with the surgeons although he does refer to the impartiality with which they treat soldiers on both sides. In the first two lines, the author asks unanswerable questions. Epithets (see the "Glossary of Literary Terms" beginning on page 467) describe significant qualities of the nouns they modify. We find "horrid" wounds and "desperate" contest, "fierce and savage" demons, as well as such poetic epithets as "melancholy," "draperied" night. The bloody battle is indeed contrasted with the "placid," "heavenly" sky. Gruesome detail abounds in the selection.

3. **3** This relatively easy question contains many clues to the answer. "Scent" and "odour" are synonyms of smell. While "pungent" may refer to both taste and smell, it is the smell of smoke rather than its taste that is obviously referred to here. Perfume, of course, is something that is smelled. The correct choice is 3 because "the radiance of the moon" refers to the sense of sight and not the sense of smell.
4. **1** Careful attention to the details of the passage reveals that the soldiers are referred to as "poor fellows," "some mere boys," "flitting souls," and "fierce and savage demons." The term "butchers' shambles" compares the camp of the wounded with a butchers' slaughterhouse and does not refer at all to the soldiers.
5. **4** The question identifies the specific place where the answer may be found—the final sentence. Study of that sentence gives us two clues to the author's feeling for the soldiers. They are "fierce and savage demons." "Courage and scorn of death" is typical of their fighting. The author does not pity the soldiers in this sentence, nor does he show any indifference to their "desperate" plight. There is no evidence that he is resigned to their having to continue the battle. While he does allude to their ferocity and savagery, he does not show contempt or scorn for the soldiers. Rather, he emphasizes their courage, since it is true that almost all display it in the fierce battle. Therefore, his feeling is one of admiration.
6. **4** What details would lead you, the reader, to conclude that any writer has the qualities of a poet? The "Glossary of Literary Terms" beginning on page 467 defines a poem as literature which has "deep emotion; highly imaginative language with figures of speech; distinctive rhythm; . . . words which mean more than they apparently say," among others. Mere description, comment, and conclusion are not poetic qualities. A good reporter does all of this. Anger, while it is a deep emotion, is not as good a clue to the fact that the author is a poet as a highly unusual sensitivity to "the radiance of the moon," "those buoyant upper oceans," (referring to the sky), "the melancholy, draperied night above." The scene is viewed by the moon, the sky is compared to a sea, and the night is compared to a hanging curtain in a way that only a poet could succeed in doing.

Summary of Prose Interpretation

What have we learned thus far from our study of prose with respect to skills of interpretation?

1. *Read the selection carefully.*
2. *In **selecting a title** that expresses the main idea, go back to the selection constantly. Arrive at the correct answer by a process of elimination.* Eliminate the possibilities which are clearly incorrect. Usually one will fall into this category. Eliminate the possibilities which are based on minor details. One or two of these will be given. From the remaining choices, you must select the one that expresses the main rather than the subordinate idea.
3. *In **drawing inferences,** find the clues in the passage from which you can draw the proper conclusion.* The clue may be a name, a place, an adjective, an object, an unusual word. You may have to reread the selection a few times before you locate the clue or the two details which can be linked to make a clue.
4. *In **determining purpose**, ask yourself why the author wrote the passage; what he wanted you, the reader, to understand or feel.* After you have read the passage several times, try to define the *total impression* you get from your reading. The purposes of authors at various times may be to inform, to arouse anger, to poke fun at, to evoke pity, to amuse, and to urge to action, among others. Which of these predominates?
5. *In **determining mood,** try to find words which either create an atmosphere or evoke an emotion.* This is related to the author's purpose but may not necessarily be his main purpose. *There are two main guides to determining atmosphere: selection of details and use of adjectives and adverbs.*

Reading Poetry

Reading poetry requires a special set of skills because the poet uses both a special language and special writing techniques.

In poetry, words are not used in their normal, literal sense. They are used in such a way that you, the reader, must use your imagination to fully understand them. Let's consider these experiences.

"I almost blew my top."

The words "blew" and "top" are not used in their regular meaning, but they are used figuratively to express the idea that I almost lost my temper.

"My fiancée is a knockout."

The word "knockout" has nothing to do with boxing. In this figurative use, it means that my fiancée is very attractive. In each case, there is an implied comparison—anger with a head blowing off; knockout with attractiveness or its effect.

> **Skill One.** In poetry, words are often used in a figurative sense. Do not take these words literally. Add your imagination in order to understand them as the poet uses them.

In poetry, meaning is frequently compressed into a few words by the use of figures of speech such as metaphors. (See the "Glossary of Literary Terms," page 467.)

"The road was a ribbon of moonlight."

In seven words, the poet tells us that the time is night, the moon is shining, and the road is the lighted area surrounded by darker ones.

"The moon was a ghostly galleon."

In six words, the poet tells us that the moon is like a ship, the sky is like an ocean, and the moon creates an eerie, supernatural feeling as it moves across the sky.

> **Skill Two.** In poetry, words often compress or condense extended meanings and pictures into a few words, usually by the use of figures of speech such as metaphors. Add to the words you read the implied meanings and pictures they create.

In poetry, meaning is closely related to rhythm. That is why it helps to read poetry aloud.

"Ĭ múst ğo dówn ťo tȟe séas ăgaín ťo tȟe lónelў séa aňd tȟe sǩy."

The combination of iambs (˘´) and anapests (˘˘´) creates for you, the reader, the actual rhythm of the waves. In the next example, a series of dactyls (´˘˘) describes the rhythm of the pounding of horses' hooves on a stone courtyard of an inn.

"Óvĕr tȟe cóbblĕs ȟe cláttеřed aňd claśhed ĭn tȟe dárk iňn yăгd."

> **Skill Three.** Read the poem aloud, paying attention to the rhythm, because the rhythm of the poem will help you understand its meaning.

In poetry, in addition to rhythm, which is always present, you will frequently encounter rhyme. Rhyme, too, helps to convey meaning. In Edgar Allan Poe's poem "The Raven," the rhyme sound is that contained in "door," "more," "Lenore," "forevermore," and "nevermore."

"'Tis some visitor,' I muttered, 'tapping at my chamber door: Only this and nothing more.'" The sound itself adds to the atmosphere of mystery.

> **Skill Four.** As you read the poem aloud, note the rhyme as well as the rhythm, since both add to the meaning and feelings expressed.

In poetry, the poet uses sounds in addition to rhyme to help convey meaning. The same poet who wrote of the sea above describes the effect of the wind with a series of "w" and "wh" sounds.

He wants to return

"To the gull's *w*ay and the *wh*ale's *w*ay *wh*ere the *w*ind's like a *wh*etted knife."

This technique is known as alliteration. (See the "Glossary of Literary Terms," page 467.)

Another technique is the use of words whose sounds correspond to their meaning. Here is the way one poet describes the movement of the waters of a river.

"And rushing and flushing and brushing and gushing,
And flapping and rapping and clapping and slapping . . ."

Skill Five. As you read the poem aloud, note the sounds of the words as well as their rhyme and their rhythm, since each adds to the meaning and feelings expressed by the poet.

In poetry, the poem itself has a certain shape or form. The poem can be in a very definite form such as the sonnet or in a very loose form called free verse. "The New Colossus," by Emma Lazarus, is a sonnet with a definite rhythm and a definite rhyme scheme. The form of the poem "The New Colossus" is appropriate because it lends itself to the main ideas expressed in each of the two stanzas of the poem.

Skill Six. As you read the poem, study its form and structure. If it is divided into stanzas or paragraph units, try to determine what each stanza adds to the meaning of the poem. The poem's form is another aid to your understanding its meaning. Consult the "Glossary of Literary Terms," page 467, for blank verse, free verse, octet, quatrain, sestet, sonnet, and stanza, all of which relate to poetic form and structure.

Now let us turn to one representative passage from poetry. Read the poem carefully and answer the questions based on it. Compare your answers with the answer key; then study the analysis of the answers, particularly those which you may have answered incorrectly.

Poetry Illustration—Classical

WHAT DOES THE NEW STATUE REPRESENT?

The New Colossus

Not like the brazen giant of Greek fame,
With conquering limbs astride from land to land;
Here at our sea-washed, sunset gates shall stand
A mighty woman with a torch, whose flame
Is the imprisoned lightning, and her name
Mother of Exiles. From her beacon-hand
Glows world-wide welcome; her mild eyes command
The air-bridged harbour that twin cities frame.

"Keep, ancient lands, your storied pomp!" cries she
with silent lips. "Give me your tired, your poor,
Your huddled masses yearning to breathe free,
The wretched refuse of your teeming shore.
Send these, the homeless, tempest-tost, to me.
I lift my lamp beside the golden door!"

—Emma Lazarus

1. The main idea of the poem is that
(1) the ancient lands of Europe should serve as a beacon to America
(2) the Greek statue serves as a model for the American statue
(3) the mighty are asked to come to these shores
(4) America welcomes all persecuted freedom-lovers
(5) the lamp guides those who come to the golden door

1. 1 2 3 4 5
|| || || || ||

2. The incorrectly paired words are
(1) brazen—of brass
(2) sunset—east
(3) beacon—guiding light
(4) refuse—trash
(5) pomp—splendour

2. 1 2 3 4 5
|| || || || ||

3. The "mighty woman" and "Mother of Exiles" is the
(1) United States of America
(2) city of New York
(3) Statue of Liberty
(4) Plymouth Rock
(5) Golden Gate

3. 1 2 3 4 5
|| || || || ||

4. The title of this poem, "The New Colossus," implies
(1) similarity to the old
(2) replacement of the old
(3) difference from the old
(4) inferiority to the old
(5) acceptance of the old

4. 1 2 3 4 5
|| || || || ||

5. The *incorrectly* matched phrase from the poem with the figure of speech or poetic device it demonstrates is
(1) "From her beacon-hand Glows"—enjambement
(2) "'Keep, ancient lands, your storied pomp!' cries she"—personification
(3) "shall stand a mighty woman"—inversion
(4) "world-wide welcome"—alliteration
(5) "flame is the imprisoned lightning"—simile

5. 1 2 3 4 5
|| || || || ||

6. The form of the poem is that of a(n)
(1) ballad
(2) octet
(3) ode
(4) sestet
(5) sonnet

6. 1 2 3 4 5
|| || || || ||

ANSWER KEY

1. **4** 2. **2** 3. **3** 4. **3** 5. **5** 6. **5**

ANSWER ANALYSIS

1. **4** Choice 1 is not correct because the reverse is actually true—that America's "beacon-hand" as represented in the statue is a beacon to the exiles from the ancient lands of Europe. Nor is choice 2 correct since the opening line begins "Not like" the Greek statue is the American statue. Choice 3 is incorrect. It is the "tired," "poor," and "homeless" who are welcomed to these shores. While choice 5 is true as far as it goes, it is not the main idea.

> *REMEMBER: You must read the selection carefully.* ***In selecting the main idea,*** *you must go back to the selection several times. Arrive at the correct answer by a process of elimination.*

2. **2** While this question is seemingly a vocabulary question which requires you to recall the meanings of the words in the five possible answers, the poem does provide hints or context clues to the meanings of several of the words. "From her *beacon*-hand glows world-wide welcome" indicates that light is going forth. The *refuse* is described as *wretched*. *Pomp* is contrasted with the *poor* and the *refuse*. So you can conclude that these words are correctly paired. If you deduce from the first verse that an ancient statue is being described, the meaning *of brass* for *brazen* seems logical. But even if you can't, "our"—meaning America's—"sunset gates" must be located in the west where the sun sets. Choice 2 is the correct answer because sunset is always associated with the west rather than the east.

> *REMEMBER: Never give up on a question.* ***Where the meaning of words is involved,*** *carefully study the clues to their meaning given by other nearby words in the passage.*

3. **3** To answer this question, you must draw an inference or conclusion from what is stated indirectly in the poem. What does the poem tell us about the "mighty woman" and "Mother of Exiles"? We learn that she stands "with a torch"; we also learn that "her mild eyes command the . . . harbour." These facts rule out all possible choices except 3. The United States of America and the city of New York do not, even symbolically, stand "with a torch." Neither Plymouth Rock (a rock) nor the Golden Gate (a bridge) fits the clues contained in the poem.

> *REMEMBER:* ***In drawing inferences or making deductions*** *from the text, find the clues which can help you. You may have to reread the selection a few times before you find them. This is a difficult kind of question but the answer is in the text if you have the patience to find it.*

4. **3** This is not a difficult question if you read the poem with care from the very beginning. The New Colossus is "not like" the old, according to the very first verse. So choices 1 and 2 are immediately ruled out. To find the correct answer, you must determine how the poet feels about this New Colossus. Since she is "mighty" and since her eyes are "mild," it is obvious that the poet admires the New Colossus and finds it superior to the Old (which the poet rejects). So choices 4 and 5 are also incorrect. It is the "difference" and the fact that the new is "not like" the old that is stressed. Therefore, choice 3 is correct.
5. **5** It is important for you to refer to the "Glossary of Literary Terms" beginning on page 467 if you haven't mastered it already because all of the five possible answers are defined in that vocabulary. *Enjambement* is the continuing of a line into the next without a stop at the end of the line, so choice 1 contains a correctly matched pair. *Personification*, the act of attributing human qualities to a "thing" (in this case the power of speech to a statue), is correctly paired with the quotation from the poem. *Inversion*, reversal of normal word order, applies to "shall stand a mighty woman" because the normal order is "a mighty woman shall stand." "World-wide welcome" is a perfect example of *alliteration* since the same consonant sound, "w," is repeated at the beginning of two words which follow one another. By elimination, choice 5 is correct since *simile* is *incorrectly* paired with "flame is the imprisoned lightning." "Like" or "as" is *not* used to make the comparison, so "flame is the imprisoned lightning" is properly called a *metaphor*.
6. **5** Where the form of a poem is required to answer a question, first count the number of verses (lines). Then figure out the rhyme scheme. Here there are 14 lines with a rhyme scheme as follows:

fame	—*a*
land	—*b*
stand	—*b*
flame	—*a*
name	—*a*
hand	—*b*
command	—*b*
frame	—*a*
she	—*c*
poor	—*d*
free	—*c*
shore	—*d*
me	—*c*
door	—*d*

If you consult the "Glossary of Literary Terms" beginning on page 467, you will find that this form cannot fit the definitions of a ballad (which deals with a simple story) or an ode (which is a lengthy lyric poem). Since it has 14 lines, it cannot be an octet (eight lines) or a sestet (six lines). The correct answer must be choice 5, a sonnet. This poem is actually only a fairly good example of an Italian sonnet. The octet, or first eight lines, present the main idea—the contrast between the new colossus which represents a welcome to the exiles and the old colossus which symbolized conquest—and is in the exact rhyme scheme required. The sestet, or second six lines, expands the idea by stressing the freedom and opportunity offered to the exiles in contrast to their rejection by the countries from which they came. The rhyme scheme, instead of rigidly following the *c d e c d e* of the Italian sonnet, confines itself to *c d c d c d*, one of the possible combinations.

It should be noted that the sestet of this famous sonnet is inscribed on the base of the Statue of Liberty and is one of the most quoted American poems.

It is also a more difficult poem than average because of its vocabulary and its compound words (sea-washed, beacon-hand, tempest-tost). If you did well, you should have no trouble with the poetry on the actual test. If you did not, concentrate on the poetry selections which follow in this chapter.

Summary of Interpretation of Poetry

The skills in reading and interpreting poetry call for you to

1. Try to get the extended meaning of words used figuratively by using your imagination to add to the usual meaning of the words.
2. Since poetry compresses meaning and description into a few words, fill in the suggested meanings and pictures they create by studying the figures of speech used, such as similes and metaphors.
3. Read the poem aloud, since the rhythm will help you determine its meaning.
4. Note the rhymes used, since they will also help you get meaning and feeling from the poem.
5. Note the sounds of the words, since they reinforce meaning.
6. Study the form of the poem, since its subdivisions (stanzas) can help you understand it better.

Note: Read the poem through quickly to get an overall idea of its meaning and feeling. Don't be discouraged if you don't understand it all at first. Then go back to read it closely after you have read the questions based on it.

Reading Drama

Earlier, we indicated how character can be inferred from words or actions, since direct description, as in prose, is not possible. It is true that, of all the forms of literature, plays are among the most difficult to read. The playwright does not speak directly to the reader in modern drama as do the novelist and short story writer. Sometimes he or she sets the scene for those who produce or read the play. Sometimes he or she includes instructions to the actor about mood or action; but, for the most part, the playwright leaves it to the actor and the reader to figure out appearance, character, actions, and feelings. The only real help the playwright should and must give is through the dialogue, the conversation between the characters. From this dialogue alone, you must *imagine the setting, visualize the action*, including "hearing" the speech of the actors, and *draw conclusions about their character and motives*. In addition, you must understand the nature of the essence of drama, which is conflict between ideas or characters. This is made clear only through the dialogue. A final point: you may also be asked to predict what is likely to happen on the basis of what you have read.

An analysis of the following scene from a classical American play will illustrate the skills you will need to read and understand drama. (This excerpt is longer than the selections on the actual test.)

Drama Illustration—Classical

HOW ARE OLSON'S DREAMS DESTROYED?

OLSON. [*After a pause—worriedly*] I tank I should go after dem. Cocky iss very drunk, too, and Drisc—

FREDA. Aar! The big Irish is all right. Don't yer 'ear 'im say as 'ow they'd surely come back 'ere, an' fur you to wait fur 'em?

OLSON. Yes; but if dey don't come soon I tank I go see if dey are in boarding house all right.

FREDA. Where is the boardin' 'ouse?

OLSON. Yust little way back from street here.

FREDA. You stayin' there, too?

OLSON. Yes—until steamer sail for Stockholm—in two day.

FREDA. [*She is alternatingly looking at JOE and feverishly trying to keep* OLSON *talking so he will forget about going away after the others.*] Yer mother won't be arf glad to see yer agen, will she? [OLSON *smiles.*] Does she know yer comin'?

OLSON. No. I tought I would yust give her surprise. I write to her from Bonos Eres but I don't tell her I come home.

FREDA. Must be old, ain't she, yer ole lady?

OLSON. She iss eighty-two. [*He smiles reminiscently.*] You know, Miss Freda, I don't see my mother or my brother in—let me tank—[*He counts laboriously on his fingers.*] must be more than ten year. I write once in while and she write many time; and my brother he write me, too. My mother say in all letter I should come home right away. My brother he write same ting, too. He want me to help him on farm. I write back always I come soon; and I mean all time to go back home at end of voyage. But I come ashore, I take one drink, I take many drinks, I get drunk, I spend all money, I have to ship away for other voyage. So dis time I say to myself; Don't drink one drink, Ollie, or, sure, you don't get home. And I want go home dis time. I feel homesick for farm and to see my people again. [*He smiles.*] Yust like little boy, I feel homesick. Dat's why I don't drink noting to-night but dis-belly-wash! [*He roars with childish laughter, then suddenly becomes serious.*] You know, Miss Freda, my mother get very old, and I want see her. She might die and I would never—

FREDA. [*Moved a lot in spite of herself*] Ow, don't talk like that! I jest 'ates to 'ear any one speakin' abaht dyin'. [*The door to the street is opened and* NICK *enters, followed by two rough-looking, shabbily-dressed men, wearing mufflers, with caps pulled down over their eyes. They sit at the table nearest to the door.* JOE *brings them three beers, and there is a whispered consultation, with many glances in the direction of* OLSON:]

OLSON. [*Starting to get up—worriedly*] I tank I go around to boarding house. I tank something go wrong with Drisc and Cocky.

FREDA. Ow, down't go. They kin take care of theyselves. They ain't babies. Wait 'arf a mo'. You ain't 'ad yer drink yet.

JOE. [*Coming hastily over to the table, indicates the men in the rear with a jerk of his thumb*] One of them blokes wants yer to 'ave a wet wiv 'im.

FREDA. Righto! [*To* OLSON] Let's drink this. [*She raises her glass. He does the same.*] 'Ere's a toast fur yer: Success to yer bloomin' farm an' may yer live long an' 'appy on it. Skoal! [*She tosses down her brandy. He swallows half his glass of ginger beer and makes a wry face.*]

OLSON. Skoal! [*He puts down his glass.*]

FREDA. [*With feigned indignation*] Down't yer like my toast?

OLSON. [*Grinning*] Yes. It iss very kind, Miss Freda.

FREDA. Then drink it all like I done.

OLSEN. Well—[*He gulps down the rest.*] Dere! [*He laughs.*]

FREDA. Done like a sport!

ONE OF THE ROUGHS. [*With a laugh*] Amindra, ahoy!

NICK. [*Warningly*] Sssshh!

OLSON. [*Turns around in his chair*] Amindra? Iss she in port? I sail on her once long time ago—three mast, full rig, skys'l yarder? Iss dat ship you mean?

THE ROUGH. [*Grinning*] Yus; right you are.

OLSON. [*Angrily*] I know dat damn ship—worst ship dat sail to sea. Rotten grub and dey make you work all time—and the Captain and Mate wus Bluenose devils. No sailor who know anything ever ship on her. Where iss she bound from here?

THE ROUGH. Round Cape 'Orn—sails at daybreak.

OLSON. Py yingo, I pity poor fallers make dat trip round Cape Stiff dis time year. I bet you some of dem never see port once again. [*He passes his hand over his eyes in a dazed way. His voice grows weaker.*] Py golly, I feel dizzy. All the room go round and round like I was drunk. [*He gets weakly to his feet.*] Good night, Miss Freda. I bane feeling sick. Tell Drisc—I go home. [*He takes a step forward and suddenly collapses over a chair, rolls to the floor, and lies there unconscious.*]

JOE. [*From behind the bar*] Quick, nawh! [NICK *darts forward with* JOE *following.* FREDA *is already beside the unconscious man and has taken the roll of money from his inside pocket. She strips off a note furtively and shoves it into her bosom, trying to conceal her action, but* JOE *sees her. She hands the roll to* JOE, *who pockets it.* NICK *goes through all the other pockets and lays a handful of change on the table.*]

JOE. [*Impatiently*] 'Urry, 'urry, can't yer? The other blokes'll be 'ere in 'arf a mo'. [*The two roughs come forward.*] 'Ere, you two, tike 'im in under the arms like 'e was drunk: [*They do so.*] Tike 'im to the Amindra—yer knows that, don't yer?—two docks above. Nick'll show yer. An' you, Nick, down't yer leave the bleedin' ship till the capt'n guvs yer this bloke's advance—full month's pay—five quid, d'yer 'ear?

NICK. I knows me bizness, ole bird. [*They support* OLSON *to the door.*]

THE ROUGH. [*As they are going out*] This silly bloke'll 'ave the s'prise of 'is life when 'e wakes up on board of 'er. [*They laugh. The door closes behind them.*]

—Eugene O'Neill

1. The playwright creates mood by his effective use of all EXCEPT
(1) stage directions
(2) names of characters
(3) dialogue
(4) dialect
(5) humour

1. 1 2 3 4 5 ‖ ‖ ‖ ‖ ‖

2. The main purpose of the playwright is to describe
(1) a sailor's life in port
(2) the frustrated longings of a sailor
(3) the weakness of character of a sailor
(4) how a sailor is exploited
(5) his admiration for sailors

2. 1 2 3 4 5 ‖ ‖ ‖ ‖ ‖

3. Olson's mood is best described as one of
(1) bitterness
(2) nostalgia
(3) happiness
(4) resignation
(5) despair

3. 1 2 3 4 5 ‖ ‖ ‖ ‖ ‖

4. Sympathy for Olson is created by the playwright by all of the following EXCEPT his
(1) devotion to his family
(2) abandonment by his shipmates
(3) resolution to stay sober
(4) courtesy to Freda
(5) description of the *Amindra*

4. 1 2 3 4 5

5. The reader can correctly infer from the incident all of the following EXCEPT
(1) Joe, Nick, Freda, and the two roughs plotted against Olson
(2) Olson may never get to see his mother
(3) Olson's life on board the *Amindra* will be difficult
(4) Olson's drink was spiked
(5) Freda regretted her role in the incident

5. 1 2 3 4 5

6. Suspense is created by all the following EXCEPT
(1) Drisc and Cocky's departure
(2) Freda's encouraging Olson to stay
(3) the entry of Nick and the roughs
(4) Olson's reluctance to take a drink
(5) Olson's talk about the *Amindra*

6. 1 2 3 4 5

7. The playwright
(1) feels sorry for Olson
(2) criticizes the habitual drinking of the sailors
(3) despises Joe, Nick, Freda, and the roughs
(4) describes the action with no comment
(5) feels life is unfair

7. 1 2 3 4 5

ANSWER KEY

1. **5** 2. **2** 3. **2** 4. **2** 5. **5** 6. **1** 7. **4**

ANSWER ANALYSIS

1. **5** The playwright uses stage directions to help create a mood of impending trouble in a waterfront saloon: "*Nick enters, followed by two rough-looking, shabbily-dressed men, wearing mufflers, with caps pulled down over their eyes.*" The names of the characters add to the mood: Cocky, Drisc, Big Irish, and The Rough. The dialogue, too, contributes: "I know dat damn ship—worst ship dat sail to sea. . . ." The dialect of the waterfront is most effective: ". . . down't yer leave the bleedin' ship till the capt'n guvs yer this bloke's advance." Choice 5 is correct because it is the exception among the five choices. There is no humour in the selection.
2. **2** The key word in this question is *main*, since the question calls for the *main* purpose of the playwright. Only choice 2 is the *main* theme of the scene—how Olson's longing to return home is thwarted. "I feel homesick for farm," says Olson and his plan to go back is made to fail. Choice 5 is obviously wrong since no admiration for sailors is present. Choices 1, 3, and 4 are partially correct—a brief period in a sailor's life in port is depicted; Olson's weakness of character is shown, since he cannot resist a drink; Olson is exploited, as are others on the *Amindra*.
3. **2** Choice 2 is correct because *nostalgia* best describes the homesickness Olson feels. He isn't bitter or despairing. "*He smiles reminiscently*" and has plans to return to see his mother. He isn't resigned either. Although he roars with laughter, he can't be considered happy.
4. **2** A great playwright succeeds in getting the viewer or the reader involved with the characters he creates. We cannot help sympathizing with Olson because he is a decent person, one

who is courteous ("Miss Freda"), devoted to his family (he wants to see his mother and help his brother), full of good intentions to stay sober ("Dat's why I don't drink noting to-night"). The playwright cleverly lets us in on the fate awaiting Olson on the "worst ship dat sail to sea." Only choice 2 doesn't contribute to our sympathy since the reason for his shipmates' leaving isn't given.

5. **5** This question calls for a number of inferences. There is evidence that the five plotted against Olson ("*. . . there is a whispered consultation, with many glances in the direction of Olson*"); since voyages lasted many months and Olson's mother is 82, Olson may never get to see her; from his description of life on the *Amindra* ("rotten grub and dey make you work all time"), we know Olson's life will be difficult; after the drink, Olson falls unconscious, so it must have been spiked. Only choice 5 isn't true; Freda stole money from the unconscious Olson.

6. **1** The incident is concerned with Olson's future, and suspense begins with Freda's encouraging Olson to stay. It continues with Nick's entrance with the others, and with Olson's reactions to Freda and the mention of the *Amindra*. Only choice 1 does not build suspense in the scene.

7. **4** Since every effort is made by the playwright to be realistic, he carefully refrains from injecting his own views.

Summary of Interpretation of Drama Reading

The skills in reading and interpreting drama call for you to

1. Try to imagine the setting. If no stage directions are given, deduce from the speech and dialogue of the characters where the action is taking place.
2. Visualize the action. As the characters speak, figure out *what they are doing* while they are speaking.
3. Determine their motives. Why are the characters speaking as they do? *Why are they doing what they do?*
4. Determine their character and personality. What sort of person talks and acts the way he or she does? Why?
5. Determine the conflict that is taking place. Since the essence of drama is conflict, who or what is in conflict with whom or what? Is the conflict physical? Is it emotional? Is it a conflict of ideas?
6. Try to predict on the basis of all of the above what is most likely to happen next.
7. Read the scene aloud, trying to project yourself into the character of each of the roles.

BASICS ON READING COMMENTARY ON THE ARTS

Selections that fall under the term *commentary* are limited to those aspects of contemporary writing that deal with the arts—music, art, theatre, movies, television, literature, and dance. They are further limited to selections in which the author comments critically on the arts, discussing the value of the content and the style of these means of artistic expression.

In these selections, try to determine the point of view of the writer and whether his evaluation of the artist, the musician, the author, the playwright, the film, the television programme, or the dancer is favourable or unfavourable. Also look for the insights of the critic into the meaning and emotion conveyed by the artist or the medium (movie, television, film).

The writing style will parallel that of the author of a piece of popular literature so that sentence structure and vocabulary should not be too hard to handle. *Here is a helpful hint*. Since critics who comment on the arts are describing their reactions, they will resort to many adjectives that give their judgment. Here are a couple of dozen of such adjectives: adept, authentic, candid, credible, dynamic, eloquent, exquisite, graphic, inane, inept, laudable, lucid, naive, poignant, prosaic, spontaneous, superb, superlative, tedious, timeless, tiresome, trite, vivacious, witty. Study the meanings of these words and similar adjectives which are included in the 500 Useful Adjectives section of *A Basic 1,100 Word Vocabulary* on page 202.

Commentary on the Arts Illustration

WHAT WAS THE CONTRIBUTION OF FRED ASTAIRE TO THE DANCE?

Astaire was far too subtle a figure to be caught in a net of loose superlatives. He was many contradictory things at once. Look at him. He was an odd little elf with pipe-cleaner limbs, a head like a Bartlett pear turned upside down and a big sad donkey face that ended in a peninsular chin; yet he was a thing of ineffable beauty when he moved: the Ariel of the age, a sprite who could fly without wings. Listen to him. He was a man with hardly enough voice to gargle with; yet he introduced more all-time hit songs (among them *Night and Day*, *The Way You Look Tonight* and *One For My Baby*) than any other singer of his day. Consider his creative achievement. He was a fellow of conservative tastes and utmost modesty; yet he demolished the long-standing Busby Berkeley tradition of movie musicals, reconstructed that popular art form nearer to his art's desire and set the '30s afire with mass Astairea. And reflect on his private character. He was the son of an immigrant and grew up in rough-scuff vaudeville houses, yet he became a man of elegant manners and cultivated sensibilities who was equally at home in a barnyard or a royal mansion . . .

Together they (Ginger Rogers and he) gave millions a vision of emotion in motion that liberates the heart as wings liberate a bird.

The emotion is released in dozens of moods and rhythms. In the twirling amorous languor of *Cheek to Cheek*, in the angry, "ratcheting tap clusters" (as one critic called them) of *Let Yourself Go*, in the slap-happy clatter of *Nice Work If You Can Get It*. And in the wavelike movements of desire and withdrawal that surge through *Never Gonna Dance*, that elegant little agon of approach-avoidance that many consider Astaire and Rogers' finest moment.

Even finer for Astaire addicts are his footloose soliloquies, those astonishing moments when he dances alone, unimpeded by the need to trim his talent to a partner's capacities, imagination running wild, he dances on chairs, on tables, on firecrackers, on walls, on ceilings; in and out of revolving doors, across plazas of thin air; with golf clubs, with hat racks, with noisy squadrons of unpopulated shoes. And all the dances, no matter how fantastic, make a story point, have an emotional meaning. Belong.

1. The attitude of the author to Astaire is full of
(1) subtlety
(2) contradiction
(3) appreciation
(4) sensibilities
(5) emotion

1. 1 2 3 4 5
|| || || || ||

2. Which of the following statements, according to the article, is true?
(1) Astaire's training prepared him for his movie personality
(2) Astaire was an artist who is easy to understand
(3) Astaire's appearance belied his dancing talent
(4) Astaire adjusted well to traditional artistic forms
(5) Astaire was endowed with an outstanding voice

2. 1 2 3 4 5
|| || || || ||

3. The author of the article **3.** 1 2 3 4 5
(1) involves the reader in his critical commentary
(2) makes unsupported judgments of Astaire's abilities
(3) points out only the favourable facts about Astaire
(4) confines his comments to Astaire as a dancer
(5) confines his comments to Astaire and Ginger Rogers

4. Astaire's finest dance with Ginger Rogers, according to the article, is **4.** 1 2 3 4 5
(1) *Cheek to Cheek*
(2) *Let Yourself Go*
(3) *Nice Work If You Can Get It*
(4) *Never Gonna Dance*
(5) *Night and Day*

5. Astaire's conservative tastes and his break with the traditional movie musical are cited as examples of his **5.** 1 2 3 4 5
(1) subtlety
(2) manners
(3) character
(4) sensibilities
(5) contradictions

6. The element common to all of Astaire's dances, according to the author, is **6.** 1 2 3 4 5
(1) amorous languor
(2) angry tap clusters
(3) slap-happy clatter
(4) approach-avoidance
(5) emotional meaning

ANSWER KEY

1. **3** 2. **3** 3. **1** 4. **4** 5. **5** 6. **5**

ANSWER ANALYSIS

1. **3** The author mentions the "beauty when he moved," "his creative achievement," "the astonishing moments when he dances alone," among the other admirable qualities of Fred Astaire. The other possible answers are wrong because it is Astaire who is contradictory, not the author; it is Astaire who portrayed emotion in motion; it is Astaire who is subtle, not the author; it is Astaire who has the sensibilities.
2. **3** Astaire's appearance—"an odd little elf with pipe-cleaner limbs"—does not lead one to expect the unspeakable beauty of his movements. Choice 1 is wrong because his training was in "rough-scuff vaudeville houses." Choice 2 is wrong because Astaire is portrayed as "subtle" and "contradictory." Choice 4 is wrong because Astaire "demolished" the traditional musical. Choice 5 is wrong because his voice was "hardly enough" to "gargle with."
3. **1** There are many examples of this. "Look at him," "Listen to him," "Consider his creative achievement," "And reflect on his private character." Choice 2 is wrong because the author documents each judgment. Choice 3 is wrong because he also points up the weaknesses in his appearance and voice. Choices 4 and 5 are wrong because the author mentions his voice and his solo dancing.
4. **4** The author specifically calls *Never Gonna Dance* Astaire and Rogers' finest moment, although the other dances are cited as examples of the moods and rhythms through which the dancers released emotion.
5. **5** The author points up Astaire's "conservative tastes," "yet he demolished the long-standing tradition of movie musicals," a definite contradiction. The other qualities of Astaire mentioned in the other choices are cited in different contexts.

6. **5** At the end of the selection, the author states "all the dances . . . have an emotional meaning." The other choices refer to individual dances mentioned earlier in the selection.

GLOSSARY OF LITERARY TERMS

To help you further in interpreting literary materials, we have included a comprehensive list of words used frequently in discussing literature. You are not expected to know *all* of these terms, but it will help you considerably to have a knowledge of many of them. Use this glossary for reference when you are in doubt about a question involving literary terms. Develop the habit of referring to this list as you read the passages that follow this section.

ACCENT The emphasis given to a syllable or syllables of a word. Accent is used primarily with reference to poetry. This term is also used for the mark which shows this emphasis. (′)

ALLEGORY Presentation in concrete terms of an abstract idea or series of abstract ideas. (In *Pilgrim's Progress*, Christian proceeds via Vanity Fair to the Celestial City.)

ALLITERATION The repetition of the same consonant sound at the beginning of two or more words in close proximity. ("The fair *b*reeze *b*lew, the white *f*oam *f*lew . . .")

ALLUSION Offhand reference to a famous figure or event in literature or history. ("He opened a Pandora's box.")

ANAPEST A poetic foot consisting of three syllables with two unaccented syllables followed by an accented one. ("tŏ thĕ stóre")

ANTITHESIS Strong contrast in ideas. (". . . wretches hang that jury-men may dine.")

APHORISM Brief statement of an idea or guide to conduct. ("Honesty is the best policy.")

APOSTROPHE Words addressed to someone or something absent as if he or it were present. (". . . sail on, O Ship of State!")

AUTOBIOGRAPHY Story of a person's life written by himself. (Franklin's *Autobiography*)

BALLAD Verse form which presents in simple story form a single dramatic or exciting episode and stresses such feelings as love, courage, patriotism and loyalty. ("Sir Patrick Spens")

BIOGRAPHY Story of a person's life written by someone else. (Boswell's *Life of Johnson*)

BLANK VERSE Unrhymed lines, ten syllables each, whose second, fourth, sixth, eighth, tenth syllables are accented. The lines consist of five iambs and are in iambic pentameter. ("Was this the face that launched a thousand ships . . .")

CLIMAX High point in the telling of a story, be it in fictional, poetic, or dramatic form. (An example is the appearance of Banquo's ghost in *Macbeth*.)

COMEDY Light form of drama which tries to amuse and/or instruct us and which ends happily. (*All's Well That Ends Well*)

COUPLET Two lines of poetry which rhyme and tend to form an independent thought.
("Hope springs eternal in the human breast:
Man never is, but always to be, blest.")

DACTYL Poetic foot consisting of one accented syllable followed by two unaccented syllables. ("Rísing and . . .")

DENOUEMENT Final unraveling of the plot in a play or novel. Included is an explanation of all the complications and mysteries of the plot.

DIALOGUE Conversation between people in a play.

DIDACTIC VERSE Verse whose main purpose is to teach a moral lesson. ("Ode to Duty")

ELEGY Lyric poem expressing a poet's ideas concerning death. (Gray's "Elegy Written in a Country Churchyard")

ENJAMBEMENT Continuing of a sentence from one line or couplet into the next without a stop at the end of the line. This is also known as a *Run-on Line*.
("'Tis the majority
In this, as all, prevails.")

ENVOY Concluding stanza added to certain forms of poems, usually to a French verse form called a ballade.

EPIC A long poem which tells a story about noble people and their adventures centring around one character who is the hero. The poem is usually closely tied to a single country and serves a patriotic purpose. (Greece—*The Iliad*; Rome—*The Aeneid*)

EPIGRAM A short poem with a witty or satirical point. This term also refers to a brief saying. ("Man proposes but God disposes.")

EPITHET Adjective which effectively identifies a significant quality of the noun it describes. (Alexander the Great)

ESSAY Prose writing which can be recognized by its incomplete treatment of any topic, no matter how unimportant, and by its approach—*formal* (containing an analysis with a moral) or *informal* (revealing the personality of the author through his humour, bias, and style). (*Formal*: Bacon, "Of Friendship"; *informal*: Lamb, "A Dissertation on Roast Pig")

FIGURE OF SPEECH Expression used to appeal to the reader's emotions and imagination by presenting words in unusual meaning or context. ("My love's like a red, red rose. . . .")

FOOT Certain number of syllables making up a unit in a verse of poetry. The four main kinds are the iamb, the trochee, the anapest, and the dactyl—each defined separately.

FREE VERSE Verse that has an irregular pattern of meter and has a variety of rhythmical effects. Stanza form is irregular and rhyme is usually absent. ("Chicago" by Carl Sandburg)

HEXAMETER A line of six metric feet.

HYPERBOLE Figure of speech used by a writer who purposely wants to exaggerate. ("rivers of blood")

IAMB A poetic foot consisting of two syllables with an unaccented syllable preceding an accented syllable ("ĭmpróve . . .")

IAMBIC PENTAMETER Line of ten syllables divided into five feet of two syllables, one unaccented and one accented, in that order. ("Shăll Í cŏmpáre thĕe to ă súmmĕr's dáy?")

IMAGE A figure of speech, especially a simile or a metaphor. See the definitions of those terms.

INVERSION Reversal of the normal order of words in a sentence. ("A king of men am I.")

IRONY Figure of speech in which the writer or speaker uses words meaning the exact opposite of what he really thinks. (In *Julius Caesar*, Antony attacks Brutus with the words, "Brutus is an honourable man.")

LIMERICK Jingle in verse containing five lines, with lines 1, 2, and 5 rhyming and lines 3 and 4 rhyming.

LYRIC Short poem expressing deep emotion in highly melodic and imaginative verse. ("The Daffodils")

MEDIAL RHYME Rhyme occurring within a line. ("Once upon a midnight *dreary*, while I pondered weak and *weary* . . .")

METAPHOR Figure of speech which compares two things, or a person and a thing, by using a quality of one applied to the other. *Like* or *as* is omitted. ("All the world's a stage.")

METER Rhythm resulting from the repetition of one of several kinds of poetic feet. (See *Iamb*, *Trochee*, *Anapest*, and *Dactyl*.)

METONYMY A figure of speech using a commonly associated word to describe the object. ("He likes Shakespeare." In reality, he likes Shakespeare's plays.)

MYTH Story of unknown origin, religious in character, which tries to interpret the natural world, usually in terms of supernatural events. (the story of Atlas)

NARRATIVE A story of events or experiences, true or fictitious. A poem may be narrative, as "The Rime of the Ancient Mariner."

NOVEL Lengthy prose story dealing with imaginary characters and settings which creates the illusion of real life. (Scott's *Ivanhoe*)

OCTET The first eight lines of a sonnet, particularly the Italian sonnet, which generally state the theme of the poem. (See Milton's sonnets)

ODE Lyric poem of particularly serious purpose written in language which is dignified and inspired. (Keats' "Ode on a Grecian Urn")

ONOMATOPOEIA Use of words whose sounds resemble and/or suggest their meaning. (e.g., buzz; hiss)

PARADOX A statement which seems contradictory, but which may, in fact, be true. (In *The Pirates of Penzance*, the hero had only five birthdays although he was 21 years old. He was born on February 29th of a leap year!)

PARODY Writing which pokes fun at a serious work by using exaggeration or broad humour in an imitation of the serious work.

PATHETIC FALLACY An expression that gives human feelings to natural or inhuman things. ("The waves danced with glee.")

PERSONIFICATION Figure of speech where an idea or a thing is given human qualities. ("Death, be not proud . . .")

POEM Literature which has any or all of the following qualities to a high degree: deep emotion; highly imaginative language with figures of speech; distinctive rhythm; compression of thought; use of the familiar in a symbolic sense; some kind of rhyme scheme; words which mean more than they apparently say.

QUATRAIN A stanza of four lines.

REFRAIN A word or group of words repeated regularly in a poem, usually at the end of a stanza. ("Nevermore" from "The Raven").

REPETITION The restating of a phrase or line for emphasis.
("And miles to go before I sleep
And miles to go before I sleep.")

RHYME In poetry, agreement in the final sounds of two or more words at the ends of lines. (June, moon; crunch on, luncheon)

RHYTHM In poetry and certain kinds of prose, patterns of stress or accent in the units which make up the verse or sentence.

SARCASM A figure of speech which is harsh in tone and expresses meaning by use of the opposite. ("Excellent" said when a mistake is made.)

SATIRE Work which makes fun of a person, an idea, or a social custom or institution by stressing its foolishness or lack of reasonableness. (Swift's *Gulliver's Travels*)

SCANNING Division of a verse into feet by finding the accents to determine its meter ("Ĭ thínk thăt Í shăll névĕr sée"—˘ ´ ˘ ´ ˘ ´ ˘ ´—verse contains four iambs)

SESTET The last six lines of a sonnet, generally making comment on the theme set in the first eight lines.

SHORT STORY Short prose narrative dealing with imaginary characters usually in a single setting, often relating a single incident, and striving for a single effect such as terror. (Poe's "The Pit and the Pendulum")

SIMILE Figure of speech in which two things essentially unlike are compared, with *like* or *as* being used to make the comparison. (". . . a poem lovely as a tree")

SOLILOQUY Speech of a character in a play uttered when he is alone on the stage and in which he informs the audience of his thoughts or of knowledge it needs to follow the action of the play. (Hamlet's "To be or not to be . . .")

SONNET A form of poetry consisting of fourteen verses in which two aspects of an idea are presented.

In the *Italian or Petrarchan sonnet*, the first aspect of the idea or theme is presented in the first eight lines, which rhyme *a b b a a b b a*; the second aspect of the idea or commentary on the theme is presented in the second six lines, which rhyme (in various combinations) *c d e c d e*. The first eight lines are the *octet*; the second six lines the *sestet*.

In the *Shakespearean sonnet*, the first aspect is presented in the first twelve lines, which rhyme *a b a b c d c d e f e f*; the second aspect is presented in the last two lines, which rhyme *g g*.

STANZA A unit in a poem, similar to a paragraph in a piece of prose writing, usually consisting of four or more lines.

SYMBOL An object that represents ideas, either psychological, philosophical, social, or religious. (The cross represents Christianity; the Star of David is the symbol of Judaism.)

SYNECHDOCHE A figure of speech that uses the part to stand for the whole. ("All *hands* perished when the ship sank.")

TETRAMETER A line of verse consisting of four feet.

TRAGEDY Form of drama which has any or all of the following qualities: conflict of character that ends in disaster; a person of great and noble character who meets his downfall because of his own weakness; drama that appeals to our emotions of pity and fear. (*Othello*)

TROCHEE A poetic foot, consisting of two syllables, with an accented syllable preceding an unaccented syllable. ("Glóry̆ . . .")

VERSE A single line of poetry.

PRACTICE IN LANGUAGE ARTS, READING (INTERPRETING LITERATURE AND THE ARTS)

Directions

The Language Arts, Reading (Interpreting Literature and the Arts) Test consists of excerpts from various time periods in literature. Since the skills remain the same, we have retained the older divisions. Each excerpt is followed by multiple-choice questions about the reading material.

Read each excerpt first and then answer the questions following it. Refer to the reading material as often as necessary in answering the questions.

Each excerpt is preceded by a "purpose question." The purpose question gives a reason for reading the material. Use these purpose questions to help focus your reading. You are not required to answer these purpose questions. They are given only to help you concentrate on the ideas presented in the reading materials.

Choose the one best answer to each item.

—IN POPULAR LITERATURE

Items 1 to 5 refer to the following selection.

A SUMMER OF CONTENTMENT?

The summer before Quebec's second referendum on independence in October 1995 was a particularly glorious one. Day followed day, week followed week of blue skies and clear nights, with just enough rain to keep the farmers happy and the wells from running dry. Biking along the ridge of Chemin Jordan with its panoramic view south across rolling fields and forests to the hills of Vermont, I sometimes used to wonder if this halcyon summer would be remembered like that of 1914, before the guns of August shattered the peace of Europe. But, literally and figuratively, there were no dark clouds on the horizon.

Everyone looked tanned and relaxed, far from aggrieved or oppressed. Indeed, it was rare to find anyone, anglophone or francophone, who wanted to waste the all-too-fleeting splendour of such a summer arguing the never-ending politics that filled the newspapers. There would be enough grim and blustery days ahead for that. As a result, I was lulled into an optimistic faith that a substantial majority of French-speaking Quebeckers would vote, as they had in 1980, to remain within Canada. There was nothing, not even the polls, to make me suspect that my home and native land might be in real danger of passing away—as ephemeral as a summer idyll.

—Ron Graham

1. While the coming referendum would be of critical importance to the future of Quebec
(1) people just seemed to be enjoying the summer
(2) many were very anxious about the future
(3) most French-speakers would vote to leave Canada
(4) dark clouds were beginning to form on the horizon
(5) farmers were upset because of the lack of rain

1. 1 2 3 4 5

2. Citizens became aware of the coming referendum
(1) by arguing with their neighbours
(2) by studying the history of the previous referendum
(3) by political reporting in the newspapers
(4) by holding local meetings to discuss the issues
(5) by watching television with their families

2. 1 2 3 4 5

3. The narrator was spending the summer
(1) working in the fields
(2) biking through the countryside
(3) debating the issue with his neighbours
(4) vacationing in Vermont
(5) reading about the First World War

3. 1 2 3 4 5

4. He was optimistic about the future because
(1) he felt most French-speakers would again vote to remain in Canada
(2) English-speakers formed the majority of voters
(3) most people would not bother to vote anyway
(4) people were sick of politics
(5) the weather made everyone happy

4. 1 2 3 4 5

5. The mood of most people might be described as
(1) argumentative
(2) frightened
(3) carefree
(4) oppressed
(5) suspicious

5. 1 2 3 4 5

Items 6 to 10 refer to the following selection.

WHAT ARE SOME OF THE EFFECTS OF THE HOLOCAUST?

She walked along the river until a constable stopped her. It was one o'clock, he said. Not the best time to be walking alone by the side of a half-frozen river. He smiled at her, then offered to walk her home. It was the first day of the new year, 1946, eight and a half months after the British tanks had rumbled into Bergen-Belsen.

That February, my mother turned twenty-six. It was difficult for strangers to believe that she had ever been a concentration camp inmate. Her face was smooth and round. She wore lipstick and applied mascara to her large dark eyes. She dressed fashionably. But when she looked into the mirror in the mornings before leaving for work, my mother saw a shell, a mannequin who moved and spoke but who bore only a superficial resemblance to her real self. The people closest to her had vanished. She had no proof that they were truly dead. No eyewitnesses had survived to vouch for her husband's death. There was no one living who had seen her parents die. The lack of confirmation haunted her. At night before she went to sleep and during the day as she stood pinning dresses she wondered if, by some chance, her parents had gotten past the Germans or had crawled out of the mass grave into which they had been shot and were living, old and helpless, somewhere in Poland. What if only one of them had died? What if they had survived and had died of cold or hunger after she had been liberated, while she was in Celle dancing with British officers?

She did not talk to anyone about these things. No one, she thought, wanted to hear them. She woke up in the mornings, went to work, bought groceries, went to the Jewish Community Centre and to the housing office like a robot.

6. The constable stopped the author's mother from walking along the river because
(1) the river was dangerous
(2) it was the wrong time of day
(3) it was still wartime
(4) it was too cold
(5) it was forbidden to do so

6. 1 2 3 4 5

7. The author states that her mother thought about her parents when she
(1) walked along the river
(2) thought about death
(3) danced with the officers
(4) was at work
(5) looked into the mirror

7. 1 2 3 4 5

8. When the author mentions her mother's dancing with British officers, she implies that her mother
(1) compared her dancing to the suffering of her parents
(2) had clearly put her troubles behind her
(3) felt it was her duty to dance with them
(4) felt guilty about dancing
(5) wanted to escape from her past

8. 1 2 3 4 5

9. The mother did not discuss her concerns about her loved ones with anyone because she
(1) thought no one was interested
(2) felt it was no one's business
(3) was too shy
(4) did not know anyone
(5) didn't want to hurt them

9. 1 2 3 4 5

10. The author's purpose in writing this selection is most likely to
(1) inform people about atrocities in the concentration camp
(2) explain the long-range effects of a traumatic emotional experience
(3) enlist active participation in refugee affairs
(4) encourage people to prosecute former concentration camp guards
(5) gain sympathy from her readers

10. 1 2 3 4 5

Items 11 to 15 refer to the following selection.

THE APPRENTICE SPY

When I was twelve years old, my parents rented a cottage on the shores of Lake Couchiching. The weather for the two weeks was very poor. My mother translated couchiching, from the Ojibway, as "lake which the sun only shines on one side of," because the far coast was always brilliantly lit, while we lived in shadow and struggled on under turbulent black cloud. So, because we could not pursue outdoorsy activities, the family made several excursions by automobile to local tourist attractions.

At this time I read voraciously, which is to say piggishly, cramming stuff into my brain that rendered me pimple-faced and pudgy. I was a great connoisseur of espionage novels, and had determined that I would one day be a spy. There are very few ways for a twelve-year-old boy to apprentice as a spy in southern Ontario. About all I could manage was to sit in the backseat on automobile voyages with my head stuck out the window, allowing the wind to burn my forehead and flap my cheeks, so that some day, when espionage was possible, I would possess the requisite "weather-beaten" features.

—Paul Quarrington

11. The Ojibway called the lake "couchiching" because
(1) it was a local tourist attraction
(2) it was a good location to write novels
(3) the sun only shines on one side
(4) the weather is always poor
(5) it is a good place to rent a cottage

11. 1 2 3 4 5

12. Outdoor activities were not possible because
(1) they enjoyed reading
(2) the weather was so bad
(3) local attractions were more fun
(4) the car would not start
(5) the sun was too bright

12. 1 2 3 4 5

13. The narrator might best be described as
(1) an active outdoorsman
(2) a willing traveller
(3) a youthful athlete
(4) a voracious reader
(5) an unimaginative thinker

13. 1 2 3 4 5

14. He prepared himself to be a spy by
(1) visiting tourist attractions
(2) specializing in espionage novels
(3) swimming in Lake Couchiching
(4) studying the Ojibway language
(5) taking long automobile rides

14. 1 2 3 4 5

15. He rode in the backseat on car trips to
(1) enjoy the scenery
(2) read a novel
(3) catch up on his sleep
(4) change his appearance
(5) continue his studies

15. 1 2 3 4 5

Items 16 to 20 refer to the following selection.

HOW DID THE AUTHOR'S MOTHER VIEW SCIENTIFIC PROGRESS?

I recall that during my youth, in the 1920s, my mother thought—or, rather, knew—that it was dangerous to drive an automobile without gasoline; it fried the valves, or something. "Now don't you dare drive all over town without gasoline!" she would say to us when we started off. Gasoline, oil, and water were much the same to her, a fact that made her life both confusing and perilous. Her greatest dread, however, was the Victrola. She had an idea that the phonograph might blow up. It alarmed her, rather than reassured her, to explain that the phonograph was run neither by gasoline nor by electricity. She could only suppose that it was propelled by some newfangled and untested apparatus which was likely to let go at any minute, making us all the victims and martyrs of the wildeyed Edison's dangerous experiments. The telephone she was comparatively at peace with, except, of course, during storms, when for some reason or other she always took the receiver off the hook and let it hang. She came naturally by her confused and groundless fears, for her own mother lived the latter years of her life in the horrible suspicion that electricity was dripping invisibly all over the house. It leaked, she contended, out of empty sockets if the wall switch had been left on. She would go around screwing in bulbs, and if they lighted up she would hastily and fearfully turn off the wall switch, happy in the satisfaction that she had stopped not only a costly but a dangerous leakage. Nothing could ever clear this up for her.

16. The narrator implies that his mother's beliefs about how automobiles operate were based on

(1) intuition
(2) misunderstanding
(3) inexperience
(4) suspicion
(5) education

16. 1 2 3 4 5

17. Attempts to explain how the Victrola worked resulted in his mother's becoming more

(1) upset
(2) curious
(3) shocked
(4) confused
(5) understanding

17. 1 2 3 4 5

18. Which is an example of his mother's "confused and groundless fears" (lines 15–16)?

(1) She would not let her children drive a car
(2) She took the telephone receiver off its hook during a storm
(3) She used gasoline, oil, and water interchangeably
(4) She replaced light bulbs on a regular basis
(5) She turned off the electricity

18. 1 2 3 4 5

19. The narrator excuses his mother's fears on the basis of her

(1) ignorance
(2) health
(3) upbringing
(4) superstitions
(5) nature

19. 1 2 3 4 5

20. Which element of the selection do the words "Victrola" (line 7) and "newfangled" (line 10) help to establish?
(1) theme
(2) plot
(3) setting
(4) point of view
(5) character

20. 1 2 3 4 5

Items 21 to 25 refer to the following poem.

IN HIGH FLIGHT

Oh, I have slipped the surly bonds of earth,
And danced the skies on laughter-silvered wings:
Sunward I've climbed and joined the tumbling mirth
Of sun-split clouds—and done a hundred things
You have not dreamed of—wheeled and soared and swung
High in the sunlit silence. Hov'ring there,
I've chased the shouting wind along and flung
My eager craft through footless halls of air.
Up, up the long delirious, burning blue
I've topped the wind-swept heights with easy grace,
Where never lark, or even eagle, flew;
And, while with silent, lifting mind I've trod
The high untrespassed sanctity of space,
Put out my hand and touched the face of God.

—John Gillespie Magee Jr.

21. In line 1 "slipped the surly bonds" means
(1) untied a knot
(2) lost control of the aircraft
(3) gone out of sight
(4) escaped the forces of gravity
(5) landed the plane

21. 1 2 3 4 5

22. In line 3 "tumbling mirth" refers to
(1) fluffy white cloud formations
(2) other aircraft in the squadron
(3) jokes told by pilots
(4) a nose dive
(5) aerobatics

22. 1 2 3 4 5

23. In line 10 "wind-swept heights" means
(1) high up in the clouds
(2) above the highest mountain tops
(3) flying into the wind
(4) losing altitude
(5) chasing other planes

23. 1 2 3 4 5

24. In line 13 "untrespassed sanctity of space" refers to
(1) returning to the airfield
(2) flying into the sun
(3) flying faster than before
(4) a place where no one has ever been
(5) losing sight of the earth

24. 1 2 3 4 5

25. "In High Flight" is a 14-verse poem called a
(1) ballad
(2) biography
(3) allegory
(4) elegy
(5) sonnet

25. 1 2 3 4 5
|| || || || ||

Items 26 to 30 refer to the following passage from a play.

WHY DO POOR PEOPLE MAKE SUCH EXPENSIVE FUNERALS?

SALESMAN: [*Chewing*] I really don't understand . . . wherever you look, in all the newspapers, you read the most horrible stories about conditions among the weavers, and you get the impression that all the people here are half-starved. And then you see such a funeral! Just as I came into the village, there were brass bands, schoolteachers, children, the pastor, and a whole string of people; my God, you'd think the Emperor of China was being buried. If these people can pay for that . . . ! [*He drinks his beer. Then he puts his glass down and suddenly speaks in a frivolous tone*.] Isn't that so, Miss? Don't you agree with me?

[ANNA *smiles, embarrassed, and continues busily with her embroidery.*]

SALESMAN: Those must be slippers for Papa.

WELZEL: Oh, I don't like to wear them things.

SALESMAN: Just listen to that! I'd give half my fortune if those slippers were for me.

MRS. WELZEL: He just don't appreciate such things.

WIEGAND: [*After he has coughed several times and moved his chair about, as if he wanted to speak*] The gentleman has expressed himself mighty well about the funeral. Now tell us, young lady, isn't that just a small funeral?

SALESMAN: Yes, I must say . . . That must cost a tremendous amount of money. Where do these people get the money for it?

WIEGAND: You'll forgive me for sayin' it, sir, there is no such folly among the poorer classes hereabouts. If you don't mind my sayin' so, they have such exaggerated ideas of the dutiful respect and the obligations that's due the deceased and the blessed dead. And when it's a matter of deceased parents, they are so superstitious that the descendants and the next of kin scrape together their last penny. And what the children can't raise, they borrow from the nearest moneylender. And then they're in debts up to their necks; they'll be owing His Reverence the Pastor, the sexton, and everybody else in the neighbourhood. And drinks and victuals and all the other necessary things. Oh, yes, I approve of respectful duty on the part of children toward their parents, but not so that the mourners are burdened down the rest of their lives by such obligations.

SALESMAN: I beg your pardon, but I should think the pastor would talk them out of it.

WIEGAND: Beggin' your pardon, sir, but there I would like to interpose that every little congregation has its ecclesiastical house of worship and must support its reverend pastor. The high clergy get a wonderful revenue and profit from such a big funeral. The more elaborate such a funeral can be arranged, the more profitable is the offeratory that flows from it. Whoever knows the conditions of the workers hereabouts can, with unauthoritative certainty, affirm that the pastors only with reluctance tolerate small and quiet funerals.

26. Which character in the passage seems to see things most clearly?
(1) the salesman
(2) Mrs. Welzel
(3) Welzel
(4) Wiegand
(5) Anna

26. 1 2 3 4 5
|| || || || ||

27. What do the italicized portions in the passage signify?
(1) directions to the actors
(2) asides to the actors
(3) directions to the cameraman
(4) important parts of the dialogue
(5) comments by the playwright

27. 1 2 3 4 5 || || || || ||

28. Why do the townspeople apparently have such elaborate funerals?
(1) They have more money than the public has been led to believe.
(2) They have strong ideas of the respect due to the dead.
(3) They look upon the funerals as holiday occasions.
(4) They wish to impress their neighbours.
(5) They wish to defy the advice of their parents.

28. 1 2 3 4 5 || || || || ||

29. Wiegand's speech about the church suggests that he views it as an institution that is
(1) sympathetic to the weavers' needs
(2) interested only in formal worship
(3) in favour of small and quiet funerals, rather than large, boisterous ones
(4) organized to do God's work on Earth
(5) interested in making money from the people

29. 1 2 3 4 5 || || || || ||

30. From this passage, the reader can most safely conclude that Anna is
(1) Weigand's wife
(2) Welzel's daughter
(3) the salesman's friend
(4) a worker in the weaving mills
(5) a servant

30. 1 2 3 4 5 || || || || ||

—IN CLASSICAL LITERATURE

Items 31 to 35 refer to the following selection.

WHY DID THE AUTHOR GO TO THE WOODS?

I went to the woods because I wished to live deliberately, to front only the essential facts of life, and see if I could not learn what it had to teach, and not, when I came to die, discover that I had not lived. I did not wish to live what was not life, living is so dear; nor did I wish to practice resignation, unless it was quite necessary. I wanted to live deep and suck out all the marrow of life, to live so sturdily and Spartan-like as to put to rout all that was not life, to cut a broad swath and shave close, to drive life into a corner, and reduce it to its lowest terms, and, if it proved to be mean, why then to get the whole and genuine meanness of it, and publish its meanness to the world; or if it were sublime, to know it by experience, and be able to give a true account of it in my next excursion. For most men, it appears to me, are in a strange uncertainty about it, whether it is of the devil or of God, and have somewhat hastily concluded that it is the chief end of man here to "glorify God and enjoy him forever."

Still we live meanly, like ants; though the fable tells us that we were long ago changed into men; like pygmies we fight with cranes; it is error upon error, and clout upon clout, and our best virtue has for its occasion a superfluous and evitable wretchedness. Our life is frittered away by detail. An honest man has hardly need to count more than his ten fingers, or in extreme cases he may add his ten toes, and lump the rest. Simplicity, simplicity, simplicity! I say, let your affairs be as two or three, and not a hundred or a thousand; instead of a million count half a dozen, and keep your accounts on your thumb-nail.

—Henry D. Thoreau

31. The best statement of why the author went to the woods is that he went to
(1) discover that he had not lived
(2) live meanly, like ants
(3) practice resignation
(4) reduce life to its simplest terms
(5) glorify God

31. 1 2 3 4 5 || || || || ||

32. The author thinks that life should be *all* of the following EXCEPT
(1) Spartan-like
(2) complicated
(3) creative
(4) noble
(5) moral

32. 1 2 3 4 5 || || || || ||

33. All of the following words as used in this selection are correctly defined EXCEPT
(1) *deliberately*—unhurriedly
(2) *front*—confront
(3) *swath*—space
(4) *mean*—nasty
(5) *frittered*—wasted

33. 1 2 3 4 5 || || || || ||

34. The tone of the selection is
(1) bitter cynicism
(2) moral indignation
(3) flippant humour
(4) quiet resignation
(5) self-congratulation

34. 1 2 3 4 5 || || || || ||

35. The author
(1) wishes to learn from nature
(2) is afraid of death
(3) has little regard for life
(4) seeks reconciliation with God
(5) celebrates man's life style

35. 1 2 3 4 5 || || || || ||

Items 36 to 40 refer to the following poem.

IN FLANDERS FIELDS

In Flanders fields the poppies blow
Between the crosses, row on row,
That mark our place; and in the sky
The larks, still bravely singing, fly
Scarce heard amid the guns below.
We are the Dead. Short days ago
We lived, felt dawn, saw sunset glow.
Loved, and were loved, and now we lie
In Flanders fields.
Take up our quarrel with the foe:
To you from failing hands we throw
The torch; be yours to hold it high.
If ye break faith with us who die
We shall not sleep, though poppies grow
In Flanders fields.

—John McCrae

36. In line 2 "between the crosses" refers to

(1) a battlefield
(2) telephone poles
(3) a flower garden
(4) a burial ground
(5) a farmer's field

36. 1 2 3 4 5

37. In line 5 the larks aren't heard because

(1) people aren't paying attention
(2) they are too far away
(3) the sound of the guns drowns out the singing
(4) they have all flown away
(5) all the soldiers are gone

37. 1 2 3 4 5

38. In line 6 "We are the Dead" refers to

(1) soldiers buried in the cemetery
(2) a battlefield
(3) a military parade
(4) a tourist attraction
(5) ancient ruins

38. 1 2 3 4 5

39. In lines 11 and 12—"throw the torch" means

(1) running in a relay race
(2) leading a procession
(3) lighting the way
(4) passing on military duties to the next generation
(5) clearing the field

39. 1 2 3 4 5

40. In line 14 "We shall not sleep" means

(1) the sound of battle keeps people awake
(2) the guns are too loud
(3) the fighting continues
(4) the ghosts of the departed won't rest
(5) the war is over

40. 1 2 3 4 5

Items 41 to 45 refer to this excerpt from a play.

WHY DO ELIZA AND EUGENE DISAGREE?

ELIZA. [*Sits beside EUGENE, his back still turned to her*] Gene. You know what I'd do if I were you? I'd just show her I was a good sport, that's what! I wouldn't let on to her that it affected me one bit. I'd write her just as big as you please and laugh about the whole thing.

EUGENE. Oh, God, Mama, please, leave me alone, leave me alone!

ELIZA. Why, I'd be ashamed to let any girl get my goat like that. When you get older, you'll just look back on this and laugh. You'll see. You'll be going to college next year, and you won't remember a thing about it. [*EUGENE turns, looks at her.*] I told you I'd sold that Stumptown property, and I have. This year's term has started already but next year—

EUGENE. Mama, *now! Now!* I've wasted enough time!

ELIZA. What are you talking about? Why, you're a child yet, there's plenty of time yet—

EUGENE. [*Rises, walks about her, beggingly*] Mama, Mama, what is it? What more do you want from me? Do you want to strangle and drown me completely? Do you want more string? Do you want me to collect more bottles? Tell me what you want! Do you want more property? Do you want the town? Is that it?

ELIZA. Why, I don't know what you're talking about, boy. If I hadn't tried to accumulate a little something, none of you would have a roof to call your own.

41. It apparently seems to the mother that she has fulfilled her obligations by
(1) always loving Eugene
(2) recognizing how much a child Eugene still is
(3) retaining her sense of humour in spite of adversity
(4) passing on her values to Eugene
(5) providing for the material needs of the family

41. 1 2 3 4 5

42. In this scene, Eugene reacts to the situation with
(1) suppressed calm
(2) wry humour
(3) growing desperation
(4) vague indifference
(5) thoughtful objectivity

42. 1 2 3 4 5

43. In this scene, Eugene's lines most strongly suggest that he
(1) envies his mother's good fortune
(2) desires independence from his mother
(3) is anxious about earning money for himself
(4) is aware of his own humility
(5) is concerned about his newest romantic attachment

43. 1 2 3 4 5

44. In this scene, the mother's attitude toward Eugene is one of
(1) dismay because of his growing greed
(2) admiration for his courage
(3) disgust at his lack of a sense of humour
(4) resentment at his lack of consideration
(5) disappointment at his lack of interest in college

44. 1 2 3 4 5

45. It is most probable that immediately preceding this scene
(1) Eugene has forgotten to write to a girl
(2) Eugene has just returned from a trip
(3) the mother has received a letter from a girl
(4) a girl has hurt Eugene
(5) Eugene has inherited some property

45. 1 2 3 4 5
|| || || || ||

—IN COMMENTARY ON THE ARTS

Items 46 to 50 refer to the following selection on literature.

WHAT IS THE SIGNIFICANCE OF *BILLY BUDD*?

Next to his towering masterpiece, *Moby Dick*, *Billy Budd* is Melville's greatest work. It has the tone of a last testament, and the manuscript was neatly tied up by his wife, Elizabeth, and kept in a trunk for some thirty years. It was not until 1924 that it was first published. Slowly it has become recognized as the remarkable work it is. *Billy Budd* has been dramatized for Broadway, done on T.V., made into an opera, and reached a highly satisfying form in Ustinov's movie.

Scholars disagree, somewhat violently, about what Melville was trying to say. He did make it pretty clear that he was recounting a duel between Good and Evil.

Several times he remarked that Billy Budd is as innocent and ignorant as Adam before the fall. His enemy is like Satan in Milton's *Paradise Lost*.

When Billy Budd destroys the letter, and is sentenced to be hanged according to the letter of the law, controversy exists as to whether the Captain is simply a mortal man preserving order, or a Jehovah-like figure, dispensing cruel justice.

Melville, it is claimed, cleverly took pains to hide his heretical feelings. *Billy Budd* is written as if told by a pious, God-loving man.

Ironically, Melville's iconoclasm has largely misfired, for the story today is accepted as either one of simple suspense or a reverent parable of God, Satan, and Adam. Meanwhile the scholars are still arguing, and *Billy Budd* remains like a porcupine, thorny, with interesting ambiguities.

46. *Billy Budd*, according to the article,
(1) brought Melville fame
(2) was Melville's greatest work
(3) reads like Melville's final work
(4) remained neglected
(5) was not successful as a book

46. 1 2 3 4 5
|| || || || ||

47. The meaning of *Billy Budd* is
(1) unclear to Melville
(2) generally understood
(3) subject to debate
(4) widely recognized
(5) based on fact

47. 1 2 3 4 5
|| || || || ||

48. Melville, according to the article, felt that Billy Budd was
(1) deserving of his fate
(2) unjustly punished
(3) well aware of his action's consequences
(4) the victim of a duel
(5) the victim of a vengeful Captain

48. 1 2 3 4 5

49. Melville disguised his
(1) intentions
(2) love of God
(3) piety
(4) true beliefs
(5) bias

49. 1 2 3 4 5

50. According to the article, Melville's original intention was later
(1) understood
(2) forgotten
(3) achieved
(4) accepted
(5) distorted

50. 1 2 3 4 5

Items 51 to 55 refer to the following passage on television.

The cultural and communications critic Marshall McLuhan called it a "cool" medium for the burgeoning "electronic village," but even those who did not look upon the phenomenon so dispassionately saw that television was having a great effect on society in the second half of the 20th century. Other countries would soon catch up, as new viewers around the world found themselves gaping at the fleeting pictures on "the boob tube" by the hour. While its potential for enriching lives was accepted, the reality of its contents was soon subject to suspicion or outright condemnation. In 1961, for instance, Newton Minow, a member of the United States Federal Communications Commission, described American TV as "a vast wasteland," for its vapid offerings. By 1963 Great Britain's government was establishing a special committee to inquire into the "moral impact" of TV on the young, and in the years to come many United States groups would study the effects of violence on the young. But if McLuhan was right, none of these well-intentioned criticisms or investigations is truly pertinent. "The medium is the message," he declared, meaning that the content of any single programme is not as significant as the fact that people are looking at television. Put another way, it did not matter whether television gained access to your living room in blue jeans or a tuxedo: it was going to make a change.

51. According to the article, there is general agreement on
(1) the quality of TV
(2) the need for TV
(3) the techniques of TV
(4) the effect of TV
(5) the advantages of TV

51. 1 2 3 4 5

52. Marshall McLuhan emphasized the fact that
(1) TV programming was important
(2) TV programming was poor
(3) TV was being viewed
(4) TV was being criticized
(5) TV was changing

52. 1 2 3 4 5

53. TV is called all of the following EXCEPT
(1) a "cool" medium
(2) an "urban village"
(3) "the boob tub"
(4) "a vaste wasteland"
(5) "the message"

53. 1 2 3 4 5

54. The content of TV programmes was suspected of all of the following EXCEPT
(1) emptiness
(2) silliness
(3) immorality
(4) violence
(5) inaccuracy

54. 1 2 3 4 5

55. According to McLuhan, investigations on the effects of TV are
(1) significant
(2) necessary
(3) long overdue
(4) too limited
(5) irrelevant

55. 1 2 3 4 5

Items 56 to 60 refer to the following selection on music.

WHAT MAKES A CONDUCTOR GREAT?

What makes a conductor great?

He must have so complete a command of the specialized techniques of conducting that he can play upon the musicians seated before him as though beneath his hands they were the keyboard of one gigantic, unimaginable instrument. He must have so deep and intimate an understanding of the music of the composers of more than two centuries that he can summon it to life from millions of soundless symbols on paper. He must project a public personality, a stage presence, that will capture and hold the worshipful attention of perhaps the most critical audiences in the world. He must be a surpassing executive, a subtle master of personal relations, and the shrewd centrally placed diplomat in a constantly explosive set of circumstances. And though he often is not, he should be the most intelligent and informed musician in his community, which today may be nation-wide or even world-wide.

What makes a conductor great is the many-faceted ability to make listeners experience music with joy and then leave the music believing that much of the joy experienced has been made possible by the man on the podium. Conducting is not a science, but an art, a method of communication. Like all other artists, conductors must respect the materials in which they work, or run the risk that those materials will turn on them destructively. Certainly the conductor must respect composers and their creations. But unless he also uses those creations to communicate with his listeners, unless he passionately shapes them into living entities, they will remain inert and he will fail. A selfish conductor is often bad, but a truly selfless one would be a monstrosity.

56. The writer implies that the conductor works in a
(1) difficult environment
(2) world-wide community
(3) nation-wide community
(4) diplomatic post
(5) atmosphere of adoration

56. 1 2 3 4 5

57. The writer implies that the least important quality of a conductor is his
(1) technique
(2) understanding of music
(3) personality
(4) tact
(5) intelligence

57. 1 2 3 4 5

58. The writer implies that working with an orchestra requires
(1) knowledge of the keyboard
(2) strong discipline
(3) self-effacing personality
(4) astute diplomacy
(5) public approval

58. 1 2 3 4 5

59. The writer implies that the most important outcome of conducting is
(1) audience contentment
(2) fine technique
(3) new approaches
(4) scientific accuracy
(5) good materials

59. 1 2 3 4 5

60. A great conductor's *most important function* is to
(1) remain faithful to his materials
(2) respect the composers
(3) respect the composers' creations
(4) change composers' creations
(5) avoid being selfish

60. 1 2 3 4 5

See the answer key below and the answer analysis on page 484.

What's Your Score?

_______right, _______wrong

Excellent	54–60
Good	48–54
Fair	42–47

If your score was low, the explanation of the correct answers which follows will help you. Analyze your errors. Then, reread the section on Basic Reading Skills (beginning on page 441) and Basics on Reading Literature (page 443).

ANSWER KEY

Practice in Popular Literature/Page 469

1. **1**	7. **4**	13. **4**	19. **5**	25. **5**
2. **3**	8. **4**	14. **2**	20. **3**	26. **4**
3. **2**	9. **1**	15. **4**	21. **4**	27. **1**
4. **1**	10. **2**	16. **2**	22. **1**	28. **2**
5. **3**	11. **3**	17. **1**	23. **2**	29. **5**
6. **2**	12. **2**	18. **2**	24. **4**	30. **2**

Practice in Classical Literature/Page 476

31. **4**	34. **2**	37. **3**	40. **4**	43. **2**
32. **2**	35. **1**	38. **1**	41. **5**	44. **4**
33. **4**	36. **4**	39. **4**	42. **3**	45. **4**

Practice in Commentary on the Arts/Page 480

46. **3**	49. **4**	52. **3**	55. **5**	58. **4**
47. **3**	50. **5**	53. **2**	56. **1**	59. **1**
48. **2**	51. **4**	54. **5**	57. **5**	60. **4**

ANSWER ANALYSIS

Practice in Popular Literature/Page 469

1. **1** People were enjoying the summer weather so much that they seemed to have little interest in politics or in the coming referendum.
2. **3** The newspapers were full of political debate.
3. **2** The narrator rode his bicycle along the Chemin Jordan enjoying the view.
4. **1** He felt that, as in 1980, Quebecers would vote to stay in Canada.
5. **3** He was carefree and relaxed.
6. **2** The selection states it was "not the best time to be walking alone by the side of a half-frozen river."
7. **4** The phrase "during the day as she stood pinning dresses" indicates that this activity took place regularly. Pinning dresses, therefore, must have been her work.
8. **4** The sentence "What if they . . . had died of cold or hunger . . . while she was . . . dancing with British officers?" communicates a sense of guilt.
9. **1** "No one, she thought, wanted to hear them," states the selection. This indicates that she believed others were not interested, not that she did not want to tell them. The fact that she continued to go to the Jewish Community Centre proves that answer choices 3 and 4 are incorrect.
10. **2** The last paragraph describes the effect of this incident. That is what the reader is meant to remember and to understand.
11. **3** The Ojibway word *couchiching* means "the sun only shines on one side."
12. **2** Their side of the lake was under a turbulent black cloud.
13. **4** He crammed his brain with reading.
14. **2** Spy novels were his passion.
15. **4** He hung his head out the window to get a wind-burned weather-beaten look.
16. **2** Since "Gasoline, oil and water were much the same to her," she had little understanding of the mechanics of automobiles.
17. **1** The fact that she was upset is obvious from the sentence "It alarmed her . . . to explain that the phonograph was run neither by gasoline nor by electricity."
18. **2** The passage states that "she always took the receiver off the hook" during storms.
19. **5** The author states that "She came naturally by her confused and groundless fears."
20. **3** Since these words are not used today, the author's use of them is designed to indicate the time or setting of the incidents he relates.
21. **4** The speed of the plane is more powerful than the force of gravity pulling the plane back to earth.
22. **1** The clouds are white puff balls shining in the sun.
23. **2** Heights refers to the highest mountaintops where even birds can't fly.
24. **4** The pilot has flown higher than anyone has ever before.
25. **5** "In High Flight" is a sonnet with 14 verses divided into an octet and a sestet.
26. **4** Wiegand is the only character who can clarify matters for the salesman. The others hardly talk.
27. **1** These portions call for actions by the actors.

28. **2** Wiegand refers to their "exaggerated ideas of the dutiful respect" for the dead.
29. **5** Wiegand mentions that the clergy get revenue and profit from big funerals.
30. **2** Anna is embroidering slippers for Papa and Welzel says he doesn't like to wear them.

Practice in Classical Literature/Page 476

31. **4** The author states "I went to the woods . . . to front only the essential facts of life . . ."
32. **2** The author says, "Our life is frittered away by detail . . . Simplicity, simplicity, simplicity! . . . keep your accounts on your thumb-nail."
33. **4** *Mean* is used here to imply the opposite of *sublime* (used in the next phrase), i.e., lowly, or unthinkingly busy, "like ants."
34. **2** The author implies that men do not know how to live properly, but they should learn.
35. **1** He wanted to see if he could not learn what the woods had to teach.
36. **4** The rows of crosses comprise a military cemetery.
37. **3** The booming of the guns is louder than the singing.
38. **1** The dead soldiers' graves are symbols of remembrance of their sacrifice.
39. **4** The young must take up the responsibilities of the older soldiers who have died.
40. **4** If their sacrifice is not remembered the ghosts of the fallen will haunt succeeding generations.
41. **5** Eliza refers to accumulating money to provide a roof for her son.
42. **3** Eugene's growing desperation is revealed by the nine consecutive questions he asks of his mother.
43. **2** Two of the questions centre on his desire for independence: "Do you want to strangle and drown me completely?" "Do you want more string?"
44. **4** The mother repeats, at two points, "What are you talking about?"
45. **4** The mother said she'd be "ashamed to let any girl get my goat like that."

Practice in Commentary on the Arts/Page 480

46. **3** The passage states that *Billy Budd* has the tone of a last testament.
47. **3** It is stated that scholars disagree about what Melville was trying to say.
48. **2** We are told that several times Melville remarked that Billy Budd is innocent.
49. **4** Melville clearly took pains to hide his heretical feelings.
50. **5** It is stated that Melville's shattering of customarily held beliefs has largely misfired, i.e., has had a different effect.
51. **4** Even those who viewed television emotionally agreed on its having a great effect.
52. **3** Nothing is as important as the fact that people are looking at television.
53. **2** Television is a medium *for* but it is not *the* "urban village."
54. **5** All the others are mentioned. Inaccuracy is not.
55. **5** McLuhan says that none of the investigations is pertinent.
56. **1** The author refers to critical audiences and a constantly explosive set of circumstances.
57. **5** Intelligence comes after technique, understanding of music, personality, and diplomacy.
58. **4** It is stated that the conductor must be a master of personal relations and a shrewd diplomat.
59. **1** The conductor must make the listeners experience music with joy.
60. **4** The conductor must shape the composers' creations to communicate with his audience.

9

MATHEMATICS

AN OVERVIEW

This section describes the content and format of the GED Mathematics Test and the skills and abilities required for success.

HOW TO READ AND SOLVE VERBAL PROBLEMS

Steps to a reasoned analysis and solution of verbal problems.

ARITHMETIC

This section reviews whole numbers, fractions, decimals, and percents. Business applications such as profit and loss, interest, taxation, and investments receive attention. This section also includes scientific notation, probability, and the mean and the median.

ALGEBRA

This section presents fundamental concepts of algebra.

GEOMETRY

This section includes problems that give extensive experience with geometric concepts.

MEASURES

Measures of length, time, and mass, liquid and dry measure, and the metric system are discussed.

TESTING TACTICS IN MATHEMATICS

This section gives practical hints for achieving a maximum score on this GED test.

FIVE PRACTICE MATHEMATICS TESTS

Each test has the standard 56 questions with explained answers. You are referred to sections in Chapter 9 to refresh your understanding of questions answered incorrectly.

AN OVERVIEW

The content outline and description of format and skills for the Mathematics Test are reprinted with permission of the GED Testing Service of the American Council on Education.

CONTENT

The Mathematics Test covers three major content areas: arithmetic, algebra, and geometry. Arithmetic questions may be further classified under the subtopics measurement, number relationships, and data analysis. The content percentages on the test are as follows:

Content Area	Percent of Test
Arithmetic	
Measurement	30
Number Relationships	10
Data Analysis	10
Algebra	30
Geometry	20

The specific skills to be tested within each content area are listed below. The page references indicate the sections of this book where a thorough treatment of the required skills can be found.

The contexts of the mathematics questions are generally realistic rather than academic and reflect tasks with which the adult student has had considerable experience. The situations are natural, rather than contrived, and deal with the world of work, the consumer, family experiences, etc.

FORMAT

The 50 mathematics test items are multiple-choice questions based on either a brief written (verbal) stimulus or a graphic stimulus (e.g. graphs, tables, charts, diagrams). Two thirds of the questions have written stimuli, and one third have graphic stimuli. Single items consist of up to about 50 words or a graphic stimulus. Item sets consist of up to about 100 words or a graphic stimulus accompanied by 2–4 questions.

Also included in the mathematics test is a page of formulas. The student will be required to (1) identify which concept is being tested and (2) select the correct formula from the formula page. This appropriately fits the student's experiences—the need to use reference materials when faced with a problem in a real setting.

SKILLS

The GED Mathematics Test includes higher level thinking skills and problem-solving ability. There is greater emphasis on problems involving solutions that have more than one step. In algebra, students are challenged by moderate to difficult word problems, and are required to translate contexts into algebraic language, and to represent a sequence of operations in arithmetic and algebraic language. The student must be able to differentiate between sufficient and insufficient data, and between relevant and extraneous data, and to determine the necessary sequence of steps in solving a problem.

The student will find it helpful to have a systematic method of approach to problem solving. Such a method is described and is then applied to problems in arithmetic, algebra, and geometry.

How to Use This Chapter

From the results of your diagnostic test, you should be aware of your strengths and weaknesses. If you are in a class where every topic is covered, prepare ahead so that you can ask questions about problems you may have in any areas of weakness. In any classroom situation a prepared student learns the most. You can use your prescription as a study guide during the lessons and in your own review before the examinations.

If you are using this book on your own, review your prescription. Make a plan for covering your areas of weakness and reviewing your areas of strength.

The final portion of this chapter contains five typical mathematics tests, with both answers and explanations of answers. In conjunction with each test item in the five practice tests, there is a key system appended to each correct answer choice. This key system refers you to the section of the chapter where you will find explanations and additional practice on the problems with which you had difficulty.

HOW TO READ AND SOLVE VERBAL PROBLEMS

Verbal problems appear in all areas of mathematics. A systematic approach to problem solving is essential for success in mathematics.

Plan for Solving Verbal Problems

Verbal problems can present obstacles for anyone preparing for the GED examinations. They are an essential part of writing a successful examination. In order to make solving verbal problems easier, we suggest the following complete plan of action:

1. Read the problem carefully.
2. Decide what the answer will be.
3. Represent the answer by a variable.
4. Collect the relevant information given in the problem.
5. Develop a path from the answer through the relevant information to the problem.
6. Follow your path from the problem to the answer.
7. Check your answer.

This plan may seem unnecessarily complex for simple problems, and after you become familiar with it, we will show you shortcuts for easier problems. You can also adapt the plan to your own level of competence and comfort. The plan is written on paper and can be adapted to suit your needs. It works well with complex problems and is too complex for simple problems. Learn to work with it, and then you can decide which of its forms to use.

Consider the following verbal problems:

Example 1
An Arithmetic Problem
Mrs. Bates bought a jacket and a shirt at a sale where all items were reduced 25% below the marked price. If the marked price of the jacket was $200 and the marked price of the shirt was $35, how much did she save by buying at the sale?

1. **Read the problem carefully.** Mrs. Bates is shopping for bargains and expects to save 25% on each purchase. She bought two items. Logically, the price she pays should be less than the marked price.

2. **Decide what the answer will be.** The answer will be the amount in dollars that Mrs. Bates will save by buying these items on sale.

3. **Represent the answer by a variable.** The answer will be $*X*.

4. **Collect the relevant information given in the problem.**

	Marked Price	Discount Percent
Jacket	$200	25%
Shirt	$35	25%

5. **Develop a path from the answer through the relevant information to the problem.**
   A. I want to calculate the amount of her savings in dollars.
   B. Since the discount is the same for all items, I can calculate the amount she saves by taking the percentage discount of her total purchases.
   C. I can calculate her total purchases by adding the marked prices of the purchases.

6. **Follow your path from the problem to the answer.**
   C. Total purchases = $200 + $35 = $235
   B. Percentage discount = 25%
   A. Amount of discount = 25% of $235 = (.25 × 235) = $58.75
   Mrs. Bates saved $58.75 by buying the items on sale.

7. **Check your answer.**
Savings on jacket = 25% of \$200 = \$50
Savings on shirt = 25% of \$35 = \$8.75
Total savings = \$50 + \$8.75 = \$58.75
HINT: You can always check your answer by following a parallel path.

Example 2
An Algebra Problem
A father is 15 years more than twice the age of his daughter. If the sum of the ages of the father and the daughter is 48 years, what is the age of the daughter?

1. **Read the problem carefully.** A father and daughter's ages are related, and we are given the relationship. We want to know the age of the daughter in years.

2. **Decide what the answer will be.** The answer will be the age of the daughter in years.

3. **Represent the answer by a variable.** The age of the daughter in years is Y.
HINT: Any letter can be used as a variable.

4. **Collect the relevant information.**
Age of father = twice age of daughter + 15
Age of father + age of daughter = 48

5. **Develop a path from the answer through the relevant information to the problem.**
A. The age of the daughter in years is Y.
B. I know that the age of the father in years plus the age of the daughter in years equals 48.
C. I can calculate the age of the father by subtracting the age of the daughter in years from 48.
D. Since the age of the father is twice the age of the daughter plus 15, I can calculate twice the age of the father by adding 15 to twice the age of the daughter.
E. Since the age of the father is constant, 48 minus the age of the daughter equals 15 plus twice the age of the daughter.

6. **Follow your path from the problem to the answer.** Let the age of the daughter in years be Y
$$48 - Y = 15 + 2Y$$
$$-Y - 3Y = 15 - 48$$
HINT: Collect all the variables on one side of the equation.
$$-3Y = -33$$
HINT: You can multiply the entire equation by the same number to simplify it. In this case, the number is –1.
$$3Y = 33$$
$$Y = 11$$
The daughter's age is 11 years.

7. **Check your answer.**
Age of daughter = 11 years
Thus, age of father = 2 × 11 + 15 = 37 years
Age of daughter in years plus age of father in years equals 48
$$11 + 37 = 48$$

Example 3
A Geometry Problem
A room is 7 m long, 5 m wide, and 3 m high. If the walls and ceiling of the room are to be painted, how many square metres must be covered with paint?

1. **Read the problem carefully.** Someone wants to paint four walls and the ceiling of a room.

2. **Decide what the answer will be.** Since the surface area is being painted, the answer will be the sum of the areas of the front and back walls, the two side walls, and the ceiling in square metres.

3. **Represent the answer by a variable.** The total area to be painted in square metres is *P*.

4. **Collect the relevant information given in the problem.**
HINT: It is usually helpful to draw a diagram to represent the information given.

In this case we have:

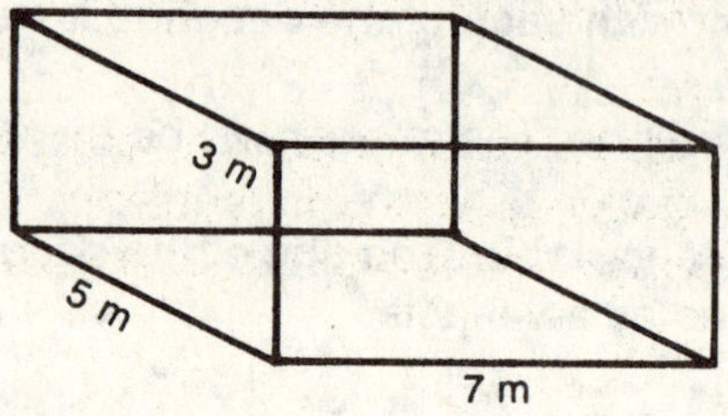

Front and back of room.

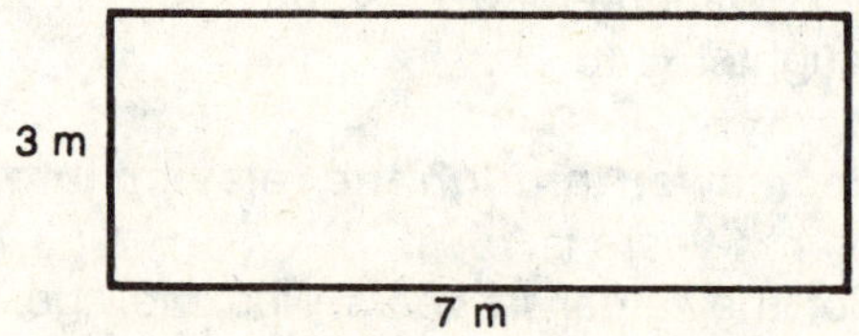

Sides of room.

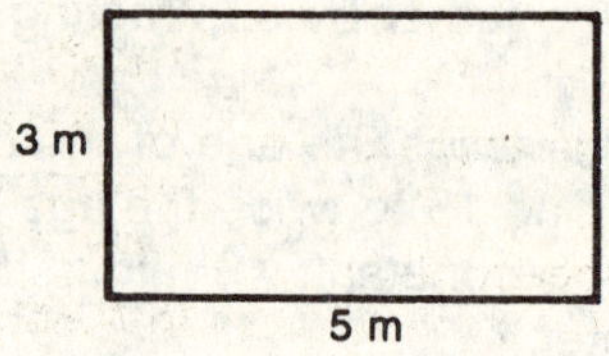

Ceiling of room.

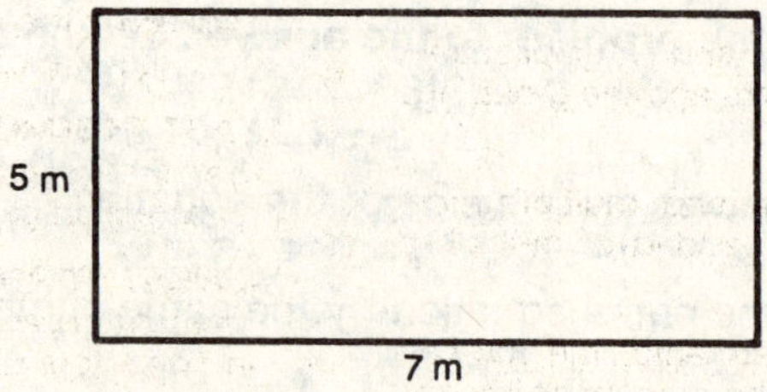

Side	Length (metres)	Height (metres)
Left side	5	3
Right side	5	3
Front	7	3
Back	7	3
Ceiling	7	length = 5

5. **Develop a path from the answer to the relevant information to the problem.**
   A. Since paint covers the area of a surface, the answer is the area of the four walls plus that of the ceiling.
   B. The total area to be covered is the sum of the areas of the four walls plus that of the ceiling.
   C. The area of each wall and the ceiling is calculated by multiplying the length by the height or width.

6. **Follow your path from the problem to the answer.**

$$\text{Area of front wall} = 7 \times 3 = 21\,\text{m}^2$$
$$\text{Area of back wall} = 7 \times 3 = 21\,\text{m}^2$$
$$\text{Area of left side} = 5 \times 3 = 15\,\text{m}^2$$
$$\text{Area of right side} = 5 \times 3 = 15\,\text{m}^2$$
$$\text{Area of ceiling} = 7 \times 5 = 35\,\text{m}^2$$
$$\text{Total area} = 21 + 21 + 15 + 15 + 35 = 107\,\text{m}^2$$

7. **Check your answer.** You can check your answer by going over the work, making sure that there are no mechanical errors and that the answer seems reasonable.

   HINT: Try estimating the answer and see if it is close to the calculated answer.

   For a simple problem, we can rewrite the plan as follows:

   1. Read the problem carefully.
   2. Decide what the answer will be and if necessary represent it by a variable.
   3. Collect the relevant information given in the problem.
   4. Decide how to use the relevant information to go from the information to the answer.
   5. Check your answer.

Try some of the examples given to learn how to use this plan.

I. ARITHMETIC

GLOSSARY

< less than

> greater than

AMOUNT in investments, the sum of the principal and the interest

ASSESSED VALUE a value for real property determined by a government

ASSESSMENT see assessed value

ASSOCIATIVE LAW in addition and multiplication, there is freedom to group numbers and the groupings do not affect the answer

COMMUTATIVE LAW in addition and multiplication, the order in which numbers are added or multiplied does not change the answer

COMPOUND INTEREST in investments, the method of calculating interest whereby the amount of interest is added to the principal at the end of a period and the next interest amount is calculated on the sum

COUNTING NUMBER the number used for counting (There is no 0.)

DECIMAL FRACTION a fraction whose denominator is a power of 10

DENOMINATOR he bottom number in a fraction (the number of parts of the whole)

DISCOUNT the amount by which a price is reduced

DISTRIBUTIVE LAW in multiplication, where a, b, and c are numbers, $a \times (b + c) = a \times b + a \times c$

DIVIDEND in division, the number or quantity that is divided

DIVISOR in division, the number or quantity that is dividing

EVEN NUMBER a number that has 2 as a factor

FRACTION a form of rational number written as a numerator divided by a denominator

IMPROPER FRACTION a fraction in which the numerator is equal to or greater than the denominator

INCOME TAX a tax on earnings determined by a government

INTEREST the amount of money paid or charged for the use of money

LEAST COMMON DENOMINATOR the smallest number into which the denominators in an addition or subtraction can be divided evenly

LOWEST TERMS the form of a fraction in which the numerator and denominator no longer have any common factors other than 1

MILL in realty taxes, 1 mill = $1 per $1000 of assessed value or assessment

MIXED NUMBER an expression consisting of the sum of a whole number and a fraction

NET EARNINGS the amount of money paid to an employee after all deductions have been made by the employer

NET PRICE the price after applying a discount (sometimes called a selling price)

NUMERATOR the top number of a fraction (the number of parts being considered)

ODD NUMBER a number that does not have 2 as a factor

PERCENT a fraction whose denominator is always 100

PREMIUM in insurance, the amount of money paid for insurance for a set period

PRIME NUMBER a number that has only itself and 1 as factors

PRINCIPAL in investments, the amount of money invested

PROPER FRACTION a fraction in which the numerator is less than the denominator

RATE in investments, the percentage of the principal paid to the investor each period, usually one year

RATIONAL NUMBER a number obtained by dividing a counting number or zero by a counting number

REALTY TAX a tax on real property

REMAINDER in division, the number or quantity left after division

SUCCESSIVE DISCOUNTS two or more discounts applied one after the other

TIME in investments, the period of time usually stated in years

I. A. Calculations

The content area of Arithmetic represents 50% of the questions in the GED Mathematics examination. One of the most important skills needed to pass the Arithmetic portion is calculation. Although calculators are now allowed in one part of the examinations, you should still practice doing calculations in your head. Now is the time to take a few minutes and make sure that you know all the various tables for addition, subtraction, multiplication, and division of numbers less than twelve. These should be completely automatic, so that you do not waste valuable time calculating. If you are unsure of your calculations, or are slow with calculations, try this:

a. buy a set of 3″ × 5″ recipe cards
b. on one side of each card, write the facts you are unsure of, such as "7 × 8"
c. on the other side, write the answer, "56"
d. working with a friend, have your friend show you the question side
e. you reply with the answer

For any question that you get incorrect or hesitate before answering, replace the card in the pile. Shuffling regularly will ensure that the questions do not always come up in the same order. Two weeks or so of regular practice will improve your calculation skills greatly.

Estimating:

The GED examination questions are multiple choice, and in Mathematics, that means that estimating is as important as calculating. You will be faced with a choice of five answers, only one of which is correct. If you can eliminate one or more of the choices, you have fewer possibilities from which to choose. After reading the question carefully, eliminate as many obviously incorrect answers as you can. Then look at the remaining numbers and use your estimating skills.

For example: 4214 ÷ 68. If we look carefully at the numbers, 4214 is about 4200 and 68 is about 70. 4200 ÷ 70 = 60. If the possible answer "62" appeared as an option, you would select it because it is so close to your estimate. (The answer is 61.97 to two decimal points.) If you compare calculating and estimating, you will see how much faster estimating is. With practice you can become quite accurate. One way of practicing is to estimate bills whenever you shop for anything. If you see a sale, try estimating the price you would pay after the discount. If the items are not on sale, estimate the sales tax. Another way is to look at menus and estimate the cost of items with tax and tip. Estimate at every opportunity and you will become quite good at it.

The easiest way to teach estimating is to teach a set of rules that work in all cases. Unfortunately, there is only one rule: there are no hard and fast rules.

A-1

Rounding. In order to make estimating easier and more accurate, we must convert numbers to approximate numbers that can be calculated in our heads. For example, 502 is almost the same as 500. If we have to use 502 in a calculation, we could use 500 to estimate the answer. If we had to use 587 in a calculation, then 600 would produce a number we could use to estimate and still calculate in our heads. The closer the actual number is to the number used for estimating, the greater the accuracy of the answer. If we were faced with 559 as a number in a problem, either 500 or 600 might do for estimating, but neither would produce an accurate estimate. Using $5^1/_2$ hundred would give a more accurate estimate. Although there are conventions for rounding, there are none for estimating. You have to choose numbers for estimating based on experience and guess the size of the answer.

For each of the numbers, write a number that is rounded and could be used in calculation with a minimum of error. Remember that you should be able to manipulate a rounded number in your head.

NUMBER	ROUNDED NUMBER
843	
26.4	
$^{21}/_{76}$	
26%	
4651	
0.00062	
459	
0.4	
181%	
5.19	

A-2

Estimating the Answer in a Calculation. Every time you do a calculation, you should try to estimate the size of the answer. If you multiplied 45 × 1.2 and got an answer of over 500, you should immediately realize that it is impossible since 45 × 1 is 45. Practice this type of estimating with each calculation.

In the following questions, use estimating techniques to arrive at an answer. Try this several times. Calculate the correct answer and compare it with each of your estimates. Develop a personal rule for estimating that most often gives you a number closest to the correct answer.

QUESTION	ESTIMATE 1	ESTIMATE 2	ESTIMATE 3	CALCULATED ANSWER
278 + 351				
27 × 68				
987 − 108				
621 ÷ 32				
967 ÷ 1.04				
35.1 + 86.9				
32.55 − 15.89				
98 × 21				
$3^{87}/_{98} \times 5$				
19% of 792				

A-3

Estimating the Answer in a Word Problem. Each time you do a word problem, ask yourself what size the answer should be. If Tony were buying a CD for $19.95 at a 20% off sale, you should immediately know some things about the answer. First it should be smaller than $19.95 since there is a discount, and secondly $19.95 is almost $20 and a 20% discount is $\frac{1}{5}$. Thus $20 minus $\frac{1}{5}$ of $20 is $16. Any answer that is near $16 is probably correct. (The answer is $15.96.)

If you have understood the idea of estimating and have obtained reasonable answers in the above questions, go on to try some of the questions in this chapter. If not, return and practice until you get more accurate in estimating.

A-4

The Acid Test for Answers. Answers must be reasonable and within our experience. If we calculate a room temperature to be 43°C, we know that is not reasonable. If the age of the eldest child in an age problem is 206, we have made a mistake. If we estimate that we must study 73 hours a day to complete an assignment, either our estimating is very wrong or we are in big trouble with the assignment. If, after estimating an answer, the numbers seem impossible, check your estimating. Quite often, the position of the decimal is causing part or all of the problem.

I. B. Numbers

We are surrounded by a world of numbers. Most of the numbers we use are counting numbers, such as 1, 2, 3, 4, and so on. There are many other types of numbers that we use every day and don't even think about. The most common set of numbers that appear in our everyday lives are real numbers. This is the set of numbers we are going to concentrate on.

Note: Real numbers consist of rational and irrational numbers and can be represented by distinct points on a number line.

B-1

Whole Numbers. The set of whole numbers sprang from necessity. In the early history of civilization, people needed only to count. They might have wanted to know how many animals they had hunted or if they had enough rocks for seating for their family. The numbers used for counting are called *natural numbers*. In simpler times, simpler numbers were all that were needed. The first time one of our ancestors who had six sheep lost six sheep to a disaster of one kind or another, a problem arose. They could count the number of sheep they originally had using natural numbers. They could count the number of sheep they lost using their memory and natural numbers. They couldn't count the number of sheep they presently owned because they didn't have a number that represented none. Since no one wanted to just add another number to the set of natural numbers, they needed a new set. The set of natural numbers and zero was called the set of *whole numbers*.

B-2

Integers. After the passage of thousands of years, people began to realize that additional numbers were needed. If Ned had five cattle and Zed had seven cattle, then Zed had two more than Ned. Ned, on the other hand had two cattle less, but a number was needed for that. Enter the negative numbers, which allowed people to do mathematics that were impossible with whole numbers. Again, no one wanted to just add numbers to a perfectly good set, so a new set was needed. The set of whole numbers and negative numbers was called the set of *integers*.

B-3

Brackets. In mathematics, brackets are often used to indicate an operation. For example, $+(-2)$ indicates adding the negative number -2; this can be written as -2. And $-(+5)$ indicates subtracting the positive number $+5$; this can be written as -5.

Brackets can also be used to indicate multiplication. For example, $(5)(7)$ indicates multiplying 5 by 7 to produce 35. As we go through the basic operations, we shall find more examples of the use of brackets.

I. C. Rational Numbers

C-1

A *counting number* is a number obtained by counting. The counting numbers are 1, 2, 3, 4, 5, . . . A number obtained when a counting number or 0 is divided by a counting number is called a positive *rational number*. For example, 2/3, 9/7 and 5/1 (or 5) are rational numbers. Zero is also a rational number since 0 may be written as 0/6.

A *fraction* is a form in which a rational number may be written. That is, 2/3 is a rational number in fractional form. But 4 is a rational number which is not in fractional form. A fraction is a form which has a numerator and a denominator. For example, in the fraction 4/5, 4 is the numerator and 5 is the denominator. Every rational number has fractional names. For example, the rational number 5 has the fractional names 5/1, 10/2, etc.

All counting numbers and 0 are rational numbers. They and all other rational numbers may be located on the number line, as shown below.

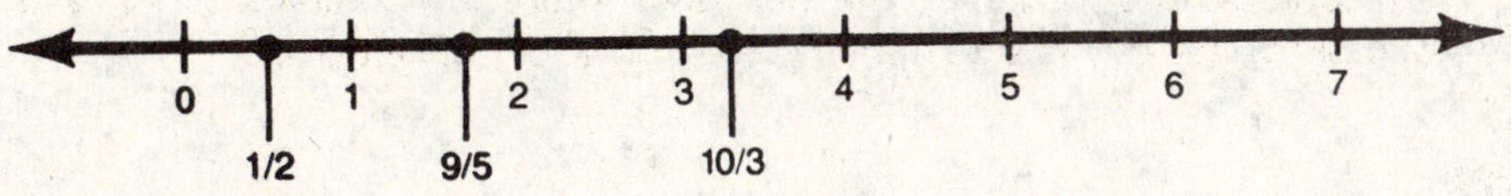

I. D. Fractions

D-1

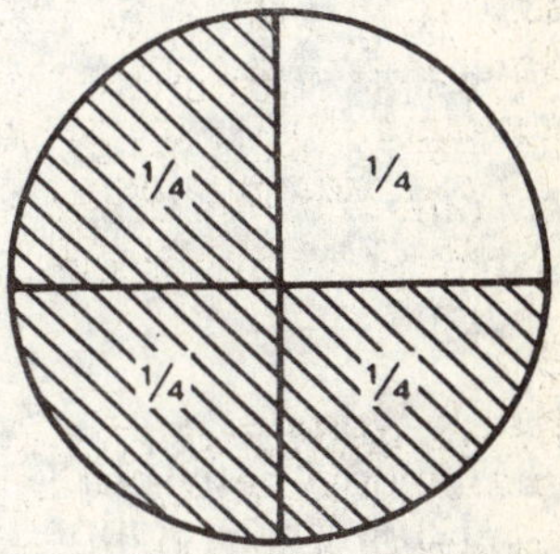

In counting, we need only whole numbers. However, when we measure, we frequently have parts, and we need fractions. For example, consider the circle at right. The circle is divided into four equal parts; each part is 1/4 of the circle. Since the shaded portion contains three of these parts, we say that the shaded portion is 3/4 of the circle. In this case, the denominator (4) tells us that the circle is divided into four equal parts. The numerator (3) tells us that we are considering 3 of these parts. In this section, you will obtain some practice in understanding the meaning of fraction.

EXAMPLE: A baseball team won 37 games and lost 15 games. What fractional part of the games played did the team win?

The required fraction is

$$\frac{\text{number of games won}}{\text{total number of games played}} = \frac{37}{37+15} = \frac{37}{52}$$

EXAMPLE: A certain school has an enrollment of 500 students. Of these students, X are girls. What fractional part of the enrollment consists of boys?

Since the total enrollment is 500 and X students are girls, the number of boys is obtained by subtracting the number X from 500. Thus, the number of boys enrolled in the school is $500 - X$.

The required fraction is

$$\frac{\text{number of boys}}{\text{total enrollment}} = \frac{500 - X}{500}$$

PRACTICE

Directions: Solve the following problems and blacken the space at the right under the number which corresponds to the one you have selected as the correct answer.

1. The Star Theatre has 650 seats. At one performance 67 seats were not occupied. What fractional part of the theatre seats were occupied?

(1) 67/650
(2) 583/650
(3) 67/588
(4) 67/717
(5) 583/717

1. 1 2 3 4 5
|| || || || ||

2. Alina parked her car at 2:45 P.M. in a one-hour parking zone. If she drove away at 3:08 P.M., during what fractional part of an hour was her car parked?

(1) 63/100
(2) 53/60
(3) 45/60
(4) 8/60
(5) 23/60

2. 1 2 3 4 5
|| || || || ||

3. Mr. Barnes spent *a* dollars for a jacket and $38 for a pair of slacks. What fractional part of the money spent was spent for the jacket?

(1) $\frac{a}{38}$
(2) $\frac{38}{a}$
(3) $\frac{38}{a+38}$
(4) $\frac{a}{a+38}$
(5) $\frac{a+38}{38}$

3. 1 2 3 4 5
|| || || || ||

4. Laurie planned to drive a distance of *x* kilometres. After driving 120 km, she stopped for gas. What fractional part of the trip had she covered when she stopped?

(1) $\frac{x}{120}$
(2) $\frac{120}{x}$
(3) $\frac{x}{x+120}$
(4) $\frac{120}{x+120}$
(5) $\frac{x+120}{x}$

4. 1 2 3 4 5
|| || || || ||

5. On a test taken by 80 students, *y* students failed. What fractional part of the students passed the test?

(1) $\frac{80-y}{80}$
(2) $\frac{y}{80}$
(3) $\frac{80}{y}$
(4) $\frac{y-80}{80}$
(5) $\frac{80}{80-y}$

5. 1 2 3 4 5
|| || || || ||

6. A dealer bought a shipment of 150 suits. Of these, 67 were blue, 39 were brown, and the rest were grey. What fractional part of the shipment was made up of grey suits?

(1) $\frac{67}{150}$
(2) $\frac{106}{150}$
(3) $\frac{39}{150}$
(4) $\frac{44}{150}$
(5) $\frac{83}{150}$

6. 1 2 3 4 5
|| || || || ||

7. A carpenter cut strips x centimetres wide from a board 60 cm wide. After she had cut 5 strips, what fractional part of the board was left? (Do not allow for waste.)

7. 1 2 3 4 5

(1) $\frac{5x}{60}$
(2) $\frac{60-5x}{60}$
(3) $\frac{5}{60-x}$
(4) $\frac{5}{60x}$
(5) $\frac{5x-60}{60}$

8. A class has 35 students. If y pupils were absent, what fractional part of the class was present?

8. 1 2 3 4 5

(1) $\frac{y}{35}$
(2) $\frac{35}{y}$
(3) $\frac{35-y}{35}$
(4) $\frac{y-35}{35}$
(5) $\frac{y}{35+y}$

9. A family spent a dollars for food, b dollars for rent, and c dollars for all other expenses. What fractional part of the money spent was spent for food?

9. 1 2 3 4 5

(1) $\frac{a+b+c}{a}$
(2) $\frac{a}{a+b+c}$
(3) $\frac{a}{a+b}$
(4) $\frac{b}{a+c}$
(5) $\frac{a+c}{a+b+c}$

10. A master painter can complete the side of a house in 8 hours. A helper could complete this task in 16 hours. How long would it take if both worked on the job?

10. 1 2 3 4 5

(1) $5\frac{1}{3}$ hours
(2) 6 hours
(3) 7 hours
(4) 12 hours
(5) 24 hours

11. A table and four chairs cost $735. If the cost of each chair was z dollars, what fractional part of the total cost was spent for chairs?

11. 1 2 3 4 5

(1) $\frac{z}{735}$
(2) $\frac{735}{z}$
(3) $\frac{4z}{735}$
(4) $\frac{735}{4z}$
(5) $\frac{735-4z}{4z}$

12. A hockey team won 8 games, lost 3 games, and tied x games. What fractional part of the games played were won?

12. 1 2 3 4 5

(1) $\frac{8}{11+x}$
(2) $\frac{8}{11}$
(3) $\frac{8+x}{11+x}$
(4) $\frac{8}{x+3}$
(5) $\frac{11}{11+x}$

ANSWERS:

1. 2 3. 4 5. 1 7. 2 9. 2 11. 3
2. 5 4. 2 6. 4 8. 3 10. 1 12. 1

I. E. Basic Operations

Note: In the following questions, do not use a calculator to find the answer. In the 2002 GED Tests, calculators will be allowed, however, doing these questions without a calculator gives you a chance to remember your basic skills. If you find yourself making many errors in basic operations, take a bit of time to practice the basic addition and multiplication skills. Then practice the basic subtraction and division skills. If necessary, make yourself sets of flash cards using recipe cards with additions such as 1 + 3 = ? on the front and 1 + 3 = 4 on the back. You can practice with these until you are confident of the basic facts.

E-1
***Introduction:* The Four Basic Operations**

A. Addition

You can think about addition as the combining of one or more numbers to produce a larger number or a sum.

1. Whole Numbers

1. Two Positive Numbers
If you are adding two positive numbers, the sum will be positive and larger than each individual number. If you find 4 tokens on Monday and 7 tokens on Tuesday, then by Wednesday you will have more tokens than on either day. You will have 4 + 7 = 11 tokens.

2. More Than Two Positive Numbers
When you add more than two positive numbers, the sum will be positive and larger than each individual number. If you find 2 tokens on Monday, 9 tokens on Tuesday, 6 tokens on Wednesday, and 3 tokens on Thursday, by Friday you will have more tokens than you had on any single day. You will have 2 + 9 + 6 + 3 = 20 tokens. An interesting concept about adding more than two positive numbers is that the order in which you add them doesn't matter. In the example above, you could add 3 + 6 + 9 + 2 to get 20, or 2 + 3 + 9 + 6 to get 20. This is useful in a test since you can add the numbers in the order that makes it simplest for you, or you can use another order to check your answer. In the above example, you could add 2 + 3 to get 5, and 9 + 6 to get 15. Then you could add 5 + 15 to get 20.

3. Two Negative Numbers
If you add two negative numbers, the sum will be negative and smaller than either number. If you are really careless and lose 4 tokens on Tuesday and 2 tokens on Thursday, by Friday you will have lost 6 tokens. You can write the number of tokens you had on Friday as (–4) + (–2) or –2 – 4 = –6.

4. More Than Two Negative Numbers
If you add more than two negative numbers, the sum will be negative and smaller than each of the numbers. For example, (–3) + (–8) + (–2) + (–7) + (–4) = –24. As with positive numbers, the order does not matter; you can add negative numbers in the order that makes it simplest for you, or you can add in another order to check your answer. In the above example, you could add (–3) + (–7) to get –10, and (–8) + (–2) to get –10. Add (–10), (–10), and (–4) to get –24.

5. Numbers with Mixed Signs
When adding numbers with both positive and negative signs, the sum will be determined by the sum of the larger of the positive or negative sums. For example, (5) + (–8) + (2) = –1 because 5 + 2 = 7 and 7 + (–8) = –1.

2. Fractions

Note: Common denominators. The bottom number of a commonly written fraction is called the denominator. When you add fractions with the same denominators, you add the numerators to arrive at the sum. For example, 3/7 + 2/7 = 5/7. Since the denominators are both 7, you add the numerators 3 + 2 = 5 and the sum of the fractions is 5/7. The numerator can exceed the denominator, in which case the fraction is called an *improper fraction* and must be simplified to a mixed number. A *mixed number* contains both an integer and a fraction. For example, 4/9 + 7/9 = 11/9, which can be written as 1 2/9. This is calculated by removing whole numbers from the improper fraction, and so 11/9 can be written as 9/9 + 2/9, or 1 2/9.

If the denominators of the fractions you are adding are different, an operation must be performed before the fractions can be added. The denominators must be manipulated so that they are the same. For example, to add 3/5 and 4/7, you have to find an equivalent denominator for both fractions. The simplest method is to multiply the denominators and use the product as the common denominator. In this case, 5 × 7 = 35 and the question becomes

(3)(7)/(5)(7) + (4)(5)/(5)(7) =	Multiply the numerator and denominator by the same number.
21/35 + 20/35 =	Perform the multiplication and add the numerators.
41/35 =	This is an improper fraction and should be simplified by removing whole numbers to get 35/35 + 6/35 = 1 + 6/35.
1 6/35	Answer.

Note: Simplification. If the numerator and denominator can both be divided by the same factor, the fraction can be simplified. For example, the fraction 9/15 can be written (3)(3)/(3)(5). If both the numerator and denominator are divided by the common factor, then the fraction becomes 3/5.

1. Two Positive Fractions

If you are adding two positive fractions, the sum will be positive and larger than each individual fraction. If you eat 1/5 of a pie on Monday and 3/5 of the pie on Tuesday, then by Wednesday you will have eaten more pie than on either day. You will have eaten 1/5 + 3/5 = 4/5 of the pie. Review the section on common denominators before attempting to answer the following questions.

PRACTICE

Choose the one best answer.

1. 2/5 + 1/5
(1) 3/10
(2) 3/5
(3) 2/25
(4) 6/7
(5) 7/6

1. 1 2 3 4 5
|| || || || ||

2. 4/9 + 2/3
(1) 1/2
(2) 8/27
(3) 6/12
(4) 10/9
(5) 5/4

2. 1 2 3 4 5
|| || || || ||

3. 7/16 + 1/4
(1) 11/16
(2) 8/20
(3) 7/64
(4) 2/5
(5) None of the above

3. 1 2 3 4 5
|| || || || ||

4. 2 1/6 + 4 1/3
(1) 6 2/9
(2) 6 1/18
(3) 62/9
(4) 6 1/2
(5) 61/2

4. 1 2 3 4 5
|| || || || ||

5. 13 8/9 + 12 5/7
(1) 18 13/16
(2) 12 5/17
(3) 156 8/7
(4) 25
(5) None of the above

5. 1 2 3 4 5
|| || || || ||

ANSWERS:

1\. **2** 2. **4** 3. **1** 4. **4** 5. **5**

2. More Than Two Positive Fractions

When you add more than two positive fractions, the sum will be positive and larger than each individual fraction. If you find 2/33 of a 33-piece puzzle on Monday, 9/33 on Tuesday, 6/33 on Wednesday, and 3/33 on Thursday, by Friday you will have more pieces of the puzzle than you had on any single day. You will have 2/33 + 9/33 + 6/33 + 3/33 = 20/33 of the puzzle. (Please note that for simplicity in the example, common denominators are used.) An interesting concept about adding more than two positive fractions is that the order in which you add them doesn't matter. In the example above, you could add 3/33 + 6/33 + 9/33 + 2/33 to get 20/33, or 2/33 + 3/33 + 9/33 + 6/33 to get 20/33. This is useful in a test since you can add the fractions in the order that makes it simplest for you, or use another order to check your answer. Review the section on common denominators before attempting to answer the questions.

PRACTICE

Indicate the sum of each of the following additions.

1. 2/3 + 1/4 + 1/6
(1) 4/13
(2) 1 4/12
(3) 1 1/12
(4) 6/6
(5) 13/4

1. 1 2 3 4 5

2. Bill ate some pie every day at dinner. On Monday he ate 1/5 of a pie, on Tuesday he ate 1/4 of a pie, and on Wednesday, he ate 1/10 of a pie. How much pie had he eaten by Thursday morning?
(1) 3/10
(2) 3/19
(3) 1/200
(4) 11/20
(5) None of the above

2. 1 2 3 4 5

3. Achmed decided to begin reading regularly. On Wednesday he read 3/20 of a book, on Friday he read 1/5 of the book, and over the weekend he read 1/4 of the book. How many pages of the book had he read by Tuesday?
(1) 5/29
(2) 29
(3) 240
(4) 3/5
(5) None of the above

3. 1 2 3 4 5

4. 1 3/7 + 4 2/3 + 11/21
(1) 6 13/21
(2) 66/31
(3) 5 16/31
(4) 5 13/21
(5) 6 13/20

4. 1 2 3 4 5

5. Sally began to run for exercise. On Monday she ran for $\frac{1}{2}$ hour, on Tuesday she ran for $\frac{3}{4}$ hour, on Wednesday she ran for 1 hour, and on Thursday she ran for $1\frac{1}{3}$ hour. How many hours had she run in total by Friday?
(1) 2 7/12
(2) 4/9
(3) 3 19/12
(4) 3 7/12
(5) 37/12

5. 1 2 3 4 5

ANSWERS:

1\. **3** 2. **4** 3. **4** 4. **1** 5. **4**

1. Two Negative Fractions
If you add two negative fractions, the sum will be negative and smaller than either fraction. If you spend 4/10 of your allowance on Monday and 3/10 on Wednesday, by Thursday you will have spent more than on either day. You could represent the fraction of your allowance you spent by Thursday as (–4/10) + (–3/10) = –7/10. (Note that for simplicity common denominators are used in the example.) Review the section on common denominators before attempting to answer the following questions.

PRACTICE

1. (–5/7) + (–2/3) — **1.** 1 2 3 4 5
(1) –7/10
(2) –1 8/21
(3) –1 3/7
(4) 1 8/21
(5) –2/3

2. (–5/9) + (–1/18) — **2.** 1 2 3 4 5
(1) –11/18
(2) –6/27
(3) –4/9
(4) 11/18
(5) 10/19

3. (–3 2/3) + (–1 5/6) — **3.** 1 2 3 4 5
(1) –4 7/9
(2) –5 1/2
(3) 5 1/2
(4) 4 7/9
(5) None of the above

4. (–2/3) + (–4 1/2) — **4.** 1 2 3 4 5
(1) 5 1/6
(2) –4 3/5
(3) 4 3/5
(4) –5 1/6
(5) 4 3/6

5. (–2 3/4) + (–3 7/8) — **5.** 1 2 3 4 5
(1) –5 5/6
(2) 1 1/2
(3) 5 5/6
(4) –1 1/2
(5) None of the above

ANSWERS:

1. **2** 2. **1** 3. **2** 4. **4** 5. **5**

1. More Than Two Negative Fractions
If you add more than two negative fractions, the sum will be negative and smaller than each of the numbers. For example, (–3/47) + (–8/47) + (–2/47) + (–7/47) + (–4/47) = –24/47. (Note that for simplicity common denominators are used in the example.) Review the section on common denominators before attempting to answer the following questions.

PRACTICE

1. (–3/7) + (–2/3) + (–2 5/21) — **1.** 1 2 3 4 5
(1) 2 10/41
(2) –3 1/3
(3) –2 10/41
(4) 3 1/3
(5) 3 10/41

2. (–3 3/5) + (–2 2/3) + (–3/4) + (–1 7/15) — **2.** 1 2 3 4 5
(1) 8 29/60
(2) –6 23/27
(3) –8 29/60
(4) 6 23/27
(5) 14

3. Mario was serving cake for dessert. Although he really liked dessert, he was very considerate. He gave his mother 1/10 of the cake, his father 1/5 of the cake, his brother 1/10 of the cake, and his sister 1/4 of the cake. How much cake had he served before he served himself?

(1) –13/20
(2) –4/20
(3) –7/10
(4) 7/20
(5) 7/13

3. 1 2 3 4 5
|| || || || ||

4. Simcha's father was interested in the stock market. He was following the price of a share of Consolidated Widgets. At 10:00 A.M., the stock fell 1/4 point, and by 11:00 A.M. it had fallen a further 1/3 point. By 1:00 P.M. it had fallen a further 2/3 point, and it finished the day falling a further 5/6 point. How many points had it lost by dinner time?

(1) 9/16
(2) 1 1/2
(3) 2/3
(4) 11/2
(5) None of the above

4. 1 2 3 4 5
|| || || || ||

5. (–2/5) + (–3/10) + (–1/2)

(1) –6/17
(2) 6/5
(3) –5/6
(4) –7/12
(5) None of the above

5. 1 2 3 4 5
|| || || || ||

ANSWERS:

1. **2** 2. **3** 3. **1** 4. **5** 5. **5**

1. Fractions with Mixed Signs
If you are adding fractions with both positive and negative signs, the sign will be determined by the sign of the larger positive or negative sum. For example, (5/13) + (–8/13) + (2/13) = –1/13 because adding the numerators 5 + 2 = 7 and 7 + (–8) = –1.

PRACTICE

1. (2/5) + (–1/4) + (–3/10)

(1) 3/10
(2) 6/19
(3) –6/19
(4) –3/20
(5) 1/3

1. 1 2 3 4 5
|| || || || ||

2. (–5 1/6) + (3 2/3) + (–1/4)

(1) –2 0/7
(2) –1 3/4
(3) –3 5/6
(4) 1 2/3
(5) None of the above

2. 1 2 3 4 5
|| || || || ||

3. (3 4/5) + (2 1/3) + (–3 7/10)

(1) 8 2/3
(2) –2/10
(3) 2 13/30
(4) 5 5/8
(5) 2 10/13

3. 1 2 3 4 5
|| || || || ||

4. (3/13) + (–1/2) + (–1/3) + (1)

(1) 31/78
(2) –46/78
(3) 5/18
(4) 39/78
(5) 78/46

4. 1 2 3 4 5
|| || || || ||

5. (3/4) + –(2 2/3) + (1 11/12)
(1) –1
(2) 0
(3) 12
(4) 7
(5) 5

5. 1 2 3 4 5

ANSWERS:

1. 4 **2. 4** **3. 3** **4. 1** **5. 2**

1. Decimal Fractions

Note: Since the decimal fractions most of us are familiar with involve currency, the examples below use currency for the purpose of illustration. There are many other uses of decimal fractions, and these will be explored later in examples and practice questions.

1. Two Positive Decimal Fractions
If you add two positive decimal fractions, the sum will be positive and larger than each individual decimal fraction. If you spend $0.75 on Monday and $0.15 on Tuesday, then by Wednesday you will have spent more money than on either day. You will have spent $0.75 + $0.15 = $0.90.

PRACTICE

1. 0.33 + 3.78
(1) 3.11
(2) 4.01
(3) 4.11
(4) 3.78
(5) None of the above

1. 1 2 3 4 5

2. 3.12 + 4.006
(1) 7.126
(2) 7.18
(3) 7.018
(4) 7.72
(5) 7.27

2. 1 2 3 4 5

3. 0.005 + 0.037
(1) 0.537
(2) 0.420
(3) 0.087
(4) 0.042
(5) None of the above

3. 1 2 3 4 5

4. 1.04 + 4.25
(1) 5.65
(2) 5.09
(3) 5.029
(4) 5.53
(5) None of the above

4. 1 2 3 4 5

5. 0.007 + 0.063
(1) 0.700
(2) 0.070
(3) 0.763
(4) 0.728
(5) None of the above

5. 1 2 3 4 5

ANSWERS:

1. 3 **2. 1** **3. 4** **4. 5** **5. 2**

1. More Than Two Positive Decimal Fractions
When you add more than two positive decimal fractions, the sum is positive and larger than each individual decimal fraction. If you earn $12.45 on Monday, $10.29 on Tuesday, $15.22 on Wednesday, and $8.61 on Thursday, by Friday you will have earned more than you had on any single day. You will have earned $12.45 + $10.29 + $15.22 + $8.61 = $46.57. An interest-

ing concept about adding more than two positive decimal fractions is that the order in which you add them doesn't matter. In the example above, you could have added any two decimal fractions together and then added the sums together to get the final sum. This is useful in a test since you can add the decimal fractions in the order that makes it simplest for you, or you can use another order to check your answer.

PRACTICE

1. 8.937 + 0.050 + 2.006 + 0.028

(1) 10.021
(2) 11.021
(3) 11.827
(4) 10.987
(5) None of the above

1. 1 2 3 4 5

2. 0.003 + 1.200 + 4.058

(1) 5.253
(2) 5.251
(3) 5.428
(4) 5.261
(5) None of the above

2. 1 2 3 4 5

3. 1.29 + 1.333 + 0.046

(1) 2.669
(2) 1.397
(3) 2.346
(4) 3.618
(5) None of the above

3. 1 2 3 4 5

4. 9.083 + 14 + 2.004

(1) 11.087
(2) 25.087
(3) 14.586
(4) 26.364
(5) None of the above

4. 1 2 3 4 5

5. 12.00 + 2.395 + 1.508

(1) 16.003
(2) 15.898
(3) 15.903
(4) 16.758
(5) None of the above

5. 1 2 3 4 5

ANSWERS:

1. **2** 2. **4** 3. **1** 4. **2** 5. **3**

1. Two Negative Decimal Fractions
If you add two negative decimal fractions, the sum will be negative and smaller than either of the decimal fractions. For example, (–0.37) + (–0.29) = –0.66.

PRACTICE

1. (–4.340) + (–2.003)

(1) –6.640
(2) –6.370
(3) –6.353
(4) –6.343
(5) None of the above

1. 1 2 3 4 5

2. (–0.0003) + (–0.0009)

(1) –0.0039
(2) –0.0012
(3) –0.0093
(4) 0.0903
(5) 0.930

2. 1 2 3 4 5

3. (–2) + (–3.47)

(1) –5.47
(2) –3.47
(3) –3.27
(4) –5.36
(5) –3.65

3. 1 2 3 4 5

4. (–44.7) + (–0.0087)
(1) –44.0094
(2) –44.0157
(3) –44.7087
(4) –44.7870
(5) –45.846

4. 1 2 3 4 5

5. (–1.0009) + (–2.085)
(1) –3.0859
(2) –3.0958
(3) –3.9850
(4) –3.7281
(5) –37.281

5. 1 2 3 4 5

ANSWERS:

1. 4 **2. 2** **3. 1** **4. 3** **5. 1**

1. More Than Two Negative Decimal Fractions

If you add more than two negative decimal fractions, the sum will be negative and smaller than each of the fractions. For example, (–0.3) + (–0.8) + (–0.2) + (–0.7) + (–0.4) = –2.4. As with positive numbers the order does not matter; you can add negative numbers in the order that makes it simplest for you, or you can add in another order to check your answer. In the above example, you could add (–0.3) + (–0.7) to get –1.0, and (–0.8) + (–0.2) to get –1.0. Add (–1.0), (–1.0), and (–0.4) to get –2.4.

PRACTICE

1. (–7.0) + (–3.034) + (–2.0008)
(1) –12.3480
(2) –12.0348
(3) –12.0420
(4) –12.5076
(5) None of the above

1. 1 2 3 4 5

2. (–1.0073) + (–0.0024) + (–2.0004)
(1) –3.1001
(2) –3.0110
(3) –3.0011
(4) –3.0101
(5) None of the above

2. 1 2 3 4 5

3. (–7.6) + (–2.3) + (–1.8) + (–2.01)
(1) –1.371
(2) –137.1
(3) –13.71
(4) –1371
(5) None of the above

3. 1 2 3 4 5

4. (–34.76) + (–10.01) + (–26) + (–0.09)
(1) –70.086
(2) –70.68
(3) –708.6
(4) –7.086
(5) None of the above

4. 1 2 3 4 5

5. (–3.100) + (–3.010) + (–3.001)
(1) –9.111
(2) –91.11
(3) –9.011
(4) –9.101
(5) –9.110

5. 1 2 3 4 5

ANSWERS:

1. 2 **2. 4** **3. 3** **4. 5** **5. 1**

1. Decimal Fractions with Mixed Signs

If you add decimal fractions with both positive and negative signs, the sign will be determined by the sign of the larger of the positive or negative sum. For example, (0.5) + (–0.8) + (0.2) = –0.1 because 0.5 + 0.2 = 0.7 and 0.7 + (–0.8) = –0.1.

PRACTICE

1. (3.47) + (–3.74) + (3.03) + (–3.029)
(1) –0.296
(2) –13.269
(3) –0.269
(4) –12.254
(5) None of the above

1. 1 2 3 4 5

2. (–3.002) + (2.983) + (1.7) + (–4.2)
(1) –2.519
(2) 2.519
(3) –2.591
(4) 2.591
(5) None of the above

2. 1 2 3 4 5

3. Brunella was trying to balance her cheque book. She started with a balance of $29.05 and made deposits of $5.60, $19.00, and $5.39. She withdrew $2.77 and $14.00. What was her new balance?
(1) $7.83
(2) $4.25
(3) $41.24
(4) $42.47
(5) None of the above

3. 1 2 3 4 5

4. (3.00009) + (–2.9) + (–1.0003) + (0.00086)
(1) 8.99351
(2) 0.08376
(3) –0.00057
(4) –1.00054
(5) None of the above

4. 1 2 3 4 5

5. (–6.00009) + (4.00002) + (0.00004) + (2.00001)
(1) 0.00002
(2) –0.00002
(3) 0.0002
(4) –0.0002
(5) –2

5. 1 2 3 4 5

ANSWERS:

1. **3** 2. **1** 3. **5** 4. **5** 5. **2**

1. Subtraction
   1. Whole Numbers
      1. Two Positive Numbers

When you subtract two positive numbers, the sign following the subtraction sign (–) must be changed. Then the appropriate operation can be performed. For example, (+5) – (+1) = 5 – 1 = 4. (The + sign in front of the 1 was changed to –.)

PRACTICE

1. 58 – 29
(1) 58
(2) 29
(3) 39
(4) 19
(5) 47

1. 1 2 3 4 5

2. 153 – 48
(1) 115
(2) 151
(3) 15
(4) 105
(5) 5

2. 1 2 3 4 5

3. 2894 – 1634
(1) 1260
(2) 1620
(3) 1026
(4) 1060
(5) 1002

3. 1 2 3 4 5

4. Cho's room is 65 square metres in area. He wants to put a rug of 37 square metres on the floor. What area of floor in square metres will be left uncovered?

(1) 82
(2) 28
(3) 22
(4) 102
(5) 12

4. 1 2 3 4 5

5. Alex has to drain 16 cubic metres out of a fish tank holding 30 cubic metres. How many cubic metres of water will be left in the tank?

(1) 46
(2) 41
(3) 14
(4) 13
(5) 28

5. 1 2 3 4 5

ANSWERS:

1. 2 **2. 4** **3. 1** **4. 2** **5. 3**

1. Two Negative Numbers
When you subtract two negative numbers, the sign following the subtraction sign (–) must be changed. Then the appropriate operation can be performed. For example, (–8) – (–5) = –8 + 5 = –3. (The – sign in front of the 5 was changed to a + sign.)

PRACTICE

1. (–45) – (–23)

(1) –22
(2) –68
(3) –86
(4) –28
(5) None of the above

1. 1 2 3 4 5

2. (–294) – (–29)

(1) –265
(2) –256
(3) –323
(4) –332
(5) None of the above

2. 1 2 3 4 5

3. (–27) – (–32)

(1) –5
(2) 5
(3) –59
(4) 27
(5) None of the above

3. 1 2 3 4 5

4. (–1286) – (–1231)

(1) 50
(2) 55
(3) –55
(4) –60
(5) None of the above

4. 1 2 3 4 5

5. (–3719) – (–2928)

(1) –719
(2) 719
(3) 791
(4) –791
(5) None of the above

5. 1 2 3 4 5

ANSWERS:

1. 1 **2. 1** **3. 2** **4. 3** **5. 4**

1. Numbers with Mixed Signs
When you subtract two numbers with mixed signs, the sign following the subtraction sign (–) must be changed. Then the appropriate operation can be performed. For example, (–9) – (+6) = –9 – 6 = –15.

PRACTICE

1. (–459) – (294)
(1) –735
(2) –165
(3) –753
(4) –743
(5) –615

2. (777) – (–382)
(1) 1159
(2) 395
(3) 1519
(4) 1681
(5) 1861

3. (–12) – (2739)
(1) 2277
(2) 7227
(3) 2772
(4) 2727
(5) 2222

4. (3928) – (–26)
(1) 3902
(2) 3209
(3) 3290
(4) 3029
(5) None of the above

5. (–7) – (–3720)
(1) 3727
(2) 3713
(3) 3731
(4) 3772
(5) None of the above

ANSWERS:

1. **3** 2. **1** 3. **4** 4. **5** 5. **2**

1. Fractions

Note: Review the sections on fractions under addition. The rules for common denominators, simplification, and mixed numbers apply to subtraction as well.

1. Two Positive Fractions
When you subtract two positive fractions, the sign following the subtraction sign (–) must be changed. Then the appropriate operation can be performed. For example, (+5/7) – (+1/7) = 5/7–1/7 = 4/7. (The + sign in front of the 1/7 was changed to a – sign.)

PRACTICE

1. 3/4 – 1/2
(1) 2/2
(2) 4/6
(3) 1/5
(4) 1/4
(5) None of the above

2. 1 5/6 – 7/8
(1) 1 23/24
(2) 22/24
(3) 11/12
(4) 1 2/3
(5) None of the above

3. 3 4/9 – 1 2/3

(1) 1 7/9
(2) 2 1/3
(3) 2 7/9
(4) 1 5/9
(5) None of the above

3. 1 2 3 4 5

4. 2 3/7 – 3 2/3

(1) 1 1/4
(2) –1 5/21
(3) –1 1/4
(4) 1 5/21
(5) None of the above

4. 1 2 3 4 5

5. 23 8/11 – 22 9/11

(1) 1 5/6
(2) 9/11
(3) 10/11
(4) 1 1/11
(5) None of the above

5. 1 2 3 4 5

ANSWERS:

1. **4** 2. **5** 3. **1** 4. **2** 5. **3**

1. Two Negative Franctions
When you subtract two negative fractions, the sign following the subtraction sign (–) must be changed. Then the appropriate operation can be performed. For example, (–8/9) – (–5/9) = –8/9 + 5/9 = –3/9, which can be simplified to –1/3. (The – sign in front of the 5/9 was changed to a + sign.

PRACTICE

1. (–2 4/5) – (–1 2/3)

(1) –1
(2) –1 2/15
(3) 1 2/15
(4) 1 3/7
(5) None of the above

1. 1 2 3 4 5

2. (–9/13) – (–2/3)

(1) 1/39
(2) 3/39
(3) –3/39
(4) –1/39
(5) None of the above

2. 1 2 3 4 5

3. (–5/16) – (–3/4)

(1) 7/16
(2) 1/2
(3) 3/8
(4) –1/6
(5) –3/8

3. 1 2 3 4 5

4. (–3 7/12) – (–3 3/4)

(1) –1/3
(2) 1/6
(3) 6 5/8
(4) 1/2
(5) 1/3

4. 1 2 3 4 5

5. (–234 6/7) – (–234 1/3)

(1) 11/21
(2) 5/4
(3) –11/21
(4) –5/4
(5) 5/21

5. 1 2 3 4 5

ANSWERS:

1. **2** 2. **4** 3. **1** 4. **2** 5. **3**

1. Fractions with Mixed Signs

When you subtract two fractions with mixed signs, the sign following the subtraction sign (–) must be changed. Then the appropriate operation can be performed. For example, (–9/17) – (+6/17) = –9/17 – 6/17 = –15/17.

PRACTICE

1. (5/7) – (–7/5)

(1) –1
(2) –24/35
(3) 2 5/7
(4) 2 4/35
(5) None of the above

1. 1 2 3 4 5

2. (1 4/9) – (–2/3)

(1) 2 1/3
(2) 2 1/9
(3) –2 1/9
(4) –2 1/3
(5) None of the above

2. 1 2 3 4 5

3. (–7 8/11) – (–3 3/4)

(1) –3 43/44
(2) 4 5/7
(3) –4 5/7
(4) 3 43/44
(5) None of the above

3. 1 2 3 4 5

4. (5 8/9) – (–2 5/6)

(1) –8 13/18
(2) 7 13/15
(3) 8 13/18
(4) –7 13/15
(5) None of the above

4. 1 2 3 4 5

5. (–27/35) – (7 4/7)

(1) –8 12/35
(2) 1 24/35
(3) –1 24/35
(4) 8 12/35
(5) None of the above

5. 1 2 3 4 5

ANSWERS:

1. **4** 2. **2** 3. **1** 4. **3** 5. **1**

1. Decimal Fractions

1. Two Positive Decimal Fractions

When you subtract two positive decimal fractions, the sign following the subtraction sign (–) must be changed. Then the appropriate operation can be performed. For example, (+0.57) – (+0.17) = 0.57 – 0.17 = 0.40. (The + sign in front of the 0.17 was changed to a – sign.)

PRACTICE

1. (0.763) – (7.10)

(1) –7.530
(2) –6.337
(3) –7.673
(4) –6.373
(5) 6.337

1. 1 2 3 4 5

2. (2.38) – (2.09)

(1) 2.90
(2) 2.09
(3) 0.92
(4) 0.29
(5) 20.9

2. 1 2 3 4 5

3. (3.781) – (4.030)
(1) –.0249
(2) –2.490
(3) –0.249
(4) 0.294
(5) None of the above

3. 1 2 3 4 5

4. (89.3) – (104.9)
(1) 15.6
(2) –1.56
(3) –93.4
(4) –51.6
(5) None of the above

4. 1 2 3 4 5

5. (99.1) – (91.1)
(1) 8
(2) 9
(3) 7
(4) 3
(5) 6

5. 1 2 3 4 5

ANSWERS:

1. 2 2. 4 3. 3 4. 5 5. 1

1. Two Negative Decimal Fractions
When you subtract two negative decimal fractions, the sign following the subtraction sign (–) must be changed. Then the appropriate operation can be performed. For example, (–0.89) – (–0.59) = –0.89 + 0.59 = –0.30. (The – sign in front of the 0.59 was changed to a + sign.)

PRACTICE

1. (–3.760) – (–1.002)
(1) –2.578
(2) –2.758
(3) –2.785
(4) –2.587
(5) None of the above

1. 1 2 3 4 5

2. (–27.48) – (–36.1)
(1) –7.48
(2) –8.62
(3) 9.51
(4) 8.62
(5) None of the above

2. 1 2 3 4 5

3. (–.0010) – (–.0001)
(1) –0.0900
(2) –0.0009
(3) –0.0090
(4) –0.9000
(5) None of the above

3. 1 2 3 4 5

4. (–66.667) – (–7.776)
(1) 74.443
(2) 7.443
(3) –58.891
(4) 58.891
(5) None of the above

4. 1 2 3 4 5

5. (–3.1416) – (–2.09)
(1) –1.0516
(2) –5.2346
(3) 1.0516
(4) 5.2316
(5) None of the above

5. 1 2 3 4 5

ANSWERS:

1. 2 2. 4 3. 2 4. 3 5. 1

1. Two Decimal Fractions with Mixed Signs
When you subtract two decimal fractions with mixed signs, the sign following the subtraction sign (–) must be changed. Then the appropriate operation can be performed. For example, (–0.97) – (+0.61) = –0.97 – 0.61 = –0.36.

PRACTICE

1. (+4.702) – (–0.4702)
(1) 0.5791
(2) 5.1722
(3) 6.7349
(4) 4.7634
(5) None of the above

1. 1 2 3 4 5

2. (–387.8) – (+2.003)
(1) –398.803
(2) –385.803
(3) –385.830
(4) –389.803
(5) –368.482

2. 1 2 3 4 5

3. (+34.0034) – (–43.0034)
(1) 77.0086
(2) 77.0068
(3) 78.0068
(4) 78.0086
(5) 79.0568

3. 1 2 3 4 5

4. (+34.56) – (–7.891)
(1) 26.669
(2) 26.696
(3) 27.669
(4) 27.966
(5) None of the above

4. 1 2 3 4 5

5. (–4.00001) – (+2.09048)
(1) –6.09841
(2) –7.09481
(3) –6.09049
(4) –5.09841
(5) –8.0483

5. 1 2 3 4 5

ANSWERS:

1. **2** 2. **4** 3. **1** 4. **5** 5. **3**

1. Multiplication

Note: Multiplication by 0 always produces a product of 0, and 0 is neither positive or negative.

1. Whole Numbers

1. Two Positive Whole Numbers
When you multiply two positive whole numbers, the product is always positive and larger than either of the factors. For example, +5 × +8 = +40. (Note that the + sign is sometimes not written in front of a number when it can be assumed to be positive. The equation could have been written 5 × 8 = 40.)

PRACTICE

1. 21 × 3
(1) 63
(2) 36
(3) 46
(4) 53
(5) None of the above

1. 1 2 3 4 5

2. 571 × 39
(1) 22 840
(2) 22 296
(3) 22 926
(4) 22 269
(5) None of the above

2. 1 2 3 4 5

3. 29 × 861
(1) 24 869
(2) 24 996
(3) 24 969
(4) 24 956
(5) None of the above

3. 1 2 3 4 5

4. 11 × 17
(1) 177
(2) 187
(3) 207
(4) 167
(5) None of the above

4. 1 2 3 4 5

5. 7 × 43
(1) 101
(2) 281
(3) 251
(4) 301
(5) None of the above

5. 1 2 3 4 5

ANSWERS:

1. 1 **2. 4** **3. 3** **4. 2** **5. 4**

1. More Than Two Positive Whole Numbers
When you multiply more than two positive whole numbers, the product is always positive and larger than each of the factors. For example 9 × 5 × 2 = 90.

PRACTICE

1. 7 × 9 × 4
(1) 225
(2) 252
(3) 452
(4) 212
(5) None of the above

1. 1 2 3 4 5

2. 12 × 3 × 10
(1) 630
(2) 306
(3) 603
(4) 360
(5) None of the above

2. 1 2 3 4 5

3. 43 × 5 × 20
(1) 4030
(2) 4003
(3) 4300
(4) 4000
(5) None of the above

3. 1 2 3 4 5

4. 71 × 22 × 8
(1) 12 320
(2) 12 230
(3) 12 023
(4) 12 032
(5) None of the above

4. 1 2 3 4 5

5. 3 × 45 × 39
(1) 5 265
(2) 5 625
(3) 5 562
(4) 5 652
(5) None of the above

5. 1 2 3 4 5

ANSWERS:

1. 2 **2. 4** **3. 3** **4. 5** **5. 1**

1. Two Negative Whole Numbers
When you multiply two negative whole numbers, the product is always positive and larger than either of the factors. For example $-7 \times -3 = +21$.

PRACTICE

1. -25×-5

(1) 135
(2) 152
(3) 155
(4) 125
(5) -152

1. 1 2 3 4 5

2. -123×-4

(1) 482
(2) 422
(3) 462
(4) 492
(5) 942

2. 1 2 3 4 5

3. -21×-77

(1) 1617
(2) 1716
(3) 1761
(4) 1671
(5) 1551

3. 1 2 3 4 5

4. -121×-44

(1) 5234
(2) 5432
(3) 5324
(4) 5422
(5) 5438

4. 1 2 3 4 5

5. $-151 \times - 25$

(1) 3775
(2) 3770
(3) 2645
(4) 3577
(5) 6458

5. 1 2 3 4 5

ANSWERS:

1. **4** 2. **4** 3. **1** 4. **3** 5. **1**

1. More Than Two Negative Whole Numbers
When you multiply more than two negative whole numbers, the product is negative if there is an odd number of factors, and positive if there is an even number of factors. For example, $-3 \times -2 \times -5 = -30$ since there are three factors and 3 is an odd number. $-3 \times -2 \times -5 \times -4 = +120$ since there are four factors and 4 is an even number.

PRACTICE

1. $-5 \times -3 \times - 2 \times -40$

(1) -1200
(2) $+1200$
(3) $+120$
(4) -120
(5) None of the above

1. 1 2 3 4 5

2. $-21 \times -7 \times -11$

(1) $+1617$
(2) -1716
(3) $+1716$
(4) -1617
(5) None of the above

2. 1 2 3 4 5

3. $-12 \times -4 \times -5 \times -2$

(1) $+480$
(2) -440
(3) $+440$
(4) -480
(5) None of the above

3. 1 2 3 4 5

4. −66 × −33 × −1
(1) −2718
(2) −2178
(3) −2817
(4) −2871
(5) None of the above

4. 1 2 3 4 5

5. −3 × −4 × 0 × −6
(1) −12
(2) −72
(3) 0
(4) −27
(5) None of the above

5. 1 2 3 4 5

ANSWERS:

1. 2 2. 4 3. 1 4. 2 5. 3

1. Whole Numbers with Mixed Signs
When you multiply a series of whole numbers, the product is negative if the number of negative factors is odd, and positive if the number of negative factors is even. For example, −3 × +5 × −2 × −5 = −150 since there are three negative factors (−3, −2, and −5) and 3 is an odd number. And −3 × +5 × −2 = +30 since there are two negative factors (−3 and −5) and 2 is an even number.

PRACTICE

1. −4 × −8 × −2
(1) −34
(2) −66
(3) −46
(4) −64
(5) 66

1. 1 2 3 4 5

2. −11 × −3 × −4 × −1
(1) 123
(2) 132
(3) 192
(4) 129
(5) 321

2. 1 2 3 4 5

3. 23 × 41 × 0 × −3
(1) 0
(2) 2829
(3) −2829
(4) −2289
(5) −2222

3. 1 2 3 4 5

4. 25 × −4 × −2 × −6
(1) −37
(2) −1020
(3) −1200
(4) −1250
(5) −6428

4. 1 2 3 4 5

5. −12 × 4 × −3 × 2
(1) 288
(2) −288
(3) 300
(4) −300
(5) 642

5. 1 2 3 4 5

ANSWERS:

1. 4 2. 2 3. 1 4. 3 5. 1

1. Fractions

Note: When multiplying fractions, look for common factors in the numerators and denominators. If there is a common denominator in the numerators and denominators, dividing both by that factor will simplify the question. For example, 3/4 × 8/9 × 1/2 = (3 × 8 × 1)/(4 × 9 × 2) = [3 × (**2** × **2** × 2) × 1]/[(**2** × **2**) × (3 × 3) × **2**]. In this example there are two factors of 2 and one factor of 3 common to both numerator and denominator. Dividing numerator and denominator by (2 × 2 × 2 × 3) produces 1/3 as the product. If there are negative fractions, use the negative sign with a factor in either the numerator or the denominator. This will allow you to do some of the more difficult questions much faster than multiplying everything and simplifying the product.

1. Two Positive Fractions

When you multiply two positive fractions, the product is always positive and larger than either of the factors. To arrive at the product, multiply the numerator by the numerator, and the denominator by the denominator. For example, +5/11 × +8/9 = +40/99. (Note that the + sign is sometimes not written in front of a number that can be assumed to be positive. The equation could have been written 5/11 × 8/9 = 40/99.)

PRACTICE

1. (+2/3) × (+3/4)
(1) 5/7
(2) 6/11
(3) 1/2
(4) +3/4
(5) None of the above

1. 1 2 3 4 5 || || || || ||

2. 7/9 × 3/4
(1) 7/12
(2) 21/9
(3) 12/7
(4) 10/13
(5) None of the above

2. 1 2 3 4 5 || || || || ||

3. 11/12 × 2/3
(1) 13/15
(2) 1 9/12
(3) 2
(4) 11/18
(5) None of the above

3. 1 2 3 4 5 || || || || ||

4. 1 1/2 × 3 1/3
(1) 4 1/2
(2) 3 1/3
(3) 0
(4) 5/6
(5) None of the above

4. 1 2 3 4 5 || || || || ||

5. 4 1/3 × 3 1/4
(1) 13 11/12
(2) 14 1/12
(3) 14 1/6
(4) 15
(5) None of the above

5. 1 2 3 4 5 || || || || ||

ANSWERS:

1. **3** 2. **1** 3. **4** 4. **5** 5. **2**

1. More Than Two Positive Fractions

When you multiply more than two fractions, the product is always positive and larger than each of the factors. To arrive at the product, multiply the numerator by the numerator, and the denominator by the denominator. For example, 9/11 × 5/6 × 2/3 = 90/198, which can be simplified to 90/198 = 2 × 3 × 3 × 5/2 × 3 × 3 × 11 or 15/33. (Divide the numerator and denominator by 2 × 3 or by 6.)

PRACTICE

1. 2/3 × 4/5 × 1/3 — **1.** 1 2 3 4 5

(1) 7/11
(2) 8/45
(3) 9/45
(4) 45/8
(5) None of the above

2. 4/3 × 3/4 × 7/8 × 8/7 — **2.** 1 2 3 4 5

(1) 1
(2) 3
(3) 24/28
(4) 21/32
(5) None of the above

3. 7/9 × 1/2 × 3/7 — **3.** 1 2 3 4 5

(1) 1/9
(2) 2/7
(3) 7/63
(4) 1/6
(5) None of the above

4. 5/6 × 6/7 × 2/5 — **4.** 1 2 3 4 5

(1) 2/7
(2) 13/18
(3) 1/3
(4) 2/5
(5) None of the above

5. 9/11 × 3/4 × 11/18 × 2/3 — **5.** 1 2 3 4 5

(1) 1/2
(2) 2/3
(3) 1/4
(4) 3/4
(5) None of the above

ANSWERS:

1. **2** 2. **1** 3. **4** 4. **1** 5. **3**

1. Two Negative Fractions

When you multiply two negative fractions, the product is always positive and larger than either of the factors. To arrive at the product, multiply the numerator by the numerator, and the denominator by the denominator. For example, –7/8 × –3/5 = +21/40.

PRACTICE

1. –2/3 × –3/4 — **1.** 1 2 3 4 5

(1) –1/2
(2) 5/7
(3) 1/2
(4) –5/7
(5) 2/7

2. –1 2/3 × –5/7 — **2.** 1 2 3 4 5

(1) –14/21
(2) –1 1/5
(3) 1 1/5
(4) 1 4/21
(5) –1 5/21

3. –5/11 × –11/17 — **3.** 1 2 3 4 5

(1) 16/28
(2) 6/17
(3) 5/17
(4) 54/187
(5) 6/18

4. –8/11 × –3/5 — **4.** 1 2 3 4 5

(1) 24/55
(2) 11/16
(3) 33/40
(4) 5/8
(5) –5/8

5. −7/11 × −13/2

(1) −4 3/22
(2) 4 3/22
(3) 13/20
(4) 4 5/22
(5) 1 3/23

5. 1 2 3 4 5

ANSWERS:

1. 3 2. 4 3. 3 4. 1 5. 2

1. More Than Two Negative Fractions

When you multiply more than two negative fractions, the product is negative if there is an odd number of factors, and positive if there is an even number of factors. To arrive at the product, multiply the numerator by the numerator, and the denominator by the denominator. For example, −3/4 × −2/3 × −5/6 = −30/72 since there are three factors and 3 is an odd number. Then −30/72 can be simplified as −(2 × 3 × 5)/(2 × 2 × 2 × 3 × 3) = −5/12. (Divide the numerator and denominator by 2 × 3 or by 6.)

PRACTICE

1. −2/3 × −3/4 × −4/5

(1) 2/5
(2) 3/4
(3) −2/5
(4) −3/4
(5) None of the above

1. 1 2 3 4 5

2. −7/11 × −3/5 × −11/13 × −13/14

(1) −3/10
(2) 3001/10010
(3) −3001/10010
(4) 3/10
(5) None of the above

2. 1 2 3 4 5

3. −9/10 × −5/7 × −2/3

(1) −2/5
(2) −9/20
(3) −3/7
(4) −1/3
(5) None of the above

3. 1 2 3 4 5

4. −5/7 × −7/11 × −11/21 × −3/4

(1) 5/28
(2) 10/57
(3) 5/27
(4) 1 150/6468
(5) None of the above

4. 1 2 3 4 5

5. −2 1/3 × −4 1/5 × −1 5/9

(1) −15 1/4
(2) −15 11/45
(3) −15 2/9
(4) −8 5/135
(5) None of the above

5. 1 2 3 4 5

ANSWERS:

1. 3 2. 4 3. 3 4. 1 5. 2

1. Fractions with Mixed Signs

When you multiply a series of fractions, the product is negative if the number of negative factors is odd, and positive if the number of negative factors is even. For example, −3/5 × +5/3 × −2/3 × 5/2 = 150/90 since there are two negative factors (−3/5, −2/3) and 2 is an even number. 150/90 is an improper fraction which can be written as 90/90 + 60/90 or as 1 60/90 which can be simplified as 1 (2 × 2 × 3 × 5)/(2 × 3 × 3 × 5) = 1 2/3. (Divide the numerator and denominator by 2 × 3 × 5 or 30.)

PRACTICE

1. −1/2 × 3/4 × −5/7

(1) 13/56
(2) 15/56
(3) −13/56
(4) −15/56
(5) None of the above

1. 1 2 3 4 5

2. 5/7 × 3/4 × −7/10

(1) −3/4
(2) −1/2
(3) −5/8
(4) −3/8
(5) None of the above

2. 1 2 3 4 5

3. 5/13 × −26/35 × −14/17

(1) 82/119
(2) 28/191
(3) 28/119
(4) 82/191
(5) None of the above

3. 1 2 3 4 5

4. −2 3/4 × −5/6 × −8/11

(1) 1 2/3
(2) −1 3/4
(3) 2 2/3
(4) −1 4/11
(5) None of the above

4. 1 2 3 4 5

5. 7/17 × −3 2/5 × 4/7

(1) −4/5
(2) 4/6
(3) −3/5
(4) 2/3
(5) None of the above

5. 1 2 3 4 5

ANSWERS:

1. **2** 2. **4** 3. **3** 4. **5** 5. **1**

1. Decimal Fractions

Note: The number of decimal places in the product should be the total of the number of decimal places in the factors. For example, 0.3 × 0.5 = 0.15. Since 0.3 has one decimal place and 0.5 has one decimal place, the product must have two decimal places, thus 0.15.

1. Two Positive Decimal Fractions

When you multiply two positive decimal fractions, the product is always positive and larger than either of the factors. For example, +0.5 × +0.8 = +0.40. (Note that the + sign is sometimes not written in front of a number that can be assumed to be positive. The equation could have been written 0.5 × 0.8 = 0.40.)

PRACTICE

1. 0.38 × 1.02

(1) 0.3876
(2) 0.3867
(3) 0.3687
(4) 0.3768
(5) 3.7642

1. 1 2 3 4 5

2. 2.009 × 4.2

(1) 8.3478
(2) 8.8743
(3) 8.0378
(4) 8.4378
(5) 8.4982

2. 1 2 3 4 5

3. 1.9 × 3.06

(1) 3.814
(2) 4.814
(3) 5.814
(4) 6.814
(5) 7.814

3. 1 2 3 4 5

4. 0.003×0.003
(1) 0.0009
(2) 0.000009
(3) 0.00009
(4) 0.9
(5) 9.0

4. 1 2 3 4 5

5. 9.12×0.001
(1) 0.00812
(2) 0.0912
(3) 0.912
(4) 0.00912
(5) 0.921

5. 1 2 3 4 5

ANSWERS:

1. **1** 2. **4** 3. **3** 4. **2** 5. **4**

1. More Than Two Positive Decimal Fractions
When you multiply more than two decimal fractions, the product is always positive and larger than each of the factors. For example, $0.9 \times 0.5 \times 0.2 = 0.090$. (The number of decimal places in the product should be the total of the number of decimal places in the factors. 0.9 has one decimal place, 0.5 has one decimal place, and 0.2 has one decimal place. $1 + 1 + 1 = 3$. The product must have three decimal places, thus 0.090.)

PRACTICE

1. $0.2 \times 5.1 \times 1.1$
(1) 11.120
(2) 1.122
(3) 1.121
(4) 5.112
(5) None of the above

1. 1 2 3 4 5

2. $2.10 \times 1.002 \times 0.001$
(1) 0.021420
(2) 0.002412
(3) 0.002142
(4) 0.201424
(5) None of the above

2. 1 2 3 4 5

3. What is the volume of a cube that is 2.1 cm long, 3.7 cm wide, and 1.2 cm high in cubic centimeters?
(1) 9.322
(2) 9.234
(3) 9.432
(4) 9.324
(5) None of the above

3. 1 2 3 4 5

4. $2.1 \times 2.01 \times 2.01$
(1) 8.48412
(2) 8.44812
(3) 8.48124
(4) 8.48421
(5) None of the above

4. 1 2 3 4 5

5. $0.3 \times 0.4 \times 0.001$
(1) 0.00012
(2) 0.00120
(3) 0.01200
(4) 0.12000
(5) None of the above

5. 1 2 3 4 5

ANSWERS:

1. **2** 2. **5** 3. **4** 4. **4** 5. **1**

1. Two Negative Decimal Fractions
When you multiply two negative decimal fractions, the product is always positive and larger than either of the factors. For example, –0.7 × –0.3 = +0.21.

PRACTICE

1. –2.3 × –4.8
(1) 1.102
(2) 0.1102
(3) 110.2
(4) 11.04
(5) None of the above

1. 1 2 3 4 5

2. –0.007 × –0.0021
(1) 0.0147
(2) 0.00147
(3) 0.000147
(4) 0.147
(5) None of the above

2. 1 2 3 4 5

3. –234.5 × –0.001
(1) 0.2345
(2) 2.345
(3) 23.45
(4) 234.5
(5) None of the above

3. 1 2 3 4 5

4. –29.3 × –56.1
(1) 1634.73
(2) 1643.73
(3) 1463.73
(4) 1346.73
(5) None of the above

4. 1 2 3 4 5

5. –7.001 × –3.02
(1) 21.14320
(2) 21.41302
(3) 21.14302
(4) 21.43102
(5) None of the above

5. 1 2 3 4 5

ANSWERS:

1. **4** 2. **5** 3. **1** 4. **2** 5. **3**

1. More Than Two Negative Decimal Fractions
When you multiply more than two negative decimal fractions, the product is negative if there is an odd number of factors, and positive if there is an even number of factors. For example, –0.3 × –0.2 × –0.5 = –0.030 since there are three factors and 3 is an odd number. –0.3 × –0.2 × –0.5 × –0.4 = +0.0120 since there are four factors and 4 is an even number.

PRACTICE

1. –2.30 × –3.1 × –1.1
(1) +7.483
(2) –7.483
(3) +7.843
(4) –7.843
(5) +7.348

1. 1 2 3 4 5

2. –2.1 × –4.2 × –5.0
(1) 44.100
(2) –44.100
(3) –40.200
(4) 40.200
(5) 42.900

2. 1 2 3 4 5

3. −11.1 × −2.2 × −3.1 **3.** 1 2 3 4 5
(1) −75.702
(2) −66.702
(3) −75.072
(4) −16.121
(5) −61.121

4. −1.01 × −1.01 × −1.01 **4.** 1 2 3 4 5
(1) −1.303001
(2) −10.30301
(3) −1.030301
(4) −1.303010
(5) −13.32742

5. −2.1 × −3.3 × −1.7 × −2.1 **5.** 1 2 3 4 5
(1) 24.7401
(2) 24.7010
(3) 24.7104
(4) 24.1704
(5) 24.4017

ANSWERS:

1. **4** 2. **2** 3. **1** 4. **3** 5. **1**

1. Decimal Fractions with Mixed Signs
When you multiply a series of decimal fractions, the product is negative if the number of negative factors is odd, and positive if the number of negative factors is even. For example, −0.6 × +1.3 × −2.33 × +52.1 = 94.68654 since there are two negative factors (−3/5, −2/3) and 2 is an even number.

PRACTICE

1. 0.002 × −3.2 × 1.01 **1.** 1 2 3 4 5
(1) −0.06464
(2) −0.006464
(3) −0.4646
(4) −0.004646
(5) None of the above

2. 2.4 × −4.1 × −2.9 **2.** 1 2 3 4 5
(1) 18.536
(2) 26.536
(3) 16.536
(4) 28.536
(5) None of the above

3. 0.1 × −0.1 × −0.1 × 0.1 **3.** 1 2 3 4 5
(1) 0.0001
(2) 0.001
(3) 0.01
(4) 0.1
(5) None of the above

4. −2.1 × −2.2 × −2.3 × 2.4 **4.** 1 2 3 4 5
(1) −25.5204
(2) −25.5024
(3) −25.5402
(4) −25.4502
(5) None of the above

5. −0.02 × −0.3 × 0.01 × −0.7 **5.** 1 2 3 4 5
(1) −0.042
(2) −0.00042
(3) −0.000042
(4) −0.0042
(5) None of the above

ANSWERS:

1. **2** 2. **4** 3. **1** 4. **2** 5. **3**

1. Division
   1. Whole Numbers
      1. Two Positive Whole Numbers

When you divide one positive whole number by another positive whole number, the quotient is positive. For example, 18 ÷ 6 = 3.

PRACTICE

1. 36 ÷ 4

(1) 9
(2) 10
(3) 11
(4) 12
(5) None of the above

1. 1 2 3 4 5

2. 108 ÷ 4

(1) 25
(2) 72
(3) 27
(4) 71
(5) None of the above

2. 1 2 3 4 5

3. 121 ÷ 11

(1) 9
(2) 10
(3) 11
(4) 12
(5) None of the above

3. 1 2 3 4 5

4. 144 ÷ 6

(1) 21
(3) 22
(3) 23
(4) 24
(5) None of the above

4. 1 2 3 4 5

5. 256 ÷ 8

(1) 23
(2) 32
(3) 41
(4) 28
(5) None of the above

5. 1 2 3 4 5

ANSWERS:

1. **1** 2. **3** 3. **3** 4. **4** 5. **2**

1. Two Negative Whole Numbers

When you divide one negative whole number by another negative whole number, the quotient is positive. For example, –24/–8 = 3.

PRACTICE

1. (–28) ÷ (–7)

(1) –4
(2) 40
(3) –40
(4) 4
(5) None of the above

1. 1 2 3 4 5

2. (–236) ÷ (–4)

(1) 95
(2) 64
(3) 73
(4) 59
(5) None of the above

2. 1 2 3 4 5

3. (–3276) ÷ (–52)

(1) 65
(2) 63
(3) 66
(4) 61
(5) None of the above

3. 1 2 3 4 5

4. (−1323) ÷ (−49)
   (1) 17
   (2) 72
   (3) 27
   (4) 36
   (5) None of the above

4. 1 2 3 4 5

5. (−2403) ÷ (−27)
   (1) 89
   (2) 98
   (3) 76
   (4) 68
   (5) None of the above

5. 1 2 3 4 5

ANSWERS:

1. **4** 2. **4** 3. **2** 4. **3** 5. **1**

1. Whole Numbers with Mixed Signs

When you divide one whole number by another, if one is positive and the other is negative, the quotient is negative. For example, −8/4 = −2.

PRACTICE

1. (357) ÷ (−17)
   (1) 22
   (2) −21
   (3) −25
   (4) −23
   (5) None of the above

1. 1 2 3 4 5

2. (−1769) ÷ (61)
   (1) −29
   (2) 29
   (3) −92
   (4) 92
   (5) None of the above

2. 1 2 3 4 5

3. (+3630) ÷ (−55)
   (1) −77
   (2) −65
   (3) −67
   (4) −66
   (5) None of the above

3. 1 2 3 4 5

4. (−3159) ÷ (39)
   (1) −81
   (2) −18
   (3) 81
   (4) −28
   (5) None of the above

4. 1 2 3 4 5

5. (3159) ÷ (−39)
   (1) −81
   (2) −18
   (3) −80
   (4) −28
   (5) None of the above

5. 1 2 3 4 5

ANSWERS:

1. **2** 2. **1** 3. **4** 4. **1** 5. **1**

1. Fractions

Note: To divide one fraction by another, invert the second fraction and multiply. For example, to divide 2/3 by 3/4, invert 3/4 to get 4/3 and then multiply. The question becomes 2/3 × 4/3 = 8/9.

1. Two Positive Fractions

When you divide one positive fraction by another positive fraction, the quotient is positive. For example, 5/6 divided by 3/4 is 5/6 × 4/3 = 20/18 which is equivalent to 10/9.

PRACTICE

1. 3/5 ÷ 1/2
(1) 1 1/2
(2) 1 1/5
(3) 1 2/5
(4) 1 1/3
(5) None of the above

1. 1 2 3 4 5

2. 5/11 ÷ 4/5
(1) 44/25
(2) 6/11
(3) 13/22
(4) 25/44
(5) None of the above

2. 1 2 3 4 5

3. 1 3/7 ÷ 10/13
(1) 1 6/7
(2) 1 3/4
(3) 1 5/7
(4) 100/91
(5) None of the above

3. 1 2 3 4 5

4. 2 3/4 ÷ 1 2/3
(1) 1 6/10
(2) 1 7/10
(3) 1 13/20
(4) 1 3/4
(5) None of the above

4. 1 2 3 4 5

5. 55/56 ÷ 5/11
(1) 15/6
(2) 1 5/6
(3) 1 2/3
(4) 2 1/2
(5) None of the above

5. 1 2 3 4 5

ANSWERS:

1. **2**   2. **4**   3. **1**   4. **3**   5. **5**

1. Two Negative Fractions
When you divide one negative fraction by another negative fraction, the quotient is positive. For example, –6/7 divided by –3/2 is –6/7 × –2/3 = +12/21 which is equivalent to +4/7.

PRACTICE

1. (–4/5) ÷ (–2/3)
(1) –1 1/5
(2) 1 1/5
(3) 1 1/15
(4) –1 1/15
(5) None of the above

1. 1 2 3 4 5

2. (–12/17) ÷ (–3/4)
(1) 1 1/16
(2) 15/17
(3) 8/9
(4) 16/17
(5) None of the above

2. 1 2 3 4 5

3. (–1 3/5) ÷ (–5/9)
(1) 2 22/25
(2) 1 22/25
(3) 2 4/5
(4) 1 4/5
(5) None of the above

3. 1 2 3 4 5

4. (–3/4) ÷ (–3 1/2)
(1) 3/4
(2) 3/41
(3) 3/14
(4) 3/1
(5) None of the above

4. 1 2 3 4 5

5. (–3 4/7) ÷ (–2 4/9)
(1) 1 17/154
(2) 1 71/154
(3) 1 71/145
(4) 1 17/145
(5) None of the above

5. 1 2 3 4 5

ANSWERS:

1. 2 **2.** 4 **3.** 1 **4.** 3 **5.** 2

1. Fractions with Mixed Signs

When you divide one fraction by another, if one is positive and the other is negative, the quotient is negative. For example, 8/3 divided by 4/7 is 8/3 × 7/4 = 56/12 = 4 8/12 which is equivalent to 4 2/3.

PRACTICE

1. (–5/6) ÷ (3/4)
(1) 1 1/24
(2) –1/9
(3) –1 1/9
(4) 2/3
(5) None of the above

1. 1 2 3 4 5

2. (3/8) ÷ (–13/15)
(1) 45/104
(2) –45/104
(3) –45/140
(4) 45/140
(5) None of the above

2. 1 2 3 4 5

3. (1 2/5) ÷ (–7/9)
(1) –1 2/3
(2) –2 1/4
(3) 7/16
(4) –1 4/5
(5) None of the above

3. 1 2 3 4 5

4. (–2 3/19) ÷ (23/29)
(1) –2 315/437
(2) –2 351/437
(3) –2 315/473
(4) –2 351/473
(5) None of the above

4. 1 2 3 4 5

5. (+22 1/2) ÷ (–45/49)
(1) 2 1/2
(2) 22 3/4
(3) 23 1/2
(4) 24 1/2
(5) None of the above

5. 1 2 3 4 5

ANSWERS:

1. 3 **2.** 2 **3.** 4 **4.** 1 **5.** 5

1. Decimal Fractions

Note: To divide decimal fractions,

1. Write the numbers in standard division form

$$0.3\overline{)55.2}$$

2. Count the number of decimal places in the divisor, in this case 1.
3. Move the decimal point over the same number of places in the divisor and in the dividend.

4. The question becomes

$$3\sqrt{552}$$

5. The answer is 184.

1. Two Positive Decimal Fractions
When you divide one positive decimal fraction by another positive decimal fraction, the quotient is positive. For example, 0.56 divided by 0.4 = 1.4.

PRACTICE

1. (0.1025) ÷ (0.25)
(1) 4.10
(2) 0.41
(3) 0.04
(4) 0.01
(5) None of the above

1. 1 2 3 4 5

2. (1.7664) ÷ (2.3)
(1) 0.786
(2) 0.867
(3) 0.768
(4) 0.678
(5) None of the above

2. 1 2 3 4 5

3. (11.89) ÷ (4.1)
(1) 0.29
(2) 29
(3) 2.9
(4) 9.2
(5) None of the above

3. 1 2 3 4 5

4. (0.0004872) ÷ (0.21)
(1) 0.00232
(2) 0.02320
(3) 0.20320
(4) 2.32000
(5) None of the above

4. 1 2 3 4 5

5. (11.36568) ÷ (56.8)
(1) 2.0010
(2) 0.0201
(3) 2.0100
(4) 0.2001
(5) None of the above

5. 1 2 3 4 5

ANSWERS:

1. **2** 2. **3** 3. **3** 4. **1** 5. **4**

1. Two Negative Decimal Fractions
When you divide one negative decimal fraction by another negative decimal fraction, the quotient is positive. For example, –6.7 divided by –0.32 is +7.02.

PRACTICE

1. (–1.14) ÷ (–0.6)
(1) –1.9
(2) 0.19
(3) +1.9
(4) –0.19
(5) None of the above

1. 1 2 3 4 5

2. (–0.42864) ÷ (–56.4)
(1) 0.0076
(2) 0.0760
(3) 0.7060
(4) 0.7600
(5) None of the above

2. 1 2 3 4 5

3. (–0.131763) ÷ (–0.00501)
(1) 23.6
(2) 26.3
(3) 2.63
(4) 2.36
(5) None of the above

3. 1 2 3 4 5

4. (–142.457) ÷ (–65.8)
(1) 2.615
(2) 3.672
(3) 2.265
(4) 2.165
(5) None of the above

4. 1 2 3 4 5

5. (–14 811.852) ÷ (–22.22)
(1) –0.666
(2) –6.666
(3) –66.66
(4) –666.6
(5) None of the above

5. 1 2 3 4 5

ANSWERS:

1. **3** 2. **1** 3. **2** 4. **4** 5. **5**

1. Decimal Fractions with Mixed Signs
When you divide one decimal fraction by another, if one is positive and the other is negative, the quotient is negative. For example, +0.85 divided by –0.05 is 17.

PRACTICE

1. (–0.2184) ÷ (0.26)
(1) –0.84
(2) –0.44
(3) –0.67
(4) –0.48
(5) None of the above

1. 1 2 3 4 5

2. (2.968) ÷ (–0.53)
(1) –6.5
(2) 5.6
(3) 6.5
(4) –5.6
(5) None of the above

2. 1 2 3 4 5

3. (–0.00009) ÷ (0.001)
(1) –0.900
(2) –0.090
(3) –0.009
(4) –9.000
(5) None of the above

3. 1 2 3 4 5

4. (–6.121812) ÷ (2.02)
(1) 3.0306
(2) 3.3006
(3) 3.0036
(4) 3.0603
(5) None of the above

4. 1 2 3 4 5

5. (26.5512) ÷ (–8.51)
(1) –3.21
(2) +3.21
(3) –3.12
(4) +3.12
(5) None of the above

5. 1 2 3 4 5

ANSWERS:

1. **1** 2. **4** 3. **2** 4. **5** 5. **3**

MIXED PRACTICE

1. 0.593 − 3.671
(1) −3.078
(2) −4.264
(3) −3.708
(4) −3.807
(5) None of the above

1. 1 2 3 4 5

2. 359 + 140
(1) 599
(2) 949
(3) 499
(4) 399
(5) None of the above

2. 1 2 3 4 5

3. 3/7 × 8/11
(1) 22/77
(2) 23/77
(3) 24/77
(4) 25/77
(5) None of the above

3. 1 2 3 4 5

4. 1 3/5 ÷ 6/13
(1) 1/6
(2) 3 1/2
(3) 3 8/15
(4) 3 7/15
(5) None of the above

4. 1 2 3 4 5

5. 23 1/2 + 3 6/7
(1) 26 5/14
(2) 27 5/14
(3) 27 4/14
(4) 26 4/14
(5) None of the above

5. 1 2 3 4 5

6. 254 − 198
(1) 65
(2) 56
(3) 55
(4) 60
(5) None of the above

6. 1 2 3 4 5

7. 1.974749 ÷ −4.9
(1) −0.40301
(2) −0.41030
(3) −0.43100
(4) −0.42001
(5) None of the above

7. 1 2 3 4 5

8. 0.8996 ÷ 3.46
(1) 0.026
(2) 2.600
(3) 0.062
(4) 0.260
(5) None of the above

8. 1 2 3 4 5

9. (−358) × (−78)
(1) 29 724
(2) −35 000
(3) 27 924
(4) 27 429
(5) None of the above

9. 1 2 3 4 5

10. (34) × (12) × (−9)
(1) −3672
(2) −408
(3) −3762
(4) 3762
(5) None of the above

10. 1 2 3 4 5

11. (−754) ÷ (13)
(1) −85
(2) −58
(3) −75
(4) −57
(5) None of the above

11. 1 2 3 4 5

12. 935 – 386

(1) 576
(2) 667
(3) 651
(4) 549
(5) None of the above

12. 1 2 3 4 5

13. –2 4/5 × –3 4/7

(1) 10
(2) 6 8/15
(3) –15
(4) –6 2/3
(5) None of the above

13. 1 2 3 4 5

14. (4 7/8) ÷ (–13/16)

(1) –4
(2) –5
(3) –6
(4) –7
(5) None of the above

14. 1 2 3 4 5

15. –9999 × 11

(1) 190 989
(2) –109 989
(3) –190 989
(4) 109 989
(5) None of the above

15. 1 2 3 4 5

ANSWERS:

1. **1** 3. **3** 5. **2** 7. **1** 9. **3** 11. **2** 13. **1** 15. **2**

2. **3** 4. **4** 6. **2** 8. **4** 10. **1** 12. **4** 14. **3**

I. F. Order of Operations

In a question with different operations, if everyone were to decide individually the order for performing the operations, there would be many different answers. That is never acceptable in mathematics, where each question should have one correct answer. Thus we need a standard order of operations. The one that is used is summarized as follows:

1. Operations within brackets
2. Multiplication and division from left to right
3. Addition and subtraction from left to right.

A simple way of remembering this is BDMAS: B for brackets, D for division, M for multiplication, A for addition, and S for subtraction.

EXAMPLE: 4 + 8 – 9 ÷ 3
Division first: 9 ÷ 3 = 3
Addition next: 4 + 8 = 12
Subtraction next: 12 – 3 = 9

EXAMPLE: (3 × 7 + 5 × 2) – 12
Brackets first:
Inside bracket, multiplication first: 3 × 7 = 21
5 × 2 = 10
Addition next: 21 + 10 = 31
Subtraction next: 31 – 12 = 19

EXAMPLE: $(2 + 8 - 3 + 8 \div 4) + 33 \times 2$

Brackets first:

Inside bracket, division first: $8 \div 4 = 2$

Addition next: $2 + 8 + 2 = 12$

Subtraction next: $12 - 3 = 9$

Multiplication next: $33 \times 2 = 66$

Addition next: $9 + 66 = 75$

This procedure looks far more complex when it is written out. If you remember to use BDMAS, you will get the correct answers.

F-1

Problems Involving Fractions. In general, there are three types of problems involving fractions.

1. To find a number that is a fractional part of a number.

EXAMPLE: A dealer sold 70 television sets one month. If 2/5 of the sets were colour sets, how many colour sets were sold?

The word *of* indicates that we are to multiply 70 by 2/5.

$$\frac{70}{1} \times \frac{2}{5} = \frac{\cancel{70}^{14}}{1} \times \frac{2}{\cancel{5}_1} = 28$$

The dealer sold 28 colour television sets.

2. To find what fractional part one number is of another.

EXAMPLE: A hotel has 70 guest rooms. Of these, 15 are single rooms. What fractional part of the total number of rooms are the single rooms?

We form a fraction as follows:

$$\frac{\text{number of single rooms}}{\text{total number of rooms}} = \frac{15}{70}, \text{ or } \frac{3}{14}$$

3. To find a number when a fractional part of the number is known.

EXAMPLE: In a town election, only 2/3 of the registered voters cast ballots. If there were 1620 cast, how many registered voters were there?

2/3 of the registered voters = 1620.

1/3 of the registered voters $= \frac{1620}{2} = 810$

Then, 3/3 or the total number of registered voters $= 810 \times 3 = 2430$.

There were 2430 registered voters.

Note that the two operations above are equivalent to dividing 1620 by $\frac{2}{3}$, that is,

$$1620 \div \frac{2}{3} = \frac{1620}{1} \times \frac{3}{2} = \frac{810}{1} \times \frac{3}{1} = 2430.$$

This is a method for finding a total number when a part of it is known and the fractional part it represents is known: divide the part by the fraction it represents.

PRACTICE

Directions: Solve the following problems and blacken the space at the right under the number which corresponds to the one you have selected as the correct answer.

1. The Globe Theatre has 600 seats. At one showing, $\frac{4}{5}$ of the seats were taken. How many seats were taken?
(1) 400
(2) 420
(3) 450
(4) 480
(5) 750

1. 1 2 3 4 5

2. An oil tank holds 160 L. When the tank is $\frac{3}{8}$ full, the number of litres of oil in the tank is
(1) 60
(2) 80
(3) 85
(4) 100
(5) 110

2. 1 2 3 4 5

3. A football team scored 35 points in a game. If the team scored 21 points in the first half, the fractional part of the total scored in the second half was
(1) $\frac{3}{5}$
(2) $\frac{7}{12}$
(3) $\frac{1}{5}$
(4) $\frac{2}{5}$
(5) $\frac{3}{7}$

3. 1 2 3 4 5

4. The Star Company employs 17 engineers. If this is $\frac{1}{3}$ of the total work force, the number of employees of the Star Company is
(1) 20
(2) 41
(3) 47
(4) 23
(5) 51

4. 1 2 3 4 5

5. The Mills family saves n dollars per year. The number of dollars saved in 5 months is
(1) $5n$
(2) $\frac{5n}{12}$
(3) $12n$
(4) $n + 5$
(5) $\frac{5}{12}$

5. 1 2 3 4 5

6. A baseball player hit 90 singles in one season. If this was $\frac{3}{5}$ of his total number of hits, the number of hits the player made that season was
(1) 54
(2) 150
(3) 540
(4) 144
(5) 154

6. 1 2 3 4 5

7. During a sale on stereos, $\frac{1}{4}$ of the stock was sold the first day. The next day, $\frac{2}{3}$ of the remaining stereos were sold. The fractional part of the total stock sold during the second day was
(1) $\frac{2}{3}$
(2) $\frac{1}{4}$
(3) $\frac{1}{6}$
(4) $\frac{1}{2}$
(5) $\frac{1}{12}$

7. 1 2 3 4 5

8. It takes n hours to complete a job. The fractional part of the job that can be completed in 3 hours is
(1) $3n$
(2) $\frac{3}{n}$
(3) $\frac{n}{3}$
(4) $3 + n$
(5) $\frac{1}{n+3}$

8. 1 2 3 4 5

9. The regular price for hats is x dollars each. If they are reduced by $\frac{1}{5}$ of the regular price, the new price is
(1) $\frac{x}{5}$
(2) $x + \frac{1}{5}$
(3) $4\frac{x}{5}$
(4) $x - \frac{1}{5}$
(5) $5x$

9. 1 2 3 4 5

10. The Khan Shoe Company received a shipment of 288 pairs of shoes composed equally of black and brown shoes. If 36 pairs of the brown shoes are returned and replaced by pairs of black shoes, the fractional part of the shipment now consisting of black shoes is
(1) $\frac{3}{8}$
(2) $\frac{5}{8}$
(3) $\frac{7}{12}$
(4) $\frac{1}{8}$
(5) $\frac{3}{4}$

10. 1 2 3 4 5

11. Mr. Benson is on a diet. For breakfast and lunch he consumed $\frac{4}{9}$ of his allowable number of calories. If he still had 1000 calories left for the day, his daily allowance in calories was
(1) 1500
(2) 1800
(3) 1200
(4) 2250
(5) $444\frac{4}{9}$

11. 1 2 3 4 5

12. In her will, Ms. Mancini left $\frac{1}{2}$ her estate to her husband, $\frac{1}{3}$ to her daughter, and the balance, consisting of $12 000, to her son. The value of Ms. Mancini's estate was
(1) $24 000
(2) $60 000
(3) $14 400
(4) $65 000
(5) $72 000

12. 1 2 3 4 5

13. An oil tank is $\frac{3}{10}$ full. It takes 105 litres more to fill the tank. The number of litres the tank holds is
(1) 150
(2) 120
(3) 210
(4) 315
(5) 250

13. 1 2 3 4 5

14. A family spends $\frac{1}{4}$ of its income for rent and $\frac{1}{5}$ for food. The fractional part of its income left is
(1) $\frac{9}{20}$
(2) $\frac{19}{20}$
(3) $\frac{11}{20}$
(4) $\frac{4}{5}$
(5) $\frac{8}{9}$

14. 1 2 3 4 5

ANSWERS:

1. **4**	4. **5**	7. **4**	10. **2**	13. **1**
2. **1**	5. **2**	8. **2**	11. **2**	14. **3**
3. **4**	6. **2**	9. **3**	12. **5**	

F-2

Arranging Fractions in Order. We know that $\frac{1}{2}$ and $\frac{3}{6}$ are equivalent fractions. This can be checked as follows:

$$1 \times 6 = 2 \times 3$$

We know that $\frac{3}{4}$ is greater than $\frac{2}{5}$. This can be checked as follows:

3 × 5 is greater than 4 × 2.

The symbol > means *is greater than*.
Thus, we may write $\frac{3}{4} > \frac{2}{5}$ because 15 > 8.

We know that $\frac{3}{7}$ is less than $\frac{5}{6}$. This can be checked as follows:

3 × 6 is less than 7 × 5.

The symbol < means *is less than*.
Thus, we may write $\frac{3}{7} < \frac{5}{6}$ because 18 < 35.

PRACTICE

In each case, use the symbol =, >, or < to show the relationship between the given fractions:

1.	$\frac{3}{4}$	$\frac{7}{10}$	**4.**	$\frac{5}{8}$	$\frac{4}{7}$	**7.**	$\frac{7}{11}$	$\frac{13}{19}$	**10.**	$\frac{8}{13}$	$\frac{5}{8}$	**13.**	$\frac{15}{35}$	$\frac{12}{28}$
2.	$\frac{6}{9}$	$\frac{40}{60}$	**5.**	$\frac{4}{9}$	$\frac{7}{15}$	**8.**	$\frac{7}{9}$	$\frac{15}{17}$	**11.**	$\frac{5}{16}$	$\frac{10}{31}$	**14.**	$\frac{6}{13}$	$\frac{11}{20}$
3.	$\frac{2}{3}$	$\frac{11}{16}$	**6.**	$\frac{12}{20}$	$\frac{3}{5}$	**9.**	$\frac{21}{28}$	$\frac{24}{32}$	**12.**	$\frac{4}{11}$	$\frac{8}{21}$	**15.**	$\frac{9}{17}$	$\frac{5}{7}$

ANSWERS:

1. $\frac{3}{4} > \frac{7}{10}$	4. $\frac{5}{8} > \frac{4}{7}$	7. $\frac{7}{11} < \frac{13}{19}$	10. $\frac{8}{13} < \frac{5}{8}$	13. $\frac{15}{35} = \frac{12}{28}$
2. $\frac{6}{9} = \frac{40}{60}$	5. $\frac{4}{9} < \frac{7}{15}$	8. $\frac{7}{9} < \frac{15}{17}$	11. $\frac{5}{16} < \frac{10}{31}$	14. $\frac{6}{13} < \frac{11}{20}$
3. $\frac{2}{3} < \frac{11}{16}$	6. $\frac{12}{20} = \frac{3}{5}$	9. $\frac{21}{28} = \frac{24}{32}$	12. $\frac{4}{11} < \frac{8}{21}$	15. $\frac{9}{17} < \frac{5}{7}$

Sometimes, we wish to arrange three fractions in order of size, such as $\frac{1}{4}$, $\frac{1}{2}$, and $\frac{5}{6}$. We may write $\frac{1}{4} < \frac{1}{2}$ and $\frac{1}{2} < \frac{5}{6}$. However, these two comparisons may be combined and written as $\frac{1}{4} < \frac{1}{2} < \frac{5}{6}$. This is read as "$\frac{1}{4}$ is less than $\frac{1}{2}$ *and* $\frac{1}{2}$ is less than $\frac{5}{6}$." Or, we may write $\frac{5}{6} > \frac{1}{2} > \frac{1}{4}$. This is read as "$\frac{5}{6}$ is greater than $\frac{1}{2}$ and $\frac{1}{2}$ is greater than $\frac{1}{4}$."

EXAMPLE: Use symbols to write "$\frac{9}{10}$ is greater than $\frac{3}{5}$ and $\frac{3}{5}$ is greater than $\frac{2}{7}$."

$$\frac{9}{10} > \frac{3}{5} > \frac{2}{7}.$$

EXAMPLE: Use the symbol < to arrange the fractions $\frac{5}{8}$, $\frac{3}{4}$, and $\frac{1}{6}$ in order of magnitude.

$\frac{1}{6} < \frac{5}{8}$ since $8 \times 1 < 5 \times 6$ $\quad$ $\frac{5}{8} < \frac{3}{4}$ since $5 \times 4 < 3 \times 8$

We may write this result as $\frac{1}{6} < \frac{5}{8} < \frac{3}{4}$.

PRACTICE

Use the symbol > to arrange the following sets of fractions in order of magnitude:

1. $\frac{1}{3}$, $\frac{6}{7}$, $\frac{3}{5}$

2. $\frac{3}{7}$, $\frac{7}{9}$, $\frac{1}{4}$

3. $\frac{7}{10}$, $\frac{3}{8}$, $\frac{5}{6}$

Use the symbol < to arrange the following sets of fractions in order of magnitude:

4. $\frac{2}{3}, \frac{1}{6}, \frac{3}{5}$

5. $\frac{4}{7}, \frac{8}{9}, \frac{5}{8}$

6. $\frac{7}{10}, \frac{2}{9}, \frac{1}{2}$

ANSWERS:

1. $\frac{6}{7} > \frac{3}{5} > \frac{1}{3}$
2. $\frac{7}{8} > \frac{3}{7} > \frac{1}{4}$
3. $\frac{5}{6} > \frac{7}{10} > \frac{3}{8}$
4. $\frac{1}{6} < \frac{3}{5} < \frac{2}{3}$
5. $\frac{4}{7} < \frac{5}{8} < \frac{8}{9}$
6. $\frac{2}{9} < \frac{1}{2} < \frac{7}{10}$

I. G. Percent

We see percent all the time. Sometimes we enjoy seeing it, such as at an 80% off sale. Sometimes we don't like seeing it, such as when an airline surcharges our tickets by 2%. Whether we like to use percent or not doesn't matter. Percent problems surround us, and we should become familiar with them.

A *percent* is a ratio between a number and 100. For example, 25% is an expression of the ratio between 25 and 100. Similarly, the expression of the ratio between 43 and 100 is 43%.

There are some words we need to know to work with percentages. If we see a sign announcing a 50% off sale, we know that we can save $8.50 on a $17.00 CD we want by buying it at the sale. The 50% is the rate, the price of the CD before a discount, $17.00, is the *base*, and the savings of $8.50 is the percentage.

The two words that can be confused are "percent" and "percentage." *Percent* is the rate. In this case it is the rate of saving. If a sales tax of 7% were added to the sale, the percent or rate would be 7.

Percentage is the quantity or amount. The percentage or amount of the savings is $8.50 on the CD transaction. The sales tax is $1.19 since that is the amount of additional money charged.

Percent, percentage, and base are related. The percent of the base is equal to the percentage, and the percentage of the amount is expressed as the percent.

If we wish to find 25% of 160, we multiply 160 by 25%:

$$160 \times 25/100 = 40 \text{ or}$$
$$160 \times 0.25 = 40$$

Percent, percentage, and base are also related by a proportion:

$$\text{Percent}/100 = \text{percentage}/\text{base}$$

Or to use common terminology,

$$P/100 = A/W$$

where P is percent, A is percentage, and W is base or amount.

This gives us a way to solve problems involving percent. For example, if Jolie wants to save 30% of her $15.00 allowance each week, how much does she have to deposit in her savings account? We could write

$$P = 30\%$$
$$A = ?$$
$$W = \$15.00$$

Using our proportion, 30/100 = ?/15, we calculate ? = 4.50. Jolie has to deposit $4.50 in her savings account each week.

Note: To solve a question stated as a proportion, cross-multiply. To solve the proportion $A/5 = 24/30$, multiply $A \times 30$ and set the product equal to 5×24:

$$30A = 120$$
$$A = 120/30 = 4$$

PRACTICE

Reminder: *Percentage* is *x percent* of the *base,* where *x* is any number.

Calculate a value for the question mark in each row.

NO.	PERCENTAGE	RATE (%)	BASE
1	40	10	?
2	?	25	160
3	13	?	65
4	225	50	?
5	?	12	150

ANSWERS:

1. **400** 2. **40** 3. **20%** 4. **450** 5. **18**

PRACTICE

Select the correct answer for each of the following questions.

1. Dennis has decided that he really needs a room 20% longer than his to hold all the stuff he has collected. If his present room is 5 m long, how long would his ideal room be?
(1) 5 m
(2) 4 m
(3) 100 m
(4) 25 m
(5) 6 m

1. 1 2 3 4 5
|| || || || ||

2. Polly wants to save for a new saw by putting away 25% of its $32.00 price each week. How much should she put away each week?
(1) $12.00
(2) $8.00
(3) $6.00
(4) $24.00
(5) $5.00

2. 1 2 3 4 5
|| || || || ||

3. Abbis saw a wonderful Father's Day gift, but it cost $52.00 and all he had was $46.80. He thought he would wait for a sale to buy it. How much of a discount must the store offer before Abbis can afford the gift?
(1) 10%
(2) 15%
(3) 20%
(4) 25%
(5) 30%

3. 1 2 3 4 5
|| || || || ||

4. Gina was looking for a bank in which to deposit her money. Bank A offered her 4% annual interest. Bank B said they would pay her $1.00 for every $50.00 she had in her account for a year. Bank C said that they would offer her $0.24 annually for every $8.00 on deposit. Which bank offered her the best rate of interest?

(1) Both Bank A and Bank C
(2) Bank B
(3) Both Bank B and Bank C
(4) Bank C
(5) Bank A

4. 1 2 3 4 5

5. Darren was told to drink 10 large glasses of water each day. If he drank 2 large glasses of water with breakfast, what percent of his daily water requirement was left to drink?

(1) 20%
(2) 80%
(3) 60%
(4) 100%
(5) 25%

5. 1 2 3 4 5

ANSWERS:

1. 5 **2.** 2 **3.** 1 **4.** 5 **5.** 2

PRACTICE

Fill in the blanks in each of the following. Write the answers to the nearest hundredth.

	FRACTION	DECIMAL	PERCENT
1.	$\frac{1}{2}$	____	____
2.	____	0.35	____
3.	____	____	36%
4.	$\frac{3}{7}$	____	____
5.	____	0.24	____
6.	____	____	$4\frac{1}{2}$%
7.	$\frac{5}{9}$	____	____
8.	____	0.38	____
9.	____	____	$83\frac{1}{3}$%
10.	$1\frac{1}{5}$	____	____

ANSWERS:

	FRACTION	DECIMAL	PERCENT
1.	$\frac{1}{2}$	0.50	50%
2.	$\frac{35}{100} = \frac{7}{20}$	0.35	35%
3.	$\frac{36}{100} = \frac{9}{25}$	0.36	36%
4.	$\frac{3}{7}$	0.43	43%
5.	$\frac{6}{25}$	0.24	24%
6.	$\frac{4\frac{1}{2}}{100} = \frac{9}{200}$	0.04	4%
7.	$\frac{5}{9}$	0.56	56%
8.	$\frac{37\frac{1}{2}}{100} = \frac{75}{200} = \frac{3}{8}$	0.38	38%
9.	$\frac{83\frac{1}{3}}{100} = \frac{250}{300} = \frac{5}{6}$	0.83	83%
10.	$1\frac{1}{5}$	1.2	120%

Certain fractions and their equivalent percents are used frequently.

Helpful Equivalents to Memorize

$\frac{1}{2} = 50\%$	$\frac{3}{4} = 75\%$	$\frac{4}{5} = 80\%$	$\frac{3}{8} = 37\frac{1}{2}\%$
$\frac{1}{3} = 33\frac{1}{3}\%$	$\frac{1}{5} = 20\%$	$\frac{1}{6} = 16\frac{2}{3}\%$	$\frac{5}{8} = 62\frac{1}{2}\%$
$\frac{2}{3} = 66\frac{2}{3}\%$	$\frac{2}{5} = 40\%$	$\frac{5}{6} = 83\frac{1}{3}\%$	$\frac{7}{8} = 87\frac{1}{2}\%$
$\frac{1}{4} = 25\%$	$\frac{3}{5} = 60\%$	$\frac{1}{8} = 12\frac{1}{2}\%$	

G-1

Problems on Percents. Since percents are fractions in another form, problems involving percents are similar to problems involving fractions.

1. To find a percent of a given number.

EXAMPLE: In a factory, 4775 machine parts were manufactured. When these were tested, 4% of them were found to be defective. How many machine parts were defective?

In this case, the word *of* indicates that we are to multiply 4775 by 4%. Since 4% = 0.04, we have

$$\begin{array}{rl} 4775 & \text{parts manufactured} \\ \underline{\times\, 0.04} & \text{percent defective} \\ 191.00 & \text{number of defective parts} \end{array}$$

191 machine parts were defective.

2. To find what percent one number is of another.

EXAMPLE: During the season, a professional basketball player tried 108 foul shots, and made 81 of them. What percent of the shots tried were made?

We form a fraction as follows:

$$\frac{\text{number of shots made}}{\text{total number of shots tried}} = \frac{81}{108}$$

This fraction may be expressed as a percent by changing $^{81}/_{108}$ to a decimal and then to a percent:

$$\begin{array}{r} 0.75 \\ 108\overline{)81.00} \\ \underline{75\ 6} \\ 5\ 40 \\ \underline{5\ 40} \end{array}$$

$$^{81}/_{108} \times 0.75 = 75\%$$

or directly to a percent:

$$\frac{81}{108} \times 100 = 75\%$$

The player made 75% of the shots.

3. To find a number when a percent of it is given.

EXAMPLE: A business owner decided to spend 16% of her expense budget for advertising. If she spent $2400, what was her total expense?

We know that 16%, or $^{16}/_{100}$, of her expenses amounted to $2400.

$$^{16}/_{100} \text{ of expense} = 2400$$

$$^{1}/_{100} \text{ of expense} = {}^{2,400}/_{16} = 150$$

$$\text{then } ^{100}/_{100} \text{ or total expense} = 150 \times 100 = \$15000.$$

PRACTICE

Directions: Solve the following problems and blacken the space at the right under the number which corresponds to the one you have selected as the right answer.

1. A TV dealer made 20% of his annual sales during the month before Christmas. If he sold 130 sets during this month, the number of sets he sold during the year was
(1) 650 (2) 260 (3) 1300 (4) 520 (5) 390

1. 1 2 3 4 5

2. Of 600 students in a high school graduating class, 85% plan to go on to college. The number of students planning to go on to college is
(1) 5100 (2) 51 (3) 540 (4) 500 (5) 510

2. 1 2 3 4 5

3. A motorist planned a trip covering 720 km. After 600 km, what percent of the trip was completed?
(1) 80% (2) $83\frac{1}{3}$% (3) 60% (4) $16\frac{2}{3}$% (5) 85%

3. 1 2 3 4 5

4. A school library contained 3200 books. Of these, 48% were books of fiction. The number of books of fiction that the library contained was
(1) 1200 (2) 1208 (3) 1536 (4) 1380 (5) 1300

4. 1 2 3 4 5

5. The fire insurance premium on a house is $320. If the premium is calculated at 32 cents per $100, what is the amount of money for which the house is insured?
(1) $1000 (2) $3200 (3) $10 000 (4) $100 000 (5) $32 000

5. 1 2 3 4 5

6. The value of a new car decreases 35% during the first year. Mr. LaMarr paid $25 600 for a new car. The value of the car at the end of the first year was
(1) $8960 (2) $10 040 (3) $9140 (4) $14 520 (5) $10 140

6. 1 2 3 4 5

7. In a large housing development there are 1250 apartments. Of these, 250 were three-room apartments. The percent of three-room apartments in the development is
(1) $16\frac{2}{3}$% (2) 25% (3) 20% (4) 24% (5) 30%

7. 1 2 3 4 5

8. Ms. George bought a dining room suite for $800. She agreed to pay 25% down and the rest in installments. Her down payment was

(1) $400
(2) $200
(3) $150
(4) $100
(5) $250

8. 1 2 3 4 5

9. A water tank contains 560 L. After 210 L of water were used, the percent of water left in the tank was

(1) $37\frac{1}{2}\%$
(2) 40%
(3) 60%
(4) $62\frac{1}{2}\%$
(5) 58%

9. 1 2 3 4 5

10. When Ms. Lau had paid $600 for her printer, she had paid 40% of the total cost. The total cost of her printer was

(1) $1000
(2) $1200
(3) $1500
(4) $2400
(5) $1800

10. 1 2 3 4 5

11. Mr. Richman left an estate amounting to $24 000. By his will, 10% was to be given to a college, 15% to a church, and the remainder to be divided equally among 3 nieces. How much money did each niece receive?

(1) $6120
(2) $2000
(3) $6333.33
(4) $6000
(5) $8000

11. 1 2 3 4 5

12. A bookstore sold 800 copies of a popular cookbook at $14 each. If the dealer made a profit of 40% on each sale, the total profit on the sale of the cookbooks was

(1) $4048
(2) $11 200
(3) $112
(4) $448
(5) $4480

12. 1 2 3 4 5

13. At an evening performance, $83\frac{1}{3}\%$ of the seats in a movie theatre were occupied. If 500 people attended this performance, the seating capacity of the movie theatre was

(1) 600
(2) 500
(3) 583
(4) 650
(5) 750

13. 1 2 3 4 5

14. A baseball team won 56 games and lost 28 games. The percent of the games won by the team was

(1) 50%
(2) $66\frac{2}{3}\%$
(3) $33\frac{1}{3}\%$
(4) 40%
(5) 36%

14. 1 2 3 4 5

15. The Star Motel had 60 rooms occupied one night. This was 80% of the total number of rooms. The total number of rooms in the motel was

(1) 80
(2) 48
(3) 140
(4) 75
(5) 100

15. 1 2 3 4 5

ANSWERS:

1. 1	4. 3	7. 3	10. 3	13. 1
2. 5	5. 4	8. 2	11. 4	14. 2
3. 2	6. 5	9. 4	12. 5	15. 4

G-2

Business Applications of Percentage. Manufacturers will frequently suggest a price for which an article is to be sold. This is called the *list price*. Dealers will sometimes reduce the price in order to meet competition. The amount by which the price is reduced is called the discount. And the reduced price is called the *net price*, or *selling price*.

EXAMPLE: In a department store, a chair was marked as follows: "List Price $45. For sale at $31.50." What was the rate of discount?

The discount was $45.00 – $31.50 = $13.50.
To find the rate of discount we use the fraction

$$\frac{\text{Discount}}{\text{List Price}} = \frac{13.50}{45.00}$$
$$= \frac{135}{450}$$
$$= \frac{3}{10}$$
$$= 30\%$$

The rate of discount was 30%.

PRACTICE

Directions: Solve the following problems and blacken the space at the right under the number which corresponds to the one you have selected as the correct answer.

1. The list price of a coat was $240. Mr. Wlasiuk bought the coat at a discount of 10%. The net price of the coat was
(1) $264
(2) $24
(3) $216
(4) $236
(5) $200

1. 1 2 3 4 5

2. A men's store advertises a shirt that usually sells for $32 at a special price of $24. The rate of discount is
(1) $33\frac{1}{3}$%
(2) 25%
(3) 20%
(4) 40%
(5) 35%

2. 1 2 3 4 5

3. A portable stereo is sold at a discount of $12\frac{1}{2}$%. If the discount amounts to $6, the list price of the portable stereo is
(1) $42
(2) $45
(3) $54
(4) $50
(5) $48

3. 1 2 3 4 5

4. An electric toaster has a list price of $36. If it is sold at a discount of $33\frac{1}{3}$% the net price is
(1) $7
(2) $28
(3) $24
(4) $25
(5) $16

4. 1 2 3 4 5

5. The net price of a watch was $40 after a discount of 20%. The list price of the watch was

(1) $50
(2) $30
(3) $48
(4) $35.20
(5) $45

5. 1 2 3 4 5 || || || || ||

ANSWERS:

1. 3 2. 2 3. 5 4. 3 5. 1

Sometimes a manufacturer will allow a *trade discount* and an additional discount on top of the trade discount. *Two or more discounts are called successive discounts*.

EXAMPLE: Mr. Boyd bought a table from a dealer. The list price was $180, and he was allowed a discount of 15%. In addition, he received a 2% discount for payment within 10 days.

How much did Mr. Boyd pay for the table?

$180	list price
×0.15	rate of discount
900	
180	
$27.00	amount of discount

$180.00	list price
−27.00	amount of discount
$153.00	cost price

When we compute the second discount, we base it on the price after the first discount is taken off.

$153	cost price
×0.02	rate of discount
$3.06	discount for early payment

$153.00	cost price
−3.06	discount for early payment
$149.94	actual payment

This result may be obtained more directly by noting that a discount of 15% means that Mr. Boyd pays 85% of the list price. A further discount of 2% means that Mr. Boyd pays 98% of the first discounted price. Thus, the doubly discounted price may be obtained as follows:

$$\$180 \times 0.85 \times 0.98 = \$149.94$$

PRACTICE

Directions: Solve the following problems and blacken the space at the right under the number which corresponds to the one you have selected as the correct answer.

1. Ms. Mack bought a television set. The list price was $400. She was allowed successive discounts of 10% and 5%. How much did Ms. Mack actually pay for the television?

(1) $340
(2) $350
(3) $352
(4) $342
(5) $324

1. 1 2 3 4 5 || || || || ||

2. Ms. Schatten bought a shipment of books. The list price of the books was \$180. If Ms. Schatten was allowed discounts of 15% and 5%, how much did she actually pay for the books?

(1) \$153.00
(2) \$171.00
(3) \$144.00
(4) \$150.00
(5) \$145.35

2. 1 2 3 4 5

3. On a purchase of \$500, how much is saved by taking discounts of 20% and 10%, rather than discounts of 10% and 15%?

(1) \$40.00
(2) \$23.50
(3) \$22.50
(4) \$32.50
(5) \$35.00

3. 1 2 3 4 5

4. Mr. Lucyk bought a boat which had a list price of \$1200. He was allowed a $12\frac{1}{2}$% discount and an additional 2% discount for cash. How much did Mr. Lucyk pay for the boat?

(1) \$1029
(2) \$1039
(3) \$1129
(4) \$989
(5) \$1050

4. 1 2 3 4 5

ANSWERS:

1. 4 2. 5 3. 3 4. 1

When a businessperson decides upon the price at which to sell an article, he or she must consider a number of items. First, the cost of the article is noted. Then such items as rent, sales help salaries, and other expenses must be considered. This is called *overhead*. Then the profit must be added on. Thus,

Selling Price = Cost + Overhead + Profit

EXAMPLE: One week the Town Shoe Shop's sales amounted to \$1590. The merchandise sold cost \$820, and the overhead was 20% of the sales. What was the profit?

20% = 0.20
The overhead was \$1590 × 0.20 = \$318.

To obtain the profit, we must subtract the sum of the cost and the overhead from the selling price.

\$820	cost of merchandise
+ 318	overhead
\$1138	cost + overhead
\$1590	selling price
− 1138	cost + overhead
\$ 452	profit

The profit was \$452.

PRACTICE

Directions: Solve the following problems and blacken the space at the right under the number which corresponds to the one you have selected as the right answer.

1. The cost of a lawn chair is \$68. The overhead is \$10, and the profit is \$18. The selling price is
   (1) \$77.50
   (2) \$86.50
   (3) \$95
   (4) \$96
   (5) \$92

1. 1 2 3 4 5
|| || || || ||

2. A merchant buys small appliances at \$43.50. She sells them at retail for \$75. If her overhead is 12% of the selling price, her profit is
   (1) \$9
   (2) \$22.50
   (3) \$23.50
   (4) \$61.50
   (5) \$31.50

2. 1 2 3 4 5
|| || || || ||

3. A merchant bought a shipment of assorted tools at a cost of \$1600 and sold the shipment for \$2500. If the profit was 25% of the cost of the shipment, her overhead expenses were
   (1) \$900
   (2) \$400
   (3) \$650
   (4) \$500
   (5) \$4100

3. 1 2 3 4 5
|| || || || ||

4. Dress shirts cost a dealer \$25 each. He plans to sell them at a profit of 30% of the cost. If his overhead on each sale is \$2, the selling price of each shirt is
   (1) \$32.50
   (2) \$30.50
   (3) \$34.50
   (4) \$7.50
   (5) \$35.10

4. 1 2 3 4 5
|| || || || ||

5. The receipts of the Village Cafeteria for one week were \$4250. The cost of the merchandise sold was \$1560 and the overhead was 34% of the receipts. The profit was
   (1) \$3005
   (2) \$1245
   (3) \$1445
   (4) \$1545
   (5) \$1255

5. 1 2 3 4 5
|| || || || ||

ANSWERS:

1. 4 **2. 2** **3. 4** **4. 3** **5. 2**

We are often interested in finding the percent of increase or decrease.

EXAMPLE: The price of a bus ride was increased from \$1.20 to \$1.35. What was the percent of increase?

\$1.35	new fare
− 1.20	original fare
\$0.15	increase in fare

To find the percent of increase we form the following fraction:

$$\frac{0.15}{1.20} = \frac{\text{increase in fare}}{\text{original fare}}$$

We now change this fraction to a percent, as follows:

$$\frac{0.15}{1.20} = \frac{15}{120} = \frac{3}{24} = \frac{1}{8}$$

$$\begin{array}{r} 0.125 \\ 8\overline{)1.000} \end{array}$$

The percent of increase was 12.5%.

EXAMPLE: During the past ten years the population of a small town decreased from 1250 to 1000. What was the percent of decrease?

$$\begin{array}{rl} 1250 & \text{original population} \\ \underline{-1000} & \text{population after decrease} \\ 250 & \text{actual decrease} \end{array}$$

To find the percent of decrease we form the following fraction:

$$\frac{250}{1250} = \frac{\text{actual decrease}}{\text{original population}}$$

We now change this fraction to a percent as follows:

$$\begin{array}{r} 0.20 \\ 1250\overline{)250.00} \\ \underline{250\ 0} \\ 0 \end{array}$$

The percent of decrease was 20%.

Sometimes we have occasion to work with percents greater than 100%.

EXAMPLE: The profit of the X Corporation this year was 108% of its profit last year. If its profit last year was $250 000, what was its profit this year?

$$\begin{array}{rl} \$250\,000 & \text{profit last year} \\ \underline{\times\ 1.08} & \text{percent this year} \\ 20\,000\ 00 & \\ \underline{250\,000\ 0} & \\ \$270\,000.00 & \end{array}$$

Its profit this year was $270 000.

EXAMPLE: Ms. Graziano bought some stock at $40 per share. Three years later Ms. Graziano sold the stock at $90 per share. What percent of profit did Ms. Graziano make?

$$\begin{array}{rl} \$90 & \text{selling price of stock per share} \\ \underline{-40} & \text{cost of stock per share} \\ \$50 & \text{profit per share} \end{array}$$

$$\frac{50}{40} = \frac{\text{profit per share}}{\text{original cost per share}}$$

$$\begin{array}{r} 1.25 \\ 40\overline{)50.00} \\ \underline{40} \\ 100 \\ \underline{80} \\ 200 \\ \underline{200} \end{array}$$

Ms. Graziano made a profit of 125%.

PRACTICE

Directions: Solve the following problems and blacken the space at the right under the number which corresponds to the one you have selected as the right answer.

1. A couple bought a condominium for \$80 000. Eight years later they sold it for \$128 000. What percent of profit did they make?
(1) 40%
(2) $37\frac{1}{2}$%
(3) 50%
(4) 60%
(5) 75%

1. 1 2 3 4 5

2. During a sale a jacket was reduced from \$120 to \$102. What was the percent of reduction?
(1) 18%
(2) 15%
(3) 50%
(4) 12%
(5) 16%

2. 1 2 3 4 5

3. A dealer sold a clock at 130% of his cost. If the sale price was \$39, how much did the clock cost the dealer?
(1) \$5.70
(2) \$11.70
(3) \$16.50
(4) \$30
(5) \$89.70

3. 1 2 3 4 5

4. Dieter earned \$210 per week at his part-time job. He received a promotion and his earnings rose to \$375 per week. The percent of increase, to the nearest percent, is
(1) 79%
(2) 80%
(3) 78%
(4) 179%
(5) 178%

4. 1 2 3 4 5

5. $137\frac{1}{2}$% of what number is 55?
(1) 50
(2) 39
(3) 40
(4) 45
(5) 42

5. 1 2 3 4 5

ANSWERS:

1. **4** 2. **2** 3. **4** 4. **1** 5. **3**

I. H. Insurance

H-1

The amount of money paid for insurance is called the *premium*. It is usually paid annually. On many types of insurance the premium rate is stated as so many dollars per \$100 or per \$1000 of insurance bought.

There are several types of life insurance sold. The ordinary life policy provides that the person buying the insurance continues to pay a premium for many years to come although dividends may reduce the premium as time goes on. The twenty-payment life policy provides that the person insured will pay the premium over a period of 20 years. The endowment policy provides that a person will pay premiums for a stated number of years. At the end of the period, he or she will receive a lump sum. During the period of the policy, he or she is protected by insurance. The rates are determined by the insurance company and are given to the agent in tabular form. For example, the figures below are a portion of such a table.

Age in Years	Ordinary Life Premium per $1000 of Insurance	Twenty-Payment Life Premium per $1000 of Insurance	Endowment Premium per $1000 of Insurance
20	$17.50	$23.40	$26.50
25	19.75	25.60	29.10
30	22.60	29.80	34.40
35	25.40	34.75	38.50
40	30.20	40.50	43.10

EXAMPLE: At the age of 30, a man buys a twenty-payment life policy for $7500. What is his annual premium?

At age 30, the table indicates that the rate is $29.80 per $1000. In 7500 there are 7.5 thousands. His annual premium is $7.5 \times \$29.80 = \$223.50$.

PRACTICE

Directions: Solve the following problems and blacken the space at the right under the number which corresponds to the one you have selected as the right answer.

1. The annual premium rate on $65 000 worth of an ordinary life insurance policy is $28.24 per $1000. The annual premium is
(1) $183.50
(2) $1735.50
(3) $1835.60
(4) $1835.50
(5) $1845.50

1. 1 2 3 4 5
|| || || || ||

2. A house is insured against fire for 70% of its value. If the house has a value of $48 000 and the premium rate is $2.30 per $1000, the annual premium is
(1) $772.80
(2) $77.28
(3) $75.28
(4) $77.08
(5) $75.08

2. 1 2 3 4 5
|| || || || ||

3. A used car is insured for fire and theft for $5700. If the annual premium rate is $1.04 per $100, the annual premium is
(1) $59.28
(2) $79.80
(3) $58.24
(4) $60.32
(5) $79.28

3. 1 2 3 4 5
|| || || || ||

4. The annual premium rate for a twenty-payment life policy is $36.40 per $1000. The total amount paid in premiums over a twenty-year period for a $6500 policy is
(1) $236.60
(2) $573.20
(3) $4532
(4) $6532
(5) $4732

4. 1 2 3 4 5
|| || || || ||

5. The annual premium on a fire insurance policy for $12 000 is $22.80. The premium rate per $100 is
(1) $1.90
(2) $3.74
(3) $0.19
(4) $37.46
(5) $0.29

5. 1 2 3 4 5
|| || || || ||

ANSWERS:

1. 3 **2.** 2 **3.** 1 **4.** 5 **5.** 3

I. I. Investments

I-1

A common form of investment is the placement of money in a savings account where it draws interest. In order to compute interest, we use the following formula.

Interest = Principal × Rate × Time

which is often written

$$I = P \times R \times T, \text{ or } I = PRT$$

The principal is the amount invested, the annual rate is the percent of the principal given to the investor each year, and the time is stated in years.

EXAMPLE: What is the interest on \$1200 at $5\frac{1}{2}$% for 9 months?

$$\text{In this case, } \begin{cases} I = PRT \\ P = 1200 \\ R = \dfrac{5\frac{1}{2}}{100} \\ T = \dfrac{9}{12} \text{ or } \dfrac{3}{4} \end{cases}$$

$$\text{Therefore,} \quad I = 1200 \times \frac{5\frac{1}{2}}{100} \times \frac{3}{4}$$

Then, if you multiply the numerator and the denominator of

$\dfrac{5\frac{1}{2}}{100}$ by 2, you have $\dfrac{11}{200}$.

$$I = 1200 \times \frac{11}{200} \times \frac{3}{4}$$

$$I = {}^{3}\!\not{6}\,\not{1200} \times \frac{11}{\not{200}_1} \times \frac{3}{\not{4}_2} = \frac{99}{2} \text{ or } 49\tfrac{1}{2}$$

The interest is \$49.50.

If the interest is added to the principal we have the *amount*.

In this case, the amount is \$1200 + \$49.50, or \$1249.50.

Many banks *compound interest* quarterly or every three months. That is, they add the interest to the principal at the end of three months. Then they compute interest for the next three months on an increased principal. This computation is made by a program on their computer or from tables. Interest that is not compounded is called *simple interest*.

A corporation is owned by stockholders who own shares of stock. Many such shares are traded on a stock exchange and are listed in the newspapers with current prices in dollars and fractions of dollars which are either halves, quarters, or eighths. For example,

General Teletype—$40\frac{1}{2}$ (\$40.50)
Modern Electric—$52\frac{1}{4}$ (\$52.25)

Stocks such as these pay dividends based upon the earnings of the company.

A corporation may borrow money by selling *bonds* to the public. Bonds carry a fixed rate of interest and are issued for a certain number of years. At the *maturity date* of the bond the corporation pays back the borrowed amount to the bondholder. Thus, a shareholder is a part owner of a company but a bondholder is a creditor.

EXAMPLE: Mrs. Wojnar owns 45 shares of stock in Company A. The stock pays an annual dividend of $1.60 per share. How much does Mrs. Wojnar receive in dividends per year?

To obtain the amount of dividends we multiply 45 by $1.60.

$$45 \times 1.60 = \$72$$

Mrs. Wojnar receives $72 in dividends.

EXAMPLE: Mr. Glenn owns six $1000 bonds that pay 8½% interest each year. How much does Mr. Glenn receive in interest each year?

This is a problem in computing simple interest. The principal is 6 × 1000 or $6000, the rate is 8½% and the period is 1 year.

$$\text{Interest} = 6000 \times \frac{8\frac{1}{2}}{100} \times 1$$
$$= 6000 \times \frac{17}{200} \times 1$$
$$= \overset{30}{\cancel{6000}} \times \frac{17}{\cancel{200}_1} \times 1 = 510$$

Mr. Glenn receives $510 in interest.

PRACTICE

Directions: Solve the following problems and blacken the space at the right under the number which corresponds to the one you have selected as the right answer.

1. Simple interest on $2400 at 4½% for 3 years is
(1) $288
(2) $32.40
(3) $3240
(4) $324
(5) $314

1. 1 2 3 4 5

2. Mr. Payne borrowed $5200 from a friend for 1 year and 3 months. He agreed to pay 5½% simple interest on the loan. The amount of money that he paid back at the end of the loan period was
(1) $5553.50
(2) $357.50
(3) $5557.50
(4) $4842.50
(5) $5000

2. 1 2 3 4 5

3. Lee Holden kept $3800 in a savings bank for 9 months at 5½% simple interest. The interest on her money was
(1) $156.75
(2) $156.50
(3) $140.75
(4) $157.75
(5) $160.50

3. 1 2 3 4 5

4. Mrs. Turcotte bought 80 shares of X Corporation at 28¾ and sold the shares a year later at 31½. Her profit, before paying commission, was
(1) $22
(2) $220
(3) $140
(4) $180
(5) $242

4. 1 2 3 4 5

5. Mr. Seto owns 120 shares of Y Corporation. The corporation declared a dividend of $1.35 per share. The amount Mr. Seto received in dividends was
(1) $16.20
(2) $121.35
(3) $135
(4) $162
(5) $1620

5. 1 2 3 4 5

6. Mr. Cooper owns 280 shares of Z Corporation. The corporation pays a quarterly dividend of $0.35 per share. The amount Mr. Cooper receives in dividends for the year is
(1) $98
(2) $9.80
(3) $392
(4) $196
(5) $280

6. 1 2 3 4 5

7. Mrs. Ross owns eight $1000 bonds that pay $8\frac{1}{2}$% interest each year. The amount of interest Mrs. Ross receives each year is
(1) $645
(2) $680
(3) $68
(4) $640
(5) $85

7. 1 2 3 4 5

8. Maurice borrows $960 from a friend at $7\frac{1}{2}$% for 3 months. The total amount that he will have to repay is
(1) $1032
(2) $942
(3) $1140
(4) $978
(5) $967.50

8. 1 2 3 4 5

ANSWERS:

1. 4 **2. 3** **3. 1** **4. 2** **5. 4** **6. 3** **7. 2** **8. 4**

I. J. Taxation

J-1

We ordinarily pay many kinds of taxes. In this section we will consider the more common types of taxes.

Prince Edward Island imposes a 10% sales tax on all accommodations (other than camping fees). This tax also applies to meals over $2.00 and is in addition to the 7% GST. In New Brunswick there is an 11% sales tax for hotel and restaurant bills plus the GST of 7%.

A homeowner must pay a *realty tax*. This tax is based on the assessed valuation of the home. The assessed valuation of a home is determined by town or city authorities. Taxes are based on a mill rate (1 mill = $1 per $1000 of assessment). A school tax, also based on the assessed valuation of the home, is part of the total realty tax.

EXAMPLE: Mr. Martin's home is assessed at $43 500. His realty tax is $1 per $1000. What is Mr. Martin's realty tax on his home?

We note that there are 43.5 thousands in $43 500 since $43500 = 43.5 \times 1000$.

The realty tax is $43.5 \times 1 = 43.50$

Tax $43.50

The federal government levies an *income tax*. Every person or business with an income above a certain minimum amount must file a tax return. The tax is based upon taxable income which is obtained after certain allowable deductions are taken off the gross income. For income tax purposes and some province income taxes, employers are required to withhold part of a worker's wages. Employers are also required to deduct a certain amount for social insurance taxes. After all deductions are made, the amount the employee gets is called her *net earnings* or "take-home pay."

EXAMPLE: Marnie's weekly salary is $285. Each week her employer deducts 5.9% of her salary for social insurance. He also deducts $15.70 for income tax. What is Marnie's weekly take-home pay?

5.9% of $285 = $16.82
Total deductions = $16.82 + $15.70 = $32.52
Marnie's take-home pay is $285 – $32.52 = $252.48.

EXAMPLE: A student earns $16 400 per year. In paying her tax, she has allowable deductions of $3750. She pays 17% on her taxable income, and a surtax of 3% on taxable income. A provincial tax of 58% of the federal tax before the surtax also must be paid. How much income tax does she pay?

The taxable income:	$16 400	(Gross income)
	– 3 750	(Allowable deductions)
	$12 650	(Taxable income)
Tax on $12 650 at 17%:	$12 650	
	× 0.17	
	$2150.50	
Surtax on $12 650 at 3%:	$12 650	
	× 0.03	
	$379.50	
Provincial tax on $2150.50 at 58%:	$2150.50	
	× 0.58	
	$1247.29	
Total Tax =	$2150.50	
	379.50	
	+ 1247.29	
	$3777.29	

PRACTICE

Directions: Solve the following problems and blacken the space at the right under the number which corresponds to the one you have selected as the right answer.

1. What is the cost of an item marked $220 plus 8% sales tax?
(1) $203
(2) $237.60
(3) $238
(4) $238.60
(5) $239

1. 1 2 3 4 5

2. On a purchase of a table for $64, Mr. Morton paid a sales tax of $5.12. The rate of sales tax was
(1) 3%
(2) 3½%
(3) 2%
(4) 2½%
(5) 8%

2. 1 2 3 4 5

3. Jan bought a mobile home for $32 000. It was assessed at 80% of her purchase price. If the regional tax is about 5% of the assessed value, Jan's regional tax was
(1) $1280
(2) $1600
(3) $128
(4) $160
(5) $12.80

3. 1 2 3 4 5

4. Carole works part-time and has a gross income of \$26650 per year. Her deductions amount to \$3650. Her federal tax is 17% of her taxable income with a 3% surcharge on her taxable income. Her provincial tax is 58% of her federal tax. Her total tax, rounded to the nearest dollar, is

(1) \$4830
(2) \$7225
(3) \$6868
(4) \$7268
(5) \$4600

4. 1 2 3 4 5
|| || || || ||

5. Yogurt is sold for 60 cents a cup plus 7% GST. If you buy the 6-cup pack, you do not pay GST. How much do you save if you buy the 6-cup pack at 50¢ a cup instead of 6 separate cups?

(1) \$0.75
(2) \$0.80
(3) \$0.85
(4) \$0.10
(5) \$0.61

5. 1 2 3 4 5
|| || || || ||

6. The hotel rate of \$64.20 per day includes the 7% federal tax (GST). What is the rate before tax?

(1) \$60
(2) \$56
(3) \$56.20
(4) \$44.94
(5) \$45

6. 1 2 3 4 5
|| || || || ||

ANSWERS:

1. **2** 2. **5** 3. **1** 4. **3** 5. **2** 6. **1**

I. K. Factors and Prime Numbers

Numbers can be divided into three groups: prime numbers, products, and one. *One* is neither a prime number nor a product. A *prime number* is a number that has only itself and 1 as factors.

For example, 11 is a prime number. Only 11 and 1 can be multiplied together to equal 11.

The small prime numbers are 2, 3, 5, 7, 11, 13, 17, 19, 23, and so on. It is a good idea to memorize the small prime numbers, which makes answering questions a bit faster.

A *product* can be expressed as the product of prime factors.

For example, 12 is a product of the factors 3 and 4 since $3 \times 4 = 12$. 12 is also a product of the factors 3, 2, and 2 since $3 \times 2 \times 2 = 12$.

Since 3, 2, and 2 are also prime numbers, they are called prime factors.

For example, the prime factors of 54 are 2, 3, 3, and 3 since $2 \times 3 \times 3 \times 3 = 54$.

In answering questions about the factors of products, you can save time and energy by memorizing a few simple rules:

1. All even numbers have 2 as a prime factor.
2. All numbers ending in 5 or 0 have 5 as a prime factor.
3. If the digits of a number add to a multiple of 3, the number has 3 as a prime factor. For example, 63. Since $6 + 3 = 9$, and 9 is a multiple of 3, then 63 has 3 as a prime factor; i.e., $63 = 3 \times 21$.
4. Multiples of 11 have a distinctive appearance. For example, $11 \times 11 = 121$ and $11 \times 5 = 55$.

PRACTICE

Directions: Blacken the space at the right under the number which corresponds to the one you have selected as the correct answer.

1. A factor of 15 is
(1) 4
(2) 6
(3) 5
(4) 10
(5) 9

1. 1 2 3 4 5

2. An example of a prime number is
(1) 6
(2) 1
(3) 17
(4) 10
(5) 39

2. 1 2 3 4 5

3. When an odd number and an even number are added, the sum is a(an)
(1) odd number
(2) prime number
(3) even number
(4) factor
(5) coordinate

3. 1 2 3 4 5

4. A factor of every even number is
(1) 3
(2) 4
(3) 6
(4) 2
(5) 7

4. 1 2 3 4 5

5. The next prime number in the series of prime numbers 7, 11, 13, 17 is
(1) 18
(2) 23
(3) 19
(4) 20
(5) 21

5. 1 2 3 4 5

ANSWERS:

1. **3** 2. **3** 3. **1** 4. **4** 5. **3**

I. L. Properties of Operations

L-1
We know that

$$7 + 2 = 9$$
and
$$2 + 7 = 9$$

The order in which we add two numbers does not matter as far as obtaining the correct sum is concerned. This mathematical principle is called the *commutative law of addition*. We state this law as follows:

> COMMUTATIVE LAW OF ADDITION
> If a and b are numbers, then $a + b = b + a$.

We also know that

$$4 \times 6 = 24$$
and
$$6 \times 4 = 24.$$

The order in which we multiply two numbers does not matter as far as obtaining the correct product is concerned. This mathematical principle is called the *commutative law of multiplication*. We state this law as follows:

> COMMUTATIVE LAW OF MULTIPLICATION
> If a and b are numbers, then $a \times b = b \times a$.

If we are required to find the sum of 3 + 6 + 5, we would add 3 + 6 to obtain 9 and then add 5 to the result to obtain 14. We may indicate this process by using parentheses to group 3 and 6 for addition before adding 5 to the result, as follows:

$$(3+6)+5=9+5=14$$

Could we have arranged our grouping differently? If we group 6 and 5 for addition before adding 3 to the result, we have

$$3+(6+5)=3+11=14$$

Thus,

$$(3+6)+5=3+(6+5)$$

This freedom in grouping is called the *associative law of addition*. We state the law as follows:

> ASSOCIATIVE LAW OF ADDITION
> If a, b, and c are numbers, then $(a + b) + c = a + (b + c)$.

If we are required to multiply the numbers $4 \times 5 \times 7$, we would multiply 4×5 to obtain 20 and then multiply the result by 7 to obtain $20 \times 7 = 140$. We may indicate this process by using parentheses to group 4 and 5 for multiplication before multiplying the result by 7, as follows:

$$(4 \times 5) \times 7 = 20 \times 7 = 140$$

Could we have arranged our grouping differently? If we group 5 and 7 for multiplication before multiplying by 4, we have

$$4 \times (5 \times 7) = 4 \times 35 = 140$$

Thus,

$$(4 \times 5) \times 7 = 4 \times (5 \times 7)$$

This freedom in grouping is called the *associative law of multiplication*. We state the law as follows:

> ASSOCIATIVE LAW OF MULTIPLICATION
> If a, b, and c are numbers, then $(a \times b) \times c = a \times (b \times c)$.

EXAMPLE: A sales clerk earns $8.00 per hour. He works 7 hours on Friday and 4 hours on Saturday. How much does he earn on these two days?

We can compute his earnings as follows:

$8 \times 7 = \$56$ for Friday
$8 \times 4 = \underline{\$32}$ for Saturday
Total: $88

We may compute the earnings more simply as follows:

$7 + 4 = 11$ (total hours worked)
$8 \times (7+4) = 8 \times 11 = \$88$ (total earnings)

Thus,

$$8 \times (7+4) = 8 \times 7 + 8 \times 4$$

The principle described above is called the *distributive law of multiplication with respect to addition*. It is usually simply called the *distributive law*. We state the law as follows:

DISTRIBUTIVE LAW
If a, b, and c are numbers, then $a \times (b + c) = a \times b + a \times c$.

PRACTICE

Answer the following questions:

1. In each case, identify the law illustrated.

a. $(8 \times 5) \times 2 = 8 \times (5 \times 2)$ ______
b. $3 \times 7 = 7 \times 3$ ______
c. $(5 + 6) + 9 = 5 + (6 + 9)$ ______
d. $7(6 + 8) = 7 \times 6 + 7 \times 8$ ______
e. $4 + 5 = 5 + 4$ ______
f. $6 \times (3 \times 7) = (6 \times 3) \times 7$ ______
g. $3 \times 5 + 3 \times 7 = 3(5 + 7)$ ______
h. $7 \times 8 = 8 \times 7$ ______
i. $(3 + 8) + 7 = 3 + (8 + 7)$ ______
j. $4 + 7 = 7 + 4$ ______
k. $5(4 + 8) = 5 \times 4 + 5 \times 8$ ______
l. $6 \times 9 = 9 \times 6$ ______
m. $4 \times (6 \times 3) = (4 \times 6) \times 3$ ______
n. $8(2 + 5) = 8 \times 2 + 8 \times 5$ ______
o. $7 + (5 + 4) = (7 + 5) + 4$ ______

2. In each case, indicate whether the statement is true or false.

a. $4 \times 6 = 6 + 4$ ______
b. $7(5 + 2) = 7 \times 5 + 2$ ______
c. $6 \times (8 \times 9) = (6 \times 8) \times 9$ ______
d. $8 + 3 = 3 + 8$ ______
e. $2 + (7 + 9) = (2 + 7) + 9$ ______
f. $(6 \times 8) + 4 = 6 \times 8 + 6 \times 4$ ______
g. $3 \times 8 + 3 \times 7 = 3(8 + 7)$ ______
h. $5 + 9 = 9 \times 5$ ______
i. $6(5 + 3) = 6 \times 5 + 6$ ______
j. $(3 \times 7) \times 5 = 3 \times 7 + 3 \times 5$ ______

3. Check (✓) the expression that is equal to $67(83 + 59)$.

a. $67 \times 83 + 59$ ______
b. $67 + 83 + 67 \times 59$ ______
c. $83 + 67 \times 59$ ______
d. $67 \times 83 + 67 \times 59$ ______
e. $67 \times (83 \times 59)$ ______

4. A motorist drove at an average speed of 70 km/h for 3 hours before lunch. After lunch he continued at 70 km/h for another 5 hours. Check (✓) the expression that gives the number of kilometres covered by the motorist.

a. $70 + 3 \times 5$ _____
b. $70 \times 3 + 5$ _____
c. $3 \times 70 + 5 \times 70$ _____
d. $3 + 5 \times 70$ _____
e. $5 \times 70 + 3$ _____

ANSWERS:

1. a. **Associative Law of Multiplication**
b. **Commutative Law of Multiplication**
c. **Associative Law of Addition**
d. **Distributive Law**
e. **Commutative Law of Addition**
f. **Associative Law of Multiplication**
g. **Distributive Law**
h. **Commutative Law of Multiplication**
i. **Associative Law of Addition**
j. **Commutative Law of Addition**
k. **Distributive Law**
l. **Commutative Law of Multiplication**
m. **Associative Law of Multiplication**
n. **Distributive Law**
o. **Associative Law of Addition**

2. a. **false** f. **false**
b. **false** g. **true**
c. **true** h. **false**
d. **true** i. **false**
e. **true** j. **false**

3. **The correct choice is (d).**

4. **The correct choice is (c).**

II. ALGEBRA

GLOSSARY

BASE a number, letter, or symbol which is to be multiplied by itself. The exponent indicates the number of times this operation is performed.

BINOMIAL an algebraic expression that contains two terms connected by plus or minus signs

CONSTANT a letter or number representing a quantity that stays the same throughout operations on an equation

EQUATION a mathematical statement that two quantities are equal

EXPONENT a number, letter, or symbol indicating the number of times the base is multiplied by itself

EXTREMES in a proportion, the two outside terms

FACTOR in multiplication, one or more of the quantities being multiplied to form a product

FORMULA a fact expressed in algebraic terms

GREATEST COMMON FACTOR the largest number that can be divided evenly into a series of numbers

INEQUALITY a mathematical statement that two quantities are unequal

MEAN of a set of *N* numbers, the average obtained by adding these numbers and dividing by *N*

MEANS in a proportion, the two inside terms

MEDIAN the number in the middle of a set of numbers arranged in order of magnitude

MONOMIAL an algebraic expression that contains one term

POLYNOMIAL an algebraic expression that contains more than one term connected by a plus or minus sign

PROBABILITY the chance of a specific event occurring, usually written as a fraction with the numerator indicating the number of successful outcomes and the denominator indicating the number of possible outcomes

PRODUCT in multiplication, the quantity produced by multiplying two or more factors

PROPORTION a comparison of more than two quantities

QUADRATIC EQUATION an equation consisting of a number of terms one of which has the exponent 2, usually written in the form $ax^2 + bx + c = 0$, where a, b, and c are constants and $c \neq 0$.

RATIO a comparison of two quantities

ROOT OF AN EQUATION a quantity which when substituted for the variable satisfies the equation

TERM a number, variable, or combination of numerals and variables that are connected by symbols of multiplication, division, or both

TRINOMIAL an algebraic expression that contains three terms connected by plus or minus signs

VARIABLE a letter or symbol used to represent a number or quantity

II. A. Fundamentals

A-1

As we have seen earlier, we frequently use letters to represent variables in algebra. For example, in the formula

$$I = P \times R \times T$$

I represents interest, *P* represents principal, *R* represents rate, and *T* represents time.
This is done because it enables us to solve many kinds of problems. That is, *P* may be $5 000 in one problem and $786 in another problem. In indicating multiplication in arithmetic we also use the × sign. For example, 5 × 6. In indicating multiplication in algebra, three methods are used:

1. Use the multiplication symbol. For example, $P \times R$.
2. Use a raised dot. For example, $P \cdot R$.
3. Place the numbers and letters next to each other. For example, $7a$ means $7 \times a$ or $7 \cdot a$; bc means $b \times c$ or $b \cdot c$.

For other operations we use the same symbols as are used in arithmetic. In order to use algebra effectively, you must learn how to translate from ordinary language into symbols and letters.

EXAMPLE: John is *x* years old. How old will he be 7 years from now?
ANSWER: $x + 7$

EXAMPLE: An apple costs *a* cents. What is the cost of 6 apples?
ANSWER: $6 \times a$, or $6 \cdot a$, or $6a$ ($6a$ is preferred)

EXAMPLE: Alice had a mass of *y* kilograms a year ago. Since then she has lost 5 kg. What is her present mass?
ANSWER: $y - 5$

EXAMPLE: Take a number *z*. Increase it by 2. Multiply the result by 6.
ANSWER: $6(z + 2)$. Notice that the number represented by $(z + 2)$ is to be multiplied by 6. The answer might also be written $(z + 2)6$.

PRACTICE

Directions: Solve the following problems and blacken the space at the right under the number which corresponds to the one you have selected as the right answer.

1. A car travels *y* kilometres per hour. The distance, in kilometres, covered by the car in *z* hours is
   (1) $y + z$
   (2) $y - z$
   (3) yz
   (4) $y \div z$
   (5) $z \div y$

   1. 1 2 3 4 5 || || || || ||

2. Bob had $15 and spent *x* dollars. The amount he had left, in dollars, was
   (1) $x - 15$
   (2) $15x$
   (3) $15 \div x$
   (4) $x \div 15$
   (5) $15 - x$

   2. 1 2 3 4 5 || || || || ||

3. If 12 eggs cost *a* cents, the cost of one egg, in cents, is
   (1) $12a$
   (2) $^{12}/_{a}$
   (3) $^{a}/_{12}$
   (4) $12 + a$
   (5) $a - 12$

   3. 1 2 3 4 5 || || || || ||

4. Mr. Barry bought a suit for y dollars. The sales tax rate on the purchase was 7%. The sales tax, in dollars, was

(1) $0.07y$
(2) $7y$
(3) $0.07 + y$
(4) $y \div 7$
(5) $y + 0.07y$

4. 1 2 3 4 5

5. Bill had y dollars. He bought a articles at b dollars each. The number of dollars Bill had left was

(1) $ab - y$
(2) $ab + y$
(3) $y - ab$
(4) $y/_{ab}$
(5) aby

5. 1 2 3 4 5

ANSWERS:

1. 3 2. 5 3. 3 4. 1 5. 3

II. B. Exponents and Evaluations

B-1

There are times when we wish to multiply a number by itself. Of course, if we wish to multiply 7 by itself, we can write 7×7. However, in modern science where we may have occasion to multiply a number by itself many times, it becomes awkward to write such numbers as $7 \times 7 \times 7 \times 7 \times 7 \times 7 \times 7 \times 7 \times 7$. Instead, we use a shortcut and write the product of nine 7's as 7^9. In this case, 9 is known as the *exponent* and 7 is called the *base*.

EXAMPLES: 6^3 means $6 \times 6 \times 6$.
a^5 means $a \times a \times a \times a \times a$.
$3b^4$ means $3 \times b \times b \times b \times b$.

We often wish to find the numerical value of an algebraic expression when we know the numerical value assigned to each letter of the expression.

To find the value of an algebraic expression:

1. Substitute the given values for the letters.
2. In moving from left to right, do all the multiplications and divisions first. Then do all the additions and subtractions.

EXAMPLE: Find the value of $5x + 3y - 7z$ if $x = 6$, $y = 4$, and $z = 1$.

$$\begin{aligned} 5x + 3y - 7z &= (5 \cdot 6) + (3 \cdot 4) - (7 \cdot 1) \\ &= 30 + 12 - 7 \\ &= 42 - 7 = 35 \end{aligned}$$

EXAMPLE: Find the value of $4a^3 - 9c^2 \div 4b$ if $a = 5$, $b = 3$, and $c = 2$.

$$\begin{aligned} 4a^3 - 9c^2 \div 4b &= (4 \cdot 5^3) - (9 \cdot 2^2) \div (4 \cdot 3) \\ &= (4 \cdot 125) - (9 \cdot 4) \div (4 \cdot 3) \\ &= 500 - 36 \div 12 \\ &= 500 - 3 = 497 \end{aligned}$$

EXAMPLE: Find the value of $5(x^3 - 2y^2)$ when $x = 4$ and $y = 3$.

$$\begin{aligned} 5(x^3 - 2y^2) &= 5(4^3 - 2 \cdot 3^2) = 5(64 - 18) \\ &= 5 \cdot 46 \\ &= 230 \end{aligned}$$

PRACTICE

Directions: Solve the following problems and blacken the space at the right under the number which corresponds to the one you have selected as the correct answer.

In the following examples $x = 5$, $y = 4$, $z = 3$, $a = 2$, and $b = 1$.

1. The value of $2x^3 + 3y$ is
(1) 112
(2) 32
(3) 47
(4) 262
(5) 98

1. 1 2 3 4 5

2. The value of $3x + 5a - 7b$ is
(1) 18
(2) 17
(3) 15
(4) 20
(5) 37

2. 1 2 3 4 5

3. The value of $3ab + x^2y$ is
(1) 9
(2) 32
(3) 11
(4) 15
(5) 106

3. 1 2 3 4 5

4. The value of $2x^2 - y^2 + 5ab$ is
(1) 54
(2) 94
(3) 44
(4) 92
(5) 78

4. 1 2 3 4 5

5. The value of $3x^2y^3z$ is
(1) 8100
(2) 14400
(3) 96
(4) 900
(5) 1800

5. 1 2 3 4 5

6. The value of $\frac{y^2}{a^2}$ is
(1) 8
(2) 2
(3) 16
(4) 4
(5) 36

6. 1 2 3 4 5

7. The value of $\frac{a^3}{y} + 2xz$ is
(1) 23
(2) 31
(3) 9
(4) 32
(5) 54

7. 1 2 3 4 5

8. The value of $\frac{4x^3}{5a} + 3y^2 - z^3$ is
(1) 21
(2) 29
(3) 32
(4) 46
(5) 31

8. 1 2 3 4 5

ANSWERS:

1. 4 2. 1 3. 5 4. 3 5. 2 6. 4 7. 4 8. 5

II. C. Operations with Exponents, and Scientific Notation

C-1

Multiplication and Division with Exponents. We know that $a^3 = a \times a \times a$ and $a^4 = a \times a \times a \times a$. The product of a^3 and $a^4 = a \times a \times a \times a \times a \times a \times a = a^7$. Similarly, $a^6 \times a^5 = a^{6+5} = a^{11}$. In general, $a^p \times a^q = a^{p+q}$.

PRACTICE

Find the following products:

1. $c^5 \cdot c^3$
2. $y^2 \times y^5$
3. $a^4 \times a$
4. $b \times b^3$
5. $x^3 \cdot x^7$
6. $z^3 \cdot z^8$

ANSWERS:

1. c^8 2. y^7 3. a^5 4. b^4 5. x^{10} 6. z^{11}

If we divide $a^6 \div a^2$ $(a \neq 0)$ we have $(a \times a \times a \times a \times a \times a) \div (a \times a)$ or

$$\frac{a \times a \times a \times a \times a \times a}{a \times a} = a^4$$

If we divide $y^8 \div y^3$ $(y \neq 0)$ we have

$$\frac{y \times y \times y \times y \times y \times y \times y \times y}{y \times y \times y} = y^5$$

Consider these two division results:

$$\frac{a^6}{a^2} = a^4 \text{ and } \frac{y^8}{y^3} = y^5$$

It is not always convenient to use the method of obtaining these results shown above. For example, the method shown above would not be convenient in the division $x^{47} \div x^{28}$. Our two examples above suggest that we may achieve the division result by retaining the base and subtracting exponents. That is, $a^6 \div a^2 = a^{6-2} = a^4$ and $y^8 \div y^3 = y^{8-3} = y^5$. Also, $x^{47} \div x^{28} = x^{19}$. In general, $x^p \div x^q$ $(x \neq 0) = x^{p-q}$.

PRACTICE

In exercises 1–6, no variable takes on the value 0. Find the following quotients:

1. $x^5 \div x^2$
2. $y^6 \div y^3$
3. $n^5 \div n$
4. $b^{12} \div b^3$
5. $x^6 \div x^2$
6. $z^9 \div z^6$

ANSWERS:

1. x^3 2. y^3 3. n^4 4. b^9 5. x^4 6. z^3

Consider the quotient $y^2 \div y^5$ $(y \neq 0)$. We may write this as $(y \times y) \div (y \times y \times y \times y \times y)$, or

$$\frac{y \times y}{y \times y \times y \times y \times y} = \frac{1}{y^3}$$

If we were to find this quotient by subtracting exponents, we would have

$$y^2 \div y^5 = y^{2-5} = y^{-3}$$

Since the two results represent the same quotient we conclude that

$$\frac{1}{y^3} = y^{-3}$$

Similarly, $z^3 \div z^8 = z^{3-8} = z^{-5}$ and $z^{-5} = \frac{1}{z^5}$

In general, $x^{-p} = \frac{1}{x^p} (x \neq 0)$.

EXAMPLE: Write y^{-6} $(y \neq 0)$ as an equivalent expression with a positive exponent.

$$y^{-6} = \frac{1}{y^6}$$

EXAMPLE: Find the quotient $a^5 \div a^7$ $(a \neq 0)$ and express the result with a positive exponent.

$$a^5 \div a^7 = a^{5-7} = a^{-2}$$

$$a^{-2} = \frac{1}{a^2}$$

PRACTICE

In exercises 1–8, no variable takes on the value 0. Find the following quotients and express the result with a positive exponent:

1. $y^8 \div y^2$
2. $a^{10} \div a^5$
3. $x^7 \div x$
4. $b^9 \div b^6$
5. $x^2 \div x^5$
6. $y^4 \div y^{12}$
7. $10^2 \div 10^5$
8. $a \div a^3$

ANSWERS:

1. y^6 2. a^5 3. x^6 4. b^3 5. $\frac{1}{x^3}$ 6. $\frac{1}{y^8}$ 7. $\frac{1}{10^3}$ 8. $\frac{1}{a^2}$

C-2

Expressing Large Numbers in Scientific Notation. Scientists such as astronomers and space engineers frequently deal with very large numbers in their work. In order for scientists to be able to write these numbers conveniently and to use them effectively, the *scientific notation* system was developed. The definition of scientific notation for writing a number is given below.

DEFINITION: When a number is written in scientific notation it is written as the product of two numbers:

a. a number equal to 1, or greater than 1 but less than 10
b. a power of 10

EXAMPLE: The distance between two planets is 460 000 000 000 kilometres. Write this number in scientific notation.

The first number between 1 and 10 is 4.6. When we go from 4.6 to 460 000 000 000 we move the decimal point 11 places to the right. Each move of the decimal point to the right represents multiplication by 10. For example 46 is 10 times 4.6. Thus, a move of the decimal point 11 places to the right is equivalent to multiplication by 10^{11}.

Therefore, $460\,000\,000\,000 = 4.6 \times 10^{11}$.

EXAMPLE: Express 875 000 000 in scientific notation.

The first number between 1 and 10 is 8.75. When we go from 8.75 to 875 000 000 we move the decimal point 8 places to the right. When we move the decimal point 8 places to the right we multiply 8.75 by 10^8.

Therefore, $875\,000\,000 = 8.75 \times 10^8$

PRACTICE

Write each of the following in ordinary extended form:

1. 6×10^5
2. 3.2×10^7
3. 5.89×10^9
4. 4.75×10^6
5. 3.14×10^3
6. 6.5×10^8

Write each of the following in scientific notation:

7. 8 200 000 000
8. 76 000 000 000
9. 45 800 000 000 000
10. 7 000 000
11. 9 020 000 000 000
12. 86 000 000 000

ANSWERS:

1. **600 000**
2. **32 000 000**
3. **5 890 000 000**
4. **4 750 000**
5. **3140**
6. **650 000 000**
7. **8.2×10^9**
8. **7.6×10^{10}**
9. **4.58×10^{13}**
10. **7×10^6**
11. **9.02×10^{12}**
12. **8.6×10^{10}**

C-3

Expressing Small Numbers in Scientific Notation. Atomic scientists and other physicists have occasion to work with very small numbers. Expressing these small numbers in scientific notation is a great convenience. The definition given above applies to very small numbers as well as to very large numbers.

EXAMPLE: Write 7.9×10^{-4} in ordinary decimal notation.

$$10^{-4} = \frac{1}{10^4}$$

Thus, we are multiplying 7.9 by $\frac{1}{10^4}$ or by $\frac{1}{10\,000}$

Multiplying 7.9 by $\frac{1}{10}$, we have 0.79

Multiplying 7.9 by $\frac{1}{100}$, we have 0.079

Multiplying 7.9 by $\frac{1}{1000}$, we have 0.0079

Multiplying 7.9 by $\frac{1}{10\,000}$, we have 0.00079

We may obtain this result more simply by noting that each multiplication by $\frac{1}{10}$ or 10^{-1} moves the decimal point one place to the left. Thus, when we multiply 7.9 by $\frac{1}{10\,000}$ or 10^{-4}, we move the decimal point four places to the left.

EXAMPLE: The length of a wave or violet light is about 0.000040 cm. Express this number in scientific notation.

The first number is 4.0. When we go from 4.0 to 0.000040, we move the decimal point 5 places to the left. Each move of the decimal point to the left represents division by 10, or multiplication by 10^{-1}. When we move the decimal point 5 places to the left, we multiply 4.0 by 10^{-5}. Therefore, $0.000\,040\text{ cm} = 4.0 \times 10^{-5}\text{ cm}$.

PRACTICE

Write each of the following in ordinary extended form:

1. 3×10^{-4}
2. 8.5×10^{-6}
3. 650×10^{-2}
4. 79×10^{-5}
5. 3.14×10^{-3}
6. 6.78×10^{-1}

Write each of the following in scientific notation.

7. 0.0069
8. 0.000 000 37
9. 0.000 85
10. 0.000 0076
11. 0.000 000 0057
12. 0.000 045

ANSWERS:

1. **0.0003**
2. **0.0000085**
3. **6.5**
4. **0.00079**
5. **0.00314**
6. **0.678**
7. **6.9×10^{-3}**
8. **3.7×10^{-7}**
9. **8.5×10^{-4}**
10. **7.6×10^{-6}**
11. **5.7×10^{-9}**
12. **4.5×10^{-5}**

C-4

The following set of practice exercises is a review of the entire topic of operations with exponents, and scientific notation.

PRACTICE

Find the following products:

1. $x^2 \cdot x^3$
2. $y \cdot y^2$
3. $z^5 \cdot z^2$
4. $b^4 \cdot b^4$

In exercises 5–8, no variable takes on the value zero. Express the result with positive exponents. Find the following quotients:

5. $x^6 \div x^2$
6. $y^3 \div y$
7. $z^2 \div z^8$
8. $a \div a^4$

9. The distance from the earth to the sun is approximately 149 000 000 km. Write this number in scientific notation.
10. If the federal government deficit amounts to $43 000 000 000, how would this number be written in scientific notation?
11. Express 2.4×10^5 in ordinary extended form.
12. The wave length of red light is approximately 0.0065 metre. Express this number in scientific notation.
13. Express 0.000032 in scientific notation.
14. The radius of an electron is approximately 0.000 000 000 05 metre. Express this number in scientific notation.
15. Express 2.4×10^{-8} in decimal form.

Express each of the following numbers in scientific notation:

16. 640 000
17. 59 000 000 000
18. 0.000 37
19. 0.000 000 000 165
20. 780 000 000 000
21. 0.000 000 000 34

ANSWERS:

1. x^5
2. y^3
3. z^7
4. b^8
5. x^4
6. y^2
7. $\frac{1}{z^6}$
8. $\frac{1}{a^3}$
9. 1.49×10^7
10. 43×10^{11}
11. **240 000**
12. 6.5×10^{-3}
13. 3.2×10^{-5}
14. 5×10^{-11}
15. **0.000 000 024**
16. 6.4×10^5
17. 5.9×10^{10}
18. 3.7×10^{-4}
19. 1.65×10^{-10}
20. 7.8×10^{11}
21. 3.4×10^{-10}

II. D. Formulae

D-1

A mathematics formula is a statement expressed in algebraic symbols.

EXAMPLE: You are driving to a relative's home in the United States. From the border the distance is 328 miles. How many kilometres is it?

We use the formula

$$m = 1.6k$$

In this case, $m = 328$

$$k = 1.6 \times 328$$
$$= 524.8\,\text{km}$$

PRACTICE

Directions: Solve the following problems and blacken the space at the right under the number which corresponds to the one you have selected as the right answer.

1. In the formula $V = \ell wh$, find V when $\ell = 2$, $w = 3$, and $h = 4$.

(1) 9
(2) 10
(3) 12
(4) 24
(5) 36

1. 1 2 3 4 5

2. The formula $A = \dfrac{a+b+c}{3}$ is used to find the average (A) of three numbers a, b, and c. The average of 95, 119, and 104 is

(1) 108
(2) 106
(3) 160
(4) $104\frac{2}{3}$
(5) 110

2. 1 2 3 4 5

3. The formula $C = 80 + 15(n - 4)$ is used to find the cost, C, of a taxi ride where n represents the number of 0.25 km of the ride. The cost of a taxi ride of 2.75 km is

(1) \$0.95
(2) \$3
(3) \$1.65
(4) \$1.85
(5) \$2

3. 1 2 3 4 5

4. The formula $C = 120m + 56h$ is used to find the daily labour cost, in dollars, of a job in carpentry. The letter m represents the number of master carpenters; h represents the number of helpers. (Note that a master carpenter earns \$120 per day and a helper earns \$56 per day.) On a certain job, 6 master carpenters are used and 4 helpers are used. The daily labour cost in dollars is

(1) \$846
(2) \$950
(3) \$650
(4) \$1064
(5) \$944

4. 1 2 3 4 5

5. The formula for the relationship between the length (L) and width (W) of a certain flag is $L = 1.8W$. A flag has a width of 2 m. Its length in metres is

(1) 2.3
(2) 3.6
(3) 90
(4) 1.3
(5) 8

5. 1 2 3 4 5

6. In the formula $V = \pi r^2 h$, what is the volume (V) when $r = 7$ and $h = 2$ (use $\pi = 22/7$)?

(1) 34
(2) 44
(3) 144
(4) 154
(5) 308

6. 1 2 3 4 5

ANSWERS:

1. 4 **2. 2** **3. 4** **4. 5** **5. 2** **6. 5**

II. E. Solving Equations

Review "How to Read and Solve Verbal Problems" on page 489.

E-1

The ability to solve equations is important because it enables us to solve many different types of problems. In this section, you will learn how to solve some of the simpler kinds of equations. In a later section you will apply these skills in problems solving.

> An equation states that two quantities are equal.

Consider the equation

$$3x + 2 = 20$$

This tells us that $3x + 2$ and 20 name the same number. If this is so, then x must represent the number 6 since

$$3 \times 6 + 2 = 20$$

And 6 is the only number which will replace x and make $3x + 2$ equal 20. The number 6, which makes the statement $3x + 2 = 20$ true, is called the *root of the equation* and is said to satisfy the equation, or to *balance* the equation.

PRACTICE

Directions: Solve the following problems and blacken the space at the right under the number which corresponds to the one you have selected as the correct answer.

In each case, select the root of the equation.

1. $x + 2 = 9$
(1) 5
(2) 9
(3) 7
(4) 3
(5) 10

1. 1 2 3 4 5

2. $x - 3 = 5$
(1) 5
(2) 3
(3) 2
(4) 10
(5) 8

2. 1 2 3 4 5

3. $2x = 10$
(1) 8
(2) 5
(3) 20
(4) $\frac{1}{5}$
(5) 9

3. 1 2 3 4 5

4. $\frac{x}{3} = 4$
(1) 12
(2) $\frac{4}{3}$
(3) $\frac{3}{4}$
(4) 1
(5) 6

4. 1 2 3 4 5

5. $2x + 1 = 7$
(1) 4
(2) $3\frac{1}{2}$
(3) 5
(4) 3
(5) 6

5. 1 2 3 4 5

6. $2x - 1 = 9$

(1) 10
(2) 8
(3) 5
(4) 4
(5) 3

6. 1 2 3 4 5
|| || || || ||

7. $\frac{x}{2} + 3 = 7$

(1) 4
(2) 8
(3) $1\frac{1}{2}$
(4) $2\frac{1}{2}$
(5) 20

7. 1 2 3 4 5
|| || || || ||

8. $\frac{x}{3} - 1 = 5$

(1) 18
(2) 12
(3) 2
(4) 6
(5) 15

8. 1 2 3 4 5
|| || || || ||

9. $\frac{2x}{5} + 1 = 9$

(1) 8
(2) 50
(3) 20
(4) 6
(5) 4

9. 1 2 3 4 5
|| || || || ||

10. $\frac{3x}{4} - 2 = 1$

(1) 5
(2) 6
(3) 12
(4) 4
(5) 9

10. 1 2 3 4 5
|| || || || ||

11. $2x + 3 = 10$

(1) 4
(2) $6\frac{1}{2}$
(3) $3\frac{1}{2}$
(4) $7\frac{1}{2}$
(5) 5

11. 1 2 3 4 5
|| || || || ||

12. $3x - 4 = 6$

(1) $3\frac{1}{3}$
(2) $\frac{2}{3}$
(3) 2
(4) $3\frac{1}{2}$
(5) 7

12. 1 2 3 4 5
|| || || || ||

ANSWERS:

1. **3** 2. **5** 3. **2** 4. **1** 5. **4** 6. **3** 7. **2** 8. **1** 9. **3** 10. **4** 11. **3** 12. **1**

We will now study systematic methods of finding the root of an equation.

Consider the equation $x + 2 = 5$. This tells us that a certain number added to 2 will give us the result of 5. We can see that $x = 3$. Now, how can we get from

$$x + 2 = 5$$

to $x = 3$?

Remember, we must perform the same operation with the same numbers on each side of the equation. To get from $x + 2$ to x, we need only to subtract 2 from $x + 2$. Thus, $x + 2 - 2 = x$. Since $x + 2$ and 5 name the same number, we may subtract the same number from $x + 2$ and from 5 and obtain equal results:

$$x + 2 - 2 = 5 - 2$$

or $x = 3$

Consider the equation $x - 1 = 5$. In order to obtain x on the left side of the equation, we add 1 to $x - 1$. Since $x - 1$ and 5 name the same number, we may add 1 to both $x - 1$ and 5 to obtain equal results:

$$x - 1 + 1 = 5 + 1$$
$$\text{or } x = 6$$

Consider the equation $2x = 12$. In order to obtain x on the left side of the equation, we must divide $2x$ (twice x) by 2. Since $2x$ and 12 name the same number, we divide both $2x$ and 12 by 2 to obtain equal results:

$$2x = 12$$
$$\frac{2x}{2} = \frac{12}{2}$$
$$1x, \text{ or } x = 6$$

Consider the equation $y/3 = 4$. In order to obtain y on the left side of the equation, we must multiply $y/3$, or $\frac{1}{3}$ of y, by 3. Since $y/3$ and 4 name the same number, we multiply both $y/3$ and 4 to obtain equal results:

$$\frac{y}{3} = 4$$
$$3 \times \frac{y}{3} = 3 \times 4$$
$$y = 12$$

The above procedures may be more easily remembered if we note the following.

Method of Finding the Root of an Equation

1. Subtract when there is a sum. For example, in $x + 2 = 5$, $x + 2 - 2 = 5 - 2$.
2. Add when there is a difference. For example, in $x - 1 = 5$, $x - 1 + 1 = 5 + 1$.
3. Divide when there is a product. For example, in $2x = 12$, $\frac{2x}{2} = \frac{12}{2}$.
4. Multiply when there is a quotient. For example, in $\frac{y}{3} = 4$, $3\left(\frac{y}{3}\right) = 3 \times 4$.

PRACTICE

Solve the following equations:

1. $x + 1 = 3$, $x =$ ___
2. $x - 2 = 4$, $x =$ ___
3. $3x = 12$, $x =$ ___
4. $x/2 = 5$, $x =$ ___
5. $x + 5 = 7$, $x =$ ___
6. $x - 3 = 4$, $x =$ ___
7. $5x = 10$, $x =$ ___
8. $x/4 = 2$, $x =$ ___
9. $x + 2 = 9$, $x =$ ___
10. $5x = 15$, $x =$ ___
11. $x - 2 = 9$, $x =$ ___
12. $x + 4 = 7$, $x =$ ___
13. $x/5 = 2$, $x =$ ___
14. $3x = 18$, $x =$ ___
15. $x + 9 = 11$, $x =$ ___
16. $x - 1 = 5$, $x =$ ___
17. $3x = 21$, $x =$ ___
18. $x + 4 = 7$, $x =$ ___
19. $x/4 = 3$, $x =$ ___
20. $x - 5 = 11$, $x =$ ___

ANSWERS:

1. **2**
2. **6**
3. **4**
4. **10**
5. **2**
6. **7**
7. **2**
8. **8**
9. **7**
10. **3**
11. **11**
12. **3**
13. **10**
14. **6**
15. **2**
16. **6**
17. **7**
18. **3**
19. **12**
20. **16**

E-2

Solving More Difficult Equations. In order to solve interesting problems, it is necessary to be able to solve more difficult equations.

EXAMPLE: Solve the equation $5x + 2x = 28$.

Since $5x + 2x = 7x$, we have

$$7x = 28$$
$$x = 28/7$$
$$x = 4$$

EXAMPLE: Solve the equation $\frac{2}{3}x = 16$.

In order to obtain x on the left side, we must multiply $\frac{2}{3}x$ by $\frac{3}{2}$. Since $\frac{2}{3}x$ and 16 name the same number, we multiply both $\frac{2}{3}x$ and 16 to obtain equal results.

$$\frac{\not{3}}{\not{2}} \cdot \frac{\not{2}}{\not{3}} x = \frac{3}{2} \cdot 16$$
$$x = 24$$

EXAMPLE: Solve the equation $2x + 3 = 15$.

$$2x + 3 = 15$$
$$2x + 3 - 3 = 15 - 3$$
$$2x = 12$$
$$\frac{2x}{2} = \frac{12}{2}$$
$$x = 6$$

EXAMPLE: Solve the equation $\frac{3}{5}x - 1 = 8$.

$$\frac{3}{5}x - 1 = 8$$
$$\frac{3}{5}x - 1 + 1 = 8 + 1$$
$$\frac{3}{5}x = 9$$
$$\frac{\not{5}}{\not{3}} \cdot \frac{\not{3}}{\not{5}} x = \frac{5}{3} \cdot 9$$
$$x = 15$$

PRACTICE

Solve the following equations:

1. $2x + 3x = 40$, $x =$ ____
2. $\frac{2}{3}x = 12$, $x =$ ____
3. $4x - 1 = 27$, $x =$ ____
4. $x/5 + 4 = 6$, $x =$ ____
5. $3x - 5 = 16$, $x =$ ____
6. $3x + 7 = 37$, $x =$ ____
7. $4x - 2 = 22$, $x =$ ____
8. $x/2 - 3 = 5$, $x =$ ____
9. $2x + x + 5 = 17$, $x =$ ____
10. $\frac{4}{5}x + 2 = 30$, $x =$ ____
11. $\frac{2}{3}x + 5 = 7$, $x =$ ____
12. $5x - 2x + 4 = 31$, $x =$ ____
13. $x/7 + 5 = 6$, $x =$ ____
14. $3x + 2x + 1 = 21$, $x =$ ____
15. $2x + x - 3 = 12$, $x =$ ____
16. $\frac{3}{4}x - 7 = 8$, $x =$ ____

ANSWERS:

1. **8**
2. **18**
3. **7**
4. **10**
5. **7**
6. **10**
7. **6**
8. **16**
9. **4**
10. **35**
11. **3**
12. **9**
13. **7**
14. **4**
15. **5**
16. **20**

II. F. Solving Problems

We may use equations to solve problems such as the following.

EXAMPLE: A plumber must cut a pipe 50 cm long into two pieces so that one piece will be 12 cm longer than the other piece. Find the length of each piece.

Let x = the length of one piece in cm
And $x + 12$ = the length of the other piece in cm
Since the sum of the two pieces is 50 cm, we have

$$x + x + 12 = 50$$
$$2x + 12 = 50$$
$$2x + 12 - 12 = 50 - 12$$
$$2x = 38$$
$$\frac{2x}{2} = \frac{38}{2}$$
$$x = 19$$

One piece is 19 cm long and the other piece is 31 cm long.

EXAMPLE: Divide an estate of $46 000 among three sons so that the second son receives $6000 more than the youngest, and the eldest son receives three times as much as the youngest.

Let x = amount the youngest son receives in dollars
And $x + 6000$ = amount the second son receives in dollars
And $3x$ = amount the eldest son receives in dollars

$$x + x + 6000 + 3x = 46\,000$$
$$5x + 6000 = 46\,000$$
$$5x + 6000 - 6000 = 46\,000 - 6000$$
$$5x = 40\,000$$
$$\frac{5x}{5} = \frac{40000}{5}$$
$$x = 8000$$

The youngest son gets $8000.
The second son gets $8000 + $6000 = $14 000.
The eldest son gets 3 × $8000 = $24 000.

EXAMPLE: Eighteen coins, consisting of nickels and dimes, have a total value of $1.25. How many dimes are there?

Let x = the number of dimes
And $18 - x$ = the number of nickels
$10x$ = the value of the dimes in cents
$5(18 - x)$ = the value of the nickels in cents

$$10x + 5(18 - x) = 125$$
$$10x + 90 - 5x = 125$$
$$5x + 90 = 125$$
$$5x + 90 - 90 = 125 - 90$$
$$\frac{5x}{5x} = \frac{35}{35}$$
$$x = 7$$

There are 7 dimes.

EXAMPLE: At a track meet the total score for each event was 20 points. First place counted twice as much as second place, and third place counted 4 points less than second place. How many points did first place count?

Let x = the number of points for second place
Then $2x$ = the number of points for first place
And $x - 4$ = the number of points for third place

$$x + 2x + x - 4 = 20$$
$$4x - 4 = 20$$
$$4x - 4 + 4 = 20 + 4$$
$$4x = 24$$
$$x = 6$$
$2x = 12$, the number of points for first place

EXAMPLE: An investment of \$12 500, part at 8% and part at 7%, earns a yearly income of \$955. Find the amount invested at each rate in dollars.

Let x = the amount invested at 8% in dollars
And $12\,500 - x$ = the amount invested at 7% in dollars
$0.08x$ = the income on the 8% investment in dollars
$0.07(12\,500 - x)$ = the income on the 7% investment in dollars

$$0.08x + 0.07(12500 - x) = 955$$
$$0.08x + 875 - 0.07x = 955$$
$$0.01x + 875 = 955$$
$$0.01x + 875 - 875 = 955 - 875$$
$$0.01x = 80$$

Multiply both sides of the equation by 100 to obtain
$$x = 8000$$

\$8000 was invested at 8%.
\$12 500 − \$8000 = \$4500 was invested at 7%.

EXAMPLE: Two cars start at the same time from two cities which are 480 km apart and travel toward each other. One car averages 35 km/h, and the other car averages 45 km/h. In how many hours will the two cars meet?

Let x = the number of hours it takes the two cars to meet.

In problems involving motion, it is convenient to collect our information in a box as shown on the next page, with the formula Rate × Time = Distance.

RATE × TIME = DISTANCE

FIRST CAR	35	x	$35x$
SECOND CAR	45	x	$45x$

Since the sum of the two distances covered is 480 km, we have

$$35x + 45x = 480$$
$$80x = 480$$
$$\frac{80x}{80} = \frac{480}{80}$$
$$x = 6$$

The cars will meet in 6 hours.

PRACTICE

Solve the following problems:

1. Two partners in a business earn $60000 one year. If the senior partner's share is 3 times that of the junior partner, what is the junior partner's share in dollars? ________
2. A wooden beam is 58 m long. A carpenter must cut the beam so that the longer part is 8 m longer than the shorter part. How long is the shorter part in m? ________
3. A certain kind of concrete contains five times as much gravel as cement. How many m^3 of each of these materials will there be in 426 m^3 of the concrete? ________
4. The length of a field is 3 times its width. If the perimeter (distance around the field) of the field is 312 m, what is the width of the field in m? ________
5. A master carpenter earns $5 more per hour than his helper. Together they earn $119 for a 7-hour job. How much does the helper earn per hour in dollars? ________
6. A boy has $3.75 in nickels and dimes. If he has 6 more dimes than nickels, how many dimes does he have? ________
7. Mr. Dale asked his son to deposit $495 in the bank. There were exactly 70 bills, consisting of 10-dollar bills and 5-dollar bills. Find the number of 10-dollar bills he had to deposit. ________
8. The perimeter of a triangle is 27 cm. One side is 3 cm longer than the shortest side, and the longest side is twice the length of the shortest side. What is the length of the shorter side in cm? ________
9. The sum of two numbers is 50. If the larger one is 5 more than twice the smaller number, what is the smaller number? ________
10. Frank had ¼ as much money as Angel. Together they had $125. How much money, in dollars, did Frank have? ________
11. Mr. Chu invests $20000, part at 5% and the rest at 4%. If he obtains an annual income of $920, how much does he invest, in dollars, at each rate? ________
12. The Rivera family has an annual income of $48000. Of this, $45000 consists of salaries and the balance is obtained by an investment that pays 8% annually. How much, in dollars, is invested at 8%? ________
13. At a sale, some radios were sold for $50 each and the rest for $35 each. If 175 radios were sold and the receipts were $7250, how many $50 radios were sold? ________

14. Mr. Carter invested a sum of money at 4%. He invested a second sum, $400 more than the first sum, at 6%. If the total annual income was $184, how much did he invest, in dollars, at each rate? ________

15. On a fishing trip José caught 8 more fish than Joe. Together they caught 32 fish. Which of the following equations may be used to find how many fish José caught?
(1) $x + 8x = 32$ (2) $x + 32 = 8x$ (3) $x + x + 8 = 32$
(4) $8x - x = 32$ (5) $x + 32 + x = 8$ ________

16. A sofa was marked for sale at $270. This was a discount of 25% on the original sale price. What was the original sale price in dollars? ________

17. The sum of the ages of a father and son is 62. If the father is 11 years more than twice the age of the son, how old is the son? ________

18. A girl has $4.35 in nickels and dimes. If she has 12 more dimes than nickels, how many nickels does she have? ________

19. The perimeter of a rectangular field is 204 m. If the length is 3 m less than 4 times the width, what is the width of the field in m? ________

20. A college football squad of 50 payers consisted of seniors, juniors, and sophomores. If there were twice as many seniors as sophomores, and 14 more juniors than sophomores, which of the following equations may be used to find how many sophomores were on the squad?
(1) $x + 2x + 14 = 50$ (2) $x + 2x - 14 = 50$ (3) $x + 2x + 14x = 50$
(4) $x + 2x + x + 14 = 50$ (5) $x + x + 14 + x = 50$ ________

21. Two cars start at the same time to travel toward each other from points 440 km apart. If the first car averages 84 km/h and the second car averages 92 km/h per hour, in how many hours will they meet? ________

22. Two trains start at the same time from the same place and travel in opposite directions. The first train averages 78 km/h and the second train averages 86 km/h. In how many hours are the trains 574 km apart? ________

23. Two trains are 800 km apart. They start at 9:00 A.M. traveling toward each other. One train travels at an average rate of 90 km/h and the other train travels at an average rate of 110 km/h. At what time do the trains meet? ________

24. Two motorboats start at the same time from the same place and travel in opposite directions. If their rates are 24 km/h and 32 km/h respectively, in how many hours will they be 140 km apart? ________

ANSWERS:

1. **$15000**
2. **25 m**
3. **71 m³ of cement**
   355 m³ of gravel
4. **39 m**
5. **$6.00**
6. **27**
7. **29**
8. **6 cm**
9. **15**
10. **25**
11. **$12000 at 5%**
    $8000 at 4%
12. **$37500**
13. **75**
14. **$1600 at 4%**
    $2000 at 6%
15. **(3)**
16. **$360**
17. **17**
18. **21**
19. **21 m**
20. **(4)**
21. **2.5 hours**
22. **3.5 hours**
23. **1 P.M.**
24. **2.5 hours**

II. G. Solving Inequalities

G-1

Recall that the symbol > means *is greater than* and that the symbol < means *is less than*. For example, $9 > 5$ and $3 < 8$.

An inequality is a statement in which two quantities are unequal. Consider the inequality

$$3x + 1 > 7$$

This tells us that $3x + 1$ names a number that is greater than 7. If this is so, then x must represent a number that is greater than 2. If $x = 2$, we have $3 \cdot 2 + 1 = 7$. When $x > 2$, $3x + 1 > 7$. For example, when $x = 5$, $3x + 1 = 16$. Thus, the solution of the inequality $3x + 1 > 7$ is $x > 2$. Note that the inequality $3x + 1 > 7$ has an infinite number of solutions. For example, some solutions are 2.1, 4, $5\frac{1}{2}$, 7, and 8.67 since the replacement of x by any of these numbers will make the inequality true.

The symbol $\geqslant$ means is greater than or equal to, and the symbol $\leqslant$ means is less than or equal to.

EXAMPLE: If x is a positive integer and $x \geqslant 5$, then the roots of this equation are 5, 6, 7 . . .

EXAMPLE: If x is a positive integer and $x \leqslant 3$, then the roots of this equation are 1, 2, 3 . . .

PRACTICE

Directions: In each case, select the number which is a solution of the given inequality.

1. $2x + 3 > 11$
(1) 4
(2) 1
(3) $2\frac{1}{2}$
(4) 5
(5) 3

1. 1 2 3 4 5 || || || || ||

2. $3x - 1 > 5$
(1) 1
(2) 2
(3) 6
(4) $1\frac{1}{2}$
(5) 0

2. 1 2 3 4 5 || || || || ||

3. $x + 2 < 7$
(1) 6
(2) 8
(3) 5
(4) 3
(5) 10

3. 1 2 3 4 5 || || || || ||

4. $2x - 3 < 5$
(1) 2
(2) 5
(3) 7
(4) 6
(5) 4

4. 1 2 3 4 5 || || || || ||

5. $5x + 2 > 17$
(1) 1
(2) 3
(3) 4
(4) 2
(5) 0

5. 1 2 3 4 5 || || || || ||

6. $4x - 3 < 9$
(1) 5
(2) 2
(3) 4
(4) 7
(5) 9

6. 1 2 3 4 5 || || || || ||

7. $x + 2 \geqslant 5$
(1) 2
(2) 0
(3) 2.5
(4) 3
(5) 1

7. 1 2 3 4 5 || || || || ||

8. $3x - 2 \leqslant 10$

(1) 2
(2) 5
(3) 7
(4) 6.5
(5) 8

8. 1 2 3 4 5
|| || || || ||

9. $2x + 5 \geqslant 15$

(1) 3
(2) 0
(3) 6
(4) 4
(5) 2

9. 1 2 3 4 5
|| || || || ||

10. $4x + 1 \leqslant 9$

(1) 6
(2) 3
(3) 4
(4) 8
(5) 2

10. 1 2 3 4 5
|| || || || ||

ANSWERS:

1. **4** 2. **3** 3. **4** 4. **1** 5. **3** 6. **2** 7. **4** 8. **1** 9. **3** 10. **5**

We will now study systematic methods of solving inequalities.

Consider the inequality $x + 3 > 7$. This tells us that when certain numbers are added to 3, the result is greater than 7. We can see that x must be greater than 4, or $x > 4$. Now, how can we get from

$$x + 3 > 7$$
$$\text{to } x > 4?$$

To get from $x + 3$ to x we need only to subtract 3 from $x + 3$. Since subtracting the same quantity from both members of an inequality does not change the sense of the inequality, we may subtract 3 from 7 to get the result

$$x + 3 - 3 > 7 - 3$$
$$x > 4$$

Consider the inequality $x - 2 < 4$. In order to obtain x on the left side, we add 2 to $x - 2$. Since adding the same quantity to both members of an inequality does not change the sense of the inequality, we may add 2 to 4 to obtain the result

$$x - 2 + 2 < 4 + 2$$
$$x < 6$$

Consider the inequality $2x < 10$. In order to obtain x on the left side of the inequality, we must divide $2x$ by 2. Since dividing both members of an inequality by a positive number does not change the sense of the inequality, we may divide 10 by 2 to obtain the result

$$\frac{2x}{2} < \frac{10}{2}$$
$$x < 5$$

Consider the inequality $\frac{y}{3} > 2$. In order to obtain y on the left side of the inequality, we must multiply $\frac{y}{3}$ by 3. Since multiplying both members of an inequality by a positive number does not change the sense of the inequality, we may multiply 2 by 3 to obtain the result.

$$3 \times \frac{y}{3} > 3 \times 2$$
$$y > 6$$

EXAMPLE: Solve the inequality $x + 5 > 7$.

$$x + 5 > 7$$
$$x + 5 - 5 > 7 - 5$$
$$x > 2$$

EXAMPLE: Solve the inequality $y - 1 < 4$.

$$y - 1 < 4$$
$$y - 1 + 1 < 4 + 1$$
$$y < 5$$

EXAMPLE: Solve the inequality $3x < 18$.

$$3x < 18$$
$$\frac{3x}{3} < \frac{18}{3}$$
$$x < 6$$

EXAMPLE: Solve the inequality $\frac{y}{4} > 2$.

$$\frac{y}{4} > 2$$
$$4 + \frac{y}{4} > 4 \times 2$$
$$y > 8$$

PRACTICE

Solve the following inequalities:

1. $x + 2 > 5$, $x >$ ________
2. $x - 3 > 1$, $x >$ ________
3. $2y < 8$, $y <$ ________
4. $y/2 > 6$, $y >$ ________
5. $y - 3 < 2$, $y <$ ________
6. $y/4 > 3$, $y >$ ________
7. $x - 5 > 2$, $x >$ ________
8. $2y < 12$, $y <$ ________
9. $y + 1 < 10$, $y <$ ________
10. $x - 3 < 4$, $x <$ ________

ANSWERS:

1. $x > 3$
2. $x > 4$
3. $y < 4$
4. $y > 12$
5. $y < 5$
6. $y > 12$
7. $x > 7$
8. $y < 6$
9. $y < 9$
10. $x < 7$

G-2

Solving More Difficult Inequalities.

EXAMPLE: Solve the inequality $2y + 3 > 11$.

$$2y + 3 - 3 > 11 - 3$$
$$2y > 8$$
$$\frac{2y}{2} > \frac{8}{2}$$
$$y > 4$$

EXAMPLE: Solve the inequality $\frac{y}{4} - 1 < 5.$

$$\frac{y}{4} - 1 < 5$$

$$\frac{y}{4} - 1 + 1 < 5 + 1$$

$$\frac{y}{4} < 6$$

$$4 \times \frac{y}{4} < 4 \times 6$$

$$y < 24$$

PRACTICE

Solve the following inequalities:

1. $2x + 1 > 7$, $x >$ _______
2. $3y - 2 < 4$, $y <$ _______
3. $4x - 7 > 5$, $x >$ _______
4. $y/2 + 1 < 5$, $y <$ _______
5. $y/3 - 4 > 1$, $y >$ _______
6. $5y + 1 < 6$, $y <$ _______
7. $7y - 2 > 19$, $y >$ _______
8. $y/4 + 3 > 5$, $y >$ _______
9. $2x + 3 \geq 11$, $x \geq$ _______
10. $3y - 2 \geq 16$, $y \geq$ _______
11. $2x + 1 \leq 7$, $x \leq$ _______
12. $4x - 5 \leq 15$, $x \leq$ _______

ANSWERS:

1. $x > 3$
2. $y < 2$
3. $x > 3$
4. $y < 8$
5. $y > 15$
6. $y < 1$
7. $y > 3$
8. $y > 8$
9. $x \geq 4$
10. $y \geq 6$
11. $x \leq 3$
12. $x \leq 5$

II. H. Ratio and Proportion

H-1

We may compare two numbers by subtraction or by division. For example, Mr. Carson earns $48 per day and Mr. Burns earns $36 per day. We may say that Mr. Carson earns $12 per day more than Mr. Burns. Or, we may say that the ratio of Mr. Carson's earnings per day to Mr. Burns' earnings per day is $^{48}/_{36}$. We may reduce $^{48}/_{36}$ to $^{4}/_{3}$ which indicates that Mr. Carson earns $1\frac{1}{3}$ times as much per day as Mr. Burns.

The comparison of the two pay rates may be written as $^{48}/_{36}$ or as 48:36. In general, the ratio of a number *a* to a number *b* (*b* cannot be 0) is *a/b*, or *a*:*b*.

EXAMPLE: At a party there are 12 men and 8 women. What is the ratio of men to women?
The ratio is $^{12}/_{8}$ or 12:8. In simplest form, this is $^{3}/_{2}$, or 3:2.

EXAMPLE: At the same party, what is the ratio of women to men?
The ratio is $^{8}/_{12}$ or 8:12. In simplest form, this is $^{2}/_{3}$, or 2:3.

EXAMPLE: At the same party, what is the ratio of men to the number of people at the party?
The ratio is $^{12}/_{20}$ or 12:20. In simplest form, this is $^{3}/_{5}$, or 3:5.

EXAMPLE:

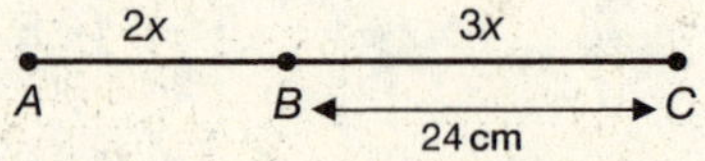

If $AB:BC = 2:3$ and if $BC = 24$ cm, what is the length of AB?

Let $AB = 2x$
And $BC = 3x$

We know that $3x = 24$

$$\tfrac{1}{3}(3x) = \tfrac{1}{3}(24)$$
$$x = 8$$

Since $x = 8$, $2x$ (which is AB) $= 2 \cdot 8 = 16$
Therefore, $AB = 16$ cm

Consider the following problem:

A baseball team wins 15 games out of 30 games played. If the team continues to win at the same rate, how many games will it win out of 40 games played?

Let n = number of games team will win in 40 games played.

The ratio of games won to games already played is $^{15}/_{30}$. Since the ratio of games won to games played is to remain the same, we may write this ratio as $n/40$. These ratios may also be written as $15:30$ and $n:40$.

We may now write the equation $^{15}/_{30} = n/40$. Such an equation which tells us that one ratio is equal to another ratio is called a *proportion*. Of course, in this case we know that $n = 20$, since the team wins $^1/_2$ of the games it plays.

Proportions have a very useful property which we will investigate. Consider the proportion

$$\tfrac{1}{3} = \tfrac{2}{6} \text{ or } 1:3 = 2:6$$

The two inside terms (3 and 2) are called the *means* of the proportion, and the two outside terms (1 and 6) are called the *extremes* of the proportion. Notice that if we multiply the two means, we obtain $3 \times 2 = 6$. Also, if we multiply the two extremes, we obtain $1 \times 6 = 6$. This illustrates the following property of proportions:

In a proportion, the product of the means is equal to the product of the extremes.

This property is very useful in solving problems.

EXAMPLE: The ratio of alcohol to water in a certain type of antifreeze is 3:4. If a tank contains 24 L of alcohol, how many litres of water must be added to make the antifreeze mixture?

Let x = the number of litres of water needed.

$$\frac{\text{alcohol}}{\text{water}} = \frac{3}{4} = \frac{24}{x}$$

Now, we may use the property of proportions to find x.

$$3:4 = 24:x$$
$$3x = 4 \times 24$$
$$3x = 96$$
$$\tfrac{1}{3}(3x) = \tfrac{1}{3}(96)$$
$$x = 32 \text{ L of water}$$

Note: We may use the same property in the form

$$\frac{3}{4} \times \frac{24}{x}$$
$$3x = 4 \times 24$$
$$3x = 96$$
$$x = 32$$

The following examples will indicate how we may use ratio and proportion to solve problems.

EXAMPLE: If 3 ties cost \$12.57, what is the cost of 5 ties at the same rate?

Let x = the cost of 5 ties.
We form the proportion

$$3:12.57 = 5:x$$
$$\frac{3}{12.57} = \frac{5}{x}$$
$$3x = 5 \times 12.57 = 62.85$$
$$\tfrac{1}{3}(3x) = \tfrac{1}{3}(62.85)$$
$$x = \$20.95$$

5 ties cost \$20.95 at the same rate.

EXAMPLE: The scale on a map is 1 cm to 60 km. If the distance between two cities is 2.75 cm on the map, what is the actual distance between the two cities?

Let d = the actual distance between the cities.

$$1:60 = 2.75:d$$
$$1 \times d = 60 \times 2.75$$
$$d = 60 \times 2.75 = 165$$

The actual distance is 165 km.

EXAMPLE: Two numbers are in the ratio 9:5. Their difference is 28. Find the numbers.

Let $9x$ = the larger number
And $5x$ = the smaller number

Then $9x - 5x = 28$
$$4x = 28$$
$$\tfrac{1}{4}(4x) = \tfrac{1}{4}(28)$$
$$x = 7$$

The larger number is $9x$, or $9 \cdot 7 = 63$.
The smaller number is $5x$, or $5 \cdot 7 = 35$.

EXAMPLE: The numerator and denominator of a fraction are in the ratio 3:7. If 2 is added to both the numerator and the denominator, the ratio becomes 1:2. Find the original fraction.

Let $3n$ = the numerator of the fraction.
And $7n$ = the denominator of the fraction.

If we add 2 to both the numerator and the denominator, the numerator becomes $3n + 2$ and the denominator becomes $7n + 2$. Thus, we have

$$\frac{3n+2}{7n+2} = \frac{1}{2}$$
$$1(7n+2) = 2(3n+2)$$
$$7n + 2 = 6n + 4$$
$$7n + 2 - 2 = 6n + 4 - 2$$
$$7n - 6n = 6n - 6n + 2$$
$$n = 2$$

The original denominator was $3n$, or $3 \times 2 = 6$.
The original numerator was $7n$, or $7 \times 2 = 14$.
The original fraction was $^6/_{14}$.

PRACTICE

Directions: Solve the following problems and blacken the space at the right under the number which corresponds to the one you have selected as the correct answer.

1. At a dance, the ratio of the number of boys to the number of girls is 4:3. If there are 32 boys present, the number of girls present is
(1) 36
(2) 40
(3) 20
(4) 24
(5) 28

1. 1 2 3 4 5

2. John earned \$150 one week and spent \$120. The ratio of the amount John saved to the amount John spent is
(1) 1:5
(2) 1:4
(3) 4:1
(4) 4:5
(5) 5:4

2. 1 2 3 4 5

3. On a trip, a motorist drove x kilometres on a local road and y kilometres on a parkway. The ratio of the number of kilometres driven on the parkway to the total number of kilometres driven was
(1) $\frac{y}{x}$
(2) $\frac{x}{y}$
(3) $\frac{y}{x+y}$
(4) $\frac{x}{x+y}$
(5) $\frac{x+y}{y}$

3. 1 2 3 4 5

4. The ratio of a mother's age to her daughter's age is 9:2. If the daughter's age is 12 years, the age of the mother, in years, is
(1) 45
(2) 36
(3) 63
(4) 50
(5) 54

4. 1 2 3 4 5

5. On the line segment $\overline{RS}$, $RT = 4$ and $RT:TS = 2:5$. The length of $\overline{RS}$ is

(1) 10
(2) 12
(3) 7
(4) 9
(5) 14

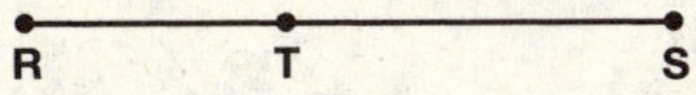

5. 1 2 3 4 5

6. A picture measures 20 cm by 15 cm. If the picture is enlarged so that the 20 cm dimension becomes 30 cm, the other dimension becomes

(1) 22.5 cm
(2) 22.8 cm
(3) 22 cm
(4) 21.75 cm
(5) 23.25 cm

6. 1 2 3 4 5

7. If 3 shirts cost $53, the cost of a dozen shirts at the same rate is

(1) $159
(2) $75
(3) $65
(4) $212
(5) $250

7. 1 2 3 4 5

8. On a map, the scale is 1 cm to 80 km. The actual distance between two cities is 200 km. The distance between the cities, on the map, is

(1) 2 cm
(2) 3 cm
(3) 2.5 cm
(4) 3.5 cm
(5) 4 cm

8. 1 2 3 4 5

9. A certain recipe that will yield 4 portions calls for 375 mL ($1\frac{1}{2}$ cups) of sugar. If the recipe is used to yield 6 portions, then the amount of sugar needed is

(1) 625 mL ($2\frac{1}{2}$ cups)
(2) 562.5 mL ($2\frac{1}{4}$ cups)
(3) 687.5 mL ($2\frac{3}{4}$ cups)
(4) 500 mL (2 cups)
(5) 750 mL (3 cups)

9. 1 2 3 4 5

10. If 0.006% of the body mass is iron, how many grams of iron are there in the body of a 70-kilogram woman? (1000 grams = 1 kilogram)

(1) 0.42
(2) 4.2
(3) 11.67
(4) 420
(5) 11 666

10. 1 2 3 4 5

11. If a car can be driven 42 km on a litre of gasoline, how many litres will be needed to drive this car m kilometres?

(1) $42m$
(2) $\frac{m}{42}$
(3) $42 + m$
(4) $\frac{42}{m}$
(5) $m - 42$

11. 1 2 3 4 5

12. Mr. Ash finds that he spends $47.50 for gas for each 1000 km that he drives his car. One month he drives his car 1800 km. The amount he spends for gas during that month is

(1) $855
(2) $95
(3) $82.50
(4) $85.50
(5) $8.55

12. 1 2 3 4 5

13. If a sheep's blood makes a complete circuit with 26 heart beats, and a complete circuit takes 14 seconds, what is the sheep's heart rate (in beats per minute)?
(1) 32
(2) 111
(3) 140
(4) 182
(5) 364

13. 1 2 3 4 5

14. A recipe for chocolate fudge calls for 187.5 mL ($\frac{3}{4}$ cup) of corn syrup and 2.5 mL of salt. If 250 mL (1 cup) of corn syrup is used, the number of millilitres of salt to be used is
(1) 3.3
(2) 10.3
(3) 4.6
(4) 15.75
(5) 3.75

14. 1 2 3 4 5

15. It takes a train *c* hours to cover *d* kilometres. If the train travels *k* kilometres at the same rate, the number of hours it takes is
(1) cdk
(2) $\frac{d}{ck}$
(3) $\frac{dk}{c}$
(4) $\frac{ck}{d}$
(5) $\frac{cd}{k}$

15. 1 2 3 4 5

16. A man finds that he spends a total of *y* dollars per month for heating oil during 7 months of cold weather. If he wishes to prorate his cost over a 12-month period, the cost per month is
(1) $\frac{12}{7y}$
(2) $\frac{y}{12}$
(3) $\frac{12y}{7}$
(4) $\frac{7y}{12}$
(5) $84y$

16. 1 2 3 4 5

17. A 25-ha field yields 375 metric tonnes of wheat. How many hectares should be planted to yield 525 metric tonnes of wheat?
(1) 33
(2) 32
(3) 45
(4) 35
(5) 75

17. 1 2 3 4 5

18. A house which is assessed at $30 000 is taxed $1170. At the same rate, the tax on a house which is assessed for $40 000 is
(1) $992.50
(2) $156
(3) $1560
(4) $2340
(5) $1360

18. 1 2 3 4 5

19. A family consumes *L* litres of milk each week. The number of litres this family consumes in 10 days is
(1) $\frac{7L}{10}$
(2) $\frac{10L}{7}$
(3) $\frac{70}{L}$
(4) $\frac{10}{7L}$
(5) $\frac{L}{70}$

19. 1 2 3 4 5

20. In making a certain type of concrete, the ratio of cement to sand used is 1 : 4. In making x barrels of this concrete, the number of barrels of cement used is

20. 1 2 3 4 5

(1) $\frac{x}{5}$

(2) $\frac{x}{4}$

(3) x

(4) $4x$

(5) $\frac{1}{5x}$

ANSWERS:

1. **4**	5. **5**	9. **2**	13. **2**	17. **4**
2. **2**	6. **1**	10. **2**	14. **1**	18. **3**
3. **3**	7. **4**	11. **2**	15. **4**	19. **2**
4. **5**	8. **3**	12. **4**	16. **4**	20. **1**

II. I. Signed Numbers

I-1

On a cold day it is announced on the radio that the temperature is 5 degrees below zero. In the weather report printed in the newspaper the temperature is listed as –5°. We often have occasion to talk about quantities that have opposite meanings. For example,

Profit of \$5 = +5, or 5 in dollars	Loss of \$5 = –5 in dollars
Gain of 3 kg = +3, or 3 in kg	Loss of 3 kg = –3 in kg
50 km north = +50, or 50 in km	50 km south = –50 in km

The numbers –5, –3, and –50 are called *negative integers*. The numbers +5, +3, and +50 are called *positive integers*. The negative, or minus, sign must always appear; the positive, or plus, sign may be omitted.

In working with the number line, we have paired points to the right of zero with numbers. May we pair points to the left of zero with numbers? Yes, we pair points to the left of zero with negative numbers, as shown below.

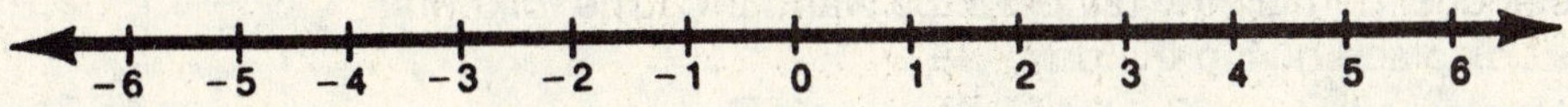

The set {. . . , –5, –4, –3, –2, –1, 0, 1, 2, 3, 4, 5, . . .} is called the set of integers. Notice that the set of positive integers {1, 2, 3, 4, 5, . . .} is an infinite set. Also the set of negative integers {. . . , –5, –4, –3, –2, –1} is an infinite set.

EXAMPLE: A man went on a diet. The changes in his mass for five consecutive months were

–3, +1, –5, +2, –7

How much did the man gain or lose over the five-month period in kg?
He gained 1 kg and 2 kg. The total gain was +3 kg.
He lost 3 kg represented by –3, 5 kg represented by –5, and 7 kg represented by –7.
The total loss was 15 kg represented by –15.

To obtain his net gain or loss, we subtract the smaller total from the larger total 15 – 3 = 12. Next, we give the answer the sign of the larger total. In this case, since –15 is the larger total, our answer is –12.

The man lost 12 kg over the five-month period.

EXAMPLE: The owner of a small store kept a record of her income by using positive numbers and her expenses by using negative numbers. During one day her record in dollars was

–17, +26, +6, –18, +41, –6

In dollars, her income was +26, +6, +41 = +73.
Her expenses were –17, –18, –6 = –41
73 – 41 = 32
Since +73 is the larger total, the result is +32.
The net result was an income of $32

PRACTICE

Directions: Solve the following problems and blacken the space at the right under the number which corresponds to the one you have selected as the right answer.

1. The sum of –6, +8, –3, +2, –1, –5 is
(1) 5
(2) –5
(3) 25
(4) –25
(5) –4

1. 1 2 3 4 5

2. The sum of –19, +3, –5, +18, –1, +7 is
(1) 53
(2) –3
(3) –2
(4) 0
(5) 3

2. 1 2 3 4 5

3. Mr. Egan's bank balance was $1247. It changed as follows over a four-month period.
–$152, +$384, –$516, +$217
His bank balance at the end of the four-month period was
(1) $67
(2) $601
(3) $459
(4) $1180
(5) $1296

3. 1 2 3 4 5

4. At 8 o'clock one morning the temperature was 12°C. The following changes took place during the day.

Noon	+8°C	8 P.M.	–9°C
4 P.M.	+5°C	12 midnight	–7°C

The temperature at midnight was
(1) 15°C
(2) –9°C
(3) 9°C
(4) –15°C
(5) 0°C

4. 1 2 3 4 5

5. In Manitoba the average temperature in summer is 33.9°C. The average temperature in winter is –7.2°C. What is the difference?
(1) 32.9°C
(2) 28.7°C
(3) 41.1°C
(4) 43.3°C
(5) 43.4°C

5. 1 2 3 4 5

6. Mr. Dunn bought some stock in the XYZ Corporation at 41. During the next week its market price changed as follows:
–2, +1, $-\frac{1}{2}$, $-1\frac{1}{2}$, $+\frac{1}{2}$
The price of the stock at the end of the week was
(1) $39\frac{1}{2}$
(2) $38\frac{1}{2}$
(3) $40\frac{1}{2}$
(4) $37\frac{1}{2}$
(5) 38

6. 1 2 3 4 5

7. During a flight the change in altitude of a plane, in metres, is given by the following signed numbers.

$$-876, +902, -195, +463, -785$$

The total change in altitude, in metres is

(1) –491 (4) –501
(2) 491 (5) 591
(3) –591

7. 1 2 3 4 5
|| || || || ||

8. At a movie theatre the changes in daily attendance for one week over the previous week were

$$-49, +146, -73, -227, +65, -87, +91$$

The change in attendance for the week was

(1) +134 (4) –134
(2) 302 (5) +638
(3) –436

8. 1 2 3 4 5
|| || || || ||

ANSWERS:

1. 2 **2. 5** **3. 4** **4. 3** **5. 3** **6. 2** **7. 1** **8. 4**

II. J. Factoring and the Solution of Quadratic Equations

J-1

The Meaning of Factoring. When we multiply two numbers such as 5 and 7, the result, 35, is called the *product*. The numbers which yield a product when multiplied are called *factors* of the product, 35. Similarly, 3 and 5 are factors of 15, and 6 and 4 are factors of 24. And 7, 2, x, and y are factors of $14xy$.

In a product any factor is the coefficient of the remaining factor or factors. For example:

In the product $6bc$
6 is the coefficient of bc
$6b$ is the coefficient of c
$6c$ is the coefficient of b

A common factor of two numbers is a number which is a factor of the two numbers. For example:

2 is a common factor of 6 and 10
3 is a common factor of 9 and 12

The greatest common factor of two or more numbers is the largest number which is a factor of the numbers. For example:

4 is the greatest common factor of 12 and 20
12 is the greatest common factor of 60 and 84
18 is the greatest common factor of 18 and 36
xy is the greatest common factor of $7x^2y$ and $9xy^2$
$6a^2b^2$ is the greatest common factor of $18a^3b^3$ and $24a^2b^2$

J-2

Finding the Greatest Common Factor. We will now consider a systematic method of finding the *greatest common factor* of two or more numbers. Consider the numbers 108 and 144. If we write each of these numbers as the product of prime numbers we have:

$$108 = 2 \times 2 \times 3 \times 3 \times 3, \text{ or } 2^2 \times 3^3$$
$$144 = 2 \times 2 \times 2 \times 2 \times 3 \times 3, \text{ or } 2^4 \times 3^2$$

The factor 2^2 is the highest power of 2 that appears in both 108 and 144. The factor 3^2 is the highest power of 3 that appears in both 108 and 144. The greatest common factor of 108 and 144 is $2^2 \times 3^2$, or 4×9, or 36.

EXAMPLE: Find the greatest common factor of 72 and 120.

$$72 = 2 \times 2 \times 2 \times 3 \times 3 = 2^3 \times 3^2$$
$$120 = 2 \times 2 \times 2 \times 3 \times 5 = 2^3 \times 3 \times 5$$

The greatest common factor of 72 and 120 is $2^3 \times 3 = 24$.

EXAMPLE: Find the greatest common factor of $42a^2b^3$ and $28ab^2$.

We will first consider the numerical coefficients

$$42 = 2 \times 3 \times 7$$
$$28 = 2 \times 2 \times 7 = 2^2 \times 7$$

The greatest common factor of 42 and 28 is 2×7, or 14.
The greatest common factor of a^2b^3 and ab^2 is ab^2.
The greatest common factor of $42a^2b^3$ and $28ab^2$ is $14ab^2$.

PRACTICE

In each case, find the greatest common factor:

1. 48 and 80
2. x^3y^4 and x^2y^3
3. $8a^2b^2$ and $20a^2b$
4. $15c^3$ and $10c$
5. $7ab$ and $7bc$
6. $28x^3z$ and $63xz^3$
7. $16c^3d$ and $24c^2d^2$
8. $35a^2b$ and $14ab^2$

ANSWERS:

1. 16 **2.** x^2y^3 **3.** $4a^2b$ **4.** $5c$ **5.** $7b$ **6.** $7xz$ **7.** $8c^2d$ **8.** $7ab$

J-3

Factoring Polynomials That Have a Common Monomial Factor. A *term* is a numeral, variable, or a combination of numerals and variables that are connected by symbols of multiplication or division, or both. For examples, 5, y, $7a$, and $16c^2d$ are terms.

An algebraic expression that contains one term is called a *monomial*. For example, 9, $16a$, $17b^2$, and $5c^2d^3$ are monomials.

An algebraic expression that contains two terms is called a *binomial*. For example, $2a - 3b$, and $7x^2 - 9xy^2$ are binomials.

An algebraic expression that contains more than one term connected by plus or minus signs is called a *polynomial*.

In factoring a polynomial we first find the greatest common factor of the terms of the polynomial and then divide each term of the polynomial by this greatest common factor to find the other factor.

EXAMPLE: Factor $7x + 7y$

The greatest common factor of $7x$ and $7y$ is 7. When we divide each term of $7x + 7y$ by 7 we have:

$$7x + 7y = 7(x + y)$$

$7(x + y)$ is called the factored form of $7x + 7y$.

EXAMPLE: Factor $24a^2 - 16a$

The greatest common factor of $24a^2$ and $16a$ is $8a$. When we divide each term of $24a^2$ and $16a$ by $8a$ we have:

$$24a^2 - 16a = 8a(3a - 2)$$

PRACTICE

Factor each of the following expressions:

1. $5a + 5b$
2. $x^2 - xy$
3. $3ab^2 + 6a^2b$
4. $3xy - 12y^2$
5. $8ab - 12a^2$
6. $6c^2 + 12cd$
7. $ab + ac$
8. $3 + 3a^2$
9. $2x^2 + 8x$
10. $24a^2c - 16ac^2$

ANSWERS:

1. **$5(a + b)$**
2. **$x(x - y)$**
3. **$3ab(b + 2a)$**
4. **$3y(x - 4y)$**
5. **$4a(2b - 3a)$**
6. **$6c(c + 2d)$**
7. **$a(b + c)$**
8. **$3(1 + a^2)$**
9. **$2x(x + 4)$**
10. **$8ac(3a - 2c)$**

J-4

Factoring the Difference of Two Squares. Consider the product of the binomial $(x + y)$ and the binomial $(x - y)$. To complete the multiplication we must multiply $x - y$ by x and $x - y$ by y and combine the results. We use the following arrangements to carry out the multiplication.

$$\begin{array}{r} x - y \\ \underline{x + y} \\ x^2 - xy \\ \underline{+xy - y^2} \\ x^2 \qquad -y^2 \end{array}$$

That is, $(x + y)(x - y) = x^2 - y^2$.

If we were to multiply the sum of any two terms (such as $x + y$) and the difference of the same two terms $(x - y)$ the result will always be the difference of the squares of the two terms (in this case $x^2 - y^2$). For example $(2c + d)(2c - d) = 4c^2 - d^2$.

In effect, we have a method of factoring an expression which is the difference of two squares. For example:

$$a^2 - b^2 = (a + b)(a - b)$$

$$x^2 - 4 = (x + 2)(x - 2)$$

$$25 - z^2 = (5 + z)(5 - z)$$

$$9c^2 - 16 = (3c + 4)(3c - 4)$$

PRACTICE

In each case, factor the expression:

1. $c^2 - d^2$
2. $y^2 - 9$
3. $x^2 - 100$
4. $36 - b^2$
5. $9a^2 - 16$
6. $49 - 4x^2$

7. $b^2 - 64$
8. $x^2 - 16y^2$
9. $4d^2 - 1$
10. $81 - 25p^2$
11. $100 - 9x^2$
12. $a^2b^2 - 49$

ANSWERS:

1. $(c + d)(c - d)$
2. $(y + 3)(y - 3)$
3. $(x + 10)(x - 10)$
4. $(6 + b)(6 - b)$
5. $(3a + 4)(3a - 4)$
6. $(7 + 2x)(7 - 2x)$
7. $(b + 8)(b - 8)$
8. $(x + 4y)(x - 4y)$
9. $(2d + 1)(2d - 1)$
10. $(9 + 5p)(9 - 5p)$
11. $(10 + 3x)(10 - 3x)$
12. $(ab + 7)(ab - 7)$

J-5

Factoring Trinomials. Consider the product of the two binomials $(y + 2)$ and $(y + 3)$. We arrange our work as follows:

$$\begin{array}{r} y+3 \\ \underline{y+2} \\ y^2+3y \\ \underline{+2y+6} \\ y^2+5y+6 \end{array}$$

In obtaining this trinomial result, we note that:

1. The first term of the product (y^2) is obtained by multiplying the first terms of the binomial $(y \times y)$.
2. The last term in the product $(+6)$ is obtained by multiplying the second terms of the binomials $(+3 \times +2)$.
3. The middle term of the product $(+5y)$ is the sum of the cross-products $(y \times +3) + (y \times +2) = 3y + 2y = 5y$.

If the binomials are written horizontally the middle term may be found mentally by obtaining the algebraic sum of the products of the terms shown by the arrows.

$$(y+2)(y+3) = y^2 + 3y + 2y + 6 = y^2 + 5y + 6$$

EXAMPLE: Find the product $(x + 5)(x - 2)$

$$(x+5)(x-2) = x^2 - 2x + 5x - 10 = x^2 + 3x - 10$$

EXAMPLE: Find the product $(2y + 3)(y - 5)$

$$(2y+3)(y-5) = 2y^2 - 10y + 3y - 15 = 2y^2 - 7y - 15$$

PRACTICE

Find the following products:

1. $(y + 2)(y + 1)$
2. $(a + 3)(a + 4)$
3. $(x - 3)(x - 1)$
4. $(y + 4)(y - 3)$
5. $(a - 7)(a + 2)$
6. $(z + 3)(z - 6)$
7. $(x - 4)(x - 3)$
8. $(y + 6)(y - 3)$
9. $(2y - 3)(y + 7)$
10. $(x + 5)(2x - 3)$

ANSWERS:

1. $y^2 + 3y + 2$
2. $a^2 + 7a + 12$
3. $x^2 - 4x + 3$
4. $y^2 + y - 12$
5. $a^2 - 5a - 14$
6. $z^2 - 3z - 18$
7. $x^2 - 7x + 12$
8. $y^2 + 3y - 18$
9. $2y^2 + 11y - 21$
10. $2x^2 + 7x - 15$

We have noticed that the product of two binomials may be a trinomial. For example, $(x + 5)(x + 7) = x^2 + 12x + 35$. In solving some equations it is necessary to write a trinomial as the product of two binomials. For example, $y^2 + 7y + 10 = (y + 5)(y + 2)$. This process of writing a trinomial as the product of two binomials is called factoring the trinomial. The following examples will illustrate the method of factoring a trinomial.

EXAMPLE: Factor the trinomial $y^2 + 8y + 15$.

The product of the first terms of the two binomials must be y^2. Therefore, each first term must be y. Thus, we may write

$$y^2 + 8y + 15 = (y \qquad)(y \qquad)$$

where the second term of each binomial is still to be determined.

The product of the last two terms of the binomials must be +15. Thus, these last two terms must both be positive or both negative. The possible pairs of factors may be $(+15) \times (+1)$ or $(+5) \times (+3)$ or $(-15) \times (-1)$ or $(-5) \times (-3)$. We may test the pairs to select the pair that will yield the correct middle term as follows.

$$(y + 15)(y + 1): 15y + y = 16y \text{ for the middle term}$$

This is rejected.

$$(y + 5)(y + 3): 5y + 3y = 8y \text{ for the middle term}$$

This is the correct choice.

Thus, $y^2 + 8y + 15 = (y + 5)(y + 3)$.

EXAMPLE: Factor the trinomial $a^2 - 3a + 2$.
The possible choices are: $(a + 2)(a + 1)$ or $(a - 2)(a - 1)$
If we check these choices we have

$$(a + 2)(a + 1): 2a + a = +3a \text{ for the middle term}$$

This choice is rejected.

$$(a - 2)(a - 1): -2a - a = -3a \text{ for the middle term}$$

This is the correct choice. Thus, $a^2 - 3a + 2 = (a - 2)(a - 1)$.

EXAMPLE: Factor the trinomial $y^2 - 3y - 10$.
The possible choices are:

$(y - 10)(y + 1): -10y + y = -9y$, reject

$(y + 10)(y - 1): 10y - y = +9y$, reject

$(y + 5)(y - 2): 5y - 2y = +3y$, reject

$(y - 5)(y + 2): -5y + 2y = -3y$, correct

Thus, $y^2 - 3y - 10 = (y - 5)(y + 2)$.

EXAMPLE: Factor the trinomial $2a^2 - 9a - 5$.
The possible choices are:

$$(2a-1)(a+5): -a+10a=+9a, \text{ reject}$$

$$(2a+5)(a-1): 5a-2a=+3a, \text{ reject}$$

$$(2a-5)(a+1): -5a+2a=-3a, \text{ reject}$$

$$(2a+1)(a-5): a-10a=-9a, \text{ correct}$$

Thus, $2a^2 - 9a - 5 = (2a + 1)(a - 5)$

PRACTICE

Factor the following trinomials:

1. $y^2 + 3y + 2$
2. $a^2 + 4a + 3$
3. $x^2 + 5x + 6$
4. $y^2 + 7y + 6$
5. $b^2 - 4b + 3$
6. $z^2 - 6z + 5$
7. $x^2 - x - 2$
8. $y^2 - 3y - 4$
9. $a^2 - a - 6$
10. $x^2 - 2x - 15$
11. $a^2 + 6a + 9$
12. $y^2 - 2y - 8$
13. $x^2 + x - 20$
14. $a^2 + a - 6$
15. $x^2 + 6x - 7$
16. $y^2 - y - 12$
17. $z^2 + 2z - 8$
18. $2y^2 + 3y - 5$
19. $x^2 + 5x - 14$
20. $2x^2 + 5x - 3$

ANSWERS:

1. $(y + 2)(y + 1)$
2. $(a + 3)(a + 1)$
3. $(x + 3)(x + 2)$
4. $(y + 6)(y + 1)$
5. $(b - 3)(b - 1)$
6. $(z - 5)(z - 1)$
7. $(x - 2)(x + 1)$
8. $(y - 4)(y + 1)$
9. $(a - 3)(a + 2)$
10. $(x - 5)(x + 3)$
11. $(a + 3)(a + 3)$
12. $(y - 4)(y + 2)$
13. $(x + 5)(x - 4)$
14. $(a + 3)(a - 2)$
15. $(x + 7)(x - 1)$
16. $(y - 4)(y + 3)$
17. $(z + 4)(z - 2)$
18. $(2y + 5)(y - 1)$
19. $(x + 7)(x - 2)$
20. $(2x - 1)(x + 3)$

J-6

Solving Quadratic Equations by Factoring. A quadratic equation is an equation which may be written in the form $ax^2 + bx + c = 0$, where a, b, and c are constants and $c \neq 0$.
For example: 1. $x^2 - 6x + 8 = 0$
2. $3x^2 - x - 2 = 0$
3. $x^2 = 4x + 5$ which becomes $x^2 - 4x - 5 = 0$ when written in the form $ax^2 + bx + c = 0$
4. $x^2 - 9 = 0$ which is in the required form but has $b = 0$.

If a quadratic equation is written in the form $ax^2 + bx + c = 0$ and the left side of the equation can be factored, then the equation may readily be solved. In solving quadratic equations by factoring we make use of the following properties of zero.

1. The product of 0 and any real number is 0. For example: $7 \times 0 = 0$, and $0 \times .3 = 0$. This property is called the multiplication property of 0.

2. If the product of two real numbers is 0, then at least one of these real numbers must be 0. For example: if $a \times b = 0$, then either a or b must be 0; both a and b may be 0.

The method of solving quadratic equations by factoring is illustrated by the examples below.

EXAMPLE: Solve the equation $x^2 - 2x - 15 = 0$
When we factor the left side of this equation we have $(x - 5)(x + 3) = 0$.
Since the product $(x - 5)(x + 3)$ is 0, at least one of the factors must be zero.
If $x - 5 = 0$, then $x = 5$. If $x + 3 = 0$, then $x = -3$.

The roots of the equation are 5 and –3. The roots are checked as follows.

Check for $x = 5$

$$x^2 - 2x - 15 = 0$$
$$5^2 - 2(5) - 15 = 0$$
$$25 - 10 - 15 = 0$$
$$0 = 0$$

Check for $x = -3$

$$x^2 - 2x - 15 = 0$$
$$(-3)^2 - 2(-3) - 15 = 0$$
$$9 + 6 - 15 = 0$$
$$0 = 0$$

EXAMPLE: Solve the equation $2x^2 + 7x - 4 = 0$.

When we factor the left side of the equation we have $(2x - 1)(x + 4) = 0$.

$$\text{If } 2x - 1 = 0$$
$$2x = 1$$
$$x = \frac{1}{2}$$

$$\text{If } x + 4 = 0$$
$$x = -4$$

The roots of the equation are ½ and –4.

Check for $x = \frac{1}{2}$

$$2x^2 + 7x - 4 = 0$$
$$2\left(\frac{1}{2}\right)^2 + 7\left(\frac{1}{2}\right) - 4 = 0$$
$$2\left(\frac{1}{4}\right) + \frac{7}{2} - 4 = 0$$
$$\frac{1}{2} + \frac{7}{2} - 4 = 0$$
$$4 - 4 = 0$$

Check for $x = -4$

$$2x^2 + 7x - 4 = 0$$
$$2(-4)^2 + 7(-4) - 4 = 0$$
$$2(16) - 28 - 4 = 0$$
$$32 - 28 - 4 = 0$$
$$0 = 0$$

PRACTICE

Solve and check each of the following equations:

1. $y^2 - 3y + 2 = 0$
2. $x^2 - 4x + 3 = 0$
3. $a^2 + 5a + 4 = 0$
4. $z^2 + 4z + 3 = 0$
5. $c^2 - 5c + 6 = 0$
6. $x^2 + x - 6 = 0$
7. $y^2 + 2y - 8 = 0$
8. $a^2 - a - 12 = 0$
9. $x^2 - 4x - 12 = 0$
10. $z^2 - z - 20 = 0$
11. $y^2 + 2y - 15 = 0$
12. $x^2 - 5x + 4 = 0$
13. $x^2 - 3x - 10 = 0$
14. $y^2 - 3y - 18 = 0$
15. $y^2 - 8y - 9 = 0$
16. $a^2 + a - 20 = 0$
17. $c^2 + 4c - 21 = 0$
18. $y^2 - y - 30 = 0$
19. $2x^2 - 7x + 3 = 0$
20. $2x^2 + 9x - 5 = 0$

ANSWERS:

1. **2, 1**
2. **3, 1**
3. **–4, –1**
4. **–3, –1**
5. **3, 2**
6. **–3, 2**
7. **–4, 2**
8. **4, –3**
9. **6, –2**
10. **5, –4**
11. **–5, 3**
12. **4, 1**
13. **5, –2**
14. **6, –3**
15. **9, –1**
16. **–5, 4**
17. **–7, 3**
18. **6, –5**
19. **½, 3**
20. **½, –5**

J-7

Using Quadratic Equations to Solve Problems. Quadratic equations may be used to solve problems.

EXAMPLE: A room, rectangular in shape, is 5 m longer than it is wide. If the area of the room is 300 m^2, find the dimensions of the room.

Let x = width of the room, in metres.
Then $x + 5$ = length of the room, in metres.

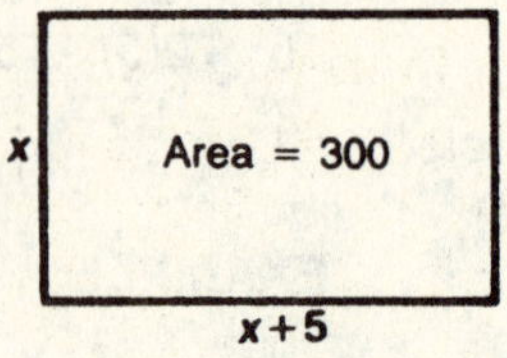

$$x(x+5) = 300$$
$$x^2 + 5x = 300$$
$$x^2 + 5x - 300 = 0$$
$$(x-15)(x+20) = 0$$

If $x - 15 = 0$, $\quad$ If $x + 20 = 0$
$x = 15$ $\quad$ $x = -20$, reject

Thus, the width of the room is 15 m and the length of the room is $x + 5$, or $15 + 5$, or 20 m.

Check your answer
If the room is 20 m long and 15 m wide, the area of the room is $20 \times 15 = 300\,m^2$.

PRACTICE

Solve the following problems:

1. A rectangular garden plot is 4 m longer than it is wide. If the area of the garden plot is 96 m^2, what are the dimensions of the garden plot?
2. When the square of a positive number is added to the number the result is 42. Find the number.
3. An auditorium has 192 seats. The number of seats in each row is 4 less than the number of rows. Find the number of seats in each row.
4. A sail is triangular in shape and has an area of 24 m^2. If the base of the sail is 2 m greater than the altitude of the sail, what is the altitude of the sail?
5. Take a positive whole number and square it. To this square add twice the original number. If the result is 99, find the original number.

ANSWERS:

1. **12m long, 8m wide**
2. **6**
3. **12 seats in each row**
4. **6m**
5. **9**

II. K. Probability

K-1

If you toss a coin in the air, it may land heads up or tails up. In fact, the chance that the coin will land heads up is equal to the chance that the coin will land tails up. That is, the chance that the coin will land heads up is one out of 2. We say that the *probability* of obtaining a head is $\frac{1}{2}$. Similarly, the probability of obtaining a tail is $\frac{1}{2}$.

Suppose that you are a member of a social club that conducts raffles with one prize to be given. The club sells 100 raffle tickets and you buy 3 of these tickets. What are your chances of winning the prize? In this case, if the prize ticket is drawn you have 3 chances out of 100 that you will be the winner. We say that your probability of success is $\frac{3}{100}$.

In general, we write the probability of an event as a fraction with the numerator indicating the number of successful outcomes and the denominator indicating the number of possible outcomes. That is,

$$P(\text{probability}) = \frac{\text{number of successful outcomes}}{\text{number of possible outcomes}}$$

EXAMPLE: John has a blue tie and a red tie, a brown tie, and a grey tie. If John selects a tie at random, what is the probability he selects a blue tie?

In selecting a tie John may select any one of four colours. Therefore, the probability that John selects a blue tie is $\frac{1}{4}$. Or,

$$P = \frac{1}{4}$$

EXAMPLE: A football squad consists of 29 linemen and 15 backfield men. If one man on the squad is chosen to be captain, what is the probability that the man chosen is a lineman?

In all, there are 29 + 15, or 44 men on the squad. Of the 44 men, 29 are linemen. Therefore, the probability that the choice is a lineman is $\frac{29}{44}$. Or,

$$P = \frac{29}{44}$$

EXAMPLE: Vida had 3 dimes and 2 quarters in her purse. If she selected a coin at random from her purse, what is the probability that the coin chosen was a nickel?

Since Vida did not have a nickel in her purse it was impossible for her to have withdrawn a nickel. In such a case, we say that the probability is zero. Or,

$$P = 0$$

Notice that the number of successful outcomes is 0 and the number of possible outcomes is 5. But $\frac{0}{5} = 0$.

EXAMPLE: A group of 8 executives is attending a committee meeting. During the meeting one of them is called to the telephone. What is the probability that the one called to the telephone is an executive?

In this case, the one called to the telephone is one of the group of executives. Thus it is certain that the one called to the telephone is an executive. Or.

$$P = 1$$

Notice that the number of successful outcomes is 8 and the number of possible outcomes is also 8. $\frac{8}{8} = 1$.

PRACTICE

Solve the following problems:

1. Ms. Finestone had two blue suits, three grey suits, and two brown suits. If she selects a suit at random, what is the probability that
   a. she selects a grey suit?
   b. she selects a brown suit?

2. A purse contains 4 quarters, 3 dimes, and 5 pennies. If a coin is drawn at random from the purse, what is the probability that it is a penny?

3. A class has 17 boys and 15 girls. If the teacher calls on a member of the class to recite, what is the probability that the teacher calls on a girl?

4. There are ten digits in our system of numeration: 0, 1, 2, 3, 4, 5, 6, 7, 8, 9. If we select a digit without looking,
a. what is the probability that the digit is 7?
b. what is the probability that the digit is an odd number?
c. what is the probability that the digit is less than 5?
d. what is the probability that the digit is greater than 12?

5. An ordinary deck of playing cards consists of 52 cards. These 52 cards are divided into four suits of 13 cards each (spades, hearts, diamonds, clubs). If a card is selected at random, what is the probability
a. that the card is the 8 of spades?
b. that the card is a heart?
c. that the card is an ace?

6. The third shelf of my bookcase contains only science books. If I select a book at random from the third shelf of my bookcase, what is the probability that the selection is a science book?

7. A jar contains 10 blue marbles, 9 red marbles, and 7 yellow marbles. If a marble is selected at random from the jar, what is the probability that the choice is
a. a red marble?
b. a yellow marble?
c. a white marble?

8. A jar contains 15 green marbles. If one marble is drawn at random from the jar, what is the probability that the marble chosen is green?

Directions: Solve the following problems and blacken the space at the right under the number which corresponds to the one you have selected as the right answer.

9. A man has 5 white shirts, 4 blue shirts, and 3 grey shirts. One white shirt cannot be worn because it needs laundering. If the man chooses one of the other shirts what is the probability that he chooses a blue shirt?

(1) $\frac{4}{12}$ (4) $\frac{4}{11}$

(2) $\frac{1}{3}$ (5) $\frac{3}{11}$

(3) $\frac{4}{7}$

9. 1 2 3 4 5
|| || || || ||

10. A large department store has 6 doors. Two doors are marked exit 1, and exit 2. The other doors are marked entrance 1, entrance 2, entrance 3, and entrance 4. If a customer enters the store through an entrance door, what is the probability that he enters through entrance 2?

(1) $\frac{2}{6}$ (4) $\frac{5}{6}$

(2) $\frac{3}{4}$ (5) $\frac{1}{4}$

(3) $\frac{4}{6}$

10. 1 2 3 4 5

11. A baseball squad consists of 7 infielders, 5 outfielders, and 10 battery persons. A player who is not a battery person is chosen to pinch hit. What is the probability that the player chosen is an infielder?

(1) $\frac{7}{22}$ (4) $\frac{7}{10}$

(2) $\frac{7}{12}$ (5) $\frac{5}{7}$

(3) $\frac{7}{15}$

11. 1 2 3 4 5

12. A class consists of 16 boys and 12 girls. If a boy and a girl are absent what is the probability that a girl is called upon to recite?

(1) $\frac{12}{27}$ (4) $\frac{12}{26}$

(2) $\frac{11}{27}$ (5) $\frac{11}{28}$

(3) $\frac{11}{26}$

12. 1 2 3 4 5

ANSWERS:

1a. $\mathbf{\frac{3}{7}}$
b. $\mathbf{\frac{2}{7}}$
2. $\mathbf{\frac{5}{12}}$
3. $\mathbf{\frac{15}{32}}$
4a. $\mathbf{\frac{1}{10}}$
b. $\mathbf{\frac{1}{2}}$
c. $\mathbf{\frac{1}{2}}$
d. **0**

5a. $\mathbf{\frac{1}{52}}$
b. $\mathbf{\frac{1}{4}}$
c. $\mathbf{\frac{1}{13}}$
6. **1**
7a. $\mathbf{\frac{9}{26}}$
b. $\mathbf{\frac{7}{26}}$
c. **0**
8. **1**

9. **(4)**
10. **(5)**
11. **(2)**
12. **(3)**

II. L. The Mean and the Median

L-1

In reading a newspaper, a magazine, or a book we frequently come across such expressions as "the average person," "average rainfall," "batting average," "average weight" and "average family." Unless we agree upon a specific mathematical procedure for finding these averages their meanings will be vague and their usefulness limited. Usually, when we use the word "average" we have in mind a group of people or objects arranged in order of size; the *average* then is the person or object which stands in the middle of the size order.

Since there are several kinds of averages used in mathematics and statistics, each determined by a specific procedure, we call the averages, in general, measures of central tendency. In this section, we will discuss two measures of central tendency, the *mean* and the *median*.

L-2

The Mean. The *mean* of a set of N numbers is the average obtained by adding these numbers and dividing this sum by N.

EXAMPLE: Mary's grades on a series of tests in history were 75, 90, 80, 65, and 70. What was the average, or mean, of Mary's grades?

To find the mean we first add the scores:

$$75 + 90 + 80 + 65 + 70 = 380$$

Then we divide this sum by the number of scores. In this case, we divide by 5.

$$380 \div 5 = 76$$

The mean of Mary's grades was 76.

EXAMPLE: In its first five games the Cardinal Basketball Team scored 58, 49, 62, 53, and 41 points. How many points must the team score in its sixth game to achieve a mean score of 56 points for the six games?

Let X = the number of points the team must score in its sixth game.

$$\text{Then, } (58+49+62+53+41+X) \div 6 = 56$$

$$\frac{263+X}{6} = 56$$

$$263 + X = 6 \cdot 56 = 336$$

$$263 + X - 263 = 336 - 263$$

$$X = 73$$

Thus, the team must score 73 points in its sixth game in order to have a mean score of 56 points for the six games.

L-3

The Median. When we arrange a set of numbers in order of magnitude, the number in the middle is called the *median*.

EXAMPLE: The masses of the starting team of the Madison Football Team are 84, 88, 94, 78, 87, 91, 107, 103, 90, 98, and 81. What is the median mass of the members of this team?

We arrange the masses in order of magnitude starting with the greatest mass. In finding the median we may arrange the masses starting with the least mass without affecting the result.

107, 103, 98, 94, 91, 90, 88, 87, 84, 81, 78

↓

median

In this case, the median is the sixth score either counting from left to right or from the right to left.

EXAMPLE: Find the median of the following set of numbers.
47, 56, 79, 83, 45, 64, 72, 53

First we arrange the numbers in order of magnitude:
83, 79, 72, 64, 56, 53, 47, 45

In this case, we have two middle numbers (64 and 56). To find the median we take the average (or mean) of the two middle numbers. $(64 + 56) \div 2 = 120 \div 2 = 60$.

The median is 60.

***Note*:** In all cases where we have an even number of scores we will have two middle scores. To find the median we take the average (or mean) of the two middle scores.

PRACTICE

Solve the following problems:

1. The heights of the members of a professional basketball squad, in centimetres, were 190, 198, 208, 205, 193, 203 and 195. Find the median height of the members of this team.

2. During a special sale on TV sets the number of sales for six days were 124, 96, 87, 91, 58, and 47. Find the median number of sales.

3. Andrea's marks on six mathematics tests were 83, 74, 68, 85, 91, and 78. What mark must she get on a seventh test in order to obtain an average (mean) of 80 for the seven tests?

4. In each case, find the mean for the following sets of numbers.
a. 102, 86, 79, 115, 94, 82
b. 17, 29, 43, 38, 51, 31, 49, 30
c. 41, 52, 39, 68, 27, 59, 46, 53, 38

5. In each case, find the median for the following sets of numbers.
a. 63, 42, 59, 37, 64, 87, 51
b. 105, 69, 94, 38, 112, 96, 83, 97, 38
c. 24, 36, 29, 18, 31, 37, 27, 35

6. The average (mean) weekly earnings of John, Frank, and Fred are $360. If John earns $375 per week, and Frank earns $350 per week, what are Fred's weekly earnings?

7. A laboratory employs six technicians and one scientist. The technicians each receive salaries of $420 per week and the scientist receives a salary of $1260 per week.
a. What is the mean salary of the seven employees?
b. What is the median salary of the seven employees?
c. Is the mean or the median a more representative measure of central tendency in this case? Why?

ANSWERS:

1. **198cm**
2. **89**
3. **81**
4. a. **93** b. **36** c. **47**
5. a. **59** b. **94** c. **30**
6. **$355**
7. a. **$540** b. **$420** c. **The median because it represents the salaries of six of the seven workers.**

III. GEOMETRY

GLOSSARY

ABSCISSA the first number of the ordered pair of numbers given to a point and measuring the number of units to the right or left of the *y*-axis

ACUTE ANGLE an angle whose measure is less than 90°

ADJACENT ANGLES angles having the same vertex and a common side between them

ANGLE a set of points consisting of two rays having the same endpoint

AREA the measure of the surface enclosed by a plane figure

BAR GRAPH graph in which a series of lines are used to represent numbers

CIRCLE a plane figure defined by a set of points at an equal distance from a fixed point

CIRCLE GRAPH graph in which segments of a circle are used to represent numbers

CIRCUMFERENCE the length of the curved line forming a circle

COMPLEMENTARY ANGLES adjacent angles whose sum is 90°

CONGRUENT TRIANGLES triangles that have exactly the same size and shape

COORDINATES the ordered pair of numbers given to a point to indicate its location on a graph

CUBE a solid figure formed by six squares all at right angles

CYLINDER a solid figure with a circle forming the top and bottom and a rectangle forming the sides

DIAMETER a line segment that passes through the centre of a circle having its endpoints on the circle

ENDPOINTS either end of a line segment

EQUILATERAL TRIANGLE a triangle with three equal sides

HEXAGON a plane figure with six sides

HYPOTENUSE in a right triangle, the side opposite the right angle

IRRATIONAL NUMBER a number that cannot be written exactly in fractional or decimal form

ISOSCELES TRIANGLE a triangle with two equal sides

LINE a set of points extending infinitely in either direction. In geometry, lines are always straight lines.

LINE GRAPH graph in which a line is used to represent a series of numbers

OBTUSE ANGLE an angle whose measure is greater than 90°

ORDINATE the second number of an ordered pair of numbers given to a point and measuring the number of units above or below the *x*-axis

ORIGIN the point where the axes meet

PARALLEL LINES lines in a plane that do not meet no matter how far they are extended

PENTAGON a plane figure with five sides

PERIMETER the distance around a plane figure

PICTOGRAPH graph in which objects are used to represent numbers

PLANE a set of points making up a perfectly flat surface

PLANE FIGURE a figure all of whose points lie in the same plane

POINT a definite location in space with no length, width, or thickness

PYTHAGOREAN THEOREM in a right triangle, the square of the length of the hypotenuse is equal to the sum of the lengths of the other two sides

QUADRANT one of four regions into which the *x*- and *y*-axes divide a plane

RADIUS a line segment from the centre of a circle to any point on the circle

RAY a straight line extending from an endpoint

RECTANGLE a plane figure with four sides and four right angles

RIGHT ANGLE an angle whose measure is 90°

RIGHT TRIANGLE a triangle containing a right angle

SEGMENT a definite part of a line

SIMILAR TRIANGLES triangles having the same shape

SLOPE OF A LINE the distance the line rises between two points as compared with the horizontal distance between the two points

SOLID FIGURE a figure whose points lie in more than one plane

SPACE the set of all points

SQUARE a plane figure with four equal sides and four right angles

SQUARE ROOT one of two equal numbers that can be multiplied together to equal a square

STRAIGHT ANGLE an angle whose measure is 180°

SUPPLEMENTARY ANGLES adjacent angles whose sum is 180°

TRANSVERSAL a line intersecting parallel lines

TRIANGLE a plane figure with three sides

VERTICAL ANGLES angles formed by the intersection of two lines

VOLUME the measure of the space within a solid figure

***X*-AXIS** one of two perpendicular lines used in locating points in space—usually drawn horizontally

***Y*-AXIS** one of two perpendicular lines used in locating points in space—usually drawn vertically

III. A. Points, Lines, and Space

A-1

By a *point* in geometry we mean a definite location in space. A point has no length, width, or thickness. We usually name a point with a capital letter.

When we use the word *line* in geometry, we always mean a straight line. Moreover, a line extends infinitely, in either direction. For this reason, arrows are frequently shown on a line, as follows:

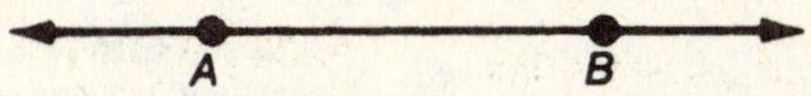

We can think of a line as a special set of points. A line is usually named by naming two points on the line with a double-arrowed symbol. For example, the line above may be named $\overleftrightarrow{AB}$.

We often have occasion to deal with a definite part of a line. Such a part of a line is called a *segment.* We can think of a segment as two points on a line, together with the set of points between these two points. *The two points are called the endpoints of the segment. We usually name a segment by naming the endpoints and place a bar above.* For example, the segment below is called $\overline{CD}$.

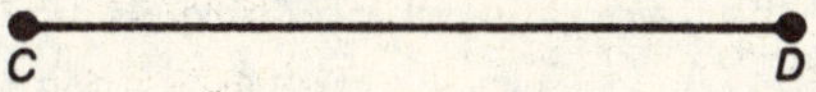

By a *ray* in geometry we mean the set of points, *A* and all the points on a straight line through *A*, that are on one side of *A.* Point *A* is called the endpoint of the ray. We name a ray by naming its endpoint and another point on the ray with an arrow symbol. For example, the ray shown below is called $\overrightarrow{AE}$.

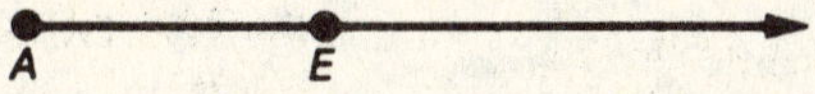

We can think of a *plane* in geometry as a set of points making up a perfectly flat surface. A plane is suggested by the floor of a room or the cover of a book.

By *space* in geometry, we mean the set of all points.

III. B. Geometric Figures

B-1

Geometric figures may be classified in two groups, plane figures and solid figures. *If all the points of a figure lie in the same plane, it is called a plane figure.* By a plane we mean a perfectly flat surface. *If the points of a figure lie in more than one plane, it is called a solid figure.* Below we have diagrams of some important plane and solid figures.

Plane Figures

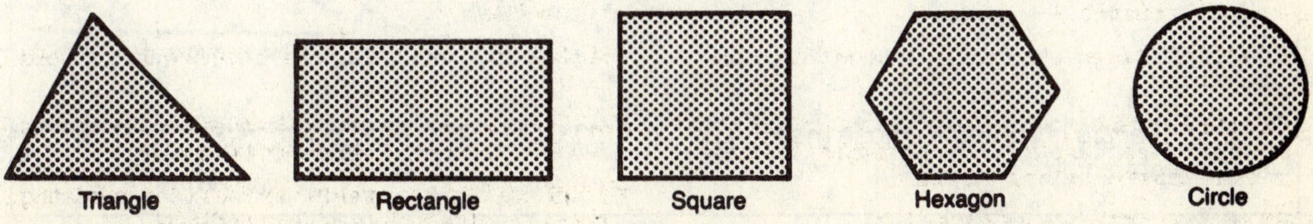

Solid Figures

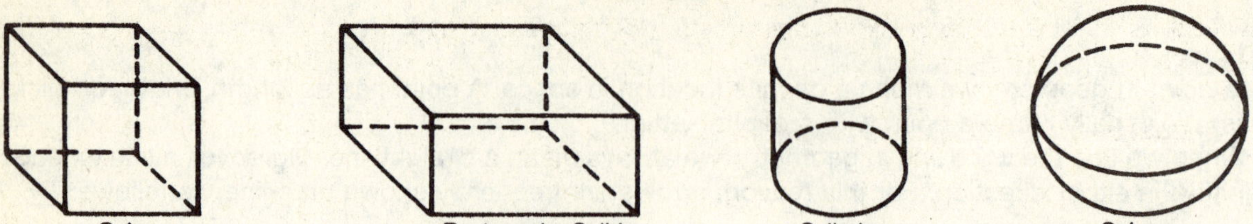

Cube | Rectangular Solid or Box | Cylinder | Sphere

III. C. Geometric Concepts and Relationships

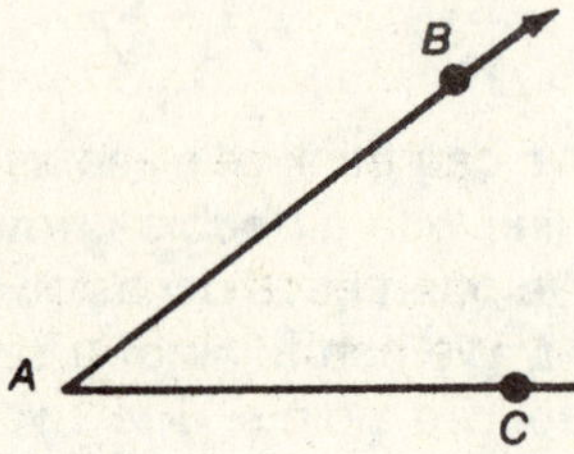

C-1

Angles. An *angle* is a set of points consisting of two rays having the same endpoint. For example, the rays $\overrightarrow{AB}$ and $\overrightarrow{AC}$ having the same endpoint, *A*, form the angle shown. We name an angle by naming a point on one ray, then the common endpoint, and finally a point on the other ray. The symbol for angle is ∠. The angle shown may be called ∠*BAC*, or ∠*CAB.* When there is no ambiguity in meaning, an angle may be named by naming its vertex, the origin of the two rays which form its sides. Thus, ∠*BAC* may be called ∠*A.*

An angle may be measured by using a protractor. As shown in the figure the measure of ∠*AOB* is 70°.

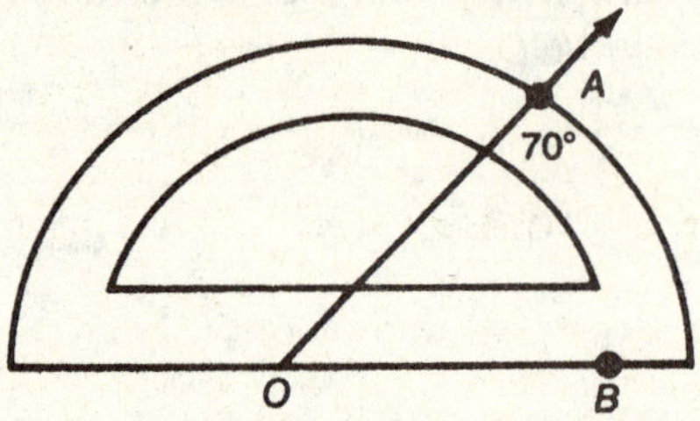

Basics on Angles

An *acute angle* is an angle whose measure is less than 90°. ∠*RST* is an acute angle.

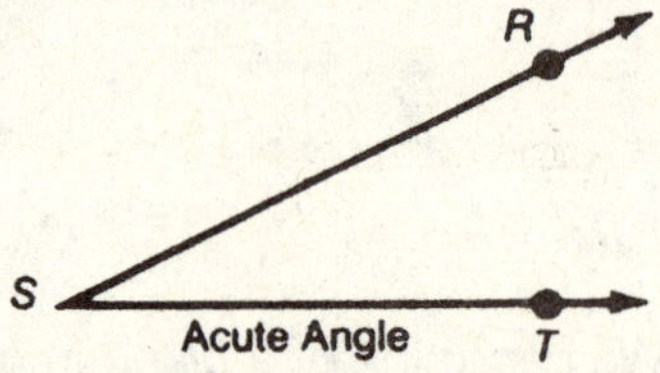

A *right angle* is an angle whose measure is 90°. ∠*VWX* is a right angle.

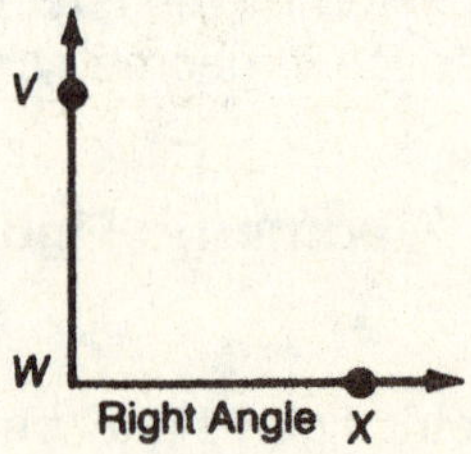

An *obtuse angle* is an angle whose measure is greater than 90° and less than 180°. ∠*OFG* is an obtuse angle.

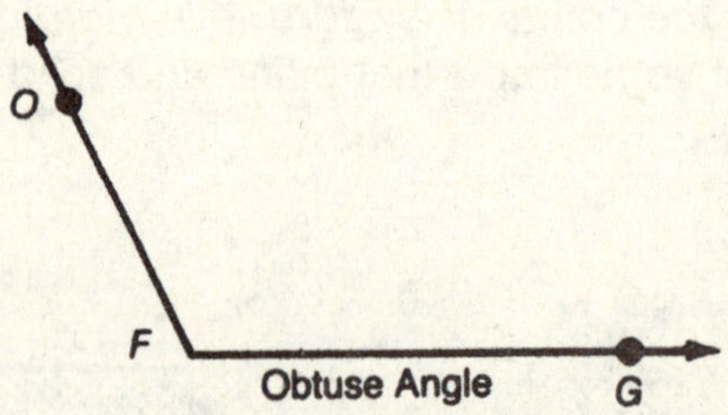

A *straight angle* is an angle whose measure is 180°. ∠*LOC* is a straight angle.

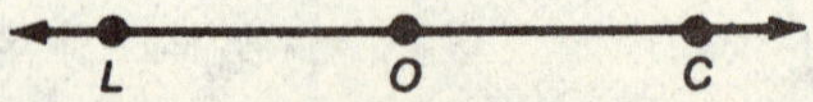

Straight Angle

When two lines meet to form right angles, we say that the lines are *perpendicular* to each other. The symbol ⊥ is used to indicate perpendicular lines. In the diagram, $\overleftrightarrow{DE}$ is perpendicular to $\overleftrightarrow{BC}$, this may be expressed as $\overleftrightarrow{DE} \perp \overleftrightarrow{BC}$. The four right angles formed are ∠*DAB*, ∠*DAC*, ∠*EAB*, and ∠*EAC*.

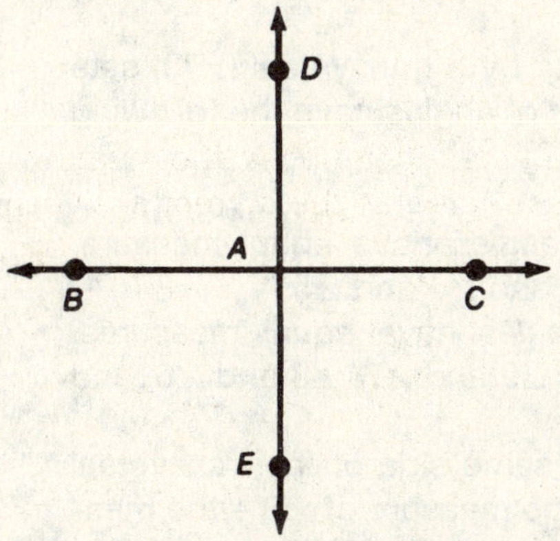

Two angles are *adjacent* if they have the same vertex and have a common side between them. In the diagram, ∠*ABC* and ∠*DBC* are adjacent angles.

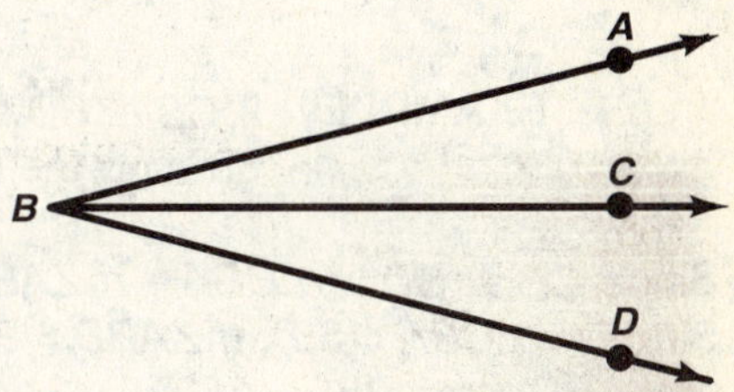

Two angles are *supplementary* if the sum of their measures is 180°. In the diagram, ∠*RST* and ∠*VST* are supplementary.

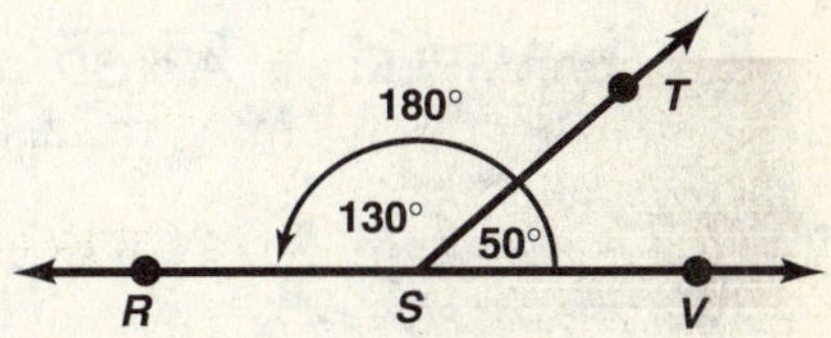

Two angles are *complementary* if the sum of their measures is 90°. In the diagram, $\overleftrightarrow{AB} \perp \overleftrightarrow{DC}$, and ∠*ABE* and ∠*CBE* are complementary.

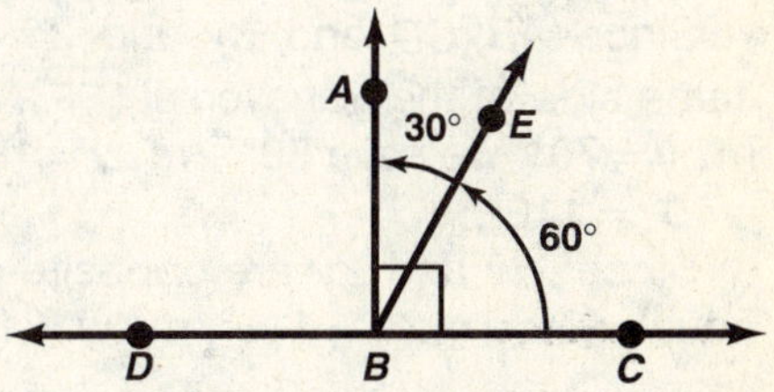

Two intersecting lines form two pairs of *opposite angles*. In the diagram ∠1 and ∠3 are opposite angles and ∠2 and ∠4 are opposite angles. Opposite angles have equal measures.

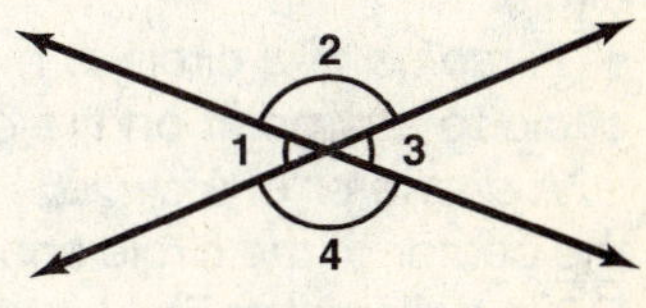

When two lines in the same plane do not meet no matter how far they are extended in either direction the lines are said to be *parallel* to each other. The symbol || is used to indicate parallel lines.

In the diagram $\overleftrightarrow{RS} \parallel \overleftrightarrow{PQ}$.

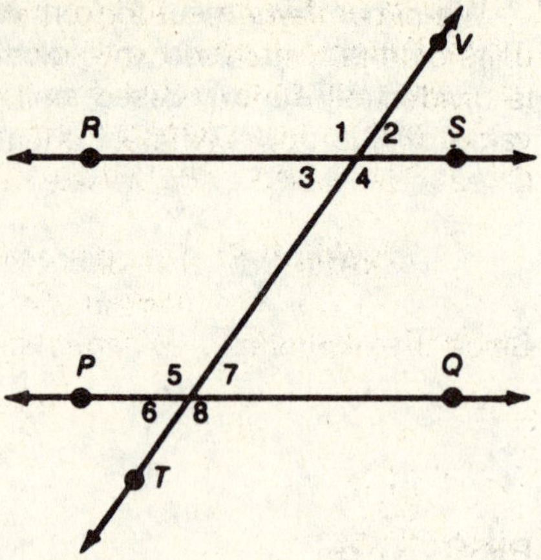

When two parallel lines are cut by a transversal ($\overleftrightarrow{VT}$), sets of angles are formed. These sets of angles have the following relationships:

1. Pairs of *alternate interior angles* have equal measure. Such pairs are ∠3 and ∠7, and ∠4 and ∠5.
2. Pairs of *corresponding angles* have equal measures. Such pairs are ∠1 and ∠5, ∠2 and ∠7, ∠3 and ∠6, and ∠4 and ∠8.
3. Two interior angles on the same side of the transversal are *supplementary*. Thus, the measure of ∠3 + the measure of ∠5 = 180°. And m∠4 + m∠7 = 180°.

EXAMPLE: If $\overleftrightarrow{CB} \perp \overleftrightarrow{BD}$ and the measure of $\angle CBA$ = 38° find the measure of $\angle DBE$.

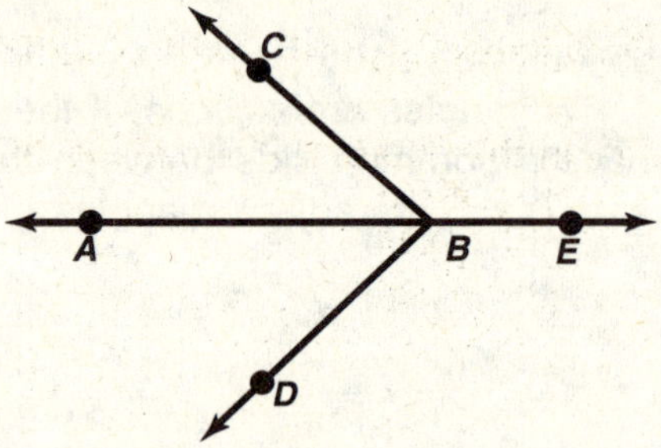

Since $\overleftrightarrow{CB} \perp \overleftrightarrow{BD}$, $m\angle CBA + m\angle ABD = 90°$
Since $m\angle CBA = 38°$, $m\angle ABD = 90° - 38° = 52°$.
$m\angle ABD + m\angle DBE = 180°$.
$52° + m\angle DBE = 180°$
$m\angle DBE = 180° - 52° = 128°$

EXAMPLE: If $\overleftrightarrow{AB} \parallel \overleftrightarrow{CD}$ and $m\angle 1 = 70°$ find $m\angle x$, $m\angle y$, $m\angle z$, $m\angle v$ and $m\angle w$.

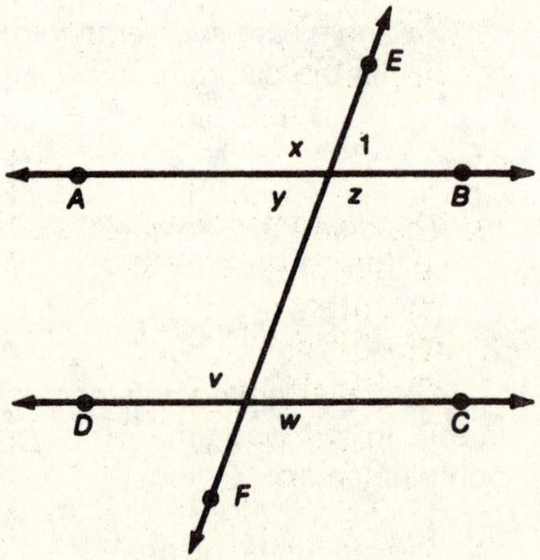

$m\angle x + m\angle 1 = 180°$.
$m\angle x + 70° = 180°$
$m\angle x = 180° - 70° = 110°$

Since $\angle y$ and $\angle 1$ are vertical angles, $m\angle y = m\angle 1 = 70°$
Since $\angle x$ and $\angle z$ are vertical angles, $m\angle z = m\angle x = 110°$
Since $\overleftrightarrow{AB} \parallel \overleftrightarrow{CD}$ and $\angle y$ and $\angle v$ are interior angles on the same side of the transversal ($\overleftrightarrow{EF}$), $m\angle y + m\angle v = 180°$. Since $m\angle y = 70°$, we have $70° + m\angle v = 180°$. Therefore, $m\angle v = 180° - 70° = 110°$.

Since $\angle w$ and $\angle v$ are opposite angles, their measures are equal. Since $m\angle v = 110°$, $m\angle w = 110°$.

C-2

Circles. There are some important terms associated with the circle.

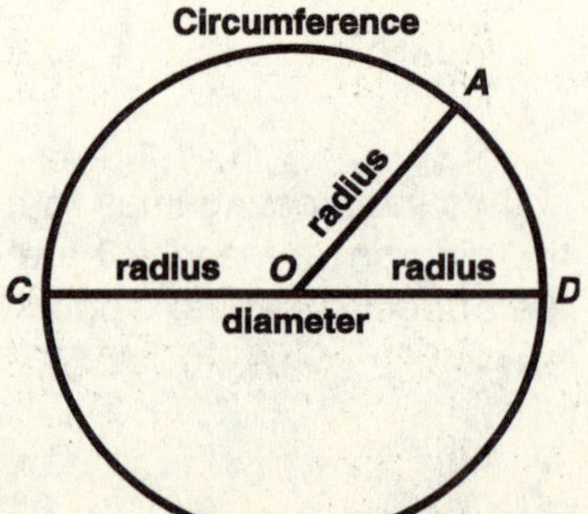

A *radius* of a circle is a line segment from the center of the circle to any point on the circle. $\overline{OA}$ is a radius.

A *diameter* of a circle is a line segment that passes through the center of the circle and has its two endpoints on the circle. $\overline{CD}$ is a diameter. The length of the diameter of a circle is twice the length of the radius of the circle.

The *circumference* of a circle is the length of the curved line forming the circle; it is measured in units of length such as centimetres or metres. If the number of units in the circumference of a circle is divided by the number of units in the diameter of the circle, the result is π (pi). The numerical value of π is approximately equal to 3.14 or $^{22}/_{7}$. *The formula for the circumference of a circle is* $C = 2 \times \pi \times r$, or $C = 2\pi r$ *where r is the radius of the circle.*

EXAMPLE: The diameter of a circle is 12 centimetres. Find the circumference of the circle. (Use $\pi = 3.14$.)

Since the diameter is 12 centimetres, the radius is 6 centimetres.

$$C = 2\pi r$$
$$C = 2 \times 3.14 \times 6 = 37.68 \text{ centimetres}$$

PRACTICE

DIRECTIONS: Blacken the space at the right under the number that corresponds to the one you have selected as the correct answer.

Questions 1–2 refer to the diagram at right.

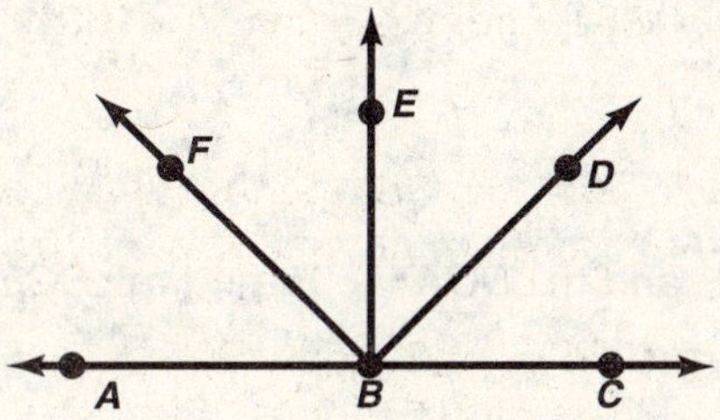

1. In the figure, $\overleftrightarrow{EB} \perp \overleftrightarrow{AC}$. A right angle is
(1) ∠*FBA*
(2) ∠*DBF*
(3) ∠*CBE*
(4) ∠*EBD*
(5) ∠*ABC*

1. 1 2 3 4 5
|| || || || ||

2. An obtuse angle is
(1) ∠*EBA*
(2) ∠*DBE*
(3) ∠*CBA*
(4) ∠*FBC*
(5) ∠*EBC*

2. 1 2 3 4 5
|| || || || ||

3. The diameter of a circle is 30 cm in length. The length of the radius of the same circle is
(1) 60 cm
(2) 60π cm
(3) 15 cm
(4) 15π cm
(5) 7.5 cm

3. 1 2 3 4 5
|| || || || ||

4. The diameter of a circle is 20 cm. If $\pi = 3.14$, then the circumference of the circle (in centimetres) is
(1) 3.14
(2) 62.8
(3) 3.4
(4) 6.28
(5) 31.4

4. 1 2 3 4 5
|| || || || ||

5. The distance around a circular flower bed is 22 m. If $\pi = {}^{22}/_{7}$, the radius of the garden bed (in metres) is
(1) 7
(2) 14
(3) 11
(4) 22
(5) 3.5

5. 1 2 3 4 5
|| || || || ||

Answer the following questions:

6. If $\overleftrightarrow{AB} \perp \overleftrightarrow{DE}$ and $m\angle CBE = 57°$ find $m\angle ABC$.

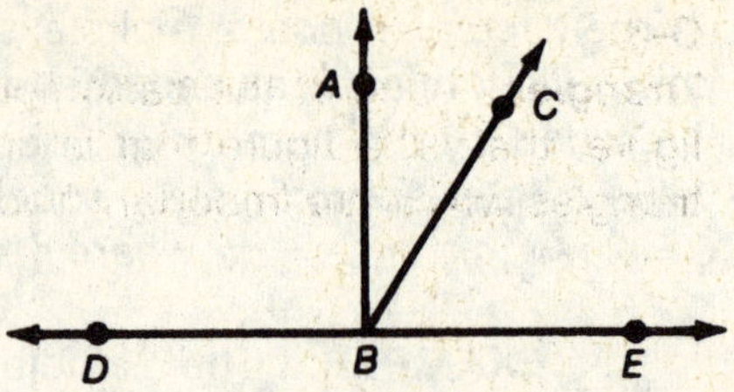

7. If $m\angle 1 = 140°$, find $m\angle x$, given that $\overleftrightarrow{CD} \parallel \overleftrightarrow{TE}$.

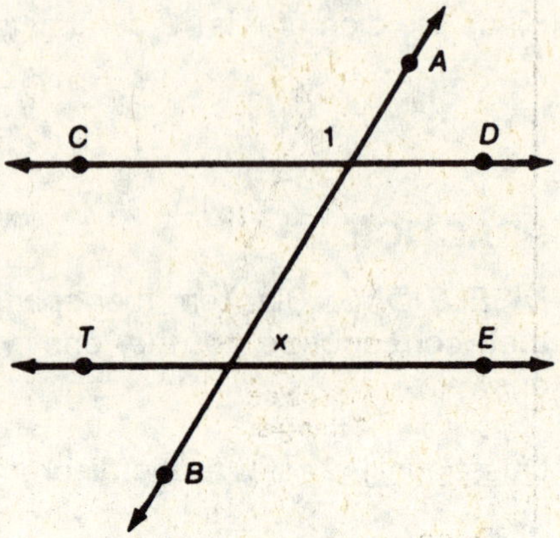

8. If $\overleftrightarrow{CD} \perp \overleftrightarrow{CE}$ and $m\angle DCA = 60°$, find $m\angle BCE$.

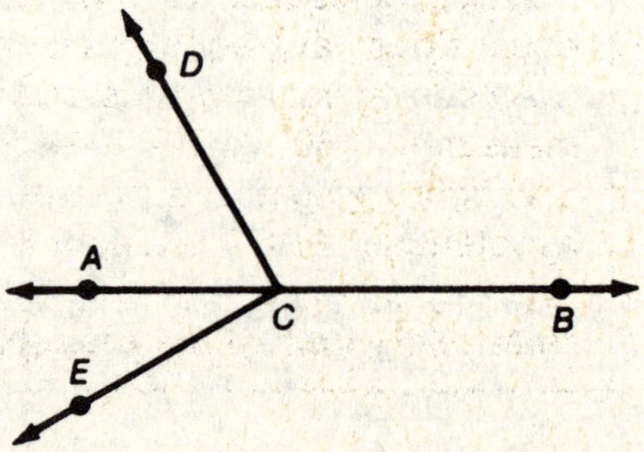

9. If $\overleftrightarrow{AB} \parallel \overleftrightarrow{DE}$, BC bisects $\angle ABD$, and $m\angle ABC = 62°$, find $m\angle BDE$.

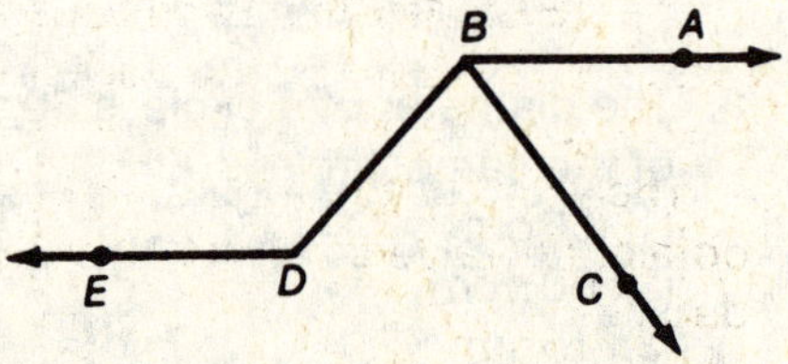

10. If $\overleftrightarrow{AB} \parallel \overleftrightarrow{DC}$, $\overleftrightarrow{BC} \perp \overleftrightarrow{CD}$, and $m\angle D = 68°$, find (a) $m\angle A$ (b) $m\angle B$.

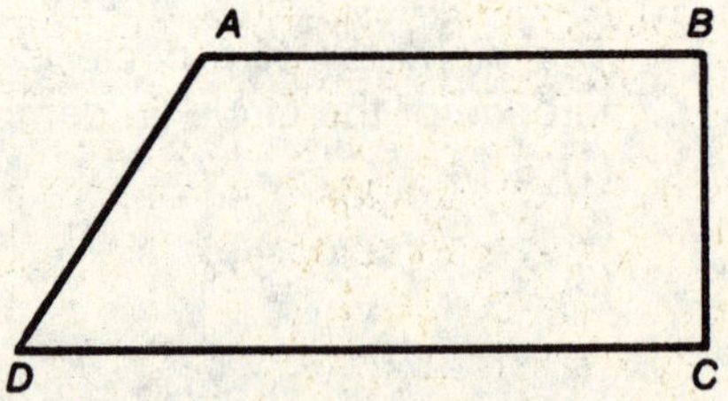

ANSWERS:

1. **3**
2. **4**
3. **3**
4. **2**
5. **5**
6. **33°**
7. **40°**
8. **150°**
9. **124°**
10. **112°, 90°**

C-3

Triangles. One of the basic figures in the study of geometry is the triangle. Because it is a rigid figure, that is, a figure that is firm, it is used for braces and supports. There are three kinds of triangles which are important because they occur frequently.

Basics on Triangles

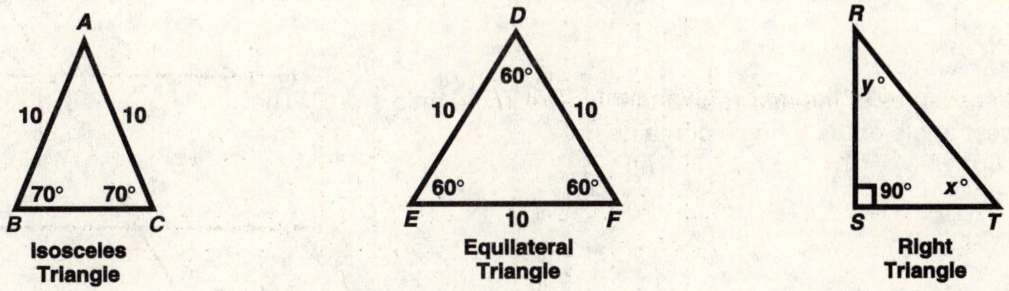

Types:

An *isosceles triangle* is a triangle which has two sides of equal length; the angles opposite the equal sides have equal measures. $\triangle ABC$ is isosceles.

An *equilateral triangle* is a triangle which has three sides of equal length; the angles have equal measures of 60°. $\triangle DEF$ is equilateral.

A *right triangle* is a triangle which has one right angle (90°). The longest side is called the hypotenuse. $\triangle RST$ is a right triangle.

Note: The sum of the measures of the angles of a triangle is 180°.

EXAMPLE: Each base angle of an isosceles triangle contains x°. How many degrees does the third angle of the triangle contain?

The sum of the two base angles is $2x$°. Since the sum of the three angles is 180°, we may obtain the value of the third angle by subtracting $2x$° from 180°. The third angle contains $(180 - 2x)$ degrees.

PRACTICE

DIRECTIONS: Blacken the space at the right under the number which corresponds to the one you have selected as the correct answer.

1. If two angles of a triangle measure 65° and 79°, the third angle of the triangle contains
(1) 56°
(2) 144°
(3) 115°
(4) 36°
(5) 101°

1. 1 2 3 4 5
|| || || || ||

2. One acute angle of a right triangle contains n°, The other acute angle contains
(1) $2n$°
(2) $(90 - n)$°
(3) 90°
(4) $(90 + n)$°
(5) $(180 - n)$°

2. 1 2 3 4 5
|| || || || ||

3. One angle of an isosceles triangle contains 102°. Each of the other angles contains

(1) 78°
(2) 34°
(3) 39°
(4) 49°
(5) 35°

3. 1 2 3 4 5

4. The measures of two acute angles of a right triangle are in the ratio 2:3. The smallest angle of the triangle contains

(1) 36°
(2) 54°
(3) 30°
(4) 70°
(5) 24°

4. 1 2 3 4 5

5. The measures of the angles of a triangle are in the ratio 1:2:3. The largest angle of the triangle contains

(1) 60°
(2) 90°
(3) 120°
(4) 100°
(5) 150°

5. 1 2 3 4 5

ANSWERS:

1. **4** 2. **2** 3. **3** 4. **1** 5. **2**

Note: Review "How to Read and Solve Verbal Problems" on page 489.

III. D. Indirect Measurement

D-1

If we wish to measure a length, we ordinarily use a ruler. However, this would not be practical if we wish to find the height of a mountain or the distance across a river. Such measurements are made indirectly. In this section, we will discuss some of the methods of indirect measurement.

Consider the following problem:

EXAMPLE: A nature group hikes 8 km east and then 6 km north. How many kilometres is the group from its starting point?

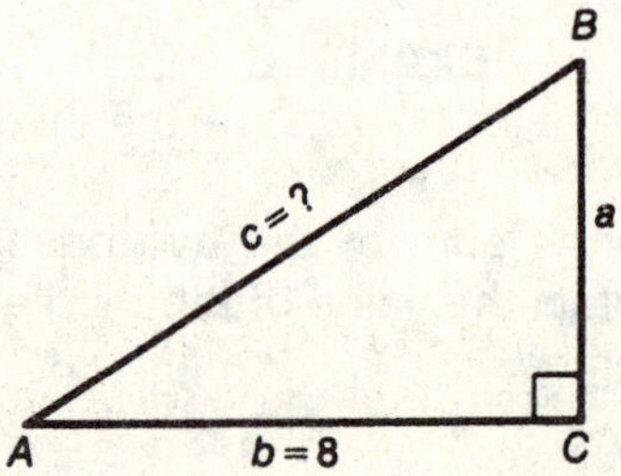

If we look at the diagram, we see that the triangle formed by the hikers is a right triangle. We will make use of a well-known property of right triangles called the Pythagorean Theorem.

D-2

PYTHAGOREAN THEOREM. *This theorem states that in a right triangle, the square of the length of the hypotenuse is equal to the sum of the squares of the lengths of the other two sides.*

To answer the EXAMPLE under section D-1, we must use both the diagram shown and the *Pythagorean Theorem* as follows:

$$c^2 = a^2 + b^2$$
$$c^2 = (6)^2 + (8)^2$$
$$c^2 = 36 + 64$$
$$c^2 = 100$$

The equation $c^2 = 100$ asks the question, "What number multiplied by itself is equal to 100?" The number that makes this statement true is $c = 10$. Thus, the nature group is 10 km from its starting point.

EXAMPLE: Next, suppose that the nature group had hiked 7 km east and then 5 km north. How many kilometres would the nature group be from the starting point?

According to the Pythagorean Theorem (see the diagram),

$$c^2 = a^2 + b^2$$
$$c^2 = (7)^2 + (5)^2$$
$$c^2 = 49 + 25$$
$$c^2 = 74$$

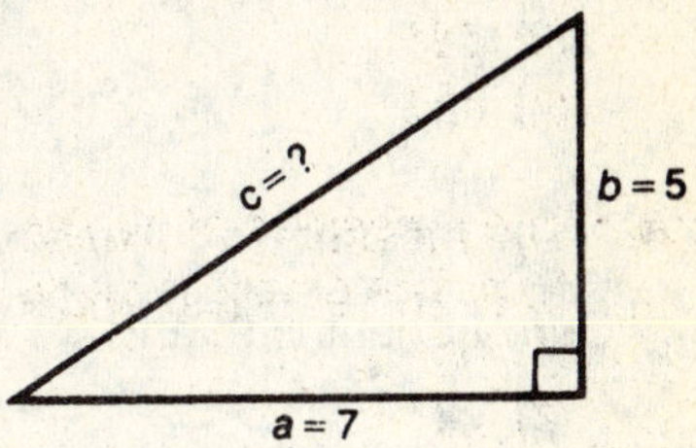

We must now find the number which, when multiplied by itself, is equal to 74. We write this number as $\sqrt{74}$ and we can estimate that the required number is between 8 and 9 since

$$8^2 = 64 \text{ and } 9^2 = 81$$

Therefore, $\sqrt{74}$ is an *irrational number* since it cannot be written exactly in fraction form or in decimal form; but we can find its value correct to the nearest tenth, the nearest hundredth, etc. $\sqrt{74} = 8.6$ correct to the nearest tenth. Note that $(8.6)^2 = 73.96$.

The following is a method for finding the square root of a number. *It is sometimes called "the divide and average method."*

D-3
Finding the Square Root of a Number.

EXAMPLE: Find $\sqrt{196}$.

We first estimate the answer. Suppose we estimate that the answer is 12. We then divide 12 into 196.

$$\begin{array}{r} 16 \\ 12\overline{)196} \\ \underline{12} \\ 76 \\ \underline{72} \\ 4 \end{array} \quad \rightarrow \text{quotient}$$

If 12 had been our answer, we would have obtained a quotient of 12. Since we did not, we get the average of the divisor (12) and the quotient (16).

$$\text{Average} = \frac{12+16}{2} = \frac{28}{2} = 14$$

Next, we use 14 as the divisor

$$\begin{array}{r} 14 \\ 14\overline{)196} \\ \underline{14} \\ 56 \\ \underline{56} \end{array}$$

Thus, $\sqrt{196} = 14$.

EXAMPLE: Find $\sqrt{74}$ to the nearest tenth.

Our first estimate is 8.2 since we wish to find the result to the nearest tenth. Next, we divide

$$\begin{array}{r} 9. \\ 8.2\overline{)74.0} \\ \underline{73\,8} \\ 2 \end{array}$$

Our quotient is 9, and we average

$$\frac{8.2+9}{2}=\frac{17.2}{2}=8.6$$

$$\begin{array}{r} 8.6 \\ 8.6.\overline{)74.0.} \\ \underline{68\,8} \\ 5\,20 \\ \underline{5\,16} \end{array}$$

Since the divisor and the quotient are identical, we have our result correct to the nearest tenth.

Irrational numbers are clearly different from rational numbers. Rational numbers may be expressed in fractional form with the numerator an integer and the denominator an integer other than zero. Irrational numbers cannot be expressed in this way. However, irrational numbers may be paired with points on the number line. For example.

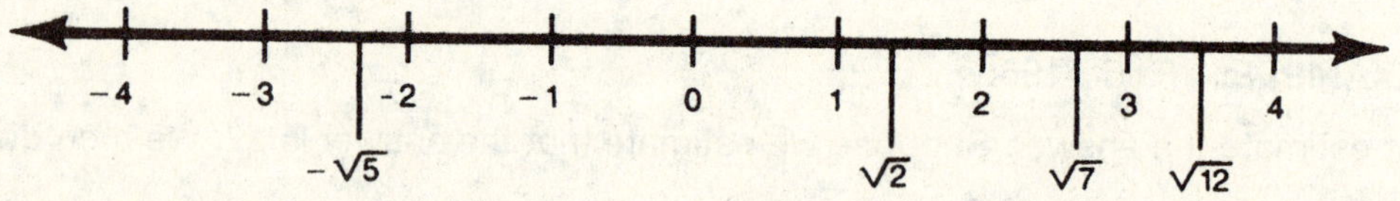

The set of rational numbers together with the set of irrational numbers is called the set of *real numbers.* We can think of a real number as a number which can be paired with a point on the number line.

PRACTICE

Solve the following problems:

1. Find the square root of each of the following.
   a. 169 ______ c. 289 ______ e. 841 ______
   b. 225 ______ d. 1156 ______ f. 1369 ______

2. Find the square root of each of the following correct to the nearest tenth.
   a. 59 ______ c. 42 ______ e. 112 ______
   b. 30 ______ d. 85 ______ f. 97 ______

3. A ladder leans against a building and just reaches the ledge of a window 20 m above the ground. If the foot of the ladder is 15 m from the foot of the building, what is the length of the ladder? __________

4. A wire stretches from the top of a pole 15 m high to a stake in the ground which is 8 m from the pole. Find the length of the wire. __________

5. A plot of ground in the form of a rectangle is 48 m long and 20 m wide. A path extends diagonally across the plot of ground. What is the length of this path? __________

6. What is the length of the ramp in the figure at the right? __________

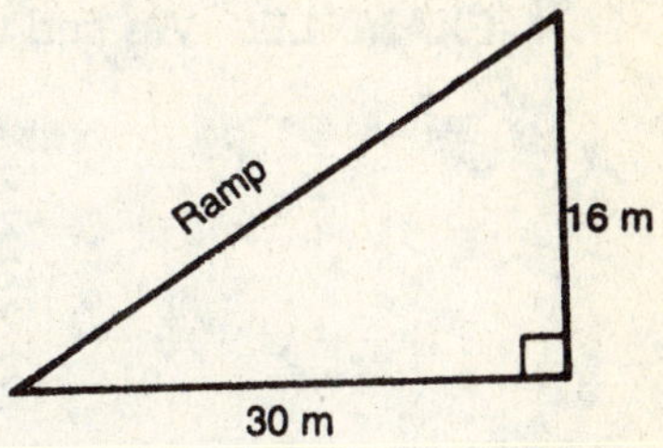

7. A baseball infield is a square 27.5 m on each side. Find, correct to the nearest 0.1 m, the distance from home plate to second base. __________

8. Find, correct to the nearest centimetre, the diameter of a round table top that can just be taken through a doorway that measures 1.5 m in width and 2.5 m in length. __________

9. A boat sails 8 km due east and then 15 km due north. How many kilometres is the boat from its starting point? __________

10. A box is 16 cm wide and 12 cm long. What is the length of a cord which joins two opposite corners of the box? __________

ANSWERS:

1. a. **13**
   b. **15**
   c. **17**
   d. **34**
   e. **29**
   f. **37**
2. a. **7.7**
   b. **5.5**
   c. **6.5**
   d. **9.2**
   e. **10.6**
   f. **9.8**
3. **25m**
4. **17m**
5. **52m**
6. **34m**
7. **38.9m**
8. **2.84m**
9. **17km**
10. **20cm**

III. E. Congruence and Similarity

E-1

Two geometric figures are said to be *congruent* if they have exactly the same size and the same shape. The symbol for congruence is ≅. The two triangles shown in the diagram are congruent. That is △ABC ≅ △DEF. Since congruent triangles can be made to fit if one is placed on top of the other, corresponding sides have the same length. For example, in the figure *AB* = *DE*, *AC* = *DF*, and *BC* = *EF*. Congruent triangles can be used to make measurements indirectly.

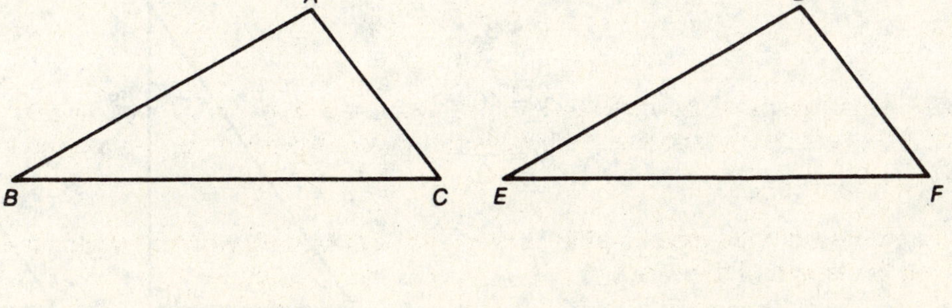

EXAMPLE: We find the distance (*DE*) across the river shown in the diagram as follows:

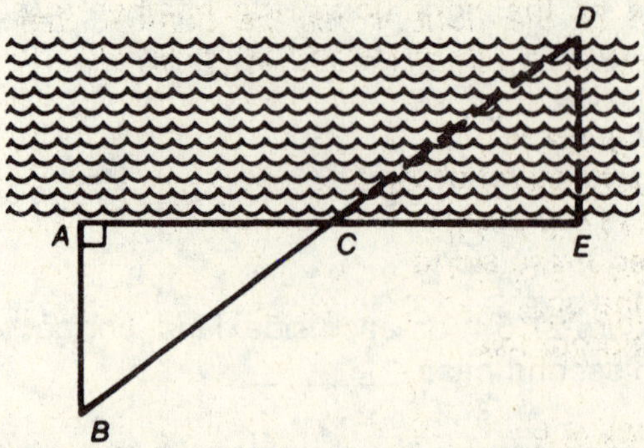

At point *E* sight a point *D* on the other bank of the river. Measure *EA* at right angles to *ED*. At *C*, the midpoint of *EA*, set a stake. Then mark off distance *AB* so that $\angle A$ is a right angle and point *B* lines up with points *C* and *D*. It can be shown that $\triangle BAC \cong \triangle DEC$ and that *AB* and *DE* are corresponding sides. Thus, the distance *AB*, which can be measured, is equal to *DE*, the distance across the river.

Two geometric figures are said to be *similar* if they have the same shape. Because similar figures have the same shape, their corresponding angles have equal measures and the lengths of their corresponding sides are in proportion. The symbol for similarity is ~. The two triangles shown in the following figure are similar. That is, $\triangle ABC \sim \triangle DEF$. Since the lengths of corresponding sides of similar triangles are in proportion, we have

$$\frac{AB}{DE} = \frac{AC}{DF} = \frac{BC}{EF}$$

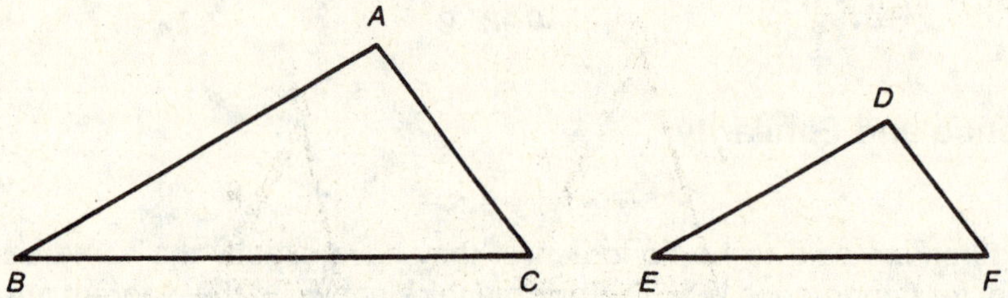

Similar triangles can be used to make measurements indirectly.

EXAMPLE: At a certain hour, a tree casts a shadow 8 m long. At the same time, a post 5 m high casts a shadow 2 m long. What is the height of the tree?

Since the triangles are similar, the lengths of their corresponding sides are in proportion. That is,

$$\frac{y}{5} = \frac{8}{2}$$

$$2y = 40$$

$$y = \frac{40}{2} = 20$$

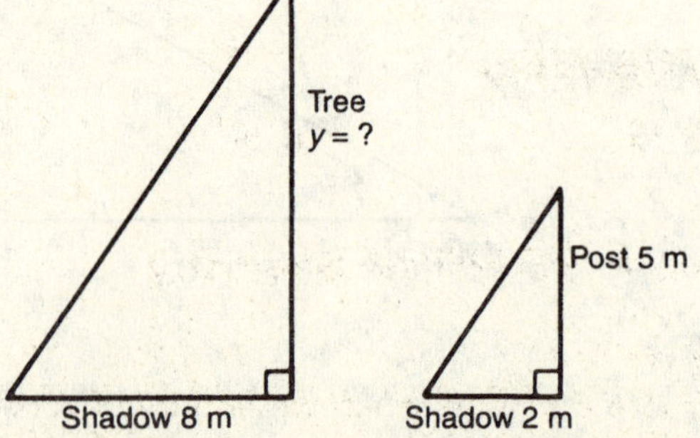

The tree is 20 m high.

PRACTICE

Directions: Blacken the space at the right under the number that corresponds to the one you have selected as the correct answer.

1. An example of congruent figures is
(1) a right triangle and an equilateral triangle
(2) a room and a blueprint of the room
(3) two of your long-sleeved dress shirts
(4) a ship and a model of the ship
(5) a person and his/her photograph

1. 1 2 3 4 5 || || || || ||

2. An example of similar figures is a
(1) square and a triangle
(2) picture and an enlargement of the same picture
(3) person and his/her dog
(4) house and a garage
(5) tennis ball and a tennis racket

2. 1 2 3 4 5 || || || || ||

3. If $\triangle ABC \cong \triangle DEF$, then $x =$
(1) 7
(2) 8
(3) 15
(4) 9
(5) 17

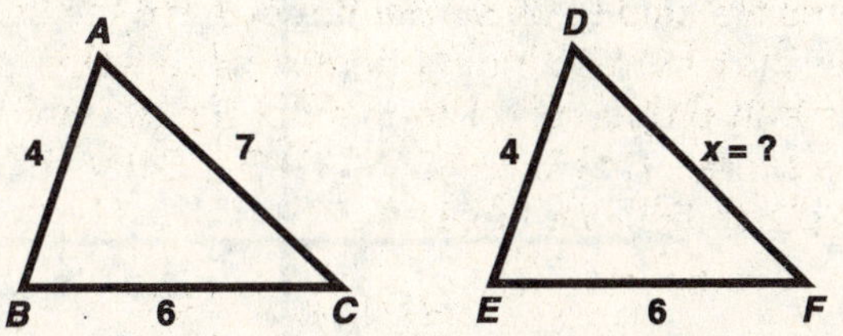

3. 1 2 3 4 5 || || || || ||

4. If $\triangle KLP \sim \triangle RST$, then $y =$
(1) 5
(2) 7
(3) 8
(4) 12
(5) 3

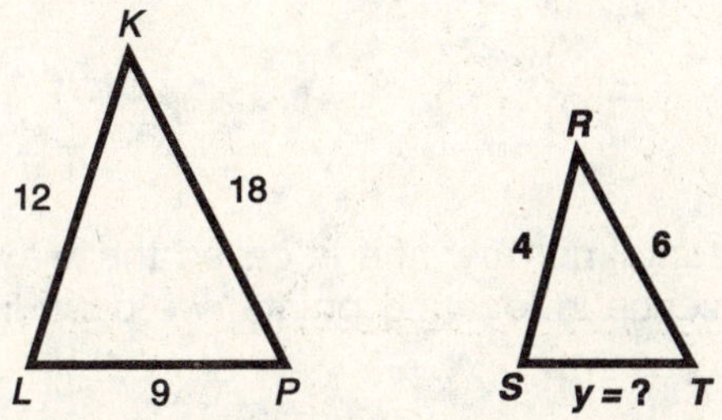

4. 1 2 3 4 5 || || || || ||

5. A tower casts a shadow of 48 m. At the same time, a pole 6 m high casts a shadow of 4 m. The height of the tower, in metres, is
(1) 24
(2) 32
(3) 96
(4) 72
(5) 64

5. 1 2 3 4 5 || || || || ||

ANSWERS:

1. **3** 2. **2** 3. **1** 4. **5** 5. **4**

III. F. Coordinate Geometry

F-1

There are times when we find it convenient to use pairs of numbers to locate points. For example, suppose you make an appointment to meet a friend. You might say, "Meet me at the corner of 5th Avenue and 3rd Street." We write this number pair as (5,3) where it is understood that the first number (5) locates the avenue and the second number (3) locates the street of the meeting. Thus, if we were to write (3,5) we would mean that we are to meet at the corner of 3rd Avenue and 5th Street. The order in which the numbers are written is important. For this reason, such pairs of numbers are called *ordered number pairs.*

Recall that we can locate points on the number line. For example,

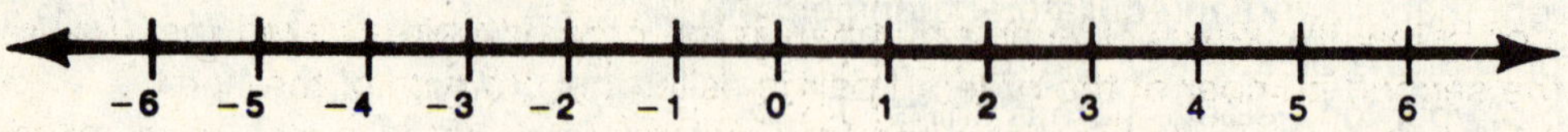

However, we may wish to locate points in the plane that are *not* on the number line. In order to do this, we use two number lines which are perpendicular to each other as shown below:

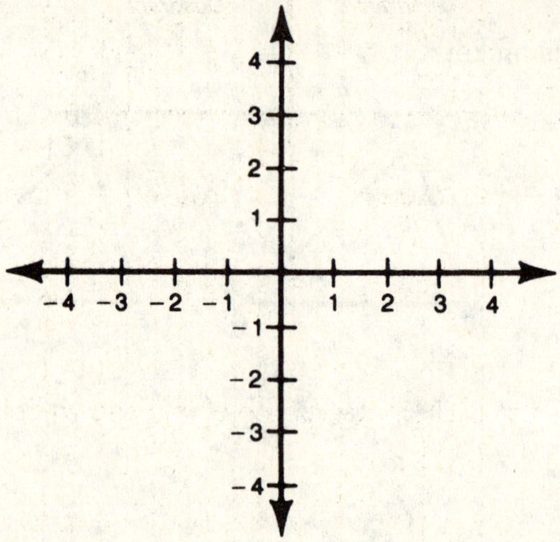

Used in this way, the horizontal number line is called the x-axis, and the vertical number line is called the y-axis. For convenience in locating points, we draw lines parallel to the axes to form a graph chart as shown below:

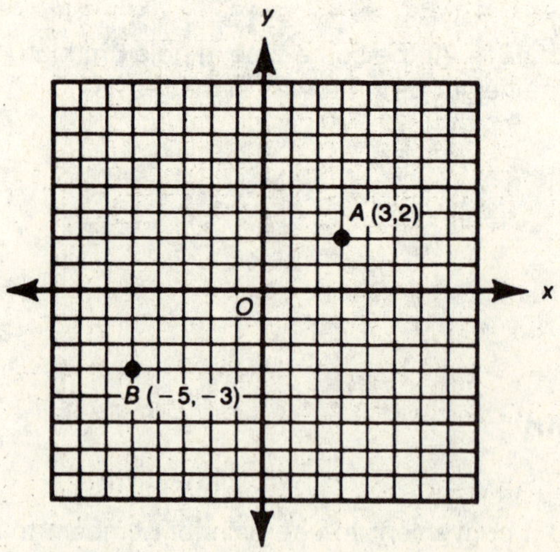

Consider point *A*. We locate point *A* in the plane by using the number pair (3,2). This indicates that point *A* is 3 units to the right of the *y*-axis and 2 units above the *x*-axis.

Consider point *B*. Point *B* is 5 units to the left of the *y*-axis and 3 units below the *x*-axis. Its number pair is (–5,–3).

In order to avoid confusion, we agree that the first number of the ordered pair will measure the number of units to the right or left of the *y*-axis and the second number will measure the number of units above or below the *x*-axis. The first number of the ordered pair is called the *abscissa* of the point, and the second number of the ordered pair is called the *ordinate* of the point.

Note that the two axes divide the plane into four regions. Each of these regions is called a *quadrant.* The quadrants are numbered I, II, III, and IV. The point where the coordinate axes meet is called the *origin*. The coordinates, or number pair, of the origin are (0,0).

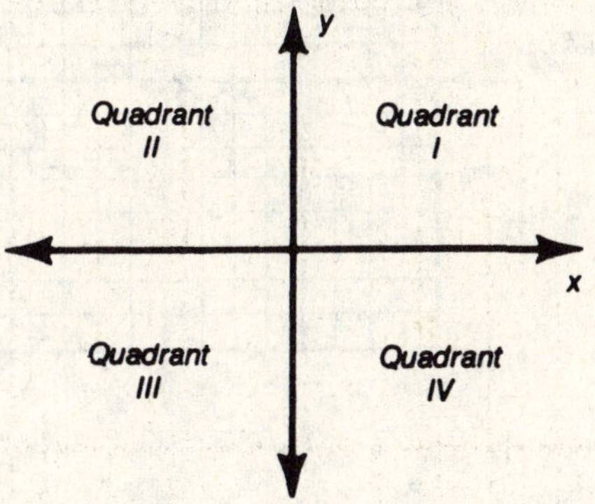

EXAMPLE: What are the coordinates of the points shown below?

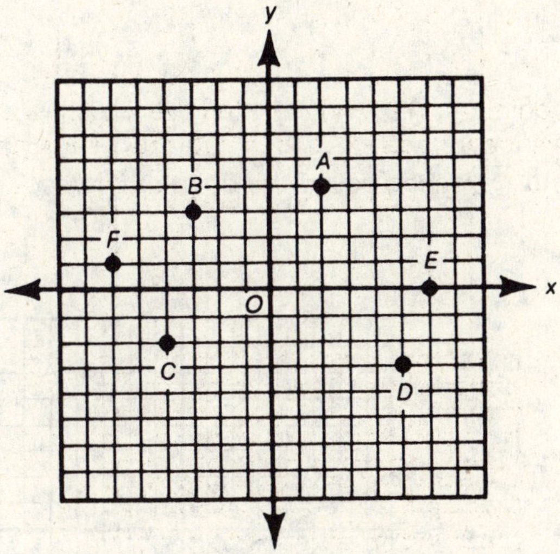

Point *A* (2, 4), Point *B* (–3, 3), Point *C* (–4, –2),
Point *D* (5, –3), Point *E* (6, 0), Point *F* (–6, 1)

PRACTICE

Directions: Blacken the space at the right under the number which corresponds to the one you have selected as the correct answer.

Questions 1–4 refer to the graph at right.

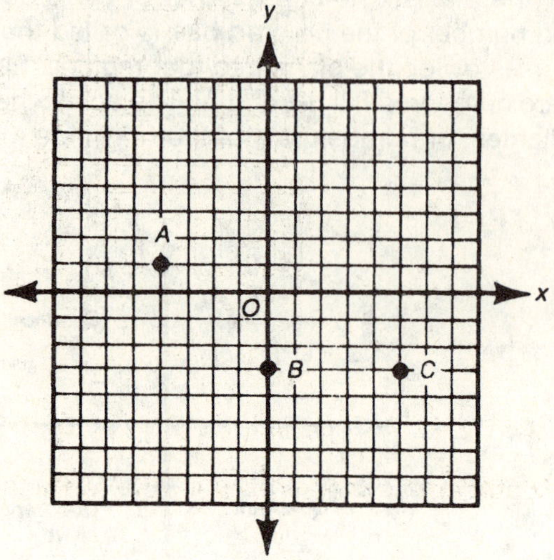

1. The coordinates of point *A* are
(1) (4,–1)
(2) (–4,–1)
(3) (–4,1)
(4) (–4,0)
(5) (4,1)

1. 1 2 3 4 5

2. The coordinates of point *B* are
(1) (0,3)
(2) (–3,0)
(3) (1,3)
(4) (0,0)
(5) (0,–3)

2. 1 2 3 4 5

3. The coordinates of point *C* are
(1) (5,3)
(2) (5,–3)
(3) (3,–5)
(4) (3,5)
(5) (5,–5)

3. 1 2 3 4 5

4. The point (–1,–3) is in Quadrant
(1) I
(2) II
(3) III
(4) IV
(5) O

4. 1 2 3 4 5

5. The point in which $\overleftrightarrow{AB}$ and $\overleftrightarrow{CD}$ meet, called the *point of intersection* of the two lines, is
(1) (2,–1)
(2) (–2,1)
(3) (–1,–2)
(4) (–2,–1)
(5) (–1,2)

5. 1 2 3 4 5

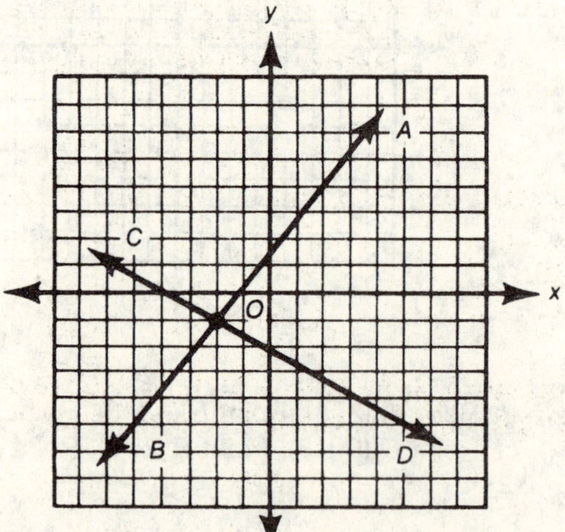

6. The point of intersection of $\overleftrightarrow{CD}$ and $\overleftrightarrow{EF}$ is
(1) (–2,–4)
(2) (–4,–2)
(3) (2,–4)
(4) (4,–2)
(5) (4,0)

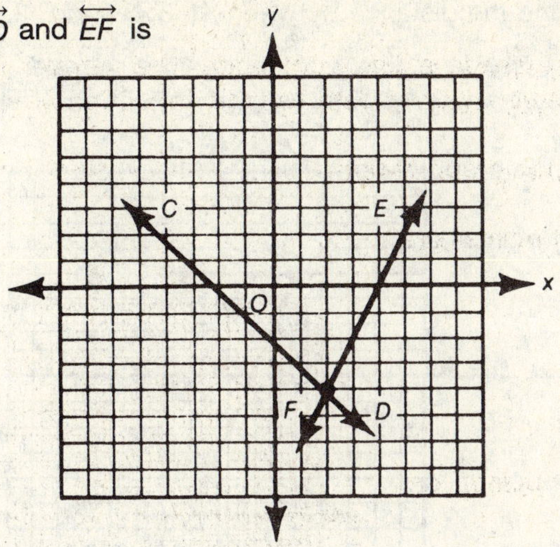

6. 1 2 3 4 5
|| || || || ||

ANSWERS

1. 3 2. 5 3. 2 4. 3 5. 4 6. 3

We may use the Pythagorean Theorem to find the distance between two points whose coordinates are given.

EXAMPLE: Find the distance between the points $A(2,1)$ and $B(6,4)$.

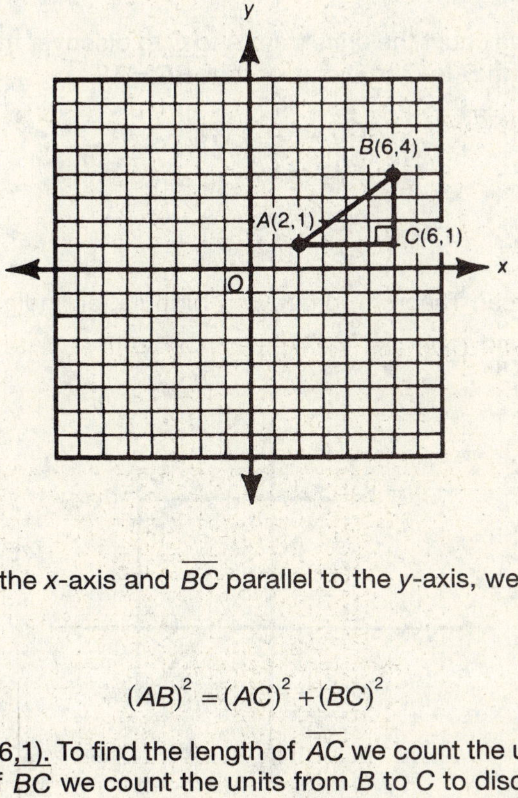

If we draw $\overline{AC}$ parallel to the x-axis and $\overline{BC}$ parallel to the y-axis, we have the right triangle ACB with the hypotenuse $\overline{AB}$.

In right triangle ACB,

$$(AB)^2 = (AC)^2 + (BC)^2$$

The coordinates of C are (6,1). To find the length of $\overline{AC}$ we count the units from A to C to discover $AC = 4$. To find the length of BC we count the units from B to C to discover that $BC = 3$.

$$(AB)^2 = (3)^2 + (4)^2$$
$$(AB)^2 = 9 + 16$$
$$(AB)^2 = 25$$
$$AB = \sqrt{25}$$
$$AB = 5$$

The length of $\overline{AB} = 5$.

EXAMPLE: Find the distance between $A(-3,4)$ and $B(2,-8)$.

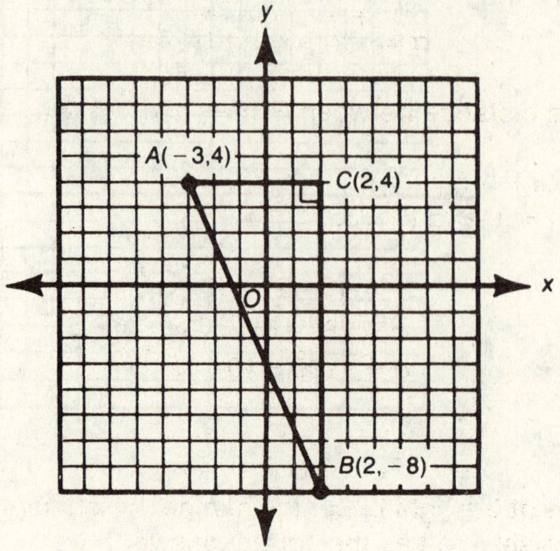

If we draw $\overline{AC}$ parallel to the x-axis and $\overline{BC}$ parallel to the y-axis, we have the right triangle ACB with hypotenuse $\overline{AB}$. The coordinates of point C are (2,4).

In right triangle ACB,

$$(AB)^2 = (AC)^2 + (BC)^2$$

To find the length of $\overline{AC}$, we count the units from A to C to discover that $\overline{AC} = 5$. To find the length of BC, we count the units from B to C to discover that $BC = 12$.

$$(AB)^2 = (5)^2 + (12)^2$$
$$(AB)^2 = 25 + 144 = 169$$
$$AB = \sqrt{169}$$
$$AB = 13$$

We may use the Pythagorean Theorem to derive a formula for finding the distance between two points $A(x_1,y_1)$ and $B(x_2,y_2)$.

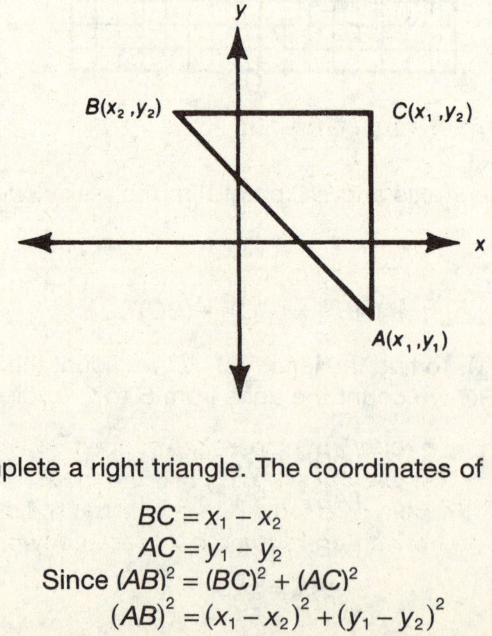

We draw $\overline{AC}$ and $\overline{BC}$ to complete a right triangle. The coordinates of point C are (x_1,y_2).

$$BC = x_1 - x_2$$
$$AC = y_1 - y_2$$
Since $(AB)^2 = (BC)^2 + (AC)^2$
$$(AB)^2 = (x_1 - x_2)^2 + (y_1 - y_2)^2$$

If we let $AB = d$, we have

$$d^2 = (x_1 - x_2)^2 + (y_1 - y_2)^2$$
$$d = \sqrt{(x_1 - x_2)^2 + (y_1 - y_2)^2}$$

EXAMPLE: Find the distance between $P(10,9)$ and $Q(2,3)$.

We use the formula $d^2 = (x_1 - x_2)^2 + (y_1 - y_2)^2$.
In this case, $x_1 = 10$, $x_2 = 2$, $y_1 = 9$, and $y_2 = 3$.

$$d^2 = (10-2)^2 + (9-3)^2$$
$$d = \sqrt{8^2 + 6^2} = \sqrt{64+36}$$
$$d = \sqrt{100} = 10$$

PRACTICE

Directions: Blacken the space at the right under the number which corresponds to the one you have selected as the correct answer.

1. The distance between $A(0,0)$ and $B(3,4)$ is

(1) 3
(2) 4
(3) 2
(4) 5
(5) 1

1. 1 2 3 4 5

2. The distance between $R(-2,1)$ and $S(4,9)$ is

(1) 7
(2) 10
(3) 5
(4) 9
(5) 4

2. 1 2 3 4 5

3. The distance between $C(5,7)$ and $D(5,1)$ is

(1) 6
(2) 0
(3) 5
(4) 8
(5) 10

3. 1 2 3 4 5

4. The distance between $P(-5,-3)$ and $Q(7,6)$ is

(1) 10
(2) 15
(3) 12
(4) 14
(5) 20

4. 1 2 3 4 5

5. The distance between $K(-5,-3)$ and $L(-2,-3)$ is

(1) 3
(2) 5
(3) 7
(4) 8
(5) 10

5. 1 2 3 4 5

ANSWERS:

1. **4** 2. **2** 3. **1** 4. **2** 5. **1**

F-2

The Slope of a Line. In designing roads, engineers are concerned with the steepness, or slope, of the road. In this section, we will discuss the meaning and the measurement of the slope of a line.

The *slope of a line* between two points on the line is defined as the distance the line rises between the points as compared with the horizontal distance between the two points. For example, see the following diagram.

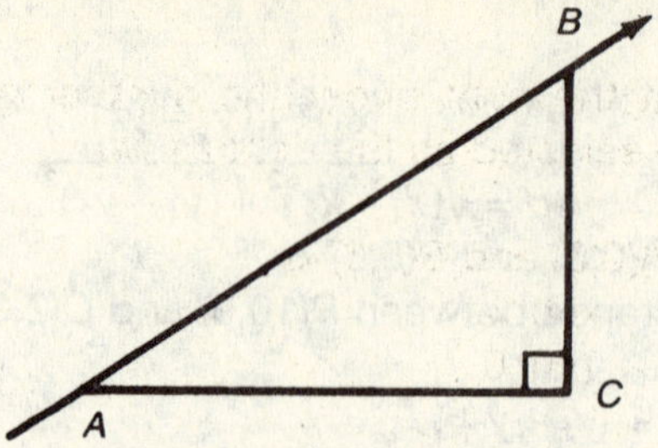

If BC represents the distance the line rises between points A and B, and AC represents the horizontal distance covered between points A and B, then the slope of AB is $\frac{5}{8}$.

In general, we can define the slope of a line as the change in the y-coordinates divided by the change in the x-coordinates of the two points.

EXAMPLE 1: Find the slope of $\overline{OB}$.

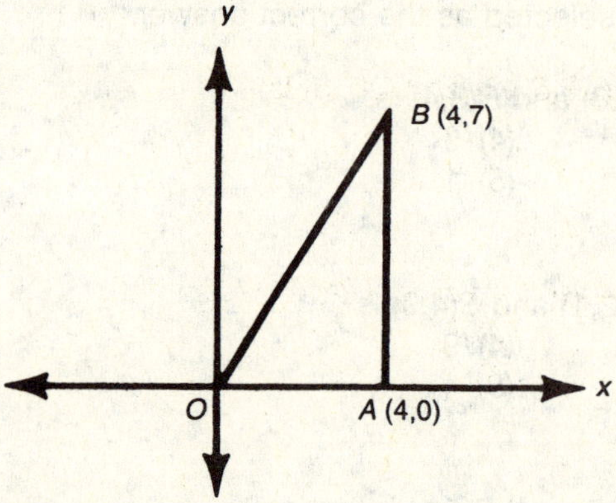

In this case,

$$\frac{\text{change in } y-\text{coordinates}}{\text{change in } x-\text{coordinates}} = \frac{7-0}{4-0} = \frac{7}{4}$$

EXAMPLE 2: Find the slope of the line joining the points $A(2,1)$ and $B(5,8)$.

We draw $\overline{AC}$ parallel to the x-axis and $\overline{BC}$ parallel to the y-axis.

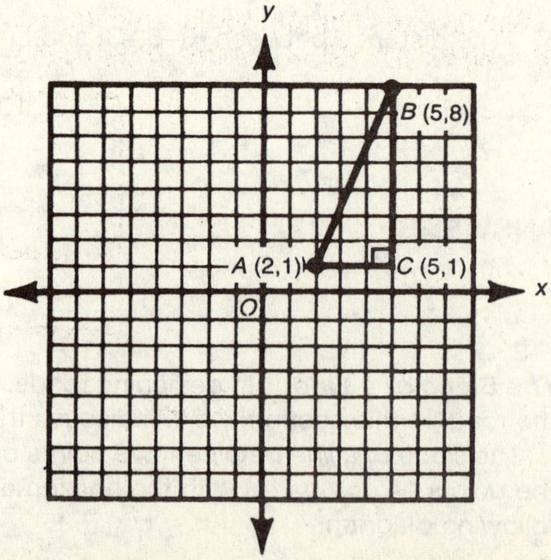

$$\text{The slope of } \overline{AB} = \frac{\text{change in } y-\text{coordinates}}{\text{change in } x-\text{coordinates}} = \frac{CB}{AC}$$

By counting, we find that $CB = 7$ and that $AC = 3$.

$$\text{slope of } \overline{AB} = \frac{CB}{AC} = \frac{7}{3}.$$

PRACTICE

Directions: Blacken the space at the right under the number which corresponds to the one you have selected as the right answer.

1. The slope of the line joining $A(0,0)$ and $B(5,6)$ is

(1) 5
(2) 6
(3) $\frac{5}{6}$
(4) $\frac{6}{5}$
(5) 0

1. 1 2 3 4 5

2. The slope of the line joining $C(3,2)$ and $D(6,7)$ is

(1) $\frac{3}{5}$
(2) $\frac{5}{3}$
(3) $\frac{7}{5}$
(4) $\frac{5}{7}$
(5) $\frac{7}{6}$

2. 1 2 3 4 5

3. The slope of the line joining $R(-1,5)$ and $S(4,7)$ is

(1) $\frac{5}{2}$
(2) $\frac{2}{3}$
(3) $\frac{2}{5}$
(4) 5
(5) $\frac{3}{2}$

3. 1 2 3 4 5

4. The slope of the line joining $P(5,-3)$ and $Q(7,5)$ is

(1) 4
(2) $\frac{1}{4}$
(3) 1
(4) $\frac{2}{7}$
(5) $\frac{5}{2}$

4. 1 2 3 4 5

5. The slope of the line joining $K(-2,-1)$ and $L(2,3)$ is

(1) 3
(2) 1
(3) $\frac{1}{3}$
(4) $\frac{2}{3}$
(5) $\frac{3}{2}$

5. 1 2 3 4 5

ANSWERS:

1. 4 **2. 2** **3. 3** **4. 1** **5. 2**

III. G. Perimeters

G-1

Mr. Wells had a garden 18 m long and 12 m wide. He wished to fence in the garden. How many metres of fencing did he need?

We can see that Mr. Wells needed two lengths of 18 m each and two widths of 12 m each. Thus, he needed $(2 \times 18) + (2 \times 12)$, or $36 + 24 = 60$ m.

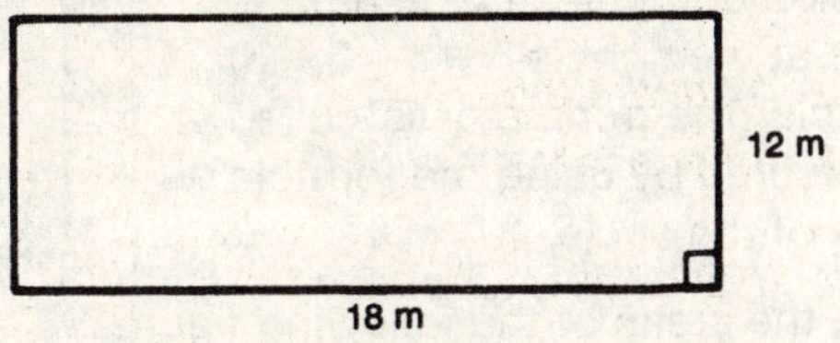

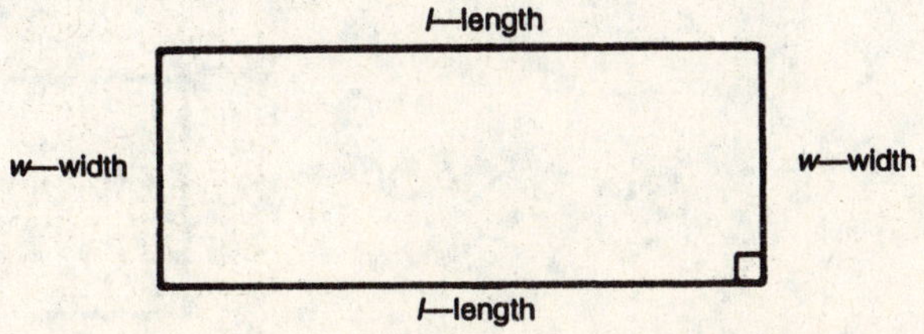

Now, suppose that we wish to find a formula to find the distance around the *rectangle* (called "the *perimeter*"). A rectangle is a figure having four sides and four right angles. If we represent the perimeter by P, the length by l, and the width by w,

Perimeter of a Rectangle
$P = l + w + l + w$
or $P = 2l + 2w$

We can write this as $P = 2(l + w)$.
$P = 2l + 2w$ or $P = 2(l + w)$ is an example of a *formula* in mathematics.

PRACTICE

Solve the following problems.

1. Ms. Chung wishes to fence in a rectangular lawn which is 60 metres long and 30 metres wide. She uses the formula $P = 2(l + w)$ to obtain the result. Find the perimeter.
2. Use the formula $P = 2(l + w)$ to find the perimeters (P) of rectangles whose lengths (l) and widths (w) are given.
   a. $l = 15$, $w = 8$
   b. $l = 17$, $w = 12$
   c. $l = 19.5$, $w = 7$
   d. $l = 16.4$, $w = 5.1$
3. If a, b and c represent the lengths of the sides of a triangle, the formula $P = a + b + c$ gives the perimeter of the triangle. Use this formula to find the perimeter of the triangles the lengths of whose sides are given below.
   a. $a = 5$, $b = 7$, $c = 8$
   b. $a = 17$, $b = 12$, $c = 15$
   c. $a = 9$, $b = 11$, $c = 15$

ANSWERS:

1. **180m**
2. a. **46** b. **58** c. **53** d. **43**
3. a. **20** b. **44** c. **35**

III. H. Areas

H-1

We have seen that the perimeter of a plane geometric figure is a measure of its outside boundary. For example, the perimeter of the rectangle at the right is $3 + 8 + 3 + 8$, or 22 m. In the case of a circle, the perimeter is called the circumference and is measured by using the formula $C = 2\pi r$, where r is the radius of the circle.

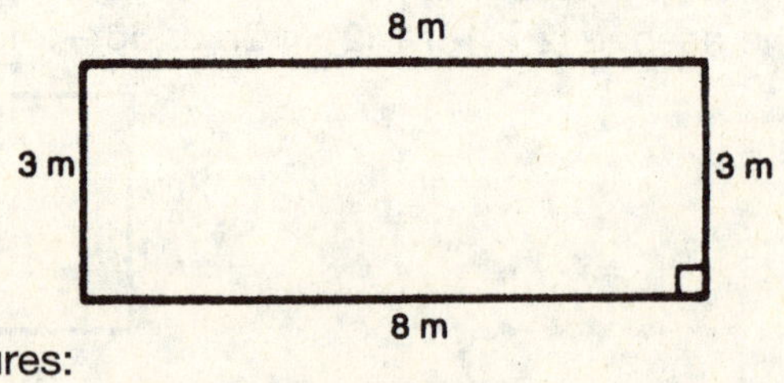

We will be concerned with the areas of the following figures:

Rectangle

Rectangle

$A = l \times w$

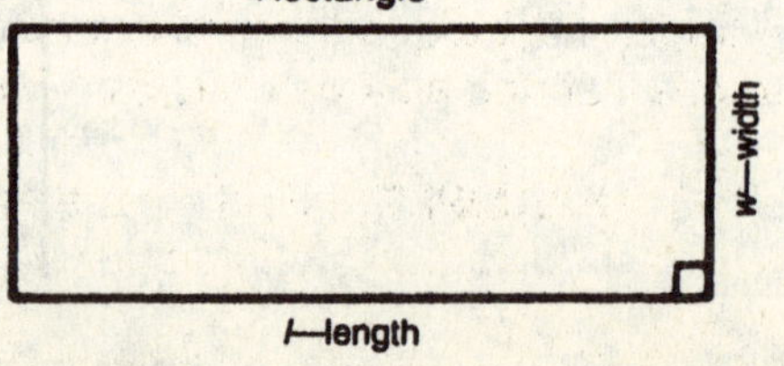

The *area of a rectangle* is found by multiplying the number of units in the length by the number of units in the width.

Triangle

$A = \frac{1}{2}b \times h$

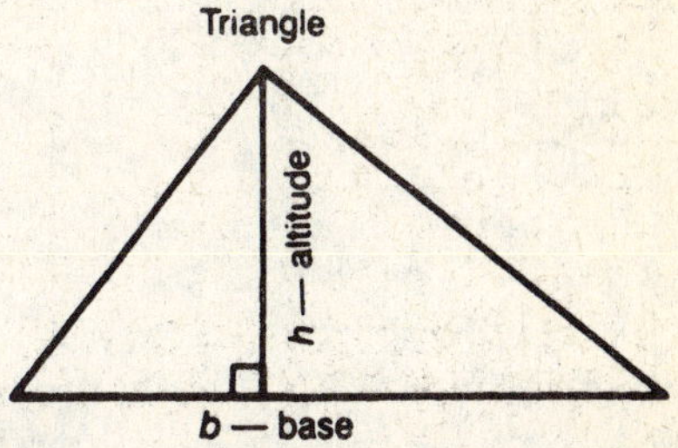

The *area of a triangle* is equal to one-half the product of the number of units in its base and the number of units in its altitude (*height*).

Square

$A = s \times s = s^2$

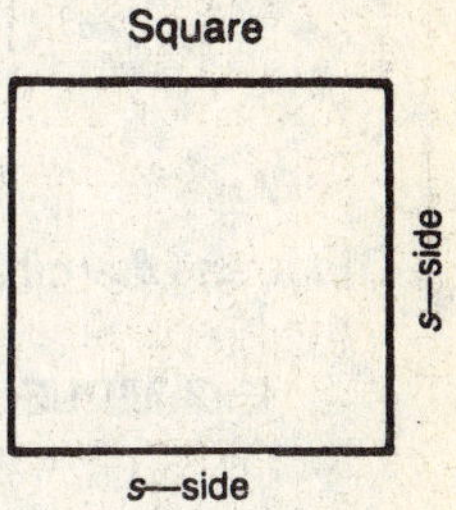

The *area of a square* is equal to the square of the number of units in a side of the square.

Parallelogram

$A = b \times h$

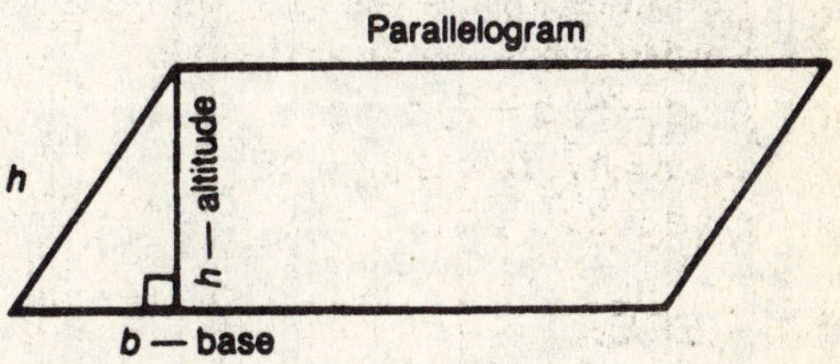

A parallelogram is a quadrilateral (4-sided figure) whose opposite sides are parallel. The *area of a parallelogram* is equal to the product of the number of units in its base and the number of units in its altitude. The altitude is a line segment drawn from a vertex perpendicular to the opposite side (called the base).

Trapezoid

$A = \frac{1}{2}h\,(b + a)$

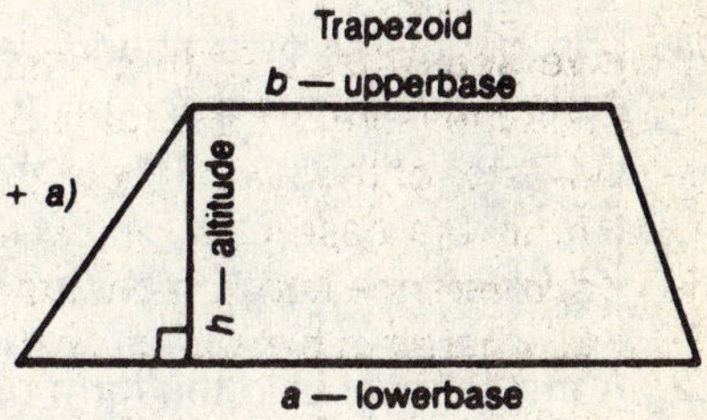

A trapezoid is a quadrilateral having two and only two sides parallel. The *areas of a trapezoid* is equal to one-half the altitude multiplied by the sum of the bases.

EXAMPLE: Find the area of a trapezoid whose altitude is 8 cm and whose bases are 12 cm and 7 cm.

$$A = \tfrac{1}{2}h(b+a)$$

In this case, $h = 8$, $b = 12$, and $a = 7$.

$$A = \tfrac{1}{2} \cdot 8(12+7)$$
$$A = 4(19) = 76\,\text{cm}^2$$

Circle

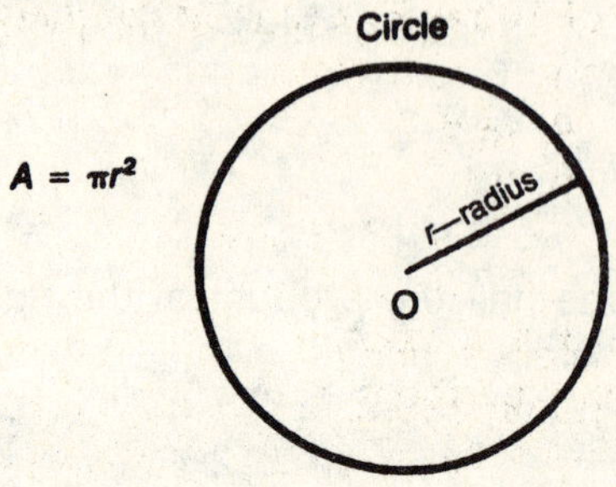

The *area of a circle* is equal to the product of π and the square of the radius.

EXAMPLE: Find the area of a circle whose radius is 14 cm

$$A = \pi r^2$$
$$A = \pi \times 14 \times 14 = 196\pi$$

If we wish to obtain a more useful answer, we must take an approximate value for π. The approximate values of π usually used are $^{22}\!/_7$ and 3.14.

If $\pi = {}^{22}\!/_7$, we have

$$\text{Area} = 196 \times \frac{22}{7} = {}^{28}\cancel{196} \times \frac{22}{\cancel{7}} = 616\,\text{cm}^2$$

If $\pi = 3.14$, we have

$$\text{Area} = 196 \times 3.14 = 615.44\,\text{cm}^2$$

The answers differ slightly because the approximations for π are slightly different in value.

PRACTICE

Directions: Blacken the space at the right under the number that corresponds to the one you have selected as the correct answer.

1. The perimeter of a square is 24 cm. The area of the square (in square centimetres) is
(1) 576
(2) 16
(3) 64
(4) 36
(5) 100

1. 1 2 3 4 5 || || || || ||

2. A metal sheet is in the form of a trapezoid whose bases are 20 cm and 15 cm and whose altitude is 8 cm. The area of the metal sheet (in square centimetres) is
(1) 420
(2) 270
(3) 140
(4) 110
(5) 47

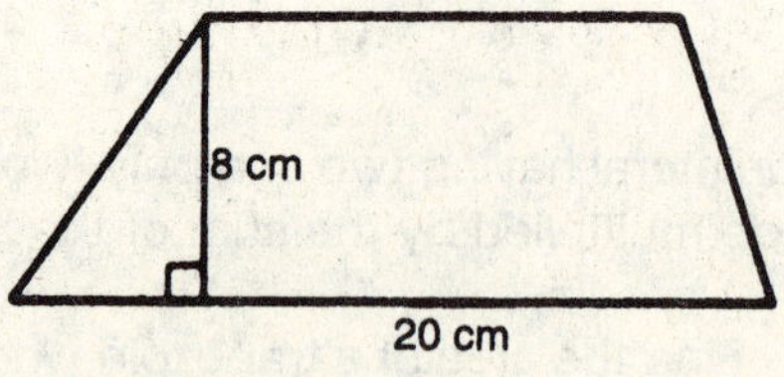

2. 1 2 3 4 5 || || || || ||

3. A rectangle and a square have equal areas. The length of the rectangle is 20 cm, and its width is 5 cm. A side of the square measures (in centimetres)
(1) 100
(2) 10
(3) 20
(4) 40
(5) 12

3. 1 2 3 4 5

4. A circular mirror has a diameter of 14 cm. The area of the mirror (in square centimetres) is [use $\pi = {}^{22}\!/_{7}$]
(1) 154
(2) 144
(3) 616
(4) 308
(5) 88

4. 1 2 3 4 5

5. Management is planning to install a floor moulding in this L-shaped banquet room. Find the perimeter (in metres).
(1) 67
(2) 77
(3) 93
(4) 108
(5) 118

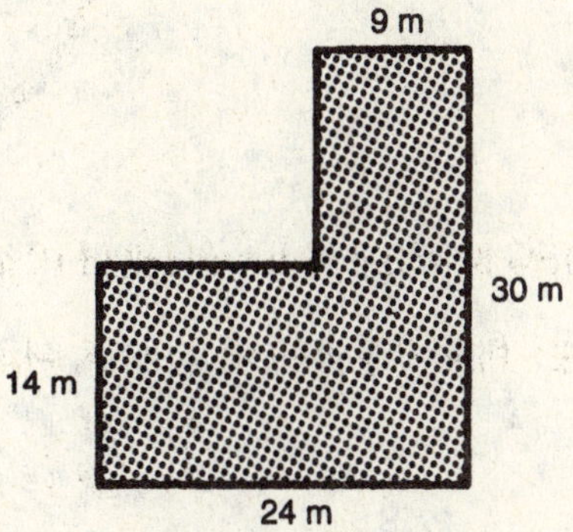

5. 1 2 3 4 5

6. The diagram at the right is a cross-section of a pipe. If the radius of the outer circle is 10 cm and the radius of the inner circle is 6 cm, the area (in square centimetres) of the cross-section is [use $\pi = 3.14$]
(1) 314
(2) 200.96
(3) 110.04
(4) 157
(5) 220.08

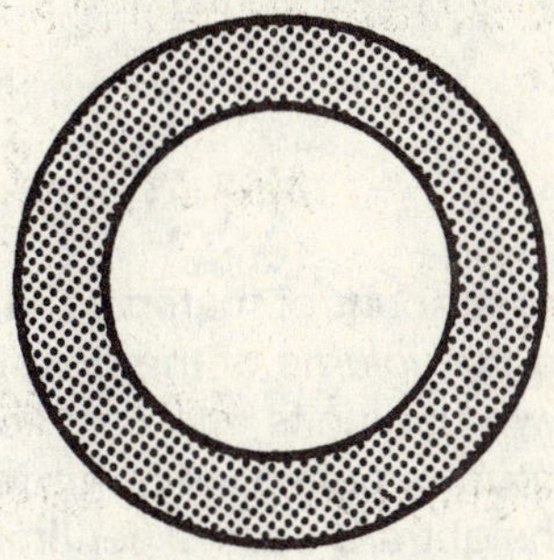

6. 1 2 3 4 5

7. A city park has a lawn 40 m long and 32 m wide. Flower beds 4 m in width are built around the lawn. The area of the flower beds, in square metres, is
(1) 1920
(2) 16
(3) 1124
(4) 640
(5) 500

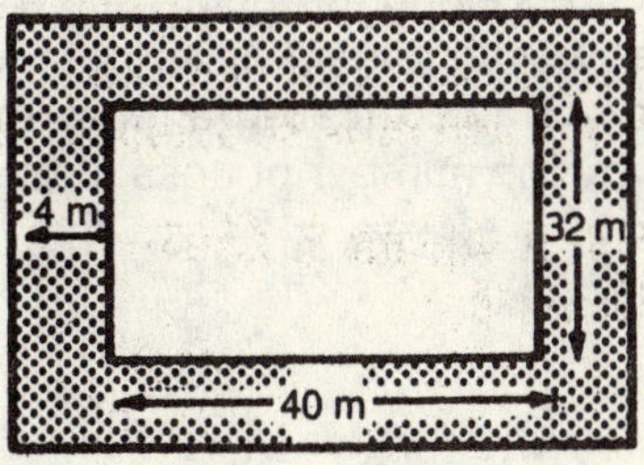

7. 1 2 3 4 5

8. The area of the figure at the right, in square centimetres, is
(1) 96
(2) 48
(3) 72
(4) 66
(5) 90

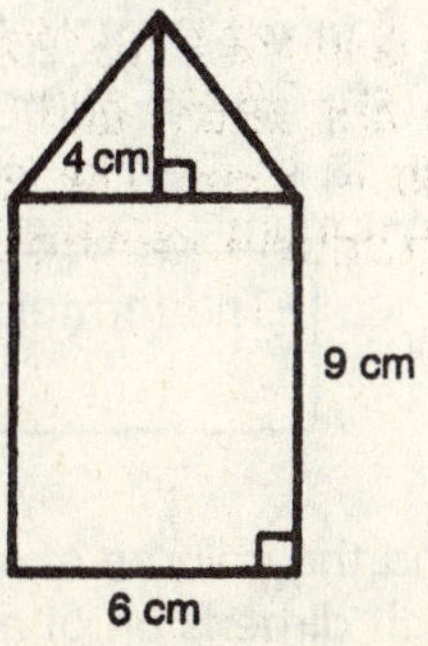

8. 1 2 3 4 5

9. A square is 8 m on a side. If its length is increased by 4 metres and its width decreased by 3 m, then the area of the square (in square metres) is decreased by
(1) 7
(2) 1
(3) 9
(4) 4
(5) 5

9. 1 2 3 4 5
‖ ‖ ‖ ‖ ‖

10. The design on the right is a square with quarter-circles drawn at each vertex. The area of the shaded portion, in square metres, is
(1) $36 - 6\pi$
(2) $36 - 9\pi$
(3) $36 - 4\pi$
(4) $36 + 9\pi$
(5) $36 + 4\pi$

10. 1 2 3 4 5
‖ ‖ ‖ ‖ ‖

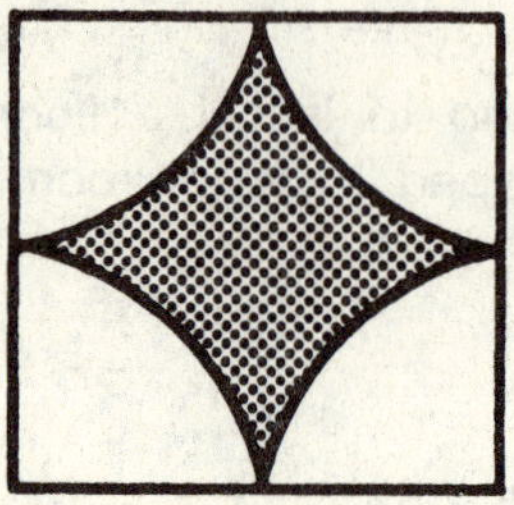

ANSWERS:

1. 4 **3. 2** **5. 4** **7. 4** **9. 4**
2. 3 **4. 1** **6. 2** **8. 4** **10. 2**

III. I. Volumes

I-1
If we wish to find the amount of material that can be fitted into the box shown below right, we have a problem in finding the *volume* of the box. In finding a length, we use units such as 1 cm, 1 m, etc. In finding an area, we use units such as 1 cm^2, 1 m^2, etc. In finding volume, we use units such as cubic centimetres, cubic metres, etc. A sketch of a cubic centimetre follows. It is a cube whose length, width, and height are each 1 centimetre. Thus, if we wish to find the number of cubic centimetres in the box shown, we must find the number of cubes that can be fitted into the box. In this case, we can fit 4 cubes along the length and 3 cubes along the width. We can therefore fit 12 cubes in one layer. Since we can place 2 layers in the box, the volume of the box is $2 \times 12 = 24\,cm^3$. In general, the volume of a box (called a rectangular solid) is obtained by multiplying the number of units in the length by the number of units in the width by the number of units in the height: volume $= 4 \times 3 \times 2 = 24\,cm^3$.

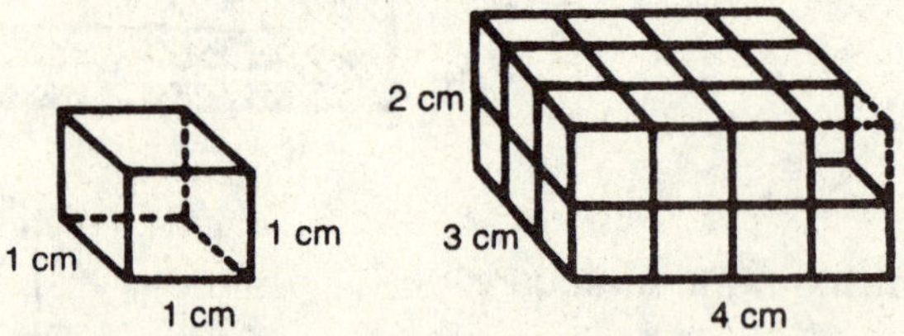

The formula for the *volume* of a *rectangular solid* is
$V = l \times w \times h$, or $V = lwh$.

If we wish to find the volume of a cube, we note that, in a cube, the length, width, and height are equal. If we let each dimension of a cube be represented by *s*, we have

> the formula for the *volume of a cube*:
> $V = s \times s \times s$, or $V = s^3$.

EXAMPLE: A coal bin is in the form of a rectangular solid. The bin is 4 m long, 2 m wide, and 2 m high. To find the volume use the formula

$$\text{Volume of bin} = lwh = 4 \times 2 \times 2 = 16\,\text{m}^3$$

An important solid figure which we find in constant use is the *cylinder*. In a cylinder, the upper and lower bases are circles which lie in parallel planes. The volume of a cylinder is obtained by multiplying the area of the base by the altitude.

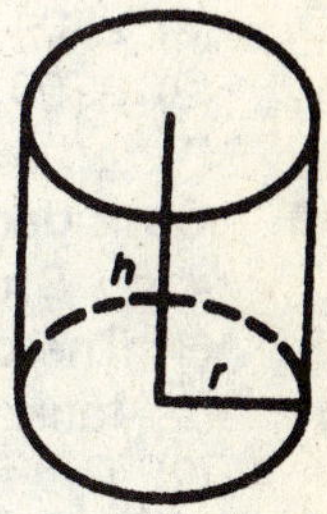

> The formula for the volume of a cylinder is
> $V = \pi r^2 \times h$, or $V = \pi r^2 h$.

EXAMPLE: A storage oil tank in the form of a cylinder is three quarters full. The radius of the base of the tank is 4 m, and the height of the tank is 7 m. Find the number of litres of oil in the tank if each cubic metre of space holds 1000 litres of oil. [Use $\pi = {}^{22}\!/_7$.]

$$\begin{aligned}\text{Volume of cylinder} &= \pi r^2 h \\ &= {}^{22}\!/_7 \times 4 \times 4 \times 7 \\ &= 352\,\text{m}^3\end{aligned}$$

Since the tank is three-fourths full, we have

$$^3\!/_4 \times 352 = 264\,\text{m}^3 \text{ of oil}$$

To find the number of litres of oil we multiply 264 by 1000.
The tank contains 264 000 litres of oil.

PRACTICE

Directions: Blacken the space at the right under the number that corresponds to the one you have selected as the correct answer.

1. A box was made in the form of a cube. If a second cubical box has inside dimensions three times those of the first box, how many times as much can it hold?

(1) 3
(2) 9
(3) 12
(4) 27
(5) 8

1. 1 2 3 4 5

2. The foundation of a building is in the form of a rectangular solid. The length of the foundation is 15 m, the width is 12 m, and the height is 2 m. The number of loads of soil to be carted away from the foundation if each load contains 4.5 m^3 is

(1) 360
(2) 80
(3) 1620
(4) 130.5
(5) 6.4

2. 1 2 3 4 5

3. How much earth had to be removed to make an excavation 30 m long, 21 m wide, and 6 m deep?

(1) 1260 m^3
(2) 3780 m^3
(3) 140 m^3
(4) 420 m^3
(5) 70 m^3

3. 1 2 3 4 5

4. A food can in the form of a cylinder has a base radius of 5 cm and a height of 7 cm. The number of cubic centimetres in the can is [use $\pi = 22/7$]

(1) 550
(2) 280
(3) 2200
(4) 320
(5) 575

4. 1 2 3 4 5

5. Consider these tanks. One is 3 m × 4 m × 5 m. The other is 5 m × 4 m × 3 m. Which of the following is a correct statement?

(1) The capacity of the second tank is 25% greater than the first tank.
(2) The first tank has a capacity of 25% greater than the second tank.
(3) The second tank has a capacity of 50% greater than the first tank.
(4) The first tank has a capacity of 50% greater than the second tank.
(5) Both tanks have the same capacity.

5. 1 2 3 4 5

ANSWERS:

1. 4 **2.** 2 **3.** 2 **4.** 1 **5.** 5

III. J. Areas of Surfaces of Solids

J-1

We are sometimes interested in the area of the surface of a solid figure. For example, a room is in the form of a rectangular solid. If we wish to paint the room, we would be interested in the area of the walls and ceiling. Also, the label on a can (or *cylinder*) covers only the area on the side of the can.

We can see that the area of the surface of the rectangular solid in the diagram is obtained by adding lw (bottom) + lw (top) + wh (side) + wh (side) + lh (front) + lh (back).

As a formula for the *area of the surface of a rectangular solid*, we have $A = 2lw + 2wh + 2lh$.

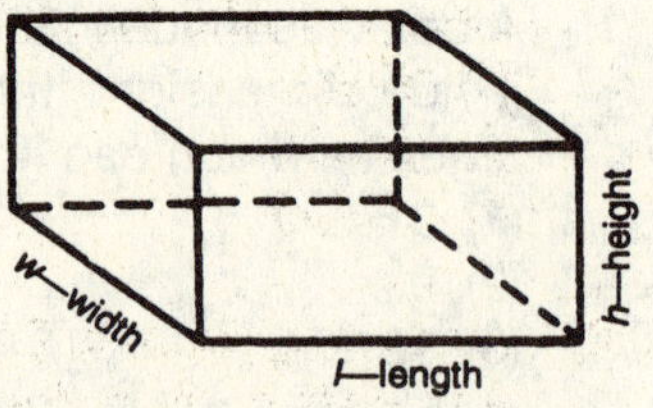

The formula for the *side area of a cylinder*, called the lateral area, is $A = 2\pi rh$.

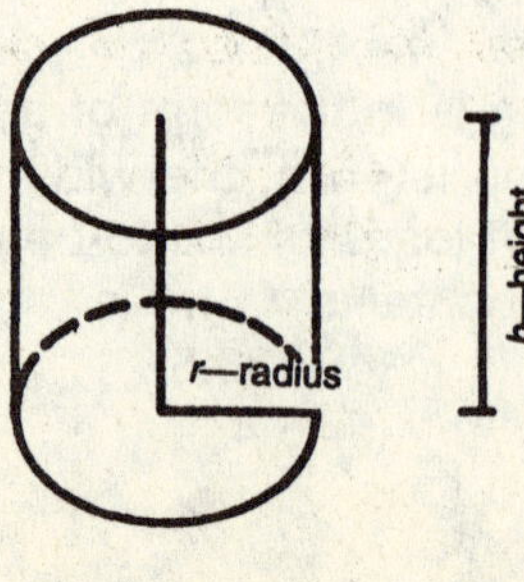

EXAMPLE: Find the number of square metres of cardboard used in making a carton 4 metres long, 3 metres wide, and 2 metres high.

We use the formula

$$A = 2lw + 2wh + 2lh$$

In this case, $l = 4$, $w = 3$, and $h = 2$:

$$A = 2 \times 4 \times 3 + 2 \times 3 \times 2 + 2 \times 4 \times 2$$
$$A = 24 + 12 + 16 = 52$$

52 m^2 of cardboard are used.

EXAMPLE: A can has a radius of 7 cm and is 12 cm high. What is the area of the label used on the can? [Use $\pi = 22/7$.]

$$\text{Lateral area of cylinder} = 2\pi rh$$
$$= 2 \times 22/7 \times 7 \times 12$$
$$= 528$$

528 cm^2 of paper are used on the label.

PRACTICE

Directions: Blacken the space at the right under the number that corresponds to the one you have selected as the correct answer.

1. A room is 7 m long, 4 m wide, and 2.5 m high. The number of square metres of wallpaper needed to paper the walls of this room is

1. 1 2 3 4 5

HINT: We do not include the floor and the ceiling. Thus, the formula we use is $A = 2wh + 2lh$.

(1) 98
(2) 70
(3) 136
(4) 55
(5) 144

2. A safe in the form of a rectangular solid is made of steel. The safe measures 80 cm in length, 50 cm in width, and 40 cm in height. The number of square centimetres on the outer surface of the steel used to make the safe is

2. 1 2 3 4 5

(1) 32 000
(2) 53 400
(3) 18 400
(4) 160 000
(5) 9300

3. A meeting room is 24 m long, 15 m wide, and 3 m high. If the walls and ceiling are to be painted, the number of square metres to be covered is

3. 1 2 3 4 5

(1) 594
(2) 549
(3) 3240
(4) 1080
(5) 1132

4. A cylindrical stovepipe has a radius of 14 cm and is 96 cm long. Its surface area is [use $\pi = {}^{22}\!/_7$]

(1) 8112 cm^2
(2) 44 998 cm^2
(3) 3825 cm^2
(4) 8448 cm^2
(5) 59 136 cm^2

4. 1 2 3 4 5

5. An open cylindrical pail has a metal base and plastic sides. The radius of the pail is 14 cm, and its height is 40 cm. The number of square centimetres of the plastic surface used in making the pail is [use $\pi = {}^{22}\!/_7$]

(1) 1760
(2) 3520
(3) 7040
(4) 6160
(5) 3420

5. 1 2 3 4 5

ANSWERS:

1. **4** 2. **3** 3. **1** 4. **4** 5. **2**

IV. MEASURES

IV. A. Time

A-1

The most *common measures of time* are

60 seconds = 1 minute	12 months = 1 year
60 minutes = 1 hour	365 days = 1 year

EXAMPLE: A man works from 9:45 A.M. until 1:30 P.M. How many hours does he work?

From 9:45 A.M. to 10:00 A.M. is 15 minutes, or $\frac{1}{4}$ hour.
From 10:00 A.M. to 1:00 P.M. is 3 hours.
From 1:00 P.M. to 1:30 P.M. is 30 minutes, or $\frac{1}{2}$ hour.
The time the man worked is $\frac{1}{4} + 3 + \frac{1}{2} = 3\frac{3}{4}$ hours.

PRACTICE

Directions: Blacken the space at the right under the number that corresponds to the one you have selected as the correct answer.

1. A food server is paid $7.50 per hour. He works from 10:45 A.M. until 3:15 P.M. He earns

(1) $30.50
(2) $43.25
(3) $37.50
(4) $39.75
(5) $73.50

1. 1 2 3 4 5

2. A bell rings every 45 minutes. The number of times the bell rings in 15 hours is

(1) 18
(2) 20
(3) 11
(4) 12
(5) 25

2. 1 2 3 4 5

3. A traveller leaves New York on a plane at 10:40 A.M. bound for Los Angeles. If she gains 3 hours in time and the trip takes 5 hours and 50 minutes, she arrives in Los Angeles at

(1) 1:30 P.M.   (4) 3:10 P.M.
(2) 2:30 P.M.   (5) 2:50 P.M.
(3) 3:30 P.M.

3. 1 2 3 4 5
‖ ‖ ‖ ‖ ‖

4. In flight, a plane covers 2 km in 10 seconds. At the same rate of speed, the number of kilometres the plane covers in 1 hour is

(1) 200   (4) 600
(2) 3400   (5) 720
(3) 1440

4. 1 2 3 4 5
‖ ‖ ‖ ‖ ‖

5. On March 5, a borrower obtains $900 from a bank for 90 days. The money must be repaid on

(1) June 1   (4) June 8
(2) June 5   (5) June 9
(3) June 3

5. 1 2 3 4 5
‖ ‖ ‖ ‖ ‖

ANSWERS:

1. 3   2. 2   3. 1   4. 5   5. 3

IV. B. The Metric System

B-1

The *metric system* of measures is used in most parts of the developed world, except the United States, and in scientific work. The metric system is used to some degree in the United States for nonscientific measurements. It is especially useful because its units are related by powers of 10. In this section we will consider the most frequently used metric measures and will cover those aspects of the metric system that may appear on the GED test.

B-2

Measure of:	Basic Unit
length	metre
mass	gram
liquid measure	litre

Prefix	Value
kilo	1000
hecto	100
deka	10
NONE	1
deci	1/10
centi	1/100
milli	1/1000

Units of Length. In the metric system the basic unit of length is the *metre* (m). In fact, 1 metre ≈ 39.37 inches.

For measuring large distances, like the distance between New York and Los Angeles, the *kilometre* (km) is used. One kilometre = 1000 metres and is approximately ⅝ of a mile.

For measuring short lengths the *centimetre* (cm) is used.

One centimetre = $\frac{1}{100}$ of a metre

For measuring very short lengths the *millimetre* (mm) is used.

One millimetre = $\frac{1}{1000}$ of a metre

Less frequently used measures of length in the metric system are the *hectometre* (100 metres), the *decametre* (10 metres) and the *decimetre* ($\frac{1}{10}$ of a metre).

In the metric system, six prefixes are used to name the units of measures, as shown below.

PREFIX	UNIT	VALUE
kilo	kilometre (km)	1000 metres
hecto	hectometre (hm)	100 metres
deca	decametre (dam)	10 metres
	metre (m)	1 metre
deci	decimetre (dm)	$\frac{1}{10}$ metre
centi	centimetre (cm)	$\frac{1}{100}$ metre
milli	millimetre (mm)	$\frac{1}{1000}$ metre

EXAMPLE: How many metres are there in 5 km? From the table we see that 1 km = 1000 m. Therefore, 5 km = 5 × 1000 = 5000 m.

EXAMPLE: How many centimetres are there in 8000 mm?

$$1\text{ mm} = \tfrac{1}{10}\text{ of a cm}$$
$$8000\text{ mm} = 8000 \times \tfrac{1}{10} = 800\text{ cm}$$

PRACTICE

In each case, replace the blank space with a number that makes the statement true:

1. 1 km = __________ m
2. 1 mm = __________ m
3. 1 m = __________ cm
4. 1 cm = __________ mm
5. 1 km = __________ cm
6. 500 mm = __________ cm

ANSWERS:

1. **1000**
2. $\frac{1}{1000}$
3. **100**
4. **10**
5. **100000**
6. **50**

B-3

Metric Units of Mass. The basic unit of mass is the *gram* (g). One gram is very light, about the mass of a small button.

For measuring heavy masses, such as the mass of a person, the *kilogram* (kg) is used. The kilogram = 1000 g and is approximately equal to 2.2 pounds.

For measuring very light objects, like small quantities of drugs the pharmacist uses, the *milligram* (mg) is used. The milligram is equal to $\frac{1}{1000}$ g.

Thus, the three widely used measures of mass in the metric system are the milligram, the gram, and the kilogram. They are related as follows:

$$1\text{ kg} = 1000\text{ g}$$
$$1\text{ mg} = \tfrac{1}{1000}\text{ g}$$

EXAMPLE: A cake has a mass of 250 grams. How many kilograms is this?

$$1\text{ g} = \tfrac{1}{1000}\text{ of a kg}$$
$$250\text{ g} = 250\left(\tfrac{1}{1000}\right)\text{kg}$$
$$= \tfrac{250}{1000}\text{, or } 0.25\text{ kg}$$

B-4

Metric Units of Liquid Measure. The basic unit of liquid measure is the *litre* (L). The litre contains a little more than a quart. Items such as milk and gasoline are sold in litre units.

For measuring very large liquid quantities, the *kilolitre* (1000 L) may be used. This measure is used infrequently.

It is convenient to remember the following,

$$1\,\text{L} = 1000\,\text{mL, or } 1\,\text{mL} = \tfrac{1}{1000}\,\text{L}$$

EXAMPLE: A glass contains 0.5 L of milk. How many millilitres is this?

$$1\,\text{L} = 1000\,\text{mL}$$
$$0.5\,\text{L} = 0.5\,(1000) = 500\,\text{mL}$$

PRACTICE

In each case, replace the blank space with a number that makes the statement true:

1. 1 kg = __________ g
2. 1 g = __________ mg
3. 1 mL = __________ L
4. 500 g = __________ kg
5. 1 mg = __________ g
6. 1 L = __________ mL

ANSWERS:

1. **1000**
2. **1000**
3. $\frac{1}{1000}$
4. **0.5**
5. $\frac{1}{1000}$
6. **1000**

B-5

The following set of practice exercises is a review of units of length, mass, and liquid measure.

PRACTICE

In each case, replace the blank space with a suitable unit of measure:

1. Each day John drinks one __________ of milk.
2. The speed limit on Canadian highways is 100 __________ per hour.
3. Mr. Alfieri takes a pill that has a mass of 80 __________.
4. Frank Sloan is the centre on his basketball team. His height is two __________.
5. Jane Morris bought a chicken that had a mass of 1.5 __________.
6. The distance between Vancouver and Toronto is approximately 4500 __________.
7. A bunch of grapes has a mass of 200 __________.
8. The length of my pencil is 14 __________.

ANSWERS:

1. **L (litre)**
2. **km (kilometres)**
3. **mg (milligrams)**
4. **m (metres)**
5. **kg (kilograms)**
6. **km (kilometres)**
7. **g (grams)**
8. **cm (centimetres)**

B-6

Area and Volume. In the metric system, measures of area include the square millimetre, the square centimetre, and the square metre. The square kilometre or the hectare are used as a measure of large tracts of land; that is, 100 hectares = 1 square kilometre.

Measures of volume include the cubic millimetre, the cubic centimetre, and the cubic metre.

PRACTICE

Directions: Blacken the space at the right under the number that corresponds to the one you have selected as the correct answer.

1. 1 cm =
(1) 100 m
(2) 10 km
(3) 5 L
(4) 0.01 m
(5) 0.1 m

1. 1 2 3 4 5
|| || || || ||

2. 4000 g =
(1) 4 km
(2) 4 cm
(3) 40 cm
(4) 4 mg
(5) 4 kg

2. 1 2 3 4 5
|| || || || ||

3. A suitable unit of measuring the distance between Montreal and Ottawa is
(1) a millimetre
(2) a kilometre
(3) a milligram
(4) a kilogram
(5) a litre

3. 1 2 3 4 5
|| || || || ||

4. A pear has a mass of
(1) 2 mg
(2) 0.2 kg
(3) 15 g
(4) 5 mL
(5) 0.5 L

4. 1 2 3 4 5
|| || || || ||

5. The quantity of gasoline needed to fill an almost empty automobile tank is
(1) 500 g
(2) 250 L
(3) 50 L
(4) 5 L
(5) 25 mL

5. 1 2 3 4 5
|| || || || ||

6. Mr. Ledoux bought a turkey that had a mass of
(1) 5 mg
(2) 5 kg
(3) 7 km
(4) 9 L
(5) 200 mg

6. 1 2 3 4 5
|| || || || ||

7. The length of a dining room table is
(1) 2 km
(2) 100 g
(3) 8 mm
(4) 3 m
(5) 6 cm

7. 1 2 3 4 5
|| || || || ||

8. 80 mg is equal to
(1) 0.008 g
(2) 0.08 g
(3) 0.8 g
(4) 80 g
(5) 800 g

8. 1 2 3 4 5
|| || || || ||

9. The approximate quantity of milk used daily by a family of four people is

(1) 1 kL
(2) 5 kg
(3) 15 L
(4) 2 L
(5) 6 mL

9. 1 2 3 4 5

10. How many centimetres are equivalent to 3 km?

(1) 30
(2) 300
(3) 3000
(4) 30 000
(5) 300 000

10. 1 2 3 4 5

11. Ed Hall is a professional football player. His mass is

(1) 200 g
(2) 220 L
(3) 105 kg
(4) 205 m
(5) 210 mg

11. 1 2 3 4 5

12. An airplane's flying speed, per hour, was

(1) 1200 m
(2) 340 km
(3) 5000 mm
(4) 1500 cm
(5) 48 km

12. 1 2 3 4 5

ANSWERS:

1. **4**	5. **3**	9. **4**
2. **5**	6. **2**	10. **5**
3. **2**	7. **4**	11. **3**
4. **2**	8. **2**	12. **2**

TESTING TACTICS IN MATHEMATICS

TACTIC 1: Answer the easy and familiar questions first. As you tackle the mathematics questions, you will find some questions that are easy and familiar. Answer these questions first, skipping, for the time being, questions that seem difficult. Answering the easier questions can be done quickly. You will then have more time to go back over the more difficult questions.

TACTIC 2: Be sure that you are answering the question that is asked.

In the excitement of taking the test you may neglect to complete a problem and lose credit for a solution that is easy for you. Consider the following problem:

A mechanic and his helper earn a total of \$30 per hour. The mechanic earns \$6 more per hour than his helper. How much does the mechanic earn per hour?

Let x = number of dollars the helper earns
And $x + 6$ = number of dollars the mechanic earns

$$x + x + 6 = 30$$
$$2x + 6 = 30$$
$$2x + 6 - 6 = 30 - 6$$
$$2x = 24$$
$$x = 12$$

The choices are:

(1) 12 (2) 15 (3) 16 (4) 18 (5) 24

You may carelessly choose (1) as your answer. On more careful consideration, you see that (4) is the correct choice; that is, the mechanic's earnings are required.

TACTIC 3: Do not assume any fact that is not specifically stated.

If two lines on a geometric figure appear to be perpendicular, do not assume that they are perpendicular unless this fact is given.

TACTIC 4: Give the answer to a problem in the units demanded. You may work out a problem perfectly but unless you give the answer in the units asked for in the problem your answer will be incorrect. Consider the following problem:

A plumber has a piece of pipe 1 m in length. She cuts off 4 pieces of pipe each 18 cm in length. How many centimetres of pipe does she have left?

The correct answer is 28 cm. If you express this answer as 28 m you will lose credit for the problem.

TACTIC 5: Do not get discouraged if you find that you cannot answer some questions.

You do not have to answer all questions to get a passing mark. Tests are usually constructed so that only the most skilled applicants can answer all questions.

TACTIC 6: Draw diagrams and sketches if this will help you think through a problem.

TACTIC 7: Do not spend too much time on any one problem. If you feel that you are not making progress in solving a problem, leave it and go back to it later if you have the time.

TACTIC 8: You need not memorize formulae. If you need a formula to solve a problem you may select the formula you need from the list of formulae provided on the examination question paper.

TACTIC 9: After you carefully read the questions and the possible answers, cross out obviously incorrect answers. You will then be considering only those options that have a chance of being correct. If you must guess at an answer, your chances of guessing a correct answer will be increased.

FORMULAE

Description	Formula
AREA (A) of a:	
square	$A = s^2$; where s = side
rectangle	$A = lw$; where l = length, w = width
parallelogram	$A = bh$; where b = base, h = height
triangle	$A = \frac{1}{2} bh$; where b = base, h = height
circle	$A = \pi r^2$; where $\pi = 3.14$, r = radius
PERIMETER (P) of a:	
square	$P = 4s$; where s = side
rectangle	$P = 2l + 2w$; where l = length, w = width
triangle	$P = a + b + c$; where a, b, and c are the sides
circumference (C) of a circle	$C = \pi d$; where $\pi = 3.14$, d = diameter
VOLUME (V) of a:	
cube	$V = s^3$; where s = side
rectangular container	$V = lwh$; where l = length, w = width, h = height
cylinder	$V = \pi r^2 h$; where $\pi = 3.14$, r = radius, h = height

Pythagorean relationship	$c^2 = a^2 + b^2$; where c = hypotenuse, a and b are legs of a right triangle
distance (d) between two points in a plane	$d = \sqrt{(x_2 - x_1)^2 + (y_2 - y_1)^2}$; where (x_1, y_1) and (x_2, y_2) are two points in a plane
slope of a line (m)	$m = \dfrac{y_2 - y_1}{x_2 - x_1}$; where (x_1, y_1) and (x_2, y_2) are two points in a plane
mean	$mean = \dfrac{x_1 + x_2 + \ldots + x_n}{n}$; where the x's are the values for which a mean is desired, and n = number of values in the series
median	median = the point in an ordered set of numbers at which half of the numbers are above and half of the numbers are below this value
simple interest (i)	$i = prt$; where p = principal, r = rate, t = time
distance (d) as function of rate and time	$d = rt$; where r = rate, t = time
total cost (c)	$c = nr$; where n = number of units, r = cost per unit

FIVE PRACTICE MATHEMATICS TESTS

This section is designed to give you practice in taking the mathematics section of the High School Equivalency Test. In taking each of these practice tests, try to give yourself the benefit of good working conditions. Select a quiet place and allow yourself one hour for each test. You may be able to complete a test in less time.

After you have completed a test, check your answers. Then use the answers to find your score. It is wise to study the solutions and explanations. You may discover new ways to attack problems. Also, you will obtain help on the questions that you could not answer and you will be able to correct any errors that you might have made. Remember that you do not have to get a perfect score to pass the test. If you find that you are weak on a certain topic you should review the material in the text on that topic.

PRACTICE TEST ONE

Directions: Blacken the space at the right under the number that corresponds to the one you have selected as the correct answer.

1. A dealer pays \$70 for 6 shirts. How much does he pay for a shipment of 150 shirts at the same price?
(1) \$420
(2) \$1050
(3) \$1200
(4) \$1750
(5) \$187

1. 1 2 3 4 5
‖ ‖ ‖ ‖ ‖

2. Eight barrels of oil are needed to sprinkle 0.5 km of roadway. How many barrels of oil are needed to sprinkle 3.5 km of roadway?
(1) 7
(2) 15
(3) 50
(4) 52
(5) 56

2. 1 2 3 4 5
‖ ‖ ‖ ‖ ‖

3. A solution of the equation $x^2 - 2x - 3 = 0$ is
(1) 0
(2) 1
(3) 2
(4) -3
(5) 3

3. 1 2 3 4 5
‖ ‖ ‖ ‖ ‖

4. Mr. Blair's bank balance was $2674. His bank balance changed as follows over a four-month period:

–$348, +$765, +$802, –$518

His bank balance at the end of the four month period was
(1) $3275
(2) $3375
(3) $3475
(4) $4241
(5) $5107

4. 1 2 3 4 5

5. An oil tank is $\frac{5}{8}$ full. It takes 360 L more to fill the tank. The number of litres the tank holds is
(1) 135
(2) 220
(3) 900
(4) 960
(5) Not enough information is given

5. 1 2 3 4 5

6. The graph below shows the lengths of some rivers correct to the nearest hundred kilometres.
Which one of the following statements is correct?
(1) The Yukon is about one-half as long as the Churchill.
(2) The Nelson is 2600 km long.
(3) The Yukon is about 250 km longer than the Nelson.
(4) The Columbia is about 4000 km longer than the Churchill.
(5) The St. Lawrence is about 300 km long.

6. 1 2 3 4 5

LENGTHS OF RIVERS

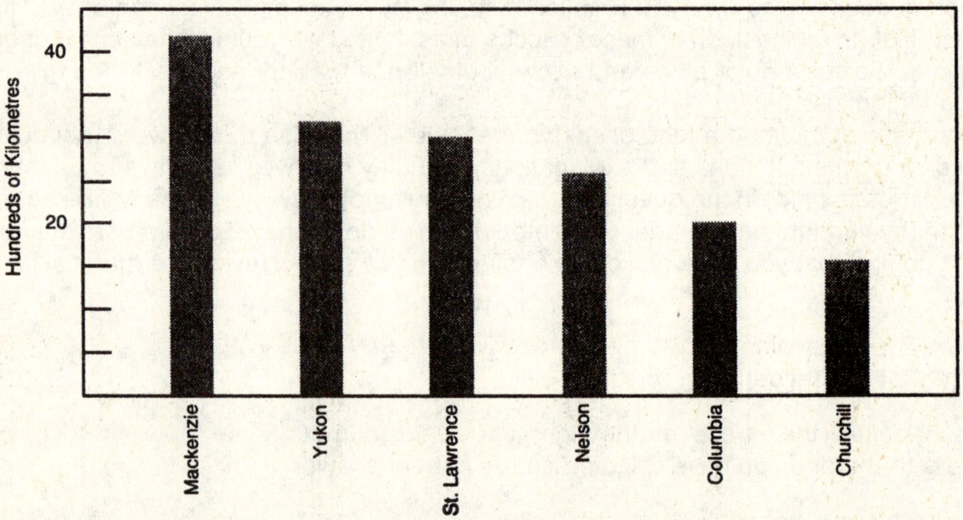

7. A professional basketball team scored 25% of its points in the first quarter, 15% in the second quarter, and 40% in the third quarter. If the team scored 21 points in the fourth quarter, how many points did the team score during the game?
(1) 84
(2) 96
(3) 100
(4) 105
(5) 121

7. 1 2 3 4 5

8. The perimeter of the figure on the right is
(1) $(C + D)(3C + D)$
(2) $7C + 10D$
(3) $8C + 9D$
(4) $8C + 10D$
(5) $9C + 8D$

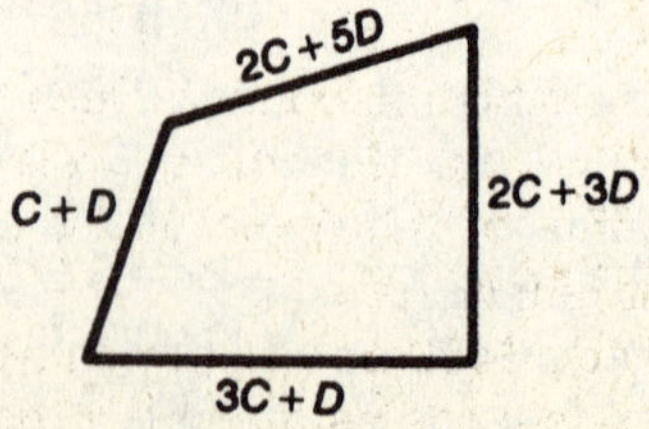

8. 1 2 3 4 5

9. If $2x + 1 > 7$ then x must be greater than
(1) 3
(2) 4
(3) 5
(4) 6
(5) 10

9. 1 2 3 4 5
|| || || || ||

10. Mr. Egan owns a men's clothing store. During a sale he sold 69 jackets at $158 each on the first day of the sale. On the second day of the sale he sold 47 jackets at $158 each. Which of the following expressions gives the number of dollars he took in during these two days?
(1) (158)(69) + 47
(2) 69 + (47)(158)
(3) 69(158 + 47)
(4) 158(69 + 47)
(5) 47 + 69(158)

10. 1 2 3 4 5
|| || || || ||

11. In the figure $\overline{AB} \parallel \overline{CD}$ and $\overline{AD} \parallel \overline{BC}$, $m\angle 1 = 62°$ and $m\angle 2 = 48°$. Find $m\angle D$.
(1) 62°
(2) 48°
(3) 70°
(4) 110°
(5) 112°

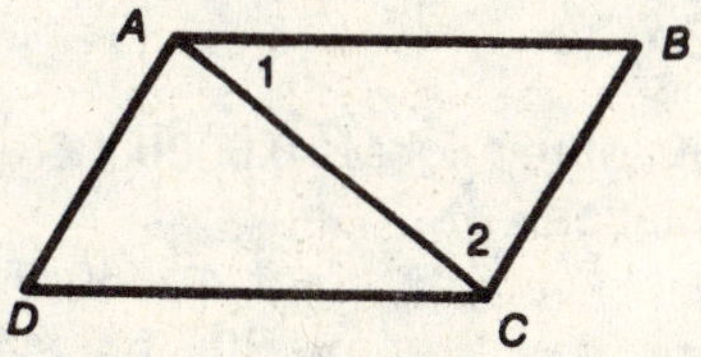

11. 1 2 3 4 5
|| || || || ||

12. Joseph Mercredi is a salesman working on a commission basis. His earnings for a 5-week period were $379, $426, $514, $489, and $362. What were his mean (average) earnings?
(1) $420
(2) $434
(3) $435
(4) $440
(5) $462

12. 1 2 3 4 5
|| || || || ||

13. An individual's taxable income is $30 000 which means that income tax payable is as follows: 17% of taxable income, a 3% individual surtax on taxable income, and a provincial tax that is 58% of the 17% federal tax. How much tax does that person pay?
(1) $7740
(2) $8958
(3) $23 400
(4) $5341.74
(5) $5100

13. 1 2 3 4 5
|| || || || ||

14. An experimenter planted 120 seeds, of which 90 sprouted. What percent of the seeds failed to sprout?
(1) 24%
(2) 25%
(3) 30%
(4) 45%
(5) 75%

14. 1 2 3 4 5
|| || || || ||

15. A snapshot 8 cm long and 6 cm wide is enlarged so that its length is 12 cm. How many centimetres wide is the enlarged snapshot?
(1) 6
(2) 8
(3) 9
(4) 10
(5) 12

15. 1 2 3 4 5
|| || || || ||

16. Sally has an after-tax income of $3000 per month. The graph shows how this income is allotted. Which of the following statements is incorrect?
(1) Food and clothing account for less than one-half of the income.
(2) The monthly cost of clothing is $360.
(3) The measure of the angle at the centre of the circle used to represent rent is 90°.
(4) Sally spends $450 per month on health and recreation.
(5) Sally spends twice as much per month on rent as on clothing.

16. 1 2 3 4 5
|| || || || ||

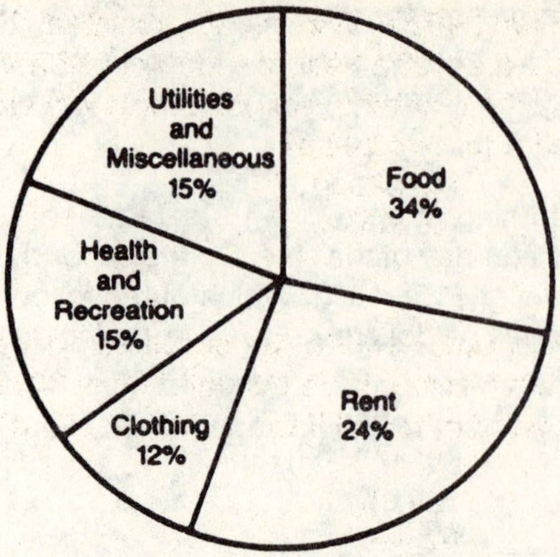

17. The wavelength of red light is 0.00000065 m. Express this number in scientific notation.
(1) 6.5×10^{-7}
(2) 6.5×10^{7}
(3) 65×10^{-6}
(4) 650×10^{5}
(5) 6.5×10^{-6}

17. 1 2 3 4 5

18. An airplane traveled 1000 km in 2 hours and 30 minutes. What was the average speed of the plane, in kilometres per hour?
(1) 200
(2) 300
(3) 350
(4) 400
(5) 600

18. 1 2 3 4 5

19. If the length of a rectangle is increased by 40% and the width is increased by 10%, the area is increased by
(1) 4%
(2) 15.4%
(3) 50%
(4) 54%
(5) 400%

19. 1 2 3 4 5

20. What is the total area of all surfaces of a rectangular solid with dimensions s, $2s$, $3s$?
(1) $6s^2$
(2) $11s^2$
(3) $14s^2$
(4) $22s^2$
(5) $49s^2$

20. 1 2 3 4 5

21. 1 mm =
(1) 1000 m
(2) 10 km
(3) 0.01 m
(4) 0.001 m
(5) 100 cm

21. 1 2 3 4 5

22. In which equation is 2 the value of x?
(1) $2x - 1 = 2$
(2) $x^2 + x = 3$
(3) $\frac{x}{3} = 2$
(4) $3x - 1 = 5$
(5) $8x = 24$

22. 1 2 3 4 5

23. If 5 shirts and 3 ties cost \$226.50 and each tie costs \$18, what is the cost of a shirt?
(1) \$40
(2) \$34.50
(3) \$32.50
(4) \$24.50
(5) \$36

23. 1 2 3 4 5

24. Evan bought a used car for $4000. The car depreciated 25% during the first year. After the second year, the depreciation was 20% of its value at the beginning of that year. What was the value of the car after Evan owned it for two years?

(1) $1800
(2) $2200
(3) $2400
(4) $2500
(5) $3000

24. 1 2 3 4 5

25. A boy who sells newspapers sent $140 to the circulation department after deducting his commission. If his commission is 30% of sales, how many newspapers did he sell if the price of each copy is 50 cents?

(1) 40
(2) 84
(3) 280
(4) 400
(5) 840

25. 1 2 3 4 5

26. $7a + 14b =$

(1) $7(a + 14b)$
(2) $14(2a + b)$
(3) $7ab(1 + 2b)$
(4) $7(a + 2b)$
(5) $2(7a + 7b)$

26. 1 2 3 4 5

27. An orchard contains *x* rows of trees with *y* trees in each row. If *n* represents the number of trees in the orchard, write an equation expressing the number of trees in terms of *x* and *y*.

(1) $n = x + y$
(2) $n = xy$
(3) $x = n + y$
(4) $y = nx$
(5) $x = ny$

27. 1 2 3 4 5

28. Question 28 refers to the number line below.

28. 1 2 3 4 5

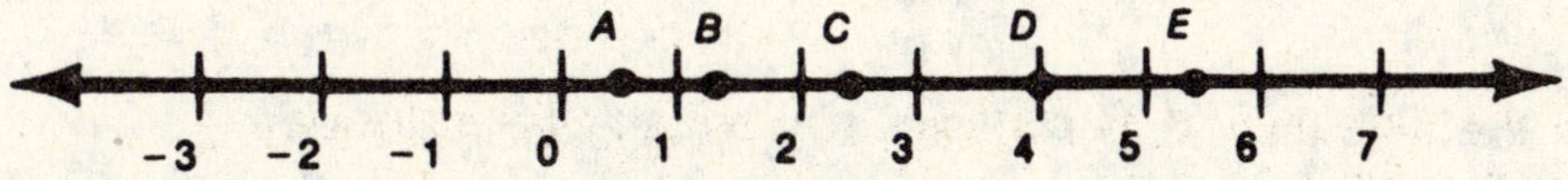

Which letter on the number line corresponds to $1\frac{5}{8} + \frac{3}{4}$?

(1) *A*
(2) *B*
(3) *C*
(4) *D*
(5) *E*

29. The Wongs purchased a table for $840 on the installment plan. They had to make a down payment of 25% of the cost and pay the remainder in 7 equal monthly payments. How much was each monthly payment?

(1) $70
(2) $75
(3) $80
(4) $90
(5) $100

29. 1 2 3 4 5

30. A woman bought a suit at a sale. The regular price of the suit was $180, but the sale price was 20% less. If the woman paid a 5% sales tax on the sale price, how much did the suit cost her?

(1) $136.80
(2) $142.30
(3) $144.00
(4) $151.20
(5) $153.00

30. 1 2 3 4 5

31. It requires 2.25 m of material to make a set of drapes. How many metres of material are needed to make 7 sets of drapes?
(1) 14.25
(2) 14.57
(3) 15.25
(4) 15.5
(5) 15.75

31. 1 2 3 4 5

32. The senior class at St. John's High School has 460 members. If 95% of the class graduates, how many students fail to graduate?
(1) 23
(2) 46
(3) 400
(4) 414
(5) 437

32. 1 2 3 4 5

33. A carpenter and his helper together earn \$48 per hour. If the carpenter earns twice as much as his helper, how many dollars does the carpenter earn per hour?
(1) \$24
(2) \$28
(3) \$32
(4) \$34
(5) \$36

33. 1 2 3 4 5

34. An article costing *c* dollars, requires a down payment of *d* dollars. The balance is paid in *n* equal installments. The amount of each installment is
(1) $n-(c-d)$
(2) $\frac{c-d}{n}$
(3) $\frac{c+d}{n}$
(4) $n(c-d)$
(5) $\frac{d-c}{n}$

34. 1 2 3 4 5

35. A field is in the form of a rectangle whose length is 8 m greater than its width. If the perimeter of the field is 128 m, what is the length of the field in metres?
(1) 28
(2) 36
(3) 40
(4) 48
(5) 96

35. 1 2 3 4 5

36. If $a = 2b(c - 4)$ find the value of *a* if $b = 3$ and $c = 9$.
(1) 11
(2) 15
(3) 30
(4) 36
(5) 48

36. 1 2 3 4 5

37. A rectangle and a square have equal areas. The length of the rectangle is 16 m and its width is 9 m. If the length of a side of the square is *x* metres, an equation which may be used to find *x* is
(1) $x^2 = 9x + 16x$
(2) $x^2 = 9 + 16$
(3) $x^2 = 9 \cdot 16$
(4) $x = \sqrt{16+9}$
(5) $x^2 + 9^2 = 16^2$

37. 1 2 3 4 5

38. Mrs. Holmes buys 3 kg of apples at *y* cents per kilogram and a melon for *z* cents. If she gives the merchant two \$2 coins and a dollar coin, how much is her change in cents?
(1) $5 - 3y - z$
(2) $500 - 2x + z$
(3) $5 - 2x - z$
(4) $500 - 3y - z$
(5) $500 + 2x - z$

38. 1 2 3 4 5

39. Gisela earns $2 per hour more than Don, and Don earns $5 per hour less than Ivan. If Ivan earns $14 per hour, how much does Gisela earn per hour?

(1) $7
(2) $8
(3) $9
(4) $10
(5) $11

39. 1 2 3 4 5

40. During a sale on television sets, $\frac{1}{3}$ of the sets were sold the first day. During the second day, $\frac{1}{2}$ of the remaining sets were sold. What fractional part of the sets were left unsold after the second day?

(1) $\frac{1}{8}$
(2) $\frac{1}{5}$
(3) $\frac{1}{4}$
(4) $\frac{1}{3}$
(5) $\frac{1}{2}$

40. 1 2 3 4 5

41. One-half a construction job is done is 5 hours and 42 minutes. How many hours does it take to do this entire job?

(1) $11\frac{2}{5}$
(2) 10.1
(3) 11.2
(4) 2.85
(5) 2.4

41. 1 2 3 4 5

42. If $AB = AC$, $\overline{BD} \perp \overline{AC}$, and $m\angle C = 64°$, find $m\angle ABD$.

(1) 26°
(2) 30°
(3) 38°
(4) 40°
(5) 42°

42. 1 2 3 4 5

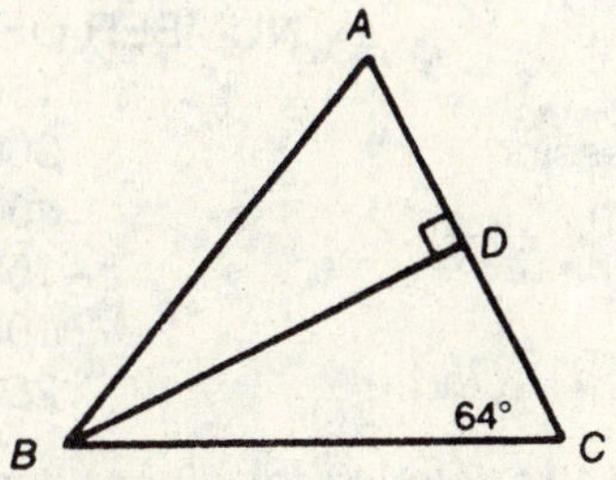

43. Approximately 40% of the mass of an adult is made up of substances other than water. If $\frac{2}{3}$ of the body water is found inside cells, and $\frac{1}{4}$ of the remainder is found in blood plasma, what fraction of body mass is the water in blood plasma?

(1) $\frac{3}{20}$
(2) $\frac{1}{20}$
(3) $\frac{1}{15}$
(4) $\frac{2}{25}$
(5) $\frac{1}{10}$

43. 1 2 3 4 5

44. In the figure, the radius of the large circle is R and the radius of each small circle is r. Write a formula that may be used to find the area (A) of the shaded portion.

(1) $A = \pi R^2 - \pi r^2$
(2) $A = 2\pi R - 2\pi r$
(3) $A = \pi R^2 - 3\pi r^2$
(4) $A = \pi R - \pi r$
(5) $A = 3\pi R^2 - \pi r$

44. 1 2 3 4 5

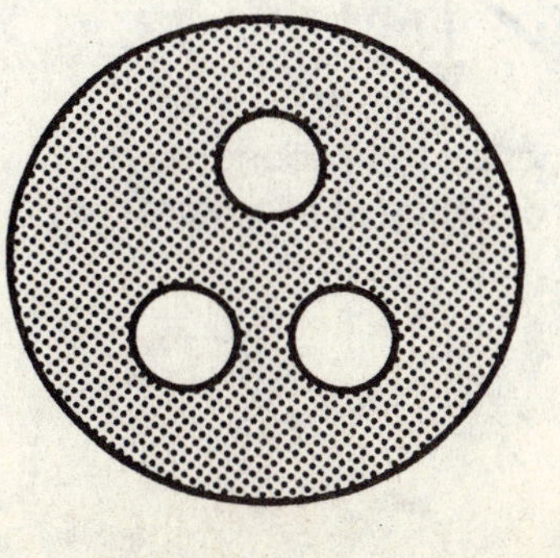

45. A man had 8 white shirts and 4 blue shirts. Of these shirts, 3 white and 2 blue shirts are in the laundry. If he selects a shirt at random from the remaining shirts, what is the probability that his selection will be a white shirt?

(1) $\frac{8}{12}$
(2) $\frac{5}{12}$
(3) $\frac{2}{7}$
(4) $\frac{5}{7}$
(5) $\frac{5}{9}$

45. 1 2 3 4 5

46. Corner $\triangle AFE$ is cut from the rectangle as shown in the figure. The area of the remaining figure, in square centimetres, is

(1) 29
(2) 68
(3) 78
(4) 88
(5) 89

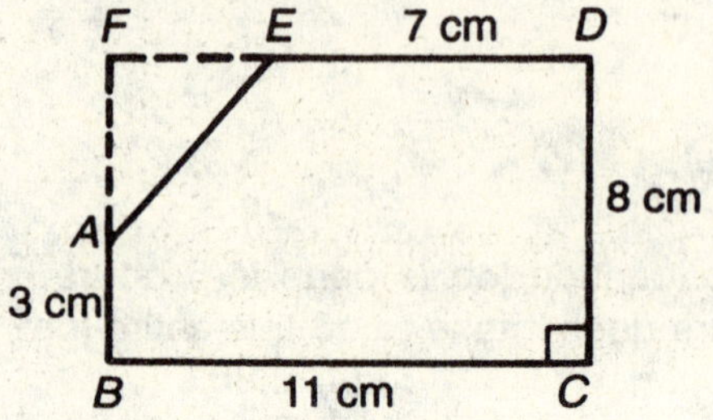

46. 1 2 3 4 5

47. Albert Dotson is on a diet which limits his food intake to 2300 calories per day. He follows the diet faithfully. One day his dinner menu was as follows:

FOOD	NUMBER OF CALORIES
Soup	150
Salad with Dressing	300
Baked Chicken	450
Baked Potato	150
String Beans	100
Apple Pie	250

If Albert consumed 1400 calories for dinner and his calorie count for lunch was twice as much as his calorie count for breakfast, what was his calorie count for lunch?

(1) 300
(2) 450
(3) 600
(4) 900
(5) Not enough information is given.

47. 1 2 3 4 5

48. If the slope of $\overleftrightarrow{AB}$ is 3, what is the value of y?

(1) 3
(2) 4
(3) 5
(4) 7
(5) 9

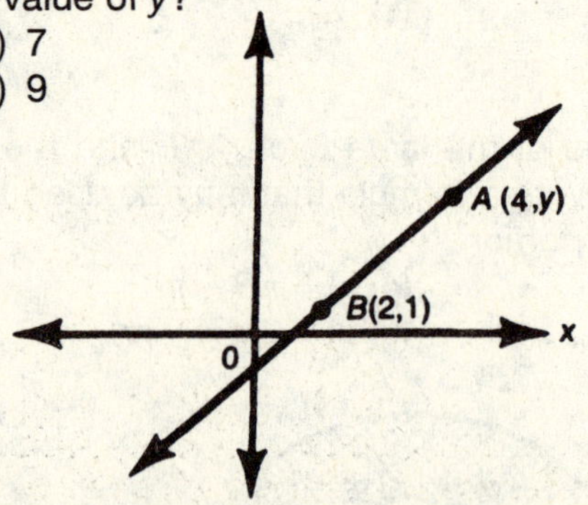

48. 1 2 3 4 5

49. A ship sails x kilometres the first day, y kilometres the second day, and z kilometres the third day. The average distance in kilometres covered per day is

(1) $\frac{xyz}{3}$
(2) $\frac{x+y+z}{3}$
(3) $3xyz$
(4) $\frac{xy+z}{3}$
(5) $3(x+y+z)$

49. 1 2 3 4 5

50. $x = 6 \cdot 10^5 \div 3 \cdot 10^2$. Find the value of x.
(1) 8
(2) 20
(3) 200
(4) 2000
(5) 4000

50. 1 2 3 4 5

51. The diameter of a wheelbarrow wheel is 30 cm. Approximately, how many centimetres does the wheelbarrow move when the wheel makes one complete revolution? [Use $\pi = 3.14$.]
(1) 88
(2) 90
(3) 94
(4) 97
(5) Not enough information is given

51. 1 2 3 4 5

52. A tree 17 m long falls against a building and touches the ledge of a window. If the bottom of the tree is 8 m from the foot of the building, how high is the window ledge above the ground, to the nearest metre?
(1) 9
(2) 10
(3) 12
(4) 15
(5) 20

52. 1 2 3 4 5

53. The distance between point *A* (8,11) and point *B* (3,5) is approximately
(1) 6
(2) 6.5
(3) 7
(4) 7.8
(5) 9

53. 1 2 3 4 5

54. Lesia and Fred bought the same number of bonds. Lesia still has all of his but Fred sold ⅓ of his. Together they still have 75 bonds. Find the number of bonds each purchased.
(1) 30
(2) 45
(3) 48
(4) 50
(5) 56

54. 1 2 3 4 5

55. If $3y = 15$ and $2x + y = 19$, find the value of x.
(1) 5
(2) 6.5
(3) 7
(4) 10
(5) 12

55. 1 2 3 4 5

56. A student has marks of 73 in English, 80 in French, and 89 in geometry. What mark must be obtained in history to have an average of 85?
(1) 84
(2) 88
(3) 92
(4) 96
(5) 98

56. 1 2 3 4 5

Turn to the answer key and the answer analysis which follow.

What's Your Score?

_________ right, _________ wrong

Excellent	51–56
Good	44–50
Fair	38–43

Be sure to refer to page 646, where these answers are explained. You may obtain additional help and practice by referring to the review material in this chapter.

ANSWER KEY

The number following each question is the correct answer. The numbers and letters in parentheses refer to the sections of this chapter which explain necessary mathematics principles. A more detailed explanation of all answers follows.

Practice Test One/Page 637

1. **4(I-F)**
2. **5(I-E)**
3. **5(II-E)**
4. **2(II-I)**
5. **4(I-E)**
6. **2(IV-B)**
7. **4(I-E)**
8. **4(III-G)**
9. **1(II-G)**
10. **4(I-K)**
11. **3(III-C)**
12. **2(II-L)**
13. **2(I-J)**
14. **2(I-G)**
15. **3(II-H)**
16. **3(IV-D)**
17. **1(II-C)**
18. **4(I-E)**
19. **4(III)**
20. **4(III)**
21. **4(V-F)**
22. **4(II-E)**
23. **2(I-C)**
24. **3(I-G)**
25. **4(I-G)**
26. **4(II-J)**
27. **2(II-A)**
28. **3(I-A)**
29. **4(I-C)**
30. **4(I-G)**
31. **5(V-G)**
32. **1(I-G)**
33. **3(II-F)**
34. **2(II)**
35. **2(II-F)**
36. **3(II-B)**
37. **3(II-F)**
38. **4(II-A)**
39. **5(I-C)**
40. **4(I-E)**
41. **1(II-F)**
42. **3(III-C)**
43. **2(I-J)**
44. **3(III-G)**
45. **4(II-K)**
46. **3(III-H)**
47. **3(II-F)**
48. **4(III-F)**
49. **2(II-L)**
50. **4(II-B)**
51. **3(III-C)**
52. **4(III-D)**
53. **4(III-E)**
54. **2(II-F)**
55. **3(II-E)**
56. **5(II-L)**

ANSWER ANALYSIS

Practice Test One/Page 637

1. **4** Let x = the cost of 150 shirts.

   We set up the proportion $\frac{6}{70} = \frac{150}{x}$.

   $6x = 70(150) = 10\,500$

   $x = \frac{10500}{6} = 1750$

2. **5** $3\frac{1}{2} \div \frac{1}{2} = \frac{7}{2} + \frac{1}{2} = \frac{7}{2} \times \frac{2}{1} = 7$

   That is, there are seven 0.5 km units in 3.5.
   For each 0.5 km unit, 8 barrels of oil are needed.
   For 7 0.5 units, $7 \times 8 = 56$ barrels of oil are needed.

3. **5** If we substitute 3 for x in the equation $x^2 - 2x - 3 = 0$, we have

   $(3)^2 - 2(3) - (3) = 0$

   $9 - 6 - 3 = 0$

   $9 - 9 = 0$

   Of the numbers given, 3 is the only one which, when substituted for x, will satisfy the equation.

4. **2** Deposits = \$765 + \$802 = \$1567
   Withdrawals = –\$348 + (–\$518) = –\$866
   Difference between deposits and withdrawals
   \$1567 – \$866 = \$701 in favor of deposits
   Therefore, \$2674 + \$701 = \$3375, new balance.

5. **4** $\frac{8}{8} - \frac{5}{8} = \frac{3}{8}$ (part of tank that is empty)

$\frac{3}{8}$ of tank = 360 L

$\frac{1}{8}$ of tank = 120 L

$\frac{8}{8}$ of tank (or full tank) = $8 \times 120 = 960$ L

6. **2** Note that each subdivision line on the vertical axis represents 500 km.
The Nelson is a little more than 2500 km. It is about 2600 km.

7. **4** 25% + 15% + 40% = 80% of the points were scored in the first three quarters.
100% − 80% = 20% of the points were scored in the fourth quarter.
Let x = the number of points scored in the game.

$$20\% \text{ of } x = 21$$
$$0.2x = 21$$
$$x = \frac{21}{0.2}$$
$$x = \frac{210}{2} = 105 \text{ points}$$

8. **4** To find the perimeter of the figure we add the lengths of the four sides of the figure.
Perimeter = $C + D + 2C + 5D + 2C + 3D + 3C + D$
Perimeter = $8C + 10D$

9. **1** $2x + 1 > 7$
$2x > 7 - 1$
$2x > 6$
$x > 3$
Note that x may be $3\frac{1}{2}$; x *need not* be greater than 4, 5, 6, or 10.

10. **4** To find the number of dollars taken in the first day we find the product 158×69. To find the number of dollars taken in the second day we find the product 158×47.
To find the sum taken in on both days we have $158 \times 69 + 158 \times 47$ which may be written as $158\,(69 + 47)$.

11. **3** Since $\overline{AB} \parallel \overline{CD}$, $m\angle y = m\angle 1 = 62°$
Since $\overline{AD} \parallel \overline{BC}$, $m\angle x = m\angle 2 = 48°$
$m\angle D + m\angle x + m\angle y = 180°$
$m\angle D + 62 + 48 = 180$
$m\angle D + 110 = 180$
$m\angle D = 180 - 110 = 70°$

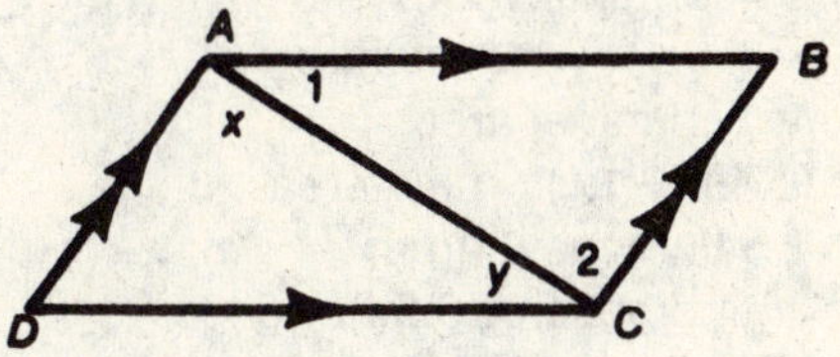

12. **2** To find the average of these 5 numbers we find their sum and divide this result by 5.
$379 + 426 + 514 + 489 + 362 = 2170$ $\quad$ $\$2170 \div 5 = \$434$

13. **2** 17% of \$30 000 = $0.17 \times$ \$30 000 = \$5100
3% of \$30 000 = $0.03 \times$ \$30 000 = \$900
58% of \$5100 = $0.58 \times$ \$5100 = \$2958
Total = \$5100 + \$900 + \$2958 = \$8958

14. **2** The number of seeds that failed to sprout is $120 - 90 = 30$. The fractional part of the seeds that failed to sprout is $\frac{30}{120}$.

$$\frac{30}{120} = \frac{1}{4} = 25\%$$

15. **3** Since the picture and its enlargement are similar figures, the two lengths have the same ratio as the two widths.

$$\frac{\text{length of picture}}{\text{length of enlargement}} = \frac{\text{width of picture}}{\text{width of enlargement}}$$

$$\frac{8}{12} = \frac{6}{\text{width of enlargement}}$$

$$8 \times \text{width of enlargement} = 12 \times 6 = 72$$

$$\text{width of enlargement} = \frac{72}{8} = 9$$

16. **3** Consider statement (3). Since the sum of the measures of the angles at the centre of the circle is 360°, the measure of the angle of the sector representing the rent is 24% of $360 = 0.24 \times 360 = 86.4°$. The statement that the measure of the angle at the centre of the circle used to represent rent is 90° is false. The other four choices are true.

17. **1** To write a number in scientific notation we write it as the product of a number between 1 and 10 and a power of 10.
In this case, the number between 1 and 10 is 6.5. In going from 6.5 to 0.000 000 65 we move the decimal point 7 places to the left. Therefore

$$0.000\,000\,65 = 6.5 \times 10^{-7}$$

18. **4** To find the average rate of speed of the plane we must divide 1000 by the time consumed ($2\frac{1}{2}$ hours).

$$\frac{1000}{2\frac{1}{2}} = \frac{1000}{\frac{5}{2}} = \frac{2(1000)}{5}$$

$$\frac{2000}{5} = 400$$

19. **4** l = original length
$l + 0.4l$ = new length
w = original width
$w + 0.1w$ = new width
lw = original area
$(1.4l)(1.1w)$ = new area
$1.54lw$ = new area,
an increase of 0.54 or 54%

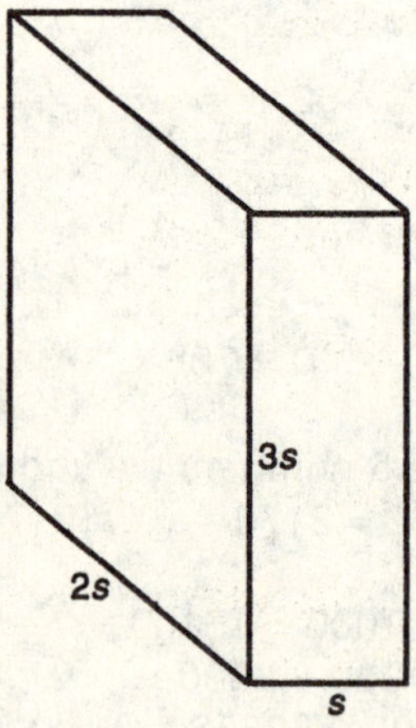

20. **4** Front—$2 \times (3s)(s) = 6s^2$
Side—$2 \times (3s)(2s) = 12s^2$
Top—$2 \times (2s)(s) = 4s^2$
Total $22s^2$

21. **4** 1000 mm = 1 m
or 1 mm = 0.001 m

22. **4** If we replace x by 2 in the equation $3x - 1 = 5$ we have $3(2) - 1 = 5$, or $6 - 1 = 5$. Thus, 2 is the value of x in the equation $3x - 1 = 5$.
2 does not balance any of the other given equations.

23. **2** If each tie costs \$18, then 3 ties cost \$54. The shirts cost \$226.50 – \$54 = \$172.50.
If 5 shirts cost \$172.50, then 1 shirt costs \$172.50 ÷ 5 = \$34.50.

24. **3** 25% = $\frac{1}{4}$, $\frac{1}{4}$ of \$4000 = \$1000
The car is worth \$4000 – \$1000 = \$3000 at the end of the first year.
20% = $\frac{1}{5}$, $\frac{1}{5}$ of \$3000 = \$600
\$3000 – \$600 = \$2400. The car is worth \$2400 at the end of two years.

25. **4** Let x = number of papers sold
$0.50x$ dollars = money collected for x copies
70% or 0.70 of $0.50x = 140$
$0.70 \times 0.50x = 140$
$0.35x = 140$

$$x = \frac{140}{0.35} = \frac{14000}{35} = 400$$

26. **4** We factor the binomial $7a + 14b$. Since 7 is a common factor, $7a + 14b = 7(a + 2b)$

27. **2** In order to find the number (n) of trees in the orchard we multiply the number of rows (x) by the number of trees (y) in each row, or $n = xy$.

28. **3** $1\frac{5}{8} = \frac{13}{8}$
$\frac{13}{8} + \frac{3}{4} = \frac{13}{8} + \frac{6}{8} = \frac{19}{8}$
$\frac{19}{8} = 2\frac{3}{8}$

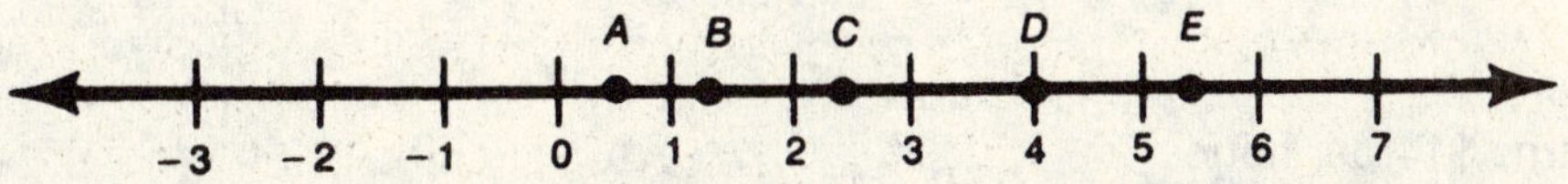

We locate $2\frac{3}{8}$ on the number line slightly to the left of the midpoint between 2 and 3. The location is point C.

29. **4** 25% = $\frac{1}{4}$, $\frac{1}{4}$ of \$840 = \$$\frac{840}{4}$ = \$210, down payment
\$840 – \$210 = \$630 to be paid in 7 monthly payments
\$630 ÷ 7 = \$90, each payment

30. **4** 20% = $\frac{1}{5}$, $\frac{1}{5}$ of 180 = $\frac{180}{5}$ = \$36, reduction
\$180 – \$36 = \$144, reduced price of suit
\$144(.05) = \$7.20, sales tax
\$144 + \$7.20 = \$151.20, final cost

31. **5** $2.25 \times 7 = 15.75$
15.75 m of material are needed.

32. **1** 95% of 460 = $.95 \times 460 = 437$, graduate
$460 - 437 = 23$ fail to graduate

33. **3** Let x = number of dollars earned by helper
And $2x$ = number of dollars earned by carpenter
$x + 2x = 48$
$3x = 48$
$x = 48 \div 3$ = \$16, earned by helper
$2x = 2 \times 16$ = \$32, earned by carpenter

34. **2** Having paid d dollars, $c - d$ is still owed. Since this balance is to be divided by n equal payments, each installment will be $\frac{c-d}{n}$.

35. **2** Let x = width of the rectangle
And $x + 8$ = the length of the rectangle
Perimeter = 128

$$x + x + 8 + x + x + 8 = 128$$
$$4x + 16 = 128$$
$$4x = 128 - 16 = 112$$
$$x = \frac{112}{4} = 28$$
$$x + 8 = \text{length} = 36$$

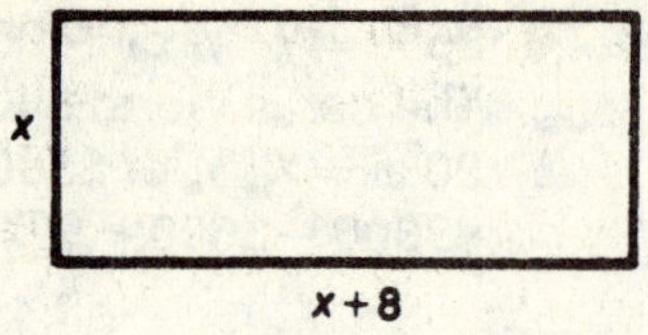

36. **3** $a = 2b(c - 4)$
$a = 2(3)(9 - 4)$
$a = 2(3)(5) = 30$

37. **3** Since the areas are equal we have $x^2 = 9 \cdot 16$.

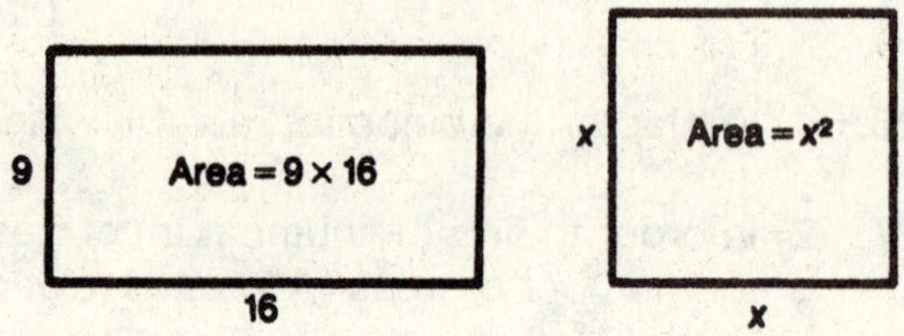

38. **4** Mrs. Holmes buys the apples for $3y$ cents and a melon for z cents. She gives the merchant \$5.00, or 500 cents. When Mrs. Holmes gets her change it is 500 minus $3y$ cents and z cents. Or, the change is $500 - 3y - z$.

39. **5** Ivan earns \$14 per hour.
Don earns \$5 less per hour than Ivan, or \$9 per hour.
Gisela earns \$2 more per hour than Don, or \$11 per hour.

40. **4** $\frac{1}{3}$ of the sets were sold the first day.
$\frac{2}{3}$ of the sets were left unsold after the first day.
$\frac{1}{2}$ of $\frac{2}{3}$, or $\frac{1}{3}$ of the sets were sold during the second day.
Thus, $\frac{1}{3}$ of the sets were sold the first day and $\frac{1}{3}$ of the sets were sold the second day.
Since $\frac{1}{3} + \frac{1}{3} = \frac{2}{3}$ of the sets were sold, then $\frac{1}{3}$ of the sets were left unsold.

41. **1** 2(5 hours and 42 minutes) = 10 hours and 84 minutes, or 11 hours and 24 minutes, or $11\frac{24}{60} = 11\frac{2}{5}$ hours.

42. **3** Since $\overline{AB} = \overline{AC}$, m$\angle ABC$ = m$\angle C$ = 64°.
In $\triangle BDC$, $\overline{BD} \perp \overline{AC}$ and m$\angle CDB$ = 90°.
m$\angle DBC$ = 90° − 64° = 26°
m$\angle ABD$ = m$\angle ABC$ − m$\angle DBC$ = 64° − 26° = 38°

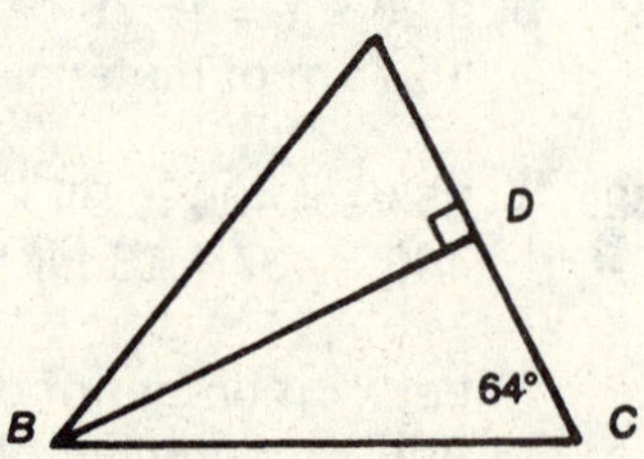

43. **2** If 60% of the mass is water and $\frac{2}{3}$ of that is found in the cells, that leaves $\frac{1}{3}$ of the 60% (or 20%) for water found elsewhere outside the cells. One fourth of this 20% (or 5%), is found in blood plasma.

$$5\% = \frac{5}{100} = \frac{1}{20}$$

44. **3** To find a formula for the area of the shaded portion, we find the area of the large circle and subtract from this result the sum of the areas of the small circles.

Area of large circle = πR^2
Area of each small circle = πr^2
Sum of areas of 3 small circles = $3\pi r^2$
Therefore, area of shaded portion = $\pi R^2 - 3\pi r^2$

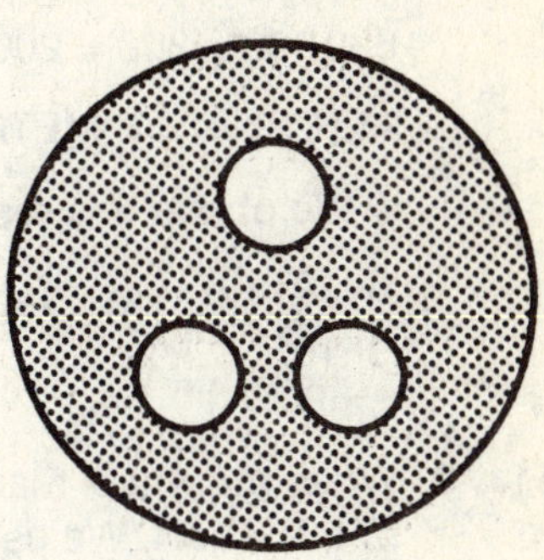

45. **4** The man had available 5 white shirts and 2 blue shirts.

$$\text{Probability} = \frac{\text{number of successful outcomes}}{\text{number of possible outcomes}}$$

In this case, the number of successful outcomes is 5 and the number of possible outcomes is 7.

The probability of the selection of a white shirt is $5/7$.

46. **3** We will find the area of the rectangle *BCDF* and subtract from this the area of triangle *AFE*.

Area of rectangle $BCDF = BC \times CD$
$= 11 \times 8 = 88\,\text{cm}^2$

Since $AF = 8 - 3 = 5\,\text{cm}$ and since $FE = 11 - 7 = 4\,\text{cm}$, then area of triangle

$AF = \frac{1}{2}(AF \times EF)$
$= \frac{1}{2}(5 \times 4)$
$= \frac{1}{2}(20) = 10\,\text{cm}^2$

The area of the remaining figure is
$88 - 10 = 78\,\text{cm}^2$

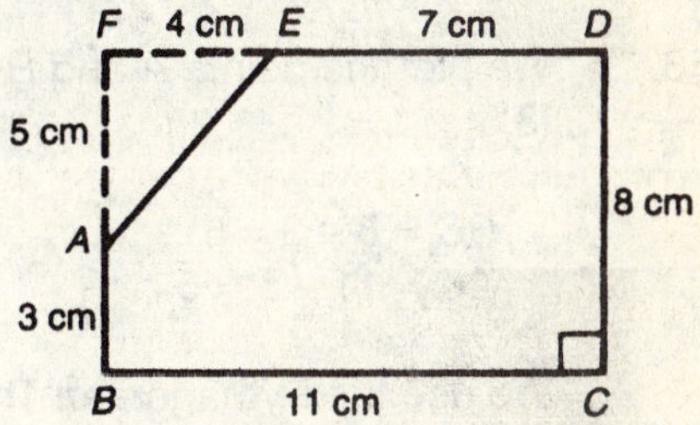

47. **3** $2300 - 1400 = 900$ calories for lunch and breakfast

Let x = number of calories for breakfast
and $2x$ = number of calories for lunch
$x + 2x = 900$
$3x = 900$
$x = 300$
$2x = 600$ calories for lunch

48. **4** Slope of $\overline{AB} = \dfrac{\text{change in } y\text{-coordinates}}{\text{change in } x\text{-coordinates}} = \dfrac{y-1}{4-2}$

Thus, $\dfrac{y-1}{2} = 3$
$y - 1 = 6$
$y = 6 + 1 = 7$

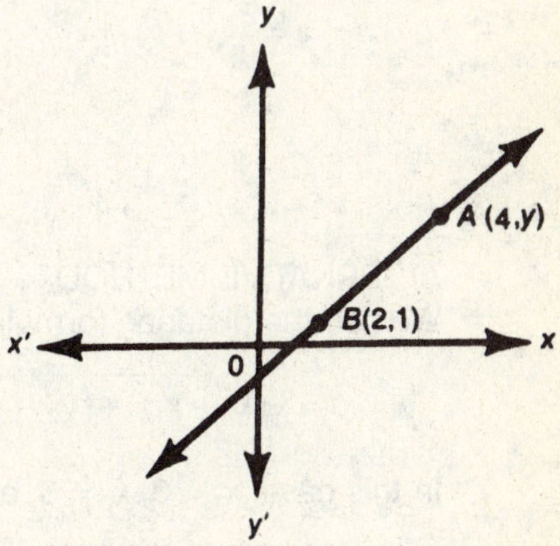

49. **2** In order to find the average of three quantities we add the three quantities and divide this sum by 3. Thus, the average of x, y and z is $(x + y + z) \div 3$.

50. **4** $6 \cdot 10^5 = 6(100\,000) = 600\,000$
$3 \cdot 10^2 = 3(100) = 300$
$600\,000 \div 300 = 2000$

ALTERNATIVE METHOD

We obtain this result more directly as follows,

$$\frac{6 \cdot 10^5}{3 \cdot 10^2} = 2 \cdot 10^3 = 2(1000) = 2000$$

51. **3** When the wheel makes one complete revolution, the wheelbarrow moves one circumference of the wheel. We use the formula $C = \pi D$, where D is the diameter.
$C = (3.14)(30) = 94.20$, or 94 cm to the nearest centimetre.

52. **4** In right triangle ACB we use the Pythagorean Theorem

$$x^2 + 8^2 = 17^2$$
$$x^2 + 64 = 289$$
$$x^2 = 289 - 64 = 225$$
$$x = \sqrt{225} = 15$$

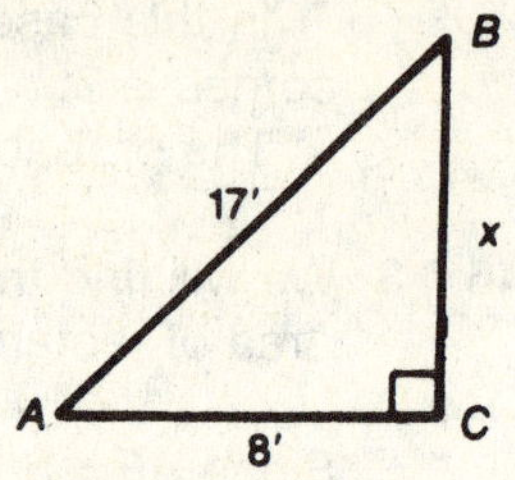

53. **4** We plot the points A and B and complete right triangle ACB. The coordinates of point C are (8,5).

$BC = 8 - 3 = 5$
$AC = 11 - 5 = 6$

We use the Pythagorean Theorem to obtain

$$(AB)^2 = (BC)^2 + (AC)^2$$
$$(AB)^2 = 5^2 + 6^2 = 25 + 36 = 61$$
$$AB = \sqrt{61} = 7.8 \text{ approximately}$$

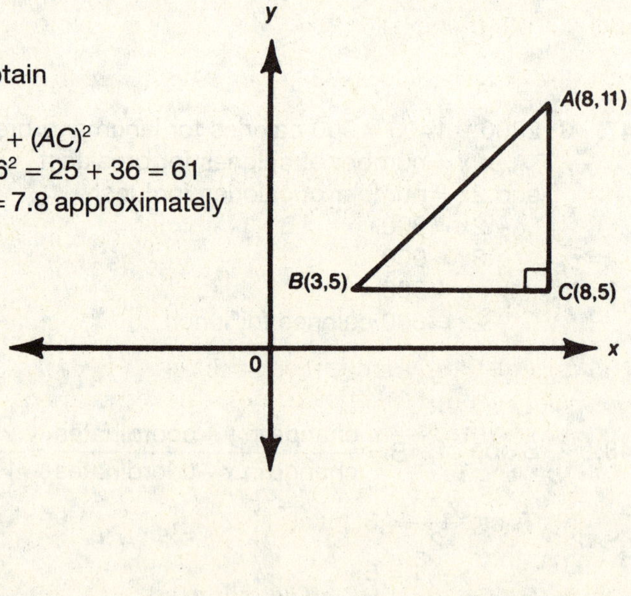

ALTERNATIVE METHOD
We use the distance formula

$$d = \sqrt{(x_2 - x_1)^2 + (y_2 - y_1)^2}$$

In this case, $x_1 = 3$, $x_2 = 8$, and $y_1 = 5$, $y_2 = 11$

$$d = \sqrt{(8-3)^2 + (11-5)^2}$$
$$d = \sqrt{5^2 + 6^2} = \sqrt{25+36}$$
$$d = \sqrt{61} = 7.8 \text{ approximately}$$

54. **2** Let x = number of bonds Lesia has

And $\frac{2x}{3}$ = number of bonds Fred has

$$x+\frac{2x}{3}=75$$

If we multiply both sides of this equation by 3 we have

$$3x + 2x = 3(75) = 225$$
$$5x = 225$$
$$x = 225 \div 5 = 45$$

Each purchased 45 bonds originally.

55. **3** $3y = 15, y = 15 \div 3 = 5$
$2x + y = 19, 2x + 5 = 19$
$2x = 19 - 5 = 14$
$x = 14 \div 2 = 7$

56. **5** Let x = mark to be attained in history

To find an average of a set of marks we divide the sum of the marks by the number of marks. This leads to the equation

$$\frac{73+80+89+x}{4}=85$$
$$\frac{242+x}{4}=85$$
$$242 + x = 4(85) = 340$$
$$x = 340 - 242 = 98$$

PRACTICE TEST TWO

Directions: Blacken the space at the right under the number that corresponds to the one you have selected as the correct answer.

1. In a theatre audience of 650 people, 80% were adults. How many children were in the audience?
(1) 130
(2) 150
(3) 450
(4) 500
(5) 520

1. 1 2 3 4 5

2. A scale on a map is 1 cm = 60 km. If two towns are 255 km apart what is the distance between the towns on the map, in centimetres?
(1) 4
(2) 4.25
(3) 4.5
(4) 4.75
(5) 5

2. 1 2 3 4 5

3. Mrs. Adams left an estate amounting to \$24 000. According to the will, 10% was to be given to a college, 15% to a church, and the remainder was to be divided equally among 3 nieces. How much money did each niece receive?
(1) \$6120
(2) \$2000
(3) \$6333.33
(4) \$6000
(5) \$18 000

3. 1 2 3 4 5

4. How many square metres of cardboard are used in making a closed carton 2 m long, 1.5 m wide, and 0.5 m high?
(1) 1.5
(2) 6.5
(3) 4.75
(4) 8.75
(5) 9.5

4. 1 2 3 4 5

5. After selling one-third of the apple crop, a farmer sold the remainder at the same price per metric tonne for \$600. What was the value of the crop?
(1) \$1000
(2) \$1200
(3) \$1800
(4) \$800
(5) \$900

5. 1 2 3 4 5

6. If O is the centre of the circle and m $\angle B = 52°$ find m$\angle O$.
(1) 52°
(2) 76°
(3) 80°
(4) 94°
(5) 128°

6. 1 2 3 4 5

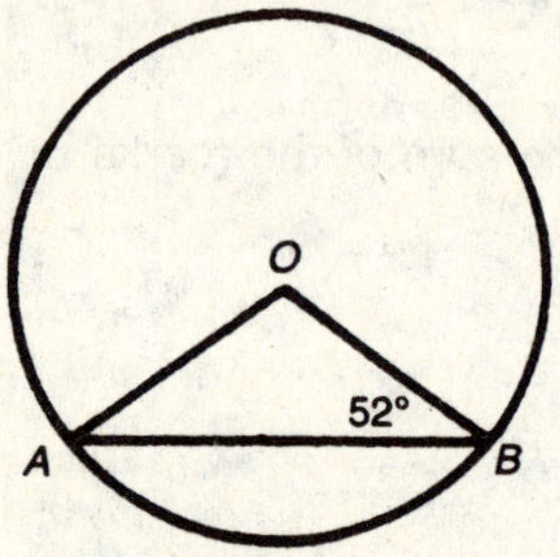

7. On the line segment $\overline{AC}$, $AB:BC = 3:5$ and $BC = 20$ cm. The length of $\overline{AB}$, in centimetres is
(1) 3
(2) 10
(3) 12
(4) 15
(5) 16

7. 1 2 3 4 5

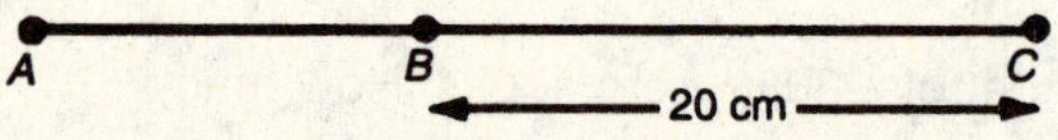

8. A cross-section of a pipe is shown. Find the thickness (in centimetres) of the pipe if the diameter of the outer circle is 7.5 cm and the diameter of the inner circle is 4.5 cm.
(1) 1
(2) 1.25
(3) 1.5
(4) 2
(5) 3

8. 1 2 3 4 5

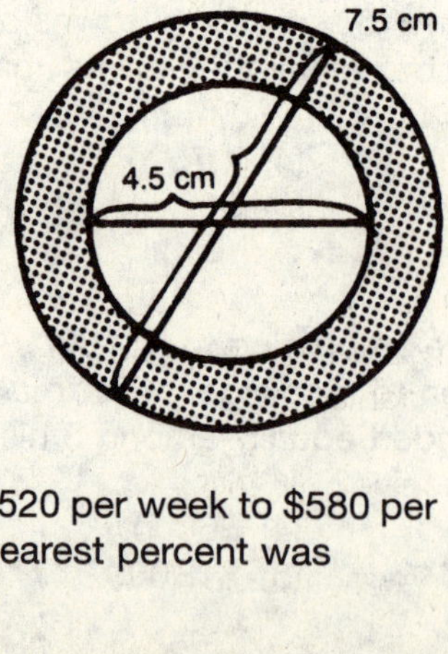

9. Lori's weekly salary was increased from \$520 per week to \$580 per week. The increase in her salary, to the nearest percent was
(1) 10%
(2) 11%
(3) 12%
(4) 14%
(5) 15%

9. 1 2 3 4 5

10. A shopper buys a loaf of bread at x cents and 0.5 kg of coffee at y cents per kilogram. If she pays with a \$5 bill, the number of cents she receives in change is

(1) $500 - x - y$
(2) $500 - (x - y)$
(3) $500 - x + 0.5y$
(4) $500 - x - 0.5y$
(5) $x + 0.5y - 500$

10. 1 2 3 4 5

11. The area of a rectangular living room is 96 m^2. If the length of the room is 12 m, what is the perimeter of the room, in metres?

(1) 12
(2) 32
(3) 50
(4) 40
(5) 60

11. 1 2 3 4 5

12. The Centre Cinema charges \$4 for matinee performances and \$8 for evening performances. On one day 267 matinee tickets and 329 evening tickets were sold. An expression which represents the total receipts for that day is

(1) 8(267) + 4(329)
(2) 4(267) + 8(329)
(3) 12(267 + 329)
(4) 4(267 + 329) + 8(267 + 329)
(5) 8(267 + 329)

12. 1 2 3 4 5

13. A crew of painters can paint an apartment in $4\frac{1}{2}$ hours. What part of the apartment can they paint in $2\frac{1}{2}$ hours?

(1) $\frac{5}{9}$
(2) $\frac{5}{7}$
(3) $\frac{2}{3}$
(4) $\frac{5}{6}$
(5) $\frac{7}{8}$

13. 1 2 3 4 5

14. Which of the following expresses 2 347 516 in scientific notation?

(1) 2.347516×10^5
(2) 23.47516×10^5
(3) 234.7516×10^4
(4) 23.47516×10^6
(5) 2.347516×10^6

14. 1 2 3 4 5

15. $x^2 - 5x + 6$ may be written as

(1) $(x + 3)(x + 2)$
(2) $(x + 3)(x - 2)$
(3) $(x - 3)(x - 2)$
(4) $(x - 3)(x + 2)$
(5) $x(5x + 6)$

15. 1 2 3 4 5

16. A class has 32 students. On a certain day x students are absent. What fractional part of the class was present on that day?

(1) $\frac{x}{32}$
(2) $\frac{32-x}{x}$
(3) $\frac{x}{32-x}$
(4) $\frac{32-x}{32}$
(5) $\frac{32-x}{32+x}$

16. 1 2 3 4 5

17. At a Calgary high school there are 402 students taking Spanish or French. If twice as many students take Spanish as take French, how many students take Spanish?

(1) 134
(2) 150
(3) 200
(4) 258
(5) 268

17. 1 2 3 4 5

18. Look at the graph below. Which of the following is correct?

(1) The change in temperature between 7 A.M. and noon was 8°C.
(2) The highest temperature reached during the day was 10°C.
(3) The change in temperature between 8 A.M. and noon was −10°C.
(4) The temperature did not change between 7 A.M. and 8 A.M.
(5) The temperature at noon was 8°C.

18. 1 2 3 4 5

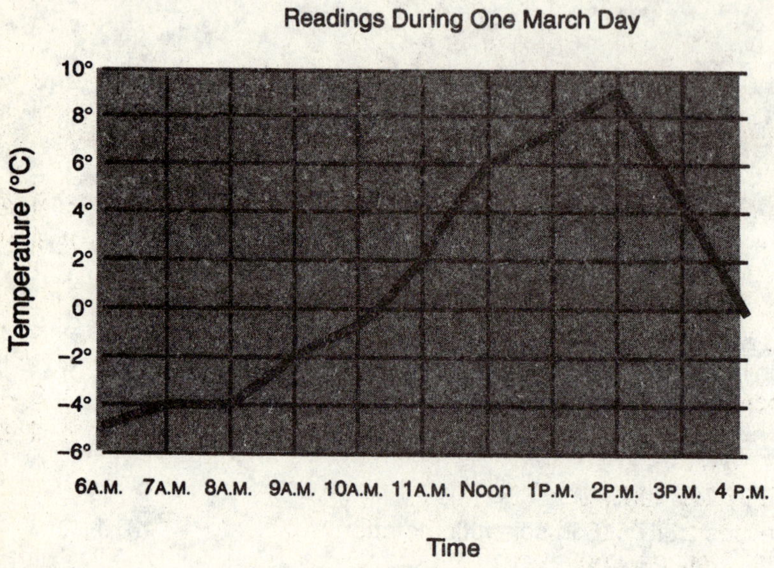

19. A team won w games and lost 5 games, what part of their games did they win?

(1) $\frac{w}{w+5}$
(2) $\frac{w}{5}$
(3) $\frac{5}{w}$
(4) $\frac{5}{w+5}$
(5) $\frac{w+5}{w}$

19. 1 2 3 4 5

20. A ship sails 8 km due east and then 15 km due north. At this point, how many kilometres is the ship from its starting point?

(1) 17
(2) 19
(3) 20
(4) 24
(5) 25

20. 1 2 3 4 5

21. A book sales representative earns 12% commission on sales. Last month she sold a set of 385 textbooks at $23 per book, a group of 18 art books at $49 per book, and a shipment of 396 novels at $18 per book. What was her commission for the month, to the nearest dollar?

(1) $202
(2) $2000
(3) $2020
(4) $2024
(5) $2100

21. 1 2 3 4 5

22. Mrs. Alvin bought 120 shares of RST Corporation at $32\frac{3}{4}$ and sold these shares a year later at $36\frac{1}{2}$. Her profit before paying commission and taxes was
(1) $400
(2) $450
(3) $480
(4) $520
(5) $560

22. 1 2 3 4 5

23. If the ratio of $x:y:z$ is 1:2:2, then $x + y$ equals
(1) 108
(2) 144
(3) 72
(4) 106
(5) 216

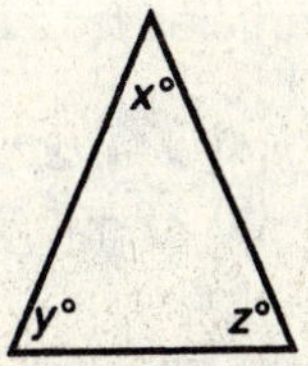

23. 1 2 3 4 5

24. In a class of 34 students, there are 6 more girls than boys. How many girls are in the class?
(1) 14
(2) 15
(3) 18
(4) 20
(5) 22

24. 1 2 3 4 5

25. Express the number of kilometres per hour needed to cover 120 km in x hours.
(1) $\frac{120}{x}$
(2) $\frac{x}{120}$
(3) $120x$
(4) $120 + x$
(5) $x - 120$

25. 1 2 3 4 5

26. In five years the population of a town increased from 2800 to 3500. The percent of increase was
(1) 20%
(2) 25%
(3) 30%
(4) 40%
(5) 70%

26. 1 2 3 4 5

27. Mr. Haines insured his building against fire for $90 000 at the annual rate of $.39 per $100. After he rebuilt the wooden section of the building with fireproof materials he found that his insurance rate was reduced to $.34 per $100. How much did Mr. Haines save yearly by making the repair?
(1) $45
(2) $450
(3) $495
(4) $4500
(5) Not enough information is given to solve the problem.

27. 1 2 3 4 5

28. If the length and the width of a rectangle are both tripled, the ratio of the area of the original rectangle to the area of the enlarged rectangle is
(1) $1:1\frac{1}{3}$
(2) 1:3
(3) 1:6
(4) 1:12
(5) 1:9

28. 1 2 3 4 5

29. Sara has h hours of homework. After working for 3 hours, what part of her homework is still left undone?

29. 1 2 3 4 5

(1) $\frac{h-3}{h}$
(2) $\frac{h}{3}$
(3) $\frac{3}{h}$
(4) $\frac{2}{h}$
(5) $\frac{h}{2}$

30. Ade had x dollars. He bought y articles for z dollars each. The number of dollars Ade had left was

30. 1 2 3 4 5

(1) $yz - x$
(2) $yx - z$
(3) $x - yz$
(4) $x + yz$
(5) $xy + z$

31. A crew of 12 takes 15 working hours to complete a job. If the crew is reduced to 9, how many hours will it take the reduced crew to complete the job?

31. 1 2 3 4 5

(1) $11\frac{1}{4}$
(2) 12
(3) 15
(4) 18
(5) 20

32. A worker earns x dollars per month and spends y dollars per month. How many dollars will he save in one year?

32. 1 2 3 4 5

(1) $12xy$
(2) $12x - y$
(3) $12(x - y)$
(4) $x - 12y$
(5) $12y - x$

33. A semicircle surmounts a rectangle whose length is $2a$ and whose width is a. A formula for finding A, the area of the whole figure, is

33. 1 2 3 4 5

(1) $A = 2a^2 + \frac{1}{2}\pi a^2$
(2) $A = 2\pi a^2$
(3) $A = 3\pi a^2$
(4) $A = 2a^2 + \pi a^2$
(5) $A = 4a + \pi a^2$

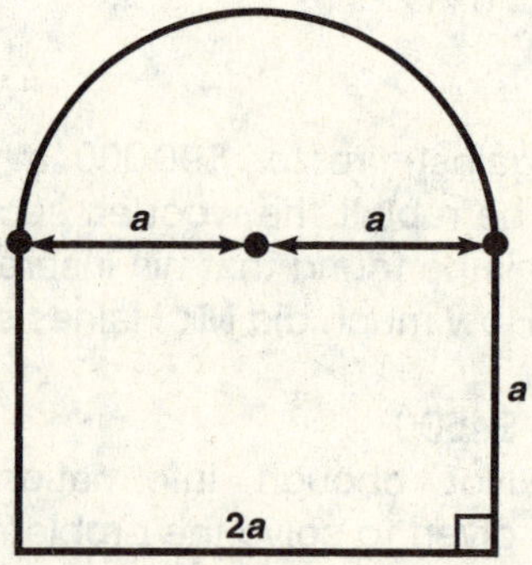

34. The graph indicates the way a person spends a day. Which one of the following statements is correct?

34. 1 2 3 4 5

(1) The person works 8 hours per day.
(2) The person spends 1 hour more on meals than on travel.
(3) The person sleeps 7 hours per day.
(4) The person spends half the time on work and travel.
(5) The person spends 4 hours on meals.

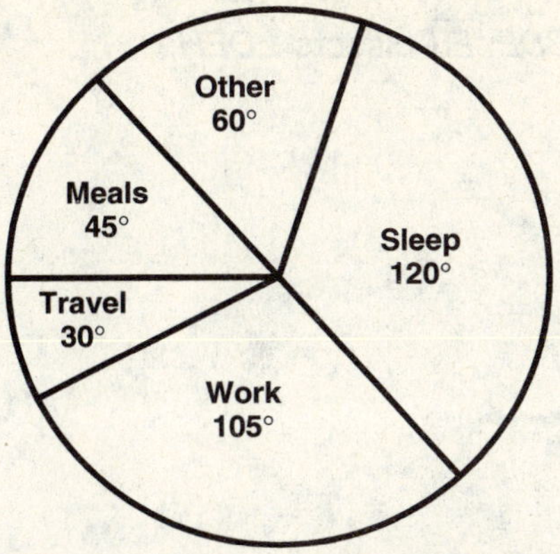

35. A storage oil tank in the form of a cylinder is full of oil. The radius of the base of the tank is 7 m and the height of the tank is 6 m. Find the number of litres of oil in the tank if each cubic metre of space holds 1000 litres of oil. [Use $\pi = {}^{22}\!/_{7}$.]
(1) 924
(2) 9240
(3) 92 400
(4) 924 000
(5) 9 240 000

35. 1 2 3 4 5
|| || || || ||

36. If $y = 2x^2(z - 3)$ find the value of y if $x = 5$ and $z = 7$.
(1) 54
(2) 150
(3) 180
(4) 200
(5) 400

36. 1 2 3 4 5
|| || || || ||

37. The fare for the 40 km ride from the Halifax International Airport to a downtown hotel by taxi is $30. The same trip by City Shuttle bus is $11. What is the percent saved by taking the City Shuttle?
(1) 11%
(2) 19%
(3) 29%
(4) 30%
(5) 63%

37. 1 2 3 4 5
|| || || || ||

38. The table gives the annual premiums for a life insurance policy taken out at various ages.

AGE IN YEARS	PREMIUM PER $1000
22	$18
30	$22
38	$28
46	$38

If the policy is fully paid up after 20 years, how much is saved by taking out a $10 000 policy at age 30 rather than at age 46?
(1) $160
(2) $320
(3) $400
(4) $3200
(5) $4000

38. 1 2 3 4 5
|| || || || ||

39. In a right triangle, the ratio of the two acute angles is 3:2. The number of degrees in the larger acute angle is
(1) 36
(2) 54
(3) 72
(4) 90
(5) 105

39. 1 2 3 4 5
|| || || || ||

40. If $3x - 1 < 5$ then x must be
(1) greater than 2
(2) less than 2
(3) greater than 3
(4) less than 0
(5) greater than 5

40. 1 2 3 4 5
|| || || || ||

41. If $\overleftrightarrow{AB} \parallel \overleftrightarrow{GH}$, $m\angle BDE = 100°$, $\overline{DJ}$ bisects $\angle BDE$, $\overline{EJ}$ bisects $\angle DEH$, find $m\angle J$.

(1) 40°
(2) 60°
(3) 65°
(4) 75°
(5) 90°

41. 1 2 3 4 5
|| || || || ||

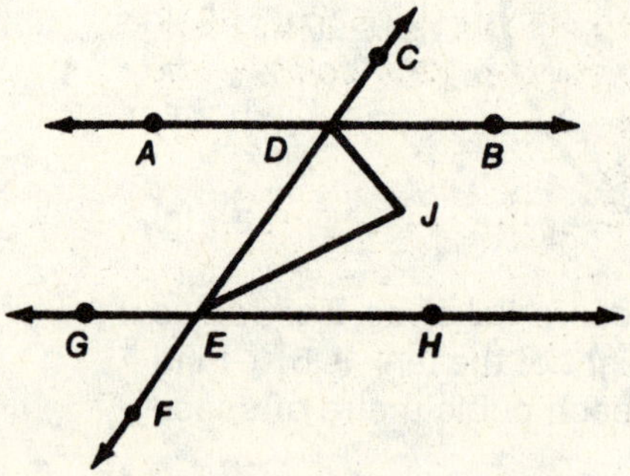

42. A chair was marked for sale at $315. This was a discount of 25% off the original price. What was the original price of the chair?

(1) $236.50
(2) $390
(3) $420
(4) $450
(5) $520

42. 1 2 3 4 5
|| || || || ||

43. There are 48 couples at a dance. Each couple consists of 1 male and 1 female. Mr. Fowler selects a female dancing partner for the next dance at random. What is the probability that Mr. Fowler selects his wife?

(1) $\frac{1}{50}$
(2) $\frac{1}{48}$
(3) $\frac{2}{48}$
(4) $\frac{1}{2}$
(5) $\frac{2}{3}$

43. 1 2 3 4 5
|| || || || ||

44. Which of the following arrangements is set up correctly?

(1) $\frac{4}{5} > \frac{2}{3} > \frac{5}{7}$
(2) $\frac{5}{7} > \frac{2}{3} > \frac{4}{5}$
(3) $\frac{4}{5} > \frac{5}{7} > \frac{2}{3}$
(4) $\frac{2}{3} > \frac{4}{5} > \frac{5}{7}$
(5) $\frac{5}{7} > \frac{4}{5} > \frac{2}{3}$

44. 1 2 3 4 5
|| || || || ||

45. If *k* kilograms of oranges can be bought for *c* cents, how many kilograms can be bought for 98 cents?

(1) $\frac{98c}{k}$
(2) $98ck$
(3) $\frac{ck}{98}$
(4) $\frac{98k}{c}$
(5) $\frac{k}{98c}$

45. 1 2 3 4 5
|| || || || ||

46. A man invests $6000 in a stock that pays dividends amounting to 5% annually on his investment. How much more must he invest in a stock that pays 6% annually in dividends so that his annual income from both investments is $900?

(1) $3000
(2) $5000
(3) $8000
(4) $10 000
(5) $12 000

46. 1 2 3 4 5
|| || || || ||

47. A tree is 16 m tall and cast a shadow of 6 m. At the same time a tower casts a shadow of 18 m. What is the height of the tower, in metres?
(1) 36
(2) 48
(3) 60
(4) 72
(5) 80

47. 1 2 3 4 5
|| || || || ||

48. Mr. Burns is on a diet. For breakfast and lunch he consumes 40% of his allowable number of calories. If he still has 1200 calories left for the day, his daily calorie allowance is
(1) 2000
(2) 2200
(3) 2400
(4) 2500
(5) 2800

48. 1 2 3 4 5
|| || || || ||

49. If $3x - y = 11$ and $2y = 8$ then $x =$
(1) 3
(2) 4
(3) $4\frac{1}{2}$
(4) 5
(5) 6

49. 1 2 3 4 5
|| || || || ||

50. Mr Clay pays $4800 in income taxes. If this is 15% of his annual income, what is his annual income?
(1) $25 000
(2) $30 000
(3) $32 000
(4) $36 000
(5) $40 000

50. 1 2 3 4 5
|| || || || ||

51. A side of a square is n m in length. Each side of the square is increased by 2 m thus creating a new square whose area exceeds that of the original square by 48 m^2. An equation which expresses the relationship between the areas of the two squares is
(1) $n^2 = (n + 2)^2 + 48$
(2) $(n + 2)^2 = n^2 + 48$
(3) $n^2 + (n + 2)^2 = 48$
(4) $n^2 - (n + 2)^2 = 48$
(5) $(n + 4)^2 - n^2 = 48$

51. 1 2 3 4 5
|| || || || ||

52. A woman invests part of $10 000 at 6% and the rest at 8%. Her annual income from both investments is $720. If x represents the amount invested at 6%, which one of the following equations may be used to find the value of x?
(1) $0.06x + 0.08(10\,000 - x) = 720$
(2) $6x + 8(10\,000 - x) = 720$
(3) $0.06x + 0.08x + 720 = 10\,000$
(4) $0.06x + 0.08(x - 10\,000) = 720$
(5) $0.06(x - 10\,000) + 0.08x = 720$

52. 1 2 3 4 5
|| || || || ||

53. A family spent $\frac{1}{4}$ of its income for rent and $\frac{1}{5}$ of its income for food. What percent of its income remains?
(1) 40%
(2) 45%
(3) 50%
(4) 52%
(5) 55%

53. 1 2 3 4 5
|| || || || ||

54. The perimeter of a triangle is 42 cm. If the second side of the triangle is 6 cm longer than the first side and the third side is double the size of the first side, find the length of the first side (in centimetres).
(1) 8
(2) 9
(3) 10
(4) 12
(5) 15

54. 1 2 3 4 5
|| || || || ||

55. On the number line $\sqrt{7}$ is located at point
(1) A
(2) B
(3) C
(4) D
(5) E

55. 1 2 3 4 5

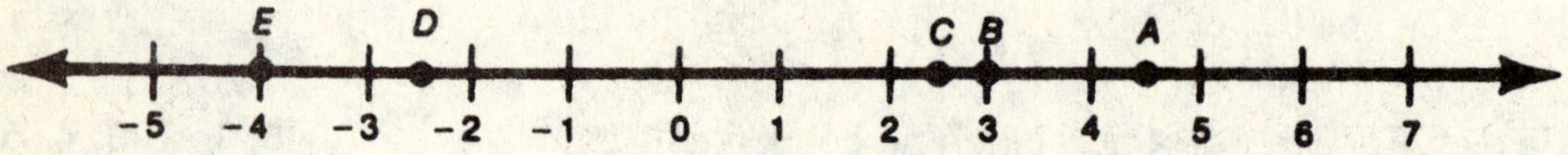

56. A certain recipe that will yield 4 portions calls for 1.5 mL of sugar. If the recipe is used to yield 10 portions, then the amount of sugar needed, in millilitres, is
(1) 3.5
(2) 3.75
(3) 4
(4) 4.25
(5) 4.75

56. 1 2 3 4 5

Turn to the answer key and the answer analysis which follow.

What's Your Score?

_________ right, _________ wrong

Excellent	51–56
Good	44–50
Fair	38–43

Be sure to refer to page 663, where these answers are explained. You may obtain additional help and practice by referring to the review material in this chapter.

ANSWER KEY

The number following each question is the correct answer. The numbers and letters in parentheses refer to the sections of this chapter which explain necessary mathematics principles. A more detailed explanation of all answers follows.

Practice Test Two/Page 653

1. **1(I-G)**
2. **2(II-H)**
3. **4(I-G)**
4. **5(III-H)**
5. **5(I-E)**
6. **2(III-C)**
7. **3(II-H)**
8. **3(III-H)**
9. **3(I-G)**
10. **4(II-A)**
11. **4(III-H)**
12. **2(I-K)**
13. **1(I-E)**
14. **5(II-C)**
15. **3(II-J)**
16. **4(II-A)**
17. **5(II-F)**
18. **4(IV-C)**
19. **1(I-E)**
20. **1(III-D)**
21. **4(I-G)**
22. **2(I-E)**
23. **1(III-H)**
24. **4(II-F)**
25. **1(II-A)**
26. **2(I-G)**
27. **1(I-H)**
28. **5(III-H)**
29. **1(I-E)**
30. **3(II-A)**
31. **5(I-C)**
32. **3(II-A)**
33. **1(III-H)**
34. **2(IV-D)**
35. **4(III-I)**
36. **4(II-B)**
37. **5(I-G)**
38. **4(I-H)**
39. **2(III-C)**
40. **2(II-G)**
41. **5(III-C)**
42. **3(I-G)**
43. **2(II-K)**
44. **3(I-E)**
45. **4(II-A)**
46. **4(I-I)**
47. **2(III-E)**
48. **1(II-F)**
49. **4(II-E)**
50. **3(I-G)**
51. **2(II-F)**
52. **1(II-F)**
53. **5(I-E)**
54. **2(II-F)**
55. **3(I-A)**
56. **2(II-H)**

ANSWER ANALYSIS

Practice Test Two/Page 653

1. **1** If 80% of the audience were adults then 100% − 80% = 20% were children.

$$20\% = \frac{1}{5}, \quad \frac{1}{5} \text{ of } 650 = 130$$

2. **2** Let x = number of centimetres between the towns on the map.

$$\text{Use the proportion } \frac{1\text{cm}}{x\,\text{cm}} = \frac{60\text{km}}{255\text{km}}$$

$$60x = 255$$

$$x = \frac{255}{60} = \frac{255 \div 15}{60 \div 15} = \frac{17}{4} = 4.25$$

The distance on the map is 4.25 cm.

3. **4** 10% of \$24 000 = \$2400
15% of \$24 000 = \$3600
\$2400 + \$3600 = \$6000
\$24 000 − \$6000 = \$18 000
\$18 000 ÷ 3 = \$6000

4. **5** To find the amount of cardboard needed we must find the surface area of the rectangular solid.

Area of bottom = 2 × 1.5 = 3 m^2
Area of top = 3 m^2
Area of front = 2 × 0.5 = 1 m^2
Area of back = 3 m^2
Area of side = 1.5 × 0.5 = 0.75 m^2
Area of other side = 0.75 m^2

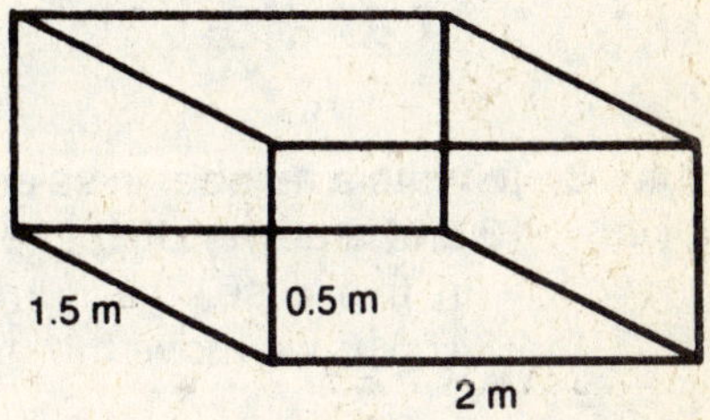

Total area = 3 + 3 + 1 + 1 + 0.75 + 0.75 = 9.5 m^2

5. **5** If ⅔ of the crop sells for \$600, ⅓ of the crop sells for \$300. So the whole crop, ⅓ + ⅔, sells for \$600 + \$300 = \$900.

6. **2** $OA = OB$
$m\angle A = m\angle B = 52°$
$m\angle A + m\angle B + m\angle O = 180°$
$52 + 52 + m\angle O = 180$
$m\angle O = 180 - 52 - 52 = 76°$

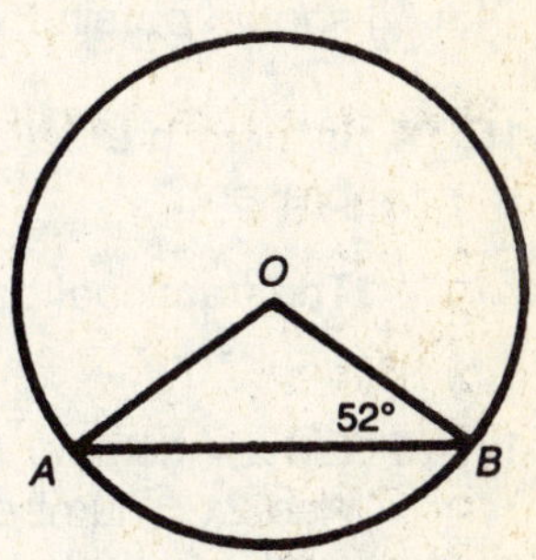

7. **3** Let $AB = 3x$
And $BC = 5x$
$5x = 20$
$x = 4$
$AB = 3x = 3(4) = 12$

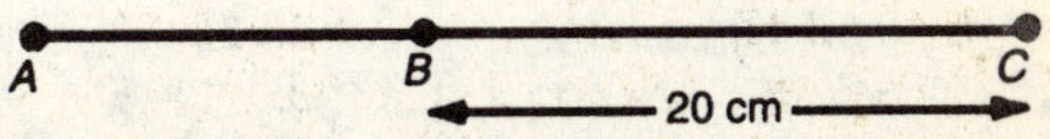

8. **3** The width of the pipe can be found by subtracting the radius of the smaller circle from the radius of the larger circle.
Diameter of larger circle = 7.5 cm
Radius of larger circle = 3.75 cm
Diameter of smaller circle = 4.5 cm
Radius of smaller circle = 2.25 cm
Thickness of pipe = 3.75 − 2.25 = 1.5 cm

9. **3** Increase in salary = \$580 – \$520 = \$60 per week

Rate of increase = $\frac{60}{520}$ which is equal to $\frac{3}{26}$.

If we divide 3 by 26 we have 0.115

0.115 = 11.5% or 12% to the nearest percent.

10. **4** The shopper gives the storekeeper \$5 or 500 cents. From this amount the storekeeper takes out x cents for the bread and $0.5y$ cents for the coffee.

The result is $500 - x - 0.5y$

11. **4** To find the width of the room we divide the area of the room (96 m^2) by the length of the room (12 m).

96 ÷ 12 = 8 m, width of the room

Perimeter of room = $2(l + w) = 2(12 + 8)$

$2(12 + 8) = 2(20) = 40$ m

12. **2** To find the total receipts we find the receipts of the matinee performances and add to this the receipts of the evening performances.

Receipts of the matinee performances = 4(267)

Receipts of the evening performances = 8(329)

Total receipts = 4(267) + 8(329)

13. **1** We can express the part of the apartment painted in $2\frac{1}{2}$ hours as

$$\frac{2\frac{1}{2}}{4\frac{1}{2}} = \frac{5}{2} \div \frac{9}{2} = \frac{5}{2} \times \frac{2}{9}, \text{ or } \frac{5}{9}$$

14. **5** To write a number in scientific notation we write it as the product of a number between 1 and 10 and a power of 10.

In this case, the number between 1 and 10 is 2.347516. In going from 2.347516 to 2 347 516 we move the decimal point 6 places to the right. Therefore,

$$2\,347\,516 = 2.347516 \times 10^6$$

15. **3** When we factor $x^2 - 5x + 6$ we obtain the product of two binomials $(x - 3)(x - 2)$.

We may check this result by multiplying the two binomials. If the factoring is correct we should obtain the original trinomial as a result.

16. **4** If there are 32 students in the class and x students are absent then $32 - x$ students are present.

The fractional part of the students present is $\frac{32 - x}{32}$.

17. **5** Let x = number of students taking French.

And $2x$ = number of students taking Spanish.

$$x + 2x = 402$$
$$3x = 402$$
$$x = 402 \div 3 = 134$$
$$2x = 2(134) = 268$$

18. **4** If we examine the graph we note that the temperature was –4°C at 7 A.M. and –4°C at 8 A.M. Thus, there was no change in temperature between 7 A.M. and 8 A.M. This conclusion may be verified by observing that the line graph neither rises nor falls between 7 A.M. and 8 A.M.

19. **1** They played $w + 5$ games and won w games. Therefore, $\frac{w}{w+5}$ = part of games won.

20. **1** We use the Pythagorean Theorem.
$x^2 = 8^2 + 15^2$
$x^2 = 64 + 225$
$x^2 = 289$
$x = \sqrt{289} = 17$

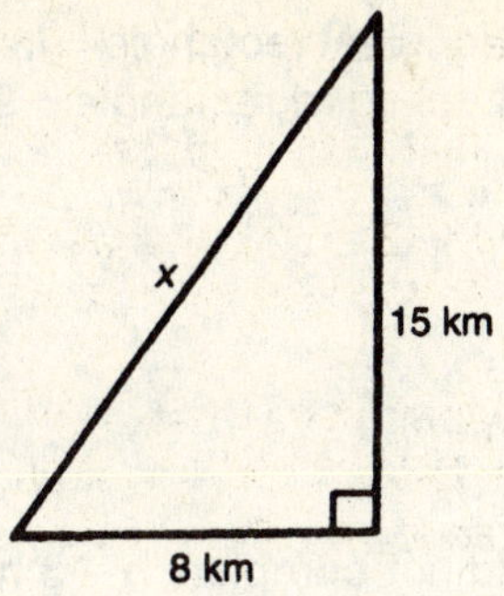

21. **4** 385 × \$23 = \$8855, textbook sales
18 × \$49 = \$882, art book sales
396 × \$18 = \$7128, novel sales
Total sales = \$16 865
Commission = 0.12 × \$16 865 = \$2024 to the nearest dollar

22. **2** $36\frac{1}{2} - 32\frac{3}{4} = 3\frac{3}{4}$, profit per share
$3\frac{3}{4} = 3.75$, \$3.75 × 120 = \$450, total profit

23. **1** $x = (\frac{1}{5})(180°) = 36°$
$y = (\frac{2}{5})(180°) = 72°$
$z = (\frac{2}{5})(180°) = 72°$
$x + y = 108°$

24. **4** Let x = the number of boys
And $x + 6$ = the number of girls
$x + x + 6 = 34$
$2x + 6 = 34$
$2x = 34 - 6 = 28$
$x = 28 \div 2 = 14$
$x + 6 = 14 + 6 = 20$ girls

25. **1** We use the relationship
Rate × Time = Distance
or Rate = $\frac{\text{Distance}}{\text{Time}}$
In this case, distance = 120 and time = x
Therefore, the number of kilometres per hour is $\frac{120}{x}$.

26. **2** 3500 − 2800 = 700, increase of population
Rate of increase $\frac{700}{2800} = \frac{1}{4}$
$\frac{1}{4}$ = 25%, increase expressed as a percent

27. **1** \$90 000 = 900 × \$100
Cost of original insurance = 900 × \$.39 = \$351
Cost of new insurance = 900 × \$.34 = \$306
\$351 − \$306 = \$45, saved

28. **5** Area of original rectangle = lw
Area of enlarged rectangle = $9lw$

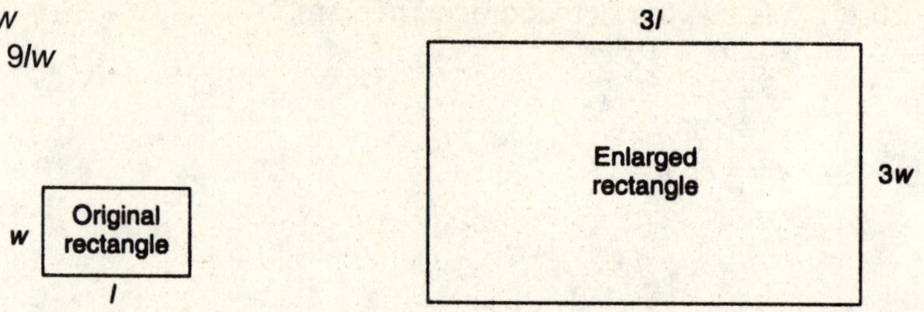

29. **1** Sara did not complete $h - 3$ hours of the *total* of h hours.

$$\frac{h-3}{h}$$

30. **3** Ade spent $y \times z$, or yz dollars
If we subtract yz from x, we have $x - yz$.

31. **5** 12 people working 15 hours = $12 \times 15 = 180$ hours to complete the job.
Let x = number of hours it takes reduced crew to complete the job.
$9x$ = the number of hours to complete the job.
$9x = 180$
$x = 180 \div 9 = 20$ hours

32. **3** If the worker earns x dollars per month and spends y dollars per month then he saves $(x - y)$ dollars per month. In one year the man saves $12(x - y)$ dollars.

33. **1** The area of the rectangle = $2a \times a = 2a^2$
The radius of the semicircle is $\frac{1}{2}(2a) = a$.
The formula for the area of a circle is $A = \pi r^2$.
The area of the semicircle is $\frac{1}{2}(\pi a^2)$.
The area of the whole figure = $2a^2 + \frac{1}{2}\pi a^2$.

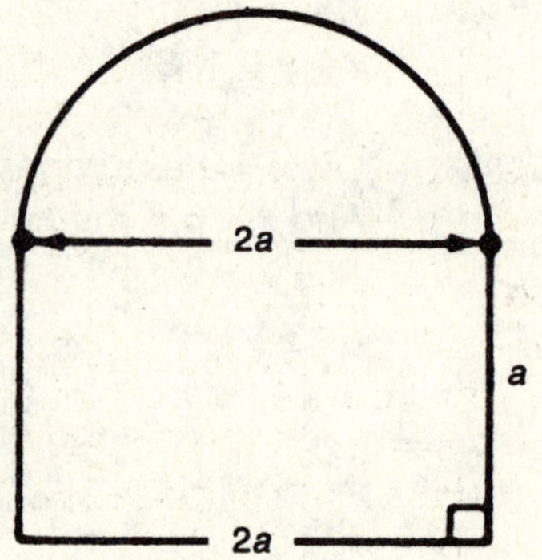

34. **2** The person spends $\frac{45}{360} = \frac{1}{8}$ of a day on meals. $\frac{1}{8}$ of a day $= \frac{1}{8} \times 24 = 3$ hours.
The person spends $\frac{30}{360} = \frac{1}{12}$ of a day on travel. $\frac{1}{12}$ of a day $= \frac{1}{12} \times 24 = 2$ hours.
The person spends 1 hour more on meals than on travel. It can be shown that the other statements are incorrect. For example, consider statement (1).

$$\frac{105}{360} = \frac{7}{24}, \frac{7}{24} \times 24 = 7$$

That is, the person works 7 hours per day, not 8 hours.

35. **4** We use the formula for the volume of a cylinder:
$V = \pi r^2 h$
In this case, $\pi = \frac{22}{7}$, $r = 7$, and $h = 6$.

$$V = \frac{22}{7} \times 7 \times 7 \times 6 = 924\text{m}^3$$

$924 \times 1000 = 924\,000$

36. **4** $y = 2x^2(z - 3)$
$y = 2(5)(5)(7 - 3)$
$y = 2(5)(5)(4)$
$y = 200$

37. **5** A saving of \$19 out of \$30
or $\frac{19}{30} = 0.6333$ or 63%

38. **4** At age 30, the policy costs 22(10) = \$220 per year.
At age 46, the policy costs 38(10) = \$380 per year.
Thus, \$380 − \$220 = \$160 saved per year.
In 20 years, the savings is 160(20) = \$3200

39. **2** Let $3x$ = number of degrees in larger angle
And $2x$ = number of degrees in smaller acute angle
$3x + 2x = 90$
$5x = 90$
$x = 90 \div 5 = 18$
$3x = 3(18) = 54°$

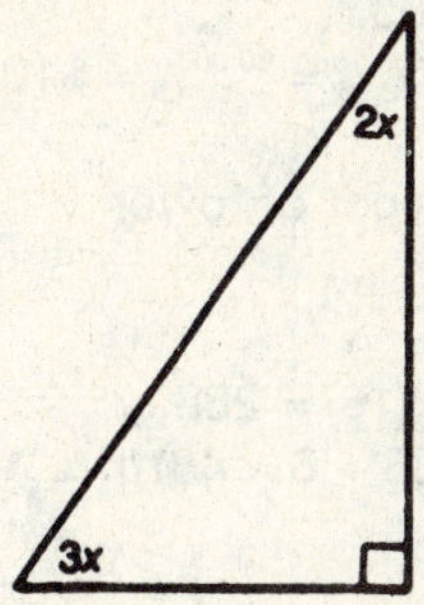

40. **2** $3x - 1 < 5$
$3x < 5 + 1$
$3x < 6$
$x < 2$
x must be less than 2.

41. **5** $m\angle BDE = 100°$
Since $\overleftrightarrow{AB} \parallel \overleftrightarrow{GH}$, $m\angle BDE + m\angle DEH = 180°$
$100 + m\angle DEH = 180$
$m\angle DEH = 180 - 100 = 80°$
$m\angle JDE = \frac{1}{2}m\angle BDE = 50°$
$m\angle DEJ = \frac{1}{2}m\angle DEH = 40°$
$m\angle J + 50 + 40 = 180$
$m\angle J = 180 - 50 - 40 = 90°$

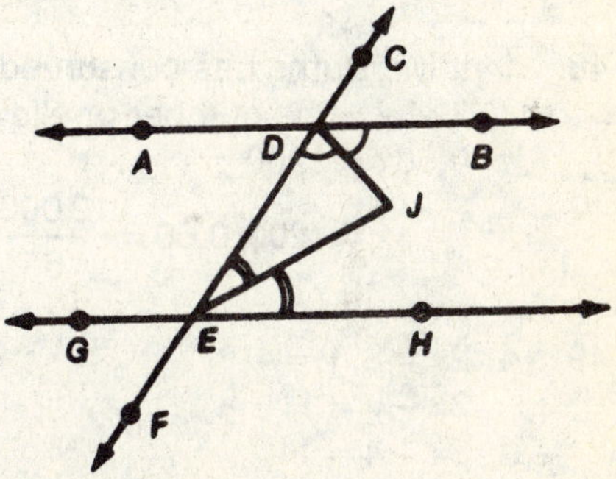

42. **3** $25\% = \frac{1}{4}$. The selling price of the chair was $\frac{3}{4}$ of the original selling price.
Let x = the original selling price
$\frac{3}{4}x = \$315$
$x = \$315 \div \frac{3}{4} = \$315 \times \frac{4}{3} = \$420$

43. **2** $\text{Probability} = \frac{\text{number of successful outcomes}}{\text{number of possible outcomes}}$

In this case, the number of successful outcomes is 1 since there is only 1 wife of Mr. Fowles out of the 48 women present. The number of possible outcomes is 48 since there are 48 possible women partners.

Probability = $\frac{1}{48}$

44. **3** $\frac{4}{5} > \frac{5}{7}$ because $4 \times 7 > 5 \times 5$
$\frac{5}{7} > \frac{2}{3}$ because $5 \times 3 > 7 \times 2$
Thus, $\frac{4}{5} > \frac{5}{7} > \frac{2}{3}$ is correct.

ALTERNATIVE METHOD

If we convert the three fractions to decimals, to the nearest hundredth, we have $\frac{5}{7} = 0.71$, $\frac{4}{5} = 0.80$, $\frac{2}{3} = 0.67$
Therefore, $\frac{4}{5} > \frac{5}{7} > \frac{2}{3}$

45. **4** If k kilograms of oranges can be bought for c cents then 1 kg of oranges can be bought for $\frac{c}{k}$ cents.

To find the number of kilograms of oranges that can be bought for 98 cents we must divide 98 by $\frac{c}{k}$.

$$98 \div \frac{c}{k} = 98 \times \frac{k}{c} = \frac{98k}{c}$$

46. **4** \$6000 at 5% = \$6000 × .05 = \$300 income
The man needs \$900 – \$300 = \$600 more in income.
6% of the new amount needed = \$600
Let x = the new amount needed
$0.06x = 600$
$x = 600/0.06 = 60\,000/6 = \$10\,000$

47. **2** Let x = height of tower
$\frac{x}{16} = \frac{18}{6}$
$6x = 18(16) = 288$
$x = 288 \div 6 = 48$ m

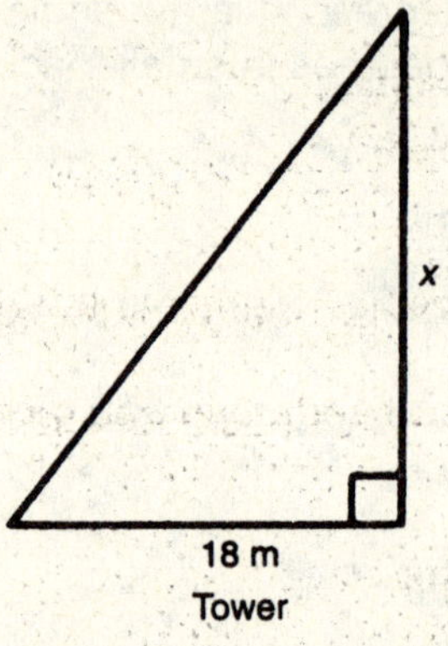

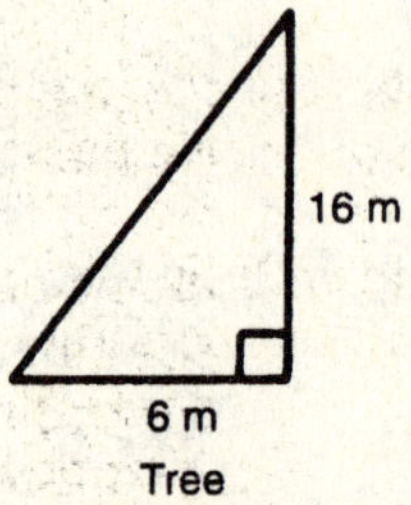

48. **1** If Mr. Burns has consumed 40% of his allowable calories he has 60% left.
Let x = the number of allowable daily calories
$0.60x = 1200$
$$x = 1200/0.60 = \frac{12\,000}{6} = 2000$$

49. **4** $2y = 8, y = 4$
$3x - y = 11$
$3x - 4 = 11$
$3x = 11 + 4 = 15$
$x = 15 \div 3 = 5$

50. **3** Let x = Mr. Clay's annual income
$0.15x = \$4800$
$x = \$4800/0.15 = \$480\,000/15 = \$32\,000$ income

51. **2** Area of enlarged square = $(n + 2)(n + 2)$
Area of original square = n^2
We use the relationship,
Enlarged square area = Original square area + 48
$(n + 2)^2 = n^2 + 48$

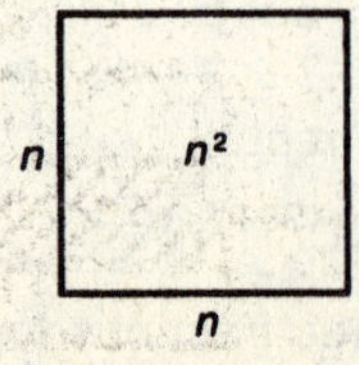

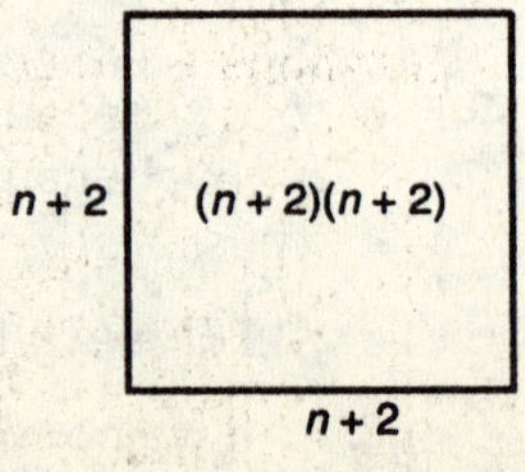

52. **1** $0.06x$ = income on 6% investment
$0.08(10\,000 - x)$ = income on 8% investment
We use the relationship,
Income on 6% investment + Income on 8% investment = \$720
$0.06x + 0.08(10\,000 - x) = 720$

53. **5** $\frac{1}{4} = \frac{5}{20}$, $\frac{1}{5} = \frac{4}{20}$
$\frac{1}{4} + \frac{1}{5} = \frac{5}{20} + \frac{4}{20} = \frac{9}{20}$, rent & food expense
$1 - \frac{9}{20} = \frac{20}{20} - \frac{9}{20} = \frac{11}{20}$, remaining income
$\frac{11}{20} = 0.55 = 55\%$

54. **2** Let x = length of first side
And $x + 6$ = length of second side
And $2x$ = length of third side
$x + x + 6 + 2x = 42$
$4x + 6 = 42$
$4x = 42 - 6 = 36$
$x = 36 \div 4 = 9$

55. **3** $\sqrt{7} = 2.6$ approximately
C names the point which is slightly to the right of the 2.5 point.

56. **2** The amount of sugar needed for 10 portions is equal to 2.5 the amount needed for 4 portions.
$2.5 \times 1.5 = 3.75$
3.75 mL of sugar needed.

PRACTICE TEST THREE

Directions: Blacken the space at the right under the number that corresponds to the one you have selected as the correct answer.

1. An oil tank contained 960 L. After 360 L were used, the percent of oil left in the tank was

(1) $37\frac{1}{2}\%$
(2) 62%
(3) $62\frac{1}{2}\%$
(4) 65%
(5) $83\frac{1}{3}\%$

1. 1 2 3 4 5 || || || || ||

2. In Halifax, the Scotia Garage charges \$1.35 per hour for parking (tax included). What is the charge for same day parking from 9:55 A.M. to 12:55 P.M.?

(1) \$1.35
(2) \$1.50
(3) \$3
(4) \$3.55
(5) \$4.05

2. 1 2 3 4 5 || || || || ||

3. The drawing is part of a bar graph showing the population of a small town. How many people lived in the town in 1994?

(1) 2500
(2) 2800
(3) 3000
(4) 3500
(5) 250 000

3. 1 2 3 4 5 || || || || ||

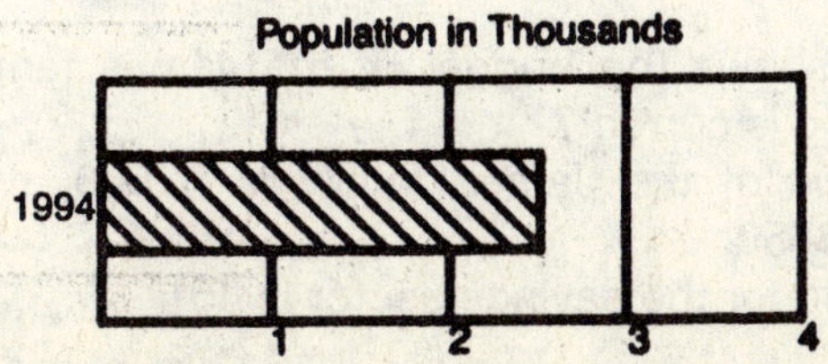

4. The charges for admission to The New Brunswick Museum are: \$2.00 for adults, and 50¢ for children. However, there is a maximum family charge of \$4. How much will Mrs. Cooke pay when she enters with her five children?

(1) \$2.50
(2) \$3
(3) \$3.50
(4) \$4
(5) \$4.50

4. 1 2 3 4 5

5. A bookcase has 3 shelves. Two of the shelves each have x books on them. The third shelf has y books on it. What is the total number of books in the bookcase?

(1) $2xy$
(2) $x + 2y$
(3) $2(x + y)$
(4) $2x + y$
(5) $2 + x + y$

5. 1 2 3 4 5

6. A front lawn measures 7 m in length and 6 m in width. The back lawn of the same house measures 14 m in length and 14 m in width. What is the ratio of the area of the front lawn to the area of the back lawn?

(1) 1:14
(2) 1:5
(3) 3:14
(4) 7:10
(5) 7:9

6. 1 2 3 4 5

7. A flask is full of lemonade. At lunch, $\frac{1}{3}$ of the flask is emptied. At dinner, $\frac{3}{4}$ of the remainder is used. What fractional part of the lemonade is left?

(1) none
(2) $\frac{1}{12}$
(3) $\frac{1}{6}$
(4) $\frac{1}{5}$
(5) $\frac{1}{4}$

7. 1 2 3 4 5

8. A farmer is making a rectangular barn door 3 m high and 4 m wide. How long (in metres) is the diagonal piece which he used to strengthen the door?

(1) 5
(2) 6
(3) 7
(4) 8
(5) 5.5

8. 1 2 3 4 5

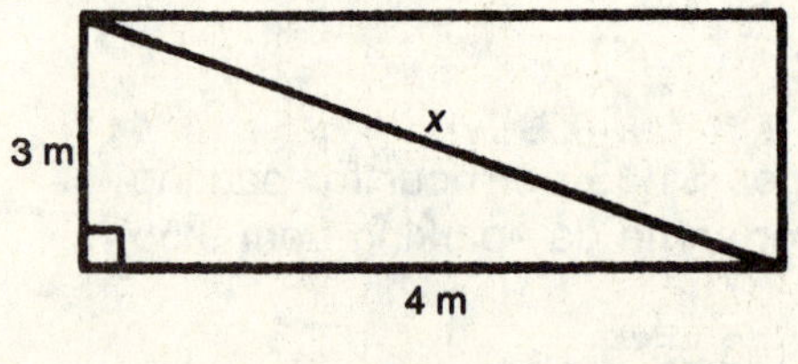

9. A television set priced at \$400 was reduced 25% in price just before a new model came out. In addition, a 2% discount is allowed for cash. What was the actual cash price the buyer paid for this television set?

(1) \$292
(2) \$293
(3) \$294
(4) \$297
(5) \$298

9. 1 2 3 4 5

10. The circle graph below shows the budget of the James family. Which one of the following is correct?

(1) If the monthly income of the James family is \$2500, their allowance for rent is \$650.
(2) The angle at the centre for the savings sector is 45°.

10. 1 2 3 4 5

(3) More than one-half of the James family budget is spent on food and rent.
(4) If the monthly income is $2500 the James family saves more than $5000 per year.
(5) Less than ⅓ of its income is spent on clothing and savings.

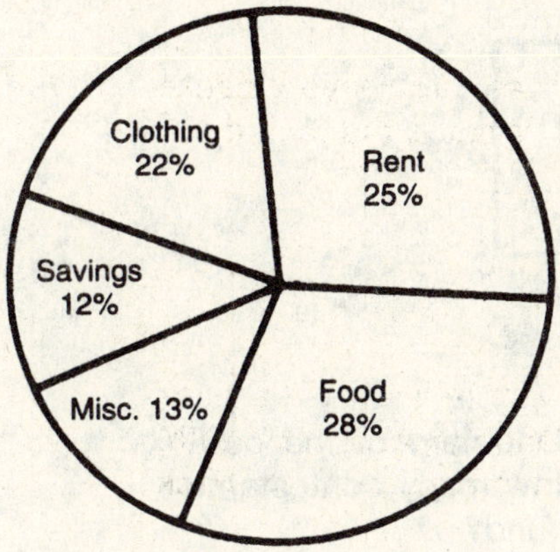

11. I can complete a job in *h* hours. What part of this task would I complete in *x* hours?

(1) $\frac{h}{x}$
(2) $\frac{1}{hx}$
(3) $\frac{h+x}{hx}$
(4) $\frac{x}{h}$
(5) $\frac{1}{h-x}$

11. 1 2 3 4 5

12. A corporation reported a profit of 28 million dollars as compared with a profit of 35 million dollars for the previous year. This represents a decrease of

(1) 7%
(2) 20%
(3) 25%
(4) 70%
(5) 80%

12. 1 2 3 4 5

13. The length of a small particle is 0.0000017 mm. Express this number in scientific notation.

(1) 1.7×10^{-5}
(2) 1.7×10^{-6}
(3) 17×10^{-4}
(4) 1.7^{6}
(5) 1.7^{-3}

13. 1 2 3 4 5

14. A melon has an approximate mass of

(1) 1000 mg
(2) 2 L
(3) 0.7 kg
(4) 50 g
(5) 1 km

14. 1 2 3 4 5

15. In the diagram, if $AC = 24$ and $AB = 6$, the ratio $AB:BC$ is

(1) 1:4
(2) 1:3
(3) 1:2
(4) 2:1
(5) 3:1

15. 1 2 3 4 5

16. *ABCD* is a rectangle. The ratio of the area of $\triangle EDC$ to the area of the rectangle *ABCD* is

(1) 1:4
(2) 1:3
(3) 1:2
(4) 3:5
(5) 3:4

16. 1 2 3 4 5

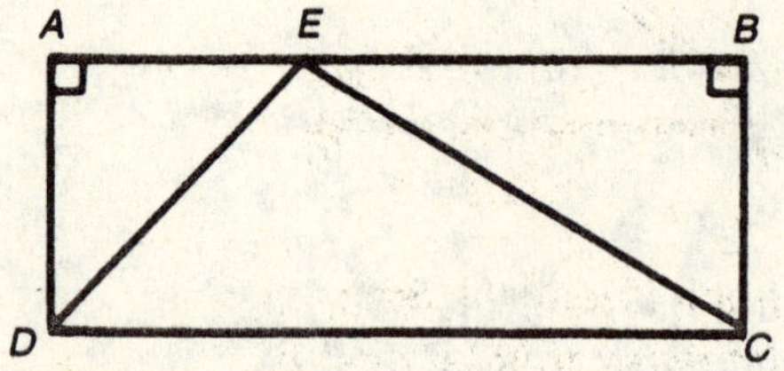

17. There are 216 competitors in a contest. One-third of the contestants are eliminated after each round. How many contestants will be eligible for a prize after the second round?

(1) 24
(2) 46
(3) 48
(4) 96
(5) 98

17. 1 2 3 4 5

18. If 5 is subtracted from twice a number, the result is equal to 3 more than the number. An equation that may be used to solve this problem is

(1) $5 - 2x = x + 3$
(2) $2x - 5 = x - 3$
(3) $2x - 5 = x + 3$
(4) $x = 5 - 2x + 3$
(5) $x = 2x - 5 + 3$

18. 1 2 3 4 5

19. I spend $\frac{1}{5}$ of my earnings for rent and $\frac{3}{8}$ of the remainder for other necessities. What part of my total income is left for savings and entertainment?

(1) $\frac{1}{2}$
(2) $\frac{5}{8}$
(3) $\frac{4}{5}$
(4) $\frac{3}{4}$
(5) $\frac{3}{10}$

19. 1 2 3 4 5

20. The Stones purchased a building lot for \$15000 on which they built a house costing \$60000. What percent of the total cost was the cost of the lot?

(1) 20%
(2) 25%
(3) 40%
(4) 75%
(5) 80%

20. 1 2 3 4 5

21. Ann earns \$8 per hour for a 40-hour week. One week she works 9 hours overtime and receives $1\frac{1}{2}$ times her regular pay per hour. An expression which states her total pay is

(1) $8(40) + 4\frac{1}{2}(8)$
(2) $8(40) + 4\frac{1}{2}(12)$
(3) $8(60) + 9(12)$
(4) $8(40) + 9(12)$
(5) $8(60) + 4\frac{1}{2}(12)$

21. 1 2 3 4 5

22. I spent twice as much on a jacket as on a pair of slacks. In all, I spent \$162. How much did I pay for the jacket?

(1) \$54
(2) \$62
(3) \$70
(4) \$96
(5) \$108

22. 1 2 3 4 5

23. In a right triangle *ABC*, *AC* = *BC*. The measure of $\angle A$ is

(1) 30°
(2) 35°
(3) 45°
(4) 50°
(5) 60°

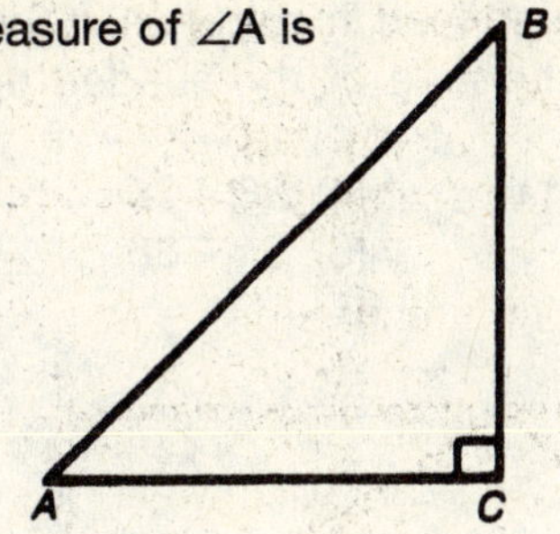

23. 1 2 3 4 5

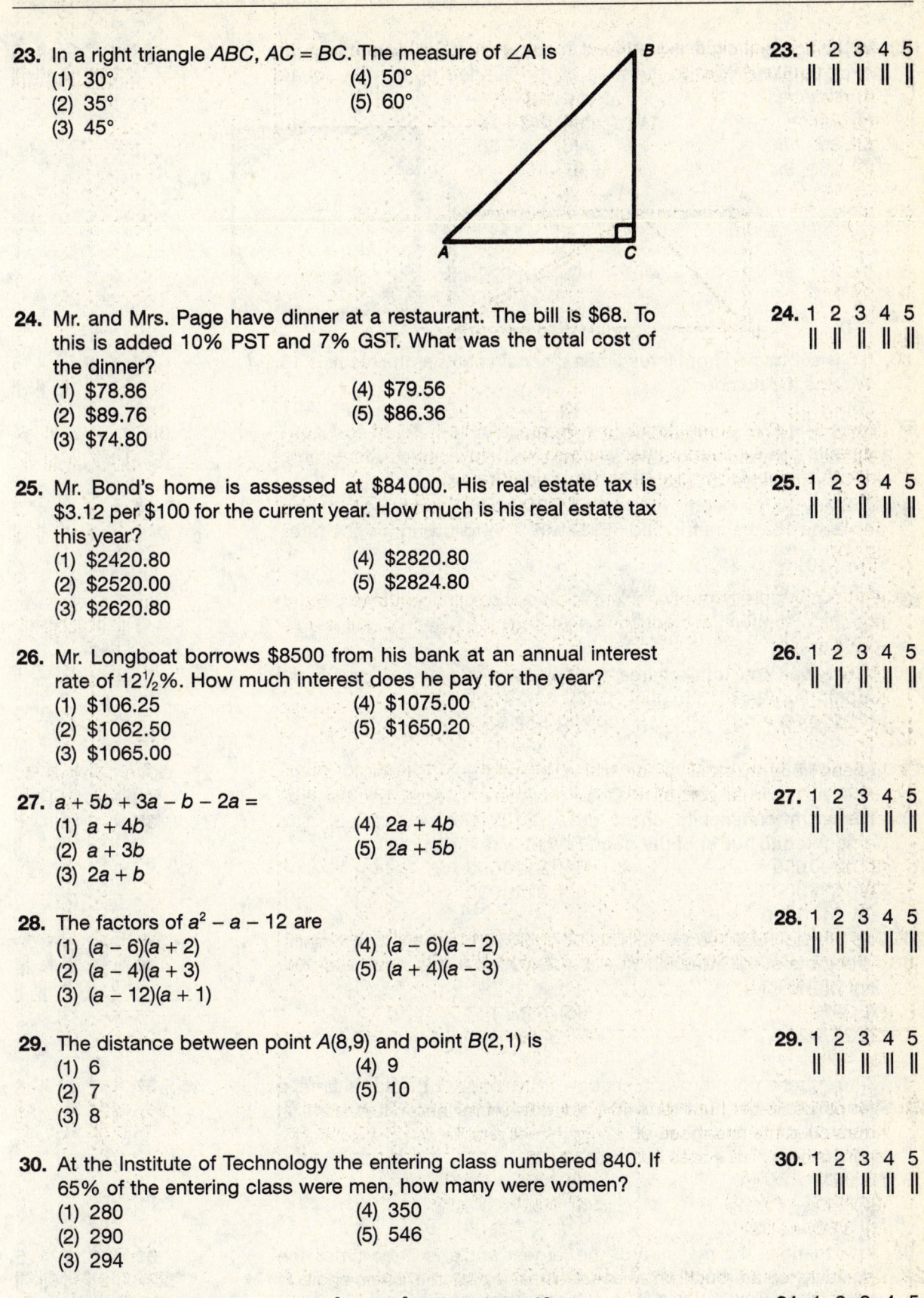

24. Mr. and Mrs. Page have dinner at a restaurant. The bill is $68. To this is added 10% PST and 7% GST. What was the total cost of the dinner?

(1) $78.86
(2) $89.76
(3) $74.80
(4) $79.56
(5) $86.36

24. 1 2 3 4 5

25. Mr. Bond's home is assessed at $84 000. His real estate tax is $3.12 per $100 for the current year. How much is his real estate tax this year?

(1) $2420.80
(2) $2520.00
(3) $2620.80
(4) $2820.80
(5) $2824.80

25. 1 2 3 4 5

26. Mr. Longboat borrows $8500 from his bank at an annual interest rate of $12\frac{1}{2}$%. How much interest does he pay for the year?

(1) $106.25
(2) $1062.50
(3) $1065.00
(4) $1075.00
(5) $1650.20

26. 1 2 3 4 5

27. $a + 5b + 3a - b - 2a =$

(1) $a + 4b$
(2) $a + 3b$
(3) $2a + b$
(4) $2a + 4b$
(5) $2a + 5b$

27. 1 2 3 4 5

28. The factors of $a^2 - a - 12$ are

(1) $(a - 6)(a + 2)$
(2) $(a - 4)(a + 3)$
(3) $(a - 12)(a + 1)$
(4) $(a - 6)(a - 2)$
(5) $(a + 4)(a - 3)$

28. 1 2 3 4 5

29. The distance between point $A(8,9)$ and point $B(2,1)$ is

(1) 6
(2) 7
(3) 8
(4) 9
(5) 10

29. 1 2 3 4 5

30. At the Institute of Technology the entering class numbered 840. If 65% of the entering class were men, how many were women?

(1) 280
(2) 290
(3) 294
(4) 350
(5) 546

30. 1 2 3 4 5

31. What is the value of x if $x = 3a^2 + a(2a^3 - 5)$ and $a = 4$?

(1) 450
(2) 540
(3) 2096
(4) 2196
(5) 2406

31. 1 2 3 4 5

32. In the figure, a circle is inscribed in a square. If the diameter of the circle is 6 cm, what is the area of the shaded portion, in square centimetres?

(1) 9π
(2) $36 - 9\pi$
(3) $36 + 9\pi$
(4) $36 - 36\pi$
(5) $9\pi - 36$

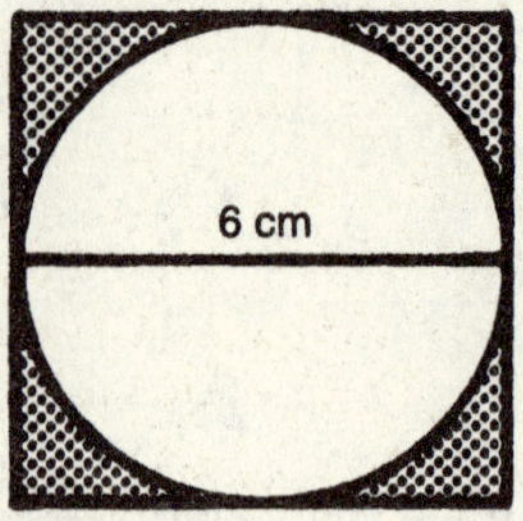

32. 1 2 3 4 5

33. If 5 is subtracted from three times a certain number the result is 16. What is the number?

(1) –4
(2) 3
(3) 0
(4) 7
(5) 9

33. 1 2 3 4 5

34. On May 15, an electric metre read 5472 kw.h. The following month, on June 15, the metre read 5698 kw.h. The following are the rates

First 10 kw.h – $2.72
Next 45 kw.h – $.22 per kw.h
Next 55 kw.h – $.19 per kw.h
Over 110 kw.h – $.16 per kw.h

What was the total charge for the kw.h consumed during the month from May 15 to June 15?

(1) $22.60
(2) $40.63
(3) $41.63
(4) $52.36
(5) $64.63

34. 1 2 3 4 5

35. During a community chest drive, $105 000 was raised. This amounted to 105% of the quota. What was the quota?

(1) $90 000
(2) $95 000
(3) $100 000
(4) $110 000
(5) $120 000

35. 1 2 3 4 5

36. The roots of the equation $x^2 - 2x - 8 = 0$ are

(1) 2, –4
(2) –2, –4
(3) 4, –2
(4) 8, 1
(5) (–8, 1)

36. 1 2 3 4 5

37. A telephone pole throws a shadow 28 m long. At the same time, a fence post 3 m high throws a shadow 4 cm long. How high (in metres) is the telephone pole?

(1) 16
(2) 21
(3) 28
(4) 35
(5) 40

37. 1 2 3 4 5

38. In a triangle, the measure of the largest angle is three times the measure of the smallest, and the measure of the other angle is twice the measure of the smallest. What is the measure of the largest angle of the triangle?

(1) 60°
(2) 65°
(3) 75°
(4) 80°
(5) 90°

38. 1 2 3 4 5

39. What is the area of the machine part below? Each end curve is a semi-circle. [Use $\pi = {}^{22}/_{7}$.]

(1) $38.5\,cm^2$
(2) $66.5\,cm^2$
(3) $105\,cm^2$
(4) $108\,cm^2$
(5) $100\,cm^2$

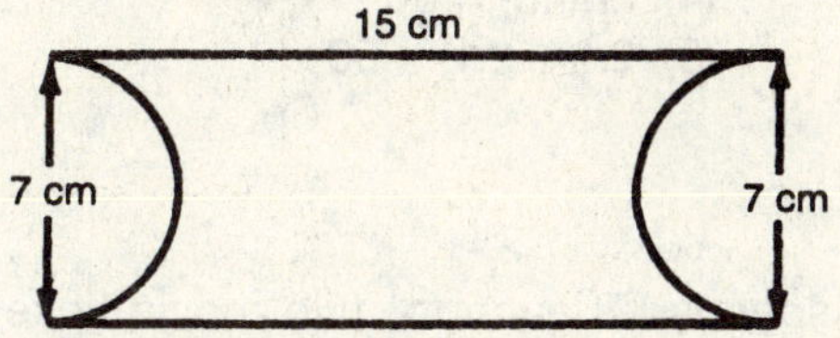

39. 1 2 3 4 5

40. A chair was marked for sale at $240. This was a discount of 25% on the original sale price. What was the original sale price?

(1) $300
(2) $280
(3) $290
(4) $320
(5) $315

40. 1 2 3 4 5

41. In order to raise funds the Atlas Club is conducting a lottery. The club is selling 500 tickets at $5 each and is awarding one prize. Mrs. Allen, a member of the club, buys 7 tickets. What is the probability that Mrs. Allen wins the prize?

(1) ${}^{7}/_{500}$
(2) ${}^{5}/_{7}$
(3) ${}^{5}/_{500}$
(4) ${}^{500}/_{7}$
(5) ${}^{1}/_{500}$

41. 1 2 3 4 5

42. Of the following numbers, the one which is closest to $\sqrt{7}$ is

(1) 2
(2) 2.4
(3) 2.6
(4) 3.1
(5) 3.4

42. 1 2 3 4 5

43. The slope of the line joining the points (4, *y*) and (2, 3) is 2. What is the value of *y*?

(1) 3
(2) 4
(3) 5
(4) 6
(5) 7

43. 1 2 3 4 5

44. There are 7 employees working in a small business firm. The average (mean) weekly salary of these workers is $584. If three of the workers each earn $450 per week and three others each earn $600 per week, how much does the seventh worker earn?

(1) $450
(2) $525
(3) $850
(4) $908
(5) $938

44. 1 2 3 4 5

45. Sara invested $12 000 at 7% annual interest. How much more must she invest at 8% so that her total annual income is $1560?

(1) $6000
(2) $8000
(3) $9000
(4) $10 000
(5) $15 000

45. 1 2 3 4 5

46. At a concert, orchestra seats sell for $15 each and balcony seats sell for $10 each. If 324 orchestra seats were sold and the box office collected $7540, how many balcony seats were sold?

(1) 249
(2) 268
(3) 275
(4) 279
(5) 281

46. 1 2 3 4 5

47. In a triangle, the length of the altitude is equal to one-half the length of the base. If n represents the length of the altitude and the area of the triangle is $50\,m^2$, an equation that expresses this relationship is

(1) $n(2n) = 50$
(2) $\frac{1}{2}(n)(2n) = 50$
(3) $\frac{n^2}{2} = 50$
(4) $2n(4n) = 50$
(5) $2n(n + 1) = 50$

47. 1 2 3 4 5

48. Demetro has x dollars. He spends $8 each for two movie tickets and y dollars at a cafe. Which of the following expresses the number of dollars he has left?

(1) $2x - 16 + y$
(2) $x - 16 + y$
(3) $x - (16 - y)$
(4) $x - 16 - y$
(5) $x + y + 16$

48. 1 2 3 4 5

49. For which values of x is the inequality $2x + 3 \geq 11$ true?

(1) 0,3
(2) 1,2
(3) 2,5
(4) 3,6
(5) 4,10

49. 1 2 3 4 5

50. If $\overleftrightarrow{AB} \parallel \overleftrightarrow{CD}$ and the ratio of $m\angle D$ to $m\angle A$ is 3:2 then $m\angle D =$

(1) 36°
(2) 72°
(3) 90°
(4) 108°
(5) 120°

50. 1 2 3 4 5

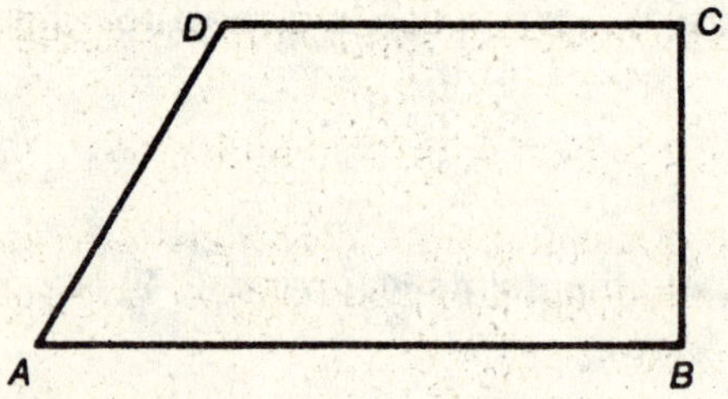

51. Lori drives a distance of 540 km in 6 hours. During the first two hours she averages 80 km/h. What was her average speed for the remaining four hours (in kilometres per hour)?

(1) 75
(2) 80
(3) 85
(4) 90
(5) 95

51. 1 2 3 4 5

52. Ben has $35 more than Joe. If Ben gives Joe $5, Ben will have twice as much as Joe. How much does Joe have?

(1) $10
(2) $15
(3) $18
(4) $20
(5) $25

52. 1 2 3 4 5

53. If $2x + 3y = 15$ and $4y = 20$ then $x =$

(1) 0
(2) −2
(3) 1
(4) 3
(5) 5

53. 1 2 3 4 5

54. A man left $\frac{1}{3}$ of his estate to his wife and divided the balance of the estate equally among his four children. What part of the estate does each child obtain?

(1) $\frac{1}{4}$
(2) $\frac{1}{5}$
(3) $\frac{1}{3}$
(4) $\frac{1}{6}$
(5) $\frac{1}{8}$

54. 1 2 3 4 5

55. A basketball team has won 12 games and lost 6. Of its 32 remaining games how many must the team win in order to have a winning percentage of 64%?

(1) 12
(2) 20
(3) 22
(4) 24
(5) 25

55. 1 2 3 4 5
|| || || || ||

56. Robert earns x dollars per month and his brother, Tom, earns y dollars per month. The number of dollars both men earn in one year is

(1) $x + y$
(2) $12x + y$
(3) $x + 12y$
(4) $12(x + y)$
(5) $x - y$

56. 1 2 3 4 5
|| || || || ||

Turn to the answer key and the answer analysis which follow.

What's Your Score?

_________ right, _________ wrong

Excellent	51–56
Good	44–50
Fair	38–43

Be sure to refer to page 677, where these answers are explained. You may obtain additional help and practice by referring to the review material in this chapter.

ANSWER KEY

The number following each question is the correct answer. The numbers and letters in parentheses refer to the sections of this chapter which explain necessary mathematics principles. A more detailed explanation of all answers follows.

Practice Test Three/Page 669

1. **3(I-G)**
2. **5(I-C)**
3. **1(IV-B)**
4. **4(I-C)**
5. **4(II-A)**
6. **3(III-H)**
7. **3(I-E)**
8. **1(III-D)**
9. **3(I-G)**
10. **3(IV-D)**
11. **4(II-F)**
12. **2(II-F)**
13. **2(II-C)**
14. **3(V-B)**
15. **2(II-H)**
16. **3(III-H)**
17. **4(I-C)**
18. **3(II-F)**
19. **1(I-E)**
20. **1(I-G)**
21. **4(I-K)**
22. **5(II-F)**
23. **3(III-C)**
24. **4(I-G)**
25. **3(I-J)**
26. **2(I-J)**
27. **4(II-A)**
28. **2(II-J)**
29. **5(III-F)**
30. **3(I-G)**
31. **2(II-B)**
32. **2(III-H)**
33. **4(II-F)**
34. **3(I-F)**
35. **3(I-G)**
36. **3(II-E)**
37. **2(III-D)**
38. **5(III-C)**
39. **2(III-H)**
40. **4(I-G)**
41. **1(II-E)**
42. **3(II-D)**
43. **5(III-F)**
44. **5(II-L)**
45. **3(I-G)**
46. **2(I-C)**
47. **2(II-F)**
48. **4(I-A)**
49. **5(II-G)**
50. **4(III-C)**
51. **5(I-C)**
52. **4(II-F)**
53. **1(II-E)**
54. **4(I-E)**
55. **2(I-G)**
56. **4(II-A)**

ANSWER ANALYSIS

Practice Test Three/Page 669

1. **3** There are $960 - 360 = 600$ L left in the tank.
$600/960 = 5/8 = 62\frac{1}{2}\%$ of oil left in the tank

2. **5** 9:55 A.M. to 12:55 P.M. = 3 hours
(3) ($1.35) = $4.05

3. **1** Note that the solid bar ends midway between the 2 and the 3.
That is, the population was 2.5 thousand, or 2500.

4. **4** $4. The maximum family charge applies.

5. **4** Two shelves have x books each for a total of $2x$ books.
The third shelf has y books.
The total is $2x + y$ books.

6. **3** Area of front lawn = $7 \times 6 = 42\,m^2$
Area of back lawn = $14 \times 14 = 196\,m^2$
Ratio of front lawn to back lawn = $42:196 = 3:14$

7. **3** At lunch, $\frac{1}{3}$ of the lemonade was used.
At dinner $\frac{3}{4} \times \frac{2}{3} = \frac{1}{2}$ of the lemonade was used.
$\frac{1}{3} + \frac{1}{2} = \frac{2}{6} + \frac{3}{6} = \frac{5}{6}$ of the lemonade was used.
Therefore, $\frac{6}{6} - \frac{5}{6} = \frac{1}{6}$ of the lemonade remained.

8. **1** We use the Pythagorean Theorem.
$x^2 = 3^2 + 4^2$
$x^2 = 9 + 16 = 25$
$x = \sqrt{25}$
$x = 5\,m$

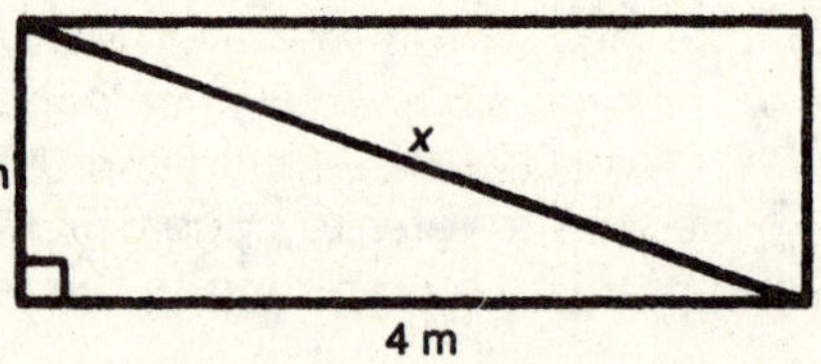

9. **3** 25% = $\frac{1}{4}$, $\frac{1}{4}$ of $400 = $100, reduction
$400 – $100 = $300, sale price
$300(.02) = $6, reduction for cash
$300 – $6 = $294, net price

10. **3** Cost of food is 28% of budget
Cost of rent is 25% of budget
28% + 25% = 53%, more than half of budget

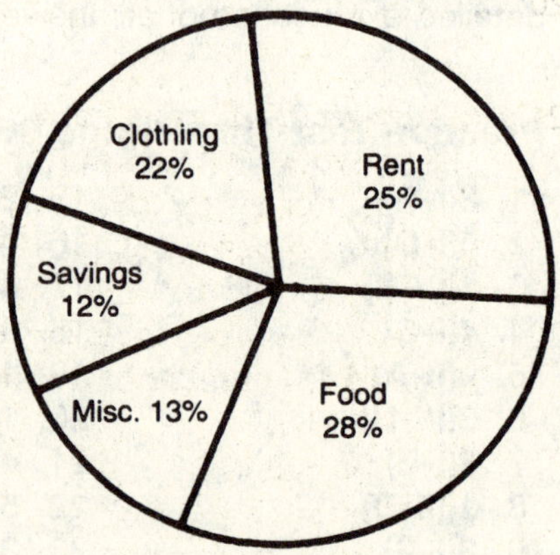

11. **4** In 1 hour I would complete $\frac{1}{h}$ part of the task.
In x hours I complete $\frac{x}{h}$ part of the task.

12. **2** $\frac{\text{Change}}{\text{Original}} \times 100 = \text{decrease in percent. } \frac{7}{35} = \frac{1}{5} = 20\%$

13. **2** To write a number in scientific notation we write it as the product of a number between 1 and 10 and a power of 10.

In this case, the number between 1 and 10 is 1.7. In going from 1.7 to 0.0000017 the decimal point is moved 6 places to the left. Therefore, $0.0000017 = 1.7 \times 10^{-6}$.

14. **3** Of the choices listed only (1), (3) and (4) are measures of mass.
Only 0.7 kg is a reasonable mass for a melon.

15. **2** Since $AC = 24$ and $AB = 6$, $BC = 24 - 6 = 18$
$AB:BC = 6:18 = 1:3$.

16. **3** Area of $\triangle EDC = \frac{1}{2}(DC) \times$ (altitude $= AD$)
Area of rectangle $ABCD = DC \times AD$
Thus, the area of $\triangle EDC$ is equal to one-half the area of rectangle $ABCD$. The ratio of the area of $\triangle EDC$ to the area of rectangle $ABCD = 1:2$.

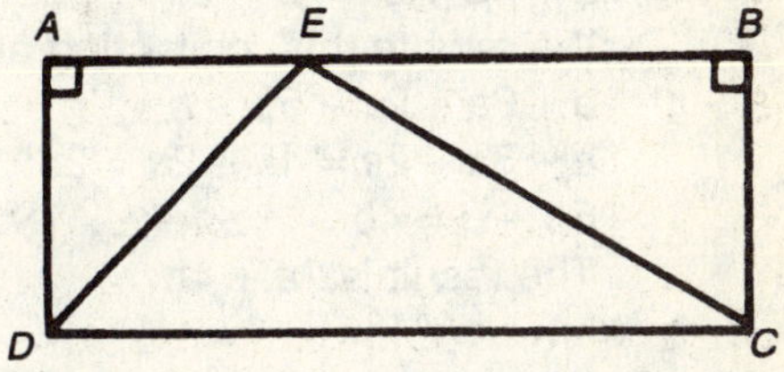

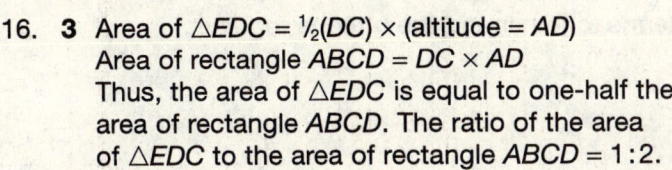

17. **4** After the first round $\frac{216}{3}$, or 72, are eliminated. There are 216 – 72, or 144, eligible for the second round. During this round, $\frac{144}{3}$, or 48, are eliminated, leaving 144 – 48, or 96, eligible for a prize after the second round.

18. **3** Let x = the number to be found
And $2x$ = twice the number
If we subtract 5 from twice the number we have $2x - 5$.
This $(2x - 5)$ is equal to 3 more than the number $(x + 3)$.
Thus, the equation to be used is
$2x - 5 = x + 3$

19. **1** Because I spend $\frac{1}{5}$ for rent, $\frac{4}{5}$ is left. Since I spend $\frac{3}{8}$ of what remains, I have $\frac{5}{8}$ of the $\frac{1}{5}$ for savings and entertainment. $\frac{5}{8}$ of $\frac{4}{5}$ equals $\frac{4}{8}$ or $\frac{1}{2}$ for savings and entertainment.

20. **1** Total cost = \$75 000. $\frac{\$15\,000}{\$75\,000} = \frac{1}{5} = 20\%$

21. **4** Ann works 40 hours at \$8 per hour. Thus, her salary for regular working time = 8(40).
Ann works 9 hours at $(1\frac{1}{2} \times 8)$ or \$12 per hour.
Thus, her salary for overtime work is 9(12).
Her total salary = 8(40) + 9(12) dollars.

22. **5** Let n = number of dollars spent on slacks
And $2n$ = number of dollars spent on jacket
$n + 2n = 81$
$3n = 81$
$n = 81 \div 3 = 27$
$2n = 2(27) = \$54$

23. **3** Since $AC = BC$, $m\angle A = m\angle B$
$m\angle A + m\angle B + m\angle C = 180$
$m\angle A + m\angle B + 90 = 180$
$m\angle A + m\angle B = 180 - 90 = 90$
Since $m\angle A = m\angle B$, $m\angle A = \frac{1}{2}(90) = 45°$

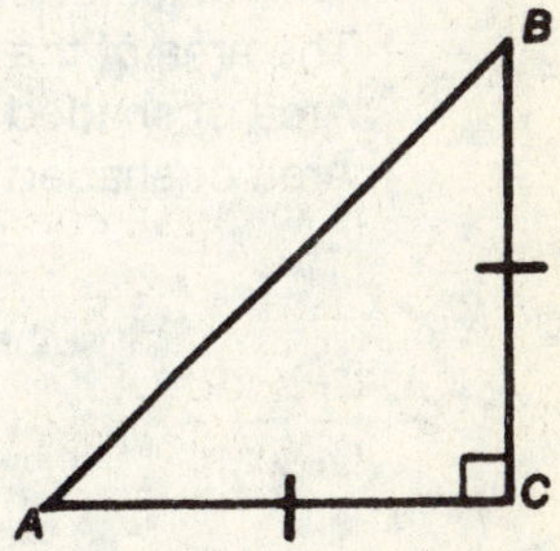

24. **4** The basic bill is \$68. To this is added 10% of \$68, or 0.10 × \$68 = \$6.80. \$68 + \$6.80 = \$74.80. Then 7% GST is added. 0.07 × \$68 = \$4.76. \$74.80 + \$4.76 = \$79.56. Total cost = \$79.56.

25. **3** In 84 000 there are 840 hundreds. The tax is \$3.12 per \$100 of assessed valuation. (3.12)(840) = \$2620.80, real estate tax

26. **2** $12\frac{1}{2}\% = .125$
0.125(\$8500) = \$1062.50

27. **4** $a + 5b + 3a - b - 2a$
We rewrite this, collecting all the *a* terms together and the *b* terms together.
$a + 3a - 2a + 5b - b$
$a + 3a - 2a = 4a - 2a = 2a$
$5b - b = 4b$
The result is $2a + 4b$.

28. **2** When we factor $a^2 - a - 12$ we obtain the result $(a - 4)(a + 3)$.
We may verify this result by finding the product of $(a - 4)$ and $(a + 3)$. This product is $a^2 - a - 12$.

29. **5** We use the distance formula
$d = \sqrt{(x_1 - x_2)^2 + (y_1 - y_2)^2}$
In this case, $x_1 = 8$, $x_2 = 2$, $y_1 = 9$, and $y_2 = 1$.
$d = \sqrt{(8-2)^2 + (9-1)^2}$
$d = \sqrt{(6)^2 + (8)^2} = \sqrt{36+64}$
$d = \sqrt{100}$
$d = 10$

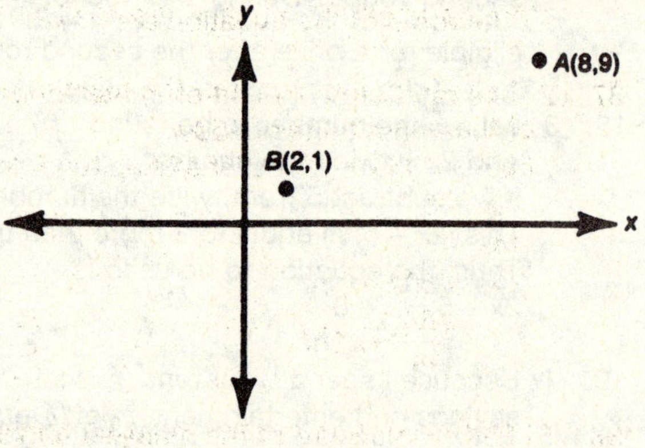

30. **3** 100% − 65% = 35% of the entering class were women (.35)(840) = 294 women

31. **2** $x = 3a^2 + a(2a^3 - 5)$
$x = 3(4)^2 + 4(2 \cdot 4^3 - 5)$
$x = 3(16) + 4(128 - 5)$
$x = 48 + 4(123) = 48 + 492$
$x = 540$

32. **2** Each side of the square is 6 cm. The area of the square is 36 cm^2.
The radius of the circle is $\frac{1}{2}(6) = 3$ cm
The area of the circle = $\pi r^2 = \pi \cdot 3 \cdot 3 = 9\pi$ cm^2
Area of shaded portion = Area of square − Area of circle
Area of shaded portion = $36 - 9\pi$

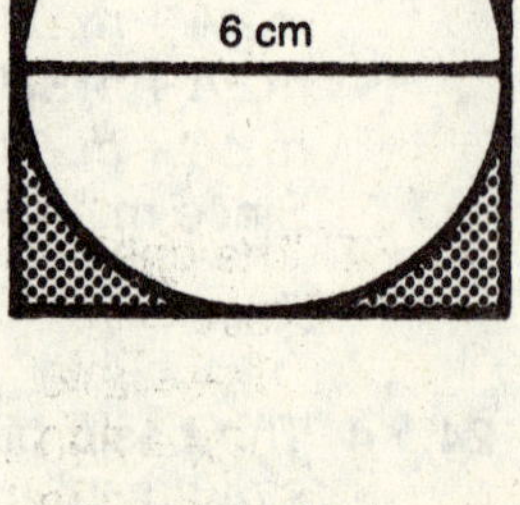

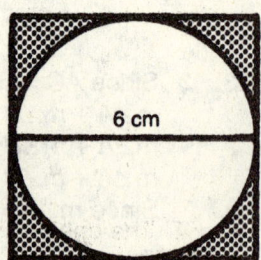

33. **4** Let x = the number.
$3x - 5 = 16$
$3x = 16 + 5 = 21$
$x = 21 \div 3 = 7$

34. **3** 5698 − 5472 = 226 kw.h used
First 10 kw.h cost \$2.72
Next 45 kw.h at \$22 per kw.h = \$9.90
Next 55 kw.h at \$.19 per kw.h = \$10.45
10 + 45 + 55 = 110 kw.h
226 − 110 = 116 kw.h at \$.16 per kw.h = \$18.56
\$2.72 + \$9.90 + \$10.45 + \$18.56 = \$41.63

35. **3** Let x = the quota.
$1.05x = 105\,000$

$$x = \frac{105\,000}{1.05} = \frac{10\,500\,000}{105} = \$100\,000$$

36. **3** $x^2 - 2x - 8 = 0$
$(x - 4)(x + 2) = 0$
$x - 4 = 0 \qquad x + 2 = 0$
$x = 4 \qquad x = -2$
The roots of the equation are 4, −2.

37. **2** The ratio of the height of the telephone pole to its shadow is equal to the ratio of the length of the post to its shadow.
Let x = the height of the telephone pole.

$$\frac{x}{48} = \frac{3}{4}$$

$4x = 3(28) = 84$

$$x = \frac{84}{4} = 21\text{m}$$

38. **5** Let x = measure of the smallest angle
And $3x$ = measure of the largest angle
And $2x$ = measure of the other angle
$x + 3x + 2x = 180$
$6x = 180$
$x = 180 \div 6 = 30$
$3x = 3(30) = 90°$

39. **2** We may regard this figure as a rectangle with two semicircles cut out. Or, we may regard the figure as a rectangle with one circle cut out.
Area of rectangle = 7 × 15 = 105 cm^2
Area of circle = $\pi r^2 = {}^{22}/_7 \times {}^7/_2 \times {}^7/_2 = {}^{77}/_2$, or 38.5 cm^2
Area of machine part = 105 − 38.5 = 66.5 cm^2

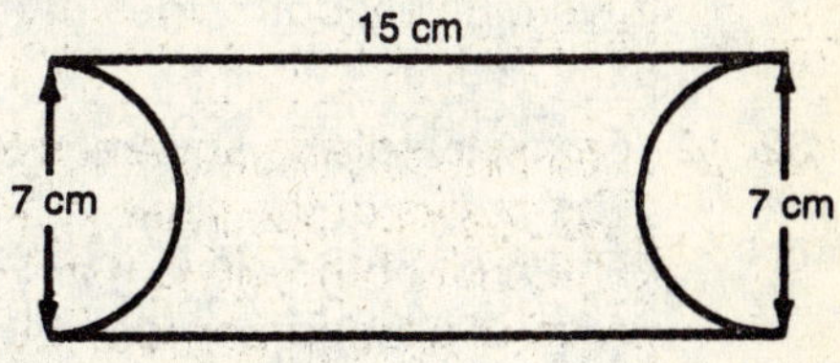

40. **4** The chair cost 100% − 25% = 75% of the original price.
$75\% = {}^3/_4$
${}^3/_4 x = 240$
$x = 240 \div {}^3/_4$
$x = 240 \times {}^4/_3$
$x = \$320$, original sale price

41. **1** Probability = $\frac{\text{number of successful events}}{\text{number of possible events}}$
In this case, the number of successful events is 7 since Mrs. Allen bought 7 tickets and the number of possible events is 500.
Probability = $\frac{7}{500}$

42. **3** $\sqrt{7} = 2.65$, correct to the nearest hundredth.
Of the choices given 2.6 is the closest.

43. **5** The slope of the line = $\frac{\text{increase in } y \text{ coordinates}}{\text{increase in } x \text{ coordinates}} = \frac{y_1 - y_2}{x_1 - x_2}$
In this case, $y_1 = y$, $y_2 = 3$, $x_1 = 4$, and $x_2 = 2$.
Slope = $\frac{y-3}{4-2} = \frac{y-3}{2}$
Since the slope of the line is 2, we have
$\frac{y-3}{2} = 2$
$y - 3 = 4$
$y = 4 + 3 = 7$

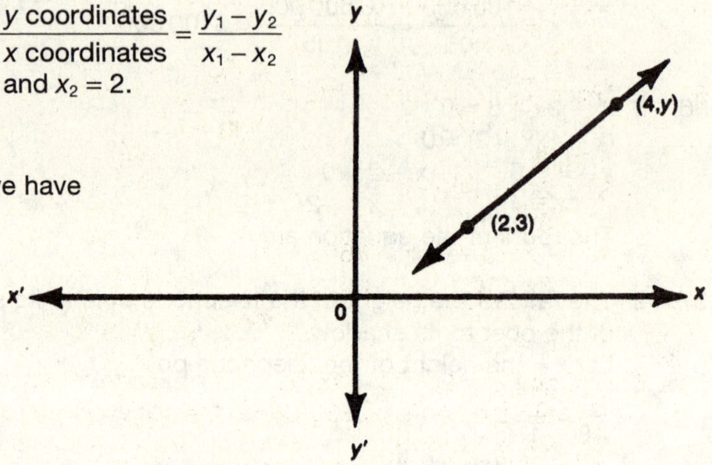

44. **5** The weekly payroll of the business firm is 7 × \$584 = \$4088.
Three workers earn 3 × \$450 = \$1350 weekly.
Three other workers earn 3 × \$600 = \$1800 weekly.
Six of the seven workers earn \$1350 + \$1800 = \$3150.
The seventh worker earns \$4088 – \$3150 = \$938.

45. **3** On her 7% investment Sara gets \$12 000 × 0.07 = \$840 per year. She wishes to get \$1560, or \$720 more.
Let x = the amount to be invested at 8%.
Let $0.08x = 720$.
If we multiply both sides of this equation by 100 we have
$8x = 72\,000$
$x = 72\,000 \div 8 = \$9000$

46. **2** 324 orchestra seats at \$15 each = \$4860
\$7540 – \$4860 = \$2680 collected for balcony seats
2680 ÷ \$10 = 268 balcony seats sold

47. **2** Since the length (n) of the altitude is equal to one-half the length of the base, the length of the base is $2n$.
Area of the triangle = $\frac{1}{2}bh$
Area of the triangle = $\frac{1}{2}(2n)(n)$, or $\frac{1}{2}(n)(2n)$.
Since the area is 50, $\frac{1}{2}(n)(2n) = 50$.

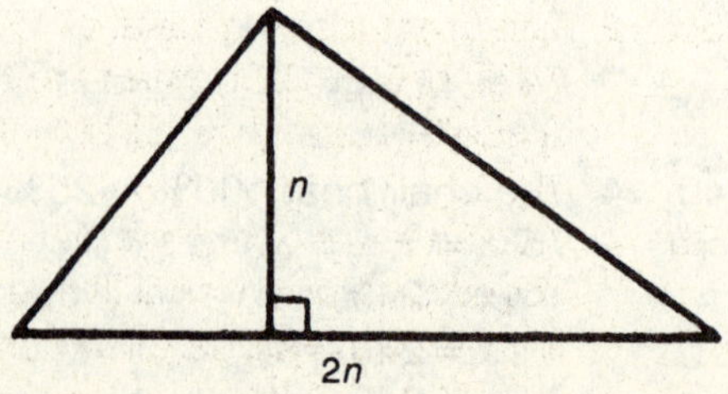

48. **4** To find the number of dollars Demetro has left we must subtract the amount he spent from x dollars.
$\$8 \times 2 = \$16$, spent for movie tickets
y dollars, spent at cafe
Amount left $x - 16 - y$

49. **5** $2x + 3 \geq 11$
$2x \geq 11 - 3$
$2x \geq 8$
$x \geq 4$
Of the choices given only the pair of values, 4 and 10, satisfy the inquality.

50. **4** Since $\overleftrightarrow{AB} \| \overleftrightarrow{CD}$ $m\angle A + m\angle D = 180°$
Let $3x = m\angle D$
And $2x = m\angle A$
$3x + 2x = 180$
$5x = 180$
$x = 180 \div 5 = 36°$
$3x = 3(36) = 108°$

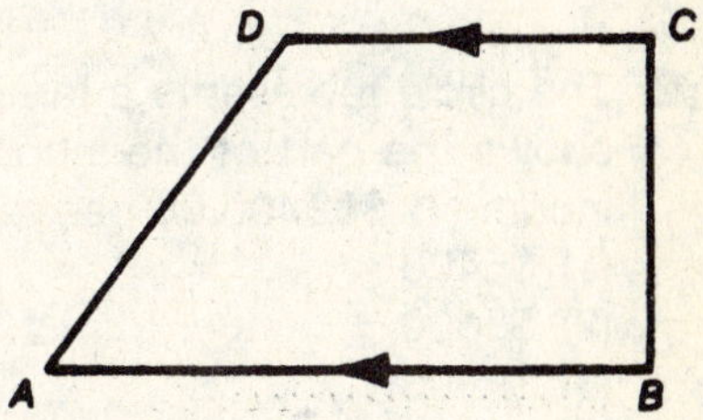

51. **5** Lori covered $2 \times 80 = 160$ km during the first two hours.
This left $540 - 160 = 380$ km for the remaining 4 hours.
$380 \div 4 = 95$ km/h.

52. **4** Let x = number of dollars Joe has
And $x + 35$ = number of dollars Ben has
$x + 35 - 5 = x + 30$ = number of dollars Ben has after giving Joe \$5
$x + 5$ = number of dollars Joe has after receiving \$5 from Ben
Ben now has twice as much as Joe
↓ ↓ ↓
$x + 30 = \quad 2 \quad (x + 5)$
$x + 30 = 2x + 10$
$30 - 10 = 2x - x$
$20 = x$, or $x = \$20$, Joe has

53. **1** If $4y = 20$, $y = 20 \div 4$, $y = 5$
$2x + 3y = 15$
$2x + 3(5) = 15$
$2x + 15 = 15$
$2x = 15 - 15 = 0$
$x = 0$

54. **4** $1 - \frac{1}{3} = \frac{2}{3}$ of the estate is left to 4 children
$\frac{2}{3} \div 4 = \frac{2}{3} \times \frac{1}{4} = \frac{1}{6}$

55. **2** The team plays a total of $18 + 32 = 50$ games.
64% of 50 = 32 games the team must win.
Since the team has already won 12 games it must win $32 - 12$, or 20 of the remaining games.

56. **4** Robert earns x dollars per month and Tom earns y dollars per month.
Together, Robert and Tom earn $x + y$ dollars per month.
In one year, Robert and Tom earn $12(x + y)$ dollars.

PRACTICE TEST FOUR

Directions: Blacken the space at the right under the number which corresponds to the one you have selected as the correct answer.

1. Janice looked at the gauge (measuring device) on her heating oil tank on November 1. The gauge showed that the tank was $\frac{7}{8}$ full. On December 1 she checked the gauge again and found that the tank was $\frac{1}{4}$ full. The tank holds 800 L when full. At $1.06 per litre, what was the cost of the oil used during the month of November?

(1) $312.00
(2) $486.00
(3) $508.00
(4) $530.00
(5) $848.00

1. 1 2 3 4 5

2. The circle represents a family's total income. The shaded section shows the part of the income that is spent for rent. If the family income is $32 400.00 per year, the amount spent for rent is

(1) $5400
(2) $5500
(3) $6400
(4) $7200
(5) $10 800

2. 1 2 3 4 5

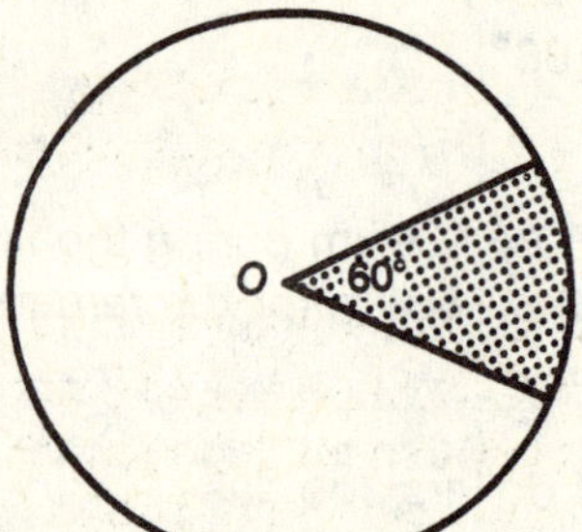

3. A driver travelled for 2 hours, averaging 75 km per hour. During the next 3 hours the driver covered 225 km. His average speed for the entire trip, in kilometres per hour, was

(1) 65
(2) 75
(3) 78
(4) 80
(5) 84

3. 1 2 3 4 5

4. The graph shows the population of Springville (in thousands) for each five-year period between 1975 and 1995 inclusive. During which five year period did the population of Springville remain the same?

(1) 1975–1980
(2) 1980–1985
(3) 1985–1990
(4) 1990–1995
(5) none of these

4. 1 2 3 4 5

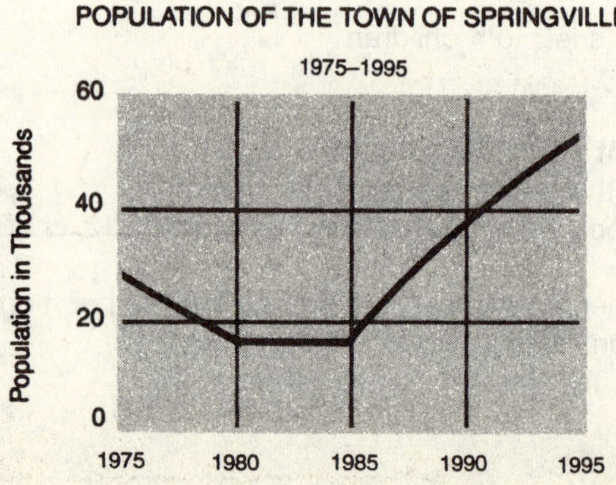

5. If the measures of two angles of a triangle are 40° and 70°, the triangle is
(1) equilateral
(2) right
(3) isosceles
(4) obtuse
(5) equiangular

5. 1 2 3 4 5

6. A woman wishes to buy a set of tools for her workshop. Dealer x lists the tools at $440 with a 25% discount. Dealer y lists the same set of tools for $400, subject to discounts of 10% and 5%. How much does the woman save by taking the better offer?
(1) $10
(2) $12
(3) $15
(4) $16
(5) $18

6. 1 2 3 4 5

7. In Nova Scotia the Grey Line has a city tour for which the charges are as follows: adults $13, senior citizens (over 65) $10.75, children (6 to 12) $6.50, and children under 6 go free. Mr. and Mrs. Kolbrener and their four children take the city tour. What is the total charge for the two adults and Lori age 11, Mark age 8, Meri age 6, and Michael age 5?
(1) $26
(2) $32.50
(3) $40.75
(4) $45.50
(5) $51.50

7. 1 2 3 4 5

8. A family spends 20% of its monthly income on rent, 23% on food, 42% on other expenses, and saves the balance. If the family saves $300 per month, what is its monthly income?
(1) $200
(2) $2000
(3) $2400
(4) $3000
(5) $20 000

8. 1 2 3 4 5

9. Find the value of $8y^2 - y(7y - 1)$ if $y = 5$.
(1) 10
(2) 15
(3) 18
(4) 25
(5) 30

9. 1 2 3 4 5

10. If $2x + 7 = 19$, the value of x is
(1) 3
(2) 5
(3) 6
(4) 7
(5) 10

10. 1 2 3 4 5

11. A rectangular garden is 80 metres long and 60 metres wide. What is the diagonal distance (in metres) across the garden?
(1) 70
(2) 75
(3) 90
(4) 100
(5) 140

11. 1 2 3 4 5

12. The perimeter of rectangle $ABCD$ is
(1) $(x + 5) + (2x + 3)$
(2) $2(2x + 3) + (x + 5)$
(3) $(2x + 3) + 2(x + 5)$
(4) $2(2x + 3) + 2(x + 5)$
(5) $3x + 8$

12. 1 2 3 4 5

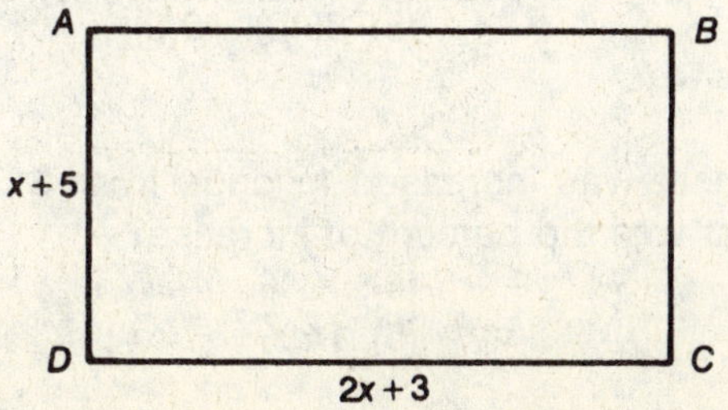

13. A hotel has 120 rooms. The number of double rooms in the hotel is three times as many as the number of single rooms. How many double rooms does the hotel have?

(1) 30
(2) 50
(3) 80
(4) 90
(5) 100

13. 1 2 3 4 5

14. What is the average speed (in kilometres per hour) of a plane that covers 240 km in one hour and twenty minutes?

(1) 120
(2) 160
(3) 180
(4) 320
(5) 380

14. 1 2 3 4 5

15. A man invests $\frac{1}{5}$ of his money in stocks, $\frac{1}{3}$ of his money in bonds, and keeps the rest in the bank. What fractional part of his money does he keep in the bank?

(1) $\frac{7}{15}$
(2) $\frac{1}{2}$
(3) $\frac{8}{15}$
(4) $\frac{5}{6}$
(5) $\frac{14}{15}$

15. 1 2 3 4 5

16. On a bar graph, a bar $3\frac{1}{2}$ units high represents $840. On the same graph, a bar $5\frac{1}{2}$ units high represents

(1) $240
(2) $480
(3) $960
(4) $1320
(5) $1500

16. 1 2 3 4 5

17. The Tiger basketball team has 10 players. The season scores of each of the players are shown below

Grant—189 points
Weber—214 points
Albert—197 points
Grimes—203 points
Chen—219 points
Wojtow—179 points
Nablo—191 points
Mason—223 points
Damon—193 points
Kostic—215 points

The median score is

(1) 197
(2) 200
(3) 203
(4) 204
(5) 205

17. 1 2 3 4 5

18. The cost of 6 shirts and 5 ties is $136. If each tie costs $8, what is the cost of a shirt in dollars?

(1) 12
(2) 13
(3) 14
(4) 15
(5) 16

18. 1 2 3 4 5

19. Joan earns $8 per hour for a 40-hour week and she is paid $1\frac{1}{2}$ times as much for overtime work. Which of the following expresses her earnings, in dollars, for a week when she works 49 hours?

(1) $8(40) = 1\frac{1}{2}(9)$
(2) $8(49) + 12$
(3) $8(40) + 12(9)$
(4) $8(49) + 1\frac{1}{2}(9)$
(5) $8(40) + 9(9)$

19. 1 2 3 4 5

20. Specialty cold meat was increased in price from $1.75/100 g to $1.89/100 g. What was the percent of increase?

(1) 6%
(2) $7\frac{1}{2}$%
(3) 8%
(4) 12%
(5) 14%

20. 1 2 3 4 5

21. A TV set sells for $584. Its price is increased by 5%. The new price of the TV set may be represented in dollars as

(1) 584 + 5
(2) 584 + 0.05
(3) 584 + 0.05(584)
(4) 584 + 584 ÷ 0.05
(5) 584 + 5(584)

21. 1 2 3 4 5

22. Mrs. Leach buys a refrigerator for $619.75. In addition, she has to pay a sales tax of 7%. Her total bill, to the nearest cent, is

(1) $646.94
(2) $656.93
(3) $663.13
(4) $664.94
(5) $665.34

22. 1 2 3 4 5

23. Which letter on the number line corresponds to –4?

(1) *A*
(2) *B*
(3) *C*
(4) *D*
(5) *E*

23. 1 2 3 4 5

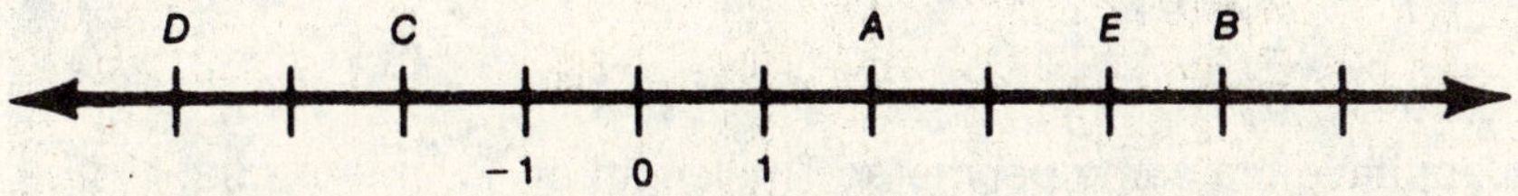

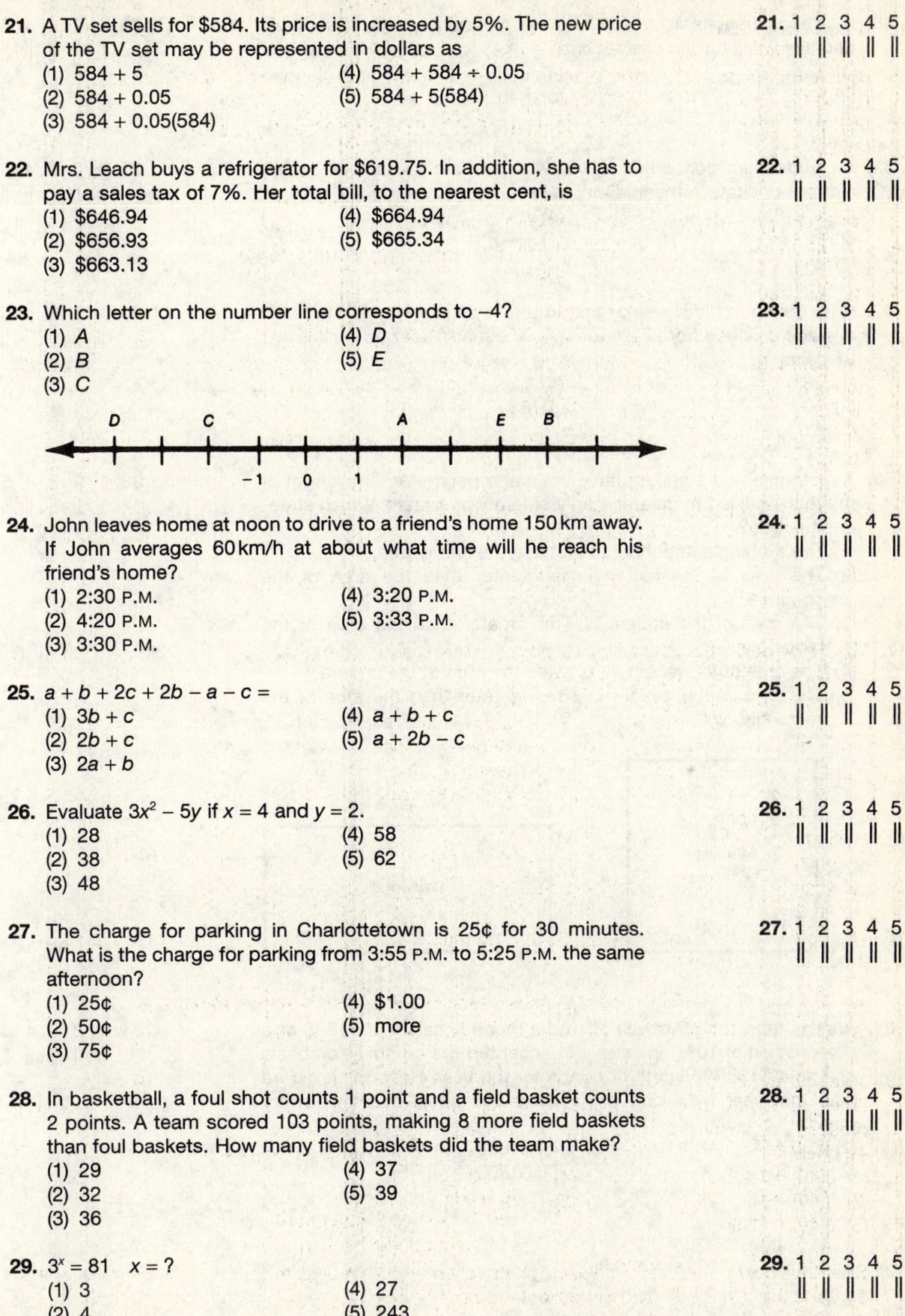

24. John leaves home at noon to drive to a friend's home 150 km away. If John averages 60 km/h at about what time will he reach his friend's home?

(1) 2:30 P.M.
(2) 4:20 P.M.
(3) 3:30 P.M.
(4) 3:20 P.M.
(5) 3:33 P.M.

24. 1 2 3 4 5

25. $a + b + 2c + 2b - a - c =$

(1) $3b + c$
(2) $2b + c$
(3) $2a + b$
(4) $a + b + c$
(5) $a + 2b - c$

25. 1 2 3 4 5

26. Evaluate $3x^2 - 5y$ if $x = 4$ and $y = 2$.

(1) 28
(2) 38
(3) 48
(4) 58
(5) 62

26. 1 2 3 4 5

27. The charge for parking in Charlottetown is 25¢ for 30 minutes. What is the charge for parking from 3:55 P.M. to 5:25 P.M. the same afternoon?

(1) 25¢
(2) 50¢
(3) 75¢
(4) $1.00
(5) more

27. 1 2 3 4 5

28. In basketball, a foul shot counts 1 point and a field basket counts 2 points. A team scored 103 points, making 8 more field baskets than foul baskets. How many field baskets did the team make?

(1) 29
(2) 32
(3) 36
(4) 37
(5) 39

28. 1 2 3 4 5

29. $3^x = 81 \quad x = ?$

(1) 3
(2) 4
(3) 9
(4) 27
(5) 243

29. 1 2 3 4 5

30. If a record makes 45 revolutions per minute, through how many degrees will it turn in one second?

(1) 8
(2) 80
(3) 120
(4) 270
(5) 540

30. 1 2 3 4 5

31. An auditorium contains x rows, with y seats in each row. The number of seats in the auditorium is

(1) $x+y$
(2) xy
(3) $x-y$
(4) $x \div y$
(5) $y-x$

31. 1 2 3 4 5

32. After taking the fifth weekly test in a foreign language a student's average dropped from 72% to 70%. The mark received on this last test was

(1) 59
(2) 60
(3) 61
(4) 62
(5) 63

32. 1 2 3 4 5

33. A rectangle and a square have the same perimeter. The length of the rectangle is 2 m greater than a side of the square. Which statement is true?

(1) The rectangle and the square have the same area.
(2) The area of the rectangle is greater than the area of the square.
(3) The area of the square is $4\,m^2$ greater than the area of the rectangle.
(4) The area of the rectangle is twice the area of the square.
(5) The area of the square is $16\,m^2$ greater than the area of the rectangle.

33. 1 2 3 4 5

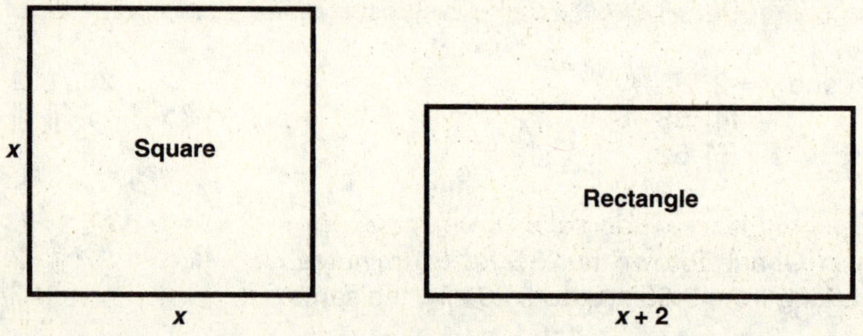

34. A sales representative was offered a monthly salary of \$1500 or a commission of 10% on sales. He accepted the commission basis and sold \$198 000 worth of goods for the year. How much did he gain that year by taking the commission basis over the salary basis?

(1) \$800
(2) \$1000
(3) \$1500
(4) \$1600
(5) \$1800

34. 1 2 3 4 5

35. Below is a table for premiums on ordinary life insurance.

IF TAKEN OUT AT AGE	ANNUAL PREMIUM PER $1000 OF INSURANCE
20	$18
25	$20
30	$24
35	$28
40	$33

Marie took out four of these insurance policies as follows: $1000 at age 20; $2000 at age 25; $2000 at age 30; $5000 at age 35.

Find the total premium she pays per year on the four policies if Marie is now 37 years of age.

(1) $246
(2) $248
(3) $256
(4) $268
(5) $276

35. 1 2 3 4 5

36. If 2 apples cost 29 cents, what is the cost of 2 dozen apples at the same rate?

(1) $1.74
(2) $2.61
(3) $2.76
(4) $3.24
(5) $3.48

36. 1 2 3 4 5

37. The roof of a building is a square measuring 40 m on a side. It costs $1400 to replace this roof. At the same rate, the cost of replacing the roof of another building, a square measuring 80 m on a side is

(1) $2800
(2) $3500
(3) $4000
(4) $5600
(5) $6400

37. 1 2 3 4 5

38. The value of a car decreases 35% the first year and 20% the second year. If a new car costs $12 000, what is its value at the end of two years?

(1) $5400
(2) $5800
(3) $6080
(4) $6240
(5) $6440

38. 1 2 3 4 5

39. The measure of the smallest angle of a triangle is 20° less than the measure of the second angle, and 40° less than the measure of the third angle of the triangle. What is the measure of the smallest angle of the triangle?

(1) 40°
(2) 42°
(3) 45°
(4) 50°
(5) 55°

39. 1 2 3 4 5

40. A solution of the inequality $2x + 1 < 3$ is

(1) 0
(2) 4
(3) 5
(4) 7
(5) 10

40. 1 2 3 4 5

41. At a certain hour, a tree casts a shadow 32 m long. At the same time, a post 5 m high casts a shadow 4 m long. What is the height of the tree in metres?

(1) $25\frac{3}{5}$
(2) 30
(3) 36
(4) 40
(5) 60

41. 1 2 3 4 5

42. A family has an income of $2500 per month. The family spends x dollars for food and rent and y dollars for other expenses per month. How many dollars does the family save per month?

(1) $2500 - x + y$
(2) $2500 + x - y$
(3) $2500 - (x + y)$
(4) $x + y - 2500$
(5) $x + 2500 - y$

42. 1 2 3 4 5
‖ ‖ ‖ ‖ ‖

43. A college club meeting was attended by 7 sophomores, 5 juniors and 11 seniors. One student was selected as chairman of the meeting. What was the probability that the student chosen was a senior?

(1) $^1/_{11}$
(2) $^{11}/_{23}$
(3) $^7/_{16}$
(4) $^{10}/_{23}$
(5) $^{11}/_{12}$

43. 1 2 3 4 5
‖ ‖ ‖ ‖ ‖

44. Together A and B have 14 marbles. Together, B and C have 10 marbles. Together A and C have 12 marbles. What is the maximum number of marbles that any one of these players has?

(1) 7
(2) 8
(3) 9
(4) 10
(5) 11

44. 1 2 3 4 5
‖ ‖ ‖ ‖ ‖

45. The population of the earth is approximately 5 000 000 000 people. This number, written in scientific notation is

(1) 5×10^9
(2) 50×10^8
(3) 0.5×10^8
(4) 0.5×10^{10}
(5) 500×10^7

45. 1 2 3 4 5
‖ ‖ ‖ ‖ ‖

46. A line segment connects two points whose coordinates are (5,6) and (–3,6). The length of the line segment, in graph units, is

(1) 2
(2) 3
(3) 5
(4) 8
(5) 12

46. 1 2 3 4 5
‖ ‖ ‖ ‖ ‖

47. If $C = \frac{5}{9}(F - 32)$ the value of C when $F = 50$ is

(1) 0
(2) 10
(3) 18
(4) 40
(5) 90

47. 1 2 3 4 5
‖ ‖ ‖ ‖ ‖

48. A sailboat travels 8 km due east. Then it travels 15 km due north. How far, in kilometres, is the sailboat from its starting point?

(1) 16
(2) 17
(3) 18
(4) 19
(5) 20

48. 1 2 3 4 5
‖ ‖ ‖ ‖ ‖

49. When a certain number is divided by 15, the quotient is 8 and the remainder is 7. The number is

(1) 71
(2) 113
(3) 123
(4) 127
(5) 225

49. 1 2 3 4 5
‖ ‖ ‖ ‖ ‖

50. The ratio of two numbers is 8 : 5. If the difference of the numbers is 21, what is the larger number?

(1) 35
(2) 39
(3) 56
(4) 85
(5) 91

50. 1 2 3 4 5
‖ ‖ ‖ ‖ ‖

51. Two prizes worth a total of $1000 were awarded in a radio game show. If the first prize was $200 less than three times as much as the second prize, what was the value of the first prize?

(1) $300
(2) $400
(3) $600
(4) $700
(5) $800

51. 1 2 3 4 5

52. A water tank is in the form of a cylinder. The diameter of the circular base is 12 m and the height of the tank is 10 m. An expression that gives the approximate volume of the tank in cubic metres is

(1) $(3.14)(12)^2(10)$
(2) $(3.14)(6)^2(10)$
(3) $(3.14)(6)(10)$
(4) $(3.14)(6)(10)^2$
(5) $(3.14)(12)(10)^2$

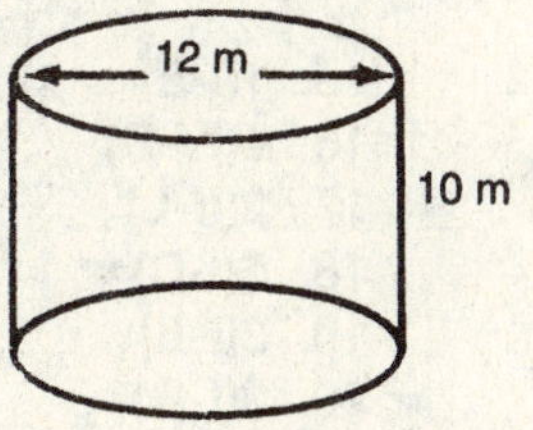

52. 1 2 3 4 5

53. The roots of the equation $x^2 - 5x + 6 = 0$ are

(1) 3,2
(2) –3,–2
(3) 3,–2
(4) –3,2
(5) 1,6

53. 1 2 3 4 5

54. If *O* is the centre of the circle and m$\angle BOC$ = 86°, what is m$\angle A$?

(1) 24°
(2) 43°
(3) 45°
(4) 50°
(5) 86°

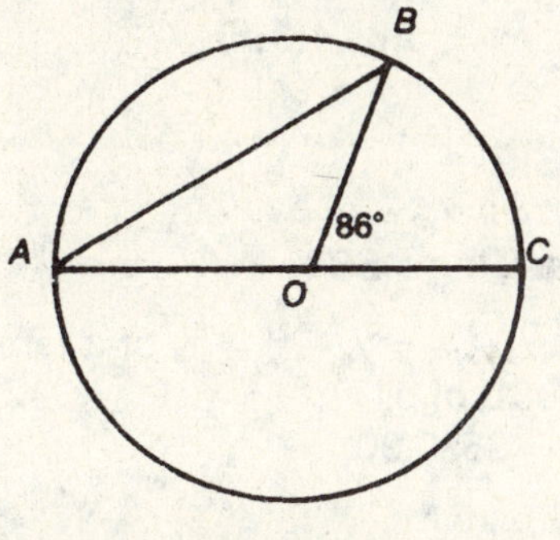

54. 1 2 3 4 5

55. A team has played 104 games. It has won 8 more games than it has lost. How many games has the team won?

(1) 40
(2) 42
(3) 50
(4) 54
(5) 56

55. 1 2 3 4 5

56. Otto has twice as much money as Fran. If Otto gives Fran $12, the two children will have equal amounts of money. How much did Otto have, in dollars, before he gave money to Fran?

(1) 24
(2) 28
(3) 30
(4) 36
(5) 48

56. 1 2 3 4 5

Turn to the answer key and the answer analysis which follow.

What's Your Score?

_________ right, _________ wrong

Excellent	51–56
Good	44–50
Fair	38–43

Be sure to refer to page 692 where these answers are explained. You may obtain additional help and practice by referring to the review material in this chapter.

ANSWER KEY

The number following each question is the correct answer. The numbers and letters in parentheses refer to the sections of this chapter which explain necessary mathematics principles. A more detailed explanation of all answers follows.

Practice Test Four/Page 684

1. **4(I-E)**
2. **1(III-C)**
3. **2(1-C)**
4. **2(IV-C)**
5. **3(III-C)**
6. **2(I-G)**
7. **4(I-C)**
8. **2(I-G)**
9. **5(II-B)**
10. **3(II-E)**
11. **4(III-D)**
12. **4(III-G)**
13. **4(II-F)**
14. **3(II-D)**
15. **1(I-E)**
16. **4(IV-B)**
17. **2(II-L)**
18. **5(I-C)**
19. **3(I-E)**
20. **3(I-G)**
21. **3(I-G)**
22. **3(I-G)**
23. **4(I-A)**
24. **1(I-E)**
25. **1(II-A)**
26. **2(II-B)**
27. **3(I-C)**
28. **4(II-F)**
29. **2(II-E)**
30. **4(III)**
31. **2(II-A)**
32. **4(I-G)**
33. **3(III-H)**
34. **5(II-B)**
35. **1(I-C)**
36. **5(I-F)**
37. **4(III-H)**
38. **4(I-G)**
39. **1(II-F)**
40. **1(II-G)**
41. **4(III-D)**
42. **3(II-A)**
43. **2(II-K)**
44. **2(II-E)**
45. **1(II-G)**
46. **4(III-F)**
47. **2(II-D)**
48. **2(III-D)**
49. **4(II-F)**
50. **3(II-H)**
51. **4(II-F)**
52. **2(III-I)**
53. **1(II-E)**
54. **2(III-C)**
55. **5(II-F)**
56. **5(II-F)**

ANSWER ANALYSIS

Practice Test Four/Page 684

1. **4** Janice used $\frac{7}{8} - \frac{1}{4} = \frac{7}{8} - \frac{2}{8} = \frac{5}{8}$ of a tank of oil
$\frac{5}{8} \times 800 = 500$ L of oil
$500 \times \$1.06 = \$530.00$

2. **1** The sum of the measures of the angles around a point in a plane is 360°. In this case, the sum of the measures of the angles around point *O* is 360°. Thus, the sector of the circle containing an angle whose measure is 60° is $\frac{60}{360}$, or $\frac{1}{6}$ of the circle.
The amount spent for rent is $\frac{1}{6}$($32 400.00), or $5400.

3. **2** To obtain the average speed, we divide the total distance covered by the total time consumed.
Distance covered = 2 × 75 + 225 = 150 + 225 = 375 km
Total time consumed = 5 hours
375 ÷ 5 = 75 km/h average speed

4. **2** Between 1980 and 1985 there was no change in population. The graph is parallel to the base line.

5. **3** The sum of the measures of the angles of a triangle is 180°. The measure of the third angle of the triangle is 180° – (40 + 70) = 180° – 110 = 70°. Since the triangle has two angles whose measures are 70°, the triangle is isosceles.

6. **2** Dealer *x* offers $440 – 0.25($440) = $440 – $110 = $330, net cost
Dealer *y* offers $400 – 0.10($400) = $400 – $40 = $360.
A further discount of 5% is offered. Therefore, $360 – 0.05($360) = $360 – $18 = $342, net cost.
The total savings are $342 – $330 = $12, buying from dealer *x*.

7. **4** Charge for the parents = (\$13)(2) = \$26.
Charge for the 3 children (age at least 6) = \$19.50.
Note: no charge for Michael. Total = \$45.50

8. **2** 20% + 23% + 43% = 85%
Thus, the family saves 100% − 85% = 15% of its income.
Let x = family income
$0.15x = 300$
$15x = 30000$
$x = 30000 \div 15 = \$2000$, monthly income

9. **5** $8y^2 - y(7y - 1)$
$8(5)^2 - 5(7 \times 5 - 1)$
$8(25) - 5(35 - 1) = 200 - 5(34)$
$= 200 - 170 = 30$

10. **3** $2x + 7 = 19$
$2x = 19 - 7 = 12$
$x = 12 \div 2 = 6$

11. **4** We use the Pythagorean Theorem.
$x^2 = 80^2 + 60^2$
$x^2 = 6400 + 3600$
$x^2 = 10000$
$x = \sqrt{10000}$
$x = 100\text{m}$

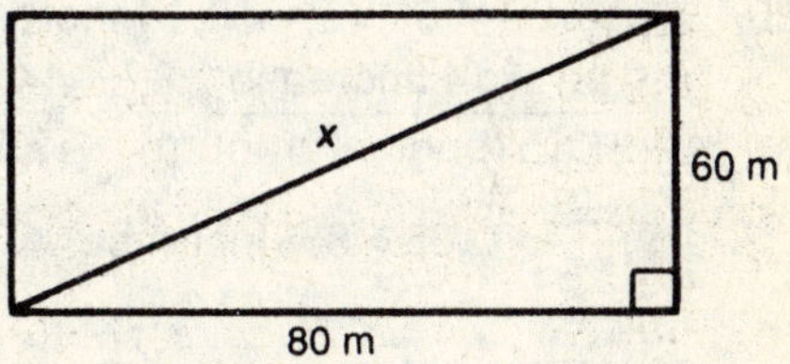

12. **4** Since the opposite sides of a rectangle are equal in length, the perimeter of this rectangle is $2(x + 5) + 2(2x + 3)$

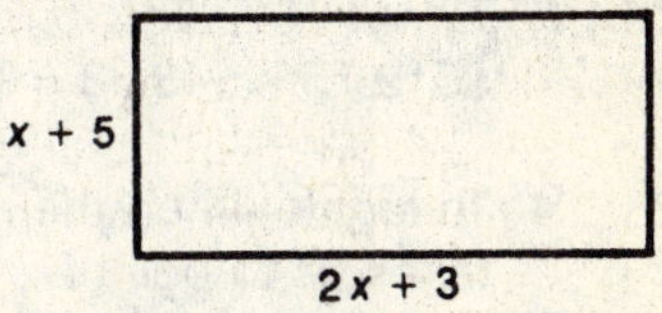

13. **4** Let x = the number of single rooms
And $3x$ = the number of double rooms
$x + 3x = 120$
$4x = 120$
$x = 120 \div 4 = 30$, number of single rooms
$3x = 3(30) = 90$, number of double rooms

14. **3** 1 hour and twenty minutes = $1\frac{1}{3}$ hours. Use formula
$R = \frac{D}{T}$ or $R = \frac{240}{4/3} = (240)\left(\frac{3}{4}\right) = 180\text{ km/h}$.

15. **1** $\frac{1}{5} = \frac{3}{15}$, $\frac{1}{3} = \frac{5}{15}$
$\frac{1}{5} + \frac{1}{3} = \frac{3}{15} + \frac{5}{15} = \frac{8}{15}$ invested in stocks and bonds
$\frac{15}{15}$ (total) − $\frac{8}{15} = \frac{7}{15}$, kept in bank

16. **4** The ratio of the height of a bar to the amount it represents is the same as the ratio of the height of any other bar to the amount it represents.
Let x = amount represented by the $5\frac{1}{2}$ unit bar

$$\frac{3\frac{1}{2}}{5\frac{1}{2}} = \frac{840}{x}$$
$$3\tfrac{1}{2}x = 5\tfrac{1}{2} \times 840 = 4620$$
$$\tfrac{7}{2}x = 4620$$
$$x = 4620 \div \tfrac{7}{2} = 4620 \times \tfrac{2}{7}$$
$$x = \$1320$$

17. **2** To find the median score we arrange the scores in order of magnitude.
223, 219, 215, 214, 203, 197, 193, 191, 189, 179
The median score is the middle score when the scores are arranged in order of magnitude. In this case, there are 10 scores. The median score is midway between the 5th and 6th scores.
$\frac{203+197}{2} = \frac{400}{2} = 200$, median score, median score

18. **5** If each tie costs \$8, then 5 ties cost 5 × \$8 = \$40
Therefore, \$136 – \$40 = \$96, cost of the shirts
If 6 shirts cost \$96, then 1 shirt costs 96 ÷ 6 = \$16

19. **3** Joan earns \$8 an hour for the first 40 hours.
Joan earns $(1\frac{1}{2})(8)$ = \$12 an hour for each hour over 40 hours per week.
When she works 49 hours in a week she earns
8(40) for the first 40 hours
12(9) for 9 hours of overtime work
Total earnings = 8(40) + 12(9)

20. **3** \$1.89 – \$1.75 = \$0.14 increase
$\frac{0.14 \text{ (increase)}}{1.75 \text{ (original amount)}} = \frac{14}{175} = \frac{2}{25}$
$\frac{2}{25} = 0.08 = 8\%$ increase

21. **3** 5% of 584 = 0.05(584)
New price = old price + 0.05(584)
New price = 584 + 0.05(584)

22. **3** 7% of \$619.75 = 0.07 × \$619.75 = \$43.38, to the nearest cent
\$619.75 + \$43.38 = \$663.13

23. **4** To locate –4 on the number line we start at the *0* point and count 4 spaces to the left. This takes us to point *D*.

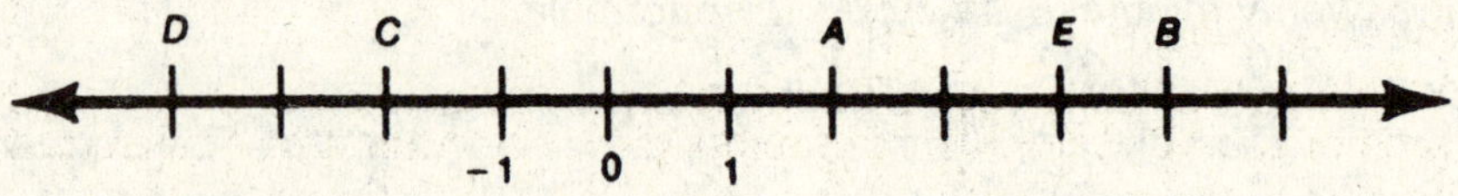

24. **1** To find the number of hours it takes John to drive 150 km we divide 150 by 60.
$\frac{150}{60} = \frac{5}{2} = 2\frac{1}{2}$ h
Since $\frac{1}{2}$ hour = $\frac{1}{2}$ of 60 = 30 minutes it takes John 2 hours and 30 minutes to complete the trip.
John arrives at 2:30 P.M.

25. **1** $a + b + 2c + 2b - a - c$
$= a - a + b + 2b + 2c - c$
$= 0 + 3b + c$
$= 3b + c$

26. **2** $3x^2 - 5y$
$= 3(4)^2 - 5(2)$
$= 3(16) - 10$
$= 48 - 10 = 38$

27. **3** 3:55 P.M. to 5:25 P.M. = $1\frac{1}{2}$ or $\frac{3}{2}$ hours (3/2) (25¢) = 75¢.

28. **4** Let x = the number of foul baskets
And $x + 8$ = the number of field baskets
x = the number of foul basket points
$2(x + 8)$ = the number of field basket points
$x + 2(x + 8) = 103$
$x + 2x + 16 = 103$
$3x + 16 = 103$
$3x = 103 - 16 = 87$
$x = 87 \div 3 = 29$
$x + 8 = 29 + 8 = 37$
There were 37 field baskets.

29. **2** $3^x = 81$. Because $(3)(3)(3)(3) = 81$
$3^4 = 81$ and $x = 4$

30. **4** There are 45 revolutions in one minute (60 seconds) and there are $\frac{45}{60}$ revolution in one second. 1 revolution = 360°

$$\left(\frac{45}{60}\right)(360°) = (45)(6°) = 270°$$

31. **2** To find the number of seats in the auditorium, we multiply the number of rows (x) by the number of seats (y) in each row. The result is xy.

32. **4** 72×4 tests = 288
70×5 tests = 350
$350 - 288 = 62\%$

33. **3** The area of the square = x^2.
Note that if the length of the rectangle is 2 m greater than a side of the square, the width of the rectangle must be 2 m less than a side of the square, since the rectangle and the square have equal perimeters.
The area of the rectangle = $(x + 2)(x - 2) = x^2 - 4$.
Since area of square = x^2 and area of rectangle = $x^2 - 4$, the area of the square is 4 m² greater than the area of the rectangle.

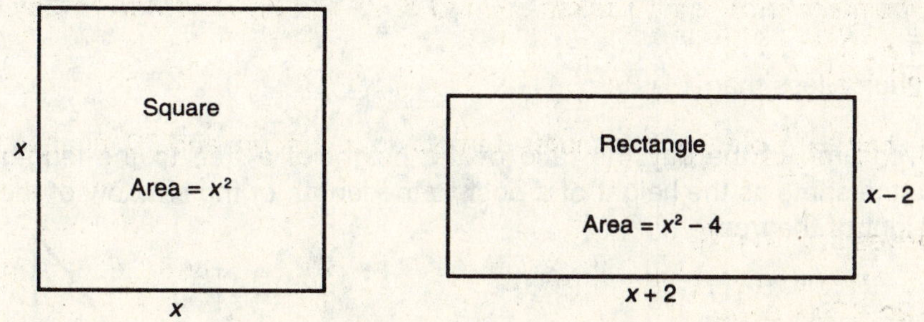

34. **5** At \$1500 per month the sales representative would earn $12 \times \$1500 = \$18000$ per year.
At 10% of sales, the representative earned $0.1 \times \$198000 = \$19800$ per year.
The salesman gained $\$19800 - \$18000 = \$1800$ by taking the commission basis.

35. **1** \$1000 policy at age 20 costs \$18
\$2000 policy at age 25 costs 2(\$20) = \$40
\$2000 policy at age 30 costs 2(\$24) = \$48
\$5000 policy at age 35 costs 5(\$28) = \$140
Total = \$246

36. **5** If 2 apples cost 29 cents, each apple cost $^{29}/_2$ cents.
Two dozen, or 24 apples cost $24(^{29}/_2) = 12 \times 29 = 348$ cents = \$3.48

37. **4** The area of the smaller square is $40 \times 40 = 1600\,m^2$
The area of the larger square is $80 \times 80 = 6400\,m^2$
$$\frac{6400}{1600} = \frac{4}{1}$$

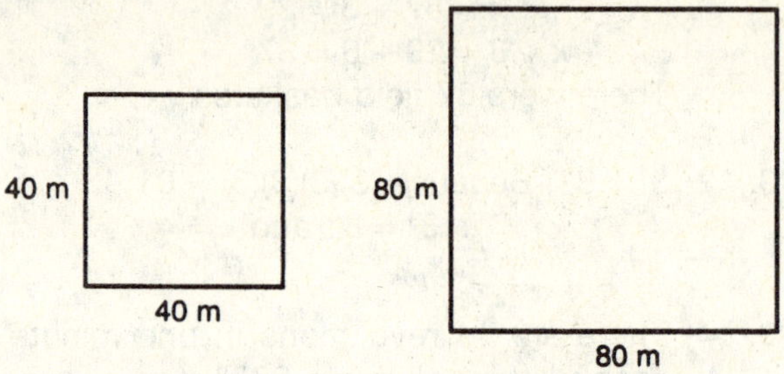

Thus, the area of the larger square is 4 times the area of the smaller square. Since the cost of replacing the smaller roof is \$1400, the cost of replacing the larger roof is $4 \times \$1400 =$ \$5600.

38. **4** $\$12000 \times 0.35 = \$4200$ decrease in value the first year
$\$12000 - \$4200 = \$7800$ value after the first year
$\$7800 \times 0.20 = \$1560$ decrease in value the second year
$\$7800 - \$1560 = \$6240$ value after the second year

39. **1** Let x = the measure of the smallest angle
And $x + 20$ = the measure of the second angle
And $x + 40$ = the measure of the third angle
$x + (x + 20) + (x + 40) = 180$
$3x + 60 = 180$
$3x = 180 - 60 = 120$
$x = 120 \div 3 = 40$

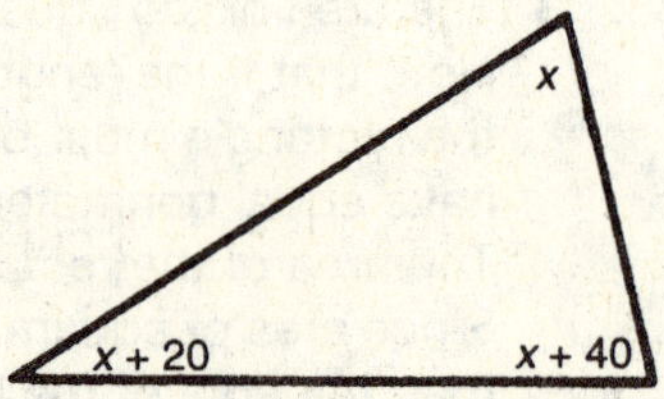

40. **1** $2x + 1 < 3$
$2x < 3 - 1$
$2x < 2$
$x < 1$
The only choice less than 1 is 0.

41. **4** At any given time of the day the ratio of the height of a tree to the length of the tree's shadow is the same as the height of a post to the length of the shadow of the post
Let x = height of the tree
$$\frac{x}{32} = \frac{5}{4}$$
$4x = 5(32) = 160$
$x = 160 \div 4 = 40\,m$

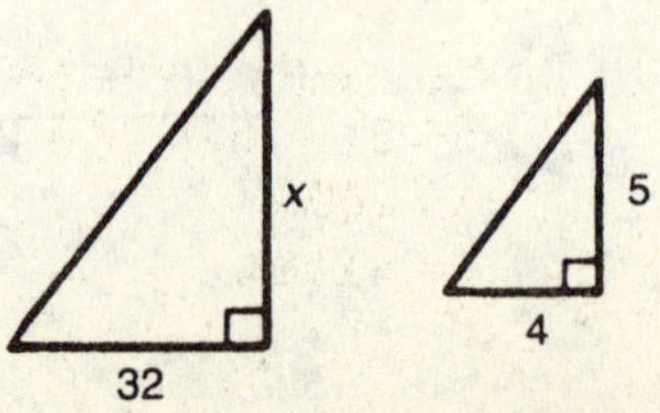

42. **3** The family's income is \$2500 per month.
x = expenses for food and rent per month
y = other expenses per month
$x + y$ = total expenses per month
$2500 - (x + y)$ = savings per month

43. **2** $\text{Probability} = \dfrac{\text{number of successful outcomes}}{\text{number of possible outcomes}}$
Of the 23 students present 11 were seniors. Thus, the probability of selecting a senior was 11 out of 23. That is, in this case there were 11 successful outcomes and 23 possible outcomes. Thus, the probability is $^{11}/_{23}$.

44. **2** $A + B = 14$ [1]
$C + B = 10$ [2]
$C + A = 12$ [3]
$A - C = 4$ [1] minus [2]
$A + C = 12$ [3]

$2A = 16$ (addition)
$A = 8$
$8 + B = 14$ [1]
$B = 6$
$C + 8 = 12$ [3]
$C = 4$

45. **1** To write a number in scientific notation we write it as the product of a number between 1 and 10 and a power of 10.
In the case of 5 000 000 000 the number between 1 and 10 is 5.
In going from 5 to 5 000 000 000 we move the decimal point 9 places to the right. That is, we multiply 5 by 10^9.
Thus, $5\,000\,000\,000 = 5 \times 10^9$.

46. **4** We plot the points (5,6) and (–3,6) and draw the line segment between the points. When the number of graph units are counted along the line it is found that the required distance is 8 units.

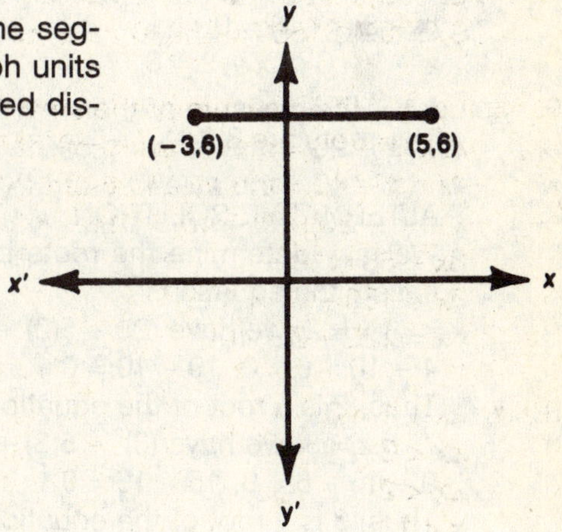

47. **2** $C = \frac{5}{9}(F - 32)$
when we subsitute 50 for F in the equation, we have
$C = \frac{5}{9}(50 - 32)$
$C = \frac{5}{9}(18)$
$C = 10$

48. **2** We use the Pythagorean Theorem to obtain
$x^2 = 8^2 + 15^2 = 64 + 225$
$x^2 = 289$
$x = \sqrt{289}$
$x = 17$

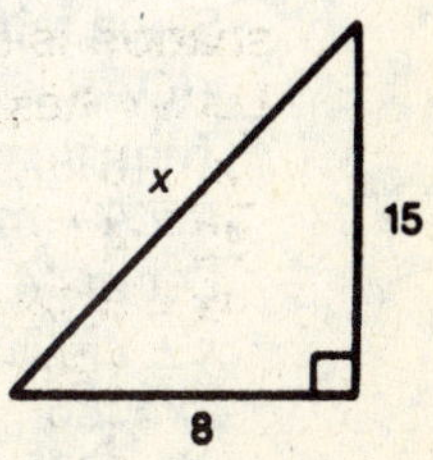

49. **4** Let x = the number

$$\frac{x}{15} = 8 + \frac{7}{15}$$

If we multiply both sides of this equation by 15 we have

$$15\left(\frac{x}{15}\right) = 15(8) + 15\left(\frac{7}{15}\right)$$

$x = 120 + 7 = 127$

50. **3** Let $8x$ = the larger number
And $5x$ = the smaller number
$8x - 5x = 21$
$3x = 21$
$x = 21 \div 3 = 7$
$8x = 8(7) = 56$

51. **4** Let x = value of second prize in dollars
And $3x - 200$ = value of first prize in dollars
The sum of the two prizes is 1000 dollars.
$x + (3x - 200) = 1000$
$4x - 200 = 1000$
$4x = 1000 + 200 = 1200$
$x = 1200 \div 4 = 300$
$3x - 200 = 3(300) - 200 = 900 - 200 = 700$
The value of the first prize was $700.

52. **2** We use the formula $V = \pi r^2 h$.
In this formula $\pi = 3.14$ approximately. In this case $r = \frac{1}{2}(12) = 6$ and $h = 10$.
Thus, $V = 3.14(6)^2(10)$

53. **1** $x^2 - 5x + 6 = 0$
When we factor the left side of the equation we have
$(x - 3)(x - 2) = 0$
$x - 3 = 0$ or $x - 2 = 0$
$x = 3$ or $x = 2$
The roots are 3,2.

ALTERNATIVE SOLUTION
We may determine the roots by substituting the choices and determining which numbers satisfy the equation.
If $x = 2$, we have $(2)^2 - 5(2) + 6 = 0$
$4 - 10 + 6 = 0, 10 - 10 = 0$
Thus, 2 is a root of the equation.
If $x = 3$, we have $(3)^2 - 5(3) + 6 = 0$
$9 - 15 + 6 = 0, 15 - 15 = 0$
Thus, 3 is a root of the equation.
The other choices do not satisfy the equation.

54. **2** $m\angle AOB = 180° - 86° = 94°$
Since radii of the same circle are equal in length $OB = OA$.
$\triangle OAB$ is isosceles and the base angles have equal measures.
That is, $m\angle A = m\angle B$.
$m\angle A + m\angle B = 180° - 94° = 86°$
Let $m\angle A = x$.
$x + x = 86°$
$2x = 86°$
$x = 86° \div 2 = 43°$

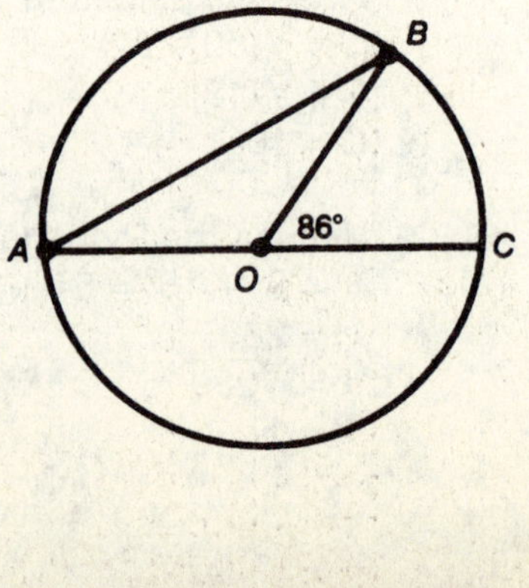

55. **5** Let x = number of games lost
And $x + 8$ = number of games won
$x + x + 8 = 104$
$2x + 8 = 104$
$2x = 104 - 8 = 96$
$x = 96 \div 2 = 48$
$x + 8 = 48 + 8 = 56$

56. **5** Let x = amount of money Fran has in dollars
And $2x$ = amount of money Otto has in dollars
$x + 12$ = amount of money Fran has after she gets \$12
$2x - 12$ = amount of money Otto has after he gives \$12
$2x - 12 = x + 12$
$2x - x = 12 + 12$
$x = 24$
$2x = 2(24) = 48$
Otto has \$48.

PRACTICE TEST FIVE

Directions: Blacken the space at the right under the number that corresponds to the one you have selected as the correct answer.

1. Larry bought a used car for \$5000. He could either pay cash or make a down payment of 20% of the price of the car and pay 24 monthly installments of \$200 each. How much did he save by paying cash?
(1) \$400
(2) \$500
(3) \$600
(4) \$800
(5) \$850

1. 1 2 3 4 5

2. O is the centre of the circle and $m\angle O = 72°$. What part of the circle is the sector OAB?
(1) $\frac{1}{10}$
(2) $\frac{1}{5}$
(3) $\frac{3}{10}$
(4) $\frac{3}{8}$
(5) 0.72

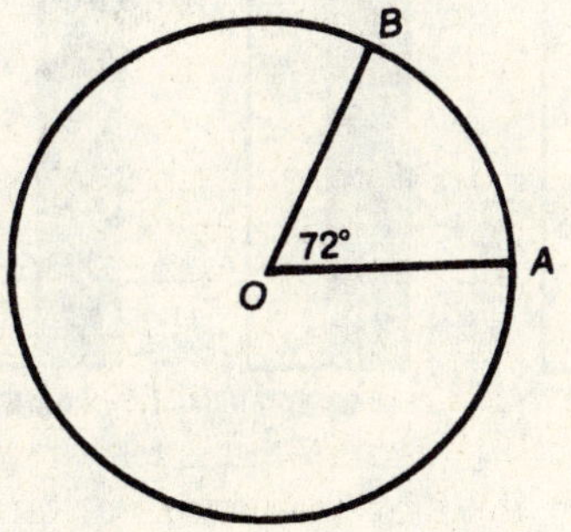

2. 1 2 3 4 5

3. After the price of a chair was raised 20%, its price was \$180. What was the price before the increase?
(1) \$150
(2) \$160
(3) \$175
(4) \$216
(5) \$236

3. 1 2 3 4 5

4. A shelf contains 7 science books, 8 fiction books, and 4 history books. If one book is selected from this shelf at random what is the probability that the book selected is a science book?
(1) $\frac{7}{15}$
(2) $\frac{4}{7}$
(3) $\frac{8}{19}$
(4) $\frac{7}{19}$
(5) $\frac{4}{15}$

4. 1 2 3 4 5

5. If 1250 wooden pegs cost *R* dollars, how many pegs can be bought for *S* dollars?

(1) $\frac{1250}{RS}$ (4) $\frac{1250S}{R}$

(2) $\frac{1250R}{S}$ (5) 1250 *RS*

(3) $\frac{1250}{R+S}$

5. 1 2 3 4 5

6. A certain store advertised: "All stock reduced 25%. No down payment. Pay, ½ on February 10, ⅓ on March 10, and the balance on April 10." Mr. Hill bought a coat which was marked $200 before the sale. What was his payment on April 10?

(1) $10 (4) $25
(2) $15 (5) $30
(3) $20

6. 1 2 3 4 5

7. The graph shows the receipts and expenses for the years shown. The receipts are designated by shaded bars and expenses by lined bars. The year in which receipts exceeded expenses by $100 000 was

(1) 1994 (4) 1997
(2) 1995 (5) 1998
(3) 1996

7. 1 2 3 4 5

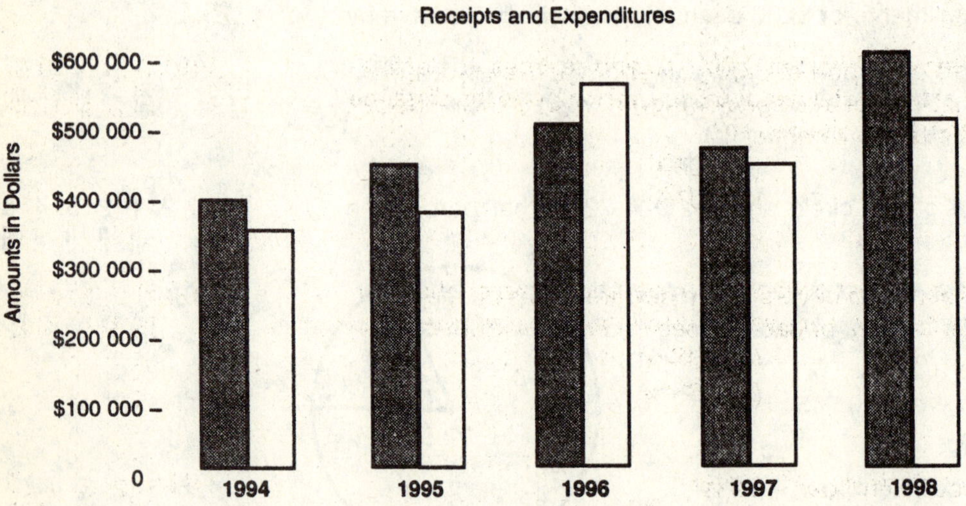

8. A church spire casts a shadow 29 m long when a pole 6 m high casts a shadow 2 m long. Find the height of the spire in metres.

(1) 9⅔ (4) 87
(2) 58 (5) 90
(3) 85

8. 1 2 3 4 5

9. The measure of one angle of a triangle is 84°. If the ratio of the measures of the other two angles is 1 : 1, then the measures of the other two angles are

(1) 40° and 40° (4) 60° and 60°
(2) 48° and 48° (5) 64° and 64°
(3) 58° and 58°

9. 1 2 3 4 5

10. A work crew can complete a job in $4\frac{1}{2}$ hours. What part of the job can this crew complete in 45 minutes?

(1) $\frac{1}{9}$
(2) $\frac{1}{8}$
(3) $\frac{1}{6}$
(4) $\frac{2}{9}$
(5) $\frac{3}{8}$

10. 1 2 3 4 5

11. If $3x + 1 \geqslant 16$ which pair of the following numbers satisfies the inequality?

(1) 6,5
(2) 3,5
(3) 2,4
(4) 0,6
(5) 3,$4\frac{1}{2}$

11. 1 2 3 4 5

12. A solution of the equation $2x^2 - x - 6 = 0$ is

(1) 0
(2) $\frac{1}{2}$
(3) 2
(4) 4
(5) 6

12. 1 2 3 4 5

13. At a track meet, first place winners are awarded 5 points, second place is awarded 3 points, and third place is awarded 1 point. If P represents the total number of points scored by a team, F represents the number of first place winners, S represents the number of second places, and T represents the number of third places, a formula stating the total number of points scored by a team is

(1) $P = F + S + T$
(2) $P = 5F + S + T$
(3) $P = F + 3S + T$
(4) $P = 5F + 3S + T$
(5) $P = 5 + 3S + T$

13. 1 2 3 4 5

14. An airplane leaves an airport at 9:30 A.M. and reaches its destination at 1:20 P.M. If the pilot averaged 540 km/h, what is the distance between the airports, in kilometres?

(1) 1925
(2) 1954
(3) 1985
(4) 2050
(5) 2070

14. 1 2 3 4 5

15. Mr Ames finds that his car covers 16 km per litre of gas on the open road. The number of litres of gas he uses in driving x kilometres is

(1) $x \div 16$
(2) $16x$
(3) $x + 16$
(4) $16 - x$
(5) $16 \div x$

15. 1 2 3 4 5

16. An expression equivalent to $x^2 - 25$ is

(1) $(x + 5)(x + 5)$
(2) $x(x - 25)$
(3) $(x - 5)(x - 5)$
(4) $(x + 5)(x - 5)$
(5) $x(5 - x)$

16. 1 2 3 4 5

17. Ms. Spadafora owns \$6000 worth of bonds that pay $8\frac{1}{2}$% interest annually. How much interest does Ms. Spadafora receive from her bonds annually?

(1) \$450
(2) \$480
(3) \$500
(4) \$510
(5) \$850

17. 1 2 3 4 5

18. During a season a professional basketball player tried 320 shots and made 272 of them. What percent of the shots tried were unsuccessful?

(1) 10%
(2) 12%
(3) 15%
(4) 18%
(5) 20%

18. 1 2 3 4 5

19. If an airplane can carry p passengers, how many airplanes are needed for xp passengers?

(1) x
(2) xp^2
(3) $\frac{1}{x}$
(2) $\frac{x^2}{p}$
(5) $\frac{1}{xp}$

19. 1 2 3 4 5

20. The perimeter of the figure is

(1) $6a + 4b$
(2) $7a + 5b$
(3) $5a + 6b$
(4) $3a + 7b$
(5) $5a + 7b$

20. 1 2 3 4 5

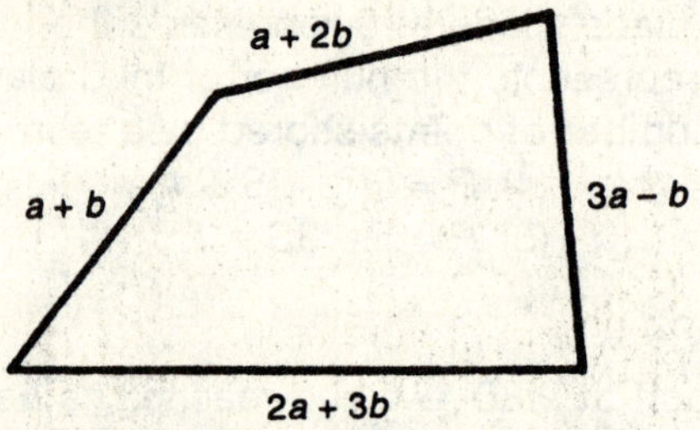

21. If $\overline{AB} \perp \overline{CB}$, $\overline{AD} \parallel \overline{BC}$, and $m\angle CAB = 49°$, then $m\angle x =$

(1) 41°
(2) 49°
(3) 50°
(4) 52°
(5) 54°

21. 1 2 3 4 5

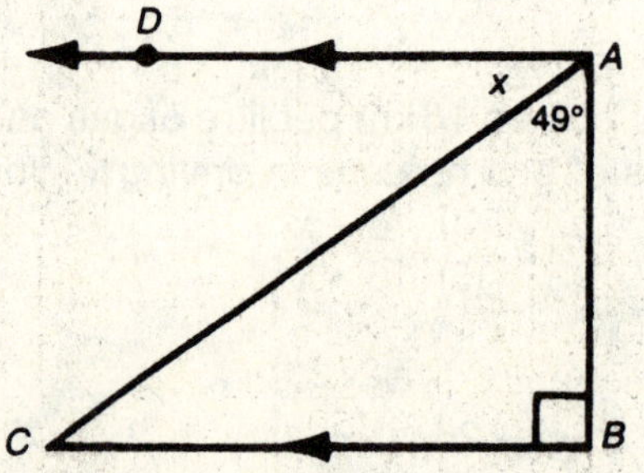

22. The area (in square metres) of the figure is

(1) 200
(2) 240
(3) 260
(4) 280
(5) 320

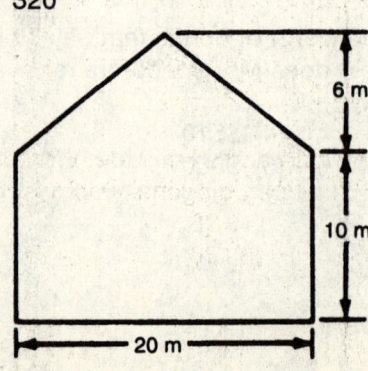

22. 1 2 3 4 5

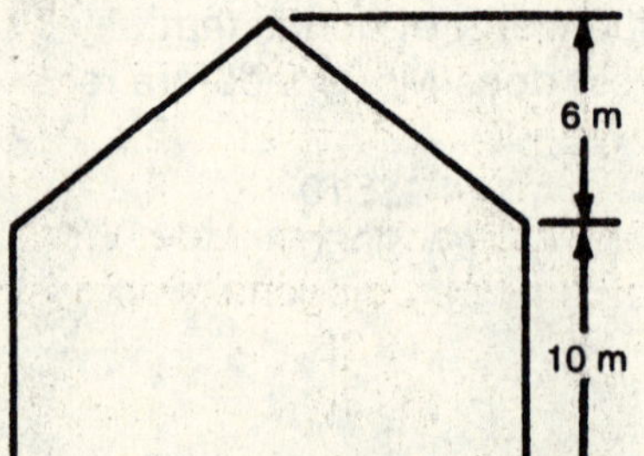

23. The wholesale price of a watch is \$50. A dealer bought a shipment of watches at a discount of 20% and sold the watches at 10% above the wholesale price. What was the profit on each watch?
(1) \$8
(2) \$10
(3) \$12
(4) \$15
(5) \$18

23. 1 2 3 4 5

24. A man's will provided that his wife receive ½ of his estate, and his three sons divide the rest equally. If each son's share was \$8000, what was the value of the estate?
(1) \$24 000
(2) \$32 000
(3) \$40 000
(4) \$48 000
(5) \$50 000

24. 1 2 3 4 5

25. In a store where the selling price is 40% above cost, how much did the store pay for an article that was marked to sell for \$28?
(1) \$16
(2) \$18
(3) \$20
(4) \$22
(5) \$24

25. 1 2 3 4 5

26. On a cold day, the following temperature readings were taken
6:00 A.M. −12°C
7:00 A.M. −7°C
8:00 A.M. −2°C
9:00 A.M. 0°C
10:00 A.M. +6°C
What is the average of these temperature readings?
(1) 0°C
(2) 2°C
(3) −3°C
(4) 3°C
(5) −1°C

26. 1 2 3 4 5

27. $(a - b)^2 = 16$
$a^2 + b^2 = 58$
$ab = ?$
(1) 16
(2) 21
(3) 42
(4) 64
(5) 74

27. 1 2 3 4 5

28. Find the value of $3y^2 - 2(y - 1)$ if $y = 5$.
(1) 53
(2) 67
(3) 83
(4) 233
(5) 250

28. 1 2 3 4 5

29. It takes a crew of 20 workers 36 days to do a construction job. How long would it take a crew of 24 to do the same job?
(1) 25 days
(2) 30 days
(3) 32 days
(4) 40 days
(5) 44 days

29. 1 2 3 4 5

30. A rectangular park is 28 m long and 21 m wide. What is the length (in metres) of a walk that is placed diagonally across the park?
(1) 25
(2) 30
(3) 32
(4) 35
(5) 36

30. 1 2 3 4 5

31. A man buys x litres of gasoline at y cents per litre. He gives the attendant a 10-dollar bill. How many cents does he receive in change?
(1) $10 - xy$
(2) $xy - 10$
(3) $10 - (x + y)$
(4) $1000 - x + y$
(5) $1000 - xy$

31. 1 2 3 4 5

32. A store advertises a sale with savings from 20% to $33\frac{1}{3}$%. If an article is on sale for $15 what is the lowest price it could have had just before reduction?
(1) $15.20
(2) $18
(3) $18.75
(4) $20
(5) $22.50

32. 1 2 3 4 5

33. A recipe calls for 0.5 kg of sugar and 2 kg of rhubarb. If 5 kg of rhubarb are used, how many kilograms of sugar are needed?
(1) 1.2
(2) 1.25
(3) 1.5
(4) 1.75
(5) 2.25

33. 1 2 3 4 5

34. A dealer buys a shipment of shirts. She pays $8 per shirt for the first 100 shirts and $7 per shirt for additional purchases. Which of the following expressions gives the total cost of a purchase of 168 shirts?
(1) 8(100) + 7(100 – 68)
(2) 7(68) + 8(100)
(3) 8(100) – 7(68)
(4) 168(8) – 7(68)
(5) 8(168 – 100) + 7(68)

34. 1 2 3 4 5

35. Which of the following represents a scale of 1 : 12?
(1) 20 cm to 1 m
(2) 2 cm to 24 m
(3) 1 cm to 0.25 km
(4) 100 m to 1.2 km
(5) 1 cm to 1 km

35. 1 2 3 4 5

36. In the figure, the length of each side of the square is 10 cm. The curves are quarter circles. What is the area of the shaded portion?
(1) $100 - 100\pi$
(2) $100 - 50\pi$
(3) $100 - 25\pi$
(4) $100 - 10\pi$
(5) $100 + 25\pi$

36. 1 2 3 4 5

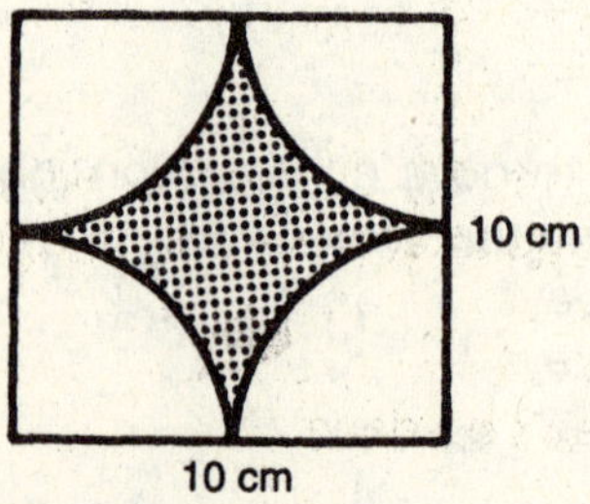

37. A man paid $8.12 for 1.75 kg of fish. The cost of fish per kilogram was
(1) $4.54
(2) $4.64
(3) $5.12
(4) $5.38
(5) $5.70

37. 1 2 3 4 5

38. A rectangular solid is 5 m in length, 4 m in width, and x m high. The volume of the solid is 50 cubic metres. Which of the following equations may be used to find the height of the rectangular solid?

(1) $5 + 4 + x = 50$
(2) $4x + 5 = 50$
(3) $5x + 4 = 50$
(4) $50x = 20$
(5) $20x = 50$

38. 1 2 3 4 5
|| || || || ||

39. The line joining point $A(2,y)$ and point $B(4,9)$ has a slope of 3. Find the value of y.

(1) 2
(2) 3
(3) 4
(4) 5
(5) 10

39. 1 2 3 4 5
|| || || || ||

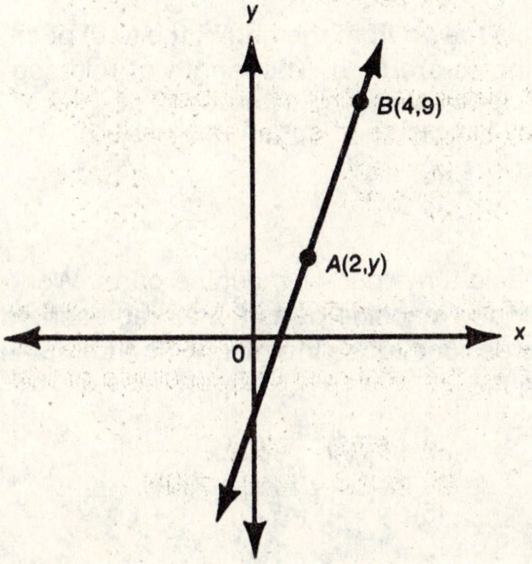

40. Joan purchased a belt for $2.19. She returned the belt the next day and selected a better one costing $2.89. She gave the clerk a one-dollar coin to pay for the difference in price. How many cents in change should she receive?

(1) 3
(2) 30
(3) 40
(4) 50
(5) 70

40. 1 2 3 4 5
|| || || || ||

41. The length of a wave of light is 0.0004622 mm. Express this number in scientific notation.

(1) 46.22×10^{-3}
(2) 4.622×10^{-4}
(3) 462.2×10^{-6}
(4) 0.4622×10^{-5}
(5) 46.22×10^{-5}

41. 1 2 3 4 5
|| || || || ||

42. Ed's scores in percent on 5 tests are 75, 70, 80, 65, and 85. What must be his score in percent on a sixth test to achieve an average of 80% on all 6 tests?

(1) 85
(2) 90
(3) 95
(4) 100
(5) It can't be done.

42. 1 2 3 4 5
|| || || || ||

43. A sales representative receives a base salary of $500 per week plus a commission of 2% on sales. What were her sales for a week when she earned $640?

(1) $700
(2) $6000
(3) $7000
(4) $9000
(5) $70 000

43. 1 2 3 4 5
|| || || || ||

44. An auditorium is 24 m long, 15 m wide, and 8 m high. How many square metres of wallpaper are needed to paper the four walls of this room?

(1) 480
(2) 624
(3) 764
(4) 984
(5) 1104

44. 1 2 3 4 5

45. If $37\frac{1}{2}\%$ of a number is 141, what is 125% of the number?

(1) $58\frac{3}{4}$
(2) 250
(3) 470
(4) 510
(5) 690

45. 1 2 3 4 5

46. On a graph, a line segment is drawn from the origin, the (0,0) point, to the point whose coordinates are (6,8). The length of this segment, in graph units, is

(1) 4
(2) 6
(3) 8
(4) 10
(5) 14

46. 1 2 3 4 5

47. In 8 hours of work a mechanic turns out 47 machine parts. Working at the same rate how many machine parts (y), as represented by one of the following expressions, does the mechanic turn out in 11 hours?

(1) $y = \frac{11}{47}(8)$
(2) $y = \frac{8}{11}(47)$
(3) $y = 8(47)(11)$
(4) $y = \frac{8}{47 \times 11}$
(5) $y = \frac{11}{8}(47)$

47. 1 2 3 4 5

48. Young's Rule states that the children's dose of a drug is approximately the adult dose $\times \frac{\text{body mass in kg}}{150\text{ kg}}$

If the adult dose of codeine is 20 mg and the children's dose is 6 mg, according to Young's Rule, how many kilograms of mass does the child have?

(1) 30
(2) 45
(3) 50
(4) 105
(5) 120

48. 1 2 3 4 5

49. If $2x + 5y = 25$ and $4y = 12$ then $x =$

(1) 1
(2) 2
(3) 3
(4) 4
(5) 5

49. 1 2 3 4 5

50. At a concert, seats in the orchestra sold for \$12 and seats in the balcony sold for \$8. If 600 tickets were sold for a total of \$6400, how many orchestra seats were sold? An equation which may be used to solve this problem is

(1) $12x + 8x = 6400$
(2) $12x + 8(x + 600) = 6400$
(3) $12(x - 600) + 8(x + 600) = 6400$
(4) $12x + 8(600 - x) = 6400$
(5) $12(600) + 8x = 6400$

50. 1 2 3 4 5

51. Salme has \$5 more than Yan and Frank has \$10 less than Yan. If Salme, Yan and Frank have a total of \$115, how much does Yan have?
(1) \$20
(2) \$30
(3) \$35
(4) \$40
(5) \$50

51. 1 2 3 4 5

52. The regular price for a certain type of jacket is x dollars. If the price is reduced by 20% of the regular price, the new price is
(1) $x/5$
(2) $x + 1/5$
(3) $4x/5$
(4) $x - 1/8$
(5) $5x$

52. 1 2 3 4 5

53. A family has an income of x dollars per month and spends y dollars per year. The yearly savings of the family are
(1) $12x + y$
(2) $x + 12y$
(3) $12(x - y)$
(4) $12x - y$
(5) $x - 12y$

53. 1 2 3 4 5

54. If $\overleftrightarrow{AB} \perp \overleftrightarrow{AC}$ and m$\angle BAD$ = 120°, find m$\angle EAC$.
(1) 30°
(2) 40°
(3) 45°
(4) 60°
(5) 75°

54. 1 2 3 4 5

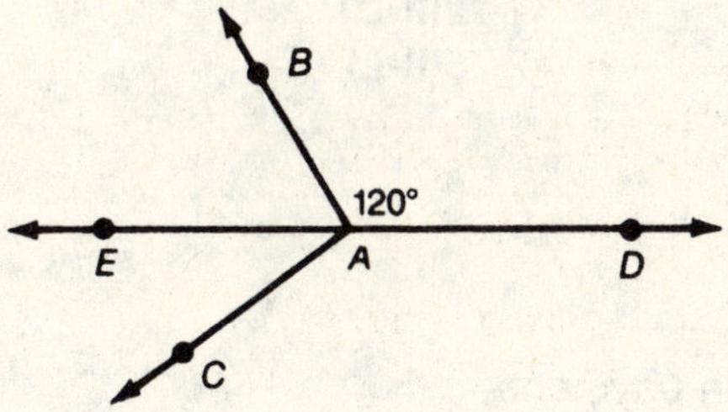

55. On a motor trip Mr. Shore covered $2/7$ of his total trip distance during the first day by driving 384 km. The total distance to be covered, in kilometres, was
(1) 98
(2) 1244
(3) 1306
(4) 1344
(5) 1500

55. 1 2 3 4 5

56. In selling TV sets, Jacek sold twice as many as Elijah, while Pierre sold 4 sets fewer than Elijah. Together they sold a total of 60 TV sets. How many TV sets did Elijah sell?
(1) 12
(2) 14
(3) 15
(4) 16
(5) 20

56. 1 2 3 4 5

Turn to the answer key and the answer analysis which follow.

What's Your Score?

________ right,	________ wrong
Excellent	51–56
Good	44–50
Fair	38–43

Be sure to refer to page 708, where these answers are explained. You may obtain additional help and practice by referring to the review material in this chapter.

ANSWER KEY

The number following each question is the correct answer. The numbers and letters in parentheses refer to the sections of this chapter which explain necessary mathematics principles. A more detailed explanation of all answers follows.

Practice Test Five/Page 699

1. **4(I-G)**	15. **1(II-A)**	29. **2(I-C)**	43. **3(I-G)**
2. **2(III-C)**	16. **4(II-J)**	30. **4(III-D)**	44. **2(III-J)**
3. **1(I-G)**	17. **4(I-I)**	31. **5(II-A)**	45. **3(I-G)**
4. **4(II-K)**	18. **3(I-G)**	32. **3(I-G)**	46. **4(III-F)**
5. **4(II-H)**	19. **1(II-A)**	33. **2(II-H)**	47. **5(II-F)**
6. **4(I-E)**	20. **2(III-G)**	34. **2(I-C)**	48. **2(II-E)**
7. **5(IV-B)**	21. **1(III-C)**	35. **4(II-H)**	49. **5(II-E)**
8. **4(III-E)**	22. **3(III-H)**	36. **3(III-H)**	50. **4(II-F)**
9. **2(III-C)**	23. **4(I-G)**	37. **2(II-H)**	51. **4(II-F)**
10. **3(II-H)**	24. **4(I-E)**	38. **5(II-F)**	52. **3(II-A)**
11. **1(II-G)**	25. **3(I-G)**	39. **2(III-F)**	53. **4(II-A)**
12. **3(II-E)**	26. **3(II-I)**	40. **2(I-C)**	54. **1(II-C)**
13. **4(II-D)**	27. **2(II-J)**	41. **2(II-C)**	55. **4(I-E)**
14. **5(I-E)**	28. **2(II-B)**	42. **5(II-L)**	56. **4(II-F)**

ANSWER ANALYSIS

Practice Test Five/Page 699

1. **4** 20% of 5000 = $\frac{1}{5} \times 5000$ = \$1000 down payment
24 × \$200 = \$4800 in monthly installments
\$1000 + \$4800 = \$5800 total payment for car
\$5800 − \$5000 = \$800 saved by paying cash

2. **2** The sum of the measures of the angles around a point in a plane is 360°

$$\frac{72}{360} = \frac{1}{5}$$

In this case, the angle whose measure is 72° cuts off a sector that is $\frac{1}{5}$ of the circle.

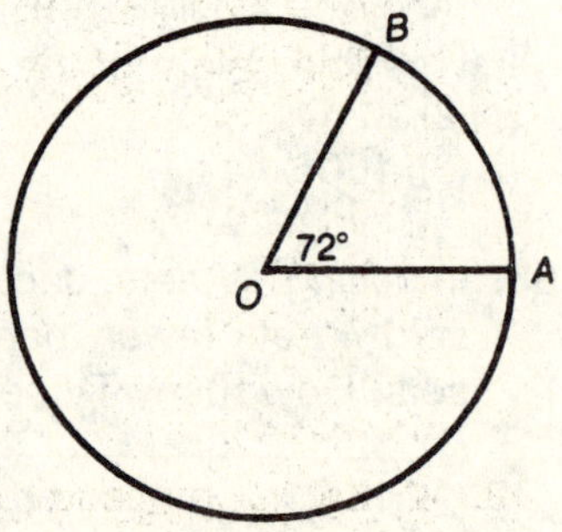

3. **1** Let x = price of chair before increase.
20% = 0.2
Let $0.2x$ = price increase of chair.

$$x + 0.2x = 180$$
$$1.2x = 180$$
$$12x = 1800$$
$$x = 1800 \div 12 = \$150$$

4. **4** Probability $= \dfrac{\text{number of successful outcomes}}{\text{number of possible outcomes}}$

In this case, the number of successful outcomes is 7 since there are 7 science books on the shelf. The number of possible outcomes is 19 since the total number of books on the shelf is 19.

Probability = $7/19$

5. **4** $\dfrac{\text{Number of pegs}}{\text{Cost in dollars}}\ \dfrac{1250}{R} = \dfrac{?}{S}$

$R(?) = 1250S$

$? = \dfrac{1250S}{R}$

6. **4** $\frac{1}{4}$ of \$200 = \$50

\$200 − \$50 = \$150, cost of coat

$\frac{1}{2}$ paid on February 10

$\frac{1}{3}$ paid on March 10

$\frac{1}{2} + \frac{1}{3} = \frac{3}{6} + \frac{2}{6} = \frac{5}{6}$, total paid on February 10 and March 10

Mr. Hill had $\frac{6}{6} - \frac{5}{6} = \frac{1}{6}$ of the cost to pay on April 10

$\frac{1}{6} \times$ \$150 = \$25, paid on April 10.

7. **5** In 1998, the receipts were \$600 000 and the expenses were \$500 000. In 1998, the excess of receipts over expenses was \$100 000.

8. **4** The ratio of the length of the pole to the length of its shadow is 6:2 or 3:1. That is, the pole is three times as long as its shadow.

The spire is also three times as long as its shadow. Therefore, the height of the spire is $3 \times 29 = 87$ m.

ALTERNATIVE METHOD

Let x = height of spire in metres

$\dfrac{x}{29} = \dfrac{6}{2}$

$2x = 6(29) = 174$

$x = 174 \div 2 = 87$

The height of the spire is 87 m.

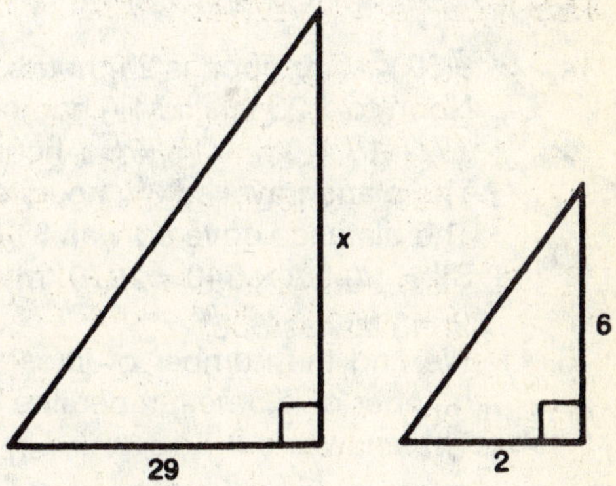

9. **2** Let x = measure of second angle of triangle

And x = measure of third angle of triangle

$x + x + 84 = 180$

$2x + 84 = 180$

$2x = 180 - 84 = 96$

$x = 96° \div 2 = 48°$

The measures of the other two angles are 48° and 48°

10. **3** 45 minutes $= \dfrac{45}{60}$, or $\dfrac{3}{4}$ of an hour

The part of the job that the crew can complete in 45 minutes is

$\dfrac{3/4}{4\frac{1}{2}} = \dfrac{3/4}{9/2}$

$\frac{3}{4} \div \frac{9}{2} = \frac{3}{4} \times \frac{2}{9} = \frac{1}{6}$

11. **1** $3x + 1 \geqslant 16$

$3x \geqslant 16 - 1$

$3x \geqslant 15$

$x \geqslant 5$

That is, x is equal to 5 or x is greater than 5. Each member of the pair 6,5 satisfies the inequality.

12. **3** $2x^2 - x - 6 = 0$

$(x - 2)(2x + 3) = 0$

$x - 2 = 0 \qquad 2x + 3 = 0$

$x = 2 \qquad 2x = -3$

$x = -3/2$

ALTERNATIVE METHOD

A solution of the equation must satisfy the equation. We substitute 2 for x to obtain

$2(2)^2 - 2 - 6 = 0$

$2(4) - 2 - 6 = 0$

$8 - 2 - 6 = 0$

$0 = 0$

Thus, 2 is a root of the equation. Substitution of the other choices does not satisfy the equation.

13. **4** Each first place yields 5 points. All first places yield $5F$ points.
Each second place yields 3 points. All second places yield $3S$ points.
Each third place yields 1 point. All third places yield T points.
The formula for stating the total number of points is

$P = 5F + 3S + T$

14. **5** 9:30 A.M. to noon is $2\frac{1}{2}$ hours.
Noon to 1:20 P.M. is $1\frac{1}{3}$ hours.
$2\frac{1}{2} + 1\frac{1}{3} = 2\frac{3}{6} + 1\frac{2}{6} = 3\frac{5}{6}$ hours
The plane travelled $3\frac{5}{6}$ hours at the rate of 540 km/h
The distance covered was $3\frac{5}{6}(540)$.
$3\frac{5}{6} = \frac{23}{6}$, $\frac{23}{6} \times 540 = 2070$ km

15. **1** We find the number of litres used by dividing the number of kilometres driven (x) by the number of kilometres per litre of gas used (16).
The answer is $x \div 16$

16. **4** $x^2 - 25$ is the difference of two squares. When we factor $x^2 - 25$ we have
$x^2 - 25 = (x + 5)(x - 5)$

17. **4** Interest = \$6000 × 0.085 = \$510, annual interest

18. **3** We set up the fraction $\frac{272}{320}$ and convert this fraction to a percent.
272 ÷ 320 = 0.85
0.85 = 85% successful
100% − 85% = 15% unsuccessful

19. **1** $$\frac{1\text{ plane}}{p\text{ passengers}} = \frac{?\text{ planes}}{xp\text{ passengers}}$$

$$p? = xp$$

$$? = \frac{xp}{p} = x$$

20. **2** To find the perimeter of the figure we find the sum of the lengths of the sides.
$a + b + a + 2b + 3a - b + 2a + 3b$
$= (a + a + 3a + 2a) + (b + 2b - b + 3b)$
$= 7a + 5b$

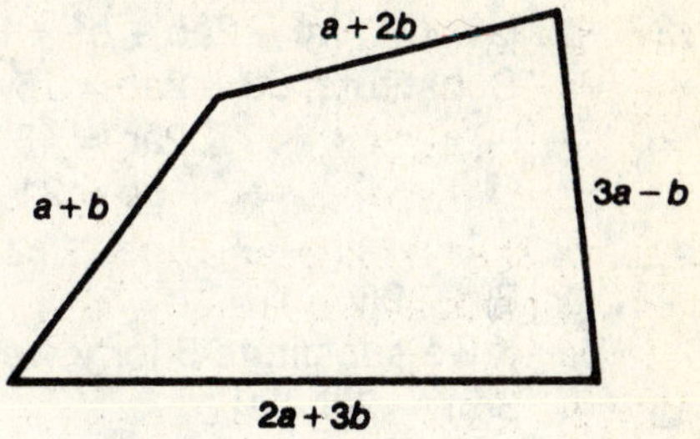

21. **1** Since $\overline{AB} \perp \overline{BC}$, $m\angle B = 90°$
$m\angle C + m\angle CAB = 90°$
$m\angle C + 49° = 90°$
$m\angle C = 90° - 49° = 41°$
Since $\overline{AD} \parallel \overline{CB}$, $m\angle x = m\angle C$
Since $m\angle C = 41°$, $m\angle x = 41°$

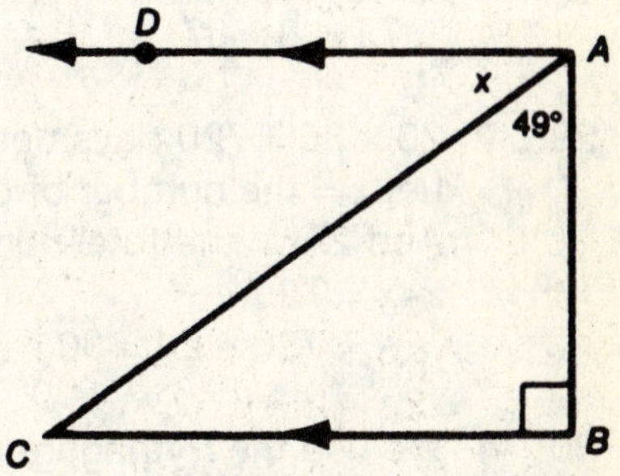

22. **3** The figure is composed of a rectangle surmounted by a triangle. To find the area of the rectangle we note that its base measures 20 m and its height measures 10 m.
Area of rectangle = $20 \times 10 = 200\,m^2$
To find the area of the triangle we note that its base measures 20 m and its altitude measures 6 m.
Area of triangle = $\frac{1}{2}$ base $\times$ altitude
Area of triangle = $\frac{1}{2}(20)(6) = 60\,m^2$
Area of figure = $200 + 60 = 260\,m^2$

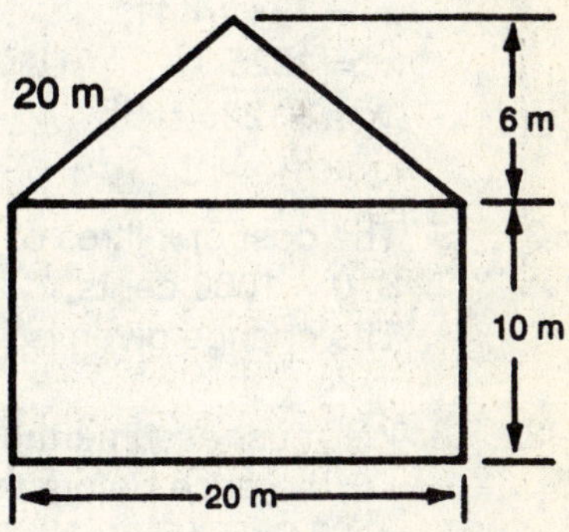

23. **4** 20% of \$50 = 0.2 × \$50 = \$10 discount
\$50 – \$10 = \$40 cost of watch to dealer
10% of \$50 = 0.1 × \$50 = \$5
\$50 + \$5 = \$55, selling price of watch
\$55 – \$40 = \$15 profit

24. **4** \$8000 = 1 son's share
3 × \$8000 = \$24 000, share left to three sons
\$24 000 = ½ of the estate
2(\$24 000) = \$48 000, the value of the full estate

25. **3** Let x = cost to store in dollars.
40% = 0.4
Selling price of article = $x + 0.4x = 1.4x$
$1.4x = 28$
$14x = 280$
$x = 280 \div 14 = 20$, cost of article
The cost to the store is \$20.

26. **3** There are five readings. To obtain the average we add the five readings and divide the sum by 5.
Add $-12 + (-7) + (-2) + 0 + 6$
$= -21 + 6 = -15$
$-15 \div 5 = -3$

27. **2** $(a-b)^2 = a^2 - 2ab + b^2 = 16$
Substitute: $58 - 2ab = 16$
$2ab = 42$
$ab = 21$

28. **2** $3y^2 - 2(y-1)$
If we substitute 5 for y we have
$3(5)^2 - 2(5-1)$
$3(25) - 2(4)$
$75 - 8 = 67$

29. **2** $20 \times 36 = 720$ days needed to do the job
Let x = the number of days it takes 24 workers to do the job.
And $24x$ = the total number of work days.
$24x = 720$
$x = 720 \div 24 = 30$

30. **4** We use the Pythagorean Theorem.
$x^2 = 28^2 + 21^2$
$x^2 = 784 + 441$
$x^2 = 1225$
$x = \sqrt{1225} = 35$

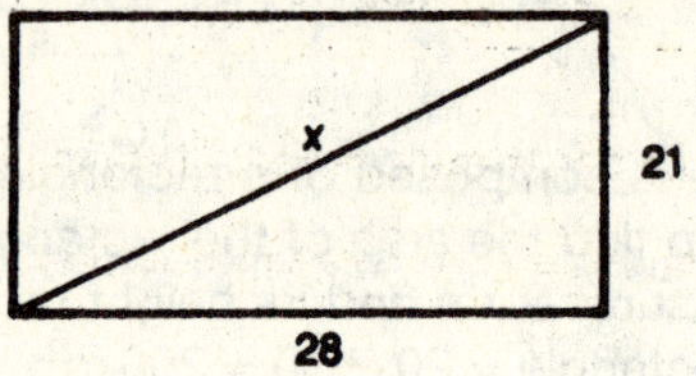

31. **5** The cost of x litres of gasoline at y cents per litre is xy cents.
$10 = 1000 cents
The change given is $(1000 - xy)$ cents.

32. **3** We must assume the least saving (20%) to find the lowest price before the reduction. Let x = the price before the sale in dollars.
$x - 0.2x = 15$
$0.8x = 15$
$8x = 150$
$x = 18.75$

33. **2** Since $\frac{5}{2}$ as much rhubarb is used as is called for in the recipe, we must use $\frac{5}{2}$ as much sugar as was called for in the recipe.
$\frac{5}{2} \times \frac{1}{2} = \frac{5}{4}$, or 1.25 kg

34. **2** The first 100 shirts cost 8(100) dollars.
The next 68 shirts cost 7(68) dollars.
The correct choice is 7(68) + 8(100).

35. **4** 1 km = 1000 m; 1.2 km = 1200 m; 100 m : 1200 m
The scale 100 m to 1.2 km is equivalent to the ratio 1 : 12.

36. **3** To obtain the area of the shaded portion, we find the area of the square and subtract from it the sum of the areas of the 4 quarter circles.

Area of the square = $10 \times 10 = 100\,\text{cm}^2$
Area of the 4 quarter circles is the same as the area of one complete circle. Since the radius of each quarter circle is 5 cm, the area of the 4 quarter circles is πr^2, or $\pi \times 5 \times 5 = 25\pi$.
The area of the shaded portion is $100 - 25\pi$.

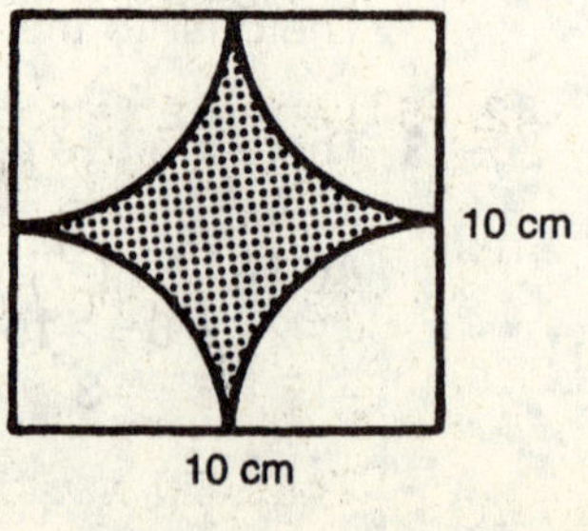

37. **2** $\frac{\text{kg}}{\text{cost}}\ \frac{1.75}{8.12} = \frac{1}{n}$

$1.75n = 8.12$

$n = \frac{8.12}{1.75}$

$n = \$4.64$

38. **5** x = height of solid.
We use the formula $V = lwh$.
In this case, $V = 50$, $l = 5$, $w = 4$, and $h = x$.
$50 = 5(4)x$
$50 = 20x$, or $20x = 50$

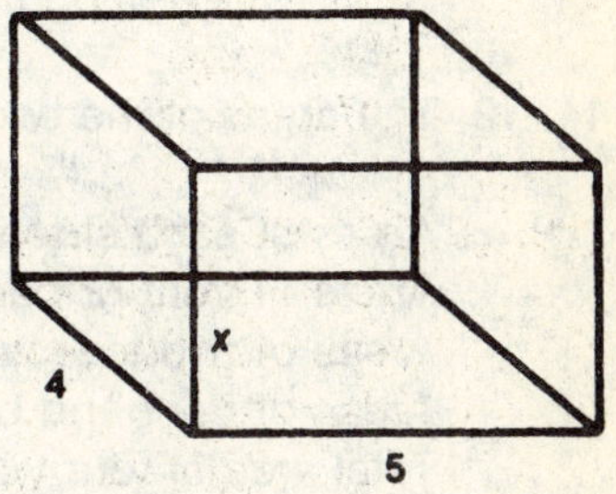

39. **2** The formula for the slope of a line is $m = \frac{y_2 - y_1}{x_2 - x_1}$.
In this case, $y_2 = 9$, $y_1 = y$, $x_2 = 4$ and $x_1 = 2$.

$m = \frac{9-y}{4-2} = \frac{9-y}{2}$

$\frac{9-y}{2} = 3$

$9 - y = 6$

$9 - 6 = y$

$3 = y$

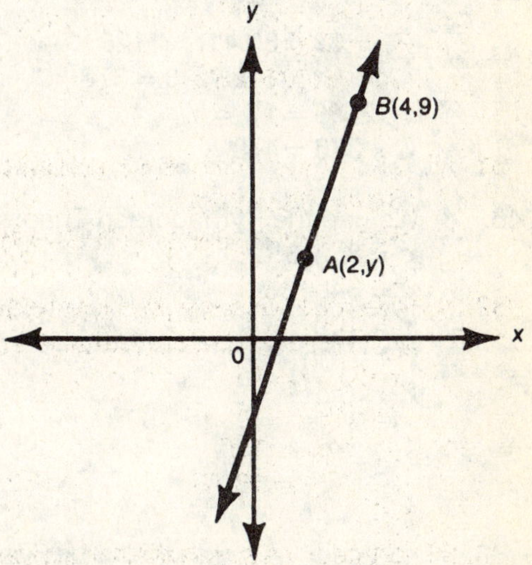

40. **2** The difference in price = \$2.89 – \$2.19, or 70¢. She would receive 30 cents change for the dollar bill.

41. **2** To express a number in scientific notation we express it as the product of a number between 1 and 10 and a power of 10. In this case, the number between 1 and 10 is 4.622. In going from 4.622 to 0.0004622 we move the decimal point 4 places to the left. This represents multiplication by 10^{-4}. Thus,
$0.0004622 = 4.622 \times 10^{-4}$

42. **5** Let x = Ed's score on the sixth test in percent.

$\frac{75+70+80+65+85+x}{6} = 80$

$75 + 70 + 80 + 65 + 85 + x = 6(80) = 480$

$375 + x = 480$

$x = 480 - 375 = 105$

Thus, Ed would have to achieve a score of 105% on the sixth test, an impossibility.

43. **3** \$640 − \$500 = \$140 earned on commission
$2\% = 0.02$
Let x = value of sales.
$0.02x = 140$
If we multiply both sides of the equation by 100 we have
$100(0.02x) = 100(140)$
$2x = 14000$
$x = \$7000$, sales

44. **2** The areas of the two pairs of opposite walls are equal.
$A = lw$
Areas of each side wall = $8 \times 5 = 120\,m^2$
Areas of front or back wall = $8 \times 24 = 192\,m^2$
Areas of two side walls = $2 \times 120 = 240\,m^2$
Areas of front and back walls = $2 \times 192 = 384\,m^2$
Total area of four walls = $240 + 384 = 624\,m^2$

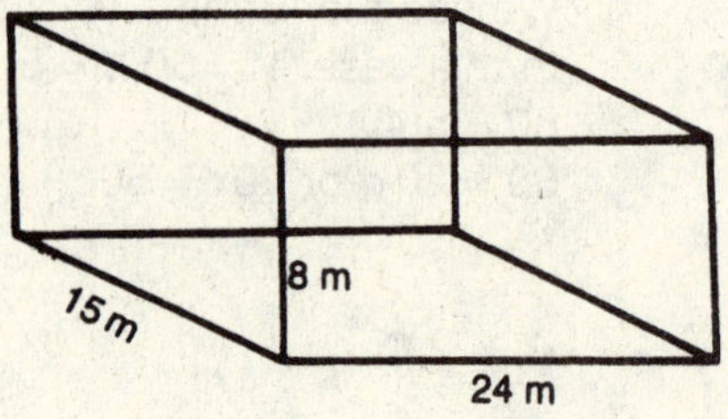

45. **3** $37\tfrac{1}{2}\% = \tfrac{3}{8}$
Let x = the number.
$\tfrac{3}{8}x = 141$
$3x = 8(141) = 1128$
$x = 1128 \div 3 = 376$
$125\% = 1\tfrac{1}{4} = \tfrac{5}{4}$
$\tfrac{5}{4} \times 376 = 470$

46. **4** We use the Pythagorean Theorem.
$x^2 = 8^2 + 6^2$
$x^2 = 64 + 36$
$x^2 = 100$
$x = \sqrt{100}$
$x = 10$

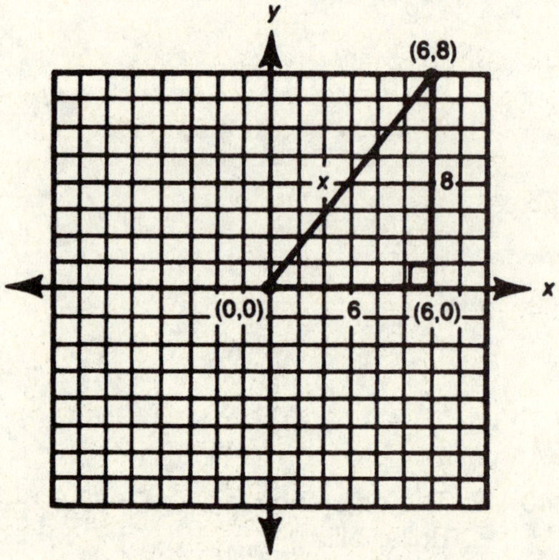

47. **5** We set up the proportion
$$\frac{8}{47} = \frac{11}{y}$$
$8y = 11(47)$
$$y = \frac{11}{8}(47)$$

48. **2** Let x = the child's mass in kg.
$$20\left(\frac{x}{150}\right) = 6$$
$$\frac{20x}{150} = 6$$
$20x = 900$
$x = 45$
The child's mass is 45 kg.

49. **5**

$$4y = 12$$
$$y = 12 \div 4 = 3$$
$$2x + 5y = 25$$
$$2x + 5(3) = 25$$
$$2x + 15 = 25$$
$$2x = 25 - 15 = 10$$
$$x = 10 \div 2 = 5$$

50. **4** Let x = number of orchestra seats sold.
And $600 - x$ = number of balcony seats sold.
$12x$ = value of orchestra seats sold
$8(600 - x)$ = value of balcony seats sold
We use the following relationship to write an equation
Value of orchestra seats + Value of balcony seats = 6400
$12x + 8(600 - x) = 6400$

51. **4** Let x = amount of money that Yan has.
And $x + 5$ = amount of money that Salme has.
And $x - 10$ = amount of money that Frank has.

$$x + x + 5 + x - 10 = 115$$
$$3x - 5 = 115$$
$$3x = 115 + 5 = 120$$
$$x = 120 + 3 = 40$$

Yan has \$40.

52. **3** $20\% = \frac{1}{5}$
The reduced price is $\frac{4}{5}$ of the regular price.
$\frac{4}{5}$ of the regular price $= \frac{4x}{5}$.

53. **4** If a family has an income of x dollars per month it has an income of $12x$ dollars per year. Since the family spends y dollars per year it saves $12x - y$ dollars per year.

54. **1** Since $\overleftrightarrow{AB} \perp \overleftrightarrow{AC}$, $m\angle BAC = 90$

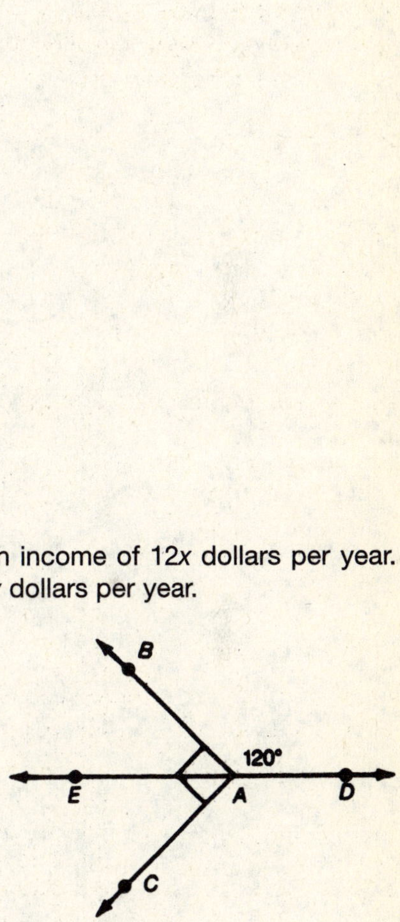

$$m\angle BAD + m\angle BAE = 180$$
$$120 + m\angle BAE = 180$$
$$m\angle BAE = 180 - 120 = 60$$
$$m\angle BAE + m\angle EAC = 90$$
$$60 + m\angle EAC = 90$$
$$m\angle EAC = 90 - 60 = 30$$
$$m\angle EAC = 30^\circ$$

55. **4** Let x = total distance to be covered.

$$\tfrac{2}{7}x = 384$$
$$2x = 7(384) = 2688$$
$$x = 2688 \div 2 = 1344$$

56. **4** Let x = number of sets sold by Elijah
And $2x$ = number of sets sold by Jacek
And $x - 4$ = number of sets sold by Pierre

$$x + 2x + x - 4 = 60$$
$$4x - 4 = 60$$
$$4x = 60 + 4 = 64$$
$$x = 64 = 64 \div 4 = 16$$

10

GRAPHS, TABLES, MAPS, AND DIAGRAMS

AN OVERVIEW

Examples of graphs, tables, maps, and diagrams from mathematics, science, and social studies have been compiled to form Chapter 10. Included are practice exercises and explanations.

GRAPHS

Line graphs, bar graphs, pictographs, circle graphs, and formula graphs are explained with opportunities for practice.

TABLES

The presentation of data with tables is outlined and explained and practice is provided.

MAPS

Information can be presented through the use of maps. Decoding this information and using it to answer questions is the skill emphasized in this section. Practice in this skill is provided.

DIAGRAMS

Diagrams help explain and present information. Examples, explanations, and practice are provided.

PRACTICE IN INTERPRETING GRAPHS, TABLES, MAPS, AND DIAGRAMS

Sample questions are provided to allow sufficient practice to master these skills.

AN OVERVIEW

There are many ways of presenting information. This chapter focuses on the most common ones: graphs, tables, maps, and diagrams. If your diagnostic tests indicate a weakness in this area, it would be to your benefit to work through the entire chapter. The skills needed to deal with information presented in these forms are not determined by subject areas. What you learn from working with a graph in social studies will help you in mathematics. Answers are included, as is analysis of the process for determining the right answer.

We suggest that you work through a question or set of questions. Check your answers. If you have marked all the right answers, congratulate yourself on a job well done. If there are errors, look back at the question, the analysis, and the instructions that preceded the question. Find out why you got it wrong. Don't be discouraged. Keep going until you understand the skills involved in answering the questions correctly. That way, no matter what question is presented to you on the exam, you will have the skills needed to correctly answer it.

If you have difficulty with the vocabulary used in the questions or answers, go back to the glossaries and learn the words and concepts. You may have to divide the glossary into sections and learn one section each day. You should be able to work the words into a conversation in a meaningful way. Working with other people studying for the GED exam makes working these words into a conversation much easier.

GRAPHS

Pictures or graphs are often used in reports, magazines, and newspapers to present a set of numerical facts. This enables the viewer to make comparisons and to draw quick conclusions. In this section, we will learn how to interpret *line graphs*, *bar graphs*, *pictographs*, *circle graphs*, and *formula graphs.*

LINE GRAPHS

A line graph is the most common way of representing data visually. It is a way of expressing the relationship between two variables. The independent variable is marked out on a linear scale along the bottom of the graph. Frequently, the independent variable is time, in one form or another. For example, it may be expressed in specific seconds, hours of the day, or months of the year; it may also be expressed in number of seconds, hours, or months. Other independent variables can have any sort of unit at all.

The dependent variable is marked out on a vertical scale along the left side of the graph. The scale is usually linear; it may or may not start at zero.

If you are given a line graph, start by studying it. What are the variables? How is the scale marked off? What are the units of measure? If there is more than one line on the graph, what do the various lines represent?

Once you know what the graph *means*, get a rough idea of what it *says*. Do not bother with a detailed analysis; you will do that when you answer the questions.

Here is a sample for you to work on:

EXAMPLE: The graph below represents the temperatures of a white sidewalk and a black asphalt driveway on a sunny day. The surfaces are side by side, and the measurements were made during a 24-hour period. The solid line represents the sidewalk, and the dash line the driveway.

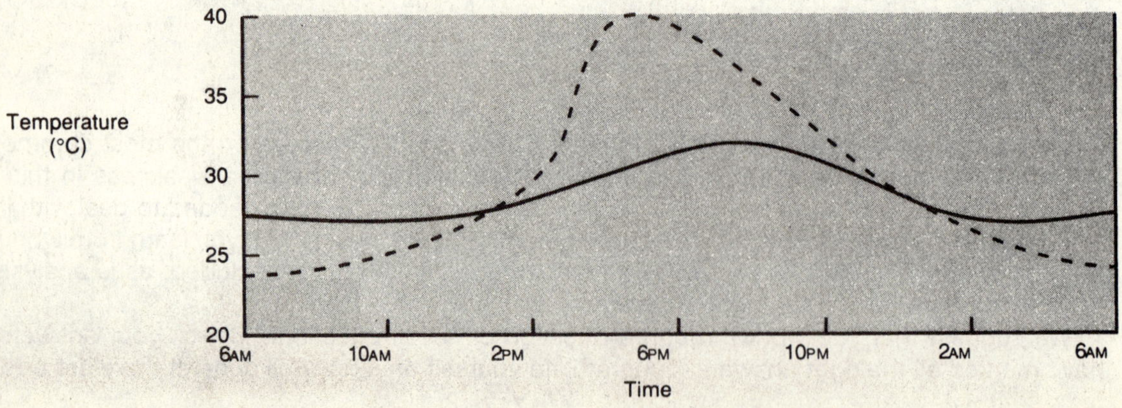

What are the features of this graph? The independent variable is the time of day. The scale is marked at 4-hour intervals and covers the full 24 hours. The dependent variable is the temperature, marked in Celsius degrees, at 5-degree intervals, from 20°C to 40°C. The solid line represents the variation in the temperature of a white sidewalk during a 24-hour period, and the dash line does the same for a black asphalt driveway. Both temperatures increase during the daylight hours, and start to decrease in the afternoon or early evening. Fine.

Now you are ready for the questions.

1. At noon, what was the temperature of the driveway?
(1) 22°C
(2) 26°C
(3) 28°C
(4) 30°C
(5) 32°C

Noon is halfway between 10 A.M. and 2 P.M., so start by placing the point of your pencil halfway between these two points on the horizontal scale. Move it straight up until it meets the dash line, which represents the driveway. Now move it to the left to find that it meets the temperature scale at 26°; the answer is choice 2.

2. What is the difference in the times when the two surfaces reach their maximum temperatures?
(1) The driveway reaches its maximum about 4 hours before the sidewalk.
(2) The sidewalk reaches its maximum about 4 hours before the driveway.
(3) The driveway reaches its maximum about 2 hours before the sidewalk.
(4) The sidewalk reaches its maximum about 2 hours before the driveway.
(5) Both surfaces reach their maximums at the same time.

The dash line (driveway) peaks at about 4 P.M. halfway between 2 P.M. and 6 P.M. The solid line (sidewalk) peaks a little before 8 P.M. The difference is fairly close to 4 hours, so the answer is choice 1.

3. Where and when was the temperature increasing most rapidly?
(1) the driveway at 4:30 P.M.
(2) the sidewalk at 5 P.M.
(3) the sidewalk at 7:30 P.M.
(4) the driveway at noon
(5) the driveway at 3 P.M.

The most rapid change is shown as the steepest slope of the graph. This occurs on the dash line at about 3 P.M., so the answer is choice 5.

4. How do the temperature patterns of the two surfaces compare?
(1) The driveway is always warmer than the sidewalk.
(2) The sidewalk is warmer than the driveway at night and cooler in the afternoon.
(3) The two surfaces are never at the same temperature.
(4) The sidewalk changes temperature faster than the driveway.
(5) The driveway is always cooler than the sidewalk.

Choices 1 and 5 are wrong by inspection of the graph. Choice 2 is right, because the graph for the driveway rises above the one for the sidewalk at about 1:30 P.M. and falls below it at midnight. Choice 3 is wrong because the two lines coincide at two times. Choice 4 is wrong because the line for the driveway is always steeper than that for the sidewalk.

5. What hypothesis might be advanced on the basis of this graph?
(1) Radiant heat flows in either direction more easily through a black surface than through a white one.
(2) Black objects tend to retain heat, while white ones lose it more easily.
(3) White objects tend to absorb heat more rapidly than black objects do.
(4) Black objects are always cooler at night than in the daytime.
(5) White objects are usually cooler than black ones.

Since the black surface both warms up and cools down faster than the white one, the answer is choice 1. Choice 2 is wrong because the black surface cools down faster than the white one. Choice 3 is wrong because the white surface warms up more slowly than the black one. Choices 4 and 5 are wrong because they do not take into account the conditions of the experiment, on which the graph was based, namely, that the two surfaces were in sunlight during the day.

As an example in social studies, let us construct a line graph charting the Consumer Price Index, an index that represents changes in the cost of selected key consumer items, given in percentages, as they relate to a given date or base period arbitrarily set at 100. We will use the following data:

EXAMPLE:

YEAR	PERCENTAGE	YEAR	PERCENTAGE	YEAR	PERCENTAGE	YEAR	PERCENTAGE
1961	23.9	1969	30.0	1977	51.3	1985	96.0
1962	24.2	1970	31.0	1978	55.9	1986	100.0
1963	24.6	1971	31.9	1979	61.0	1987	104.4
1964	25.1	1972	33.4	1980	67.2	1988	108.6
1965	25.7	1973	36.0	1981	75.5	1989	114.0
1966	26.6	1974	39.9	1982	83.7	1990	119.5
1967	27.6	1975	44.2	1983	88.5	1991	126.2
1968	28.7	1976	47.5	1984	92.4	1992	132.8

To construct the graph, we let the
—horizontal line (technically known as the *abscissa*) represent the period from 1961 to 1983 in two-year intervals.
—vertical line (technically known as the *ordinate*) represent percentage units for the Consumer Price Index, in intervals of ten from 50 to 310.

The basic graph, without any data recorded, looks like this:

EXAMPLE:

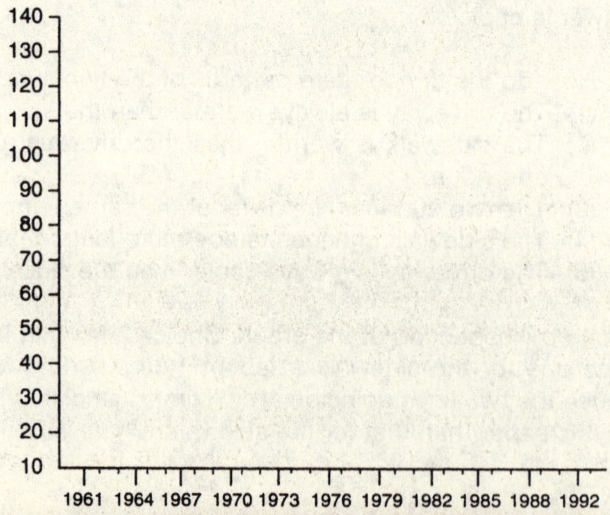

To plot the line graph, start with the first line of data—year 1961, CPI 23.9. Go to the ordinate at 1961; point to 23.9 and place a mark there. Then find the next date on the abscissa (horizontal axis). Trace a line vertically until you reach 24.6 (the CPI for 1963) and place a mark there. Continue to do the same until you have recorded all of the percentages given. Then link all of your marks to produce a graph that looks like the following:

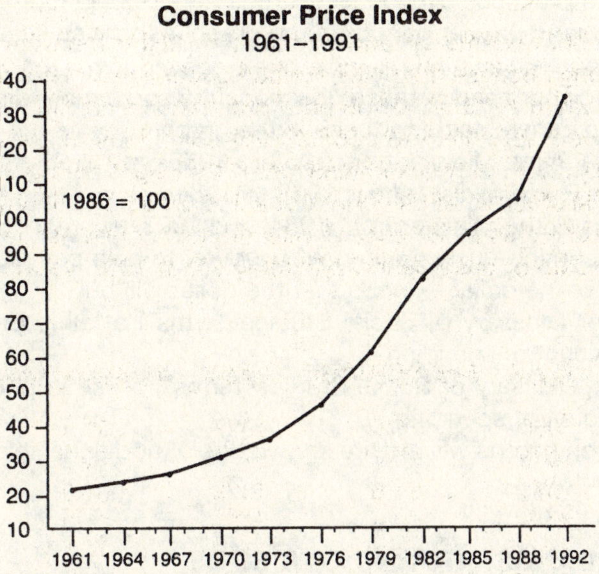

What can you see or visualize from a line graph? Try these questions.

QUESTIONS

1. What was the direction in the trend of consumer prices from 1961 to 1965?
2. When was the consumer price index (CPI) equal to exactly 100?
3. In which half decade was the increase the greatest?
4. During which half decade did prices change least?

ANSWER KEY

1. slightly upward
2. 1986
3. 1981–1985
4. 1961–1965

ANSWER ANALYSIS

Visual inspection of the graph gives you the answers.

1. From 1961 to 1965, the plotted line of consumer prices is in an upward trend; that is, the line slants upward from the left to the right. Note also that the trend is slight.
2. This requires you to draw a horizontal line from the 100 point on the vertical axis to intersect the graph line. Then drop a line vertically from the point of intersection to intersect the horizontal axis to identify the year. In many instances the "base year" is specifically indicated as in this graph ("1986 = 100").
3. A half decade is the period representing the first half or the second half of any given decade. For example, 1971 to 1975 or 1976 to 1980. You can calculate the change for each half decade as follows:

1966 (27) minus 1961 (24) = 3

During this period the Consumer Price Index rose 3 points. Or, 1980 (67) minus 1976 (47) = 30. During this period the CPI rose 30 points.

By doing this for each half decade, we can identify during which one the CPI increased most. Or you can look at the steepest parts of the graph and see if they correspond with a particular half decade. If this does not give you a clear answer, it is best to do the calculations.

4. The plotted graph line is almost level between 1961 and 1965 (a four-year period) showing very little change. In no other four-year period on the graph is there so little change.

Now that you have tried your hand at these questions, try some more difficult ones. These require you to apply the following general facts to those in the graph:

—Lester Pearson was Prime Minister from 1963 to 1968
—Pierre Trudeau was Prime Minister from 1968 to 1984
—Brian Mulroney was Prime Minister from 1984 until 1993
—Cost-of-living adjustment—increase in pay to worker to help pay higher prices for goods
—Purchasing power of the dollar—goods that the dollar will buy
—Deflation—(see the "Glossary of Social Studies Terms") a fall in prices brought about by a decrease in the amount of spending
—Inflation—(see the "Glossary of Social Studies Terms") a rise in prices brought about by an increase in the amount of spending

Nearly every question on graphs will require knowledge of additional information from your social studies background.

QUESTIONS REQUIRING GENERAL KNOWLEDGE

1. The graph shows that the Consumer Price Index
(1) increased sharply from 1961 to 1965
(2) was double that of 1971 in 1965
(3) was half that of 1971 in 1965
(4) rose sharply while Prime Minister Trudeau was in office
(5) declined while Prime Minister Pearson was in office

1. 1 2 3 4 5
|| || || || ||

2. Which conclusion can best be drawn from the graph?
(1) Labour unions asked for cost-of-living adjustments to wages during the 1970s.
(2) The purchasing power of the dollar was stable before 1970.
(3) The average homeowner with a mortgage obtained in 1961 found it easier to pay his interest in 1981.
(4) A man who cashed in his 10-year Canada Savings Bond in 1983 received more purchasing power per dollar than he had when he bought the bond.
(5) Canadian living standards rose during the 1980s.

2. 1 2 3 4 5
|| || || || ||

3. By looking at the graph for the period 1985 to 1992, one might expect that for the following five years
(1) deflation would set in
(2) current social security retirement benefits would be adequate to meet the future needs of pensioners
(3) wages and salaries would decline
(4) inflation would threaten the economy
(5) conditions would remain stable

3. 1 2 3 4 5
|| || || || ||

4. Which statement could NOT be verified by evidence drawn from the graph?

(1) The Pearson era was marked by falling prices.
(2) Inflation was a feature of the economy in the sixties, seventies, and eighties.
(3) In the sixties prices rose less than in the seventies.
(4) Inflationary forces are best controlled through government regulation of prices.
(5) Prices have been rising steadily since 1961.

4. 1 2 3 4 5
|| || || || ||

ANSWER KEY

1. **4** 2. **3** 3. **4** 4. **4**

ANSWER ANALYSIS

1. **4** Prices rose slightly, not sharply, between 1961 and 1965 so choice 1 is not correct. Choices 2 and 3 are inaccurate statements (the calculations are wrong) so these choices are not correct. Choice 5 is wrong since prices rose while Mr. Pearson was in office. Choice 4 is the only accurate statement and hence the only one shown by the graph.
2. **3** This is a difficult question. There is no way of knowing from the graph what the labour unions asked for during the seventies. Choice 1 cannot be correct. Nor is choice 2 correct since the CPI rose more than 20% in the decade before 1970. Between 1973 and 1983 the CPI more than doubled so each dollar received would have less than 50 percent of the purchasing power of a 1973 dollar. Choice 3 is correct because if a person bought a home when the Consumer Price Index was low, the mortgage debt would be low, and the payments would be made when prices (and the borrower's income) would be higher.
3. **4** This question calls for you to make a projection from the graph. Since prices were rising from 1985 to 1992, it can only mean, by our definition of inflation, that inflation will increase. Choice 4 is correct.
4. **4** The graph deals with prices—the Consumer Price Index. It gives us information on 1, 2, 3, and 5 but it does not deal with how to control prices. Choice 4 is correct.

In mathematics, a line graph is especially helpful in showing changes over a period of time.

EXAMPLE: The graph below shows the growth in motor vehicle registration in a certain province.

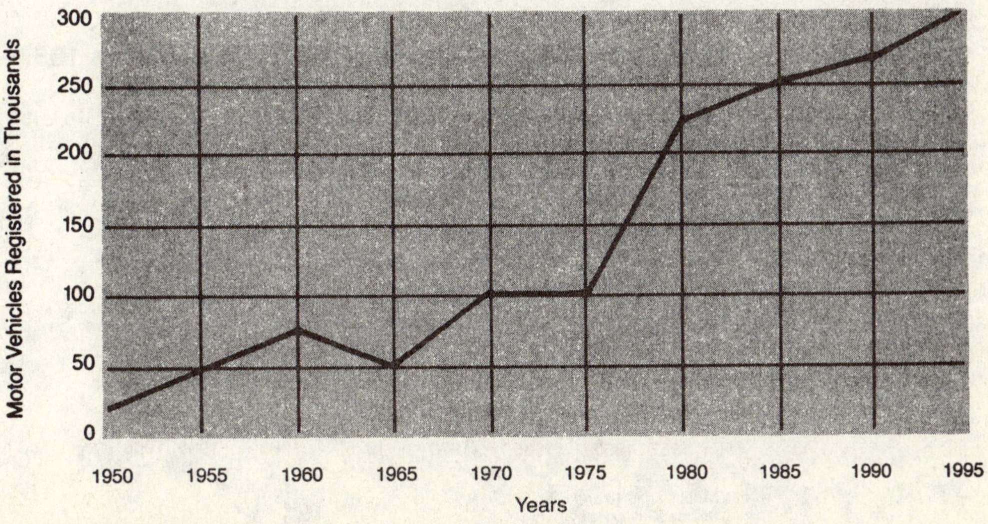

1. Approximately how many motor vehicles were registered in 1980?
ANSWER: We cannot tell exactly from the graph, but a good estimate is 220 000.

2. Approximately how many times as many motor vehicles were registered in 1985 as in 1955?
ANSWER: Registered in 1985—250 000
Registered in 1955—50 000
There were 5 times as many motor vehicles registered in 1985 as in 1955.

3. What percent of increase in registration took place between 1965 and 1995?
ANSWER: Registered in 1965—50 000
Registered in 1995—300 000
Increase in registration—250 000

$$\text{Percent of increase} = \frac{\text{Increase}}{\text{Original}} = \frac{250\,000}{50\,000} = \frac{5}{1}, \text{ or } 500\%$$

4. Between what two periods shown was the increase the greatest?
ANSWER: Between 1975 and 1980. This is shown on the graph by the sharpest rise in the line.

5. Between what two periods shown was there no increase?
ANSWER: Between 1970 and 1975. This is shown by the horizontal (or flat) line between 1970 and 1975.

BAR GRAPHS

A bar graph is very much like the line graph we have just studied. There is the same visual presentation of one set of facts in relation to another set. There is the same horizontal line (*abscissa*) representing one set of facts. The same vertical line (*ordinate*) represents the other set.

For a bar graph, however, you do not put a dot at the point which represents one fact in relation to another, nor do you connect those points by lines. You simply make bars of equal width which you draw up to a point to show the relationship. Thus we could change the line graph we just worked on to a bar graph by making bars for each point identified.

The two graphs below show the contrast between a line graph and a bar graph.

EXAMPLE:

Church or synagogue attendance,[1] Canada and United States 1957–1988

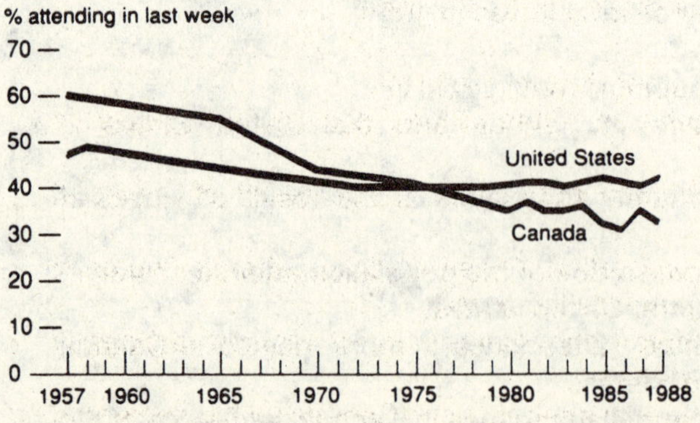

[1]Adults aged 18 and over.
Source: Gallup Poll.

Percentage of people attending religious services or meetings at least once a week, by region, 1985—1990

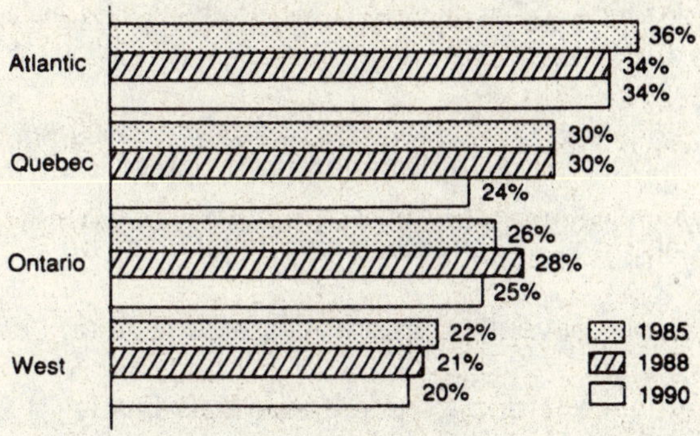

Source: Statistics Canada, General Social Survey.

Note the titles. The line graph is entitled "Church or Synagogue Attendance, Canada and the United States, 1957–1988." It gives the percentage of church attendance on the vertical line (ordinate) for each year shown on the horizontal line (abscissa).

The bar graph is entitled "Percentage of people attending religious services or meetings in Canada at least once a week, by region, 1985–1990." The vertical line represents the percentage of the entire population. The horizontal line shows the three years covered by the graph as well as the regions.

Use these graphs to answer the following practice questions.

QUESTIONS

1. In 1960, what percentage of Canadians attended religious services regularly?
(1) 75%
(2) more than 75%
(3) almost 60%
(4) about 50%
(5) less than 50%

1. 1 2 3 4 5
|| || || || ||

2. In 1988, attendance at religious services in Canada was
(1) about the same as in 1957
(2) slightly more than half what it was in 1957
(3) less than half what it was in 1957
(4) more than what it was in 1957
(5) about one quarter of what it was in 1957

2. 1 2 3 4 5
|| || || || ||

3. Which statement is supported by graph 1?
(1) Church attendance in Canada and the United States is increasing.
(2) The change in church attendance is the result of weekend sports.
(3) About the same proportion of the population attends church in both Canada and the United States.
(4) The decline in church attendance is more marked in Canada than in the United States.
(5) There will be no church attendance in Canada by the end of the century.

3. 1 2 3 4 5
|| || || || ||

4. The bar graph shows that attendance at religious services is
(1) highest in Atlantic Canada
(2) lowest in Atlantic Canada
(3) about the same in all regions
(4) highest in the West
(5) lowest in Quebec

4. 1 2 3 4 5
|| || || || ||

5. Which statement is NOT supported by information from one of the graphs?
(1) Today, more Americans than Canadians are likely to be churchgoers.
(2) As recently as the early seventies, more Canadians than Americans attended church.
(3) Declining church attendance is due to recent scandals involving leaders of various faiths.
(4) Over the last half of the eighties, church attendance declined most sharply in Quebec.
(5) Westerners are more likely to be churchgoers than other Canadians.

5. 1 2 3 4 5
|| || || || ||

6. Which statement concerning church attendance can be supported by the bar graph?
(1) Few people in the West believe in God.
(2) The rate of decrease in church attendance in these years was greatest in Ontario.
(3) In 1990, the proportion of the population attending church in the Atlantic region was twice that in Quebec.
(4) Most churches and synagogues in Canada are in the Atlantic region.
(5) In 1990, attendance at religious services was lower in all regions than in 1985.

6. 1 2 3 4 5
|| || || || ||

ANSWER KEY

1. **3** 2. **2** 3. **4** 4. **1** 5. **3** 6. **5**

ANSWER ANALYSIS

4. **1** When looking at question 4, remember that each bar represents a definite quantity in percentages. Simply through inspection, it is possible to see which bars are higher and, therefore, represent the larger percentages. The bars for the Atlantic region are the highest for all three years. Answer 1 is correct.

5. **3** The search here is for the answer for which the graphs provide no evidence. We can tell that there is evidence for answer 1 from the line graph which shows that in 1988 more Americans attended church. Check the line graph at 1970 for both countries. Note that the Canadian line is higher than the American, so there is also evidence to support answer 2. From the bar graph we can see also that the decline in the rate of attendance is indeed greatest in Quebec (from 30% to 24%) so answer 4 is not the correct choice. Choice 5 is supported by evidence from the graphs; indeed, the evidence shows that the opposite of the statement would be true. As for choice 3, there is no evidence anywhere in the graphs pointing to the cause of lower church attendance so this is the correct answer.

6. **5** This question requires you to go through the reverse process from the previous one. You have to find an answer for which there is clear support in the graphs. Sometimes the information will be inaccurate and sometimes there will not be sufficient information in the graph

to support the statement. Answer 1 gives an explanation of why fewer people in the West attend church but there is no way to tell from the information on the graph whether it is true. Choices 2 and 3 are inaccurate readings of the graph. Answer 4 is an inference that is not warranted. While the proportion of the population attending church in this region may be greater, it is also the region with the smallest population, and, in fact, the smallest number of churches and synagogues. Answer 5 is correct. By inspecting the information for each region we can see that attendance was lower in all of them in 1990 than in 1985: for example, in the Atlantic region it was 36% in 1985 and 34% in 1990.

Bar graphs are used to show relationships in a set of quantities.

EXAMPLE: In a recent year, a large industrial concern used each dollar of its sales income as shown in the graph below.

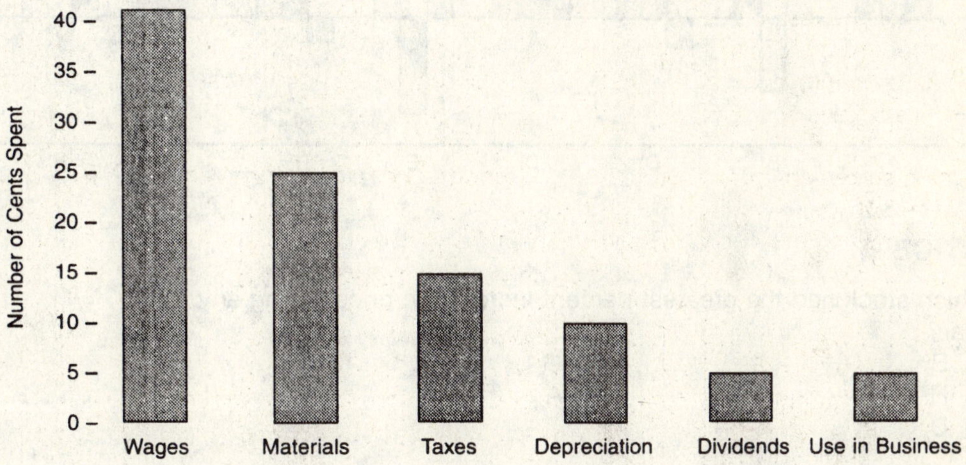

1. How many cents of each dollar of sales income did the company use to pay wages?
ANSWER: $0.40

2. How many more cents of each sales dollar were spent on wages than on materials?
ANSWER: $0.15

3. What percent of the sales dollar was spent for depreciation and dividends?
ANSWER: 15%

4. The amount of money the company paid in taxes was how many times the amount of money it paid in dividends?
ANSWER: 3 times

5. What percent of the sales dollar was spent on wages, materials, and taxes?
ANSWER: Wages, 40%
Materials, 25%
Taxes, 15%
Total, 80%

EXAMPLE:

Percent Change in Certain Stock Prices for the Years 1995–1997

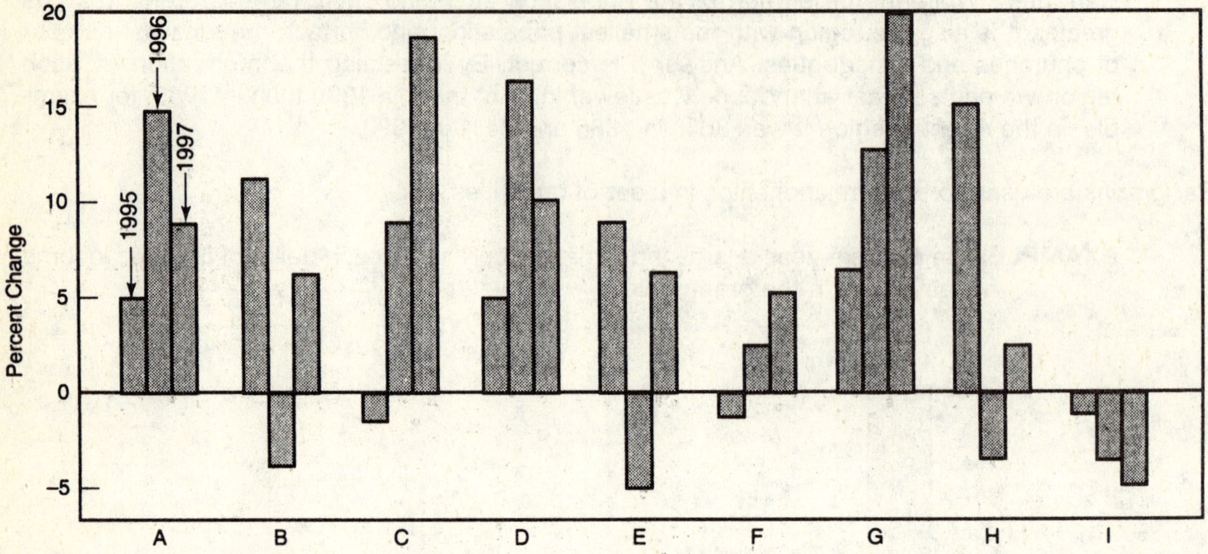

PRACTICE

1. Which stock had the greatest percent increase in price during any year?
(1) B
(2) H
(3) D
(4) G
(5) A

1. 1 2 3 4 5

2. Which of the following pairs of stocks gained in price during each of the years 1995, 1996, and 1997?
(1) H and I
(2) A and D
(3) B and E
(4) C and G
(5) F and I

2. 1 2 3 4 5

3. Which stock had the smallest average percent change in the years 1995, 1996, and 1997?
(1) I
(2) A
(3) C
(4) G
(5) H

3. 1 2 3 4 5

4. Which stock had the greatest percent decrease in price between two consecutive years?
(1) B
(2) D
(3) F
(4) H
(5) A

4. 1 2 3 4 5

ANSWERS:

1. **3** 2. **4** 3. **1** 4. **4**

Approach a bar graph as you would a line graph. The first question is, What exactly is represented by each bar? This will be indicated for each bar. Then you should ask yourself, What is the quantitative value of each bar? The longer the bar, the greater is the value. The value is read against the scale.

EXAMPLE: The bar graphs show the percentages by volume of the sediment sizes that are found in four different sediment deposits, A, B, C, and D.

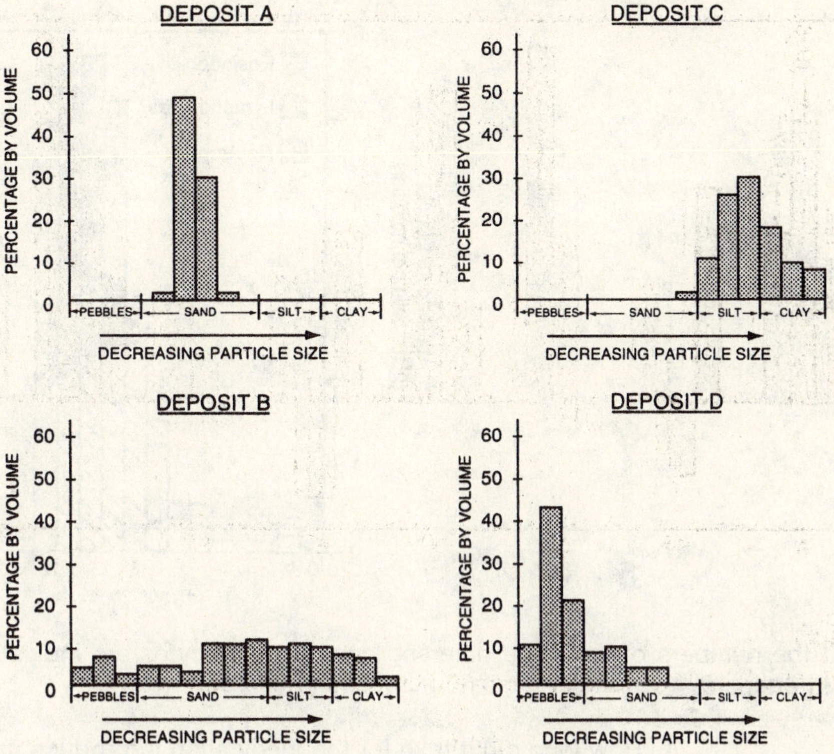

1. What is the total percentage of silt in deposit B?
(1) 5%
(2) 9%
(3) 27%
(4) 48%
(5) 54%

In deposit B there are three bars representing silt. Each deposit is 10% or slightly less. Adding the three deposits of silt together produces a total of a little less than 30%.

2. What was the most probable agent of erosion that deposited the unsorted sediments in deposit B?
(1) a stream
(2) a glacier
(3) wind
(4) ocean waves
(5) a river

Glaciers carry a wide range of particle sizes. When the ice melts, this mixture of materials is deposited. The deposit will contain a wide range of particle sizes that reflects the mixture of material carried by the glacier.

3. Which deposit or deposits contain the highest percentage of sediments that would stay in suspension for the longest time before settling?
(1) deposit A
(2) deposit B
(3) deposit C
(4) deposit C
(5) deposits A or B

Smaller particles will tend to remain in suspension for longer periods of time. Deposit C contains mostly silt and clay, which are the smallest particles. The materials in deposit C will therefore tend to remain in suspension for the longest period of time.

EXAMPLE: The graph below represents the counts of three kinds of leukocytes (white blood cells) in an animal that was administered a standard dose of a drug starting on day 4.

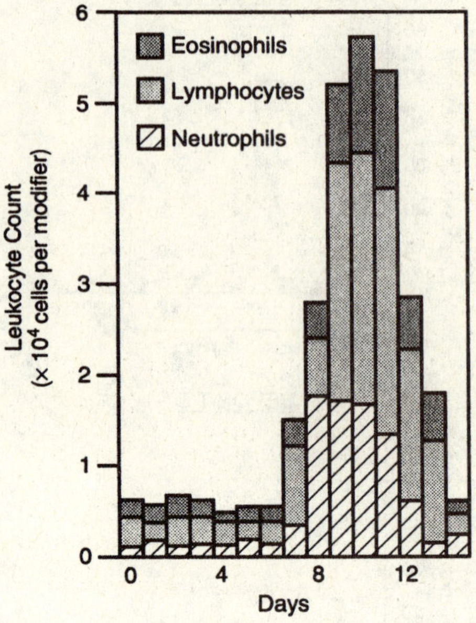

Note that the numbers of the three different kinds of leukocytes are indicated by using different patterns in the bars.

1. How long did it take for the medication to produce its maximum effect?
(1) 4 days
(2) 7 days
(3) 10 days
(4) 12 days
(5) 14 days

The peak of leukocyte production was reached on day 10, after starting on day 4—a total of 7 days. The correct answer is choice 2.

2. How did the relative amounts of the three different kinds of leukocytes react to the medication?
(1) All three increased in roughly the same proportion.
(2) The neutrophils increased proportionally more than the others.
(3) The eosinophils increased proportionally more than the others.
(4) There was proportionally less increase in the eosinophils.
(5) There was proportionally less increase in the lymphocytes.

At the peak, the ratios were about 1/4 neutrophils and 1/5 eosinophils, which were not much different from the starting ratios. The answer is choice 1.

3. What do the data suggest as to the potential usefulness of this drug?
(1) It might be used to produce an increase in the leukocyte count in someone suffering from a long-time shortage of leukocytes.
(2) It is completely useless because the improvement is temporary.
(3) It is too dangerous because the increase in the leukocyte count is so great.
(4) It might be useful in producing a large, temporary increase in the availability of leukocytes.
(5) It is dangerous because, after the effect wears off, the leukocyte count is extremely low.

If there is some condition, perhaps a systemic infection, in which the body has a sudden demand for an exceptionally large, temporary supply of leukocytes, this drug might be useful. The answer is choice 4.

4. What is the probable reason that the drug was administered from day 4 instead of at the very start of the experiment?
(1) This was done to allow the animal to become used to its cage and other conditions of its surroundings.
(2) This might have been done because the drug was not available for the first 3 days.
(3) This was necessary to allow the leukocyte count to rise to normal levels before beginning the experiment.
(4) This had to be done to allow the experimenter to determine the correct dosage.
(5) This was a control to establish the pattern of leukocyte count before the drug was given.

Before beginning the experiment, the scientist had to make sure that any changes in the leukocyte count were the result of the medication, and not something else. The answer is choice 5.

PICTOGRAPHS

A *pictograph* is a graph in which objects are used to represent numbers.

EXAMPLE:

Population of Various Cities

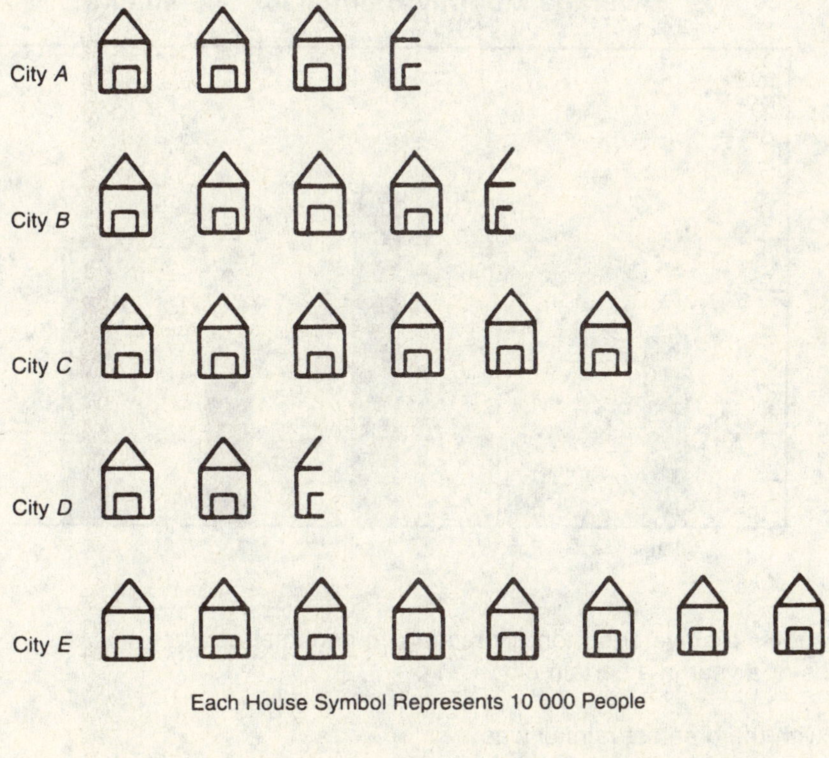

Each House Symbol Represents 10 000 People

1. Which city has the largest population:
ANSWER: City E

2. By how many people does the population of the largest city exceed the population of the next largest city?
ANSWER: City E has 80 000 people.
City C has 60 000 people.
City E has 20 000 people more than City C.

3. What is the ratio of the population of City B to City C?
ANSWER: City B has a population of 45 000.
City C has a population of 60 000.
Ratio is 45 000:60 000.
This ratio can be simplified to 3:4.

4. If City D's population is increased by 40%, what will its population be?
ANSWER: City D has a population of 25 000. If the population is increased by 40%, we have $25000 \times 0.4 = 10000$ more people.
City D's population will become 35 000.

PRACTICE

Directions: **Blacken the space at the right under the number that corresponds to the one you have selected as the correct answer.**

Questions 1–3 refer to the following bar graph.

Average Monthly Rainfall for Six Months

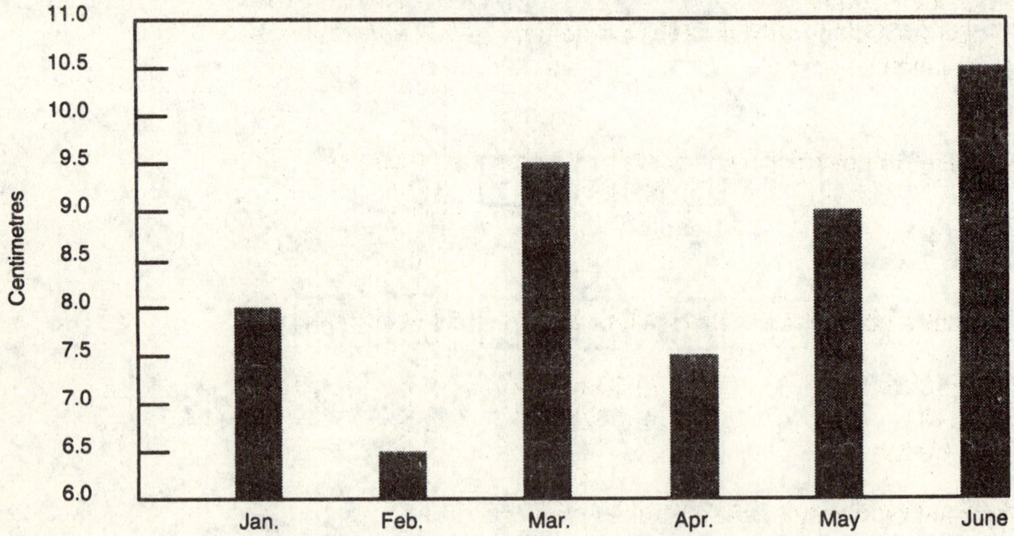

This bar graph shows the average monthly rainfall, in centimetres, for the first 6 months of a year in a certain city.

1. The month with the greatest rainfall was
(1) February
(2) March
(3) May
(4) June
(5) January

1. 1 2 3 4 5
|| || || || ||

2. The total rainfall for the 6 months was
(1) 25.5 cm
(2) 48 cm
(3) 49.5 cm
(4) 51 cm
(5) 46 cm

2. 1 2 3 4 5

3. The average monthly rainfall for the 6-month period was
(1) 8 cm
(2) 8.5 cm
(3) 306 cm
(4) 6.75 cm
(5) 310 cm

3. 1 2 3 4 5

Questions 4–7 refer to the following graph.

How the Taxes Were Spent

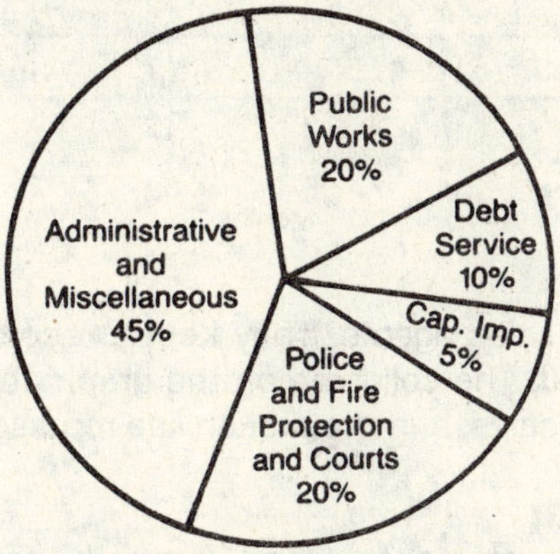

In a large city, the breakdown of the $30 000 000 raised by means of real estate taxes for all purposes, except schools, is shown in the graph. To raise this sum, the tax rate was set at $21.95 per $1000 of assessed valuation.

4. The angle at the center for the public works sector measures
(1) 90°
(2) 72°
(3) 100°
(4) 80°
(5) 75°

4. 1 2 3 4 5

5. Mr. Mitchell's home is assessed at $18 000. His real estate tax bill is
(1) $385.10
(2) $394.10
(3) $3951.00
(4) $395.10
(5) $375.00

5. 1 2 3 4 5

6. The amount of money spent for public works is
(1) $5 000 000
(2) $1 500 000
(3) $6 000 000
(4) $3 000 000
(5) $2 500 000

6. 1 2 3 4 5

7. The ratio of money spent for administrative and miscellaneous to the money spent for public works is
(1) 9:4
(2) 4:9
(3) 9:5
(4) 5:9
(5) 2:1

7. 1 2 3 4 5

Questions 8–10 refer to the following graph.

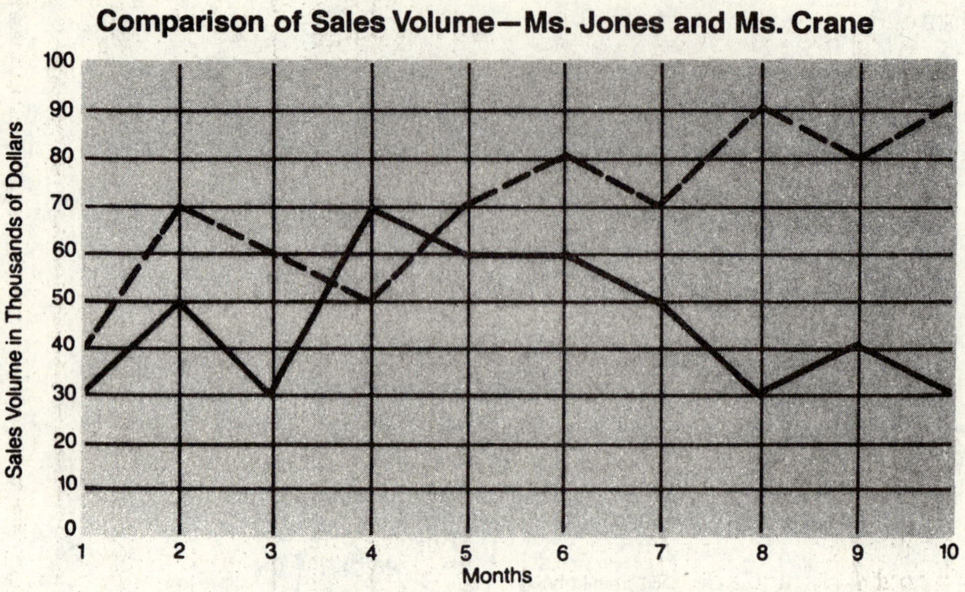

Ms. Jones and Ms. Crane are sales agents. They kept a record of their sales over a 10-month period. The solid line on the graph above represents Ms. Jones's volume of sales, and the broken line represents Ms. Crane's volume of sales.

8. Ms. Jones's greatest sales volume for the 10-month period occurred on the month numbered

(1) 3
(2) 4
(3) 7
(4) 6
(5) 9

8. 1 2 3 4 5
|| || || || ||

9. How much greater volume was Ms. Crane's best month over Ms. Jones's best month? (in thousands of dollars)

(1) 10
(2) 30
(3) 50
(4) 90
(5) 20

9. 1 2 3 4 5
|| || || || ||

10. How much greater was Ms. Crane's average for the 10 months than Ms. Jones's average for this period? (in thousands)

(1) 44
(2) 70
(3) 25
(4) 36
(5) 16

10. 1 2 3 4 5
|| || || || ||

Questions 11–13 refer to the following pictograph.

The Blue Jays professional baseball team opens its season at the beginning of May and closes its season at the end of September. The pictograph below shows the average attendance for each month of the 1987 season. Each ⚾ represents an attendance of 4000 fans.

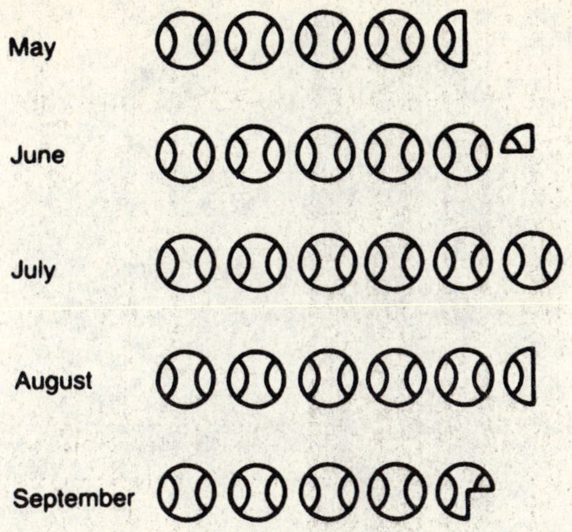

11. What was the average attendance in May?
(1) 4500
(2) 16000
(3) 18000
(4) 19000
(5) 22000

11. 1 2 3 4 5
|| || || || ||

12. What was the average attendance in September?
(1) 16000
(2) 18000
(3) 18500
(4) 19000
(5) 23000

12. 1 2 3 4 5
|| || || || ||

13. By how many fans did the August attendance exceed the June attendance?
(1) 250
(2) 500
(3) 750
(4) 800
(5) 1000

13. 1 2 3 4 5
|| || || || ||

ANSWERS:

1. **4**	5. **4**	9. **5**	13. **5**
2. **4**	6. **3**	10. **3**	
3. **2**	7. **1**	11. **3**	
4. **2**	8. **2**	12. **4**	

CIRCLE GRAPHS OR PIE CHARTS

These are circular graphs, in which the circle is divided into sectors. They are used when the important information is the fraction of the total that applies to each part. Each sector is a proportional part of the whole. The first thing to notice on a pie chart is the labels, which indicate what each sector represents. Next, look carefully at the proportional sizes of the sectors to get some idea of which are largest and which smallest. Recall that a complete revolution is divided in 360°. Thus, if we wish to mark off one-quarter of the circle, the angle at the centre must be $^1/_4 \times 360°$, or 90°. For the same reason, a part of the circle with an angle at the centre of 60° will be $^{80}/_{360}$, or $^1/_6$ of the circle.

EXAMPLE: The following chart indicates the cost of the electricity, in thousands of dollars per year, used in each of the various functions in a factory.

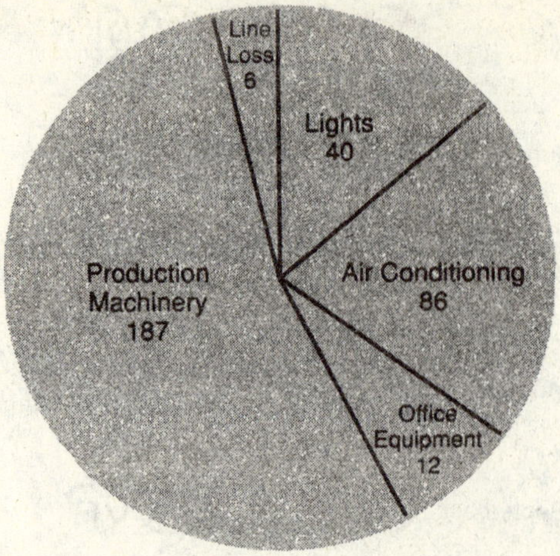

Note at once that production is the biggest part, over half, with all the other functions costing less.

1. What part of the total cost for electricity is used in the production machinery?
(1) 25%
(2) 40%
(3) 53%
(4) 66%
(5) 75%

The sector for production machinery is a little over half, so the answer is choice 3.

2. If an engineer found a way to air condition the place for $35 000 a year, how would next year's pie chart be different?
(1) The whole circle would be smaller.
(2) The sector for air-conditioning would be smaller, but the rest would be unchanged.
(3) The chart would look the same, but the number in the air conditioning sector would be 35, not 86.
(4) The number in the air-conditioning sector would be 35, and all the other numbers would be larger.
(5) All the other sectors would be larger, but only the number in the air-conditioning sector would change.

The size of each sector represents the fraction of the total cost that it represents. If nothing changed but the cost of air-conditioning, each of the other sectors would be a larger fraction of the (smaller) total. The answer is choice 5. Choice 1 is wrong because the size of the circle indicates nothing. Choice 2 is wrong because it is not possible to shrink one part without enlarging the others; the total must be 360°. Choice 3 is wrong because the air conditioning would now be a smaller part of the total. Choice 4 is wrong because nothing would have happened to change the amounts of electricity used by other parts of the system.

The circle graph can also help you to compare visually two sets of facts. Here is a pair of circle graphs.

EXAMPLE:

Canadian International Trade, 1991
(in millions of dollars)

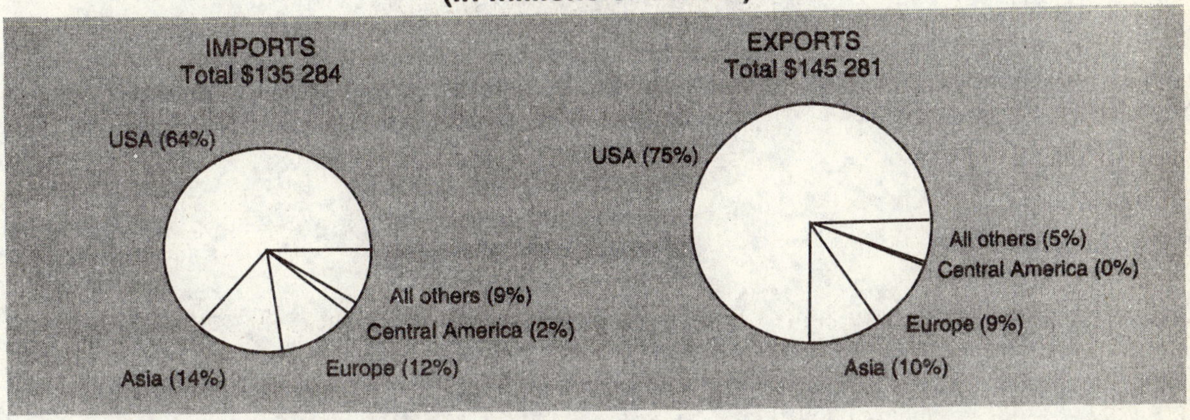

Note the title—"Canadian International Trade, 1991."
Note the unit used—millions of dollars.
Note the titles of the two circle graphs—"Imports" and "Exports."
Note the total number of millions of dollars imported and exported—$135 284 million imports, and $145 281 million exports. Note that while similar in size, the two circles are not exactly the same size, reflecting the difference in the dollar values of all imports and all exports.

Now, study both graphs carefully and answer the following questions.

QUESTIONS

1. Which country is Canada's most important trading partner?
2. Which regions contribute a greater proportion of Canada's imports than they receive from Canada as a proportion of exports?
3. Which one of the trading regions listed has the largest percentage trade deficit with Canada?

ANSWER KEY

1. The U.S.A., which in 1991 received 75.4% of all of Canada's exports and contributed 63.7% of all of Canada's imports, is by far its most important trading partner.
2. Everywhere except the U.S.A. All of these regions had a trading surplus with Canada in 1991.
3. The U.S.A. was the only one of the trading partners shown that experienced a trade deficit with Canada in 1991.

FORMULA GRAPHS

In working with a formula we may have occasion to obtain a number of bits of information. Instead of using the formula each time it may be easier to work from a graph of the formula (*formula graph*).

In most of the developed world except the United States and in all scientific work, the scale used to measure temperature is the Celsius scale. In the United States, the Fahrenheit scale is still used but mention is frequently made of the Celsius scale. We sometimes find it necessary to convert from one scale to the other. The following graph shows how the scales are related.

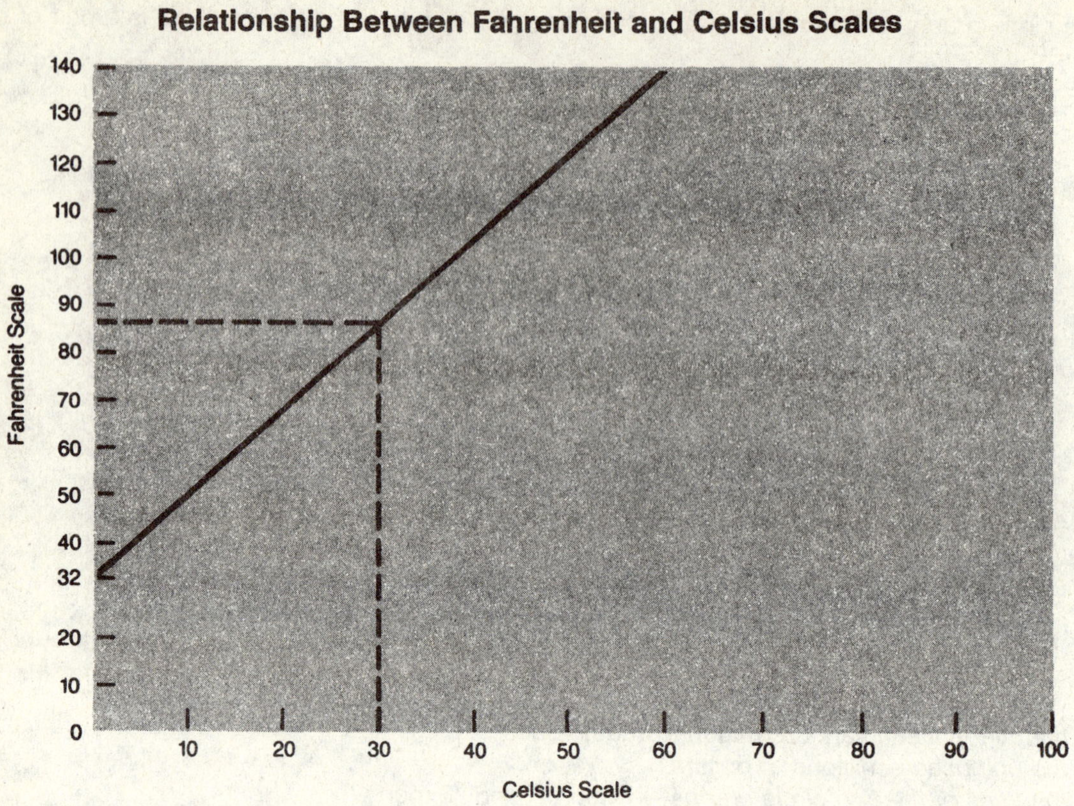

1. A weather report in Paris indicated that the temperature was 30° Celsius. What was the corresponding Fahrenheit temperature?

ANSWER: Locate 30° on the Celsius scale (the horizontal scale). At this point draw a line so that it is perpendicular to the Celsius scale line (as shown in the diagram). You can read the corresponding Fahrenheit temperature by drawing a line perpendicular to the Fahrenheit scale line from the point where the first line cuts the graph. The answer is 86°.

2. What Celsius reading corresponds to a Fahrenheit reading of 77?

ANSWER: 25°

3. During one day the temperature rose from 41° to 68° Fahrenheit. What was the corresponding rise in the temperature on the Celsius scale?

ANSWER: The Celsius temperature rose from 5° to 20°.

TABLES

What is a table? It is an arrangement of figures, usually in one or more columns, which is intended to show some relationship between the figures. In political science, a table may show the growth of the number of eligible voters in national elections. In economics, a table may show the annual income of various groups within the population of a country. A table may also show the relationship between two factors, for example, between the amount of education of various groups as related to their annual income.

Just how do you read a table? First you read the title of the table to determine just what figures are being presented. The title is usually at the top of the column or columns of figures. Let us use the following table as a typical illustration.

EXAMPLE:

CANADIAN IMMIGRANTS, 1981 AND 1991 BY PLACE OF BIRTH

	1981		1991	
	NUMBER	%	NUMBER	%
Europe	44784	34.8	46651	20.2
Great Britain	18912	14.7	6383	2.8
Portugal	3292	2.6	5837	2.5
France	1681	1.3	2619	1.1
Greece	924	0.7	618	0.3
Italy	2057	1.6	775	0.3
Poland	4093	3.2	15737	6.8
Other	13825	10.7	14682	6.4
Africa	5901	4.6	16530	7.2
Asia	50759	39.5	122228	53.0
Philippines	5978	4.6	12626	5.5
India	9415	7.3	14248	6.2
Hong Kong	4039	3.1	16425	7.1
China	9798	7.6	20621	8.9
The Middle East	5409	4.2	24497	10.6
Other	16120	12.5	33811	14.7
North and Central America	10183	7.9	18899	8.2
United States	8695	6.8	5270	2.3
Other	1488	1.2	13629	5.9
The Caribbean and Bermuda	8797	6.8	13046	5.7
Australasia	1020	0.8	735	0.3
South America	6114	4.8	10468	4.5
Oceania	1024	0.8	2213	1.0
Other	36	—	11	—
Total	128618	100.0	230781	100.0

First note the title of the table. This one is entitled:

"Canadian Immigrants, 1981 and 1991, by place of birth."

Now, look at the headings of each column of the columns in the table,

There are two *major headings*: 1981 and 1991. The information under 1981 gives information about that year; the information under 1991 gives information about that year.

Under each of the major headings there are two *sub-headings*: number and percentage (%). Number gives the exact number of immigrants to Canada from a given area in 1981 and in 1991; % gives the percentage of total immigrants in 1981 and 1991 from each of the identified countries.

Next, locate the rows to which the columns are related. In this case there are nine major areas of the world (Europe, Africa, Asia, North and Central America, The Caribbean and Bermuda, Australasia, South America, Oceania, and Other). Some individual countries are also given. Each row gives the number of immigrants and the percentage of the total coming to Canada from that country or region in 1981 and 1991.

Having identified the title, the column headings, and the rows that make up points of reference, you are now in a position to *locate facts*. See if you can locate the following facts.

QUESTIONS ON LOCATING FACTS

1. How many immigrants came from Poland in 1981?
2. Which country of birth produced the most immigrants to Canada in 1981?
3. What was the total number of immigrants in 1991?
4. What percentage of 1991 immigrants came from India?
5. Which country accounted for 6.8% of immigration in 1981 and 2.3% in 1991?

ANSWER KEY

1. 4093
2. Great Britain
3. 230781
4. 6.2%
5. United States

ANSWER ANALYSIS

1. Question 1 asks for the number of immigrants from Poland in 1981. Go to the major heading indicating 1981 and locate under that the sub-heading "number," which gives you the number of immigrants from various countries and regions in 1981. Put your finger on the top of that column and run it down the column until it is opposite Poland—4093.
2. Question 2 asks which country of birth produced the most immigrants to Canada in 1981. Locate the column that shows the number of immigrants in 1981. Run your finger down the column trying to identify the largest number. The largest number is 50759 for Asia, but Asia is a continent and the question asked for a country. The largest number for a country is 18912, indicating Great Britain.
3. Question 3 asks for the total number of immigrants in 1991. Totals are given in the bottom row. Run your finger across the totals row until you reach the number for 1991—230781.
4. Question 4 puts the focus on percentages rather than numbers. Find the percentage column under 1991 and run down the column until you are opposite the row for India—6.2%.
5. This question requires information from two columns in order to answer. First locate the country that accounted for 6.8% of immigration in 1981. Did it also account for 2.3% of immigration in 1991? If it did then this is the correct response—the United States.

QUESTIONS ON FINDING RELATIONSHIPS BETWEEN FACTS

1. Which of the European countries listed show a decrease in the number of immigrants to Canada between 1981 and 1991?
2. Which country shows the largest increase in the number of immigrants between 1981 and 1991?
3. Which country shows the greatest drop in the number of immigrants?
4. Which continent accounted for more than 50% of immigration to Canada in 1991?

ANSWER KEY

1. Great Britain, Greece, and Italy
2. China
3. Great Britain
4. Asia

ANSWER ANALYSIS

1. This question asks for a comparison of information about European countries from the columns that give numbers for 1981 and 1991. There are three countries for which the numbers for 1991 are smaller than for 1981—Great Britain, Greece, and Italy.

2. This question asks you to identify which countries increased their number of immigrants into Canada between 1981 and 1991 AND then to identify which one of those had the largest increase. Both Poland and China had large increases; Poland's is larger.
3. This question asks you to do the same as question 2 but this time you have to identify the country that had the largest drop in immigration into Canada—Great Britain.
4. This question asks you to compare the numbers of immigrants from the different continents in 1991 with the total number of immigrants. Since the total number of immigrants in 1991 was 230781, a continent accounting for more than 50% of total immigration would have to have provided more than 115391 immigrants. Looking down the numbers column for 1991, we find that only Asia can be the correct response.

Summary of How to Read a Table

1. Note the title.
2. Look at the column headings.
3. Locate the column to which the other columns are related.
4. Locate facts.
5. Find relationships between facts.
6. Infer conclusions from the facts presented.

EXAMPLE: The following table gives the atomic numbers and average atomic weights of the commonest elements in the earth's crust. The atomic number is the number of protons in the atom.

ELEMENT	ATOMIC NUMBER	ATOMIC WEIGHT (DALTONS)
aluminum	13	27.0
calcium	20	40.1
carbon	6	12.0
iron	26	55.8
magnesium	12	24.3
oxygen	8	16.0
potassium	13	39.1
silicon	14	28.1
sodium	11	23.0

1. How many protons are there in a molecule of magnesium oxide (MgO)?
   (1) 4
   (2) 8
   (3) 12
   (4) 16
   (5) 20

Just add the 12 in magnesium to the 8 in oxygen; the answer is choice 5.

2. Which of the following groups is arranged in order of increasing atomic weight?
   (1) calcium, iron, potassium
   (2) carbon, oxygen, silicon
   (3) aluminum, carbon, magnesium
   (4) iron, silicon, sodium
   (5) oxygen, calcium, silicon

Choice 2 gives carbon, at 12.0 daltons (D); oxygen, at 16.0 D; and silicon at 28.1 D, and is the answer.

MAPS

A map is a visual representation of all or part of the surface of the earth. This map may or may not include a number of clues to help us visualize the surface it is depicting. It will always include a *title*. If the map uses symbols, it will always include a *legend* (or key) to give the meaning of those symbols. It may also include

—latitude and longitude to indicate direction and help you to find a specific location;
—a scale of kilometres (miles) to indicate what distance on the map equals a specific distance in kilometres or miles on land;
—a grid, or square, usually identified by a set of letters on one axis (vertical or horizontal) and a set of numbers on the other (so that a place can be found in, for example, a grid identified as F3 or H7);
—relief or differences in height of land shown by lines.

The two important clues that you must learn to use in order to read a map are its *title* and its *legend* (or key). Let us look at a map which is in many respects typical of the maps you will encounter. These questions will sharpen your skills in map reading.

QUESTIONS

1. What is the title of the map?
2. What four indicators make up the legend (or key)?
3. What does the figure in ( ) mean?
4. What is the per capita gross domestic product in Ontario?

EXAMPLE:

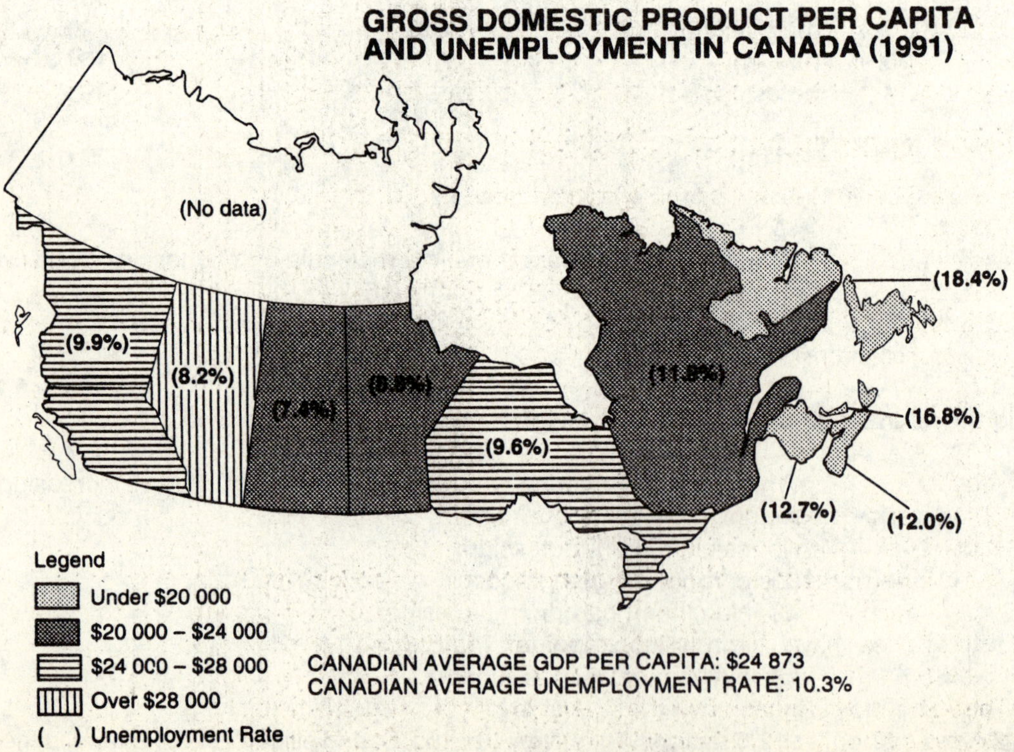

5. What is the per capita gross domestic product in Alberta?
6. Which province has the larger per capita gross domestic product, Quebec or Ontario?
7. Does this information refer to today?

Note:

In order to answer these questions, you will need to be able to correctly locate each of the provinces. If you cannot do this, make sure that you consult an appropriate atlas.

ANSWER KEY AND ANALYSIS

1. The title of the map is "Gross Domestic Product Per Capita (dollars) and Unemployment in Canada (1991)." See the heading above the map.
2. The four indicators are patterns of shading showing different levels of per capita Gross Domestic Product (GDP). See below and left of the map. Sometimes the word "legend" will be left out.
3. The figures in ( ) are unemployment rates. This is also included as part of the legend. Sometimes an explanation will not be included in the legend. It will be left to you to recognize that, in this case, the dollar amounts refer to GDP and percentages refer to unemployment.
4. By comparing the pattern of shading for Ontario on the map with the patterns in the legend, we can see that its GDP per capita is between $24 000 and $28 000.
5. Similarly, by comparing the patterns on the map with those in the legend, we can see that Alberta's per capita GDP is over $28 000.
6. Since the pattern of shading indicates that Ontario has a per capita GDP between $24 000 and $28 000, and that the corresponding figure for Quebec is between $20 000 and $24 000, Ontario has a higher per capita GDP than Quebec.
7. No! Read the title carefully. Note that the information is identified as referring to 1991.

This map is a little more complicated than most that you will be asked to interpret in that it shows information on two topics: per capita GDP and unemployment rates. Some of the questions below ask you to consider both of them.

ADDITIONAL QUESTIONS

1. Per capita GDP in British Columbia is most nearly equal to
   (1) Alberta
   (2) Ontario
   (3) Manitoba
   (4) Quebec
   (5) Newfoundland and Labrador

1. 1 2 3 4 5
|| || || || ||

2. Which generalization is best supported by the map?
   (1) All of the Atlantic provinces have per capita GDP's over $20 000.
   (2) Ontario and British Columbia have the highest levels of productivity in the country.
   (3) The Western provinces have the highest levels of productivity in the country.
   (4) The Prairies have the lowest levels of productivity in the country.
   (5) The Atlantic provinces have the lowest levels of productivity in the country.

2. 1 2 3 4 5
|| || || || ||

3. The lowest unemployment rates are found in
(1) the Atlantic region
(2) Quebec
(3) Ontario
(4) the Prairies
(5) British Columbia

3. 1 2 3 4 5

4. Low world demand for wheat would contribute to unemployment mainly in
(1) the Atlantic region
(2) Quebec
(3) Ontario
(4) the Prairies
(5) British Columbia

4. 1 2 3 4 5

5. Which province has both a per capita GDP of under $20 000 and an unemployment rate of 12.7%?
(1) New Brunswick
(2) Alberta
(3) Ontario
(4) Quebec
(5) Prince Edward Island

5. 1 2 3 4 5

6. Unemployment is less of a problem in Quebec than it is in
(1) British Columbia
(2) Saskatchewan
(3) Manitoba
(4) Ontario
(5) Prince Edward Island

6. 1 2 3 4 5

7. Which conclusion concerning the province of Saskatchewan is best supported by the map?
(1) It is larger than Nova Scotia and has higher productivity than Alberta.
(2) It has less unemployment than British Columbia and has higher productivity than Nova Scotia.
(3) It has productivity similar to Quebec and has higher unemployment than Alberta.
(4) It has lower unemployment than Prince Edward Island and is smaller than New Brunswick.
(5) It is smaller than Ontario and has lower productivity than Quebec.

7. 1 2 3 4 5

8. The two adjacent provinces that show the greatest contrast in unemployment are
(1) British Columbia and Alberta
(2) Newfoundland and Quebec
(3) Manitoba and Ontario
(4) Saskatchewan and Quebec
(5) Prince Edward Island and New Brunswick

8. 1 2 3 4 5

ANSWER KEY

1. **2** 2. **5** 3. **4** 4. **4** 5. **1** 6. **5** 7. **2** 8. **5**

ANSWER ANALYSIS

1. **2** The correct answer is choice 2 since Ontario is the only choice listed that shows the same pattern of shading on the map. Both British Columbia and Ontario have per capita GDPs between \$24 000 and \$28 000.
2. **5** This question requires you to know that the Atlantic provinces comprise Newfoundland and Labrador, Prince Edward Island, Nova Scotia, and New Brunswick, and to observe from the map that the per capita GDP in all of them is lower than any other part of the country.
3. **4** This question requires you to know that the Prairies consist of Alberta, Saskatchewan, and Manitoba, and to observe from the map that their unemployment rates are lower than any other region.
4. **4** You need to know here that the Prairie provinces are the country's major wheat producers and would, therefore, be most affected by a low world demand for their product.
5. **1** This question requires you to locate those provinces that have a per capita GDP of under \$20 000. By comparing the shading patterns on the map with the legend, we can see that only the four Atlantic provinces are possible responses. Of these possibilities, only New Brunswick meets the second requirement of an unemployment rate of 12.7%.
6. **5** This requires you to interpret the question correctly so that you are searching for a province that has a higher unemployment rate than Quebec. Of those listed, only Prince Edward Island has a higher unemployment rate. Hence, unemployment is less of a problem in Quebec than it is in PEI. Choice 5 is the correct answer.
7. **2** This question requires you to use the information on the map to compare Saskatchewan with some of the other provinces in terms of their size, their per capita GDP, and their unemployment rates. You will need to work carefully through each choice to see if it meets the requirements specified in the question. Only choice 5 offers a correct statement about the province of Saskatchewan.
8. **5** Here you will need to use the unemployment figures from the map to calculate the differences in unemployment rates for the provinces listed. You may note that the largest difference is between Newfoundland and Saskatchewan but the question is asked about adjacent provinces and these two are not adjacent. Prince Edward Island and New Brunswick are the two adjacent provinces with the greatest contrast in unemployment rates.

DIAGRAMS

A diagram is not a picture; it is a conventional way of showing the relationship between parts. Some parts are inside others, or connected to others, or completely apart. When you see a diagram, the first thing to look for is the connections.

EXAMPLE: The following diagram represents the human ear. Empty spaces are shown in black.

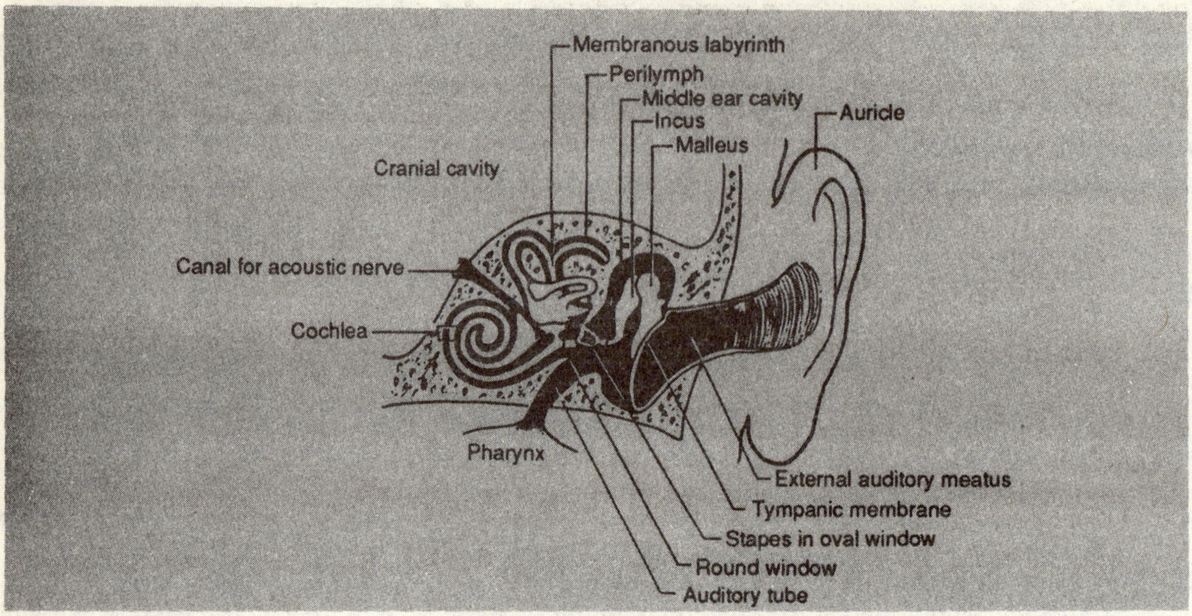

You should see at once that the external auditory meatus is a space separated from the middle ear cavity by the tympanic membrane. The middle ear cavity contains three bones.

1. The incus is inside the
(1) malleus
(2) middle ear cavity
(3) tympanic membrane
(4) round window
(5) auditory tube

The label *Incus* points to something white, a bone. The label *Middle ear cavity* leads to a black area, a cavity. The answer is choice 2.

2. For a sound wave to get from the external auditory meatus into the pharynx, it would have to go through
(1) the malleus, incus, and stapes only
(2) the tympanic membrane, malleus, and middle ear cavity only
(3) the tympanic membrane, middle ear cavity, and auditory tube only
(4) the middle ear cavity, round window, and cochlea only
(5) the tympanic membrane and auditory tube only

The path to the pharynx leads through the auditory tube, so that must be included. Since there is no way to get to the auditory tube without passing through the tympanic membrane and middle ear cavity, the answer is choice 3.

3. Ear wax is deposited in the
(1) auditory tube
(2) auricle
(3) middle ear cavity
(4) pharynx
(5) external auditory meatus

The canal from the outside through the auricle leads into the external auditory meatus, where the wax is found. The answer is choice 5.

PRACTICE IN INTERPRETING GRAPHS, TABLES, MAPS, AND DIAGRAMS

Directions: **Read each of the following questions carefully. Select the best answer. Then blacken the appropriate space in the answer column to the right.**

Questions 1–6 are based on the following map.

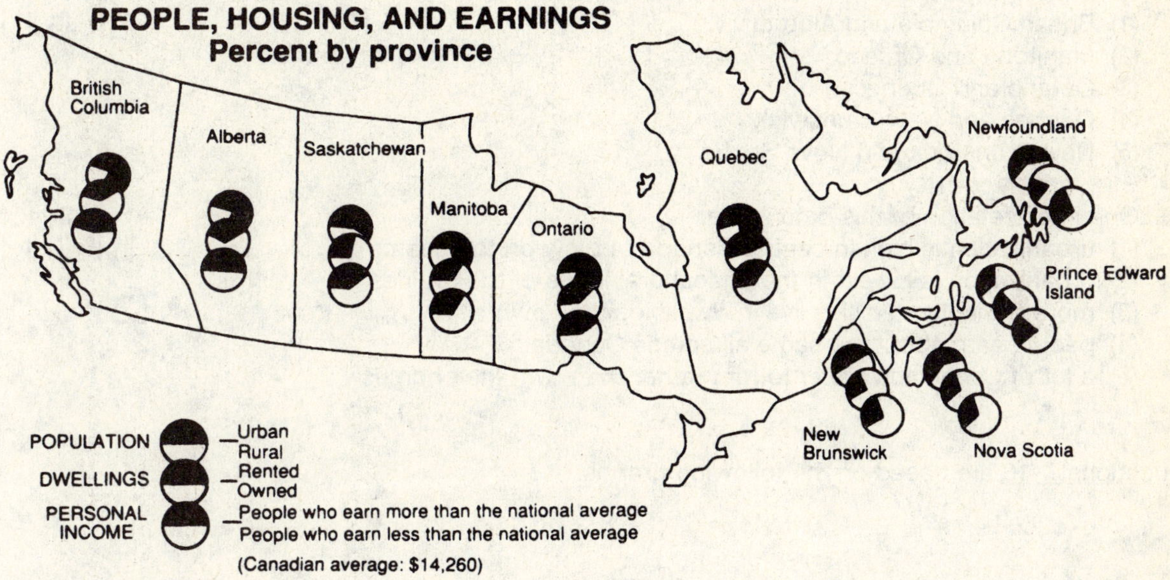

1. The LEAST urban region of Canada, not counting the Yukon and the Northwest Territories, is
(1) the Atlantic
(2) Quebec
(3) Ontario
(4) the Prairies
(5) British Columbia

1. 1 2 3 4 5

2. The province where the highest percentage of people own their own dwelling is
(1) British Columbia
(2) Saskatchewan
(3) Ontario
(4) New Brunswick
(5) Newfoundland and Labrador

2. 1 2 3 4 5

3. What is the only province where more people live in rural areas than in urban areas?
(1) Nova Scotia
(2) Prince Edward Island
(3) Manitoba
(4) Saskatchewan
(5) Alberta

3. 1 2 3 4 5

4. Which conclusion concerning Quebec is best supported by information on the map?
(1) It is more urban in character than Manitoba but less so than Ontario.
(2) More of its people earn below the national average income than in New Brunswick.
(3) It has fewer renters than any other province.
(4) It has more urban dwellers and more dwelling owners than Saskatchewan.
(5) Most of its citizens are rich property owners.

4. 1 2 3 4 5

5. Which two adjacent provinces are most urbanized?
(1) British Columbia and Alberta
(2) Manitoba and Ontario
(3) Ontario and Quebec
(4) Quebec and New Brunswick
(5) New Brunswick and Nova Scotia

5. 1 2 3 4 5

6. One interpretation of this data is that
(1) urbanization is high in central Canada but low on the coasts
(2) urbanization is lowest in the agricultural lands of the Prairies
(3) more Canadian families live in dwellings they own
(4) people earn about the same all across Canada
(5) a lot of Canadians prefer to rent rather than own their homes

6. 1 2 3 4 5

<u>Questions 7–13</u> are based on the following graphs.

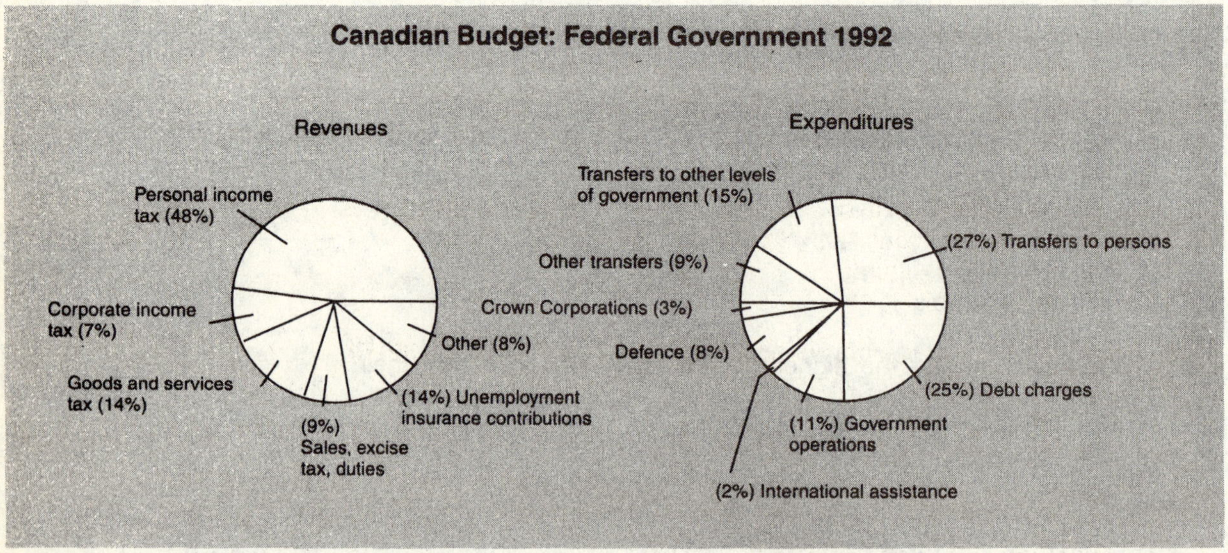

7. Forty-eight percent of the national income is derived from
(1) personal income tax
(2) personal income tax and corporation income tax
(3) corporation income tax and sales taxes
(4) corporation income tax together with sales taxes and duties
(5) other sources

7. 1 2 3 4 5

8. The largest amount of the national income is expended on
(1) transfers to persons
(2) defence
(3) government operations
(4) debt charges
(5) transfer payments to other levels of government

8. 1 2 3 4 5

9. Two areas on which an equal amount of the income is expended are
(1) transfer payments and national defence
(2) government operations and transfer payments
(3) debt charges and transfers to persons
(4) international assistance and defence
(5) crown corporations and transfers to other levels of government

9. 1 2 3 4 5

10. The percentage of income received from corporate income tax most closely equals the percentage expended for
(1) debt charges
(2) international assistance
(3) transfers of all kinds
(4) government operations
(5) defence

10. 1 2 3 4 5

11. What is the biggest source of income for the federal government?
(1) sales, excise taxes, and duties
(2) corporation income tax
(3) personal income tax
(4) the goods and services tax
(5) other sources

11. 1 2 3 4 5

12. The combined expenditure on government operations and transfers to other levels of government just about equals that of
(1) defence
(2) debt charges
(3) international assistance
(4) crown corporations
(5) all other expenditures

12. 1 2 3 4 5

13. The revenue from the goods and services tax as a percentage of the total is the same as that from
(1) personal income tax
(2) corporate income tax
(3) other
(4) sales, excise taxes, and duties
(5) unemployment insurance contributions

13. 1 2 3 4 5

Questions 14–17 are based on the following graphs.

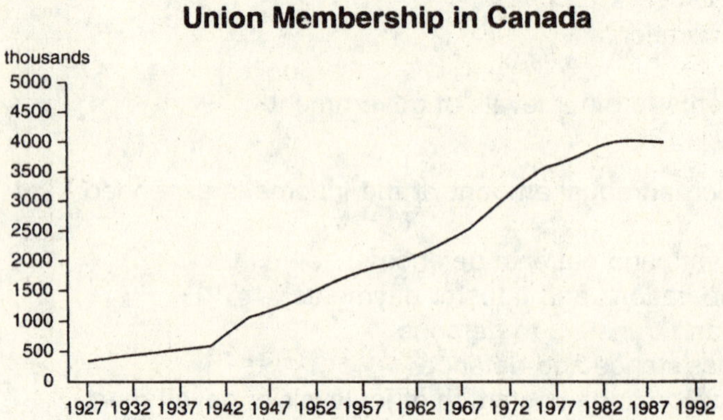

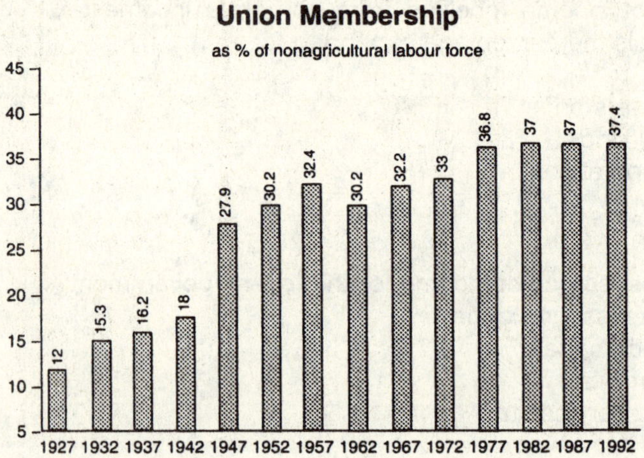

The two graphs represent (1) trends in total labour union membership and (2) union members as a percentage of the nonagricultural labour force.

14. According to the graphs, during the period 1927–1937, total union membership
(1) remained the same
(2) increased slowly
(3) increased sharply
(4) decreased sharply
(5) decreased slowly

14. 1 2 3 4 5

15. In the period covered by the graphs, the total membership in unions grew by almost
(1) one million
(2) two million
(3) two and a half million
(4) three million
(5) more than three and a half million

15. 1 2 3 4 5

16. The greatest increase in total union membership, as indicated by the graphs, occurred during the period
(1) 1932–42
(2) 1942–52
(3) 1952–62
(4) 1962–72
(5) 1982–92

16. 1 2 3 4 5

17. According to the graph, it may be concluded that the proportion of union members in the nonagricultural labor force

(1) rose sharply between 1932 and 1937
(2) decreased between 1962 and 1967
(3) in 1977 was more than triple what it had been just before the Great Depression
(4) doubled between 1957 and 1977
(5) remained stable between 1937 and 1947

17. 1 2 3 4 5

Questions 18–20 are based on the following graph.

Balance of Trade in Great Britain

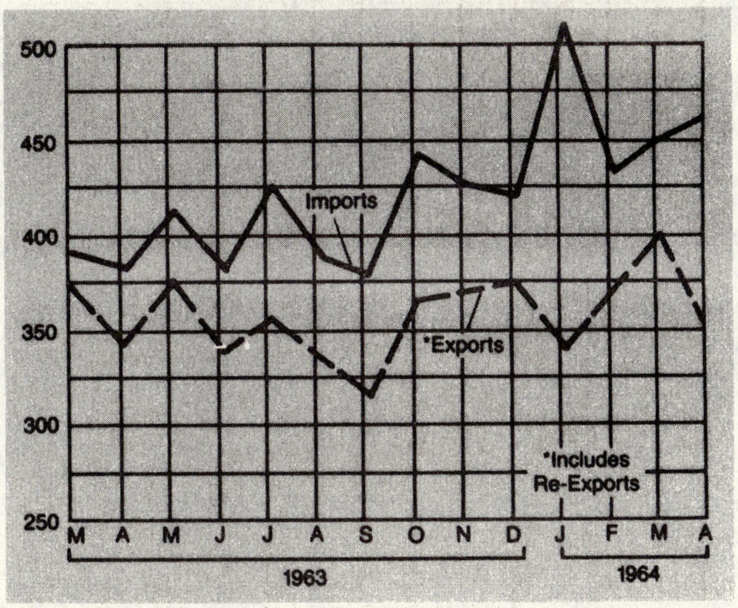

18. The graph shows that the balance of trade was LEAST favourable to Great Britain in

(1) March 1963
(2) September 1963
(3) January 1964
(4) April 1964
(5) July 1963

18. 1 2 3 4 5

19. Which conclusion can best be drawn from the graph?

(1) Great Britain is fast becoming a creditor nation.
(2) Great Britain had fewer exports than West Germany in 1963.
(3) The value of the pound sterling is rising.
(4) The trend is toward an outflow of sterling from Great Britain.
(5) The balance of payments in Great Britain is favourable.

19. 1 2 3 4 5

20. If this graph had appeared about 1700, the directors of a trading company would most likely have urged the British government to

(1) raise tariffs
(2) license foreign ships
(3) consider a laissez-faire policy
(4) encourage the colonists to industrialize at a faster pace
(5) import more

20. 1 2 3 4 5

Questions 21–24 are based on the following illustrations.

Crude oil pipelines and refineries in Canada (1973)

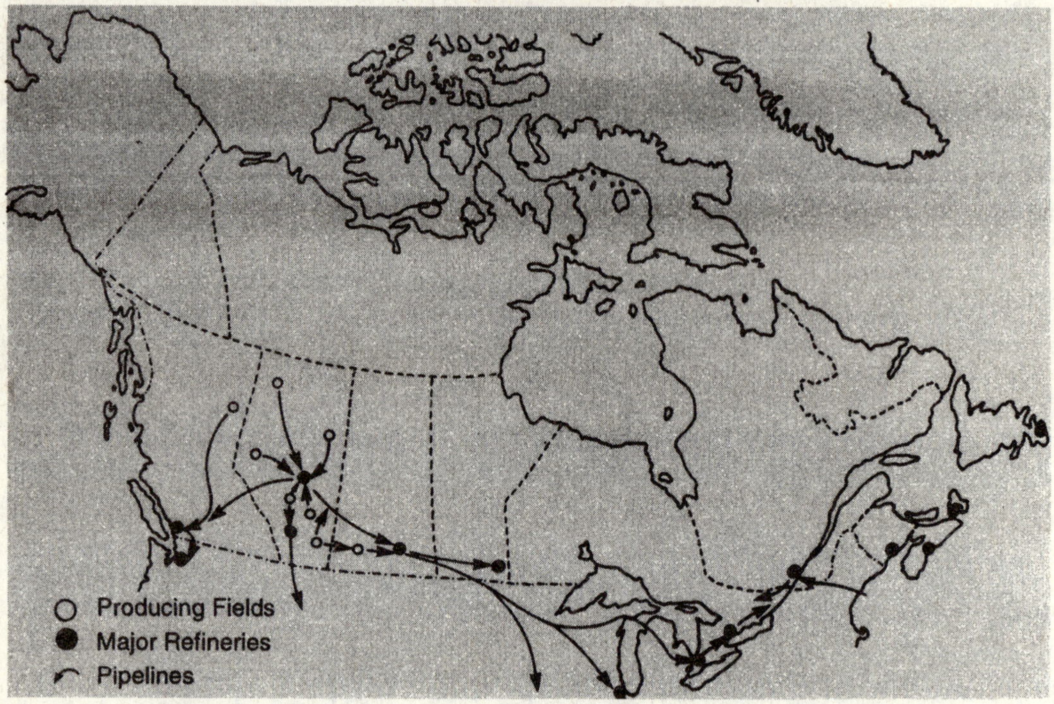

21. According to the map, the highest concentration of producing oil fields in Canada in 1973 was in

(1) British Columbia
(2) Alberta
(3) Saskatchewan
(4) Manitoba
(5) Ontario

21. 1 2 3 4 5

22. Which ONE of the following statements concerning oil produced in Alberta is NOT supported by evidence in the map?

(1) It supplied only Alberta refineries.
(2) It supplied refineries throughout Western Canada.
(3) It supplied refineries in all parts of Canada.
(4) It supplied refineries as far east as Ontario.
(5) It supplied refineries in some parts of the United States.

22. 1 2 3 4 5

23. The map shows a pipeline traveling through the state of Maine to supply refineries in

(1) Halifax
(2) Saint John
(3) Montreal
(4) Ottawa
(5) Toronto

23. 1 2 3 4 5

24. In 1973, which of the following provinces relied primarily on imported oil?
(1) New Brunswick
(2) Ontario
(3) British Columbia
(4) Manitoba
(5) Saskatchewan

24. 1 2 3 4 5

Questions 25–27 are based on the following graph.

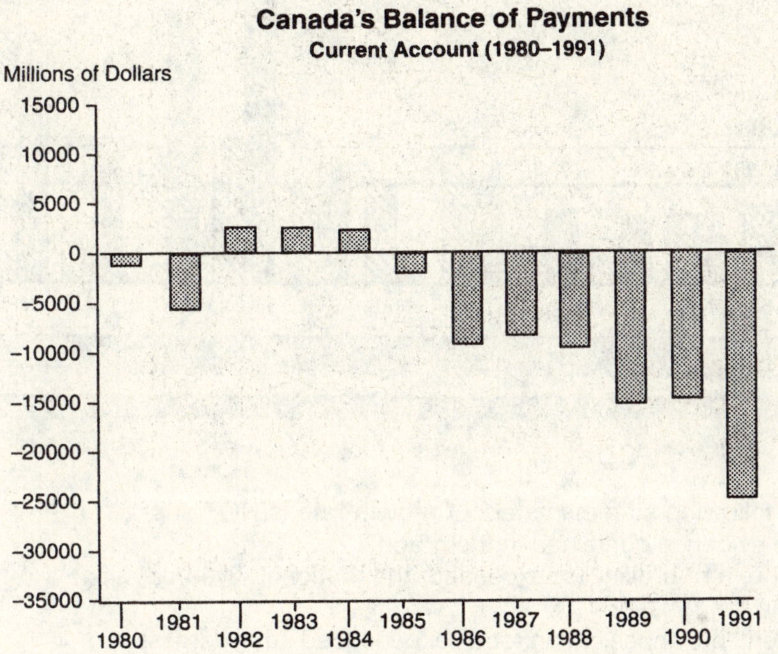

25. The graph illustrates Canada's
(1) net value of all goods and services exported and imported
(2) dollar contributions to the United Nations
(3) cost of military expenditures
(4) total dollar investments abroad
(5) net value of exports

25. 1 2 3 4 5

26. According to the graph, the year of greatest deficit in the current account balance of payments was
(1) 1980
(2) 1983
(3) 1986
(4) 1988
(5) 1991

26. 1 2 3 4 5

27. The deficits shown in the graph for 1985 to 1991 tend to decrease with an increase in
(1) unemployment in Canada
(2) aid to Third World countries
(3) Canadian tourism abroad
(4) Canadian exports
(5) Canadian imports

27. 1 2 3 4 5

Questions 28–29 are based on the following graph.

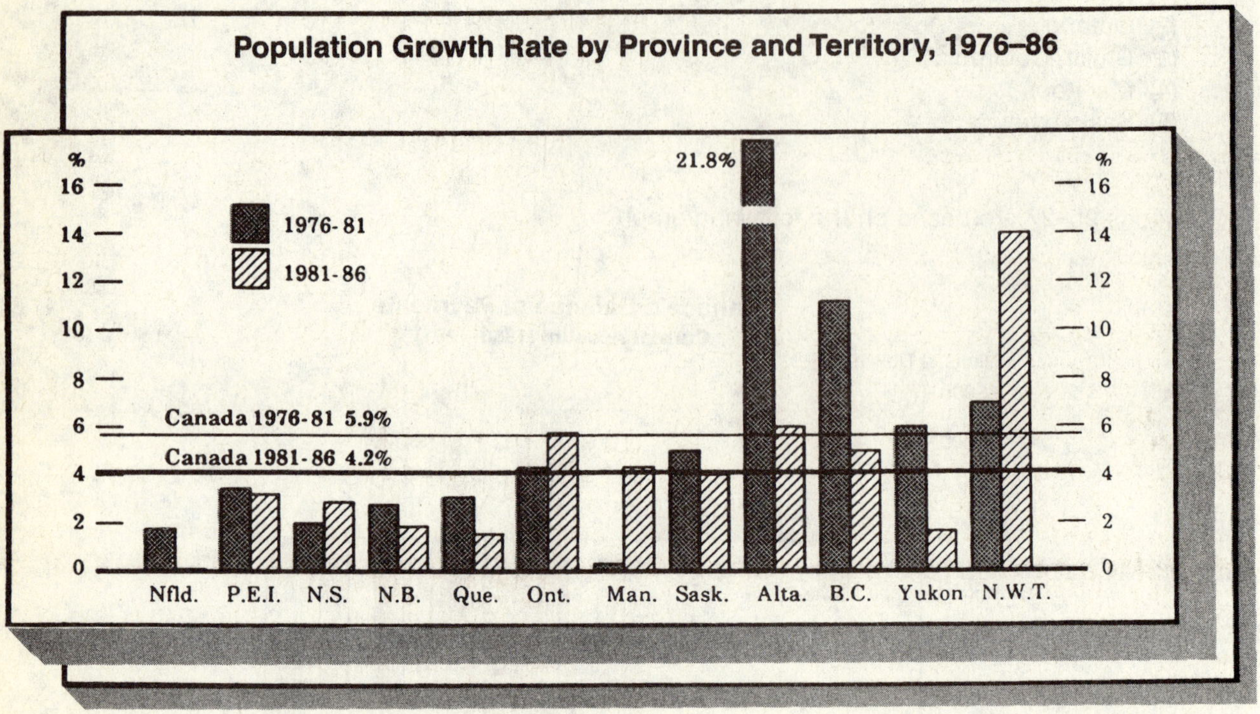

28. Which of the following statements about growth rate is NOT supported by the evidence contained in the graph?

(1) Five of the ten provinces exceeded the national five-year growth rate for 1981–86.
(2) Of the ten provinces, Manitoba experienced the largest increase in growth rate between the 1976–81 period and the 1981–86 period.
(3) Prince Edward Island, New Brunswick, and Quebec experienced a decline in growth rate between the two periods.
(4) The growth rate for 1981–86 in the Northwest Territories almost doubled the 1976–81 rate.
(5) The growth rate in all provinces west of Ontario declined in 1981–86 from 1967–81.

28. 1 2 3 4 5

29. Which statement would appear to be a future result of the trends in the graph?

(1) The Western provinces will seek to join the United States.
(2) All parts of the country will support Senate reform.
(3) The Western provinces will seek greater representation in Parliament.
(4) Quebec will become independent.
(5) The federal government will enact legislation restricting immigration into the Western provinces.

29. 1 2 3 4 5

Questions 30–33 are based on the following chart.

Number and Average Income in Constant (1985) Dollars of Census Families in Canada, 1980 and 1985

	Number of families			Average family income		
	1980	1985	Percent change	1980	1985	Percent change
Total	**6325315**	**6733845**	**6.5**	**38276**	**37827**	**–1.2**
Husband-wife families	5611495	5880550	4.8	40335	40222	–0.3
– Wife with employment income	3101375	3464815	11.7	46187	46221	0.0
– Wife without employment income	2510125	2415735	–3.8	33104	31618	–4.5
Single-parent families	713815	853300	19.5	22090	21321	–3.5
– Male single-parent	124380	151485	21.8	33261	31252	–6.0
– Female single-parent	589435	701815	19.1	19733	19177	–2.8

30. Which statement is NOT supported by information from the chart?
(1) The number of single-parent families increased by almost 20% between 1980 and 1985.
(2) Average family income declined between 1980 and 1985.
(3) Husband-wife families where the wife had no employment income had a lower family income in 1985 than in 1980.
(4) All families improved their incomes between 1980 and 1985.
(5) Single-parent families had a lower income in 1985 than in 1980.

30. 1 2 3 4 5

31. What is the most likely explanation of the higher number of single-parent families in 1985?
(1) increases in teenage pregnancy
(2) a higher divorce rate
(3) the economic recession of the early eighties
(4) increased immigration
(5) lower fertility rates

31. 1 2 3 4 5

32. From the evidence in the chart, what phrase best describes the economic status of Canadian families in 1985?
(1) It is improving slowly.
(2) It is improving rapidly.
(3) It is remaining stable.
(4) It is declining slowly.
(5) It is declining rapidly.

32. 1 2 3 4 5

33. Which of the following statements is best supported by the evidence presented in the chart?
(1) All families were improving their income position.
(2) Only two-income families were able to maintain their income level.
(3) The increase in the number of single-parent families was the result of the economic recession in the early eighties.
(4) In order to survive, families have to have two incomes.
(5) Few single-parent families are headed by a woman.

33. 1 2 3 4 5

Turn to the answer key and the answer analysis which follow.

What's Your Score?

_______ right, _______ wrong

Excellent	28–33
Good	24–27
Fair	20–23

If your score was low, you may need more review. Reread the basics on interpreting graphs (page 718), tables (page 738), maps (page 742), and diagrams (page 745), and try again.

ANSWER KEY

Practice in Interpreting Graphs, Tables, Maps, and Diagrams/Page 747

1. **1**	8. **1**	15. **5**	22. **3**	29. **2**
2. **5**	9. **3**	16. **4**	23. **3**	30. **4**
3. **2**	10. **5**	17. **3**	24. **1**	31. **2**
4. **1**	11. **3**	18. **3**	25. **1**	32. **4**
5. **3**	12. **2**	19. **4**	26. **5**	33. **2**
6. **3**	13. **5**	20. **1**	27. **4**	
7. **1**	14. **2**	21. **2**	28. **1**	

ANSWER ANALYSIS

Practice in Interpreting Graphs, Tables, Maps, and Diagrams/Page 747

1. **1** The legend shows that the urban/rural population is displayed in the uppermost of the three circles in each group. Examination of this circle for each of the Atlantic provinces shows that they have the least urban populations.
2. **5** Ownership of dwellings is displayed in the middle circle of the group. Almost 80% of Newfoundlanders own their own dwelling.
3. **2** Only for Prince Edward Island is more than half of the circle "rural."
4. **1** This is the only choice supported by information on the map. While Quebec, with an urban population of more than 75% is more urban than Manitoba, it is less urban than Ontario where the urban population is in excess of 80% of the total.
5. **3** Ontario is the most urban province and Quebec ranks second. The two of them together are more urban in character than any other two provinces.
6. **3** In all provinces, the owned/rented circle shows more than 50% owned.
7. **1** Forty-eight percent of the revenues pie is specifically designated as personal income tax.
8. **1** This is the largest item (27%). The next largest is debt charges at 25%.
9. **3** Debt charges at 25% and transfers to persons at 27% are the expenditures that are most nearly equal of those listed. International assistance (2%) and Crown Corporations (3%) are close but were not listed. This would be a much harder question if they had been listed. While the two are only 1 percentage point different in terms of total government expenditures, Crown Corporations actually receive 50% more than international assistance. (The 3% figure is reached by multiplying 2% by 1.5.)
10. **5** The amount of corporate income tax is 7%. Defence at 8% of expenditures is the closest of those listed.
11. **3** No other source of revenue exceeds 48%.
12. **2** Expenditures on government operations and transfers to other levels of government equals 26%. Debt charges amount to 25% of expenditures. None of the other choices is as close.
13. **5** Revenue from the goods and services tax is 14% of the total as is the revenue from unemployment insurance contributions.
14. **2** The black line indicating union membership rose only slightly between 1927 and 1937.
15. **5** The graph line starts at just over 250 000 in 1927 and rises to over 4 million by 1992, an increase of "more than three and a half million."

16. **4** The increase of over a million members between 1962 and 1972 is not equalled by any of the other ten year periods listed.
17. **3** Union membership in the nonagricultural labour force is indicated by the shaded bars. In 1977, the indicated percentage is 38. The bar representing membership "just before the Great Depression," which started in 1929, is the one for 1927. It indicates 12%. Membership in 1977 was "more than triple" what it was in 1927.
18. **3** An unfavourable balance of trade exists when imports are high and exports are low. This was most true in January 1964.
19. **4** Since the gap between exports and imports is widening in favour of increased imports, Britain must pay out more in sterling to pay for its imports.
20. **1** One way to cut down on imports and improve the balance is to raise tariffs, making the price of imported goods higher.
21. **2** Check the legend on the map for the symbol indicating "producing field." Refer to the map and note that six of these are found in Alberta and not more than one in any other province.
22. **3** The legend shows that an arrow line indicates a pipeline. Note that these can be traced eastward from Alberta as far as Ontario. There is no evidence on the map to show that Alberta oil is supplied to Quebec or the Atlantic region.
23. **3** This requires you to locate a relatively short pipeline running from the coast of the state of Maine to the Saint Lawrence River. The terminus is Montreal.
24. **1** Of the provinces listed, Ontario, British Columbia, Manitoba, and Saskatchewan can all receive oil from Canadian sources through the pipeline system. The map shows that New Brunswick is not connected to this system and must rely on oil supplied from overseas.
25. **1** This requires you to correctly interpret the term "Balance of Payments" as used on the graph. Note that the reference is to the "Current Account." The current account keeps track of all Canadian payments for imported goods and services and of all money received for Canadian exports of goods and services. When exports exceed imports there is a surplus or profit. When imports exceed exports, there is a deficit or loss. Losses are shown on the graph by bars below the 0 or break-even line.
26. **5** Check the bars below the 0 line. These represent deficits or losses. The largest of these is the line representing 1991.
27. **4** Losses will decrease if Canada exports more goods and services. Increased aid to other countries and more Canadians vacationing abroad will take money out of the country and worsen the balance of payments situation.
28. **1** Manitoba is one of the provinces located west of Ontario. Its growth rate increased in 1981–86 over 1976–81. So the statement that the growth rate decreased in all provinces west of Ontario cannot be sustained.
29. **2** One of the principles of democracy in Canada is "representation by population." This means that populations of approximately the same size should have the same number of representatives in Parliament. If the population in the West grows substantially, it would seem likely that it would lead to a demand for greater representation in Parliament.
30. **4** No families increased their income in the period represented by the chart.
31. **2** A very high proportion of divorces produces single-parent families. A much smaller proportion of teenage pregnancies has the same result. The other choices are simply not related to the number of single-parent families.
32. **4** No family incomes showed an improvement over this period. Most were in a slow decline.
33. **2** All families had lower incomes in the second period except for two-income families which reported no change.

11

TWO PRACTICE EXAMINATIONS

PRACTICE EXAMINATION ONE

This examination contains five sub-tests: Writing Skills (Part I), Writing Skills (Part II), Social Studies, Science, Interpreting Literature and the Arts, and Mathematics.

ANSWER KEYS, SUMMARIES OF RESULTS, AND SELF-APPRAISAL CHARTS

For each of the five tests, you will find an answer key to score yourself. You can summarize your results and locate where you made errors.

ANSWER ANALYSIS

Each answer is completely explained. There are two full model essays on the assigned topic, one *for* the problems discussed and one *against*.

PRACTICE EXAMINATION TWO

This second practice examination provides additional practice.

ANSWER KEYS, SUMMARIES OF RESULTS, AND SELF-APPRAISAL CHARTS

You can again score yourself, summarize results, and locate your errors.

ANSWER ANALYSIS

In addition to the fully explained answers, there are two more complete essays, one *for* and one *against* the subject at issue.

Answer Sheet—Practice Examination

Test 1: The Language Arts, Writing (Writing Skills) Test ______________________

1. ① ② ③ ④ ⑤
2. ① ② ③ ④ ⑤
3. ① ② ③ ④ ⑤
4. ① ② ③ ④ ⑤
5. ① ② ③ ④ ⑤
6. ① ② ③ ④ ⑤
7. ① ② ③ ④ ⑤
8. ① ② ③ ④ ⑤
9. ① ② ③ ④ ⑤
10. ① ② ③ ④ ⑤
11. ① ② ③ ④ ⑤
12. ① ② ③ ④ ⑤
13. ① ② ③ ④ ⑤
14. ① ② ③ ④ ⑤
15. ① ② ③ ④ ⑤
16. ① ② ③ ④ ⑤
17. ① ② ③ ④ ⑤
18. ① ② ③ ④ ⑤
19. ① ② ③ ④ ⑤
20. ① ② ③ ④ ⑤
21. ① ② ③ ④ ⑤
22. ① ② ③ ④ ⑤
23. ① ② ③ ④ ⑤
24. ① ② ③ ④ ⑤
25. ① ② ③ ④ ⑤
26. ① ② ③ ④ ⑤
27. ① ② ③ ④ ⑤
28. ① ② ③ ④ ⑤
29. ① ② ③ ④ ⑤
30. ① ② ③ ④ ⑤
31. ① ② ③ ④ ⑤
32. ① ② ③ ④ ⑤
33. ① ② ③ ④ ⑤
34. ① ② ③ ④ ⑤
35. ① ② ③ ④ ⑤
36. ① ② ③ ④ ⑤
37. ① ② ③ ④ ⑤
38. ① ② ③ ④ ⑤
39. ① ② ③ ④ ⑤
40. ① ② ③ ④ ⑤
41. ① ② ③ ④ ⑤
42. ① ② ③ ④ ⑤
43. ① ② ③ ④ ⑤
44. ① ② ③ ④ ⑤
45. ① ② ③ ④ ⑤
46. ① ② ③ ④ ⑤
47. ① ② ③ ④ ⑤
48. ① ② ③ ④ ⑤
49. ① ② ③ ④ ⑤
50. ① ② ③ ④ ⑤
51. ① ② ③ ④ ⑤
52. ① ② ③ ④ ⑤
53. ① ② ③ ④ ⑤
54. ① ② ③ ④ ⑤
55. ① ② ③ ④ ⑤

Test 2: The Social Studies Test ______________________

1. ① ② ③ ④ ⑤
2. ① ② ③ ④ ⑤
3. ① ② ③ ④ ⑤
4. ① ② ③ ④ ⑤
5. ① ② ③ ④ ⑤
6. ① ② ③ ④ ⑤
7. ① ② ③ ④ ⑤
8. ① ② ③ ④ ⑤
9. ① ② ③ ④ ⑤
10. ① ② ③ ④ ⑤
11. ① ② ③ ④ ⑤
12. ① ② ③ ④ ⑤
13. ① ② ③ ④ ⑤
14. ① ② ③ ④ ⑤
15. ① ② ③ ④ ⑤
16. ① ② ③ ④ ⑤
17. ① ② ③ ④ ⑤
18. ① ② ③ ④ ⑤
19. ① ② ③ ④ ⑤
20. ① ② ③ ④ ⑤
21. ① ② ③ ④ ⑤
22. ① ② ③ ④ ⑤
23. ① ② ③ ④ ⑤
24. ① ② ③ ④ ⑤
25. ① ② ③ ④ ⑤
26. ① ② ③ ④ ⑤
27. ① ② ③ ④ ⑤
28. ① ② ③ ④ ⑤
29. ① ② ③ ④ ⑤
30. ① ② ③ ④ ⑤
31. ① ② ③ ④ ⑤
32. ① ② ③ ④ ⑤
33. ① ② ③ ④ ⑤
34. ① ② ③ ④ ⑤
35. ① ② ③ ④ ⑤
36. ① ② ③ ④ ⑤
37. ① ② ③ ④ ⑤
38. ① ② ③ ④ ⑤
39. ① ② ③ ④ ⑤
40. ① ② ③ ④ ⑤
41. ① ② ③ ④ ⑤
42. ① ② ③ ④ ⑤
43. ① ② ③ ④ ⑤
44. ① ② ③ ④ ⑤
45. ① ② ③ ④ ⑤
46. ① ② ③ ④ ⑤
47. ① ② ③ ④ ⑤
48. ① ② ③ ④ ⑤
49. ① ② ③ ④ ⑤
50. ① ② ③ ④ ⑤
51. ① ② ③ ④ ⑤
52. ① ② ③ ④ ⑤
53. ① ② ③ ④ ⑤
54. ① ② ③ ④ ⑤
55. ① ② ③ ④ ⑤
56. ① ② ③ ④ ⑤
57. ① ② ③ ④ ⑤
58. ① ② ③ ④ ⑤
59. ① ② ③ ④ ⑤
60. ① ② ③ ④ ⑤
61. ① ② ③ ④ ⑤
62. ① ② ③ ④ ⑤
63. ① ② ③ ④ ⑤
64. ① ② ③ ④ ⑤

Test 3: The Science Test

1. ① ② ③ ④ ⑤
2. ① ② ③ ④ ⑤
3. ① ② ③ ④ ⑤
4. ① ② ③ ④ ⑤
5. ① ② ③ ④ ⑤
6. ① ② ③ ④ ⑤
7. ① ② ③ ④ ⑤
8. ① ② ③ ④ ⑤
9. ① ② ③ ④ ⑤
10. ① ② ③ ④ ⑤
11. ① ② ③ ④ ⑤
12. ① ② ③ ④ ⑤
13. ① ② ③ ④ ⑤
14. ① ② ③ ④ ⑤
15. ① ② ③ ④ ⑤
16. ① ② ③ ④ ⑤
17. ① ② ③ ④ ⑤
18. ① ② ③ ④ ⑤
19. ① ② ③ ④ ⑤
20. ① ② ③ ④ ⑤
21. ① ② ③ ④ ⑤
22. ① ② ③ ④ ⑤
23. ① ② ③ ④ ⑤
24. ① ② ③ ④ ⑤
25. ① ② ③ ④ ⑤
26. ① ② ③ ④ ⑤
27. ① ② ③ ④ ⑤
28. ① ② ③ ④ ⑤
29. ① ② ③ ④ ⑤
30. ① ② ③ ④ ⑤
31. ① ② ③ ④ ⑤
32. ① ② ③ ④ ⑤
33. ① ② ③ ④ ⑤
34. ① ② ③ ④ ⑤
35. ① ② ③ ④ ⑤
36. ① ② ③ ④ ⑤
37. ① ② ③ ④ ⑤
38. ① ② ③ ④ ⑤
39. ① ② ③ ④ ⑤
40. ① ② ③ ④ ⑤
41. ① ② ③ ④ ⑤
42. ① ② ③ ④ ⑤
43. ① ② ③ ④ ⑤
44. ① ② ③ ④ ⑤
45. ① ② ③ ④ ⑤
46. ① ② ③ ④ ⑤
47. ① ② ③ ④ ⑤
48. ① ② ③ ④ ⑤
49. ① ② ③ ④ ⑤
50. ① ② ③ ④ ⑤
51. ① ② ③ ④ ⑤
52. ① ② ③ ④ ⑤
53. ① ② ③ ④ ⑤
54. ① ② ③ ④ ⑤
55. ① ② ③ ④ ⑤
56. ① ② ③ ④ ⑤
57. ① ② ③ ④ ⑤
58. ① ② ③ ④ ⑤
59. ① ② ③ ④ ⑤
60. ① ② ③ ④ ⑤
61. ① ② ③ ④ ⑤
62. ① ② ③ ④ ⑤
63. ① ② ③ ④ ⑤
64. ① ② ③ ④ ⑤
65. ① ② ③ ④ ⑤
66. ① ② ③ ④ ⑤

Test 4: The Language Arts, Reading (Interpreting Literature and the Arts) Test

1. ① ② ③ ④ ⑤
2. ① ② ③ ④ ⑤
3. ① ② ③ ④ ⑤
4. ① ② ③ ④ ⑤
5. ① ② ③ ④ ⑤
6. ① ② ③ ④ ⑤
7. ① ② ③ ④ ⑤
8. ① ② ③ ④ ⑤
9. ① ② ③ ④ ⑤
10. ① ② ③ ④ ⑤
11. ① ② ③ ④ ⑤
12. ① ② ③ ④ ⑤
13. ① ② ③ ④ ⑤
14. ① ② ③ ④ ⑤
15. ① ② ③ ④ ⑤
16. ① ② ③ ④ ⑤
17. ① ② ③ ④ ⑤
18. ① ② ③ ④ ⑤
19. ① ② ③ ④ ⑤
20. ① ② ③ ④ ⑤
21. ① ② ③ ④ ⑤
22. ① ② ③ ④ ⑤
23. ① ② ③ ④ ⑤
24. ① ② ③ ④ ⑤
25. ① ② ③ ④ ⑤
26. ① ② ③ ④ ⑤
27. ① ② ③ ④ ⑤
28. ① ② ③ ④ ⑤
29. ① ② ③ ④ ⑤
30. ① ② ③ ④ ⑤
31. ① ② ③ ④ ⑤
32. ① ② ③ ④ ⑤
33. ① ② ③ ④ ⑤
34. ① ② ③ ④ ⑤
35. ① ② ③ ④ ⑤
36. ① ② ③ ④ ⑤
37. ① ② ③ ④ ⑤
38. ① ② ③ ④ ⑤
39. ① ② ③ ④ ⑤
40. ① ② ③ ④ ⑤
41. ① ② ③ ④ ⑤
42. ① ② ③ ④ ⑤
43. ① ② ③ ④ ⑤
44. ① ② ③ ④ ⑤
45. ① ② ③ ④ ⑤

Test 5: The Mathematics Test ______________________________

1.	①	②	③	④	⑤
2.	①	②	③	④	⑤
3.	①	②	③	④	⑤
4.	①	②	③	④	⑤
5.	①	②	③	④	⑤
6.	①	②	③	④	⑤
7.	①	②	③	④	⑤
8.	①	②	③	④	⑤
9.	①	②	③	④	⑤
10.	①	②	③	④	⑤
11.	①	②	③	④	⑤
12.	①	②	③	④	⑤
13.	①	②	③	④	⑤
14.	①	②	③	④	⑤
15.	①	②	③	④	⑤
16.	①	②	③	④	⑤
17.	①	②	③	④	⑤
18.	①	②	③	④	⑤
19.	①	②	③	④	⑤
20.	①	②	③	④	⑤
21.	①	②	③	④	⑤
22.	①	②	③	④	⑤
23.	①	②	③	④	⑤
24.	①	②	③	④	⑤
25.	①	②	③	④	⑤
26.	①	②	③	④	⑤
27.	①	②	③	④	⑤
28.	①	②	③	④	⑤
29.	①	②	③	④	⑤
30.	①	②	③	④	⑤
31.	①	②	③	④	⑤
32.	①	②	③	④	⑤
33.	①	②	③	④	⑤
34.	①	②	③	④	⑤
35.	①	②	③	④	⑤
36.	①	②	③	④	⑤
37.	①	②	③	④	⑤
38.	①	②	③	④	⑤
39.	①	②	③	④	⑤
40.	①	②	③	④	⑤
41.	①	②	③	④	⑤
42.	①	②	③	④	⑤
43.	①	②	③	④	⑤
44.	①	②	③	④	⑤
45.	①	②	③	④	⑤
46.	①	②	③	④	⑤
47.	①	②	③	④	⑤
48.	①	②	③	④	⑤
49.	①	②	③	④	⑤
50.	①	②	③	④	⑤
51.	①	②	③	④	⑤
52.	①	②	③	④	⑤
53.	①	②	③	④	⑤
54.	①	②	③	④	⑤
55.	①	②	③	④	⑤
56.	①	②	③	④	⑤

The direction sheets, mathematics formulas, and question formats of the following examinations are constructed like the actual test you will take. Each examination consists of five parts:

	TESTS	QUESTIONS	TIME ALLOWANCE
Test 1:	The Language Arts, Writing (Writing Skills) Test, Part I	55	1 hour, 15 minutes
	The Language Arts, Writing (Writing Skills) Test, Part II	Essay	45 minutes
Test 2:	The Social Studies Test	64	1 hour, 25 minutes
Test 3:	The Science Test	66	1 hour, 35 minutes
Test 4:	The Language Arts, Reading (Interpreting Literature and the Arts) Test	45	1 hour, 5 minutes
Test 5:	The Mathematics Test	56	1 hour, 30 minutes
		Total:	7 hours, 35 minutes

For each test in the two practice examinations we have included an Answer Key, a Score Yourself chart, an Evaluate Your Score section, and an Analyze Your Errors section. Mark yourself on each test, checking your answers against the answer key. Count the number of questions you answered correctly. Then refer to the Score Yourself chart to find your rating: Excellent, Good, or Fair. The Evaluate Your Score section will indicate the minimum number of correct answers considered safe to pass this part of the examination. The Analyze Your Errors section will help you identify your weaknesses more precisely so that you can do the necessary follow-up study.

The purpose of these two practice examinations is to give you the experience in taking a test which is similar to the actual one you will take. IMPORTANT: You should spend more time studying those chapters which deal with the tests in which you are weakest. In that way, you will improve your score when you take the actual examination.

SIMULATE TEST CONDITIONS

To make conditions similar to those on the actual examination, do not take more time than that allowed for each test.

PRACTICE EXAMINATION ONE

TEST 1: LANGUAGE ARTS, WRITING (WRITING SKILLS) TEST, PART I

Directions

Allotted time: 75 minutes

This part of the Language Arts, Writing (Writing Skills) test contains **55 multiple-choice questions** that test your ability to write English correctly and effectively.

The multiple-choice questions are based on numbered sentences in paragraphs. These sentences may be correct as written (if so, choose option 1), or they will contain an error in sentence structure, grammar and usage, punctuation, capitalization, or spelling. You must choose the option that either corrects the error, indicates the best way to write a portion of the sentence, combines two sentences effectively, or provides another way in which the sentence can be rewritten.

Since 55 questions must be answered in 75 minutes, if there are six paragraphs, spend no more than 12 minutes on each set of questions based on each paragraph. Do not devote more than a few minutes to any one question. If there is time left, you may go back to a question.

Answer all questions. Do not leave any blanks since there is no penalty for incorrect answers. Your score will be the number of your correct responses.

You may go on to Language Arts, Writing (Writing Skills), Part II, the essay, when you complete Part I.

Decide which is the best answer and mark the numbered space on the answer sheet beside the number that corresponds to the question in the test.

Make no mark on your answer sheet other than your choice of the correct answer. If you change your answer, erase your first mark completely. Only *one* answer space should be marked for each question.

EXAMPLE:

In the future, people will need to learn to turn to their computer for assistence.

What correction should be made to this sentence?

(1) remove the comma after future
(2) change will need to need
(3) change the spelling of their to they're
(4) change the spelling of assistence to assistance
(5) no correction is necessary

① ② ③ ● ⑤

In this sentence, the correct spelling is "assistance," so mark answer 4 on the answer sheet.

Directions: Choose the one best answer to each item.

Items 1 to 9 refer to the following paragraphs.

(1) Safe food must be planned and not left to chance, for the consumer, food safety begins in the marketplace. (2) All cooperative efforts made by states and the U.S. department of agriculture to make available a clean, safe, wholesome food supply will be in vain unless the consumer takes certain precautions to keep it that way. (3) The precautions to be taken by the consumer include care in buying, storing, handling, and cooking food.

(4) Shop for groceries last after all other errands have been run. (5) Take foods home immediately and don't leave them unattended for a long period of time. (6) Suficient light in grocery stores is necessary to enable you to adequately view foods for proper selection. (7) Store personnel should make sure that foods are replaced frequently in order to keep them as fresh as possible.

(8) Under no circumstances buy swollen or leaking cans. (9) The food in a swollen or leaking can may be dangerous to eat or even to taste.

(10) Ask the checkout clerk to bag cold foods together so that they keep cold longer; interspersed with room temperature foods, they may warm up quickly.

1. Sentence 1: **Safe food must be planned and not left to chance, for the consumer, food safety begins in the marketplace.**

Which of the following is the best way to write the underlined portion of this sentence? If you think the original is the best way, choose option (1).

(1) chance, for
(2) chance: for
(3) chance; for
(4) chance, For
(5) chance. For

2. Sentence 2: **All cooperative efforts made by states and the U.S. department of agriculture to make available a clean, safe, wholesome food supply will be in vain unless the consumer takes certain precautions to keep it that way.**

What correction should be made to this sentence?

(1) insert a hyphen in cooperative
(2) capitalize department and agriculture
(3) remove the comma after clean
(4) change it to them
(5) no correction is necessary

3. Sentence 3: **The precautions to be taken by the consumer include care in buying, storing, handling, and cooking food.**

   If you rewrote sentence 3 beginning with

   Care in buying, storing, handling, and cooking food

   the next words should be

   (1) include
   (2) is
   (3) is among
   (4) would be among
   (5) will be among

4. Sentence 4: **Shop for groceries last after all other errands have been run.**

   What correction should be made to this sentence?

   (1) insert a comma after last
   (2) remove the word other
   (3) change have been to will have been
   (4) change run to ran
   (5) no correction is necessary

5. Sentence 5: **Take foods home immediately and don't leave them unattended for a long period of time.**

   Which of the following is the best way to write the underlined portion of this sentence? If you think the original is the best way, choose option (1).

   (1) and don't
   (2) also don't
   (3) but don't
   (4) however don't
   (5) nevertheless don't

6. Sentence 6: **Suficient light in grocery stores is necessary to enable you to adequately view foods for proper selection.**

   What correction should be made to this sentence?

   (1) change the spelling of suficient to sufficient
   (2) insert a comma after stores
   (3) change the spelling of necessary to necessery
   (4) insert a comma after foods
   (5) no correction is necessary

7. Sentence 7: **Store personnel should make sure that foods are replaced frequently in order to keep them as fresh as possible.**

   What correction should be made to this sentence?

   (1) change the spelling of personnel to personal
   (2) change should to might
   (3) change them to it
   (4) change fresh to freshly
   (5) no change is necessary

8. Sentences 8 and 9: **Under no circumstances buy swollen or leaking cans. The food in a swollen or leaking can may be dangerous to eat or even to taste.**

   The most effective combination of sentences 8 and 9 would include which of the following groups of words?

   (1) which contain food that may be
   (2) and the food in a swollen can
   (3) since the food in a swollen can
   (4) being dangerous to eat
   (5) that may be dangerous to eat

9. Sentence 10: **Ask the checkout clerk to bag cold foods together so that they keep cold longer; interspersed with room temperature foods, they may warm up quickly.**

   Which of the following is the best way to write the underlined portion of this sentence? If you think the original is the best way, choose option (1).

   (1) longer; interspersed
   (2) longer. interspersed
   (3) longer: interspersed
   (4) longer, interspersed
   (5) longer, interspersed

Items 10 to 18 refer to the following paragraphs.

(1) The traditional family grouping will remain dominant, although the people in the family may change because of divorce, separation, and remarriage.

(2) The family with dual careers, both husband and wife working, will increase—particularly among the young. (3) The husband and wife family with no children will also increase.

(4) Some couples will choose to remain childless, others will spend the major part of their lifetime with no children present because of the possibilities for spacing and limiting family size.

(5) An increasing number of single parent families will be formed as a result of divorce, death, abandonment, or the choice of the unwed to rear their children alone. (6) In most cases, the single parent family will have an employed woman at its head.

(7) Because of increased acceptability, more individuals may remain unmarried and establish single households. (8) The single adult living alone will establish close kin or simulated kin networks, relying upon and sharing with others economic and emotional resources to fulfill parent-like roles in an "aunt-uncle" capacity.

(9) These family forms, will present different issues and problems for family members.

(10) Families will need information to select wisely the family pattern they want to pursue.

10. Sentence 1: **The traditional family grouping will remain <u>dominant, although</u> the people in the family may change because of divorce, separation, and remarriage.**

Which of the following is the best way to write the underlined portion of this sentence? If you think the original is the best way, choose option (1).

(1) dominant, although
(2) dominant, indeed
(3) dominant, so
(4) dominant, therefore
(5) dominant, nevertheless

11. Sentences 2 and 3: **The family with dual careers, both husband and wife working, will increase—particularly among the young. The husband and wife family with no children will also increase.**

The most effective combination of sentences 2 and 3 would include which of the following groups of words?

(1) as well as
(2) but
(3) although
(4) nevertheless
(5) therefore

12. Sentence 4: **Some couples will choose to remain <u>childless, others</u> will spend the major part of their lifetime with no children present because of the possibilities for spacing and limiting family size.**

Which of the following is the best way to write the underlined portion of this sentence? If you think the original is the best way, choose option (1).

(1) childless, others
(2) childless. others
(3) childless. Others
(4) childless; Others
(5) childless: others

13. Sentence 5: **An increasing number of single parent families will be formed as a result of divorce, death, abandonment, or the choice of the unwed to rear their children alone.**

if you rewrote sentence 5 beginning with

<u>As a result of</u> . . . <u>alone</u>

the next words should be

(1) an increasing number
(2) single parent families
(3) divorce, death, abandonment
(4) the choice of the unwed
(5) to rear their children

14. Sentence 6: **In most cases, the single parent family will have an employed woman as its head.**

What correction should be made to this sentence?

(1) remove comma after <u>cases</u>
(2) insert a hyphen in <u>single parent</u>
(3) change <u>will have</u> to <u>has</u>
(4) change <u>its</u> to <u>it's</u>
(5) no change is necessary

15. Sentence 7: **Because of increased acceptability, more individuals may remain unmarried and establish single households.**

What correction should be made to this sentence?

(1) change the spelling of <u>acceptability</u> to <u>acceptibility</u>
(2) remove the comma after <u>acceptability</u>
(3) change <u>may remain</u> to <u>will remain</u>
(4) insert a comma after <u>unmarried</u>
(5) no correction is necessary

16. Sentence 8: **The single adult living alone will establish close kin or simulated kin networks, relying upon and sharing with others economic and emotional resources to fulfill parent-like roles in an "aunt-uncle" capacity.**

What correction should be made to this sentence?

(1) add a comma after close kin
(2) remove the comma after networks
(3) change the spelling of resources to resourses
(4) change to fulfill to fulfilling
(5) no correction is necessary

17. Sentence 9: **These family forms, will present different issues and problems for family members.**

What correction should be made to this sentence?

(1) remove the comma after forms
(2) change will present to will have presented
(3) insert a comma after issues
(4) insert a comma after problems
(5) no correction is necessary

18. Sentence 10: **Families will need information to select wisely the family pattern they want to pursue.**

What correction should be made to this sentence?

(1) change will need to will be needing
(2) change select wisely to wisely select
(3) change the spelling of pattern to pattren
(4) change the spelling of pursue to persue
(5) no correction is necessary

Items 19 to 27 refer to the following paragraphs.

(1) Drug abuse is like a communicable disease. (2) It spreads—by example, by word of mouth, and by imitation. (3) Drug abuse is certainly increasing, but so is the number of young people who have tried drugs and want out. (4) As we provide treatment services for them, these young people become able to tell other youth that the drug scene is not as great as they thought it was, before they got hooked. (5) And, of greater importance, they are beleived by their contemporaries before experimentation becomes habit.

(6) Parents can help prevent drug usage by setting an example, by knowledge, and by understanding. (7) If they are to talk to their children about drugs they must be informed. (8) usually they know far less about drugs than do their children. (9) Ideally, before their child is tempted to experiment, they will be able to explain to him the undesirability of the drugged life. (10) What is even more convincing to young people, they will have been able to communicate to him the actual damage that a drug abuser does to their body.

19. Sentences 1 and 2: **Drug abuse is like a communicable disease. It spreads—by example, by word of mouth, and by imitation.**

The most effective combination of sentences 1 and 2 would include which of the following groups of words?

(1) disease. it spreads
(2) disease although it spreads
(3) disease yet it spreads
(4) disease which spreads
(5) disease having spread

20. Sentence 3: **Drug abuse is certainly increasing, but so is the number of young people who have tried drugs and want out.**

What correction should be made to this sentence?

(1) remove the comma after increasing
(2) change but to and
(3) change number to amount
(4) insert a comma after people
(5) no correction is necessary

21. Sentence 4: **As we provide treatment services for them, these young people become able to tell other youth that the drug scene is not as great as they thought it was, before they got hooked.**

What correction should be made to this sentence?

(1) change As to Although
(2) remove the comma after them
(3) change become to became
(4) change thought to think
(5) no correction is necessary

22. Sentence 5: **And, of greater importance, they are beleived by their contemporaries before experimentation becomes habit.**

    What correction should be made to this sentence?

    (1) remove the commas before of and after importance
    (2) change beleived to believed
    (3) insert commas before by and after contemporaries
    (4) change becomes to will become
    (5) no correction is necessary

23. Sentence 6: **Parents can help prevent drug usage by setting an example, by knowledge, and by understanding.**

    What correction should be made to this sentence?

    (1) change can to could
    (2) change by setting an example to by example
    (3) change the spelling of knowledge to knowlege
    (4) remove the comma before and
    (5) no correction is necessary

24. Sentence 7: **If they are to talk to their children about drugs they must be informed.**

    What correction should be made to this sentence?

    (1) change are to to would
    (2) change their to they're
    (3) insert a comma after drugs
    (4) change informed to informative
    (5) no correction is necessary

25. Sentences 7 and 8: **If they are to talk to their children about drugs they must be informed. usually they know far less about drugs than do their children.**

    Which of the following is the best way to write the underlined portion of this sentence? If you think the original is the best way, choose option (1).

    (1) informed. usually
    (2) informed usually
    (3) informed : usually
    (4) informed – Usually
    (5) informed. Usually

26. Sentence 9: **Ideally, before their child is tempted to experiment, they will be able to explain to him the undesirability of the drugged life.**

    What correction should be made to this sentence?

    (1) change the spelling of ideally to idealy
    (2) remove the comma before before
    (3) change be able to have been able
    (4) change the spelling of undesirability to undesireability
    (5) no correction is necessary

27. Sentence 10: **What is even more convincing to young people, they will have been able to communicate to him the actual damage that a drug abuser does to their body.**

    What correction should be made to this sentence?

    (1) move even to after convincing
    (2) remove the comma after people
    (3) change the spelling of communicate to comunicate
    (4) change their to his
    (5) no change is necessary

Items 28 to 37 refer to the following paragraphs.

(1) Statistically, by far the most common type of home accidents are falls. (2) Each year thousands of canadians meet death in this way, within the four walls of their home or in yards around their house. (3) Nine out of ten of the victims are over 65 but people of all ages experience serious injuries as a result of home falls. (4) It is impossable to estimate how many injuries result from falls, but they must run into the millions.

(5) Falls can be a problem for all ages. (6) In the process of growing up, children or teenagers often will fall. (7) Fortunately their bodies are supple, so they may suffer only skinned knees bumps, and bruises. (8) But in an older person, the same fall may cause a broken arm, leg, hip, or other injury that requires hospitalization or medical care. (9) As you get older, you may not fall any more often, but the results usually are more serious and may even be fatal.

(10) Adults fall because they don't look where they're going, are in a hurry, are careless, or thinking about something else.

(11) A few inexpensive items such as a suction-type rubber mat or safety strips in the tub, a non-slip mat on the floor, and bathtub handholds can go a long way toward eliminating falls in the bathroom.

28. Sentence 1: **Statistically, by far the most common type of home accidents are falls.**

    What correction should be made to this sentence?

    (1) change the spelling of Statistically to Statisticly
    (2) remove the comma before by
    (3) insert a comma after accidents
    (4) change are to is
    (5) no correction is necessary

29. Sentence 2: **Each year thousands of americans meet death in this way, within the four walls of their home or in yards around their house.**

    What correction should be made to this sentence?

    (1) change canadians to Canadians
    (2) remove to comma after way
    (3) change within to in
    (4) insert a comma after home
    (5) no correction is necessary

30. Sentence 3: **Nine out of ten of the victims are over 65 but people of all ages experience serious injuries as a result of home falls.**

    What correction should be made to this sentence?

    (1) change are to is
    (2) insert a comma after 65
    (3) change but to and
    (4) change experience to experiance
    (5) no correction is necessary

31. Sentence 4: **It is impossable to estimate how many injuries result from falls, but they must run into the millions.**

    What correction should be made to this sentence?

    (1) change the spelling of impossable to impossible
    (2) change result to results
    (3) remove the comma after falls
    (4) change but to since
    (5) no correction is necessary

32. Sentences 5 and 6: **Falls can be a problem for all ages. In the process of growing up, children or teenagers often will fall.**

    Which of the following is the best way to write the underlined portion of this sentence? If you think the original is the best way, choose option (1).

    (1) ages. In
    (2) ages. in
    (3) ages : In
    (4) ages : in
    (5) ages; In

33. Sentence 7: **Fortunately their bodies are supple, so they may suffer only skinned knees bumps, and bruises.**

    What correction should be made to this sentence?

    (1) change the spelling of Fortunately to Fortunitely
    (2) remove the comma after supple
    (3) change suffer only to only suffer
    (4) insert a comma after knees
    (5) no comma is necessary

34. Sentence 8: **But in an older person, the same fall may cause a broken arm, leg, hip, or other injury that requires hospitalization or medical care.**

    What correction should be made to this sentence?

    (1) change But to Although
    (2) insert a colon after cause
    (3) insert a comma after injury
    (4) change requires to require
    (5) no correction is necessary

35. Sentence 9: **As you get older, you may not fall any more often, but the results usually are more serious and may even be fatal.**

    What correction should be made to this sentence?

    (1) change As to When
    (2) change get to will get
    (3) change but to and
    (4) change more to most
    (5) no correction is necessary

36. Sentence 10: **Adults fall because they don't look where they're going, are in a hurry, are careless, or thinking about something else.**

What correction should be made to this sentence?

(1) change don't to doesn't
(2) change they're to there
(3) remove the comma after hurry
(4) insert are before thinking
(5) no correction is necessary

37. Sentence 11: **A few inexpensive items such as a suction-type rubber mat or safety strips in the tub, a non-slip mat on the floor, and bathtub handholds can go a long way toward eliminating falls in the bathroom.**

If you rewrote sentence 11 beginning with

To eliminate falls in the bathroom

the next words should be

(1) a few inexpensive items
(2) a suction-type rubber mat
(3) safety strips
(4) a non-slip mat
(5) bathtub handles

Items 38 to 46 refer to the following paragraphs.

(1) The only known cure for bikomania, a highly contagious fever, sweeping the country from coast to coast, is to ride a bike. (2) Nearly 100 million happy victims, including mom and pop and the kids, now are taking this delightful treatment and pedaling their two-wheelers into an exciting new world of fun and adventure.

(3) Why buy a bike? Partly because riding a bike benefits both you and your enviroment. (4) A bike doesn't foul up the air, makes no noise, keeps you in top physical shape, takes up little room on the road. and is easy to park in a small space. (5) With apropriate accessories—such as saddle bags, luggage racks, or baskets—a bike can be used on shopping missions, picnic excursions, or bicycle tours.

(6) What kind of bike should you get? (7) Bewildered by the tantalizing display of racing models with 10-speed gearshifts and lots of fancy gimmicks, your apt to plunge into something you really don't need. (8) Best advice: buy the simplest model that meets your transportation requirements. (9) You need not invest in dropped handlebars, multigear ratios, and special frames that may be too complicated for your purposes.

(10) Try renting a bike before you buy one. (11) Spend a couple of weekends pedaling various makes over typical terrain in your area; this tryout will answer many of your questions.

38. Sentence 1: **The only know cure for bikomania, a highly contagious fever, sweeping the country from coast to coast, is to ride a bike.**

What correction should be made to this sentence?

(1) remove the comma after bikomania
(2) change the spelling of contagious to contageous
(3) remove the comma after fever
(4) remove the comma after coast
(5) no correction is necessary

39. Sentence 2: **Nearly 100 million happy victims, including mom and pop and the kids, now are taking this delightful treatment and pedaling their two-wheelers into an exciting new world of fun and adventure.**

What correction should be made to this sentence?

(1) remove the comma after victims
(2) capitalize mom, pop
(3) capitalize kids
(4) change the spelling of exciting to exsiting
(5) no correction is necessary

40. Sentence 3: **Why buy a bike? Partly because riding a bike benefits both you and your enviroment.**

What correction should be made to this sentence?

(1) remove the question mark after bike
(2) change the spelling of benefits to benifits
(3) change your to you're
(4) change the spelling of enviroment to environment
(5) no correction is necessary

41. Sentence 4: **A bike doesn't foul up the air, makes no noise, keeps you in top physical shape, takes up little room on the road. and is easy to park in a small space.**

Which of the following is the best way to write the underlined portion of this sentence? If you think the original is the best way, choose option (1).

(1) road. and
(2) road. And
(3) road, and
(4) road, And
(5) road: and

42. Sentence 5: **With apropriate accessories—such as saddle bags, luggage racks, or baskets—a bike can be used on shopping missions, picnic excursions, or bicycle tours.**

What correction should be made to this sentence?

(1) change the spelling of apropriate to appropriate
(2) remove the dashes before such and after baskets
(3) remove the comma after bags
(4) change the spelling of excursions to excurshuns
(5) no change is necessary

43. Sentence 7: **Bewildered by the tantalizing display of racing models with 10-speed gearshifts and lots of fancy gimmicks, your apt to plunge into something you really don't need.**

What correction should be made to this sentence?

(1) insert commas before with and after gearshifts
(2) remove the comma after gimmicks
(3) change the spelling of your to you're
(4) change the spelling of really to realy
(5) no correction is necessary

44. Sentence 8: **Best advice: buy the simplest model that meets your transportation requirements.**

Which of the following is the best way to write the underlined portion of this sentence? If you think the original is the best way, choose option (1).

(1) Best advice: buy
(2) Best advice; Buy
(3) Best advice; buy
(4) Best advice, Buy
(5) Best advice, buy

45. Sentence 9: **You need not invest in dropped handlebars, multigear ratios, and special frames that may be too complicated for your purposes.**

If you rewrote sentence 9 beginning with

Nor need you

the next words should be

(1) invest in
(2) dropped handlebars
(3) multigear ratios
(4) that may be
(5) for your purposes

46. Sentence 11: **Spend a couple of weekends pedaling various makes over typical terrain in your area; this tryout will answer many of your questions.**

Which of the following is the best way to write the underlined portion of this sentence? If you think the original is the best way, choose option (1).

(1) area; this
(2) area: this
(3) area, this
(4) area. this
(5) area this

Items 47 to 55 refer to the following paragraphs.

(1) At every stage of development, clothes can help establish a person's identity for himself and for those with who he interacts. (2) The childhood game of "dressing up" in parents' clothes provides the opportunity for the child to practise the roles he will be expected to play in adult life.

(3) The degree to which a person choses clothes that fit the roles will affect his performance in those roles.

(4) Clothes are an important factor in developing feelings of self-confidence and self-respect. (5) When you look good, you feel good. (6) For most people, clothes are often a source of positive reaction from others, since in our culture we are more apt to compliment a person on his appearance than on other aspects of the "self."

(7) Most Canadians also recognize that a proper appearance and proper dress are the keys to association with the right crowd, which in turn opens the door to job advancement increased income and greater prestige.

(8) Our clothing needs are influenced by a multitude of circumstances. (9) Buying motives are seldom simple.

(10) The first step in the decision-making process is to make a conscious ordering of the things that are important to us. (11) If a person recognizes and accepts the priorities of his values—e.g., that his status and prestige may be more important than his physical comfort—his choice of clothing is not only simplified, but more likely to bring him greater satisfaction.

47. Sentence 1: **At every stage of development, clothes can help establish a person's identity for himself and for those with who he interacts.**

What correction should be made to this sentence?

(1) change the spelling of development to developement
(2) remove the comma after development
(3) insert a comma after himself
(4) change who to whom
(5) no correction is necessary

48. Sentence 2: **The childhood game of "dressing up" in parents' clothes provides the opportunity for the child to practise the roles he will be expected to play in adult life.**

What correction should be made to this sentence?

(1) remove the quotation marks around "dressing up"
(2) change parents' to parent's
(3) change provides to provide
(4) change the spelling of practise to practice
(5) no correction is necessary

49. Sentence 3: **The degree to which a person choses clothes that fit the roles will affect his performance in those roles.**

What correction should be made to this sentence?

(1) remove the word to
(2) change the spelling of choses to chooses
(3) insert a comma after roles
(4) change the spelling of affect to effect
(5) no correction is necessary

50. Sentences 4 and 5: **Clothes are an important factor in developing feelings of self-confidence and self-respect. When you look good, you feel good.**

The most effective combination of sentences 4 and 5 would include which of the following groups of words?

(1) self-respect, moreover, when
(2) self-respect, although, when
(3) self-respect, nevertheless, when
(4) self-respect, therefore, when
(5) self-respect, since, when

51. Sentence 6: **For most people, clothes are often a source of positive reaction from others, since in our culture we are more apt to compliment a person on his appearance than on other aspects of the "self."**

What correction should be made to this sentence?

(1) remove the comma after people
(2) change the spelling of compliment to complement
(3) change the spelling of appearance to appearence
(4) change than to then
(5) no correction is necessary

52. Sentence 7: **Most Canadians also recognize that a proper appearance and proper dress are the keys to association with the right crowd, which in turn opens the doors to job advancement increased income, and greater prestige.**

What correction should be made to this sentence?

(1) change Canadians to canadians
(2) change the spelling of recognize to reconize
(3) remove the comma after crowd
(4) insert a comma after advancement
(5) no correction is necessary

53. Sentences 8 and 9: **Our clothing needs are influenced by a multitude of circumstances. Buying motives are seldom simple.**

The most effective combination of sentences 8 and 9 would include which of the following groups of words?

(1) circumstances, although buying
(2) circumstances, because buying
(3) circumstances, but buying
(4) circumstances, that is, buying
(5) circumstances, however, buying

54. Sentence 10: **The first step in the decision-making process is to make a conscious ordering of the things that are important to us.**

If you rewrote sentence 10 beginning with

Making a conscious ordering . . . to us the next word(s) should be

(1) the first step
(2) in the decision-making process
(3) is
(4) are
(5) things that are

55. Sentence 11: **If a person recognizes and accepts the priorities of his values—e.g., that his status and prestige may be more important than his physical comfort—his choice of clothing is not only simplified, but more likely to bring him greater satisfaction.**

What correction should be made to this sentence?

(1) change the spelling of accepts to excepts
(2) remove the comma after e.g.
(3) change may to might
(4) remove the comma after simplified
(5) no correction is necessary

TEST 1: LANGUAGE ARTS, WRITING (WRITING SKILLS) TEST, PART II

Directions

Allotted time: 45 minutes

Part II of the Writing Skills Test will test your ability to write by having you write an essay in which you either take and defend a position on a debatable topic or explain how something affects our lives.

Remember to:

- follow the directions
- read the topic on which your essay will be based
- be careful to write your essay on the separate answer sheet, confining your notes to scratch paper
- reread your essay, revising it where necessary to improve what you have written
- correct any errors you find in paragraphing, sentence structure, capitalization, punctuation, spelling and usage.

You must:

- write the letter of the topic in the box at the upper right corner of the answer sheet where you write your essay
- write your essay on the given topic legibly on the lined pages of the answer sheet in the 45 minutes allotted. Use a ballpoint pen. Your notes on scratch paper will not be considered.

You will have 45 minutes to write on the topic below.

The computer is one of the most important technological developments in the twentieth century. Our lives have been vastly affected by computers, from the giant supercomputer to the small personal computer.

There exist widely differing views about the computer's contribution to the quality of our life. Some regard it as indispensable; others consider it a liability. Write a composition of about 200 words in which you present your view on this issue giving reasons and examples to support your position.

END OF EXAMINATION

TEST 2: SOCIAL STUDIES

Directions

Allotted time: 85 minutes

This test consists of **64 multiple-choice questions** designed to measure your knowledge of the general ideas or concepts of social studies: history, geography, economics, political science and behavioural sciences.

You will be given information in the form of readings, some of which will be accompanied by a map, chart, or graph. Study the given information and answer the questions based on it.

Since you are allowed 85 minutes, be careful not to spend too much time on each question.

Make no mark on the answer sheet other than your choice of the correct answer. If you change your answer, erase your first mark completely. Only *one* answer space should be marked for each question.

EXAMPLE:

Changes in occupational titles from busboy to dining room attendant and stewardess to flight attendant illustrate an attempt to deal with the problem of

(1) racism
(2) ethnocentrism
(3) sexism
(4) age bias
(5) unionism

① ② ● ④ ⑤

The changes in occupational titles are evidence that sex indications, such as boy and stewardess, are being removed and that sexism, the exploitation and domination of one sex by the other, is being given attention. Therefore, the correct answer is 3, and 3 should be marked on the answer sheet.

Directions: Choose the one best answer to each item.

Items 1 to 3 refer to the following passage.

Another "elite" is developing. The "have" and the "have-nots" of the Industrial Age have been replaced by the "know" and the "know-nots" of the Communications Age. The gap between the masses of techno-peasants and the new elite will grow ever wider as the new age progresses. Because the more we know makes it even easier to know more. Those who are behind at the start of the race may never catch up.

1. This passage is chiefly about

(1) the "haves" and the "have-nots"
(2) the widening gap between the techno-elites and the techno-peasants
(3) the Industrial Age
(4) the Communications Age
(5) knowledge for the masses

2. Techno-peasants refer to

(1) industrial age elites
(2) the gap between the masses
(3) new age "haves"
(4) those who have not acquired communication skills
(5) competitors in the race

3. Techno-elites may be described as

(1) casualties of the Industrial Age
(2) Communications Age "knows"
(3) the opposite of "have-nots"
(4) knowing more than ever
(5) "know-nots"

Items 4 to 6 are based on the following passage.

Late in 1941 the Japanese entered the war against the Allies. For people of Japanese descent in Canada it was the beginning of a nightmare, for soon after that the Canadian government introduced a policy of "internment."

At this time there were 23,000 people of Japanese ancestry in Canada. Of these, 6,000 were Japanese nationals, 3,000 were naturalized Canadians, and 14,000 were native-born Canadians of Japanese descent. Most of these people were sent to internment camps. They were often separated from friends and family, and their belongings and businesses were sold with little provided to them by way of compensation.

Why did Canada treat these Japanese people so harshly? Because we let panic get in the way of justice. We threw aside everything we were supposed to be fighting for and trampled on the rights of Canadians. The Canadian government gave in to pressure from British Columbians whose fear of the new war in the Pacific revived and strengthened old feelings of bigotry against Asians. The records of the Canadian Cabinet show that what the government feared was not subversive activity by Japanese Canadians but serious racial attacks on them by the white population.

4. Most of the Japanese people interned in Canada during the Second World War were born

(1) in Japan
(2) en route from Japan to Canada
(3) in internment camps
(4) in Canada
(5) in other countries

5. According to the passage, why did the Canadian government introduce a policy of internment?

(1) fear that the Japanese people in Canada would act as spies for Japan
(2) because the Japanese acted harshly in attacking Pearl Harbor and entering the war
(3) in order to curb successful Japanese business ventures
(4) fear of attacks on the Japanese community by the white population
(5) because the Japanese were not loyal to Canada

6. Which of the following terms best describes the attitudes of Canadians toward the Japanese people who were interned?

(1) tolerant
(2) accepting
(3) racist
(4) impartial
(5) open-minded

---

7. The most useful indicator of the degree of democracy reached by a particular society would be whether it has a

(1) formal method whereby people can effect changes in government policy
(2) system of government checks and balances
(3) two-house legislature
(4) system of liberal and humane courts
(5) civilian government

8. "The Liberal and Conservative parties have assumed an important place in Canadian political culture for almost a century but their claim to the status of national parties has often been tenuous. The Conservatives have often been virtually excluded from Quebec and the Liberals have found it hard to establish a permanent presence in the West." The author of this statement probably means to suggest that

(1) political parties in Canada tend to represent language interests
(2) each of the major political parties appeals to a different social class
(3) there is no significant difference between the Conservatives and the Liberals
(4) the two major parties do not have a broadly based appeal in all parts of the country
(5) only a two-party system can function in a democracy

Item 9 is based on the following drawing

	HUNTER	COUREUR de BOIS	TRADING COMPANY	ARTISAN	MERCHANT	BUYER
activity	producer of raw material	carrier and middleman	middleman	producer of finished product	middleman	consumer
productive % labour	65%	5%	0%	30%	0%	
% profits	.01%	4.99%	60%	5%	30%	

"The Fur Trade"

9. Which contributor to the fur trade did the most work and earned the least profit?

(1) the hunter
(2) the coureur de bois
(3) the trading company
(4) the artisan
(5) the merchant

Items 10 and 11 are based on the following passage.

Increased growth through acquisition by the largest corporations has resulted in a situation where western economies will be dominated by virtually independent economic giants. Growth of these vast corporate structures, even though accompanied by an increase in the number of much smaller and less powerful companies that operate under their control, foretells the creation of monopoly-like structures throughout the business world.

In general, the major acquisitions by the sample companies were corporate organizations that were profitable and successful before acquisition. The main effect of the merger or acquisition was to transfer control and management of an already successful enterprise to a new group. Profitability ratios, which provide a measure of management performance, for some of the major acquired companies for the year immediately preceding acquisition when compared to the years after acquisition, indicate that, in most instances, the acquired companies operated less efficiently after acquisition.

10. Where mergers took place, the companies which were added had
(1) low profitability ratios
(2) inferior corporate values
(3) achieved success
(4) poor productivity
(5) management difficulties

11. According to the passage, one measure of management performance is a corporation's

(1) geographic market
(2) available capital
(3) corporate values
(4) profitability ratio
(5) cartel-like structure

Items 12 and 13 are based on the following graph.

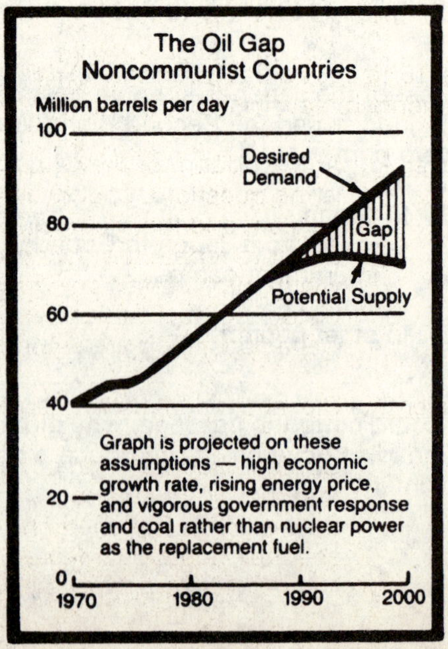

12. Based on the information in the graph, the demand of noncommunist countries for oil will begin to exceed the supply of oil in about the year

(1) 1980
(2) 1985
(3) 1990
(4) 1995
(5) 2000

13. A valid conclusion that can be drawn from the data in the graph is that the noncommunist countries will

(1) have serious economic problems if alternate sources of energy are not developed
(2) avoid any gap between oil supply and demand by increasing oil production
(3) have until the year 2000 to make any major changes in energy policies
(4) be unable to solve their energy problems
(5) use less oil because of its high price

---

14. A study of the causes of the American Revolution of 1776, the French Revolution of 1789, and the Russian Revolution of 1917 best supports the generalization that revolution is most likely to occur when

(1) those in power are resistant to change
(2) a society has a lower standard of living than those around it
(3) a society has become industrialized
(4) stable governments are in power
(5) people are given too much voice in their government

Items 15 to 17 are based on the following statements by four historians.

Speaker A: At the bottom of the whole affair is the question of nationality and religion, and the Metis seemed about to repeat the dark pages which mark certain periods in the history of the Acadians and the Canadians, their ancestors.

Speaker B: Riel and his Metis wanted to belong to the Canadian Confederation, but on condition that they were able to negotiate their entry as free men and to see their rights guaranteed.

Speaker C: Riel, from the beginning, when he went into the country, until he left, went there for the purpose of making money. He came there for the most sordid purposes possible . . . and he told all kinds of lies.

Speaker D: Riel wanted it understood that the Metis did not fight for two hundred and forty acres of land. He wanted it to be clear that there were two societies that treated together. One was small, but in its smallness had its rights. The other was great, but in its greatness had no greater rights than the rights of the small.

15. Which speakers would be most likely to agree that the Riel Rebellions represented a struggle for freedom and justice?

(1) A and C
(2) B and D
(3) C and D
(4) A and D
(5) B and C

16. With which statement about Riel would Speaker B most likely agree?

(1) He was a fanatic who would go to any length to secure an upper hand for the French language and the Catholic faith.
(2) He was a patriot who fought and secured the rights of his people.
(3) He was a murderer whose hands were stained with innocent blood.
(4) He was a schemer who wanted to take the Canadian west into the United States.
(5) His major goal was to keep settlers out of the West.

17. The most valid inference to be drawn from the statements of the four speakers is that

(1) all the facts should be known before a conclusion is drawn
(2) historians must be free of personal bias
(3) a study of history enables people to predict future events
(4) historians disagree over interpretation of events
(5) only one of the speakers is correct in his views

Item 18 is based on the following chart.

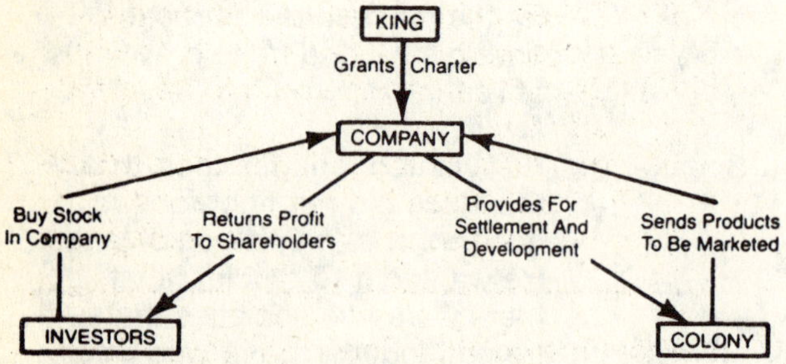

18. Which is a valid conclusion that can be drawn from the information in the chart?

(1) The main purpose of the system was to benefit the colonies.
(2) Nationalism was the motivating factor in English colonization.
(3) The profit motive was a strong force in colonization.
(4) The opportunity to own land attracted many settlers to the colonies.
(5) Inducements were offered to prospective settlers.

Items 19 and 20 are based on the following passage.

The first fur traders came to Canada along with fishermen in the early 1600s. When the fishermen came ashore to dry and salt their catches they often received food from the Indians as well as help in building shelter. It was from these first contacts that the fur trade arose. In 1635 Jacques Cartier wrote ". . . the Indians made frequent signs to us to come on shore, holding up to us some furs on sticks . . . and the two parties traded together. They bartered all they had to such an extent that all went back naked without anything on them; and they made signs to us that they would return on the morrow with more furs."

19. What sort of trade does Cartier mean when he says that "they bartered."

(1) the exchange of goods without the use of money
(2) the two parties would haggle over the price
(3) the sale of an item at a fixed price
(4) the illegal transfer of goods
(5) trading without paying the proper taxes

20. Cartier's description of the trading process implies that

(1) the French traders succeeded in exploiting the Indians
(2) the Indians thought that the prices offered for the furs were too low
(3) fur trading provided an opportunity to plan permanent colonization of the New World
(4) both the French and the Indians thought that they benefited from the fur trade
(5) the Indians used fur trading as a cover to plan an attack

---

Items 21 and 22 are based on the following cartoon.

"WE'D BE PERFECTLY WILLING TO USE SOME OF OUR EXTRA PROFITS TO EXPLORE WAYS OF MAKING MORE EXTRA PROFITS"

from Herblock On All Fronts (New American Library, 1980)

21. A member of Parliament who shared the cartoonist's viewpoint would be most likely to vote for

(1) tax incentives to encourage corporations to diversify
(2) decreased corporate income taxes
(3) stronger laws regulating monopolies
(4) reduced taxes on dividends paid to corporate stockholders
(5) restraints of trade by corporations

22. The cartoon suggests that the oil companies have used their profits to

(1) build conglomerates
(2) develop more efficient and safer consumer products
(3) establish cooperatives
(4) improve the standard of living in Canada
(5) subsidize the media

Items 23 to 25 are based on the following chart.

Canada: Population Changes

	1901	1991
Urban population (percent of total)	35%	76.6%
Rural population (percent of total)	65%	23.4%
Farm employment (percent of total employed)	16.1%	3.3%
Per capita gross domestic product	$410	$24,873

23. Which statement concerning population changes is best supported by the data in the chart?

(1) Urbanization has accompanied economic growth.
(2) There is little connection between population changes and prosperity levels.
(3) Urban workers earn more money than rural workers.
(4) The decrease in farm employment resulted in increased urban unemployment.
(5) Urban population growth was in line with growth in per capita gross national product.

24. Which situation would most likely account for the changes in population shown in the chart?

(1) Greater educational opportunities were available in the cities.
(2) Greater economic opportunities were available in the cities.
(3) The crime rate was lower in rural areas.
(4) Housing became scarce in rural areas.
(5) Farmers received government subsidies.

25. Which factor would best explain the change in farm employment?

(1) Immigration was restricted after 1901.
(2) The amount of available farmland decreased.
(3) Mechanization reduced the need for farm workers.
(4) Imports provided a higher percentage of food needs.
(5) The birthrate in rural areas decreased.

---

26. From the point of view of an environmentalist, which is probably the most significant argument against offshore drilling for oil?

(1) There is little need to take such natural resources from the ocean waters.
(2) Oil corporations are falsely advertising an oil shortage in order to expand their drilling operations.
(3) The potential oil to be found is not worth the capital investment needed to extract it.
(4) The possible harm to the balance of nature is more important than a gain in energy.
(5) Coal is a preferable resource to oil.

27. Topography deals with surface features of a region including its landforms and rivers, lakes, etc., and with man-made features such as canals, bridges, and roads. According to this, the topography of a region would include its

(1) climate
(2) plants
(3) animals
(4) mountains
(5) inhabitants

Items 28 to 30 are based on the following passage.

In the late 1930s, when it was still reeling from the effects of the Great Depression, the federal government appointed a Royal Commission to examine the fiscal relationship that existed between the federal and provincial levels of government. In their report, the Commissioners commented that "Since the Great War, the Great Depression has been the chief stimulus to labour legislation and social insurance. The note sounded has not been so much the ideal of social justice as political and economic expediency. For instance, the shorter working week was favoured in unexpected quarters, not because it would give workers more leisure and possibilities for a fuller life, but because it would spread work; and the current singling out of unemployment insurance for governmental attention in many countries is dictated by the appalling costs of direct relief and the hope that unemployment insurance benefits will give some protection to public treasuries in future depressions and will, by sustaining purchasing power, tend to mitigate these depressions."

28. The passage deals principally with

(1) the causes of the Great Depression
(2) the need for social justice
(3) the benefits of unemployment insurance
(4) support for labour legislation and social insurance
(5) the consequences of the Great War

29. According to the commissioners, social reforms were accepted as a means to

(1) promote social equality
(2) redistribute wealth
(3) stabilize the economy
(4) win votes
(5) ensure a booming economy

30. Which one of the following was the focus of the Royal Commission?

(1) historical concerns
(2) economic relations
(3) social problems
(4) environmental issues
(5) political problems

Items 31 to 33 are based on the following passage.

For some time, the absence of women in the elected assemblies of western democracies was attributed to physiological factors, although "hormone-based" explanations find little support today. The continued exclusion of women from the ranks of political decision-makers has also been attributed to a male conspiracy that subjugates women to a subordinate and dependent social status. Overall, however, the "socialization paradigm" and gender role constraints have become the most popular explanations for division of political power by gender.

The "socialization" explanation contends that women do not seek elected office because, in western democracies, women are socialized to be apolitical. Young girls are taught differently from young boys. Females are encouraged, directly through example and indirectly through cultural prescriptions and sanctions, that politics is better left to men.

31. The term *apolitical* as used in the second paragraph means

(1) to have strong political views
(2) to be politically open-minded
(3) not to stick with one political party
(4) to be faithful to one political party
(5) to have no concern at all for politics

32. According to the passage, which of the following is the most widely accepted explanation for the comparative under-representation in the elected assemblies of western democracies?

(1) the socialization explanation
(2) the "hormone-based" explanation
(3) the male conspiracy theory explanation
(4) the male superiority explanation
(5) the female lack of interest explanation

33. Which one of the following is an implication of the "hormone-based" explanation?

(1) Women's upbringing teaches them that politics is "a man's world."
(2) Men systematically plot to keep women out of politics.
(3) Women are not emotionally suited to the hard knocks of everyday political life.
(4) Women have too many family responsibilities to be involved politically.
(5) Women should be legally excluded from extensive political involvement.

Items 34 and 35 are based on the following cartoon.

34. According to the cartoon, how has the federal government viewed the Atlantic provinces?

(1) as a region needing aggressive development
(2) as not being of much interest
(3) as a political liability
(4) as an economic asset
(5) as an economic liability

35. Which ONE of the following statements is likely to be true of the cartoonist?

(1) He supported the federal government's policies toward the Atlantic region.
(2) He thought the federal government was sympathetic toward the Atlantic region.
(3) He did not have much sympathy for the Atlantic region.
(4) He viewed federal policy toward the Atlantic region as generally too little, too late.
(5) He thought a Royal Commission would be the best thing for the Atlantic region.

---

36. Which statement best illustrates the principle of multiple causation of human behavior?

(1) To each according to his or her needs.
(2) Environment and heredity are constantly interacting.
(3) Geographic differences account for variations in civilizations.
(4) Wealth and power go together.
(5) Habit results from repeated acts.

Items 37 and 38 are based on the following passage.

Since 1750, about the beginning of the Age of Steam, the earth's population has more than tripled. This increase has not been an evolutionary phenomenon with biological causes. Yet there was an evolution—it took place in the world's economic organization. Thus 1,500,000,000 more human beings can now remain alive on the earth's surface, can support themselves by working for others who in turn work for them. This extraordinary tripling of human population in six short generations is explained by the speeded-up economic unification which took place during the same period. Thus, most of us are now kept alive by this vast cooperative unified world society.

37. The writer considers trade necessary for

(1) travel
(2) democracy
(3) political unity
(4) self-preservation
(5) the theory of evolution

38. The basic change which led to the greatly increased population concerns

(1) new explorations
(2) economic factors
(3) biological factors
(4) an increase in travel
(5) the growth of world government

---

39. It sometimes seems to Indians that Canada shows more interest in preserving its rare whooping cranes than its Indians. And Canada, the Indian notes, does not ask its cranes to become Canada geese. It just wants to preserve them as whooping cranes. Indians hold no grudge against the big, beautiful, nearly extinct birds, but we would like to know how they managed their deal. Whooping cranes can remain whooping cranes, but Indians are to become brown white men.

The major concern of the author is

(1) protecting the natural environment
(2) native land claims
(3) Indian assimilation into the white culture
(4) poverty on Indian reserves
(5) protecting aboriginal languages

40. "The parties agree than an armed attack against one or more of them in Europe or North America shall be considered an attack against them all . . ."

This quotation is most closely associated with which concept?

(1) collective security
(2) intervention
(3) ultimatum
(4) appeasement
(5) aggression

41. Social mobility refers to a situation in which an individual can and often does change in social status. Which best illustrates social mobility in Canada?

(1) A farm family in Southern Ontario buys a farm in the Okanagan valley of British Columbia.
(2) The son of a president of a large manufacturing plant becomes a company executive.
(3) The daughter of an unskilled immigrant worker becomes a teacher.
(4) A woman whose parents are both university professors receives a graduate degree.
(5) A Montrealer moves to Vancouver.

42. Cultural diversity, a variety of cultural patterns, is generally the result of

(1) actions by the government of the area
(2) the desire of the inhabitants to develop original ideas and styles
(3) competition among the people for control of food sources
(4) migrations to the area by various groups
(5) reciprocal regional agreements

43. Culture shock is the confusion experienced by someone encountering unfamiliar surroundings, a strange community, or a different culture. Which situation is the best example of culture shock?

(1) the refusal of some religious groups to allow blood transfusion
(2) the hippies' rejection of the "Establishment" in the 1960s
(3) the differences in life-styles between the early European explorers and Canada's native peoples
(4) the initial reaction of a Canadian aid worker arriving in a developing nation
(5) the generation gap

44. An extended family is a group of relatives by blood, marriage, or adoption living in close proximity or together, especially if three generations are involved.

Which is usually a characteristic of societies that have the extended family as their basic unit?

(1) The society tends to be highly industrialized.
(2) The roles of the family members are economically and socially interdependent.
(3) The government usually provides incentives to increase family size.
(4) The functions of the family unit are defined mainly by the government.
(5) The family becomes widely dispersed geographically.

45. Pluralism is the existence within a society of groups distinctive in ethnic origin, cultural patterns, or religion. Maintaining stability in a pluralistic society is difficult because

(1) individuals are often forced to deal with the views of others which may challenge their own ideas
(2) there is usually no well-defined order of governmental authority
(3) new members in the society are often unwilling to obey established laws of the society
(4) the wide variety of citizens' abilities hinders the management of labour resources
(5) there are differing degrees of respect for authority

<u>Items 46 and 47</u> refer to the following passage.

It is not difficult to get into trouble in school. Being part of a group of people, some of whom are feeling very different emotions at the same time, can easily lead to misunderstandings. Telling a joke to someone who is feeling happy will lead to both of you laughing. The same joke told to someone who is feeling angry can lead to an argument.

When the teacher is one of the people involved, the situation can get out of hand. As the authority figure in the class, the wrong word said to an angry student can lead to an ugly incident. The right word to that same student can diffuse a situation. The best choice in a group is to be aware of the emotional state of the people around you.

46. Telling a joke

(1) is always fun
(2) is never fun
(3) can be inappropriate
(4) is alright outside of school
(5) can make a class interesting

47. Teachers must be especially careful of what they say because they

(1) are authority figures
(2) can give you detentions
(3) have poor senses of humour
(4) are older than most of the class
(5) speak loudly

48. Mountains and coasts have served to restrict settlements; rivers and plains, to extend them. Each of these natural features has placed a characteristic imprint on the society which it dominated, largely fashioning its mode of life, its customs, morals, and temperament.

The passage implies that

(1) mountains and coasts are unfriendly to man
(2) mountains and rivers exert an equal influence on society
(3) mountains and plains have similar effects on settlement
(4) natural features result from the society which evolves within them
(5) geographic features influence the society mankind develops

Items 49 and 50 are based on the following tables.

Table A

Question: "Here are two suggestions that people have made to improve stability and order in this country. For each, would you favour or oppose such a step being taken?"

SUGGESTIONS	PERCENT OF PUBLIC		
	FAVOUR	OPPOSE	NOT SURE
A law should be passed allowing police officers to search a home without a warrant in an emergency, such as when they are looking for drugs.	32	65	3
The government should be given authority to use wiretaps and other electronic surveillance to gather evidence against citizens suspected of criminal activity, even if a court does not authorize such activity.	27	68	5

Table B

Question: "Do you feel the federal government should be allowed to engage in wiretapping and electronic surveillance, if in each case it had to go to court beforehand to obtain court permission, or don't you feel the federal government should ever be allowed to engage in wiretapping or electronic surveillance?"

RESPONSE	PERCENT OF PUBLIC
Should be allowed	63
Should not be allowed	28
Not sure	9

49. The information in Table A indicates that most people questioned

(1) were undecided on the issues in question
(2) supported the idea of a search without a warrant only in an emergency
(3) favoured protecting their privacy
(4) favoured permitting the government to investigate their lives
(5) favoured electronic eavesdropping over searches

50. A valid conclusion based on both tables is that the results of opinion surveys

(1) tend to obscure the issues
(2) are purposely biased by the pollsters
(3) can vary according to the way the issue is presented
(4) show that public attitudes are generally consistent
(5) tend to be inconclusive

Items 51 and 52 are based on the following chart.

THE AGRICULTURAL MARKETING SYSTEM

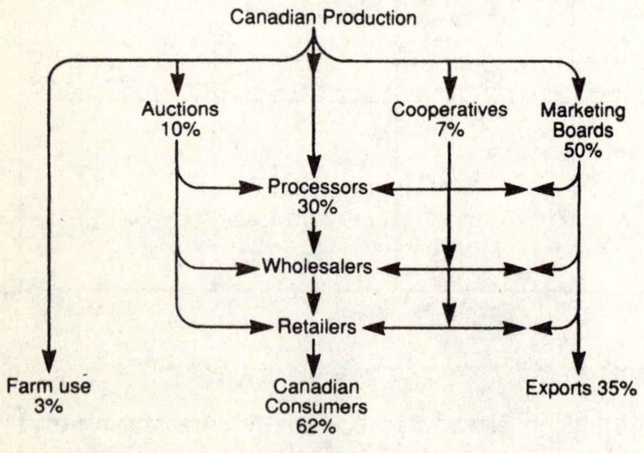

51. According to the chart, which ONE of the following plays the most important role with respect to the initial purchase of agriculture products?

(1) marketing boards
(2) cooperatives
(3) processors
(4) consumers
(5) retailers

52. A conclusion that can be drawn from the information presented on the chart is that

(1) almost all Canadian agricultural production is controlled through marketing boards
(2) retailers make the most profit from the agriculture sector
(3) most Canadian agricultural production is consumed in Canada
(4) most Canadian agricultural production is exported
(5) too much Canadian agricultural production is consumed domestically

---

Items 53 and 54 are based on the following graphs.

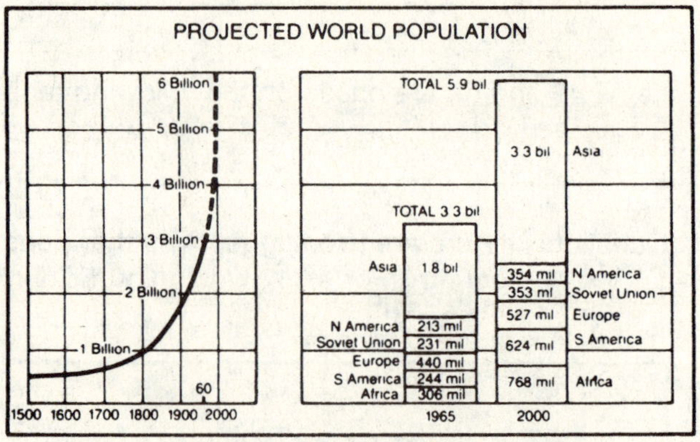

53. Which conclusion is best supported by the data in the graphs?

(1) In 1965 the populations of Asia and Africa were about equal.
(2) The world population was relatively stable until after World War II.
(3) The population of North America is growing faster than the population of South America.
(4) The population of the world will have almost tripled between 1900 and 2000.
(5) The population of the Soviet Union has been stable.

54. Which prediction is best supported by the data in the graphs?

(1) Population changes will reduce international tensions in the future.
(2) The rate of world population growth will peak before 2000.
(3) Asian influence in world affairs is likely to increase.
(4) The influence of older people in world politics will increase by the year 2000.
(5) There will be fewer population problems in the year 2000 because of population growth.

<u>Items 55 and 56</u> are based on the following map.

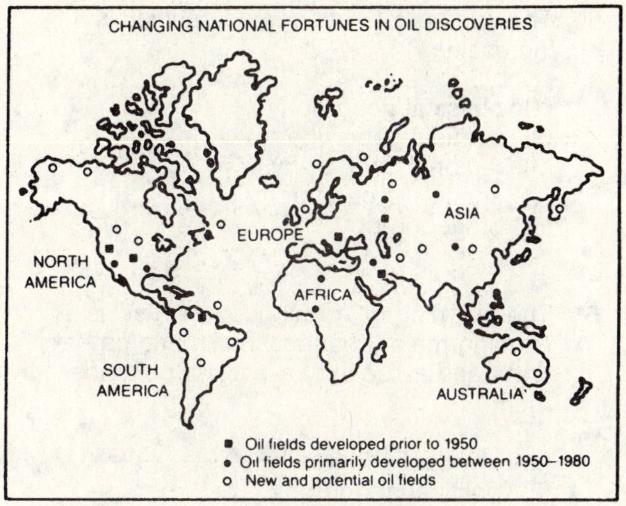

55. Which pair of continents has the greatest potential for new oil production?

(1) Australia and Europe
(2) Asia and North America
(3) South America and Africa
(4) Africa and Australia
(5) North America and South America

56. Which prediction is best supported by the information included on the map?

(1) North America will become less dependent upon the Arab nations for its oil.
(2) There will be continuing major rises in the price of oil throughout the world.
(3) There will be a ban on nuclear energy development.
(4) Africa and Europe will become the major oil exporters in the world.
(5) Asia will become less important as a supplier of oil.

<u>Items 57 and 58</u> are based on the following information

Rate per 100 000 Population of Violent Crime Offences, Canada and the Provinces/Territories, 1980 and 1990

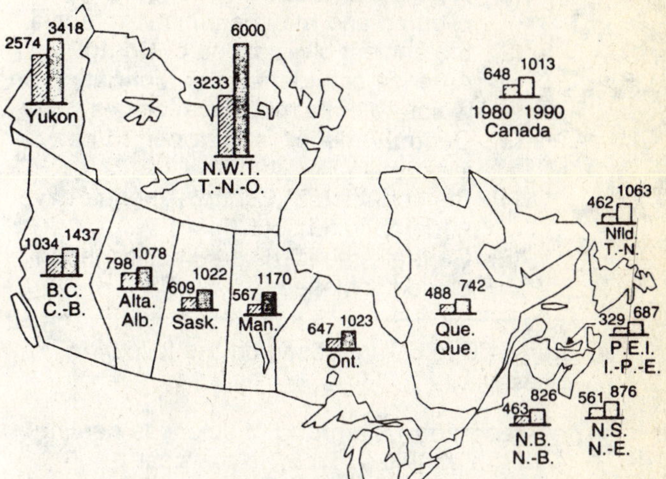

57. The evidence in the bar graph disproves the commonly held belief that

(1) the violent crime rate in Newfoundland and Labrador is below the Canadian average
(2) large seaports attract criminal elements
(3) Quebec has the highest rate of violent crime in Canada
(4) British Columbia is the centre of drug-related crime in Canada
(5) most crimes do not involve violence

58. The highest percentage increase in violent crime in Canada between 1980 and 1990 was in

(1) Prince Edward Island
(2) Newfoundland and Labrador
(3) the Yukon
(4) Alberta
(5) Manitoba

<u>Item 59</u> is based on the following cartoon.

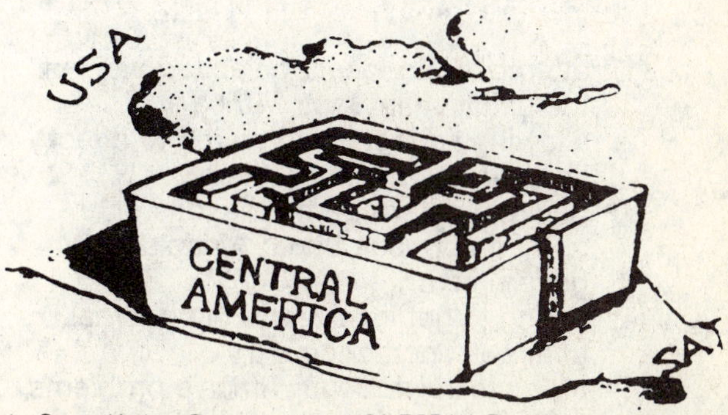

by Susan Harlan. Copyright 1984, USA TODAY. Reprinted with permission.

59. The main idea of the cartoon is that
    (1) problems in Central America are complicated and may be difficult to solve
    (2) the ancient civilizations of Central America provide a weak foundation on which to build modern societies
    (3) Central America is not open to new ideas
    (4) the countries of Central America have undemocratic societies
    (5) Central Americans are imprisoned in closed societies

Items 60 to 62 are based on the following passage.

Geography is a group of sciences dealing with the earth's surface, its physical structures, and the distribution of life on earth. Among the many branches of geography are:
(1) physical geography, which deals with the physical features of the earth and includes climatology and oceanography
(2) political geography, which deals with the world as divided into nations
(3) regional geography, which deals with the world in terms of regions separated by physical rather than national boundaries
(4) economic geography, which deals with the patterns of the world's commerce in terms of production, trade, and transportation
(5) biogeography, which is concerned with the distribution of life, both plant and animal (including man), around the world

For each of the following concerns, identify the branch of geography involved.

60. The number of endangered species is increasing.
    (1) physical geography
    (2) political geography
    (3) regional geography
    (4) economic geography
    (5) biogeography

61. The warming or "greenhouse effect" is causing major changes in climatic patterns and a rise in sea level as polar ice melts.
    (1) physical geography
    (2) political geography
    (3) regional geography
    (4) economic geography
    (5) biogeography

62. Drought conditions have caused malnutrition in East Africa.
    (1) physical geography
    (2) political geography
    (3) regional geography
    (4) economic geography
    (5) biogeography

Items 63 and 64 are based on the following cartoon.

Tom Joles in The Buffalo News

63. The cartoon implies that Western governments are
    (1) attempting to take a balanced view of the situation in South Africa
    (2) allowing economic concerns to affect its view of a moral problem
    (3) being threatened with the loss of an ally if it opposes South Africa's government
    (4) willing to get involved in the internal affairs of another country
    (5) trying to solve South Africa's problems

64. The major South African issue referred to in the cartoon is
    (1) apartheid
    (2) reciprocal trade agreements
    (3) civil unrest
    (4) majority rights in a democracy
    (5) deteriorating financial conditions

END OF EXAMINATION

TEST 3: SCIENCE

Directions

Allotted time: 95 minutes

The **66 multiple-choice questions** in this test measure the general concepts in science. You may find a graph, a chart, or a table included with some questions.

Study the information given. Decide which is the best answer and mark the numbered space on the answer sheet beside the number that corresponds to the question in the test.

Answer all questions. Do not leave any blanks since there is no penalty for incorrect answers. Your score will be determined by the number of your correct responses.

EXAMPLE:

Which of the following is the smallest unit?

(1) element
(2) compound
(3) atom
(4) mixture
(5) molecule

① ② ● ④ ⑤

The correct answer is “atom”; therefore, answer space 3 would be marked on the answer sheet.

Directions: Choose the one best answer to each item.

Items 1 to 6 are based on the following article.

The study of ecology, the branch of biology that deals with the interrelations between living things and their environment, is most important today. The environment of living things must be considered from the point of view of the physical factors, such as temperature, soil, and water, and the biotic factors, which are the effects of other living things.

Ecologists organize groups of living things into populations, communities, ecological systems, and the biosphere. A *population* consists of organisms of the same species living together in a given location, such as all the oak trees in a forest or all the frogs of the same species in a pond. A *community* consists of populations of different species, living together and interacting with each other. The accompanying diagram illustrates a simple community. It pictures a large bottle with a layer of mud on the bottom. The bottle was filled with pond water and several fish and some green plants were added. The bottle was then made airtight. The members of this community will thrive as long as the balance is maintained.

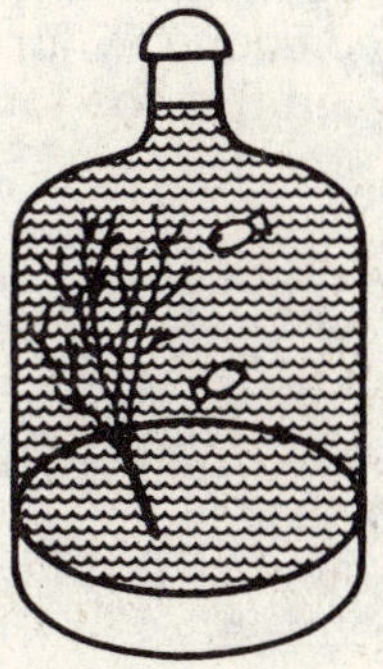

1. Which of the following consists of a single species?

(1) biosphere
(2) community
(3) ecosystem
(4) biome
(5) population

2. The fact that living things can survive in the airtight bottle illustrates the

(1) need for green plants in our environment
(2) need for physical factors in a community
(3) balance within a population
(4) need for biotic factors in a community
(5) interrelations between living things and the physical and biotic factors of the environment

3. When species of plants and animals are introduced into a new habitat, they often become pests in the new habitat, even though they were not pests in their native habitats. The most probable reason for this is that in the new habitat they

(1) have fewer natural enemies
(2) have a much lower mutation rate
(3) develop better resistance to the new climate
(4) learn to use different foods
(5) have more predators

4. If this airtight container and its contents were weighed each day for several days, it would be found that the total weight would

(1) increase gradually
(2) remain the same
(3) decrease gradually
(4) decrease for the first few days and then increase
(5) increase for the first few days and then decrease

5. All of the following are biotic factors affecting the balance of the airtight container EXCEPT

(1) the concentration of minerals in solution
(2) the number of fishes
(3) the kinds of protozoa in the water
(4) the kinds of plants
(5) the presence of crustaceans in the mud

6. Many different species of organisms interacting in a particular environment is an example of a

(1) population
(2) biosphere
(3) community
(4) biome
(5) species

Items 7 to 10 refer to the following article.

The present-day horse is an animal whose evolution can be traced through complete series of fossil ancestors. The first horse, or dawn horse, was called *Eohippus* and lived about 60,000,000 years ago. It was but a foot high, had four toes on each front foot, and three on each hind foot. Each toe had a toenail, which was a primitive hoof. The teeth were small, with little if any ridges. It had a short neck and a small skull. Descendents of this first horse include a slightly larger *Mesohippus*. The Mesohippus had three toes on each foot, but the middle toe was large and carried most of the weight. The teeth had well-developed ridges. A still later fossil had a foot much like the horse today, but there were still two small side toes that were in evidence that did not touch the ground. It was still smaller than the modern horse. The modern horse has but tiny splints remaining of the two toes on the sides of the legs.

7. The author draws the facts from the study of

(1) toes
(2) fossils
(3) teeth
(4) splints
(5) body size

8. Organisms often possess structures that are useless to the individual but are thought to have been functional in their remote ancestors. Such structures are called *vestigial*. An example of a vestigial structure is the

(1) four toes of Eohippus
(2) toenail of Eohippus
(3) large toe of Mesohippus
(4) splints of the modern horse
(5) hoof of the modern horse

9. Which of the following statements is true of Equus, the modern horse?

   (1) It lived 60 million years ago.
   (2) It has few ridges on its teeth.
   (3) It resembles Eohippus more than Mesohippus.
   (4) It walks on its splints.
   (5) It walks on the remains of a middle toe.

10. Mesohippus differs from Eohippus in that

    (1) Mesohippus disappeared before Eohippus evolved.
    (2) Eohippus had three toes on each foot.
    (3) Mesohippus had two small side toes that didn't touch the ground.
    (4) Mesohippus had a more highly developed tooth structure.
    (5) Eohippus had a larger middle toe.

Items 11 to 14 refer to the following information.

A dog was placed in a special room free of unrelated stimuli. On repeated trials a tone was sounded for 5 seconds; approximately 2 seconds later the dog was given powdered food. Trials 1, 10, 20, 30, 40, and 50 were test trials; that is, the tone was sounded for 30 seconds and no food powder was given. The following data were collected:

Test Trial Number	Drops of Saliva Secreted	Number of Seconds Between Onset of Tone and Salivation
1	0	
10	6	18
20	20	9
30	60	2
40	62	1
50	59	2

11. The experimenter is most probably studying

    (1) salivary digestion
    (2) instinctive behaviour
    (3) unlearned behaviour
    (4) effects of sound on animal behaviour
    (5) changed or conditioned responses

12. Of the following, which is similar to the type of response mentioned in the experiment?

    (1) A spider spins a web.
    (2) You automatically pull your hand away from a hot object.
    (3) A rat is taught to solve a maze.
    (4) A person becomes an efficient typist.
    (5) Your mouth waters at the sight of certain foods.

13. The greatest increase in the number of drops of saliva secreted occurred between test trials

    (1) 1 and 10
    (2) 1 and 20
    (3) 10 and 20
    (4) 20 and 30
    (5) 30 and 40

14. At test trial number 60, the number of drops of saliva secreted would probably be closest to

    (1) 25
    (2) 35
    (3) 55
    (4) 62
    (5) 75

Items 15 and 16 refer to the following article.

A question puzzling humans is—How did life originate? We agree that all life comes from pre-existing life, but to answer this question we must consider a time when there was no life. We must seek an explanation of the origin of the complex organic compounds, since we know that our present-day complex organic compounds are the results of life processes.

Any consideration of the origin of life must be concerned with the element carbon since organic substances are carbon compounds. We must also consider amino acids, the building blocks of protein and protoplasm—the living substance. One explanation tells us that simple chemical elements of the atmosphere were combined to form an amino acid that later may have been synthesized into a more complex bit of "stuff" that we now call protoplasm. The energy needed to cause this chemical synthesis, they say, might have been furnished by lightning or by the ultraviolet energy of the sun.

15. All living matter contains the chemical element

    (1) water
    (2) phosphorus
    (3) carbon
    (4) carbon dioxide
    (5) protein

16. The problem of explaining the origin of life on earth involves an answer to the question of the origin of

    (1) ultraviolet rays
    (2) proteins
    (3) atoms
    (4) molecules
    (5) inorganic carbon

Items 17 to 22 refer to the following information.

Scientists at a California Administration Medical Center performed an experiment to determine whether learning efficiency is related to feeding. Two groups of 20 mice each, all taken from the same pure-bred strain, were deprived of food for three days and then given a standard learning session in running through a maze. They were trained by giving them a mild electric shock whenever they took a wrong turn. One group was fed immediately after each learning session, and the other was not. A week later, all mice were tested to see whether they could still run the maze correctly. The group that was fed could still do it, but the other group could not.

The questions that follow consist of statements about the experiment. Classify each of the statements into one of the categories defined as follows. More than one statement may have the same classification.

(1) the problem—the main issue or subject being investigated in this study
(2) a method—a procedure used to conduct this investigation
(3) a finding—a proven result obtained as part of this investigation
(4) an assumption—a supporting idea, theory, or belief for which no proof is provided in the study
(5) irrelevant information—material that does not directly help or provide an understanding of the problem

17. The practice of using all mice from the same pure-bred strain is a(n)

    (1) assumption
    (2) hypothesis
    (3) conclusion
    (4) problem statement
    (5) control

18. The report of this experiment states that mice remember better if fed immediately after each training session. This statement is a(n)

    (1) irrelevancy
    (2) hypothesis
    (3) experimental finding
    (4) item of data
    (5) law of nature

19. The practice of using an electric shock in the teaching process is a(n)

    (1) experimental finding
    (2) experimental design element
    (3) theory
    (4) irrelevancy
    (5) observation

20. The authors say the experiment suggests that memory may be improved by hormones released from the stomach during feeding. This is a(n)

    (1) observation
    (2) experimental result
    (3) control
    (4) hypothesis
    (5) experimental design element

21. The experiment was suggested by the idea that memory might be helpful to animals in finding food. This is a(n)

    (1) experimental design element
    (2) irrelevancy
    (3) observation
    (4) experimental result
    (5) assumption

22. It is noted that mice can learn to run a maze more readily if the maze is well illuminated. This is a(n)

    (1) irrelevancy
    (2) experimental design element
    (3) assumption
    (4) experimental result
    (5) problem

Items 23 and 24 are based on the following diagram.

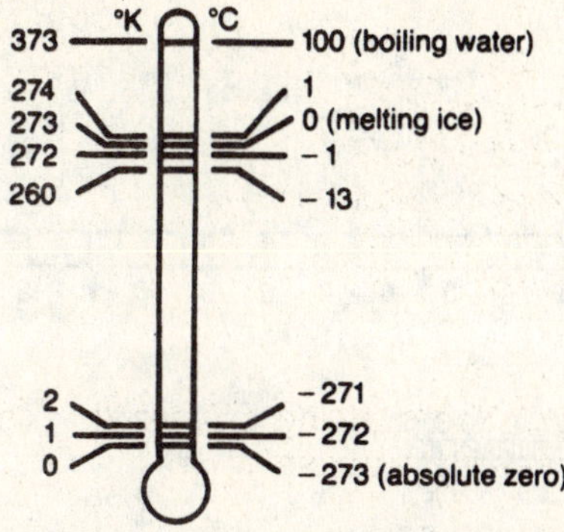

The diagram shows the connection between the Kelvin and the Celsius scales.

23. Which temperature is the same as –13° Celsius?

(1) 260 K
(2) 272 K
(3) 286 K
(4) 747 K
(5) 773 K

24. If the Celsius temperature of an object is increased 90°, its increase on the Kelvin scale is

(1) 50°
(2) 90°
(3) 162°
(4) 271°
(5) 273°

25. When an object is in free fall with no air resistance, its speed increases in direct proportion to the time of fall. If an astronaut on the moon drops his phasor, which of the following graphs best represents its motion?

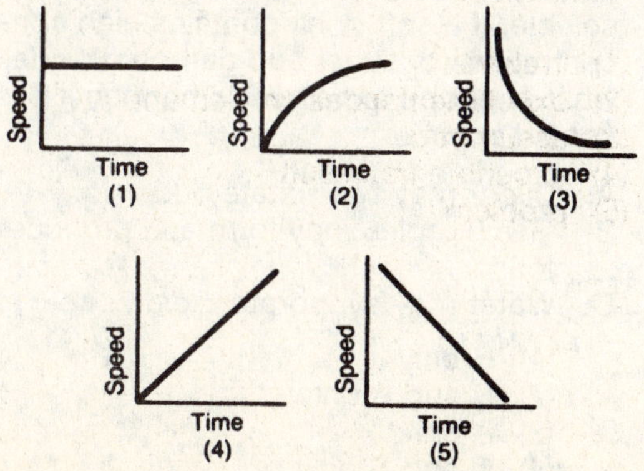

26. Electrical resistance is a property of electrical conductors, such as metals. The greater the resistance, the less current will flow in a given situation. The following table gives the resistance of ten meters of #22 wires of various metals:

aluminum:	0.87 ohms
brass:	2.15 ohms
copper:	0.53 ohms
iron:	3.1 ohms
platinum:	3.1 ohms
magnesium:	1.4 ohms

If each of these wires is connected in turn to a battery, which two will carry the most current?

(1) copper and aluminum
(2) magnesium and brass
(3) iron and platinum
(4) aluminum and magnesium
(5) copper and brass

Items 27 to 32 refer to the following article.

Acid deposition, commonly called "acid rain," is a complex and serious environmental problem. It can mean two things: sulphur and nitrogen pollutants in the atmosphere react with water in the air and form acid precipitation or sulphur and nitrogen pollutants are directly deposited on the surface of the earth where they react with water, forming acid substances.

Either way, the increased acidity changes the chemistry of both land and water environments. Two main causes of acid deposition are the burning of fossil fuels (such as coal, oil, and gasoline) and natural sources (such as volcanoes and bacterial decay.)

Water in pollution-free environments is actually slightly acidic. It has an average pH of 5.6. So a pH of 5.6 is a standard that may be used to judge whether water in the environment (rain, lakes, etc.) is truly more acidic than usual.

In cases of acid deposition, pH values from 3 to 5 are common, with some as low as 1.5. An important factor is *where* the acid deposition occurs. Other substances in the environment can neutralize the acid. For example, in one area the acid might be neutralized by the presence of calcium compounds or ammonia.

Evidence shows that acid deposition has an adverse effect on the environment. In lakes with increasing acidity, scientists have observed a decrease in the fish population. The acidity appears to reduce the fishes' ability to reproduce and the ability of the young fish to survive. It also seems to decrease the productivity of the plankton (the free-floating, usually microscopic, organisms found near the surface of the water) and to encourage the growth of more acid-resistant types of plants. On land, increased acidity can damage trees and change the chemistry of the soil.

27. Which substance may neutralize acidic conditions in the environment?

(1) carbon dioxide
(2) nitrogen
(3) sulphur
(4) carbon
(5) calcium carbonate

28. Which of the following is <u>not</u> a possible source of acid deposition?

(1) gasoline exhaust
(2) diesel exhaust
(3) a water-powered electric generating plant
(4) a volcanic eruption
(5) burning of coal in industry

29. Acid deposition can serve as

(1) a promoter of growth of algae
(2) a growth accelerator for fish
(3) an agent to produce alkaline soil
(4) a biotic factor in the environment
(5) a selective agent in the environment

30. Which of the following is an abiotic factor that relates to the acid deposition problem?

(1) plankton
(2) sulphur
(3) fish
(4) trees
(5) algae

31. Which of the following represents a rational, direct approach to reducing acid deposition?

(1) allowing lakes to continue to acidify indefinitely
(2) restocking the lakes where affected species exist
(3) altering weather patterns to prevent precipitation
(4) controlling air pollution at the source
(5) seeding the clouds to produce rain artificially

32. The accompanying scale shows the pH of five substances. Acid rain has a pH closest to that of which of these substances?

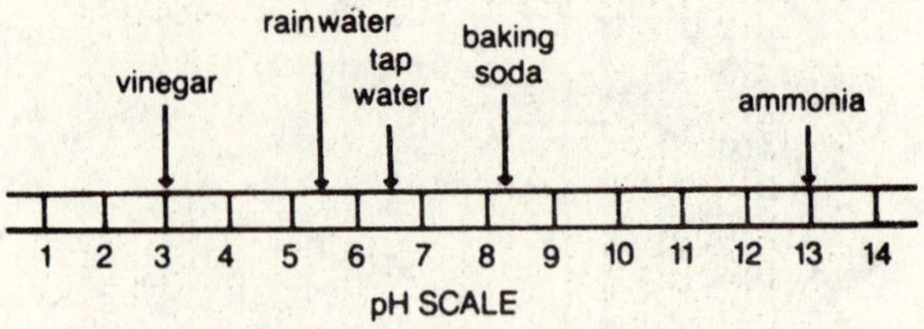

(1) ammonia
(2) tap water
(3) baking soda
(4) vinegar
(5) rainwater

33. Chemical fertilizers stimulate plant growth, but if the concentration is too high, they may damage roots. What precautions concerning chemical fertilizers must a gardener take?

(1) Use them only on some of his plants.
(2) Use only the amount recommended.
(3) Do not apply chemical fertilizers.
(4) Apply as much as possible without damaging roots.
(5) Give the plants only tiny amounts.

34. Amniote vertebrates are generally classified into three orders: Reptilia, Aves (birds), and Mammalia. Of the following, which group of three animals contains one member of each order?

(1) ostrich, American robin, Norway rat
(2) Beluga whale, black-footed ferret, box turtle
(3) timber rattlesnake, fence lizard, leopard
(4) African lion, sea otter, herring gull
(5) house sparrow, garter snake, African elephant

35. As temperature rises, solids become more soluble in water, but gases become less soluble. If a soft drink contains high concentrations of sugar and carbon dioxide, what might be expected to happen if it is cooled down?

A. Sugar may precipitate out.
B. Gas bubbles may form and produce foam.
C. Water may evaporate rapidly.

(1) B only
(2) B and A only
(3) A only
(4) C and B only
(5) A and C only

Item 36 is based on the following graph.

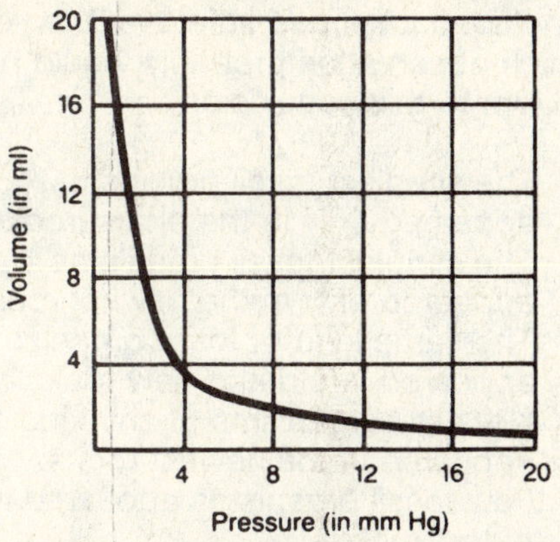

36. This graph represents the relationship of the pressure and volume of a given mass of a gas at constant temperature. When the pressure equals 8 mm of mercury (Hg), what is the volume in milliliters?

(1) 1
(2) 2
(3) 4
(4) 8
(5) 16

---

37. Clouds block the passage of radiant heat, which comes from the sun to the earth in the daytime and passes from the earth into outer space at night. How does cloud cover affect the surface temperature?

A. It makes days warmer.
B. It makes days cooler.
C. It makes nights warmer.
D. It makes nights cooler.

(1) B only
(2) D only
(3) A and C only
(4) B and D only
(5) B and C only

38. An object accelerates (changes its speed) only if the forces acting on it in one direction are greater than the forces in the opposite direction. All of the following objects will accelerate EXCEPT

(1) a gas balloon in which the buoyant force is greater than its weight and air resistance.
(2) a man in a parachute when the air resistance is less than his weight.
(3) an airplane in horizontal flight when the thrust of the engine is equal to the drag of the air.
(4) a ball striking a wall, in which the force of the ball on the wall is equal to the force of the wall on the ball.
(5) a rocket fired straight up, when the engine thrust is equal to the air resistance.

39. The four giant planets, Jupiter, Saturn, Uranus, and Neptune (in that order), are very far from the sun; only the small planet Pluto is farther. The *Voyager* space explorer found that Neptune and Uranus are surrounded by rings like those of Saturn. What hypothesis would be suggested by the discovery that Pluto has no rings?

(1) All large planets have rings, and small ones do not.
(2) Rings are present around any planet that is far enough from the sun.
(3) Rings are distributed at random, regardless of the size or position of the planet.
(4) Large planets may have rings, but small ones cannot.
(5) Pluto has lost its rings because it is so far from the sun.

40. Wind can carry dry sand, blowing it against bedrock and eroding the rock into fantastic shapes. What kind of ecosystem is most likely to have wind-eroded rocks?

(1) seashore
(2) desert
(3) prairie
(4) tundra
(5) deciduous forest

41. In a tank with water contaminated with bacteria, a surgical wound in a frog's skin heals much more rapidly than a similar wound in a fish. Any of the following might be a possible explanation EXCEPT

(1) The bacteria in the tank are not harmful to frogs.
(2) Some chemical in the frog's skin defends against bacteria.
(3) The frog's immune system responds efficiently to the bacteria.
(4) Frog skin has a much better ability to regenerate than the skin of a fish.
(5) The water contains some chemical substance that promotes healing.

Items 42 and 43 are based on the following table.

Mass of salt (g)	Heating time (min)
5.0	0.0
4.1	5.0
3.1	10.
3.0	15.
3.0	30.
3.0	60.

The table shows the data collected during the heating of a 5.0-gram sample of a hydrated salt.

42. After 60 minutes, how many grams of water appear to remain in the salt?

(1) 0.00
(2) 0.9
(3) 1.9
(4) 2.0
(5) 3.0

43. What is the percentage of water in the original sample?

(1) 30%
(2) 40%
(3) 50%
(4) 60%
(5) 82%

---

44. In a reflex, an impulse starts at a sense organ, passes through sensory neurons to the brain or spinal cord, then goes through motor neurons to a muscle or a gland. What is the sequence of organs in the reflex that causes tears to flow when the cornea of the eye is irritated?

(1) cornea–tear gland–brain–sensory neuron–motor neuron
(2) cornea–brain–motor neuron–sensory neuron–tear gland
(3) cornea–sensory neuron–brain–motor neuron–tear gland
(4) tear gland–cornea–motor neuron–brain–sensory neuron
(5) brain–cornea–sensory neuron–motor neuron–tear gland

45. In a certain area, DDT-resistant mosquitoes now exist in greater numbers than 10 years ago. What is the most probable explanation for this increase in numbers?

(1) DDT causes sterility in mosquitoes.
(2) Mosquito eggs were most likely to have been fertilized when exposed to DDT.
(3) DDT acted as a reproductive hormone for previous generations of mosquitoes.
(4) DDT serves as a new source of nutrition.
(5) Genetic differences permitted some mosquitoes to survive DDT use.

46. A scientist studying fossils in undisturbed layers of rock identified a species that, he concluded, changed little over the years. Which observation probably would have led him to this conclusion?

(1) The simplest fossil organisms appeared only in the oldest rocks.
(2) The simplest fossil organisms appeared only in the newest rocks.
(3) The same kind of fossil organisms appeared in old and new rocks.
(4) No fossil organisms of any kind appeared in the newest rocks.
(5) Few fossil organisms appeared in the oldest rock.

47. The pollen grain of a wheat plant produces a sperm nucleus with 14 chromosomes. How many chromosomes would there be in the egg nucleus and in a leaf cell?

(1) 14 in the egg nucleus, 28 in a leaf cell
(2) 14 in both the egg nucleus and leaf cells
(3) 28 in both the egg nucleus and leaf cells
(4) 7 in the egg nucleus and 14 in a leaf cell
(5) 7 in the egg nucleus and 28 in a leaf cell

48. A salmon will die after laying thousands of eggs, depositing them in the open water. A robin lays about 4 eggs and cares for the young when they hatch. It is reasonable to assume that

(1) there are far more salmon than robins in the world
(2) far more salmon than robins die before reaching adulthood
(3) there is more food available for growing salmon than for young robins
(4) salmon do not reproduce until they are much older than adult robins
(5) robins are better parents than salmon

49. Corn plants that are grown in the dark will be white and usually much taller than genetically identical corn plants grown in light, which will be green and shorter. The most probable explanation for this is that the

(1) Corn plants grown in the dark are all mutants for colour and height.
(2) The expression of a gene may be dependent on the environment.
(3) Plants grown in the dark will always be genetically albino.
(4) The phenotype of a plant is independent of its genotype.
(5) The genotype is independent of its phenotype.

50. Potatoes can be reproduced either by cuttings of the tubers or by seed formed sexually. Why would an agriculture specialist decide to go to the trouble of growing potatoes from seed?

(1) to produce the largest possible crop
(2) to try out a new fertilizer
(3) to reduce the difficulty of planting
(4) to produce new varieties
(5) to protect the new plants from insects

51. Element *A* and element *B* chemically combine to form substance *C*. Substance *C* must be

(1) a solution
(2) a compound
(3) an element
(4) a mixture
(5) an isotope

Items 52 to 54 refer to the following article.

Perhaps if it weren't for Joseph Priestley's work about 200 years ago, we would have no ice-cream sodas today. For it was he who experimented with the gas carbon dioxide that the chemist Joseph Black had prepared by pouring acid on chalk. By dissolving this gas in water he actually was the first to make carbonated water. His interest in the properties of gases led him to his famous experiment of heating mercuric oxide. This resulted in the formation of a silvery film deposited on the inside of the glass container and the liberation of a gas that we now call oxygen.

52. In addition to releasing oxygen, heating mercuric oxide produces

(1) nitrogen
(2) silver
(3) charcoal
(4) mercury
(5) carbon dioxide

53. Dissolving carbon dioxide in water forms

(1) chalk
(2) acid
(3) sodium
(4) carbonic acid
(5) heavy water

54. When acid is poured on chalk, the fizz is due to the presence of

(1) carbon dioxide
(2) mercuric oxide
(3) oxygen
(4) water
(5) mercury

---

55. The half-life of an isotope of an element is the time required for one-half of the nuclei of a sample of that isotope to break up. The half-life of thorium is 24 days. What amount of a 12-gram sample would remain after 96 days?

(1) 0.5 gram
(2) 0.75 gram
(3) 1 gram
(4) 1.5 grams
(5) 6 grams

Items 56 and 57 refer to the following information.

All organic compounds contain the element carbon. Since carbon does not give up the four electrons in its outermost shell and does not accept four electrons from other elements, it shares electrons. This sharing of electrons forms covalent bonds. This is characteristic of all organic compounds.

56. The number of covalent bonds in a molecule of methane is

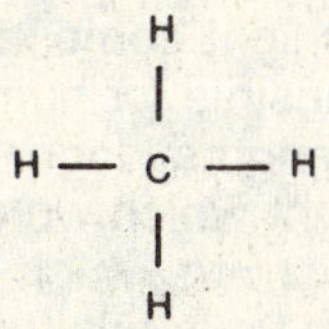

Methane

(1) one
(2) two
(3) three
(4) four
(5) five

57. Which, if any, of the following would be organic compounds?

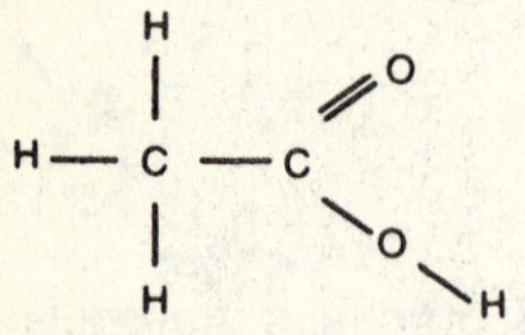

(A)

(B)

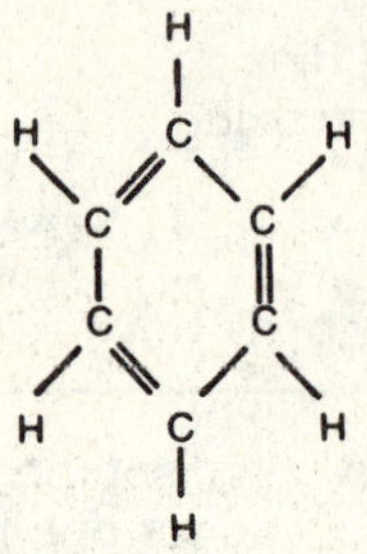

(C)

(1) only A and C
(2) only B and C
(3) only A and B
(4) A, B, and C
(5) none of these

Items 58 to 61 refer to the following article.

Recent findings by psychologists seem to indicate that exposure to different colours of light as well as different sources of light affect one's well-being. What are light rays? Light rays are forms of electromagnetic radiation—wave motion in ether—differing from one another in wavelength and frequency. For example, violet has the shortest wavelength, measured in angstrom units (A), violet has a wavelength of less than 4500A. Red has the longest wavelength of more than 6000A. The colours in between, that is from about 4000A in deep violet to the 7500A in the deep red is the visible spectrum. Light with wave lengths shorter than violet is called ultraviolet light. A great deal of this light comes to us from the sun and is responsible for human sunburn. Light with wavelengths longer than red is called infrared light which we cannot see but we can feel its warmth. Much of the sun's warmth comes to us in this form.

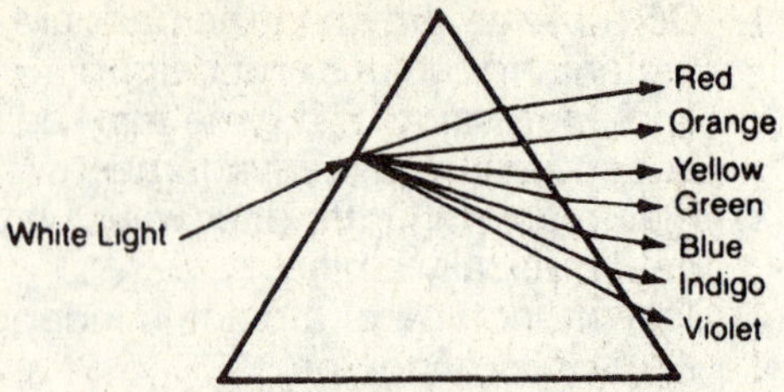

When a beam of white light is passed through a prism, it is split up into its components, forming a band having all the colours of the rainbow. Each of these colours, according to psychologists, has a particular effect on living things. Photography is also concerned with this phenomenon as it uses different filters to absorb certain colours of the spectrum, while allowing other colours to pass. Thus a filter that absorbs blue and red is green but one that absorbs only blue appears yellow because it transmits the combination of green and red.

58. Which of the following is the wavelength of red light?

(1) less 4500A
(2) 4500A
(3) 6000A
(4) 7500A
(5) more than 7500A

59. A photographer would use a blue filter to

(1) form a prism
(2) absorb blue light
(3) transmit green light
(4) absorb green light
(5) transmit blue light

60. Yellow glass to be used as a filter must

(1) absorb yellow light
(2) transmit all colours but yellow
(3) transmit blue light
(4) absorb rays in the wavelength range of 450–500 μm
(5) absorb rays in the wavelength range of 500–600 μm

61. Which of the following is the wavelength of infrared rays?

(1) less than 4500A
(2) 4500A
(3) 6000A
(4) 6500A
(5) more than 7500A

62. Electric power, the energy converted per second, is found by multiplying potential difference (in volts) by current (in amperes). Of the following, which consumes the LEAST amount of electric power?

(1) a starter motor using 50 amperes at 12 volts for 10 seconds
(2) a clock using 0.002 amperes at 120 volts for a year
(3) a TV set using 2.5 amperes at 120 volts for 6 hours
(4) an air conditioner using 3 amperes at 240 volts for an hour
(5) a flashlight bulb using 0.20 amperes at 3 volts for a half hour

63. The work done on an object is the product of the force applied to it and the distance it moves in the direction of the force. In which of the following situations is the greatest amount of work done?

(1) A force of 1200 newtons is applied to a wall for 15 minutes.
(2) A box weighting 500 newtons is carried horizontally a distance of 10 metres.
(3) A box weighing 200 newtons is shoved along a floor a distance of 3 metres, using a force of 100 newtons.
(4) A box weighing 300 newtons is lifted vertically a distance of 2 metres.
(5) A box weighing 500 newtons is put on a wagon and moved along a floor a distance of 5 metres, using a force of 50 newtons.

64. A ringing electric bell is placed inside a bell jar, and the air in the jar is evacuated. As the air is removed, the sound heard gets softer, and eventually cannot be heard at all. What is the most reasonable explanation?

(1) Electricity cannot travel through a vacuum.
(2) The clapper of the bell cannot vibrate without air.
(3) The glass of the bell jar blocks the passage of sound.
(4) The ability to hear depends on the presence of air.
(5) Sound waves need air to travel.

Item 65 is based on the following diagram

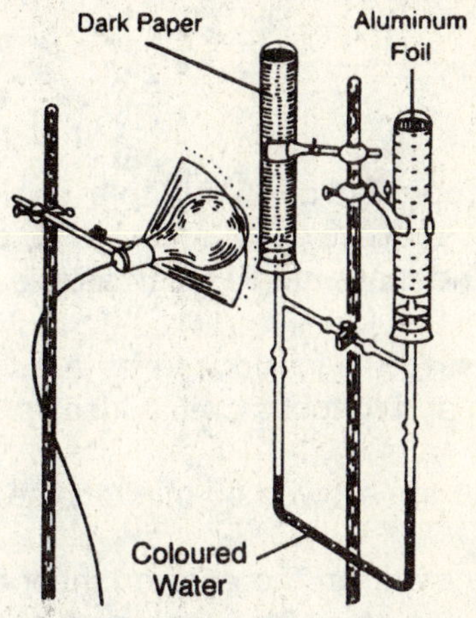

65. The difference in the level of the coloured water in the U-tube can best be explained by the principle of

(1) atmospheric pressure at different levels
(2) absorption of radiant energy by light and dark objects
(3) gravitational force
(4) convection of air currents
(5) conduction of heat energy

Item 66 is based on the following diagram.

66. The result of holding the two flashlights at different angles demonstrates which of the following principles?

(1) Light intensity depends upon source.
(2) The more vertical the light rays are, the less intense is the illumination.
(3) The more nearly vertical rays of the summer sun account for the summer's heat.
(4) The more concentrated a given number of light rays, the less is the heat energy released.
(5) Intensity of light is directly proportional to distance from source.

END OF EXAMINATION

TEST 4: LANGUAGE ARTS, READING (INTERPRETING LITERATURE AND THE ARTS)

Directions

Allotted time: 65 minutes

This test consists of **45 multiple-choice questions** based on passages from classical and popular literature, prose, poetry, and drama, as well as from articles about literature and the arts—music, dance, and mass media, such as television.

Each passage is introduced by a question designed to help you locate the main purpose of the selection and to focus on the ideas presented to achieve that purpose.

Since you are allowed 65 minutes, be careful not to spend too much time on any one question.

Make no mark on the answer sheet other than your choice of the correct answer. If you change your answer, erase your first mark completely. Only *one* answer space should be marked for each question.

EXAMPLE:

I went to the woods because I wished to live deliberately, to front only the essential facts of life, and see if I could not learn what it had to teach, and not, when I came to die, discover that I had not lived.

The author

(1) wishes to learn from nature
(2) is afraid of death
(3) has little regard for life
(4) seeks life's pleasures
(5) wishes to avoid life's problems.

● ② ③ ④ ⑤

The author states that he wanted to "learn what it (the woods, that is, nature) had to teach" so 1 is the correct answer and 1 should be marked on the answer paper.

Directions: Choose the one best answer to each item.

Items 1 to 5 refer to the following passage.

WHAT IS THE RESULT OF THE NARRATOR'S SHAMEFUL ACTION?

When I arrived at a few minutes before seven, I found the platoon assembled and ready to go. It was cold, and in the ranks the men were shivering. I was only the second-in-command of the platoon at that time. Punctually at seven I said to Broadhurst, "March off, Sergeant. To the aerodrome, at the double."

Broadhurst asked doubtfully whether we hadn't better wait for the platoon commander. I said, "No, march off. The men are cold." We doubled off.

Three or four minutes later the platoon commander, who had about fourteen years of service, appeared. He rushed straight up to Broadhurst and asked him furiously what he meant by marching off without permission.

Broadhurst said, "I'm sorry sir."

I looked at Broadhurst, but he was busy. After parade I apologized to him, but I never explained to the lieutenant. Broadhurst told me the incident wasn't worth worrying about.

Does this seem a small crime to remember all one's life? I don't think so. It was the worst thing that I ever did in the army, because in it I showed cowardice and disloyalty. It has a result, though. I had been frightened of the lieutenant, frightened of being reprimanded, frightened of failure even in the smallest endeavour. I discovered now that being ashamed of yourself is worse than any fear. Duty, orders, loyalty, obedience—all things boiled down to one simple idea: whatever the consequences, a man must act so that he can live with himself.

1. The narrator most probably gave the order to march off because he

(1) wanted a chance to show his authority
(2) was considerate of the troops
(3) wanted to show himself superior to Broadhurst
(4) secretly wanted Broadhurst to receive a reprimand
(5) wanted to be in good favour with the troops

2. From the passage the reader can most safely conclude that the narrator never explained the truth to the platoon commander because

(1) army custom forbade his doing so
(2) he felt that the incident was unimportant
(3) he hoped that Broadhurst would do it for him
(4) he feared the reaction of the platoon commander
(5) the episode had happened too quickly

3. In the passage, Broadhurst seems to be a man who

(1) has the courage to stand up for his rights
(2) is willing to overlook an error
(3) greatly resents authority
(4) wants to protect his men from the cold
(5) cannot understand other people's mistakes

4. From the passage the reader can most safely conclude that Broadhurst was

(1) familiar with army routine
(2) proud of the platoon
(3) friendly with the platoon commander
(4) higher in rank than the platoon commander
(5) inconsiderate of the narrator

5. The narrator is a person who gives evidence of

(1) callousness
(2) inefficiency
(3) indecisiveness
(4) loyalty
(5) self-criticism

Items 6 to 10 refer to the following passage.

WHAT LESSONS HAD JOEY LEARNED AT THE POND?

It was raining the next morning when Joey awoke, and he didn't get up right away.[2] He couldn't hear Mr. Ben moving about and thought that probably the old man felt the same way he felt himself: satisfied to lie still, warm and comfortable, and listen to the rain on the roof for awhile.[3] He fell into a half-dreamy state, and fragments of things that had happened to him since he had come to the Pond without grownups drifted through his mind; he made a sort of recapitulation.[4] He had learned some things.[5] He had been lost in a swamp and had been frightened and had found his way out again, and now he would keep track of where he was in the woods; the big bass had shown him an unsuspected meanness in his nature that he would probably manage better when it appeared again. Sharbee and his raccoon had been another lesson, and Mr. Ben had helped him there; he still wanted the raccoon, but he understood why it wouldn't be fair to take it. He learned from the Johnson boys as well. . . . It was the first time he had encountered and realized that there were ways of life different from his own and that boys were caught in it.

6. Which phrase best expresses the main ideas of this passage?

(1) a lifetime goal
(2) freedom from responsibility
(3) respect for authority
(4) lessons in living
(5) the great outdoors

7. What is the relationship of sentence 5 to sentence 4?

(1) It adds to the mood created in sentence 4.
(2) It presents an alternative to the idea in sentence 4.
(3) It contradicts sentence 4 with counter arguments.
(4) It summarizes the idea in sentence 4.
(5) It supports sentence 4 with examples.

8. In staying at the Pond, Joey learned to

(1) value living more than going to school
(2) respect law and order more than before
(3) cope with unexpected situations
(4) appreciate the fine upbringing he had had
(5) apply what he had learned at school to new situations

9. At the Pond, Joey came to realize that

(1) people have differing values
(2) he was independent
(3) the imaginary world was better than the real one
(4) he was too much inclined to daydream
(5) he was trapped

10. Which did Joey not learn about at the Pond?

(1) fishing
(2) getting lost
(3) himself
(4) swimming
(5) raccoons

Items 11 to 15 refer to the following passage.

WHY IS THE YOUNG GIRL UNHAPPY?

Every night she listened to her father going around the house, locking the doors and windows. She listened: the back door closed, she could hear the catch of the kitchen window click, and the restless pad of his feet going back to try the front door. It wasn't only the outside doors he locked: he locked the empty rooms, the bathroom, the lavatory. He was locking something out, but obviously it was something capable of penetrating his first defense. He raised his second line all the way up to bed.

In fifteen years, she thought unhappily, the house will be his; he had paid twenty-five pounds down and the rest he was paying month by month as rent. "Of course," he was in the habit of saying, "I've improved the property." "Yes," he repeated, "I've improved the property," looking around for a nail to drive in, a weed to be uprooted. It was more than a sense of property; it was a sense of honesty. Some people who bought their homes through the society let them go to rack and ruin and then cleared out.

She stood with her ear against the wall, a small dark, furious, immature figure. There was no more to be heard from the other room; but in her inner ear she still heard the chorus of a property owner, the tap-tap of a hammer, the scrape of a spade, the whistle of radiator steam, a key turning, a bolt pushed home, the little trivial sounds of men building barricades. She stood planning. . . .

11. In this passage, the father is shown to be

(1) unkind to his daughter
(2) suspicious of home improvements
(3) methodical in his actions
(4) friendly to his neighbors
(5) confident of others' good will

12. In this passage, the girl's attitude is one of

(1) grateful acceptance
(2) great resentment
(3) mild distaste
(4) stupid indifference
(5) vague dislike

13. This passage *as a whole* conveys a feeling of

(1) heartlessness
(2) envy
(3) peace
(4) greed
(5) tenseness

14. The last sentence of this passage conveys a feeling of

(1) simple faith
(2) great unconcern
(3) joyous anticipation
(4) vague foreboding
(5) constructive criticism

15. The author feels that the father is

(1) greedy
(2) loving
(3) self-sacrificing
(4) secure
(5) honest

Items 16 to 20 refer to the following poem.

HOW DOES THE POET FEEL ABOUT TELEVISION?

The crooked crosses overhead proclaim
High homage to the god-of-living-rooms;
As silently as Pharaohs in their tombs
Men sit before the sacrificial flame.
The incense from the king-size cigarettes
Is wafted idly toward the altar box
Where current ministers harangue their flocks
With tired wit and lively murder threats.
Tonight I shall not play the pious role
Nor join the dead who once had been so quick;
But I shall try to walk, strange heretic,
Among neglected precincts of my soul.

16. The "crooked crosses" (line 1) are

(1) church towers
(2) ceiling beams
(3) telephone poles
(4) television antennae
(5) altar decorations

17. The poet criticizes television programs in

(1) line 4
(2) line 6
(3) line 8
(4) line 10
(5) line 12

18. The poet has decided not to watch television, but to devote the evening to

(1) prayer
(2) repentance
(3) self-education
(4) self-contemplation
(5) physical conditioning

19. In line 3, there is an example of a (an)

(1) simile
(2) metaphor
(3) epithet
(4) alliteration
(5) onomatopoeia

20. In lines 6 and 12, there are examples of

(1) similes
(2) metaphors
(3) epithets
(4) alliteration
(5) onomatopoeia

Items 21 to 25 refer to the following poem.

WHAT CRITICISM IS THE POET MAKING OF CONTEMPORARY SOCIETY?

I have known the inexorable sadness of pencils,
Neat in their boxes, dolor of pad and paper-weight,
All the misery of manila folders and mucilage,
Desolation in immaculate public places,
Lonely reception room, lavatory, switchboard,
The unalterable pathos of basin and pitcher,
Ritual of multigraph, paper-clip, comma,
Endless duplication of lives and objects.
And I have seen dust from the walls of institutions,
Finer than flour, alive, more dangerous than silica,
Sift, almost invisible, through long afternoons of tedium,
Dropping a fine film on nails and delicate eyebrows,
Glazing the pale hair, the duplicate gray standard faces.

21. The phrase that best expresses the main ideas of this poem is

(1) the public place
(2) keeping up appearances
(3) why employers are miserable
(4) the look of sameness
(5) the danger of silica

22. The poet chooses as a reflection of modern life the world of the

(1) dead
(2) office
(3) movie
(4) elementary school
(5) dust

23. A sense of powerlessness is created by the use of such words as

(1) inexorable and unalterable
(2) sadness and dolor
(3) misery and desolation
(4) lives and objects
(5) pale and standard

24. The mood of the poem is

(1) somber
(2) resigned
(3) pathetic
(4) hopeful
(5) bored

25. In line 3, "the misery of manila folders and mucilage" is an example of

(1) simile
(2) metaphor
(3) onomatopoeia
(4) alliteration
(5) hyperbole

Items 26 to 30 refer to the following excerpt from a play.

WHAT ARE THE TWO VIEWS OF CAPITAL?

ROBERTS. [*The crowd sags nearer, looking eagerly up. With withering scorn.*] You've felt the pinch o't in your bellies. You've forgotten what that fight 'as been. . . . Capital! A thing that buys the sweat o' men's brows, and the tortures o' their brains, at its own price. *Don't* I know that? Wasn't the work o' *my* brains bought for seven hundred pounds, and hasn't one hundred thousand pounds been gained them by that seven hundred without the stirring of a finger. . . . That's *Capital!* A thing that will say—"I'm very sorry for you, poor fellows—you have a cruel time of it, I know," but will not give one sixpence of its dividends to help you have a better time. That's Capital! Tell me, for all their talk, is there one of them that will consent to another penny on the Income Tax to help the poor? That's Capital! A white-faced, stony-hearted monster! Ye have got it on its knees; are ye to give up at the last minute to save your miserable bodies pain?

ANTHONY. The men have been treated justly, they have had fair wages, we have always been ready to listen to complaints. It has been said that times have changed; if they have, I have not changed with them. Neither will I. It has been said that masters and men are equal! There can only be one master in a house! Where two men meet the better man will rule. . . . [*He pauses. . . .*] There is only one way of treating "men"—with *the iron hand*. This half and half business, the half and half manners of this generation, has brought all this upon us. Sentiment and softness, and what this young man, no doubt, would call his social policy. You can't eat cake and have it! This middle-class sentiment, or socialism, or whatever it may be, is rotten. Masters are masters, men are men!

—John Galsworthy

26. Roberts' main purpose in his speech is to
    (1) condemn capital
    (2) gain revenge
    (3) revise the Income Tax
    (4) rally his listeners
    (5) vindicate his position

27. Roberts does all of the following to achieve his purpose EXCEPT
    (1) recall past experiences of his audience
    (2) cite his own experience
    (3) put words in the mouth of Capital
    (4) ask questions which require no answer
    (5) present Capital's position

28. Anthony's purpose in his speech is to inform his audience that he will
    (1) stick to his guns
    (2) compromise with Labour
    (3) accept Labour's terms
    (4) give in to shareholders
    (5) accept criticism of himself

29. Anthony disagrees with all of the following EXCEPT
    (1) sentiment
    (2) socialism
    (3) class distinctions
    (4) equality of men
    (5) softness

30. What has happened before the two speakers present their views?
    (1) Roberts' followers have gone out on strike.
    (2) Roberts' followers have given up their strike.
    (3) Roberts and Anthony agree to have the workers' complaints heard.
    (4) Anthony has defended the middle class.
    (5) Anthony has indicated a willingness to debate the issues.

Items 31 to 35 refer to the following passage.

A YOUNG TEACHER'S LESSON

Fall is a nervous time for a new teacher. I was never sure of what I was about to do, and lacked the experience to have a bag of tricks to fall back on. I guess I had a bag, but it was mostly empty. If it were not for a most cooperative class, I would have been in big trouble.

One Tuesday morning, as I was coming to an important point in a mathematics lesson, the door burst open. Standing there was a stocky child with tousled blond hair, and a smile wider than the door.

"Sophie!" came from her mouth without interrupting the smile. "Sophie!" I approached, welcomed her, introduced her to the class, and suggested she put her jacket in the cloakroom.

Sophie was very quiet and accepting. She smiled. Sophie volunteered no answers, and often feigned deafness to deflect questions. I could almost hear her praying for a less patient pupil to blurt out the answer as she smiled and waited. I tried to remember her voice from that first day, but it was becoming more difficult. Sophie was becoming only a smile, but a smile radiating enough warmth to heat the room.

In the middle of January, I thought that I should begin to teach the solution of word problems. With my notes on scraps of paper, I was ready to teach a lesson to remember. I slowly wrote on the blackboard.

"Jane and George went shopping. Together they had twenty dollars.

Jane wanted a jacket for eleven dollars, and George wanted a baseball for five dollars and a baseball glove for six dollars. Could Jane and George both have everything they wanted?"

"What do we know?" I looked around for answers.

"Two kids went shopping."

"They only had twenty bucks."

"Not bad for two kids!"

"They don't have enough money."

"He has five bucks in his back pocket."

After a few minutes, I realized we might be on a tangent. "Let's make a list" I suggested.

Joey rose to announce, "We don't need no list. They can't afford all that stuff. She can't get her jacket. He gets two baseballs, one glove and some gum."

Sophie's smile disappeared. She shot up, and stared at me. "Not enough money?"

I looked at Sophie, serious for the first time since her arrival. A tear started to fall from her left eye. "What they do now? Not enough money! Oh! What they do now?"

Sophie slumped into her seat. The smile replaced by a serious frown. She was very upset. I tried explaining that this was just a mathematics problem. I tried to show her the solution. I tried everything. Finally, I went down the row to her seat.

Sophie's sorrowful face lifted to look me in the eye. "Not enough money. What we do now?"

—Murray Shukyn

31. Another suitable title for this selection is

(1) "Solving Word Problems"
(2) "First Day at School"
(3) "Shopping"
(4) "A Personal Problem"
(5) "A Mathematics Lesson"

32. From their use in the passage, all of the following words are correctly paired EXCEPT

(1) *feigned*—pretended
(2) *patient*—long-suffering
(3) *stocky*—thickset
(4) *radiating*—emitting
(5) *tousled*—streaked

33. The teacher regarded Sophie as all of the following EXCEPT

(1) quiet
(2) patient
(3) boisterous
(4) shy
(5) obedient

34. The point of the story is

(1) Sophie thought Jane should buy her jacket.
(2) Sophie couldn't do mathematics problems.
(3) The word problem triggered strong feelings within Sophie.
(4) The mathematics problem was too complex for the class.
(5) The other students were misbehaving.

35. What made Sophie cry?

(1) fear of the teacher
(2) sympathy for Jane
(3) being asked a question
(4) the other students teasing her
(5) a sad memory about not having money

Items 36 to 40 refer to the following passage on music.

WHAT IS THE DIFFERENCE BETWEEN CLASSICAL AND POPULAR MUSIC?

There is another way to divide music into two categories that usually creates more problems than it solves. This is the division into popular or light music and classical or serious music. Most people have some idea of what is meant by these terms and could probably decide, for example, that a rock tune in the "top 40" or a theme song from a current film would belong in the first category, while a piano concerto by Tchaikovsky or a symphony by Haydn would belong in the second. However, no adequate terms to describe these categories have yet been found. If we measure popularity by the total number of enthusiastic listeners through the years and not just during one year, then the Tchaikovsky Concerto No. 1 for Piano would be more "popular" than the rock song. A theme song from a movie might be quite serious and a Haydn symphony may be light in character. The term "classical" is probably best reserved for a specific period of music history (roughly from 1750 to 1825); for a general stylistic tendency marked by such characteristics as balance, clarity, stability, or restraint; or for a notable accomplishment as when a symphony is called a classic example of colourful orchestration.

Above all, the distinction between popular and classical music, as well as a similar dichotomy between folk music and art music, all too often has implications and connotations of value, integrity, and level of technical achievement that are highly inappropriate. No single type of music has a monopoly on worth, sincerity, or craftsmanship, and no single type of music can be dismissed categorically as inferiour, insincere, or incompetent. Like Sir Donald Tovey, the perceptive British music critic, we are not sure if there is such a thing as bad music, but if there is, then we prefer "good bad music" to "bad good music."

36. According to the article, the difference between classical and popular music is

(1) important
(2) clear
(3) well-understood
(4) confusing
(5) helpful

37. According to the passage,

(1) only popular music can be popular
(2) only classical music can be classic
(3) classical music can be popular
(4) popular music is best confined to a single era
(5) both popular and classical music have balance and restraint

38. The passage implies that most people, in their view of classical and popular music,

(1) are using imprecise terms
(2) can distinguish between popular and classical
(3) prefer light music to serious music
(4) are limited by experience
(5) make mistakes in their classification

39. The author feels that

(1) classical music is preferable to popular
(2) popular music is preferable to classical
(3) both are similar
(4) any music can be worthwhile
(5) some music is inferior to other music

40. The passage states that distinctions between folk music and art music lead to

(1) greater integrity
(2) higher technical achievement
(3) inferior music
(4) monopolies
(5) invalid judgments

Items 41 to 45 refer to the following passage on the theatre.

WHAT IS THE PLACE OF THEATRE AMONG THE ENTERTAINMENT MEDIA?

The fact that the theatre is closely linked with TV and the movies is not in itself an element of weakness. It is true that Hollywood and Madison Avenue exploit Broadway by buying its plays and offering jackpots to the successful playwrights, hiring them much as the Roman conquerors hired the Greek intellectuals to teach them philosophy and art. But despite the swagger and brashness of the Hollywood money one may question which is the main stream and which the tributary. There is a wholeness in a play which neither the movies nor TV offers—a wholeness of experience for playwright, actor, and audience alike.

When several arts are linked together, as is true of the theatre, the movies, and TV, they may fertilize one another, and each of them may profit from the connection. The era of dramatic creativeness in America coincides curiously with the emergence of the movies and TV. I do not say that these are the only forces at work, but they help. The knowledge of a playwright that his play, while first produced on Broadway for a limited audience, may ultimately reach millions of people, must prove a stimulus to his imagination. Some of the people he ultimately reaches may lack sensibility, but this will not be true of all of them. The fact is that an Elizabethan audience showed a sense of excitement even when the crowd in the pit applauded and derided at the wrong passages. They sensed that new things were happening in their world, and the theatre gave a concrete dramatic form to this awareness. The Americans too have an awareness of new things happening: And although millions of them flock to the movies and watch TV, while only thousands go to the theatre, the fact is that, for writers and actors alike, the prestige attaches to the theatre and not to the big media. No great theatre is possible in any culture unless the people consider it a great art—a place of great writing, poetry, and mime, and a place for the enactment of ideas and passions.

41. The author feels that the artistic medium which offers the audience the most rewarding experience is

(1) television
(2) movies
(3) theatre
(4) philosophy
(5) art

42. The author feels that television, movies, and theatre

(1) compete with one another
(2) harm one another
(3) benefit one another
(4) are viewed by equal numbers of people
(5) are equally creative

43. The author implies that

(1) the movies stimulate the theatre
(2) television stimulates the movies
(3) the movies stimulate television
(4) the movies and television stimulate the theatre
(5) the theatre stimulates the movies and television

44. The author is critical of

(1) the emergence of movies and television
(2) dramatic creativeness in America
(3) the Broadway playwright
(4) movie and television audiences
(5) theatre audiences

45. The most important factor in the greatness of theatre, according to the passage, is

(1) Hollwood and Madison Avenue
(2) successful playwrights
(3) intellectuals
(4) money
(5) the audience

END OF EXAMINATION

TEST 5: MATHEMATICS

Directions

Allotted time: 90 minutes

This test consists of **56 multiple-choice questions** designed to measure general mathematics skills and problem-solving ability. Some questions include a graph, chart, or figure, along with a short reading upon which the question is based. You may not use a calculator during the test.

Some questions require the application of a formula. Page 809 has any of the formulae you may need.

There will be some questions that give more information than you need to solve the problem. Other questions do not furnish enough information to solve the problem. In such cases, choose the answer "Not enough information is given."

Work carefully but do not spend too much time on any one question. Record your answer on the answer sheet by marking the numbered space beside the number that corresponds to the question in the test. Answer *all* questions since there is no penalty for incorrect answers. Your score will depend on the number of correct responses.

EXAMPLE:

I purchased five 45¢ postage stamps with two $2 bills. How much change should be returned? (Do not calculate GST.)

(1) $.29
(2) $.54
(3) $.55
(4) $1.45
(5) $1.75

① ② ③ ④ ●

The correct answer is $1.75; therefore, answer space 5 should be marked on the answer sheet.

FORMULAE

Description	Formula
AREA (A) of a:	
square	$A = s^2$; where s = side
rectangle	$A = lw$; where l = length, w = width
parallelogram	$A = bh$; where b = base, h = height
triangle	$A = \frac{1}{2} bh$; where b = base, h = height
circle	$A = \pi r^2$; where $\pi = 3.14$, r = radius
PERIMETER (P) of a:	
square	$P = 4s$; where s = side
rectangle	$P = 2l + 2w$; where l = length, w = width
triangle	$P = a + b + c$; where a, b, and c are the sides
circumference (C) of a circle	$C = \pi d$; where $\pi = 3.14$, d = diameter
VOLUME (V) of a:	
cube	$V = s^3$; where s = side
rectangular container	$V = lwh$; where l = length, w = width, h = height
cylinder	$V = \pi r^2 h$; where $\pi = 3.14$, r = radius, h = height
Pythagorean relationship	$c^2 = a^2 + b^2$; where c = hypotenuse, a and b are legs of a right triangle
distance (d) between two points in a plane	$d = \sqrt{(x_2 - x_1)^2 + (y_2 - y_1)^2}$; where (x_1, y_1) and (x_2, y_2) are two points in a plane
slope of a line (m)	$m = \frac{y_2 - y_1}{x_2 - x_1}$; where (x_1, y_1) and (x_2, y_2) are two points in a plane
mean	$mean = \frac{x_1 + x_2 + \cdots + x_n}{n}$; where the x's are the value for which a mean is desired, and n = number of values in the series
median	median = the point in an ordered set of numbers at which half of the numbers are above and half of the numbers are below this value
simple interest (i)	$i = prt$; where p = principal, r = rate, t = time
distance (d) as function of rate and time	$d = rt$; where r = rate, t = time
total cost (c)	$c = nr$; where n = number of units, r = cost per unit

Directions: Choose the one best answer to each item.

1. Luisa worked 40 hours and earned \$6.30 per hour. Her friend Joan earned \$8.40 per hour at her job. How many hours did Joan have to work in order to equal Luisa's earnings for 40 hours?

(1) 252
(2) 20
(3) 30
(4) 25
(5) Not enough information is given.

Item 2 is based on the following figure.

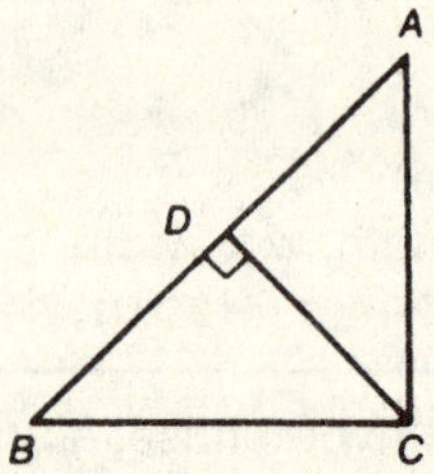

2. $\triangle ABC$ is a right triangle and $\overline{CD} \perp \overline{AB}$. If the measure of $\angle CAD = 40°$, what is the measure of $\angle DCB$?

(1) 10°
(2) 20°
(3) 40°
(4) 50°
(5) 90°

---

3. The number of students in a class is x. One day 5 students were absent. What fractional part of the class was present?

(1) $\frac{x}{5}$
(2) $\frac{5}{x}$
(3) $\frac{5}{x-5}$
(4) $\frac{x+5}{5}$
(5) $\frac{x-5}{x}$

4. The gasoline gauge shows that a gasoline tank is $\frac{1}{3}$ full. In order to fill the tank, 24 L of gasoline are added. How many litres of gasoline does the tank hold when full?

(1) 30
(2) 36
(3) 45
(4) 48
(5) 72

Item 5 is based on the following figure.

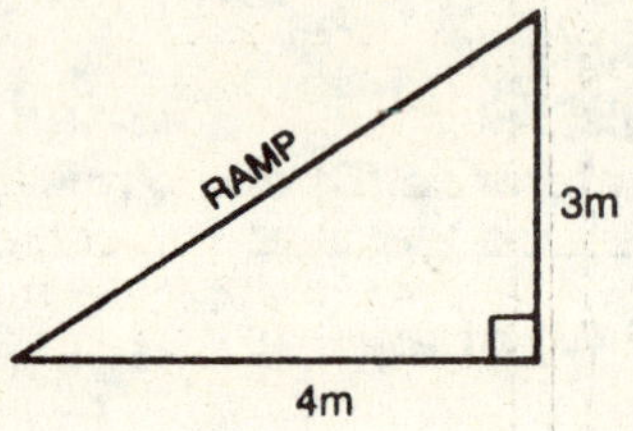

5. What is the length of the ramp in metres?

(1) 5
(2) 7
(3) 9
(4) 16
(5) Not enough information is given.

---

6. The dial of a meter is divided into equal divisions from 0 to 60. When the needle points to 48, the meter registers 80 amperes. What is the maximum number of amperes that the meter will register?

(1) 92
(2) 98
(3) 100
(4) 102
(5) 120

7. If $5x - 1 = 34$, then $2\frac{1}{2}x$ is equal to

(1) 7
(2) 14
(3) $16\frac{2}{3}$
(4) 17
(5) $17\frac{1}{2}$

Item 8 is based on the following figure.

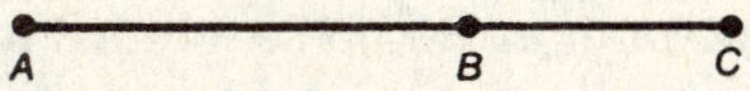

8. If $AC = 18$ cm and $BC = 8$ cm, then the ratio $AB:BC$ is equal to

(1) 2:1
(2) 4:5
(3) 3:2
(4) 5:4
(5) Not enough information is given.

---

9. A rectangular lobby has a floor area of 322 m². If the length of the lobby is 23 m, how many metres are there in the perimeter of the lobby?

(1) 28
(2) 37
(3) 45
(4) 60
(5) 74

10. Lugin Dolewski priced a TV set at $280 at the Triangle Store. He then saw an advertisement for the same TV set at the *ABC* Store announcing 20% off all merchandise. What additional information does Lugin need in order to make a wise buying decision?

(1) The Triangle Store has a better reputation than the *ABC* Store.
(2) The sales tax on TV purchases is 15%.
(3) Both stores have a $5 delivery charge.
(4) The name of the manufacturer of the TV set.
(5) The price from which the *ABC* Store deducts 20%.

11. A crew can load a truck in 3 hours. What part of the truck can they load in 45 minutes?

(1) $\frac{1}{8}$
(2) $\frac{1}{4}$
(3) $\frac{1}{3}$
(4) $\frac{1}{2}$
(5) Not enough information is given.

12. Given the equation $x^2 + x - 6 = 0$, which of the following choices give(s) a complete solution of the equation?

A. 2
B. −2
C. 3
D. −3

(1) A only
(2) A and D
(3) B and C
(4) A and C
(5) C and D

Item 13 is based on the following figure.

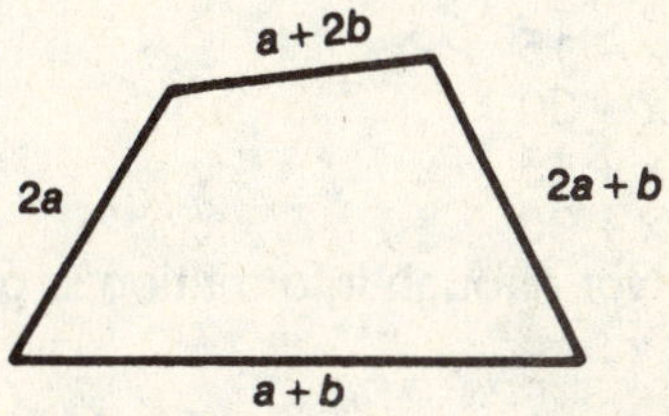

13. What is the perimeter of the figure?

(1) $6a + b$
(2) $5a + 5b$
(3) $6a + 4b$
(4) $4a + 4b$
(5) $3a + 5b$

---

14. Henry has $5 more than Bob. If Henry's money is added to twice Bob's money the sum will be $65. How much money did Bob have?

(1) $10
(2) $12
(3) $15
(4) $20
(5) Not enough information is given.

15. A motel charges $48 per day for a double room. In addition, there is a 5% PST. How much does a couple pay for several days stay?

(1) $144.00
(2) $151.20
(3) $156.20
(4) $158.40
(5) Not enough information is given.

16. If the square of a number is added to the number increased by 4, the result is 60. If n represents the number, which equation can be used to find n?

(1) $n^2 + 4 = 60$
(2) $n^2 + 4n = 60$
(3) $n^2 + n + 4 = 60$
(4) $n^2 + 60 = 4n + 4$
(5) $n^2 + n = 64$

17. A box of cereal is priced at x cents per box. A customer has a 15 cents off coupon. If the store reduces prices by doubling the value of each coupon, how much does the customer pay for the box of cereal, in cents?

(1) $x - 15$
(2) $x - 30$
(3) $x + 15$
(4) $x + 30$
(5) Not enough information is given.

18. The measures of the angles of a triangle are in the ratio 3:2:1. What is the measure of the largest angle of the triangle?

(1) 65°
(2) 70°
(3) 72°
(4) 80°
(5) 90°

Item 19 is based on the following figure.

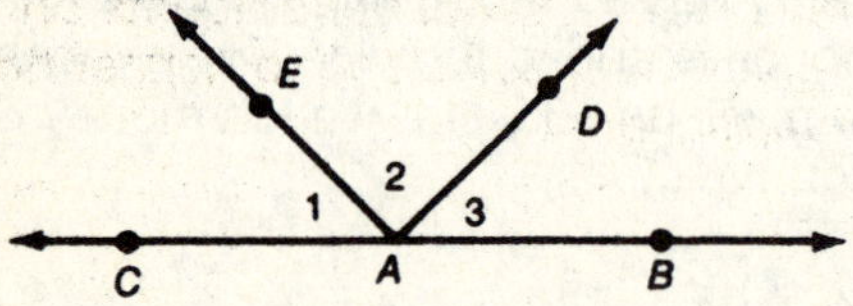

19. If m $\angle 1 = 36°$ and m $\angle 2 = 2(\text{m } \angle 3)$, then m $\angle 3$ equals

(1) 36°
(2) 40°
(3) 44°
(4) 48°
(5) Not enough information is given.

---

20. If $8x$ represents the perimeter of a rectangle and $2x + 3$ represents its length, what is its width?

(1) $10x + 3$
(2) $2x - 3$
(3) 3
(4) $6x - 3$
(5) $3x - 2$

21. A clerk earns \$16 per hour and the assistant earns half as much. Which of the following expressions represent how many dollars both earned on a job that took 9 hours?

(1) $9(16) + 9(\frac{1}{2})$
(2) $9(16) + 9(10)$
(3) $16(8) + 9(9)$
(4) $16(\frac{1}{2}) + 9(\frac{1}{2})$
(5) $9(16) + 9(8)$

22. The distance between two heavenly bodies is 63 150 000 000 km. What is the number expressed in scientific notation?

(1) 631.5×10^8
(2) 63.15×10^9
(3) 6315×10^7
(4) 6.315×10^{10}
(5) 6.315×10^{-10}

23. An English class has an enrollment of 14 boys and 12 girls. On a rainy day 4 boys and 3 girls are absent. If a student is called at random to recite, what is the probability that the student called is a girl?

(1) $\frac{9}{19}$
(2) $\frac{10}{19}$
(3) $\frac{12}{26}$
(4) $\frac{9}{14}$
(5) Not enough information is given.

24. Ms. Doucette has invested \$12 000 in bonds that pay interest at the rate of 9% annually. What is Ms. Doucette's annual income from this investment?

(1) \$108
(2) \$180
(3) \$1080
(4) \$10 800
(5) \$12 000

25. For which value of x is the inequality $3x + 2 < 14$ true?

(1) 3
(2) 4
(3) 5
(4) 6
(5) 7

Item 26 is based on the following graph.

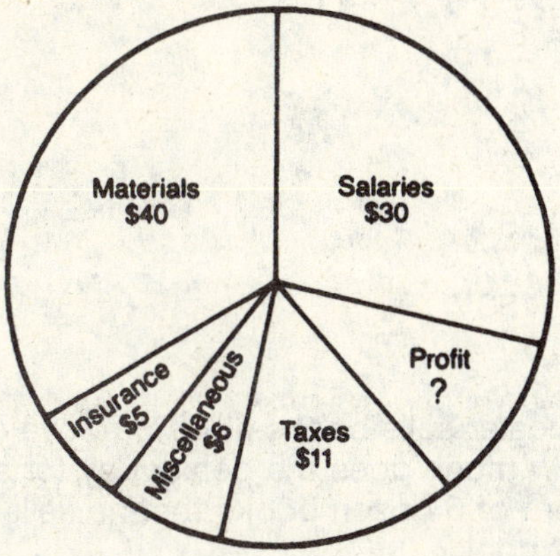

26. The graph shows what happened to each \$100 taken in by a small business firm. How many dollars out of each \$100 taken in represented profit?

(1) \$5
(2) \$6
(3) \$7
(4) \$7.5
(5) \$8

27. Over a period of 5 months Joan saved \$659. At the same rate of saving, which expression below represents what she saved over a period of 9 months? Let y represent savings for 9 months.

(1) $y = 9(659)$
(2) $y = \frac{5(659)}{9}$
(3) $y = 5(659)$
(4) $y = \frac{9(659)}{5}$
(5) $y = 5(9)(659)$

28. Ben scored 7 more points than Jack in a basketball game. Paola scored 2 points less than Jack in the same game. If the three boys scored a total of 38 points, how many points did Jack score?

(1) 5
(2) 9
(3) 11
(4) 14
(5) 15

29. A box in the form of a rectangular solid has a square base 5 m in length and a height of h metres. If the volume of the rectangular solid is 200 m^3, which of the following equations may be used to find h?

(1) $5h = 200$
(2) $5h^2 = 200$
(3) $25h = 200$
(4) $h = 200 \div 5$
(5) $h = 5(200)$

Item 30 is based on the following figure.

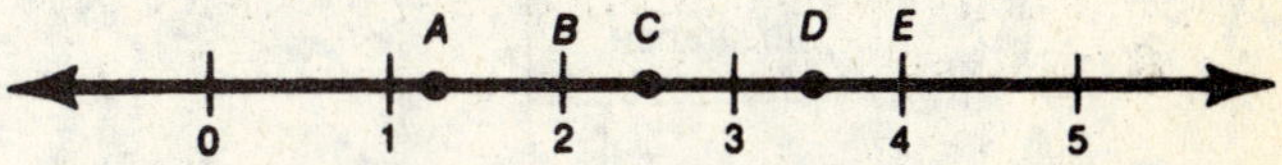

30. Which point on the number line represents the closest approximation to the square root of 12?

(1) A
(2) B
(3) C
(4) D
(5) E

31. Of the 12 students on the Student Council, one-half belong to the Scholastic Honour Society, one-third belong to the Varsity Athletic Club, and one-fourth are members of both these honour organisations. How many of the students on the Student Council belong to neither honour organisations?

(1) 3
(2) 4
(3) 6
(4) 5
(5) 8

32. If one plane can carry x passengers, how many planes will be needed to carry y passengers?

(1) xy
(2) $\frac{x}{y}$
(3) $\frac{y}{x}$
(4) $\frac{1}{xy}$
(5) $x + y$

Item 33 is based on the following bar graph.

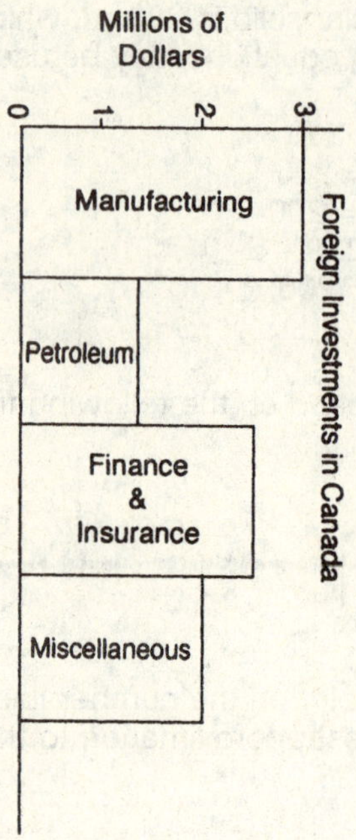

33. By what amount does the investment in manufacturing exceed the amount invested in petroleum?

(1) $\$1\frac{1}{2}$ billion
(2) $\$3\frac{1}{2}$ million
(3) \$0.5 million
(4) $\$1\frac{1}{2}$ million
(5) $\$3\frac{1}{2}$ billion

34. If the point (x, 3) is on the graph of an equation $x + y = 7$, what is the value of x?

(1) 4
(2) 3
(3) 7
(4) 1
(5) 0

35. What percent of x is y?

(1) $\frac{y}{x}$
(2) $\frac{x}{y}$
(3) $\frac{100x}{y}$
(4) $\frac{y}{100x}$
(5) $\frac{100y}{x}$

36. $X = 3Y$

$\frac{1}{4}X$ equals (?)% of Y

(1) $\frac{3}{4}$
(1) $\frac{4}{3}$
(3) 75
(4) $7\frac{1}{2}$
(5) $133\frac{1}{3}$

37. A dealer sells books at 40% above cost. How much does the dealer pay for a shipment of 6 dozen books that he sells for \$7 per book?

(1) \$360
(2) \$380
(3) \$450
(4) \$504
(5) \$520

Item 38 is based on the following figure.

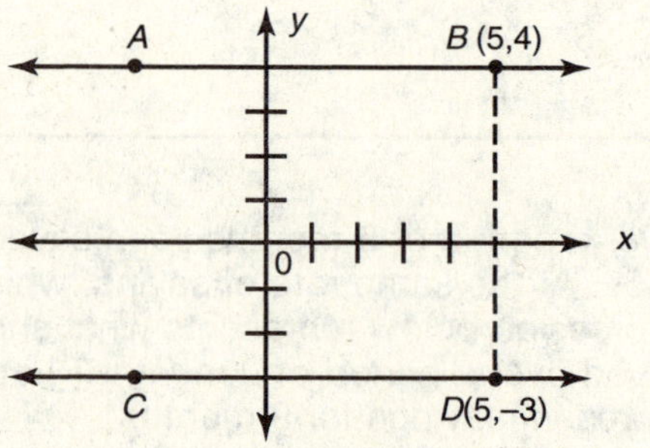

38. In the figure, $\overleftrightarrow{AB}$ and $\overleftrightarrow{CD}$ are parallel to the x-axis. The coordinates of B are (5, 4) and the coordinates of D are (5, –3). The perpendicular distance between $\overleftrightarrow{AB}$ and $\overleftrightarrow{CD}$ is

(1) –2
(2) 5
(3) 6
(4) 7
(5) 10

39. Evaluate $(6 \times 10^5) \div (4 \times 10^3)$.

(1) 20
(2) 100
(3) 150
(4) 1500
(5) 2000

Item 40 is based on the following graph.

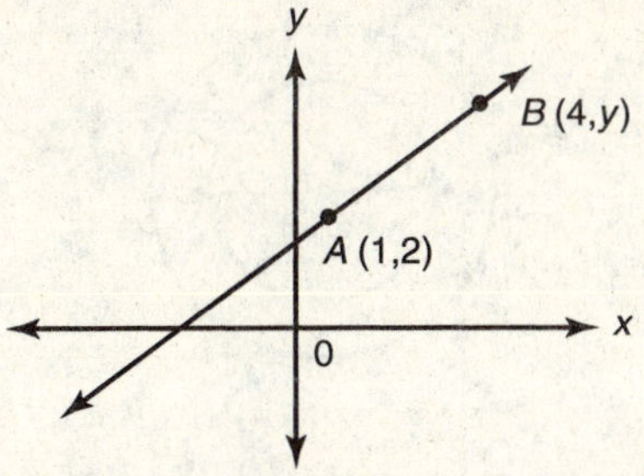

40. If the slope of $\overleftrightarrow{AB}$ is 1, what is the value of y?

(1) 1
(2) 2
(3) 3
(4) 4
(5) 5

---

41. Evaluate $2x^2 - 3(x - 4)$ if $x = 6$.

(1) 15
(2) 48
(3) 66
(4) 78
(5) 138

42. If $a < b$ and $c < d$ then

(1) $a + c > b + d$
(2) $bd > ac$
(3) $a + c = b + d$
(4) $b + d > a + c$
(5) $ac > bd$

43. A small business employs 10 clerks at \$380 per week, 1 assistant manager at \$480 per week, and 1 manager at \$604 per week. What is the average (mean) weekly salary paid by this business?

(1) \$47
(2) \$122
(3) \$407
(4) \$488
(5) Not enough information is given

Item 44 is based on the following figure.

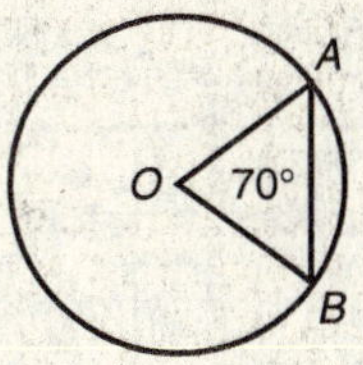

44. O is the centre of the circle and the measure of $\angle O$ is 70°. What is the measure of $\angle OAB$?

(1) 55°
(2) 60°
(3) 65°
(4) 70°
(5) 75°

Item 45 is based on the following table.

TIME	3:00 P.M.	4:00 P.M.	5:00 P.M.
Distance covered in kilometres	80	164	248

45. Sylvia took an automobile trip. The table shows the distance she covered during one afternoon. If she drove at a steady rate, how many kilometres had she covered at 4:15 P.M.?

(1) 84
(2) 125
(3) 185
(4) 220
(5) Not enough information given.

---

46. The following is a list of ingredients used in making cornmeal crisps:

250 mL yellow cornmeal
125 mL of sifted flour
2.5 mL salt
1.25 mL baking powder
30 mL melted shortening
$\frac{1}{3}$ cup of milk

If Joan finds that she cannot accurately measure $\frac{1}{3}$ cup of milk and decides to use 250 mL of milk, then she will have to use

(1) 250 mL of sifted flour
(2) 7.5 mL of salt
(3) 15 mL of baking powder
(4) 45 mL of melted shortening
(5) 625 mL of yellow cornmeal

Item 47 is based on the following graph.

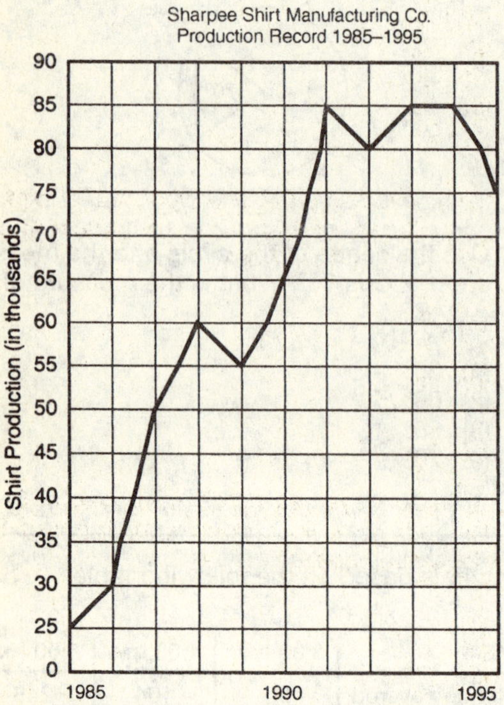

47. What was the number of shirts produced in 1990?

(1) 2500
(2) 6500
(3) 25 000
(4) 65 000
(5) 70 000

48. A house and a lot cost $120 000. If the house cost three times as much as the lot, how much did the house cost?

(1) $30 000
(2) $40 000
(3) $60 000
(4) $90 000
(5) $100 000

49. A bookcase has 3 large shelves and 4 small shelves. Each large shelf contains 8 more books than each small shelf. If the bookcase contains 297 books, how many books does each small shelf hold?

(1) 29
(2) 31
(3) 32
(4) 35
(5) 39

Item 50 is based on the following figure.

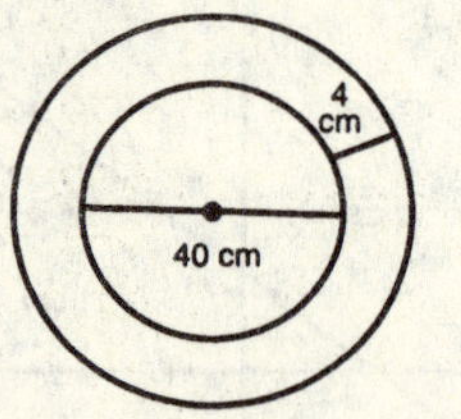

50. A wheel is surrounded by a rubber tire. If the diameter of the wheel is 40 cm and the width of the tire is 4 cm, what is the area of the tire in square centimetres? (Leave your answer in terms of π.)

(1) 16π
(2) 176π
(3) 180π
(4) 200π
(5) 240π

51. If x is an odd integer, what is the result if the next consecutive odd integer is divided by x?

(1) 1
(2) 2
(3) $1+\frac{1}{x}$
(4) $1+\frac{2}{x}$
(5) x

52. The hypotenuse of a right triangle whose legs are represented by $2x - 1$ and $2x + 1$ is

(1) $(2x-1)^2-(2x+1)^2$
(2) $\sqrt{8x^2+2}$
(3) $4x^2$
(4) $4x^2-1$
(5) $(4x-1)^2$

Item 53 is based on the following figure.

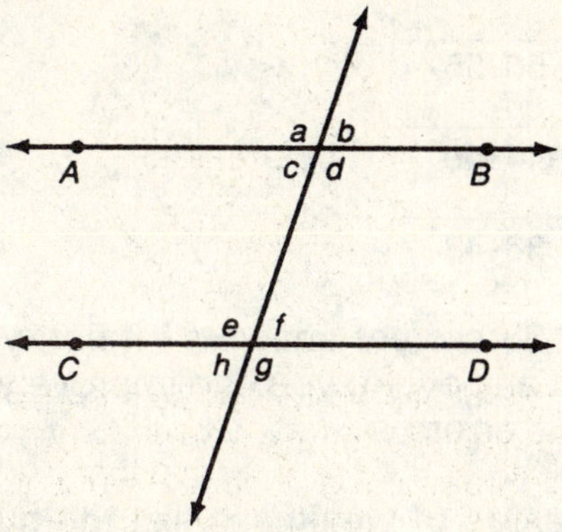

53. If $\overleftrightarrow{AB}$ is parallel to $\overleftrightarrow{CD}$, the angles in each of the following pairs are congruent EXCEPT

(1) $\angle a \cong \angle d$
(2) $\angle b \cong \angle f$
(3) $\angle c \cong \angle b$
(4) $\angle f \cong \angle c$
(5) $\angle b \cong \angle g$

54. $A + B + C = 180$. If $A = B$ and $B = 2C$, then the value of C is

(1) 36
(2) 45
(3) 60
(4) 72
(5) 90

55. Point *A* is east of *B* and west of *C*. Point *X* is southeast of *A* and *Z* is southwest of *B*. Which is farthest west?

(1) *X*
(2) *Z*
(3) *A*
(4) *B*
(5) *C*

56. A dealer buys ties which are priced at 6 for $39. How much does a shipment of 15 dozen ties cost?

(1) $234
(2) $585
(3) $785
(4) $1070
(5) $1170

END OF EXAMINATION

ANSWER KEYS, SUMMARIES OF RESULTS, AND SELF-APPRAISAL CHARTS

TEST 1: The Language Arts, Writing (Writing Skills) Test, Part I/Page 765

I. CHECK YOUR ANSWERS, using the following answer key:

1. **5**	12. **3**	23. **2**	34. **5**	45. **1**
2. **2**	13. **1**	24. **3**	35. **5**	46. **1**
3. **3**	14. **5**	25. **5**	36. **4**	47. **4**
4. **5**	15. **5**	26. **3**	37. **1**	48. **4**
5. **1**	16. **5**	27. **4**	38. **3**	49. **2**
6. **1**	17. **1**	28. **4**	39. **2**	50. **5**
7. **5**	18. **5**	29. **1**	40. **4**	51. **5**
8. **1**	19. **1**	30. **2**	41. **3**	52. **4**
9. **1**	20. **5**	31. **1**	42. **1**	53. **2**
10. **1**	21. **5**	32. **1**	43. **3**	54. **3**
11. **1**	22. **2**	33. **4**	44. **1**	55. **5**

II. SCORE YOURSELF:

Number correct:

Excellent	______ 50–55
Good	______ 44–49
Fair	______ 38–43

III. EVALUATE YOUR SCORE: Did you get at least 38 correct answers? If not, you need more practice for the Writing Skills, Part I Test. In any event, you can improve your performance to Excellent or Good by analyzing your errors.

IV. ANALYZE YOUR ERRORS: To determine your areas of weakness, list the number of correct answers you had under each of the following categories (which correspond to the content areas of the Writing Skills, Part I Test), and compare your score with the average scores in the right-hand column. Review the answer analysis section beginning on page 823 for each of the questions you got wrong, and give yourself more practice in your weak areas with the appropriate material in Chapter 4 before attempting Practice Examination Two.

CONTENT AREAS	ITEMS	YOUR SCORE	AVERAGE SCORE
Sentence Structure	1, 3, 5, 8, 10–13, 19, 25, 32, 37, 45, 50, 53–54		11
Usage	16, 23, 26–28, 36, 43, 47		6
Mechanics			
Spelling	6, 22, 31, 40, 42, 48–49		5
Punctuation	9, 17, 24, 30, 33, 38, 41, 44, 46, 52		7
Capitalization	2, 29, 39		2
No correction	4, 7, 14–15, 18, 20–21, 34–35, 51, 55		8

Total ______

TEST 2: The Social Studies Test/Page 776

I. CHECK YOUR ANSWERS, using the following answer key:

1. **2**	14. **1**	27. **4**	40. **1**	53. **4**
2. **4**	15. **2**	28. **4**	41. **3**	54. **3**
3. **2**	16. **2**	29. **3**	42. **4**	55. **2**
4. **4**	17. **4**	30. **2**	43. **4**	56. **1**
5. **4**	18. **3**	31. **5**	44. **2**	57. **3**
6. **3**	19. **1**	32. **1**	45. **1**	58. **2**
7. **1**	20. **4**	33. **1**	46. **3**	59. **1**
8. **4**	21. **3**	34. **2**	47. **1**	60. **5**
9. **1**	22. **1**	35. **4**	48. **5**	61. **1**
10. **3**	23. **1**	36. **2**	49. **3**	62. **3**
11. **4**	24. **2**	37. **4**	50. **3**	63. **2**
12. **3**	25. **3**	38. **2**	51. **1**	64. **1**
13. **1**	26. **4**	39. **3**	52. **3**	

II. SCORE YOURSELF:

Number correct:

Excellent	57–64
Good	51–56
Fair	45–50

III. EVALUATE YOUR SCORE: Did you get at least 45 correct answers? If not, you need more practice for the Social Studies Test. In any event, you can improve your performance to Excellent or Good by analyzing your errors.

IV. ANALYZE YOUR ERRORS: To determine your specific weaknesses, list the number of correct answers you had under each of the following categories (which correspond to the content areas of the Social Studies Test), and compare your score with the average scores specified in the right-hand column. Review the answer analysis section beginning on page 826 for each of the questions you got wrong, and give yourself more practice in your weak areas with the appropriate material in Chapter 6 (including the "Glossary of Social Studies Terms"), before attempting Practice Examination Two.

CONTENT AREAS	ITEMS	YOUR SCORE	AVERAGE SCORE
Political Science	1–3, 7–8, 31–35, 49–50		8
Economics	10–13, 19–22		6
History	4–6, 9, 14–18, 28–33, 40, 51–52, 59, 63–64		15
Geography	23–25, 26–27, 37–38, 48, 53–56, 60–62		11
Behavioural Science	36, 39, 41–47, 57–58		8

Total ________

TEST 3: The Science Test/Page 789

I. CHECK YOUR ANSWERS, using the following answer key:

1. **5**	15. **3**	29. **5**	43. **2**	57. **4**
2. **5**	16. **2**	30. **2**	44. **3**	58. **3**
3. **1**	17. **5**	31. **4**	45. **5**	59. **5**
4. **2**	18. **3**	32. **4**	46. **1**	60. **4**
5. **1**	19. **2**	33. **2**	47. **1**	61. **5**
6. **3**	20. **4**	34. **5**	48. **2**	62. **2**
7. **2**	21. **5**	35. **3**	49. **2**	63. **4**
8. **4**	22. **1**	36. **2**	50. **4**	64. **5**
9. **5**	23. **1**	37. **5**	51. **2**	65. **2**
10. **4**	24. **2**	38. **3**	52. **4**	66. **3**
11. **5**	25. **4**	39. **4**	53. **4**	
12. **5**	26. **1**	40. **2**	54. **1**	
13. **4**	27. **5**	41. **5**	55. **2**	
14. **3**	28. **3**	42. **1**	56. **4**	

II. SCORE YOURSELF:

Number correct:

Excellent	60–66
Good	49–59
Fair	40–48

III. EVALUATE YOUR SCORE: Did you get at least 40 correct answers? If not, you need more practice for the Science Test. In any event, you can improve your performance to Excellent or Good by analyzing your errors.

IV. ANALYZE YOUR ERRORS: To determine your specific weaknesses, encircle the number of each question you got wrong. This will reveal the specific science area that needs emphasis in planning your study program. After studying the answer analysis section beginning on page 829 for each of the questions you got wrong, list the terms that you feel need further explanation and study them in the "Glossary of Scientific Terms" beginning on page 362. Then give yourself more practice in your weak areas with the appropriate material in Chapter 7 before attempting Practice Examination Two.

CONTENT AREAS	ITEMS	YOUR SCORE	AVERAGE SCORE
Biology	1–22, 33, 34, 41, 44, 45, 47–50		22
Earth Science	37, 39, 40, 46, 66		3
Chemistry	24, 27–32, 35, 42, 43, 51–57		12
Physics	23, 25, 26, 36, 38, 58–65		9

Total ________

TEST 4: Language Arts, Reading (Interpreting Literature and the Arts)/Page 800

I. CHECK YOUR ANSWERS, using the following answer key:

1. **2**	10. **4**	19. **1**	28. **1**	37. **3**
2. **4**	11. **3**	20. **2**	29. **3**	38. **1**
3. **2**	12. **2**	21. **4**	30. **1**	39. **4**
4. **1**	13. **5**	22. **2**	31. **4**	40. **5**
5. **5**	14. **4**	23. **1**	32. **5**	41. **3**
6. **4**	15. **5**	24. **1**	33. **3**	42. **3**
7. **5**	16. **4**	25. **4**	34. **3**	43. **5**
8. **3**	17. **3**	26. **4**	35. **5**	44. **4**
9. **1**	18. **4**	27. **5**	36. **4**	45. **5**

II. SCORE YOURSELF:

Number correct:

Excellent ______ 41–45

Good ______ 36–40

Fair ______ 31–35

III. EVALUATE YOUR SCORE: Did you get at least 31 correct answers? If not, you need more practice for the Test on Interpreting Literature and the Arts. You can improve your performance to Excellent or Good by analyzing your errors.

IV. ANALYZE YOUR ERRORS: To determine your specific weaknesses, list the number of correct answers you had under each of the following categories and compare your score with the average scores in the right-hand column. After studying the answer analysis section beginning on page 832 for each of the questions you answered incorrectly, study the material in the section on *Basic Reading Skills* and the section *Basics on Reading Literature—Prose, Poetry, Drama* in Chapter 8 as well as the "Glossary of Literary Terms" to strengthen your weak areas before attempting Practice Examination Two.

READING SKILLS	ITEMS	YOUR SCORE	AVERAGE SCORE
Locating the Main Idea	6, 21, 26, 28, 31		4
Finding Details	1, 3, 8–9, 12, 15, 19–20, 25, 27, 29–30, 33–34, 36–37, 40–42, 44–45		14
Inferring Meaning	16, 18, 23, 32, 35		4
Making Inferences	2, 4, 7, 11, 17, 22, 38–39, 43		6
Determining Tone and Mood	13–14, 24		2
Inferring Character	5		1

Total ______

Now to see how your scores in the content areas of Interpreting Literature and the Arts Test compare with the average scores in the right-hand column, list your score for each of the following:

CONTENT AREAS	ITEMS	YOUR SCORE	AVERAGE SCORE
Popular Literature	1–25		17
Classical Literature	26–35		7
Commentary	36–45		7

Total _______

LITERARY FORMS	ITEMS	YOUR SCORE	AVERAGE SCORE
Prose Fiction	1–15		11
Prose Nonfiction	31–35		3
Prose Nonfiction (Commentary)	36–45		7
Poetry	16–25		7
Drama	26–30		3

Total _______

Note: While Commentary on the Arts is a content area in itself, the commentary, as written, is in the form of prose nonfiction.

TEST 5: The Mathematics Test/Page 808

I. CHECK YOUR ANSWERS, using the following answer key. The number following each question number is the correct answer. The numbers in parentheses (the *Mathematics Answer Key*) refer to the sections in the Mathematics Review (Chapter 9) which explain the necessary mathematics principles. A more detailed explanation of all answers follows in the Answer Analysis section beginning on page 834.

1. **3**	15. **5**	29. **3**	43. **3**
2. **3**	16. **3**	30. **4**	44. **1**
3. **5**	17. **2**	31. **4**	45. **3**
4. **2**	18. **5**	32. **3**	46. **2**
5. **1**	19. **4**	33. **4**	47. **4**
6. **3**	20. **2**	34. **1**	48. **4**
7. **5**	21. **5**	35. **5**	49. **5**
8. **4**	22. **4**	36. **3**	50. **2**
9. **5**	23. **1**	37. **1**	51. **4**
10. **5**	24. **3**	38. **4**	52. **2**
11. **2**	25. **1**	39. **3**	53. **5**
12. **2**	26. **5**	40. **5**	54. **1**
13. **3**	27. **4**	41. **3**	55. **2**
14. **4**	28. **3**	42. **4**	56. **5**

II. SCORE YOURSELF:

	Number correct:
Excellent	______ 51–56
Good	______ 44–50
Fair	______ 38–43

III. EVALUATE YOUR SCORE: Did you get at least 38 correct answers? If not, you need more practice for the Mathematics Test. In any event, you can improve your performance to Excellent or Good by analyzing your errors.

IV. ANALYZE YOUR ERRORS: To determine your specific weaknesses, list the number of correct answers you had under each of the following categories (which correspond to the *Mathematics Answer Key* just discussed in item I), and compare your score with the average scores in the right-hand column. After studying the answer analysis section beginning on this page for each of the questions you got wrong, give yourself more practice in your weak area with the appropriate material in Chapter 9 before attempting Practice Examination Two. (Note again the *Mathematics Answer Key* explanation in item I.)

CONTENT AREAS	ITEMS	YOUR SCORE	AVERAGE SCORE
I. Arithmetic	1, 4, 6, 8, 10–11, 15, 18, 21–24, 26–27, 30, 33, 35–37, 39, 42–43, 45–47, 51, 55–56		18
II. Algebra	3, 6, 7, 12–14, 16–17, 25, 28, 31, 32, 34, 41, 48–49, 54		11
III. Geometry	2, 5, 9, 19, 20, 29, 31, 36, 38, 40, 44, 50, 52, 53		8

Total ______

YOUR TOTAL GED SCORE

The Writing Skills Test	______
The Social Studies Test	______
The Science Test	______
The Literature and the Arts Test	______
The Mathematics Test	______
Total	______

ANSWER ANALYSIS

TEST 1: The Language Arts, Writing (Writing Skills) Test, Part I/Page 765

1. **5** This change is necessary to correct the run-on sentence.
2. **2** *D*epartment of *A*griculture must be capitalized.
3. **3** The singular subject *Care* requires the singular verb *is. Among* is necessary because the verb *include* implies other precautions that are not mentioned.

4. **5** No correction is necessary.
5. **1** The original is correct because two equally important ideas require two independent clauses connected by *and*.
6. **1** The correct spelling is *sufficient*.
7. **5** No correction is necessary.
8. **1** The use of the adjective clause *which contains food that may* avoids the repetition of *swollen or leaking can*.
9. **1** The original is correct because the semicolon separates two independent clauses in the same sentence.
10. **1** The original is correct because the second idea "the people in the family may change" is in opposition to the first, so *although* is necessary. The comma after *dominant* must be retained.
11. **1** This combination eliminates repetition of the words *will also increase*.
12. **3** This is necessary to avoid the run-on sentence.
13. **1** Following the rewritten sentence's introductory clause should come the subject of the sentence *an increased number.*
14. **5** No correction is necessary.
15. **5** No correction is necessary.
16. **5** No correction is necessary.
17. **1** A comma is never used immediately after the subject and before its verb.
18. **5** No correction is necessary.
19. **4** The sentences are best combined by an adjective clause *which spreads* which modifies *disease*.
20. **5** No correction is necessary.
21. **5** No correction is necessary.
22. **2** The correct spelling is *believed*.
23. **2** To achieve parallelism with *knowledge* and *understanding*, a noun, *example*, must be used.
24. **3** A comma is needed after a lengthy introductory clause.
25. **5** This is necessary to prevent a run-on sentence.
26. **3** The proper sequence of tenses requires the future perfect tense *will have been* since this action precedes *is tempted*.
27. **4** The pronoun must agree in number with its antecedent *his*.
28. **4** The verb should be singular because its subject, *type*, is singular.
29. **1** *Canadians* should be capitalized.
30. **2** A comma is used to separate independent clauses in a compound sentence joined by a conjunction, *but*.
31. **1** The correct spelling is *impossible*.
32. **1** The original is correct because two distinctly different sentences are involved.
33. **4** A comma is used to separate items in a series.
34. **5** No correction is necessary.
35. **5** No correction is necessary.
36. **4** The insertion of *are* is necessary to parallel *are in a hurry* and *are careless*.
37. **1** The subject of the sentence should follow the introductory clause.
38. **3** No comma is necessary between *fever* and *sweeping*.
39. **2** *Mom* and *Pop* should be capitalized since they are proper nouns.
40. **4** The correct spelling is *environment*.
41. **3** A comma is necessary before the final clause in the series.
42. **1** The correct spelling is *appropriate*.
43. **3** *You're* which is a contraction of *you are*, is required in this sentence.
44. **1** The original is the best way. The colon is used because it states the advice.
45. **1** *Invest in* is required by the sense of the sentence.
46. **1** The original is correct because the semicolon is used to separate independent clauses in the same sentence.
47. **4** *Whom* is necessary since it is the object of the preposition *with* and .... in the objective case.
48. **4** The correct spelling is *practice*.

49. **2** The correct spelling is *chooses*.
50. **5** *Since* is required because the second sentence is the result of the first.
51. **5** No correction is necessary.
52. **4** A comma is needed to separate items in a series.
53. **2** *Because* is needed since the second sentence gives a cause (reason) for the first.
54. **3** *Is* is the verb which must follow the noun clause *Making a conscious ordering*.
55. **5** No correction is necessary.

TEST 1: The Language Arts, Writing (Writing Skills) Test, Part II/Page 775

SAMPLE ESSAYS

For the computer

The advent of the computer has vastly improved life in the twentieth century.

Thanks to the computer, it is now possible to do away with much of the drudgery of data handling. The combination of computer, printer, copier saves many hours of routine typing since it is now easy to obtain from a one-time input of data as many copies as one needs.

Thanks to the computer, it is now possible to store important data and to summon the data up when necessary. Files can be set up for hundreds of subjects and the stored data are instantly available.

Thanks to the computer, it is possible to have endless hours of enjoyment from entertaining and educational games. Learning becomes a joy with computer-aided instruction.

Thanks to the computer, engineers and architects can work out their problems more efficiently using computer-assisted design programs.

Thanks to the computer, families can monitor their budgets and keep financial and family records.

Thanks to the computer's word processing capabilities, authors can avoid much monotony in editing and revising works in progress.

Thanks to the computer built-in spelling and dictionary programs, computers make letter writing much less burdensome.

Thanks to the computer and an almost infinite variety of software programs, data can be structured to meet nearly every conceivable need.

These are only a few of the many ways the computer has made the world a better place in which to live.

Summary of reasons *for* the computer:

The computer

1. makes data handling less burdensome;
2. stores and makes data readily available;
3. aids instruction and provides entertainment;
4. aids engineers and architects in their designs;
5. aids families in keeping personal records;
6. aids authors through word processing;
7. makes letter writing more efficient;
8. makes data available in varied ways by means of software programs.

Against the computer

> The computer has brought nothing but problems to the world of the twentieth century.
>
> Chief among the problems has been the dehumanization of society. People are no longer human. Each of us is a series of numbers, numbers to be fed into computers. There are our credit card numbers, our bank account numbers, our social security numbers, our telephone and electricity numbers—the computer number game is endless.
>
> What happens to these computerized numbers? They are distributed to a network of government agencies and businesses which can use them to invade our privacy. The Internal Revenue Service stores millions of facts about every citizen. Credit agencies exchange information on the spending and saving practices of nearly every American adult. Mailing lists are made available by computers to dozens of organizations, public and private, who bombard us with unwanted mail.
>
> Just let the computer which stores data concerning our accounts, let us say with a credit card company, make an error and it is almost impossible to correct it. The result is an avalanche of bills, threats, and loss of credit standing.
>
> The computer has thrown thousands of people out of work. The gamut of computer-generated unemployed runs from highly skilled technicians to typists.
>
> These are some of the reasons why I feel that the advent of the computer has been detrimental to the quality of our life in the twentieth century.

Summary of reasons *against* the computer:

1. The computer has dehumanized society.
2. The computer has invaded our privacy in many ways.
3. Computer errors have caused great hardship to many unfortunate individuals.
4. The computer has thrown many people out of work.

TEST 2: The Social Studies Test/Page 776

1. **2** Just as the Industrial Age saw a widening gap between "haves and have-nots" the Communications Age foresees a developing gap between the techno-elites (knows) and techno-peasants (know-nots).
2. **4** Techno-peasants are the "know nots" who have not acquired communication skills to be successful in the new Communication Age.
3. **2** Techno-elites are the "knows" who have acquired the necessary skills to be successful in the new age.
4. **4** The second paragraph points out that 14,000 of the people of Japanese ancestry in Canada were native born.
5. **4** It has been commonly believed that the Canadian Japanese were interned because they posed a threat as spies or subversives. This passage refers to Canadian cabinet documents that indicate the real reason was to maintain civil order by avoiding racial attacks on the Japanese by the white population.
6. **3** The passage refers to the war giving rise to old feelings of bigotry, especially on the West Coast.
7. **1** Some of these methods include frequent elections, an impartial court system, freedom of the press, the right to petition for a hearing of grievances, and the right to oust corrupt officials through prosecution or impeachment.
8. **4** Historically, both the Liberals and the Conservatives have found it difficult to maintain any kind of national basis.
9. **1** The chart shows that native peoples performed 65% of the labour related to the fur trade and received only one tenth of one percent of the profit.

10. **3** The added companies are described as already successful enterprises.
11. **4** The passage states that profitability ratios provide a measure of management performance.
12. **3** The gap between the fast-rising "desired demand" and the "potential supply," which levels off, is first noticeable at about 1990 on the graph.
13. **1** Western European countries and Japan would lack fuel for their industries, and production would drop, with resultant unemployment and depression.
14. **1** Such resistance is often expressed by *denying* the formal methods for peaceful change. Failure to permit evolutionary change may result in revolution. An example of such a dangerous situation today exists in South Africa.
15. **2** Speaker B emphasized ideas of "free men' and "guaranteed rights." Speaker D emphasizes equality of rights independent of strength.
16. **2** Speaker B sees Riel as a leader in a just cause.
17. **4** The different historical perspective of each will assign differing causes and results to the same major events.
18. **3** The joint stock company's charter gave it a monopoly over colonization and trade in an area, with profits being shared by the shareholders and the King.
19. **1** The Indian people had no experience in the use of money, so trade was carried on by exchanging one type of goods for another.
20. **4** Both the Indians and the French were willing to trade and they made plans to return and do it all again "on the morrow."
21. **3** The expansion of oil companies into unrelated fields, making them some of the largest conglomerates in the world, has led to the call for stronger laws regulating monopolies.
22. **1** Conglomerates are companies which own a controlling interest in other companies, generally in more than one industry. Oil companies have been purchasing control of such unrelated businesses.
23. **1** One measure of economic growth is the change in the GNP—the value of all goods and services produced in a given year. The table shows an increase in both urbanization and GNP for the years 1901 and 1971.
24. **2** Population moves to where economic growth and opportunity are greater. The chart suggests that the cities attracted people from the farms.
25. **3** Farm machinery replaced manpower on the farms.
26. **4** Oil spills have repeatedly ruined the recreational value of beaches and destroyed fish and birdlife, causing both economic and ecological damage.
27. **4** Topography deals with the surface features of a region.
28. **4** The passage focuses on reasons why governments supported labour legislation and social insurance programs in the years of the Great Depression whereas they had previously resisted them. It was not because of commitment to the ideals of social justice but rather because it was politically useful to do so.
29. **3** The emphasis became one of bringing stability to economies that had just been through the turmoil of the greatest periods of boom and bust in their histories.
30. **2** The major concern of the period was to restore economic prosperity.
31. **5** Apolitical as used here means having no interest at all in politics.
32. **1** Other theories are not well accepted. Most analysts see the absence of women from any aspects of political life as being something that results from the formal and informal processes of socialization in our society.
33. **3** There is much in how both girls and boys are raised that implies to them that political life should be the preserve of men.
34. **2** Note the epitaph on the tombstone, "Died of Neglect."
35. **4** Clearly the medical doctor is not going to be of much use to a patient who is already dead; it is too little, too late.
36. **2** Heredity and environment each represents various contributing factors to the behaviour of individuals and groups. No *single* factor can be isolated and identified as determining human actions.
37. **4** It is trade which keeps us alive.

38. **2** Increased population is caused by a speeded-up economic unification.
39. **3** The concern expressed is the expectation on the part of the wider society that Indians should become "brown, white men;" that is, that they should become assimilated and adopt the ways of the dominant culture.
40. **1** Collective security calls for nations to coordinate their military strength to protect one another from aggression.
41. **3** Social mobility is the movement of individuals up or down in social and economic status in society, largely on ability and effort. This is an example of social mobility.
42. **4** Cultural diversity, a variety of cultural patterns, exists where different peoples come together frequently and intermingle. Migration is a principal means of bringing this about.
43. **4** Cultural shock results from rapid social change—movement to a more developed society or movement to a less developed one. The latter is the example given in this question.
44. **2** An extended family includes grandparents, uncles, aunts, and cousins. Out of economic necessity, they may live together and survive because of their dependence on one another.
45. **1** A pluralistic society encourages coexistence of peoples of various ethnic heritages, usually holding differing views on important issues.
46. **3** The author says that jokes can sometimes be inappropriate.
47. **1** The author says that teachers are authority figures.
48. **5** This passage states that geographic natural features leave their imprint on society.
49. **3** In Table A, 65% opposed home searches without a specific warrant; 68% opposed any electronic surveillance of citizens without a court order.
50. **3** Table B shows that 63% would allow the federal government to eavesdrop with specific court permission. When the same question was asked negatively in Table A, 68% opposed electronic eavesdropping without such permission.
51. **1** Fifty percent of Canadian agricultural production goes initially to marketing boards.
52. **3** Eventually 62% of Canadian production is consumed by Canadians.
53. **4** The graph on the left shows the world population to be approximately two billion people in 1900. By the year 2000, it projects the population to be six billion.
54. **3** Although the proportion of Asians to the rest of the world will not increase greatly, their numbers will equal the total world population of 1965. Much of this growth will take place in China, now trying to industrialize. The combination of these two factors could make China a world power equal to the United States and the former Soviet Union.
55. **2** Asia and North America have the greatest potential for new oil production as shown by the new and potential oil fields on the map.
56. **1** New oil finds in North America will cause less dependence upon Arab nations.
57. **3** Contrary to popular belief, the chart shows that Quebec has one of the lowest rates of violent crime in the country. In fact, it is below the national average.
58. **2** This requires you to combine the rates of the three types of crime to get an overall crime rate, and then to find the two provinces with the highest rates. Saskatchewan and Alberta have the highest crime rates in the country.
59. **1** The cartoon indicates that the problems of Central America are as complicated as a maze and they elude solution.
60. **5** Biogeography is concerned with the destruction of animal life on earth, and the increasing number of endangered species of animals is of concern to the biogeographer.
61. **1** Physical geography deals with climatology, the study of climate and climatic phenomena, and with oceanography, the study of the environment in the oceans. The "greenhouse effect" would be of importance to the physical geographer.
62. **3** Drought conditions in the region of East Africa would fall into the domain of the regional geographer since it involves a region and a number of countries in it, Ethiopia and the Sudan as examples.
63. **2** The cartoon implies that Western countries are allowing economic interests (green refers to money) to colour their views on moral opposition to the policy of apartheid in South Africa.

64. **1** Apartheid, the South African policy of separation of the races, is referred to by the term "black and white."

TEST 3: The Science Test/Page 789

1. **5** The selection defines population as a group of organisms of the same species living together in a given location. An ecosystem (or ecological system) consists of the living community of a region and its nonliving environment. The biosphere is that portion of the earth in which ecosystems function. A community consists of populations of different species.
2. **5** The diagram illustrates a simple community consisting of populations of different species living together and interacting with each other.
3. **1** The factor that helps to keep a population in check is natural *predators*. Both predators and prey are adapted to each other and to the environment. If an organism is introduced into a new habitat, it will have few natural enemies or predators. Its population increases.
4. **2** In this simple community the plants carry on photosynthesis, whereby they give off oxygen and make food for themselves and the fish. The fish breathe and supply carbon dioxide to the plants, which they need for the process of photosynthesis. The wastes produced by the fish are acted upon by bacteria in the mud and produce nitrates for the plant.
5. **1** A biotic factor is one concerned with living things. Minerals are not living.
6. **3** A *community* is a particular environment in which organisms of different species live and interact. A community is a self-maintaining unit in which energy and food materials are recycled.
7. **2** Since these ancestors of Equus (the modern horse) have long disappeared, they only evidence of their structure comes from fossils.
8. **4** Refer to the last sentence of this passage.
9. **5** The horse's hoof is the toenail of a middle toe.
10. **4** Eohippus had teeth without ridges. Mesohippus had teeth with well-developed ridges.
11. **5** The original reflex was the production of saliva when the dog was given food. The dog associated another stimulus (the sound of the tone) with the sight of food. After a number of repetitions, the dog salivated when the new stimulus was presented. This was a case of a changed or conditioned response.
12. **5** Choices (1) and (2) are inborn responses. Choices (3) and (4) are learned responses that require a great deal of practice. The correct answer is choice (5) since salivation normally requires contact of food in the mouth but now the sight of certain food causes the response.
13. **4** Between trials 1 and 10, six drops were secreted. Between trials 1 and 20, 26 drops were secreted. Between trials 10 and 20, 14 drops were secreted. Between trials 20 and 30, 40 drops were secreted—the correct choice. Between trials 30 and 40, two drops were secreted.
14. **3** One of the factors involved in the permanent acquisition of a conditioned response is the element of satisfaction. At the test trials no food was given. Note that there were fewer drops of saliva secreted at test trial 50 than 40. It is reasonable to expect fewer drops at test trial 60.
15. **3** Water, carbon dioxide, and protein are chemical compounds. Not all living things have the chemical element phosphorus.
16. **2** Protoplasm is a complex protein.
17. **5** If the effect of one variable is to be tested (feeding in this case) all other variables must be the same on both groups. A control is a factor that is kept the same in both groups.
18. **3** The data obtained in the experiment clearly give an answer to the question raised by the experiment, so this is an experimental finding.
19. **2** In designing the experiment, the scientist had to set it up in such a way that the mice would learn the maze.
20. **4** There is no evidence that this is the reason for the results obtained in the experiment, but the scientist might guess that this is a possibility. It would be tested by further experiments.
21. **5** An assumption is a reasonable guess, based on available knowledge, that is used as a basis for the experimental design.

22. **1** While this statement may be true, it has nothing to do with this experiment.
23. **1** Note that the temperature in the Kelvin scale is equal to the Celsius degrees plus 273: K = °C + 273 or K = (–13°C) + 273 = 260.
24. **2** Each Kelvin degree represents the same CHANGE in temperature as the Celsius degree. Therefore, a change of 90° on the Celsius is also a change of 90° on the Kelvin scale.
25. **4** A straight line with a positive slope and passing through the origin is the graph representing two variables in direct proportion to each other.
26. **1** The wires with the least resistance will carry the most current. Only aluminum and copper have resistances of less than 1 ohm.
27. **5** Since calcium compounds neutralize acidic conditions, calcium carbonate is the only correct choice.
28. **3** Pollutants are the sources of acid deposition. Water is a natural part of the environment. No polluting gases are produced by the use of water power to generate electricity.
29. **5** Selective agents work for or against living organisms in the environment. Acid deposition works against fish and plankton and favors the growth of more acid-loving types of plants.
30. **2** Abiotic factors are nonliving factors in the environment. Sulfur is the abiotic factor related to the acid deposition problem.
31. **4** Since acid deposition results from pollutants that come from burning fossil fuels, the best approach to reducing acid deposition is to control air pollution.
32. **4** Household vinegar is about 2 percent acetic acid.
33. **2** All plants might benefit, but the only way the gardener can know how much to use is to follow the instructions given.
34. **5** Reptilia: garter snake; Aves: house sparrow; Mammalia: African elephant.
35. **3** The sugar becomes less soluble, and might come out of solution as a solid. The gas becomes more soluble, and will remain in solution. If anything, the water will evaporate more slowly at lower temperatures.
36. **2** Locate the given pressure along the horizontal axis. Read up to the curve and then read to the left to the vertical axis. Since the pressure is 8 mm, read up to the 8 mm line until the graph curve is reached. Read to the left, and you will find that the volume at this point is approximately 2 ml.

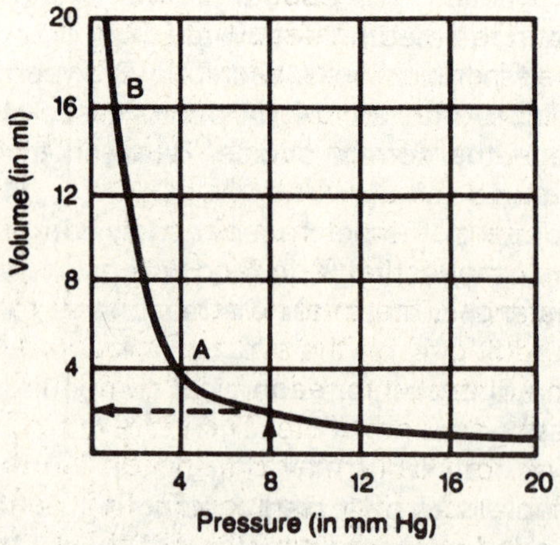

37. **5** The clouds block the entry of radiant heat in the daytime, so the days will be cooler. Since they block the escape of radiant heat at night, the nights will be warmer.
38. **3** In horizontal flight, the engine thrust pushes the plane forward and air drag holds it back; if they are equal, there will be no change in speed. In choices (1) and (2) one of the vertical forces is greater than the other. Choice (4) is wrong because the force acting on the wall has nothing to do with the speed of the ball. Choice (5) is wrong because it takes no account of the pull of gravity.

39. **4** No small planets have rings, but all the large planets except Jupiter have them. Choice (1) is wrong because Jupiter has no rings. Choice (2) is wrong because Pluto has none. Choice (3) is wrong because there is a definite trend. Choice (5) is wrong because there is no reason to believe that Pluto ever had rings.

40. **2** It is only in deserts that dry sand is on the surface, where it can be picked up and carried by the wind.

41. **5** If there is some such substance, there is no reason to suppose that it would affect frogs differently from fish.

42. **1** Hydrated salt is a salt that contains water attached to its molecules. This water is easily removed by heating, leaving only the pure salt (anhydrous = without water). The original 5.0g of this hydrated salt contained pure salt and water. As heating proceeds we see the sample losing weight as the water is driven out. After 15 minutes the sample weighs 3.0g. After this there is no further loss of weight, even after heating for a whole hour. We must assume all the water has been driven out of the material. By 15 minutes, by 30 minutes, certainly by 60 minutes of heating, there are 0.00g of water left in the hydrated salt.

43. **2**

Mass of hydrated salt	= 5.0 g
Mass of dried salt	= 3.0 g
Mass of water removed from salt	= 2.0 g

$$\%\ \text{Water} = \frac{\text{mass of water in hydrated salt}}{\text{mass of hydrated salt sample}} \times 100$$

$$\%\ \text{Water} = \frac{2.0\ \text{g of } H_2O \text{ in sample}}{5.0\ \text{g of sample taken}} \times 100$$

$$\%\ \text{Water} = 0.40 \times 100 = 40.\%$$

44. **3** The impulse starts with irritation of the cornea, goes to the brain through a sensory neuron, and then returns to the tear gland through a motor neuron.

45. **5** That DDT-resistant mosquitoes now exist in greater numbers than 10 years ago means that genetic differences permitted some mosquitoes to survive DDT use. These mosquitoes lived and reproduced others of their kind. Mosquitoes that did not survive DDT use died off. Those with survival power lived and reproduced others with similar survival power. The result was an increase in the numbers of DDT-resistant mosquitoes in the species.

46. **1** Fossils are found in sedimentary rocks, which are laid down in layers. The oldest layers are closest to the earth's crust and the youngest layers are near the surface. To conclude that a species had not changed very much over the years, the unchanged fossils of that species must have been distributed throughout the layers.

47. **1** Gametes—eggs and sperms—have half as many chromosomes as somatic cells. The somatic cell number is produced at fertilization.

48. **2** Under normal circumstances, the total number of adult robins or of adult salmon does not change rapidly. Each adult pair, on the average, produces enough eggs to replace itself, so only 2 eggs survive to adulthood for each adult pair.

49. **2** Corn plants grown in the dark are white. The most probable explanation for this is that the expression of the gene for colour may depend on the environment. The plants have the genetic information for chlorophyll production. This can be assumed because they are genetically identical to the plants grown in the light. Light is needed to activate the chlorophyll gene.

50. **4** In sexual reproduction, new properties are produced by recombination of the genes of the two parents.

51. **2** When two or more elements "chemically combine" they produce a compound. "Chemically combine" means that the individual properties of the original elements are lost when these elements combine. The new material has new, different properties and it is called a compound. In solutions and mixtures the various components have not lost their individual properties nor have they formed a new material.

52. **4** Heating mercuric oxide yields oxygen and mercury, the silvery film mentioned in the passage.
53. **4** The production of the carbonated water mentioned in the passage can be explained by the equation $CO_2 + H_2O \rightarrow H_2CO_3$.
54. **1** As mentioned in the selection, chalk ($CaCO_3$) plus acid, in this case hydrochloric acid (HCl), yields the gas carbon dioxide. In the chemical reaction of Choice (1) the product shown is H_2CO_3 (carbonic acid), but this unstable product quickly breaks up into CO_2 and H_2O.
55. **2** After 24 days one-half of the 12 grams or six grams is left. After 48 days one-half of the six grams or three grams is left. After 72 days one-half of the three grams or 1.5 grams is left. After 96 days one-half of the 1.5 grams or 0.75 gram is left.
56. **4** Each bond holds a hydrogen atom to the carbon atom.
57. **4** A represents acetic acid, B represents acetylene, and C represents benzene. Each has at least one carbon atom with sharing electrons (bonding) with other carbon atoms and/or hydrogen atoms.
58. **3** The selection mentions that red light has a wavelength of 6000A.
59. **5** In order for a particular colour to be transmitted, the other colours of the spectrum must be absorbed.
60. **4** Since the blue rays are absorbed, the green and red rays are transmitted. This gives the yellow appearance, as mentioned in the closing sentence of the selection.
61. **5** Observe the diagram, which shows how white light is broken up into its components by a prism. Red light has the longest wavelength. Infrared rays are even longer and, therefore, are not visible to the human eye. Also note that the violet rays are the shortest. Ultraviolet rays are even shorter and are not visible to the human eye. The selection mentions the range within which the eye can detect light rays.
62. **2** The time is irrelevant because power expresses only the rate of using energy, not the total amount of energy used. The smallest power consumption of those given is (0.002 A) (120 V) = 0.24 watts.
63. **4** The box is being lifted, so the force on it is its weight; the work done is 300 newtons times 2 metres = 600 joules. Choice (1) is wrong because there is no movement, so no work is done. Choice (2) is wrong because the force is upward, holding the box up, not in the direction of motion. In Choice (3), the work is 100 newtons times 3 metres = 300 joules; the weight of the box is irrelevant. Similarly, in Choice (5), the work is only 250 joules.
64. **5** Choice (1) is wrong because the electricity is traveling to the bell in wires; air is irrelevant. The movement of the clapper is independent of the air, so Choice (2) is wrong. Choice (3) is wrong because the bell was heard through the glass as long as there was air in the jar. Choice (4) is wrong because the observer's ears are still in air. This leaves only Choice (5).
65. **2** Since light objects reflect radiant heat and dark objects absorb radiant heat, the test tube on the left will be warmer than the one on the right. Therefore, the air in the U-tube on the left will cause the coloured water to rise to a higher level at the right side.
66. **3** The diagram illustrates the point that the more vertical the angle at which light rays hit the surface, the more intense is the concentration of rays.

TEST 4: Language Arts, Reading (Interpreting Literature and the Arts)/Page 800

1. **2** The passage states that the men were shivering in the cold.
2. **4** He says he "had been frightened of the platoon commander."
3. **2** Broadhurst said "the incident wasn't worth worrying about."
4. **1** This conclusion is warranted by Broadhurst's request that the narrator wait until marching the men off.
5. **5** The narrator concludes from the incident that he "showed cowardice and disloyalty."
6. **4** The passage mentions four situations and people from which and from whom Joey learned.
7. **5** The fifth sentence gives illustrations of what Joey learned.

8. **3** Joey mentions that he would do things in the future which he learned were necessary when he was in the woods and fishing.
9. **1** Joey is described as realizing there were different ways of life from his own.
10. **4** The passage mentions fishing, getting lost, and raccoons. Joey learned much about himself. Only swimming is not mentioned.
11. **3** He locked the doors and windows in a definite order.
12. **2** The words "she thought unhappily" and "furious" indicate how the girl felt.
13. **5** Tension is created by the vagueness—"locking something out"—and the eavesdropping—"her ear against the wall."
14. **4** We are not told what she is planning, but the future is dimly involved.
15. **5** The passage refers to the father's "sense of honesty."
16. **4** The crooked crosses are the poet's metaphorical depiction of television antennas.
17. **3** The poet calls television humour "tired" and criticizes the violence of its programs.
18. **4** The poet will "walk . . ./Among neglected precincts of my soul"; that is, commune with his own spirit.
19. **1** "As silently as Pharoahs" is a simile.
20. **2** Reference to the television set as "the altar box" and to personal spiritual matters as "precincts of my soul" are metaphors.
21. **4** The words "duplication," "duplicate," and "standard" indicate the look of sameness.
22. **2** He uses such objects as pencils, pad, multigraph, among others.
23. **1** The words mean "unable to be stopped or changed"; therefore, powerlessness.
24. **1** The mood is set by the use of such words as "sadness," "dolor," and "desolation," among others.
25. **4** The letter "m" is used three times in the line, a perfect example of alliteration.
26. **4** The purpose of Roberts' speech is revealed in the final sentence—to rally the strikers.
27. **5** He does all the things mentioned, but he does not present a single argument for capital.
28. **1** Anthony indicates there can only be one master in the capital-labour struggle—capital.
29. **3** The final line indicates the need for class distinctions, in Anthony's view.
30. **1** Roberts mentions "that fight 'as been" and "Ye have got it (capital) on its knees," both of which indicate the men have been on strike.
31. **4** Sophie's reaction and the repetition of "What we do now?" in various forms shows that this was a personal problem for Sophie.
32. **5** "Tousled" means "disordered" not "streaked."
33. **3** "Boisterous" means "noisy and given to outbursts" which is the exact opposite of the description of Sophie.
34. **3** The situation of being without enough money triggered troubling memories for Sophie and she cried.
35. **5** The first four choices are unsupported by anything in the story. Sophie's tears indicate that the memory was sad.
36. **4** The article states that "no adequate terms to describe these categories have yet been found."
37. **3** The article cites the Tchaikovsky Piano Concerto as having enjoyed great popularity.
38. **1** Besides indicating the inadequacy of the terminology, the article mentions the problems division into classical and popular creates.
39. **4** It is stated that "no single type of music has a monopoly on worth."
40. **5** The passage says that the distinction between classical and popular music leads to inappropriate implications of value.
41. **3** It is stated that "there is a wholeness in a play which neither the movies nor TV offers."
42. **3** The author states that the three media "may fertilize one another."
43. **5** The author states that Hollywood and Madison Avenue exploit Broadway.
44. **4** The author feels that "some of the people" reached by the movies and TV "may lack sensibility."
45. **5** The author concludes that "no great theatre is possible . . . unless the people consider it a great art."

TEST 5: The Mathematics Test/Page 808

1. **3** Luisa earned a total of 40($6.30) = $252. To find the number of hours it would take Joan to earn $252, we must divide $252 by $8.40.
   $252.00 \div 8.40 = 30$ hours

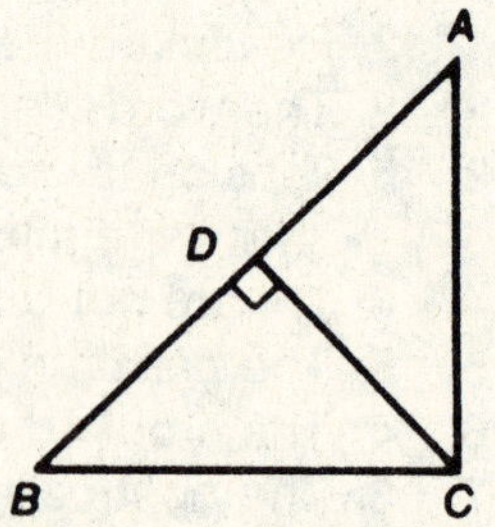

2. **3** Since $m\angle ACB = 90°$ and $m\angle CAD = 40°$
   then $m\angle B = 180° - 90° - 40° = 50°$.
   In $\triangle BCD$, $m\angle CDB = 90°$ and $m\angle B = 50°$.
   Therefore, $m\angle DCB = 180° - 90° - 50° = 40°$.

3. **5** If the class has x students and 5 students are absent then $x - 5$ students are present.
   $$\frac{x-5}{x} = \frac{\text{number of students present}}{\text{number of students in class}}$$

4. **2** If the gauge shows $^1/_3$ full, then the tank is $^2/_3$ empty.
   $^2/_3$ of the tank = 24 L
   $^1/_3$ of the tank = 1/2(24) = 12 L
   $^3/_3$ of the tank = 3(12) = 36 L

5. **1** Let x = length of ramp.
   We use the Pythagorean Theorem to obtain the equation
   $x^2 = 3^2 + 4^2$
   $x^2 = 9 + 16 = 25$
   $x = \sqrt{25} = 5$

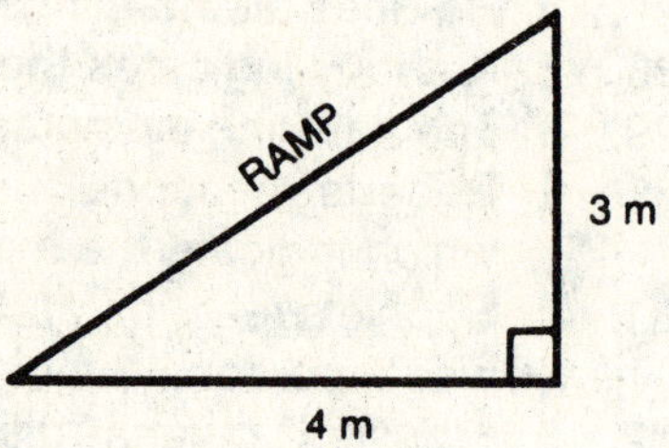

6. **3** A reading of 48 corresponds to 80 amperes.
   Let x represent the maximum number of amperes.
   $\frac{48}{80} = \frac{60}{x}$ [Direct ratio]
   $48x = 4800$ $x = 100$

7. **5** $5x - 1 = 34$
   $5x = 34 + 1 = 35$
   $x = 35 \div 5 = 7$
   $2\ 1/2x = 5x/2 = {}^5/_2 \times 7 = {}^{35}/_2$, or $17^1/_2$

8. **4** If $AC = 18$ and $BC = 8$ then $AB = 18 - 8 = 10$.
   The ratio $AB:BC = 10:8$, or $5:4$.

9. **5** let x = width of the lobby
   $23x = 322$ (area)
   $x = 322 \div 23 = 14$
   Perimeter = 23 + 14 + 23 + 14 = 74 m

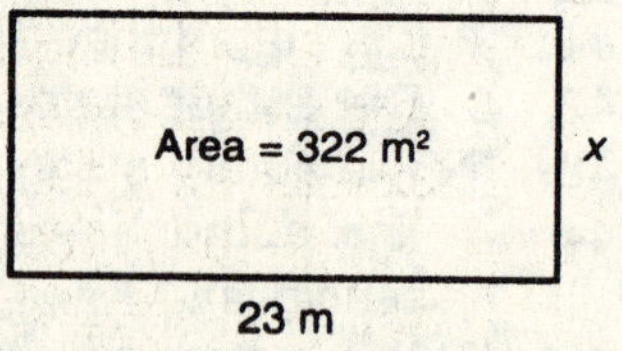

10. **5** In order to determine the price that the *ABC* Store charges for the TV set, Lugin must know the price from which the store deducts 20%.

11. **2** If a crew can load a truck in 3 hours, than it can load $\frac{1}{3}$ of the truck in 1 hour. In 45 minutes, or $\frac{3}{4}$ of an hour, the crew can load $\frac{3}{4} \times \frac{1}{3} = \frac{1}{4}$ of the truck.

12. **2**

$$x^2 + x - 6 = 0$$
$$(x + 3)(x - 2) = 0$$
$$x + 3 = 0 \quad \text{or} \quad x - 2 = 0$$
$$x + 3 - 3 = 0 - 3 \quad\quad x - 2 + 2 = 0 + 2$$
$$x = -3 \quad\quad x = 2$$

The correct choice is (2).

13. **3** To find the perimeter of the figure we must find the sum of the lengths of its sides.
$2a + a + b + 2a + b + a + 2b$
$= 6a + 4b$

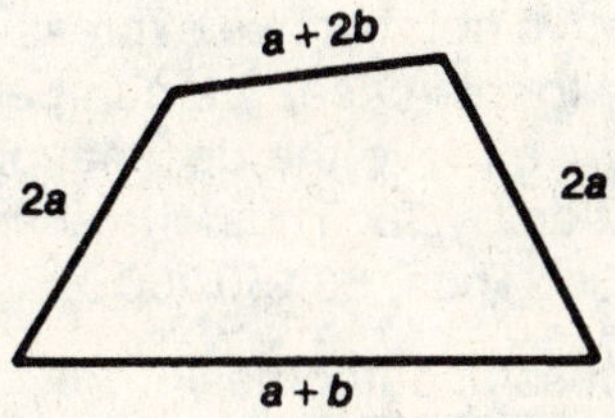

14. **4** Let x = Bob's money.
And $x + 5$ = Henry's money.

$$x + 5 + 2x = 65$$
$$3x + 5 = 65$$
$$3x = 65 - 5 = 60$$
$$x = 60 \div 3 = \$20$$

15. **5** We cannot compute the cost unless we are told the number of days that the couple stays at the motel. This information is not given.

16. **3** Let n = the number.
Then n^2 = the square of the number.
And $n + 4$ = the number increased by 4.
The equation is $n^2 + n + 4 = 60$.

17. **2** Because the coupon has double value, the reduction in price is 2(15¢) = 30 cents.
The cost of the cereal is $x - 30$.

18. **5** Let $3x$ = the measure of the largest angle.
And $2x$ = the measure of the second angle.
And x = the measure of the third angle.

$$3x + 2x + x = 180$$
$$6x = 180$$
$$x = 180 \div 6 = 30$$
$$3x = 3(30) = 90°$$

19. **4** Let $x = m\angle 3$.
And $2x = m\angle 2$.
$m\angle 1 + m\angle 2 + m\angle 3 = 180°$
$36 + 2x + x = 180$
$3x + 36 = 180$
$3x = 180 - 36 = 144$
$x = 144 \div 3 = 48°$

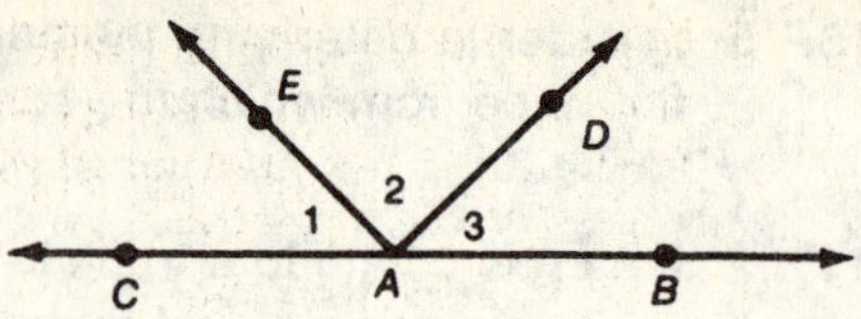

20. **2** Perimeter = 2 (Length + Width)
Let y = Width
$8x = 2\,(2x + 3 + y)$
Solve for y:
$8x = 4x + 6 + 2y$
$4x - 6 = 2y$
$2x - 3 = y$ [Divide by 2]

21. **5** The clerk earns \$16 per hour or 9(16) dollars for 9 hours of work.
The assistant earns \$8 per hour or 9(8) for 9 hours of work.
The two together earned 9(16) + 9(8) dollars.

22. **4** To express a number in scientific notation we express it as the product of a number between 1 and 10 and a power of 10. In this case, the number between 1 and 10 is 6.315. In going from 6.315 to 63 150 000 000 we move the decimal point 10 places to the right. Each such move represents a multiplication by 10. Thus, the entire movement of the decimal point represents a multiplication by 10^{10}. Thus, $63\,150\,000\,000 = 6.315 \times 10^{10}$.

23. **1** $\text{Probability} = \dfrac{\text{number of successful outcomes}}{\text{total number of outcomes}}$
In this case, there are 9 girls who could have been called upon.
The total number of students who could have been called upon was 19.
$\text{Probability} = \dfrac{9}{19}$

24. **3** $\$12\,000 \times 0.09 = \$1080$

25. **1** $3x + 2 < 14$
$3x < 14 - 2$
$3x < 12$
$x < 4$
The only choice less than 4 is answer (1) 3.
Thus, the substitution of 3 for x satisfies the inequality. Note that the substitution of any of the other values given for x would make the statement of the inequality untrue.

26. **5** If we add the amounts given
$11 + 6 + 5 + 40 + 30 = \$92$
This leaves \$8 for profit.

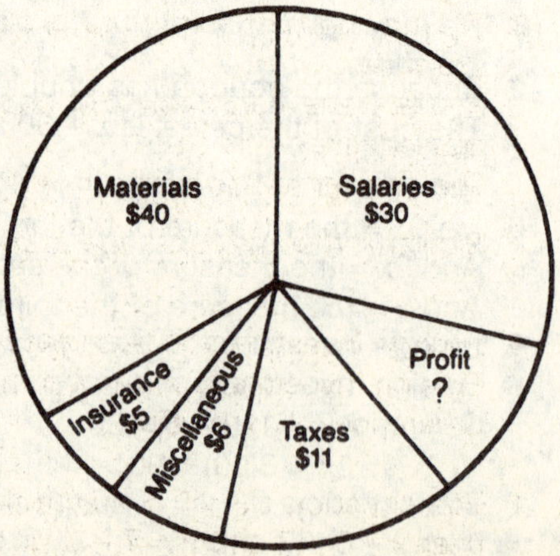

27. **4** We set up the proportion
$\dfrac{5}{659} = \dfrac{9}{y}$
$5y = 9(659)$
$y = \dfrac{9(659)}{5}$

28. **3** Let x = the number of points scored by Jack.
And $x + 7$ = the number of points scored by Ben.
And $x - 2$ = the number of points scored by Paolo.

$$x + x + 7 + x - 2 = 38$$
$$3x + 5 = 38$$
$$3x = 38 - 5 = 33$$
$$x = 33 \div 3 = 11$$

29. **3** We use the formula $V = lwh$
In this case, $l = 5$, $w = 5$, and $h = h$.
Therefore, $V = 5 \times 5 \times h$
$V = 25h$
And $25h = 200$

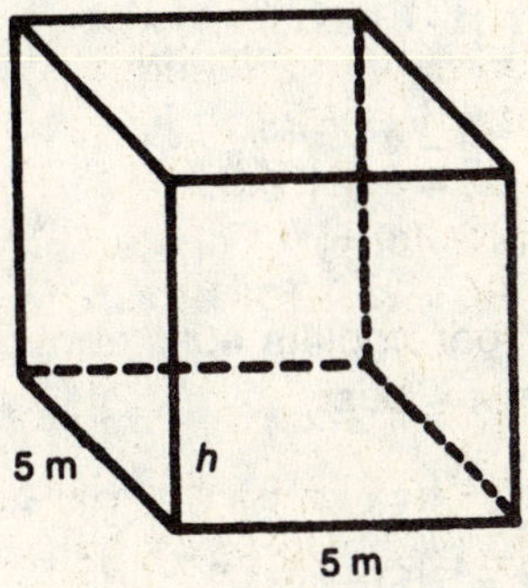

30. **4** $\sqrt{12} = 3.46$, or 3.5 to the nearest tenth
Point D is paired with 3.5 on the number line.

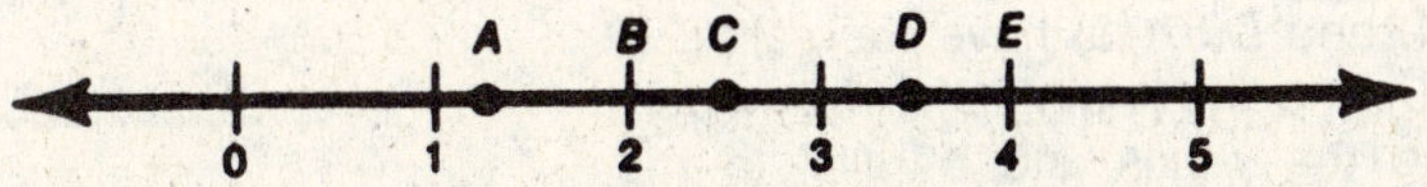

31. **4** Notice the diagram shows $^1/_4$ of 12 or 3 students who belong to both clubs, and 3 students, the remainder of $^1/_2$(12), who belong to the Scholastic Honour Society only, and 1 student, the remainder of $^1/_3$(12), belongs to Varsity Athletic only. Thus we have accounted for 7 of the 12 students. Therefore, 5 students belong to neither organisation.

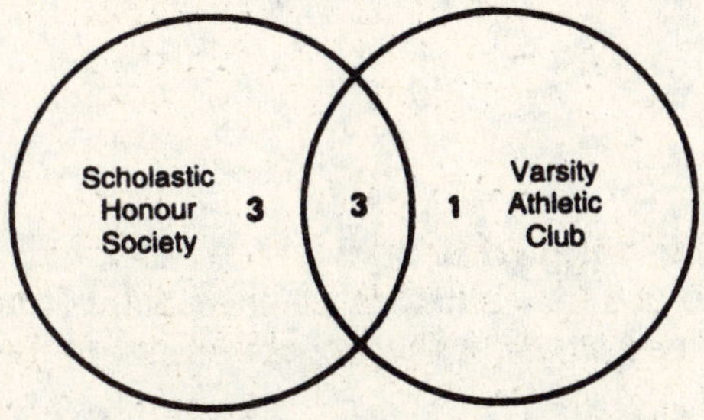

32. **3** We may develop a method of solving this problem by replacing the letters by numbers. For example,
If one plane can carry 200 passengers, how many planes will be needed to carry 1000 passengers?
The answer to this problem is obtained by dividing 1000 by 200.
Similarly, the answer to the original problem is $\frac{y}{x}$.

33. **4** Foreign investment in manufacturing = \$2$^1/_2$ million
Foreign investment in petroleum = \$1 million
Difference = \$1$^1/_2$ million

34. **1** The equation $x + y = 7$ states that the sum of two numbers is 7. Since the value of y is 3, then $x + 3 = 7$ and $x = 7 - 3$, or 4.

35. **5** $\frac{y}{x}$ = what part x is of y

$\left(\frac{y}{x}\right)(100) = \frac{100y}{x}$ = what percent x is of y

36. **3** Substitute $X = 3Y$

$\left(\frac{1}{4}\right)(3Y) = (?)\%$ of Y

$\frac{3}{4}Y = 75\%$ of Y

37. **1** \$7 per book is 40% above cost or 140% of cost. 140% may be expressed as $1\frac{2}{5}$ or $\frac{7}{5}$.
Let x = cost.

$\frac{7x}{5} = 7$

$7x = 7(5) = 35$

$x = 35 \div 7 = 5$

The dealer's cost is \$5 per book.
Six dozen books = $6 \times 12 = 72$ books
$\$5 \times 72 = \$360$, cost of books

38. **4** Since $B(5, 4)$ and $D(5, -3)$ have the same x-coordinate (5), the line joining B and D is perpendicular to the x-axis and parallel to the y-axis. The distance from point B to the x-axis is 4, since the y-coordinate of B is 4. Since the y-coordinate of D is -3, the distance from the x-axis to D is 3.
The total distance from B to D is $4 + 3 = 7$.

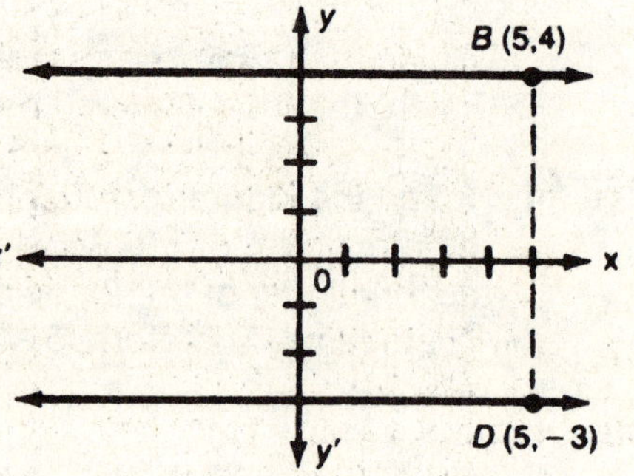

39. **3** $6 \times 10^5 = 600\,000$
$4 \times 10^3 = 4000$
$600\,000 \div 4000 = 600 \div 4 = 150$

40. **5** slope $= \frac{y_1 - y_2}{x_1 - x_2}$

In this case, $y_1 = y$, $y_2 = 2$, $x_1 = 4$, and $x_2 = 1$.

Therefore, $\frac{y-2}{4-1} = 1$

$\frac{y-2}{3} = 1$

$y - 2 = 3$

$y = 3 + 2 = 5$

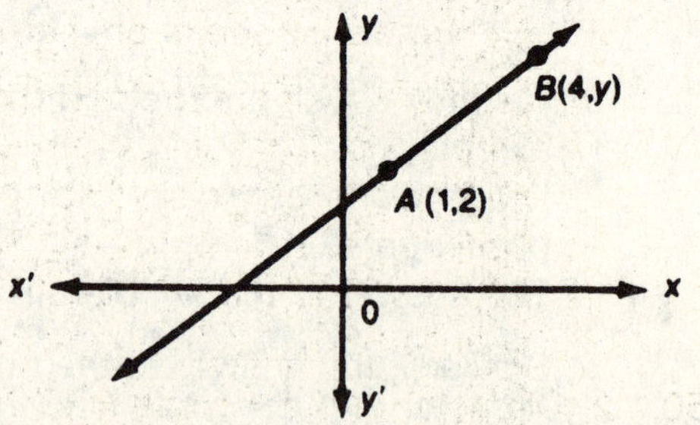

41. **3** $2x^2 - 3(x - 4)$
If $x = 6$ we have
$2(6)(6) - 3(6 - 4)$
$2(6)(6) - 3(2)$
$72 - 6 = 66$

42. **4** $a < b$
$c < d$
$a + c < b + d$, or $b + d > a + c$
Two inequalities may be added, if the inequality signs have the same direction, by simply adding the left side and adding the right side and keeping the same inequality sign.

43. **3** Average (mean) $= \dfrac{\text{sum of all wages paid}}{\text{number of workers}}$

10 clerks at \$380 per week = 10(380)	= \$3800
1 assistant manager at \$480 per week	= \$ 480
1 manager at \$604 per week	= \$ 604
Total wages paid	\$4884

$4884 \div 12 = 407$
Average salary is \$407 per week

44. **1** Let x = measure of m$\angle OAB$
$OA = OB$ since radii of the same circle have equal measures.
Therefore, m$\angle OAB$ = m$\angle OBA$:

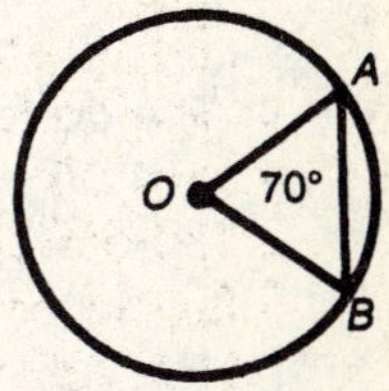

$$x + x + 70 = 180$$
$$2x + 70 = 180$$
$$2x = 180 - 70 = 110$$
$$x = 110 \div 2 = 55$$

45. **3** Up to 4:00 P.M., Sylvia had traveled 164 km. From the table we see that she was traveling at a steady rate of 164 − 80 = 84 km/h. In $\frac{1}{4}$ hour Sylvia traveled $\frac{1}{4} \times 84 = 21$ km. Thus, at 4:15 P.M. Sylvia had covered 164 + 21 = 185 km.

46. **2** If Joan uses 250 mL of milk instead of $\frac{1}{3}$ of a cup she must multiply the measure of each ingredient by 3.
3(2.5 mL of salt) = 7.5 mL of salt

47. **4** This information can be read directly on the graph.

48. **4** Let x = cost of lot.
And $3x$ = cost of house.
$$x + 3x = 120\,000$$
$$4x = 120\,000$$
$$x = 120\,000 \div 4 = 30\,000$$
$$3x = 3(30\,000) = \$90\,000$$

49. **5** Let x = number of books on small shelf.
And $x + 8$ = number of books on large shelf.
$4x$ = number of books on 4 small shelves
$3(x + 8)$ = number of books on 3 large shelves
$$4x + 3(x + 8) = 297$$
$$4x + 3x + 24 = 297$$
$$7x + 24 = 297$$
$$7x = 297 - 24 = 273$$
$$x = 273 \div 7 = 39$$

50. **2** Diameter of outer circle = 40 + 4 + 4 = 48 cm
Radius of outer circle = $\frac{1}{2}(48)$ = 24 cm
Diameter of inner circle = 40 cm
Radius of inner circle = 20 cm
We use the formula $A = \pi r^2$
Area of outer circle = $\pi \times 24 \times 24 = 576\pi$
Area of inner circle = $\pi \times 20 \times 20 = 400\pi$
Area of border = $576\pi - 400\pi = 176\pi$

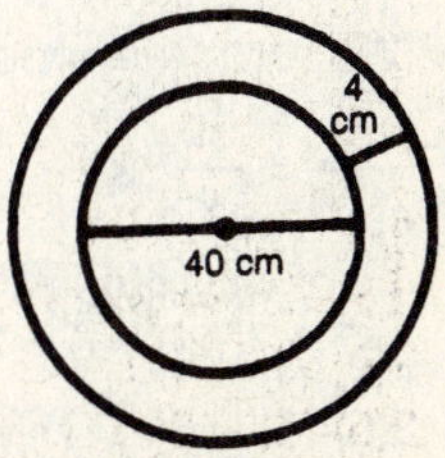

51. **4** The next odd integer is $x + 2$.

$$\frac{x+2}{x} = \frac{x}{x} + \frac{2}{x} = 1 + \frac{2}{x}.$$

52. **2** By the Pythagorean theorem

$$(2x - 1)^2 + (2x + 1)^2 = (\text{hypotenuse})^2$$
$$(4x^2 - 4x + 1) + (4x^2 + 4x + 1) = (\text{hypotenuse})^2$$
$$8x^2 + 2 = (\text{hypotenuse})^2$$
$$\sqrt{8x^2 + 2} = \text{hypotenuse}$$

53. **5** We check each pair of angles for congruence.

$\angle a \cong \angle d$. Opposite angles are congruent.
$\angle b \cong \angle f$. Corresponding angles of parallel lines are congruent.
$\angle c \cong \angle b$. Opposite angles are congruent.
$\angle f \cong \angle c$. Alternate interior angles of parallel lines are congruent.
There is no basis for saying that $\angle b$ is congruent to $\angle g$.

The correct choice is (5).

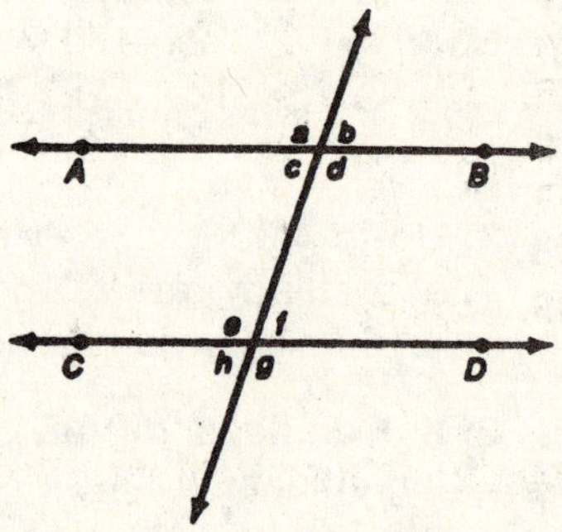

54. **1** $A + B + C = 180$
Since $A = B$, we may write
$B + B + C = 180$
Since $B = 2C$, we may write
$2C + 2C + C = 180$
$5C = 180$
$C = 180 \div 5 = 36$

55. **2** Point Z is farthest west.

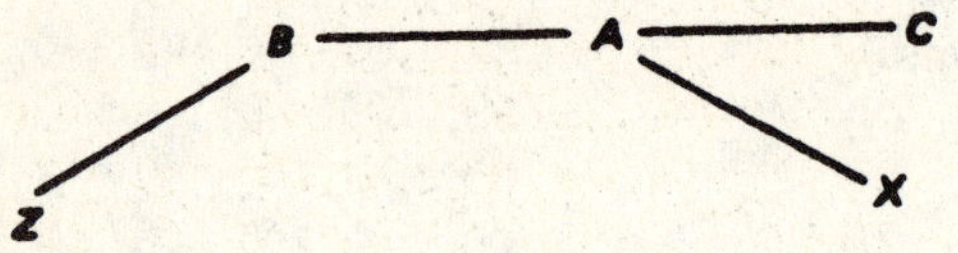

56. **5** 15 dozen = $15 \times 12 = 180$
We form the proportion

$$\frac{6}{180} = \frac{39}{x}$$

$6x = 39(180) = 7020$
$x = 7020 \div 6 = \$1170$

Answer Sheet—Practice Examination

Test 1: The Language Arts, Writing (Writing Skills) Test ________________

1. ① ② ③ ④ ⑤
2. ① ② ③ ④ ⑤
3. ① ② ③ ④ ⑤
4. ① ② ③ ④ ⑤
5. ① ② ③ ④ ⑤
6. ① ② ③ ④ ⑤
7. ① ② ③ ④ ⑤
8. ① ② ③ ④ ⑤
9. ① ② ③ ④ ⑤
10. ① ② ③ ④ ⑤
11. ① ② ③ ④ ⑤
12. ① ② ③ ④ ⑤
13. ① ② ③ ④ ⑤
14. ① ② ③ ④ ⑤
15. ① ② ③ ④ ⑤
16. ① ② ③ ④ ⑤
17. ① ② ③ ④ ⑤
18. ① ② ③ ④ ⑤
19. ① ② ③ ④ ⑤
20. ① ② ③ ④ ⑤
21. ① ② ③ ④ ⑤
22. ① ② ③ ④ ⑤
23. ① ② ③ ④ ⑤
24. ① ② ③ ④ ⑤
25. ① ② ③ ④ ⑤
26. ① ② ③ ④ ⑤
27. ① ② ③ ④ ⑤
28. ① ② ③ ④ ⑤
29. ① ② ③ ④ ⑤
30. ① ② ③ ④ ⑤
31. ① ② ③ ④ ⑤
32. ① ② ③ ④ ⑤
33. ① ② ③ ④ ⑤
34. ① ② ③ ④ ⑤
35. ① ② ③ ④ ⑤
36. ① ② ③ ④ ⑤
37. ① ② ③ ④ ⑤
38. ① ② ③ ④ ⑤
39. ① ② ③ ④ ⑤
40. ① ② ③ ④ ⑤
41. ① ② ③ ④ ⑤
42. ① ② ③ ④ ⑤
43. ① ② ③ ④ ⑤
44. ① ② ③ ④ ⑤
45. ① ② ③ ④ ⑤
46. ① ② ③ ④ ⑤
47. ① ② ③ ④ ⑤
48. ① ② ③ ④ ⑤
49. ① ② ③ ④ ⑤
50. ① ② ③ ④ ⑤
51. ① ② ③ ④ ⑤
52. ① ② ③ ④ ⑤
53. ① ② ③ ④ ⑤
54. ① ② ③ ④ ⑤
55. ① ② ③ ④ ⑤

Test 2: The Social Studies Test ________________

1. ① ② ③ ④ ⑤
2. ① ② ③ ④ ⑤
3. ① ② ③ ④ ⑤
4. ① ② ③ ④ ⑤
5. ① ② ③ ④ ⑤
6. ① ② ③ ④ ⑤
7. ① ② ③ ④ ⑤
8. ① ② ③ ④ ⑤
9. ① ② ③ ④ ⑤
10. ① ② ③ ④ ⑤
11. ① ② ③ ④ ⑤
12. ① ② ③ ④ ⑤
13. ① ② ③ ④ ⑤
14. ① ② ③ ④ ⑤
15. ① ② ③ ④ ⑤
16. ① ② ③ ④ ⑤
17. ① ② ③ ④ ⑤
18. ① ② ③ ④ ⑤
19. ① ② ③ ④ ⑤
20. ① ② ③ ④ ⑤
21. ① ② ③ ④ ⑤
22. ① ② ③ ④ ⑤
23. ① ② ③ ④ ⑤
24. ① ② ③ ④ ⑤
25. ① ② ③ ④ ⑤
26. ① ② ③ ④ ⑤
27. ① ② ③ ④ ⑤
28. ① ② ③ ④ ⑤
29. ① ② ③ ④ ⑤
30. ① ② ③ ④ ⑤
31. ① ② ③ ④ ⑤
32. ① ② ③ ④ ⑤
33. ① ② ③ ④ ⑤
34. ① ② ③ ④ ⑤
35. ① ② ③ ④ ⑤
36. ① ② ③ ④ ⑤
37. ① ② ③ ④ ⑤
38. ① ② ③ ④ ⑤
39. ① ② ③ ④ ⑤
40. ① ② ③ ④ ⑤
41. ① ② ③ ④ ⑤
42. ① ② ③ ④ ⑤
43. ① ② ③ ④ ⑤
44. ① ② ③ ④ ⑤
45. ① ② ③ ④ ⑤
46. ① ② ③ ④ ⑤
47. ① ② ③ ④ ⑤
48. ① ② ③ ④ ⑤
49. ① ② ③ ④ ⑤
50. ① ② ③ ④ ⑤
51. ① ② ③ ④ ⑤
52. ① ② ③ ④ ⑤
53. ① ② ③ ④ ⑤
54. ① ② ③ ④ ⑤
55. ① ② ③ ④ ⑤
56. ① ② ③ ④ ⑤
57. ① ② ③ ④ ⑤
58. ① ② ③ ④ ⑤
59. ① ② ③ ④ ⑤
60. ① ② ③ ④ ⑤
61. ① ② ③ ④ ⑤
62. ① ② ③ ④ ⑤
63. ① ② ③ ④ ⑤
64. ① ② ③ ④ ⑤

Test 3: The Science Test ____________________

1. ① ② ③ ④ ⑤
2. ① ② ③ ④ ⑤
3. ① ② ③ ④ ⑤
4. ① ② ③ ④ ⑤
5. ① ② ③ ④ ⑤
6. ① ② ③ ④ ⑤
7. ① ② ③ ④ ⑤
8. ① ② ③ ④ ⑤
9. ① ② ③ ④ ⑤
10. ① ② ③ ④ ⑤
11. ① ② ③ ④ ⑤
12. ① ② ③ ④ ⑤
13. ① ② ③ ④ ⑤
14. ① ② ③ ④ ⑤
15. ① ② ③ ④ ⑤
16. ① ② ③ ④ ⑤
17. ① ② ③ ④ ⑤
18. ① ② ③ ④ ⑤
19. ① ② ③ ④ ⑤
20. ① ② ③ ④ ⑤
21. ① ② ③ ④ ⑤
22. ① ② ③ ④ ⑤
23. ① ② ③ ④ ⑤
24. ① ② ③ ④ ⑤
25. ① ② ③ ④ ⑤
26. ① ② ③ ④ ⑤
27. ① ② ③ ④ ⑤
28. ① ② ③ ④ ⑤
29. ① ② ③ ④ ⑤
30. ① ② ③ ④ ⑤
31. ① ② ③ ④ ⑤
32. ① ② ③ ④ ⑤
33. ① ② ③ ④ ⑤
34. ① ② ③ ④ ⑤
35. ① ② ③ ④ ⑤
36. ① ② ③ ④ ⑤
37. ① ② ③ ④ ⑤
38. ① ② ③ ④ ⑤
39. ① ② ③ ④ ⑤
40. ① ② ③ ④ ⑤
41. ① ② ③ ④ ⑤
42. ① ② ③ ④ ⑤
43. ① ② ③ ④ ⑤
44. ① ② ③ ④ ⑤
45. ① ② ③ ④ ⑤
46. ① ② ③ ④ ⑤
47. ① ② ③ ④ ⑤
48. ① ② ③ ④ ⑤
49. ① ② ③ ④ ⑤
50. ① ② ③ ④ ⑤
51. ① ② ③ ④ ⑤
52. ① ② ③ ④ ⑤
53. ① ② ③ ④ ⑤
54. ① ② ③ ④ ⑤
55. ① ② ③ ④ ⑤
56. ① ② ③ ④ ⑤
57. ① ② ③ ④ ⑤
58. ① ② ③ ④ ⑤
59. ① ② ③ ④ ⑤
60. ① ② ③ ④ ⑤
61. ① ② ③ ④ ⑤
62. ① ② ③ ④ ⑤
63. ① ② ③ ④ ⑤
64. ① ② ③ ④ ⑤
65. ① ② ③ ④ ⑤
66. ① ② ③ ④ ⑤

Test 4: The Language Arts, Reading (Interpreting Literature and the Arts) Test ____________

1. ① ② ③ ④ ⑤
2. ① ② ③ ④ ⑤
3. ① ② ③ ④ ⑤
4. ① ② ③ ④ ⑤
5. ① ② ③ ④ ⑤
6. ① ② ③ ④ ⑤
7. ① ② ③ ④ ⑤
8. ① ② ③ ④ ⑤
9. ① ② ③ ④ ⑤
10. ① ② ③ ④ ⑤
11. ① ② ③ ④ ⑤
12. ① ② ③ ④ ⑤
13. ① ② ③ ④ ⑤
14. ① ② ③ ④ ⑤
15. ① ② ③ ④ ⑤
16. ① ② ③ ④ ⑤
17. ① ② ③ ④ ⑤
18. ① ② ③ ④ ⑤
19. ① ② ③ ④ ⑤
20. ① ② ③ ④ ⑤
21. ① ② ③ ④ ⑤
22. ① ② ③ ④ ⑤
23. ① ② ③ ④ ⑤
24. ① ② ③ ④ ⑤
25. ① ② ③ ④ ⑤
26. ① ② ③ ④ ⑤
27. ① ② ③ ④ ⑤
28. ① ② ③ ④ ⑤
29. ① ② ③ ④ ⑤
30. ① ② ③ ④ ⑤
31. ① ② ③ ④ ⑤
32. ① ② ③ ④ ⑤
33. ① ② ③ ④ ⑤
34. ① ② ③ ④ ⑤
35. ① ② ③ ④ ⑤
36. ① ② ③ ④ ⑤
37. ① ② ③ ④ ⑤
38. ① ② ③ ④ ⑤
39. ① ② ③ ④ ⑤
40. ① ② ③ ④ ⑤
41. ① ② ③ ④ ⑤
42. ① ② ③ ④ ⑤
43. ① ② ③ ④ ⑤
44. ① ② ③ ④ ⑤
45. ① ② ③ ④ ⑤

Test 5: The Mathematics Test

1.	①	②	③	④	⑤
2.	①	②	③	④	⑤
3.	①	②	③	④	⑤
4.	①	②	③	④	⑤
5.	①	②	③	④	⑤
6.	①	②	③	④	⑤
7.	①	②	③	④	⑤
8.	①	②	③	④	⑤
9.	①	②	③	④	⑤
10.	①	②	③	④	⑤
11.	①	②	③	④	⑤
12.	①	②	③	④	⑤
13.	①	②	③	④	⑤
14.	①	②	③	④	⑤
15.	①	②	③	④	⑤
16.	①	②	③	④	⑤
17.	①	②	③	④	⑤
18.	①	②	③	④	⑤
19.	①	②	③	④	⑤
20.	①	②	③	④	⑤
21.	①	②	③	④	⑤
22.	①	②	③	④	⑤
23.	①	②	③	④	⑤
24.	①	②	③	④	⑤
25.	①	②	③	④	⑤
26.	①	②	③	④	⑤
27.	①	②	③	④	⑤
28.	①	②	③	④	⑤
29.	①	②	③	④	⑤
30.	①	②	③	④	⑤
31.	①	②	③	④	⑤
32.	①	②	③	④	⑤
33.	①	②	③	④	⑤
34.	①	②	③	④	⑤
35.	①	②	③	④	⑤
36.	①	②	③	④	⑤
37.	①	②	③	④	⑤
38.	①	②	③	④	⑤
39.	①	②	③	④	⑤
40.	①	②	③	④	⑤
41.	①	②	③	④	⑤
42.	①	②	③	④	⑤
43.	①	②	③	④	⑤
44.	①	②	③	④	⑤
45.	①	②	③	④	⑤
46.	①	②	③	④	⑤
47.	①	②	③	④	⑤
48.	①	②	③	④	⑤
49.	①	②	③	④	⑤
50.	①	②	③	④	⑤
51.	①	②	③	④	⑤
52.	①	②	③	④	⑤
53.	①	②	③	④	⑤
54.	①	②	③	④	⑤
55.	①	②	③	④	⑤
56.	①	②	③	④	⑤

PRACTICE EXAMINATION TWO

TEST 1: LANGUAGE ARTS, WRITING (WRITING SKILLS), PART I

Directions

Allotted time: 75 minutes

This part of the Language Arts, Writing (Writing Skills) test contains **55 multiple-choice questions** that test your ability to write English correctly and effectively.

The multiple-choice questions are based on numbered sentences in paragraphs. These sentences may be correct as written (if so, choose option 1), or they will contain an error in sentence structure, grammar and usage, punctuation, capitalization, or spelling. You must choose the option that either corrects the error, indicates the best way to write a portion of the sentence, combines two sentences effectively, or provides another way in which the sentence can be rewritten.

Since 55 questions must be answered in 75 minutes, if there are six paragraphs, spend no more than 12 minutes on each set of questions based on each paragraph. Do not devote more than a few minutes to any one question. If there is time left, you may go back to a question.

Answer all questions. Do not leave any blanks since there is no penalty for incorrect answers. Your score will be the number of your correct responses.

Decide which is the best answer and mark the numbered space on the answer sheet beside the number that corresponds to the question in the test.

You may go on to Writing Skills, Part II, the essay, when you complete Part I.

Make no mark on the answer sheet other than your choice of the correct answer. If you change your answer, erase your first mark completely. Only *one* answer space should be marked for each question.

EXAMPLE:

In the future, people will need to learn to turn to their computer for assistence.

What corrections should be made to this sentence?

(1) remove the comma after future
(2) change will need to need
(3) change the spelling of their to they're
(4) change the spelling of assistence to assistance
(5) no correction is necessary

① ② ③ ● ⑤

In this sentence, the correct spelling is "assistance," so mark answer 4 on the answer sheet.

Directions: Choose the one best answer to each item.

Items 1–10 refer to the following paragraphs.

(1) Each year more young men and young women are recognizing the rewards in nursing and enroll in nursing programs, but the demand for nurses continues to outstrip the supply.

(2) If you join the personnel of a hospital you can choose among absorbing fields. (3) You can concentrate on work with children, in obstetrics, in surgery, or on the fascinating new techniques of orthopedics which calls so heavily for a nurse's skill and imagination.

(4) Since Florence Nightingale went to the crimea over a hundred years ago, nurses have been an enormously mobile group. (5) If one wants to travel, many posts are open to you, both in this country and abroad. (6) You can choose foreign service with the World Health Organization, with our own goverment's foreign operations or with one of our armed services.

(7) Schools need nurses. (8) Many married nurses who want time in the afternoon with their own children find part-time positions ideal and easy to get. (9) Private practice brings its special rewards in choice of hours and cases.

(10) Opportunities in community and public health programs which require a bachelor's degree from an accredited school are growing rapidly. (11) A visiting nurse has a fascinating career, moving through many homes each day and leaving order and comfort behind.

1. Sentence 1: **Each year more young men and young women are recognizing the rewards in nursing and enroll in nursing programs, but the demand for nurses continues to outstrip the supply.**

   What correction should be made to this sentence?

   (1) change the spelling of recognizing to reconizing
   (2) change enroll to are enrolling
   (3) remove the comma before but
   (4) change but to and
   (5) no correction is necessary

2. Sentence 2: **If you join the personnel of a hospital you can choose among absorbing fields.**

   What correction should be made to this sentence?

   (1) change join to will join
   (2) change the spelling of personnel to personel
   (3) insert a comma after hospital
   (4) change the spelling of choose to chose
   (5) no correction is necessary

3. Sentence 3: **You can concentrate on work with children, in obstetrics, in surgery, or on the fascinating new technlques of orthopedics which calls so heavily for a nurse's skill and imagination.**

   What correction should be made to this sentence?

   (1) change the spelling of concentrate to consentrate
   (2) change the spelling of children to childern
   (3) remove the comma after surgery
   (4) change calls to call
   (5) no correction is necessary

4. Sentence 4: **Since Florence Nightingale went to the crimea over a hundred years ago, nurses have been an enormously mobile group.**

   What correction should be made to this sentence?

   (1) change went to had gone
   (2) capitalize crimea
   (3) remove the comma after ago
   (4) change the spelling of enormously to enormusly
   (5) no correction is necessary

5. Sentence 5: **If one wants to travel, many posts are available to you, both in this country and abroad.**

   What correction should be made to this sentence?

   (1) change one wants to you want
   (2) remove the comma after travel
   (3) change the spelling of available to availible
   (4) remove the comma after you
   (5) no correction is necessary

6. Sentence 6: **You can choose foreign service with the World Health Organization, with our own goverment's foreign operations, or with one of our armed services.**

   What correction should be made to this sentence?

   (1) change the spelling of foreign to forign
   (2) remove the capitals from World Health Organization
   (3) remove the comma after Organization
   (4) change the spelling of goverment's to government's
   (5) no correction is necessary

7. Sentences 7 and 8: **Schools need nurses. Many married nurses who want time in the afternoon with their own children find part-time positions ideal and easy to get.**

   The most effective combination of sentences 7 and 8 would include which of the following groups of words?

   (1) nurses and many
   (2) nurses because many
   (3) nurses if many
   (4) nurses since many
   (5) nurses, so many

8. Sentence 9: **Private practice brings its special rewards in choice of hours and cases.**

   What correction should be made to this sentence?

   (1) change the spelling of practice to practise
   (2) change its to it's
   (3) change the spelling of special to speshal
   (4) insert a comma after rewards
   (5) no correction is necessary

9. Sentence 10: **Opportunities in community and public health programs which require a bachelor's degree from an accredited school are growing rapidly.**

   Which of the following is the best way to write the underlined portion of this sentence? If you think the original is the best way, choose option (1).

   (1) programs which require
   (2) programs who require
   (3) programs which do require
   (4) programs which are requiring
   (5) programs which will require

10. Sentence 11: **A visiting nurse has a fascinating career, moving through many homes each day and leaving order and comfort behind.**

    What correction should be made to this sentence?

    (1) change the spelling of fascinating to fasinating
    (2) remove the comma after career
    (3) change the spelling of through to thorough
    (4) insert a comma after order
    (5) no correction is necessary

Items 11 to 19 refer to the following paragraphs.

(1) Nutritional food buying emphasizes the "Basic Four". (2) Backpacking also has its basic four, these being in order of importance: (1) hiking shoes, (2) the backpack, (3) sleeping gear, and (4) shelter.

(3) Selection of hiking shoes should be your first concern. (4) Even a one-day hike can be misery without comfortable shoes.

(5) Today's hikers prefer a shoe that is six inches high, is made of leather, and thick sturdy composition soles. (6) Break the shoes in thoroughly on short walks before going on any extended hike.

(7) When purchasing a backpack, you will find an almost bewildering array of makes, styles, and materiels to choose from. (8) The backpacking frame must have both shoulder straps and a waist strap. The latter strap being of such design as to permit much of the weight of the pack to rest on the sturdy hip bones rather than on the more fragile shoulder bones.

(9) The sleeping bag and its two accessories (ground cloth and mattress) are next on the list of basics.

(10) The fourth and last of the basic four is the tent or other emergency shelter. (11) An inexpensive shelter is the plastic tube tent.

11. Sentence 1: **Nutritional food buying emphasizes the "Basic Four".**

    What correction should be made to this sentence?

    (1) insert a hyphen in food buying
    (2) change emphasizes to emphasize
    (3) remove the capital from Four
    (4) place the period within the quotation marks
    (5) no correction is necessary

12. Sentence 2: **Backpacking also has its basic four, these being in order of importance: (1) hiking shoes, (2) the backpack, (3) sleeping gear, and (4) shelter.**

What correction should be made to this sentence?

(1) change its to it's
(2) change the colon to a semicolon
(3) change being to are
(4) remove the comma after gear
(5) no correction is necessary

13. Sentences 3 and 4: **Selection of hiking shoes should be your first concern. Even a one-day hike can be misery without comfortable shoes.**

The most effective combination of sentences 3 and 4 would include which of the following groups of words?

(1) concern, also even
(2) concern, although even
(3) concern, because even
(4) concern, if even
(5) concern, whereas even

14. Sentence 5: **Today's hikers prefer a shoe that is six inches high, is made of leather, and thick sturdy composition soles.**

What correction should be made to this sentence?

(1) remove the apostrophe from today's
(2) insert a comma after shoe
(3) remove the comma after high
(4) insert has before thick
(5) no correction is necessary

15. Sentence 6: **Break the shoes in thoroughly on short walks before going on any extended hike.**

Which of the following is the best way to write the underlined portion of this sentence? If you think the original is the best way, choose option (1).

(1) walks before
(2) walks, before
(3) walks: before
(4) walks. before
(5) walks. Before

16. Sentence 7: **When purchasing a backpack, you will find an almost bewildering array of makes, styles, and materiels to choose from.**

What correction should be made to this sentence?

(1) remove the comma after backpack
(2) change the spelling of almost to allmost
(3) remove the comma after makes
(4) change the spelling of materiels to materials
(5) no correction is necessary

17. Sentence 8: **The backpacking frame must have both shoulder straps and a waist strap. The latter strap being of such design as to permit much of the weight of the pack to rest on the sturdy hip bones rather than on the more fragile shoulder bones.**

Which of the following is the best way to write the underlined portion of these sentences? If you think the original is the best way, choose option (1).

(1) strap. The
(2) strap. the
(3) strap, The
(4) strap, the
(5) strap: the

18. Sentence 9: **The sleeping bag and its two accessories (ground cloth and mattress) are next on the list of basics.**

If you rewrote sentence 9 beginning with

Next on the list of basics

the next word should be

(1) the sleeping bag
(2) its two accessories
(3) ground cloth and mattress
(4) are
(5) is

19. Sentences 10 and 11: **The fourth and last of the basic four is the tent or other emergency shelter. An inexpensive shelter is the plastic tube tent.**

The most effective combination of sentences 10 and 11 would include which of the following groups of words?

(1) shelter of which an inexpensive shelter is
(2) shelter such as the inexpensive plastic tube tent
(3) shelter whose inexpensive shelter is
(4) shelter: an inexpensive shelter is
(5) shelter; an inexpensive shelter is

Items 20 to 27 refer to the following paragraphs.

(1) We were born to be creative in a world rich in creative design rich in natural resources rich with innovative people who consider creativity fun and a responsibility, in a world of rich endowments from nature and man's creative urge. (2) Crafts are one of the rich heritages of our nation. (3) In pioneer days the itinerant craftsman traveled from home to home, selling his wares and earning his bed and board by weaving fabric or a coverlet or handcarving wooden items for the kitchen or barn.

(4) If people become involved in these early crafts, they may become interested in "trying their hand." (5) They have not only all the rich natural resources and related contemporary subject matter, but they also have manmade materials and efficient, fast equipment to aid them in their creativity (6) Their products are limited only by their imagination, skill, and knowledge of design.

(7) If they live in a wooded area and like to collect the unusual from nature's wonders, they may begin to reproduce the pine and nut "Kissing balls" and christmas wreaths. (8) If the male member of their family loves to hunt, they may create with feathers. (9) Feather wreaths were made at an early date.

20. Sentence 1: **We were born to be creative in a world rich in creative design rich in natural resources rich with innovative people who consider creativity fun and a responsibility, in a world of rich endowments from nature and man's creative urge.**

What correction should be made to this sentence?

(1) insert commas after design and resources
(2) change the spelling of innovative to inovative
(3) remove the comma after responsibility
(4) insert a comma after nature
(5) no correction is necessary

21. Sentences 2 and 3: **Crafts are one of the rich heritages of our nation. In pioneer days the itinerant craftsman traveled from home to home, selling his wares and earning his bed and board by weaving fabric or a coverlet or handcarving wooden items for the kitchen or barn.**

Which of the following is the best way to write the underlined portion of this sentence? If you think the original is the best way, choose option (1).

(1) nation. In
(2) nation: in
(3) nation: In
(4) nation, In
(5) nation, in

22. Sentence 3: **In pioneer days the itinerant craftsman traveled from home to home, selling his wares and earning his bed and board by weaving fabric or a coverlet or handcarving wooden items for the kitchen or barn.**

What correction should be made to this sentence?

(1) insert a comma after craftsman
(2) change the spelling of traveled to travelled
(3) change wares to wears
(4) insert a comma after fabric
(5) no correction is necessary

23. Sentence 4: **If people become involved in these early crafts, they may become interested in "trying their hand."**

What correction should be made to this sentence?

(1) change become to became
(2) change they to one
(3) change may to might
(4) change hand." to hand".
(5) no correction is necessary

24. Sentence 5: **They have not only all the rich natural resources and related contemporary subject matter, but they also have manmade materials and efficient, fast equipment to aid them in their creativity.**

What correction should be made to this sentence?

(1) place not only before have
(2) change the spelling of contemporary to contemperary
(3) change but to although
(4) change the spelling of equipment to equiptment
(5) no correction is necessary

25. Sentences 5 and 6: **They have not only all the rich natural resources and related contemporary subject matter, but they also have manmade materials and efficient, fast equipment to aid them in their creativity Their products are limited only by their imagination, skill, and knowledge of design.**

Which of the following is the best way to write the underlined portion of this sentence? If you think the original is the best way, choose option (1).

(1) creativity Their
(2) creativity, their
(3) creativity. their
(4) creativity. Their
(5) creativity: Their

26. Sentence 7: **If they live in a wooded area and like to collect the unusual from nature's wonders, they may begin to reproduce the pine and nut "Kissing balls" and christmas wreaths.**

What correction should be made to this sentence?

(1) change live to lived
(2) change like to would like
(3) remove the comma after wonders
(4) capitalize christmas
(5) no correction is necessary

27. Sentences 8 and 9: **If the male member of the family loves to hunt, they may create with feathers. Feather wreaths were made at an early date.**

The most effective combination of sentences 8 and 9 would include which of the following groups of words?

(1) feather and feather wreaths
(2) feathers because feather wreaths
(3) feathers although feather wreaths
(4) feathers which were made into wreaths
(5) feathers made at an early date

Items 28 to 36 refer to the following paragraphs.

(1) Housing is the hub of the family's private world, the nature of housing has a direct effect on the quality of family life. (2) It effects health, time, and energy required in rearing a family and caring for its members, self-related attitudes, morale, and satisfaction with one's station in life. (3) It also affects the way in which one family relates to another, to the neighborhood, and to the community.

(4) Families do not want, expect, or require dwellings that is identical. (5) Families with limited means are more interested in securing clean, safe, and reasonably comfortable housing than to find quarters that are especially psychologically stimulating. (6) At the same time many families having greater incomes can take basic shelter for granted and proceed to satisfy higher level needs in housing.

(7) Nevertheless, as a nation we are being more and more concerned with housing that does far more than support physical survival. (8) In other words, essentially all American families are upgrading their housing goals and expectations. (9) And the dominant housing image remains the single-family house.

(10) Only when families are more articulate in identifying their needs and when builders and public policy become more sensitive to human needs will the nation have a variety of good housing designed, built, and serviced in line with family purposes.

28. Sentence 1: **Housing is the hub of the family's private world, the nature of housing has a direct effect on the quality of family life.**

Which of the following is the best way to write the underlined portion of this sentence? If you think the original is the best way, choose option (1).

(1) world, the
(2) world. the
(3) world; the
(4) world: The
(5) world. The

29. Sentence 2: **It effects health, time, and energy required in rearing a family and caring for its members, self-related attitudes, morale, and satisfaction with one's station in life.**

What correction should be made to this sentence?

(1) change the spelling of effects to affects
(2) change the spelling of its to it's
(3) remove the comma after members
(4) change the spelling of morale to moral
(5) no correction is necessary

30. Sentence 3: **It also affects the way in which one family relates to another, to the neighborhood, and to the community.**

What correction should be made to this sentence?

(1) change also to nevertheless
(2) insert a comma after way
(3) remove the comma after another
(4) change the spelling of neighborhood to nieghborhood
(5) no correction is necessary

31. Sentence 4: **Families do not want, expect, or require dwellings that is identical.**

What correction should be made to this sentence?

(1) change the spelling of families to family's
(2) remove the comma after want
(3) change is to are
(4) change the spelling of identical to identicle
(5) no correction is necessary

32. Sentence 5: **Families with limited means are more interested in securing clean, safe, and reasonably comfortable housing than to find quarters that are especially psychologically stimulating.**

What correction should be made to this sentence?

(1) remove the comma after clean
(2) change to find to in finding
(3) change the spelling of especially to especialy
(4) change the spelling of psychologically to phsycologically
(5) no correction is necessary

33. Sentence 6: **At the same time many families having greater incomes can take basic shelter for granted and proceed to satisfy higher level needs in housing.**

What correction should be made to this sentence?

(1) insert a comma after incomes
(2) change can to must
(3) insert a comma after granted
(4) change the spelling of proceed to procede
(5) no correction is necessary

34. Sentence 7: **Nevertheless, as a nation we are being more and more concerned with housing that does far more than support physical survival.**

If you rewrote sentence 7 beginning with

Housing that does far more than support physical survival

the next words would be

(1) as a nation
(2) we are being
(3) we, as a nation,
(4) concerns us, as a nation,
(5) we are concerned

35. Sentences 8 and 9: **In other words, essentially all American families are upgrading their housing goals and expectations. And the dominant housing image remains the single-family house.**

The most effective combination of sentences 8 and 9 would include which of the following groups of words?

(1) expectations but the single-family house remains
(2) expectations since the single-family house remains
(3) expectations although the single-family house remains
(4) expectations with the single-family house remaining
(5) expectations despite the single-family house remaining

36. Sentence 10: **Only when families are more articulate in identifying their needs and when builders and public policy become more sensitive to human needs will the nation have a variety of good housing designed, built, and serviced in line with family purposes.**

If you rewrote sentence 10 beginning with

The nation

the next words should be

(1) are more articulate
(2) identifying their needs
(3) become more sensitive
(4) will have
(5) serviced in line

Items 37 to 45 refer to the following paragraphs.

(1) Auto insurance can be bought in the form of a bundle of coverage or each section in the bundle can be bought seperately.

(2) Liability the core of an auto policy pays for bodily injury and property damage to others when you are legally responsible for the accident. (3) Liability coverage, stated separately for bodily injury and property damage, pays for other people's injuries—not yours.

(4) Medical payments cover your and your passengers medical fees regardless of who was to blame for the accident.

(5) The uninsured motorist coverage offers protection to you, your spouse, and resident children if you are struck by an uninsured motorist or a hit and run driver while driving or walking.

(6) Collision pays for damage to your car when you hit another vehicle or an object like a tree, telephone pole etc. (7) Collision coverage is usually sold in the form of a deductible. (8) The larger the amount of the deductible, the less the premium.

(9) Losses caused by fire, wind, theft, vandalism, collision with animals, explosions, flood, and lightning are covered by the comprehensive coverage feature.

(10) Accidental death and dismemberment coverage pays a lump sum for death in a car accident, loss of a limb, blindness, fractures, and dislocations, plus a disability benifit each week.

37. Sentence 1: **Auto insurance can be bought in the form of a bundle of coverage or each section in the bundle can be bought seperately.**

What correction should be made to this sentence?

(1) change the spelling of insurance to insurence
(2) insert a comma after bought
(3) change or to and
(4) change the spelling of seperately to separately
(5) no correction is necessary

38. Sentence 2: **Liability the core of an auto policy pays for bodily injury and property damage to others when you are legally responsible for the accident.**

What correction should be made to this sentence?

(1) insert commas before the and after policy
(2) insert a comma after injury
(3) change the spelling of legally to legaly
(4) change the spelling of responsible to responsable
(5) no correction is necessary

39. Sentence 3: **Liability coverage, stated separately for bodily injury and property damage, pays for other people's injuries—not yours.**

What correction should be made to this sentence?

(1) remove the comma before stated and after damage
(2) change pays to pay
(3) change people's to peoples'
(4) change yours to your's
(5) no correction is necessary

40. Sentence 4: **Medical payments cover your and your passengers medical fees regardless of who was to blame for the accident.**

What correction should be made to this sentence?

(1) change cover to covers
(2) change your to you're
(3) add an apostrophe after passengers
(4) change who to whom
(5) no correction is necessary

41. Sentence 5: **The uninsured motorist coverage offers protection to you, your spouse, and resident children if you are struck by an uninsured motorist or a hit and run driver while driving or walking.**

What correction should be made to this sentence?

(1) insert a hyphen in uninsured
(2) remove the comma after you
(3) change struck to stricken
(4) insert hyphens into hit and run
(5) no correction is necessary

42. Sentence 6: **Collision pays for damage to your car when you hit another vehicle or an object like a tree, telephone pole etc.**

What correction should be made to this sentence?

(1) change the spelling of vehicle to vehical
(2) change like to as
(3) insert a comma after pole
(4) remove the period after etc.
(5) no correction is necessary

43. Sentences 7 and 8: **Collision coverage is usually sold in the form of a deductible. The larger the amount of the deductible, the less the premium.**

Which of the following is the best way to write the underlined portion of this sentence? If you think the original is the best way, choose option (1).

(1) deductible. The
(2) deductible. the
(3) deductible; The
(4) deductible; the
(5) deductible, The

44. Sentence 9: **Losses caused by fire, wind, theft, vandalism, collision with animals, explosions, flood, and lightning are covered by the comprehensive coverage feature.**

If you rewrote sentence 9 beginning with

The comprehensive coverage feature

the next words would be

(1) losses caused
(2) causes losses
(3) collision
(4) explosions
(5) covers

45. Sentence 10: **Accidental death and dismemberment coverage pays a lump sum for death in a car accident, loss of a limb, blindness, fractures, and dislocations, plus a disability benifit each week.**

What correction should be made to this sentence?

(1) change the spelling of accidental to acidental
(2) change pays to pay
(3) remove the comma after dislocations
(4) change the spelling of benifit to benefit
(5) no correction is necessary

Items 46 to 55 refer to the following paragraphs.

(1) How do you find help, when you require it, in your community, assuming that you or your family just cannot meet your own needs or solve your own problems.

(2) It's not easy, but it can be done. (3) Most Americans, in most communities, can find most of the kinds of help they may need within their local area.

(4) In just about every city in the Nation, there is a classified phone directory called the Yellow Pages and, if any public, voluntary, or private (for profit) services agencies exist, they will be listed under the heading: "Social Services Organizations."

(5) Using the Washington, D.C., directory as an example, the organizations under this heading number in the hundreds and range from Big Brothers through Family Service to Young Adult Rehabilitation Council. (6) In your phone book there may only be four agencies listed where you can call for help, or there may be 400. (7) The longer the list, unfortunately, the more difficult it is to decide from organization names which one can help you with your particular problem.

(8) Strangely enough, the best place to call or see is your county or local public welfare office (in some areas called social services or public assistence), whether you can or cannot afford to pay for the help you need. (9) Under the Social Security Act, all Federally funded local welfare agencies provide information and referral services without regard for welfare eligibility by reason of poverty, etc.

(10) Just a word about a very special problem: the problem of where a non-English-speaking person can be sent for help. (11) Because of the increasing awareness of such a problem, a number of self-help organizations have recently come into existence in communities where there are a number of ethnic minorities.

46. Sentence 1: **How do you find help, when you require it, in your community, assuming that you or your family just cannot meet your own needs or solve your own problems.**

What correction should be made to this sentence?

(1) remove the comma after help
(2) remove the comma after it
(3) remove the comma after community
(4) place a question mark after problems
(5) no correction is necessary

47. Sentences 2 and 3: **It's not easy, but it can be done. Most Americans, in most communities, can find most of the kinds of help they may need within their local area.**

The most effective combination of sentences 2 and 3 would include which of the following groups of words?

(1) done, most
(2) done, although most
(3) done, but most
(4) done, nevertheless, most
(5) done, since most

48. Sentence 4: **In just about every city in the Nation, there is a classified phone directory called the Yellow Pages and, if any public, voluntary, or private (for profit) services agencies exist, they will be listed under the heading: "Social Services Organizations."**

What correction should be made to this sentence?

(1) remove the capital in Nation
(2) change the spelling of directory to directry
(3) remove the capitals in Yellow Pages
(4) change the colon to a semicolon after heading
(5) no correction is necessary

49. Sentence 5: **Using the Washington, D.C., directory as an example, the organizations under this heading number in the hundreds and range from Big Brothers through Family Service to Young Adult Rehabilitation Council.**

What correction should be made to this sentence?

(1) remove the comma after Washington
(2) remove the comma after D.C.
(3) remove the comma after example
(4) remove the capital from Brothers
(5) no correction is necessary

50. Sentence 6: **In your phone book there may only be four agencies listed where you can call for help, or there may be 400.**

If you rewrote sentence 6 beginning with

Only four agencies

the next words would be

(1) in your phone book
(2) may be
(3) there may be
(4) or there may be
(5) to where you can call

51. Sentence 7: **The longer the list, unfortunately, the more difficult it is to decide from organization names which one can help you with your particular problem.**

What correction should be made to this sentence?

(1) remove the comma after list
(2) remove the comma after unfortunately
(3) change the spelling of difficult to dificult
(4) insert a comma after names
(5) no correction is necessary

52. Sentence 8: **Strangely enough, the best place to call or see is your county or local public welfare office (in some areas called social services or public assistence), whether you can or cannot afford to pay for the help you need.**

What correction should be made to this sentence?

(1) capitalize county
(2) capitalize local public welfare
(3) remove the parentheses before in and before whether
(4) change the spelling of assistence to assistance
(5) no correction is necessary

53. Sentence 9: **Under the Social Security Act, all Federally funded local welfare agencies provide information and referral services without regard for welfare eligibility by reason of poverty, etc.**

What correction should be made to this sentence?

(1) remove the capital from Act
(2) capitalize funded
(3) remove the capital from Federally funded
(4) add and before etc.
(5) no correction is necessary

54. Sentence 10: **Just a word about a very special problem: the problem of where a non-English-speaking person can be sent for help.**

What correction should be made to this sentence?

(1) add Here is before Just
(2) remove the colon after problem
(3) remove the hyphens in non-English-speaking
(4) remove the capital from English
(5) no correction is necessary

55. Sentence 11: **Because of the increasing awareness of such a problem, a number of self-help organizations have recently come into existence in communities where there are a number of ethnic minorities.**

What correction should be made to this sentence?

(1) change Because of to Despite
(2) remove the comma after problem
(3) remove the hyphen in self-help
(4) change the spelling of existence to existance
(5) no correction is necessary

TEST 1: LANGUAGE ARTS, WRITING (WRITING SKILLS), PART II

Directions

Allotted time: 45 minutes

Part II of the Language Arts, Writing (Writing Skills) Test will test your ability to write by having you write an essay in which you either take and defend a position on a debatable topic or explain how something affects our lives.

Remember to:
- follow the directions
- read the topic on which your essay will be based
- be careful to write your essay on the separate answer sheet, confining your notes to scratch paper
- reread your essay, revising it where necessary to improve what you have written
- correct any errors you find in paragraphing, sentence structure, capitalization, punctuation, spelling and usage.

You must
- write the letter of the topic in the box at the upper right corner of the answer sheet where you write your essay
- write your essay on the given topic legibly on the lined pages of the answer sheet in the 45 minutes allotted. Use a ballpoint pen. Your notes on scratch paper will not be considered.

You will have 45 minutes to write on the topic below.

Canada's youth has always been a major concern of the Canadian people.

Opinions on the youth of our nation differ widely. Some have a high regard for Canada's young. Others wonder "what the youth of Canada is coming to."

In an essay of about 200 words, present your views on Canada's youth today. Your evaluation may include positive or negative arguments or both. Support your views with appropriate reasons and examples.

END OF EXAMINATION

TEST 2: SOCIAL STUDIES

Directions

Allotted time: 85 minutes

This test consists of **64 multiple-choice questions** designed to measure your knowledge of the general ideas or concepts of social studies: history, geography, economics, political science, and behavioural sciences.

You will be given information in the form of readings, some of which will be accompanied by a map, chart, or graph. Study the given information and answer the questions based on it.

Since you are allowed 85 minutes, do not spend more than a suitable time on any one question.

Make no mark on the answer sheet other than your choice of the correct answer. If you change your answer, erase your first mark completely. Only *one* answer space should be marked for each question.

EXAMPLE:

Early colonists of North America looked for settlement sites that had adequate water supplies and were accessible by ship. For this reason, many early towns were built near

(1) mountains
(2) prairies
(3) rivers
(4) glaciers
(5) plateaus

① ② ● ④ ⑤

The correct answer is "rivers"; therefore, answer space 3 would be marked on the answer sheet.

Directions: Choose the one best answer to each item.

Items 1 to 3 refer to the following passage.

Not only the corporate world was in trouble. Years of overfishing off the Atlantic Coast by domestic and foreign fleets, compounded by changes in the water temperature, had their inevitable outcome. After years of reports, warnings, and denial from the industry and its workers, Canada finally agreed to ban most offshore fishing, beginning with Newfoundland's northern cod and gradually extending along almost the entire Atlantic Coast. Not only the economic staple of the region but also the way of life for hundreds of communities was finished for at least a decade, perhaps forever. Meanwhile, farming faced a comparable challenge as Prairie wheat growers in the early 1990s watched prices fall before the cost of production. The United States and the European Community could afford the subsidies of a grain price war; like other smaller-producing countries, Canada could not. Wheat farmers could hope for a settlement as part of a major agreement until the General Agreement on Tariffs and Trade (GATT). If that happened, dairy, egg, and poultry producers, chiefly in Quebec and Ontario, would lose their system of supply-management and only huge corporate production units could hope to survive.

1. What was the result of overfishing off the Atlantic Coast?
   (1) reports, warnings, and denials
   (2) the temperature of the water changed
   (3) Canada had trouble with foreign fleets
   (4) fishing was banned and communities declined
   (5) Newfoundland was finished.

2. Prairie wheat growers suffered because
   (1) the United States started a price war
   (2) the European Community wouldn't cooperate
   (3) grain prices rose sharply
   (4) of the General Agreement on Tariffs and Trade
   (5) Canada could not afford to subsidize her farmers

3. The above passage is chiefly about
   (1) Canada's difficulty in competing in world markets
   (2) the end of offshore fishing
   (3) the General Agreement on Tariffs and Trade
   (4) a grain price war
   (5) how only huge production units can survive

Items 4 to 6 are based on the following passage.

The Prime Minister is normally the leader of the party that has a majority of the seats in the House of Commons. The Prime Minister and his personally selected Cabinet form the government. All of them are members of Parliament and they are simultaneously members of both the legislature and the executive. In contrast is the American presidential form of government, wherein there is a clear separation of executive and legislative powers. The presidential/congressional system of checks and balances creates an atmosphere of public political bargaining not found in Canada. For example, in the United States the executive must rely on Congress to authorize funds to implement policy, and the Senate must ratify presidential appointments to the Cabinet, the diplomatic service, federal courts and other boards and commissions.

Also in contrast to the Canadian Constitution, the American chief executive is elected independently by the people at large, and his tenure in office is in no way dependent on the fate of his legislative program. The executive can frustrate Congress because, for instance, Congress is dependent on the President to implement its policies, and the executive often controls the information needed to formulate effective policies in Congress. On the other hand, the American legislature can and often does reject executive proposals, an exceedingly rare event in Canada, where such rejection could cause the government to fall and a new election to be held.

4. A Canadian Prime Minister takes office when
   (1) elected independently by the people at large
   (2) selected by the House of Commons
   (3) elected by the Commons and Senate together
   (4) appointed by the Premiers of the provinces
   (5) the Governor General appoints the leader of the party with the most seats in the House of Commons

5. Which of the following features of Canadian government would you not find in the United States?
   (1) a cabinet appointed by the chief executive
   (2) the chief executive speaking on behalf of the country concerning international affairs
   (3) the appointment of Supreme Court justices by the chief executive
   (4) the chief executive and cabinet sitting in the legislature
   (5) the formulation of legislative programs by the chief executive and the Cabinet

6. It can be inferred from the passage that

(1) the Canadian form of government is much superior to that of the United States
(2) not all democratic governments take precisely the same form
(3) the United States and Canada are in conflict over their forms of government
(4) Presidents are much more powerful than Prime Ministers
(5) legislatures are not very important in influencing government policy.

Items 7 and 8 are based on the following cartoon.

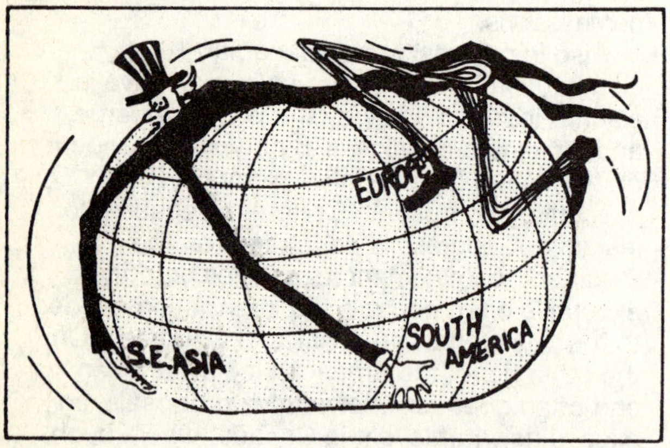

7. The United States involvement in Europe indicated in the cartoon most probably refers to the role of the United States in the

(1) Alliance for Progress
(2) Common Market
(3) Nuclear Test-Ban Agreement
(4) North Atlantic Treaty Organization
(5) Helsinki Agreement

8. On the basis of the cartoon, it can be concluded that the cartoonist

(1) questions the United States role of "world policeman"
(2) favors United States imperialism
(3) supports the foreign policy of the United States
(4) opposes a return to an isolationist policy
(5) is expressing concern for world survival

9. "To accept passively an unjust system is to cooperate with that system. . . . Noncooperation with evil is as much an obligation as is cooperation with good. But [violence] solves no social problem: it merely creates new and more complicated ones." The author of this statement is expressing a belief in

(1) religious toleration
(2) civil disobedience
(3) situational ethics
(4) anarchy
(5) socialism

Items 10 to 12 refer to the following graph.

SUICIDE IN CANADA, 1984–1988

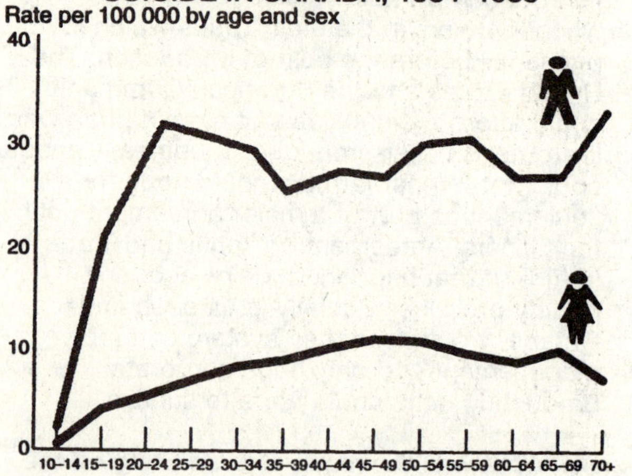

Source: Suicide Information & Education Centre

10. The suicide rate in this period for females aged 50–54 was

(1) approximately 30 per 100 000 population
(2) approximately 20 per 100 000 population
(3) approximately 10 per 100 000 population
(4) approximately 8 per 100 000 population
(5) approximately 5 per 100 000 population

11. Based on the data in the graph, which one of the following is not a valid statement?

(1) The suicide rate in Canada increases steadily with age.
(2) The suicide rate for women was lower than that for men.
(3) The suicide rate for men is lowest among children.
(4) The suicide rate for women does not fluctuate as much between age groups as it does for men.
(5) The suicide rate for males is highest for young men and old men.

12. Based on the data in the graph, which of the following statements is true?

    (1) Women's increasing participation in the workforce has affected suicide rates.
    (2) The suicide rate in Canada is not a major cause for concern.
    (3) The suicide rate for both men and women is affected by the same causes.
    (4) About the same number of 40-year-old and 60-year-old men are victims of suicide each year.
    (5) The suicide rate for women is less than half that for men.

Item 13 is based on the following cartoon.

GIVE ME
YOUR SCIENTISTS,
YOUR DOCTORS,
YOUR TEACHERS,
BUT KEEP YOUR
HUDDLED MASSES
TO YOURSELVES.
Adapted from World Press Review. November 1980

13. The above cartoon, which appeared in a newspaper published in India, is using the statement attributed to the Statue of Liberty to

    (1) convince the reader of the value of education in the United States
    (2) criticize the United States for not accepting poor immigrants
    (3) deplore the immigration policies in less developed countries
    (4) publicize the need for professionals in the United States
    (5) support the imposition of immigration quotas for professionals

---

Items 14 to 16 are based on the following passage.

It is said that growth by merger adds nothing to the economy in the way of new investment, whereas so-called "grass roots" growth does. This, too, is not necessarily so. In many cases, a company has the available capital and several other ingredients of success for a new venture, but can only get some missing ingredient—such as qualified technical manpower—by acquiring another company. In such a case the merging of two companies means a new investment which would not have taken place by the "grass roots" method.

Actually, corporate diversification in the past has served to enhance competition, and it will continue to do so. No company today can confidently look upon its established competitors as being its only future competitors. Tomorrow their ranks may be joined by others now in wholly unrelated industries. If new competitors do enter by acquisition or otherwise, it will be only because they think in the long run they can market a better product, or sell at a lower price, and make a profit by doing so.

14. A reason which is offered for the need to merge is to

    (1) meet new competition
    (2) increase diversification
    (3) increase available capital
    (4) provide for "grass roots" growth
    (5) extend consumer choice

15. The author maintains that growth by merger is sometimes necessary to

    (1) acquire capital
    (2) reduce competition
    (3) make a new investment
    (4) gain technically qualified personnel
    (5) add to the economy

16. Motivations for merger mentioned in this passage include all EXCEPT

    (1) marketing a better product
    (2) selling at a lower price
    (3) making a profit
    (4) getting a missing ingredient
    (5) meeting current competition

Item 17 to 19 are based on the following passage.

. . . Of the Anglo-Saxon we are not in the least afraid, but when we consider that last year (1912) over twenty-one percent of all the incomers to Canada were non-Anglo-Saxons . . . then we begin to understand what a task is ours as a nation.

. . . From southern Italy, 56 of every 100 are illiterate. The illiteracy of the Russian Jew runs about 23 percent, and he is perhaps the hardest of all to assimilate. He is industrious, hardworking and sober, but from the viewpoint of national digestion is like Jonah of old, still indigestible.

All authorities agree that intemperance is the great curse of the Slav wherever you find him.

. . . In many cases they bring with them a sort of atheistic socialism which casts a blight of death over any country where it takes root. Often they underbid the labor market, driving out the white man. They raise vexing municipal questions, they strain our charitable organizations, sometimes to the breaking point, they expose healthy people to disease, and often herd themselves together in certain localities of the cities, constituting a real problem of the slums . . .

Rev. W.D. Reid, Presbyterian Congress, 1913

17. The attitude of the author toward non-Anglo-Saxon immigrants is one of

(1) caution
(2) enthusiastic approval
(3) intolerance
(4) warmth
(5) support

18. The author would likely support

(1) an open-door immigration policy
(2) multiculturalism
(3) a highly restrictive immigration policy
(4) building a cultural mosaic
(5) legislation prohibiting discrimination on the basis of religious or ethnic background.

19. Which one of the following objectives of the 1978 Immigration Act would not be acceptable to the author of the passage?

(1) fostering the development of a strong and viable economy
(2) maintaining and protecting health, safety and good order in Canadian society
(3) denying admission to Canada to people who would be likely to engage in criminal activity
(4) facilitating entry for the purposes of fostering trade, commerce, and tourism
(5) ensuring that there is no consideration of race, national or ethnic origin, religion, or sex in assessing potential immigrants

20. Which has been an important result of improved means of communication and travel?

(1) Changes in one part of the world can greatly affect other parts of the world.
(2) Countries have become more nationalistic.
(3) Barriers to international trade have been abolished.
(4) There is less need for international organizations.
(5) Isolationism has been eradicated.

21. An extended family is a group of relatives by blood, marriage, or adoption living in close proximity or together, especially if three generations are involved. A nuclear family as the basic social unit consists of parents and their children living in one household.

A major difference between the two is that in the extended family

(1) age and sex roles are not clearly defined
(2) the family ties are weak
(3) intermarriage among close relatives is allowed
(4) there is a sharing of residence and income among several generations
(5) the mother is the dominant figure

Items 22 and 23 are based on the following graph.

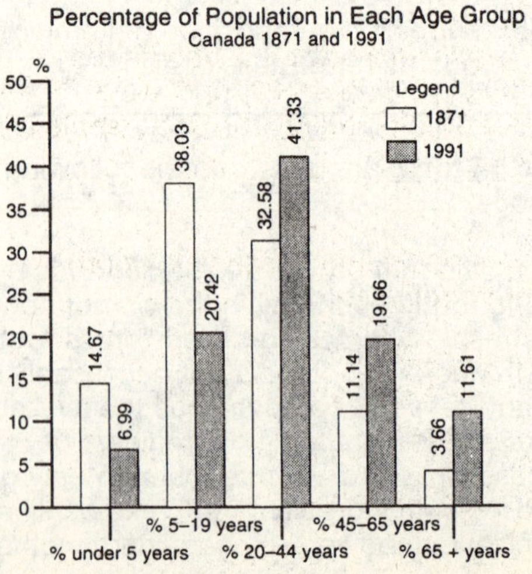

22. In proportional terms, the greatest population change between 1871 and 1991 occurred in which age group?

(1) under 5 years
(2) 5–19 years
(3) 20–44 years
(4) 45–65 years
(5) 65+ years

23. The information in the graph would be immediately useful to Canadian government officials concerned with

(1) finding alternative energy resources
(2) financing the Social Security system
(3) planning defense projects
(4) developing public works programs
(5) subsidizing farmers

Items 24 to 26 are based on the following statement.

Anthropology may be subdivided into several areas of study. In the study of *physical anthropology* the emphasis is on the study of physical characteristics and social behaviour of humans past and present. Anthropologists in this area may study fossil remains or observe how people live in their natural habitats.

In *archaeology* the stress is placed upon the study of material remains of cultures. Central to archaeology are the interrelationships between technological development and economic, social and ideational factors.

In *anthropological linguistics* the basic concern is for how groups of people use language. Linguists study both the forms of language and what is meaningful to the people as evidenced in formal and informal speech.

Cultural anthropology concerns the description of different groups' ways of life. Daily patterns of interaction of a people are studied.

24. The focus in the passage is upon anthropology's

(1) growth
(2) importance
(3) scope
(4) role
(5) principles

25. The difference among the four areas of anthropology described is one of

(1) subjectivity
(2) importance
(3) emphasis
(4) recency
(5) objectivity

26. A person who excavates sites looking for tools and other artifacts from previous cultures would be

(1) a physical anthropologist
(2) a scientist
(3) an anthropological linguist
(4) a cultural anthropologist
(5) an archaeologist

Items 27 and 28 are based on the following passage.

A map is a presentation on flat surface of all, or a part of, the earth's surface, drawn to scale. A map, in order to accomplish fully the objectives for which it was intended, should generally possess certain essentials. These are a title, a legend, direction, scale, latitude and longitude, and a date . . .

A legend should define the symbols used on a map to explain the colors or patterns employed . . . Since a legend unlocks map details, key is probably an appropriate synonym.

Scale may be defined as the ratio between map distance and earth distance. Scale may be shown as a fraction, for example, 1/62,500, that is, one unit on the map represents 62,500 units on the earth's surface . . .

A compass rose showing direction is a desirable feature on every map. This directional feature can be eliminated on certain maps where both parallels indicating latitude and meridians indicating longitude are straight lines at right angles to each other.

27. "Drawn to scale" as used in this passage means

(1) the direction of the parallels and meridians
(2) the relationship between map distance and earth distance
(3) linear scales
(4) verbal scales
(5) latitude and longitude

28. A compass rose is associated with

(1) a map title
(2) a legend
(3) scale
(4) direction
(5) latitude and longitude

Item 29 is based on the following passage.

McDonald's of Canada, the fast food giant, announced recently that it would phase out its plastic foam food containers in favor of paper wrappers. The big company was bowing to environmental pressure, and spearheading the attack were Ms. Dziadyk's grade 6 students in Kew Beach public school in Toronto. Going into direct action, pupils visiting McDonald's would ask to have their "McFood" served on napkins rather than in the foam. Class members became a symbol, winning wide coverage for their new children's crusade. Eventually, they got to see senior executives of McDonald's.

29. From the passage it can be concluded that

(1) consumer action groups can influence the policies of large corporations
(2) large corporations are sympathetic toward the views of children
(3) teachers act in their own self interest
(4) paper wrappers are more environmentally sound than plastic containers
(5) large corporations disregard the views of their clients

---

30. In 1980, in the case of *Belzberg v. British Columbia Television Broadcasting* a television reporter did not want to reveal the name of a person who had provided information for a news report. However, the British Columbia Supreme Court ruled that the overriding public interest required that the name of the informant be revealed so that the person could testify in Court.

This Court's decision reflects the view that freedom of the press is

(1) guaranteed by the Charter of Rights and Freedoms
(2) subject to limitations
(3) clearly dangerous and evil
(4) the most important consideration in court cases
(5) impossible to protect

31. ". . . the welfare of Canada requires the adoption of a National Policy, which, by a judicious readjustment of the Tariff, will benefit and foster the agricultural, the mining, the manufacturing and other interests of the Dominion; that such a policy will retain in Canada thousands of our fellow countrymen now obliged to expatriate themselves in search of the employment denied them at home."

Sir John A. Macdonald, 1878.

Which of the following would Macdonald not have claimed as a likely benefit of the National Policy?

(1) an increase in the Gross National Product
(2) a decrease in the trade deficit
(3) increased employment
(4) an increased balance of payments deficit
(5) reduced emigration

Item 32 is based on the following cartoon.

32. According to the cartoonist, which is a likely result of permitting an Energy Mobilization Board to determine government policy?

(1) a massive rebuilding program to aid urban areas
(2) nullification of the benefits of current environmental laws
(3) an increase in lumbering to lessen our dependence on foreign oil
(4) landclearing and home building projects to relieve unemployment among construction workers
(5) government-sponsored work projects to combat inflation

Items 33 and 34 are based on the following graph, which shows the relationship of supply and demand for consumer goods and services in five model economies.

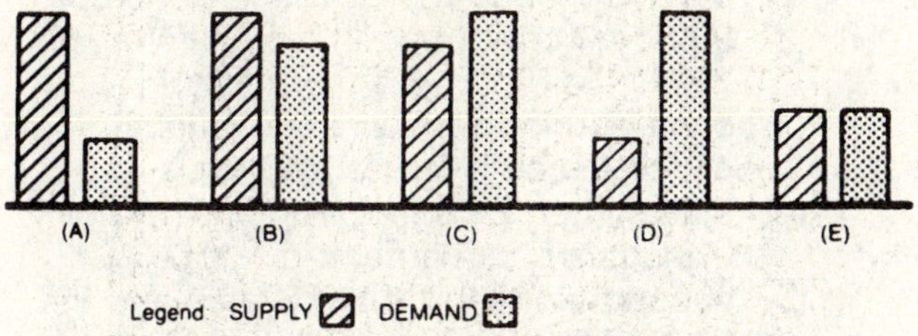

33. If model *B* were representative of the economy of Canada, which government action would most likely lead to a balance between supply and demand?

    (1) freeze on wages
    (2) limits on consumer credit
    (3) decrease in income tax rates
    (4) increase in sales taxes
    (5) increase in interest rates

34. Which model economy is most similar to the economic situation in Canada during the years 1929–1939?

    (1) *A*
    (2) *B*
    (3) *C*
    (4) *D*
    (5) *E*

Items 35 and 36 refer to the following passage.

Latin America has a rich and varied cultural heritage. It was brought into world history by Columbus, was colonized and made a part of Western culture by European powers, and was successful (with a few exceptions) in securing independence during the revolutionary era of George Washington and Simon Bolivar. Latin America differs, however, from North America in carrying over from pre-Columbian times an Indian population whose cultural influence has intermingled with that of the European. Latin America was colonized primarily by Spanish and Portuguese. They brought to the area a Catholic religious tradition, an agricultural way of life with a land-owning wealthy class, and an influential military class. Independence resulted in twenty separate countries, the Spanish-speaking portion alone being divided into eighteen states, the Portuguese portion being represented by Brazil, and Haiti, which emerged from a long period of French rule.

35. The countries that colonized Latin America brought all of the following EXCEPT

    (1) a religious tradition
    (2) an agricultural way of life
    (3) a military class
    (4) a largely Spanish-speaking population
    (5) an Indian population

36. All of the following peoples are represented in the population of Latin America EXCEPT

    (1) Spanish
    (2) Portuguese
    (3) North America
    (4) French
    (5) Indian

Items 37 to 39 refer to the following passage.

The main conclusion arrived at in this work, namely that man is descended from some lowly-organized form, will, I regret to think, be highly distasteful to many persons. The astonishment which I felt on first seeing a party of Fuegians, South American Indians, on a wild and broken shore will never be forgotten by me, for the thought at once rushed into my mind—such were our ancestors. He who has seen a savage in his native land will not feel much shame if forced to acknowledge that the blood of some more humble creatures flows in his veins.

Man may be excused for feeling some pride at having risen, though not through his own exertions, to the very summit of the organic scale; and the fact of his having thus risen, instead of having been originally placed there, may give him hopes for a still higher destiny in the distant future. But we are not here concerned with hopes or fears, only with the truth as far as our reason allows us to discover it. I have given the evidence to the best of my ability; and we must acknowledge, as it seems to me, that man, with all his noble qualities, still bears in his bodily frame the indelible stamp of his lowly origin.

37. The author is aware that his conclusions about man are

    (1) unscientific
    (2) pessimistic
    (3) unpleasant
    (4) astonishing
    (5) regretful

38. The author states that his conclusions are based on

(1) religious faith
(2) personal intuition
(3) hope
(4) fear
(5) reason

39. With regard to the future, the author of the selection feels that man should be

(1) optimistic
(2) noncommittal
(3) anxious
(4) depressed
(5) concerned

---

40. Which situation in Canada is an illustration of lobbying, that is, attempting to influence legislators to support bills which favour a special group?

(1) A defeated candidate for Parliament is appointed by the Prime Minister to head up a crown corporation.
(2) A corporation hires a person to present its views to certain members of Parliament.
(3) Federal projects are awarded to a province in return for certain political actions by the province's government.
(4) The opposition agrees to support the government's legislation.
(5) A member of the government party votes against a government bill.

41. Since World War II, Canada's security policy has rested on three complementary foundations:
(a) prevention of war and deterence of aggression through collective defense arrangements.
(b) pursuit of disarmament controls and verifiable arms control.
(c) commitment to the peaceful settlement of disputes and collective efforts to resolve the underlying causes of international tensions.

Which action best illustrates section (c)?

(1) allowing the United States to test unarmed Cruise missiles over Canadian territory
(2) participation in the Coalition of Forces that confronted Iraq in the Gulf War of 1991
(3) contributing to the United Nations peace-keeping forces in Cyprus
(4) stationing troops in Europe as part of Canada's commitment to NATO
(5) encouraging the United States and the Soviet Union in their Strategic Arms Limitation Talks

42. In North America, changes in occupational titles from busboy to dining room attendant and stewardess to flight attendant illustrate an attempt to deal with the problem of

(1) racism
(2) ethnocentrism
(3) sexism
(4) age bias
(5) unionism

Item 43 is based on the following chart.

YEAR	CORN PRODUCTION (THOUSANDS OF BUSHELS)	PRICE OF CORN (CENTS PER BUSHEL)
1875	1,450	41.9
1880	1,706	39.0
1885	2,058	32.2

43. The data in the chart could best be used to illustrate which economic concept?

(1) inflation
(2) interdependence
(3) free enterprise
(4) deflation
(5) supply and demand

Items 44 to 46 are based on the following passage.

In the future, our planet may be organized by tribes. These tribes or clans may replace the current concept of country. Ethnic rivalries are re-emerging all over the world as artificial national borders come to mean less and less. The former Soviet Union split up more into tribes than neat geographical divisions.

Modern communication enables people to communicate around the globe. They can now reach out to people who have the same belief structures without being concerned about where they live. People can share beliefs and aspirations across geographical borders. People sharing common values, beliefs and aspirations may join an existing tribe with similar values or try to form a new one. A tribe can provide support and reinforcement of beliefs. A tribe can also provide intellectual if not physical defense from outside beliefs and values.

44. People can share views easier today thanks to

(1) modern communication
(2) denser cities
(3) modern subways
(4) higher literacy
(5) better schools

45. Earth may become organized in the future into

(1) the United Nations
(2) NATO
(3) multi-national corporations
(4) tribes
(5) countries

46. People sharing common values may be considered a

(1) city
(2) clan
(3) country
(4) corporation
(5) community

Item 47 is based on the following table.

Tax Table

Income	*Tax Percentage Rate*
$0–3,000	0
3,001–8,000	10
8,001–14,000	20
14,001–20,000	25

47. The income tax shown in the table above is best described as

(1) graduated
(2) negative
(3) proportional
(4) regressive
(5) universal

48. "We must bring the benefits of Western civilization and Christianity to the less fortunate."

This idea has been used to justify

(1) imperialism
(2) nationalism
(3) socialism
(4) feudalism
(5) regionalism

49. "Nations strive to prevent any one country from becoming all-powerful and domineering."

Which concept is referred to by this statement?

(1) militarism
(2) imperialism
(3) national sovereignty
(4) balance of power
(5) appeasement

Items 50 and 51 are based on the following chart.

CITIES RANKED BY POPULATION

1976 rank	City	Population	Percent change (1961–1978)
1	Toronto	2,803,000	+53.6
2	Montreal	2,802,000	+32.9
3	Vancouver	1,166,400	+47.6
4	Ottawa	693,400	+61.3
5	Winnipeg	578,300	+21.6
6	Edmonton	554,200	+45.7
7	Quebec	542,200	+51.6
8	Hamilton	529,300	+33.9
9	Calgary	469,900	+68.4
10	Kitchener	272,100	+75.7
11	London	270,300	+49.1
12	Halifax	268,000	+45.7

50. According to the chart, the fastest-growing city, among those listed, during the period 1961–1978 was

(1) Kitchener
(2) Toronto
(3) Ottawa
(4) Calgary
(5) Vancouver

51. According to the chart, the cities in which province experienced the greatest average growth?

(1) Nova Scotia
(2) Quebec
(3) Ontario
(4) Alberta
(5) British Columbia

Items 52 to 54 are based on the following statements.

During the two world wars, the issue of conscription precipitated national crises in Canada. Here are four statements from political leaders of the time.

Speaker A: The will of the majority must be respected and it must prevail. But I trust that, here in Canada, the majority will always assert that will only after giving due consideration to the feelings and views of the minority.

Speaker B: The wealthy classes and the big business interests of the East are perfectly willing to see the poor man put all his capital, that is to say, his blood and sinews, on the altar to aid in winning the war. But they block every procedure that would entail equivalent sacrifices of conscription of wealth and material resources.

Speaker C: How many soldiers would France, or even England, send to America if Canada were attacked by the United States? It is useless to disguise the truth: two million French-Canadians are united against conscription.

Speaker D: It is no answer to say that we must have conscription or "quit." Australia rejected conscription and Australia did not "quit." Australia is still in the fight under the voluntary system.

52. With which statement would speaker B likely agree?

(1) The war was simply another opportunity for the manufacturing classes to grow richer.
(2) The disagreements over conscription were simply the continuation of the long-standing hostility between the French and the English people in Canada.
(3) All Canadians should serve if called upon.
(4) Compulsory military service should not be necessary in a democratic country.
(5) Canada should quit the war.

53. A leading opponent of conscription, Henri Bourassa, published five reasons to oppose it. Which one of them is implied by speaker C?

(1) Canada had already made a greater contribution in men and money than any other nation engaged in the war.
(2) Sending more men overseas would weaken agricultural and other essential industries in Canada.
(3) Conscription would weaken Canada's war effort by causing domestic disunion and strife.
(4) Increasing the war budget to support conscription would bankrupt the country.
(5) Conscription would threaten the economic life of the country and, eventually, its political independence.

54. If the four speakers were on a television news program, the moderator would probably introduce the topic of their discussion as:

(1) support for our Allies
(2) the need for democratic decision-making
(3) how to win the war
(4) compulsory or voluntary military service?
(5) Australia's example

Item 55 is based on the following cartoon.

"Miss Jones, weren't there any founding MOTHERS?"

55. Which statement best expresses the main idea of the cartoon?

(1) Women have increasingly difficult choices in a modern society
(2) More emphasis should be placed on the role of women in Canadian history
(3) Women made few significant contributions to society until the 20th century
(4) Free public education in Canada was established primarily by women
(5) Women are the dominant force in Canadian education today

Items 56 and 57 are based on the following table.

REPRESENTATION IN THE HOUSE OF COMMONS

Year	*Liberal*	*Conservative*	*New Democrat*	*Social Credit*	*Bloc Quebecois*	*Reform?*
1949	193	41	13	10	n/a	n/a
1953	171	51	23	15	n/a	n/a
1957	105	112	25	19	n/a	n/a
1958	49	208	8	0	n/a	n/a
1962	100	116	19	30	n/a	n/a
1963	129	95	17	24	n/a	n/a
1965	131	97	21	14	n/a	n/a
1968	155	72	22	14	n/a	n/a
1972	109	107	31	15	n/a	n/a
1974	141	95	16	11	n/a	n/a
1979	114	136	26	6	n/a	n/a
1980	147	103	32	0	n/a	n/a
1984	40	211	30	0	n/a	n/a
1988	82	169	20	0	n/a	n/a
1993	177	2	9	0	54	52

56. Which statement is best supported by information in the table?

(1) Since 1949 the Liberals have usually been the party with the majority of seats in the House of Commons.
(2) The major parties have been losing influence over the period shown on the chart.
(3) Support for the New Democratic Party has grown steadily since the fifties.
(4) Social Credit supporters moved to the Conservatives during the 1980s.
(5) The Liberal party has been steadily losing its influence in Parliament.

57. Which of the following results is most likely based on the trend in evidence in the table?

(1) Canada will end up with only one political party.
(2) The New Democratic Party will develop to the point where it will be a serious threat to the two main parties.
(3) Interest in politics will increase.
(4) Control of the government is likely to fluctuate between the two major parties.
(5) There will be a proliferation of political parties.

58. During the War in the Gulf in 1991, Western newspapers used all of the following terms to describe the situation for their readers:

They have	**We have**
censorship	reporting guidelines
propaganda	press briefings
They launch	**We launch**
sneak missile attacks	preemptive strikes

Their men are	**Our men are**
hordes	lads
Their soldiers are	**Our soldiers are**
brainwashed	lionhearted
cowardly	cautious
blindly obedient	loyal
fanatical	brave
Their missiles cause	**Our missiles cause**
civilian casualties	collateral damage
They	**We**
fire wildly at anything	precision bomb
Their leader is	**Our leader is**
demented	statesmanlike

The news coverage of the war illustrates that

(1) you should never believe anything you read in a newspaper
(2) a free press ensures comprehensive and objective coverage of the issues
(3) we were fighting in a good cause
(4) Iraq did not have a very good military
(5) the press often serves a propaganda purpose

Items 59 and 60 are based on the following graph.

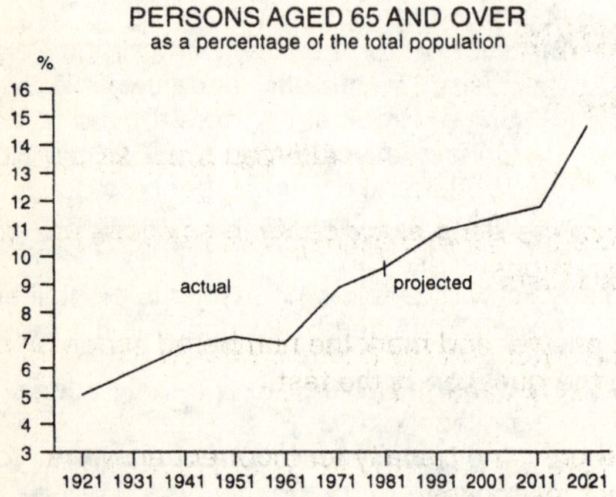

Source: Statistics Canada

59. Which statement is supported by the data in the graph?

(1) The birth rate increased steadily between 1950 and 1980.
(2) While the percentage of elderly is increasing, the total population is actually decreasing.
(3) Policies concerning the elderly will have to be reviewed and revised.
(4) Voters under age 30 will have proportionately more political power during the next 40 years.
(5) The rate of increase in the percentage of persons aged 65 and over is slowing.

60. If the projection in the graph is correct, a probable consequence will be a decrease in the percentage of

(1) marriages ending in divorce
(2) individuals living alone
(3) Americans below the poverty level
(4) full-time workers
(5) welfare cases

Items 61 and 62 are based on the following passage.

There are four ways of thinking about the production of goods and services in Canada. Activities that depend upon the direct use of natural products such as mining, forestry, and farming are *primary production*. *Secondary production* consists of manufacturing and construction along with any activity that has a tangible end product. *Tertiary production* involves the performance of services rather than the production of goods and consists of transportation, utilities, the selling and servicing of goods, as well as the professions, public administration, and the whole range of personal services. Activities which are related exclusively to research and development are often viewed as *quaternary production*.

61. To which of the categories of production would health care belong?

(1) primary
(2) secondary
(3) tertiary
(4) quaternary
(5) both secondary and tertiary

62. The province of New Brunswick relies greatly upon agriculture, fishing, mining, and forestry. Which kind of production do these activities reflect?

(1) primary production
(2) secondary production
(3) tertiary production
(4) quaternary production
(5) both secondary and tertiary production

---

63. Down to 1800 the majority of artisans laboured in their own houses and in the bosoms of their families . . . The artisan generally earned wages which were sufficient not only to live comfortably on, but which enabled him to rent a few acres of land.

This passage refers to life in England before

(1) feudalism
(2) mercantilism
(3) protectionism
(4) the industrial revolution
(5) cottage industry

Item 64 is based on the following cartoon.

64. Which statement best expresses the main idea of the cartoon?

(1) There are subtle ways to practice discrimination.
(2) Affirmative action programs have practically eliminated sex discrimination in business.
(3) It is legal and right to give men and women different job titles for the same work.
(4) The job title rather than the job should determine the salary.
(5) Discriminatory attitudes are more commonly found among lower paid employees than among executives.

END OF EXAMINATION

TEST 3: SCIENCE

Directions

Allotted time: 95 minutes

The **66 multiple-choice questions** in this test measure the general concepts in science. You may find a graph, a chart, or a table included with some questions.

Study the information given. Decide which is the best answer and mark the numbered space on the answer sheet beside the number that corresponds to the question in the test.

Answer all questions. Do not leave any blanks since there is no penalty for incorrect answers. Your score will be determined by the number of your correct responses.

EXAMPLE:

Which of the following is the smallest unit?

(1) element
(2) compound
(3) atom
(4) mixture
(5) molecule

① ② ● ④ ⑤

The correct answer is "atom"; therefore, answer space 3 would be marked on the answer sheet.

Directions: Choose the one best answer to each item.

Items 1 to 3 refer to the following article.

In the mammal, the fertilized egg becomes implanted in the wall of the uterus. As it develops, it becomes surrounded by several protective membranes. It obtains its food and oxygen from the mother's bloodstream through the placenta. This structure is well supplied with many blood vessels that carry blood from the mother's circulation in close proximity to the embryo's bloodstream. Wastes diffuse into the parent's blood from the embryo's bloodstream.

1. The process by which materials are exchanged between mother and embryo is known as

   (1) circulation
   (2) adsorption
   (3) secretion
   (4) diffusion
   (5) excretion

2. The human embryo develops is the

   (1) egg
   (2) zygote
   (3) placenta
   (4) uterus
   (5) protective membrane

3. Which of the following would pass from the embryo to the mother's bloodstream?

   (1) wastes
   (2) digested food
   (3) oxygen
   (4) blood
   (5) all of these

Items 4 to 7 refer to the following article.

Sodium chloride, by far the largest constituent of the mineral matter of the blood, assumes special significance in the regulation of water exchanges in the organism. And, as Cannon has emphasized repeatedly, these latter are more extensive and more important than may at first have been thought. He points out "there are a number of circulations of the fluid out of the body and back again, without loss." Thus, for example, it is estimated that from a quart to a quart and one-half of water daily "leaves the body" when it enters the mouth as saliva: another one or two quarts are passed out as gastric juice; and perhaps the same amount is contained in the bile and the secretions of the pancreas and the intestinal wall. This large volume of water enters the digestive processes, and practically all of it is reabsorbed through the intestinal wall, where it performs the equally important function of carrying in the digested foodstuffs. These and other instances of what Cannon calls "the conservative use of water in our bodies" involve essentially osmotic pressure relationships in which the concentration of sodium chloride plays an important part.

4. This passage implies that

   (1) substances can pass through the intestinal wall in only one direction
   (2) water cannot be absorbed by the body unless it contains sodium choloride
   (3) every particle of water ingested is used over and over again
   (4) sodium chloride does not actually enter the body
   (5) regulation of water exchanges in the organism is controlled by the concentration of sodium chloride

5. One of the processes occurring in the small intestine makes it unnecessary for us to

   (1) drink large quantities of water
   (2) digest our food completely
   (3) consume large amounts of salt
   (4) secrete a variety of digestive juices
   (5) reuse the body water

6. Sodium chloride is an important constituent of

   (1) gastric juice
   (2) bile
   (3) pancreatic juice
   (4) intestinal juice
   (5) blood

7. The importance of water in the intestine is its ability to

   (1) form saliva
   (2) dilute the gastric juice
   (3) form bile
   (4) act as a vehicle for digested food
   (5) dissolve sodium chloride

Items 8 to 11 refer to the following article.

The process of mitosis has been studied very carefully. Scientists hope some light will be shed on the abnormal cell division that occurs in malignancies by observing the normal process of cell division. Also, research in mitosis is important to the science of genetics. The chromosomes—long, thin strands—are carriers of nucleoprotein, which is made up of DNA molecules. Chromosomes are visible only when the cell is undergoing division. Biologists have observed that the number of chromosomes counted during mitosis is characteristic of the species. For example, in the fruit fly, this number is eight except in the sex cells or gametes. Only four chromosomes are found in the egg cell or sperm cell of the fruit fly. However, during the union of these cells in fertilization, the normal, characteristic number is restored.

Scientists may be guilty of errors. However, they are constantly checking and make revisions where necessary. It was long believed that the normal number of human chromosomes is 48. Recent research on tissue culture has made it necessary to revise the figure to 46.

Tissue culture is the technique by which cells can be grown artificially outside the body. By special procedures, human dividing cells were permitted to reach the metaphase but prevented from developing further. The material with many metaphase cells was squashed, the cells were spread out and the chromosomes photographed through a microscope. The photographs showed 23 pairs of chromosomes in each cell. Today we refer to the normal number of human chromosomes as 46.

8. The correct number of chromosomes normally found in the human egg cell is

(1) 8
(2) 23
(3) 24
(4) 46
(5) 48

9. The number of chromosomes in the body cells is how many times that of the reproductive cells?

(1) ½
(2) ⅛
(3) ¼
(4) twice
(5) the same

10. The process by which cells normally divide is called

(1) mitosis
(2) fertilization
(3) gamete formation
(4) tissue culture
(5) chromosomes

11. Abnormal cell division is most important for research in

(1) plants
(2) chromosome composition
(3) cancer
(4) guinea pigs
(5) fruit flies

Items 12 to 14 refer to the following article.

What was the earth's climate like half a million years ago? Fossil studies of radiolaria, a group of one-celled animals characterized by silicon-containing shells, have given scientists a fairly accurate account of climatic conditions in the distant past. Geologists found these microorganisms preserved in cores of sediment taken beneath the floor of the Indian Ocean. The cores penetrated deep enough to provide a record going back about 450,000 years. The cycles of climatic changes were determined by the alternating layers of species of warm- and cold-preferring radiolaria. These climatic changes were compared with cycles of changes in the shape, tilt, and seasonal positions of the earth's orbit, which other scientists studied by investigating past changes in global ice volume. We now have confirmation of the theory that states that changes in the earth's orbital geometry caused the ice ages.

12. Fossil studies of radiolaria are possible because they

(1) live in the depths of the ocean
(2) are one-celled
(3) have survived through the ages
(4) have a shell surrounding the cell
(5) react to cold and warmth

13. The scientists mentioned in this passage were most probably climatologists, oceanographers and

(1) anthropologists
(2) protozoologists
(3) geologists
(4) archaeologists
(5) zoologists

14. The fundamental cause of the ice ages is

(1) periodic changes in the earth's orbit around the sun
(2) fossil remains of one-celled animals
(3) accumulation of global ice
(4) alternating cold and warm seasons
(5) changes in distance of the earth from the sun

Items 15 to 17 refer to the following article.

This diagram represents a sealed plastic container with two Celsius thermometers, one of which is in a glass cup containing ice and water. A heating coil is available to vary the temperature of the sealed container. The purpose of this demonstration is to study the behaviour of water vapour and temperature at which air becomes saturated by water (dew point).

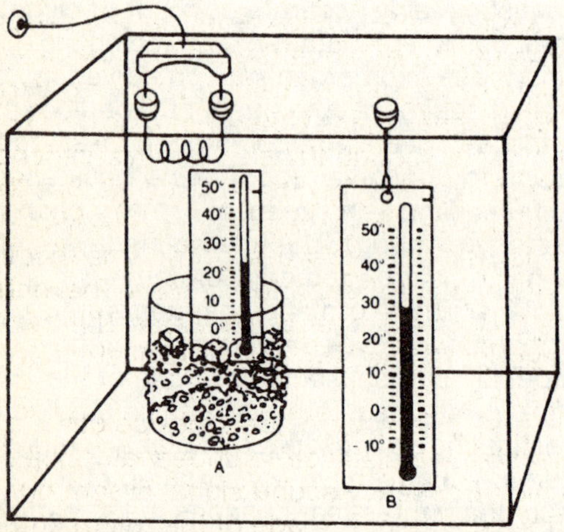

15. What is the temperature of the air in the box?

(1) 23.0°C
(2) 25.0°C
(3) 26.0°C
(4) 28.0°C
(5) 29.0°C

16. Why have droplets of water formed on the outside of the glass cup?

(1) Glass cups always accumulate water droplets on the outside when they are filled with water.
(2) The air near the glass cup has become saturated.
(3) Water has seeped through the pore spaces in the glass cup.
(4) The relative humidity of the air near the glass cup is approaching 0 percent.
(5) The dew point temperature was not reached.

17. If the water droplets have just appeared on the glass cup, what is the dew point temperature?

(1) 6.5°C
(2) 23.0°C
(3) 28.0°C
(4) 29.0°C
(5) 50°C

Items 18 to 20 refer to the following article.

Although we often observe the condensation of water vapour on cold surfaces, we seldom think of solid substances going directly to the vapour state. This is possible when some solid substances are heated under atmospheric pressure. They do not melt but change directly from the solid to the vapour state. In these solids, the intermolecular forces are weak and they exhibit measurable vapour pressures at room temperature. Because of these low intermolecular forces, many of them, such as naphthalene (mothballs), evaporate rather easily. Sublimation may also be described as the complete process of a solid passing directly into the vapour state without melting and recondensation of the vapour into the solid state.

18. Condensation is a change from the

(1) gaseous phase to the solid phase
(2) gaseous phase to the liquid phase
(3) liquid phase to the gaseous phase
(4) liquid phase to the solid phase
(5) solid phase to the liquid phase

19. Some substances evaporate more easily than others because they

(1) condense on cold surfaces
(2) can be heated at atmospheric pressure
(3) do not change from solid to liquid
(4) pass from solid state to vapour state
(5) have weak intermolecular forces

20. Sublimation is a change directly from the

(1) solid phase to the gaseous phase
(2) solid phase to the liquid phase
(3) liquid phase to the gaseous phase
(4) gaseous phase to the liquid phase
(5) liquid phase to the solid phase

Items 21 to 23 refer to the following article.

Without Archimedes' Principle, the invention of the submarine would have been impossible. According to this principle, when an object is submerged, it is buoyed up by a force equal to the weight of the volume of liquid it displaces. Therefore, when a body sinks, its weight is greater than the buoyant force or weight of the liquid that it displaces.

For a submarine to rise to the surface, water is pumped from the inside of the ballast tanks until the weight of the submarine is less than the upward buoyant force exerted by the water outside. To sink, the submarine takes on water until its weight is greater than the buoyant forces.

21. This selection illustrates the principle of

(1) Newton
(2) Archimedes
(3) Einstein
(4) Galileo
(5) Boyle

22. An object has a volume of $2\,m^3$ and it has a mass of 100 kg. It will float on water because when it is submerged it displaces

(1) $2\,m^3$ of water
(2) 100 kg of water
(3) less than 100 kg of water
(4) more than $2\,m^3$ of water
(5) more than 100 kg of water

23. Water wings and lifesaving jackets are useful in times of danger in water because they

(1) act as fins for nonswimmers
(2) protect from excess wetting and soaking
(3) increase one's volume
(4) increase one's mass
(5) decrease one's volume

Items 24 and 26 refer to the following article.

Water is a good conductor of sound waves. If you were swimming under water while someone struck two rocks together under water 3 m away, you would be surprised at how loud the sound was. The U.S. Navy makes use of this knowledge in detecting enemy submarines. During World War II, it was found that the sound of propellers or of a hammer being dropped inside a submarine could be heard hundreds of yards away with the use of sensitive listening devices.

Sound waves under water can be used to measure the depth of the water beneath a ship. This is done by sending a sound wave downward from the bottom of a ship. It is known that sound travels 1440 m a second through water. When the sound reaches the sea floor, it is reflected back up. Careful measurements are made of the time required for the echo to return to the ship. The longer the time, the deeper is the water. The depth of water under the ship is read directly on a gauge.

In a similar way, a sonar device can measure the distance to underwater objects. A high-frequency sound signal is sent out, and a measurement is made of the return time for the echo. Since many fish make sounds in water, the presence of a school of fish can be detected, by sonar, by a fishing fleet.

24. Of the following, which can best be concluded from this selection?

(1) Fish cannot hear ordinary sounds.
(2) Submarines cannot detect sound waves.
(3) The propeller of a submarine distorts sound waves.
(4) Sound waves become compressed in very deep water.
(5) Water is a good conductor of sound waves.

25. Underwater objects can be detected by sonar, which uses

(1) high-frequency sounds
(2) low-frequency sounds
(3) radar
(4) high-intensity light waves
(5) ultra-high-frequency television

26. A sound wave is sent downward from the bottom of a ship; an echo is received six seconds later. The depth of the water is most likely

(1) 2400 m
(2) 2900 m
(3) 3400 m
(4) 4320 m
(5) 4500 m

Items 27 to 29 refer to the following article.

This diagram, which represents a vertical cross-section showing a stream profile, is useful in studying how gravity acts on a boulder rolling down to a lower elevation. Actually, gravity is responsible for all erosion, and the rate of erosion depends upon the slope of the incline. Moving materials have kinetic energy. The faster they move, the greater is their kinetic energy until they reach an obstacle such as the lake in this diagram. As they slow down, they lose kinetic energy and deposit some of the sediment. The large particles can be carried along only where the water is flowing more rapidly.

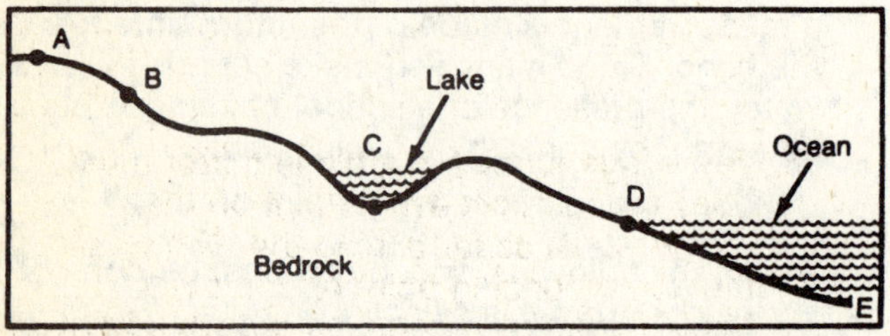

27. At which point would erosion most likely be greatest?

(1) A
(2) B
(3) C
(4) D
(5) E

28. Deposition in the lake at point C is most likely caused by a

(1) loss of potential energy by the lake
(2) loss of kinetic energy by the sediments
(3) gain of potential energy by the lake
(4) gain of kinetic energy by the sediments
(5) gain of potential energy by the sediments

29. At which point would the finest suspended particles settle out?

(1) A
(2) B
(3) C
(4) D
(5) E

Items 30 to 32 are based on the following graphs.

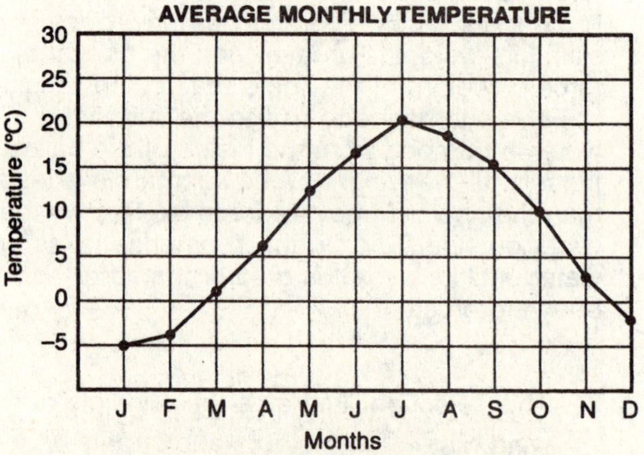

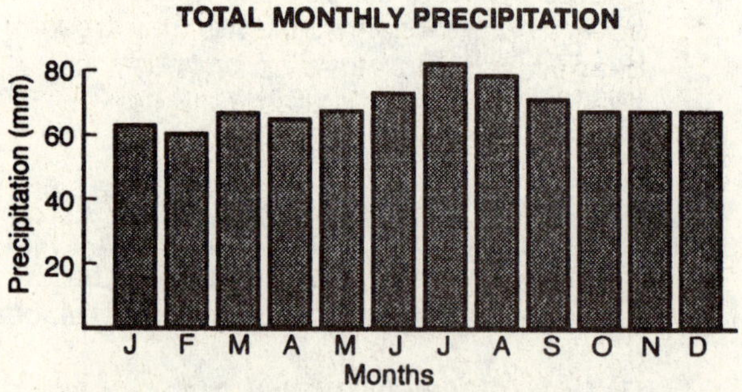

The two graphs represent average monthly temperature and total monthly precipitation from January through December for a city located near the centre of a continent.

30. Between which two consecutive months is there the least change in the average temperature?

(1) January and February
(2) February and March
(3) May and June
(4) October and November
(5) December and January

31. The average temperature and the total precipitation during the month of September, marked S in the graph, were

(1) 7°C; 63 mm
(2) 16°C; 63 mm
(3) 16°C; 68 mm
(4) 21°C; 68 mm
(5) 21°C; 80 mm

32. Which best describes the climate pattern of this location?

(1) hotter and wetter in summer than in winter
(2) hotter in summer than in winter, with no pronounced wet or dry season
(3) wetter in summer than in winter, with fairly constant temperature throughout the year
(4) dry and cold during the winter months
(5) dry and warm during the summer months

33. In temperate climates, flowers are pollinated either by insects or by the wind. The bright colours and strong odours of many flowers are forms of advertising to attract insects. Oak trees bear flowers that have no brightly coloured petals. It is reasonable to assume that the oak flowers

(1) can be pollinated either by insects or by wind
(2) have a strong odour
(3) do not have to be pollinated
(4) are wind-pollinated
(5) cannot be wind-pollinated

34. Green plants absorb carbon dioxide from the air and release oxygen; animals use oxygen and produce carbon dioxide. In a completely sealed aquarium, it is found that the oxygen level drops. The reason might be

A. too many plants
B. not enough plants
C. too many fishes
D. not enough fishes

(1) B only
(2) D only
(3) B or D
(4) B or C
(5) A or C

35. Pure water has a pH of 7. Acids have pH values lower than 7 and alkalis have values higher than 7. A gardener knows that the plants she grows need soil with a pH of 7.5. If the pH of the soil is 6.5, what action might she take?

(1) Use only pure water in watering the plants.
(2) Add a mild acid to the soil.
(3) Add a mild alkali to the soil.
(4) Water with tap water, which has a pH of 6.5.
(5) Use an organic fertilizer that becomes acid when it decays.

Item 36 is based on the following diagram.

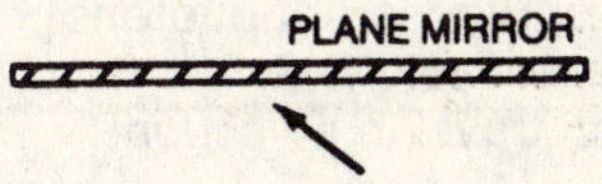

36. The image formed in a plane mirror must obey the rule that every point on the image is just as far behind the mirror as the corresponding point on the object. The diagram represents an object in front of a plane mirror. Which of the following arrows represents the image?

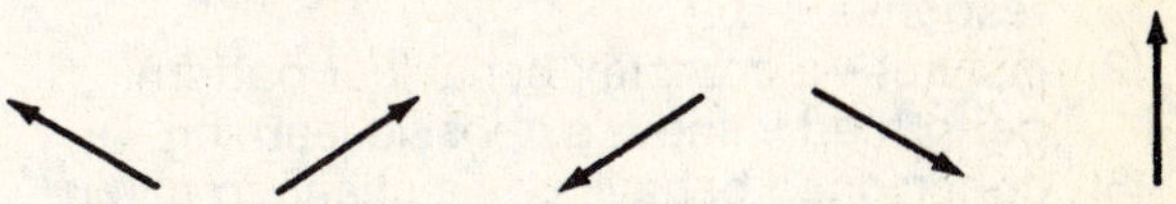

(1) (2) (3) (4) (5)

37. An object will not change the speed or direction of its motion unless acted on by an unbalanced force. In which of the following cases can it be assumed that there is no unbalanced force?

(1) A rock breaks from the side of a cliff and falls.
(2) A hot-air balloon is released and starts to rise.
(3) A car with its engine on climbs a hill at 80 km/h.
(4) A car going 80 km an hour turns a corner.
(5) A car on a level road shifts to neutral and coasts.

38. In a household circuit, an electric current will flow only if there is a complete circuit going from one terminal of the wall outlet to the other. All of the following will stop the flow of current EXCEPT

(1) opening the switch of a hair dryer
(2) overheating of an electric toaster
(3) burning out of a light bulb
(4) melting of a fuse
(5) removing a plug from the wall socket

39. If an opaque object is placed between a light bulb and a wall, the shadow on the wall is a faithful copy of the shape of the object. This is evidence that light

(1) is a type of wave
(2) travels in straight lines
(3) is composed of photons
(4) travels very fast
(5) can travel in a vacuum

<u>Items 40 to 49</u> are based on the following information.

Behaviour in living organisms is the pattern of activities in response to stimuli of the environment. Below are five types of behaviour.

(1) reflex act—a simple, inborn, automatic response
(2) instinct—a complex behaviour pattern performed without extensive learning
(3) conditioned behaviour—a changed stimulus producess the original response
(4) habit—a conscious response becomes automatic after constant repetition
(5) learned behaviour—a complex process involving reasoning and insight

Each of the following items refers to one of these types of behaviour. For each item choose the category that best describes the one type of behaviour. A category may be used more than once in answering the following questions.

40. In January, I find myself dating checks with the old calendar year. This type of behaviour is best described as

(1) reflex act
(2) instinct
(3) conditioned behaviour
(4) habit
(5) learned behaviour

41. The pupils are asked to write their names as many times as they can within two minutes. Then they are asked to do the same using the other hand. Comparisons are made regarding quality of performance and number of copies made. This type of behaviour is best described as

(1) reflex act
(2) instinct
(3) conditioned behaviour
(4) habit
(5) learned behaviour

42. The brain of a frog is destroyed in a painless fashion. Some absorbent cotton is dipped in vinegar (two percent acetic acid) and then placed on the frog's thigh. The leg reacts. This type of behaviour is best described as

(1) reflex act
(2) instinct
(3) conditioned behaviour
(4) habit
(5) learned behaviour

43. Joan holds a square of wire mesh closely to her face. Although Martin warns her that he is about to throw a wad of paper at her, when he throws the ball of paper at her she blinks. This type of behaviour is best described as

(1) reflex act
(2) instinct
(3) conditioned behaviour
(4) habit
(5) learned behaviour

44. Stanley and Lynda finish a difficult crossword puzzle in 60 minutes. Florence and Regina need more time to do the same puzzle. This type of behaviour is best described as

(1) reflex act
(2) instinct
(3) conditioned behaviour
(4) habit
(5) learned behaviour

45. A robin raised in an incubator builds a nest much like those of wild robins. This type of behaviour is best described as

(1) reflex act
(2) instinct
(3) conditioned behaviour
(4) habit
(5) learned behaviour

46. A newborn baby cries when it is uncomfortable, but an older baby will cry just to get attention. This type of behaviour is best described as

(1) reflex act
(2) instinct
(3) conditioned behaviour
(4) habit
(5) learned behaviour

47. A dolphin is rewarded with extra food each time it performs a trick. This type of behaviour is best described as

(1) reflex act
(2) instinct
(3) conditioned behaviour
(4) habit
(5) learned behaviour

48. After a passage is read to a class very slowly, it is read so that the class could copy what they hear but they are told NOT to cross the t's and NOT to dot the i's. Then the number of errors are reported. What is the kind of behaviour that causes the errors?

(1) reflex act
(2) instinct
(3) conditioned behaviour
(4) habit
(5) learned behaviour

49. Persons who have used this book to prepare for the GED have attained satisfactory scores on the test. This type of behaviour is best described as

(1) reflex act
(2) instinct
(3) conditioned behaviour
(4) habit
(5) learned behaviour

Items 50 to 56 refer to the following information.

About 100 years ago, two German scientists studying the function of the pancreas as an organ of digestion removed the entire pancreas from several dogs. A short time later some assistants observed that swarms of flies hovered around those cages that housed these dogs. Many regard this as the initial, but accidental, step in diabetes research. However, it was not until 1922 that Banting and Best showed that the pancreas produces the hormone insulin, which is essential for the proper use by the body of sugar. They concluded that if insulin is lacking, diabetes results.

50. The cages around the group of dogs not given the pancreas surgery did not seem to attract as many flies. This statement should be classified as

(1) the problem statement
(2) a hypothesis
(3) an observation
(4) an assumption
(5) irrelevant information

51. The urine of all dogs was tested for the presence of sugar. The dogs that had the pancreas removed produced urine that gave a positive test for sugar. This statement should be classified as

(1) a hypothesis
(2) the experimental design
(3) an experimental finding
(4) an assumption
(5) a law of nature

52. The dogs in both groups were approximately of the same age, weight, and breed. This statement should be classified as

(1) irrelevant information
(2) the experimental design
(3) a theory
(4) a problem statement
(5) a fact proved by experiment

53. The two German scientists whose work with pancreas is described in the passage should have shared the honours with Banting and Best for discovering the cure for diabetes. This statement should be classified as

(1) an experimental design
(2) an experimental finding
(3) a hypothesis
(4) an assumption
(5) irrelevant information

54. Before removing the entire pancreas from the dogs, these researchers experimented several times by removing a segment of this gland. This statement should be classified as

(1) a theory of physiology
(2) the experimental design
(3) an observation
(4) an assumption
(5) irrelevant information

55. The number and nature of the secretions of the pancreas have puzzled scientists for many years. This statement should be classified as

(1) an area for research
(2) an experiment
(3) a theory
(4) an assumption
(5) irrelevant information

56. After completing the experiments on dogs, the scientists suggested that human diabetes may be the result of a deficiency of the pancreas. This was a(n)

(1) experimental finding
(2) irrelevant statement
(3) observation
(4) assumption
(5) experimental design

Items 57 to 61 are based on the following diagrams.

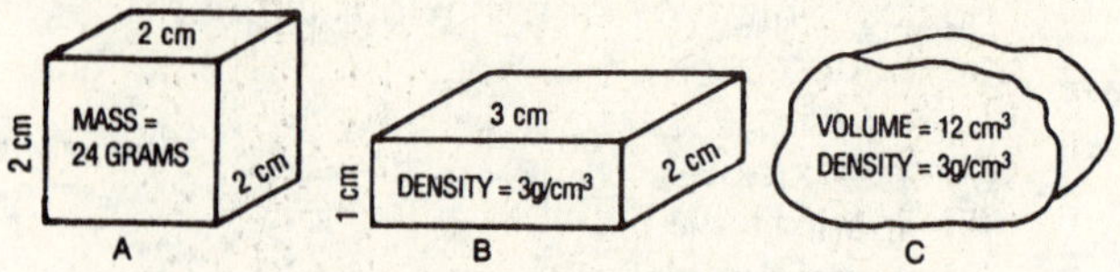

These diagrams, not drawn to scale, represent three samples of the same substance each having different size and shape. The following formulas are involved:

$$\text{Volume} = \text{length} \times \text{height} \times \text{width}$$

$$\text{Density} = \frac{\text{mass}}{\text{volume}}$$

57. What is the density of sample *A*?

(1) $0.33\,g/cm^3$
(2) $2.0\,g/cm^3$
(3) $3.0\,g/cm^3$
(4) $4.0\,g/cm^3$
(5) $8.0\,g/cm^3$

58. If sample *B* were split in half, what would be the density of each piece?

(1) $1.0\,g/cm^3$
(2) $1.5\,g/cm^3$
(3) $3.0\,g/cm^3$
(4) $6.0\,g/cm^3$
(5) $8.0\,g/cm^3$

59. Which graph best represents the relationship between the mass and the volume of the substance?

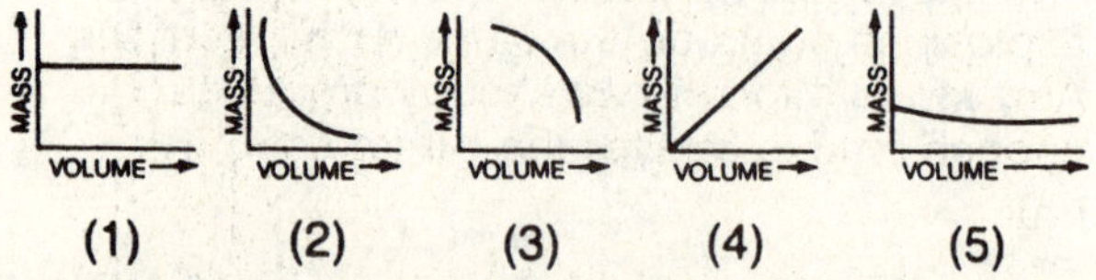

60. If sample *C* were compressed, which would probably occur?

(1) The volume would decrease and the density would decrease.
(2) The volume would decrease and the density would increase.
(3) The volume would increase and the density would increase.
(4) The volume would increase and the density would decrease.
(5) The volume would decrease and the density would remain the same.

61. Which order of letters ranks the samples by volume from largest to smallest?

(1) A, B, C
(2) A, C, B
(3) B, C, A
(4) C, B, A
(5) C, A, B

Items 62 to 65 refer to the following article.

Weather changes daily, but in any given region, it follows certain definite patterns that we call the climate of the region. Regions far north and south of the equator will have colder weather than those of low latitude. The reason is that the earth is warmed by the radiant energy received from the sun. Near the equator, these rays arrive nearly vertically most of the year. At higher latitudes, the rays strike the surface at a high angle, and thus their energy is spread out over wider areas. This is the same reason that it is warmer in the middle of the day, when the sun is nearly overhead, than in the morning or evening.

Proximity to large bodies of water has a strong influence on climate. Water has a high specific heat, so that it warms up and cools down much more slowly than land areas. The result is that places near the ocean have much more uniform temperatures than inland regions. The oceans may have another important influence on climate. Cold currents in the ocean will lower the temperatures of adjacent land areas, and warm currents have the opposite effect.

Accidental phenomena may have far-reaching effects on climate. A volcanic explosion may put so much dust in the air that the sun's rays are partially blocked for years. There is reason to believe that nuclear explosions could do the same. Burning of the Amazon rain forest has already produced enough smoke to alter the climate of the region.

62. Climate can best be defined as

(1) the state of the atmosphere at any given time
(2) atmospheric conditions at a given location
(3) weather conditions over a long period of time
(4) insolation
(5) nearness to bodies of water

63. As compared with coastal regions in the same latitude, regions that are located at great distances from oceans are likely to have

(1) hotter summers and colder winters
(2) hotter summers and warmer winters
(3) cooler summers and warmer winters
(4) cooler summers and colder winters
(5) any of these combinations, depending upon weather conditions

64. The process by which heat is transmitted from the sun to the earth is

(1) conduction
(2) convection
(3) radiation
(4) weathering
(5) cosmic disturbances

65. Humans can interfere with nature in creating changes in climate by influencing

(1) topography
(2) altitude
(3) winds and storms
(4) radiation by atomic experimentation
(5) direction of ocean currents

Item 66 is based on the following graph.

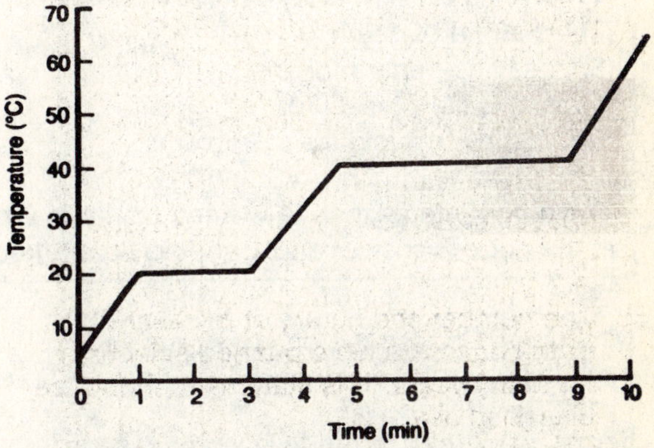

66. While a substance is absorbing heat and undergoing a change of state, its temperature remains constant. The graph above shows the temperature of a substance during a period of time in which heat is being added at a steady rate. The material melts and then boils. What is its boiling temperature?

(1) 0°C
(2) 20°C
(3) 70°C
(4) 40°C
(5) 30°C

END OF EXAMINATION

TEST 4: LANGUAGE ARTS, READING (INTERPRETING LITERATURE AND THE ARTS)

Directions

Allotted time: 65 minutes

This test consists of **45 multiple-choice questions** based on passages from classical and popular literature, prose, poetry, and drama, as well as from articles about literature and the arts—music, dance, and mass media, such as television.

Each passage is introduced by a question designed to help you locate the main purpose of the selection and to focus on the ideas presented to achieve that purpose.

Since you are allowed 65 minutes, be careful not to spend too much time on each question.

Make no mark on the answer sheet other than your choice of the correct answer. If you change your answer, erase your first mark completely. Only *one* answer space should be marked for each question.

EXAMPLE:

I went to the woods because I wished to live deliberately, to front only the essential facts of life, and see if I could not learn what it had to teach, and not, when I came to die, discover that I had not lived.

The author

(1) wishes to learn from nature
(2) is afraid of death
(3) has little regard for life
(4) seeks life's pleasures
(5) wishes to avoid life's problems.

● ② ③ ④ ⑤

The author states that he wanted to "learn what it (the woods, that is, nature) had to teach" so 1 is the correct answer and 1 should be marked on the answer paper.

Directions: Choose the one best answer to each item.

Items 1 to 5 refer to the following passage.

NO HOME TOWN

Between 1936 and 1948 my parents moved twenty times. Sometimes between two fixed points—to a city in the late fall, to the forest in the early spring; sometimes it was from one city to another. My mother and father were from Nova Scotia, and that was *home* to them. But it wasn't where I was. So where was I?

Here and there, but never both at once. Home was not a place but a trajectory; it was the dotted line that marked our trail. It would appear out of boxes and suitcases, be packed away, appear again in a different form, in a different room, after a long and uncomfortable journey, hundreds of miles in the back of a car stuffed full of bundles and packages, then on the bottom of a canoe with the rain dribbling down your neck or on a sleigh drawn by horses over the creaking ice. You couldn't count on home. You couldn't count on it to stay put.

What has become of them, those provisional homes—the second-floor apartment in Ottawa with its long dark hallways, and the French Canadian and the English Canadian who lived below, and were always squabbling, and were married to each other? Or the drafty mansion in Sault Ste. Marie, which was falling apart and stood in a field of cabbages, with the hole in the ceiling through which we dropped crayons onto the stove to melt in puddles of smelly colour? Or the one house that was torn down, or the other one that burned down; or the tent whose roof you weren't supposed to touch for fear of leaks? That tent had no floor, and the mice always got in; they knew a good home when they saw it.

—Margaret Atwood

1. How would you best describe the author's family?

(1) at home in Nova Scotia
(2) liked apartments rather than houses
(3) always on the move
(4) enjoyed camping
(5) had interesting neighbours

2. How did the author feel about her early life?

(1) enjoyed travelling
(2) had many adventures
(3) didn't like noisy neighbours
(4) longed for a stable sense of homelife
(5) felt at home in the woods

3. Why do you think the family moved so often?

(1) to seek better opportunities for employment
(2) enjoyed travelling
(3) wanted to see the country
(4) hated to stay in one place
(5) to give the children more experiences

4. How would you best describe their housing?

(1) interesting
(2) exciting
(3) mobile
(4) precarious
(5) satisfactory

5. What word would you use to describe the author's early life?

(1) disorganized
(2) happy
(3) determined
(4) comfortable
(5) predictable

Items 6 to 10 refer to the following passage.

WHAT ARE THE ADVANTAGES OF A NEW MODEL CAR?

Frantic Motors has embodied some of the motorist's most cherished ideals in the design of its latest model, the Sloth.

You won't find advertisements for the Sloth in these pages, because Frantic learned through its experience with the Dugong, the only car able to be refueled from a truck without stopping, that the public is not quite ready for its breakthroughs.

And yet the Sloth promises comfort, security, and cleanliness to a degree yet unmatched in vehicular history. After studying gasoline and the environment, ecologically minded Frantic engineers have fitted the Sloth with sails, a feature that supplements the engines and is to be used when entering large communities in which pollution is a problem.

Such cities are usually congested, and road tests have proved that the Sloth, under a full head of sail, moves as fast as anything else in a traffic-snarled street—somewhat faster in Chicago, for that matter, where brisk winds off Lake Michigan occasionally heel the Sloth sharply around the Loop. The savings in fuel are obviously large with kicking canvas, and there have been unconfirmed reports that Nader's Raiders are looking with favour on the Sloth's rigging, which includes a bosun's chair with safety belt.

6. Which does the author *not* indicate as a characteristic of the Sloth?

(1) economy of operation
(2) safety belt
(3) appeal to buyer's beliefs
(4) protection of the environment
(5) beauty of appearance

7. On the basis of the passage, which statement can most safely be made?

(1) The Sloth is the first car produced by Frantic Motors.
(2) The Sloth has had minimum exposure.
(3) The Sloth has hundreds of supporters.
(4) The Sloth will undersell its competition.
(5) The Sloth will sell well in Chicago.

8. The use of the names Frantic and Sloth would appear to indicate that the author's real purpose in writing the passage is

(1) educational
(2) promotional
(3) satirical
(4) rhetorical
(5) ideological

9. After he reads the passage, the reader's most logical conclusion would be that the Sloth

(1) will disappoint the public
(2) has many critics
(3) is primarily built to last
(4) will not be widely distributed
(5) has no special features

10. The author indicates that the reason the Sloth can keep up with other traffic in cities is that

 (1) the Sloth does not need engines
 (2) most cities are noted for their brisk winds
 (3) the sails only supplement the engine
 (4) the Sloth helps prevent pollution
 (5) city traffic moves slowly

Items 11 to 15 refer to the following passage.

HOW DID ONE VILLAGE BRING DISASTER ON ITSELF?

On a morning in early spring, 1873, the people of Oberfest left their houses and took refuge in the town hall. No one knows why, precisely. A number of rumours had raced through the town during recent weeks, were passed on and converted to news; predictions become certainties. On this particular morning, fear turned into terror, and people rushed through the narrow streets, carrying their most precious possessions, pulling their children and dashing into the great hall. The doors were nailed shut, and men took their turns watching out the window. Two days passed. When no disaster came, the fear grew worse, because the people began to suspect that the danger was already in the hall, locked inside. No one spoke to anybody else; people watched each other, looking for signs. It was the children who rang the great bell in the first bell tower—a small band of bored children found the bell rope and swung on it—set the bell clanging. This was the traditional signal of alarm, and in a moment the elders were dashing in panic to all the other bell towers and ringing the bells. For nearly an hour, the valley reverberated with the wild clangor—and then, a thousand feet above, the snow began to crack, and the avalanche began; a massive cataract of ice and snow thundered down and buried the town, silencing the bells. There is no trace of Oberfest today, not even a spire, because the snow is so deep; and, in the shadow of the mountains, it is very cold.

11. Which element is especially significant in this passage?

 (1) dialogue
 (2) setting
 (3) illustrations
 (4) levels of usage
 (5) rhythm

12. Which is the most valid conclusion regarding the *theme* of the passage?

 (1) It is a minor feature of the passage.
 (2) It is not related to the plot.
 (3) It is related to the topic sentence.
 (4) It is stated, rather than implied.
 (5) It is implied, but not stated.

13. That the alarm, sounded to avert danger, became the apparent cause of the avalanche is an example of

 (1) irony
 (2) simile
 (3) satire
 (4) personification
 (5) exaggeration

14. The effect of the last phrase of the passage, "it is very cold," depends mainly on

 (1) rhythm
 (2) rhyme
 (3) comparison
 (4) connotation
 (5) sound

15. Which word best expresses the main idea of the passage?

 (1) faith
 (2) suspicion
 (3) nostalgia
 (4) disaster
 (5) rumours

Items 16 to 20 refer to the following poem.

HOW DOES THIS POET FEEL ABOUT HIMSELF?

Every Good Boy Does Fine

I practiced my cornet in a cold garage
Where I could blast it till the oil in drums
Boomed back; tossed free-throws till I
 couldn't move my thumbs;
Sprinted through tires, tackling a headless
 dummy.

In my first contest, playing a wobbly solo,
I blew up in the coda, alone on stage,
And twisting like my hand-tied necktie, saw
 the judge
Letting my silence dwindle down his scale.

At my first basketball game, gangling away from home
A hundred miles by bus to a dressing room,
Under the showering voice of the coach, I stood in a towel,
Having forgotten shoes, socks, uniform.

In my first football game, the first play under the lights
I intercepted a pass. For seventy yards, I ran
Through music and squeals, surging, lifting my cleats,
Only to be brought down by the safety man.

I took my second chances with less care, but in dreams
I saw the bald judge slumped in the front row,
The coach and team at the doorway, the safety man
Galloping loud at my heels. They watch me now.

You who have always horned your way through passages,
Sat safe on the bench while some came naked to court,
Slipped out of arms to win in the long run,
Consider this poem a failure, sprawling flat on a page.

16. The "I," or speaking voice of the poem, probably regards himself mainly as a(n)

(1) athlete
(2) musician
(3) loser
(4) wit
(5) critic

17. In relation to the content of the poem, its title is an example of

(1) personification
(2) allegory
(3) sensory language
(4) irony
(5) an epithet

18. In the final stanza, the reader is asked to

(1) make an improper judgment
(2) feel sorry for the poet
(3) feel superior to the poet
(4) agree with the poet
(5) admire the poet

19. In line 7, "twisting like my hand-tied necktie" is an example of

(1) a striking contrast
(2) a vague reference
(3) an implied meaning
(4) an overused symbol
(5) a vivid comparison

20. With which group of words does the poet address the reader directly?

(1) "I practiced my cornet" (line 1)
(2) "In my first contest" (line 5)
(3) "in dreams I saw the bald judge" (lines 17 and 18)
(4) "some came naked to court" (line 22)
(5) "Consider this poem a failure" (line 24)

Items 21 to 25 refer to the following poem.

HOW WILL AMERICANS FACE UP TO THEIR DOOM?

The Civic Banquet

Pompeians buried by surprise
In parlours, bedrooms, baths and hallways,
At least we could breathe their final sighs
As warm as always.
But should Americans face doom
I know how we will be positioned:
All frozen in some banquet room
That's air-conditioned.

The frost is on the pumpkin pie,
It chilled the soup, congealed the dinner
And kept the butter hard and dry,
The only winner,
While ladies who can see their breath,
In evening dress turn blue and colder,
Exposing to the kiss of death
A naked shoulder.

The arctic blasts are filtered clear;
Two thousand diners can't pollute them
Nor can the speakers we must hear
And then salute them.

Ah! We will die and make world news
From cold, increasing slow but steady,
While listening to those men whose views
We knew already.

21. The poet unifies the stanzas of the poem through the use of

(1) refrain and onomatopoeia
(2) rhythm and rhyme
(3) alliteration and assonance
(4) symbol and connotation
(5) simile and metaphor

22. The poet views the dinner guests with

    (1) helpless rage
    (2) great envy
    (3) happy approval
    (4) amused pity
    (5) vague annoyance

23. The attitude of the poet is most clearly revealed by the

    (1) listing of historical references
    (2) quoting of authorities
    (3) description of humorous examples
    (4) quoting of proverbs
    (5) taking of a solemn oath

24. The poet's intention in stanza 1 seems to be to

    (1) suggest contrast
    (2) develop characters
    (3) establish diction
    (4) create conflict
    (5) introduce facts

25. The title of the poem refers to the

    (1) plot
    (2) mood
    (3) setting
    (4) hero
    (5) interpretation

Items 26 to 30 refer to the following excerpt from a play.

HOW DO HER SUITORS REACT TO CANDIDA'S DECISION?

MORELL: [*with proud humility*] I have nothing to offer but my strength for your defence, my honesty for your surety, my ability and industry for your livelihood, and my authority and position for your dignity. That is all it becomes a man to offer to a woman.

CANDIDA: [*quite quietly*] And you, Eugene? What do you offer?

MARCHBANKS: My weakness. My desolation. My heart's need.

CANDIDA: [*impressed*] That's a good bid, Eugene. Now I know how to make my choice. *She pauses and looks curiously from one to the other, as if weighing them. Morell, whose lofty confidence has changed into heartbreaking dread at Eugene's bid, loses all power of concealing his anxiety. Eugene, strung to the highest tension, does not move a muscle.*

MORELL: [*in a suffocated voice: the appeal bursting from the depths of his anguish*] Candida!

MARCHBANKS: [*aside, in a flash of contempt*] Coward!

CANDIDA: [*significantly*] I give myself to the weaker of the two.

EUGENE: *divines her meaning at once; his face whitens like steel in a furnace.*

MORELL: [*bowing his head with the calm collapse*] I accept your sentence, Candida.

CANDIDA: Do *you* understand, Eugene?

MARCHBANKS: Oh, I feel I'm lost. He cannot bear the burden.

MORELL: [*incredulously, raising his head and voice with comic abruptness*] Do you mean *me*, Candida?

CANDIDA: [*smiling a little*] Let us sit and talk comfortably over it like three friends. [**To MORELL**] Sit down, dear. [**MORELL**, quite lost, takes the chair from the fireside: the children's chair]. Bring me that chair, Eugene. [*She indicates the easy chair. He fetches it silently, even with something like cold strength, and places it next to* **MORELL**, *a little behind him. She sits down. He takes the visitor's chair himself, and sits, inscrutable. When they are all settled she begins, throwing a spell of quietness on them by her calm, sane, tender tone*]. You remember what you told me about yourself, Eugene: how nobody has cared for you since your old nurse died: how those clever fashionable sisters and successful brothers of yours were your mother's and father's pets: how miserable you were at Eton: how your father is trying to starve you into returning to Oxford: how you have to live without comfort or welcome or refuge: always lonely, and nearly always disliked and misunderstood, poor boy!

MARCHBANKS: [*faithful to the nobility of his lot*] I had my books. I had Nature. And at last I met you.

CANDIDA: Never mind that just at present. Now I want you to look at this other boy here: *my* boy! spoiled from his cradle. We go once a fortnight to see his parents. . . . [*With deepening gravity*] Ask James's mother and his three sisters what it cost to save James the trouble of doing anything but be strong and clever and happy. Ask *me* what it costs to be James's mother and three sisters and wife and mother to his children all in one. . . . I build a castle of comfort and indulgence and love for him, and stand sentinel always to keep little vulgar cares out. I make him master here, though he does not know it, and could not only tell you a moment ago how it came to be so.

MORELL: [*quite overcome, kneeling beside her chair and embracing her with boyish ingenuousness*] It's all true, every word. What I am you have made me with the labour of your hands and the love of your heart. You are my wife, my mother, my sister: you are the sum of all loving care to me.

CANDIDA: [*in his arms, smiling to* **EUGENE**] Am I *your* mother and sisters to you, Eugene?

MARCHBANKS: [*rising with a fierce gesture of disgust*] Ah, never. Out, then, into the night with me!

CANDIDA: [*rising quickly*] You are not going like that, Eugene?

MARCHBANKS: [*with the ring of a man's voice—no longer a boy's—in the words*] I know the hour when it strikes. I am impatient to do what must be done.

MORELL: [*who has also risen*] Candida: don't let him do anything rash.

CANDIDA: [*confident, smiling at* **EUGENE**] Oh, there is no fear. He has learnt to live without happiness.

MARCHBANKS: I no longer desire happiness: life is nobler than that. Parson James: I give you my happiness with both hands. I love you because you have filled the heart of the woman I loved. Goodbye.

—George Bernard Shaw, *Candida*

26. The incident which is dramatized portrays a(n)

(1) conflict between Candida and Morell
(2) conflict between Morell and Marchbanks
(3) conflict between Candida and Marchbanks
(4) choice by Candida between Morell and Marchbanks
(5) agreement by Candida with Morell and Marchbanks

27. The atmosphere is one of

(1) light humour
(2) mock heroics
(3) desperate self-sacrifice
(4) sentimental tear-jerking
(5) good-natured fun

28. Candida tells Marchbanks how she spoiled Morell in order to

(1) impress him
(2) gain his sympathy
(3) exasperate him
(4) justify her decision
(5) embarrass him

29. Marchbanks' departure may best be described as

(1) noble
(2) spiteful
(3) timid
(4) childish
(5) predictable

30. Candida's decision may be considered to be

(1) impulsive
(2) unfair
(3) ironic
(4) misunderstood
(5) sentimental

Items 31 to 35 refer to the following passage.

HOW DOES THE AUTHOR FEEL ABOUT PRIZE FIGHT CROWDS?

The fight crowd is a beast that lurks in the darkness behind the fringe of white light shed over the first six rows by the incandescents atop the ring, and is not to be trusted with pop bottles or other hardware.

People who go to prize fights are sadistic.

When two prominent pugilists are scheduled to pummel one another in public on a summer's evening, men and women file into the stadium in the guise of human beings, and thereafter become a part of a gray thing that squats in the dark until, at the conclusion of the bloodletting, they may be seen leaving the arena in the same guise they wore when they entered. . . .

As a rule, the mob that gathers to see men fight is unjust, vindictive, swept by intense, unreasoning hatreds, proud of its swift recognition of what it believes to be sportsmanship. It is quick to greet the purely phony move of the boxer who extends his gloves to his rival, who has slipped or been pushed to the floor, and to reward this stimulating but still baloney gesture with a pattering of hands which indicates the following: "You are a good sport. We recognize that you are a good sport, and we know a sporting gesture when we see one. Therefore we are all good sports, too. Hurrah for us!"

The same crowd doesn't see the same boxer stick his thumb in his opponent's eye or try to cut him with the laces of his glove, butt him or dig him a low one when the referee isn't in a position to see. It roots consistently for the smaller man, and never for a moment considers the desperate psychological dilemma of the larger of the two. It howls with glee at a good finisher making his kill. The Roman hordes were more civilized. Their gladiators asked them whether the final blow should be administered or not. The main attraction at the modern prize fight is the spectacle of a man clubbing a helpless and vanquished opponent into complete insensibility. The referee who stops a bout to save a slugged and punch-drunken man from the final ignominy is hissed by the assembled sportsmen.

31. The writer of this passage is

(1) disgusted
(2) jovial
(3) matter-of-fact
(4) satiric
(5) optimistic

32. As used in line 26, which action is referred to as the "baloney gesture"?

(1) pushing the opponent to the floor
(2) shaking hands with the opponent
(3) touching gloves with the downed opponent
(4) smiling at the opponent
(5) digging the opponent a low one

33. The dilemma of the bigger man in line 40 is caused by the crowd's

(1) rooting for the smaller man, but cheering a good finisher
(2) cheering a good finisher, but hissing at the referee
(3) applauding a friendly gesture, but rooting for the smaller man
(4) hissing at the referee, but howling at a good finisher
(5) applauding a friendly gesture, but cheering a helpless opponent

34. Which group of words best indicates the author's opinion?

(1) "referee," "opponent," "finisher"
(2) "gladiators," "slugged," "sporting gesture"
(3) "stimulating," "hissing," "pattering"
(4) "best," "lurks," "gray thing"
(5) "spectacle," "psychological dilemma," "sportsmen"

35. The author states that the prize fight audience is

(1) sportsmanlike
(2) fair
(3) civilized
(4) uninvolved
(5) vengeful

Items 36 to 40 refer to the following commentary on literature.

A NATIONAL TREASURE

Leonard Cohen is a national treasure. He has made a significant contribution to the Arts, from the publication in 1956 of *Let Us Compare Mythologies* to his next book of poetry or CD of music. He has created magic for almost half a century.

Leonard Cohen is not an unknown poet and singer. Many of his books have sold over 800,000 copies throughout the world, and many of his music albums have become number one hits. Reactions to his albums from the early *Life of Leonard Cohen* to the latest work from this gravelly-voiced singer have spoken to the inner person in all of us. It is difficult to say if they are poetry set to music or a unique variation on a ballad. In any case, his albums and books have become best sellers.

Recognition has come to Leonard Cohen for his works. From the 1955 MacNaughton Prize for Creative Writing to the 1993 Governor General's Performing Arts Award, he has been recognized by his peers and the public. He has been honored with five Juno Awards, two honorary degrees and other awards and prizes. His career has spanned the sixties to the present. He has something to say to people of all ages and all times. He has also been heard, which is the ultimate compliment for any artist.

Looking at the person behind the persona reveals an interesting story. Leonard Cohen has traveled extensively, explored religions and countries and incorporated all the changes in himself and the society around him into his poetry and songs.

In an interview with Arthur Kurzweil and Pamela Roth in the *Jewish Book News* Leonard Cohen ties to explain poetry.

"In its *(poetry's)* pure form it's like bee pollen. . . . The honey of poetry is all over the place. It is in the writing of the *National Geographic*, when an idea is absolutely clear and beautiful; it's in movies; it's all over because the taste of significance is that which we call poetry, when something resonates with a particular kind of significance. We may not call it poetry but we've experienced poetry. It's got something to do with truth and rhythm and authority and music." Even his explanations are rich and require repeated reading.

36. The author implies that Leonard Cohen is popular because

(1) he speaks to a large audience
(2) his books sell a lot of copies
(3) his records sell a lot of copies
(4) he has performed for many years
(5) people like the sound of his voice

37. The number of Junos won by Leonard Cohen is:

(1) one
(2) two
(3) three
(4) four
(5) five

38. Leonard Cohen's first book was published in

(1) 1955
(2) 1993
(3) 1960
(4) 1956
(5) 1965

39. Writing can be considered poetry when

(1) it rhymes
(2) It can be put to music
(3) no one understands it
(4) it is full of emotion and meaning
(5) it is absolutely clear and beautiful

40. Poetry can be part of everyday communication when

(1) people speak with difficult words
(2) the words form a pattern
(3) the words have hidden meanings
(4) there is truth, rhythm, authority, and music in the words
(5) people want it to be

Items 41 to 45 refer to the following commentary on entertainment.

JUNO WHO'S THE BEST

Stan Klees and Walt Grealis had an idea in 1970 to honour Canadian musical talent. Originally called the Gold Leaf Awards, it became the Junos just a year later. These awards were to honour the best in a series of categories. For the first five years of the awards, they were an industry celebration, but television changed all that.

People love to see musicians on television playing themselves. Television gives the audience a chance to do this by broadcasting award shows. In 1975, the presentation of the Junos was televised and the Canadian Academy of Recording Arts and Sciences was founded. The Junos had arrived on television screens across the country.

Winning one of the Junos is a long process. Between October 1 and November 14, submission forms have to be procured, completed and returned. Artists must be Canadian citizens who have lived in Canada for the year and recordings must have been released and available for purchase at retail outlets between the beginning of September and the middle of November of the following year. Some categories are based on total sales and sales figures for the period must be calculated and submitted to be verified. Other categories are juried. This means that the winner is chosen by a jury of his or her peers.

An advisory committee selects judges to sit on the juries. These judges can only sit for one year and their identities are confidential until the night of the awards. Each judge receives a CD from each of the nominees, and must base his or her decision on the recorded performance. Votes are by secret ballot returned to an accounting firm which verifies and totals the votes. The voting establishes the five nominees in each category who are announced in February to the media. All the members of the Canadian Academy of Recording Arts and Sciences vote for the winner. This process is followed for each of 15 categories.

There are an additional 21 craft categories. These are the people who work behind the scenes to make a winning CD. For these categories, the judges vote on the winner and submit their ballots to the accounting firm which tabulates the results.

All of this comes together on the night of the show when winners are announced with great fanfare.

41. The author of this passage is

(1) objective
(2) critical
(3) laudatory
(4) humourous
(5) nationalistic

42. The Junos are a tribute to the vision of

(1) the Canadian Academy of Recording Arts and Sciences
(2) the television stations
(3) the Backstreet Boys
(4) Stan Klees and Walt Grealis
(5) Trevor Guthrie and George Pimentel

43. The winers of the craft awards are chosen by

(1) members of the Academy
(2) members of the audience
(3) the Prime Minister
(4) the Advisory Committee
(5) members of the juries

44. Winning one of the Junos begins on

(1) November 14
(2) January 1
(3) the night of the broadcast
(4) October 1
(5) the release date of the CD

45. The number of craft awards is

(1) 19
(2) 20
(3) 21
(4) 22
(5) 23

END OF EXAMINATION

TEST 5: MATHEMATICS

Directions

Allotted time: 90 minutes

This test consists of **56 multiple-choice questions** designed to measure general mathematics skills and problem-solving ability. Some questions include a graph, chart, or figure, along with a short reading upon which the question is based. You may not use a calculator during the test.

Some questions require the application of a formula. Page 890 has any of the formulae you may need.

There will be some questions that give more information than you need to solve the problem. Other questions do not furnish enough information to solve the problem. In such cases, choose the answer "Not enough information is given."

Work carefully but do not spend too much time on any one question. Record your answer on the answer sheet by marking the numbered space beside the number that corresponds to the question in the test. Answer *all* questions since there is no penalty for incorrect answers. Your score will depend on the number of correct responses.

EXAMPLE:

If I purchase five 45¢ postage stamps with two $2 coins, how much change should be returned? (Do not calculate GST.)

(1) $.29
(2) $.54
(3) $.55
(4) $1.45
(5) $1.75

① ② ③ ④ ●

The correct answer is $1.75; therefore, answer space 5 should be marked on the answer sheet.

FORMULAE

Description	Formula
AREA (A) of a:	
square	$A = s^2$; where s = side
rectangle	$A = lw$; where l = length, w = width
parallelogram	$A = bh$; where b = base, h = height
triangle	$A = \frac{1}{2} bh$; where b = base, h = height
circle	$A = \pi r^2$; where $\pi = 3.14$, r = radius
PERIMETER (P) of a:	
square	$P = 4s$; where s = side
rectangle	$P = 2l + 2w$; where l = length, w = width
triangle	$P = a + b + c$; where a, b, and c are the sides
circumference (C) of a circle	$C = \pi d$; where $\pi = 3.14$, d = diameter
VOLUME (V) of a:	
cube	$V = s^3$; where s = side
rectangular container	$V = lwh$; where l = length, w = width, h = height
cylinder	$V = \pi r^2 h$; where $\pi = 3.14$, r = radius, h = height
Pythagorean relationship	$c^2 = a^2 + b^2$; where c = hypotenuse, a and b are legs of a right triangle
distance (d) between two points in a plane	$d = \sqrt{(x_2 - x_1)^2 + (y_2 - y_1)^2}$; where (x_1, y_1) and (x_2, y_2) are two points in a plane
slope of a line (m)	$m = \frac{y_2 - y_1}{x_2 - x_1}$; where (x_1, y_1) and (x_2, y_2) are two points in a plane
mean	$mean = \frac{x_1 + x_2 + \cdots + x_n}{n}$; where the x's are the value for which a mean is desired, and n = number of values in the series
median	median = the point in an ordered set of numbers at which half of the numbers are above and half of the numbers are below this value
simple interest (i)	$i = prt$; where p = principal, r = rate, t = time
distance (d) as function of rate and time	$d = rt$; where r = rate, t = time
total cost (c)	$c = nr$; where n = number of units, r = cost per unit

Directions: Choose the one best answer for each item.

1. A salesman earns \$200 per week plus a 5% commission on all sales over \$8000. One week, his sales amounted to \$15 000. What were his earnings that week?

(1) \$200
(2) \$350
(3) \$500
(4) \$550
(5) \$600

2. A carton can hold c cans of processed meat. How many cartons will be needed for x cans of this meat?

(1) cx
(2) $\frac{c}{x}$
(3) $\frac{x}{c}$
(4) $\frac{1}{cx}$
(5) $c + x$

3. One morning Martin drove 180 km in 2 hours. After lunch, he covered 250 km more in 3 hours. What was his average rate of speed, in kilometres per hour, for the entire trip?

(1) 75
(2) 86
(3) 90
(4) 90.5
(5) Not enough information is given.

4. A photograph 8 cm long and 6 cm wide is to be enlarged so that its length will be 12 cm. What is the width of the enlargement in centimetres?

(1) 9
(2) 10
(3) 12
(4) 14
(5) 16

5. An investor bought *ABC* stock at $19\frac{5}{8}$ and sold it as $23\frac{1}{4}$. What was the profit on 80 shares before deductions for commission and taxes?

(1) \$29
(2) \$240
(3) \$255
(4) \$290
(5) \$358

6. A solution of the inequality $3x - 1 < 5$ is

(1) 3
(2) 2
(3) 1
(4) 5
(5) $2\frac{1}{2}$

7. A theatre has 850 seats, 60% of which are in the orchestra. How many seats are in the balcony?

(1) 240
(2) 260
(3) 320
(4) 340
(5) 510

8. In a right triangle, the ratio of the measures of the two acute angles is 4:1. What is the measure of the larger acute angle in degrees?

(1) 50°
(2) 54°
(3) 70°
(4) 72°
(5) Not enough information given.

9. Two sides of a triangle are each $\frac{2}{3}$ of the base, b. The perimeter is

(1) $\frac{4b}{9}$
(2) $\frac{4b}{3}$
(3) $\frac{5b}{3}$
(4) $\frac{7b}{3}$
(5) 7b

10. Bill earns m dollars per month and Antonio earns n dollars per month. How many dollars do both men earn in 1 year?

(1) $12mn$
(2) $12m + n$
(3) $12(m + n)$
(4) $12n + m$
(5) $12n - m$

Item 11 is based on the following figure.

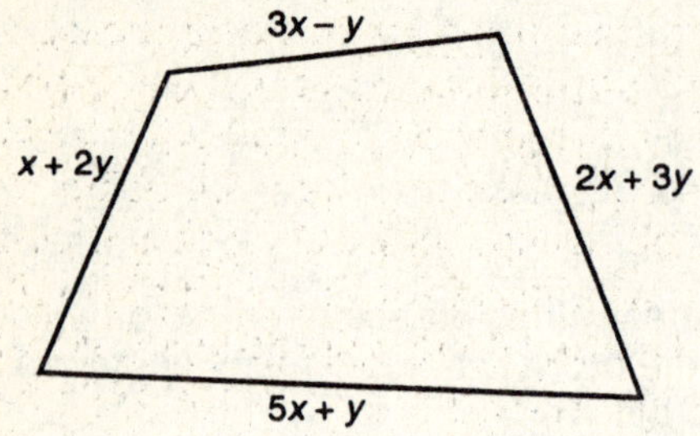

11. What is the perimeter of the figure?

(1) $11x + 5y$
(2) $10x + 5y$
(3) $11x + 4y$
(4) $9x - y$
(5) $8x + 3y$

12. Joan and Ahmed earn money by babysitting. If Joan earns twice as much as Ahmed and the two girls earn a total of $42, how much does Ahmed earn?

(1) $8
(2) $10
(3) $12
(4) $14
(5) Not enough information is given.

Item 13 is based on the following table.

An income tax form gives the following instructions.

If your taxable income is

At least	But not more than	Your tax is
0	$3499	2% of the amount
$3500	$4499	$70 plus 3% of any amount above $3500
$4500	$7499	$100 plus 5% of any amount above $4500
$7500		$250 plus 7% of any amount above $7500

13. How much tax is due on a taxable income of $5800?

(1) $120
(2) $135
(3) $150
(4) $165
(5) $175

14. Given the formula $x = 2a(b + 7)$, find x if $a = 3$ and $b = 5$.

(1) 13
(2) 72
(3) 108
(4) 120
(5) 210

15. The mass of each of the eleven men on the Panthers football team is 91, 90, 88, 96, 93, 94, 89, 97, 90, 92, and 84 kg. What is the median mass (in kilograms) of a player on this team?

(1) 89
(2) 90
(3) 91
(4) 92
(5) 93

16. A committee consists of 7 women and 4 men. If one member of the committee is chosen to act as chairman, what is the probability that the choice is a woman?

(1) $\frac{1}{11}$
(2) $\frac{1}{7}$
(3) $\frac{4}{7}$
(4) $\frac{7}{11}$
(5) $\frac{10}{11}$

17. On line segment AB, points C and D are so located that $AC = CD = DB$. What part of AD is CD?

(1) $\frac{1}{4}$
(2) $\frac{1}{3}$
(3) $\frac{1}{2}$
(4) $\frac{2}{3}$
(5) $\frac{3}{2}$

Item 18 is based on the following figure.

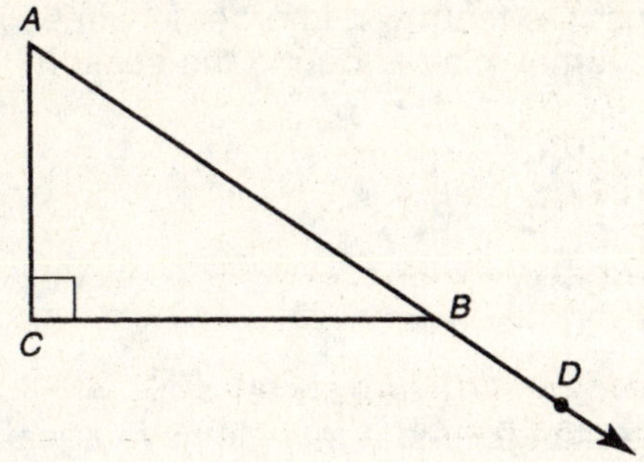

18. If $\overleftrightarrow{AC}$ is perpendicular to $\overleftrightarrow{CB}$ and $m\angle CBD = 125°$ then $m\angle A$ equals

(1) 15°
(2) 20°
(3) 35°
(4) 45°
(5) Not enough information is given.

---

19. In a large class 80 students took a test. When the test papers were rated, it was found that 10% of the students had *A* papers, 25% of the students had *B* papers, 30% of the students had *C* papers, 15% of the students had *D* papers and the rest failed. How many students failed the test?

(1) 10
(2) 12
(3) 15
(4) 16
(5) Not enough information is given.

20. An investor obtains an annual interest of 7% on $20 000 and 7½% on $12 000. What was his annual income on the two investments?

(1) $1400
(2) $1500
(3) $2000
(4) $2300
(5) $2800

21. A dozen eggs cost *x* cents. What is the cost of 3 eggs at the same rate in cents?

(1) $\frac{x}{3}$
(2) $\frac{x}{4}$
(3) $\frac{3x}{4}$
(4) $\frac{x}{12}$
(5) $3x$

22. Pete Rossini has just graduated from university with honours. He has been offered desirable jobs with the following pay provisions:

A. $27 000 for the first year
B. $570 per week for the first year
C. $2250 per month for the first year
D. $2000 per month for the first 6 months and an increase of 10% for the last 6 months

Which of the above offers will give Pete Rossini the greatest income for the first year?

(1) A
(2) B
(3) C
(4) D
(5) Not enough information is given.

23. A dealer bought two dozen jackets at $48 each. The next month he bought 15 more jackets at $48 each. Which of the following expressions gives the number of dollars the dealer spent for the jackets?

(1) $24 \times 48 + 15$
(2) $(24 \times 48) \times 15$
(3) $24 + 48 \times 15$
(4) $48(24 + 15)$
(5) $24 + (48 + 15)$

24. One car travels at an average speed of 96 km/h. A slower car travels at an average speed of 72 km/h. How many more kilometres does the faster car travel than the slower car in 45 minutes?

(1) 18
(2) 10
(3) 12
(4) 27
(5) 36

Item 25 is based on the following graph.

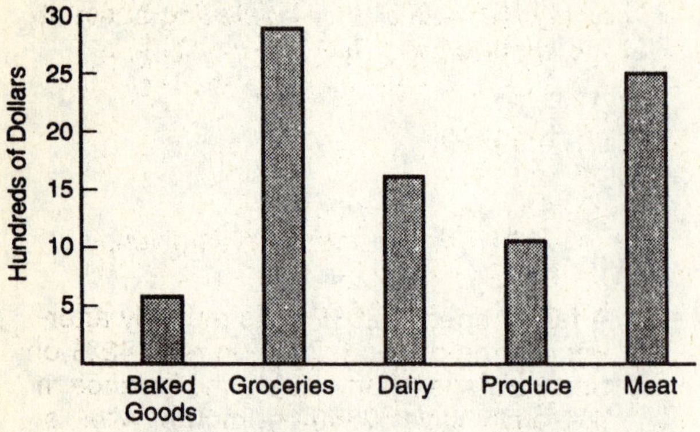

25. By how many dollars do the sales in the meat department exceed the sales in the dairy department?

(1) \$100
(2) \$1000
(3) \$1500
(4) \$1800
(5) \$10 000

---

26. A boat travels due east for a distance of 15 km. It then travels due north for a distance of 20 km, at which point it drops anchor. How many kilometres is the boat from its starting point?

(1) 23
(2) 25
(3) 29
(4) 30
(5) 35

27. If the average of the ages of three individuals is 44 years, and no one of them is less than 42 years old, what is the maximum age of any of them?

(1) 46
(2) 47
(3) 48
(4) 49
(5) 50

28. Express 2 750 389 in scientific notation.

(1) 27.50389×10^5
(2) 275.0389×10^3
(3) 27.50389×10^6
(4) 0.2750389×10^7
(5) 2.750389×10^6

29. A basketball team has won 50 games of 75 played. The team still has 45 games to play. How many of the games left to play must the team win in order in win 60% of all games played during the season?

(1) 20
(2) 21
(3) 22
(4) 25
(5) 30

30. A rectangle and a triangle have equal areas. The length of the rectangle measures 12 cm and its width measures 8 cm. If the base of the triangle measures 32 cm, what is the measure of the altitude in centimetres?

(1) 6
(2) 8
(3) 9
(4) 12
(5) 16

31. A school has 18 classes with 35 students in each class. In order to reduce class size to 30, how many new classes must be formed?

(1) 2
(2) 3
(3) 5
(4) 6
(5) 8

Item 32 is based on the following graph.

Distribution of expenses for sales of \$240,000 Ace Manufacturing Company

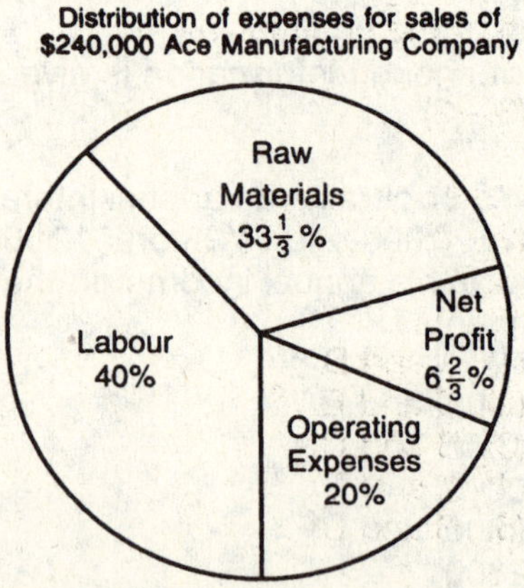

32. How many dollars were spent for labour?

(1) \$4800
(2) \$9600
(3) \$48 000
(4) \$96 000
(5) \$960 000

<u>Item 33</u> is based on the following graph.

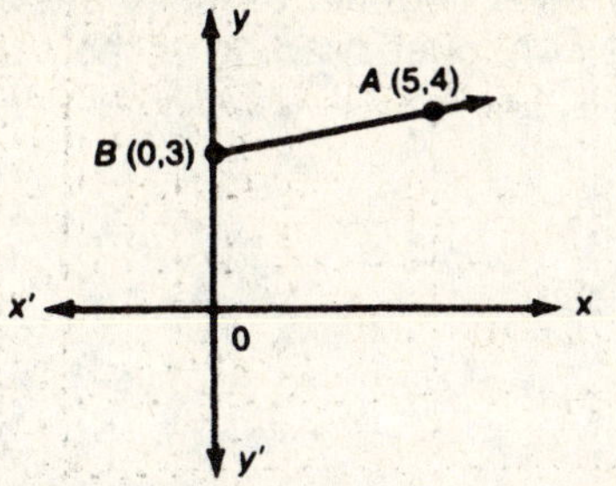

33. What is the slope of the line joining point $A(5,4)$ and point $B(0,3)$?

(1) $\frac{1}{10}$
(2) $\frac{1}{5}$
(3) $\frac{3}{5}$
(4) $\frac{4}{5}$
(5) 5

---

34. Barbara can input one report in twenty minutes and a second report in fifteen minutes. The average time (in hours) for both reports is

(1) $\frac{1}{7}$
(2) $\frac{2}{7}$
(3) $\frac{7}{24}$
(4) $\frac{1}{12}$
(5) $\frac{7}{12}$

35. Given the equation $3x - y = 2$, which of the following pairs of points lie on the graph of the equation?

A. (3, –2)
B. (1, 5)
C. (2, 4)
D. (2, –3)
E. (3, 7)

(1) A and B
(2) C and E
(3) B and C
(4) A and E
(5) B and D

36. If $3x - 1 = 11$, what is the value of $x^2 + x$?

(1) 12
(2) 15
(3) 16
(4) 18
(5) 20

37. A bell rings every 2 hours, a second bell rings every 3 hours, and a third bell rings every 4 hours. If all three bells ring at 9:00 A.M., when will all three bells ring again at the same time?

(1) noon
(2) 6:00 P.M.
(3) 9:00 P.M.
(4) 10 P.M.
(5) Not enough information is given.

38. A family spends 20% of its monthly after-tax income on food, 23% on rent, 42% on other expenses, and saves the balance. If the family saves \$360 per month, what is its monthly after-tax income?

(1) \$2000
(2) \$2200
(3) \$2400
(4) \$2599
(5) \$28800

<u>Item 39</u> is based on the following figure.

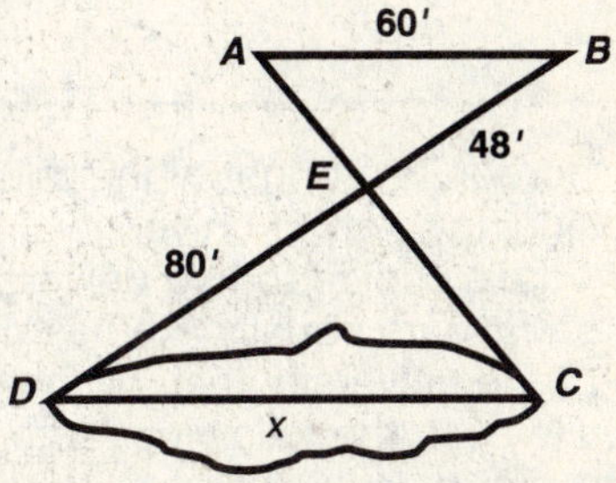

39. In order to measure the distance across a pond (DC), a surveyor takes points A and B so that $\overleftrightarrow{AB}$ is parallel to $\overleftrightarrow{DC}$. If AB = 60 m, EB = 48 m, and ED = 80 m, find DC.

(1) 72 m
(2) 84 m
(3) 96 m
(4) 100 m
(5) Not enough information is given.

---

40. If $x = \frac{1}{a+b}$ then $\frac{3}{x}$ is equal to

(1) $3(a+b)$
(2) $\frac{3}{a+b}$
(3) $\frac{3}{a} + \frac{3}{b}$
(4) $\frac{a+b}{3}$
(5) $\frac{a+b}{3ab}$

41. Each of the numbers below is a solution of the inequality $2x + 3 > 7$ EXCEPT

(1) 5
(2) 4
(3) 3
(4) 10
(5) 0

Item 42 is based on the following figure.

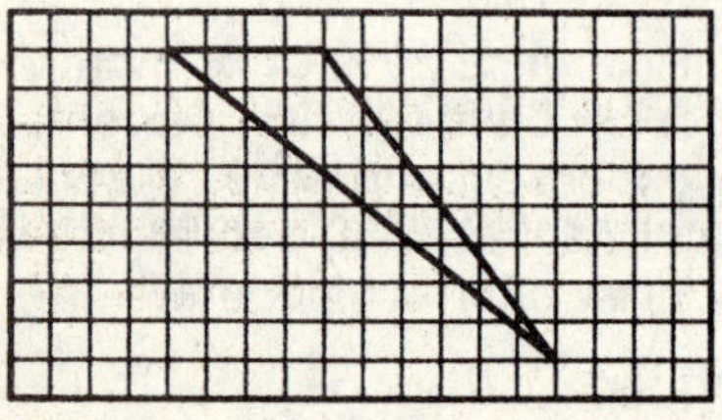

42. What is the area of the triangle in square graph units?

(1) 8
(2) 10
(3) 16
(4) 32
(5) 48

43. David Gordon is a bright high school student planning to go to university. He has narrowed his choice to two universities which he favours equally. He has decided to select the university that will be less costly. He used the following facts to help him arrive at a decision.

UNIVERSITY *A*

Tuition—$9480, Board and Lodging—$6320. Books and incidentals—$1200.

David has been offered a scholarship of $4200 per year.

UNIVERSITY *B*

Tuition—$9200, Board and Lodging—$6150. Books and incidentals—$1200.

David has been offered a scholarship of $3200 per year.

David has also been offered a part time job working in the university library.

What information does David need in order to make a choice?

(1) How many kilometres does he live from each university?
(2) Which university has the better reputation?
(3) How many scholarships does each university grant?
(4) How much can David earn by working in the university library at University *B*?
(5) Which university has better athletic facilities?

44. Maral reads one-third of her book in 2 hours and 42 minutes. How many more hours will it take her to finish the book if she continues reading at the same rate?

(1) 2.7
(2) 5.1
(3) 5.22
(4) 5.4
(5) 8.1

45. A driver covers *x* kilometres the first day, *y* kilometres the second day, and *z* kilometres the third day. The average distance in kilometres covered per day is

(1) $\frac{xyz}{3}$
(2) $\frac{xy+z}{3}$
(3) $x+y+z$
(4) $\frac{x+y+z}{3}$
(5) $3xyz$

46. The diameter of a bundle buggy wheel is 28 cm. How many centimetres does the bundle buggy move when the wheel makes 10 complete revolutions? (Let $\pi = {}^{22}/_{7}$.)

(1) 88
(2) 440
(3) 540
(4) 750
(5) 880

47. After working 4 hours Rosina has made 21 machine parts. At the same rate, which expression below represents what she can accomplish in 7 hours? (Let x represent the number of machine parts Rosina can make in 7 hours.)

(1) $x = \frac{7(21)}{4}$
(2) $x = \frac{7(4)}{21}$
(3) $x = 7(21)$
(4) $x = \frac{4(21)}{7}$
(5) $x = 7(4)\,(21)$

48. A storage box in a form of a rectangular solid has a square base. If V represents the volume of the box, x represents the length of the base, and y represents the height of the box, which of the following equations expresses the relationship among V, x, and y?

(1) $V = 2xy$
(2) $V = xy^2$
(3) $V = 2xy^2$
(4) $V = x^2y$
(5) $V = x + xy$

49. In her will, Ms. Adams left $\frac{1}{4}$ of her estate to her husband and divided the balance between her son and daughter. If the son received $36 000 as his share, what was the total value of the estate?

(1) $45 000
(2) $72 000
(3) $80 000
(4) $90 000
(5) Not enough information is given.

50. One month the Gorman family spent a total of $1044 for food and rent. If the outlay for rent was three times as much as the outlay for food, how much was spent for food during that month?

(1) $261
(2) $348
(3) $350
(4) $360
(5) Not enough information is given.

51. At a dance, the ratio of the number of boys to the number of girls was 5:4. If 48 girls were at the dance, how many boys were at the dance?

(1) 25
(2) 36
(3) 52
(4) 55
(5) 60

52. (1)(2)(3)(4)(5)(6)(7)(8)(9)(10)(11) = 39 916 800
(12)(11)(10)(9)(8)(7)(6)(5) = ?

(1) 9 979 200
(2) 19 958 400
(3) 39 916 800
(4) 79 833 600
(5) 479 001 600

53. A map has a scale of 1 cm to 80 km. Lakeville and Fulton are 4.5 cm apart on the map. What is the actual distance between Lakeville and Fulton, in kilometres?

(1) 190
(2) 360
(3) 310
(4) 325
(5) 350

54. The regular price of a pair of pants is y dollars. If the price is reduced by 20%, which of the following expressions indicates the cost of 3 pairs of pants?

(1) $\frac{4}{5}y$
(2) $\frac{3}{5}y$
(3) $3(\frac{4}{5}y)$
(4) $3(\frac{3}{4}y)$
(5) $3(\frac{1}{5}y)$

55. Mr. Downs is on a diet. For breakfast and lunch he consumes 40% of his allowable number of calories. If he still has 1200 calories left for the day, what is his daily allowance in calories?

(1) 800
(2) 1200
(3) 1500
(4) 1800
(5) 2000

56. The afternoon classes in a school begin at 1 P.M. and end at 3:52 P.M. There are four class periods with 4 minutes between classes. How many minutes are there in each class period?

(1) 39
(2) 40
(3) 59
(4) 60
(5) 64

END OF EXAMINATION

ANSWER KEYS, SUMMARIES OF RESULTS, AND SELF-APPRAISAL CHARTS

TEST 1: The Language Arts, Writing (Writing Skills) Test, Part I/Page 845

I. CHECK YOUR ANSWERS, using the following answer key:

1. **2**	12. **5**	23. **5**	34. **4**	45. **4**
2. **3**	13. **3**	24. **1**	35. **4**	46. **4**
3. **4**	14. **4**	25. **4**	36. **4**	47. **5**
4. **2**	15. **1**	26. **4**	37. **4**	48. **1**
5. **1**	16. **4**	27. **4**	38. **1**	49. **5**
6. **4**	17. **4**	28. **5**	39. **5**	50. **2**
7. **5**	18. **4**	29. **1**	40. **3**	51. **5**
8. **5**	19. **2**	30. **5**	41. **4**	52. **4**
9. **1**	20. **1**	31. **3**	42. **3**	53. **3**
10. **5**	21. **1**	32. **2**	43. **4**	54. **1**
11. **4**	22. **5**	33. **5**	44. **5**	55. **5**

II. SCORE YOURSELF:

Number correct:

Excellent	50–55
Good	44–49
Fair	38–43

III. EVALUATE YOUR SCORE: Did you get at least 38 correct answers? If not, you need more practice for the Writing Skills, Part I Test. In any event, you can improve your performance to Excellent or Good by analyzing your errors.

IV. ANALYZE YOUR ERRORS: To determine your areas of weakness, list the number of correct answers you had under each of the following categories (which correspond to the content areas of the Writing Skills, Part I Test), and compare your score with the average scores in the right-hand column. Review the answer analysis section beginning on page 904 for each of the questions you got wrong, and give yourself more practice in your weak areas with the appropriate material in Chapter 4 before taking the actual GED examination.

CONTENT AREAS	ITEMS	YOUR SCORE	AVERAGE SCORE
Sentence Structure	7, 9, 13, 15, 17–19, 21, 25, 27–28, 34–36, 43–44, 47, 50, 54		13
Usage	1, 3, 5, 14, 24, 31–32		5
Mechanics			
Spelling	6, 16, 29, 37, 45, 52		4
Punctuation	2, 11, 20, 22, 33, 38, 40–42, 46		7
Capitalization	4, 26, 48, 53		3
No correction	8, 10, 12, 23, 30, 39, 49, 51, 55		6

Total ______

TEST 2: The Social Studies Test/Page 856

I. CHECK YOUR ANSWERS, using the following answer key:

1. **4**	14. **1**	27. **2**	40. **2**	53. **3**
2. **5**	15. **4**	28. **4**	41. **3**	54. **4**
3. **1**	16. **5**	29. **1**	42. **3**	55. **2**
4. **5**	17. **3**	30. **2**	43. **5**	56. **1**
5. **4**	18. **3**	31. **4**	44. **1**	57. **4**
6. **2**	19. **5**	32. **2**	45. **4**	58. **5**
7. **4**	20. **1**	33. **3**	46. **2**	59. **3**
8. **1**	21. **4**	34. **1**	47. **1**	60. **4**
9. **2**	22. **5**	35. **5**	48. **1**	61. **5**
10. **3**	23. **2**	36. **3**	49. **4**	62. **4**
11. **1**	24. **3**	37. **3**	50. **1**	63. **4**
12. **5**	25. **3**	38. **5**	51. **5**	64. **1**
13. **2**	26. **5**	39. **1**	52. **1**	

II. SCORE YOURSELF:

	Number correct:
Excellent	57–64
Good	51–56
Fair	45–50

III. EVALUATE YOUR SCORE: Did you get at least 45 correct answers? If not, you need more practice for the Social Studies Test. In any event, you can improve your performance to Excellent or Good by analyzing your errors.

IV. ANALYZE YOUR ERRORS: To determine your specific weaknesses, list the number of correct answers you had under each of the following categories (which correspond to the content areas of the Social Studies Test), and compare your score with the average scores specified in the right-hand column. Review the answer analysis section beginning on page 906 for each of the questions you got wrong, and give yourself more practice in your weak areas with the appropriate material in Chapter 6 (including the "Glossary of Social Studies Terms") before taking the actual GED examination.

CONTENT AREAS	ITEMS	YOUR SCORE	AVERAGE SCORE
Political Science	1–6, 9, 24–26, 29–30, 40, 52–54, 56–57, 61–63		13
Economics	10–12, 14–16, 31, 33–34, 43, 47		8
History	7–8, 13, 17–19, 41, 48–49, 55, 58		9
Geography	20, 22–23, 27–28, 32, 50–51, 59–60		8
Behavioural Science	21, 35–39, 42, 44–46, 64		8

Total ________

TEST 3: The Science Test/Page 869

I. CHECK YOUR ANSWERS, using the following answer key:

1. **4**	15. **4**	29. **5**	43. **1**	57. **3**
2. **4**	16. **2**	30. **1**	44. **5**	58. **3**
3. **1**	17. **2**	31. **3**	45. **2**	59. **4**
4. **5**	18. **2**	32. **2**	46. **3**	60. **2**
5. **1**	19. **5**	33. **4**	47. **3**	61. **5**
6. **5**	20. **1**	34. **4**	48. **4**	62. **3**
7. **4**	21. **2**	35. **3**	49. **5**	63. **1**
8. **2**	22. **5**	36. **3**	50. **3**	64. **3**
9. **4**	23. **3**	37. **3**	51. **3**	65. **4**
10. **1**	24. **5**	38. **2**	52. **2**	66. **4**
11. **3**	25. **1**	39. **2**	53. **5**	
12. **4**	26. **4**	40. **4**	54. **2**	
13. **3**	27. **2**	41. **4**	55. **1**	
14. **1**	28. **2**	42. **1**	56. **4**	

II. SCORE YOURSELF:

Number correct:

Excellent	______ 60–66
Good	______ 49–59
Fair	______ 40–48

III. EVALUATE YOUR SCORE: Did you get at least 40 correct answers? If not, you need more practice for the Science Test. In any event, you can improve your performance to Excellent or Good by analyzing your errors.

IV. ANALYZE YOUR ERRORS: To determine your specific weaknesses, encircle the number of each question you got wrong. This will reveal the specific science area that needs emphasis in planning your study program. After studying the answer analysis section beginning on page 909 for each of the questions you got wrong, list the terms that you feel need further explanation and study them in the "Glossary of Scientific Terms" beginning on page 362. Then give yourself more practice in your weak areas with the appropriate material in Chapter 7 before taking the actual GED examination.

CONTENT AREAS	ITEMS	YOUR SCORE	AVERAGE SCORE
Biology	1–14, 33, 34, 40–56		23
Earth Science	15–17, 27–32, 62–65		9
Chemistry	18–20, 35, 66		3
Physics	21–26, 36–39, 57–61		10

Total ______

TEST 4: Language Arts, Reading (Interpreting Literature and the Arts)/Page 880

I. CHECK YOUR ANSWERS, using the following answer key:

1. **3**	10. **3**	19. **5**	28. **4**	37. **5**
2. **4**	11. **2**	20. **5**	29. **1**	38. **4**
3. **1**	12. **5**	21. **2**	30. **3**	39. **5**
4. **3**	13. **1**	22. **4**	31. **1**	40. **4**
5. **1**	14. **4**	23. **3**	32. **3**	41. **1**
6. **5**	15. **4**	24. **1**	33. **1**	42. **4**
7. **2**	16. **3**	25. **3**	34. **4**	43. **5**
8. **3**	17. **4**	26. **4**	35. **5**	44. **4**
9. **4**	18. **1**	27. **2**	36. **1**	45. **3**

II. SCORE YOURSELF:

Number correct:

Excellent	41–45
Good	36–40
Fair	31–35

III. EVALUATE YOUR SCORE: Did you get at least 31 correct answers? If not, you need more practice for the Test on Interpreting Literature and the Arts. You can improve your performance to Excellent or Good by analyzing your errors.

IV. ANALYZE YOUR ERRORS: To determine your specific weaknesses, list the number of correct answers you had under each of the following categories and compare your score with the average scores in the right-hand column. After studying the answer analysis section beginning on page 912 for each of the questions you answered incorrectly, study the material in the section on *Basic Reading Skills* and the section *Basics on Reading Literature—Prose*, *Poetry*, *Drama* in Chapter 8 as well as the "Glossary of Literary Terms" to strengthen your weak areas before taking the actual GED examination.

READING SKILLS	ITEMS	YOUR SCORE	AVERAGE SCORE
Locating the Main Idea	1, 12, 15, 25–26, 30		4
Finding Details	5–6, 10, 20, 22, 28, 32–33, 35, 37–39, 42–44		10
Inferring Meaning	2, 14, 19		2
Making Inferences	3, 4, 7, 9, 13, 17–18, 21, 24, 29, 34, 36, 40, 45		10
Determining Tone and Mood	8, 23, 27, 31, 41		3
Inferring Character	16		1
Inferring Setting	11		1

Total ________

Now to see how your scores in the content areas of Interpreting Literature and the Arts Test compare with the average scores in the right-hand column, list your score for each of the following:

CONTENT AREAS	ITEMS	YOUR SCORE	AVERAGE SCORE
Popular Literature	6–25, 31–35		17
Classical Literature	1–5, 26–30		7
Commentary	36–45		7

Total ______

LITERARY FORMS	ITEMS	YOUR SCORE	AVERAGE SCORE
Prose Fiction	1–15		11
Prose Nonfiction	31–35		3
Prose Nonfiction (Commentary)	36–45		7
Poetry	16–25		7
Drama	26–30		3

Total ______

Note: While Commentary on the Arts is a content area in itself, the commentary, as written, is in the form of prose nonfiction.

TEST 5: The Mathematics Test/Page 889

I. CHECK YOUR ANSWERS, using the following answer key. The number following each question number is the correct answer. The numbers in parentheses (the *Mathematics Answer Key*) refer to the sections in the Mathematics Review (Chapter 9) which explain the necessary mathematics principles. A more detailed explanation of all answers follows in the Answer Analysis section beginning on page 913.

1. **4**	15. **3**	29. **3**	43. **4**
2. **3**	16. **4**	30. **1**	44. **4**
3. **2**	17. **3**	31. **2**	45. **4**
4. **1**	18. **3**	32. **4**	46. **5**
5. **4**	19. **4**	33. **2**	47. **1**
6. **3**	20. **4**	34. **3**	48. **4**
7. **4**	21. **2**	35. **2**	49. **5**
8. **4**	22. **2**	36. **5**	50. **1**
9. **4**	23. **4**	37. **3**	51. **5**
10. **3**	24. **1**	38. **3**	52. **2**
11. **1**	25. **2**	39. **4**	53. **2**
12. **4**	26. **2**	40. **3**	54. **3**
13. **4**	27. **3**	41. **1**	55. **5**
14. **2**	28. **5**	42. **3**	56. **2**

II. SCORE YOURSELF:

Number correct:

Excellent	______ 51–56
Good	______ 44–50
Fair	______ 38–43

III. EVALUATE YOUR SCORE: Did you get at least 38 correct answers? If not, you need more practice for the Mathematics Test. In any event, you can improve your performance to Excellent or Good by analyzing your errors.

IV. ANALYZE YOUR ERRORS: To determine your specific weaknesses, list the number of correct answers you had under each of the following categories (which correspond to the *Mathematics Answer Key* just discussed in item I), and compare your score with the average scores specified in the right-hand column. After studying the answer analysis section beginning on page 913 for each of the questions you got wrong, give yourself more practice in your weak areas with the appropriate material in Chapter 9 before taking the actual GED examination. (Note again the *Mathematics Answer Key* explanation in item I.)

CONTENT AREAS	ITEMS	YOUR SCORE	AVERAGE SCORE
I. Arithmetic	1–3, 5, 7, 9, 12–13, 15–17, 19–20, 22, 23, 25, 27–29, 31–32, 37–38, 43, 44, 49, 52, 53, 55, 56		18
II. Algebra	6, 10–12, 14, 21, 24, 27, 29, 35, 36, 41, 45, 47–48, 50–52, 54, 56		11
III. Geometry	4, 8, 9, 17, 18, 26, 30, 33, 39, 40, 42, 46		8

Total ______

YOUR TOTAL GED SCORE

The Writing Skills Test	______
The Social Studies Test	______
The Science Test	______
The Literature and the Arts Test	______
The Mathematics Test	______
Total	______

ANSWER ANALYSIS

TEST 1: The Language Arts, Writing (Writing Skills) Test, Part I/Page 845

1. **2** *Are enrolling* is necessary to parallel *are recognizing*.
2. **3** A comma is used after an introductory clause.
3. **4** The plural verb, *call*, must be used because the plural subject is *techniques*.
4. **2** A specific place is capitalized.
5. **1** You cannot shift pronouns which refer to the same person in the same sentence. Use either *you* or *one* throughout the sentence.
6. **4** The correct spelling is *government's*.
7. **5** The second sentence is a result of the first, so the conjunction *so* must be used.
8. **5** No correction is necessary.
9. **1** The original is the best way.
10. **5** No correction is necessary.
11. **4** The period should be placed within the quotation marks.
12. **5** No correction is necessary.
13. **3** *Because* is used since the second sentence is the reason for the first.
14. **4** *Has* must be inserted to insure parallel structure with *is six inches high, is made of leather*.
15. **1** The original is the best way.
16. **4** The correct spelling is *materials*.
17. **4** This is necessary to avoid a sentence fragment beginning after *waist strap*.
18. **4** A plural is needed since *sleeping bag and its two accessories* is plural and is in the predicate nominative.
19. **2** The second sentence is an example of the *tent* mentioned in the first sentence, so *such as* is used.
20. **1** Commas are used to separate items in a series.
21. **1** The original is the best way.
22. **5** No correction is necessary.
23. **5** No correction is necessary.
24. **1** The correlatives *not only* and *but also* must be followed by parallel elements.
25. **4** This is necessary to prevent a run-on sentence.
26. **4** Holidays are capitalized.
27. **4** The relative clause is used as an adjective modifying *feathers*.
28. **5** This is necessary to avoid a run-on sentence.
29. **1** The correct spelling in this sentence is *affects*.
30. **5** No correction is necessary.
31. **3** The plural verb form *are* is needed to agree in number with *dwellings*.
32. **2** *In finding* is necessary for parallel structure with *in securing*.
33. **5** No correction is necessary.
34. **4** *Concerns* must follow since the subject is *housing*.
35. **4** A prepositional phrase is used to describe *are upgrading*.
36. **4** The sense of the sentence requires the verb *will have* after the subject *nation*.
37. **4** The correct spelling is *separately*.
38. **1** Commas are used to set off phrases inserted into a sentence.
39. **5** No correction is necessary.
40. **3** An apostrophe is needed to show possession.
41. **4** Hyphens are needed to join the parts of the adjective *hit-and-run*.
42. **3** A comma is used to set off items in a series.
43. **4** The semicolon is needed to prevent a sentence fragment starting *The larger.*
44. **5** The subject *feature* requires the verb *covers*. The feature does not cause losses.
45. **4** The correct spelling is *benefit*.
46. **4** A question mark is used after a sentence which asks a question.
47. **5** The second sentence follows as a reason for the first.

50. **2** The subject, *four agencies*, is followed by *may be*.
51. **5** No correction is necessary.
52. **4** The correct spelling is *assistance*.
53. **3** *Federally funded* is not a proper adjective.
54. **1** *Here is* is needed to change the fragment into a sentence.
55. **5** No correction is necessary.

TEST 1: The Language Arts, Writing (Writing Skills) Test, Part II/Page 855

SAMPLE ESSAYS

For Canadian youth:

Canada can well take pride in its youth.

Never have young Canadians achieved more than they are achieving now. At the high school level, Provincial Scholarships are being awarded to the elite of young high school graduates. Awards are being made to those young scientists and mathematicians who hold great promise of being tomorrow's leaders in science and technology. Competition for entry into the country's finest universities is intense. Most university graduates go on to study for graduate degrees.

In addition to educational achievement, today's youth is in the forefront of programs designed to improve the quality of life around the world. There are the scout movements, the 4H clubs and Junior Achievement, among many others. Canadian youth are in the vanguard of movements which seek to advance peace. Our youth are idealistic.

In business and technology, young Canadians are being given increasingly important positions as managers and executives. They are, in the best sense of the term, young upward mobile professionals (yuppies).

In sports, the prowess of young athletes is constantly being demonstrated, particularly in the Olympic Games. In recent years, young people like Elvis Stoyko have been leaders in the world of Olympic Figure Skating.

In the entertainment media, future leaders are more youthful, witness the success of on-air personalities like Avi Lewis.

Young Canadians are taking an active part in every part of our country's life.

Yes, indeed, Canada can well take pride in its youth.

Summary of reasons *for* Canadian youth:

1. Canadian youth is achieving at a high educational level.
2. Canadian youth is in the forefront of groups which seek to improve the quality of life in Canada and abroad.
3. Canadian youth is succeeding in business and technology.
4. Canadian youth is outstanding in sports.
5. Canadian youth leads in the field of entertainment.

Against Canadian youth:

> Canada has good reasons to be concerned about its youth.
>
> Never before have juveniles been guilty of such heinous crimes. The term youthful offender, has become part of our daily language, and the government is deliberating altering the laws to change the treatment of youth involved in crime.
>
> Thousands of young Canadians have fallen prey to drugs, from marijuana to crack, from "coke" to heroin. With addiction comes the need to turn to crime to support their habit.
>
> In education, high school dropout rates have reached 30 to 40% in urban areas and special programs have not yet stemmed this tide.
>
> Even among the more privileged of our youth there has been a decline in the work ethic. Youth today seeks instant gratification in all its activities, from its spending habits to its penchant for instant-on television.
>
> Traditional values have been flouted by sexual mores that allow for cohabitation without marriage and a casual approach to smoking results in severe health problems.
>
> This generation has been called "laid back," the "now" generation, and deservedly so. In times of plenty, it has chosen to abandon traditional values to pursue its own selfish goals.
>
> Indeed, Canada has good reason to be concerned for the future of its youth.

Summary of reasons *against* Canadian youth:

1. Younger and younger Canadians are engaged in crime.
2. Thousands of young Canadians are drug addicts.
3. Many young Canadians are school dropouts.
4. Privileged young Canadians seek instant gratification.
5. Traditional sexual mores have been flouted.
6. Traditional values have been abandoned.

TEST 2: The Social Studies Test/Page 856

1. **4** Because of overfishing by domestic and foreign fleets offshore fishing was banned and communities declined.
2. **5** Canada was not wealthy enough to subsidize farmers to survive a grain price war unlike the United States and the European Community.
3. **1** The passage describes Canada's difficulty in competing in world markets, in such areas as fishing and agriculture.
4. **5** The Prime Minister is appointed by the Governor General acting on behalf of the monarch. By convention, it is always the leader of the party that can command the majority of support in the House of Commons who is appointed.
5. **4** In the United States there is a separation of the executive and legislative functions of government so the chief executive and Cabinet would not be found in the legislature as they are in Canada.
6. **2** Canada and the United States are both democracies but their forms of government are not precisely the same.
7. **4** Of the choices given, the United States has direct involvement with Europe only in NATO, a military alliance created in 1949 as a shield against further communist expansion or aggression. Under the North Atlantic Pact, a mutual defense agreement, an attack on any NATO member is to be considered an attack on all.
8. **1** The exaggerated, uncomfortable and desperate position of Uncle Sam is meant to be critical. Note the arms crossed just below the shoulders, the left leg raised to touch Europe, dark rings under the eyes, and the outer lines beyond the globe and human figure showing both to be unstable. The implication is that the United States cannot continue in this position.
9. **2** Henry David Thoreau expressed these ideas in opposition to the United States' involvement in a war against Mexico in 1846–48. Similar sentiments have been expressed in recent times by Gandhi and by Martin Luther King, Jr. in advocating civil disobedience. Like Thoreau, they were imprisoned for their actions.

10. **3** Draw a vertical line from the point on the axis for 50–54-year-olds to intersect the graph line representing the suicide rate for females. From that point, a horizontal line to the left axis will show a rate of "approximately 10 per 100 000 population."
11. **1** The focus here must be on a statement that is "not valid." The key here is simply to note the shape of the graph. Neither of the graph lines increases "steadily with age." For males there are considerable fluctuations with age; with females there is actually a decrease in the suicide rate for the oldest group.
12. **5** The focus here must be on a statement that is "true." Note that the highest rate for females is just slightly over 10 per 100 000, whereas the rate for almost all of the male categories exceeds 25 per 100 000. If you were inclined to consider choice 4 remember that, while there were approximately 9 victims per 100 000 in each group, we do not know from the graph what size the groups are. This choice refers to the same number of victims and not to the same suicide rate.
13. **2** The quotation is a perversion of the original poem which reads "Give me your tired, your poor, your huddled masses," and which is inscribed on the Statue of Liberty. By changing it to welcome only the educated, the cartoonist is critical of the United States for not accepting the poor.
14. **1** The second paragraph points out the corporate diversification (by merger) will continue to be necessary to meet new competitors.
15. **4** It is mentioned that a company can get qualified technical manpower only by acquiring another company.
16. **5** The passage emphasizes future, rather than established, competitors as creating a motivation to merge.
17. **3** The author refers to only negative aspects of non-Anglo-Saxon immigrants.
18. **3** The author would not be in favour of any policy that would provide easier access to Canada for non-Anglo-Saxons. He would seek to severely restrict access to Canada.
19. **5** The Immigration Laws reflect other aspects of Canadian life that prohibit any discrimination against the members of minority groups.
20. **1** The world is becoming a "global village" as a result of this aspect of the Industrial Revolution.
21. **4** The nuclear family, typical in the modern industrial city, contains only the parents and their unmarried children. The extended family of more traditional, agricultural societies includes grandparents, parents, children (both married and unmarried), and often such dependents as the wife's sister *all* under one roof. In the extended family, each member has clearly defined roles, and family ties are usually much stronger than in the nuclear one.
22. **5** The 65+ age group has grown by almost 300% between 1871 and 1991; from just 3.66% of the population in 1871 to 11.61% of the population in 1991.
23. **2** The greatest proportional change is in persons over age 60, a group of vital importance of those administering the social security system. Typically, more benefits are paid out to older people.
24. **3** The focus here is on the different types of work that anthropologists do, that is, the scope of their work.
25. **3** While all anthropology is concerned with the study of cultures, its various branches emphasize different aspects of the work.
26. **5** The excavation of sites such as that of the early Norse settlements in L'Anse Aux Meadows in Newfoundland is the work of archaeologists.
27. **2** Scale is the ratio between distance as shown on a map and the actual distance on the earth.
28. **4** The passage states that a compass rose shows direction.
29. **1** The action of the grade six students made them a very effective consumer action group.
30. **2** It is sometimes said that our freedom to act as we please stops where the other person's nose begins. In this case it was judged that the freedom of the press endangered the common good and it was ruled that it was in the public interest that the journalist reveal his sources. This shows that some rights are subject to limitations.
31. **4** An increased balance of payments deficit would indicate a worsening economic picture. This would hardly be something that Macdonald would want to claim for the National Policy.
32. **2** Those who favour development of new energy sources tend to give a low priority to the need to protect our environment and to conserve our natural resources.

33. **3** Model B shows an economy which could lead to depression if supply and demand are not brought into balance. A balance could result from a decrease in income taxes, which would increase consumer demand.
34. **1** In 1929–39, there was a depression in Canada, with huge supply and little demand because of high unemployment. This is depicted in model A.
35. **5** The Indian population was carried over from the time before Columbus discovered the Americas.
36. **3** North America had no role in settling or colonizing Latin America.
37. **3** In the first sentence, the author acknowledges that his findings will be "highly distasteful to many."
38. **5** The author states his concern for truth as discovered through reason.
39. **1** The author states that man may be hopeful for a "still higher destiny" because he has already risen to the top of the organic scale.
40. **2** Lobbying is the use of politically experienced people to influence lawmakers, usually by providing information, testifying at hearings or suggesting needed legislation.
41. **3** Contributing to peacekeeping forces has been an important way that Canada has demonstrated its commitment to the peaceful settlement of disputes.
42. **3** Sexism, the exploitation and domination of one sex by the other, more traditionally of women by men, is being countered by the women's liberation movement. Women, on the basis of preference and ability, can now enter occupations previously closed to them.
43. **5** As the supply of corn increases, the selling price decreases (assuming the demand for corn to be stable).
44. **1** The author says modern communication makes it easy to share views.
45. **4** The author says the earth may be organized in tribes.
46. **2** The author says people sharing views are a clan.
47. **1** The tax is graduated because it divides the taxed population into income groups with increasing tax percentage rates by stages for groups with increasing incomes.
48. **1** Imperialism is the policy of acquiring colonies or of establishing political and economic control of foreign areas.
49. **4** Nations cooperating to prevent any one country from becoming dominant is a definition of the term *balance of power*.
50. **1** Kitchener, Ontario, grew at a rate of more than 75%, faster than any other city listed.
51. **4** The average growth rate in Alberta's two major cities, Edmonton and Calgary, was more than 57%, which exceeds the average growth of the five Ontario cities which was second largest.
52. **1** Speaker B who was from the West was presenting the view that conscription could be viewed as more than simply the drafting of soldiers to fight. Conscription, he pointed out, might also mean the conscription of wealth. Since this was not happening, the poorer classes were waging the war while business interests benefited from the economic opportunities it provided.
53. **3** By emphasizing that two million French Canadians were opposed to conscription, speaker C was alluding to the possibility of civil strife in Canada.
54. **4** The statements of all four speakers refer to the question of conscription, which is compulsory military service.
55. **2** The point of the student's question focuses attention on the role of women in history. For example, in all of the famous portraits depicting the negotiations for Confederation, there is not a single woman, hence the question "Were there no founding mothers?"
56. **1** This simply requires you to count the number of years in which each of the parties held a majority of seats.
57. **4** In the period since the end of World War II, control of the House of Commons has always rested with the Liberals and the Progressive Conservatives. In spite of the birth of new parties in the 1993 election and the virtual elimination of the Progressive Conservatives, we will not know if this is part of a long term trend until there have been a few more elections.
58. **5** Newspapers, and today other news media, often dehumanize the enemy simply through the descriptions they use. Historically, this has been an important function of propaganda.

59. **3** The projections show that the proportion of the population aged 65 and over will increase greatly in the next forty years. Therefore, much greater attention will have to be paid to them including a review of policies concerning the elderly.
60. **4** Since most people retire or continue as part-time workers after age 65, there will be a decrease in the percentage of full-time workers.
61. **3** Health care is a service provided by doctors and other health professionals and hence is classified as tertiary production.
62. **1** Agriculture, fishing, mining, and forestry all involve the direct use of natural products; therefore, New Brunswick relies mainly on primary production.
63. **4** The situation described here changed greatly with the industrial revolution with workers moving to factories rather than pursuing their crafts at home.
64. **1** Women and minority groups still face discrimination in the job market despite the fact that some progress has been made to secure for them equal pay for equal work.

TEST 3: The Science Test/Page 869

1. **4** Diffusion is the process whereby molecules of substances tend to intermingle, in this case, as they pass through the placenta.
2. **4** Refer to the statement in the opening sentence of the passage.
3. **1** Digested food and oxygen pass *to* the embryo from the mother's bloodstream. No blood as such is exchanged. Wastes from the metabolic activities of the embryo are passed into the mother's bloodstream.
4. **5** The first sentence indicates that sodium chloride assumes special significance in the regulation of water exchange in the organism.
5. **1** The water in all the digestive juices is reabsorbed into the blood in the small intestine. Without this process, we would have to replace all this water.
6. **5** The opening sentence of the passage states that sodium chloride is the largest constituent of the mineral matter of the blood.
7. **4** The digested food is dissolved in water and is absorbed through the intestinal wall.
8. **2** Since the normal number of chromosomes in human body cells is now considered 46, the number of chromosomes in the sperms and eggs would be one-half that number.
9. **4** Body cells have twice the number of chromosomes as sex cells. In fertilization (union of sex cells) the normal number of chromosomes is restored.
10. **1** By definition.
11. **3** The passage refers to malignancies as illustrations of abnormal cell division.
12. **4** Most protozoa do not lend themselves to fossilization. Only those with shells surrounding the cell will fossilize. These radiolaria have shells of silicon. Others have shells of calcium carbonate.
13. **3** Anthropologists deal with the origin, development, ethnic groups, customs, and beliefs of humanity. Protozoologists are mainly interested in live, one-celled animals. Archaeologists study the people, customs, and life of ancient times. Geologists deal with the earth's crust, the layers of which it is composed, and their history. Zoologists are biologists concerned with the animal kingdom.
14. **1** The closing sentence of the passage summarizes the basic cause of the ice ages.
15. **4** The temperature of the air is given on the thermometer marked *B*. The scale is marked in units of 10°, and the mercury has risen to the fourth subdivision between 20° and 30°, which means that the reading is 28°.
16. **2** The temperature of the ice-water mixture is lower than the temperature of the air in the box. Therefore, the air near the glass cup will be cooled below the temperature of the surrounding air. At this lower temperature, the amount of moisture the air can hold decreases. The droplets of water represent the excess moisture that has condensed out of the air.
17. **2** The dew point temperature is the temperature at which the air becomes saturated (as shown by the water droplets). Since the temperature of the air near the cup is the same as that of the ice-water mixture, the reading of 23°C is the dewpoint temperature.
18. **2** A change from the gaseous phase to the liquid phase is called condensation. A change from the liquid phase to the gaseous phase is called evaporation. A change from the solid phase to the liquid phase is called melting or fusion.

19. **5** The passage says that naphthalane, for example, vapourizes easily because of small intermolecular forces.
20. **1** The definition of sublimation is given in the closing sentence of the passage.
21. **2** Newton's Laws pertain to bodies in motion. According to Archimedes' Principle, when a body sinks, its weight is greater than the buoyant force or weight of liquid that it displaces. Einstein gave us a law that expresses mathematically the relationship between matter and energy. Galileo experimented with falling bodies. Boyle's law deals with the relationship between the volume of a gas and the pressure exerted on it.
22. **5** A body will rise to the surface if the buoyancy is greater than its weight. At the surface, the amount submerged will be just enough to displace 100 kilograms of water.
23. **3** The weight of water wings or lifesaving jackets is negligible compared with the increase in volume to the wearer. According to Archimedes' Principle, we can increase the tendency to float either by decreasing only the weight of the body or by increasing its volume.
24. **5** The passage opens with the statement that water is a good conductor of sound.
25. **1** Sonar makes use of high-frequency sounds, which are sent out and then reflected from underwater objects.
26. **4** It takes half of the total time, or three seconds, for the sound wave from the ship to reach the sea floor. Since sound travels at the rate of 1400 metres a second through water, it will travel a distance of 1440×3, or 4320 metres to the bottom of the sea before its echoes will start to return.
27. **2** The slope of the land is greatest at point *B*.
28. **2** Sediment is deposited as the particles flow down and lose kinetic energy.
29. **5** Colloidal-size particles are carried as a fine suspension in water. They tend to be deposited only when the water stops moving. As a river flows into an ocean, the largest particles will be deposited first. As the water continues to slow down, finer and finer material settles out. At a point near the coast (point *E*), the finest suspended material will settle out.
30. **1** Observe that there is almost no change in temperature between the months of January and February. The temperature in January is –5°C and in February it is just above –5°C.
31. **3** In September the average temperature was between 15°C and 20°C and can be estimated to be close to 16°C. The precipitation for September was between 60 mm and 80 mm and can be estimated to be 68 mm.
32. **2** The graph for temperature shows a pronounced rise in the summer months, while the bars for moisture are all about the same size.
33. **4** Without bright petals, the flowers could not attract insects and could be pollinated only by wind.
34. **4** Since plants produce oxygen, the level might drop because there are not enough of them. However, animals use the oxygen, so too many fishes would also lower the oxygen level.
35. **3** Since alkalis have a high pH, adding an alkali will raise the pH of the soil. Choices (2) and (5) add acid, thus lowering the pH. Pure water could raise the pH, but never higher than pH 7. The tap water has the same pH as the soil, so it would make no change at all.
36. **3** For a plane mirror, every point of the image is as far behind the mirror as the corresponding point of the object is in front. This is indicated in the sketch. Note that Choice (3) closely points in the same direction as the image.

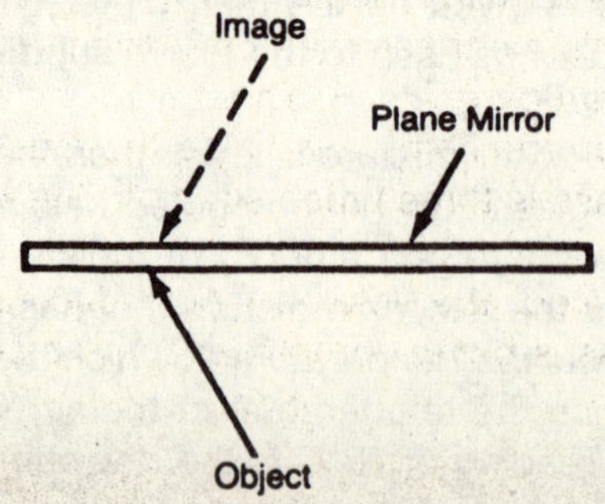

37. **3** The car is going at constant speed in a straight line, so there is no unbalanced force on it. In Choices (1) and (2), the object starts at rest and picks up speed. Choice (4) is a change of direction, which requires an unbalanced force. Choice (5) is wrong because a car in neutral will surely slow down.

38. **2** While overheating of a device is probably not good, the current continues to flow through it and the circuit is not broken.

39. **2** All of the listed properties of light are true, but only one of them explains why the shadow conforms to the shape of the object. Straight lines from the lamp to the wall are blocked by the object to form the shadow.

40. **4** After repeating the writing of the calendar year on various documents for a year it becomes automatic, and so without thinking the error is made in the early days of the new year.

41. **4** Habit formation leads to efficiency. This explains why the names were written neatly and in greater number with the normal method.

42. **1** The brain is not involved in reflex acts. A reflex is a simple, quick, automatic act that involves the neurons and the spinal cord.

43. **1** See question 42.

44. **5** Solving a crossword puzzle involves the higher senses of memory and reasoning.

45. **2** Nest building is a complex activity, involving finding materials and constructing the nest. The robin does it right the first time, even though it has never seen a nest.

46. **3** On previous occasions when the baby cried adult attention was forthcoming. The infant associated crying with getting attention, even though the original crying was in response to pain.

47. **3** All training of animals is the result of conditioning. The dolphin associated the reward (food) with the performance of the trick.

48. **4** Dotting i's and crossing t's has been learned by extensive practice, forming a habit that is hard to disobey.

49. **5** The higher senses are involved in studying and remembering.

50. **3** This is an important observation that led to further research.

51. **3** This find established that sugar attracted the flies.

52. **2** This procedure provided a control group for the experiment.

53. **5** The suggestion is open to question but is unrelated to this problem.

54. **2** This is a good description of the method used.

55. **1** There are a great many problems associated with the mysteries of the pancreas, which would be attacked only in a long series of experiments.

56. **4** There is no direct evidence that human diabetes is related to the results of the experiments on dogs, but the finding of sugar in the urine points strongly in that direction.

57. **3** Use the formula:

$$\text{Density} = \frac{\text{mass}}{\text{volume}} = \frac{24 \text{ grams}}{8 \text{ cm}^3} = 3 \text{ grams/cm}^3$$

58. **3** The diagram indicates that the density of sample *B* is 3 g/cm^3. If the sample were split in half, the density would remain the same. The density of a sample is the ratio of its volume. When the sample is cut in half, both the mass and the volume of the sample are also reduced by half. As a result, the density remains the same.

59. **4** The mass and volume for different samples of a given substance are directly proportional. This relationship is illustrated by graph 4. The density of all samples of that substance will be the same. If the mass of one sample is twice the mass of another, the volume will also be twice as great. If the mass is three times as great, the volume will also be three times as great, and so forth.

60. **2** If sample *C* were compressed, the volume would decrease. The mass would remain the same. Since the same mass is being compressed into a smaller volume, the density will be greater.

61. **5** To answer this question, the volumes of samples *A* and *B* must first be calculated.
Volume = length × width × height
for *A* Volume = $2\,cm \times 2\,cm \times 2\,cm = 8\,cm^3$
for *B* Volume = $3\,cm \times 2\,cm \times 1\,cm = 6\,cm^3$
The volume for sample *C* is given as $12\,cm^3$. Sample *C* therefore has the largest volume and sample *B* has the smallest volume.

62. **3** In the passage, weather is defined as the state of the atmosphere at any given time. Insolation is the amount of solar energy received at the earth's surface. Nearness to bodies of water may affect climate. Climate is the composite of weather conditions over a long period of time.

63. **1** Bodies of water become stabilizers of temperature. This causes the atmospheric conditions over water to be more uniform than over the land areas. Regions far from bodies of water do not enjoy the stabilizing effects and have hotter summers and colder winters.

64. **3** Radiation is heat in the form of sun rays. Conduction is the transfer of heat by direct conduct between two bodies. Convection is the transfer of heat by the motion of a gas. Weathering is the process of disintegration or decomposition of rocks at or near the surface of the earth.

65. **4** Topography is the general configuration of the earth's surface. Altitude refers to elevation. Humans cannot control winds, storms, or direction of ocean currents. Radiation from atomic experimentation may affect the atmosphere and climatic conditions.

66. **4** During the phase change, the constant temperature is represented by a horizontal line on the graph. Melting occurs at the lower of the two constant temperatures, and boiling at the higher one.

TEST 4: Language Arts, Reading (Interpreting Literature and the Arts)/Page 880

1. **3** The family moved constantly from house to apartment to tent.
2. **4** The author wished to stay in one place for a real sense of home.
3. **1** It seems obvious that the author's father was seeking more stable employment by moving westward.
4. **4** Accommodations might best be described as unstable or precarious, for instance, provisional, drafty, with a hole in the ceiling, and no floor.
5. **1** The constant travelling and changes in housing made for a very disorganized life-style.
6. **5** Large savings in fuel, safety belt, appeal to buyers' beliefs about comfort, and ecology are all mentioned. Beauty of appearance is not.
7. **2** The passage mentions the absence of advertisements.
8. **3** *Frantic* means desperate and a *sloth* is a very slow animal; both are terms that would not likely be used if the purpose were anything but satirical.
9. **4** With the stated knowledge that the public is not yet ready for its breakthroughs, it is unlikely that the Sloth will be widely distributed.
10. **3** The passage states that the sails are "a feature that supplements the engines."
11. **2** The setting of Oberfest at the foot of the snow-covered mountains is especially significant because of its contribution to the tragic ending.
12. **5** Nowhere is any theme (the essential subject) of the incident stated. The theme—that people, through their actions based on rumour and fear, bring about their own destruction—is left to the reader to deduce from the evidence presented by the author.
13. **1** In addition to the meaning given in the "Glossary of Literary Terms" on page 467, irony also refers to a combination of circumstances that results in the opposite of what might be expected to happen. That is true of this selection; the alarm which should bring help, brings the opposite—destruction.
14. **4** The word *cold* has two meanings in this context: a literal or denotative meaning of very chilly as applied to climate, and an extended or connotative meaning, lifeless.
15. **4** Oberfest was buried beneath the snow without a trace.
16. **3** He failed as a cornetist, a basketball player, and a football player.

17. **4** The title, a way of remembering E, G, B, D, F—the notes of the musical staff, describes the opposite of what happened to the poet.
18. **1** The reader is asked to consider the poem a failure, which it definitely is not.
19. **5** The poet compares his physical posture on stage to his "hand-tied necktie."
20. **5** The poet asks the reader to "consider this poem a failure."
21. **2** The poem has a definite rhyming pattern; it also has a predominant iambic tetrameter rhythm (see the "Glossary of Literary Terms" on page 467).
22. **4** The poet identifies with the suffering guests: "we must hear"; "we will die."
23. **3** Among the examples are frosted pie, ladies turning blue, and naked shoulders dying.
24. **1** The poet is contrasting the ways Pompeii did face and America might face doom.
25. **3** The poem describes an air-conditioned banquet room as the setting for our doom, should it come.
26. **4** Candida says, "I know how to make my choice."
27. **2** Marchbanks' last words indicate that he will not do anything heroic and that "smiling" Candida understands his pose is only a fake.
28. **4** She tells how she spoiled Morell to justify her choice of the weaker man.
29. **1** He says he "loves" the man who won.
30. **3** It is ironic that Candida chooses the man, superior in strength, whom she considers the weaker.
31. **1** The author's feelings are indicated by the use of such words as "beast" and "sadistic."
32. **3** The action referred to is "the purely phony move of the boxer who extends his gloves to his rival" on the floor.
33. **1** The passage states that the mob "roots consistently for the smaller man" and "howls with glee at a good finisher making his kill."
34. **4** The author's opinion is evident in the use of such words as "beast," "lurks," and "gray thing."
35. **5** The author describes the mob (audience) as vindictive.
36. **1** In the second paragraph, the author tells us that Cohen speaks to a large audience.
37. **5** This fact appears in the third paragraph.
38. **4** This fact appears in the first paragraph.
39. **5** See paragraph 6 for this point.
40. **4** See paragraph 6 for this point.
41. **1** The author describes the Junos, so he is "objective."
42. **4** The first sentence names Klees and Grealis.
43. **5** See paragraph 4 for this fact.
44. **4** The third paragraph says that the winning process begins October 1.
45. **3** The fifth paragraph says that there are 21 craft awards.

TEST 5: The Mathematics Test/Page 889

1. **4** \$15 000 – \$8000 = \$7000 sales over \$8000
   0.05 × \$7000 = \$350 commission
   \$200 + \$350 = \$550 total salary

2. **3** Total ÷ capacity of 1 = number needed: $\frac{x}{c}$.

3. **2** To obtain the average rate of speed, we divide the total distance covered by the total driving time.
   Total distance = 180 + 250 = 430 km
   Total time = 2 + 3 = 5 hours
   430 ÷ 5 = 86 km per hour, average rate of speed

4. **1** We use the following proportion

$$\frac{\text{length of photograph}}{\text{length of enlargement}} = \frac{\text{width of photograph}}{\text{width of enlargement}}$$

Let x = width of enlargement

$$\frac{8}{12} = \frac{6}{x}$$

$8x = 6(12) = 72$

$x = 72 \div 8 = 9$ cm

5. **4** $23\tfrac{1}{4} = 22 + \tfrac{4}{4} + \tfrac{1}{4} = 22\tfrac{5}{4}$

$22\tfrac{5}{4} = 22\tfrac{10}{8}$

$- 19\tfrac{5}{8}$

$3\tfrac{5}{8}$

$3\tfrac{5}{8} = \tfrac{29}{8}$

$\$\tfrac{29}{8} \times 80 = \$290$

6. **3** $3x - 1 < 5$

$3x < 5 + 1$

$3x < 6$

$x < 2$

Of the choices given the only choice less than 2 is 1.

The correct choice is (3).

7. **4** $850 \times 0.60 = 510$ seats in orchestra

$850 - 510 = 340$ seats in balcony

8. **4** Let $4x$ = the measure of the larger acute angle.

And x = the measure of the smaller acute angle.

$4x + x = 90$

$5x = 90$

$x = 90 \div 5 = 18$

$4x = 4(18) = 72°$, measure of the larger aculte angle.

9. **4** The sides are $b, \frac{2b}{3}, \frac{2b}{3} = \frac{7b}{3}$.

10. **3** Bill earns m dollars per month.

Antonio earns n dollars per month.

Together Bill and Antonio earn $(m + n)$ dollars per month.

In one year, Bill and Antonio earn $12(m + n)$ dollars.

11. **1** The perimeter of the figure is $(x + 2y) + (3x - y) + (2x + 3y) + (5x + y)$.

Perimeter $= (x + 3x + 2x + 5x) + (2y - y + 3y + y)$

Perimeter $= 11x + 5y$

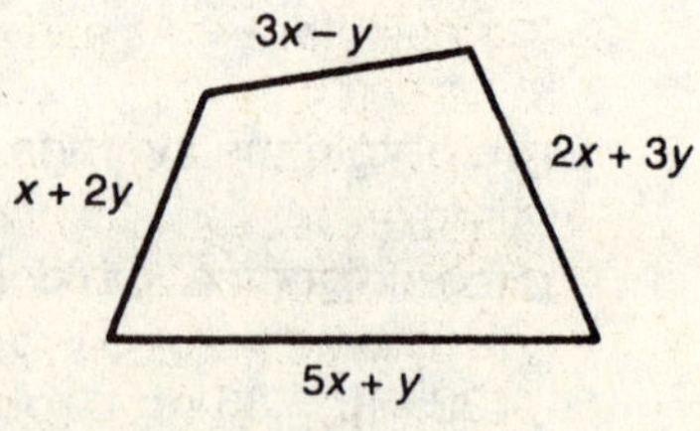

12. **4** Let x = Ahmed's earnings.

And $2x$ = Joan's earnings.

$x + 2x = 42$

$3x = 42$

$x = 42 \div 3 = \$14$, Ahmed's earnings

13. **4** $\$5800 - \$4500 = \$1300$

Tax is $\$100 + 5\%$ of $\$1300 = 100 + 0.05(1300) = 100 + 65 = \$165$

14. **2** $x = 2a(b + 7)$
$x = 2(3)(5 + 7)$
$x = 2(3)(12)$
$x = 72$

15. **3** To find the median mass we arrange the figures representing the masses in order of size and identify the middle one.
In order of size the masses are
84, 88, 89, 90, 90, 91, 92, 93, 94, 96, 97
The middle (or sixth mass) is 91.

16. **4** $\text{Probability} = \dfrac{\text{number of successful outcomes}}{\text{total number of outcomes}}$
In this case, the number of successful outcomes is 7 and the total number of outcomes is 11. Probability = $^7/_{11}$.

17. **3** $\dfrac{CD}{AD} = \dfrac{1\text{ unit}}{2\text{ units}} = \dfrac{1}{2}$

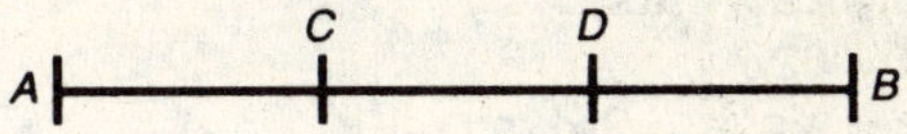

18. **3** $m\angle CBD = 125°$
$m\angle ABC = 180° - 125° = 55°$
$m\angle A + m\angle ABC = 90°$
$m\angle A + 55° = 90°$
$m\angle A = 90° - 55° = 35°$

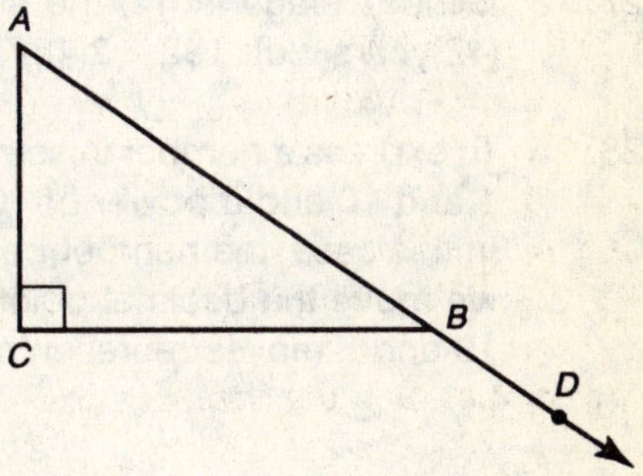

19. **4** 10% had *A* papers
25% had *B* papers
30% had *C* papers
15% had *D* papers
80% had passing papers
20% had failing papers
20% of 80 = $^1/_5(80) = 16$

20. **4** $\$20000 \times 0.07 = \$1400$
$7\frac{1}{2}\%$ written as a decimal = 0.075
$\$12000 \times 0.075 = \$900$
$\$1400 + \$900 = \$2300$

21. **2** If a dozen eggs cost *x* cents, 1 egg costs $\dfrac{1}{12}x$ cents.
3 eggs cost $3\left(\dfrac{1}{12}x\right)$, which may be written as $\dfrac{3}{12}x$.
$\dfrac{3}{12}x$ reduces to $\dfrac{1}{4}x$, or $\dfrac{x}{4}$.

22. **2** We calculate the yearly income for each choice.
A. $27000
B. $\$570 \times 52 = \$29640$
C. $\$2250 \times 12 = \$27000$
D. $6 \times \$2000 = \$12000$ for the first half-year
10% of $2000 = $200
$2000 + $200 = $2200 each month for the second six months
$6 \times \$2200 = \$13200$; $\$12000 + \$13200 = \$25200$ for the first year
The correct answer choice is (2).

23. **4** The distributive property states that $a(b + c) = a \times b + a \times c$.
We may represent the number of dollars spent by the dealer as
48(24 + 15)
Note that $48(24 + 15) = 48 \times 24 + 48 \times 15$.

24. **1** 45 minutes = 0.75 of an hour
At 96 km/h, the faster car covers 0.75×96, or 72 km.
At 72 km/h, the slower car covers 0.75×72, or 54 km.
$72 - 54 = 18$ km

25. **2** Meat department sales = \$2500
Dairy department sales = \$1500
Difference = \$1000

26. **2** We use the Pythagorean Theorem.

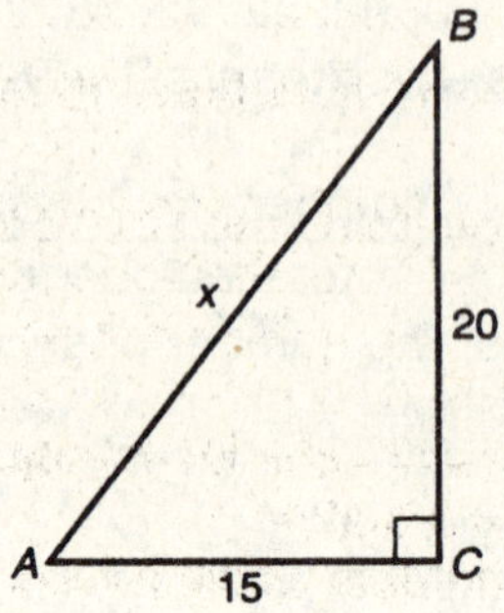

$x^2 = (15)^2 + (20)^2$
$x^2 = 225 + 400$
$x^2 = 625$
$x = \sqrt{625} = 25$ km

27. **3** If the average is 44, the sum is 132. If 2 of the individuals are the minimum as specified (42 years old), $132 - 2(42) = 48$.

28. **5** To express a number in scientific notation, we express it as the product of a number between 1 and 10 and a power of 10.
In this case, the number between 1 and 10 is 2.750389. In going from 2.750389 to 2 750 389 we move the decimal point 6 places to the right. Each move represents a multiplication by 10 and 6 moves represents a multiplication by 10^6. Thus,

$$2\,750\,389 = 2.750389 \times 10^6$$

29. **3** The team has played 75 games and will play 45 more games.
$75 + 45 = 120$
60% of $120 = 0.6 \times 120 = 72$
The team must win 72 games and it has already won 50 games.
Therefore, the team must win $72 - 50 = 22$ more games.

30. **1** The area of the rectangle =
base × altitude = $12 \times 8 = 96\text{cm}^2$.
The area of the triangle =
½ base × altitude = $\frac{1}{2}(32)(x) = 16x$
$16x = 96$
$x = 6$ cm

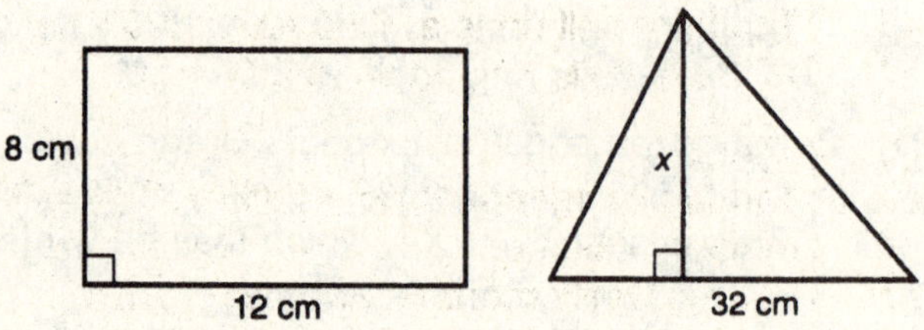

31. **2** The number of students in the school is $18 \times 35 = 630$. If there are to be 30 students in a class, the number of classes needed is $630 \div 30 = 21$.
Therefore, the number of new classes needed is $21 - 18 = 3$.

32. **4** 40% of the total expenses of \$240 000 went for labour.
40% = 0.4(\$240 000) = \$96 000

33. **2** Slope $= \dfrac{y_1 - y_2}{x_1 - x_2}$

In this case $y_1 = 4$, $y_2 = 3$, $x_1 = 5$, and $x_2 = 0$.

Slope $= \dfrac{4-3}{5-0} = \dfrac{1}{5}$

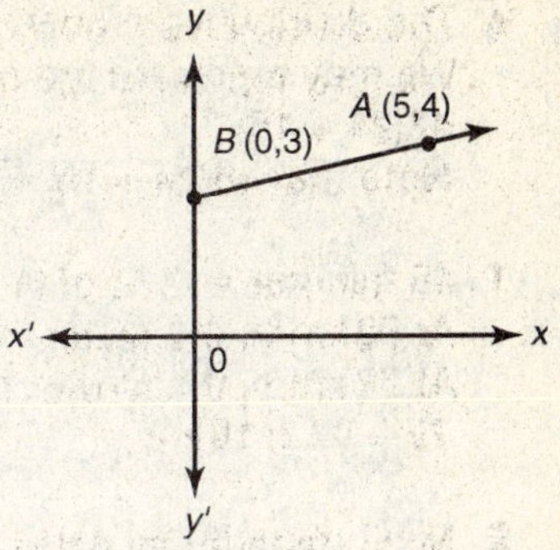

34. **3** 20 minutes + 15 minutes = 35 minutes

$\dfrac{35}{2}$ = average (minutes). Convert to hours: $\dfrac{\overset{7}{\cancel{35}}}{2} \cdot \dfrac{1}{\underset{12}{\cancel{60}}} = \dfrac{7}{24}$ hour.

35. **2** If a number pair satisfies an equation, then the point named by the number pair lies on the graph of the equation.
We try the number pairs in turn.

$$3x - y = 2$$

If $x = 3$ and $y = -2$, we have $3(3) - (-2) = 9 + 2 = 2$. Not true
If $x = 1$ and $y = 5$, we have $3(1) - (5) = 3 - 5 = 2$. Not true
If $x = 2$ and $y = 4$, we have $3(2) - (4) = 6 - 4 = 2$. True
If $x = 2$ and $y = -3$, we have $3(2) - (-3) = 6 + 3 = 2$. Not true
If $x = 3$ and $y = 7$, we have $3(3) - (7) = 9 - 7 = 2$. True
Thus, C and E are true. The correct choice is (2).

36. **5** $3x - 1 = 11$
$3x = 11 + 1 = 12$
$x = 12 \div 3 = 4$
$x^2 + x = (4)^2 + 4 = 16 + 4 = 20$

37. **3** The first bell rings at 9:00 A.M., 11:00 A.M., 1:00 P.M., 3:00 P.M., 5:00 P.M., 7:00 P.M., 9:00 P.M., 11:00 P.M., 1:00 A.M., 3:00 A.M., 5:00 A.M., 7:00 A.M.
The second bell rings at 9:00 A.M., 12 noon, 3:00 P.M., 6:00 P.M., 9:00 P.M., 12:00 midnight, 3:00 A.M., 6:00 A.M.
The third bell rings at 9:00 A.M., 1:00 P.M., 5:00 P.M., 9:00 P.M., 1:00 A.M., 5:00 A.M.
All three bells ring again at 9:00 P.M.

38. **3** The family spends 20% + 23% + 42% = 85%. The family saves 100% − 85% = 15% of its monthly income.
Let x = family monthly income
15% of $x = 0.15x$
$0.15x = 360$
$x = {}^{360}/_{0.15} = {}^{36\,000}/_{15} = \$2400$

39. **4** Let $x = DC$
Since $\triangle ABE$ is similar to $\triangle CED$, the lengths of the corresponding sides of the two triangles are in proportion.

$\dfrac{x}{60} = \dfrac{80}{48}$

$48x = 80(60) = 4800$
$x = 4800 \div 48 = 100$ m

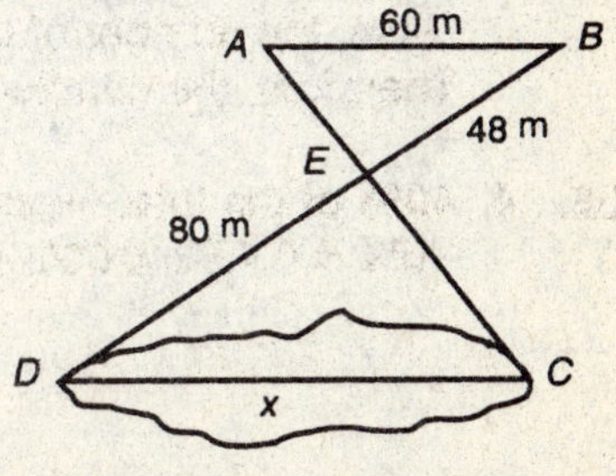

40. **1** $x = \frac{1}{a+b}$

$$\frac{3}{x} = \frac{3}{\frac{1}{a+b}} = 3 \div \frac{1}{a+b} = (3)(a+b)$$

41. **5** We check each of the numbers in turn.

$2(5) + 3 > 7$, $10 + 3 > 7$.	True
$2(4) + 3 > 7$, $8 + 3 > 7$.	True
$2(3) + 3 > 7$, $6 + 3 > 7$.	True
$2(10) + 3 > 7$, $20 + 3 > 7$.	True
$2(0) + 3 > 7$, $0 + 3 > 7$.	Not True

The correct choice is (5).

42. **3** The area of the triangle is given by the formula $A = \frac{1}{2}bh$.
In this case, $b = 4$ and $h = 8$.
Area $= \frac{1}{2}(4)(8) = 16$

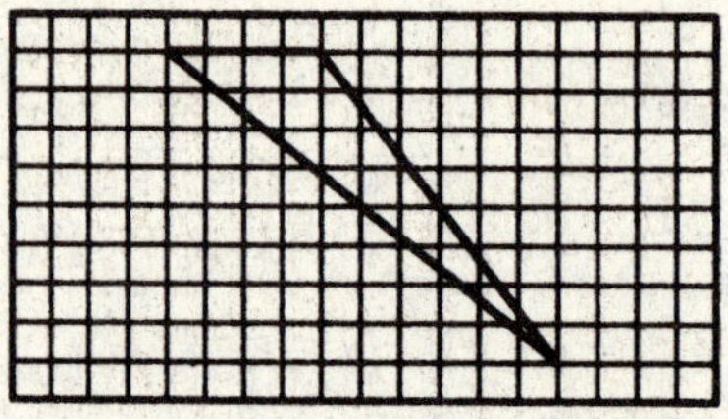

43. **4** In order to make a sound financial decision, David must know how much he can earn by working in the University *B* library.

44. **4** If she did one-third in 2 hours and 42 minutes, for two-thirds she needs 4 hours and 84 minutes, or 5 hours and 24 minutes, or $5^{24}/_{60}$, or $5^2/_5$, or 5.4 hours.

45. **4** To find the average we divide the total distance covered by the time consumed.
Total distance covered $= x + y + z$
Total time consumed = 3 days

$$\text{Average} = \frac{x+y+z}{3}$$

46. **5** To find the circumference of the wheel, we use the formula $C = \pi d$.
In this case, $\pi = {}^{22}/_7$ and $d = 28$.
$C = {}^{22}/_7 \times 28 = 88$ cm
Every time the wheel makes a complete revolution, the bundle buggy moves the distance of the circumference, or 88 cm.
In 10 complete revolutions, the bundle buggy moves $10 \times 88 = 880$ cm.

47. **1** Let x = the number of machine parts Rosina can make in 7 hours.
We use the proportion

$$\frac{4}{21} = \frac{7}{x}$$

$$4x = 7(21)$$

$$x = \frac{7(21)}{4}$$

48. **4** We use the formula $V = lwh$.
In this case, $l = x$, $w = x$, and $h = y$
$V = x(x)y$
$V = x^2y$

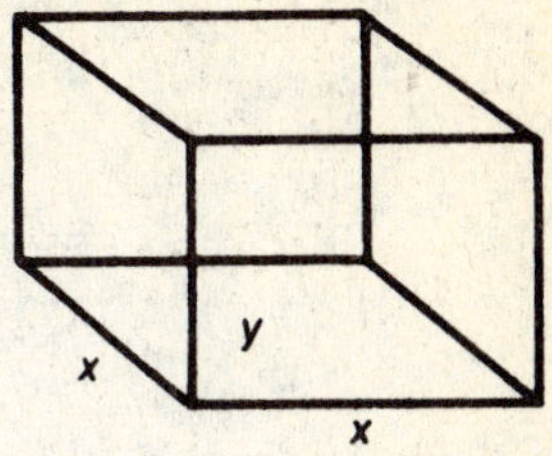

49. **5** We cannot find the value of the estate unless we know the daughter's share. This information is not given.

50. **1** Let x = outlay for food.
And $3x$ = outlay for rent.
$x + 3x = 1044$
$4x = 1044$
$x = 1044 \div 4 = \$261$

51. **5** Let $5x$ = the number of boys at the dance.
And $4x$ = the number of girls at the dance.
$4x = 48$
$x = 48 \div 4 = 12$
$5x = 5(12) = 60$ boys at the dance.

52. **2** The numbers 5 through 11 are common to both groups of numbers, leaving (1)(2)(3)(4) and (12). By cancellation, we can eliminate (3)(4) and 12, leaving only (1)(2) or 2 in the upper set, which gives a relationship that can be stated as follows: the lower set of numerals have a value equal to $\frac{1}{2}$ that of the upper set. $\frac{1}{2}$ of 39916800 is equal to 19958400.

53. **2** Lakeville and Fulton are 4.5 cm apart on the map. Since 1 cm = 80 km, 4 cm = 4(80) = 320 km.
Since 1 cm = 80 km, 0.5 cm = 0.5(80) = 40 km.
320 + 40 = 360 km

54. **3** $20\% = \frac{1}{5}$
$\frac{5}{5} - \frac{1}{5} = \frac{4}{5}$

The reduced price of a pair of pants is $\frac{4}{5}y$.

The reduced price of 3 pairs of pants is $3\left(\frac{4}{5}y\right)$.

55. **5** For breakfast and lunch Mr. Downs consumes 40% of his allowable number of calories. Thus, Mr. Downs had 60% of his allowable number of calories left for the day.
Let x = number of allowable calories per day.
$0.60x = 1200$
$x = 1200 \div 0.60$
$x = 1200/0.60 \times 100/100 = 120\,000/60 = 2000$

56. **2** From 1 P.M. to 3:52 P.M. = 2 hours and 52 minutes, or 172 minutes, less 12 minutes between classes. There are 3 intervals between 4 class periods, *not* 4. Therefore, 172 − 12 = 160 minutes left for class instruction. In each class period there are 160 ÷ 4 = 40 minutes.

12

THE HIGH SCHOOL EQUIVALENCY DIPLOMA

QUALIFICATIONS

General qualifications for taking the GED test are given. This is not an inclusive set of rules and regulations. You should check with your provincial office first. Contact numbers are provided in the accompanying chart.

CONTACTS BY PROVINCES

This chart lists the Canadian provinces that offer the GED test. A listing of all the GED administrators is provided, including addresses, phone and fax numbers, and where possible, e-mail addresses.

GED AND THE INTERNET

A source for recent information is given.

QUALIFICATIONS

PROVINCES

The GED test is offered in all provinces except Quebec.

MINIMUM AGE

The minimum age to take the test is 19 in all provinces except Alberta and the Northwest Territories, where it is 18 years of age.

MINIMUM SCORES

In order to be granted an Equivalency Certificate, the minimum score on each test must be 45, except for Newfoundland, where the minimum score on each test is 40 with a 45 average score on five tests.

WAITING PERIOD

To take the GED test, applicants must be out of public school for at least one year. In most provinces this means that the class in which you were last a member must have graduated.

RESIDENCY REQUIREMENT

Provinces except for Manitoba and New Brunswick have a residency requirement.

GED AND THE INTERNET

There is a great deal of information about the GED on the Internet. The easiest way to find everything is to enter "GED" into your favourite browser. With some refinement, you can find information about courses being offered in your province as well as general information you might want. As a start, you may want to visit http://www.nald.ca/gedblue/contact.htm.